A TRANSLATOR'S HANDBOOK ON THE GOSPEL OF LUKE

HELPS FOR TRANSLATORS

PREPARED UNDER THE AUSPICES OF THE

UNITED BIBLE SOCIETIES

VOLUME X

A TRANSLATOR'S HANDBOOK ON THE GOSPEL OF LUKE

PUBLISHED FOR THE UNITED BIBLE SOCIETIES

BY E. J. BRILL, LEIDEN

1971

A TRANSLATOR'S HANDBOOK ON THE GOSPEL OF LUKE

BY

J. REILING

AND

J. L. SWELLENGREBEL

PUBLISHED FOR THE UNITED BIBLE SOCIETIES

BY E. J. BRILL, LEIDEN

1971

PRINTED IN THE NETHERLANDS

"...I could never feel quite sure without asking Luke himself. Indeed, if I could have the privilege of a few moments' talk with the four Evangelists, I must confess it would be Luke whom I would confront with the longest list of questions."

E. V. Rieu

The Four Gospels, p. xxvi

CONTENTS

INTRODUCTION

In method and general set-up this book is in line with *A Translator's Handbook on the Gospel of Mark,* Vol. 2 of the series "Helps for Translators" (Leiden, 1961), by Robert G. Bratcher and Eugene A. Nida. It is tacitly assumed that this companion volume is in the hands of the readers of the present handbook. The same applies to the eighth volume in the same series, Eugene A. Nida and Charles R. Taber, *The Theory and Practice of Translation* (Leiden, 1969); to *A New Testament Wordbook for Translators,* in two fascicles, (1) *Some Exegetical Articles in Preliminary Form* (ABS, New York, 1964), by Robert G. Bratcher, and (2) *Some Translational Articles in Preliminary Form* (ABS, New York, 1966), by Eugene A. Nida; and to William F. Arndt and F. Wilbur Gingrich, *A Greek-English Lexicon of the New Testament (and Other Early Christian Literature)* (5th impression, Chicago, 1960).

This book is different from its predecessor on Mark in that it does not deal with problems of text and punctuation. The edition of *The Greek New Testament* (*GNT*) with its extensive critical apparatus and its punctuation apparatus makes this superfluous. Furthermore the forthcoming companion volume to *GNT* is intended to give the translators all the help and information they need with regard to textual problems. Only where the RSV follows a text different from that of *GNT* is the difference made clear in order to avoid confusion. In a few cases differences between *GNT* and Nestle are referred to.

The exegetical notes aim at making clear the meaning of the Greek text in terms of translational problems. Theological and historical questions are touched upon only when they have a direct bearing on the translation. It is assumed that one or more commentaries are always at hand, and sometimes commentaries are referred to, either in a general way or directly by the name of the author. For practical purposes references to lexicons, grammars and other scholarly literature have been restricted to those mentioned in the List of Books (see below, p. 775ff).

Ample attention has been given to an analysis of the syntactic structure of the Greek clauses. When different possible renderings or interpretations are presented, the exegete's preference is, as a rule, indicated but seldom explicitly argued. Lack of space made this imperative. To present and discuss the evidence and the main scholarly opinion would have required another volume. The absence of argument may make the preferences indicated seem arbitrary and unwarranted but they are only for the benefit of those translators who find it impossible to choose between the alternatives.

As in the Translator's Handbook on Mark the Greek text is cited in terms of primary and secondary levels of comment, with two steps of indentation. But instead of all occurrences being listed in the lexical notes, an Index of Greek words is given at the end of the volume. In the introduction to that Index the reader will learn what to look for in the Index and what not. Words occurring only once are indicated as such at their place of occurrence, and, if necessary, discussed. Words occurring twice are usually discussed at their first occurrence and the other occurrence is added. If useful, a back reference is given at the second place. Occurrences in two subsequent verses are considered as one, both in the exegetical notes and in the Index.

The discussion of the translational problems of each verse, or sequence of verses, keeps closely to the interpretation given in the preceding exegetical section; the one should not be used without the other. A secondary alternative, mentioned as possible but not preferable in *Exegesis*, has not been discussed in *Translation*, unless it appears to have been widely adopted in the versions investigated.

The translational notes aim basically at two things, (1) to help the translator not to feel himself bound to the formal linguistic features of the source language, and (2) to make him aware of the problems he may meet in his search for the closest natural equivalent in matters of lexical items, syntactic construction, clause and sentence structure, stylistic features, etc. A considerable part of the notes is taken up by examples and/or quotations, the former attempting to indicate how certain problems may be solved, the latter showing how the same or comparable problems have actually been solved by other translators. The quotations usually give a rather literal English back-translation, sometimes in a kind of "translationese". In reading and evaluating such back-translations one should be conscious that they are only approximations (as Nida rightly points out in his *Bible Translating*, p. 196).

When using the handbook the translator should not simply imitate in the receptor language the solutions suggested. He must always exercise his own judgment, taking into account the specific linguistic features and translational possibilities of the receptor language, and its typical differences from Greek and/or English. In particular he should remember that the receptor language will often require less extreme transformations, transpositions and adjustments than those reflected in the given examples and quotations, for the simple reason that the handbook tends to call attention to rather extreme solutions, in which the points to be made can be most clearly demonstrated. Many translators will have to break up, for instance, the long and involved Greek sentence found in Luke 1 : 1-4, but such break-ups will seldom be as extreme as those reflected in the quotations given in the note on that passage (below pp. 6f).

Translation may be characterized as an art made possible by a technique. This handbook aims at providing the technique, but it cannot teach the art. The latter must spring from the translator's intimate knowledge of the source in combination with his "feel" for the genius of the receptor language, his experience in using it in a creative way, and his familiarity with the life, ideals, thoughts, and culture of its speakers.

The author of the translational notes apologizes for the rather extensive use he has made of references to books on Bible translation. To repeat or summarize the relevant data found in them would probably have made for easier reading; it would, however, have added so much to the bulk of the handbook (which even now is considerable) as to defeat its own end. For the same reason back references to the discussion of a certain lexical item are not repeated if the distance from the preceding identical reference would have been less than twenty to thirty verses, and items occurring more than about twelve times are not followed by a back reference, but their occurrences can be found with the help of the English Word List (see below pp. 791f).

The English running text quoted in this book is that of the Revised Standard Version, 1946, ed. 1964; it is used by permission of the Division of Christian Education of the National Council of the Churches of Christ in the United States of America.

The authors of a handbook like this are indebted to many people: New Testament scholars, linguists, missionaries, translators. For the exegetical part this indebtedness is brought out only to a limited extent by the List of Books Quoted. Much more literature has been consulted which has not been mentioned in the notes. Valuable suggestions have been offered by Dr. M. de Jonge, professor of New Testament at the University of Leiden, and by the Rev. F. Visser, of the Netherlands Bible Society. Mr. G. W. Marchal, assistant in the New Testament Department at the University of Utrecht, has placed the writer, and the readers, in his debt by checking all references in the text of the exegetical part and by assisting the writer in the tedious work on the Index of Greek Words.

For the translational part the situation is somewhat different. Its author passes on the results of the insight, the experience, and the toil of many Bible translators of yesterday and today. Relatively few of them, however, have cared to publish books or articles about their work. The problems they met, the solutions they found, the hesitations they felt, occasionally also the false steps they made (which in several cases were found to provide rewarding material for the handbook!), had to be extracted from their translations, either by the author himself, or by others on his behalf.

Thus the material used in the translational part of this book is drawn from a number of sources, including principally:

(1) *The Bible Translator*, and books about Bible translating;
(2) field notes of Eugene A. Nida, which he kindly made available to be used by others;
(3) versions in languages the author could read and understand fairly well himself, viz. in some European and Indonesian languages;
(4) material provided by consultants on the basis of versions in languages known to them.

The consultants mentioned under (4) have been so kind as to read through continuous stretches of the first draft of the notes, and/or to answer one or more extensive questionnaires circulated amongst them. The author owes much to their comments and replies, and he wishes to thank them for their valuable help. Their names, together with the names of the language(s) they dealt with are as follows.

Ralph Covell (Sediq), Wesley J. Culshaw (some languages of India), Donald S. Deer (Kituba), Marion L. Doble (Kapauku), Faye Edgerton (Navajo, Apache), Richard Elkins (Manobo), W. H. Ford (Lokele), Vivian Forsberg (Tagabili), Fidel P. Galang (Pampango), Herbert G. Grether (Thai), C. D. Grijns (Bahasa Indonesia), Harold F. Hanlin (Ponape, Trukese), Michail Hannan (Shona), R. P. Kramers (Chinese), Houndja Lazare (Bamiléké), Paul Lewis (Lahu), James Loriot (Shipibo), P. Middelkoop (Timorese), J. Noorduyn (Sundanese), H. Perdok (East Toradja), W. Perston (Kanarese, Tamil, Telugu), T. Price (East Nyanja, Lomwe, Yao), W. Murray Rule (Foe, Huli), Fred. W. Schelander (Marathi), Lynn A. de Silva (Sinhalese), Marianna C. Slocum (Tzeltal), E. Smits (Sundanese), Arlene Spurlock (Zarma), Leslie H. Stennes (Fulani), H. van der Veen (South Toradja), J. B. Veitch (West Nyanja), J. Voorhoeve (Sranan, Bamiléké, Kilega, Nyakyusa), G. Henry Waterman (Tagalog, Cuyono), K. A. Zeefuik (Sranan).

It is to be hoped that the use made of all this material will not fall too far short of the painstaking care most consultants have given to it. At the same time it should be pointed out that only the author is responsible for the presentation of that material, for the conclusions drawn, and the (necessarily subjective) selection made from it. And he apologizes in advance for any misuse, mistake, or misjudgment that may have crept in.

The final draft of the translational notes was read through by Dr. J. Voorhoeve, professor of West African languages at the University of Leiden. Their author wishes to express his gratitude for this help and for the readiness with which it was given. All drafts and other material have been typed and retyped by Mr. E. Smits, who also handled the manuscript before it went to the printers, and read the proofs. The authors owe much to the great care and scrupulous attention he gave to the job.

A few words should be said about the language in which this book is written. The authors are not native speakers of English. Their English (or what they supposed to be so!) had to undergo careful correction, of course. The Reverend J. Williamson (chaplain of Christ Church, Amsterdam) and Miss Edyth A. Banks (UBS, London) have been so kind as to perform this task, the former for chapters 1-18, the latter for chapters 17-24. The authors have greatly benefited by their corrections and critical remarks on wording and style. Their advice has gladly and gratefully been followed except in a very few matters, especially the use of one or two technical grammatical terms, and some minor changes in wording made when the book was already going to the press, which could not be discussed because of the pressure of time.

Whoever uses this handbook should be aware of the following items.

(1) Quotations from existing translations are followed by a reference to the version from which they are taken. For versions in English and other western languages a conventional abbreviation is used (e.g. NEB), or a short indication (e.g. Zürich), or the name of the translator (e.g. Rieu); for versions in non-western languages the name of the language is given, where necessary followed by an indication of the specific version, revision or edition used. Further particulars can be found in the List of Books and the List of Languages (see below pp. 775-777 and 793-798). If the reference to the source is preceded by "cp.", this is to show that the quotation does not render or reproduce the original in all details but is more freely worded, concentrating on what is especially relevant to the

point under discussion. In some cases a quotation reflects not a final but an evolving stage of the work, and hence the translators working in the language concerned may have in the meantime modified their renderings or adopted quite different forms of expression. It has not been possible, of course, to revalidate all of these details, but the authors will certainly welcome correspondence from translators whose data is cited here and who may have now found still more satisfactory solutions.

(2) References to editions of the text and to books are given in such a form that further particulars can easily be found in the List of Books (see below, pp. 775ff).

(3) Section headings are not discussed in the body of the commentary, but a list of proposed section headings is added on pp. 769-774.

(4) Italics mark,
- (a) words quoted in Greek, or in another foreign language;
- (b) English words quoted from the *Revised Standard Version* and functioning as the beginning of an entry in the translational notes;
- (c) titles of books.

(5) Some special abbreviations and symbols are employed.
The phrase "in Luke" means, "in the Gospel of Luke" (*not* including Acts).
The abbreviation *l.c.* stands for *loco citato* (in the place already quoted).
The abbreviation *scil.* stands for *scilicet* (you may understand; supply).

"..." indicates direct quotation from an English source.

'...' reflects the (approximate) English rendering of a foreign language expression.

[...] in the running text marks English words or passages which the RSV does not have in the text but in a footnote; in *Exegesis* it encloses parts of the text which the *GNT* regards as having dubious textual validity.

(...) in the examples or quotations encloses words or phrases the addition of which is optional.

(or, ...) in the examples or quotations indicates an alternative phrase.

(†) after a Greek word marks it as occurring only once in the Gospel of Luke.

(††)	after a Greek word marks it as occurring only once in the New Testament.
.../...	indicates alternative renderings of a foreign language word or phrase.
...-...	joins together renderings that consist of more than one word but correspond to a single word in the source language.
::	stands between two words which are opposite in meaning.

J. Reiling
J. L. Swellengrebel

TREATMENT OF THE TEXT

Title: ***The Gospel according to Luke.***

Translation: For general remarks on the title of the Gospels, and on the rendering of the term *Gospel* see *TH-Mk,* pp. 1 and 3.

According to Luke, or, 'written down by Luke', 'written by Lucas-even-again' (Shipibo, implying that other writers had written other books on the same subject), 'that Luke arranged/recorded', 'as Luke told/reported it'. Whatever rendering is chosen, care should be taken to avoid three possible misunderstandings, (1) that the following narrative tells us about Luke; (2) that Luke was the person who brought the Good News; or, (3) that the story is given according to the personal views of Luke—which might be understood from "according to", *selon,* in some English and French versions.

Luke. In this and all other cases the translator has to consider the way proper names are idiomatically handled in the receptor language. Some languages, for instance, cannot use a name without a preposed particle functioning as name qualifier. In such a case, both for native and foreign names, the translator should comply with usage, giving the name in the way names are given in the receptor language. In honorific languages name qualifiers tend to be differentiated according to the person's rank or status, and may then acquire the force of titles; on the other hand, titles can function as name qualifiers, and may even become fused with the name (cp. the use of 'Saint', as discussed in *TH-Mk,* p. 1). Such a title or qualifier, though obligatory with native names, may never, or rarely, be employed with foreign names. Thus, in several languages of India a locally used polite title would sound as strange with 'Luke' as "Doctor" would sound in the English Bible; some versions have solved the problem by introducing *sadhu* (as a translation of 'saint') to do duty as name-qualifying title. That some such solution is necessary was demonstrated in one case, where in public reading the title was regularly inserted, although the text read did not have it. If an honorific title has to be used in the case of Luke, its level should be in accordance with the reverence in which the Christian church holds him as Evangelist.

Transliteration of proper names will not be discussed in detail in this Handbook. For general remarks see Nida, *Science,* 193ff,[1] mentioning two basic types, viz. phonological adjustment (for which cp. also Nida, *BT,* 244-246) and borrowing of orthographic forms, and a compromise between the two, involving a distinction between familiar and unfamiliar names. Non-linguistic factors will influence the choice between the types; cultural insecurity, for instance, may result in a deference for the orthographical forms of the source language, geographical isolation, or a long historical

[1] Now also Nida, *TAPOT,* 118f.

tradition, in a preference for phonological adjustment. Hence, if circumstances change, transliteration may change also, as in Shipibo, where names were previously written according to the Spanish tradition, but tend to be spelt in accordance with pronunciation now that more literature in the vernacular is coming out. Conversely, increasing contacts with the outside world may start a movement away from phonological adjustments, as is the case in Kapauku and South Toradja, which now write *Lukas*, although phonology would require *Dukati* (cp. *TBT*, 1.133-135, 1950) and *Luka'* respectively. Compare also the change from *Isa* and *Ibrahim*, chosen under influence of Muslim surroundings, to *Jesus* and *Abraham*, as a consequence of increasing contacts with other Christian communities (cp. on 1 : 31 and 55).

Ideally the ultimate model or base of transliteration is the Greek form of the name (or the Hebrew, or Latin form reflected by the Greek, cp. on 3 : 23ff and 2 : 2), but often the model that is best acceptable to the constituency (because it is known from previous versions in the receptor language, or from a neighbouring language of prestige) has considerably changed in form already. For Arabic models for some biblical names see below on "Aaron" in v. 5.

CHAPTER ONE

1 ***Inasmuch as many have undertaken to compile a narrative of the things which have been accomplished among us,*** 2 ***just as they were delivered to us by those who from the beginning were eyewitnesses and ministers of the word,*** 3 ***it seemed good to me also, having followed all things closely for some time past, to write an orderly account for you, most excellent Theophilus,*** 4 ***that you may know the truth concerning the things of which you have been informed.***

Exegesis: Vv. 1-4 constitute one complex sentence of which v. 3, *edoxe...grapsai* 'it seemed good...to write', is the main clause to which the clauses of v. 1 and v. 4 are subordinate. The clause of v. 1, introduced by *epeidēper* 'inasmuch as', is causal and explains why it seemed good to write; the clause of v. 4, introduced by *hina* 'in order that', is final and tells of the purpose for which the writing was undertaken. To each of these clauses one other clause is subordinate; to v. 1 the clause of v. 2, introduced by *kathōs* 'just as', is subordinate; this clause is of a comparative nature and serves to define more accurately certain aspects of v. 1 (see below on v. 2). To the final clause in v. 4 is subordinate the relative clause *peri...logōn* 'of which you have been informed', which serves to identify *logōn* 'things' in v. 4. Finally the participial phrase *parēkolouthēkoti* 'having followed' goes syntactically with *kamoi* 'to me also' but semantically with the main clause as a whole (see below on v. 3).

Many translations break down the complex sentence of vv. 1-4 into smaller sentences. The most obvious solution is to render vv. 1 and 2 together as an independent clause (cp. NEB, Kingsley Williams, Goodspeed and others). The causal relationship between v. 1 and v. 3 is then brought out by an adverbial expression at the beginning of v. 3, as "And so" (NEB), "For that reason" (Goodspeed). In this division v. 2 remains subordinate to v. 1 and v. 4 to v. 3.

The style of vv. 1-4 is in accordance with Greek literary usage. Its elaborateness does not however affect its clarity and the literary character of the passage lies more in its syntactic structure than in its choice of verbs and nouns, even if several of them do not occur elsewhere in Luke.

Translation: (1) This preface, or dedication, is addressed to a person named in the text. This may have special consequences in receptor languages which differentiate according to status, because the word 'most excellent' or 'honourable' (v. 3) shows the position of Theophilus to have been such as to entitle him to be addressed in honorific terms.

In the rest of the Gospel no indication can be detected that would show it in its totality to be addressed to Theophilus (see *Exegesis* on v. 3, *soi*). Consequently, in matters of honorifics, the dedication and the body of the

Gospel story cannot be handled in the same way. It is interesting to compare what happens in Javanese and Balinese when a story-teller addresses an audience consisting of people of superior rank. As a rule he will start with a few introductory sentences in respectful language, addressing himself directly to his noble audience, but, having thus given courtesy its due, he can forget about his hearers, so to speak, and recite the story itself in ordinary language. Where this example can be followed, it is distinctly an advantage, for one can usually be more concise and to the point in ordinary than one can in honorific vocabulary. Such an advantage, however, should never be attained at the cost of the linguistic etiquette required in the receptor language.

(2) The translator should try to carry over at least part of the stylistic flavour of this dedication, e.g., by using literary terms and a somewhat stilted way of speaking, if the receptor language not only provides such facilities but also uses them for more or less the same purpose. Stylistic *finesses* should not, however, detract from the clear expression of the contents of these verses.

(3) This is especially true of the way in which the structure of this long sentence is handled. Several old and new, western and non-western translators have tried to imitate it, even though the formal linguistic features of the language did not allow them to do so. The result is a sentence that is top-heavy and inelegant, the exact contrary of what Luke intended when he chose this literary form for his dedication.

Drastic adjustments may be necessary when, besides shifts from subordination to co-ordination and from nominal to verbal constructions, the linguistic sequence of phrases and clauses has to parallel the historical order of events. In vv. 1-4 nine linguistic entities can be discerned, which indicate phases in the historical process, viz. (1) the undertaking to compile a narrative, (2) certain things being accomplished, (3) their being delivered, (4) their being seen by eyewitnesses, (5) the action of ministers of the word—virtually identical with (3)—, (6) Luke's taking a decision, (7) his investigation of the facts, (8) his writing an account for Theophilus, (9) the results hoped for. The historical order of these phases, however, is (2) (4) (5) (3) (1) (6) (7)—or, perhaps, (7) (6), see on v. 3—(8) (9). Most of the resulting shifts and adjustments are found in the following example. 'Mr. Teofilo, as you know, certain things have been done among us. Certain people saw those things with their own eyes, beginning from beginning, and they made-known that story. They taught us that story. Afterwards, as you know also, many people have given-themselves-over to writing a story of those things. They followed (the) same way only (as the) things we received from those first witnesses. Therefore, I also, I have decided to write those things in order, on your behalf, because I have examined them good-good, since long-ago. Thus, you will know that you can have confidence (lit. put heart) in the things that they taught you' (Kituba). Yet another restructuring of the four verses is shown in the following quotation from Shipibo, where the translator had to divide the long period into several co-ordinate sentences, but could make use of an intricate system of connectives to weld the whole together.

'(V. 1) Already (a) many have tasted, to write everything nicely in paper; such as happened at ours. (V. 2) Such (b) they told us, the-ones-who-saw even when/while (c) that (d) began, and also the-ones-who-speak word. (V. 3) Thereupon (e) I also, them having-asked learned everything, in a very nice way. Thereupon (f) I learned even the having begun (g). Such being (h), I thought, to write such for you nicely on paper, strong Téofilo. (V. 4) The words they told you you know true (i)'—in which the lettered words and phrases can be specified as follows: (a) introductory conjunction; (b) relative pronoun referring to events or quotations; (c) subordinating clitic to the clause, indicating approximate circumstances; (d) relative pronoun referring ambiguously to "the things... accomplished"; (e) marker of transition from one paragraph, or actor, to another; (f) marker of transition from one kind of activity to another; (g) direct object, referring to "the things...accomplished"; (h) transitional phrase to introduce the conclusion of a logical reasoning; (i) a clause put in the hortatory mood, and functioning as a purpose clause, with a subject-actor different from that of the main clause, as indicated by a specific affix. In other languages quite different and less radical changes may be required, such as a division in two sentences (see *Exegesis*); or one in four sentences, using some introductory phrases in the second sentence (v. 2), e.g. 'that composition conformed to', 'they wrote down those things just as', and in the fourth (v. 4), e.g. 'its purpose was that', or, 'may its result be that', cp. also, "I do this so that you will know..." (TEV).

1 ***Inasmuch as many have undertaken to compile a narrative of the things which have been accomplished among us,***

Exegesis: *epeidēper* (††) 'inasmuch as', 'since', implying a reference to something which is already known to the reader, in this case to Theophilus. There is no reason to treat it as a solemn or stately conjunction (cp. Moulton-Milligan).

polloi 'many' refers to unknown members of the Christian community who have been engaged in writing a Gospel account; that the reference is to writers follows from v. 3.

epecheirēsan 'have attempted'.

epicheireō (†) 'to set one's hand to', 'to attempt'. The question whether the use of this verb with regard to the work of his predecessors implies a criticism of their work, is much debated. But it should be pointed out (1) that the verb as such is neutral in this respect (cp. Moulton-Milligan), and (2) that it was in accordance with Greek literary usage for a writer to refer to the work of predecessors in the preface of his own work (cp. A-G s.v.).

anataxasthai 'to reproduce' or 'to compile'.

anatassomai (††) either 'to repeat from memory', hence 'to reproduce' (Zahn, Moulton-Milligan) or 'to draw up', 'to compile' (modern translations, cp. A-G s.v.). Because of what follows the latter is preferable.

diēgēsin peri tōn peplērophorēmenōn en hēmin pragmatōn 'an account concerning the things which have been accomplished among us'.

diēgēsis (††) 'narrative', 'account'. The use of the preposition *peri* 'concerning' instead of a simple genitive is either due to the literary character of the passage or intentionally somewhat vague because Luke does not want to commit himself as to the completeness of the accounts of his predecessors.

plērophoreō (†) 'to fill', 'to fulfil', or 'to convince fully'. Here the participle *peplērophorēmenōn* admits of two explanations, viz.: (1) 'fulfilled', i.e. 'accomplished', which means that the events in question "lie now before us as a complete whole" (Bruce). Several versions give a rendering which is more general, as e.g. "that have happened" (NEB, Phillips), or, "which have taken place" (Kingsley Williams). The force of the past participle should however be brought out: the "things that have happened" are not described as belonging to the past (which would have been expressed by the aorist) but as something the influence of which is still felt; hence also *en hēmin* 'among us' (see below); (2) 'fully convinced', i.e. "on which there is full conviction among us" (Rengstorf; the most recent edition has "which have been fulfilled", which belongs to (1)); cp. also Schonfield, "held by us to be fact". Moffatt's "the established facts of our religion" seems to combine both interpretations; Goodspeed's "the movement which has developed among us" may imply that the preface of the Gospel was intended for both the Gospel and Acts.

en hēmin 'among us' but used in a rather broad sense, 'in our circles', 'in our group as Christians', and not denoting the writer and his contemporaries but rather the writer and his fellow Christians.

pragma (†) 'thing', 'event'.

Translation: *Inasmuch*, or 'because..., as you know', or 'because..., indeed'. When the causal connexion is not expressed here but in v. 3 (see remarks on vv. 1-4), v. 1 should still contain some expression conveying the other idea, e.g. 'indeed (or 'as you know') many people have already tried...' (Balinese, Kituba).

Have undertaken, or, 'have lifted the (writing-)brush' (Chinese UV), 'have-exerted-themselves', or, more generically, 'have begun'.

Compile a narrative of. In languages that have no detailed terminology for stages and genres of literary activity one may say, 'to gather and (or, in order to) write down', or, 'to write down the full story about'.

Things which have been accomplished among us. The verb may be rendered, 'have become complete', 'have run their full course' (NV). The aspect of continuing effect (see *Exegesis*), if not sufficiently expressed by the form of the verb, or implied in the phrase 'among us', 'in our midst', may have to be indicated by other means, e.g. by adding, 'and still affect (or, are important for) us', hence, 'the important things that became complete (or, that happened) among us', cp. "the momentous happenings in our midst" (Rieu). The other possible interpretation, 'on which there is full conviction among us', results in a clause structure that often has to be simplified, e.g. 'which have-certainty among us' (Malay), or recast, e.g. 'the reality of which is believed among us' (Balinese); when active forms must be used, it may become, 'which we know really/truly to have happened', taking 'among us' as referring to the agents. — *Us* is usually rendered as exclusive, cp. *Exegesis* on v. 3. It should be kept in mind, however, that the choice between inclusive and exclusive pronouns is not always dependent only on the question whether the audience is included or not; it may be influenced also by intersecting trends and considerations. Thus in Santali the inclusive pronoun expresses friendly respect (compare the "epistolary we"); similarly in East Toradja common knowledge and interest may induce a speaker to use the inclusive 'we' although the person addressed is not in actual fact a member of his group. On the other hand, in languages using honorifics it may be felt impolite to include the speaker and the person addressed in the same group, when the latter's status is higher than the former's, as is the case here; this would lead to the use of the exclusive 'we', even if Theophilus is supposed to have been a Christian or catechumen, i.e. a member of the speaker's group. On the use of inclusive or exclusive pronouns and its problems, see Nida, *BT*, 256f; *Science*, 204f; *TAPOT*, 116f; Beekman, *NOT*, 124-176; *TBT*, 4.86-90, 1953; 15.88-92, 1964.

2 ***just as they were delivered to us by those who from the beginning were eyewitnesses and ministers of the word,***

Exegesis: *kathōs paredosan hēmin* 'as handed down to us...'. Grammatically the object of *paredosan* is *pragmata* 'things', to be understood from *pragmatōn* in v. 1. But because, properly understood, not the *pragmata* themselves were handed down but information or tradition concerning them, several translations resort to a more free rendering as e.g. "following the traditions handed down to us" (NEB), or "basing their work on the evidence" (Phillips, cp. also Willibrord, Brouwer).

kathōs 'just as', stronger than *hōs* 'as'.

paradidōmi 'to hand over', 'to turn over'; with regard to oral or written tradition 'to hand down', 'to pass on'. Here probably of the oral transmission of the Gospel tradition.

hēmin 'to us', i.e. to Christians of a generation subsequent to those referred to in the next phrase.

hoi ap' archēs autoptai kai hupēretai genomenoi tou logou 'those who from the beginning were eyewitnesses and ministers of the word' or 'those who from the beginning were eyewitnesses and became ministers of the word' (cp. Segond, Willibrord), dependent upon the interpretation of *ap' archēs* and of the participle *genomenoi*.

ap' archēs 'from the beginning', viz. of the *pragmata* i.e. of the life and ministry of Jesus, cp. Acts 1 : 21f. Since the preaching of the Gospel did not begin until after the ministry of Jesus as defined in Acts 1 : 21f, it is best to take *ap' archēs* to refer to *autoptai* only and not to *hupēretai tou logou* as well. Furthermore the position of *genomenoi* between *hupēretai* and *logou* does not point to its going with both *autoptai* and *hupēretai*. Hence it is preferable to take *ap' archēs* to modify *autoptai* 'those who were eyewitnesses from the beginning' and *genomenoi* to go with *hupēretai tou logou* 'who became ministers of the word'.

autoptēs (††) 'eyewitness'.

hupēretēs (also 4 : 20) 'servant', here with *logos* 'word', i.e. the Gospel or the word of God (for *logos* in this sense cp. Acts 6 : 4; 11 : 19; for *hupēretēs* in this connexion cp. Acts 26 : 16; 1 Cor. 4 : 1), 'preacher of the Gospel message'.

Translation: *They were delivered to us*, or, 'we had heard them from the mouth of men who...' (Sranan). — *To deliver*, or, 'to make known' (Kanarese), 'to show causing (us) to know' (Thai), 'to cause-to-receive' (Balinese, using a verb that also has the meaning 'to bequeath an inheritance').

From the beginning, or, specifying the reference, 'from its beginning', 'since those things began to happen', 'from the very first of those things/events'.

Eyewitnesses may have to be expressed analytically, e.g. 'people/those who saw with their own eyes', 'people who witnessed with the seeing of their eyes' (East Toradja, using a current idiomatic expression for 'to see clearly', cp. 'with the hearing of the ear' for 'to hear clearly'), 'people in whose presence they happened' (Apache). The object of 'to see' is "the things accomplished", which may have to be said explicitly, e.g. adding 'those things', or a pronominal reference.

Ministers refers to those who give the word the service it needs; hence e.g., 'those who teach' (Tagabili), 'those who convey/spread', 'proclaimers of' (Pampango), 'those who preach' (Tagalog, Bolivian Quechua, similarly Chinese, lit. 'those who hand down the way', see below), or simply, 'those who tell' (Navajo, Apache).

The word is used here as a technical term. In several languages a literal rendering would be misleading, and still more so by its being combined here with the word 'minister/servant', used also in an uncommon sense; hence such renderings as, 'God's word' (Navajo, Apache), cp. on 5 : 1; or, 'Gospel/Good News' (NEB, Bahasa Indonesia, Balinese), 'the word of the gospel' (Kanarese), 'the holy word' (Tamil). Chinese uses a cultural equivalent, 'the way' (*tao*), and 'to hand down the way', in use for the teaching of the ancient sages, has become the normal term for proclaiming Christian doctrine.

3 ***it seemed good to me also, having followed all things closely for some time past, to write an orderly account for you, most excellent Theophilus,***

Exegesis: *edoxe kamoi* 'it seemed good to me also...'; here begins the main clause (see above).

dokeō 'to believe', 'to seem', also impersonal *dokei* 'it seems', or, with following infinitive 'it seems good'.

parēkolouthēkoti anōthen pasin akribōs 'having investigated from the beginning everything accurately'. This participial phrase serves to bring out the qualification of the author for his task.

parakoloutheō (†) 'to follow', 'to accompany', or 'to trace' (Phillips), 'to investigate' (Goodspeed). When taken in the former sense the word would imply that Luke had been familiar with what he described (cp. Rieu, "having kept in close touch with the whole course of these events"), that he was "a contemporary witness" (Moulton-Milligan s.v., p. 486, cp. also the literature quoted there). But this is against the general idea of the preface of Luke's Gospel, according to which Luke ranks himself with the many Gospel-writers who have to rely upon that which the original eyewitnesses have handed down to them, cp. *kamoi* 'to me also'. This has also a bearing upon the interpretation of *anōthen*.

anōthen (†) 'from the beginning', 'for a long time', syntactically going with *parēkolouthēkoti*. When interpreted as 'from the beginning' it goes semantically with the following *pasin*, 'all things', because it refers to the beginning of those things, not of the investigation, cp. "from their beginning" (Schonfield); when rendered 'for a long time' it qualifies the investigation as to its duration.

pasin, scil. *pragmasin* (cp. v. 1) 'all things'.

akribōs (†) 'accurately', qualifies *parēkolouthēkoti* when that word is interpreted as 'having investigated' (see above); when, however, *parēkolouthēkoti* is interpreted as 'having been familiar with', *akribōs* must go with *grapsai* 'to write'.

kathexēs soi grapsai 'to write for you in proper order', without grammatical direct object. Therefore several translations render the adverb *kathexēs* by means of a substantive which serves as object with *grapsai*, cp. RSV, NEB, Goodspeed.

kathexēs (also 8 : 1) 'in proper order', not necessarily chronologically but rather systematically, cp. Acts 11 : 4.

soi 'for you', i.e. 'for your benefit', as explained in v. 4, or 'in dedication to you', cp. Rieu, not 'to you', which would make the Gospel a letter to Theophilus.

graphō 'to write', 'to compose'.

kratiste Theophile 'most excellent Theophilus' or "your Excellency" (Moffatt, BFBS, and others). This title implies that Theophilus is considered to be a man of high social status. The question whether or not Theophilus was a Christian at the time when this was written is much debated but cannot be decided, since nothing is known of him beyond the mentioning of his name here and Acts 1 : 1. A majority of scholars favours the opinion that he was not (yet) a Christian (some think that the omission of *kratiste* or a similar adjective in Acts 1 : 1 implies that he became a Christian during the time between Luke's Gospel and Acts). From this supposition it follows that Theophilus is not to be included in *en hēmin* (v. 1), or in *hēmin* (v. 2), cp. *TBT*, 4.87f, 1953. *kratistos* (†).

Translation: This and the preceding verse specify in detail how Luke came to know the events he was to report in his Gospel. Such specification will be important for translators working in languages where the form of the entire narrative, or of parts of it, is dependent on the kind of evidence available to the speaker. Cp. e.g. Guaica, Warao and Shipibo, where a narrator has to indicate whether the events described and the speeches reported have been personally witnessed by him, have been told to him by others, are conjecture, or are legendary.

It seemed good to me, or, 'I was of the opinion (lit. the saying of my heart was)' (East Toradja), 'I decided' (Kituba; similarly Toba Batak, lit. 'I made-one my-mind'), 'I conceived the plan' (lit. 'it got into my head') (Sranan).

Having followed all things closely for some time past, to write... The participial phrase may be taken as having temporal or causal force. Where co-ordination is preferable one may say e.g., 'to look into all things..., to put them on paper' (Sranan); or, supposing another possible order of the events, "I..., as one who has gone over the...events, have decided to write..." (NEB), 'I also have investigated all things... Therefore I decided to write...'. *Having followed*, or, 'investigated' (see *Exegesis*); or, 'I have enquired from those who know' (East Toradja 1933). *All things*, i.e. all the things meant in v. 1; hence, 'all those events', 'all that'. — It is often not easy to reproduce this accumulation of qualifying expressions without producing a cumbersome sentence. One may bring together two terms in one phrase, e.g. "the whole course of these events" (Rieu, NEB), combining Gr. *anōthen* 'for a long time' and *pasin* 'all things'; or in one compound verb, combining the ideas 'closely' and 'investigation' (Javanese); or in one adverbial expression built on a root meaning 'complete', combining 'all things' and 'closely' (Thai). But one may not omit one or two of these qualifications, as has sometimes been done.

To write an orderly account, or, 'write one-after-another that-which happened' (Apache), 'write-completely item-by-item' (Kapauku), '...to put them on paper, to fit-everything-together just as it happened' (Sranan). In the latter case the resulting series of three co-ordinated clauses each beginning with a verb (cp. above on "having followed all things", etc.), suggests urgency and accumulation, and thus Sranan reproduces a closely equivalent stylistic effect, though using syntactic means different from those of the original.

For you, most excellent Theophilus. In languages using honorifics, pronoun and epithet may have to be combined in one honorific pronoun, or pronominal expression, cp. 'Your Excellency' in modern English versions.

The vocative, or form of address, *most excellent Theophilus*, may have to be marked as such by a preposed exclamational particle (e.g. in Toba Batak), or by a possessive (e.g. in Sranan, lit. 'my grand-master T.'). In some languages it must have another position, e.g. at the beginning of the discourse, or inserted close to the first words or phrases, e.g. 'As you know, Theophilus, many...', or must become an independent clause or phrase at the head of the dedication, e.g. 'To (lit. offered to) The Honourable Teofilus' (Balinese). In some languages the use of vocatives is restricted to special cases, for instance, to calling a person's attention when his attention has strayed (Machiguenga); then it may better be simply omitted here, or be shifted to another syntactic position, as mentioned above for Balinese. — *Most excellent*. Of this and comparable epithets or titles, such as, 'highly respected' (Navajo), 'dear' (English), 'rich/fortunate'

(Kanarese, used in addressing people of high position, socially or economically, and in Christian circles, the apostles), it is, of course, the conventional connotation that matters, not the literal meaning. Some languages, however, entirely lack such conventional epithets of polite address; then the translator has either to translate the word literally, with as result a term or phrase which by its very newness has a higher information load than the original (e.g. in Toba Batak), or to neglect it (as has been done in Toba Batak 1885, Tagabili). Usually the first solution is chosen, because of the feeling that a Bible translator should translate everything that is in the original. Yet a normal form of address with some informational loss may be preferable to an abnormal expression with an increase in information load. In Shipibo long epithets are far from polite, because they express ridicule; therefore the version simply has 'strong' here.

4 ***that you may know the truth concerning the things of which you have been informed.***

Exegesis: *hina epignōs* 'in order that you may know exactly'.

hina with following subjunctive 'in order that', here indication of purpose.

epiginōskō 'to know', 'to know exactly', 'to learn', 'to recognize'. In the present context *katēchēthēs*, however interpreted (see below), implies that Theophilus had already some knowledge of the Gospel facts but not enough to be sure of their trustworthiness. Hence *epiginōskō* carries here the nuance of 'knowing exactly'. The majority of translations do not bring out this nuance but the idea of 'knowing exactly' is also suggested by the object of *epignōs*, viz. *asphaleian* 'reliability', cp. Phillips, "that you may have reliable information". That *epiginōskō* would mean 'to have additional knowledge' is improbable.

peri hōn katēchēthēs logōn tēn asphaleian 'the reliability of the things that you have been taught'. The connexion of the whole clause is as follows: *hina epignōs tēn asphaleian* (*tōn*) *logōn peri hōn katēchēthēs*; the relative clause *peri hōn katēchēthēs logōn* (with incorporation of the antecedent *logōn*, cp. Bl-D, § 294.5) has been placed between the main verb *epignōs* and its object *asphaleian* in order to give greater emphasis to the latter, and because it is in accordance with literary usage.

katēcheō (†) 'to inform', or 'to teach'. When understood in the latter meaning the reference is to some form of instruction in the fundamentals of the Christian faith but not necessarily to what later became known as the instruction of the catechumens. In either meaning, therefore, *katēchēthēs* does not implicitly decide whether or not Theophilus was a Christian. If it is assumed that he is, then the more logical translation is 'to teach', but this assumption then is based on other grounds than the meaning of *katēcheō*, cp. on v. 3, and the most that can be argued from the present phrase is that it does not exclude the possibility that Theophilus was already a Christian at the time Luke's Gospel was written. Hence the mere fact that the meaning 'to teach' is favoured is in itself no indication of the translator's choice in this question. Both interpretations are well represented among commentators (cp. A-G s.v. 2 a) and translators, but the majority favour 'to teach'.

logos 'word'; here it must either be understood in the very general meaning 'matter', 'thing', cp. A-G s.v. 1 a ε, or in the rather special meaning 'story', preferably the former.

asphaleia (†) 'truth', 'trustworthiness', 'reliability', preferably the last.

Translation: *Know*, or, 'understand', 'discern clearly' (Chinese RC), *se rendre compte* (Jerusalem); the aspect is ingressive. In some languages 'to know/perceive' and 'to see' are rendered by the same term (Sranan); elsewhere exact knowledge is referred to by a figurative expression, 'to be clear to the self' (South Toradja).

The truth concerning the things of which you have been informed. This complex phrase usually has to be recast as a clause, e.g. 'that the things... are true', or, trying to reproduce the emphasis of the Greek, 'that the things... have actually occurred (Telugu), or, are perfectly certain (Tamil), or, are entirely reliable'. A further shift is found in Apache, 'that you may truly know the things..., how they happened'. Cp. also the Kituba and Shipibo quotations in the note on vv. 1-4. For *truth* cp. also *N.T.Wb.*/71. *The things of which you have been informed*, again, will often have to be restructured, e.g. 'what people have taught you' (Sranan), 'the words they told you' (Shipibo), 'the way you have learned' (Chinese UV), 'the things you have heard' (Tagabili).

5 ***In the days of Herod, king of Judea, there was a priest named Zechariah, of the division of Abijah; and he had a wife of the daughters of Aaron, and her name was Elizabeth.***

Exegesis: *egeneto...hiereus tis* 'there was a priest'. The narrative begins without any introductory word which connects the preface with the rest of the Gospel. *egeneto* is here equivalent to *ēn* 'was', cp. A-G s.v. *ginomai* II.

en tais hēmerais Hērōdou basileōs tēs Ioudaias 'in the days of Herod, king of Judea'.

hēmerai in the plural of the time of life as in v. 7, or activity as here. Hence Rieu translates, "in the reign of Herod".

Hērōdēs Herod I, the Great, who reigned from 37-4 B.C. as king over Palestine; appointed by the Romans, to whom he was responsible. *basileōs* is in apposition to *Hērōdou*, and without article because of the following genitive *tēs Ioudaias*.

hē Ioudaia 'Judea', properly of the southern part of Palestine, but sometimes used of the whole country inhabited by the Jewish nation, either including the Samaritans (here), or not (4 : 44; 6 : 17; 7 : 17; 23 : 5). When used in this wider meaning the name has both an administrative and a geographical connotation.

hiereus tis 'a (certain) priest'. The indefinite pronoun often serves to introduce someone or something new in the narrative, cp. e.g. 7 : 2; 10 : 31; 17 : 12.

onomati Zacharias 'of the name (of) Zechariah'. *onomati*, dative of *onoma* 'name', has adverbial function.

ex ephēmerias Abia 'belonging to the division of Abijah'.

ephēmeria (also v. 8) 'division', 'section', i.e. one of the 24 divisions into which the priests were divided for the performing of the daily service in the temple of Jerusalem, cp. 1 Chr. 24: 1-19. Each division served for one week, cp. Strack-Billerbeck II, 55ff.

kai gunē autō ek tōn thugaterōn Aarōn scil. *ēn* 'was', 'and he had a wife who belonged to the female descendants of Aaron'. Syntactically *gunē* (*ēn*) *autō* 'he had a wife' is the main clause and *ek tōn thugaterōn Aarōn* is an adjectival phrase modifying *gunē*, but semantically this phrase is the most important: not that Zechariah had a wife, but that his wife was also of priestly origin is what matters. Hence several modern translators change the syntactic pattern accordingly, cp. "his wife was a descendant of Aaron" (BFBS).

gunē 'woman', 'wife'.

thugatēr 'daughter', here in the plural denoting female descendants. The term 'belonging to the female descendants of Aaron' identifies Zechariah's wife as the daughter of a priest. This is in accordance with the rules of Jewish tradition, cp. Strack-Billerbeck II, 69f.

Translation: Above (first remark on vv. 1-4) it has been stated that Luke's directly addressing Theophilus is restricted to the dedication and does not continue in the body of the narrative. Consequently, in a language where the use of honorifics is obligatory the translator will from v. 5 onward no longer have to use the honorific forms that are required by Luke's relationship with and respect for the honourable Theophilus. But even so the translator still has a problem to solve. In the conversations he is recording he has to decide in which instances and to what degree he will make his personages use honorifics when addressing each other; in the rest of the narrative he must know how and when to refer respectfully to the persons, possessions, sayings and deeds of the participants in the events he is reporting. To that end he must study the social scene and the personal interrelationships described in the Gospel, trying to look at them from the viewpoint of the receptor culture, and then, in accordance with its norms of linguistic etiquette, to decide what are the rank and status of his personages in relation to each other and what honorifics are due to them. Some of the most common factors determining these norms are genealogical descent, occupation and age. The influence each of them has on linguistic etiquette, and the way they intermingle, differ from language to language; they may counteract each other (as in the case of a person of superior family or caste having an inferior occupation); their influence may vary with circumstances (in a public appearance, for instance, honorifics are more regularly and extensively applied than in the intimate sphere).

All this means that the use of honorifics often is not rigidly regulated and that, therefore, the translator has the responsible task of choosing between alternative renderings. If his choices are not in tune with linguistic etiquette, including its exceptions, the receptors will infer that he is an ignoramus, or, worse, they will misinterpret his intentions, supposing e.g. that he wishes to express disdain for his personages (when he does not use honorifics where they are clearly due according to receptor language norms), or to ridicule them (in the reverse case).

It is in these choices between alternatives that a subjective factor enters, viz. the point of view of the narrator, his opinion of the personages and his involvement in the narrative. The translator has to keep in mind that he has to tell the story from the viewpoint of Luke. Accordingly, he must try to view the social scene and to use the appropriate honorifics in the way a Christian of the second generation would have done had he been a member of the receptor culture. If with reference to Joseph, for instance, there is a choice between non-honorific language (because Joseph's actual position and occupation seem to have been rather low) and honorific language (because of his royal descent), he will prefer the second alternative, which agrees with the respect Luke would have felt, and the translator himself feels, for Jesus' human father. Similarly, in the case of Jesus, the hidden Messiah, he will probably prefer honorifics which agree with the fact that Jesus belonged to the Davidic clan. In recording Jesus' encounters and debates with the Pharisees he may hesitate whether to make Jesus address his adversaries in non-honorific language, or to envisage him as showing respect to the religious leaders of his people and using the honorifics due to them; he will probably be happy then, if linguistic etiquette allows him the reciprocal use of honorifics, since the public character of the occasions requires formal politeness on both sides. However, alternatives will not always be available. Thus, with reference to Jesus' disciples the actual historical circumstances described in the Gospel usually exclude the use of honorifics, even though a Christian may feel respect towards these followers and friends of his Lord.

In the following notes all this cannot be touched upon in detail, but by way of example a few problems of this kind will be discussed on the basis of some honorific languages best known to the present author, especially Balinese; cp. also on 1 : 31, 42; 68-75; 2 : 48f; 3 : 22; 4 : 3, 21, 23; 6 : 36; 15 : 21, 29; 20 : 19; 22 : 67; 23 : 3; 24 : 18, 25; etc. For a general discussion of the phenomenon of honorifics cp. also Nida, *BT*, 262f, and *TAPOT*, 117f; *TBT*, 8.52f, 56f, 211-214, 1957; 14.158-197, 1963.

The beginning of a narrative, or of a new section, may have to be marked by a specific expression, e.g. 'to-begin-with' (Malay), or a specific construction or sentence type, e.g. inversion of subject and verb. The form chosen should agree with the character of the story that follows. Thus the introductory term 'it-is-told' may suggest a fiction story in Balinese, and the same would be true in Sranan of the sentence type, 'there was a priest in the days of H....', whereas 'in the days of H.... there was a priest' is a good beginning of any story.

The introduction of a new unrelated character, either at the beginning of a narrative, as is the case here, or in the course of it, may be subject to specific rules. In Shipibo, for instance, one has to use an introducing sentence, followed by a characterizing expression in apposition to it,

'There was a man, one-whom-they-made-to-ask God (i.e. a priest)'. In Cashinahua, each new unrelated character is introduced by a one-phrase sentence, and then described. This may lead to a restructuring of the verse, so that Zechariah is mentioned first. Cp. also *TBT*, 17.16-24, 1966, on introduction of main characters and reference ties in Sateré.

In the days of Herod, king of Judea, or, '(in the time) when H. was king of (or, reigned over) J.'. The name may require an honorific name qualifier or title, e.g. 'His Majesty H.', 'king H.'. *King* (also in 7 : 25; 14 : 31; 19 : 38; 21 :12; 22 : 25; 23 : 2f, 37f), or, 'chief', 'the one in authority, or, command', 'the one who holds the country' (Kapauku, a newly coined phrase), 'the highest one-who-moves-the-head-from-side-to-side (i.e. headman)' (Navajo, see *TBT*, 13.31, 1962); cp. also *TH-Mk* on 6 : 14.

A priest, cp. *N.T.Wb.*/58f, and *TH-Mk* on 1 : 44. In a language like Balinese the rendering chosen refers to a priest of Brahmin caste, a person entitled to honorifics.

Of the division of Abijah, or, 'one of the group of Ab.', 'one of those-who-were with Ab.' (Navajo), or, 'one of those who held (i.e. were responsible) to the late Ab.' (Tagabili); cp. also 'that man, being an Abijah-ite (formed with an affix indicating membership of a group related to a person) used to work when their day of work was fulfilled' (Shipibo). *Division.* The Greek term views the referent as a group performing daily services (cp. Shipibo), but many versions have 'division' (which is formally closer to the O.T. equivalent of the term used), or, 'shift' (Thai), *classe* (Jerusalem). — Names of persons already dead may have to be marked as such, as is the case in this verse with Abijah and Aaron in Tagabili.

He had a wife of the daughters of Aaron, or, 'he had married (for which see on 14 : 20) one of the descendants of A.'; or, taking 'wife' as the subject (see *Exegesis*), 'his wife came-out (i.e. descended) from tribe of A.' (Kituba), 'his wife was of the family/clan of A.' (Hindi, Santali; Apache). For *wife* (also in 1 : 13, 18, 24; 3 : 19; 8 : 3; 14: 20, 26; 16 : 18; 17 : 32; 18 : 29; 20 : 28f, 33) cp. *N.T.Wb.*/75, WOMAN. In socially stratified communities the term used for a wife of the same caste or status as her husband (which is the case here) may differ from that for a wife of lower status. Elsewhere the term a husband uses when referring to his wife differs from the one applied by others to the wife when speaking to the husband. *Aaron* was considered the ancestor of all priestly families in Israel; hence such renderings of the clause as, "his wife also was of priestly descent (NEB), or, also belonged to a priestly family" (TEV), 'the parents of his wife Elizabeth were also priests' (Cuyono). — *Aaron* and some other biblical personages are also mentioned in the Koran, with the result that their names are rather well known to Muslims, in arabicized forms that are more or less divergent from the biblical ones. To adopt such forms, or to take them as model of transliteration, as has been done in several versions in predominantly Muslim countries, can be an acceptable procedure if the function the person in question has in the Koran is not intrinsically different from its biblical counterpart, and if the two forms of the name rather closely resemble each other (as is the case with *Harun*—for "Aaron", *Jibril* or *Jabra'il*—for "Gabriel", *Mariam*—'Maria'/"Mary",

Yusuf—"Joseph", *Nuh*—"Noah", *Da(w)ud*—"David", *Yunus*—"Jonah", *Ishak*—"Isaac", *Ya'kub*—"Jacob", *Sulaiman*—"Solomon", *Lut*—"Lot"); it is less acceptable when the differences in form are rather great (cp. *Yahya*—'Johannes'/"John"); but it is decidedly objectionable when there is a basic contrast in function of the two persons, as in the case of *Isa*—"Jesus", and *Ibrahim*—"Abraham" (cp. below on vv. 31 and 55).

The final clause, *and her name was Elizabeth* may better be embedded in the preceding sentence, as done in Cuyono (see above), Apache. For various renderings cp. *TH-Mk* on "what is your name" in 5 : 8.

6 ***And they were both righteous before God, walking in all the commandments and ordinances of the Lord blameless.***

Exegesis: *ēsan de dikaioi amphoteroi enantion tou theou* 'and they were both righteous before God'. *amphoteroi* 'both' is in apposition to the subject 'they'.

dikaios 'upright', 'righteous', i.e. he who lives and acts according to the will of God as expressed in his law, and wins his favour (cp. *N.T.Wb.*, 112/RIGHTEOUS). Here the religious aspect of the term is stressed by *enantion tou theou*, and by the appositional phrase *poreuomenoi* ... *amemptoi* 'walking ... blameless'.

enantion with genitive 'in the presence of', or 'in the sight, or, judgment of'. In the present context *enantion tou theou* means that God is the judge of their righteousness; therefore it seems less correct to render *dikaioi enantion tou theou* as "upright and devout" (NEB), or, "truly religious" (Phillips).

poreuomenoi en pasais tais entolais kai dikaiōmasin tou kuriou amemptoi 'walking in all the commandments and ordinances of the Lord blameless'.

poreuomai 'to depart', 'to go', here in the figurative sense 'to walk in', the commandments and ordinances being, as it were, the way on which one walks or goes.

entolē 'commandment', both human (cp. 15 : 29) and divine (as here).

dikaiōma (†) 'ordinance', 'requirement'. Although *entolē* and *dikaiōma* differ in gender they have in common the article *tais* and the adjective *pasais* 'all' (morphologically going with *entolais*, being the nearest of the two substantives), because they are very similar in meaning.

kurios occurs in Luke with the following meanings:

(1) 'master' (of slave or servant) in 12 : 36f, 42b-47; 14 : 21, 23; 16 : 3-13 (but cp. on 16 : 8), or 'owner' (with objective genitive) in 19 : 33 (colt); 20 : 13-15 (vineyard), or 'ruler (over)' in 6 : 5 (sabbath); 10 : 2 (harvest); 10 : 21 (heaven and earth); in this last meaning it refers either directly or implicitly to a divine ruler.

(2) in the vocative *kurie* as a polite form of address, used (a) by slaves or servants to address their master, see 13 : 8; 14 : 22; 19 : 16-20, 25. In 13 : 25 it is used by guests when addressing their host and best rendered as 'sir'; (b) to address Jesus. This may be rendered as 'Lord', or as 'lord', preferably the latter since it is a polite form of address, rather than a christological title (cp. *TWNT* III, 1085, 1092f). *kurie* in this meaning

occurs in 5 : 8, 12; 6 : 46; 7 : 6; 9 : 54, [59,] 61; 10 : 17, 40; 11 : 1; 12 : 41; 13 : 23; 17 : 37; 18 : 41; 19 : 8; 22 : 33, 38, 49.
(3) as a title ('the Lord') referring to Jesus, used by Luke under the influence of later Christian usage, with the connotation of royal power. In this meaning it occurs in 7 : 13, 19; 10 : 1, 39, 41; 11 : 39; 12 : 42; 13 : 15; 17 : 5f; 18 : 6; 19 : 8, 31, 34; 22 : 61. In 1 : 43 and 20 : 42 it is followed by the possessive pronoun *mou* 'my' and refers to the expected Messiah (which applies also to 20 : 44). For 2 : 11 see the note there.
(4) 'the Lord', following Septuagint usage, where *kurios* renders Hebrew *'adonay* when standing for Yahweh. It has this meaning in all occurrences in chs. 1 and 2 (except 1 : 43 and 2 : 11), and in 5 : 17, and furthermore in Old Testament quotations in 3 : 4; 4 : 8, 12, 18f; 10 : 27; 13 : 35; 19 : 38; 20 : 37, 42.

amemptos (†) 'blameless'. Here *amemptoi* is the complement of *dikaioi* as e.g. in Job 12 : 4. Syntactically it goes with *poreuomenoi*...*tou kuriou*, indicating the result of it: they were observing the commandments and requirements of the Lord in such a way that they were blameless. Several translations render it adverbially ("blamelessly") which is acceptable only as a second best rendering.

Translation: *They*...*both*, or more fully, 'Zechariah as well as Elizabeth', 'Z. and his wife with him' (Apache), 'the pair of them (lit. they man-woman)' (Balinese).

For *righteous* see *N.T.Wb.*/63 sub (2); *TH-Mk* on 2 : 17; 6 : 20.

Before God, or, in a verbal clause, 'as judged by God', 'as seen by God' (Shipibo); or with a further syntactic restructuring, 'God was considering both...to-be-righteous' (cp. Kituba). The phrase does not limit the righteousness ("only in God's judgment—not in that of men"), but defines and intensifies it. For *God* see *TH-Mk* on 1 : 1 and references, to which now should be added *TBT*, 7.126, 163, 1956; 8.146, 1957; 9.52, 1958; 10.102, 1959; 11.40, 1960; 13.71f, 1962; 15.118f, 1964.

Walking in, i.e. 'behaving/living according to', 'doing things according to', 'observing'. The verb is rendered by 'to follow' (Jerusalem, Kituba), 'to perform' (Thai, employing a form of 'to walk' that is mainly used metaphorically), 'to fulfil' (Shipibo, using a term of high cultural relevance that refers to the fitness of things).

Commandments and ordinances of the Lord. The two synonyms are reinforcing one another; therefore, they have sometimes been rendered by one phrase, e.g. 'words all themes', understood to mean 'commandments' because it goes with 'observe/obey' (Kapauku), 'the law the Lord had set them' (Sranan). *Commandment*, or, 'command', is often better rendered by a verbal phrase; hence e.g. 'what the Lord has commanded, or, has told people to do', 'the way the Lord put it' (Cuna), cp. also 'what he (i.e. the Lord) caused-to-follow' (the Tagabili rendering of "ordinances"). Rather often the more generic term 'word' (e.g. in Shipibo, Balinese, Hebrew), or 'spoken-word' (Maya, cp. Nida, *BT*, 198) can do duty for 'command(-ment)', since the context shows that this 'word' is spoken by one in authority and, therefore, is a command.

The Lord, see *TH-Mk* on 1 : 3 and references, to which is to be added *TBT*, 3.180-204, 1952; 8.148, 1957; 13.77f and 87f, 1962; 15.170f, 1964; *Indian Wordlist,* 116f. One should preferably use one rendering for the various occurrences of Gr. *kurios* mentioned in *Exegesis,* especially for those of the categories (2[b]), (3), (4), although this may imply the use of a rendering having a certain degree of foreignness that can only be overcome by use and teaching. Even then, however, it proves impossible in some languages to find such a *passe-partout,* especially in socially stratified cultures with correspondingly differentiated linguistic forms. In such cases there may be three, if not more, distinctive terms to render *kurios,* viz. (a) a word used with reference to a person to whom one owes allegiance, and as ordinary form of polite address, roughly covering the occurrences of categories (1) and (2[a]); (b) a word from the sphere of chieftainship or royalty to be used of the Messiah, the Davidic king of Israel, as expected by the Jews (in 1 : 43; 2 : 11; 20 : 42); and (c) a term referring to a divine Lord (such as *Rabb* in Arabic, 'Venerated-one' in Balinese), to be used in all occurrences of category (4), and, probably, in 10 : 21. The problem then is what term to choose when *kurios* refers to Jesus. In category (2[b]) one can best choose a term (d) that is more polite than the one mentioned under (a), preferably a reverent form of address. In category (3), where *kurios* characterizes Jesus as the universal king, to whom "all authority in heaven and earth has been given" (Mt. 28 : 18), one may hesitate between terms in the line of (b) or of (c), but traditionally the preference is for (c).

A solution along these lines is found in several versions, often with interesting differences in detail. Thus RSV uses, "sir", "master" in the occurrences of category (1) and (2[a]), but "Lord" in the other occurrences (and "LORD" for Yahweh in the O.T.). StV and NV make an arbitrary distinction between *heer* ('lord', 'sir') for categories (1) and (2[a]) and an archaistic form of the same, *Here* (in O.T. *HERE*) for the rest; similarly in Malay and Bahasa Indonesia (*tuan, Tuhan, TUHAN*). In Arabic, which differentiated between *Rabb* ('Lord') for God and *Sayyid* (a title of prophets and of the descendants of Mohammed) for Jesus, the revisers have shifted to *Rabb* in some occurrences of categories (2[b]) and (3). The revised Tamil version uses two words which are the same in meaning but different in form, viz. the Sanskrit word for 'Lord' when the reference is to God, and its Tamil equivalent with reference to Jesus. An interesting solution is found in Thai. In this language the usual rendering of 'God' has the basic meaning 'Lord'. This term has also been used to render *kurios* in the occurrences of category (4), but then it is specified by the addition of a familiar Thai symbol indicating that a name is to be understood with the term, which name is so well known that it need not be added specifically in writing, nor be pronounced. The same term is used when *kurios* refers to Jesus, but then the form is modified in such a way as to provide an arbitrary distinction, while preserving the basic meaning.

In honorific languages the alternative renderings discussed above may have consequences also for the level of honorifics to be used in the context.

Blameless, or, 'no one could scold them' (Shipibo), or, 'being perfect'.

In Sranan "walking in the commandments...blameless" has been rendered, 'without missing one thing of the law...'

7 ***But they had no child, because Elizabeth was barren, and both were advanced in years.***

Exegesis: *kai ouk ēn autois teknon* 'and they had no child' denoting the main aspect of their life which is relevant to what follows. To render *kai* as 'but' (cp. RSV) is to comment implicitly on the childlessness of Zechariah and Elizabeth and hence not advisable.

kathoti ēn hē Elisabet steira 'because Elizabeth was barren'.

kathoti (also 19 : 9) 'because of the fact that'.

steira 'barren'. In ancient Israel to have no children was a disgrace (cp. 1 : 25; 1 Sam. 1 : 2-2 : 10), or considered as divine punishment (cp. Lev. 20 : 20f, Jer. 22 : 30), but neither thought is implied here (cp. Gen. 18 : 11).

kai amphoteroi probebēkotes en tais hēmerais autōn ēsan 'and both were advanced in their days', not dependent upon *kathoti* but co-ordinate with *kai ouk ēn autois teknon* and adding to that phrase and the preceding one a third trait which completes the picture of Zechariah and Elizabeth: righteous, without child and beyond the hope of ever having one.

probainō 'to advance', in Luke only in the perfect and in a figurative sense, 'advanced in years', with *hēmerai* 'days', 'life', cp. on v. 5.

Translation: *They had no child*, or, 'they were childless, or, without offspring'. — *Child* has two basic components of meaning, (1) descent, in the Greek indicated by *teknon* 'child', 'offspring' (used here and in 1 : 17; 3 : 8; 11 : 13; 14 : 26; 18 : 29; 20 : 28f, 31; 23 : 28), or *sperma* 'seed', 'offspring' (20 : 28); and (2) age, in the Greek indicated by *paidion* (1 : 59, 66, 76, 80; 2 : 17, 27, 40; 7 : 32; 9 : 47f; 11 : 7; 18 : 16f), or *pais* (8 : 51, 54). Term (1) may be used for descendants in the first degree, or in further degrees (3 : 8); it can be expanded to cover other intimate human relationships, e.g. between teacher and pupil (similarly in East and South Toradja, where 'child of teacher' means 'disciple', 'pupil'), and even non-human interrelations, cp. 'children of a city' (13 : 34; 19 : 44), 'children of wisdom' (7 : 35). The word also has a component of relative age, since a person is older than his offspring. (In RSV "child" occurs moreover in "to be with child", rendering Gr. *ousē egkuō* in 2 : 5, which see, and *en gastri echousais* in 21 : 23). Term (2) usually refers to young persons; the age can vary from newly born to about 12 years, but age grades may also be specified, cp. "boy" in 2 : 43 and 9 : 42. In certain contexts this term may imply descent, since 'a person's young-ones' may refer to his offspring. Some receptor languages follow more or less the English pattern, e.g. French, Kapauku, Sranan, Bahasa Indonesia (where the use for non-human interrelations is wider, not only 'children of a city' for its inhabitants, 'children of a boat' for crew, etc., but also 'child of a gun' for bullet, 'child of a wheel' for spoke, etc.). Other languages have distinctive terms for 'offspring' (often obligatorily or preferably in the possessed form) and for 'young person', e.g. Balinese, East and South Toradja. Though the basic division may correspond with the Greek, there usually are differences in detail. Thus, a language may have more distinctive terms for age grades than the Greek, or less (see on 2 : 17). Or Gr. *paidion*, when used in close connexion with a young person's parents, may better be rendered by the term for 'offspring' (often with a possessive), e.g. in 1 : 80, or in 1 : 76 and 11 : 7 (South Toradja; similarly Balinese, which in 1 : 76 combines the two terms, 'little-one my child'). The same may be true of Gr. *pais*, when used as a friendly form of address by a person who is not the parent, cp. e.g. 'my-child/offspring' (East Toradja 1933) in 8 : 54. Reversely Balinese can in certain contexts use 'the little-one' in the sense of 'my (or, your) child/offspring'.

Was barren, or, 'one-who-did-not-bear' (Apache), 'could not give birth' (Bolivian Quechua, similarly Kituba, where the existing specific term 'sterile person' is primarily used of men). Sranan distinguishes between a term for barrenness in general, 'unable to get a child' (used here) and one for barrenness because of old age, 'closed womb/belly' (used in v. 36).

Advanced in years, or, 'old in months' (Tarascan), 'high in age' (Chinese L), 'already many their years' (Tagabili), 'about-come-to-an-end' (Navajo, in v. 18), 'past (the time of) having-children' (South Toradja). In some languages (e.g. Thai, East Toradja, Tagalog) the closest natural equivalent is simply, 'old/aged'; this fits the context in this verse, but less so in v. 18. Special problems are encountered in Shipibo, which counts age by age-grades: baby - child - adolescent - mature - old, with sex-distinction from adolescent on (hence two separate statements must be made), and prefers to use kinship terms instead of pronouns (hence 'her husband' must replace 'he'); this results in 'that woman was a-little-old-lady, and her husband was a-little-old-man'.

8 ***Now while he was serving as priest before God when his division was on duty,*** 9 ***according to the custom of the priesthood, it fell to him by lot to enter the temple of the Lord and burn incense.***

Exegesis: *egeneto de...elache* 'it happened...it fell to him by lot'. The phrase *egeneto de*, or *kai egeneto* 'and it happened' with a subordinate expression of time and followed by a verbal clause occurs 40 times in Luke's Gospel (in 8 : 40 and 10 : 38 in *Textus Receptus* only). It has come to Luke through the Septuagint where it serves to render Hebrew *wayy^{e}hi* with expression of time, followed by a verbal clause. The phrase consists of three syntactic elements, viz.

(1) introductory verb, *kai egeneto* or *egeneto de* without difference in meaning;

(2) indication of time, mostly in the form of *en* with following articular infinitive or accusative and infinitive, or in the form of a prepositional phrase, but sometimes appearing as a subordinate verbal clause or as a genitive absolute;

(3) connecting clause, in some cases linked to the introductory verb by *kai* but usually asyndetic; in 5 cases the connecting clause is an accusative

and infinitive dependent upon *egeneto*. Decisive for the translation of the *kai egeneto*-phrase is the function it has in the context of its occurrences. These functions may be classified as follows:
(1) introduction, or beginning of a narrative (24 times): (a) beginning of the narrative proper or description of the event that determines what follows (2:1; 3:21; 6:1; 7:11; 8:1, 22; 9:28, 51; 10:38 *Textus Receptus*; 11:1, 27; 18:35; 20:1), (b) description of the circumstances or the background of the narrative (5:1, 12, 17; 6:6, 12; 8:40 *Textus Receptus*; 9:18, 37; 14:1; 17:11);
(2) beginning of a narrative after preceding introduction (1:8, 59; 11:14; 19:29; 24:15);
(3) climax in a narrative (1:41; 2:6, 46; 17:14; 19:15; 24:4, 30, 51);
(4) transition in a narrative (2:15; 9:33; 16:22);
(5) close of a narrative (1:23).
None of these various functions requires a literal rendering of the *egeneto*-phrase, unless in the receptor language such a phrase exists and is used to express the semantic function in question. In many cases no such rendering is needed and it will be sufficient to use particles which have a similar function as the *egeneto*-phrase has in the case in question. For a full treatment of all New Testament materials cp. *TBT*, 16.153-163, 1965.

en tō hierateuein auton 'during his serving as a priest', articular accusative and infinitive. Most translations shift to a subordinate temporal clause e.g. RSV.

hierateuō (††) 'to perform the service of a priest'.

en tē taxei tēs ephēmerias autou 'in the turn of his division', adverbial phrase with *hierateuein*, indicating the frame within which the priestly service took place. Hence NEB, "when it was the turn of his division and he was there to take part in the divine service".

taxis (†) 'fixed succession', 'turn'.

enanti tou theou 'in the presence of God', qualifying *hierateuein* locally ('in the temple', where God was believed to dwell in the Holy of Holies) and by implication indicating to whom the service was directed.

enanti (†) 'opposite', 'before'.

(V. 9) *kata to ethos tēs hierateias* 'according to the custom of the priestly service', may go syntactically either with the preceding or with what follows. When taken with the preceding (cp. BFBS) the phrase qualifies *en tē taxei tēs ephēmerias autou* explaining that it was the custom of the priestly service that each division did its turn of temple service, but this comes near to a tautology (cp. Plummer). Therefore it is preferable to take it with the following, to qualify the casting of lots as the customary method to decide the task each priest had to do (cp. 1 Chron. 25:8). This is done by the majority of translators and commentators.

ethos 'custom', 'habit'.

hierateia (†) 'priestly service', rather than 'priestly office'. The genitive *hierateias* is qualifying.

elache tou thumiasai 'it fell to him by lot to make the incense offering'. The genitive *tou thumiasai* may be a genitive of object with *elache* (cp. Plummer) or be understood as an independent genitive of the articular infinitive complementing in free connexion the action of the main verb (cp. Bl-D, § 400.3,5).

lagchanō (†) 'to obtain by lot', 'to be chosen by lot'.

thumiaō (††) 'to make an incense offering'.

eiselthōn eis ton naon tou kuriou 'having entered the temple of the Lord', to be taken with *thumiasai* as subordinate to its (unmentioned) subject and not with *elache*, because the casting of the lots took place before the priest entered the temple (cp. Strack-Billerbeck II, 72).

naos 'temple', referring to the central building, as contrasted with *hieron* (cp. on 2 : 27) in RSV also translated 'temple' but referring to "the whole sacred area, including various auxiliary courts, side chambers and porticos" (cp. *IDB* IV, 551). Only priests were allowed to enter the *naos*.

Translation: In several cases, e.g. Kituba, Tagabili, Shipibo, the information implied in these verses must be made more explicit, and/or subordinated clauses must be changed in co-ordinate sentences. This may result in something like, 'One day it was the turn of Z.'s division, and he served as priest before God. Now the priests were accustomed to cast lots to apportion their duties (or, to decide what each had to do). When they did so on that day, it fell to Z. to enter...and to burn the incense.'

Now, or, 'one day', 'once', 'it-is-told' (Javanese), '(things) being thus' (Tamil, Kanarese), 'on a certain occasion' (Malay), all having transitional and/or introductory function.

He may be ambiguous; hence, 'Zechariah' in several versions. — Personal pronouns and pronominal reference play an important role in clause and discourse structure; their system and use are an intimate part of the linguistic structure, and differ from language to language. The translator, therefore, should not feel tied to the way Greek, or English, uses its pronouns (as done in many old versions, and even in some modern ones, unfortunately), but use, omit, add, substitute, or shift pronouns as required by receptor language usage. It is impossible in this Handbook to point out and discuss the problems in detail; only some rather general and obvious ones will be touched upon, and even those not systematically, but rather by way of example, cp. e.g., range of pronominal reference (1 : 11), full reference in a new section (2 : 22), pronoun and respect (3 : 22), sequence of pronoun and noun (4 : 5), pronoun and principal character (4 : 16). In the present verse the pronoun may have to be replaced by the proper name for several reasons, e.g., because here, where the actual narrative begins, a full reference is required; or, in languages where pronouns are neutral as to sex, because the pronoun would naturally be taken as referring to the person last mentioned in what precedes, viz. Elizabeth.

Was serving (or, acting) *as a priest*, or, 'was-priesting' (Javanese), "did his work as priest" (TEV), or simply, 'did his work', its specific kind being clear from the context.

Before God. The image is that of a servant working under the eyes of his master. Some possibly necessary semantic shifts are, to mention God's abode instead of God's person, e.g. 'in the temple' (see on 2 : 27); or to take God as the goal of the action performed in His presence, e.g. 'serving God as (his) priest', or, 'rendering priestly service to God'.

When his division was on duty, or, 'when the Abiah-priests had their turn' (Sranan), 'when the time came for him/Zechariah and his companions to work as priests'.

(V. 9) *According to the custom of the priesthood, it fell to him by lot*, or, 'as the priests used to do (or, always did), it was assigned to him by means of casting lots', 'when they (indefin.) cast lots, in-accordance-with the custom valid amongst the priests, it was he who was appointed' (Bahasa Indonesia 1968). *The priesthood* may have to be specified, 'the priests there' (Balinese), 'the priesthood in Jerusalem'. — Casting or drawing lots was probably used as a means to make the choice independent of human decisions. Often a specific idiom, or a reference to a cultural equivalent of 'to cast lots' can be used, e.g. 'to take out bamboo slips' (Chinese), 'each to pick-up which is-written (i.e. small sticks inscribed with characters and used as lots)' (Toba Batak), a term for divination by means of reed stalks (South Toradja). Elsewhere a descriptive or generic rendering must be given, e.g. 'to write on pieces of potsherd; to take one out' (Totonac, in Acts 1 : 26), or, 'to vie with each other', a reciprocal form of 'to win' (Tagabili). In some cases a cultural equivalent is not available, or it is felt to be unsuitable in this situation, e.g. in Kapauku (where 'to spin acorns' has the connotation of gambling); then one may have to state the fact without mentioning the means, e.g. 'it came to him' (Kapauku), 'it happened that he had'.

To enter the temple of the Lord and burn incense, co-ordinating the two verbal forms, and reversing their order. By this shift 'to enter' becomes directly dependent upon 'it fell to his lot', in accordance with the actual facts, appointment to burn incense in the sanctuary naturally including entering it. — *The temple* renders Gr. *naos* and *hieron* in RSV, but it is preferable to use distinctive renderings. For the latter see on 2 : 27; the former (also occurring 1 : 21f; 23 : 45) has been rendered: 'holy place', 'sanctuary', 'Shrine', 'house in which worship is carried out' (Navajo), 'inner part of the Great Temple' (Balinese, the term 'inner part' denoting the hindmost and holiest of the two or three courts that temples on Bali usually possess), 'womb (i.e. interior)-of-the-abode' (Telugu, in v. 21), or, a term denoting the main audience hall of a Buddhist temple compound (Thai). If the expression used contains a term for 'house of God', it may be possible to combine it with 'of the Lord' (cp. e.g., 'place of holiness of house-God Lord', Kituba), but often this is impossible. Then 'Lord' may have to be substituted for 'God' (Malay), or to be omitted, cp. 'deep in God's house' (Shipibo). — *To burn incense*, or "to offer the incense", 'to bring a smoke-offering' (Sranan), or, a causative verbal derivation of 'fragrance' (Tagabili). For *incense* one may use the name of some locally known sweet smelling spice or sap used for fumigation, preferably in religious ceremonies, e.g. 'benzoin' (Bahasa Indonesia), 'eightfold benzoin', an incense composed of eight ingredients, used in religious ceremonies (Balinese), or a more generic expression, e.g. 'fragrant stuff' (Thai) or, 'that-which-being-burned-smells-sweet' (Navajo).

10 ***And the whole multitude of the people were praying outside at the hour of incense.***

Exegesis: *kai* connects the clause of vv. 8f, expressing an event, with the clause of v. 10, which describes an accompanying circumstance. The relevance of mentioning this circumstance becomes clear in v. 21. Several translations shift from co-ordination of vv. 8f and 10 to subordination of v. 10 to vv. 8f, e.g. "while all the throng of people was outside" (Goodspeed, cp. also Moffatt, Brouwer, Menge).

pan to plēthos...tou laou 'the whole body of the people'.

plēthos 'large number', 'multitude' but often denoting a body of people gathered for religious fellowship or worship (cp. e.g. Acts 15 : 30; 19 : 9; also Lk. 19 : 37 where it refers to the body or community of Jesus' disciples).

laos 'people', 'crowd', in the latter meaning without religious connotation (so in the majority of occurrences in Luke). Several translators render *pan to plēthos tou laou* in one expression, as 'all the people' (20th Century, Kingsley Williams) where both *plēthos* and *laos* are taken in a non-religious meaning. Others (NEB, Rieu, Phillips) render 'the whole' or 'the crowded congregation', without indicating which Greek word is given a religious meaning. If *plēthos* is taken in its religious sense, the translation is 'the whole worshipping body of the crowd' and the genitive is definitive: 'consisting of the crowd'; if *laos* is taken to mean 'the people of God in worship', the translation is 'the whole crowd of the (worshipping) people'. Both interpretations admit of the translations of NEB, Rieu and Phillips, but the former interpretation is more probable.

ēn...proseuchomenon exō: three interpretations are possible: (1) *ēn* may be independent 'was there' or 'there was'; (2) *ēn* may go with *proseuchomenon* as a periphrastic imperfect: 'was praying' or 'was in prayer' (the use of a participle with a form of *einai* 'to be' instead of the imperfect is common in the N.T. and serves to emphasize the durative aspect, cp. Bl-D, § 353); (3) *ēn* may go with *exō*, 'was outside, praying'. The article *to* (*plēthos*) makes (1) highly improbable, and the order of the Greek words suggests (2), but translations as "stayed outside and prayed" (Rieu) do no violence to the sense of the Greek text, since the emphasis is on the fact that the people were outside while Zechariah had gone into the temple where was the scene of what was to happen.

exō 'outside', here outside the temple building (*naos*) but within the temple precincts (*hieron*).

tē hōra tou thumiamatos 'at the hour', or, 'time of the incense offering'.

hōra 'hour', here of the time when something takes place.

thumiama 'incense offering'; incense offerings were burnt at sunrise and at sunset. Probably, though not quite certain, the evening incense is meant here because of the crowd that is present, cp. Acts 3 : 1.

Translation: When the verse is rendered as an independent sentence, the transition from v. 9 to v. 10 may require special care. In some cases a connective like 'meanwhile' may suffice, but in others a more explicit transition must be made, e.g. by adding some such phrase as, 'when he was doing so'; or by moving forward the final phrase, e.g., 'while he burnt it, all the people were praying...' (Tagabili), similarly in Shipibo, which moreover has to state explicitly that Z. entered the sanctuary, and therefore renders v. 9^b as a statement not of purpose but of performance, 'And so he entered deep in God's house, in order to burn...'

The whole multitude of the people, interpreted as having no specific religious connotation, can be rendered, 'very many people', 'a very big heap of men' (Sranan), and cp. on "multitudes" in 3 : 7. If the other interpretation is followed, one may say, 'all those who gathered there for worship'. For *people* cp. below on v. 17.

Were praying. For 'pray(er)' (also in 1 : 13; 2 : 37; 3 : 21; 5 : 16, 33; 6 : 12, 28; 9 : 18, 28f; 10 : 2; 11 : 1f; 18 : 1, 10f; 19 : 46; 20 : 47; 22 : 32, 40f, 44-46) see *N.T.Wb.*/13, ASK, *TH-Mk* on 1 : 35 and references; *TBT*, 7.22f, 85f and 127, 1956.

Outside (viz. outside the place where Zechariah was officiating, i.e. the sanctuary) usually is easy to translate, but some renderings of Gr. *naos* ask for specific adjustments; thus the Balinese version uses 'in the middle court', the term indicating the court in front of the 'inner-part'.

At the hour of incense, or, 'when the incense was burnt/offered', 'when the incense-offering was made', or, 'when Zechariah burnt those things of smell of pleasantness' (Kituba).

11 ***And there appeared to him an angel of the Lord standing on the right side of the altar of incense.***

Exegesis: *ōphthē de autō* 'and there appeared to him'. The word order of the Greek, when retained in translation, necessitates expletive 'there'.

ōphthē, passive form of *horaō* 'to see', is used here and 9 : 31, 22 : 43, 24 : 34, in the meaning 'to appear', of beings who make their appearance in a supernatural manner, cp. *TH-Mk* on 9 : 4, A-G s.v. 1 a δ. The term denotes an objective appearance, not a subjective vision, as is shown by its frequent usage with reference to appearances of the risen Christ (cp. 24 : 34; Acts 13 : 31; 1 Cor. 15 : 5, 6, 7, 8).

aggelos 'angel', of celestial messengers sent by God (chs. 1 and 2; 4 : 10; 22 : 43; 24 : 23), of celestial beings who are with God in heaven (9 : 26; 12 : 8, 9; 15 : 10; 16 : 22), or of human messengers (7 : 24, 27; 9 : 52).

hestōs ek dexiōn tou thusiastēriou tou thumiamatos 'standing on the right side of the incense-altar', in apposition to *aggelos kuriou* and hence translated as a relative clause by Zürich and Menge. The emphasis is not so much on 'standing erect' as an indication of the bodily position, as on 'being there' (cp. A-G s.v. *histēmi* II 2 b β). Hence Phillips omits 'standing' and makes the rest of the phrase an adverbial expression with 'appeared'.

dexios 'right' as contrasted with left. The right side is the place of honour (cp. Mt. 25 : 33, Lk. 22 : 69, Acts 7 : 55, Rom. 8 : 34) and stresses here the dignity of the angel (cp. Lagrange and *TBT*, 2.30, 1951).

thusiastērion (also 11 : 51) 'altar'. The following genitive *tou thumiamatos* is definitive, 'the incense-offering'.

Translation: *And there appeared to him an angel...*, or, 'on that moment (or, then) an angel showed himself to him (or, came into his view)', cp. *N.T.Wb.*/11, ad (1). *Him*, or, 'Zechariah', for a reason similar to that in v. 8, or because the distance from the proper name is too long for pronominal reference, as in Thai.

Angel of the Lord. Two of the common renderings of 'angel' (see *N.T.Wb.*/9, and *TH-Mk* on 1 : 13) are 'messenger', 'sent-one', specified by 'of God', 'holy', or 'from heaven/heavenly'. In the present phrase (also in 2 : 9, and cp. "his angels" in 4 : 10, and "angels of God" in 12 : 8f; 15 : 10) the first mentioned specification is often, the second or the third in some cases, omitted, because 'of the Lord' already specifies the character of the messenger. For other occurrences of "angel" see *Exegesis*.

On the right side of. A literal rendering of this phrase may be unacceptable, because (1) the 'right side' (for which cp. *N.T.Wb.*/42 and 63, s.vs. HAND and RIGHT) has an unfavourable connotation, or (2) the phrase 'at the right, or left, side/hand' is customarily used only in speaking of living beings, but never, or only exceptionally, of objects. In case (1) the translator may substitute a functional rendering, e.g. 'at the place of honour', or he may add the function, e.g. 'at the right side of...and so honoured' (Isthmus Zapotec, in 1 Pet. 3 : 22). In case (2) the translator will try to use the indigenous way of indicating a local relationship, e.g. 'at the southern side of' (cp. *TBT*, 2.30, 1951). If such a rendering also has a favourable connotation (as 'southern (lit. upstream) side' would have in North Bali), he has translational luck; if it is unfavourable (as it would be in South Bali), he may shift the point of orientation, and say that the angel had the altar at his left (Shipibo), or, if this would exclude the figurative interpretation, he may use a functional rendering, which in Shipibo would lead to, 'nicely-beside (i.e. at the honourable side of)'.

Altar of incense, cp. *N.T.Wb.*/7. In Balinese the phrase has been rendered by a derivation of 'to smoke (fragrant spices)', viz. 'place-for-smoking'.

12 ***And Zechariah was troubled when he saw him, and fear fell upon him.***

Exegesis: *kai etarachthē Zacharias idōn* lit. 'and Zechariah having seen, was perplexed'. *idōn* in the aorist tense refers to an act preceding the event of the main verb; its object *auton* 'him' is to be understood from the preceding verse. Strictly speaking *idōn*, as a conjunctive participle, goes syntactically with *etarachthē* only, and not with the subsequent clause but semantically that clause *kai phobos epepesen ep' auton* 'and fear fell upon him' is as much determined by the fact that Zechariah saw the angel, as is *etarachthē* (cp. Phillips, Goodspeed, Willibrord).

tarassō (also 24 : 38), in the passive 'to be startled', at the sight of something supernatural.

kai phobos epepesen ep' auton 'and fear fell upon him', see above.

phobos 'fear', 'sense of awe', in Luke always of the reaction upon some supernatural happening as the appearance of an angel (1 : 12; 2 : 9), a miraculous healing (5 : 26), a raising from the dead (7 : 16) or some terrifying experience (8 : 37; 21 : 26). Because it is here parallel to *etarachthē* the emphasis is rather on 'fear' than on 'a sense of awe'.

epipiptō (also 15 : 20) 'to fall upon', 'to take hold of', here with *phobos* as in Acts 19 : 17.

Translation: For the use of *and* between clauses or sentences to express transition see *TBT*, 2.131f, 1951; 10.107-110, 1959, and Nida, *Science*, 210. The translator should ascertain what is the normal way to express transition in the receptor language, and translate accordingly. Such a procedure leads in some cases (e.g. in Malay) to the use of a transitional word, roughly to be rendered 'then', or 'next', with approximately the same frequency and regularity as in the Greek; elsewhere to the omission of such a word (as is often done in modern western versions), or, to its being replaced by a transitional construction, such as a special word, phrase, or clause order; or again to the insertion of a transitional phrase summarizing part of what precedes (cp. *TBT*, 15.18, 1964; 16.131, 1965). In some cases it is better to change from co-ordination to subordination, subordinating the 'and'-clause to what precedes, or the reverse. Finally, it is often necessary to use connectives that state the relationship between the sentences or clauses more explicitly than does the original, e.g. 'afterward' (2 : 20), 'meanwhile' (1 : 21[a]), 'consequently' (1 : 63[b]), 'at-that-moment' (4 : 17).

Was troubled, see *N.T.Wb.*/71, and below on "greatly troubled" in v. 29.

And fear fell upon him, or, 'fear gripped him' (Tamil, Kanarese, Kituba); or, avoiding the shift of subject, from Zechariah to fear, "he was...overcome with fear" (Goodspeed, similarly in Javanese). Expressions referring to fear occur rather often in this Gospel. The simplest and most frequent form is 'to fear', or, 'to be afraid' (e.g. 8 : 50; 12 : 4f; 22 : 2; or, 1 : 13; 8 : 25; 9 : 34); other phrases are used to bring out the ingressive aspect, cp. "fear came on all" (1 : 65), "fear seized them" (7 : 16), "they were frightened" (24 : 5), or a certain degree of suddenness (here) and intensity, cp. "they were filled with fear" (lit. 'they feared with a great fear', in 2 : 9), "they were filled with awe" (5 : 26), "they were seized with great fear" (8 : 37). Further occurrences of "fear" or "afraid": 1 : 13, 30, 65, 74; 2 : 10; 5 : 10; 8 : 35; 9 : 45; 12 : 7, 32; 19 : 21; 20 : 19; 21 : 26; 22 : 2. For "to fear God" see on 1 : 50. The concept 'to fear' is sometimes to be rendered by idiomatic expressions such as, 'the heart trembles' (Tzeltal), 'to feel him creep' (Valiente), 'to shiver in the liver' (Uduk), 'to have a little heart' (Tzotzil), 'to have a light heart' (Kabba Laka, contrasting with 'a hard heart' for 'courage', cp. *TBT*, 10.1, 1959); or, more strongly emotive, 'their thoughts left them', 'their hearts fell' (cp. *TH-Mk* on 4 : 41).

13 ***But the angel said to him, "Do not be afraid, Zechariah, for your prayer is heard, and your wife Elizabeth will bear you a son, and you shall call his name John.***

Exegesis: *eipen de pros auton ho aggelos* 'but the angel said to him'.

de serves here to bring out the contrast between this clause and the preceding. Luke prefers *pros auton* 'to him' to the simple dative *autō* after verbs meaning 'to say' but this has no bearing upon the meaning.

mē phobou 'do not fear (any longer)'; as in 1 : 30; 2 : 10; Mt. 28 : 10; Mk. 6 : 50; Rev. 1 : 17, he whose appearance caused people to fear reassures them so that they will stop fearing. The imperative of the present tense with the negation *mē* indicates that an existing condition should come to an end.

phobeomai 'to fear', 'to be afraid', 'to have respect for'.

dioti eisēkousthē hē deēsis sou 'because your prayer has been heard'.

dioti 'because', here equivalent to causal *hoti* (cp. Bl-D, § 456.1). The subordination of the clause introduced by *dioti* or *hoti* is often rather loose and the conjunction should be rendered 'for' (cp. RSV). Several translators do not translate it at all, taking the causal force to be implied in the sentence as a whole (cp. e.g. BFBS, NEB, Phillips). This is justified because the relationship between the two clauses is not directly causal: Zechariah's prayer has been heard and the angel is there to tell him so; this explains his presence in the temple and implies that Zechariah has nothing to be afraid of.

eisakouō (†) 'to hear'. When referring to a prayer being heard it implies that the request is, or, will be granted.

deēsis 'prayer', 'supplication', more specific than *proseuchē*. As to what Zechariah had been praying for, opinions of commentators vary considerably: (1) for the redemption of Israel and the coming of the Messiah (Plummer, Lagrange, Grundmann who compares Dan. 9 : 20), because it would not be fitting to pray for the fulfilment of private wishes when in actual priestly service; (2) for a son (Zahn, Weiss, Klostermann, Manson, Creed). There is no need to suppose that the reference is to the prayer he offered when in actual priestly service. It may well be that both interpretations supplement each other: Zechariah had prayed for a son in private and now he offered a prayer for the redemption of Israel. The angel tells him that his prayers have been heard and that he will have a son. But this son will have the task of preparing Israel for the coming redeemer. There is, therefore, no reason to press the question, but if a choice between the alternatives is necessary, (2) is preferable.

kai hē gunē sou...gennēsei huion soi 'and your wife will bear you a son'. *kai* is used here in an explicative sense, because the clause it introduces is best understood as explaining the preceding one, see above. *soi* is dative of advantage. Several translations express the relationship between these clauses by placing a colon (NEB) or semicolon (Phillips) after 'heard' without translating *kai*.

gennaō 'to beget' (1 : 35), 'to bear' (here).

kai kaleseis to onoma autou Iōannēn 'and you shall call his name John'. The future tense is not a continuation of the preceding clause referring to a future event but has the force of an imperative as often in Hebrew, cp. Bl-D, § 362.

kaleō 'to call' in several meanings. The normal Greek construction with *kaleō* when meaning 'to name' is with both the noun referring to the person to be named and the name in the accusative, cp. 1 : 59 *ekaloun auto...Zacharian* 'they were going to name him Zechariah'. Here and in 1 : 31, under the influence of Old Testament usage the noun referring to the person to be named is replaced by *to onoma autou* 'his name', cp. Gen. 17 : 19; 1 Sam. 1 : 20; Hosea 1 : 9 in the Septuagint.

Iōannēs Greek transliteration in abbreviated form of the Hebrew name *Iehochanan,* 'Yahweh is gracious'.

Translation: *Said to him.* Since Javanese and Balinese use an honorific verb, the roles of the participants are sufficiently clear, so that it becomes superfluous, and unidiomatic, to add 'to him' (cp. *TBT*, 14.161, 1963).

Be afraid, see on "fear" in v. 12.

Your prayer is heard. In many languages 'to hear a prayer, or supplication' does not imply its being granted, which concept has to be expressed by such renderings as, 'allowed' (Bahasa Indonesia), 'accepted' (South Toradja), 'received favourable hearing' (Chinese L); cp. also, 'God has accepted/granted the things you have asked-for' (Kituba).

Your wife Elizabeth. The appositional construction (for which cp. also Nida, *BT*, 271) has explicative meaning here (not distinctive meaning: 'that one of your wives called Elizabeth'). To prevent its being taken in the latter meaning it may be better to make 'your wife' appositional to 'Elizabeth'. Some languages (e.g. Shipibo, Toba Batak, Kituba) have to omit the proper name, because according to receptor language usage the mentioning of names is avoided generally, or a wife's name is not used when one speaks to her husband, or strangers should not know, or mention, the name of a person's wife, or for a combination of these reasons.

Will bear you a son. The dative of advantage *you* sounds unduly redundant in several languages; hence it is omitted e.g. in Hindi, Tagabili, Thai, Sundanese. Where 'child/son' is obligatorily possessed it may be possible to say, 'give birth to your child/son'. The expression *to bear a son* is variously rendered, e.g. 'to get a child' (Sinhalese, where the more specific term would sound indecent), 'to give-birth-to a male/a boy' (Tagabili, Navajo), 'to have-as-child a male (child)' (East Toradja), 'to cause-to-come-forth a male child' (Javanese); cp. also Nida, *BT*, 188. In some languages (such as Shipibo, which uses 'to child') it is better idiom not to specify the child's sex; this is acceptable, if the name in the next clause is a sufficient indicator of male sex. *Son* is used in the sense of offspring in the first degree (here and passim), or offspring in further degrees (see on 1 : 16); or in a figurative sense (10 : 6; 11 : 19; 16 : 8; 20 : 34 and 36, second occurrence); cp. *N.T.Wb.*/68f.

You shall call his name may have to be rendered by an optative verbal form, or equivalent phrase, because a wish often can express a kindly worded command, e.g. in South Toradja, Hindi. *Call his name*, or, 'name him', 'call him', 'give him the name', 'keep his name' (Hindi), 'make his name' (Toba Batak), 'set-up/establish (the) name (of) that son' (Thai), 'make that baby's name...for him' (Apache).

14 ***And you will have joy and gladness,
and many will rejoice at his birth;***

Exegesis: *kai estai...soi* lit. 'and there will be for you'. The meaning depends on whether *chara kai agalliasis* 'joy and exultation' (understood as one concept, see below) is (1) subject of *estai* or (2) predicate with it. When subject the meaning of *estai...soi* amounts to "you will have" (RSV, BFBS, Jerusalem, Menge) or 'will be your share' (NV, Rengstorf). When *chara kai agalliasis* is predicate, the subject is either 'he', i.e. John (Rieu, Brouwer, Segond), or 'this' (Goodspeed, Phillips) or 'it' (Moffatt) referring both to the announced birth. On the whole the former is the more acceptable interpretation.

chara kai agalliasis 'joy and exultation', best understood as expressing one concept, each word strengthening the other; hence NEB, "your heart will thrill with joy".

chara 'joy', the more general word.

agalliasis 'exultation', often with a religious connotation and, therefore, stronger than *chara*, as brought out by Willibrord, Zürich ('joy and exultation'), cp. also the verb *agalliaomai* 'to exult' (1 : 47; 10 : 21; 1 Pet. 1 : 6, 8). But because of the fact that *chara* and *agalliasis* go so closely together most translators do not differentiate sharply between them, cp. "joy and gladness" (RSV), "gladness and delight" (Goodspeed), "joy and delight" (BFBS).

kai polloi...charēsontai 'and many will be glad'. *kai* is slightly ascensive: not only you yourself will be glad but also many other people. There is no indication in the text to whom *polloi* refers.

chairō 'rejoice', 'be glad', a very common word.

epi tē genesei autou 'at his birth'. *epi* with dative indicates the cause of the gladness, cp. A-G s.v. II 1 b γ.

genesis (†) 'birth'.

Translation: *You will have joy and gladness,* or, 'you will rejoice and exult', 'you will be happy, very truly you will be happy' (Shipibo; similar emphatic repetition in Navajo, Apache); or, 'you will have great joy' (Tagalog), 'you will take-in (lit. eat) a very true pleasure' (Sranan), 'you being very happy will be overwhelmed' (Kapauku). For the close synonyms *joy* (also in 1 : 44; 2 : 10; 6 : 23; 8 : 13; 10 : 17; 15 : 7, 10; 24 : 41, 52) and *gladness* (cp. also 15 : 16, 32; 22 : 5; 23 : 8) see Nida, *GWIML*, 132; *TBT*, 3.90f, 1952; still other languages use expressions built on 'happiness of life' (Tarascan), 'to like' (Tepehua), 'the being lifted up of the heart' (East Toradja), 'warmth of the heart' (Toba Batak).

Rejoice (also in 1 : 47, 58; 6 : 23; 10 : 20f; 13 : 7; 15 : 5f, 8; 19 : 37), i.e. to have, or feel, or show joy, for which see above.

At his birth often is better rendered, 'that/because he was born', or made the subject of a causative verb, e.g. 'his birth will cause many to rejoice'. Such a restructuring may also affect the first line, because of the existing parallelism between the two, e.g. 'his birth will completely cause-happiness to you, and cause-happiness to many people' (Pampango).

15 ***for he will be great before the Lord,***
and he shall drink no wine nor strong drink,
and he will be filled with the Holy Spirit,
even from his mother's womb.

Exegesis: Vv. 15-17 form one series of co-ordinate clauses, together stating the reason for the rejoicing of Zechariah and the 'many'. Hence all clauses are determined by *gar* 'for' in v. 15. V. 15 describes John personally, vv. 16f describe his work.

megas enōpion [*tou*] *kuriou* 'great in the sight of the Lord'.

megas 'great', here in a figurative sense of rank and dignity as also indicated by *enōpion tou kuriou.*

enōpion preposition with genitive, 'before' of place, 'in the presence of', 'in the sight', or, 'the judgment of'. Here equivalent to *enantion* in v. 6.

kai oinon kai sikera ou mē piē 'and wine and strong drink he shall not drink'. There is no reason to take this clause and the next one as explaining *megas enōpion tou kuriou.* The relationship between the clauses is rather that the first describes the rank or dignity, the second the behaviour and the last the spiritual endowment of the promised child.

oinos 'wine', i.e. the fermented juice of the grape.

sikera (††) transliteration of an Aramaic word meaning 'strong drink'. The abstinence from wine and strong drink marks John as a Nazirite, i.e. a man who by a special vow had devoted himself completely to God and as an illustration of this devotion abstained from everything "that is produced by the grapevine" (cp. Num. 6 : 1-4).

ou mē piē 'he shall not drink'. *ou mē* with aorist subjunctive or future indicative is "the most definite form of negation regarding the future" (Bl-D, § 365; A-G s.v. *mē* D).

pinō 'to drink'.

pneumatos hagiou plēsthēsetai 'he will be filled with the Holy Spirit'. The endowment with the Holy Spirit characterizes John as a prophet since, according to Jewish interpretation, the Spirit was the "Spirit of prophecy" (cp. Strack-Billerbeck II, 127ff).

pneuma 'spirit' with the following meanings: (1) with *hagion* with or without article 'the Holy Spirit'; (2) *to pneuma* 'the Spirit', identical with (1); (3) the 'human spirit' (cp. on 1 : 47, 80), or 'life-spirit' (cp. 8 : 55); (4) 'evil spirit', causing bodily and/or mental illness.

pimplēmi 'to fill', except 5 : 7 always in the passive and here and 1 : 41, 67 of being filled with the Holy Spirit, i.e. the Spirit takes possession of the person who is filled by him (cp. Judg. 6 : 34) and enables him to prophesy.

eti ek koilias mētros autou 'even from his mother's womb', either 'from his leaving his mother's womb', i.e. "from his very birth" (NEB, cp. Rieu, Brouwer), or 'from the time when he was still in his mother's womb', i.e. "still in his mother's womb" (Willibrord; RSV, BFBS, Jerusalem, Segond, Zürich seem to follow this interpretation), preferably the latter (cp. Is. 49 : 1, 5; Jer. 1 : 5 LXX and A-G s.v. *eti* 1 a γ).

Translation: *Great.* Often physical size is not a metaphor for rank, cp. *N.T.Wb.*/41 and *TH-Mk* on 10 : 42f. Thus Shipibo, in view of John's function as a prophet, has 'he will have great thought', i.e. great power and ability, commanding respect; if John had been a governmental or economic figure, the rendering would have been 'precious', which refers to real or attributed worth.

For some special problems in rendering *to drink* (also in 5 : 30, 33, 39; 7 : 33f; 10 : 7; 12 : 19, 29, 45; 13 : 26; 17 : 8, 27f; 22 : 18, 30) cp. *N.T.Wb.*/31, EAT.

Wine and *strong drink,* see *N.T.Wb.*/74; *TH-Mk* on 2 : 22. If "wine" is rendered by a local equivalent, it is sometimes better given in a comparison, e.g., 'a drink like pulque (fermented agave juice)' (Mezquital Otomi); if a borrowed term is used, its meaning will become clearer when the second part of the phrase is rendered by, 'and other things that cause-to-become-dizzy/drunk' (Tagabili, similarly Kituba). Chinese versions have, 'light wine and strong wine', corresponding to the culturally well known pair 'rice wine and millet-gin'. If it is impossible to find two appropriate terms, the translator may have to use one phrase meaning 'all drinks that intoxicate', 'all fermented juices'.

He will be filled with the Holy Spirit. This clause refers to something that will happen and will induce an enduring condition. In some receptor languages 'to be full/filled' can be said only of material things; hence renderings such as, "the H. Sp. shall be with him' (cp. Tagabili), 'the H. Sp. shall entirely possess him, or, shall permeate him' (the latter in Shipibo, using a term said of medicines), 'he shall be under the control of the H. Sp.' (cp. Cuyono, for 4 : 1), 'the full strength of the H. Sp. shall stay in him' (cp. Valiente, for Acts 2 : 4), 'he shall carry the H. Sp. in his inner being' (cp. East Toradja 1933), and cp. *TBT*, 13.30, 1962. Instead of a reference to the person himself, one may have to use a term designating the centre of personality such as, 'heart' (Tzeltal). Care should be taken not to choose an expression suggesting demonic possession. For *Holy Spirit* (also in 1 : 35, 41, 67; 2 : 25f; 3 : 16, 22; 4 : 1; 10 : 21; 11 : 13; 12 : 10, 12) see *TH-Mk* on 1 : 8, and *TBT*, 7.162f, 1956; 8.146ff, 1957; and (on the word class of this term in Bantu languages) 17.32-38, 1966; for *holy* cp. *N.T.Wb.*/43-45; Nida, *BT*, 225-228; *TBT*, 7.128, 1956.

From his mother's womb. The first interpretation given in *Exegesis* may result in, 'from the moment he will come out of his mother's womb', 'from (the moment of) his birth' (Subanen, Tagalog), 'from the time his mother gives birth (to him)'; the second in, 'from the time he is/shall be in his mother's womb', 'from inside (or, beginning from when he lay in) his mother's womb' (Navajo, Apache), 'from the time his mother is-pregnant-of-him' (South Toradja), 'when he has not yet been born' (Kituba), 'from the time he (i.e. the child) causes-to-be-pregnant his mother'. Terms sounding vulgar in the receptors' ears should certainly be avoided, but the translator should keep in mind that what sounds rather too outspoken in his own ears may be perfectly acceptable and appropriate to his hearers or readers. For *mother* (also in 1 : 43, 60; 2 : 33f, 48, 51; 7 : 12, 15; 8 : 19ff, 51; 12 : 53; 14 : 26; 18 : 20; 24 : 10) cp. *N.T.Wb.*/55f.

16 *And he will turn many of the sons of Israel to the Lord their God,*

Exegesis: *pollous tōn huiōn Israēl* 'many of the descendants of Israel'.
huios 'son', here in the plural meaning 'descendants'. Hence many translators have 'Israelites' (e.g. BFBS, NEB).

epistrepsei epi kurion ton theon autōn 'will he turn to the Lord their God'.

epistrephō 'to turn', 'to return'; here in the sense of 'to bring back'. In the Septuagint the verb serves as a translation for several forms of Hebrew *šub* when denoting religious or moral conversion. Hence some translators have "he will convert" (Brouwer, NV, Rengstorf), but (1) 'to turn' keeps the metaphor of the Hebrew word better and (2) *epistrephō* is not a technical term for the description of some inner experience which may be associated with religious conversion.

kurios ho theos autōn 'the Lord their God', usually in Old Testament quotations (cp. 4 : 8, 12), but here and 1 : 32, 68 in passages strongly reminiscent of the Old Testament. The term is, therefore, to be understood from the Old Testament background as the Greek rendering of *Yahweh 'Elohim* in which *Yahweh* is a proper name and *'Elohim* a class noun.

Translation: *Turn...to.* More or less literal renderings are, 'turn them round again to' (Santali); or, 'turn their lives towards' (Sranan), 'turn-back the minds of the Israelites in order to go-in-the-direction-of' (Balinese), the words 'life' and 'mind' respectively serving to signal the metaphorical use of the verb; or again, 'bring forward (viz. to the place someone has left)' and 'lead cause them turn (and) return come seek'—closest natural equivalents in Kapauku and Thai, respectively. Possible other renderings are, 'cause to follow anew', 'cause to believe' (Shipibo), 'cause to seek/obey again'.

The sons of Israel, or, 'the people of Israel', 'the Israelites'. For *son* in the sense of offspring in further degrees (also in 16 : 25; 18 : 38f; 19 : 9; 20 : 41, 44) cp. *N.T.Wb.*/68.

The Lord their God. For these two nouns, used separately, cp. references on v. 6; for their combination in one phrase cp. *TH-Mk* on 12 : 29f. — *Their God.* In some languages the word for 'God' cannot be, or usually is not, grammatically possessed; in others the possessive pronoun conveys the wrong meaning, e.g., 'the God whom they have/possess/rule' instead of 'the God who rules/helps/guides them'; hence shifts to, 'he that is God to them', 'the One they acknowledge/obey as God', 'the God whom they worship' (Apache). Yet another pronominal problem is found in Shipibo, where the pronoun 'our' means 'your, their, and mine too', but the pronouns 'their' and 'your' imply 'not mine'; to translate 'their God', would imply that he is not the God of the angel speaking, nor the God of Zechariah. Hence the pronoun 'our' had to be used.

17 ***and he will go before him in the spirit and power of Elijah,***
to turn the hearts of the fathers to the children,
and the disobedient to the wisdom of the just,
to make ready for the Lord a people prepared."

Exegesis: The syntactic structure of this verse is rather loose. The main clause *proeleusetai enōpion autou* 'he will go before him', etc. is followed by two infinitive clauses, one (1) with the loosely attached final *epistrepsai* 'to turn', the other (2) with the unconnected final *hetoimasai* 'to prepare'. Clause (2) is either subordinate to (1), or dependent upon the main clause and then co-ordinate with (1). The former interpretation (represented by Rieu, Willibrord, Segond) seems to be slightly more probable, since clause (2) is the more general and comprehensive of the two, but the syntactic pattern is too vague to admit of clear distinctions. The semantic function of the clause beginning with *hetoimasai* however is clear: it serves to indicate with what intention John will 'turn the hearts of the fathers to the children and the disobedient to the wisdom of the just'; it is to prepare a people for the Lord.

kai autos proeleusetai enōpion autou 'and he will go before him'.

kai autos 'and he', unemphatic: there appears to be no reason for referring explicitly to the subject because it is the same as that of the preceding verb *epistrepsei* 'he will turn' (different in 1:22; 2:28, which see).

proerchomai 'to go before', as a forerunner (here) or as a leader (22 : 47), cp. A-G s.v. 2.

enōpion autou 'before him', cp. on v. 15. Here it has both a local meaning, 'some distance in front of him', and a temporal one 'going and coming sometime before him'. From the general usage of *enōpion* it follows that the local meaning is predominant, cp. A-G s.v.

en pneumati kai dunamei Ēliou 'in the spirit and power of Elijah', i.e. "possessed by the spirit and power of Elijah" (NEB). *en* means here as in 2 : 27 'under the influence of', or 'guided by'. The genitive *Ēliou* is not possessive but qualifying: John will be possessed by the same spirit as Elijah. *pneuma* does not refer to the human spirit but to the divine spirit, as usually when accompanied by a semantically related noun, cp. A-G s.v. 6 a.

dunamis 'power', often connected with *pneuma* (4 : 14; Acts 1 : 8; Rom. 15 : 13, 19; 2 Tim. 1 : 7) and here practically synonymous with it as in 1 : 35. Hence both words may be rendered as one concept, 'powerful spirit'.

epistrepsai kardias paterōn epi tekna 'to turn the hearts of the fathers to the children', a free quotation of Mal. 4 : 6 (3 : 23 in the Hebrew text); the emphasis is on the restoration of mutual relationship between fathers and children. Translations like "to reconcile father and child" (NEB, cp. Phillips, Goodspeed) are based on the idea of the Hebrew of Mal. 3 : 23 rather than on the exact wording of Lk. 1 : 17! The clause may refer to a restoration of parental affection (Plummer, Creed, Klostermann, Weiss) or to the winning of the older generation for the religious ideals of the younger generation (Zahn, Grundmann).

kai apeitheis en phronēsei dikaiōn 'and the disobedient to the wisdom of the righteous'. The phrase is still dependent upon *epistrepsai*, which implies that *en phronēsei* is equivalent to *eis phronēsin*, indicating to which John will turn the disobedient. For *dikaios* cp. on v. 6.

apeithēs (†) 'disobedient', here in the religious sense of 'disobedient towards God'.

phronēsis (†) 'way of thinking', or, 'insight', 'understanding'. The translation "wisdom" (RSV and many others) goes back to the latter, "ways" (NEB) to the former, which seems to suit the context better.

hetoimasai kuriō laon kateskeuasmenon 'to make ready for the Lord a people prepared', indicating the final purpose of the preceding clause.

hetoimazō 'to make ready', 'to prepare', virtually synonymous with *kataskeuazō*, but used with a different function: *hetoimasai*, qualified by *kuriō*, refers to the act as done by John for the Lord, *kateskeuasmenon*, past participle, refers to the outcome of the act (as brought out by BFBS, "thoroughly prepared"). Some translations take *kuriō* to go with *kateskeuasmenon* and render *hetoimasai* and *kateskeuasmenon* by one expression, cp. "to make a people perfectly ready for the Lord" (Goodspeed), but the position of *kuriō* immediately after *hetoimasai* and separated from *kateskeuasmenon* does not point to this interpretation.

kataskeuazō (also 7 : 27) 'to make ready', 'to prepare'.

Translation: *Him*, or, 'the Lord', because the mere pronoun sounds disrespectful (Malay), cp. on 3 : 22.

In the spirit and power. As shown in *Exegesis* the function of "in" often has to be described, e.g. by 'bearing', 'endowed with' (Kanarese), 'having received' (Shipibo); with necessary further shifts and expansions this may lead to such renderings of the phrase as, 'being dressed-in the spirit and having-as-attribute the power' (Javanese), 'having-as-spirit the spirit and having-as-power the power', 'having received the powerful/strong spirit', or to corresponding verbal clauses. For *spirit*, preferably to be rendered as in 'Holy Spirit', see references on v. 15; for *power* on v. 35.

Of Elijah, i.e. that (the prophet) E. had, cp. 'bespirited and bepowered as E. (was)' (Toba Batak 1885), 'his strength of spirit (will be) like the strength of spirit of E.' (East Toradja 1933), 'and the spirit and power that have influenced (or, driven/strengthened) E. also will influence (etc.) him.'

To turn the hearts of the fathers to the children repeats the verb of v. 16 but in different context; hence, the rendering may have to differ more or less radically, as in, 'make the fathers love their children' (Ponape), 'direct the hearts of the fathers towards their children' (South Toradja), 'cause men to think well again of their children' (Apache, where 'father' cannot be used without definite possessor; hence, 'men'). The plural in 'hearts' is distributive, that in 'fathers' and 'children' collective, expressing a category; in both cases some languages use a singular. For *heart* see *TH-Mk* on 2 : 6; 7 : 6, 19; *TBT*, 10.1-4, 1959; Nida, *BT*, 152f. The word (also occurring in 1 : 51, 66; 2 : 19, 35, 51; 3 : 15; 5 : 22; 6 : 45; 8 : 12, 15; 9 : 47; 10 : 27; 12 : 34; 16 : 15; 18 : 1; 21 : 34; 24 : 25, 32, 38) stands for the centre of the personality, the seat of emotions and/or intellect, etc. Here, as in some other cases, its use helps to signal the metaphorical meaning the verb has. In other languages, however, a direct reference to the person concerned is preferable, see some of the renderings quoted above. In Kituba a literal rendering would imply that a physical transaction was taking place, a quite dangerous idea in the local cultural context, which is avoided by saying, 'to return fathers to love their children'. — *Fathers.* The plural is distributive. For the noun, here used in the sense of a person's biological father (also in 1 : 59, 62, 67; 8 : 51; 9 : 42, 59; 11 : 11; 12 : 53; 14 : 26; 15 : 12, 17f, 20ff, 27ff; 16 : 27; 18 : 20; and in 2 : 33, 48, referring to Joseph, the supposed father of Jesus) see *N.T.Wb.*/33f. For *father*(*s*), i.e. 'ancestor(s)' cp. below on 1 : 32 and 55; for *Father* in the sense of Jesus' or the believers' heavenly Father on 2 : 49.

And the disobedient to the wisdom (preferably, way of thinking) *of the just.* To clarify the clause structure the verb rendering "to turn" often has to be repeated here, or a synonymous verb that fits this phrase better, cp. 'cause the hard-headed to accept the same thoughts as the people who do right' (Sranan), 'cause those who do not hear/obey to hear/obey the wisdom of the men who are good' (Apache), 'change the rebellious ones to think as the righteous think' (Tarascan). For *disobedient*, i.e. 'those who do not obey God' (Tagabili), cp. the above quotations, and Shipibo's 'the-not-to-be-talked-to', i.e. people who, though you tell them, do not want to do. For the verb 'obey' see on 2 : 51. For *just* cp. references on "righteous" in v. 6.

To make ready...prepared, or as a co-ordinated clause, 'and so (he will) make ready...prepared'. In translating this phrase the main problem is to prevent its sounding repetitive, or becoming a tautology. This will influence the way the verb and the participle must be rendered. *Make ready for the Lord,* or, 'form...for the Lord' (Willibrord, Français Courant), 'make the hearts soft for the Lord' (Huanuco Quechua); or again, because the phrase emphasizes the beneficiary, 'to put at the Lord's disposal', 'to provide the Lord with'. *A people prepared,* or, 'a people fit to be used' (Chinese UV). If the aim of preparation has to be made explicit, one may say, '...prepared for (or, to serve) him'. — *People* may have a generic meaning, 'several persons', or it may refer, as it does here, to a particular political and/or racial entity, such as Israel, and then has been rendered, 'nation' (see on 7 : 5), 'race', 'tribe', 'the hundred (sur)names' (Chinese UV, traditional for the totality of the Chinese people), or a term for the collective citizens (Chinese L). When that entity is seen in its relationship to a ruler or overlord, one may have to say, 'the subjects'. When that ruler is God, the same rendering often can be used (as is done here in Balinese), or a specific term designating a people as a religious community, e.g. the followers of a prophet or the worshippers of a god (Bahasa Indonesia). In some cases the term is used to indicate the common people in contrast to their leaders, see on 7 : 29.

18 ***And Zechariah said to the angel, "How shall I know this? For I am an old man, and my wife is advanced in years."***

Exegesis: *kata ti gnōsomai touto* lit. 'in accordance with what', i.e. 'by what sign shall I know this?', cp. A-G s.v. *kata* II 5 a γ.

ginōskō 'to come to know', 'to know'. Here it means 'to be sure of', cp. NEB, Phillips, Jerusalem.

egō gar eimi presbutēs 'for I am an old man'. The connexion with the preceding clause is as follows: Zechariah requested a sign because he could not believe what the angel had told him, and he could not believe it because he and his wife were old.

presbutēs (†) 'old man', substantive.

probebēkuia en tais hēmerais autēs 'advanced in her days', cp. on v. 7.

Translation: *Said*, often better, 'asked', because the verb introduces a question. A similar shift must often be considered before direct questions, e.g. in 1 : 34; 7 : 19 ("sent saying", i.e. 'sent to ask him'); 7 : 40 ("answering, said", i.e. 'in his turn, asked'); and, though less common, also before rhetorical questions, or exclamations having the form of a question, such as 2 : 48; 4 : 22, 36, etc.

How shall I know this?, or, 'how (or, by what means, or, by what sign) shall I know this is true', 'how (etc.) can I be sure of this (or, that this will happen)', 'how shall the certainty of this be' (Tagabili), 'relying on what can I know this thing' (Chinese).

Advanced in years, see on v. 7. If there 'old/aged' has been used, as being the closest natural equivalent, this rendering will sound repetitive in the present verse. Tagalog solves this problem by saying, 'I am very old already, and like that also is my wife'.

19 ***And the angel answered him, "I am Gabriel, who stand in the presence of God; and I was sent to speak to you, and to bring you this good news.***

Exegesis: *kai apokritheis ho aggelos eipen autō* 'and answering the angel said to him', i.e. 'and the angel answered him'.

egō eimi Gabriēl ho parestēkōs enōpion tou theou 'I am Gabriel who stand before, or, in attendance upon God', an implicit rebuke of Zechariah's unbelief by stating explicitly who he is and by whom he is sent (cp. Plummer). The participial phrase *ho parestēkōs* etc. is the more important part of the information Gabriel gives to Zechariah: not the fact that he is Gabriel but that he stands in attendance upon God is what gives him authority.

paristamai († in the perfect with intransitive meaning) 'to stand', 'to be present'. Here it expresses primarily that he is a servant of God. For *enōpion* cp. on v. 15.

kai apestalēn lalēsai pros se kai euaggelisasthai soi tauta 'and I was sent in order to speak to you and to announce to you this good news'. After introducing himself and stating his position Gabriel proceeds to describe the specific mission he is fulfilling at this moment; hence the aorist tense of the main verb and of the two dependent infinitives *lalēsai*. . .*euaggelisasthai*. Of these the former is the more general and describes in which way he was to fulfil his commission, viz. by speaking, and the second is the more specific and characterizes what he has to speak about.

apostellō 'to send away', or, 'to send out', implying the idea of a commission.

euaggelizomai 'to bring', or, 'announce good news'; the good news always concerns an act of God. When used with a specific object, as 'great joy' (2 : 10), 'the kingdom of God' (4 : 43; 8 : 1), the idea of the good news is still implied though not always expressed in translation. When used without any object of content the verb means 'to preach', as e.g. in 9 : 6; 20 : 1, but also implying the idea of the good news.

Translation: *Answered him.* In some languages the verb has to be followed by a word or phrase that introduces the direct discourse, e.g., 'thus', 'saying', 'with the words', 'its sound', 'his word (was)' etc. Since 'to answer' already implies a reference to the preceding speaker, some languages prefer to omit an explicit reference to that person.

Who stand in the presence of God, or, 'I am standing before God to serve him' (Français Courant), 'I am at God's service' (Spanish VP). The corresponding Javanese verb, lit. 'to face', refers to people who are sitting before a prince or noble, awaiting orders or seeking an opportunity to make a request, and a Balinese equivalent means 'to draw-near', 'to approach', and is the root of the term for 'servant-at-a-court'; such terms often are preferable to a literal rendering of the Greek phrase. The expression refers to a habitual state or occupation; hence one may have to add, 'used to', 'always', 'daily', cp. also "My place is at the side of" (Rieu).

I was sent to speak to you, or, 'God has sent me to tell you' (Kituba). In some languages one must take a decision about the time this happened, e.g. in Foe, which possesses a near past tense, for any event taking place on the day of speaking but prior to the moment of speaking, and a remote past tense, for anything that happened yesterday or before; in the present verse tense (1) has been chosen. For *to send* see *N.T.Wb.*/65f. The verb may have to be expressed analytically, 'to order a person to go', cp. 'being told to go, I came. . .' (Foe); if the implied direct discourse has to be made explicit, this becomes, 'to tell a person, "You must go"'. Some Indonesian languages distinguish between a verb used in reference to servants and errand-boys, and another implying a certain delegation of authority, and used e.g. in reference to Mohammed as Allah's deputy; the latter verb is employed here, of Jesus in 4 : 43, of the apostles, etc.

To speak to you, and to bring you this good news. The two verbs are closely connected; hence, 'to speak to you, announcing this good news'. Cp. also Kapauku, which uses a close-knit verb sequence, e.g. 'tell-you + give-you', which indicates a full declaration. *To bring you this good news.* Though the phrase here does not have the more specific sense mentioned in the note on 3 : 18, its rendering should preferably conform as closely as idiom allows to the rendering used in the expressions discussed in that note.

20 ***And behold, you will be silent and unable to speak until the day that these things come to pass, because you did not believe my words, which will be fulfilled in their time."***

Exegesis: *kai idou* 'and behold', imperative of *eidein* 'to see', used as a demonstrative particle, losing its force as a verb, and serving to focus the attention strongly on what follows which is usually something quite unexpected. Several translations therefore have a rendering which does not carry the idea of seeing but only arrest the attention, as "mark this" (BFBS), "listen" (NEB).

esē siōpōn kai mē dunamenos lalēsai 'you will be silent and not able to speak'. The periphrastic construction is used in order to express duration, as brought out by Phillips, "you shall live in silence", cp. Moule 18. *mē dunamenos lalēsai* indicates that Zechariah's silence will be compulsory.

siōpaō (also 19 : 40) 'to be silent', here in the sense of being unable to speak.

achri hēs hēmeras lit. 'until which day', i.e. 'until the day on which'.

anth' hōn 'in return for which' (cp. A-G s.v. *anti* 3), with loss of its relative force, 'because'.

hoitines 'which'. Some commentators (e.g. Plummer) think that the use of the indefinite relative pronoun suggests an interpretation like 'which are of such a character that...', but Moule (123f) quotes Cadbury who maintains that there is no difference in meaning between the definite and the indefinite relative pronoun.

plērōthēsontai 'will be fulfilled', i.e. what has been said will happen. When used in this meaning the verb refers mostly to the Scripture and its words, cp. A-G s.v. 4 a.

plēroō 'to make full', 'to fill', 'to complete', 'to fulfil'.

eis ton kairon autōn 'at their proper time'. *autōn* refers back to *logois* and the 'proper time' of Gabriel's words is the time which has been fixed by God for their fulfilment. *eis* 'to', 'into' refers to a future event, cp. A-G s.v. 2 a γ.

kairos 'point of time', or, 'period of time', here 'the proper time', cp. A-G s.v. 2.

Translation: In this verse five clauses can be discerned, viz., (1) "and behold", (2) "you will...to speak", (3) "until the...to pass", (4) "because you...my words", and (5), "which will be fulfilled in their time", to be taken either (a) as attributive to "my words" and characterizing them as true, or (b) as a separate piece of information referring to a future event. If the structure of the verse has to be changed in accordance with the historical oder of events, the clause order will become either, (1), (4), (5^a), (2), (3), cp. TEV, or (1), (4), (2), (3), (5^b), resulting in something like: 'But now listen. You have not believed my words. Therefore you will be...unable to speak, until...those things (or, the things I have told you) happen. They (certainly) will be fulfilled at the right time'.

And behold. For the Greek particle to be idiomatically rendered in most of its occurrences by an imperative form of a verb for 'to see' or 'to look' is the exception (on record for Kituba and Sranan) rather than the rule. Usually divergent renderings are required, dependent on what is idiomatic in the given context. A few examples must suffice. Where introducing something new, extraordinary, or unexpected, the particle has been rendered, "but now listen" (NEB), "learn then" (Rieu), 'mind-you' (Bahasa Indonesia) in the present verse, by interjections meaning, 'see, it's this way' and 'take notice' (Navajo and Apache) in v. 31, by "suddenly" (NEB, similarly Bahasa Indonesia), 'O wonder' (Low Malay), in 9 : 30; and in a verse as 13 : 30, bringing home the truth of a preceding parable, by "yes" (NEB, similarly Jerusalem), "indeed" (BFBS), "remember" (Rieu). In other verses it seems to ask for closer consideration; hence, 'now think how' (Willibrord) in 2 : 48; or to emphasize a reason, cp. "for, mark this" (BFBS, similarly Javanese, Sundanese), "for assuredly" (NEB), in 6 : 23. Or, again, the particle simply means, 'this here (or, that there) is/was', cp. "what is here is greater than Solomon" (NEB) in 11 : 31, or with a further shift, "I am the Lord's servant" (NEB and several others) in 1 : 38. Its demonstrative force may serve to mark a shift in focus, e.g. from the parents to the child Jesus (2 : 34), or from past to present, hence, 'but now' (13 : 35); or to introduce new persons (5 : 18); or to specify one person amongst many (9 : 38); or to start a new story (10 : 25) or episode (7 : 37), hence, "now there was" (Goodspeed). In some cases the particle cannot be expressed by one specific word or phrase, but is rendered by other means, e.g. by the beginning of a new paragraph, by specific word order (Jerusalem, in 5 : 18), or by an adversative connective, cp. 'whereas' (Sundanese, similarly Rieu) in 11 : 31f and cp. on 23 : 14, or, by a combination of the two latter renderings, cp. "but it is in palaces" (Rieu) in 7 : 25. Further occurrences of "behold" : 1 : 36, 44, 48; 2 : 10; 7 : 12, 24, 27, 34; 9 : 39; 10 : 3, 19; 11 : 41; 13 : 32; 14 : 2; 17: 21; 18 : 31; 19 : 8; 22 : 10, 21, 31; 23 : 15, 29; 24 : 4, 49.

In rendering the two expressions in *you will be silent and unable to speak* the translator must be on his guard against repetitiveness. In some languages it is better to combine them in one phrase, 'you will be dumb' (Thai, Tagalog), for which term see on v. 22; or one may render the second expression by a causal clause, e.g., '...silent, because you will not be able to speak', or, 'you will not speak, because you will not be able to do so.' In languages that have distinctive terms for speech as a mere faculty and as a special skill with magical or rational function, the first term should be used here.

Until the day that, or, 'awaiting the moment that', 'and this will not end before', 'up to the time that'. Here *until* implies a condition; hence, 'as-long-as-not-yet' and 'when/if not-yet' (Balinese and Javanese, in 12 : 59); or, 'only when', cp. e.g. 'only when what I said is fulfilled, you will speak again' (Shipibo, which has to add a positive reference to the return of speech; similarly in Apache). See also *TBT*, 16.134, 1965. If renderings of "until" have to be different in accordance with the length of time envisaged, as e.g. in Sranan, the more comprehensive one should be used here, since a period of more than nine months is implied.

Come to pass, or, 'happen', 'take place'.

You did not believe my words, or, if a personal object is required, 'you did not believe me when I (or, me who) spoke these words'; or again, more analytically rendered, 'you did not think, "His words are true", or, "What he just said will come true/will happen"'. Cp. also below on "faith" in 5 : 20.

Which will be fulfilled, when taken attributive to "my words", implies a contrast with Zechariah's doubt; hence several translators use an adversative or concessive connective (Kituba, Willibrord, or, Kingsley Williams, NEB). To preserve the expressiveness of the verb one may say 'surely happen' (Javanese), or, using a double negation expressing strong affirmation, 'not amiss' (South Toradja). For the verb cp. on 4 : 21.

In their time, or, "at their appointed time" (BFBS, similarly Javanese), 'at the time having-been-reached' (Balinese). In Sranan, where the equivalent expression is 'a time will come', the clause "which will be fulfilled in their time" has to be rendered, 'for yet a time will come (that) these things will come true'.

21 ***And the people were waiting for Zechariah, and they wondered at his delay in the temple.***

Exegesis: *kai ēn ho laos prosdokōn* 'and the crowd was waiting'. *kai* here introduces the description of what happened parallel with the meeting of Zechariah and the angel; hence NEB, Phillips, Willibrord render "meanwhile". The translation of *laos* depends upon the decision taken in v. 10, cp. "congregation" (Rieu) and "people" (NEB). The periphrastic construction *ēn...prosdokōn* 'was waiting' has a durative meaning.

prosdokaō 'to wait' (for something to happen), 'to wait for', 'to expect'.

kai ethaumazon 'and they wondered', in the plural because *laos* suggests the idea of many people. The imperfect expresses duration.

en tō chronizein...auton either (1) causal, 'at his staying away for a long time', hence "at his delay" (RSV), or (2) temporal, 'during his staying away for a long time', hence "while he tarried" (Plummer, Grundmann), or "during his tarrying" (Klostermann, Weiss), preferably the latter, cp. Bl-D, § 404.1. But (1) is not impossible here. The Talmud states that the priest prays only a short prayer inside the temple in order to keep the people from anxiety, cp. Strack-Billerbeck II, 77f.

chronizō (also 12 : 45) 'to stay for a long time', 'to take a long time in doing'.

Translation: *Were waiting for Zechariah*, i.e. remained standing outside till Z. came back from the sanctuary, expecting some benefit, probably Z.'s blessing; cp. *N.T.Wb.*/14, AWAIT. The durative aspect is expressed in several ways, e.g. by reduplication of the verbal root (Bahasa Indonesia), by a temporal adverb expressing duration, or by the meaning of the introductory word, e.g. 'meanwhile'.

They wondered at his delay. Aspect, see above. For the verb cp. *N.T.Wb.*/7f, AMAZE. To the figurative expressions mentioned there may be added, 'to listen quietly' (Tarahumara in Mk. 5 : 20, formally the opposite of the

Mixtec expression quoted in *N.T.Wb.*), 'to feel like dying' (Tzeltal, in Mk. 1 : 27, expressing high degree), 'to weigh heavily upon' (Sranan, with Jesus' astonishing teaching as subject, in Lk. 4 : 32), 'to cease to think with the heart' (Bulu, in Acts 2 : 7), 'to become like mute' (Sranan, in Lk. 8 : 56). South Toradja can use an expression (no longer felt to be figurative) that is related to the phrase 'the hair-on-the-body stays on end'. Where necessary the concept may be described, e.g., 'considered very strange' (Tzeltal, in Mk. 5 : 20), 'never having heard/seen/experienced anything like...', 'to say in his mind, "Is it really true that...?"' (Chontal of Tabasco, in Mk. 15 : 44). Navajo uses a similar rendering in the present verse, 'and he having-gone-into the sanctuary some-time-ago they thought, "What could have happened!"' In such a case the causal interpretation, viz. 'that/because/why he stayed so long' may become more attractive because it makes for better idiom and/or a less overloaded message; hence renderings such as, 'they said (which includes thinking), "Why does he delay in the house?"' (Shipibo), 'thinking why does he not come out yet' (Apache).

22 ***And when he came out, he could not speak to them, and they perceived that he had seen a vision in the temple; and he made signs to them and remained dumb.***

Exegesis: *exelthōn* 'having come out'; the aorist tense has pluperfect force here.

lalēsai autois 'to speak to them', refers probably to the blessing people expected from the priest (cp. Plummer).

epegnōsan 'they realized', cp. on v. 4.

hoti optasian heōraken 'that he had seen a vision'. This is a conclusion from the fact that Zechariah could not speak, not an observation on the part of the crowd.

optasia (also 24 : 23) 'vision', always of supernatural appearances.

kai autos 'and he on his part'. Different from v. 17 *kai autos* is used here emphatically and contrasts Zechariah with the crowd.

ēn dianeuōn 'he continually was making signs', periphrastic construction.

dianeuō (††) 'to beckon with the hand or with the head'.

diemenen kōphos 'he remained dumb', imperfect tense suggesting duration. *diamenō*, cp. on 22 : 28.

Translation: *When he came out* contrasts with his delay in the temple; hence, "when he did come out" (NEB), or, 'when he had arrived outside'.

He could not speak to them, echoing the wording of v. 20. In Navajo one must say, 'he tried to speak to them but could not'.

Here *and* introduces a conclusion; hence, 'thereby' (Leyden), 'so' (Javanese), '(only) then' (Chinese).

They perceived has been rendered in this context, 'it became clear to them', 'it-reached their heart', i.e. they came to the conclusion (East Toradja); Navajo uses the verb 'to think', modified by a particle expressing surprise.

Seen a vision. Several languages can use a rather generic expression, leaving the specific meaning to become clear from the context, e.g. 'to see something' (Sranan, East Toradja), 'something is made visible' (Apache), and cp. 'they knew, what he might have seen', i.e. they knew that something had been seen but not what (Shipibo). Elsewhere a specification must be added, cp. 'to see a divine sight' (Kanarese, South Toradja), 'he had seen something supernatural, which had appeared to him' (Tagabili). A term for 'vision' having the connotation of 'an illusion', suggesting unreality, should be avoided.

He made signs, or, 'he addressed (lit. talked-to) them in signs only' (Kituba), 'he made illustrations/examples' (Tagabili), 'he beckoned' (Balinese), 'he gesticulated' (Navajo). The noun refers to a motion or gesture by which a wish or command is made known or a thought expressed. The closest natural equivalent may be a term that refers to a specific gesture, cp. 'to nod' (Santali, Thai), 'to wave the hand' (Sranan). The meaning of the movement used should be carefully checked; where, for instance, 'to wave the hand up and down' means a command to draw near (as in Indonesia) it does not fit the context here.

And he remained dumb, or, 'he was dumb, he uttered no word' (South Toradja, emphasizing duration by the use of two synonymous expressions). In some languages (e.g. Balinese), the term 'dumb' includes deafness, as it does in the Greek, cp. on v. 62. In others the rendering simply is 'not able to speak' (Kituba, Navajo).

23 ***And when his time of service was ended, he went to his home.***

Exegesis: *kai egeneto* cp. on v. 8 and reference there.

hōs eplēsthēsan hai hēmerai tēs leitourgias autou 'when the days of his service were fulfilled', cp. on v. 57.

hōs 'when', cp. A-G s.v. IV 1 a.

pimplēmi 'to fill', of men filled with the Holy Spirit (1 : 15, 41, 67), with wrath (4 : 28), or fury (6 : 11), or of ships (5 : 7); in the passive 'to be fulfilled', of prophecies that come true (21 : 22), of a time that has to pass before something can happen (1 : 57; 2 : 6, 21, 22), of a period of time that comes to a close (1 : 23).

hai hēmerai 'the days', hence 'the period', cp. on v. 5.

leitourgia (†) 'service as a priest'.

apēlthen eis ton oikon autou 'he departed to his house', implying both departure from one and arrival at another place.

Translation: The verse forms the conclusion of the narrative told in vv. 8-22.

And is often not expressly rendered, because the temporal clause sufficiently marks transition. Where that is not the case an expression meaning 'soon afterwards' may be used.

When his time of service had ended, or, 'when he had finished (or, come to the end of) his term of service' (cp. *TBT*, 18.121, 1967, the rendering of "end" in Hebr. 1 : 12), 'after the last day that he had to serve (or, to work as priest, or, in the temple, or, before God, cp. on v. 8)'.

24 ***After these days his wife Elizabeth conceived, and for five months she hid herself, saying,***

Exegesis: *meta...tautas tas hēmeras* 'after these days' does not refer to the 'days' of v. 23, but to all that is told in vv. 8-23. Hence "sometime afterwards" (Jerusalem, Segond).

sunelaben 'became pregnant'.

sullambanō 'to seize', or, 'to conceive', 'to become pregnant', in the latter meaning only in Luke.

periekruben heautēn 'she kept herself hidden'. The imperfect tense suggests duration.

perikrubō (††) 'to conceal (entirely)'.

mēnas pente 'during five months', accusative of extent, answering the question 'how long'.

legousa 'saying', connecting what she said with the fact that she kept herself hidden. But this connexion is far from obvious. Some see in what follows the reason for Elizabeth hiding herself (cp. Kingsley Williams, NV) but most translators leave the connexion undefined.

Translation: *After these days*, or, 'some time later'. When rendering *day(s)* one must consider at least the following six basic components, (1) a period of light between the rising and setting of the sun, as e.g. in 21 : 37; (2) the daylight, as e.g. in 9 : 12; (3) a period of 24 hours, including the night, as e.g. in 13 : 14; (4) a unit for the reckoning of time, as e.g. in 2 : 21; (5) a certain point in time, as in 1 : 20, 80; and (6) a period of some duration, as in 17 : 24, often in the plural, as here, 1 : 39; 2 : 1, etc. Languages usually have distinctive terms for some or all of these meanings, cp. *N.T.Wb.*/22f.

Conceived. In several cases conception, or pregnancy are referred to by what are originally descriptive and/or veiled expressions, such as, 'got belly' (Sranan, similarly Kituba), 'having two bodies' (Bahasa Indonesia), 'be-of-womb' (Sinhalese), 'heavy' (Balinese), 'in-a-fortunate-state' (Toba Batak). The translator must be on his guard against possible vulgar connotations in the receptor culture, but also sensitive to the style of the narrative: euphemisms equivalent to 'in the family way' (as used in one version) are out of place here and therefore sound slightly ridiculous.

Month. A term for a period approximately corresponding with the lunar cycle from new moon to new moon (hence one word sometimes covers 'moon' and 'month'), or with one twelfth of the solar year, seems nearly always to be available. As a rule that same term can be used also in connexion with the menstrual period (cp. *TH-Mk* on "flow of blood" in 5 : 25), but exceptionally it may be necessary to introduce a specific expression or adjustment.

She hid herself. A too literal rendering may suggest furtive doings; then renderings such as 'she stayed in her house' (Tagabili), "she did not leave the house" (TEV), "she withdrew herself from view" (Rieu), will be useful models.

Sayings, or, 'and said'; or, at the head of the next sentence, 'She said' (Kituba), or, 'Meanwhile she said'.

25 ***"Thus the Lord has done to me in the days when he looked on me, to take away my reproach among men."***

Exegesis: *houtōs moi pepoiēken kurios* 'thus has the Lord dealt with me, or, treated me', cp. A-G s.v. *poieō* I 2 a β. *houtōs* refers to Elizabeth's pregnancy, and the perfect tense of *pepoiēken* shows that the emphasis is on the present results of the Lord's dealing with Elizabeth. The clause means to qualify this as an act of divine mercy; it is an exclamation rather than a statement, as brought out in Phillips' free rendering "how good is the Lord for me". Analogous exclamations in Gen. 21 : 6; 30 : 23.

en hēmerais hais 'in the days in which', 'in the time when', here used in a causal sense, "now that" (Goodspeed, Phillips).

epeiden aphelein oneidos mou 'he has looked on me, to take away my reproach', or 'has taken care, or, has deigned to take away my reproach', preferably the former; *aphelein* is a final infinitive. *epeidon* (†).

oneidos mou (††) 'my reproach' with objective genitive, cp. "the disgrace I have endured" (Goodspeed). The 'reproach' was her barrenness, cp. Gen. 30 : 23.

en anthrōpois 'among men', goes with *oneidos*.

Translation: *Thus the Lord has done to me*, or, better to bring out that the reference is to the state Elizabeth is in now, 'as-this here (is) the Lord's doing to me' (Javanese, similarly Toba Batak and cp. NEB), 'that I am like this, the Lord has done it for me' (Français Courant).

He looked on me, i.e. he cared for me, gave attention to me. In some languages closely similar expressions can have the required meaning, e.g. 'he looked-downward-on me' (East Toradja, especially said of the gods), 'his eye fell upon me' (Sranan). Elsewhere the favourable meaning must be made explicit, cp. 'to have compassion', 'to look graciously', 'to be kind' (Tagalog, Hindi, Apache).

To take away, or, 'to remove' (Kituba), 'to wipe off' (Hindi, Malay), 'to remove throw away (i.e. to remove utterly)' (Santali), 'to cause-to-disappear' (Javanese).

My reproach among men, or, 'what disgraced me in the eyes of men', 'things that were causing-to-see me shame before people' (Kituba); or, taking 'men' as the agent, 'the reason why people abased (or, laughed at) me'. The cause of the reproach or disgrace may have to be specifically mentioned, e.g. in Shipibo, which renders the whole phrase by, 'that they (indefinite) might not ever again reproach me for barrenness'. For "shame" cp. on 13 : 17.

26 ***In the sixth month the angel Gabriel was sent from God to a city of Galilee named Nazareth,***

Exegesis: *en tō mēni tō hektō* 'in the sixth month', viz. of Elizabeth's pregnancy, cp. vv. 24 and 36.

apestalē, cp. on v. 19.

apo tou theou 'from God' or 'by God'; if understood in the latter sense *apo* replaces *hupo*; if translated 'from God' *apo* denotes God as the initiator of the sending of the angel, cp. A-G s.v. V, 6.

eis polin tēs Galilaias 'to a town in (or, belonging to) Galilee'; the mentioning of Galilee gives a certain colour to the narrative since Nazareth and Galilee were despised by the Jews. For *eis* as contrasted with *pros* cp. on v. 27.

hē onoma Nazareth 'which had the name Nazareth', lit.: 'to which (was) the name'; in most modern versions rendered by 'named', or, "called" (NEB).

Translation: *In the sixth month,* if rendered literally, may easily be taken as referring to the sixth month of the calendar year. To avoid this misunderstanding one may make a more explicit reference to the events in vv. 24f, e.g. 'such-being-the-case in month six' (Timorese), *au sixième mois après ces evénements* (Français Courant), or to Elizabeth, e.g. 'in her sixth month', 'when six months of Elizabeth's time had passed'. In the latter case one may have to add an explicit reference to Elizabeth's pregnancy, making use of the idiomatic phrases the language possesses, e.g. 'when Elizabeth was with abdomen of six months' (Kituba), 'when (it was) already the sixth month of Elizabeth's carrying a person' (Tagalog); cp. also on v. 36.

Angel, cp. on v. 11. Renderings containing the expression 'sent-one' may prove troublesome in this context because the verb 'to send' occurs in the same sentence. To avoid repetition Toba Batak has, 'a heavenly-one was-sent' instead of 'a sent-one was sent'.

Was sent from God, or, 'by God' (see *Exegesis*). The first interpretation may lead to, '. . . Gabriel was sent by order of God', 'God caused. . . Gabriel to be sent'.

A city of Galilee named Nazareth, or, adding classifiers to the proper name, 'a city in the land G., named the city N.' (Low-Malay), 'a city named N., which is in the land G.', 'the city N., which is situated in (or, is part of) the region G.' The rendering should preferably not coincide with that of 'Nazareth of/in Galilee' (Mt. 21 : 11; Mk. 1 : 9), which is merely a geographic indication. — *City* (also in 1 : 39; 2 : 3f, 11, 39; 4 : 29, 31, 43; 5 : 12; 7 : 11f, 37; 8 : 1, 27, 34, 39; 9 : 10; 14 : 21; 18 : 2f; 19 : 17, 19, 41; 21 : 21; 22 : 10; 23 : 19; 24 : 49), or some such term as, 'houses which-cover-an-area' (Navajo), 'settlement', 'cluster of houses', in societies where the specific concept "city" is unknown; where it is to be distinguished from "village" (see on 5 : 17) one may say e.g., 'large settlement'. In rendering Gr. *polis* some English versions, e.g. RSV and NEB, differentiate between "cities" (for the large and/or important ones) and "towns" (in 8 : 4; 9 : 5; 10 : 1, 8, 10ff; 13 : 22; 23 : 50). If the translator follows this example he may use, 'very large settlements' and 'large settlements'; cp. also Nida, *BT*, 197. In some languages (e.g. Sranan, Bahasa Indonesia) the term used for "city" or "town" originally meant, 'fortified place'.

27 ***to a virgin betrothed to a man whose name was Joseph, of the house of David; and the virgin's name was Mary.***

Exegesis: *pros parthenon* 'to a virgin', like *eis polin* still depending on *apestalē* 'was sent' in v. 26. In this context *eis* refers to the place, *pros* to the person to whom the angel was sent.

parthenos (†) either has the general meaning 'girl', or the specific meaning 'virgin'; here the latter translation is preferable, since in v. 34 the fact that Mary has had no sexual intercourse, is stressed, cp. *TBT*, 9.97-126, 1958, esp. pp. 112f.

emnēsteumenēn andri 'betrothed to a man'.

mnēsteuō (also 2 : 5) 'to betroth', both times, as in Mt. 1 : 18, of Mary and therefore in the passive, 'to become betrothed'. According to Jewish law betrothal established a legal relationship between a man and a woman, binding upon both parties, cp. Deut. 20 : 7; 22 : 23-27. It took place after the conclusion of the marriage-contract between the parents, and was performed by the exchange of something of a certain value between the parties. The interval between betrothal and marriage was usually one year, during which time the woman and her property juridically already belonged to her future husband, and unfaithfulness on her part was considered adultery.

ex oikou Dauid 'belonging to (or, 'one of') the descendants of David', cp. A-G s.v. 3. This may refer either to Joseph alone or to both Joseph and Mary, but the former is the most probable since in the subsequent clause *kai to onoma tēs parthenou Mariam* the repetition of the word *parthenos* suggests the preceding clause refers not to Mary but to Joseph.

Mariam, Greek transliteration of the Old Testament name *Miryam*; an alternative form is *Maria*.

Translation: In some cases the verse can better be rendered as a new sentence, repeating the verb.

Virgin, see Nida, *BT*, 190; *N.T.Wb.*/75, WOMAN. Some other terms denoting 'virgin' are, 'woman that is untouched (a qualification current also for an object that never has been used)' (Toba Batak), 'a woman with a whole (i.e. unopened) body' (Timorese). In some cases, however, such terms, or descriptive phrases like, 'a woman who has not been with a man', are felt to be too outspoken. Hence, in English versions the rendering has been toned down from "virgin" (AV, RSV), *via* "maiden" (Goodspeed, Rieu), to "girl" (NEB), and in Toba Batak from 'woman that is untouched' to 'girl' (lit. 'female child'). Similar words for 'girl', 'unmarried young woman', suggesting virginity without explicitly stating it, are found in Marathi, Apache, Kituba. Cultural features naturally influence connotations of possible renderings, for instance, the child marriage customs in some Tagabili areas, where the boy and girl are made to sleep together at the initial marriage, but after that do not live together and may not see each other again for years. Hence, the closest attainable equivalent, 'female adolescent', does imply that a young girl is not living with her husband, and that she never had a child, but it leaves uncertain whether she has ever slept with a male person or not. Accordingly one has to depend on v. 34 to make clear that Mary and Joseph had not had sexual intercourse. A different problem is encountered in Pampango, where *birhen* (an adaptation of Spanish *virgen* 'virgin'), when standing alone, is a name of the Virgin Mary. To exclude this meaning the version uses 'marriageable *birhen*', thus at the same time indicating that Mary was relatively young.

Betrothed, see *N.T.Wb.*/52f, MARRY. In Israel a man's betrothed could be called 'his wife'; transposed in modern terms her condition was like that of a girl married by proxy during the period before she meets her husband; hence, a term for 'bride' may be considered. The new Pampango and Tagalog versions have adopted terms literally meaning, 'having-been-given-approval', and, 'having-been-brought-before-the-authorities', both said of a couple which has already applied to the local civil registrar or priest for a license to marry. Similarly, Tagabili uses 'braceleted', a figurative expression for the giving of property for the dowry, an act that finalizes the marriage contract. Several other versions use a term for 'promised in marriage', e.g. 'publicly pledged to marry (lit. 'reciprocally-bound')' (Timorese), a term indicating that an interchange of gifts as a pledge for marriage has taken place, and nowadays not implying secret sexual intercourse, as it did in former days. Such terms are acceptable if engagement to marriage is legally binding and officially made known in the village, as in Balinese customary law. Marriage customs, however, are changing rapidly, especially in urban centres, and the meaning of the term in question may change accordingly, e.g. from implying a strict and legal bond to a simple promise which can be broken unpunished. If the latter meaning is going to prevail, the term is too wide and loose to be used here. Descriptive renderings of the kind 'she was going to marry Joseph', 'J. had asked her to marry him', may be unsatisfactory because they lack the concept of being officially pledged or designated.

Of the house of David, i.e. a member of (or, belonging to, originating from) the house (or, lineage) of David, or, 'a descendant of David'. In some receptor languages the translator is able to keep close to the term 'house', e.g. in Marathi, which has a word meaning 'family', 'clan' from the same root as 'house'; or in Timorese, where the phrase 'old house' means 'the original family'. Usually, however, this is impossible, and a literal rendering would lead to expressions that have the wrong meaning (as in one older version, which by using 'inmates of the house' unwittingly made David a contemporary of Joseph and Mary, because in the language in question the phrase used happened to refer to people living together in the same house). In such cases a word for 'descendants', 'family/lineage/clan' is to be preferred. — *David* may have to be preceded by a title, 'King

David' (not 'Prophet D.', of course, although this is one of David's titles amongst Muslims).

28 ***And he came to her and said, "Hail, O favoured one, the Lord is with you!"***

Exegesis: *eiselthōn pros autēn eipen* 'having gone in to her said'.

eiserchomai followed by *pros* with a personal object 'to go to somebody', often with the connotation of going into somebody's house, cp. Mk. 15 : 43, Acts 10 : 3; 11 : 3; Rev. 3 : 20.

chaire, kecharitōmenē 'hail, O favoured one', play on sounds.

chaire imperative (this form †) of *chairō*, 'to be glad' (cp. on 1 : 14), used as a very common formula of greeting, its meaning ranging from 'hail to you' to 'hello', cp. A-G s.v. *chairō* 2 a. Some translators take *chaire* in the literal meaning and translate 'rejoice' with reference to Old Testament verses announcing the coming of the Messiah (Zeph. 3 : 14-17; Zech. 9 : 9). The former interpretation is preferable.

kecharitōmenē perfect participle of *charitoō* (†) here 'to bestow favour upon', 'to bless'. The precise meaning of the verb here (which to Mary is not quite clear as v. 29 shows) is explained by the angel in v. 30 'you have found favour with God', *charis* being the key to both expressions, cp. on v. 30.

ho kurios meta sou 'the Lord with you'; either with *estin* 'is' or *estō* 'be' understood. When understood with *estin* the clause is a statement, continuing and explaining the preceding vocative *kecharitōmenē* (cp. Judg. 6 : 12); when *estō* is understood the clause contains a wish (cp. Ruth 2 : 4). The former is preferable.

meta sou 'with you', *meta* with genitive here in the figurative sense of 'standing by' somebody, cp. A-G II 1 c β.

According to Jewish custom it was considered unusual to greet a woman (cp. Strack-Billerbeck II, 99); this explains Mary's bewilderment expressed in v. 29.

Translation: The verse continues the narration of events after the enumeration of additional details given in v. 27. The pronoun *he* often has to be specified, e.g. by using, 'the angel', or, 'Gabriel'.

He came to her. It may be preferable, or even obligatory, to say 'come to where she was' (Sinhalese), 'enter her vicinity/presence' (Dravidian languages), 'enter her house' (Javanese, Toba Batak, East Toradja, Sranan), 'ascend to her house' (East Toradja 1933, because the only type of house known at the time was one that was built on poles). In some languages the expression requires careful handling here, because 'entered her house', 'came to her', would suggest sexual intercourse; hence, 'he came and arrived where Mary was' (Kituba), 'he came gently to her' (Timorese).

Several versions can render *hail* by a word or formula commonly used in the language when greeting a person. Its basic meaning may be, (1) a term of well-wishing, e.g. 'peace to you' (Arabic, borrowed also in some Indonesian languages), 'you in peace' (Bambara), 'goodness' (Kituba), 'hither your soul' (South Toradja), "good morning" (Goodspeed, cp. *Problems*, 45f), 'live' (Tamil, cp. also *TH-Mk* on 15 : 18), 'be/stay well' (Balinese, Kapauku, where the use of the formula is rather recent); (2) a phrase for asking permission to enter or to depart (Toba Batak); or (3) a question like English 'how are you' (Cuyono), cp. also Sranan *odi*, a distant relative of 'how do you do'. Other versions use a form of the verb 'to greet', e.g. 'be greeted' (NV, Zürich), 'I greet you' (Français Courant). In some cases existing formulas of greeting cannot be used, as e.g. in Marathi, where the common Muslim greeting (*salaam*, lit. peace) is suspect to the Hindus in the area, whereas the Hindu formulas are objectionable to Christians, because they imply worship of the divine spirit within the person greeted; the translators solved their problem by using a neutral word for well-wishing. Elsewhere the custom of greeting and corresponding formulas do not exist (as e.g. in Tagabili, where the translator employs an interjection used to attract the attention of a person to whom one wants to speak), or terms for greeting do not refer to words but to gestures, e.g. 'to meet snapping fingers' (cp. *TH-Mk* on 9 : 15), which may lead to a rendering of "hail" by 'I meet you snapping fingers'. If the translator is of the opinion that the literal meaning of the Greek verb should prevail (see *Exegesis*), he should try at the same time to bring out its functional meaning, e.g. by using some such translation as, 'and greeted her with the words, "Be glad"', or 'and grasped fingers with her saying, "Rejoice"'. This is necessary because in v. 29 Mary expressly refers to her having been greeted.

O favoured one. In rendering the Greek construction (a passive participle used as a noun in the vocative) various shifts and/or additions may be necessary. (1) The form of address may become more natural by adding the name 'Mary', or the pronoun second person. (2) The agent, 'God', may have to be added. (3) One may have to shift from exclamation to statement, 'for you are made to rejoice' (Timorese), or (4) from passive to active voice, 'you whom God favours', or 'you who receive favour/grace' (Sranan, Bahasa Indonesia), or (5) to a combination of (3) and (4), 'God favours you'. The verb has been rendered, 'to help well' (Huanuco Quechua), 'to dispense fullness of satisfaction' (Kapauku), 'to value-highly' (Navajo), 'the breath to be with', i.e. to think of, or, to love (Tagabili); cp. also the references on v. 30.

The Lord is with you, or, 'accompanies you', 'is-near-to-you' (South Toradja), 'stands-by/takes-care-of you' (East Toradja 1933). In some languages the durative aspect is made explicit, 'continually is with you' (Tagabili).

29 ***But she was greatly troubled at the saying, and considered in her mind what sort of greeting this might be.***

Exegesis: *hē* 'she'. The article is used here as a personal pronoun (cp. Moule 123).

epi tō logō 'because of the saying'; cp. A-G *epi* II 1 b γ. The preposition indicates here that Mary's bewilderment is due to the angel's word; hence,

RSV, cp. *à ces mots* (Jerusalem) and "at what he said" (Goodspeed).

logos 'the saying', i.e. the words spoken by the angel, cp. A-G 1 a γ.

dietarachthē (††) 'she was (greatly) perplexed', probably stronger than *etarachthē* 'was perplexed' (v. 12), cp. L-Sc, s.v. *diatarassō*.

dielogizeto 'she stood there wondering'; durative imperfect after the (punctiliar) aorist *dietarachthē*.

dialogizomai 'to ponder', or, 'to argue', here the former.

potapos eiē ho aspasmos houtos, lit.: 'of what kind (or 'meaning') this greeting might be', hence: "what this greeting might mean" (NEB).

potapos (also 7 : 39) 'of what sort', always suggesting something extraordinary, either good (cp. 1 Jn. 3 : 1) or bad (cp. 7 : 39).

aspasmos 'greeting', always of formal or solemn salutations.

Translation: *But she*, or, preferably, 'thereupon she (or, Mary)'. In several languages a better transition is obtained by shifting the prepositional phrase to the head of the sentence, 'at (or, hearing) his word she...', or, 'when Mary heard what the angel was saying, she...'

Some idioms for *she was...troubled* are, 'her breath (was) anxious' (Tagabili), 'her mind was upset' (Marathi), 'she had a crumpled heart' (Bahasa Indonesia RC in 24 : 38), 'her members shook' (Navajo), and cp. *N.T.Wb.*/71. In Sranan one has to use an active construction, 'this word confused her'.

She considered in her mind, or, 'she was thinking/asking-herself', 'her heart said' (Toba Batak), 'she puzzled forth and puzzled back' (Sranan). The aspect is inceptive-continuative, for Mary started wondering and continued in that state.

What sort of greeting this might be. Direct discourse is obligatory, or preferable, in several cases, e.g. in Sediq, Kapauku, Dravidian languages. The clause is in the dubitative mood, to be expressed by modal verbal forms or particles, or by adverbial qualifications such as, "possibly" (Phillips). *Greeting.* If no specific verb for 'to greet (with words)' exists, an expression can often be used that is built on the word or formula of greeting, cp. on "hail" in v. 28; hence e.g., 'this *odi*' (Sranan), 'this well-saying' (Balinese). With some syntactic shifts this may lead to renderings such as, 'Why does he say (or, What can it possibly mean that he says) "hail" to me?' Where, however, the language does not possess a common formula of greeting, or the expression for 'to greet' refers to gestures, and not to words (cp. on v. 28), the verb may have to be rendered more generically, e.g. 'to speak (kindly, or, graciously) to'; hence, 'What in-the-world is-he-saying-to-me' (Navajo). To call attention to Gabriel's unusual behaviour (cp. *Exegesis*, last entry on v. 28) it may be advisable to use here, 'to deign to speak (kindly/graciously) to'.

30 ***And the angel said to her, "Do not be afraid, Mary, for you have found favour with God.***

Exegesis: *mē phobou* cp. on v. 13.

heures gar charin para tō theō 'for you have found grace with God', a well known Old Testament phrase; cp. Gen. 6 : 8; 18 : 3; 19 : 19; 30 : 27; 32 : 5; 33 : 8, 10, 47, 29, where the meaning usually is 'to win somebody's favour' with a view to receiving a boon; but here as in Gen. 6 : 8 and Acts 7 : 46 election for some specific divine purpose is implied.

charis 'attractiveness', 'favour', 'grace', 'goodwill', 'gratitude'.

Translation: *Do not be afraid, Mary.* The vocative, 'Mary', may have to be put at the head of the clause, e.g. in Marathi, Balinese, and/or to be preceded by an exclamatory particle. — In a language like Balinese the angel, as being God's messenger, uses non-honorific terms in addressing Mary.

You have found favour with God, or 'favour from God, or, God's favour, or, favour in God's sight'. Syntactic shifts may be preferable, e.g. 'the favour of God has happened on you' (Marathi), 'God has shown you his grace' (Kituba), "God has been gracious to you" (NEB). For *favour,* or, 'grace', cp. Nida, *BT,* 223; *TBT,* 1.120f, 1950.

31 ***And behold, you will conceive in your womb and bear a son, and you shall call his name Jesus.***

Exegesis: *kai idou* 'and behold'; cp. on v. 20. Here it emphasizes that Mary's pregnancy is proof that she has found grace with the Lord.

sullēmpsē en gastri 'you will become pregnant'; *sullambanō* 'to become pregnant' occurs with or without *en gastri* 'in the womb', without difference in meaning. *en gastri* also 21 : 23.

kai kaleseis cp. on v. 13.

Iēsoun the Greek transliteration of the Hebrew name Jeshua, and of its older form Joshua or Jehoshua, 'Yahweh saves' or 'Yahweh is saviour'; the name was both in its Hebrew and in its Greek form very common among the Jews.

Translation: The rendering of *conceive in your womb* often will coincide with that of "conceive" in v. 24, but it is stylistically preferable, of course, when the two can be differentiated, as is done e.g. in Timorese, which can use a parallelism here, 'you will conceive and become pregnant'.

Bear a son, see on v. 13, where a synonymous verb is used in the Greek.

In languages which, in addressing and referring to persons, have to differentiate words in accordance with status, the position Jesus has, and the one Mary has in relation to Gabriel, and the ensuing decisions as to the use of honorific and less or non-honorific words may form a problem. To solve it the translator should investigate more or less comparable cases in ordinary life (e.g. in Bali the case of a low caste girl married to a nobleman, a not uncommon and legitimate situation), or in folktales (where heavenly announcements to maidens about supernatural sons are not exceptional). Such a comparison will at least constitute a valid frame of reference for the discussion of the linguistic and cultural problems, and at its best may suggest an acceptable, sometimes quite unexpected, solution. Thus in Balinese the verse is in non-honorifics up to 'bear a son', but the clause "you shall call his name Jesus" is rendered in honorifics. In Thai, which has a highly developed system of honorifics and reckons with different degrees of highness, one has to take into account that Gabriel is speaking for God; this makes it unnecessary and undesirable to refer to the infant Jesus with terms of the highest level, such as would be proper for subjects to use in referring to their king's son. Whatever solution the translator chooses, however, somewhere it will probably have to be in conflict with normal usage in the receptor language, for the simple reason that the facts to be told do not fit in the normal experience of men. When the message requires it he must be ready to give theology precedence over linguistics, but in doing so he should exactly know to what extent and at what cost he deviates from usage, lest what he thinks to be a theologically sound rendering turn out to be only a nonsensical one.

As to different forms of the name *Jesus* cp. the list given in *TBT*, 4.104-106, 1953. For versions made in languages of predominantly Muslim countries 'Isa', the Arabic form of the name, as found already in the Koran, has been advocated (cp. *ibid.*, 83-86). Older versions have used it, some modern ones still do so. It is significant, though, that in course of time 'Isa', or a form based on it, has often been changed into (a form based on) 'Jesus', but that examples of the contrary procedure are less conspicuous. At least two objections can validly be made against the use of the Arabic form of the name. (1) The connotation of 'Isa' in Islam is very different from that of 'Jesus' in Christianity. It goes back to teachings of the Koran containing several statements about 'Isa', which are in open and intentional controversy with the Christian creed: he is held to be simply a prophet, one amongst many colleagues of whom Mohammed is the highest, "the seal"; it is stressed that he was nothing more than a servant, having no divine rights, and certainly not being the Son of God; he is said not to have died on the cross in his own body but in effigy only (cp. Sura 33 : 7, 40; 43 : 59; 5 : 116; 9 : 30f and 4 : 157). The name 'Isa', therefore, must be said to stand for the negation of much that 'Jesus Christ' means. Now cp. also, Nida, *TAPOT*, 83f, nt. 13. (2) The choice of 'Isa' tends to isolate its users from the rest of the Church, because 'Jesus', or forms based on it, are widely accepted all over the world.

32 ***He will be great, and will be called the Son of the Most High; and the Lord God will give to him the throne of his father David,***

Exegesis: *houtos* 'he'; the demonstrative pronoun serves here as a personal pronoun, cp. Moule 122.

huios hupsistou 'son of the Most High' is a parallel expression of 'son of God' (v. 35). The Old Testament knows only the king as son of God by adoption (Ps. 2 : 7) but Jesus will be son of God by birth, cp. v. 35.

hupsistos lit. 'highest' occurs either in the plural of the neuter (2 : 14; 19 : 38) in the meaning 'the highest places', hence 'heaven', or in the singular of the masculine as a name of God. As such it is a Septuagint translation of an Old Testament name of God which very probably also has the meaning 'highest'. Once it is combined with *theos* (8 : 28). Without *theos* it is regarded as a proper name and therefore used without article.

klēthēsetai 'will be called', refers not to a personal name as in the preceding verse but to an official appellation, hence 'will be given the title'. The agent is God. There is no contrast between *estai* 'he will be' and *klēthēsetai* as if the latter should mean 'he will only be in name', cp. A-G s.v. *kaleō* 1 a δ.

ton thronon Dauid tou patros autou 'the throne of his father David', i.e. the reign over Israel as once exercised by David. The phrase implies that the child Mary will bear is to be the Messiah. Since the expression *thronos Dauid* was well known, the apposition *tou patros autou* has predicative value and gives an additional qualification of the name *Dauid*.

patēr here 'ancestor', cp. A-G s.v. 1 b.

Translation: *Will be called the Son of the Most High.* This passive verbal form, or a corresponding impersonal active one, 'they (or, people/one) will call him...', often will be misleading, because the agent is taken to be men in general, the public. It is preferable then to use such a rendering as, "He will bear the title 'Son of the Most High'" (NEB), 'his name will be son of God (who) is in heaven' (Kituba). If an active verbal clause is obligatory, one may say, 'God will call him (or, give him the title/name) son of the Most High', or, if this would suggest that 'God' and 'Most High', have different referents, 'the Most High (God) will call him his son'. For *Son of the Most High* cp. on "Son of God" in v. 35. *The Most High*, or, 'the-one-who-is absolutely beyond-all' (Navajo, similarly in Apache, South Toradja), or a combination of two synonyms for 'high/long' (Timorese); cp. also *TH-Mk* on 5 : 7. In some languages the expression rendering "most high" cannot be nominalized; hence one may have to add a noun, e.g. 'the Highest Person' (Kapauku), 'God who (is) high/highest' (Bambara, Thai), 'the Lord on High' (East Toradja, cp. also Kituba quoted above).

The Lord God, see on v. 16. The term for "God" has to be possessed in South Toradja, 'our (inclusive)-Worshipped-one', similarly that for "Lord" in Apache.

Give him the throne of...David. In languages where 'throne' can be used metaphorically for 'rule/reign (as king)', only some minor adaptations may be necessary, such as, (1) "give him" becoming 'seat him on', 'cause him to sit on', 'cause him to possess (or, inherit)'; (2) "throne" being described, e.g. by 'large stool', 'stool/seat of the king' (Marathi), 'seat of commanding/chieftainship' (Totonac, Kituba), 'seat of the Supreme one (lit. of-him-who-has-the-umbrella)' (South Toradja, the umbrella being a well known symbol of power in various parts of South and South-East Asia), or again, 'glorious place to sit' (Kapauku); and (3) the qualitative force of the genitive "of...David" and the reference to the past being made more explicit, e.g. 'the throne that...David has sat on (or, has possessed)'. Non-metaphorically "throne" may be rendered 'kingship', 'reign/majesty/authority of king' (Balinese); where a verbal construction is preferable this may lead to, "make him a king" (TEV), 'give him that over-which...David when-he-was-ruler had-charge' (Navajo), or, 'our-

Lord God will cause Jesus to rule-over that-which David...ruled-over' (Apache).

His father David, or, if a predicative relationship cannot be expressed in the receptor language by simple apposition, '...of David, who is his (fore)father', or, '...of David. For (king) David is his (fore)father'. For *father*, in the sense of 'grandfather', 'forefather', 'ancestor' (also in 1 : 73; 3 : 8; 16 : 24, 27, 30) cp. *N.T.Wb.*/34. In some languages one usually speaks of 'forefathers' in the plural (cp. below on v. 55). Then the accompanying proper name will often be enough to qualify this collective expression as a singular; if not, it may be possible to use some phrase like, 'David (who is) one of (or, the principal one amongst) his forefathers'. In other languages, which do not possess any specific term for '(individual) ancestor', it often is possible to describe the concept, e.g. by saying, 'David, the founder of his lineage/family', 'D., the one he descends from'. In Apache it proved better only to translate the time element inherent in "forefather"; hence, "the throne of his father D." has been rendered 'that-which D. not-recently (i.e. a long time ago) ruled-over'.

33 ***and he will reign over the house of Jacob for ever; and of his kingdom there will be no end."***

Exegesis: *kai basileusei epi ton oikon Iakōb* 'and he will rule over the house of Jacob'; the subject changes abruptly from God in the preceding clause to Jesus.

basileuō 'be king', 'rule', in Luke always with *epi* followed by an accusative to indicate the king's subjects.

oikon Iakōb lit. 'the house of Jacob', i.e. 'the descendants of Jacob', cp. on v. 27.

eis tous aiōnas lit. 'into the ages', hence 'for ever'.

aiōn 'age', cp. *TH-Mk* on 3 : 29 and *N.T.Wb.*, 13f/AGE.

kai tēs basileias autou ouk estai telos lit. 'and of his reign there will be no end'. The place of the genitive *tēs basileias* at the beginning of the clause represents an attempt to carry over the dominating idea of the preceding clause (*basileusei*) into this clause.

basileia 'kingship', 'kingdom' or 'reign', 'rule'.

Translation: The verse is consecutive to v. 32^b; hence *and* may be rendered, 'then', 'thus', 'and so' (Navajo). The two clauses parallel each other, the second semantically repeating the first and thus reinforcing it.

The reference of *he* may have to be specified, e.g. by qualifying the pronoun by means of a deictic element, or by substituting 'your son', or, 'Jesus'.

Reign over, or, 'rule', 'be king/chief over', 'have power/authority over', 'command', 'hold' (Kapauku, cp. on "king" in 1 : 5).

House of Jacob refers to a group that is coextensive with the people Israel, whereas "house of David" in v. 27 refers to the royal clan; accordingly "house" may have to be rendered differently here, e.g. by 'people/tribe' (East Toradja), 'all-the-progeny' (Balinese, instead of 'descendants' in v. 27).

For ever, or, 'age after age' (Marathi), reduplication of 'age' (Telugu), reduplication of 'what-day/when' (Tamil), 'in-long-length(-of-time)' (Malay and Toba Batak); or a negative phrase, e.g. 'without an end(ing)' (Tagabili). See also *N.T.Wb.*/4f, AGE.

Of his kingdom there will be no end, or, 'the length of his being-king will be without limit' (Balinese), 'he will never stop commanding' (Bolivian Quechua), 'his chieftainship will not finish' (East Toradja), 'his reign will not come to a stopping place' (Chokwe, see *TBT*, 5.89, 1954). For *kingdom* (also in 4 : 5; 11 : 2, 17f; 12 : 31f; 21 : 10; 22 : 29f) see on "king" in 1 : 5 and on "kingdom of God" in 4 : 43. If this noun has to be rendered by a verb, e.g. 'he will rule (as king)' and/or if "forever" in the preceding clause has to be rendered by a negative phrase, e.g. 'without end', the two clauses may come to resemble each other too closely. In order to avoid repetition then the translator may try lexical differentiation, e.g. by the use of synonyms, such as 'exercise authority' after 'hold/rule' (Kapauku), 'be chieftain' after 'have-as-subjects' (cp. East Toradja 1933), and/or, 'without limit', 'unrestricted' after 'without end'; or he may try to turn repetition to advantage, and say in the second clause something like, 'indeed, reign without end he will', cp. also the Sranan rendering of this verse, 'he will be king over..., he will remain king...'.

34 ***And Mary said to the angel, "How can this be, since I have no husband?"***

Exegesis: *pōs estai touto* lit. 'how will this be'; *touto* refers to what is announced in v. 31, and the clause expresses Mary's astonishment, rather than curiosity or unbelief.

pōs 'how', inquires after the way in which something happens, but also after the possibility as in 20 : 41, 44; Jn. 12 : 34; hence the translation 'how can this be?'

epei andra ou ginōskō 'since I have no sexual relationship with a man'; *andra* means 'any man' including Joseph. The phrase does not refer to marriage (cp. on v. 27). The present tense implies that Mary expects the angel's prophecy to be fulfilled shortly. *ginōskō* denoting sexual intercourse is Hebrew usage, cp. e.g. Gen. 4 : 1, 17.

epei 'because', 'since'.

Translation: *How can this be,* or, 'how will this be possible' (Français Courant), or, "how will this be brought about" (Rieu), or more explicitly, 'how can I become pregnant' (Cuyono).

I have no husband, lit. 'I do not know a man'. In several other languages besides Hebrew and Greek the verb 'to know' can be used with reference to sexual intercourse (or especially to the first intercourse a person has), e.g. in Marathi, Sranan, Balinese, Timorese, Moré, where necessary slightly adjusting the clause, e.g. 'there is no man that knows my body' (East Toradja). In the many languages, however, where 'to know' cannot have this metaphorical meaning, another current expression for cohabitation must be used, which should be clear without being vulgar, cp. "I have not lain with any man" (Rieu), "I am a virgin" (TEV), 'I live with no man' (Bolivian Quechua), the dual form of the verb 'to stay/be-present' (Kapauku), 'I have not yet been/joined with a man' (Kituba, Thai). Cp. also *TBT*, 12.42f, 1961. In some languages a speaker has to use a specific negative particle when he knows, or supposes, that the event he is denying for the present will happen in the future. As it is normal for a betrothed girl to suppose sexual relationship in the future, several versions use 'not-yet' here, e.g. Apache, Navajo, Tagabili, Sranan, Bahasa Indonesia, Balinese, also Thai, Kituba (see above). To demonstrate the importance of this point Navajo may be cited, in which language the rendering 'my-husband yet being-lacking' conveys the intended meaning, whereas without 'yet' the phrase would suggest either, 'I have no husband', or, 'my husband is not here just now', or, 'my husband is dead'.

35 ***And the angel said to her,***
"The Holy Spirit will come upon you,
and the power of the Most High will overshadow you;
therefore the child to be born will be called holy, the Son of God.

Exegesis: *kai apokritheis ho aggelos eipen*, see on v. 19.

pneuma hagion epeleusetai epi se 'the Holy Spirit will come upon you', see on v. 15.

eperchomai 'to come over, or, upon', here (as in Acts 1 : 8) of the Holy Spirit coming down upon a person.

dunamis hupsistou 'the power of the Most High'; for *dunamis* cp. on v. 17 and for *hupsistou* on v. 32. The expression is almost synonymous with *pneuma hagion*, the difference being that *pneuma* has in view the character of divine action and *dunamis* its effectiveness.

episkiasei soi lit. "will draw its shadow over you" (Rieu).

episkiazō (also 9 : 34) 'to throw a shadow upon', used in Luke to express the divine presence (cp. Ex. 40 : 35). The literal renderings in most modern translations are due to the fact that the idiom has passed over from the Greek into modern languages. There is no reason to see in *episkiazō* a veiled reference to a divine act of begetting.

dio kai 'therefore too'.

dio (also 7 : 7) 'for that reason'; *kai* here reinforces *dio* and serves to introduce a statement that follows from the preceding (cp. Bl-D, § 442.12).

to gennōmenon hagion klēthēsetai huios theou 'that which is being begotten will be called holy (and) the Son of God'. Various interpretations are adopted:

1. *to gennōmenon hagion* is taken as the subject and *huios theou* as the predicate, e.g.: 'the holy child to be born will be called "Son of God"' (NEB). This implies that *to gennōmenon* must be interpreted as a substantive and *hagion* as its attribute, but to add an attribute to a participial substantive is without example in the Greek. The reverse interpretation, viz. to take *gennōmenon* attributive to the neuter *to hagion* and the latter in the sense of 'the holy child' is unacceptable, cp. A-G s.v. *hagios*, 2 a (α and β).

2. *to gennōmenon* is taken as the subject, *hagion* as the predicate and *huios theou* as in apposition to *hagion,* e.g. in RSV. This is accepted by several translators and commentators and by Westcott and Hort as shown by their punctuation; but it is difficult to accept this appositional construction, since the title *huios theou* does not explain or extend the statement about the nature of the child expressed by *hagion* but introduces something new.
3. *huios theou* is taken as a secondary independent predicate with *klēthēsetai*, hence, '...will be called holy (and) the Son of God', cp. also Goodspeed. This, although syntactically also somewhat uncommon, is preferable, because it does justice to the fact that *hagion* and *huios theou* belong to different categories.

to gennōmenon lit. 'that which is being begotten' or 'that which is being born', here preferably the former because of the present tense.

klēthēsetai, see on v. 32.

hagion 'holy' qualifies *to gennōmenon* as originating from and belonging to God.

huios theou 'the Son of God'. The omission of the article, here due to the syntactic function of the phrase, is common with this title, cp. *TH-Mk* on 1 : 1.

Translation: *Will come upon you,* or, 'will descend on you' (Tagalog), 'will alight-on you' (Toba Batak, using the same verb as in Mk. 1 : 10), 'to come-to' (Tagabili). Elsewhere a verb for 'to come in/to/upon' may have to be avoided, because it denotes possession by a god or demon (some Indonesian languages), or would suggest rape or sexual intercourse (Tarascan).

Power, occurring also in 1 : 17; 4 : 14, 36; 5 : 17; 6 : 19; 8 : 46; 9 : 1; 10 : 19; 12 : 5; 19 : 12, 15; 21 : 26f; 22 : 53, 69; 23 : 42; 24 : 49. In some languages one term covers the related concepts 'power', 'strength', 'force', 'authority' etc.; elsewhere the translator has to distinguish between various kinds of power, such as, bodily *versus* non-bodily, originating within oneself *versus* derived from others, exerted on another *versus* not exerted on another, human *versus* more than human, associated with religion *versus* associated with (black) magic, etc. Some seemingly obvious equivalents may have to be avoided because of connotations or associations that are undesirable in this context. In Malay, for example, the Arabic borrowing for 'Almighty Power' has the connotation of 'destiny' and a comparable term can denote the virtue of a talisman. In India the Sanskrit term *śaktī*, denoting divine power or energy operating in the world, has been used in some Indic languages for God's power (in Malayalam, Mt. 6 : 13), and for Jesus' healing power (in Marathi, Mk. 5 : 30), but in others its use has been restricted to passages such as Lk. 11 : 15; Acts 8 : 10, because it is invoked for purposes of black magic. A metaphorical rendering of 'power' is, 'God's hand' (Pame), an interesting parallel to biblical usage. In some languages the noun 'power' can best be rendered by a verb, 'to exercise-power', 'to be able'. Cp. Nida, *BT*, 197; *TH-Mk* on 5 : 30; *TBT*, 13.83, 1962; *Indian Wordlist*, 154f.

Will overshadow you, or, 'will come upon you with his shadow' (Sranan). The choice in several Indonesian languages is between (1) a phrase built on a word for 'shade', suggesting darkness, coolness, shelter from heat or danger, and (2) one built on a word for 'shadow', presupposing some entity causing the shadow; here term (1) is used. Timorese employs a parallelistic expression combining 'shelter' and 'shadow', used when asking for a chief's help and protection. Possible non-figurative renderings are, 'be (present) with', 'come-on (like a cloud passing over)' (Navajo), 'cover' (Kapauku, Sinhalese; and Thai, same verb as used in Ex. 40 : 35); Apache shifts to, 'the greatest One his-power on-you he-will-put'.

The child to be born, or, 'the one/the child you are to give birth to'. The other interpretation, preferred in *Exegesis,* viz. 'that which is being begotten', is harder to translate. Two points require special attention. (1) The clause refers to an event that is close at hand; hence the tense used should express present or near future. (2) The rendering of 'to beget', already difficult for general linguistic or cultural reasons (cp. Nida, *BT,* 191), here may prove the more so because of specific theological considerations. Therefore a more generic verb may be preferable, e.g. 'cause to exist (or, to grow)', 'give life', where the passive construction can be kept, or, 'come-into-existence' (Apache), 'grow', 'receive life', where one has to shift to the active voice; in both cases an additional qualification, e.g. 'in your womb' may be required. Or again, it may be better to describe the event from the female viewpoint; hence, 'the person you will bear' (Kapauku), 'the one you are going to conceive (or, to be pregnant of)'.

Will be called, cp. on v. 32. Taken with two predicates, as preferred in *Exegesis,* it may be necessary that the verb be repeated, as in Thai, or that both predicates be of the same class, e.g. nominal phrases, cp. 'called person of holiness and Son of God' (Kituba).

Son of God, see *N.T.Wb./*68; *TH-Mk* on 15 : 39. A literal rendering is preferable, but may be impossible; hence, '(the) One belonging to God' (Ponape, in several of the occurrences). Or it may be misleading, as in Gbandi, where it would mean 'lucky person'; hence, 'truly the Son of God'. For other occurrences of the phrase see 3 : 38; 4 : 3, 9, 41; 22 : 7; and cp. "my Son" in 3 : 22; 9 : 35; "the Son" in 10 : 22; "Son of the Most High (God)" in 1 : 32; 8 : 28.

36 ***And behold, your kinswoman Elizabeth in her old age has also conceived a son; and this is the sixth month with her who was called barren.***

Exegesis: *hē suggenis sou* 'your kinswoman'.

suggenis (††) feminine form of *suggenēs* 'of the same kin'; it implies blood-relationship but does not define its degree.

kai autē 'she also', or 'even she', (not 'herself'), serves to reinforce *Elisabet.*

suneilēphen 'has conceived', see on vv. 24 and 31 but here with object. The perfect tense refers to some fact of the past which has brought about a still prevailing situation.

en gērei autēs 'in her old age'. *gēras* (††).

kai houtos mēn hektos estin 'this is the sixth month', not 'this month is the sixth'; *houtos* takes the gender of the predicate.

autē tē kaloumenē steira 'for her who was said to be barren'; *tē kaloumenē steira* is in apposition to *autē*, but is usually translated as a relative or concessive clause.

kaloumenē 'being called'; the present participle of the passive of *kaleō*, 'to call', when not used to indicate a name, expresses what one is thought to be or what one really is (cp. Schonfield, "who was barren"), cp. A-G s.v. 1 a γ. δ. Both interpretations are possible here.

steira 'barren', see on v. 7.

Translation: *Your kinswoman* (cp. *N.T.Wb.*/33, FAMILY), or a word for 'cousin' (relative of one's own generation), or preferably, 'aunt' (in its classificatory sense indicating relatives of the generation of one's parents). If the language uses distinctive terms for relatives of patrilineal or matrilineal descent, Mary and Elizabeth can best be taken to belong to different patrilineal groups. — In languages without a category of gender it is in this context superfluous, or even slightly ridiculous, expressly to indicate the sex, as done in one version.

Has conceived a son, or, 'is pregnant with a son'. In several languages the usual expression for 'to conceive', or, 'to be pregnant' cannot take 'son/daughter' as its object or qualification. In such cases one will have to use here another rendering of the verb than in v. 24, e.g. 'there-is a male foetus (lit. what-is-carried-inside)' (Javanese), 'being-with-life-of a son' (Toba Batak), 'there-is her son that-makes-abdomen' (Tagabili), 'she is with abdomen; she will give birth to a son' (Kituba, similarly East Toradja).

In her old age, or, 'old though she is'.

This is the sixth month with her, i.e. of her pregnancy, as made explicit e.g. in 'having-conceived, it has monthed/full-mooned six-times' (Navajo, Apache), cp. also on v. 26.

Who was called barren, or, 'whom they (indefinite) regarded to be barren' (Thai), 'even though she is barren, they (indefinite) say' (Cuyono); or, reversing the clause order, 'she who formerly was called barren, now has reached her sixth month' (Balinese). For *barren* see above on v. 7.

37 ***For with God nothing will be impossible."***

Exegesis: *hoti* 'because' here introduces a clause that both explains the statement of Elizabeth's pregnancy in the preceding verse and warrants the promise to Mary of vv. 31-33 and 35.

ouk...pan rēma, a Hebraism expressing strong negation: 'none whatever', cp. Jer. 32 : 17, where both the Hebrew and the Greek have the same expression. *rēma* either 'word', 'saying', or 'thing', cp. 2 : 15; here preferably the latter.

ouk adunatēsei 'will not be (or, prove) impossible'; many translators (e.g. Phillips, Rieu, Goodspeed) have 'is impossible' or another phrase in the present tense because they take the clause primarily or even exclusively as an explanation of v. 36. The future tense, however, is preferable; because it shows that the reference is also to what will happen to Mary.

para tou theou 'from God' is either connected with *rēma*, hence, 'thing originating from God' (Weymouth), or with *adunatēsei* which is better in accordance with its position in the sentence. In the latter case some translations simplify the clause somewhat and translate: 'is (or, will be) impossible with God' (RSV, Kingsley Williams, Menge, Weissäcker)

Translation: *With God nothing will be impossible* has been rendered, 'there is no work/act which cannot be effected by God' (Tamil, similarly Tagabili), 'God not anything in-vain He-will-do-it' (Navajo, Apache). *With God*, or, 'from (the side of) God', 'for/to God' (Goodspeed, Marathi) can in this context also mean 'in the sphere of God's activity', i.e. as an indirect reference to God as agent, cp. the above quoted renderings. The double negative *nothing...impossible* sometimes is better expressed in the affirmative, 'everything...will be in his power' (cp. Kituba, Malay).

38 ***And Mary said, "Behold I am the handmaid of the Lord; let it be to me according to your word." And the angel departed from her.***

Exegesis: *idou* 'behold', with following nominative. This use of *idou* is probably a Hebraism and expresses readiness to serve or to listen, cp. 1 Sam. 3 : 5, 6, 8. Renderings like "I am" (e.g. Goodspeed), or "here I am" (NEB) make explicit what is implied in the phrase viz. that the following words refer to Mary herself.

hē doulē kuriou 'the slave (or, servant) of the Lord'.

doulē (also v. 48) 'female slave', 'bondmaid', like *doulos* often used when someone of high rank is addressed by somebody of lower rank.

genoito moi 'let it happen to me'.

genoito 'let it be', expresses Mary's readiness to serve the Lord. For *ginomai* with dative cp. A-G s.v. 3 b β.

kata to rēma sou 'according to your word', i.e. 'according to what you have told me'; *sou* refers to the angel.

Translation: *Mary said.* Just as one may better render 'said' by 'asked' where it introduces a question (see above on 1 : 18), thus it may be better to translate it by 'answered' where it introduces a sentence that clearly is a reply to a preceding utterance. This change is obligatory in some languages, preferable in others, e.g. in order to strengthen the inner structure of the dialogue. — In honorific languages Mary, in addressing the angel, has to use respectful terms; in Marathi these are honorifics of the highest degree, but not the form used to deity.

Handmaid. Often the word for 'servant' (for which see on 12 : 37) can be used, with indication of feminine sex where required. Because God is the one served the aspects of obedience, devotion, or even worship come to the fore, which may lead to the use of a term or expression meaning 'devotee' (Marathi), 'subject' (Sundanese, Balinese), cp. also, 'I am the Lord's person (i.e. subject)' (South Toradja), 'I am under the Lord', suggesting the being under God's command as well as under his protection (Sranan).

Let it be to me according to your word, or, "as you have spoken, so be it" (NEB), 'may be done to me (or, may I be given) all that you have said', 'let God send (lit. cause-to-proceed to) me that which you have just told me about now' (Tagabili). In Subanen the idiom is, 'I will allow what you said'; Apache has to use, 'yes, I say: just-what-you-said it-will-be-done-to-me'.

Departed from her. The Greek uses a term for the departure of ordinary mortals; therefore renderings such as 'faded-away' (a term for the disappearance of a supernatural being), or, 'return to heaven', are not advisable: they say more than Luke is saying.

39 ***In those days Mary arose and went with haste into the hill country, to a city of Judah,***

Exegesis: *anastasa* lit. 'having risen'.

anistēmi transitive 'to raise', intransitive (with middle forms) 'to rise', often used with weakened basic meaning to indicate the beginning of an action (usually a motion), cp. A-G s.v. 2 d; the verb is especially common of the preparation of a journey as here (cp. 15 : 18, 20; 17 : 19).

en tais hēmerais tautais lit. 'in these days', goes with the whole clause. Its meaning is of a very general nature, cp. e.g. NEB, 'about this time', but it refers usually to a somewhat shorter period than *en tais hēmerais ekeinais* (cp. 2 : 1; 9 : 36).

eis tēn oreinēn scil. *chōran* 'to the hill country', of Judea, as v. 65 shows, possibly an echo of the Hebrew *ha-har* as an indication of the mountainous part of the area of Judah (cp. e.g. Jos. 9 : 1).

meta spoudēs (†) 'with haste', qualifies *eporeuthē*; several translators render both words in one expression as e.g. "hurried off" (Phillips, Goodspeed).

eis polin Iouda 'to a town of Judah', the territory occupied by the tribe of Judah in the time before the Exile. In the New Testament in this meaning only here and Mt. 2 : 6 in a quotation from the Old Testament; here it refers to the same area as that meant in v. 65.

Translation: *Arose*, or, "set out" (NEB, similarly in Sranan, lit. 'took path', and in Bahasa Indonesia, Tagabili), 'having started-off' (Navajo), 'got ready' (Javanese).

Went...into the hill country, to a city of Judah, or in one phrase, mentioning the more specific first, cp. "went...to a town in the uplands of Judah" (NEB). *Went*, or, 'journeyed'; distance, and details such as descending or ascending, may influence the term to be chosen, cp. on 2 : 4. *The hill country* here comes near to a proper name, cp. 'the Highlands' in Scots. Some versions simply say, 'the hills/mountains', as in Hebrew. For *hill* cp. also on 3 : 5.

40 ***and she entered the house of Zechariah and greeted Elizabeth.***

Exegesis: *kai ēspasato tēn Elisabet* 'and she greeted Elizabeth'.
aspazomai (also 10 : 4) 'to greet', here of the person who enters, as the substantive *aspasmos* in 1 : 29, 41.

Translation: *And.* Because the story leaves untold Mary's arrival in the city it may be necessary to make the transition less abrupt, e.g. by preparing it in v. 39, cp. '. . .she arrived at a city in Judah, (40) and then she entered' (Navajo); or by starting v. 40 with, 'there', or, 'on her arrival there'.
She entered and greeted, or, 'having entered she greeted', 'on-entering she greeted' (Balinese). For *greeted* cp. on v. 29 and on "hail" in v. 28; Tagabili has here, 'called to', as one does when coming up the stairs of a house but not seeing anyone right away; Navajo has, 'said peace/friendship to', a common way of reporting a friendly greeting, although 'peace/friendship' is not part of the actual formula of greeting.

41 ***And when Elizabeth heard the greeting of Mary, the babe leaped in her womb; and Elizabeth was filled with the Holy Spirit,***

Exegesis: *kai egeneto hōs ēkousen. . .eskirtēsen*, cp. on v. 8.
ton aspasmon tēs Marias 'the greeting of Mary', i.e. Mary greeted Elizabeth when entering Zechariah's house. There is no reason to suppose that in her greeting Mary had told the story of the angelic visit.
eskirtēsen to brephos 'the babe leaped'.
skirtaō (only here and v. 44 in the N.T.) 'to leap', is used in the Septuagint in Gen. 25 : 22 of the struggling of the unborn twins in Rebekah's womb. Neither that meaning, nor the general meaning 'to leap', or 'to spring' are adequate here, where a sudden and vigorous stirring of the unborn child within his mother's womb is meant.
brephos either 'unborn child' as here and in v. 44, or a newly born child as in 2 : 12, 16; in 18 : 15 it has a more general meaning.
en tē koilia autēs 'in her womb'; the phrase probably goes with the preceding *to brephos*, rather than with *eskirtēsen.*
koilia 'womb'.
eplēsthē pneumatos hagiou 'was filled with the Holy Spirit'; when in the aorist tense the phrase refers to a sudden and momentary experience enabling a person to inspired utterances, as here and in v. 67. Here it marks the utterances of Elizabeth in vv. 42f as prophetic.

Translation: In rendering the verb *to hear* the following points must be kept in mind. Some receptor languages use the verb, as a rule, with an object, others do so always. In some languages the object can be both a person and the words said by a person, but elsewhere it must be either the words or the person. In the latter case the phrase in this verse will have to become 'heard Mary greeting (or, while she greeted, or, who greeted) her'. When intentional, attentive hearing is meant a specific verb (e.g. 'listen'

English, Sranan, in 9 : 35), or a specific verbal form of 'to hear' is obligatory in some languages. The same is true when 'to hear' refers to the faculty of hearing, see below on "the deaf hear" in 7 : 22.

The babe...in her womb, or, 'within/inside her (i.e. Elizabeth)' (cp. Goodspeed, Phillips, Apache). If "babe" is rendered by '(little) child' (as is idiomatic in several languages), the phrase "in the womb", taken adjectivally, qualifies the child as still unborn (cp. also 'the child that-made abdomen-her', Tagabili); if idiom requires here a more specific term for "babe", such as, 'unborn child', 'embryo' (for which see on "fruit of the womb" in v. 42), the prepositional phrase may be unduly redundant and better omitted.

Leaped. A literal rendering may sound vulgar (Gio), or unidiomatic, e.g. because the verb means only 'leaping off a surface' (Aymara, Tagabili). Current idioms for the process here mentioned are, 'trampled' (Javanese), 'shook-itself' (Kituba), 'wriggled' (Thai), 'danced' (Sediq), 'stirred' (South Toradja), 'sprawled' (Toba Batak), 'played' (Shipibo). In some cases idiom or decency requires a more generic word, e.g. 'moved' (East Toradja, Aymara, Tagalog); in Gio the clause has to be rendered, 'her stomach moved'.

And Elizabeth was filled with the Holy Spirit, or, 'now (particle indicating punctiliar action) the H. Sp. came to be/stay/live with E.' (Tagabili); cp also above on v. 15.

42 ***and she exclaimed with a loud cry, "Blessed are you among women, and blessed is the fruit of your womb!***

Exegesis: *anephōnēsen kraugē megalē* 'she exclaimed with a loud cry', showing the strong feeling of Elizabeth.

anaphōneō (††) 'to cry out', 'to shout'.

kraugē (†) 'screaming', 'loud cry'.

kai eipen 'and she said', identical action with *anephōnēsen kraugē megalē* and hence sometimes not rendered distinctly (cp. RSV).

eulogēmenē su en gunaixin 'blessed (are) you among women'. The phrase may be understood as a wish or as a statement, preferably the latter, cp. RSV. The construction with *en* is a Hebraistic periphrasis for the superlative (cp. Goodspeed).

eulogeō 'to praise', or, 'to bless' in the sense of calling God's gracious power upon somebody, or of providing with benefits; the last meaning either in the active with God or Christ as subject or in the passive as here and in the next clause, and then indicating a person that has received God's blessing.

karpos 'offspring', cp. A-G s.v. 1 b; the phrase *karpos tēs koilias* is a Hebraism, cp. Gen. 30 : 2, and the reference may be to the embryo in her womb or to the child she will bear in due time, preferably the latter. Hence the phrase should be taken as referring to the future, 'blessed will be...'

Translation: *She exclaimed with a loud cry*, usually will require adaptation, cp. "gave a great cry" (Goodspeed), 'shouted with-power' (Apache), 'making a high tone she loudly spoke' (Marathi), 'the sound of her mouth (lit. oral-cavity) cried and was loud' (East Toradja), or somewhat simplified, 'loud her-words' (Tagabili, where 'cry' or 'shout' can be used only with reference to pain, fear, or anger); cp. also on "cried out with a loud voice" in 4 : 33.

Blessed are you among women, preferably, 'blessed are you above (or, more than) all women', 'the most blessed of women you are'. The clause form should be that of an exclamation expressing strong emotion. A shift may be necessary to the active voice, taking as agent 'God', or a reference to the supernatural (Navajo); or to constructions such as, 'you get/receive a (great) blessing' (Kanarese, Sranan, Toba Batak, Thai), "God's blessing is on you" (NEB). The verb *to bless* has various uses. (1) Here, in 24 : 50f, and probably in 18 : 15, it is used, with God or Christ as agent, in the sense of 'to provide a person with benefits', 'to confer prosperity or happiness on a person'; as such it has been rendered e.g. 'to bestow favour upon', 'to favour' (for which see on vv. 28, 30), 'to think well of' (Cuna), 'to speak good to' (Ifugao), 'to make happy' (Ponape), 'to cause-to-live-as-a-chief' (Zulu), 'to sprinkle with a propitious (lit. cool) face', a poetic expression occurring in the priests' language (South Toradja). When the participle is used in an exclamatory phrase, as is the case here, its meaning comes close to that of Gr. *makarios* 'happy', for which see on v. 45. (2) With man as agent and God or Christ as object the verb means 'to praise' (see 1 : 64; 2 : 28; 24 : 53), and has been rendered e.g. 'cast the (praised person's) name abroad' (Valiente); cp. also on "praising" in 2 : 13. With this meaning too the participle is used in an exclamatory phrase (see 1 : 68; 13 : 35; 19 : 38); cp. also *TH-Mk* on 11 : 9f. (3) With man as agent, again, the verb can be used in the sense of 'to invoke divine care and favour for a person' (see 2 : 34; 6 : 28), and has been rendered e.g. 'request happiness/peace/well-being for' (cp. South Toradja, Balinese). Finally (4), with Jesus as agent, the verb can have the meaning of 'to say/call a blessing over something', 'to invoke divine power on, or to consecrate, something (by word)' (see 9 : 16; 24 : 30). Possible renderings of the verb in this sense are, 'to arrange well in the heart' (Piro), 'to speak good over' (Valiente), 'to say sweet things concerning' (Maya), 'to put one's mind on it to the father' (Cuna), 'to request strength for' (South Toradja), 'to request *merta* for' (Balinese, the term *merta*, etym. related to skr. *amṛta* 'nectar/water-of-life', referring to a vital force, e.g. the sprouting force of rice); and cp. the renderings quoted in *TH-Mk* on 6 : 41. — *Women* (passim), always referring to adult females, usually ones who are, or have been married. For problems one may encounter see *N.T.Wb.*/75.

You...your again may require a decision about honorifics. Marathi here has the familiar pronoun used to juniors; Balinese uses 'younger sister' (which is in accordance with family relationship and age), but combines this with honorific terms, thus trying also to express Elizabeth's respect for the mother of her Lord.

The fruit of your womb, or, 'that-which-will-be-born out-of your-womb' (Navajo), 'the blossom (literary for, offspring) from your womb' (Timorese), 'the one who will be born from you' (Subanen), 'the child you will give birth to', or simply, 'your child' (Goodspeed, Phillips). Taken as a reference to the still unborn child the rendering of the phrase may be identical to that of 'babe in the womb' (v. 41) or synonymous to it.

43 ***And why is this granted me, that the mother of my Lord should come to me?***

Exegesis: *kai pothen moi touto hina*... 'and whence (comes) this to me that...'. *pothen* 'whence', sometimes used to indicate surprise at the cause or reason of something: 'how is it possible that...', cp. Mk. 12 : 37. *moi* is best taken as an ethical dative with little or no emphasis. *touto* refers to the subsequent clause introduced by *hina*. *hina* originally an indication of purpose, often denotes content in the New Testament, cp. Moule 145f.

elthē 'comes' or 'has come'; the subjunctive, obligatory after *hina* has lost its modal function since *hina* has ceased to indicate purpose.

hē mētēr tou kuriou mou 'the mother of my Lord' i.e. the mother of the Messiah, cp. on v. 6 sub (3).

pros eme 'to me', emphatic.

Translation: *Why is this granted me*, or, 'how is it that it should be done to me' (Kapauku), "Who am I" (Goodspeed, NEB), "why should this great thing happen to me" (TEV), 'whence (or, who gave me) this good fortune' (Javanese, Sranan), 'whence is this honour to me?' (Marathi, where the clause has to be in final position). Elsewhere the rhetorical question may have to become a statement, introduced by some phrase like, 'it is astonishing that', 'I can't believe that'. On rhetorical questions in general see Nida, *TAPOT*, 30; *TH-Mk* on 2 : 25; 11 : 17; 12 : 10.

Lord, see on v. 6, sub (b).

Should come to me, or, 'should come to meet/visit me' (Bahasa Indonesia, Javanese); or, making explicit the speaker's humble mood, 'is so kind to come to me' (Apache, Balinese), cp. also, 'would fain visit one such as this one here that I am' (Tagabili, the circumlocutionary rendering of the object bringing out the emphatic force of the pronoun). For the verb cp. also v. 28.

44 ***For behold, when the voice of your greeting came to my ears, the babe in my womb leaped for joy.***

Exegesis: *idou* 'behold', cp. on v. 20, here emphasizes the explanatory character of the following clause; hence renderings like "I tell you" (NEB), "why" (Kingsley Williams), *vois tu* (Jerusalem).

gar 'for', introduces the explanation of what Elizabeth said in the two preceding verses.

hōs egeneto hē phōnē tou aspasmou sou eis ta ōta mou 'when the sound of your greeting came to my ears'.

egeneto... *eis ta ōta mou* 'came to my ears'; for *ginomai eis* denoting a movement cp. A-G s.v. 4 c α; the expression is rather colourless.

hē phōnē tou aspasmou sou 'the sound of your greeting'; *phōnē* 'sound' or 'voice' is added here in order to show that the reference is not to the contents of Mary's word of greeting, but merely to its sound.

en agalliasei 'in exultation', cp. on v. 14. Both the substantive *agalliasis* and the verb *agalliaomai* often denote an exultation which is due to the Holy Spirit, cp. 10 : 21, 1 Pet. 4 : 13f.

eskirtēsen . . . to brephos en tē koilia mou, see on v. 41.

Translation: *When the voice of your greeting came to my ears,* preferably, 'when the sound of your greeting came to (or, fell-on/reached/called-in) my ear(s)'; or with further adaptations needed, 'as-soon-as your well wishing resounded in my ear' (Balinese, using an onomatopoeic verb suggesting the concept sound, similarly NEB), 'when I heard your voice that greeted me'.

Leaped for joy. The verb usually can be rendered as in v. 41, but in some cases differentiation is needed, e.g. because of the adverbial qualification. *For joy,* or, 'because of its joy', 'because it rejoiced (or, exulted/was happy)'.

45 ***And blessed is she who believed that there would be a fulfilment of what was spoken to her from the Lord."***

Exegesis: *makaria* 'fortunate', 'happy', usually with a religious connotation, 'blessed'; often, as here, in a nominal clause with a participle or an adjective as its subject. The word also serves as a translation of the exclamatory Hebrew *ašrēi,* 'hail to him', or, 'Oh, the happiness of. . .', less an exclamation than a statement. The difference between *makaria* and *eulogēmenē* (v. 42) is comparable to that between German 'selig' and 'gesegnet'.

hē pisteusasa 'she who believed'; the aorist tense indicates that the reference is to a specific act of faith of a specific person rather than to faith or to believing women in general. The word then refers here either to Elizabeth (Rieu) or to Mary (most translators and commentators); the latter is preferable since v. 38 clearly implies Mary's faith.

pisteuō 'to believe', 'to have faith', includes conviction, trust and obedience.

hoti admits grammatically of two explanations: 'that' or 'for', preferably the latter.

estai teleiōsis tois lelalēmenois lit. 'there will be fulfilment for what has been said', hence 'what has been said will be fulfilled'. *teleiōsis* (†).

para kuriou 'from the Lord', i.e. 'coming from the Lord' (cp. Rieu, "the words that reached me from the Lord"), or, 'on behalf of the Lord' (cp. NV, Brouwer, Willibrord, Jerusalem, Segond).

Translation: *Blessed.* The Greek term used here should be rendered by a receptor language word used for well wishing, as opposed to cursing, cp. 6 : 20ff; that term usually has the basic meaning 'happy', 'glad', 'prosperous', 'well', 'safe'. Care should be taken that the rendering chosen is not exclusively associated with material prosperity, or gambling (cp. Nida, *GWIML*, 43), or recovery from illness (cp. *TBT*, 4.186, 1953). The terms for Gr. *makarios* (here) and *eulogēmenos* (v. 42) coincide in some languages, e.g. English. There is a difference, however, *makarios* referring to a situation of happiness and bliss as such, *eulogēmenos* more clearly envisaging such a situation as originating from God; therefore differentiation is preferable, if possible.

If *she who...to her* is taken as referring to Mary, a shift to pronouns of the second person often is preferable, e.g. in Kituba, Kanarese, Sundanese; this may also serve to bring out the specifying force the aorist has here (see *Exegesis*). In Tagabili it is possible to refer to the person addressed in the third person, but only if, in settling a case, one addresses him or her in the presence of others; since here only two seem to be present the pronoun of the second person had to be employed.

Believed that, or, 'believed for'. If Gr. *hoti* is taken to mean 'that', the next clause functions as object of 'believed' (cp. RSV), but if it is interpreted as 'for' (as preferred in *Exegesis*) an object may have to be added; hence e.g. 'believed what was said to (or, promised) her', 'considered-it-to-be-true' (South Toradja). For *to believe* see on 1 : 20.

That there would be a fulfilment of what..., preferably, 'for there will be a fulfilment of what...'; or, taking the "what"-clause as subject, 'for what...will receive fulfilment, or, will be accomplished (Kanarese), will become full (Tamil), will-be-caused-to-happen (Navajo), will come right (Sranan), will certainly take effect (Sundanese), is a certainty (Tagabili), will lack nothing'.

What was spoken to her from the Lord, or, 'the Lord's word told to her' (Kapauku), 'what the Lord had-ordered-to-speak' (Toba Batak), intimating that the Lord was the initiator, not the agent of the speaking. In some languages the actual speaker can better be made explicit, e.g. 'what the angel told you in the name of the Lord' (Kituba), 'what was spoken to her by the Lord's holy messenger' (Navajo). For *Lord*, here and in the further occurrences in this chapter, see v. 6, sub (c).

(Vv. 46-56). As there is no indication in this hymn that Mary is addressing herself to God, she can best be taken as speaking to Elizabeth (perhaps together with her household). This means that "our" (v. 55) has inclusive force, and that, in honorific languages, the translator has to use the same categories as employed in the preceding conversation between Mary and Elizabeth.

46 ***And Mary said,***
"My soul magnifies the Lord,
47 ***and my spirit rejoices in God my Saviour,***

Exegesis: *megalunei* 'magnifies'.

megalunō (also v. 58) lit. 'to make large', here used in the figurative sense, cp. "extols" (Weymouth), "exalts" (20th Century).

hē psuchē mou 'my soul'.

psuchē 'soul', 'life', is here used in the sense of the seat of the inner life of man, his feelings and emotions, and is parallel with *pneuma* (v. 47).

(V. 47) *kai ēgalliasen to pneuma mou* 'and my spirit rejoices'; the aorist tense after the present tense of *megalunei* is probably due to the influence of Hebrew poetry and need not affect the tense of the translation.

agalliaō 'to be overjoyed', 'to exult', always has a religious connotation: a joy or rejoicing due to the Holy Spirit or brought forth by an act of God (as here).

pneuma 'spirit'. As to a differentiation of *psuchē* and *pneuma, psuchē* (in v. 46) expresses what is man's own inner nature and *pneuma* the self that is not so much his own as given to him from God. Cp. also *TBT*, 4.38-40, 1953.

epi tō theō tō sōtēri mou 'in God my saviour'; *epi* followed by dative denotes here God as the origin of the rejoicing.

sōtēr (also 2 : 11) lit. 'he who saves' (from *sōzō* 'to save'), here of God, and therefore, in accordance with Old Testament usage, less a title than an agent noun.

Translation: *My soul,* cp. *TH-Mk* on 12 : 30, and *TBT*, 9.53, 1958. Languages differ in the entities regarded as centre of emotions, cp. Nida, *BT*, 151-153, and in any one language not all emotions are associated with the same centre. For some renderings used see on v. 47. In several cases it is better to use a simple reference to the first person, cp. 'Great my praising the Lord' (Tagabili), or to say something like, 'I...in my soul' (Kituba), 'I...with (all) my heart'.

Magnifies is often rendered by a declarative verbal derivation of 'great/high/excellent', such as 'tells-about-the-greatness-of' (Navajo, Apache), 'considers...great/noble' (Marathi). Other possible renderings are, 'honours' (Kituba), 'glorifies' (Malay, the same term as renders Gr. *doxazō,* e.g. in 5 : 25); see also *N.T.Wb.*/41, GREAT.

(V. 47) *My spirit.* The variation of the pair "soul"—"spirit" has primarily stylistic function here, forming an important feature of the parallelistic verse structure. One should, therefore, preferably use two synonymous terms for a person's emotional centre, cp. e.g. the following renderings of the pair, "heart"—"spirit" (Goodspeed, similarly Kituba), "heart"—"soul" (TEV, similarly East Toradja 1933), 'soul'—'insides' (Sranan), 'that-which-stands-within'—'the spirit-(lit. air)-which-stands-within' (Navajo), 'heart'—'that-which-stands-within' (Apache), 'breath/wind-of-life'—'spirit' (Kanarese, Telugu). In some languages, however, it proves impossible to differentiate.

Rejoices in God my Saviour. The preposition "in" rendered literally, may easily be misunderstood (cp. *TBT*, 9.145 and 147, 1958); the relationship is better expressed by 'over', 'because of', or by shifting to a construction like, 'God my Saviour gives me joy (or, makes me glad)'. *God my Saviour,* or, 'God who saves me'. The agent noun occurs also in 2 : 11. The verb 'to save' (also occurring in 1 : 71; 6 : 9; 7 : 50; 8 : 12; 9 : 24; 13 : 23; 18 : 26; 19 : 10; 23 : 35, 37, 39; and cp. "salvation" in 1 : 69, 77; 2 : 30; 3 : 6; 19 : 9) basically means 'to preserve or deliver from harm', such as danger, illness, death. Especially in the perfective and passive forms the focus may shift from the process to its positive result, a state of safety and well-being. In figurative extension of meaning the verb is used to indicate the preservation from (the causes of) eternal death, or positively, the grant of eternal life and the ensuing blessedness. Used in this meaning the explicit or implicit agent is God, Jesus, or faith (in God or Jesus). The receptor language rarely has one term covering the various meanings discussed. For possible ways of rendering the verb see Nida, *BT*, 222f; *TH-Mk* on 10 : 26; *TBT*, 12.2, 1961; 13.115f, 1962; 14.38, 1963; 18.185f, 1967. — In some languages there is a danger that 'God' (here) and 'Lord' (v. 46) are understood as referring to two different entities; hence in Tagabili one has to render the clause by, 'my breath/spirit is-happy in his (i.e. the Lord's) causing-to-have-life me'.

48 ***for he has regarded the low estate of his handmaiden. For behold, henceforth all generations will call me blessed;***

Exegesis: *epeblepsen epi tēn tapeinōsin tēs doulēs autou* 'he looked upon the low position of his slave'.

epiblepō epi with accusative (also 9 : 38) 'to look upon with care', with the intention of doing something about it; here the verb implies that God has changed or is about to change Mary's humble situation.

tapeinōsis (†) 'low position', 'humiliation' as a state of being.

idou gar, 'for behold', introduces here a clause that describes what will be the outcome of God's dealing with Mary.

apo tou nun 'from now on', 'henceforth'; the expression does not imply that the 'now' is the very moment of Mary's words.

makariousin me 'will call me blessed'.

makarizō (†) 'to call someone *makarios*', cp. on v. 45 *makaria*.

pasai hai geneai 'all (subsequent) generations'.

genea 'those descended from a common ancestor', 'family', 'race', or 'those born (and living) in the same age', 'generation'.

Translation: *Regarded*, or, "tenderly...looked upon" (NEB), 'his eye looked on' (Sranan), 'cast-a-kind-glance (lit. a side look)' (Telugu), all keeping close to the metaphor of the original. Some non-metaphorical renderings are, 'placed attention on' (Kanarese), 'is concerned about' (Thai), 'found' (Kapauku), "deigned to notice" (Phillips); for a shift to another metaphor cp. 'set his hand under' (Vai, an idiom for 'had concern for').

The low estate of his handmaiden, or, reorganizing the syntactic pattern, 'his lowly servant', "his servant, humble as she is" (NEB); or, 'that the condition of his servant was (a) humble (one)'. In some languages the first person reference has to be made explicit, e.g. 'I the-one-who-works-for-him who-am-not-great' (Apache), 'me his humble servant' (Kapauku); cp. also TEV, Français Courant. For *low estate* see *N.T.Wb.*/45f, HUMBLE. For *his handmaiden* cp. on v. 38. In several languages 'servant/slave' can do duty as a polite substitute for the pronoun of the first person, but in this verse the term is meant to convey more than mere polite humility. The combination of a pronoun of the first person with an appositional phrase (see above) may help to bring this out.

All generations. In the meaning of 'people of the same age' the word 'generation' may be rendered by, '(people of one) layer' (Chol, Kapauku, East Toradja, Toba Batak), 'one storey of growing' (Totonac, using a term also denoting a storey or floor of a building), 'people born/living', followed by an indication of time (Gio, Zacapoaxtla Aztec, Black Bobo, Ifugao, Sranan); some languages are as English in that one term covers both the meaning 'people of common descent' and the meaning 'people born or living in the same age', e.g. Bahasa Indonesia, Javanese. The rendering of 'all generations', i.e. those who are or will be born and living in this or subsequent ages, can usually be built on these and similar expressions, cp. e.g. 'all people in all times' (Sranan), 'all descendants of man' (Balinese, Apache), 'all those-who-will-be-being-born as-time-goes-on' (Navajo); or, changing the syntactic structure, 'doing-in-succession people will...' (South Toradja, shifting to a verb related to its word for 'descent/ descendant').

Will call me blessed, or, 'a blessed one/woman', or, 'will say that I am (a) blessed (one/woman)'; for "blessed" cp. on v. 45. The aspect is continuative, or repetitive, cp. South Toradja, which combines the main verb with a verbal form meaning 'to mention-again-and-again'. Some other renderings are, 'will praise me, calling me "blessed"' (Kanarese), 'will call my name (i.e. will honour me) highly (lit. with good)' (Sranan); 'will mention my happiness/peace' (Timorese); or an expression in direct discourse, e.g. 'a woman who-is-blessed she-is, they-will-say-about-me' (Apache, similarly in Navajo).

49 ***for he who is mighty has done great things for me, and holy is his name.***

Exegesis: *hoti,* parallel to *hoti* in the first clause of v. 48.

epoiēsen...megala 'has done great things'. The aorist tense *epoiēsen* points to the parallelism between this clause and the first clause of v. 48 (where *epeblepsen* also in the aorist). Both refer to the visit and the prophecy of the angel (vv. 26-38).

moi 'for me', but also 'to me', if necessary, preferably the latter, cp. NEB.

ho dunatos 'the mighty one'.

dunatos 'powerful', here used with the article and referring to God in accordance with Old Testament usage (cp. Ps. 45 : 3, in LXX 44 : 4).

kai hagion to onoma autou 'and holy is his name', a well known Old Testament liturgical phrase, cp. e.g. Ps. 111 : 9. Syntactically the clause is best understood as a case of Hebrew co-ordination (cp. Bl-D, § 442.6) and hence to be interpreted as a continuation of *ho dunatos,* cp. 'he whose name is holy' (Brouwer).

hagios 'holy', here denoting what is of God as opposed to everything created.

onoma 'name', here of God, a well known Old Testament expression for the personal ruling and acting of God in his revelation to man.

Translation: *He who is mighty,* or, "the Almighty" (Goodspeed, and several others), 'he-who-has-great-strength' (Navajo), 'the-One who-has-power-over all-that-exists' (South Toradja); or, 'the (al)mighty (or, powerful) God'. For 'might', 'power' see above on v. 35.

He has done great things to me, or, 'has caused-to-be (i.e. has brought about) for me great deeds' (Bahasa Indonesia, similarly in Marathi), 'has brought-to-light great works to my-person' (South Toradja); with a syntactic shift, 'amazing his-work to-me' (Tagabili); or with a more specific verb, 'he has helped me greatly'. For *great things,* or "wonders" (Goodspeed, also in Javanese), 'amazing things' (Sundanese) cp. also *N.T.Wb.*/41.

Holy is his name. The use of "name" in the sense discussed in *Exegesis* (cp. also Nida, *BT,* 178ff) is not foreign to some receptor languages, and seems to have been assimilated without too great difficulty in others. Not in all, however; hence, 'he is the Holy One', or, 'he is holy' (Lahu, where a literal rendering would have been misleading).

50 ***And his mercy is on those who fear him***
from generation to generation.

Exegesis: The verse is a nominal clause consisting of three phrases: (a) *to eleos autou* 'his mercy', subject of the clause, (b) *eis geneas kai geneas* 'for generations and generations', and (c) *tois phoboumenois auton* 'for those who fear him'. Either (b) or (c) may be interpreted as predicate of the clause, preferably the former, since the word order of the verse suggests a closer relationship between (b) and (a) than between (c) and (a).

kai to eleos autou 'and his mercy'. The verse is a free quotation of the Septuagint translation of Ps. 103 : 17.

eleos 'compassion', 'pity', in ch. 1 always of God towards man; the Hebrew word used in Ps. 103 : 17, which colours the meaning of *eleos* here, is usually understood as 'solidarity', cp. "steadfast love" (RSV).

eis geneas kai geneas 'for generations and generations' or 'for ages and ages', a well known time-phrase in the Septuagint, cp. e.g. Ps. 32 (in Hebrew 33) : 11. The phrase indicates continuation in successive generations or ages; cp. 'all generations', i.e. people in age after age, in v. 48.

tois phoboumenois auton 'for those who fear Him'.

phobeomai 'to fear' is sometimes (18 : 2, 4; 23 : 40) used with *theos* as its object as a translation of the well known 'fear of the Lord' in the Old Testament, a comprehensive expression of the relationship of man with God, with the emphasis on the reverence towards God on the side of man.

Translation: If phrase (b) is taken as the predicate (see *Exegesis*), the first line of this verse becomes, 'his mercy is from generation to generation', and expresses that God's mercy is everlasting; the second line, i.e. phrase (c), then serves to qualify that mercy by mentioning its recipients, e.g. '(that is,) to those who fear him'. If one has to shift to a verbal construction, e.g. 'he shows mercy to (or, mercy-es, i.e. has mercy on)', and the verb requires an object, one may add 'people', 'his people', 'us'; then the second line becomes an apposition to that object, or may be rendered as a subordinate clause, 'whenever they/we fear him'.

The term *mercy* often implies not only a sympathetic consciousness of another's situation but also a readiness and/or activity to help him in distress. For idioms rendering the related concepts 'mercy' and 'compassion' see *N.T.Wb.*/54; *TH-Mk* on 5 : 19.

Those who fear him. For 'to fear' cp. above on v. 12, but in the specific use found here, and in 18 : 2, 4; 23 : 4, it is often better to render it by a verb meaning 'to have respect/reverence for' (as in Subanen, Tarascan, Navajo, Javanese, Tagabili), cp. also, 'to make great before oneself' (Valiente). Kanarese can employ a compound, 'fear-devotion', that is in current use as a description of the life of piety; Apache renders the phrase by, 'those-with-whom he-is-holy'.

From generation to generation, or, 'from children to children's children' (Sranan), 'descend-descending' (a repetitive form, Bahasa Indonesia, Balinese), 'life one-layer, life one-layer' (East Toradja), 'from-those-who-have-been-being-born and-on to-those-who-will-be-being-born' (Navajo); or, 'forever' (Vai, Tarascan), 'always' (Bambara). Cp. also on v. 48.

(Vv. 51-54) The Greek aorists in these verses do not refer to something which has happened to Mary in the past (as was the case in vv. 48f), but to things which are bound to happen as a consequence of that which God did to Mary; they are therefore best understood as renderings of the Hebrew prophetic perfect which represents things of the future as already accomplished (cp. Zahn, Plummer).

Several English, Dutch, French and German versions usually render these prophetic perfects by their own perfect tense forms, hoping thus to convey the required meaning, but most ordinary users of these languages will take these perfects as referring to some event that has happened in the (near) past and, at the most, is still continuing in the present. This danger is especially great here because in the preceding verses the same verbal forms do refer to the past, and it is natural to take the subsequent ones in the same sense. In some European languages it is usually preferable to shift to the present tense (as being the most general one), or to the future tense. A few other solutions used are: verbs expressing action that is sure to happen in the near future (Pampango); progressive verbal forms denoting action taking place now and continuing in the future (Tagalog); verbal forms without tense or aspect indication, giving to the verbs the nuance of 'this is the way one is, or the kind of thing one does' (Kapauku, where the use of any past tense would imply a particular occasion with a choice between remote historical past and nearer past, contemporary with the speaker and/or hearers); or, finally, general verbal forms that do not differentiate between past, present or future (Indonesian languages). Even though such a rendering does not convey the full meaning of the prophetic perfect, it is decidedly preferable to one conveying the wrong meaning by exclusively referring to the past.

51 ***He has shown strength with his arm,***
he has scattered the proud in the imagination of their hearts,

Exegesis: *epoiēsen kratos* 'he has done a mighty deed'.

kratos (†) 'power', 'might', or 'mighty deed'. When the former meaning is accepted, *epoiēsen* is to be rendered 'he showed, or, displayed' (cp. RSV). In the latter meaning the phrase is to be understood as the rendering of the Hebrew expression 'to do strength', i.e. 'to do a mighty deed, or, mighty deeds' (cp. e.g. 1 Sam. 14:48; Ps. 60:12). This is preferable. *kratos* refers either to a single act of God and then takes up the phrase of v. 49: *epoiēsen...megala*, or to the series of acts described in the subsequent verses, preferably the latter.

en brachioni autou 'by means of his arm'; *en* with dative has here instrumental meaning as a translation of the Hebrew *be*.

brachiōn (†) 'arm', often as a symbol of God's active power, cp. Is. 52:10; Ps. 71:18; 77:16. The omission of the article before *brachioni* is due to Hebrew influence (cp. Moule 117).

dieskorpisen 'he scattered'.

diaskorpizō 'to disperse', i.e. 'to cause to fly in all directions', cp. Mt. 26:31.

huperēphanous dianoia kardias autōn 'the proud in the thought of their heart'; for the omission of the article before *dianoia* see above.

huperēphanos (†) 'arrogant', 'presumptuous'.

dianoia (also 10:27) 'understanding', 'mind', here 'thought', '(way of) thinking'; since *dianoia* in the Septuagint is one of the renderings of Hebr. *leb* (heart), of which *kardia* is the normal rendering, it follows that both words here represent virtually the same idea, cp. *TBT*, 4.38-40, 1953. *dianoia*, in the dative, is limitative and denotes as it were the area or the seat of their arrogance; hence translations like "the proudminded" (Goodspeed), 'the men with a proud heart' (Jerusalem). The people to whom the phrase refers, are probably the rulers of v. 52 and the rich of v. 53.

Translation: *He has shown strength with his arm,* preferably, 'he has done (or, he has performed/worked) mighty deeds (or, powerful works) with his arm', 'he acts powerfully with his arm'. The instrumental function which 'his arm' has in the sentence may have to be expressed by, 'he uses (or, causes) his arm to do...', or by making it the subject of the clause (Javanese). For *arm* see *N.T.Wb./42*. In some languages 'hand', or a term covering both 'hand' and 'arm', can better be used in the required metaphorical sense (e.g. in Sranan, Vai, and in Tagabili respectively). Where a metaphorical rendering is impossible one may have to say something like, 'he has power to do mighty deeds', 'strong as he is he does mighty deeds'.

He has scattered the proud..., or, 'he causes the proud... to fly in all directions', 'the proud...fled in-confusion through him' (Balinese).

The proud in the imagination of their hearts, or, "the arrogant of heart and mind" (NEB), 'those who think in their heart that they are great, or, people of bigness' (Bolivian Quechua, Kituba), 'big thoughts in the heart thinking people' (Kapauku); or rendering the phrase "imagination of their hearts" by one term, 'the proud in heart' (Marathi), 'those who have proud thoughts' (Balinese). In Tagabili the qualifying phrase has to be omitted because it would suggest a limitation of meaning; in some other languages, where the normal word or phrase for 'proud' contains a reference to the seat of pride, such as 'heart/mind/thought', the qualifying phrase has to be omitted to avoid repetition, e.g. 'the arrogant hearted men' (Bahasa Indonesia, similarly in Toba Batak), 'proud/haughty people (lit. big-memory-men)' (Sranan). For *proud* cp. *N.T.Wb.*/16, BOAST; *TH-Mk* on 7 : 22. Sundanese possesses three terms, identical in their first two syllables, and meaning respectively 'proud because of honoured position' (used here), 'proud because of strength', 'proud because of intelligence'.

52 ***he has put down the mighty from their thrones, and exalted those of low degree;***

Exegesis: *katheilen dunastas apo thronōn* 'he has torn rulers from (their) thrones', the phrase is metaphorical but a literal interpretation is not impossible.

kathaireō 'to tear', 'to bring down'; the verb suggests vigorous action.

dunastēs (†) 'ruler'; the word refers either to human sovereigns or to divine rulers; the former meaning here; hence translations like "kings" (Phillips), "monarchs" (Rieu).

thronos, cp. on v. 32.

hupsōsen tapeinous 'he has exalted the people of low position', contrasting with the preceding clause. Hence *hupsōsen* is the opposite of *katheilen apo thronōn* and *dunastas* is the opposite of *tapeinous*.

hupsoō 'to lift up', here in the figurative sense 'to raise to a high position'.

tapeinos (†) 'of low position', cp. on *tapeinōsis* in v. 48, which suggests a corresponding interpretation.

Translation: *He has put down the mighty from their thrones*, or, because of the necessity to render "throne" by a descriptive or non-metaphorical expression (cp. above on v. 32), 'he causes-to-shrink the authority of princes' (Balinese), 'he made low the titles (i.e. reputations) of men who were sitting high' (Subanen). This may reinforce the contrast between the two lines of this verse, because the renderings to be used are more directly and completely opposite to each other than is the case in the Greek, cp. e.g. 'he humbles the high, he heightens the humble' (Tagabili), 'the great ones, he has made them down, those who are not great, he has made them up' (Apache). The plurals are distributive. — *The mighty* has also been rendered, 'great rulers' (Marathi), 'possessors of power' (Telugu, Tamil).

And has adversative meaning, often expressed by 'but', or by simple juxtaposition of the two clauses.

For *exalted* see *N.T.Wb.*/28 and 60, DIMENSIONS (A) and RAISE, for *those of low degree* cp. on "low estate" in v. 48.

53 ***he has filled the hungry with good things,***
and the rich he has sent empty away.

Exegesis: *peinōntas eneplēsen agathōn* 'hungry people he has filled with good things'.

peinaō 'to be hungry', here in a figurative sense, as shown by *agathōn* and by the contrasting *ploutountas* in the next clause. The omission of the article before *peinōntas* (as compared with *hoi peinōntes* in 6 : 21) shows that no special group or class of people is referred to.

empimplēmi (also 6 : 25) 'to fill' or 'to satisfy'; both meanings are possible here.

kai ploutountas exapesteilen kenous 'and rich people he has sent away empty'.

plouteō (also 12 : 21) 'to be rich'.

exapostellō 'to send away'; in Luke the verb occurs always with the adjective *kenos* 'empty', and is construed with an accusative of object and a predicative accusative; the former indicates who is sent away and the latter indicates in what state.

kenos (also 20 : 10f) 'empty', of persons 'empty-handed', cp. A-G s.v. 1.

Translation: *He has filled the hungry with good things*, i.e. he gives the hungry plenty of good things; where 'hungry' cannot have the extended meaning required here one may have to shift to, 'he gives to those in want plenty of goods', 'he satisfies with what is good the poor' (Tagabili), 'the needy are filled with treasures' (Sundanese). For *hungry* cp. *N.T.Wb.*/46, and below on 4 : 2[b]. Sranan has here, 'the hungry-belly people'; in South Toradja the etymology of the term is 'not-satiated'.

Rich (also in 6 : 24; 12 : 16, 21; 14 : 12; 16 : 1, 19, 21f; 18 : 23, 25; 19 : 2; 21 : 1) is in some cases rendered by a derivation of 'to-be(-available)' (East Toradja, similarly Navajo, Apache), or, 'to-be-strong/firm/secure' (another Apache dialect); a possible descriptive rendering is 'having much property/money', 'having plenty'.

Has sent empty away, or, 'sends away with empty hands', or, 'without anything' (Kapauku), 'carrying nothing' (Tagalog), 'just as he is' (Navajo), 'smooth (i.e. with nothing on them)' (Apache), 'hands and hands' (Kikongo), cp. 'holding his own hands (i.e. with nothing but his own hands)' (Yipounou); or, 'sent-straight-forward-away', implying that the person can take nothing with him (Sediq).

54 ***He has helped his servant Israel,***
in remembrance of his mercy,
55 ***as he spoke to our fathers,***
to Abraham and to his posterity for ever."

Exegesis: *antelabeto Israēl paidos autou* 'he has helped Israel his servant'; *paidos autou* predicative apposition to *Israēl*. There is little direct connexion between this phrase and those of vv. 51-53; the latter refer to groups or categories of people within or outside Israel, here the reference is to the people of Israel as a whole and exclusively.

antilambanō (†) with genitive 'to lay hold of' in order to assist or to support; with an undertone of concern and care for the person whom one lays hold of.

pais 'son' or 'servant'; here of the people of Israel as set apart by God for some divine commission, cp. Is. 41 : 8; 44 : 21.

mnēsthēnai eleous 'to remember his mercy'. With a view to the Hebraistic background of the style and idiom of the hymn the infinitive is best understood as the equivalent of a Hebrew infinitive with the preposition *le* which sometimes denotes some act or happening parallel with, or motivating the act or event expressed by the preceding verb, cp. Klostermann; hence e.g., 'he has helped... ; he has remembered his mercy'.

mimnēskomai (always in the aorist tense and usually with genitive) 'to remember', 'to care for'; when said of God it often implies that He performed some act of redemption as a consequence of His remembering.

(V. 55) *kathōs elalēsen pros tous pateras hēmōn* 'as he has spoken to our forefathers'; *kathōs* refers back either to *antelabeto* or to *mnēsthēnai* or perhaps to the whole preceding verse, preferably the second.

tō Abraam kai tō spermati autou 'to Abraham and his offspring'.

The datives *tō Abraam* etc. are interpreted either as a freely construed apposition to *tous pateras hēmōn* (*laleō* is followed either by *pros* with accusative or by a dative, cp. v. 22), or as going with *mnēsthēnai* in the preceding verse and indicating the person who benefits by God's remembering of His mercy, preferably the former, since the forefathers are virtually identical with Abraham, the first to receive the promise, and his offspring, to whom the promise was subsequently renewed.

sperma (also 20 : 28) 'seed', here in the figurative sense of 'descendants' or 'offspring' of a male ancestor.

eis ton aiōna 'unto eternity', cp. on v. 33; the phrase is to be connected with *mnēsthēnai*.

Translation: *Has helped* has been rendered here by, 'takes...to his side' (Sranan), 'has taken the hand of' (Kanarese), an idiomatic expression lit. meaning 'runs for their sake' (Navajo).

His servant Israel, or, in order that this be not taken as a reference to the patriarch Israel/Jacob: 'Israel, his servants', 'the people Israel, (that is) his servant (or, that serves him)', 'the Israelites, his...servants (or, who serve him)'. That the reference is to the speaker's own people has to be made explicit in some languages, e.g. in Huixtec; this may lead to such renderings as 'we the people of Israel, his servants', 'we his servants, who are descendants of Israel'. Other occurrences of (the people) *Israel*: 1 : 68, 80; 2 : 25, 32, 34; 4 : 25, 27; 7 : 9; 22 : 30; 24 : 21. For *servant* see on 12 : 37, and for the religious connotation it has here on "handmaid" in 1 : 38.

In remembrance of his mercy, or shifting to verbs, 'and (or, because) he remembers to have-mercy/be-merciful'. With the latter verb an indication of the beneficiary may be obligatory. In that case the translator who follows the interpretation preferred in *Exegesis* can best transfer 'our (fore)fathers' to this clause, replacing it by a pronominal reference in the next. — The verb 'to remember' in the sense of 'to keep in mind for care and attention' is in some cases more idiomatically, or forcefully, rendered by 'not to forget' (NEB, Tagabili). Elsewhere (e.g. in Miskito, Karré, Moré) it can be expressed by a phrase combining 'to keep', 'to take', 'to bear' with 'in the heart/chest/stomach'.

(V. 55) The interpretation given in *Exegesis* implies taking this verse as one clause, in which 55^b is appositional to 'fathers'; this relationship is sometimes better overtly marked, e.g. 'that is (or, to wit) to Abraham...'.

As he spoke to..., or, 'in accordance with what he promised (to do) to...'; or changing the syntactic structure, 'firm in his promise to...' (cp. NEB); or again, starting a new sentence, 'So doing he performs/fulfils what he had spoken to...', 'Thus he keeps his promise to...' (cp. TEV). It may be obligatory (e.g. because the linguistic and historical order should parallel each other), or stylistically preferable, to place v. 55 before v. 54.

For *fathers*, i.e. 'ancestors' (also in 1 : 72; 6 : 23, 26; 11 : 47f) see *N.T.Wb.*/34, and cp. above on the singular in v. 32. Navajo and Apache can use 'fathers' with an enclitic that expresses the meaning 'former/who-used-to-be'. Elsewhere the forefathers are collectively referred to as, 'grand- and greatgrandparents' (Bahasa Indonesia), 'people of former days' (East and South Toradja), 'elevated-ones' (Balinese; for those in a very remote past: 'origin/beginning'), 'root' (Barrow Eskimo), 'elders of old' (Kituba), 'those from whom we descend' (Tagabili).

Abraham. In predominantly Muslim countries the Arabic form of the name, *Ibrahim*, has often been adopted. It should be remembered, however, that the Koran does not only change Abraham's name but also his character: he is the prototype of the true Muslim, a prophet whose teaching was a refutation of Jewish belief, who built the sanctuary in, and instituted the pilgrimage to Mecca (Sura 2 : 124-135, 22 : 78, etc.). Where a translator is still free to choose, he will do best to take the Hebrew form of the name as basis of transliteration.

His posterity, or, 'those who will be born from Abr. following each other in line' (Apache), 'his children-grandchildren' (Malay), 'his descendants'.

Forever can, as a rule, better be placed closer to the clause or phrase it goes with, v. 54^b.

In the other interpretation of v. 55, which takes 55^b with 54^b, line 55^a acquires the character of a parenthesis. Where parentheses are not normally used, some possible restructurings are, (1) to put 55^a at the head or the tail of the sentence; (2) to repeat part of 54^b in 55^b, cp. '...mercy-of-him, as what he promised to our ancestors, that mercy-of-him toward Abr. ...' (South Toradja); (3) to reverse the position and role of 'mercy' and of line 55^a respectively, cp. '...remembering his promise to our ancestors: (that he) would have-mercy-on Abr. ...' (Balinese, similarly Tagabili).

56 ***And Mary remained with her about three months, and returned to her home.***

Exegesis: *emeinen de Mariam sun autē* 'and Mary stayed with her'.

menō 'to stay', 'to remain', here in the meaning of 'to stay for a visit'.

de marks the transition from the hymn to the resumption of the narrative which began in v. 39.

hōs mēnas treis 'about three months'; accusative of temporal extension or duration and indicating the length of Mary's visit.

hōs here 'approximately'; the phrase implies that Mary stayed with Elizabeth till about the birth of John the Baptist, but Luke does not state explicitly that she was still present when the birth took place.

kai hupestrepsen eis ton oikon autēs 'and she returned to her (own) home'.

hupostrephō 'to turn back', 'to return'.

Translation: *With her,* i.e. 'with Elizabeth' (Jerusalem), or, 'at Elizabeth's' (Balinese), 'in Elizabeth's house' (Javanese), or simply, 'there' (East Toradja, Toba Batak).

For *about* cp. on 9: 14.

And, or, 'then', 'next', 'after that'.

57 ***Now the time came for Elizabeth to be delivered, and she gave birth to a son.***

Exegesis: *tē de Elisabet eplēsthē ho chronos tou tekein autēn* 'for Elizabeth the time of her delivery was fulfilled'. The expression 'the days, or, the time is fulfilled' as a whole (1: 23, 57; 2: 6, 21, 22) combines two ideas: (1) that a certain time must elapse before something can happen, as shown by the fact that *hēmerai* 'days', and *chronos* 'time', always denote a period, never a moment; (2) that the time has come for something to happen, as intimated by *eplēsthē* 'was fulfilled'. The construction of *tou tekein autēn* is an articular accusative and infinitive (cp. Moule 127f): the accusative is the logical subject of the action expressed by the infinitive.

ho chronos 'time', 'period of time'.

kai egennēsen huion 'and she bore a son'; *gennaō* and *tiktō* are synonymous, cp. vv. 13 and 31; here Luke's shift from the one to the other is in order to avoid repetition.

Translation: *Now* is not temporal here, but transitional, marking a new division in the narrative. Cp. also v. 8, where "now" renders Gr. *egeneto de.*

The time came for Elizabeth to be delivered. In speaking of a woman's coming delivery specific idioms are often in use, e.g. 'her month to bring-forth (a child) becomes' (Kapauku), 'the day arrives when she goes into labour (lit. day of labour-paining her abdomen)' (Tagabili), 'full the time/days of her pregnancy (lit. being-with-life)' (Toba Batak), 'complete her months to give-birth' (Bahasa Indonesia); some such idioms do not explicitly refer to the actual delivery, e.g. 'her days are fully fulfilled' (Marathi), and cp. English "her time comes".

She gave birth to a son, see on "to bear a son" in v. 13; Marathi expresses this by 'a son became to her'. Some languages must render the synonymous expressions "to be delivered" and "to give birth" by forms of the same verb, e.g. Kituba, Sundanese, East Toradja.

58 ***And her neighbours and kinsfolk heard that the Lord had shown great mercy to her, and they rejoiced with her.***

Exegesis: *hoi perioikoi* (††) lit. 'those living around (her)', 'neighbours'.
hoi suggeneis autēs "her relatives" (Goodspeed), cp. on v. 36.
hoti emegalunen kurios to eleos autou met' autēs 'that the Lord had made large his mercy with her', i.e. 'dealt with her in a very merciful way'; for *emegalunen* cp. on v. 46; for *to eleos* cp. on v. 50. *met' autēs* 'with her', a Hebraism, means that she is the one to whom God's mercy is directed.
kai sunechairon autē 'and they were glad with her'.
sugchairō 'to rejoice with someone', or 'to congratulate'; here in the former meaning, and referring not only to inner feelings of joy and delight but also to their manifestation. The imperfect suggests duration as contrasted with the momentary aspect of the aorist of *ēkousan*.

Translation: The first clause is sometimes better subordinated, e.g. 'when her neighbours...heard that the Lord..., they rejoiced', 'on hearing that the Lord..., her neighbours...rejoiced'.
Neighbours, or, 'those who lived beside her' (Apache), 'those of the same street (or, ward)', 'co-villagers' (East Toradja), 'people living-close-together around there' (South Toradja), 'the surrounding houses' (Timorese), all implying a local relationship; cp. also *TH-Mk* on 12 : 31.
Kinsfolk, i.e. those of the same family or clan; cp. *N.T.Wb.*/33, FAMILY.
That the Lord had shown great mercy to her, or, 'that the Lord had been very merciful towards her, or, had greatly mercy-ed her, or, had performed a very merciful deed for her'; cp. 'that the Lord had made his mercy come so big over her' (Sranan), 'the Lord's having been greatly kind to her' (Navajo).
Rejoiced with her. The aspect is inceptive-durative, which in Marathi is expressed by the use of an inceptive imperfect form. Javanese has, 'joined (in being) glad', which says by implication only that they were glad with Elizabeth; Bamiléké uses a compound pronoun serving to refer to a combination of two groups or of an individual with a group: 'they rejoiced they-plus-her (lit. they-with-they)', which comes close to a reciprocal expression.

59 ***And on the eighth day they came to circumcise the child; and they would have named him Zechariah after his father,***
60 ***but his mother said, "Not so; he shall be called John."***

Exegesis: *kai egeneto...ēlthon* 'and it happened...that they came'; cp. on v. 8.
en tē hēmera tē ogdoē ēlthon peritemein to paidion 'on the eighth day they

came to circumcise the child', as prescribed in Gen. 17 : 9-14. The infinitive is final; the subject of *ēlthon* must be understood from those mentioned in v. 58.

en tē hēmera tē ogdoē 'on the eighth day', or, since according to Jewish time reckoning the day of birth is counted as a full day, 'seven days after his birth'.

peritemnō (also 2 : 21) 'to circumcise', technical term for the performing of the rite of circumcision, which consists of the cutting away of the prepuce or foreskin of the newly born males, cp. Gen. 17 : 9-14, Lev. 12 : 1-3; it was a distinctive sign of the covenant relationship between Israel and God.

paidion in ch. 1 and 2 'infant', elsewhere 'child' in a general sense, referring usually to children from about three to twelve years.

kai ekaloun auto...Zacharian 'they wanted to call it Zechariah'; the imperfect tense is best understood as conative (Moule 8f, BFBS, Jerusalem, Zürich). *Zacharian* is an accusative used predicatively, i.e. to 'predicate' something of a noun (here *auto*) already in the accusative, cp. Moule 35.

epi tō onomati tou patros autou 'after the name of his father'; this profane use of the expression *epi tō onomati* is to be distinguished from its religious meaning as in 9 : 48; 21 : 8; 24 : 47, cp. A-G s.v. *onoma* 4 c ε. To call a child after the name of his father was not uncommon, though not widespread.

(V. 60) *kai apokritheisa...eipen* 'and, answering, (she) said'. *apokrinomai* is often used without a preceding question or communication addressed to its subject. In such a context it introduces the subject's reaction or comment upon (a) the situation (13 : 14; 17 : 17; 22 : 51), or (b) other peoples' thoughts or plans (1 : 60; 3 : 16; 5 : 22; 14 : 3), or (c) something said in general (9 : 49), or (d) something said to other people (5 : 31; 7 : 40; 8 : 50; 11 : 45; 13 : 15; 20 : 39; 23 : 40). The usual construction is that of a participle going with a verb of saying (except 3 : 16 and 8 : 50).

ouchi as a negative particle 'no', 'by no means'.

alla 'but', 'rather', cp. A-G s.v. 1 a.

Translation: *On the eighth day*, or, specifying the connexion with what precedes, 'the eighth day after that (or, after his/the child's birth)', 'seven nights later', 'when the child was a week old', etc.

They came to circumcise the child. The neighbours and kinsfolk were not the agents of the circumcision; hence, 'they came to join in the circumcision ceremony of the child' (Balinese), 'they came to join-in with their (referring to those directly responsible) circumcising the child' (Tagabili). For *circumcise* and 'circumcision' see Nida, *BT*, 190; the term may preferably be identified as a rite or ceremony, cp. Wonderly, *BTPU*, 107f. Some renderings are based on the act as such, e.g. 'to cut the flesh' (Quechua of Ecuador), 'to cut around' (Mixtec, Navajo), 'to clip-away' (Javanese), 'to pinch and cut', usually shortened to 'to cut' (Timorese); others are based on the rite's function, e.g. 'to put the mark' (Barrow Eskimo, Tarascan), or more explanatory, 'to put the mark in the body showing that they belong to God (Tetelcingo Aztec), or, that they have a covenant with God';

'to cause to receive the ceremony for entering *sunat*', recently proposed Thai rendering, making use of the Arabic term *sunnah* '(religious) way (of life)'. In several Indonesian languages the same Arabic borrowing is the current technical term for the Muslim rite of circumcision, and has been used for the corresponding rite mentioned in the Bible. Reactions to a bald reference to the actual operation vary from language to language; in Pampango, for instance, such a term can be used in front of women and in church, but in Tagabili teachers refuse to read publicly any portion containing the same term, although they insist in having it in the translation. Some versions have two renderings, one a rather overt term or phrase, used in only one or two occurrences, the other more veiled and used in all other occurrences, cp. Bahasa Indonesia (revision), which in Gen. 17 : 10f has 'every male...should undergo-*sunat*; his foreskin (lit. skin of circumcision, partly another Arabic borrowing) should be cut', but in most other occurrences uses '(undergo-)*sunat*'; similarly Kapauku, which in Gen. 17 uses, 'to cut the end of the member for which one fears shame', but elsewhere refers to circumcision as 'the cutting custom'; or in Tzotzil, see *TBT*, 9.90f, 1958.

They would have named him Zechariah after his father refers to an event that might have happened had it not been prevented by Elizabeth. *To name him Z. after his father* is rendered variously, cp. e.g. 'to give him the name of his father Z.' (Sranan, 'Z.' going with 'father'), 'to give him the name of his father, Z.' (Kituba, 'Z.' going with 'name'), 'call him Z. same-name(-as) his father' (South Toradja), 'name him (lit. place his name) Z. after (lit. from above, or, on) the name of his father' (Marathi).

(V. 60) *Not so*, or, 'No, no!' (Sranan). Some languages resemble the Greek in requiring a transitional term after a prohibitive word, e.g. 'No, but' (Zürich, similarly Bahasa Indonesia).

He shall be called, or, 'his name is, or, must be', 'we (inclus.) shall call him'.

61 ***And they said to her, "None of your kindred is called by this name."***

Exegesis: *hoti* marks here the beginning of direct speech, cp. A-G s.v. 2.

oudeis estin ek tēs suggeneias sou hos kaleitai tō onomati toutō 'there is nobody of your relatives who is called by that name'. *ek tēs suggeneias sou* 'of your relatives' goes with *oudeis* and stands for a partitive genitive, meaning 'belonging to', or 'being a part of'.

suggeneia (†) 'kinship', here in the concrete and collective sense 'relatives', cp. on v. 36 (*suggenis*).

Translation: *None of your kindred*. The partitive, often expressed by prepositions, cp. "in" (NEB), 'among' (Bahasa Indonesia), may also be indicated by simple juxtaposition of the collective noun and the reference to the part, e.g. 'all your-relatives no one' (Javanese, South Toradja). For *kindred* cp. on "kinsfolk" in v. 58.

None...is called by this name, or, 'not one is called/named that way'

(Apache), "there is no one...who bears that name" (Goodspeed), 'no one...we (inclus.) call thus, or, by that name'.

62 ***And they made signs to his father, inquiring what he would have him called.***

Exegesis: *eneneuon de tō patri autou* 'and they made signs to his father'.

enneuō (††; cp. *dianeuō* in v. 22) 'to nod', 'to make signs'; the use of this verb here seems to imply that Zechariah is deaf as well as dumb, which is not excluded by *kōphos* (v. 22); on the other hand the story supposes that Zechariah has heard the preceding discussion.

to ti an theloi kaleisthai auto "as to what he wished him to be called" (BFBS); the indirect question is made into a substantival phrase by prefixing the article in the neuter (cp. Bl-D, § 267.2). The connexion of this phrase with the verb in the main clause is syntactically rather loose; the article may be understood as introducing the question that is implied in *eneneuon* and explicitly stated in the substantival phrase.

thelō 'to wish', 'to desire'.

Translation: *They made signs...inquiring*, or, 'asked...by (making) signs'; the following question is often better given in direct discourse. For *to make signs* see above on v. 22; Sediq has 'to use-talk-for-the-deaf', a verbal derivation from 'deaf'.

His...he...him refer to the child, the father, and the child again, which may have to be specified, e.g. by using 'child/babe/boy' in the first and/or in the third instance.

What he would have him called, or, 'how he wanted that they/people should call the child' (Sranan), 'how he liked them to mention/call his name' (Timorese); or, taking Zechariah as the agent both of the wishing and the calling, e.g. 'how he would call his child' (East Toradja), "What name do you desire to give?" (three Dravidian languages), 'what name he wished to name him' (Kapauku, which possesses two interrogatives, the one for a choice out of two, the other for a choice out of many; though the first is not impossible, since the names Zechariah and John have been in discussion, the second interrogative has been preferred).

63 ***And he asked for a writing tablet, and wrote, "His name is John." And they all marvelled.***

Exegesis: *aitēsas pinakidion* 'having asked for a writing-tablet', by signs of course.

aiteō 'to ask', 'to ask for'.

pinakidion (††) 'writing-tablet', consisting of a small board (yew tree, according to Jewish sources) covered with wax.

egrapsen legōn lit. 'he wrote saying...', but *legōn* is a literal translation of Hebrew *le'mor* which can introduce indirect speech even when the words are not spoken but written, cp. 2 Kings 10 : 6.

Translation: *Asked for*, cp. *N.T.Wb.*/12f. In some languages the corresponding verb can only be used when speech is implied; hence e.g. 'he caused to be brought' (Kanarese).

Writing tablet, or somewhat more generically, 'board/thing-to-write-on' (Sundanese, Toba Batak), 'that on which he could write' (Tagabili); or, 'slate' (Balinese, Marathi; also East Toradja, Kituba, lit. 'stone on which-to-write').

He wrote, usually to be followed by a marker of quotation, e.g. 'thus' (East Toradja). In some cases a marker which primarily refers to quoted speech can also be used with extended meaning in reference to writing, e.g. 'its-sound' (Malay), 'saying' (Sranan, Navajo, Apache).

And they all marvelled, or, specifying the connexion with what precedes, 'therefore they all were perplexed' (Toba Batak), 'they all were astonished at it' (Jerusalem), 'that surprised them' (cp. Phillips). For *to marvel* see on "wondered" in v. 21.

64 ***And immediately his mouth was opened and his tongue loosed, and he spoke, blessing God.***

Exegesis: *aneōchthē de to stoma autou parachrēma* 'and his mouth was opened at once'.

anoigō 'to open'; when used with *stoma* 'mouth' the verb usually refers to the beginning of speech, cp. e.g. Mt. 5 : 2; 13 : 35; but here it refers to the restoration of the mouth to its proper function, cp. Mt. 20 : 33; Jn. 9 : 10, 14, 17, 26, 30, 32 (of the eyes) and Mk. 7 : 35 (of the ears).

parachrēma 'at once', 'immediately', a more literary word than the more common *euthus* or *eutheōs*. The place of *parachrēma* here between the two subjects of the clause is awkward and stresses its zeugmatic character, see next note.

kai hē glōssa autou 'and his tongue', connected with *aneōchthē* by a zeugma, i.e. a construction which joins one verb with two different subjects; the normal verb with *glōssa* would be *eluthē* 'was loosed' (cp. RSV). *glōssa* also 16 : 24.

kai elalei eulogōn ton theon 'and he spoke, praising God'; the use of the phrase *elalei eulogōn* instead of the more simple *ēulogei* 'he praised' stresses the implication that he was now again able to speak; the participle *eulogōn* qualifies Zechariah's speaking as praising God; the imperfect tense of *elalei* suggests that Zechariah continued to speak for some time.

eulogeō, see on v. 42; here it is used in a sense different from v. 42, with God as object and meaning 'to praise', cp. A-G s.v. 1.

Translation: *Immediately* (also in 4 : 39; 5 : 13, 25; 6 : 49; 8 : 44, 47; 13 : 13; 14 : 5; 18 : 43; 19 : 11; 22 : 60), or, 'at the very moment', 'right then'. Since the word introduces an event that coincides with another event, or follows it after only a very short interval, the word may also be rendered by a phrase such as, 'while he did so...', 'as soon as he had done this...'.

His mouth was opened and his tongue loosed. In some languages the zeugma of the Greek (i.e. the use of one verb with two subjects in such a manner that it applies to each in a different sense) can be preserved, cp. 'the tie which had bound the mouth and tongue having become loose' (Tamil), 'his mouth and tongue were-loosed/opened/untied' (Kituba, similarly in Javanese); since this figure of style is more or less artificial the use of a rendering that is not entirely natural in the receptor language may be considered. But even so it may prove impossible to find one verb that can do duty with both subjects; hence the addition of a second verb (cp. *Exegesis*), e.g. 'lived' (Sundanese), 'became-relaxed' (South Toradja), 'became flexible' (Lahu, where mutes are considered to have 'stiff tongues'). Some other adaptations may be needed, e.g. where a personal subject is preferable, hence, 'he could open his mouth...'; or where it must be made clear that the organs of speech, 'mouth' (or "lips", NEB, South Toradja) and/or 'tongue', refer metaphorically to the faculty of speech, cp. e.g. 'the mouth of Zechariah opened, he could use his tongue to speak' (Français Courant), "his voice and the use of his tongue were...restored" (Goodspeed), 'his tongue having straightened (an idiom used of a child that has learned to speak) he uttered-speech' (Kapauku); 'his mouth came to him (a similar idiom), his tongue became loose' (Kanarese), 'his tongue loosed' (Sediq, rendering only the second metaphor which is idiomatically acceptable in the language, and shifting the reference to 'mouth' to the next clause, 'his mouth spoke glorifying God', in order to preserve it in translation); or simply, 'his dumbness was-removed/healed' (Tagabili), 'he was able to speak again' (Cuyono, cp. TEV). For *mouth* cp. also *N.T.Wb.*/17, BODY.

He spoke, blessing God. The implications discussed in *Exegesis* are brought out in, 'his first words were to praise God' (cp. Phillips), 'as one having the power of speech, he praised God' (Kanarese). For *to bless* in the sense it is used here cp. on 1 : 42, sub (2).

65 ***And fear came on all their neighbours. And all these things were talked about through all the hill country of Judea;***

Exegesis: *kai egeneto epi pantas phobos tous perioikountas autous* 'and there came fear on all who lived in their neighbourhood'; the subject of the clause, *phobos*, is placed between *pantas* and *tous* which belong closely together. This word order is very awkward and without parallel in the New Testament. It is best explained as a stylistic means to emphasize *pantas*, cp. Bl-D, § 472.2.

kai egeneto...phobos 'and there came fear'; the expression is more general than *epepesen phobos*, 'fear fell upon (him)' in v. 12 (which stresses the unexpected and overwhelming character of what happened and is Hebraistic, cp. Gen. 35 : 5).

perioikeō with accusative (††) 'to live in the neighbourhood of somebody'; *autous* refers to Zechariah and Elizabeth.

en holē tē oreinē tēs Ioudaias 'in all the hill country of Judea'; cp. on v. 39.

hē Ioudaia, cp. on v. 5.
dielaleito panta ta rēmata tauta 'were all these things talked about'.
dialaleō (also 6 : 11) 'to talk about', 'to discuss', not 'to tell'.

Translation: *Their neighbours* in this context refers to a larger local group than in v. 58, and probably to one with fewer or no social ties. This may necessitate the use of different renderings, compare 'those in the same region' with 'neighbours' in v. 58, or, 'those living nearby' with 'those living next door' (Toba Batak).

All these things were talked about, or, 'people were talking together about these things' (Kanarese), 'these things became widely known' (Telugu), 'they-spread-the-news' (East Toradja); cp. also on "a report...went out" in 4 : 14.

Judea is used here in its proper sense (see *Exegesis* on v. 5) and refers to the same region as "Judah" in v. 39.

66 ***and all who heard them laid them up in their hearts, saying, "What then will this child be?" For the hand of the Lord was with him.***

Exegesis: *kai ethento...en tē kardia autōn* 'and (they) laid to heart'; the phrase is best understood in the light of the Hebrew expression *śim b^{e}lêb* 'to lay to heart', 'to pay heed to'. The subsequent clause indicates that the expression here refers to the astonishment caused by the birth of the child of Zechariah and Elizabeth.

ti ara to paidion touto estai 'what then will this child be'. *ara* serves here to enliven the question, cp. A-G s.v. 2. The question is rhetorical, i.e. no direct answer is given or expected, although the question itself more or less suggests an answer.

kai gar cheir kuriou ēn met' autou 'for indeed the hand of the Lord was with him', in order to help him or to stand by him, cp. A-G s.v. *meta* A II 1 c β.

kai gar, stronger than the sole *gar*, an elliptic phrase, either as "for besides all that" (Plummer, Klostermann), or, as "for indeed" (NEB, Jerusalem), preferably the latter.

cheir kuriou 'the hand of the Lord', i.e. the saving and helping power of the Lord, cp. A-G s.v. *cheir* 2 a.

einai met' autou 'to be with him'.

Translation: *All who heard them.* The pronoun "them", here and in the next clause, refers to "these things" (v. 65), i.e. the events told in the preceding narrative, cp. "the whole matter" (Phillips); in some languages idiom requires a reference to the talking heard (cp. on v. 41), e.g. 'all who heard people speak about them, or, heard the talk about that whole matter'.

Laid them up in their hearts. Many languages have formally similar expressions, but that does not warrant their referring to the same state of mind. South Toradja, for instance, possesses three comparable expressions,

(1) 'put-into the stomach (inward being)', equivalent to English 'lay to heart'; (2) 'put-into the spirit/mind', i.e. 'consider'; and (3) 'put-into the breast', i.e. 'feel offended'. Some other idioms used are, 'engraved in their heart' (Jerusalem), 'noted-down in their heart' (Sundanese).

What then will this child be, or "become" (NEB, also many other versions), or, 'whoever will this child become', an idiom suggesting that the child will be someone great (Marathi, where a comparable idiom, 'how will this child turn out', would suggest a reference to a naughty boy), 'then what will that infant be(come) in the future' (Thai, where a shorter idiom, 'what will that infant become', would be used when referring to disease or infirmity that may be in store for the child).

The hand of the Lord was with him is usually to be rendered by another metaphorical expression, such as 'he was sheltered by the hand of the Lord' (Javanese), 'the Lord carried him on the palm of His hand' (South Toradja), 'the eye of God was always on him' (Tagabili, a figurative expression used of a possession one values highly, or a person one loves dearly); or non-metaphorically, e.g. 'the Lord helped him' (Bolivian Quechua, Kituba). Most of the renderings of 'to be with' are different from those in v. 28, one of the reasons being that expressions used there with a personal subject cannot go with 'hand' or 'power'. Bamiléké uses a compound pronoun indicating individual dual (cp. on v. 58): 'the hand of the Lord was he-plus-he'. For *hand* (passim) cp. also *N.T.Wb.*/42.

67 ***And his father Zechariah was filled with the Holy Spirit, and prophesied, saying,***

Exegesis: *eplēsthē pneumatos hagiou* 'was filled with the Holy Spirit', cp. on vv. 15 and 41.

kai eprophēteusen legōn 'and prophesied, saying'; the clause refers, together with the preceding phrase, to a specific happening as is shown by the aorist tense. The participle *legōn* 'saying', when going with a main verb denoting an act of speaking (e.g. *eipon* 'they said' in 7 : 39, or *boaō* 'to shout' in 18 : 38), or an act performed by means of speaking (e.g. *prophēteuō* here, or *epitimaō* 'to rebuke' in 4 : 35, or *eperotaō* 'to ask' in 3 : 10, or *aineō* 'to praise' in 19 : 37) has no semantic value of its own but serves as a formula introducing direct speech, cp. Bl-D, § 420. Whether or not it is rendered depends on the question whether the main verb can be followed immediately by direct speech in the receptor language.

prophēteuō (also 22 : 64) 'to proclaim a divine revelation'. The verb refers primarily to the content of the divine message and not to the condition of the prophet.

Translation: *His father Zechariah,* or specifying the pronoun, 'Z., the one who was the baby's father'.

Prophesied. Often the phrase or term for 'prophet' (for which see on v. 70) contains, or is built upon, a verb that can be used here; in other cases, esp. where a borrowing (e.g. from a European language, or from Arabic, *nabi*) is used, one may have to use, 'speak like a prophet' (Sranan,

Balinese). Tagabili has, 'interpreted for God', the basic meaning of which verb is 'to put-an-extension-to something', in order to make it fulfil its purpose or make it of value, here figuratively of putting the proper extension to God's words in order to make them valuable for man. In Apache, which renders 'prophet' by 'one-whom-God-works', God has to become the subject, 'and God spoke through him (i.e. Zechariah)'.

(Vv. 68-75) For the interpretation of the aorist tenses in vv. 68 and 72 see note on vv. 51-54. The birth of John the Baptist warrants as it were the fulfilment of these prophecies.

In the Greek these eight verses form one sentence, without any full stop. Although the connexion between some of its clauses is rather loose, the syntactic structure seeks to suggest a unity: the praise offered to the Lord God of Israel in v. 68[a] is made clear in, and rings on to the very end of, the twelve subsequent lines. It is often preferable to break up the long sentence into shorter co-ordinated sentences, expressing the semantic unity by the use of transitional expressions and connective words; for details see below on the verses concerned.

In languages requiring a close parallelism between linguistic and historical sequence a more radical restructuring may be needed, in which the reference to the covenant sworn to Abraham (vv. 72[b]-75; or, following the other exegesis, only vv. 72[b]-73) and to the words of the prophets (v. 70) will have to be placed immediately after line 68[a], with ensuing adaptations.

Zechariah probably was addressing the company in his house, i.e. his wife, household, relatives and neighbours; hence, the pronouns of the first person plural occurring in these verses have inclusive force (cp. on vv. 46-56). If honorifics must be employed, they should be appropriate to the highest ranking person(s) present, in this case probably Zechariah's and Elizabeth's relatives, who were members of the honoured priestly group.

68 ***"Blessed be the Lord God of Israel,***
for he has visited and redeemed his people,

Exegesis: *eulogētos* (†) 'praised', with *eiē* 'be' (optative), or *estin* 'is' understood, preferably the latter. As distinct from *eulogēmenos* (see on v. 42), *eulogētos* in the New Testament always refers to God or to Jesus Christ.

kurios ho theos tou Israēl 'the Lord, the God of Israel'; because of the Old Testament background of the phrase it is best to understand *kurios* as representing the name Yahweh and not as a title.

hoti epeskepsato 'for he has visited (his people)' with *ton laon* understood.

episkeptomai in Luke always of God's visiting of his people in order to bestow some grace upon them, here the redemption referred to in the subsequent clause. Thus the verb here prepares, as it were, the way for that clause.

kai epoiēsen lutrōsin tō laō autou 'and he has brought about redemption for his people'. In this Hebraistic phrase the event is indicated by the verbal noun *lutrōsis*, *epoiēsen* having only an auxiliary function; hence the rendering 'redeemed' (cp. RSV).

lutrōsis (also 2 : 38) 'redemption', cp. *N.T.Wb.*, 109/.

Translation: *Blessed*, or, 'worthy of praise' (Tagalog); or, where active forms must be used, 'I wish-to praise' (Kituba), 'the Lord...should receive big name' (Sranan).

The Lord God of Israel. For "the Lord, (the) God" followed by a possessive, see above on v. 16.

Has visited. The verb 'to visit', 'to come to see' sometimes has the required connotation of 'to care for', e.g. in Trukese, Zarma. Elsewhere other verbs or phrases must be used to indicate that connotation, e.g. 'to look-(down-)upon' (East Toradja, Kituba), 'to turn-to-look-at' (Tagabili), 'to descend-upon' (Balinese in 7 : 16, a term commonly used when the gods visit their worshippers e.g. at a temple festival), 'to forget not' (Cuyono in 7 : 16), and quite explicitly, 'come to help/save' (Spanish VP, TEV). In the present verse, however, some versions use a more generic verb because of the specification given by the next verb, e.g. 'he has come to redeem his people' (cp. Navajo, Apache).

Redeemed, cp. *N.T.Wb.*/60f, RANSOM, and *TBT*, 18.80f, 1967.

In Greek or English *his people* can have two meanings, (1) 'the people he rules' (as intended here), and (2) 'the people he is member of', but in other languages the use of the possessive pronoun may suggest either (1) or (2); if (2), then another rendering must be chosen. Therefore South Toradja says 'the men He has chosen'; some other Indonesian languages use a noun that characterizes a people as the followers of a prophet or subjects of a god, and normally takes the possessive pronoun as a reference to that prophet or god. For *people* cp. above on v. 17; for making explicit that the reference is to the people to which the speaker belongs, cp. on "his servant Israel" in v. 54.

69 ***and has raised up a horn of salvation for us***
in the house of his servant David,

Exegesis: *kai ēgeiren keras sōtērias hēmin* 'and he has raised up a horn of salvation for us'.

egeirō 'to wake', 'to raise', 'to raise up' (in the active), 'to rise' (in the passive); when used with a personal object it may be rendered 'to bring into being', 'to cause to appear', and it is implied that the object will have to fulfil a task, cp. A-G s.v. 1 a ε and *N.T.Wb.*, 107/. This meaning fits the interpretation of *keras sōtērias*, given below.

keras sōtērias is translated literally by the great majority of translators. In the Old Testament 'horn' is often a symbol of might and power, cp. Jer. 48 : 25; Zech. 1 : 18ff; Ez. 29 : 21. But in 2 Sam. 22 : 3 (= Ps. 18 : 2) God is called "the horn of my salvation", and Strack-Billerbeck (II, 111) quotes ancient Jewish prayers where the same expression refers to the davidic Messiah; hence translations like "a mighty Savior" (Goodspeed, cp. *Problems* 70f, reprinted *TBT*, 3.69f, 1952, see also BFBS, NEB, Moffatt, Weymouth). *keras* (†).

en oikō Dauid paidos autou 'in the house of David, his servant'; this addition shows that the preceding clause is a reference to the davidic Messiah.

Translation: *Horn of salvation.* A literal rendering (though possible in some languages, e.g. in Timorese which can use 'horn' metaphorically for 'hero') is, as a rule, impossible. Yet the tendency seems to be strong to use such a rendering, even when unidiomatic, misleading, or incomprehensible in the language concerned, and to disregard existing acceptable cultural equivalents (e.g. 'tusk', suggesting 'champion/hero', in Balinese). In the material investigated only two translators render "horn" by another metaphor, viz. Phillips, "standard", and Knox, "sceptre". Some non-metaphorical renderings are, 'one who is very strong, who will save us/people' (cp. Apache, Tagabili), 'salvation-hero' (Kanarese); or, following the non-personal interpretation, 'token of happiness/salvation' (South Toradja), or (combining such a rendering with a simile), 'caused the help/salvation to grow like an animal's horn' (Sranan). For *salvation*, or, 'Saviour', cp. on v. 47.

In the house of, cp. on v. 27, for *his servant David*, or, 'David, who is his servant', cp. on v. 32.

70 ***as he spoke by the mouth of his holy prophets from of old,***

Exegesis: *kathōs elalēsen* 'as he spoke', subject God.

dia stomatos tōn hagiōn ap' aiōnos prophētōn autou 'through the mouth of his holy prophets of old'.

dia stomatos in Luke and Acts always (with the exception of Acts 15 : 7 where the reference is to the preaching of the Gospel) introduces a quotation of, or a reference to, a word of God in the Old Testament, cp. Acts 1 : 16, 4 : 25 (David); 3 : 18 (all the prophets).

hagios 'holy' here as an attribute of people consecrated to God, cp. A-G s.v. 1 b α.

ap' aiōnos 'of old time', either 'from the beginning of time' (cp. Zürich, 'from eternity') or 'of time gone by', 'of long ago' (so the majority of translators), preferably the latter; the phrase is attributive to *prophētōn.*

prophētēs 'prophet', i.e. the person who proclaims and interprets a divine revelation mostly by means of the spoken word.

Translation: The verse qualifies the events referred to in vv. 68^b and 69 as being the fulfilment of God's promise. It acquires the character of a parenthesis when, as preferred in *Exegesis*, v. 71 is taken with v. 69. Where such a sentence structure would be undesirable, one may make a break after v. 70, thus giving vv. 71ff the status of a new sentence, to be introduced by an appropriate connective or transitional expression (see below).

He spoke by the mouth of..., or, 'by the lips/tongue/voice of...', 'by the intermediacy of...', 'through (the words of)...', all indicating God as the initiator, but the prophets as the actual speakers; or, reorganizing the syntactic pattern, 'as he caused his holy prophets to speak' (Tagabili), or, 'as his word, uttered by...' (South Toradja). For *spoke*, or, 'promised', cp. on v. 55.

Holy, cp. references on v. 15.

Prophets from of old is, in the interpretation preferred in *Exegesis*, synonymous with "old prophets" in 9 : 8, and rendered, 'prophets of former times' (East Toradja), 'prophets who lived long ago'; cp. also *TH-Mk* on 6 : 15. For *prophet* see *TH-Mk* on 1 : 2, and cp. above on v. 67; some other renderings used are, 'person who speaks under divine impulse' (Kapauku), 'divine-word-man' (Chinese L, see *TBT*, 5.186, 1954), 'holy spokesman' (Timorese). Such renderings may have to be adjusted here because the explicit reference to God or to holiness would sound superfluous in this context. The noun occurs also in 1 : 76; 3 : 4; 4 : 17, 24, 27; 6 : 23, 26; 7 : 16, 26, 39; 9 : 8, 19; 10 : 24; 11 : 47, 49f; 13 : 28, 33f; 16 : 16, 29, 31; 18 : 31; 20 : 6; 24 : 19, 25, 27, 44; and in the feminine form, 2 : 36.

71 ***that we should be saved from our enemies,***
and from the hand of all who hate us;

Exegesis: *sōtērian ex echthrōn hēmōn* 'salvation from our enemies'. *sōtērian*, in the accusative, may be interpreted in different ways: (1) as the object of *elalēsen* in v. 70, cp. NEB; (2) as an apposition to *keras sōtērias* in v. 69, or to the whole clause of that verse; (2) is to be preferred. The phrase may be explicative (as brought out by those translators who keep the appositional construction, cp. 20th Century, Segond), or predicative, i.e. indicating the purpose of v. 69 (as brought out by a shift to an infinitive of purpose, cp. Goodspeed, BFBS).

echthros 'enemy'; in the present context the reference is to the enemies of the people of Israel.

ek cheiros pantōn tōn misountōn hēmas 'from the hand of all that hate us'.

ek cheiros 'from the hand', i.e. 'from the power' (Weymouth), cp. A-G s.v. 2 b.

miseō 'to hate', here with the accusative of the person whom one hates. The phrase is parallel to *echthrōn* and therefore to be understood in the same sense.

Translation: If this verse has to be rendered as a new sentence the connexion with what precedes has to be clarified, e.g. by saying, 'His aim was that we should be saved...', or (using terms that echo the renderings of "raised up" and "horn" in v. 69b), 'this hero appeared to save us...', 'this token was established that we should be saved...'. When the other interpretation (*sotēria* as object of *elalēsen*) is preferred, it may be better to introduce v. 71 by a form of 'to say', e.g. 'saying that we...', or, beginning a new sentence, 'He (i.e. God) said that he would save us', or, 'They said that God would save us'. For *to save* see on "saviour" in 1 : 47.

From and *from the hand* (or, power/might) *of*, are virtually synonymous here, cp. 'from the power of... from the hand of' (Leyden), "from... from" (Phillips).

Our enemies, or, 'our adversaries', 'those who fight us'. Sometimes a term built on the verb 'to hate' is used for 'enemy', e.g. in Lahu, Apache; cp. also 'professional hater' (Yipounou). Elsewhere the aspect of reciprocity has to be made explicit, cp. *TBT*, 20.27, 1969.

Who hate us. The verb expresses aversion coupled with enmity or malice. Some languages can describe the concept by the negation of its opposite, 'who do not love/like us' (cp. e.g. Kapauku), others use idiomatic phrases such as, 'who cannot see us in the eye (i.e. who cannot stand us at any price)' (Sranan), 'the ones with swelling jugular vein (because of suppressed anger)' (Timorese). If the preceding term already contains the verb 'to hate' the translator will have to use a synonymous expression in order to avoid repetition, e.g. 'the lazy to look at us' (i.e. 'the ones who can't stand the sight of us') (Lahu), 'those who would ruin us' (Apache).

72 ***to perform the mercy promised to our fathers,***
and to remember his holy covenant,

Exegesis: *poiēsai eleos meta tōn paterōn hēmōn* 'to do mercy with our fathers'. *poiēsai* is either final infinitive (cp. Plummer, BFBS), or (Hebraistic) infinitive of continuation (cp. on v. 54 and Bl-D, § 391.4), preferably the latter. *meta tōn paterōn* implies that the fathers somehow share in the blessings of the Messianic age, because they still share in the covenant.

kai mnēsthēnai diathēkēs hagias autou 'and to remember his holy covenant'; for *mnēsthēnai* see on v. 54.

diathēkē (also 22 : 20) 'covenant', not to be understood as an agreement between two parties but as a divine decree by which God binds himself and the other party involved, cp. A-G s.v. 2. This "unilateral" character of the idea of covenant is strengthened by the phrase *horkon hon ōmosen*, which serves to explain *diathēkēs* in the following verse.

hagios 'holy', i.e. 'belonging to God', as in Dan. 11 : 28, 30.

Translation: Starting a new sentence here one may say, 'Thus God performs mercy'; or when vv. 71f are taken as the contents of *elalēsen* in v. 70, 'and that he/God will have mercy...'.

Perform the mercy promised to, preferably, 'have mercy on' (Marathi), "deal mercifully with" (NEB), and cp. on v. 50.

And to remember should parallel the preceding clause both syntactically and semantically. The verb (cp. on v. 54) expresses that the covenant has been continually kept by God, cp. "keeping his sacred agreement" (Goodspeed).

Covenant, often a general term for contract or agreement, e.g. 'to put mouths equal' (Conob), 'helping promise' (Moré), 'a thing-time-bind', i.e. something agreed upon for a period of time (Vai), 'a broken-off word (viz. broken-off to be left with the person with whom the agreement has been made)' (Huastec), 'a word between' (Tchien), 'a promise which brings together' (Kiyaka); cp. also *TBT*, 3.226f, 1952; 11.26, 1960. If such a term would too strongly suggest reciprocity, it is better to employ a word like 'promise' (Javanese, Kituba).

73 ***the oath which he swore to our father Abraham,***

Exegesis: *horkon hon ōmosen* 'the oath which he swore'; *horkon* is apposition to *diathēkēs* in the preceding verse (the genitive has been changed into an accusative because of the following *hon*, inverted attraction, cp. Bl-D, § 295), or a second object to *mnēsthēnai*; the former interpretation is preferable.

horkos (†) 'oath'; the word refers here to Gen. 22 : 16; 26 : 3, cp. Ps. 105 : 8-10 and Jer. 11 : 5.

omnuō (†) 'to swear', 'to take an oath', 'to promise under oath', here followed by *pros* with accusative to indicate the party to whom the promise under oath is made.

tou dounai hēmin 'to give us', belongs to v. 73 according to the traditional division in verses, but is printed as part of the next line in Nestle, and taken with v. 74 in RSV. Syntactically vv. 74 and 75 are dependent upon it and it is, accordingly, treated with them.

Translation: The explicative function of the apposition may be indicated by, 'that is, the oath he swore...', 'how he swore with an oath...', or in a relative clause, 'which was the oath he swore...'.

The oath which he swore. The two terms are semantically related, and often also formally cognate. Therefore one of the two may better be rendered more generically, e.g. 'what he said/promised under oath', 'the oath he spoke/used' (Javanese, Malay), 'the word/promise he swore', 'what he promised, lifting up his hand' (cp. Apache), 'his oath'. If the oath complex is unknown in the culture one may say, 'the vow/promise he made (solemnly)'. A similar simplification is found in Tagabili, where the normal formula for swearing an oath, i.e. 'if I don't keep my promise to you, God will punish me', is felt to make no sense when God himself is the one making the oath. For *oath* and *swear* cp. also *TH-Mk* on 6 : 23, 26; Nida, *BT*, 228f.

74 ***to grant us***
that we, being delivered from the hand of our enemies,
might serve him without fear,
75 ***in holiness and righteousness before him all the days of our life.***

Exegesis: *tou dounai hēmin...latreuein autō* 'to give us...to worship him'. *tou dounai* is articular infinitive (cp. Moule 128f) and may be understood to indicate the content of the oath ('an oath to the effect that...') or to explain the purpose of God's dealing as described in vv. 68-73; the former seems to be preferable.

latreuō 'to serve', refers here to worship and adoration of God in general; the spirit or attitude in which this serving of God is performed is indicated by the phrase which follows *latreuein*, see below.

aphobōs (†) 'fearlessly', goes with *latreuein* and the subsequent phrase *ek cheiros echthrōn rusthentas* explains why this fearless service is possible.

ek cheiros echthrōn rusthentas 'delivered from the hand of the enemies'; *rusthentas* (in acc.) is attributive to *hēmin* (in dative), cp. Bl-D, § 410.

ruomai (†) 'to rescue', 'to save', 'to deliver'. Here the word refers back to *lutrōsis* (v. 68) and *sōtērian* (v. 71) but the fact that it is syntactically subordinated to *latreuein*, shows that the deliverance from the enemies is no end in itself but serves to make possible the service of God as described in the next verse.

(V. 75) *en hosiotēti kai dikaiosunē enōpion autou* 'in holiness and righteousness before him'.

hosiotēs occurs in the New Testament always together with *dikaiosunē*. The two nouns (both †) denote the right attitude towards God and towards man.

enōpion autou 'before him', going either with *latreuein* (cp. Plummer, NEB, Goodspeed) or with *en hosiotēti kai dikaiosunē* (cp. Lagrange, Klostermann), preferably the latter.

Translation: The syntactic structure of these verses may have to be reorganized, shifting to co-ordination (see below, and cp. the Tarascan example in Nida, *BT*, 276), and/or to direct discourse (as done e.g. in Bolivian Quechua, Marathi, Kituba). The latter requires in some cases an introductory expression, e.g. 'saying', 'which is this' (Marathi), and always changes in the references to the speaker (i.e. God) and the persons spoken of (i.e. Zechariah and his Jewish contemporaries, and in wider perspective the people of Israel in general, viewed as Abraham's descendants). This may result in something like, 'I will grant them (or, the people, or, your descendants) that they, delivered from...their enemies, will serve me... before me all the days of their life'.

The following remarks on details assume a rendering in indirect discourse; the renderings discussed can easily be adjusted to a rendering in direct discourse, if required.

To grant us that we, being delivered...might serve him... The introductory phrase, "to grant us", shows that the situation described in the next clauses is envisaged as brought about by God. In some languages the phrase is transferred to the end of the sentence, '...; so he/God will grant us' (cp. Marathi, Kanarese); in others the force of the verb is expressed otherwise and embedded in the following clauses, cp. some of the renderings given below. The sentence structure usually has to be reorganized. Some possibilities are: a transposition of the clauses, e.g. 'that he would allow/enable us to serve him..., after we (or, because we, or, as persons who) have been delivered...'; a change in the pattern of subordination, e.g. '(that) he will kindly deliver us..., so-that we can serve him...' (Balinese); or a shift to co-ordination, e.g. 'that he will save us from..., and give that we...may be able to worship him' (Tagalog, similarly TEV), or with a further, lexical shift, 'that he will enable us to escape...and to serve him...' (cp. Marathi).—Often the term used for *delivered* is identical or closely synonymous with the renderings of "redeemed" (cp. references on v. 68) and/or "saved" (cp. on v. 47). — *Serve*, or, 'carry-on-the-head', i.e. worship (Balinese), 'cause-(ourselves-)to-be-slaves to' (Tagabili), 'work for' (Apache, Bamiléké).

Without fear, or, 'fearlessly' (Marathi), 'not having a fearful heart' (Lahu).

V. 75 contains three more qualifications of "serve him". To avoid too heavy a syntactic structure, one may repeat 'to serve' here (Kituba).

In (i.e. with, or, having) *holiness and righteousness*, or, shifting to a verbal construction, e.g. 'acting holily and (acting) righteously', 'having-holiness and having-righteousness' (Toba Batak); or to an adjectival construction, e.g. 'we...as holy and righteous persons', or, 'pray-to him in worship that is holy and perfect' (cp. Kituba). For *holiness* some versions use the word that also renders Gr. *hagios* 'holy' (cp. on v. 15), but a different rendering is preferable, e.g. 'purety' (Balinese), 'perfection (lit. roundness of heart)' (East Toradja 1933), 'being-sufficient (i.e. complete, perfect, acceptable)' (Kituba), 'unreserved obedience' (Tagabili, using a noun built on the expression 'his breath/soul is conformed, lit. repeating'). For *righteousness before him* see on v. 6.

All the days of our life. The more literal "all our days" (Rieu, Phillips), *au long de nos jours* (Jerusalem) may be possible in some languages, but more often the phrase must be expanded, e.g. "all the days of our life" (TEV), or changed, "our whole life long" (NEB), 'as long as we live' (e.g. Javanese), 'as long as our breath/spirit-of-life comes' (East Toradja), 'to the end of our lives' (Lahu), 'until being short our sprout/shoot', i.e. 'until we die' (Tagabili).

(Vv. 76-79) The syntactic structure of these verses is again that of one long sentence with subordinate phrases and clauses but it is possible to discern two principal parts in it, (1) vv. 76f, describing John's future status and task, (2) vv. 78f, speaking of the origin and circumstances of his ministry. So the natural place for an incision is after v. 77; v. 78 may then begin with a transitional phrase such as, 'All that will happen because of the tender mercy...'.

76 ***And you, child, will be called the prophet of the Most High; for you will go before the Lord to prepare his ways,***

Exegesis: *kai su de, paidion* 'and you, child'. These words introduce the second part of Zechariah's prophecy, in which he addresses the child directly and speaks about his mission in the service of the Lord. The two connectives *kai* and *de* have different function: *kai* expresses the idea of continuation; John's ministry is not to be separated from the Messianic prophecies of vv. 68-75; *de* however marks the transition from the more general part of Zechariah's prophetic hymn to the part referring specifically to the child whose birth was the occasion for the hymn.

paidion 'child', see on v. 59.

prophētēs hupsistou klēthēsē 'prophet of the Most High you will be called', cp. on vv. 32 and 70.

proporeusē gar enōpion kuriou 'for you will go before the Lord'; this will be his mission as a prophet, in fulfilment of what Gabriel had said to Zechariah, and of the prophecy of Mal. 3 : 1, quoted in the next phrase.

proporeuomai (†) 'to go before somebody', equivalent to *proerchomai* in v. 17.

enōpion kuriou 'before the Lord', i.e. as his forerunner, cp. on v. 17.

hetoimasai hodous autou 'to make ready his ways'; for *hetoimazō* cp. on v. 17; here it means to bring into readiness the existing but impassable roads; the genitive *autou* suggests here primarily that the Lord himself will come along them.

Translation: For *child* see on v. 7, for *the Most High* on v. 32.

Will be called. The agent is 'God' rather than 'people'.

To prepare his ways, cp. *TH-Mk* on 1 : 2f. To make clear the function of the pronoun here it may be preferable to say, 'the way (along which) he will come', 'the way on-which-his-treading' (Javanese), or to change the syntactic pattern of the phrase, e.g. 'to prepare for-him the ways' (Jerusalem). For *ways* cp. *N.T.Wb.*/72f.

77 ***to give knowledge of salvation to his people***
in the forgiveness of their sins,

Exegesis: *tou dounai gnōsin sōtērias tō laō autou* 'to give knowledge of salvation to his people', either explains *hetoimasai,* or is parallel with it, preferably the former.

gnōsis (also 11 : 52) 'knowledge', always with a religious connotation.

sōtēria 'salvation', here in a religious sense as the subsequent clause shows.

en aphesei hamartiōn autōn 'in the forgiveness of their sins'; *autōn* refers to the individual members of the *laos* 'people'. The phrase goes either with *dounai gnōsin sōtērias* or with *sōtērias* only, preferably the latter; this means that salvation consists in the forgiveness of sins.

aphesis 'release from captivity' (4 : 18), 'remission of debt', hence 'forgiveness' in the sense of 'the act of forgiving', cp. A-G s.v. 2.

hamartia 'sin', in the plural 'sinful actions'; in Luke *hamartia* occurs always in connexion with forgiveness or forgiving and hence refers to the guilt of sin.

Translation: *To give knowledge of salvation to his people.* One or both of the verbal nouns may have to be changed into a verb, e.g. 'to make known to his people salvation', 'to cause his people to know that they are saved'; or in the active voice with appropriate adjustments 'to cause his people to know (or, to tell his people) that the Lord saves them'. For *his people,* i.e. 'the Lord's people', 'the people the Lord rules', cp. above on v. 68.

In the forgiveness of their sins. The preposition serves here to introduce that in which salvation consists, that which is the contents of salvation. This can often be expressed by equating 'salvation' and 'forgiveness'; hence, '(that is,) forgiveness...', 'which is forgiveness...' (Tagalog); or, using a verbal clause, 'that their sins are forgiven' (Balinese), 'that is, he has forgiven them their sins' (Kituba). Idiom may require minor syntactic shifts without appreciable difference of meaning, e.g. 'to forgive a person's sins', 'to forgive a person who has sinned', 'to forgive (his) sins to a person', 'to forgive a person as to (his) sins'. For *forgive(ness)* (occurring also in 3 : 3; 5 : 20f, 23f; 7 : 47ff; 11 : 4; 17 : 3f; 23 : 34; 24 : 47) see *N.T.Wb.*/39f; *TH-Mk* on 1 : 4 (pp. 13f). The verb occurs also in 7 : 42f, in the sense of 'to cancel debts', and in 6 : 37 (for Gr. *apoluō*) with a juridical connotation 'to acquit/to set free'. For *sin* (also in 3 : 3; 5 : 20f, 23f; 7 : 47ff; 11 : 4; 24 : 47; and the verb in 15 : 18, 21; 17 : 1-4) see *TH-Mk* on 1 : 4 (pp. 14f); *TBT*, 8.148, 1957; 9.53, 1958; 13.33, 1962.

78 ***through the tender mercy of our God,***
when the day shall dawn upon us from on high

Exegesis: *dia splagchna eleous theou hēmōn* 'because of the tender mercy of our God'; the phrase is to be connected either with the whole preceding clause from *proporeusē* onward, or with what immediately precedes, viz. *en aphesei hamartias* (which in its turn refers back to *sōtērias*), indicating God's motive for the forgiveness of sins; the latter is preferable.

splagchna (†) lit. 'inward parts', 'bowels', esp. heart, lungs and liver, fig. of the seat of emotions and affections; its meaning here is determined by the qualifying genitive *eleous*, lit. 'inner mercy-feelings', hence 'tender mercy'.

en hois episkepsetai hēmas anatolē ex hupsous 'with which will visit us the sunrise from on high'; *en hois* designates its antecedent *splagchna eleous* either (a) as the means "by which" (BFBS), or "through which" (Weymouth), the visiting will be brought about, or (b) as the manner or way in which it will take place, preferably the latter. For the meaning of *episkeptomai* see on v. 68.

anatolē lit. 'the rising of a star or of the sun', hence 'the region where the sun rises', 'the east', 'the orient'. In the present context however it must refer to a person because of *episkepsetai*. Hence several figurative interpretations have been given, the most important of which are the following:

1. *anatolē* is interpreted in the light of e.g. Mal. 4 : 2 and understood as referring to the rising sun as a picture of the Messiah; this is in accordance with the terms used in the first clause of v. 79, but not with *ex hupsous* because the sun does not rise from on high; but since *anatolē* is a picture of the Messiah, *ex hupsous* may refer to his coming from heaven (see below).
2. *anatolē* is taken to mean 'the scion' as in the Septuagint of Jer. 23 : 5; Zech. 3 : 8; 6 : 12 and refers to the Messiah; *ex hupsous* is either a circumlocution of the name of God or an indication of the scion's heavenly origin (cp. Dan. 7 : 13 of the coming from heaven of the Son of man). As interpretation (2) is not consistent with the idea of shining in the darkness

in the next clause which clearly should be related to *anatolē*, interpretation (1) is to be preferred; but it is possible that the idea of 'the scion' has served to strengthen the interpretation of *anatolē* as referring to a person.

Translation: *Through the tender mercy of our God*, or, 'through the kindness of God which cares for us' (Navajo), 'because (the heart of) our God is full of mercy' (cp. Phillips, Goodspeed), 'because our God tenderly mercy-es us'. For *tender mercy*, lit. 'bowels of mercy', cp. *N.T.Wb.*/17f, BODY (*splanchnon*).

When the day dawns upon us, preferably, 'by which, or, in which way the dawn/sunrise visits us', cp. *Exegesis* sub (a) and (b). On the basis of (a) it may be preferable to shift to a causative construction, taking as subject 'which' (referring to 'mercy') or, 'who' (referring to 'God'), or 'it/he', where co-ordination is required. On the basis of (b), some possible ways to express the connexion between the two lines are, '...mercy..., which is such that the sunrise will visit us', '...mercy..., and so the dawn will...' (cp. Goodspeed), '...in the tender mercy...the morning sun will...' (cp. NEB), 'God loves us dearly, in such a way that (or, so that) the dawn will...' — 'The dawn/sunrise will visit us'. To indicate more clearly that the reference is to the person of the coming Messiah, using a poetic or veiled epithet, one may mark the noun as a name, e.g. by adding a name qualifier, cp. the use of capitals in several versions. Elsewhere one has to shift to a simile, e.g. 'a light...like that of the rising sun' (Français Courant), 'as a rising light' (Timorese), 'he who is like the dawn/morning sun'. For the verb 'to visit' cp. on v. 68; Tagabili has a verb 'to come/arrive' that can also refer to the rising of the sun, and thus is usable with 'sunrise/dawn' either as a natural phenomenon or as a metaphorical reference to a person.

On high, or, 'in heaven', 'in the sky', 'in the divine palace' (Timorese); and cp. on "in the highest" in 2 : 14.

79 ***to give light to those who sit in darkness and in the shadow of death,***
to guide our feet into the way of peace."

Exegesis: *epiphanai* 'to give light'; the infinitive is final ('in order to') or consecutive ('so as to'), preferably the latter.

epiphainō (†) 'to appear', but here in a more pregnant meaning, 'to shine forth', 'to give light'.

tois en skotei kai skia thanatou kathēmenois 'to those who sit in darkness and in shadow of death', a quotation from the Septuagint of Ps. 107 : 10, cp. also Is. 9 : 2.

skotos 'darkness', here in the figurative sense of a difficult situation where no solution is visible.

skia (†) 'shadow'; *skia thanatou* renders Hebrew *ṣalmawēt* 'darkness', but the Greek expression is stronger than the Hebrew; the genitive *thanatou* is qualifying.

tou kateuthunai tous podas hēmōn 'to direct our feet'; the articular final infinitive is either subordinated to the preceding infinitive clause (cp. BFBS) or co-ordinated with it (cp. e.g. NEB), preferably the former.

kateuthunō (†) 'to make straight', 'to lead'.

pous 'foot', here representing a person in motion, cp. A-G s.v. 1 b.

eis hodon eirēnēs 'into the way of peace'; *hodos* is used here in a figurative sense; the genitive *eirēnēs* is either qualifying ('the way characterized by peace') or objective ('the way which leads to peace'), preferably the former.

eirēnē 'peace', 'well being', here of the peace of the Messianic age and therefore referring to the salvation described in vv. 71 and 74-75, cp. Richardson, *Word Book*, 165f.

Translation: Rendering the verse as a new sentence one may introduce it by, 'It/He comes (in order) to', 'Its/His aim is to'.

Those who sit, or, 'us who sit', the pronoun of the first person plural referring to virtually the same group in the next, parallel line. *Sit*, or, 'are', 'live', 'stay', the sitting position being irrelevant in this context.

In darkness, or, shifting to a locative, 'in a dark place' (Balinese, similarly in Tagabili); and cp. *N.T.Wb.*/21f. The metaphorical meaning of the phrase is made clear in the next phrase.

In the shadow of death, or using a verbal clause, 'who are-overshadowed by death' (cp. Tagabili, Toba Batak), 'shaded by the shadow of death' (South Toradja); or again, as a locative, 'where death threatens'. *Shadow of death*, an acceptable metaphor in several languages, cannot be used so in others, e.g. because it would be understood to mean 'among the ghosts' (Kituba), or because 'shadow/shade' does not suggest threat and danger but shelter and protection (cp. above on v. 35); hence shifts to an equivalent metaphor (cp. "under the cloud of death", NEB), or a non-metaphorical rendering, e.g. 'fear of death' (Vai, Kituba), 'afraid of death' (Apache), 'threat/danger of death'. If "death" cannot be rendered by an equivalent noun, it may be possible to use a personification such as 'demon-of-death', or one may have to say something like 'deadly shadow', 'danger of dying', 'where they/we are fearing that they/we will die'. For *death* (also in 2 : 26; 7 : 2; 9 : 27; 21 : 16; 22 : 2, 33; 23 : 15, 22, 32; 24 : 28), referring to the state, cause, or occasion of dying or having died, cp. *N.T.Wb.*/27, DIE.

To guide our feet into the way of peace, or non-metaphorically, 'to teach us the way-of-life that brings peace, or, behaviour that is peaceful', 'to put us right on the way of peace' (South Toradja). Where it is possible to keep to the metaphor minor adjustments are necessary in some cases, see below. *To guide*, or, "to direct" (BFBS, also Bahasa Indonesia), 'to cause-to-go/walk' (Javanese, Apache), 'to put' (Sranan, Marathi). *Our feet*, or, 'our steps' (Toba Batak, Balinese), 'our going/walking '(Kituba). *Into the way of peace*, or, 'on/upon/along (lit. following) the way of peace'. — *Peace*. In English, as in the Greek, the term has a negative aspect: lack of strife between persons, absence or cessation of war, and a positive one: fulness of well-being resting on confidence in God. The corresponding word in several western languages has, or has acquired, the same two sided-ness;

similarly in some non-western languages, e.g. in New Caledonian, where 'peace of war' proved to render the positive aspect better than 'calm' or 'quietness' would do (cp. *TBT*, 2.148f, 1951), or in Ilocano, which uses one word both for inward calm and for the state of a nation not at war (*TBT*, 11.29, 1960). Elsewhere two or more terms have to be distinguished. For the negative aspect an expression is used such as, 'the palaver has passed' (Gbeapo), 'well arranged', implying reconciliation (Totonac), 'being-good-with-each-other' (East and South Toradja), 'land and water are well' (East Toradja 1933, in Lk. 12 : 51), 'free', cp. 'to make free', used in the specific sense of 'to conclude peace' (Sranan). For the positive concept many figurative expressions are on record, built on various basic concepts, such as strength, e.g. 'strength of heart' (one of two synonymous expressions in Zacapoaxtla Aztec), 'leaning on the liver' (Karré); 'well-being/happiness', e.g. in Navajo; 'evenness', cp. South Toradja, where the term is derived from a verb 'to level', and Timorese, where the basic verb is 'to make-even/to join', and a differentiation is made between 'making-even the-land/people' (e.g. here) and 'making-even the-heart' (e.g. in 2 : 14 and in the Pauline epistles). For other idioms cp. Nida, *GWIML*, 128-130; *TH-Mk* on 9 : 50; *TBT*, 1.28, 1950; 20.27f, 1969.

80 ***And the child grew and became strong in spirit, and he was in the wilderness till the day of his manifestation to Israel.***

Exegesis: *to de paidion ēuxanen kai ekrataiouto pneumati* 'the child grew up and became strong in spirit'; the imperfect tense of the verbs expresses the process of growing and becoming strong.

auxanō 'to grow', both transitive and intransitive.

krataioō (also 2 : 40) 'to strengthen', in the passive 'to become strong'.

pneumati either 'in (his own) spirit' (most commentators and translators) or 'in the (Holy) Spirit' (Plummer, cp. Kingsley Williams, Goodspeed, Moffatt); the former interpretation is to be preferred. The dative is metaphorically local, cp. Moule 44, 46.

kai ēn en tais erēmois 'and he was in the desert'.

hai erēmoi, scil. *chōrai* 'the desert regions', cp. *N.T.Wb.*, 41/.

heōs hēmeras anadeixeōs autou pros ton Israēl 'till the day of his appearing before Israel'.

anadeixis (††) 'commissioning', 'installation' or 'public appearance', preferably the latter.

Translation: *Grew.* The verb is often rendered analytically, e.g. 'to become big' (Apache), 'his-bigness rose/increased' (Javanese), or a term built on the word 'big', and expressing the concept of increase by reduplicating that word (South Toradja). Cp. also *N.T.Wb.*/41.

Became strong in spirit. The two last words qualify "strong": 'was-made-strong as to his soul' (Sundanese), 'became spiritually strong', "gathered spiritual strength" (Rieu). In Kapauku a literal rendering would result in 'became hard-hearted', i.e. 'stubborn'; therefore the phrase had to be rendered 'became wise in his consciousness'. For similar reasons Tagabili uses an adjective meaning 'sturdy/steady/reliable', lit. 'nailed'. *Spirit*, or, 'character' (Tagabili, using a derivation of 'breath-of-life'), 'heart' (Vai, where a literal rendering of 'spirit' would suggest that John had so strong a ghost as to be able to live on some time after his death), 'consciousness' (Kapauku, a compound of 'thought' and 'speech'); and cp. above on v. 47.

Wilderness, see *N.T.Wb.*/25, DESERT.

Till the day of his manifestation, or as a verbal clause, 'until (the day) he showed/made-publicly-known himself' (Navajo, Apache, Toba Batak), 'up to the time that he appeared in public'.

CHAPTER TWO

1 ***In those days a decree went out from Caesar Augustus that all the world should be enrolled.***

Exegesis: *egeneto de...exēlthen* 'and it happened that...went out', cp. on 1 : 8.

en tais hēmerais ekeinais 'in those days' (cp. on 1 : 39) serves to bring out the temporal relationship between the narratives of ch. 1 and ch. 2 and is best understood as pointing back to *en tais hēmerais Hērōdou* in 1 : 5.

exēlthen dogma para Kaisaros Augoustou 'a decree went out from Caesar Augustus'; a general expression, not official language.

dogma (†) 'decree', usually of one issued by a person of unquestionable authority.

Kaisar, representing Latin Caesar, originally a name which the first Roman emperor acquired by adoption as the son of Julius Caesar, soon became a title. Since *Kaisar Augoustos* (here) and *Tiberios Kaisar* (3 : 1) are in accordance with the official Roman form of the names of both emperors *Kaisar* is best understood as a part of the name.

apographesthai pasan tēn oikoumenēn 'that the whole world should have itself registered', indicating the content of the imperial decree in the form of an accusative and infinitive.

apographō 'to register', here either in the middle 'to have oneself registered', or, in the passive 'to be enrolled', preferably the former, cp. Bl-D, § 317. Here *apographesthai* refers to registration for tax purposes (cp. on v. 2, *apographē*).

oikoumenē scil. *gē* lit. 'the inhabited earth', hence 'mankind'; it refers here to the inhabitants of the Roman empire as in Acts 17 : 6; the equation of *oikoumenē* to the Roman empire or its inhabitants was not uncommon.

Translation: *In those days*, or, 'in that time/period also'; care should be taken not to suggest a connexion with the day of John's manifestation to Israel (1 : 80).

A decree went out from Caesar Augustus, or, 'came down from C. A.' (Tagalog), 'was given by C. A.', cp. "a proclamation was made by C. A." (Phillips); or, 'C. A. posted a placard (Sranan), put-out strong word (i.e. order)' (Kapauku); or again, shifting to a possessive, 'there-was a proclamation of C. A.' (cp. Javanese, and Jerusalem). *A decree*. Where no specific term exists one may use 'order', 'command'. Tagabili uses a term that points to civil law in contrast to customary law. *Caesar Augustus*. If taken as part of the proper name (see *Exegesis*) "Caesar" will have to be transliterated. In some languages the use of a name qualifier or title is required with the proper name; hence e.g. 'big chief Kaisali Angustu' (Kituba), 'King-of-kings Kaisar Augustus' (cp. Balinese).

That, introducing the contents of the decree, may have to be rendered, 'saying/commanding/ordering', or, '(in it) he said/commanded/ordered', followed by direct or indirect discourse.

All the world, preferably, 'the whole kingdom' (Kanarese, Kapauku), 'all his subjects' (East Toradja, the same in Tagabili, lit. 'all persons holding to-him'), 'all people in all countries of his empire' (Kituba), 'all the people included in the Roman empire' (Cuyono). See also *TBT*, 14.150, 1963.

Should be enrolled, preferably, 'should have itself/themselves enrolled'. The middle voice is sometimes expressed by a causative, e.g. 'that all his subjects should cause-to-have-written (i.e. cause someone to write down) their name' (Tagabili), or it may have to be circumscribed, e.g. 'that in the whole kingdom people should come to those who would register them'. *To enroll,* or, 'to hold a census (lit. listing of souls)' (Bahasa Indonesia KB), 'to write names' (East and South Toradja, Kituba, Tagabili), 'to write names in a book' (Gio), 'to make a list of' (Huanuco Quechua), 'to record the number of' (Telugu), 'to count' (Kapauku).

2 ***This was the first enrollment, when Quirinius was governor of Syria.***

Exegesis: *hautē apographē prōtē egeneto hēgemoneuontos tēs Surias Kurēniou* 'this registration, the first, happened when Quirinius governed Syria'; the phrase serves to indicate (1) the time when the registration referred to in v. 1, took place, and (2) the fact that this registration was the first to happen. Hence a rendering like "this was the first registration of its kind; it took place when Quirinius was governor of Syria" (NEB, cp. Zürich) seems to cover best the full implications of the Greek text. Registrations in the Roman empire might easily extend over a period cf many years and Quirinius acted as the special representative of the Roman emperor and was engaged in a census from 12 B.C. to 16 A.D.; during this period he was also twice governor of Syria, probably in 3-2 B.C. and certainly from 6 A.D. to the end of his term as special representative; for a full discussion cp. *IDB* III, 975ff.

apographē (†) 'registration', 'census', here according to Stauffer (op. cit. p. 29) referring to "the systematic registration of all taxable persons and of all things subject to taxes"; in most cases the latter had to do with landed property, and since Joseph was of the house and lineage of David he very probably would have a share in the landed property of the descendants of David in his place of origin (op. cit. p. 33).

hēgemoneuontos tēs Surias Kurēniou 'when Quirinius governed Syria'; the phrase may either mean that the registration of Palestine took place during Quirinius' first period of actual governorship of the Roman province of Syria or contain a somewhat incorrect reference to the whole period of his activities in the East.

hēgemoneuō (also 3 : 1) 'to govern', 'to rule', a very general word, alike applicable to the Roman emperor and to his underlings in the provinces of the empire.

Kurēnios Greek transcription of the Roman name 'Quirinius'.

Translation: *This was the first enrollment,* or, shifting to a verbal construction, e.g. 'this was the first time people had to enroll themselves'; or again, using a generic reference to the verb in v. 1, 'this happened (or, was done) for the first time'. *Enrollment,* cp. on the verb in v. 1; most renderings refer only to the persons registered, some include their possessions, e.g. 'numbering-of-houses (referring to population and live-stock)' (Kanarese).

When, preferably, 'done/held when', 'it happened when'.

Quirinius. Older versions transliterate the Greek form of the name, but it is preferable to take the original Latin form as basis of transliteration; usually *qu* then can best become *k,* or its closest equivalent.

Governor. Usually one can find an appropriate equivalent in the local or national official hierarchy of the present or in a colonial one of the past (cp. Nida, *BT,* 197), e.g. 'province-ruler' (Tamil, Telugu, Kanarese), 'the exalted person' (South Toradja, using the title of the Governor-General and of provincial governors); or, since Quirinius represented the imperial government, 'representative of the government' (Bahasa Indonesia), cp. 'stood in power...representing the Emperor' (Balinese).

3 ***And all went to be enrolled, each to his own city.***

Exegesis: *kai eporeuonto pantes apographesthai* 'and all went to have themselves registered'; *kai* connects the clause with v. 1 and this connexion makes of v. 2 a parenthesis (cp. Moffatt, 20th Century).

pantes 'all people concerned', viewed in their totality; as compared with *pantes* the subsequent *hekastos* (in the singular), being a distributive pronoun, refers to the individual members of that totality.

apographesthai 'in order to be registered', final infinitive, cp. on v. 1.

hekastos eis tēn heautou polin 'each to his own town'; there is no need to translate 'the town of his birth', because one could have a claim to landed property in a place other than one's birthplace.

Translation: Because of the parenthetical character of v. 2 it may be preferable to specify the transition and/or the subject, e.g. 'therefore', 'because of that decree/command', and/or, 'all people (there)', 'all the inhabitants'.

Went, or, 'set out' (Zürich), "made their way" (NEB), 'rose to journey' (Sranan), indicating the general upheaval, the next clause indicating the individual directions. Since the journey is to the people's places of origin idiom may require 'to go home' (Balinese), 'to go back' (Bahasa Indonesia).

His own city, or, 'his settlement of origin' (Malay), 'the settlement of his ancestors' (East Toradja; properly the term refers to the settlement of female ancestors, the traditional Toradja marriage being matrilocal), 'his ancestral-house', lit. 'his seat' (South Toradja), 'his clan-origin', lit. 'the trunk of his *nangka*-tree' (Toba Batak, the strong, but slow growing *nangka,* or Jack-fruit, tree being used metaphorically of the compound of a well-to-do family which remained in the same village for generations).

4 ***And Joseph also went up from Galilee, from the city of Nazareth, to Judea, to the city of David, which is called Bethlehem, because he was of the house and lineage of David.***

Exegesis: *anebē de kai Iōsēph* 'and Joseph also went up'; *de* is purely transitional (cp. A-G s.v. 2) and *kai* refers back to *hekastos* in the preceding verse: like everyone concerned Joseph 'also' went.

anabainō 'to go up', 'to ascend', here of going to a place that is at a higher altitude, but the emphasis is more on going than on ascending. The distance between Nazareth and Bethlehem is 63 miles and the difference in height is about 1000 feet.

apo tēs Galilaias ek poleōs Nazareth 'from Galilee, from the city of Nazareth'. There is no difference in meaning between *apo* and *ek* because Nazareth is part of Galilee.

eis polin Dauid hētis kaleitai Bēthleem 'to the town of David which is called Bethlehem'; the reason for calling Bethlehem "the town of David" here is that the Messiah, who will occupy the throne of David (cp. 1 : 32) will be born in Bethlehem (cp. Mic. 5 : 1f; Jn. 7 : 42).

dia to einai auton ex oikou kai patrias Dauid 'because he was of the house and family of David', articular accusative and infinitive governed by a preposition. For *ex oikou...Dauid* cp. on 1 : 27.

patria (†) 'family', 'clan', usually the larger unit as compared with *oikos*, but here the words are best understood as a hendiadys (two semantically related words expressing the same idea and, by virtue of their coordination, emphasizing that idea), cp. NEB.

Translation: *Went up*. Departing from Nazareth Joseph and Mary actually had to descend first, either to the valley of Megiddo or to that of the Jordan, and then, having crossed the former, or followed the latter down stream to Jericho, go up again into the hills, towards Bethlehem. Now, languages differ in specifying whether a journey is to a point higher or lower than the point of departure. Some indicate the difference in elevation always, others do so only when the difference is visible or, though not visible, can easily be envisaged in the mind. In the latter cases a rendering like 'set out', 'journeyed' will in this context be more idiomatic. Cp. also *TH-Mk* on 3 : 22. — Where the combination of one verb with two contrasting prepositions is undesirable a second verb may have to be added, e.g. 'he journeyed/set-out from...and went to...' (Low Malay), or, 'he departed from village of N....in-order to go-up as-far-as...' (Kituba, cp. also Jerusalem, Toba Batak).

From Galilee, from the city of Nazareth, to Judea, to the city of David, which is called Bethlehem. The parallelism between the two locative phrases should preferably be preserved, even if the more specific name has to be put first, e.g. 'from the city (of) N. in (the region of) G., to the city of D., which is called B., in (the region of) J.'. For *Judea* see on 1 : 65.

The city of David. As David is known to have been a king, 'David's city' would normally be taken to mean his residence, or the capital of his kingdom. To avoid this one may have to use 'birthplace' instead of 'city' (Balinese).

Of, i.e. 'originating from', cp. 'came-out of' (Javanese, Kituba), 'born in' (Telugu).

House and lineage, often rendered by two synonymous terms, or by one expression (see *Exegesis*), such as, 'descent' (Kapauku), 'clan/tribe' (Kituba), and, with a further syntactic shift, 'descended from the former David' (Tagabili). For *David* and *house* cp. on 1 : 27.

5 ***to be enrolled with Mary, his betrothed, who was with child.***

Exegesis: *apograpsasthai sun Mariam tē emnēsteumenē autō* 'to have himself registered with Mary who was betrothed to him'; *apograpsasthai* depends upon *anebē* and the aorist tense refers to the specific act of Joseph's registering as contrasted with the present tense in v. 1 and v. 3, referring to the registering of 'the whole world' and of 'everyone'.

sun Mariam 'with Mary', goes either with *apograpsasthai* (RSV) or with *anebē* (NEB), preferably the latter.

ousē egkuō 'being pregnant', a second apposition to *Mariam*, best taken as preparing for the subsequent verse which describes the birth of Mary's child, the main objective of the whole narrative. But this should not be overstressed by making it the opening phrase of the next verses, cp. on v. 6.

egkuos (††) 'pregnant'.

Translation: *To be enrolled* is separated by several phrases from its immediate constituent "went up". Where this would be confusing or unidiomatic, one may have to change the word order, bringing the two verbs closer together in v. 4, e.g. 'he went up to have himself registered, (going) from...', cp. "he travelled up for this purpose from..." (Rieu), or to make v. 5 into a separate clause or sentence, repeating the reference to the journey, e.g. 'he went up there (or, he did so) in order to have himself enrolled'.

With Mary. To make it clear that this phrase goes with 'went up' (see *Exegesis*) one may have to change the word order again, cp. 'he went up with M., ..., in order to be enrolled' (Thai), or to render the phrase as a clause or sentence, e.g. "and he took with him Mary" (Rieu).

His betrothed, who was with child, two qualifications, both going with "Mary", the former mentioning a fact already known to the reader, the latter giving new information. Where both would have to be rendered as relative clauses it may be preferable to make the second one into an independent sentence, cp. 'Mary who was betrothed to him. She was pregnant'. For *his betrothed* see on 1 : 27. — *Who was with child*, or, 'was pregnant'. Often the rendering differs from that of 'to conceive' (1 : 24) only by its being without indication of the ingressive aspect, cp. 'to be pregnant' with 'to become pregnant' (Dutch versions), or 'to be with belly' with 'to receive belly' (Sranan); and cp. *TH-Mk* on 13 : 17.

6 ***And while they were there, the time came for her to be delivered.***

Exegesis: *egeneto de* marks the approach of the climax of a narrative, cp. on 1 : 8.

en tō einai autous ekei 'during their being there'; for the construction cp. on 1 : 8.

eplēsthēsan hai hēmerai tou tekein autēn 'the days of her giving-birth (i.e. for her to give birth) were fulfilled', cp. on 1 : 23; *eplēsthēsan* continues the sentence introduced by *egeneto*.

Translation: *They,* i.e. the two of them, which is made explicit where a dual form is obligatory, but also in some other languages, e.g. 'the two' (Malay, South Toradja), 'they two together' (Thai).

The time came for her to be delivered, see on 1 : 57.

7 ***And she gave birth to her first-born son and wrapped him in swaddling cloths, and laid him in a manger, because there was no place for them in the inn.***

Exegesis: *kai eteken* 'and she bore', best taken as not dependent upon *egeneto*.

ton huion autēs ton prōtotokon 'her first-born son'; *ton prōtotokon* is attributive to *huion,* and not in apposition to it.

prōtotokos (†) 'first-born', here in the literal sense as usually in the Old Testament; the word represents here the Hebrew *b^{e}kōr,* 'first-born' (cp. Ex. 13 : 2; 34 : 19; Num. 18 : 15f), which belonged to the Lord and, in the case of the human male first-born, had to be redeemed, as is done with Jesus in vv. 22-24, but serves primarily to distinguish Jesus from Mary's children that were born later (Plummer, Zahn, Klostermann).

kai esparganōsen auton 'and wrapped him up', scil. in *spargana* 'swaddling cloths'; this was a very natural procedure and the phrase suggests no special circumstances.

sparganoō (also v. 12) 'to wrap up'.

kai aneklinen auton en phatnē 'and she laid him in a manger'.

anaklinō 'to lay down', 'to cause to lie down', in the passive 'to lie down', 'to recline'.

phatnē 'manger', 'feeding trough', or 'stall' (cp. Moffatt), preferably the former.

ouk ēn autois topos 'there was no room for them'; *autois* refers to Joseph and Mary.

topos here 'place or room to stay or to live', cp. A-G s.v. 1 e.

en tō katalumati 'in the inn' or 'in the lodging'.

kataluma (also 22 : 11) 'a place to lodge', usually after a journey; in 22 : 11 the word clearly refers to a room, not to a house, and the usual word for 'inn' is not *kataluma* but *pandocheion* (cp. 10 : 34); on the other hand it seems improbable that *kataluma* refers here to the guest room of a private house; hence Klostermann thinks it indicates the common lodging-place of a caravanserai.

Translation: *Gave birth,* cp. on 1 : 57.

Her first-born son. In languages where one has to say 'male child', one must make clear that the word 'first-born' is not qualifying 'child' only, but 'male child'; hence such shifts as, 'her first(-born) child, a male-one' (East Toradja), 'child male, her first child' (Kituba). Some idiomatic renderings of *first-born* are, 'first seen' (Lengua, see *TBT*, 20.27, 1969), 'he/she that opens the gown' (in use in Toba Batak, because formerly a woman stopped wearing a gown and started using a bodice after the birth of her first child), 'he/she that damages the stalk (i.e. the body)' (Timorese); and see *TBT*, 16.86, 83f, 1965. In some receptor languages the normal equivalent of "first-born", e.g. 'eldest' (Balinese), implies that more children are expected to follow, or are known to have followed.

Wrapped him in swaddling cloths, or, 'swaddled him', or more generically, 'wrapped/enveloped him in pieces of cloth'.

Manger, or descriptive phrases like, 'trough (for) grass' (Thai), 'place (for) animals' grass' (Low Malay), 'box from which animals eat' (Sinhalese), 'place where cared-for animals eat' (Kapauku), 'place (where) they always put the food for the horse' (Tagabili, horses being the only domesticated animals kept in the area), 'thing that animals use-to-eat their food' (Kituba).

There was no place for them in the inn may better be stated affirmatively, 'the inn was-crowded' (cp. Kapauku). *The inn* is usually best described as 'guest place', 'lodging place', 'travellers place', 'place to pass the night', which leaves room for the interpretation indicated in *Exegesis.*

8 ***And in that region there were shepherds out in the field, keeping watch over their flock by night.***

Exegesis: *kai poimenes ēsan en tē chōra tē autē* 'and there were shepherds in the same region'.

poimēn 'shepherd'; according to rabbinic sources shepherds in Israel were despised and considered unreliable, cp. Strack-Billerbeck II, 113f.

chōra 'district' (as here), 'country', '(cultivated) land'; the phrase *en tē chōra tē autē* is sometimes translated less emphatically, "in that region" (RSV, cp. Kingsley Williams, Goodspeed) instead of 'in the same region'.

agraulountes kai phulassontes phulakas tēs nuktos 'staying out in the fields and keeping the night watches', appositive to *poimenes* and describing the activity of the shepherds. The accusative *phulakas* is the cognate accusative or accusative of content (cp. Bl-D, § 153.3), etymologically related to the preceding main verb *phulassontes* 'watching' and thus specifying its meaning: the shepherds keep watch over their flock by means of *phulakai. tēs nuktos* is either genitive of time (but then usually without article, cp. Bl-D, § 186.2), going with *phulassontes phulakas* 'keeping watches at night', or, preferably, qualifying genitive with *phulakas*: 'night watches'.

phulassō active: 'to watch', 'to protect', middle: 'to guard against', 'to look out for'.

phulakē 'guarding', 'watch of the night', 'prison'.

Translation: *Shepherds* usually can be described as 'men who tend (or, feed/lead/care-for/watch) the sheep'. In some cases such a rendering would lead to tautology, because the rest of the sentence comes near to a description of a shepherd's job; then it is preferable simply to render 'men'. For 'sheep' see references on 15 : 4.

Out in the field, keeping watch over their flock by night. In a context like this some languages (e.g. Javanese, Kapauku) render 'to (keep) watch' by 'to stay with'; in others the rendering requires a second verb to express the connexion with the object, e.g. 'to (keep) watch, staying-with/taking-care-of' (cp. Balinese). In some cases the language renders the phrase 'to keep watch at night' by one verb (East Toradja); elsewhere the language possesses one verb to render 'to be/stay at night', 'to pass the night'. In the latter case the structure of the sentence may better be slightly changed, cp. 'they were-passing-the-night in the fields, staying-with their flock' (Javanese, Toba Batak). — *Out in the field,* or, 'in the grass (i.e. open uncultivated areas)' (Tagabili), 'in (the-)country (i.e. brushland, suitable for grazing), but in (the-)open' (Kituba, which has to use two expressions in order to make it clear that they were not inside a house). For *flock,* i.e. a number of domesticated animals tended by a herdsman, some languages have a specific term, e.g. a word related to 'gathered group' (Lokele), or 'enclosure', by extension also used to indicate the animals normally kept there (Zarma). In other languages "their flock" has to be rendered by, 'those-they-tend/feed' (Balinese, Toba Batak), 'the sheep they had to care for', 'their sheep'. For *night* cp. *N.T.Wb.*/57.

9 ***And an angel of the Lord appeared to them, and the glory of the Lord shone around them, and they were filled with fear.***

Exegesis: *aggelos kuriou,* cp. on 1 : 11.

epestē autois 'stood by them', denoting a movement towards the shepherds, hence "came upon them" (BFBS), and implying a note of suddenness, cp. A-G s.v. 1 a.

ephistēmi usually in present or aorist tense only, 'to stand by', 'to approach', 'to appear', often of the appearing of divine beings in dreams and visions.

doxa kuriou perielampsen autous 'the splendour of the Lord shone around them'.

doxa 'brightness', 'splendour', 'magnificence', 'honour'; here it appears visibly as a radiant light, cp. Zürich, *Lichtglanz.* In the Septuagint *doxa kuriou* translates *k*^{e}*bōd yahwe(h)*, God's visible presence, cp. e.g. Ex. 16 : 10; 24 : 16; 40 : 34f.

perilampō (†) 'to shine around someone'.

kai ephobēthēsan phobon megan lit. 'and they feared (with) a great fear'; *phobon megan* is accusative of content (cp on v. 8) and here has the function of an adverb of degree, cp. "greatly afraid" (BFBS).

Translation: For *the Lord* (also in vv. 15, 22ff, 26, 29, 39) see on 1 : 6 sub (c).

Appeared to them. The verb (in the original differing from the one used in 1 : 11) has also been rendered, 'came and stood at the side (or, in the midst, or, in front) of' (cp. Sranan, Kanarese, Tagabili).

The glory of the Lord shone around them, or more analytically, 'shone-on them, it surrounded them' (Kituba). Often the expression usually rendering *glory* (cp. *TBT*, 1.28f, 1950; 4.169-72, 1953; 13.86, 153, 1962; Nida, *BT*, 192f, s.vs. "glory" and "majesty"; *TH-Mk* on 8 : 38; 10 : 37; 13 : 26) clearly conveys the concept of 'brightness', 'radiance'; then it may be better to render the verb simply by 'was around them', 'enveloped/surrounded them', cp. 'great the brightness...all around them' (Tagabili). Elsewhere the usual rendering does not go idiomatically with 'to shine'; then it may be possible to say, 'the radiance of the majesty...shone-on them all-around' (Balinese), or to shift to a simile, e.g. 'the greatness/ majesty...was around (or, enveloped) them like a flame/radiance'.

They were filled with fear, or, 'they became very afraid', refers to the effect of the two preceding events; hence a connective like, 'therefore', 'consequently', 'so' (cp. Javanese, Toba Batak).

10 ***And the angel said to them, "Be not afraid; for behold, I bring you good news of a great joy which will come to all the people;***

Exegesis: *idou gar* 'for behold', cp. on 1 : 44.

euaggelizomai humin charan megalēn 'I bring(-as)-good-news to you a great joy', cp. on 1 : 19.

hētis estai panti tō laō "which will be for all the people" (BFBS): *hētis* is here equivalent to the simple relative pronoun *hē*, cp. Bl-D, § 293.3.

panti tō laō is best understood as a dative of advantage: 'a joy which will be to the benefit of all the people'. For *laos* cp. 1 : 68, 77; the reference is not to 'people' in general, i.e. mankind, but to 'the people', i.e. Israel.

Translation: *I bring you good news of a great joy*, i.e. news that gives great joy, or, causes people to rejoice greatly. Some other restructured renderings of the phrase are, "I bring you good tidings, news of a great joy" (Rieu), "I have good news for you: there is great joy coming to..." (NEB, making 'great joy' the grammatical subject of the next clause); or, toning down the force of the verb, '...tell the news which will give great joy' (Bolivian Quechua), 'great joy word(s) wish-to-tell-you I-have-come' (Kapauku). For *to bring good news* cp. also on 1 : 19.

Which will come to all the people, or, 'which will be the share of this whole-people' (East Toradja), 'in which the whole country will take part' (Sranan), 'a blessing for all the people' (Toba Batak, using an appositional construction), 'over which all the people will be-glad' (East Toradja 1933). *The people*, or, to make it clear that here Israel is meant, 'this people', 'your people' (Balinese), 'the people in your country' (Tagabili), '(the people of) Israel'; see also on 1 : 17.

11 ***for to you is born this day in the city of David a Saviour, who is Christ the Lord.***

Exegesis: *hoti etechthē humin sēmeron sōtēr* 'for there has been born for you today a saviour', or, 'viz. that there has been born for you today a saviour', preferably the latter. Thus interpreted the clause is epexegetic to *charan megalēn* in v. 10.

humin 'for you' dative of advantage, as usual in ancient proclamations of royal births (cp. Klostermann); there is no contradiction with *panti tō laō* (v. 10) 'for all the people' because the persons addressed represent all the people concerned.

sēmeron 'today'. According to Jewish time reckoning the day begins at sunset.

sōtēr 'saviour', cp. on 1 : 47. Because of the subsequent relative clause *hos estin Christos kurios* 'who is Messiah (and) Lord' (see below), which serves to identify the *sōtēr* whose birth is announced, it is better to understand *sōtēr* not as a title but as an agent-noun.

hos estin Christos kurios 'who is Messiah (and) Lord'. The absence of a connective between *Christos* and *kurios* (for which see on 1 : 6) is awkward and has been variously explained: (1) BFBS understands the words as a hendiadys (i.e. two words expressing together one idea) and translates "the Anointed Lord" (cp. Moffatt "the Lord messiah"); (2) NEB, Segond and Zürich interpret both words as titles, cp. "the Messiah, the Lord" (NEB); (3) RSV and others understand *Christos* as a name and *kurios* as a title, cp. "Christ the Lord" (RSV). As (2) meets with less difficulties than (1) and (3) there is reason to adopt it.

en polei Dauid 'in the town of David', to be connected with *etechthē* 'was born'.

Translation: *To you is born.* In some receptor languages the translator is compelled to decide how the angels came to know the facts told. In Foe, which has six evidential aspect forms, the choice is between a form indicating a statement based on evidence the speaker has previously seen, and one indicating that the speaker describes something he can see going on; the latter is used here. Similarly in Huli a past active form is chosen, which indicates that the statement is not based on deduction but on known fact in which the speaker took part or which he saw going on. — In this position the dative of advantage is often difficult to express; hence shifts to, 'you have received to-day a saviour, (who is) born in...', 'born is your Saviour' (Javanese, similarly Kapauku).

This day, or, 'today', 'now', 'at this time', or, '(in) this night' (Kituba, Tagabili, Toba Batak).

A Saviour, i.e. 'One who saves you'.

Christ (also in 2 : 26; 3 : 15; 4 : 41; 9 : 20; 20 : 41; 22 : 67; 23 : 2, 35, 39; 24 : 26, 46). There is a strong tendency amongst translators to transliterate Gr. *christos*, both where it still is a noun or title, and where it already has become a proper name or nearly so. When that line is followed, the translator has only to consider how, and to what extent, the form of the name has to be adjusted to phonemic patterns of the receptor language, e.g.

Kedays (Tagabili), *Kaditoti* (Kapauku, but later replaced by *Keristus*, as used in the language of prestige), *Kerisitu* (East Toradja), *Klisto* (Kituba), *Chitu* (Chinese); cp. also *TBT*, 4.104-106, 1953.

Other problems arise if one tries to translate the word, where it is to be taken as a noun or title (see *Exegesis*), cp. e.g. NEB, where (*ho*) *christos* is rendered by "the Messiah", and once by "(God's) Anointed" (23 : 35), or Goodspeed, where "the Messiah" is used here and in v. 26, "an anointed (king)" in 23 : 2, and "(the) Christ" in all other passages. Working along this line the translator may have the choice of three alternatives. (1) In several languages 'Messias', 'Messiah' (a borrowing by way of Gr. *messias* and Aramaic *m^{e}shīḥā* from Hebrew *māshiaḥ* 'the anointed one') has been taken over in the sense it had acquired amongst the Jews, i.e. a God-promised or God-sent saviour-king. In that case it is possible to use the word here, in the phonemic form already existent in the receptor language. (2) In languages spoken in predominantly Muslim areas, the term (*al*)*masiḥ* may be known, going back to the form which *māshiaḥ* or *m^{e}shīḥā* took on in Arabic, where it was used by Mohammed in reference to *Isa* (Jesus) (e.g. Sura 3 : 45, 9 : 30f). This term has often been used to render 'Christ' (see e.g. the above mentioned list), on the assumption that the meaning of the borrowing and the original term are the same. This assumption, however, rather questionable in general, is especially so in this case, because in the Koran the word had fairly well lost its Old Testament meaning to become part of the name of *Isa*, the prophet of the Christians (see on 1 : 31). This may be the reason why in some receptor languages the rendering (*al*)*masih*, after having been used for some time, has been discarded afterwards, e.g. in Malay. (3) Apart from these renderings, which make use of terms originally foreign to the receptor language, attempts have been made to describe the concept in indigenous terms, e.g. 'the anointed one' (cp. *N.T.Wb.*/10), 'the consecrated one', 'the one God has inaugurated'. A cultural equivalent found in one version is, 'Son of heaven'; this interesting solution, however, is thought a questionable one by some translators (cp. *TBT*, 3.166 and 171, 1952; 4.184, 1953), especially because of undesirable associations with mythological concepts such as the holy marriage of the god of heaven with mother earth.

The opinion of the present author is that, in all passages reflecting Messianic concepts current among the Jews of Jesus' days, translation is preferable. In practice, however, transliteration will often have to prevail, e.g. because of existing tradition in the receptor language, or in a neighbouring language of prestige (cp. also Nida, *BT*, 215; *TH-Mk* on 8 : 29).

The Lord, see on 1 : 6, sub (b).

12 ***And this will be a sign for you: you will find a babe wrapped in swaddling cloths and lying in a manger."***

Exegesis: *kai touto humin to sēmeion* 'and this for you the (or 'a') sign', with either *estin* 'is' (cp. BFBS), or *estai* 'will be' (cp. Goodspeed) understood, preferably the latter. *touto* 'this' points to the subsequent description of the sign; *humin* 'for you', dative of advantage.

sēmeion 'sign', 'distinguishing mark', 'miracle'. Here the sign serves either to identify the new-born child or to prove the truth of what has been said about the child, but these interpretations do not exclude each other; the latter is preferable.

esparganōmenon kai keimenon en phatnē 'wrapped up and lying in a manger', cp. on v. 7; strictly speaking only the second part of the phrase denotes something out of the ordinary and has therefore the character of a sign.

Translation: *This will be a sign for you,* or, 'this the you-will-recognize sign' (Kapauku), 'by this you will recognize him' (Leyden), following the first interpretation mentioned in *Exegesis,* or, "this will prove it to you" (Goodspeed), following the other interpretation. For *sign* cp. also on 2 : 34.

Find. Receptor languages may distinguish between (1) 'find/come-across' (by chance), and (2) 'find/obtain' (as result of deliberate seeking), as is the case here. Cp. also *TH-Mk* on 1 : 37. In some languages one verb covers the concepts 'to see' and 'to find' (e.g. Tagabili), or, 'to see', 'to meet' and 'to find' (e.g. Balinese).

A babe wrapped in swaddling cloths and lying in a manger. The verbs used are the same as in v. 7 but the aspect is different. This may be expressed by the use of different aspect forms, or by other means, compare e.g. 'wrapped-him-up with/by-means-of swaddling-cloths', suggesting an act, in v. 7, with 'wrapped-up in swaddling-cloths', suggesting repose, here (Bahasa Indonesia KB), 'was wrapped by her in swaddling-cloths' with 'having-swaddling-cloths' (Balinese), or, 'put him in a manger' with 'lying in a manger' (Sranan). In some languages a one-word rendering such as 'wrapped-up' or 'swaddled' is more idiomatic than a literal rendering of the phrase "wrapped up in swaddling cloths". This may help to make it possible to recast the whole expression in such a way as to focus the attention on the second part, cp. 'find a wrapped-up babe which was lying in a manger' (cp. Toba Batak 1885). For *babe* cp. on v. 17.

13 ***And suddenly there was with the angel a multitude of the heavenly host praising God and saying,***

Exegesis: *kai exaiphnēs egeneto sun tō aggelō* 'and suddenly (or, 'unexpectedly') there was with the angel...'; *egeneto* is used here as a substitute for a form of *eimi* 'to be', cp. A-G s.v. *ginomai* II, 4. *exaiphnēs* also 9 : 39.

plēthos stratias ouraniou 'a great company of the heavenly army'; the genitive refers to content (to be interpreted as 'consisting of').

stratia ouranios (both words †) 'heavenly army', scil. of angels, cp. 1 Kings 22 : 19.

ainountōn ton theon kai legontōn 'praising God and saying'; both participles are appositive to the preceding *stratias ouraniou* but are in the plural as if *aggelōn* preceded, cp. Bl-D, § 134. *legontōn* 'saying' serves to introduce the content of the praise.

Translation: *There was with the angel...*, or, 'suddenly there-appeared/

became-visible near the angel' (Bahasa Indonesia KB, similarly Kapauku), 'there joined themselves to the angel...' (Jerusalem, similarly Tagalog), 'the angel was surrounded by...' (Vai), 'there came to the side of the angel...' (Sranan).

A multitude of the heavenly host, or, 'a numerous heavenly army' (Sundanese), 'many heavenly soldiers' (Toba Batak). For *multitude* cp. on 3 : 7, for *heavenly* on "heaven" in v. 15. Since in *host* the emphasis is not on the military aspect, "heavenly host" may also be rendered by 'those from heaven' (Tagabili), 'inhabitants of heaven' (Thai).

Praising God and saying. In some receptor languages words of praise are preferably not introduced by 'to say'; hence, 'they praised..., thus their praise' (Balinese, Sundanese), "praising God and singing" (Rieu). *To praise* is often rendered by a descriptive expression, e.g. 'make-great, or, make-great the name of' (East Toradja, in v. 20), 'to speak well of' (Tarascan), 'lift up the name of' (Cuna, Kpelle), 'to sing the name of' (Tepehua), 'to make good' (Totonac), 'to say good about' (Tzeltal), 'to make known something good about' (Navajo).

14 ***"Glory to God in the highest,***
and on earth peace among men with whom he is pleased!"

Exegesis: When the reading *eudokias* 'favour' in the genitive is adopted the hymn consists of two corresponding lines connected by *kai*; the parallelism between the various parts of each line is very close but does not strictly follow the word order: *doxa* 'glory' corresponds with *eirēnē* 'peace', *en hupsistois* 'in the highest' with *epi gēs* 'on earth', and *theō* 'to God' with *en anthrōpois* 'among men'. When however the reading *eudokia* in the nominative is adopted this parallelism is lost because *eudokia* is then a third predicate besides *doxa* and *eirēnē*. The reading *eudokias* is preferable, cp. Plummer and Schrenk, *TWNT*, II, 745ff.

doxa en hupsistois theō 'glory in the highest to God'; the form of the verb *einai* that is to be understood with the phrase, is either *eiē* 'may be' (optative) or *estin* 'is' (indicative), cp. Bl-D, § 128.5; neither form however expresses the meaning of the doxology adequately because a doxology is not merely a wish ('may glory be given to God') nor just a statement ('God has glory'), but rather "a statement of that which is, in terms of a praise of God" (cp. Kittel, *TWNT*, II, 251); in the present context 'that which is' is the birth of the Saviour and the doxology expresses what this birth means in heaven and on earth.

doxa 'glory', cp. on v. 9; here it does not have the connotation of 'radiant light'.

hupsista 'the highest', cp. on 1 : 32; *en hupsistois* goes with *theō* as indicating the place where God is (cp. RSV, NEB, and others) or with the phrase as a whole, indicating the place where glory is given to God (cp. BFBS, Rieu); the latter seems preferable because of the place of *en hupsistois* before *theō* and of the parallelism with *epi gēs* 'on earth'.

epi gēs eirēnē en anthrōpois eudokias 'on earth peace among men of his favour'.

gē 'soil', 'ground', 'land', 'earth'.

eirēnē 'peace', cp. on 1 : 79.

eudokia (also 10 : 21) 'good will' of men, cp. "men of good will" (Rieu), or 'favour', 'pleasure', of God, cp. "men on whom his favour rests" (NEB); the latter interpretation is adopted by the great majority of commentators and translators and supported by the repeated occurrence of the same phrase in Hebrew in the Dead Sea Scrolls, where the possessive suffix makes clear that God is the subject of the act implied in the verbal nouns 'favour' or 'pleasure', cp. Grundmann and Bl-D, § 165. The genitive is qualifying. There is no reason to assume a contradiction between *panti tō laō* 'all the people' in v. 10 and *en anthrōpois eudokias* 'among men of his favour' as if the latter would impose a restriction upon the former: it only serves to express that the initiative in establishing peace on earth is not with men but with God.

Translation: *Glory to God.* Often a verb must be added, 'praise be/is-offered to God' (Javanese), or the syntactic pattern changed, e.g. 'most exalted (is) God' (Balinese), or 'honoured should God be' (Sundanese), 'let God be greatly praised' (Bolivian Quechua).

In the highest. Some versions have to add a word for 'place' (Telugu, Sundanese). Where the context is not sufficient to show that place to be God's abode in heaven it is better to add 'heaven(s)'. Balinese uses a term, 'highest-world', referring to the highest of the layers of heaven, cp. also 'upper world' (Kanarese).

On earth. The rendering must be the normal counterpart of the term chosen for "in the highest". Thus Balinese employs 'sphere-of-mortals' (thought of as taking the middle position between heaven and netherworld and, as such, also called 'middle sphere'), because this term, not 'earth', is commonly used in one pair with 'highest-world'.

Peace among men, or, 'peace reign(s) among men', 'men (may) receive peace', 'men's condition is (or, may be) peaceful'. For *peace*, here used in its positive meaning, see on 1 : 79.

With whom he is pleased. Some versions keep closer to the Greek construction, only adding a possessive pronoun, cp. "men of his choice" (BFBS, similarly Sinhalese). Several do as RSV does, and shift to a relative verbal clause, e.g. "men he favors" (Goodspeed), 'men he rejoices in' (Chinese), 'people that he accepts/approves of' (Kituba, using a continuative present tense), 'people He likes' (Tagabili, lit. 'people where stays his breath'), 'men who are-pleasing to His heart' (Bahasa Indonesia KB), 'people who fit God's eye' (Sranan). When the verb is specific, and normally used with God as agent, it is sometimes possible to omit the indication of the agent, e.g. 'men who are elected' (Javanese). When a relative clause is impossible one may shift to, 'peace for men: he favours (or, is pleased with, or, loves) them'. For *pleased* see references on "well pleased" in 3 : 22.

In some languages incongruity between the two lines of the verse in matters of word order would destroy the meaning of the whole clause, or at least impair the stylistic impression aimed at; then the word order of the two lines should be made more closely parallel. Similar considerations may make preferable the use of more closely parallel renderings of the prepositions, e.g. 'is given to God...comes to the earth' (Sranan), "glory to God...peace to the men" (Goodspeed), 'most exalted (is) God...very peaceful (are) the men' (Balinese).

15 ***When the angels went away from them into heaven, the shepherds said to one another, "Let us go over to Bethlehem and see this thing that has happened, which the Lord has made known to us."***

Exegesis: *kai egeneto hōs apēlthon...hoi aggeloi, hoi poimenes elaloun...* lit. 'and it happened when the angels had gone away, that the shepherds said...', cp. note on 1 : 8.

hōs apēlthon ap' autōn eis ton ouranon hoi aggeloi 'when the angels had gone away from them back to heaven'; the Greek verb *aperchomai* means both 'to go away' and 'to go back' (cp on 1 : 23).

hoi poimenes elaloun pros allēlous 'the shepherds repeatedly said to one another', the imperfect tense *elaloun* marks repetition.

dielthōmen dē heōs Bēthleem 'let us then go over to Bethlehem'.

dierchomai 'to go through', 'to go', but always with the implication that a certain distance is to be traversed, cp. Moulton-Milligan 160.

dē (†) 'then', lends greater urgency to the exhortation (cp. A-G s.v.).

heōs as a preposition 'as far as' or in a more general sense 'to', cp. A-G s.v. II 2 a.

to rēma touto to gegonos 'this thing that has happened', cp. on 1 : 37; the expression is Hebraistic, cp. 1 Sam. 4 : 16, where Leroy Waterman in *An American Translation* translates "what has happened?" The participle *gegonos* 'happened' does not add to the meaning of *rēma* 'thing' but stresses the perfective aspect of the 'thing'.

ho ho kurios egnōrisen hēmin 'which the Lord has made known to us', implying that the angel has been the mouthpiece of the Lord; the first *ho* (with accent) is the relative pronoun, referring back to *to rēma.*

gnōrizō (also v. 17) 'to make known', not a specifically religious term.

Translation: *Went away from them into heaven,* one verb with two indicators of direction. Idiom may require the addition of a verb, e.g. 'they left them going (or, and went, or, to go) back to heaven' (cp. Kapauku, Telugu, Tamil, Kituba, South Toradja), or the omission of 'from them' (Tagabili, Sundanese); the latter does not mean an actual loss of information, since the point of departure is clear from the context. Some languages prefer to be more specific, saying 'went up/ascended to heaven' (e.g. Kapauku, Pampango, East Toradja). — In the Bible *heaven* may refer to the abode of God or to the vault of heaven, the firmament/sky. In the former meaning it occurs here and in 3 : 22; 6 : 23; 10 : 18 (?), 20; 11 : 16; 12 : 33; 15 : 7; 18 : 22; 19 : 38; 22 : 43, 51, and as adjective 'heavenly' in 2 : 13; 11 : 13; and metonymically, cp. on 15 : 18. The latter meaning occurs in 3 : 21; 4 : 25; 9 : 16, 54; 10 : 18 (?); 17 : 29; 18 : 13; 21 : 10, 26;

also in combination with "Hades" or with "earth" in 10 : 15 and 21 (which see). Some languages distinguish between these concepts (cp. also *TH-Mk* on 1 : 10); elsewhere the sky is seldom associated with God, e.g. in Samoan, cp. *TBT*, 18.77, 1967. In such cases a descriptive term, 'abode of God', 'place where God lives' may be an acceptable rendering. The Greek word used here is more everyday than "the highest" in v. 14, but in some languages, e.g. in Tagabili, one rendering has to cover the two terms.

Said to one another is often expressed by a reciprocal form of the verb, cp. on 4 : 36; in Bamiléké by a complex pronoun (lit. 'they-they') with reciprocal meaning, 'they among themselves said'.

In some cases the clause structure of the following direct discourse must be changed, e.g. 'The Lord has made known to us what has happened. Let us go . . . and look at it' (cp. Telugu).

Let us go over to, or, 'go (straight) to' (cp. TEV, NEB). The hortatory mood is often expressed by a specific form of the verb, e.g. an imperative (Kituba), or by the use of an interjection (cp. Sundanese), or of a combination of both. In some cases the verb must be rendered by a specific term for going from the countryside to the central town or village.

Thing that has happened, or, 'what has happened', 'event that has taken place (lit. is-born)' (Thai), 'things that have taken place (lit. have fallen) there' (Kituba); or here, 'this that they told us about just now' (Tagabili, which does not possess such a generic term as 'happened'). Considerations of sentence structure may make it preferable to render the phrase by one term, e.g. "this event" (Phillips), 'that matter' (Balinese).

Which the Lord has made known to us. Whereas the preceding relative clause is restrictive, this one is non-restrictive, cp. 'what has happened here, as has been made known...' (Javanese). God was the ultimate source of the message but the angels were the actual conveyors; therefore it may be necessary to say, 'which God has caused to be told (or, caused the angels to tell) to us'.

16 ***And they went with haste, and found Mary and Joseph, and the babe lying in a manger.***

Exegesis: *kai ēlthon speusantes* 'they went with haste'; the participle *speusantes* qualifies the action of the main verb as happening with haste or quickly (cp. RSV, NEB, Jerusalem, Zürich).

speudō (also 19 : 5f) 'to hurry', 'to make haste', in Luke always as a participle qualifying the main verb.

kai aneuron 'and they found'.

aneurō (†) 'to find out', implying a search as in Acts 21 : 4, cp. "they found their way to Mary and Joseph" (NEB).

tēn te Mariam kai ton Iōsēph kai to brephos keimenon en tē phatnē 'Mary and Joseph and the child lying in the manger'; the series of connectives *te...kai...kai* admits of the following interpretations: (1) 'Mary, Joseph and the child', i.e. *te* is taken to be followed by more than one corresponding *kai*, cp. Moffatt, A-G s.v. *te* 3 a; (2) 'Mary and Joseph, and the child', i.e. *te* is connected with the first *kai* only and this connexion expresses that

Mary and Joseph are one group as compared with the child, cp. RSV, BFBS, Phillips, Goodspeed, Zürich; (3) the second *kai* is taken to connect two co-ordinate clauses, cp. "they found...Mary and Joseph; and the baby was lying in the manger" (NEB). Of these interpretations (2) is the most probable because when *te* is followed by more than one *kai* usually *te* and the first *kai* connect concepts which are more closely related to each other than to what follows, cp. Lk. 12 : 45, Acts 1 : 8, Heb. 2 : 4; this is here supported by the fact that the participle *keimenon* 'lying' goes with *brephos* only.

Translation: *Found*, or, because of the implied search, 'they looked for and found', 'in their search they saw' (Cuyono).

Mary and Joseph, and the babe lying in a manger. To avoid the danger that the participle would be taken with the three persons mentioned, various ways are open, such as the use of different connectives, e.g. 'Mary with Joseph, and the babe...' (Bahasa Indonesia KB), 'M. and J., moreover the babe...' (Javanese, Balinese), or of a deictic element after 'Joseph', giving to the next phrase a rather independent position (Sundanese); or the repetition of the verb, cp. 'found M. with J., and found the babe lying...' (Thai); or again, a repetition of 'babe/child', cp. '...found M., J. and child; child was lying...' (Kituba).

17 ***And when they saw it they made known the saying which had been told them concerning this child;***

Exegesis: *idontes* 'having seen', the object has to be supplied from the preceding clause and is either Mary, Joseph and the child, cp. "them" (Kingsley Williams), or the child only, cp. "him" (NEB), "it" (RSV), preferably the former.

egnōrisan peri tou rēmatos tou lalēthentos autois peri tou paidiou toutou lit. 'they made known about the word that had been spoken to them about this child'; *peri tou rēmatos* has the function of a direct object in the accusative with *egnōrisan* (cp. v. 15); when connected with a form of the verb *laleō* 'to speak' *rēma* means 'word', not 'thing', but here it refers rather to the content of the word than to the word itself: hence many translators render *tou rēmatos tou lalēthentos autois* as "what had been told them" (BFBS) or a similar translation. *egnōrisan* has no indirect object, which is supplied variously: (a) "them", i.e. Mary and Joseph (Kingsley Williams); this seems the natural supplement when the omission of the indirect object is not intentional; (b) "everybody" (Phillips), this is in accordance with the following verse which presupposes that the story has been spread. In the order of the story it is only logical to think of Joseph and Mary as the first persons to receive the message of the shepherds, but Luke has already in mind what follows, i.e. the reaction of all who heard that message, and in order to prepare the reader for what follows he does not mention the indirect object of *egnōrisan* 'they made known'. According to this interpretation Luke's omission of the indirect object is intentional.

paidion 'little child', cp. on 1 : 59. The terms *brephos* 'babe' (vv. 12,

16), *paidion* (here, v. 27 and v. 40) and *pais* 'boy' (v. 43) apparently are used to suggest phases in Jesus' growth, the end of which is indicated by the use of 'Jesus' without a qualifying apposition (v. 52). But this is not to be pressed, as is shown by the facts that *brephos* can also mean 'embryo' (1 : 41, 44), and that *paidion* here has the same referent as *brephos* (v. 12), although its general range of meaning is wider, covering the whole period of childhood.

Translation: *When they saw it,* or, 'them', as preferred in *Exegesis.*

They made known, the same verb as in v. 15, probably in order to suggest that God's message brought by the angels now finds its parallel in the message brought by the shepherds. NEB has "made known" in v. 15, but here "recounted", another way to refer the reader to the first message; similarly South Toradja, 'go-along-the-whole-length', i.e. tell again, keeping exactly to the original message. Some translators, taking the indirect object here to be 'everybody' (as preferred in *Exegesis*) have chosen a somewhat more encompassing expression, 'to tell all' (Tagabili), 'to make-widely-known' (Bahasa Indonesia), 'to make known everywhere' (Kapauku).

The saying which had been told them, or, 'what the angels had told them'. Tagabili renders 'that which they had heard', probably to avoid repetition of 'to tell'.

Child, cp. on 1 : 7. The series "babe"—"child"—"boy" will require careful handling in receptor languages that have a different division and/or a different number of grades, or no grading at all, as in East Toradja. In some other cases a grading term, though existing, is unacceptable in this context for various reasons, stylistic, as in Dutch (where the usual term for the first grade, a borrowing from English "baby", would sound ridiculous), or honorific, as in Balinese (which, though possessing a word for "babe", cannot use it when referring to a child of high rank), or semantic, as in Bahasa Indonesia (where the term 'boy' came to be primarily associated with the concept 'servant').

18 ***and all who heard it wondered at what the shepherds told them.***

Exegesis: *pantes hoi akousantes* 'all who heard', without specific object; this is either the shepherds, cp. "them" (Phillips, Segond) or what the shepherds told, cp. "it" (RSV, Goodspeed, Zürich), preferably the latter.

peri tōn lalēthentōn hupo tōn poimenōn pros autous lit. 'about the things that had been told by the shepherds to them'.

Translation: Some possibly necessary changes of the sentence structure are, 'the things the shepherds had told them astonished all people who had heard them' (Sranan), 'all who heard what the shepherds told wondered (at it)'.

Wondered at, see on 1 : 21.

What (or, the things/matter) *the shepherds told them,* or, 'the words of the shepherds (to them)', 'the shepherds' story' (Javanese).

19 ***But Mary kept all these things, pondering them in her heart.***

Exegesis: *hē de Mariam* 'but Mary', in contrast with *pantes hoi akousantes* 'all who heard' in v. 18.

panta...ta rēmata tauta 'all these things'; *panta* is emphatic, as shown by its position.

rēmata 'things' (many translators) or 'words' (Dutch versions, Goodspeed, Zürich); the former interpretation implies a reference to all that Mary had seen, heard and experienced and is, therefore, wider in scope than the latter and as such preferable.

suneterei '(she) treasured up'; as compared with the aorist tense in the preceding verse the imperfect tense here suggests that Mary kept her experiences in mind not for a moment but for a long time.

suntēreō (†) 'to keep carefully', 'to treasure up in one's memory'.

sumballousa en tē kardia autēs 'pondering in her heart', scil. all these things; the object is to be taken over from *sunetērei* 'she treasured up'; *en tē kardia* may go with *sunetērei*, or with *sumballousa*; because of the word order preferably the latter.

sumballō (also 14 : 31) transitive 'to bring together', hence 'to compare', 'to interpret', or, in a more weakened sense, 'to ponder'.

Translation: *Kept all these things, pondering them in her heart.* In some receptor languages 'to keep/to treasure', in the sense intended here, requires a reference to the place where the things are kept, whereas 'to ponder' can go without; hence such transposition of the locative phrase as, 'placed in her heart and considered' (Tamil, Kanarese), 'she-put in her breath and...she-thought' (Tagabili, similarly in Tagalog). In other languages both verbs have to be qualified; hence a transposition of the object, e.g. 'kept and pondered all these things in her heart' (Bahasa Indonesia RC). — *To keep*, or, 'to keep in the heart'. A connotation of secrecy (which can slip in rather easily because of the esoteric tendencies of many religions) must be avoided. Cp. also *N.T.Wb.*/49, category (1). *Ponder*, or, 'continually think-about' (Tagabili), 'turn around in the mind' (Toba Batak), a reiterative form of 'think' (several other Indonesian languages), 'puzzle forth, puzzle back' (Sranan).

20 ***And the shepherds returned, glorifying and praising God for all they had heard and seen, as it had been told them.***

Exegesis: *kai hupestrepsan hoi poimenes* 'and the shepherds returned', to their flocks; *kai* 'and' indicates that the account of the events immediately following the birth of Christ is resumed after mentioning in v. 19 what Mary's attitude was.

doxazontes kai ainountes ton theon 'glorifying and praising God'.

doxazō, always (except 4 : 15) with God as object, 'to honour', 'to glorify'. As compared with *aineō* 'to praise' *doxazō* is the stronger of the two.

epi pasin hois ēkousan kai eidon 'for all that they had heard and seen'; *epi* followed by dative introduces here that upon which the glorifying and praising of the shepherds is based, cp. A-G s.v. II 1 b γ. The relative pronoun *hois* 'that' has been attracted into the case of the antecedent *pasin* 'all', cp. Bl-D, § 294. The verbs are in the aorist tense but are to be rendered in the pluperfect, cp. Moule 16. *ēkousan kai eidon* '(what) they had heard and seen' is best understood as one expression summing up the experience of the shepherds in Bethlehem.

kathōs elalēthē pros autous 'as it had been said to them', scil. by the angel, to be connected only with the preceding 'all that they had heard and seen'.

Translation: *The shepherds returned, glorifying and praising God*, or, changing the pattern of subordination, 'when the shepherds returned (viz. to their sheep), they were-glorifying, they were-praising God' (Kituba); or, shifting to co-ordination, 'the shepherds went back, (and) they glorified and praised God'. *Glorifying and praising.* For the first verb see *TH-Mk* on 2 : 12, and cp. Nida, *GWIML*, 162, and above v. 9 on "glory". A few other renderings are, 'to make big the precious quality of' (Kekchi), 'to holy-remember' (Chontal of Tabasco). For the second verb see above v. 13. Since in several cases the renderings of the two verbs are basically the same or closely resemble each other, their combination may require some adaptation, such as using one verb with two qualifications, e.g. 'lift up the brightness and the name', 'say that is great and good', or representing the second verb as an indication of high degree, e.g. 'to speak extremely well of', 'great their praising' (Tagabili).

All they had heard and seen, as it had been told them, or to express the relationship of the two clauses more clearly, "all that they had heard and seen in fulfilment of what they had been told" (Goodspeed), "all they had heard and seen; it had been just as the angel had told them" (TEV, similarly NEB, Willibrord).

21 ***And at the end of eight days, when he was circumcised, he was called Jesus, the name given by the angel before he was conceived in the womb.***

Exegesis: *kai hote eplēsthēsan hēmerai oktō tou peritemein auton* 'and when eight days had been fulfilled (and the time had come) for circumcising him', cp. on 1 : 57. The omission of the article before *hēmerai* is awkward because the reference is not to *a* period of eight days but to those eight days that had to elapse between birth and circumcision, cp. on 1 : 59. *tou peritemein auton* is best understood as an independent articular infinitive in the genitive with a consecutive meaning, cp. 'when eight days were fulfilled that they (indefinite) should circumcise him' (Brouwer, also Zürich).

kai eklēthē to onoma autou Iēsous 'and his name was called Jesus'; *kai* 'and' at the beginning of the apodosis when a subordinate clause precedes, is primarily due to Hebrew influence.

to klēthen hupo tou aggelou 'the (name) called, or, named by the angel', attributive to *to onoma*.

pro tou sullēmphthēnai auton en tē koilia 'before his being conceived in the womb'; the same expression in the active in 1 : 31.

Translation: *At the end of eight days, when he was circumcised.* The prepositional phrase may also be rendered, 'after eight days had passed/elapsed', 'when eight days were complete' (Sinhalese), 'when the eighth day was already broken off' (Tagabili, where people keep track of dates for certain events by tying knots in abaca strands, and breaking them off one by one, as the days successively elapse), 'after eight days'; cp. also on 1 : 59. — Other possible translations of the "when"-clause are, 'so that the child should be circumcised', 'at the time they (indefinite) should circumcise the child' (East Toradja 1933), 'at his circumcision day' (Balinese, employing a verbal derivation that is in general use for forming names of religious ceremonies, *rites de passages* etc., and thus suggests the idea of a traditionally fixed day and period). It may be preferable to avoid subordination here, cp. "Eight days later the time came to circumcise him, and he..." (NEB). — *He.* Here and in the rest of the chapter the child Jesus is often referred to by a pronoun of the third person singular. Where a noun has to be substituted (cp. on 1 : 8) care should be taken that it should agree with the grades of Jesus' growth (see above on v. 17). Thus the terms to be used in vv. 21-38 and 42-51 should agree with the rendering of "child" in v. 17, and "boy" in v. 43, respectively. — *Was circumcised.* If one cannot use a passive construction, or an active form having an indefinite subject, one may shift to, 'his parents should have him circumcised', or, 'the child/he received the mark', etc., cp. on 1 : 59.

He was called Jesus, or, 'he received the name Jesus' (Sranan), 'they/his parents called him (or, gave him the name) Jesus'; cp. also on "call his name" in 1 : 13.

The name given by the angel, translated literally, may suggest that the angel had performed some ceremony of namegiving on the unborn child. Such a misunderstanding can be avoided by saying something like, 'as the angel had said he should be called', 'the name the angel had ordered his mother to give him', or, 'had shown to Mary' (Kituba).

Before he was conceived in the womb, or, 'before his mother had begun yet her conceiving him, or, had-become-pregnant-of Him' (Tagabili, East Toradja); and see on 1 : 31.

22 ***And when the time came for their purification according to the Law of Moses, they brought him up to Jerusalem to present him to the Lord.***

Exegesis: *kai hote eplēsthēsan hai hēmerai tou katharismou autōn* 'and when the days of their purification had been fulfilled', i.e. 'when the time for their purification had come'. *eplēsthēsan hai hēmerai,* cp. on 1 : 57.

katharismos (also 5 : 14) 'purification', i.e. the restoration of ritual cleanness; according to the law of Moses a woman remained unclean for forty days after the birth of a male child. During this period she was forbidden to touch any sacred thing or to enter the temple. Ritual cleanness was restored by a burnt offering and a sin offering (cp. Lev. 12 : 1-8). *autōn* 'of them', i.e. 'their' may refer to Joseph and Mary (cp. Plummer); to Jesus and Mary (cp. Lagrange), or to the three of them (cp. Grundmann), preferably the first.

kata ton nomon Mōüseōs 'according to the law of Moses' may be connected with *eplēsthēsan* 'were fulfilled', as e.g. NEB, Kingsley Williams, or, preferably, with *tou katharismou autōn* 'of their purification', as e.g. BFBS, Phillips, Goodspeed, Moffatt.

nomos 'law', in Luke of the law of Moses only, even when his name is not added as here.

anēgagon auton eis Hierosoluma 'they brought him up to Jerusalem'.

anagō 'to bring up' from a lower to a higher place. Actually Bethlehem is lying higher than Jerusalem (cp. Plummer), but it is hardly conceivable that Luke was aware of this difference in height.

Hierosoluma 'Jerusalem'; this is the Greek form of the name. Elsewhere (e.g. v. 25) Luke uses the Hebraistic form *Ierousalēm.*

parastēsai tō kuriō 'in order to present to the Lord'; object 'him' (i.e. Jesus) to be understood from *auton,* the object of *anēgagon.*

paristēmi in the active (†) 'to present'; presentation in the temple was not part of the ritual of the redemption of the first-born sons referred to in v. 23. Ex. 13 : 2, quoted there, does not order presentation to God, but is, together with other passages, the foundation for the redemption-offering. Luke does not mention the redemption-offering at all but selects one basic aspect of it, the belonging of all male first-borns to God, in order to bring into special relief the fact that Jesus had been presented to God in the temple. This presentation is probably a reminiscence of 1 Sam. 1 : 22-28; hence translations like 'to dedicate' (Brouwer) but this dedication is to be interpreted in the sense of 'to bring in the presence of', cp. Acts 23 : 33.

V. 22 is taken up again in v. 24, the chain of thought being: (22) when the time for their purification came, they went to Jerusalem (24) to offer the prescribed sacrifice. Between these two clauses Luke inserts something else which disrupts this logical sequence and is much more important for Luke because it prepares the way for the recognition by the inspired Simeon of Jesus as Israel's Messiah.

Translation: *When the time came for their purification,* or, 'the purification day having-come' (Balinese, derivation as in v. 21, leaving the persons that are the objects of the purification unidentified), or using a verbal clause, 'on the day that they (or, his parents, or, Joseph and Mary) should be purified', 'when they must cause-themselves-to-be-purified' (Kituba), 'when (they) should do ceremony to purify self' (Thai, the subject idiomatically being left implicit). For *purification,* and 'purify', see *N.T.Wb.*/59; *TBT,* 18.36, 1967. Since removal of ritual uncleanness resulting from childbirth is rather widespread, the receptor language often provides an acceptable specific term; such a term, however, cannot be used here if its application is restricted to the purification of the mother only.

According to the law, or, 'following the law', "stipulated by the Law"

(Phillips), 'that the Law required/prescribed', 'as the law... has laid-down' (Sranan). *Law*. Receptor language terminology may differentiate between two or more of the following pairs of contrasting concepts: customary law *versus* statute law, often coinciding with the contrast oral *versus* written code; secular *versus* religious law; tribal *versus* national or supranational law, either secular (e.g. law or custom of the tribe *versus* law of the national state), or religious (tribal religion *versus* one of the world religions). Between these pairs there may be considerable overlapping. The term chosen should preferably suggest a written code of behaviour, divinely inspired, and of at least national validity. A receptor language term (such as, 'word/matter to be observed' in Kapauku, 'decision/decree', a derivation of 'to cut', in Shona 1966) may, even if originally linked up with another religion, permit sufficient expansion to cover the law of other peoples or religions, where necessary reinforced by a qualification such as 'of the Jews'. In some cases, however, such an expansion of meaning is impossible because the term in question is exclusively associated with one specific religion. For that reason, probably, technical terms for the Muslim law have often proved unsatisfactory, e.g. in languages of Indonesia. Where no technical term is existent or acceptable, one may coin a descriptive phrase, e.g. 'commands/ordinances/decisions of God', 'written command' (Moré), 'laws/rules-(contained-in-)scripture' (Marathi). Cp. also Nida, *BT*, 198; *TBT*, 8.204f, 1957.

Of Moses. For the meaning of this construction see on "the law of the Lord" in v. 23. The name may require a title, 'the prophet M.'.

They brought him up, or, 'they took Him along with them (lit. took-as-companion Him)' (East Toradja, which can use this verb even when the 'companion' is as passive as a babe of six weeks), 'they carried the child' (Sranan, Kituba); idiom may require the use of a verb specifying the way of carrying (in the arms, on the shoulder etc.).

To present him to the Lord, or, 'to place him before the Lord's face' (Sranan), 'to show him to the Lord' (East Toradja). In Malay "to present" is rendered by the causative of a verb meaning 'to be-in-front-of', hence 'to have-an-audience with', 'to pay-one's-respects to'.

23 ***(as it is written in the law of the Lord, "Every male that opens the womb shall be called holy to the Lord")***

Exegesis: *kathōs gegraptai en nomō kuriou* 'as it is written in the law of the Lord', cp. on v. 22.

hoti 'that', introduces a quotation.

pan arsen dianoigon mētran 'every male that opens the womb'.

arsēn (†) 'male'; *pan arsen* 'every male' (in the neuter) is a rendering of the Hebrew *kol zakar* (in the masculine). The neuter here suggests the idea of a collectivity; although it may include both men and animals (as shown in Ex. 13 : 2, 12, 15), in this context only the first category is important.

dianoigō 'to open'.

mētra (†) 'womb'. The expression *dianoigon mētran* 'opening the womb' denotes the first child to which a mother gives birth; it is a Hebraism, cp. Ex. 13 : 2, not on record in Greek.

hagion tō kuriō klēthēsetai 'shall be called holy to the Lord'. The future tense has the force of an imperative. For *klēthēsetai* 'shall be called' cp. on 1 : 32. *hagion tō kuriō* 'holy to the Lord' means 'his property, dedicated to his service'.

Translation: Where it is unacceptable to use a long sentence in parenthesis, it is better to give v. 23 the status of an independent sentence, e.g. 'For so it is written...' (Sranan), "This was to fulfil a requirement of the Law" (Phillips), expressing by another device the connexion between v. 22 and v. 24 (which see).

As it is written in is the standing phrase for introducing quotations from Holy Scripture. Equivalent formulas are found in several languages, e.g. 'as it says in', 'as Scripture, or, the book, or (in this passage), the Law has it', 'thus is the sound of', 'as what stands in' (Balinese), 'thus word of tradition, or, writ in' (a more archaic Balinese expression). Where such a formula is available it should be used, even if formally different from the Greek; where not, a literal rendering of the Greek will do, unless the receptor language cannot use a passive construction. Then one may have to shift to something like 'as people/we read in', or, if the author is mentioned in, or can be inferred from, the context, 'as NN has written'.

The law of the Lord and *the law of Moses* (v. 22). The preposition "of" expresses different relationships, viz. 'given by', 'originating from' and 'written down by' respectively; therefore the two phrases may have to be rendered differently, e.g. 'the commandment of the Lord' and 'the commandment God formerly wrote through Moses' (Tagabili), 'the law, commandment of the Lord' and 'the law of M.' (Balinese). Bahasa Indonesia, though using the same construction in both cases, has different terms, 'Law' and *Torat* (borrowed, *via* Arabic, from Hebrew *tōrāh*, suggesting the written form of the law, and therefore naturally going with a reference to the person who wrote it down).

Male that opens the womb. A literal rendering of this Hebraism may be dangerous: in one receptor language it would indicate sexual intercourse. The rendering often is basically the same as that of "first-born son" in v. 7 (cp. Lengua, Tagalog, Kanarese, Kituba, Javanese). Vai has, 'male child first born in the family'; Timorese uses here, 'male his-mother gives-birth-to making-an-opening-for-herself' but could also have chosen the comparable idiom found in v. 7.

Called holy to. Translators have used renderings such as, 'counted dedicated to' (Tagalog), 'called the property of' (Toba Batak), 'which-is-reserved-to...its name' (Balinese), 'called set-apart for' (South Toradja) or, in the active voice, 'they always set apart for' (Tagabili, omitting the verb 'called', probably in order to avoid the connotation 'only in name but not actually'. — For *holy* see references on 1 : 15.

24 ***and to offer a sacrifice according to what is said in the law of the Lord, "a pair of turtledoves, or two young pigeons."***

Exegesis: *kai tou dounai thusian* 'and in order to make an offering'; the articular infinitive *tou dounai* is co-ordinate with the final infinitive *parastēsai* 'in order to present' in v. 22; both are dependent upon *anēgagon* 'they brought up'. V. 24 is the continuation of v. 22. *thusia* (also 13 : 1) 'sacrifice', 'offering', either the act or the thing that is sacrificed; here the latter. *didonai thusian* 'to give, or, make an offering' is often translated 'to offer a sacrifice' (cp. RSV) but the offering of sacrifices was the task of the priest (cp. Lev. 12 : 8) and *didonai thusian* is used nowhere to denote this priestly task. The purification-offering was handed over to the priest at one of the temple-gates (cp. Strack-Billerbeck II, 119f). It is to this act that *didonai thusian* refers, not to the actual sacrificing on the altar.

kata to eirēmenon en tō nomō kuriou 'in accordance with what is said in the law of the Lord'. Quotations from the Old Testament are often introduced by this or a related formula. There is no difference in usage between expressions derived from the verb *erō* 'to say' or related verbs and those derived from *graphō* 'to write'.

zeugos trugonōn ē duo nossous peristerōn 'a pair of turtledoves or two young pigeons'. Syntactically the phrase is an apposition to *thusian* 'offering', but separated from it by *kata to eirēmenon en tō nomō kuriou* (see preceding note) which marks it as a quotation. Lev. 12 : 8 names two turtledoves or two young pigeons as the purification-sacrifices for those who cannot afford a lamb. The turtledove is a smaller migratory species of the pigeon. Pigeons and turtledoves were the only species of poultry allowed by the law as sacrificial gifts. Since the idea of an Old Testament offering was that of a gift, spent from the property of the donor, pigeons and turtledoves must have been domesticated birds in Bible times and land. That two species are mentioned is due to the fact that turtledoves were fit for sacrifice as soon as they were full grown, but doves only as long as they were young, cp. Strack-Billerbeck, II, 123. Doves were considered very clean and peaceful animals. (Communication of Dr. Jordt Jørgensen, Denmark.)

zeugos (also 14 : 19) 'yoke', 'pair', here not of male and female but simply equivalent to the numeral 'two', cp. Lev. 5 : 11.

trugōn (††) 'turtledove'.

nossos (††) 'the young (of a bird)'. Most translations render it by means of the adjective 'young'.

peristera (also 3 : 22) 'dove'.

Translation: If v. 23 has not been rendered as a parenthesis, one has to make clear that v. 24 is a continuation of v. 22, e.g. by saying, "They also went to offer a sacrifice" (TEV).

Offer a sacrifice. In some languages one can use an expression that does not specify whether the worshipper himself performs the cultic act, or the priest does so in his behalf. Elsewhere it is better to be more specific as to the role of the agent, e.g. 'give to be sacrificed to God' (cp. Tagabili), 'hand over the sacrifice to the priest', 'bring the sacrifice to the temple'. For *sacrifice* cp. Nida, *BT*, 234; *TBT*, 11.26, 1960. When the usual rendering is some descriptive phrase, e.g. 'slain offering', 'killed gift', the form will have to be adapted here, e.g. 'gifts/offerings to be killed/slain'. Some receptor languages, on the other hand, are rich in specific terms forming part of an elaborate sacrificial system, which may include purification sacrifices. Then a translator naturally will try to use such a term, which shares the principal components of meaning with the Biblical sacrifice, viz. (1) performed not for a community, but for its individual members, (2) the performer a temple priest, (3) implying the slaughter of an animal and the shedding of blood, and (4) offered in order to worship a good, celestial deity, not to exorcize demons or bad spirits. On investigation, however, it may become clear that the sacrificial vocabulary, however rich it may be, does not yield an acceptable specific term and that the translator, therefore, has to use a rather generic term, such as 'tribute-of-homage' (East Toradja, Balinese).

According to what is said in serves to introduce a quotation from Scripture in much the same way as does "as it is written in"; hence the renderings may closely resemble each other, or may coincide.

A pair of turtle doves or two young pigeons. If no two acceptable distinctive names can be found (cp. *N.T.Wb.*/34f), one may say something like, 'two small pigeons or two children of (i.e. young) pigeons of another kind', making use of the fact that difference in size is one of the distinctive features.

25 ***Now there was a man in Jerusalem, whose name was Simeon, and this man was righteous and devout, looking for the consolation of Israel, and the Holy Spirit was upon him.***

Exegesis: *kai idou anthrōpos ēn en Ierousalēm* 'and behold, there was a man in Jerusalem'. *idou* 'behold' usually serves to introduce the announcement of a new or unexpected event, but here the event is not mentioned until v. 27, the verses 25 and 26 serving only to introduce and to describe in some detail the person who acts in the event.

anthrōpos 'man', is here almost equivalent to the indefinite pronoun *tis* 'somebody', cp. A-G s.v. 3 a β.

kai ho anthrōpos houtos dikaios kai eulabēs 'and this man was righteous and devout', with *ēn* 'was' understood from the preceding clause.

eulabēs (†) 'devout', usually of Jews who live according to the law, cp. Acts 22 : 12. Here it is almost synonymous with the preceding *dikaios* for which cp. on 1 : 6.

prosdechomenos paraklēsin tou Israēl 'expecting the consolation of Israel', apposition to the preceding clause. It contains information which is new as compared with the preceding clause and is not an explanation of what precedes.

prosdechomai 'to wait for', 'to expect', or 'to receive as guests'.

paraklēsis (also 6 : 24) 'comfort', 'consolation'. Its eschatological meaning is derived from such places as Is. 40 : 1 and 61 : 2 where comforting is part of the proclamation of the eschatological restoration of Israel. Hence the expression *paraklēsin tou Israēl* 'consolation of Israel', where *tou Israēl* is objective genitive, has become "a comprehensive expression indicating the fulfilment of messianic hope" (Strack-Billerbeck II, 124); a parallel expression is found in v. 38, "all who were waiting for the redemption of Jerusalem".

kai pneuma ēn hagion ep' auton 'and the Holy Spirit was upon him'. The omission of the article before *pneuma hagion* is very common.

ep' auton 'upon him', i.e. 'resting', not 'coming upon him', denoting an enduring state which results from the descending or coming down of the Spirit, cp. *TH-Mk* on 1 : 10. Rieu's rendering *pneuma hagion* as "the spirit of prophecy", a common rabbinic paraphrase of the Old Testament phrase "the Spirit of God" (cp. Strack-Billerbeck II, 127ff), is unnecessarily interpretative.

Translation: *Righteous*, see references on 1 : 6.

Devout. Descriptive renderings are built on various concepts, e.g. (1) observance of religious duties (Tagalog, Sundanese); (2) relation with God, (a) obedience (East Toradja), (b) worship or reverence (Thai, Javanese, Tarascan, Mazahua), (c) love (Maya), (d) awe or respect (Bahasa Indonesia), (e) belief (South Toradja, Tagabili), (f) walking with God (Cuna); or (3) qualities of the heart, e.g. 'straight-hearted' (Aymara), 'good-hearted' (Huichol). The high measure of synonymy existing here between "righteous" and "devout" may lead to a combinatory phrase, such as 'serving and worshipping God', 'reverent/obedient towards God and his law'. Cp. also *N.T.Wb.*/75f, WORSHIP.

Looking for, or, '(and) he looked for'. Often the durative aspect is made explicit, cp. 'eagerly waiting for a long time' (Cuyono), "living in expectation of" (Goodspeed), 'he was in state of awaiting (Sranan). Cp. also *N.T.Wb.*/14, AWAIT.

Consolation of Israel, or, 'consolation (that is) for/to Isr.'; or, 'the time that Isr. would be consoled, or, that God would console Israel' (Kituba). A few versions use an agent-noun, 'the consoler of Isr.' (Toba Batak), 'the one to console Isr.' (Sundanese), which may be an acceptable solution when 'to look for/expect' only takes a personal object. For *to console* see *N.T.Wb.*/2f, ADMONISH, giving idiomatic expressions in several languages; an acceptable descriptive rendering in this context would be, 'to take away (or, bring to an end) Isr.'s sorrows/distress'.

Was upon him, or, 'was with him' (Tagabili), 'was near him', 'accompanied him'. In some receptor languages the image of the Spirit as a dove has led to the use of a term like 'perched on him'; in others a somewhat specific term for the influence of spiritual forces on men is used, e.g. 'impelled him' (Kanarese).

26 ***And it had been revealed to him by the Holy Spirit that he should not see death before he had seen the Lord's Christ.***

Exegesis: *kai ēn autō kechrēmatismenon* 'it had been revealed to him'.

chrēmatizō (†) 'to impart a divine revelation'; the revelation may be a promise (as here) or a warning (Mt. 2 : 12, 22).

mē idein thanaton 'that he should not see death', with *auton* 'he' (lit. 'him') understood from *autō* 'to him', cp. Bl-D, § 407. 'To see death' is a well known Old Testament phrase for 'to experience death', i.e. 'to die' (cp. Ps. 89 : 48; Acts 2 : 27, 31; 13 : 35, 37).

prin [ē] an idē ton Christon kuriou 'before he had seen the anointed one of the Lord'. The repetition of *idein* 'to see' is intentional; the aorist *idē* has here the function of a pluperfect. The expression *Christos kuriou* 'the anointed one of the Lord' is the Greek translation of a well known Hebrew expression (cp. 1 Sam. 24 : 6 and 10 (in LXX vv. 7 and 11); 26 : 9, 11, 16, 23; Lam. 4 : 20), referring to the king of Israel or Judah, as one who has been anointed by or on behalf of the Lord. For the term *Christos* cp. on v. 11.

Translation: *It had been revealed to him by the Holy Spirit.* It may be necessary to recast the structure, and/or to describe the concept 'to reveal', cp. '(the) H. Sp. had caused him to know hidden-things of God' (Sranan), '(the) H. Sp. had given him a divine announcement' (Bahasa Indonesia KB), 'there had been a word of God to him by-means-of (the) H. Sp.' (Balinese); or, making explicit the implied direct discourse, 'the H. Sp. had revealed (or simply, said) to him, "You will not..."'. It may be preferable to use a pronoun instead of a repetitive 'Holy Spirit' at so short a distance.

See death...see Christ. This play on words, using 'to see' first in its metaphorical, next in its literal sense, is possible in several languages, e.g. English, Dutch, Sinhalese, South Toradja. Elsewhere it is unacceptable and ineffective, because 'to see death' is unidiomatic. Hence many languages have to render this phrase by 'experience death' (Bahasa Indonesia, similarly Thai, lit. 'meet death', and Dravidian languages, lit. 'obtain death'), or simply, 'die' (e.g. in Sranan, Tagabili), all having to use a natural equivalent at the cost of some stylistic loss. Javanese attempts to steer a middle course, 'to experience death...to experience to see Christ'. In some cases a shift to a roughly synonymous verb may give the opportunity to preserve the play on words, cp. 'to know death...to know Christ'.

The Lord's Christ, or, "the Lord's Messiah" (NEB). To express the meaningful relationship between the two titles one may have to use 'originating from' (Balinese), 'who starts/comes from' (Tagabili, Kekchi), '(who is) sent/appointed by', cp. 'whom the Lord must send' (Kanarese); or, taking one's starting point from the Hebrew descriptive phrase mentioned in *Exegesis,* 'the-One anointed-by the-Lord' (Bahasa Indonesia RC), 'the One the Lord has (caused to be) anointed'.

27 ***And inspired by the Spirit he came into the temple; and when the parents brought in the child Jesus, to do for him according to the custom of the law,*** 28 ***he took him up in his arms and blessed God and said,***

Exegesis: *kai ēlthen* 'and he came'. With this clause the description of the event, already announced by *kai idou* 'and behold' in v. 25 (cp. note there), begins; *kai* therefore resumes the opening words of v. 25. Hence Knox translates "he now came".

en tō pneumati 'in the Spirit', i.e. "guided by the Spirit" (NEB), not on his own account or initiative.

eis to hieron 'into the temple', viz. the temple in Jerusalem.

hieron 'temple'; as compared with *naos* 'temple' (1 : 9, 21, 22) *hieron* includes the whole temple with its buildings, courts, etc. and is often used when the scene of action is not the temple building itself, cp. A-G s.v. 2.

kai en tō eisagagein tous goneis to paidion Iēsoun 'and after the parents had brought in the child Jesus', scil. *eis to hieron* 'into the temple', omitted in order to avoid repetition. *en* with following articular accusative and infinitive in the aorist tense indicates events preceding the event expressed in the main clause (cp. 9 : 36; 11 : 37; 14 : 1; 19 : 15, and Bl-D, § 404 and Plummer on 3 : 21).

eisagō 'to bring in', or, 'into'.

tou poiēsai autous kata to eithismenon tou nomou peri autou 'in order to do concerning him according to the custom of the law'. *tou* with following articular infinitive has final force and the clause expresses the purpose of their entering the temple. *autous* is the subject of the infinitive *poiēsai*, not expressed in English. *peri autou* 'concerning him' goes with *poiēsai*; the phrase does not mean that the child Jesus himself is to be submitted to a rite but only that what his parents do, concerns him.

to eithismenon (††), past participle of *ethizō* 'to accustom', lit. 'that which is accustomed' i.e. 'that which has become a custom', synonymous with *to ethos* (cp. on 1 : 8) 'custom', 'tradition'; *to eithismenon tou nomou* 'the custom of the law' is the custom which the law prescribes.

(V. 28) *kai autos* 'and he'. *autos* refers to a subject already mentioned, viz. that of *ēlthen* 'he came' (cp. A-G s.v. 2 and 1 : 22; 4 : 15; 22 : 23). *kai* is used here in a redundant way to introduce the apodosis after a subordinate clause (cp. Bl-D, § 442.7 and 2 : 21).

edexato auto eis tas agkalas 'he received it in his arms'.

dechomai 'to take', 'to receive'. The use of this verb here suggests that the initiative is not with Simeon but that the child is handed over to him.

agkalē (††) 'bent arm', usually in order to receive something.

kai eulogēsen ton theon kai eipen 'and he praised God and said'. For *eulogeō* cp. on 1 : 64. The two verbs of this clause may be taken to refer to two different acts, or to one single act, preferably the latter, cp. Rieu, "blessed God in these words".

Translation: *Inspired by the Spirit he came into the temple.* The activity of the Spirit has also been described as, "impelled by" (Rieu), 'moved by' (Kapauku), 'on instruction of' (South Toradja), 'on instigation/command of' (Tamil); or, changing the syntactic pattern, 'the Holy Spirit led him into, or, caused Simeon to enter' (Sranan, Tagabili). *Spirit* may have to be specified, cp. 'Holy Spirit', 'Spirit of God'. — *The temple* (Gr. *to hieron*, occurring in 2 : 37, 46; 4 : 9; 18 : 10; 19 : 45, 47; 20 : 1; 21 : 5, 37f; 22 : 52f; 24 : 53) is preferably to be distinguished in translation from the more specific *ho naos* (for which see on 1 : 9). Commonly used descriptive renderings are, 'Holy/Sacred House', 'Divine Abode', 'House of God'. Cp. also *TH-Mk* on 11 : 11. In order to indicate the uniqueness of Jerusalem's temple Balinese has to use 'Great Temple'. The Chinese UV did not choose the term for the temple of popular religion (in which also the participation of the state was centred), but a word (lit. 'palace') indicating the main worship hall of the Buddhists. A similar term is used in Thai to translate *ho naos,* and an expression built on that term is employed as rendering of *to hieron,* viz. 'environs-of the main-audience-hall' (preferred to the existing term for a temple compound because of the strong Buddhist connotations of the latter). Some other renderings used (most of them both for *hieron* and *naos*) are, 'God's compound' (Zarma), 'big church of the Jews' (Otomi), 'big house on top (i.e. most important)' (Zapotec of Villa Alta), 'festival longhouse of God' (Guhu-Samane, cp. *TBT*, 16.85, 1965), 'sacrosanct house', lit. 'house where-the-belly-gets-swollen' (viz. because taboo is violated) (South Toradja, using a term that is also applied to a Muslim mosque).

The parents brought in the child Jesus. Where 'parents' should preferably be possessed one may shift to, 'the child J. was brought in by his parents' (Indonesian languages), 'father and mother of that child J. brought-in him' (Kituba), or, 'Jesus' parents brought in the little one'. *Parents* is often rendered by a combination of the words for father and mother, cp. on v. 33. — *Brought in,* or, 'brought/carried enter (the temple)', 'came in there, carrying'; cp. also on "brought him up" in v. 22. — *The child Jesus.* This combination of noun and proper name is awkward in some languages; then one may have to say, 'the young/little one called Jesus', or simply, 'the little one', or, 'Jesus' (Tagabili); or again, shifting to a term for descendant (cp. on 1 : 7), 'their child (called Jesus)'.

To do for him, or, 'concerning him', 'with him'; or, 'to act/perform with regard to him'. In some languages the very generic character of the clause cannot be maintained. Since it refers backwards to v. 22[b], it is defensible in such a case to say 'to present him (to the Lord)'.

According to the custom of the law, 'as was the custom prescribed by the law', 'as the law had made them accustomed to do' (Sranan); or, making the phrase the object of 'to do', "what was customary under the Law" (NEB), 'custom required by the law' (Tagalog), 'custom that started from their own commandment/law' (Tagabili). Where 'custom' and 'law' are incompatible in an expression like this, one may have to shift to, "what the Law required" (TEV), 'the prescriptions of the Law'; then the rendering may become more similar to, or coincide with, that of "according to the law" in v. 22.

(V. 28) *He took him up in his arms.* One or both of the pronouns may have to be specified, 'Simeon' and 'the child' respectively. *To take in one's arms* (in some languages expressed by one verb), or, with a slight semantic shift 'to take/hold-to-one's-breast' (Bahasa Indonesia, Javanese). Elsewhere one has to add a verb, cp. 'he took and held-in-his-arms' (South Toradja), 'Simeon took him, held-him-to-his-breast' (Malay).

Blessed God and said, preferably, 'praised God, saying (or, in/with these words)', see on 1 : 42 sub (2).

(Vv. 29-32) Syntactically the song of Simeon is one long period, beginning with a personal prayer addressed to God (v. 29), motivated in a causal clause (v. 30); this motivation however moves beyond the realm of the personal because it has to do with *sōtērion* 'salvation' and the mention of this word is the transition from the personal to the universal: in a relative clause (vv. 31-32) the salvation is described as the work of God, realized before the eyes of the whole world, and in two parallel appositions its meaning for the Gentiles and for Israel is explained.

29 ***"Lord, now lettest thou thy servant depart in peace, according to thy word;***

Exegesis: *nun* 'now' (adverb of time), i.e. now that the divine promise that he should see the Messiah before dying had been fulfilled.

apolueis ton doulon sou, despota 'thou releasest thy servant, O master', implying that the condition for his release has been fulfilled. This, of course, does not mean that Simeon is to die immediately.

apoluō 'to set free', 'to dismiss'. Here the verb is used metaphorically and the metaphor is that of the manumission of a slave. This metaphor, however, has lost its original force and been changed into that of the release from a task. Simeon's life had been devoted to the expectation of the Messianic salvation, and now that this expectation had been fulfilled, this task had come to an end. This implies that Simeon's release from life is drawing near.

doulos 'slave', 'servant'.

despotēs (†) 'master', 'lord', in the Septuagint often used of God (cp. also Acts 4 : 24; Rev. 6 : 10).

kata to rēma sou 'according to thy word', referring back to v. 26.

en eirēnē 'in peace', going with *apolueis*. In the Old Testament *eirēnē*, when used in connexion with dying, qualifies it as a natural death (Jer. 34 : 5, in LXX 47 : 5) or as the end of a long life of happiness (Gen. 15 : 15). Here the 'peace' in which Simeon will die is due to the fact that his life's expectation had been fulfilled (cp. v. 26 and v. 30). Basic to this usage of *eirēnē*, or rather of the Hebrew *shalōm*, of which it is the Greek translation in the Septuagint, is the meaning of 'well being and harmony with God and with man' (cp. Richardson, *Word Book*, 165f).

Translation: *Lord*. Some versions use 'master', 'boss', i.e. the normal opposite of 'slave/servant'. Such a word, however, may be unacceptable as form of address to God; hence, 'Lord', in RSV and several other versions, cp. on 1 : 6, sub (a) and (c).

Lettest thou depart, or, 'you can release (from his task)', or, 'you can give his leave/discharge to' (cp. Bahasa Indonesia KB, Balinese; NEB); or, choosing expressions more clearly suggesting a euphemism for death, 'cause-to-leave' (Tagabili; when speaking of a person who has just died, the Tagabili always say 'he's left now'), 'let return' (Bahasa Indonesia, Malay, using a verb that may suggest the phrase 'return to Allah's mercy'), 'allow to go away' (Leyden, choosing a verb that can mean also 'pass away'). If it is impossible to find a term that covers both shades of meaning, the meaning 'release from a task' should be given priority.

Thy servant, or, to indicate that the reference is to the speaker, 'me, your servant' (Balinese, Kituba, Tagabili), 'this your servant' (Bahasa Indonesia KB). For *servant,* when used in connexion with God, see on 1 : 54.

In peace here refers to a state of mind, not to outward circumstances. Since it has a rather emphatic position in the sentence it is sometimes better rendered by something like 'now that I can leave in (or, having) peace', 'now that my mind is set at peace'.

According to thy word, or, 'as you said to me' (Kapauku), "as you promised" (Goodspeed); or, 'this is what you promised', cp. also 'already fulfilled your former promise' (Tagabili).

30 ***for mine eyes have seen thy salvation***
31 ***which thou hast prepared in the presence of all peoples,***
32 ***a light for revelation to the Gentiles,***
and for glory to thy people Israel."

Exegesis: *eidon hoi ophthalmoi mou* 'my eyes have seen'. The expression is stronger than a simple 'I have seen', cp. Job 19 : 27; 42 : 5.

to sōtērion sou 'thy salvation', referring back to *ton Christon kuriou* 'the anointed one of the Lord'.

sōtērion (also 3 : 6) 'salvation', synonymous with *sōtēria* (1 : 69, 71, 77).

(V. 31) *ho hētoimasas* 'which thou hast prepared'; cp. on 1 : 17. When used with God as a subject the verb often has the connotation of 'to realize', cp. 1 Cor. 2 : 9.

kata prosōpon pantōn tōn laōn 'before the face of all nations', i.e. "in full view of all the nations" (NEB), or "in the presence of" (RSV), cp. Acts 3 : 13 and A-G s.v. *prosōpon* 1 c δ.

prosōpon 'face', occurring in a variety of expressions.

The use of the plural *laōn* of a word which in the singular refers to Israel, shows that here Israel and all other nations are envisaged. The next verse refers to the nations and Israel separately.

(V. 32) *phōs eis apokalupsin ethnōn* 'light for revelation to the Gentiles', best understood as an apposition to *to sōtērion sou* 'thy salvation'. As the genitive *ethnōn* cannot refer to the object or agent of the act of revelation, the phrase *phōs eis apokalupsin ethnōn* must be understood as an amplification of the Old Testament expression 'a light to the nations' (*phōs ethnōn,* Is. 42 : 6; 49 : 6; 51 : 4), occurring in prophecies about eschatological salvation similar to that under discussion. *eis apokalupsin* (not further qualified by agent or object) indicates the character or purpose of *phōs* 'the light'; and *ethnōn* goes with the whole expression *phōs eis apokalupsin.* The phrase, lit. 'a light-to-revelation of the peoples', may be rendered then: 'a light that leads to (or: that brings; or: to be a) revelation for the peoples', or 'a revealing light for the peoples'.

phōs 'light'; here it serves as an explanation of what salvation means for the Gentiles.

apokalupsis (†) 'revelation', i.e. the act of revealing (not the contents of revelation).

kai doxan laou sou Israēl 'and glory for thy people Israel'. *doxan* is best understood as parallel with *phōs* and appositive to *sōtērion*. The Messianic salvation is 'light and glory', a light that pierces through the darkness of the gentile world and reveals to them the true God, and glory for Israel, God's people, for His salvation reveals His glory (Is. 40 : 5) and His glory means also glory for his people. The genitive *laou* 'people' refers to the persons to whom glory is given.

Translation: *Mine eyes have seen,* or, 'my own eyes have seen', 'I have seen, with eyes of me myself' (Kituba, similarly NEB, Kapauku, Telugu, Kanarese), 'I myself have seen', 'I really have seen'. A literal rendering may prove an unacceptable pleonasm in the receptor language.

Thy salvation. That the possessive pronoun refers to the actor, or rather initiator, of the saving act is made clear by renderings like, 'the salvation (that is/comes) from thee' (Tagalog, East and South Toradja), 'the salvation (that is) thy gift' (Javanese, Balinese), 'your saving (lit. giving-life-to) man' (Tagabili). Actually the phrase points to a future event, 'your coming salvation', or, in a verbal clause, 'that you are going to save (man)', cp. also, "the deliverance which thou hast made ready" (NEB). Where it is impossible to say that such an event can be seen, it is defensible to substitute a reference to the saviour, e.g. 'the saviour whom thou hast appointed' (Kanarese), 'the saviour which you have prepared' (Kituba).

(V. 31) *In the presence of all peoples,* or, 'to be seen by all peoples', 'as all peoples will witness', 'so that all peoples will see it', or an equivalent idiomatic expression, e.g. 'at the nose of all peoples' (Kapauku). *All peoples.* If the language uses distinctive terms for the speaker's own people and other peoples, one may have to say 'all men', 'all on earth' (South Toradja); cp. also on 1 : 17.

(V. 32) If a break-down into smaller units has to be made here, it may be introduced by, 'This (salvation) is (or, means/brings/produces)...'.

A light for revelation to the Gentiles, preferably, 'a light of revelation for the Gentiles' (cp. Goodspeed), or, mentioning the recipients first, 'for the G. a revealing light' (in which case the next line should be changed likewise, 'and for thy people Isr. glory'). The necessity to describe the concept "revelation" (cp. on v. 26), and shift to a verbal clause may lead to, 'a light that causes the G. to see/know', 'a light that shines-upon the G.' (Balinese), 'a light for the G. to enlighten them' (cp. Kapauku). In such cases the verb often requires an object, cp. 'bring all things to clarity' (Sranan), "to show truth" (Phillips, similarly Français Courant), "to reveal your way" (TEV).

The Gentiles, or, "the heathen" (Goodspeed), 'the outsiders' (Kapauku), 'other (or, foreign) peoples/tribes', 'people of foreign lands' (Kanarese), 'non-Jews' (Barrow Eskimo), 'non-Israel'. Where Muslim influence is strong there is a tendency to transliterate Arabic *kāfir*, a designation of the non-Muslim. This word, however, may have a connotation of strong contempt which makes it inappropriate for use in a verse like this, and/or it may be so specifically Muslim that it can only mean 'one outside Islam', not one outside another religion, as, for instance, in Balinese and South Toradja, which prefer 'other nations', and 'people being-in-darkness' (a figurative expression for people lacking cultural or religious insight). Cp. also Nida, *BT*, 185-87; *TH-Mk* on 10 : 33.

Glory to thy people Israel, or, 'honour/praise (to be given) to thy people Isr.'. For *thy people* see on 1 : 68.

33 ***And his father and his mother marvelled at what was said about him;***

Exegesis: *kai ēn ho patēr autou kai hē mētēr thaumazontes* 'and his father and mother were astonished'; *autou* goes with both *ho patēr* and *hē mētēr*. *ēn* 'was' is in the singular and *thaumazontes* 'astonished' is in the plural. When the subject of a clause consists of two co-ordinate words connected by *kai* the verb is often in the singular when it stands before the subject; when the verb stands after the second subject it is usually in the plural. Here we have a combination of these rules (cp. Bl-D, § 135). The periphrastic conjugation stresses the durative aspect of the imperfect.

epi tois laloumenois peri autou 'at what was being said about him', i.e. about Jesus. Simeon's prophecy is the first to transcend the boundaries of Israel and to stress the universal aspect of Messianic salvation (cp. Plummer).

Translation: *His father and his mother*, or, 'the child's father and mother (or, parents)'. In several languages it is possible to say 'the father and mother', in which the article, or a deictic element, virtually limits the reference to the only parents-child relationship relevant in the context. The idiomatic sequence of the two nouns is not the same in all languages; several Indonesian languages, for instance, prefer 'mother (and) father'. The translator should use the sequence that is normal in the receptor language.

Marvelled at, or making explicit the durative aspect, e.g. 'stood marvelling at' (NV); see on "wondered at" in 1 : 21.

What was said, or, 'what Simeon said', 'Simeon's words'.

34 ***and Simeon blessed them and said to Mary his mother,***
"Behold, this child is set for the fall and rising of many in Israel,
and for a sign that is spoken against

Exegesis: *kai eulogēsen autous Sumeōn* 'and Simeon blessed them', i.e. called God's gracious power upon them, cp. on 1 : 42.

idou 'behold', emphatic introduction of what follows, not translated in several versions.

houtos 'this one here', i.e. 'this child'.

keitai eis ptōsin kai anastasin pollōn en tō Israēl 'is destined for the fall and rising of many in Israel'. In this phrase 'falling' and 'rising' balance each other but the 'sign that is spoken against' in the next phrase stresses the negative reactions which the appearing of the Messiah will call forth in Israel.

keitai lit. 'is placed', or, 'is set', here with *eis* in a figurative sense, 'is destined for'.

ptōsis (†) 'falling'; *eis ptōsin* is an indication of purpose, 'in order to cause the falling'.

anastasis 'rising', 'resurrection'; *eis anastasin* 'in order to cause the rising'.

pollōn en tō Israēl 'of many in Israel', goes syntactically with both *ptōsin* and *anastasin*, but this does not necessarily mean that "many will fall and rise again" (NEB footnote); it is true that 'falling' and 'rising' occur often together (cp. e.g. Micah 7 : 8), but they do not denote two subsequent stages in the reaction of 'many' towards the Messiah. Hence the phrase goes with *ptōsin* 'fall' and *anastasin* 'rising' separately; it is perhaps best understood as a parallel to 1 : 52, and the syntactic structure is to be taken rather loosely (cp. Phillips).

kai eis sēmeion antilegomenon 'and for a sign that is spoken against'. For *sēmeion* 'sign' cp. on v. 12; here as in 11 : 29f 'sign' means a warning sign from God, not a miracle. Jesus will be a sign in person, i.e. he will confront Israel with the claim of God.

antilegō (also 20 : 27) 'to speak against', 'to oppose'. Here the word suggests that Jesus will meet with opposition to the divine claim he represents.

Translation: *Blessed them*, see on 1 : 42 sub (3). The pronoun refers to Joseph, Mary and the child.

And said does not introduce the contents of the blessing, but a prophecy that is subsequent to, and different from, it; hence, 'and then he said'.

In honorific languages one has to decide whether Simeon should address Mary in non-honorifics because he is much the older of the two, or in honorifics in order to indicate his reverence for the mother of the Messiah; the latter is probably preferable.

Is set for, or shifting to an active construction, 'God has set/destined him for (or, to be)', 'God has chosen this child to cause' (Tagabili), 'God has sent him in-order-that' (Kituba). Sometimes it is better to express the concept of necessity not by an introductory verb (as in Greek, English) but in the next phrase or clause, e.g. 'that child must bring-about the fall...' (Jerusalem); see also the South Toradja rendering quoted below.

For the fall and rising of many... The causal character of the expression may lead to the use of causative verbs, e.g. 'to cause-to-fall and to cause-to-rise many...' (Bahasa Indonesia). Such a causative derivation, however, sometimes is less easily used figuratively than its simple verb; hence, 'to bring-about that many...fall or rise' (Balinese). Elsewhere it may be preferable to shift to a simile; or to change the functions of the participants to the event, cp. 'certainly many men...will have-as-falling and have-as-rising this child' (South Toradja, rendering the force of "is set for" by the adverb 'certainly'), or, 'many will fall or stand because of him' (cp. NEB, Tagalog). Several versions indicate, or at least suggest, the disjunctive relationship between the two verbs, e.g. by using the connective 'or' (Sranan, and see above), 'or else' (Kituba), or by saying something like, "to make many fall and many rise" (Phillips). *Fall and rise* are used metaphorically here, as references to a movement away from God and a movement towards God. The translator should investigate whether the receptor language allows this figurative use of the terms. The metaphor has been rendered literally in all versions investigated except Tagabili, which has, 'cause to be made low and cause to be made high many people'.

And for a sign, or, 'and to be (or, to serve as) a sign'. Sometimes one can better begin a new sentence, repeating the equivalent of the introductory verb, cp. 'God has sent this child to be a sign' (Kituba), '. . . ; he must be a sign' (Jerusalem). — The term *sign* refers to something which indicates a fact that would not be known without the sign, cp. the Kapauku rendering 'a see not thing', i.e. something ordinarily unobservable. It may be used of something that serves to identify the child Jesus or to prove the truth of what has been said about him (2 : 12); of Jesus, who by means of his deeds and words will demonstrate God's will (here); of a remarkable, or miraculous deed that is to prove Jesus' divine power and authority (11 : 16, 29; also in 23 : 8, where, however, the reference is to the miracle rather than to the proof of divine power); of Jonah's words about what was to happen to Nineveh (11 : 29f); or of natural or supernatural phenomena or occurrences on earth or in the sky indicating coming events (17 : 20; 21 : 7, 11, 25). Cp. also Nida, *BT*, 217; *TH-Mk* on 8 : 11. If the term has to be rendered descriptively one may say here something like, 'the one who shows God's will'.

That is spoken against, or, "which many will attack" (Phillips), 'which people will mock/scorn, or, oppose' (cp. Tagabili, Kapauku).

35 ***(and a sword will pierce through your own soul also), that thoughts out of many hearts may be revealed."***

Exegesis: *kai sou [de] autēs tēn psuchēn dieleusetai romphaia* 'and as to you yourself, through your soul a sword will go'. For Mary the consequences of the destiny of her child as described in v. 34 will be that a sword will pierce through her soul; this is expressed in a clause which is syntactically co-ordinate with the preceding one. There is no need to treat it as a parenthesis.

kai . . . de. The first word marks this co-ordination and the second the contrast between the 'many in Israel' and Mary. For the combination of *kai* and *de* cp. on 1 : 76.

sou . . . autēs lit. 'of you yourself', a possessive genitive, which goes with the subsequent *tēn psuchēn* 'soul'; but its place at the very beginning of the clause and before the noun with which it goes makes a separate and emphatic rendering necessary.

romphaia 'sword' (†); here it is used figuratively for pain or anguish, cp. A-G s.v.

hopōs an apokaluphthōsin ek pollōn kardiōn dialogismoi 'in order that may be revealed out of many hearts thoughts'. *hopōs an* introduces a clause denoting an expected result.

apokaluptō 'to reveal', 'to disclose', 'to bring to light'; here not a specifically religious term.

ek pollōn kardiōn 'out of many hearts' can best be taken with the preceding verb; the use of this phrase then suggests that thoughts will be brought into the light out of the secrecy of the hearts.

dialogismos 'thought', 'reasoning', cp. on 9 : 46.

Translation: To make clear that line (a) refers to the consequences for Mary (see *Exegesis*) one may say something like, 'as to you, a sword will pierce your soul', 'but you, this will pierce your soul with a sword'.

A sword will pierce through your own soul. Often one can use a rather literal rendering; sometimes it is preferable to shift to a simile, e.g. 'as for your soul, it will be as if a sword pierced it' (Kanarese, similarly Balinese, Pampango, South Toradja); or to another metaphor; or to a non-metaphorical expression, e.g. 'you will experience anguish' (Tagabili, where a literal rendering would mean death rather than anguish). For *sword* cp. on 22 : 36. In some cases the equivalent expression does not need a term for "sword", e.g. "you...shall be pierced to the heart" (NEB), 'your heart will be stabbed' (a Cuyono expression for the heartbreak of a mother over what her child does or experiences). The rendering of *soul* (for which see on 1 : 46f) here is dependent on which term idiomatically fits the corresponding figurative phrase. Terms as 'heart', 'mind', 'inward being' are used, or the person itself is directly mentioned (Tagabili).

Line (b) is not subordinate to line (a) but to v. 34. To make sure that the receptor makes the right connexion it may be better to render line (b) as a new sentence dependent on a repetition of (part of) the rendering of "the child is set", e.g. 'he was (so) destined/appointed in order that...might be revealed', 'God sent/chose him in order that he might reveal...'.

That thoughts out of many hearts may be revealed. The implied agent is 'he/the child'; the other participants are the persons to be understood from "many hearts"; the plural of "hearts" is distributive; and something that is brought to light from a certain place can also be described as located in that place. Hence, the structure of this clause may, where necessary, be changed into something like, 'that the thoughts of many (people) may be revealed (or, come to light) out of their heart', 'that the child may reveal (or, make visible) what many think in their heart, or, what is in the inmost heart/mind of many', 'that he may reveal the secret thoughts of many people' (cp. TEV).

36 ***And there was a prophetess, Anna, the daughter of Phanuel, of the tribe of Asher; she was of a great age, having lived with her husband seven years from her virginity,*** 37 ***and as a widow till she was eighty-four. She did not depart from the temple, worshipping with fasting and prayer night and day.***

Exegesis: *kai ēn* 'and there was' or, establishing a closer connexion with v. 25, "There was also" (NEB), preferably the latter.

Hanna prophētis 'Anna, a prophetess', the apposition denotes the function or quality in which Anna acts. As such it is different from the two subsequent appositions which serve to identify Anna as to her lineage. *prophētis* (†).

In the clause which runs from *hautē* 'she' till *tessarōn* 'four', the main verb is *probebēkuia* 'advanced', scil. *ēn* 'was' and the phrase *hautē*. . .*pollais* gives the central information, viz. that Anna was very old, and the subsequent participial clause *zēsasa*. . .*tessarōn* is to be understood as a consistent whole which serves (1) to explain the preceding phrase 'well advanced in years' and (2) to inform the reader also in what status Anna had spent her long life.

hautē probebēkuia en hēmerais pollais scil. *ēn*, lit. 'she was advanced in many days', cp. 1 : 7 and 18 'advanced in their (or, her) days'. The addition here of *pollais* 'many', which is idiomatically a pleonasm, conveys the idea that Anna is very old, cp. BFBS.

zēsasa meta andros etē hepta apo tēs parthenias autēs 'having lived with a husband seven years from the time of her virginity'.

zaō 'to live' here 'to pass life', specified first as 'married life' by *meta andros* and subsequently as 'widowed life' by *autē chēra* 'on her own as widow' (v. 37[a]).

meta andros lit. 'with a man', here 'with a husband'.

parthenia (†) 'virginity', here to be understood as 'time of her virginity' and *apo* as temporal 'from the end of' or even 'after'. Hence the phrase indicates that this marriage had been her first.

(V. 37) *heōs etōn ogdoēkonta tessarōn* 'until eighty-four years' i.e. 'until the age of eighty-four', cp. Goodspeed, *Problems* 79ff.

hē ouk aphistato tou hierou 'who did not depart from the temple', a relative clause which continues the introductory description of Anna and draws a picture of her religious life. The imperfect tense is durative and the clause suggests, with exaggeration, frequent attendance in the temple, not actual residence within the temple precincts, especially since *autē tē hōra* 'at that very hour' (v. 38) would be pointless if Anna was always in the temple.

aphistamai 'to go away from', with genitive.

nēsteiais kai deēsesin latreuousa nukta kai hēmeran 'with fasting and praying serving (God) night and day'; this participial phrase serves to describe how Anna spent her time in the temple.

nēsteia (†) 'fasting', here in the plural 'times, or acts, of fasting'.

deēsis 'prayer', cp. on 1 : 13.

latreuō 'to serve', cp. on 1 : 74; the object, God, is here omitted.

Translation: *Daughter of Phanuel.* Probably Phanuel was Anna's father, not her forefather.

Of (or, belonging to/a member of/having-as-tribe) *the tribe of Asher* may syntactically go either with Anna or with Phanuel. This is immaterial where a daughter belongs to the tribe or clan of her father, as in Israel; in cultures where the genealogical system is different it is better to make clear that the phrase qualifies Anna, e.g. '. . ., a woman of the tribe. . .', and/or to indicate that Phanuel is a man's name. — *Tribe,* referring here to one of the twelve patrilineal tribes into which Israel was traditionally divided. The noun may have to be rendered by a descriptive phrase, e.g. 'those who descend from the former Asher' (Tagabili), 'those who have Asher as their ancestor'.

Of a great age, cp. on "advanced in years" in 1 : 7.

The participial phrase, *having lived* etc., is usually better rendered as a new sentence, e.g. '. . . ; (for) she had lived. . .'.

Having lived with her husband refers to the period of Anna's married life. The phrase has been rendered, 'who had-a-husband' (Toba Batak, where 'husband' is rendered 'he for-whom-one-serves food'), 'she was-together-with her-husband (lit. male)' (South Toradja), 'she had been married (lit. went with a male spouse)' (Kapauku).

From her virginity, i.e. since the end of her life as unmarried girl, or stated reversely, since the beginning of her life as married woman; hence such renderings as, "after her girlhood" (Goodspeed), 'as a girl she married' (cp. South Toradja, Sranan), "after she was first married" (NEB), 'since she entered married life (or, became a married woman/a wife)'; or, shifting to a relative clause going with 'husband', 'whom she had married in her girlhood' (cp. Français Courant). — The rendering 'since she became a virgin (i.e. reached the age of puberty)' rests on an erroneous interpretation.

(V. 37) *And,* or, 'after that time', 'afterwards' (Tagalog), 'from then onward'.

As a widow, preferably, 'on her own (or, by herself) as a widow'. The translation must indicate that the phrase is dependent on 'having lived' (e.g. by repeating that verb here, or by other devices), and that it syntactically parallels 'with a husband'; therefore, adaptations that were necessary in the lexical and/or syntactic form of the preceding phrase will usually lead to corresponding adaptations in this one. For *widow* cp. *N.T.Wb.*/53, MARRY; *TBT*, 18.187f, 1967. East Toradja distinguishes between a widow who still is under obligation of mourning, and one who is not and, therefore, may remarry, the latter term being, of course, required here. If a specific term does not exist in the receptor language, or if it can also mean 'a divorced woman' (as e.g. in Bahasa Indonesia), or has the connotation of promiscuity (as in a Chuj dialect) or grief verging on madness (Tagabili), a descriptive phrase will have to be used, e.g. 'a woman whose husband has died'. Adjustments of this phrase to the present context may result in something like, 'after her husband's death she lived unmarried' (Kituba), 'but he died and she lived on' (Vai).

Till she was eighty-four, or, "to the age of eighty-four" (NEB), 'till her years (or, winters, or, seasons, cp. *TH-Mk* on 5: 42) were eighty-four'. In some receptor languages a numeral like *eighty-four* has to be rendered by approximation, and/or by multiplication, e.g. 'seven times twelve', 'four scores', or addition, e.g. 'sixty and twenty four' (Kapauku).

She did not depart from, or, with an equivalent English hyperbole "she spent her whole life" (Phillips); or less hyperbolically, "never far from" (Rieu). Sranan has a positive rendering, qualifying the following verb, 'on and on she served God in God's house'.

Worshipping...night and day. Several versions co-ordinate this clause with what precedes, 'and she worshipped (there)...'; some reverse the pattern of subordination, see the above Sranan quotation. For *to worship* cp. on 4 : 7.

With fasting and prayer, or, 'by means of/accompanied by (Balinese)/in the way of (East Toradja) fasting and prayer', indicating the forms in which she expressed her worship. When the nouns have to be rendered as verbal clauses the three verbs often are best co-ordinated; in some cases 'to worship' has to be subordinated to the other two, e.g. 'worshipping/when she worshipped she fasted and prayed' (cp. Kapauku, Kituba), 'she fasted and prayed in order to (or, as a form of) worship'. For *to fast* see *N.T.Wb.*/46, HUNGER, *TH-Mk* on 2 : 18; *TBT*, 3.153f, 1952. The context here is clearly referring to religious ritual; hence some of the proposed descriptive phrases may be shortened or expressed more generically.

Night and day, or, 'day and night', where that is the normal sequence, or 'continually', cp. *N.T.Wb.*/57; *TH-Mk* on 5 : 5.

38 ***And coming up at that very hour she gave thanks to God, and spoke of him to all who were looking for the redemption of Jerusalem.***

Exegesis: *kai autē tē hōra* 'and at that very hour', i.e. at the time that Jesus was presented in the temple by his parents, stronger than 'at that time' and suggesting that the meeting with Anna was more than just a coincidence.

epistasa anthōmologeito tō theō 'after coming up, she returned thanks to God'. *epistasa* expresses an action which precedes the action of the main verb, and is to be connected with *autē tē hōra*. For *ephistēmi* cp. on v. 9. Here it suggests the idea of approaching somebody.

anthomologeomai (††) 'to return praise', 'to thank'; *anti* brings out that she thanked God in return for what He had done, viz. the birth of the Messiah.

kai elalei peri autou 'and she spoke about him'. The imperfect tense has durative meaning, and suggests that she spoke about Jesus till long afterwards. *autou* refers to the child.

pasin tois prosdechomenois lutrōsin Ierousalēm 'to all who were expecting the redemption of Jerusalem'. In Old Testament passages referring to Messianic redemption, Jerusalem often represents all Israel, cp. Is. 40: 2; Zeph. 3 : 14-20; Zech. 9 : 9f. For *lutrōsis* cp. on 1 : 68.

Translation: *Coming up,* or, 'coming near', or, co-ordinating the clause and specifying the participants, 'she came (to) stand on their side' (Sranan).

She gave thanks to God. Some languages can use a rendering built on their normal expression for 'thank(fulness)', for which see on "ungrateful" in 6 : 35; other languages (e.g. Bahasa Indonesia) use a specific term for thank offered to God, or say, 'she praised God' (Jerusalem, East Toradja), 'she praised God for his gift/deed, or, for that child' (Tagabili).

Spoke of him (or, 'the child'), or, 'kept on talking about him' (Kapauku).
Redemption of Jerusalem, or, '(God's) redeeming (lit. action redeem) Jerusalem' (Thai), 'that Jerusalem would be made free', 'the time that God would pull Jerusalem from its distress' (Sranan). For *redemption* see references on "redeemed" in 1 : 68.

39 ***And when they had performed everything according to the law of the Lord, they returned into Galilee, to their own city, Nazareth.***

Exegesis: *kai hōs etelesan panta ta kata ton nomon kuriou* lit. 'and when they had accomplished all the things (that were) according to the law of the Lord, i.e. all the requirements of the law of the Lord'.

teleō 'to bring to an end', 'to accomplish', 'to fulfil'.

epestrepsan eis tēn Galilaian eis polin heautōn Nazareth 'they returned to Galilee, to their own city, Nazareth'; same construction and order as in v. 4.

epistrephō here 'to turn back'; cp. A-G s.v. 1 b α.

Translation: *They,* or, 'the parents (or, the father and mother) of the child'.

Had performed everything, or, 'had done everything (or, all thing they had to do)'.

According to the law of the Lord, cp. on v. 22, and, for the meaning of the possessive construction, on v. 23.

Their own city, Nazareth, or, clarifying the possessive pronoun, 'the place where they lived, that-is the city N.' (Bahasa Indonesia RC), or, "their home town of N." (TEV).

40 ***And the child grew and became strong, filled with wisdom; and the favour of God was upon him.***

Exegesis: *to de paidion ēuxanen kai ekrataiouto plēroumenon sophia* 'the child grew up and became strong, being filled with wisdom', conclusion of the preceding narrative. *ekrataiouto* is best understood as referring to mental and moral growth because (1) this area of meaning is most widely attested in the Septuagint and other Koine texts, and (2) the similarity between this verse and 1 : 80 suggests the same meaning on both places rather than different meanings. Hence it is better to take *ekrataiouto* and *plēroumenon sophia* as semantically belonging together. Then the latter phrase either defines *ekrataiouto* ('he became strong because he was being filled with wisdom') or complements it ('he became strong and was being filled with wisdom', implying that 'becoming strong' and 'being filled with wisdom' are closely related concepts), preferably the latter.

plēroumenon sophia 'being filled with wisdom' may be derived from the idiom 'being full of the Spirit' (cp. on 4 : 1; also Acts 6 : 3, Eph. 5 : 18), and it means that the wisdom becomes more and more the dominating power of his life.

sophia 'wisdom', here simply "insight in the will and rule of God"

(Grundmann), which is not man's own achievement but imparted by God (cp. A-G s.v. 2).

charis theou ēn ep' auto 'the blessing of God was upon it'; *auto* (acc.) refers to *to paidion* 'the child'. For *einai epi* cp. on v. 25. *charis* may here refer either to God's favour, or to God's grace as a source of blessing, preferably the latter and the phrase is best understood in analogy to 'the Holy Spirit was upon him' (v. 25), and as indicating the origin of his growth in wisdom.

Translation: *And* (for Gr. *de*) here introduces a change from the parents, who were in focus in v. 39, to the child; hence renderings like 'as to the Child, its bigness increased' (Javanese).

Grew, cp. on 1 : 80.

Became strong, to be understood figuratively, of spiritual, mental strength (see *Exegesis*). In some languages (e.g. Bahasa Indonesia, Tagabili) the usual term for 'strong' does not allow the required figurative extension of meaning; hence, 'his mind developped' (Bahasa Indonesia RC). Cp. also on "became strong in spirit" in 1 : 80.

Filled with wisdom, or, 'had much wisdom', 'very wise' (Tagabili), 'was becoming abundant in wisdom' (Telugu). *Wisdom* has been rendered, '(big) mind' (Ifugao, Chontal of Tabasco), 'heart thinking' (Bulu, Kaka), 'cleverness of heart' (East Toradja). The concepts 'slyness', 'cleverness', 'knowledge', 'magic skill', and 'wisdom' sometimes are not clearly distinguished; terms may overlap considerably or even coincide for some or all of these concepts, and therefore require careful handling. This is shown e.g. by the revision in Toba Batak, where 'slyness/cleverness' was changed into 'true mind', or in Bahasa Indonesia, *hikmat* (an Arabic borrowing, meaning 'wisdom' but also 'magic skill/charm') changed into a term indicating 'practical wisdom/prudence', and even 'policy'. One should not choose a term that refers exclusively, or primarily, to book learning or keen intellect.

And the favour of God was upon him, or, changing the syntactic structure, 'and (or, because) God gave him favour/grace/blessing, or, favoured/ graced/blessed him'. For *favour*, or, 'grace', see on 1 : 30, for 'bless(ing)' on 1 : 42 sub (1).

41 ***Now his parents went to Jerusalem every year at the feast of the Passover.***

Exegesis: *kai eporeuonto hoi goneis autou* 'and his parents used to go'. The imperfect tense suggests customary action.

kat' etos 'every year'; *kata* is used here distributively, cp. A-G s.v. II 2 c.

tē heortē tou pascha 'at (the occasion of) the feast of Passover'; the dative *tē heortē* is temporal, cp. Bl-D, § 200.3.

heortē 'religious feast', 'festival'.

pascha 'the Passover', transliteration of the Aramaic *pasḥa'* (Hebrew *pesaḥ*), cp. *TH-Mk* on 14 : 1. Here the word is used in a broader sense, including the feast of the unleavened bread, taking place the subsequent days.

Translation: *Now,* cp. on 1 : 57.

Went, cp. on 1 : 39. The verb used here can refer to travel in any direction and on any occasion; it is more generic than the one used in v. 42.

At the feast of the Passover, or, 'when it was the feast of Passover', 'at the time people had-the-feast Pascha (cp. Toba Batak), or, celebrated the Passover'; and cp. *N.T.Wb.*/35f, FEASTS. In some cases "feast" is simply rendered 'day', the following name being enough to mark it as a festival (South Toradja). — *Passover.* The term is often transliterated (as is also the case in Greek), but preferably translated (as done in English), cp. 'the having passed over delivered remember day' (Kapauku), 'celebrating that (in former days) the Lord (rather than 'the angels', cp. Ex. 11 : 4f; 12 : 12, 23, 27) passed by (or, spared) the first-born sons (of Israel)'; cp. also *TH-Mk* on 14 : 1; Beekman, *NOT*, 99f, 105. When in case of transliteration the resulting form is primarily known as the name of the Christian festival of the resurrection its use here may have its drawbacks; if in case of translation a phrase or term is employed that explicitly refers to the resurrection, its use here would mean a reversal of the historical development, which is not to be recommended.

42 ***And when he was twelve years old, they went up according to custom;*** 43 ***and when the feast was ended, as they were returning, the boy Jesus stayed behind in Jerusalem. His parents did not know it,***

Exegesis: The syntactic structure of v. 42 and v. 43 is complicated. These verses contain clauses, telling successively that when Jesus had reached the age of 12 years (a), his parents went up to the feast as usual (b), completed their stay (c) and went back (d), but that Jesus stayed behind (e) and his parents did not know (f). Of these 6 clauses (a) is necessarily a subordinate clause, indicating when the events described subsequently took place, and (e) and (f) are two co-ordinate independent clauses, containing the main information; the remaining 3 clauses (b), (c) and (d) are subordinate to (e), because Luke wants to focus all attention on the fact that Jesus stayed behind without his parents' knowledge, which is the basis for the subsequent narrative. The necessary details which lead up to the focal clause *hupemeinen Iēsous* 'Jesus stayed behind' are passed over as quickly as possible: (b) and (c) are genitives absolute and (d) is a phrase in the articular infinitive (for a similar syntactic pattern cp. 3 : 21-22).

kai hote egeneto etōn dōdeka 'and when he was twelve years old'; the genitive *etōn dōdeka* is genitive of quality, '(a boy) of twelve years', cp. Bl-D, § 165. At the age of twelve a Jewish boy became a 'son of the law' and henceforth had to keep its enactments (cp. Plummer).

anabainontōn autōn kata to ethos tēs heortēs 'when they went up according to the custom of the feast'. *autōn* refers primarily to *hoi goneis autou* 'his parents' in v. 41 but may be taken to include Jesus. For *kata to ethos tēs heortēs* 'according to the custom of the feast', cp. on 1 : 9. The genitive is one of association: the custom that is associated with the feast. The present tense of *anabainontōn* suggests that they were in the habit of going to Jerusalem every year, as is said explicitly in v. 41. *anabainō* (cp. on v. 4) is often a technical term for a pilgrimage to Jerusalem (cp. 18 : 31; 19 : 28; Mt. 20 : 17; Jn. 2 : 13; 5 : 1).

(V. 43) *teleiōsantōn tas hēmeras* 'after having completed the days', of the feast. The phrase is, like the preceding one, in the genitive absolute, but the tense shifts from the present (suggesting habit, see above) to the aorist; this is done in order to describe an event which immediately precedes the event referred to by the main verb.

teleioō (also 13 : 32) 'to complete', 'to bring to an end'; *tas hēmeras*, 'the days', without further specification, refers to a fixed period, probably the period of seven days prescribed in the law (cp. Ex. 12 : 15f; Lev. 23 : 6ff; Deut. 16 : 3).

en tō hupostrephein autous 'when they were returning', articular accusative and infinitive, in the present tense because the event described is simultaneous with the event referred to by the main verb. *autous* refers to Joseph and Mary only. The verb here is best taken as durative, referring to a period that covers the first day of the journey.

hupemeinen Iēsous ho pais 'the boy Jesus stayed behind'.

hupomenō (†) 'to stay behind', while others go away.

pais 'boy', cp. on 1 : 54 and 2 : 17.

kai ouk egnōsan hoi goneis autou 'and his parents did not know'; object of *egnōsan* is, of course, the fact that Jesus stayed behind.

Translation: An attempt to imitate the syntactic pattern of the Greek may result in, 'when his age was twelve years, after they had gone according..., and after they had completed-the-festival, at the going home the son Jesus still was in Jerusalem, but Joseph and his mother didn't know' (Javanese). In most receptor languages, however, such constructions are still more heavy than they are in Javanese, or even impossible. Therefore the syntactic pattern usually has to be altered, e.g. by starting a new sentence after clause (b) or clause (c). If the pattern of subordination has to be changed more thoroughly, it is important to mark the principal item of information clearly. To give a (probably purely theoretical) example: 'In his twelfth year they went up according to the custom of the feast. They completed its days, and then returned. As for the boy Jesus, however, he stayed behind in Jerusalem, and/but his parents did not know it.'

Twelve years old, cp. *TH-Mk* on 5 : 42.

He and *the boy Jesus* (v. 43) often can better change places, 'The boy Jesus...he (or, the boy)'.

They went up. That Jesus is included is not self-evident for non-Jewish readers; hence specifications of subject such as, 'the-three-of-them' (Malay), 'they together' (Balinese); cp. also 'they-took-him-with-them upward' (East Toradja 1933). To express the specific meaning that *went up* has in this context (cp. *N.T.Wb.*/60, RAISE) some versions add a goal, e.g. "to the City" (Phillips), 'to Jerusalem' (Kituba, Balinese), 'thither' (Jerusalem, Bahasa Indonesia RC, KB); such an addition is based on translational, not on textual considerations. Cp. also "they made the pilgrimage" (NEB, taking 'feast' with this verb).

According to custom, preferably, "according to the custom of the feast" (cp. *Exegesis*), or, 'as was customary at the feast', 'as people used to do (or, which people always did) at the feast'.

(V. 43) *And when the feast was ended*, preferably 'when they had completed the days (of the feast)' (cp. *Exegesis*), or, 'they remained (there) to the end (of the feast), or, during all the days (of the feast)', cp. "and remained there for the days prescribed" (Rieu).

As they were returning. Here the pronoun does not include Jesus; if "they" in v. 42 has been specified it may here be rendered, 'his (or, the/Jesus') parents', or be taken in an indefinite meaning, e.g. 'when people were going home', cp. 'at the returning' (Balinese).

The boy Jesus, or, 'the boy called Jesus' (Sinhalese), or simply, 'the boy'; for the combination of noun and proper name cp. on v. 27. *Boy* indicates a further phase in Jesus' growth, see on v. 17.

Stayed behind, i.e. remained in the place they had left, viz. Jerusalem. The act is intentional and of his own doing, not happening by accident or through the agency of others (as suggested in some versions by a rendering that comes close to 'was left behind').

His parents did not know it, sometimes better subordinated to the preceding clause, cp. 'without his parents knowing it' (cp. Bahasa Indonesia, Toba Batak). *Know* here means 'to be aware of', 'to notice' (Tagalog).

44 ***but supposing him to be in the company they went a day's journey, and they sought him among their kinsfolk and acquaintances;*** 45 ***and when they did not find him, they returned to Jerusalem, seeking him.***

Exegesis: *nomisantes de... ēlthon* 'but, supposing... they went'; *de* 'but' contrasts *ouk egnōsan* 'they did not know' (v. 43) with *nomisantes* 'supposing...', the clause which is dependent upon *nomisantes* (viz. *auton einai en tē sunodia* 'him to be in the company') motivates their going.

nomizō (also 3 : 23) 'to believe', 'to suppose'.

en tē sunodia 'in the company of travellers'.

sunodia (††) 'group of people travelling together'.

hēmeras hodon 'a day's journey'; the accusative *hodon* 'way', hence 'journey', is of extent. Jewish sources differ considerably as to the length of a day's journey, ranging from 15 to 40 miles (cp. Strack-Billerbeck II, 149) but it is safe to assume that a caravan of pilgrims would not do more than 15-20 miles a day.

kai anezētoun auton 'and they were looking for him'. The imperfect tense of *anezētoun* is best understood as a durative or iterative imperfect: Joseph and Mary supposed Jesus to be somewhere among the company of travellers and were, therefore, looking for him during that day's journey among their relatives and friends.

anazēteō 'to look for', especially of looking for human beings, with an implication of difficulty and thoroughness.

en tois suggeneusin kai tois gnōstois 'among the relatives and acquaintances'; without a possessive pronoun or its equivalent, which is to be supplied from the context. For *suggenēs* cp. on 1 : 36.

gnōstos (also 23 : 49) 'known', hence, when used of persons, 'acquaintance', 'friend'.

(V. 45) *kai mē heurontes hupestrepsan* 'and not having found him, they returned'. Here the aorist participle *heurontes* indicates an event preceding the event referred to by the main verb *hupestrepsan* 'they returned'.

anazētountes auton 'looking for him', indicating an event which is simultaneous with the event referred to by the main verb *hupestrepsan* 'they returned'.

Translation: *Supposing him to be...they went...* Rendering the participle by a co-ordinate or subordinate clause one may say something like, 'They supposed that he was... ; so/therefore/consequently they went...', or, 'They went..., since they supposed that...'. *To suppose* implies that the author does not vouch for the opinion concerned, or even knows it to have been wrong, as brought out by East Toradja, which uses a verb basically meaning 'to substitute', 'to mistake a person for another', then, 'to suppose wrongly'. If one has to make explicit the implied direct discourse, one may say e.g. 'thinking, "Certainly he is (or, we will find him) in ..."'.

The company, or, 'group of those who-were travelling same road with them' (Kituba), 'people on-the-same-journey' (Balinese), 'people that walk in-the-same-group' (East Toradja); Bamiléké, using the same compound pronoun as in 1 : 58, has 'people who they-plus-they came'.

They went a day's journey, or, 'as much as one day they went' (Tagabili), 'they did one day on road' (Kituba), 'they travelled one-day's-measure' (Toba Batak).

And they sought him, or, expressing simultaneity, 'and in the meanwhile they sought him (or, looked for him, or, tried to find him)'.

Kinsfolk, see on 1 : 58.

Acquaintances usually refers to relationships which are somewhat less intimate than friendship. It can often be rendered by a derivation of, or a phrase built on, 'to know', cp. 'group of people who know each other' (Thai), 'people whom they-plus-they know' (Bamiléké). Elsewhere the closest natural equivalent is a more generic term, covering both intimate and casual relationships, e.g. in Kituba, Toba Batak.

(V. 45) *When they did not find him* explains what follows; hence, "They did not find him, so they went back..." (TEV).

46 ***After three days they found him in the temple, sitting among the teachers, listening to them and asking them questions;***

Exegesis: *kai egeneto...heuron auton* 'and it happened that they found him', cp. on 1 : 8 and *TBT*, 16.153-163, 1965 (esp. p. 156); here it indicates that the climax of the story is at hand: they found him, of all places, in the temple.

meta hēmeras treis 'after three days', i.e. most probably on the second day after the day of their departure from Jerusalem, because according to Jewish and Greco-Roman time-reckoning the day of departure is counted as a full day, cp. *TH-Mk* on 8 : 31.

en tō hierō 'in the temple', to be taken with *heuron auton* 'they found him'.

kathezomenon en mesō tōn didaskalōn 'sitting among the teachers'. For the correct interpretation of this phrase two considerations are important: (a) public teaching in the temple was customary, especially at the occasion of the great festivals and discussion between teachers and questions from the listeners were an essential part in Jewish teaching methods (cp. Strack-Billerbeck II, 150); hence there is nothing out of the ordinary in the scene in the temple and there is no reason to imagine Jesus as teaching the teachers; (b) *en mesō*, preferably rendered as "surrounded by" (NEB), cp. 8 : 7; 10 : 3; 22 : 27, 55; 24 : 36, is best understood from the point of view of Joseph and Mary, not of the teachers: for the parents who have been looking for him for two or three days, Jesus is in the centre of the scene. *kathezomai* (†).

kai akouonta autōn kai eperōtōnta autous 'and listening to them and asking them questions'. The first and the second *kai* are different in function, because *akouonta* 'listening' and *eperōtōnta* 'asking questions' belong together closely, as contrasted with the preceding *kathezomenon* 'sitting', and express together what Jesus was doing while sitting.

eperōtaō 'to ask a question' with the accusative of the person to whom the question is addressed. Sometimes it is used of the asking of questions in discussions, cp. 6 : 9; 20 : 21, 27; see also on next verse.

Translation: *After three days.* The idiomatic way to indicate the intended time limit often will be different (cp. on "eight" in 1 : 59); in English, for instance, one normally would say, "two days later", "the day after the next", in Balinese, 'on its after to-morrow'. It is preferable to use such an idiomatic rendering. (For a probably necessary exception see on 9 : 22, "on the third day be raised".)

Sitting, or, 'where he sat', 'as he was sitting'; or co-ordinated, 'There he sat'. — *To sit.* In some languages usage makes preferable a more generic rendering, e.g. 'to be', 'to be present', 'to stay', or even omission of any verb ('found him among the teachers'), whereas in others it tends to be more specific, e.g. 'to sit-cross-legged', 'to sit-with-the-legs-at-the-side-of-the-body'. The generic rendering is acceptable because it is not Jesus' act of sitting but the place where he was found that counts in the narrative; the specific rendering is acceptable provided that the term chosen fits the situation as envisaged according to local custom.

Teacher (also in 5 : 17; 6 : 40; 8 : 49; 22 : 11; and as polite form of address, cp. on 3 : 12). The rendering often is a phrase built on the verb 'to teach' (for which cp. below on 4 : 15), e.g. 'those who habitually/professionally teach', 'those who always taught there' (Tagabili), or an agent noun of that verb; sometimes a specific noun exists, e.g. 'guru' (in some Indic and Indonesian languages). The term usually has a connotation of status, hence Rieu's "Doctors". See also *N.T.Wb./70f.*

Listening to them and asking them questions. The two participles form a closely connected pair here, which may be indicated by the use of a stronger connective, e.g. 'and also', 'as well as', or by only once naming the object, if the syntactic structure of the receptor language allows doing so. For *to listen* cp. on "heard" in 1 : 41. *Asking them questions.* The aspect is iterative, as expressed by the plural form of the noun in English (cp. also 'many-things also he asked', East Toradja 1933), by reduplication in several Indonesian languages. That the phrase implies discussion may lead to the use of such expressions as, 'to question-answer' (Bahasa Indonesia) and 'in-turns taking-up speech' (Balinese).

47 ***and all who heard him were amazed at his understanding and his answers.***

Exegesis: *existanto de pantes hoi akouontes autou* 'all who heard him were amazed'; the clause is the last part of the description of the situation which Joseph and Mary found. This is brought out by the imperfect tense of *existanto,* 'were amazed', as compared with the aorists in v. 46 and v. 48.

existamai 'to be amazed', cp. A-G s.v. 2 b.

epi tē sunesei kai tais apokrisesin autou 'at his insight and his answers'. The latter word implies that Jesus did not only ask questions but was also questioned; this supports the idea of a discussion at which also *eperōtōnta* 'asking questions' in v. 46 hints (cp. last note on v. 46).

sunesis (†) 'insight', here best taken as referring to both questions and answers.

apokrisis (also 20 : 26) 'answer'.

Translation: *All who heard him,* or, '...heard his words', cp. on 1 : 41.

Were amazed at, or more positively, 'admired'; for the verb cp. on "wondered at" in 1 : 21.

His understanding and his answers. Though the two terms are in themselves neutral the intention in this context is clearly positive; hence the first noun may be rendered by, 'his insight', "his intelligence" (NEB), "his quick understanding" (Knox), 'his cleverness' (East Toradja 1933), 'the acuteness of his mind' (Toba Batak); and the second by, 'his wise answers', 'the rightness of his answers' (East Toradja 1933). Shifts to a verbal clause may result in something like, 'the way how he understood and answered', 'the fact that (or, because) he understood things very well and answered wisely'. For *to understand* a figurative rendering is sometimes used, e.g. 'to receive in the heart', 'to see clearly', 'to reach (or, find, or, hear) with the mind/heart'.

48 ***And when they saw him they were astonished; and his mother said to him, "Son, why have you treated us so? Behold, your father and I have been looking for you anxiously."***

Exegesis: *kai idontes auton exeplagēsan* 'and when they saw him they were astonished', resuming the subject of *heuron* in v. 46, viz. his parents.

ekplēssomai 'to be astonished', stronger than *existamai* (v. 47).

ti epoiēsas hēmin houtōs 'why have you done to us like this', i.e. "why have you treated us like this" (NEB); the phrase is clearly reproachful.

ho patēr sou kagō odunōmenoi ezētoumen se 'your father and I were looking for you in great anguish'. The subject consists of a noun in the 3rd person and a pronoun in the 1st, hence the verb is in the 1st person plural. *odunōmenoi* '(being) in great anguish' goes with the subject of the verb *ezētoumen*, and indicates the state of mind in which Joseph and Mary were during their search.

odunaomai (also 16:24) 'to feel pain', here of mental pain.

Translation: *They*, or to avoid ambiguity, 'they-two', or, 'his parents'.

Astonished, cp. on "wondered" in 1:21.

Son (lit. 'child', cp. on 1:7), or, 'my child/son/boy'; in Balinese 'ah, little-one' is the closest natural equivalent.

Why have you treated us so, or, 'why have you done this to us'; or more explicitly reproachful, by using a more specific rendering of "why", cp. 'how could you...', and/or of the verb, e.g. 'cause-trouble-to' (Balinese), 'behave badly towards', or adverb (Javanese, which adds to 'so' a particle expressing disapproval). In some languages, e.g. South Toradja, *to treat so* is rendered by a causative derivation of 'so'. The pronoun *us* must sometimes be specified, e.g. 'us, your parents'.

Your father and I have... The combination of a compound subject (consisting of a reference to a third and first person singular) with the verb may require some adaptation, such as adding the pronoun of the first person plural, e.g. 'we (or, we-two), your father and I, ...' (followed by the verb in plural or dual, where such categories exist; cp. Jerusalem); or a shift to the singular, e.g. 'I, together with your father (or, and your father also)'. In Tagabili the singular pronoun is absorbed by the plural, so to speak, cp. 'look, us two your father continually sorrowful look-for you'. *Your father* should be rendered by the term that is normally used in the receptor language by the mother when speaking about her husband to the children, e.g. 'father', treated as a proper name, as shown by the use of a name qualifier (Balinese). Similarly the pronoun *I* should be rendered by the form normally used in family life, e.g. 'mother' (in the sense of 'I, your mother') in Balinese and Sundanese. To employ the humble form used by a speaker when addressing a person of superior rank (as done by a few versions in languages using honorifics) is not advisable.

Anxiously. Versions in English and several other languages have to render the attributive participle, qualifying the state of mind of the agent, by an adverbial expression, qualifying the action performed by the agent while being in that state of mind. Elsewhere it is better to shift to a co-ordinate verbal clause, 'and we were worrying', "and have been very anxious" (Goodspeed). Several translators follow Goodspeed in using a stronger expression than RSV does, e.g. 'much distressed/troubled' (Thai, Tagalog, Kapauku, Sundanese), "in anguish and grief" (BFBS), in order to give expression to the emphatic position the word has in the clause. For *anxious*, i.e. worrying and apprehensive of ills that may happen, cp. on 10:41.

49 ***And he said to them, "How is it that you sought me? Did you not know that I must be in my Father's house?"***

Exegesis: *ti hoti ezēteite me* 'why is it that you were looking for me?'; *ti hoti,* with ellipsis of *estin* 'is', 'why (is it) that?', stronger than a simple *ti,* or *dia ti* 'why' (cp. Acts 5 : 4, 9 with Lk. 5 : 30; 19 : 23, 31, 33; 22 : 46), here expresses surprise because Jesus' parents did not know where to find him.

ouk ēdeite 'did you not know'.

oida 'to know'; when used with an object, person or thing, synonymous with *ginōskō* (cp. Moulton-Milligan 439).

hoti en tois tou patros mou dei einai me 'that it is necessary that I am in my Father's house', or 'engaged in my Father's business'. The context requires us to interpret *ta tou patros mou* (lit. 'the (things) of my father') as 'my father's house', for which a sufficient number of parallels may be quoted (cp. Moulton-Milligan 436, Goodspeed, *Problems* 81ff); the place of *en tois tou patros mou* at the beginning of the clause indicates emphasis.

dei impersonal 'it is necessary', here followed by an accusative and infinitive. Here it expresses a compulsion of duty, cp. A-G s.v. 2.

Translation: *How is it that you sought me,* or, 'how did you come (or, need) to look for me' (Goodspeed, Toba Batak). The point of the question is that, as Joseph and Mary should have expected Jesus to be in the temple, there was no reason for them to run about seeking him. To make this clear Tagabili has, 'why did you look in a different place for me?' — *You* here may have to be specified, e.g. 'mother and father' (Balinese, where the use of the pronoun would be unnatural and impolite from a son addressing his parents). Elsewhere the pronoun is omitted, 'why seek me' (Sundanese, probably for similar reasons).

I must, or, 'I have to', 'it is proper that I', or, 'as to me, not I not' (South Toradja), which often can also be used in cases like 4 : 43 and 9 : 22.

In my Father's house, or, 'at my father's' (Balinese, expressing the meaning of the phrase without using a term for 'house', as the Greek does). When 'house' must be added, the rendering will usually coincide with that of "(my Father's/thy) house" in John 2 : 16f, cp. also "house (of God)" in Lk. 6 : 4. Yet it can be argued that the expression in the present verse is more intimate. For this reason, probably, Javanese here uses the normal word for the house of a person of rank, but in Lk. 6 : 4, John 2 : 16f the more literary 'mansion' (also part of its rendering of "temple"). A rendering like 'in that which is my Father's', is an attempt to imitate the vagueness, which the Greek phrase has in our ears (but probably had not for Luke's readers or hearers); usually it implies the use of an expression that is uncommon or will not easily be understood in the right sense by the hearer or reader. *My Father,* here referring not to a human father but to the heavenly Father. For some problems inherent in this use of the word see *N.T.Wb.*/33f. In languages that differentiate according to rank the fact that both Jesus and the persons he addresses, his parents (here), or his followers (22 : 29; 24 : 49), acknowledge this heavenly Father as their

God usually leads to the use of an honorific term. Balinese, for instance, employs the term by which a prince would refer to his royal father in a conversation with his father's subjects. Other occurrences of *Father* in this meaning: 6 : 36; 9 : 26; 10 : 21f; 11 : 2, 13; 12 : 30; 22 : 42; 23 : 34, 46.

50 ***And they did not understand the saying which he spoke to them.***

Exegesis: *kai autoi ou sunēkan* 'and they did not understand'. *autoi* 'they' as contrasted with Jesus (cp. Bl-D, § 277.3).

suniēmi 'to understand', 'to comprehend'.

Translation: *Did not understand,* i.e. they were unable to grasp the full implications and real intent of the saying (cp. *TH-Mk* on 6 : 52). Some versions use here a specific verb (e.g. Pampango, a derivative verb the root of which means 'to penetrate into the inner part' and is cognate to a word for 'sharp'); others employ the general verb 'to know', but add to the object a word for 'intent/(real) meaning'; cp. also, 'but they did not know what his words...really meant (lit. the place to which his words...came-through)' (Tagabili, making use of an idiom said of people who do not know the answer to a riddle or the true meaning of an allegory).

The saying which he spoke to them, or simply, 'what he told them', "this reply" (Phillips).

51 ***And he went down with them and came to Nazareth, and was obedient to them; and his mother kept all these things in her heart.***

Exegesis: *kai katebē met' autōn* 'and he went down with them'.

katabainō 'to come down', 'to go down', here used of going away from Jerusalem (cp. 10 : 30, 31; Acts 24 : 1; 25 : 7; A-G s.v. 1 a), as contrasted with *anabainō* (cp. vv. 4 and 42), and implying going back home.

kai ēn hupotassomenos autois 'and he was obedient to them'. The imperfect tense is durative.

hupotassō 'to subject', in the passive 'to become subject', 'to obey'; here the participle is virtually equivalent to an adjective meaning 'obedient'.

kai hē mētēr autou dietērei panta ta rēmata 'and his mother kept everything'. The definite article *ta* here makes *panta ta rēmata* a summary of the events told in the preceding narrative.

diatēreō (†) 'to keep', 'to treasure', synonymous with *suntēreō,* used in a similar phrase in v. 19.

Translation: *He* (or, the boy Jesus) *went down with them and came to Nazareth,* or, 'came and-arrived in N.' (Kituba). Some versions contract the two clauses into one, e.g. "he went back with them to N." (Goodspeed). *Went down.* For movement to a lower, or a higher, level cp. on "went up" in 2 : 4. *With them,* or specifying the pronoun, 'with his parents', 'with the-two-of-them' (Malay); Balinese has 'returned together', leaving the persons in whose company he returned to be inferred from the context.

And was obedient to them. From the change of aspect it follows that this clause is not a mere continuance of the preceding pair of clauses; hence some versions prefer a major break and an explicit reference to the agent, cp. '. . . ; and he was submissive to them' (Jerusalem). The phrase may be interpreted as the description of Jesus' behaviour (i.e. he willingly did as he was ordered), or of the situation in which he found himself, cp. 'was under their authority' (cp. NEB). Where a rendering covering both possibilities is not available, the second one can best be chosen. — *Obedient.* The concept of 'obedience' may be described by 'to do what a person says', 'to accept orders', 'to follow (in a person's steps)' (Malay), 'to have an ear that listens' (Kipsigis), 'to hear a person's mouth' (Uduk). In some other languages one term covers 'to believe' and 'to obey' (Cuicatec, Tzeltal), or 'to hear/listen' and 'to obey' (Bahasa Indonesia), or, 'to listen', 'to believe' and 'to obey' (Thai).

Kept all these things in her heart, cp. on v. 19.

52 ***And Jesus increased in wisdom and in stature, and in favour with God and man.***

Exegesis: *kai Iēsous* 'and Jesus'; this is the first time that the name occurs without a qualifying apposition, indicating the last phase of his growth, cp. on v. 17.

proekopten 'increased'.

prokoptō (†) 'to progress', 'to advance'. The field in which progress is made is either indicated by a simple dative, or by *en* with dative.

[*en tē*] *sophia kai hēlikia kai chariti* 'in wisdom and stature and favour'; the three substantives belong closely together.

hēlikia either 'age' or 'bodily stature'. Since the fact that Jesus increased in age i.e. grew older is hardly relevant after his growth in wisdom, the rendering 'bodily stature' seems preferable.

charis here 'favour', not 'blessing', because of the following 'with God and man', cp. on v. 40.

Translation: Semantically the whole of this verse is closely similar to v. 40, and part of it to 1 : 80a; formally it is rather dissimilar from the two others; in the discourse structure all three verses have the same function, viz. to mark the end of a narrative by a general statement, summarizing a development stretching over several years. To preserve both the differences and the similarities may prove difficult, or even impossible: the use of an idiomatic rendering may entail more similarity of expression in one receptor language (cp. below on "increased"), or more dissimilarity in another (cp. below on "in favour with").

And Jesus, or better to bring out that the focus shifts back to Jesus and his condition, 'as to Jesus, he...' (Jerusalem; similarly Javanese).

The clause *Jesus increased in wisdom and in stature* may have to be restructured, e.g. 'Jesus' wisdom and his stature increased' (South Toradja, similarly in Tagabili), 'Jesus' wisdom and body growing' (Kapauku), 'Jesus became steadily wiser and bigger', 'Jesus became more-and-more wise and grew up'. For the verb cp. *N.T.Wb.*/41f, GROW.

And in favour with God and man. In several languages this third part of the series is better rendered as an independent clause, repeating the preceding verb or using a synonymous one, and adding a reference to Jesus, e.g. "he grew also in the love of..." (Phillips), 'moreover he became more and more the favoured-one of God and man' (Bahasa Indonesia RC). *Favour* (see on 1 : 30, and cp. on "pleased" in 2 : 14) often has to be rendered by a verbal expression, cp. 'he-was-favoured-by God and man' (Toba Batak), 'he pleased (lit. caused-to-be-happy) God and man' (Tagabili), 'his conduct pleased both God and men' (Gio), 'God and men liked/loved him, or, looked upon him for good (Kekchi, Bolivian Quechua), or, approved him' (Kapauku, subordinating the preceding phrases); or again, because in this verse the process is not related to God only, but to men also, a double rendering, 'he was-granted-grace-by God and loved-by men' (Balinese).

CHAPTER THREE

1 ***In the fifteenth year of the reign of Tiberius Caesar, Pontius Pilate being governor of Judea, and Herod being tetrarch of Galilee, and his brother Philip tetrarch of the region of Ituraea and Trachonitis, and Lysanias tetrarch of Abilene,*** 2 ***in the high-priesthood of Annas and Caiaphas, the word of God came to John the son of Zechariah in the wilderness;***

Exegesis: Vv. 1f consist of (a) a series of indications of time, serving to fix the events to be described in vv. 2ff in the setting of world and regional history, the latter both political and religious, and (b) the main clause *egeneto rēma theou epi Iōannēn* 'the word of God came to John', etc.

en etei de pentekaidekatō tēs hēgemonias Tiberiou Kaisaros 'in the fifteenth year of the reign of Tiberius Caesar'. *de* is transitional and serves to introduce a new narrative.

hēgemonia (††) 'rule', here referring to the reign of the Roman emperor but in itself as general a term as the verb *hēgemoneuō* (used in the next phrase), cp. on 2 : 2.

Tiberiou Kaisaros 'of Tiberius Caesar', cp. on 2 : 1.

tēs Ioudaias 'of Judea', cp. on 1 : 5. Here it is used in an administrative sense, including Samaria but not Galilee, as the next phrase shows.

kai tetraarchountos...Hērōdou 'and when Herod was tetrarch'.

tetrarcheō (††) 'to be tetrarch', i.e. originally the governor of one of the four provinces of Thessaly (cp. Plummer), later denoting the ruler of any small country or region who was not a king.

tēs Itouraias kai Trachōnitidos chōras 'of Ituraea and Trachonitis', both going with *chōras* which admits of many translations, cp. e.g., "district" (BFBS), "territory" (Phillips), "country" (Moffatt). Their tetrarch Philippus was Herod's older brother, of a different mother.

epi archiereōs Hanna kai Kaïapha 'in the time of the high priest Annas and Caiaphas', cp. A-G s.v. *epi* I 2. *archiereōs*, though in the singular, refers to both names mentioned, and Luke may have thought of Annas and Caiaphas as being a kind of joint high priests, cp. *N.T.Wb.*, 104f/PRIEST.

archiereus 'high priest', cp. A-G s.v. 1 b.

egeneto rēma theou epi Iōannēn 'the word of God happened, or, came to John'. This phrase occurs frequently in the Septuagint, denoting the divine inspiration of a prophet by God and the entrusting of a divine message or commission (cp. e.g. Gen. 15 : 1; 1 Sam. 15 : 10; Jer. 1 : 2). It implies that the person to whom the word of God comes, comes under the power of that word, not just that the word is communicated to him.

en tē erēmō 'in the desert', refers to the same area as *hai erēmoi* in 1 : 80.

Translation: The elaborate way in which Luke states the date of the events to be told has the stylistic function of marking that he now comes to the main part of his narrative. In several languages this can be imitated approximately, but it may be advisable then to divide the one long sentence in smaller units, introducing the main event ('the word...came...') by a recapitulating expression, e.g. "It was the fifteenth year of the rule of Emperor T.; Pontius P. was governor of Judea, Herod was ruler of G., ...It was at that time that the word of God came..." (TEV). Other languages may require an introductory word or phrase, such as, 'To-begin-with' (Malay; cp. also above on 1 : 5), 'What will be told now is this.' If according to receptor language usage the main event has to be mentioned early in the utterance, the sentence may have to be recast in such a way that first the emperor, next John and what happened to him, and last the secular and religious rulers are referred to (Manobo), whereas in a language as Sateré (see *TBT*, 17.14ff, 1966) what happened to John will have to come at the very beginning.

The noun *reign* may have to be expressed in a clause, e.g. 'when T. C. had been reigning/ruling, or, had been emperor'; and cp. on 1 : 33.

Governor, see on 2 : 2.

Tetrarch. The rendering to be chosen should denote an indigenous ruler that is subject to higher authority, cp. the following renderings of 'tetrarch' and 'emperor' respectively, 'prince'—'king-of-princes' (cp. Balinese), 'chief'—'chief of greatness' (Kituba), 'king who has been apportioned a fief', i.e. feudal Lord—'(one who is) on the throne', using a well known idiom that expresses sovereignty (Chinese UV); in Kekchi the distinction is indicated by a reference to areas of different size, e.g. 'who had power in Galilee' (etc.)—'who had power in all the land'. A cultural equivalent has been used in, 'at the time of these four chiefs: Herod in the region G., Phillip in the region I. ...' (Toba Batak, adapting an expression employed in several parts of Sumatra for groups of high dignitaries, which are called 'the four chiefs/grandees', even if their number is not complete). Attempts at a literal rendering, often a neologism in the receptor language, usually result in a long and cumbersome phrase, in some cases even a misleading one, suggesting some such meaning as 'chief over four parts', or 'fourth ruler'. The renderings of "tetrarch" and "governor" are the same in some languages (e.g. Kituba, Kapauku, Sranan); this is acceptable, because the distinction is of no relevance here (cp. the fact that in Pilate's case the Greek does not mention his precise rank).

Brother, see below on 6 : 14.

(V. 2) *In the high-priesthood of A. and C.*, or, 'when A. and C. were high-priests'. For *high priest* see *N.T.Wb.*/58f, PRIEST, and cp. *TH-Mk* on 1 : 44; 14 : 47.

The word of God came to John. Though the wording of this Hebraistic phrase should preferably be preserved, yet receptor language idiom may compel the translator to the use of more or less radical adjustments. He may have to mark the expression as a simile, e.g. 'the word of God came, as it were, to/over John'; or to rephrase it so that the connexion between 'word of God' and the verb becomes less direct, e.g. by speaking of 'the power/guidance of God's word', or so that 'the word of God' is no longer the agent, e.g. by shifting to a rendering like, 'John was-commissioned with God's word' (Javanese), or, 'John received the word of God'; or again, he may have to treat the ultimate agent, i.e. God, as subject of the sentence, e.g. 'God made J. the one to speak his (i.e. God's) words', 'God made-known his message to him' (Kituba), 'God commanded/commissioned/told John to preach'. — For *word of God* cp. on 5 : 1. In some Bantu languages the choice is between two terms for 'word', the one used in contexts of social communication in the meaning 'voice', 'word (that is heard and awaits response)', the other in that of 'word (as power, or as expression of intention)', 'command', 'message'; as the exegesis shows the latter term will usually best fit the present context. — *Came to,* has been rendered by 'came over' (Willibrord), 'took possession of' (Schonfield), 'found' (Nyakyusa), 'arrived in the heart of', indicating that John is merely an instrument of God in receiving the word (Tzeltal), 'arrived at/reached' (Shona 1963, employing a verb that, when given a suffix indicating purpose or aim, is used in ritual contexts of a god, or spirit, that takes possession of a medium).

In such phrases as *John the son of Zechariah* the appositional phrase functions approximately as does the surname in modern western languages; in some languages it forms a closely knit linguistic unit, signalled as such by a specific term or construction.

When name and apposition do not form such a unit one should make clear that *in the wilderness* does not go with Zechariah, but with John, cp. 'then God's voice found J., the son of Z., it found him in the woods' (Nyakyusa), '. . . to John there in the wilderness. This J. was the child of Z.' (Manobo); cp. also, 'at that time Z.'s son J. was in the desert (and) the word of God came down to him' (Chinese UV, locative clauses in Chinese normally preceding the part they qualify). For *wilderness* see *N.T.Wb./*25, DESERT.

3 ***and he went into all the region about the Jordan, preaching a baptism of repentance for the forgiveness of sins.***

Exegesis: *kai* 'and', i.e. as a consequence of this divine commission.

eis pasan [*tēn*] *perichōron tou Iordanou* 'into all the country around the Jordan'. The Jordan country is the area where John went to fulfil his commission, not visiting one definite place but going from place to place within this area, cp. "he went all over the Jordan valley" (NEB).

perichōros 'neighbouring', mostly used as a substantive, with *chōra* 'country' understood, and rendered 'neighbourhood'.

kērussōn baptisma metanoias eis aphesin hamartiōn 'proclaiming a baptism of repentance for the forgiveness of sins'.

kērussō 'to proclaim', 'to speak', with a connotation of authoritative proclamation. The content of John's preaching is described in the following words *baptisma metanoias eis aphesin hamartiōn.* These words belong together. For a detailed discussion of the whole phrase cp. *TH-Mk* on 1 : 4.

baptisma 'baptism' in Luke (with the exception of 12 : 50 where it is used in a figurative sense) always of the rite proclaimed and administered by John the Baptist.

metanoia 'change of mind', 'repentance', a deliberate turning from sin to God. The genitive *metanoias* here is qualifying and defines the baptism John proclaimed as an act expressing repentance. Cp. also *N.T.Wb.*, 110/REPENT.

eis aphesin hamartiōn 'for the forgiveness of sins', indicating either purpose or result, probably the former. Cp. also on 1 : 77.

Translation: *And*, or, 'then', 'accordingly'.

He went into all..., or, 'travelled-around in' (Kituba); Ponape specifies the aspect, using a reduplication of the root-word 'move' with a suffix that carries the meaning of 'doing in several places what the root-word says'; the same aspect form is used in the rendering of 'preaching'.

All the region of the Jordan, or, 'the whole area near J.', 'on both borders of the river J.' (Timorese).

Preaching. This subordinate participle may better become a second finite verb, 'and (he) preached', or even the main verb, 'and going through...he preached'. For *to preach*, i.e. 'to proclaim', 'to make widely known with authority', see *TH-Mk* on 1 : 4 (pp. 12f). In Chinese the UV had 'to hand down (the Way)', but the revision (L) uses the term for 'to propagate', "nowadays a very common word..., (which) de-specializes the term and puts it again in the midst of reality, showing with a new freshness the force of the Greek word" (*TBT*, 5.187, 1954).

A baptism of repentance for the forgiveness of sins. For often necessary transformations of this complex phrase see Nida, in *TBT*, 3.98-103, 1952, *TH-Mk* on 1 : 4 (pp. 15f), *TAPOT*, 51. For *baptism* cp. *TH-Mk* on the verb 'to baptize' in 1 : 5 (pp. 18f). Some languages that use a word for 'bath' add a qualification, cp. the compound nouns 'bath-of-enlightenment' and 'bath-of-dedication' (Tamil and Kanarese respectively). — For *repentance* and 'to repent' (also occurring in 3 : 8; 5 : 32; 10 : 13; 11 : 32; 13 : 3, 5; 15 : 7, 10; 16 : 30; 17 : 3f; 24 : 47) see *N.T.Wb.*/61f, and cp. Nida, *GWIML*, 136-138; *TBT*, 1.116-118, 1950; 5.95, 1954.

4 ***As it is written in the book of the words of Isaiah the prophet,***
"The voice of one crying in the wilderness:
Prepare the way of the Lord,
make his paths straight.

Exegesis: *hōs gegraptai* 'as it is written', the usual formula for the introduction of a quotation from the Old Testament, cp. A-G s.v. *graphō* 2 c. The subsequent quotation, here related to what precedes by the connective *hōs* 'as', serves to qualify John's ministry in a general way as the announcing of the promised salvation and has no direct bearing upon the baptism he proclaims.

en biblō logōn Ēsaïou tou prophētou 'in the book of sayings of Isaiah the prophet'.

biblos (also 20 : 42) 'book', in both places followed by a genitive which indicates the content of the book. As the synonymous *biblion* it is to be thought of as a scroll (cp. Plummer on 4 : 20).

phōnē boōntos '(the) voice of one shouting', the genitive *boōntos* makes *phōnē*, which is without article, definite. The phrase serves to draw the attention strongly to what follows, cp. Phillips' "Hark! Someone is shouting".

boaō 'to shout', 'to cry out', here of solemn proclamation.

en tē erēmō 'in the desert', goes with *boōntos*, not with what follows, as in the Hebrew text of Is. 40 : 3.

hetoimasate tēn hodon kuriou 'prepare the road of the Lord'. The underlying picture is that of preparations for an approaching visit of a king (cp. Moulton-Milligan 258): the road over which the Lord shall come must be made ready. The plural shows that the order is directed to a group but this group is not subsequently identified. The picture is that of an existing road which must be made ready.

eutheias poieite tas tribous autou 'make his paths straight'. The reference is to the elimination of curves, rather than to making the road smooth, as shown by the use of *euthus* 'straight' elsewhere (cp. L-Sc, s.v. 1, and A-G s.v. 1) and by the fact that in v. 5 the same word *eutheias* is used in contrast with *skolios* 'bent', 'curved', and distinguished from *leios* 'smooth'.

eutheia (†, from masc. *euthus*) 'straight'. In v. 5 it is used as a substantive with *hodon* 'way' understood, and meaning 'straight way'.

tribos (†) 'a beaten track', 'path'.

Translation: This verse, in the Greek subordinated to v. 3, may better become a new sentence, e.g. 'This happened just as it was written in...' (Marathi), 'This is according to what...' (cp. Manobo). A more radical shift of order is required in Telugu, which first quotes the prophecy, and concludes this quotation with the statement that these occurrences were predicted by Isaiah.

As it is written in... For this formula to introduce quotations from the Old Testament see above on 2 : 23. The pronoun *it* refers to the details of John's ministry as described in v. 3, cp. "all in accordance with" (Rieu); if necessary, one may shift to a personal reference, e.g. 'About him it has been written in...', or, 'He was like the man mentioned in...'.

The book of the words of Isaiah the prophet, i.e. the book containing the words of the prophet Isaiah, or, the book recording what the prophet Isaiah has said. Idiom may necessitate some adjustments, e.g. 'the words recorded in the book (of prophecies) of the prophet Is.' (Chinese UV, BT), or, 'the words of the prophet Is., (as) recorded/contained in his book'. If idiom, style, or decodability require a simpler wording, the rendering may be modelled on the synonymous phrase "the book of the prophet Is." (4 : 17), as done in Marathi, Balinese, or it may become, 'in the (book of the) prophecies of (Prophet) Is.' (cp. Malay and Bahasa Indonesia RC). Still further simplification will be necessary where passive constructions and subordination have to be avoided; then the whole clause "it is written ...Isaiah" may be rendered, "as the prophet Is. had written in his book" (TEV). For *book* see also on 4 : 17.

The voice of one crying in the wilderness, see *TH-Mk* on 1 : 3. *One* (or, a person) *crying* has been rendered by the more specific 'a proclaimer'

(Marathi, which also changes the phrase in a full sentence by adding a verb, 'happened'). In Manobo culture 'crying/shouting' implies anger and accordingly has to be avoided. In such a case one may shift to 'the voice of a person was widely heard'. For *wilderness* see *N.T.Wb.*/25, DESERT.

For *prepare the way of the Lord, make his paths straight* see *TH-Mk* on 1 : 3. — *Prepare the way of.* One of the renderings possible in Sranan is 'clear the overgrown tracks for (lit. wake up the lines for)'. *Way* (cp. also *N.T.Wb.*/72) and *paths*, or, 'road(s)' and 'little roads', 'path(s)' and 'by-paths/side-alleys'; or, not to overtranslate the difference, 'passage (or, place to walk)' and 'ways/paths', or a noun and a pronominal reference, e.g. 'prepare the way..., and make it straight'.

Lord, see above on 1 : 6, sub (c).

5 ***Every valley shall be filled,***
and every mountain and hill shall be brought low,
and the crooked shall be made straight,
and the rough ways shall be made smooth;

Exegesis: *pasa pharagx* 'every valley, or, ravine'. *pharagx* (††) in Is. 40 : 4 and elsewhere renders Hebrew *gai'* 'valley'. This rendering also here.

plērōthēsetai 'shall be filled'. The future tenses of v. 5 may be interpreted as imperatives (continuation of v. 4) or as referring to future events, as v. 6. The latter is preferable. For *pleroō* cp. on 1 : 20; here it is used in a literal meaning.

pan oros kai bounos tapeinōthēsetai 'every mountain and hill shall be levelled'.

bounos (also 23 : 30) 'hill'.

tapeinoō here 'to level', elsewhere 'to humble'.

kai estai ta skolia eis eutheian 'the crooked (places) shall become a straight (way)', cp. A-G s.v. *eimi* III 2. The future tense has the same meaning as that in the preceding clauses, see above.

skolios (†) 'bent', 'curved', 'crooked'. *ta skolia,* as the gender shows, does not refer to existing roads but to places that were too crooked to have any roads at all (cp. Plummer).

eutheian scil. *hodon* 'a straight road'. Other manuscripts read *eutheias*, scil. *hodous* 'straight roads', cp. Nestle.

hai tracheiai eis hodous leias 'the rough ways (shall become) smooth'. From the preceding clause a form of the verb *eimi* 'to be' has to be supplied, viz. *esontai*. Here the reference is clearly to existing roads that shall be made smooth.

trachus (†) 'rough', 'uneven'.

leios (††) 'smooth'.

Translation: Where a passive construction cannot be used one may employ such a rendering as 'every valley shall fill-up, every mountain... shall go-down. Roads that are crooked shall straighten-out, roads that are bumpy (lit. holes-holes) will be measure (= level) ones' (Kituba), or (in lines c, d) 'the crooked paths shall become straight, the bad paths shall become pleasant to walk' (Sranan), or, with an explicit reference to the agent, 'God will fill...bring low...' etc.

Be filled, or a more specific term, 'be earthed-up/filled-up' (Javanese, Balinese).

Mountain and hill, or, where such a pair of close synonyms does not exist, 'mountain and little-mountain' (Kituba), 'hill and rise in land' (Lokele), 'mountains high or low', 'hills big or small'. Hindi can use the feminine form of 'mountain' to refer to a hill. Cp. also *TH-Mk* on 9 : 2.

Brought low, or, 'caused to be low', "levelled" (NEB, Goodspeed, similarly in Javanese, East Toradja).

One, or both, of the contrastive pairs *crooked—straight, rough—smooth* may have to be rendered by a negative-positive phrase, e.g. 'the not-straight shall be made straight' and/or 'the not-smooth shall be smoothed' (the latter in South Toradja).

6 ***and all flesh shall see the salvation of God."***

Exegesis: *kai opsetai pasa sarx* 'and all mankind shall see', cp. on v. 5.

pasa sarx (†; in 24 : 39 *sarx* refers to the flesh of the human body as distinct from the bones) 'all flesh' is in the Greek a rendering of the Hebrew *kol basar,* which means either 'every living thing', or 'all mankind'. Because of the subsequent *to sōtērion tou theou* 'the salvation of God' the latter rendering is preferable.

to sōtērion tou theou 'the salvation of God'. For *to sōtērion* cp. on 2 : 30; no direct reference to the Messiah here.

Translation: *All flesh,* or, 'all mankind', 'all men/people' (Marathi, Vai), 'every human being', 'all kinds/tribes people' (Kapauku); or 'all that lives' (Timorese, the rest of the clause restricting the meaning to human beings). An older Chinese version (UV) used a time honoured idiomatic expression, 'all that has blood and breath', i.e. all living beings; a revision (RC) has 'blood and flesh' (cp. English "flesh and blood"), which has similar meaning.

See, or, 'notice', 'perceive', 'experience'; cp. also above on 2 : 26.

The salvation of God, or, clarifying the function of the genitive, 'God's work of salvation' (Ponape, Trukese), 'the salvation that God has wrought' (Marathi). Shifting to a verbal clause, one may say 'in what manner God saves people' (Kituba), 'how (but implying fact rather than manner) God saves people' (cp. Manobo); the object of such a clause may also be a pronoun referring back to the term rendering "all flesh".

7 ***He said therefore to the multitudes that came out to be baptized by him, "You brood of vipers! Who warned you to flee from the wrath to come?***

Exegesis: *elegen oun* 'and so he said'. *oun* indicates the resuming of the narrative after the interruption of vv. 4-6 (cp. A-G s.v. 2 a). The imperfect tense is best understood as introducing what may be regarded as the content or the summary of a speech, cp. Bl-D, § 329, and 6 : 20.

tois ekporeuomenois ochlois baptisthēnai hup' autou 'to the crowds who came out to get baptized by him'. The infinitive *baptisthēnai* is dependent upon the participle *ekporeuomenois* indicating the purpose of the crowds in coming out.

ekporeuomai 'to come out', without indication from where and whither. The latter is implied in v. 3 but the former remains open.

ochlos 'crowd', without unfavourable connotation. Here the plural suggests a very big crowd.

baptizō 'to dip', 'to immerse', exc. 11 : 38 and 12 : 50, in Luke always used with reference to the baptism preached and administered by John the baptist. The aorist tense implies that the rite of baptism is administered only once. As to the meaning of the passive two explanations are possible: (1) 'to be baptized', or (2) 'to get baptized', cp. *sich taufen zu lassen* (Zürich, NV), and "to have oneself baptized" (A-G s.v.). The latter fits the context better because of the final force of the infinitive *baptisthēnai*; the emphasis is on the intention of the crowds.

gennēmata echidnōn 'brood of vipers'. The exact meaning of the phrase (clearly meant as reproach) has to be determined in the light of the context. Since the crowds want to be baptized as a safeguard against the impending judgment of God, the phrase *gennēmata echidnōn* exposes them as cunning, cp. Mt. 10 : 16, and the Jewish parallels quoted by Strack-Billerbeck I, 574f on that verse.

gennēma (†) 'offspring', 'brood'.

echidna (†) 'viper', 'poisonous snake'.

tis hupedeixen humin 'who has suggested to you'. The usual meaning of *hupodeiknumi* with following infinitive is 'to warn', but this is not fitting here. The coming judgment was part of John's message (cp. v. 9) and we may assume that he called his hearers to repent before the day of judgment would dawn. The point of the passage is that people think that they can escape from judgment by being baptized without sincere repentance, and John asks the crowds who suggested that impossible idea to them.

hupodeiknumi 'to show', 'to warn'.

phugein apo tēs mellousēs orgēs 'to fly from the coming wrath'. The participle of *mellō* usually refers to events or situations of eschatological order, cp. A-G s.v. 2.

orgē (also 21 : 23) 'wrath', in Luke of the future judgment of God, cp. Richardson, *Word Book*, 289f.

mellō with present infinitive following 'to be about to', 'to be on the point of', often of that which is divinely bound to happen; with less emphasis 'to have in mind'. The participle *mellōn* (of which here the feminine form *mellousēs*) means 'future', 'coming' or 'to come'; here with the connotation that the 'coming wrath' is bound to come.

Translation: *He said.* The pronominal reference will have to be elucidated in many languages, cp. above on 1 : 8.

The multitudes that came out to be baptized by him refers to a fact that is prior to John's speaking, and essential to the understanding of what follows; hence it may be better rendered as an introductory sentence, e.g.

'people came to John in-order to be-baptized by him. He said to them...' (Kituba, cp. also TEV). — *The multitudes*. The noun (also in 1 : 10; 2 : 13; 3 : 10; 5 : 15; 6 : 17; 7 : 9; 8 : 45; 12 : 1, 13, 54; 14 : 25; 18 : 36; 19 : 37, 39; 22 : 6; 23 : 4, 27, 48) can often be rendered by 'mass', 'gathering of people', 'many people'. The plural has augmentative force here, i.e. emphasizes that the reference is to a multitude of large size; cp. *TH-Mk* on "crowds" in 10 : 1. For the force of the definite article see below on "the crowd" in 5 : 19. — *To be baptized* can often be rendered by a causative reflexive form (Manobo, see on v. 3) or phrase (Sranan), or by 'to take baptism' (Marathi), 'to receive baptism' (Hindi), 'to receive water' (Bamiléké), 'to ask him/John to baptize them'. In East Toradja one can use a verbal form with a specific prefix indicating that the subject asks for, evokes, or instigates the act of 'washing/baptism' expressed by the root-word. Cp. also the Ponape rendering mentioned below.

You here helps to identify what follows as an exclamation; one may have to add or substitute an exclamatory particle.

Brood of vipers. In languages where honorific forms of speech are normally used towards strangers, this strong term of abuse is an important clue, because it may be taken as an indication that the speaker is not in a mood to be polite. In some languages 'vipers' or, 'snakes' is not commonly used as an invective, e.g. in Balinese or Kituba, where the natural equivalent would be 'leeches' or 'insects', respectively. Even in such languages, however, translators often have kept to the literal rendering, probably because they felt that the bad connotation was sufficiently suggested by the situation. It may be advisable then to shift from metaphor to simile, adding e.g. 'like', 'as it were' etc. — The normal equivalent of *brood*, e.g. 'young ones', may rather impair the pejorative force of the expression; hence it had to be omitted in some versions. — *Vipers*, or a local equivalent, or, 'poisonous snakes', or simply, 'snakes'.

Who...? If the intention of this rhetorical question must be brought out, one may add an answer such as 'It is not I!'. The people's intention in asking for baptism (as explained in *Exegesis*) is brought out economically in Ponape by the use of a suffix which, added to 'be-baptized', suggests that the physical experience was all they came for.

Warned you, or, following the interpretation advocated in *Exegesis*, 'gave you a hint' (NV, Hindi; also Sranan, lit. 'pinched you to'); 'counselled you' (Telugu), 'pointed-out to you the way' (Bahasa Indonesia), 'showed you the means' (Tamil), 'taught you', cp. also "told you that you could" (TEV, similarly Nyakyusa).

Flee, or, 'run off/away (from danger)'; here metaphorically, 'to shun', 'to try to escape from'.

Wrath, or specified, 'God's wrath', 'divine anger' (Chinese, Balinese, Dravidian languages). Here the term does not primarily refer to the emotion felt but to the action resulting from that emotion; hence such renderings as, 'judgment', "retribution" (NEB), 'punishment' (Manobo). Cp. also *N.T.Wb.*/9f, ANGER and 59/PUNISH and *TH-Mk* on 3 : 5.

To come, or, 'impending' (Willibrord); cp. also 'wrath which God will have' (Kekchi).

8 ***Bear fruits that befit repentance, and do not begin to say to yourselves, 'We have Abraham as our father'; for I tell you, God is able from these stones to raise up children to Abraham.***

Exegesis: *poiēsate oun karpous axious tēs metanoias* 'then bear fruits that befit your repentance'. *oun* is inferential and means 'if you want to be saved, then...'. *karpoi* 'fruits' (a metaphor for *erga* 'works', 'deeds', cp. A-G s.v. *karpos* 2 a) views the deeds as the outcome of some moral or inner force. The aorist tense of *poiēsate* expresses that a change of conduct or attitude is implied, cp. Bl-D, § 337.1.

axios, of things, 'corresponding', 'consistent', of people, 'worthy'.

kai mē arxēsthe legein en heautois 'and do not begin to say to yourselves'.

archomai 'to begin', but here it has lost this meaning and has no distinct semantic function, cp. on 4:21.

patera echomen ton Abraam 'we have Abraham for our (fore)father'. According to Jewish tradition Abraham's merits could save Israel from the wrath of God, cp. Strack-Billerbeck I, 116-121.

legō...humin 'I tell you'. *legō* with following dative *humin* or *soi* serves as an emphatic introduction of a statement, which follows either in direct speech (e.g. in 6:27) or in indirect speech, connected by *hoti* (e.g. here).

dunatai ho theos ek tōn lithōn toutōn egeirai tekna tō Abraam 'God is able from these stones to raise up children for Abraham'. *ek tōn lithōn toutōn* 'from these stones' depends upon *egeirai* but is not a genitive of place but of origin; the stones are, as it were, the material from which the children could be made.

Translation: If the linguistic and the historical order should be parallel one may shift to, 'change the mind so that the fruit/result may be seen' (Valiente), 'if you (really) repent, bear fruits that show so'.

Bear fruits that befit repentance. The metaphor, though nearly dead as such, should preferably be preserved here, because the formal tie between this verse and the next exists in the echoing of the phrase 'bear fruits'. — In Marathi one does not say 'a tree bears fruit' but the idiom is, 'fruit comes to the tree'; in some other languages 'to bear fruit' is rendered by one verb, 'to fruit', 'to have-fruits'. Such a verb or idiom can in some cases not go with an expression like 'befit repentance'; then the translator may have to shift to a less obvious rendering, e.g. 'produce fruits', 'bring-to-light fruits'. — *That befit repentance*, or, 'that agree with/show repentance', 'that befit people who repent' (Sranan), 'that show you have repented'.

In some receptor languages, however, 'bear fruits' cannot be used in the required metaphorical sense, which has led several translators to the use of a non-metaphorical rendering, e.g. 'produce results'. This, however, has the drawback of destroying the formal tie between vv. 8 and 9. In order to preserve that tie it may be preferable to make explicit the simile implied in 'bear fruits', e.g. 'just as fruit trees must bear fruit, so you must do things that will show that you have repented', or, 'you are like fruit trees; the fruits you must bear are deeds that agree with your change of heart'.

Do not begin to say to yourselves (or, 'in your heart/mind'), or, 'do not think' (Kituba, Balinese); or, influenced by this specific context, 'do not put-your-hope-in (the fact) that you...' (Ponape, similarly Manobo).

We have Abraham as our father, or, 'Abraham is our father'. In the Greek such a genealogical claim can be expressed both in this form, starting from the father (cp. also John 8 : 39[a]) and in the reverse form, starting from the children (cp. the next clause, and John 8 : 39[b]); in some other languages the reverse form is idiomatically to be preferred: 'we belong to Abr.'s posterity/children', 'we are descendants of Abr.' (cp. Ponape).

The phrase *I tell you* is sometimes parenthetical; in translation it may have to be given another position in the sentence. Its function is in some cases better rendered by some such word as 'indeed', 'certainly', cp. on 12 : 51.

God is able from these stones to raise up children to Abraham. One may have to change the structure of this clause, e.g. 'God can use these stones to raise (or, to make/cause-to-exist/cause-to-be-born) children for Abr.', "God can take these rocks and make descendants for Abr." (TEV), 'God can cause these stones to change-into Abr.'s children' (Sranan). The emphasis is on "from these stones"; hence, 'from these very stones', "right out of these stones" (Goodspeed). Semantically *to Abraham* serves in this context to qualify the children rather than to indicate the beneficiary of the process; hence some versions have 'children of Abr.' (Bahasa Indonesia, cp. also Phillips), cp. also, 'children to-function-as offspring of Abr.' (Javanese).

9 ***Even now the axe is laid to the root of the trees; every tree therefore that does not bear good fruit is cut down and thrown into the fire."***

Exegesis: *ēdē de kai. de kai* is best understood as giving special emphasis to *ēdē* 'already', in order to make clear that John's call is urgent.

hē axinē (†) 'axe'.

pros tēn rizan tōn dendrōn keitai 'is lying at, or, directed towards, the root of the trees', cp. Plummer. *pros* with accusative suggests movement or direction, which, in the present context, because of *keitai* 'is lying', means a movement which has come to rest, or a direction in which the axe points. Weiss thinks that the clause refers to the moment immediately before the first blow, when the woodman puts his axe at the very place where it has to come down later. This interpretation is preferable.

riza (also 8 : 13) 'root'.

dendron 'tree'. Here and in 6 : 43f used in connexion with the picture of the tree and its fruits.

oun 'then', indicating that what follows is an inference from the preceding.

mē poioun karpon kalon 'that does not bear good fruit'. The use of *mē* with the participial phrase indicates that it has conditional force: every tree will be cut out, if it does not bear good fruit. The expression is the same as in v. 8 but here it is used in a literal sense.

kalos 'beautiful', as an indication of quality, 'good'. The good fruit to which John refers, is the fruits that befit repentance of v. 8.

ekkoptetai 'is cut down', but the present tense may well have futuristic meaning, since the context is prophetic, cp. Bl-D, § 323.

eis pur balletai 'is thrown into the fire'. For the present tense cp. preceding note. The fire is the fire of judgment, as often in the Old Testament, cp. Jer. 11 : 16; 21 : 14; 22 : 7; Ezek. 15 : 6f, and "the unquenchable fire" in v. 17.

Translation: The verse takes up the expression 'bear fruits' from v. 8[a], but now in a living and rather elaborate metaphor. If the underlying comparison of fruit trees with human beings has been made explicit in v. 8[a] (which see), the metaphor will be easily understood here; if not, it may be advisable to add such an explicit reference here, cp. 'You are like trees. The axe...' (Manobo).

The axe is laid to, or, "the axe lies ready at" (Rieu, similarly Bahasa Indonesia), 'the axe is ready to cut' (Kekchi, where a literal rendering would suggest that the axe had accidentally been left at the foot of the tree), 'the axe is-used-to-menace' (Balinese). If idiom requires a personal agent, one may say, 'some one is taking the axe towards (or, swings the axe against) the tree'; where an axe or comparable instrument is unknown the rendering of the sentence will have to become something like, 'the moment is near that the trees will be cut down, or, that some one will cause the trees to come down'. In Zarma one does not say 'to cut down a tree' but 'to kill a tree'.

Root. If a literal rendering would suggest something low down in the soil, the word can better be rendered, 'base' (Malay; similarly Kapauku, which uses a word that also can refer to the back end of a boat), 'foot' (Manobo); Toba Batak can use here a specific term for roots that have grown so big and thick as to be visible.

Thrown into the fire, or, 'lost/consumed in fire' (Ponape), or, 'burnt with/in the fire'. One version simply had 'is-burnt', but a reference to 'the fire' should preferably be preserved because of the specific meaning the term has in this context.

10 ***And the multitudes asked him, "What then shall we do?"***

Exegesis: *kai epērōtōn auton hoi ochloi* 'and the crowds asked him'. The imperfect tense *epērōtōn* suggests that this question was asked repeatedly.

legontes 'saying', has the force of a colon.

ti oun poiēsōmen 'what then are we to do?' *oun* implies that the question is a reaction to what John had said.

Translation: *What then shall we do?* The question is not a rhetorical one, expressing despair, but a real one, asking for information how to bear fruits that are good in God's eyes; hence such renderings as, 'what is it God wants us to do?' (Manobo), 'what good shall we do?' (Kekchi).

11 ***And he answered them, "He who has two coats, let him share with him who has none; and he who has food, let him do likewise."***

Exegesis: *ho echōn duo chitōnas* 'he who has two shirts'.

chitōn 'tunic', 'shirt', a garment worn next to the skin and under the *himation* as 6 : 29 shows. Travellers used to wear two shirts but the reference here seems to be to possessing, not to the wearing of two shirts at the same time.

metadotō tō mē echonti 'must share with him who has none'. As object of both *metadotō* (†) and *echonti* is to be understood *chitōna* '(one) shirt'.

brōmata (also 9 : 13) 'food'. There is no reference to an abundance of food. The mere having of food brings with it the duty of sharing with somebody who has none and is starving.

homoiōs 'likewise'.

Translation: *He* (or, the man) *who has...* (twice), 'whoever has...' (Marathi); or, 'if somebody has...' If the use of the third person would obscure the fact that John's advice is addressed to his questioners, it is better to say 'if somebody amongst you has...', 'if you have...'

Coats, see *N.T.Wb.*/20, CLOTHE. The term to be chosen should refer to a commonly used inner garment, e.g. 'shirt', 'loincloth' (Timorese); a more generic term, e.g. 'garment', '(piece of) clothing', is acceptable also.

Let him share with, or, 'he (or, you, see above) must share with', 'he must give one (of them) to' (Kituba, similarly Manobo, Marathi, Nyakyusa); for the verb cp. also *N.T.Wb.*/67.

Him who has none. Some languages can be as concise as is the Greek, or even more so, cp. '(the) not-have one' (Chinese), '(the) not-man' (Kapauku); others must expand the expression, e.g. 'person that lacks shirt' (Kituba, similarly Manobo).

Food, or, 'something-to-eat', cp. *N.T.Wb.*/38.

Let him do likewise, or, 'like that also', with marker of future (South Toradja); or expanding the phrase again, 'he must give away part of that too', 'he also must-share food of him with person that lacks food' (Kituba), 'should give to him who has none' (Manobo).

12 ***Tax collectors also came to be baptized, and said to him, "Teacher, what shall we do?"***

Exegesis: *ēlthon de kai telōnai baptisthēnai* 'tax-collectors also came to be baptized'. The aorist tense of *ēlthon* does not imply that the tax-collectors came to John only once but indicates progress in the narrative. For *baptisthēnai* cp. on v. 7.

telōnēs 'tax-collector', usually an underling, employed by Roman tax officers or Jewish tax farmers to do the actual collecting, despised because of this direct or indirect connexion with the Roman government and his reputation of enriching himself at the expense of the people.

didaskale 'teacher', Greek equivalent of Hebrew *rab* or *rabbi*, a polite form of address rather than the designation of somebody whose occupation is teaching. This applies also here since John is not a teacher of the law but a prophet.

Translation: *Tax collectors*. Terms for taxes and/or custom duties often are borrowings from the national or trade language. Where no specific term is available one may use a descriptive phrase, e.g. 'people who collect shells (i.e. money)' (Kapauku), 'those who extract (or, profit by taking) money for the government', cp. *N.T.Wb.*/70, TAX; *TH-Mk* on 2 : 15.

Teacher, cp. on 2 : 46, is used as a form of address to John (here), and to Jesus (in 7 : 40; 9 : 38; 10 : 25; 11 : 45; 12 : 13; 18 : 18; 19 : 39; 20 : 21, 28, 39; 21 : 7). If the usual rendering of 'teacher' cannot be employed in this position or context, one may have to use 'sir' (Kituba, Ponape), or another term used in polite address: Chinese (L) has an expression literally meaning '(you have been) born before (me)', which is the usual thing pupils say to their teachers in school, besides being the usual polite form of address; in Tagabili 'friend' is a respectful form of address that can often (e.g. in 7 : 40) do duty for 'teacher', which is never used in direct address.

13 ***And he said to them, "Collect no more than is appointed you."***

Exegesis: *mēden...prassete* 'exact nothing'. *mēden* is accusative of object.

prassō 'to do', of taxes 'to collect', possibly here with a slight connotation in the direction of 'to extort', cp. A-G s.v. 1 b.

pleon para to diatetagmenon humin 'beyond what has been laid down for you'. *para* with accusative has here the force of a comparative genitive, cp. Bl-D, § 185.3. *pleon* 'more' is pleonastic.

diatassō 'to order', with dative of the person to whom the orders are given.

Translation: *Do not collect more than*. The comparative can be expressed by, 'collect nothing that is not', 'only ask for what..., don't go beyond that' (cp. Kituba), 'apart from what..., you must take no more' (Chinese). For *collect* one may use a term or phrase meaning 'demand/ask money from the people', or, in order to bring out the concept of extortion, 'take away money (from the people)', 'compel people to pay money'; cp. also on "tax collector" in v. 12.

(What) is appointed you, or, '(what) you are told' (Kapauku), 'the amount designated' (Ponape); or, if an active construction is preferable, 'things somebody ordered you' (Nyakyusa), '(what) they have instructed (lit. set for) you to ask' (Sranan); cp. also *N.T.Wb.*/11, sub (4).

14 ***Soldiers also asked him, "And we, what shall we do?" And he said to them, "Rob no one by violence or by false accusation, and be content with your wages."***

Exegesis: *kai strateuomenoi* (†) 'also people in military service, or, soldiers'.

ti poiēsōmen kai hēmeis 'and we, what are we to do'. *kai* is best understood as 'even', and the clause appears to imply that the soldiers were non-Jewish, and that they asked John's advice as people who were, as it were, not entitled to it.

mēdena diaseisēte mēde sukophantēsēte 'rob no one by violence or by blackmail'. In view of the fact that in the next clause John urges the soldiers to be content with their proper pay it is reasonable to suppose that both verbs used in the present clause refer to the obtaining of money by unlawful means.

diaseiō (††) 'to shake', hence 'to use force in order to obtain something valuable', or 'to extort by violence'. The idiom is the same as that of the English slang expression 'to shake somebody down for his money'.

sukophanteō (also 19 : 8) either 'to accuse falsely', or 'to extort'. Here it is used with a personal object and this requires the rendering 'to blackmail'; thus *diaseiō* and *sukophanteō* denote two different ways of robbing people of their possessions, viz. by violence and by blackmail.

arkeisthe tois opsōniois humōn 'be content with your pay'.

arkeomai (†) 'to be content', or, 'satisfied'.

opsōnion (†) 'money paid to a soldier'.

Translation: *And we, what shall we do.* The emphatic position 'we' has in this verse may lead to a rendering that is formally rather dissimilar from the phrases used in vv. 10 and 12, e.g. 'how about us (lit. what is ours)' (Manobo).

Rob no one by violence or by false accusation, or, "don't take money from anyone by force or by false charges" (TEV). *To rob by violence,* or, 'to press/squeeze' (Bahasa Indonesia RC), 'to corner' (Timorese). Some descriptive renderings used are, 'to browbeat (lit. cause-to-fear) and overthreaten' (Lokele), 'to rob like an arrogant man (would do)' (Trukese), 'to force people to give money' (Manobo), 'to take away from another forcibly' (Tzeltal). *By false accusation,* or, 'by accusation-without-reason' (Trukese); or, shifting to a verbal construction, 'by accusing people deceitfully/treacherously', 'by saying, "He has done wrong", though he didn't'; cp. on "accuse" in 6 : 7.

Be content with your wages may be rendered by, 'do not want (or, try to get) more than your wages', 'your wages must be enough for you' (cp. Sranan). *Your wages,* or, 'what you get for your work' (Kapauku), 'the money for which you work' (Sranan), 'what they pay you (for your work)', 'your pay'.

15 ***As the people were in expectation, and all men questioned in their hearts concerning John, whether perhaps he were the Christ,*** 16 ***John answered them all, "I baptize you with water; but he who is mightier than I is coming, the thong of whose sandals I am not worthy to untie; he will baptize you with the Holy Spirit and with fire.***

Exegesis: Main clause to the two absolute genitives of v. 15 (*prosdokōntos* *tou laou* 'as people were in expectation', and *dialogizomenōn pantōn* 'as all were wondering') is the first clause of v. 16, *apekrinato*...*Iōannēs*, 'John answered'. The relationship of the two absolute genitives to one another depends on the interpretation of the first one, see next note.

(V. 15) *prosdokōntos de tou laou* 'as people were in expectation'. *de*, which has not been translated, marks the beginning of a new development. The participle *prosdokōntos* which has no object, is best understood in an absolute sense as e.g. in RSV. People were "in a great state of expectation" (Phillips), because of John's message. The clause describes the result of John's preaching, cp. Goodspeed, "as all this aroused people's expectations". Then *laos* does not refer to the people of Israel in general but to the people that came out to listen to John. For *prosdokaō* cp. on 1 : 21.

dialogizomenōn pantōn 'as all were wondering', describes a further and more specific result of John's preaching; *pantes* refers to the same people as *laos* in the preceding clause. For *dialogizomai* cp. on 1 : 29.

en tais kardiais autōn 'in their hearts', or, "in their minds" (BFBS), or, "inwardly" (Phillips).

mēpote autos eiē ho Christos 'whether perhaps he was the Messiah', cp. A-G s.v. *mēpote* 3 b α. *autos* is unemphatic 'he', referring back to John's name in the preceding clause. The optative *eiē* has no special function. Instead of 'the Messiah' RSV and several other translations have "the Christ", a transliteration of the Greek rendering of the Hebrew word. This must be regarded as a second best rendering.

(V. 16) *apekrinato legōn pasin ho Iōannēs* 'John answered saying to all', cp. on 1 : 60.

egō men hudati baptizō humas 'As to me, I am baptizing you with water'. *egō* is emphatic and *men* suggests that a contrast is to follow. *hudati* 'with water', instrumental dative, cp. Bl-D, § 195.1 (d), and *TH-Mk* on 1 : 8. The present tense *baptizō* is habitual, 'I practise water-baptism'.

erchetai de ho ischuroteros mou 'but the one who is mightier than I is coming'. *de* corresponds to *men* in the preceding clause but the clause which corresponds materially with it ('he will baptize you with the Holy Spirit and with fire') does not come until its subject, viz. the mightier one, is properly identified in his relationship to John. The clause introduces the mightier one as someone who is known, though no previous reference has occurred.

ischuros 'strong', 'mighty'.

hou...*autou* 'whose...of him'. The relative pronoun at the beginning of the clause and the personal pronoun at the end both go with *ton himanta tōn hupodēmatōn* 'the thong of the sandals' and are therefore to be rendered only once. This is probably a semitism (cp. Black, *Aramaic Approach*, 75) but also not unknown in Greek (cp. *TH-Mk* on 1 : 7).

hikanos of things 'adequate', 'considerable', of persons 'fit', 'competent', here with the connotation 'worthy for something', cp. A-G, and followed by a complementing infinitive.

lusai ton himanta tōn hupodēmatōn 'to untie the thong of the sandals'. This was considered to be the task of a slave.

luō 'to loose', 'to untie', 'to set free'.

himas (†) 'thong', or 'strap' on sandals.

hupodēma 'sandal', "a leather sole that is fastened to the foot by means of straps", A-G.

autos humas baptisei en pneumati hagiō 'he will baptize you with Holy Spirit'. *autos* 'he' is emphatic and contrasts with *egō* at the beginning of the verse. *humas* 'you' does, of course, not imply that this baptism will be limited to those who have previously received John's baptism with water, just as *humas* in the first clause of this verse does not mean that John only baptized those to whom he talked at the moment.

en pneumati hagiō 'with', rather than 'in the Holy Spirit', cp. A-G s.v. *en* I 4 c, III 1 a. The phrase 'to baptize with the Holy Spirit' occurs only in connexion with, and contrast to, John's baptism with water (Mt. 3 : 11; Mk. 1 : 8; Lk. 3 : 16; Jn. 1 : 33; Acts 1 : 5; 11 : 16) and not as an independent expression. It is therefore best understood as an analogy to the baptism with water and to be interpreted along the same lines as that phrase.

kai puri 'and with fire'. This addition also in Matthew but not in Mark. There are two interpretations: (1) the fire is the fire of judgment (Klostermann, Zahn) because of the mentioning of the fire in vv. 9 and 17 both in a picture that refers to the coming judgment; (2) the fire is the fire of purification (Plummer, Lagrange). Interpretation (1) is preferable. This implies a disjunctive relationship between *pneuma hagion* and *pur*.

Translation: It is often better not to render v. 15 as a subordinate clause, but as one separate sentence, formed by two co-ordinated clauses with or without connective, or as two such sentences.

The people, here virtually the same as 'the crowd'.

Were in expectation, or, if the expression requires an object, 'were expecting something', 'were believing that things of importance would come to pass' (Kituba). For the noun see *N.T.Wb.*/14, AWAIT.

All men, or, "they...all" (Goodspeed), 'everyone (amongst them)', referring to the subject of the first clause, cp. also, 'the multitudes', partly repeating 'the multitude of people (i.e. the crowds)' (Chinese L).

Questioned in their hearts, or, 'inquired in their minds' (Dravidian languages), 'were asking-themselves in heart of them' (Kituba), the qualifying word or phrase being required to show that no discussion with others is meant; or again, 'wondered (lit. guessed and doubted)' (Chinese UV), 'were-thinking' (Marathi, Manobo), without such a qualification.

Concerning John, whether perhaps he were the Christ may have to be restructured, e.g. '...whether perhaps J. were the Messiah', or, if the verb is to be followed by direct discourse, "Is John (or, this man, or, he) perhaps the Messiah?", "What? Might he be Christ?" (Marathi).

(V. 16) *Answered.* RSV's rendering of Gr. *apokrinomai* by a form of 'to answer' here (and in 5 : 22, 31; 7 : 40[a]; 8 : 50; 9 : 49; 11 : 45; 13 : 15) is rather unidiomatic because it does not introduce a person's reaction upon a request or statement that has been addressed to him. As a rule it is preferable in these cases to shift to another verb, e.g. 'to speak up', 'to start speaking', 'to address'; or 'to interpose'; or a combination of 'to say/

speak to' with such expressions as 'on his part', 'to this', 'again', 'then', 'thereupon', 'but', 'however', as required by the context; hence here e.g. 'But John said to them'. Such renderings have been used by RSV itself for similar occurrences of Gr. *apokrinomai* (e.g. 1 : 60, cp. also 13 : 14; 17 : 17, 37; 22 : 51), but some other translations have used 'to answer/reply' for nearly all occurrences even though decidedly unidiomatic in the language concerned. Their example is not to be followed.

For John's answer see *TH-Mk* on 1 : 7f, to which only a few points have to be added here.

I, or more emphatically, 'as for me (lit. to me), I' (Kituba, similarly Kanarese), 'I indeed' (Marathi).

He who is mightier, etc. is to be applied to the Messiah, although his name is not explicitly mentioned; hence in the references to his person and acts in vv. 16f the use of honorifics may be required in languages like Balinese and Javanese. — Comparative forms of adjectives may not be available in the receptor language. Then it is usually possible to circumscribe the comparison by 'he surpasses me (or, he is ahead) in might/power', or to use a positive-negative contrast, 'he is (really) mighty, I am not mighty'. Cp. also Nida, *BT*, 261; *TH-Mk* on 1 : 7; *TBT*, 13.29, 1962; and below on 7 : 42; 10 : 12; 15 : 7. For *mighty*, or, 'powerful', cp. on "power" in 1 : 35.

The function of the clause *the thong of whose sandals I am not worthy to untie* is to give the measure of the difference in might between John and Jesus; hence, "I am not good enough even to untie his sandals" (TEV), 'mightier than I so that (or, so much mightier than I that) I am unworthy to untie-for-him. . .'. — *Thong*, or, 'tie', 'straps'; in some cases not rendered by a separate term but implied in the verb for 'untie'. — *Sandals*, see also Nida, *BT*, 170; Trukese has to use a descriptive phrase, 'covering-of his-foot'. — *I am not worthy to*, i.e. I have not sufficient worth/value/excellence to. In Trukese, Ponape, and some Indonesian languages one says, 'it is not fitting that I. . .'; for other renderings see *TH-Mk, l.c.*

With the Holy Spirit and with fire. The rendering of this phrase should be modelled on that of 'with water', where necessary marking a shift from metaphor to simile by adding a clue like, 'as it were'. The disjunctive relationship between the two nouns may be suggested by using 'or' instead of 'and' (Kituba), or expressed more explicitly by saying, 'some of you with the Holy Spirit, others with fire', cp. 'some of you he will baptize with the H. Sp. and the rest he will baptize with fire' (Manobo).

17 ***His winnowing fork is in his hand, to clear his threshing floor, and to gather the wheat into his granary, but the chaff he will burn with unquenchable fire."***

Exegesis: The structure of v. 17 is, syntactically, as follows: *hou. . . autou* is a relative clause, 'in whose hand (is) the shovel', with *estin* 'is' understood; this is followed by two final infinitives: *diakatharai* 'in order to clean', and *sunagagein* 'in order to bring together', both dependent upon the preceding clause. Then follows an independent clause *to de achuron*

...*asbestō* 'but the chaff he will burn with unquenchable fire'. This structure, brings out that the primary purpose of the winnowing is to clean and to gather the grain (indicated by the two final infinitives), but that he will inevitably also burn the chaff (indicated by co-ordinate clause).

hou...autou 'whose...his'. The relative pronoun *hou* goes either with *to ptuon* 'whose shovel' (so, with shift from the relative to independent clause, RSV, BFBS, NEB) or with *cheiri* 'in whose hand' (so NV, Willibrord, Jerusalem, Zürich). Its antecedent is *autos* in the preceding clause and to this *autou* also refers. Clauses of this type are best understood as Hebraistic (cp. Bl-D, § 297, and Black, *Aramaic Approach*, 75) and the relative pronoun refers either in a general way to the clause as a whole (like the relative noun *'ăšer*) or is taken up again by the personal pronoun. It is therefore preferable to connect *hou* with *cheiri*, and not with *to ptuon*.

ptuon (only here and parallel Mt. 3 : 12 in the N.T.) '(winnowing) shovel', a fork-like instrument with which the threshed grain was thrown into the wind (cp. A-G s.v.). Here as in Jer. 15 : 7 the winnowing symbolizes judgment.

diakatharai tēn halōna autou 'in order to clean his threshing-floor', indicating the purpose of the winnowing announced in the preceding clause.

diakathairō (†) 'to clean out', 'to clear'.

halōn (†) 'threshing-floor', or 'threshed grain still lying on the threshing floor' (A-G s.v. 2). The latter is preferable.

sunagagein ton siton 'in order to gather the grain'.

sunagō 'to gather', 'to bring together', 'to call together'.

sitos 'grain', either a specific sort of grain such as 'wheat', or grain in general.

eis tēn apothēkēn autou 'into his barn', or, 'granary'.

apothēkē 'storage place', here for grain, 'barn', 'granary', probably a large pit with a building overhead (cp. *IDB* II, 469 s.v. 'granary').

to de achuron katakausei 'but the chaff he will burn'. The place of *achuron* in the clause indicates emphasis, cp. Jerusalem, 'and as to the chaff, he will burn it'.

achuron (†) 'chaff'.

katakauō (†) 'consume with fire', 'burn up'.

puri asbestō (†) 'with unquenchable fire' or "fire that can never go out" (NEB), i.e. the fire of everlasting judgment (cp. Is. 66 : 24), or of hell (cp. Mk. 9 : 43).

Translation: One can use this metaphor in many cultures, where necessary shifting to another cereal, such as rice, see below on "wheat". Such a shift usually entails adjustment in the rendering of the accompanying terms; in some cases the tools and processes can be referred to by terms associated with rice, although for the cereal the term 'wheat', known as a foreign product, is used. Where such rather close cultural equivalents are lacking, the translator may choose some other kind of fruit or agricultural product that is stored after its waste products have been removed, adjusting the terms for tools and processes accordingly. In some cases translators have introduced foreign terms, e.g. in Ponape and Trukese, transliterating English 'shovel' and 'wheat', and clarifying the winnowing process by illustrations.

His winnowing fork is in his hand, or, 'his hands already hold the winnowing basket' (Balinese). Often it is better to have a personal subject, e.g. 'he is holding the winnowing fork in his hands', 'he has already taken the winnowing basket' (Manobo), where necessary shifting to a simile, e.g. 'he is like a man who is holding...'. *Winnowing fork,* or, '(winnowing) basket/tray', or an instrumental derivation of 'to winnow' (Toba Batak). Where such a technical term is lacking one may use a descriptive phrase, e.g. 'dirt shaking out thing' (Kapauku), or a generic term such as 'tool' (Kekchi), 'thing' (Kituba), the specific use of which is sufficiently made clear by the subsequent clauses.

Wheat, or the (indigenous or borrowed) name of another small grain used for food in the culture or known to the receptors as being used for food in other cultures, e.g. 'rice', 'millet', 'barley', 'corn/maize'; or an expression built upon such a name, such as 'seed like rice' (Korku), 'foreign rice' (Timorese); and see *TH-Mk* on 2 : 23.

Clear his threshing floor, or, preferring the other meaning of Gr. *halōn,* 'winnow (or, sift) his threshed grain', cp. 'winnow what-has-been-threshed (lit. trodden-out)' (South Toradja), 'remove hulls of rice that he has pounded' (Kituba), or omitting the reference to threshing or its equivalent, 'clean-well skin-of wheat' (Trukese), 'fan the rice' (Sranan). Some versions apparently try to combine the two meanings that Gr. *halōn* can have, cp. 'winnow the heap on the threshing floor' (Kanarese), 'clean his wheats in their place' (Ponape).

Gather...into his granary, or, 'into his house-of storage' (Ponape, Trukese), 'into the storeroom', or simply, 'into its place'; cp. also on "barns" in 12 : 18. In some places threshing or its equivalent is not done before but after the storing in the granary, e.g. in Bali, where bunches of rice are kept in the rice-barn unpounded, and every few days the quantity needed is brought down, pounded and winnowed. Hence the phrase in question had to be rendered in Balinese by, 'the grains...he gathers and stores-away' (viz. in a big vessel in the house where the pounded rice to be used in the next days is kept).

The term *the chaff* summarizes all the waste products, i.e. empty ears, stalks and straw, and can, if necessary, be described with one or more of these terms, cp. 'its empty ones and straw' (South Toradja), 'the straw' (Manobo), 'the hulls' (Kituba, similarly Kapauku, Ponape).

Unquenchable, or, 'not to be put out', or, in active construction, 'that is not dying' (Kituba), 'that never goes out' (Nyakyusa), 'that you can't quench (lit. kill)' (Sranan).

18 ***So, with many other exhortations, he preached good news to the people.***

Exegesis: *men oun* indicates that the clause it introduces serves to summarize and bring to a close what has been described in the preceding verses, in order to form a transition to what follows, since it is a combination of the particle *oun*, which is retrospective, with *men*, which is prospective, i.e. preparing the way for a new subject to be introduced by subsequent *de* (cp. J. D. Denniston, *Greek Particles*, Oxford, 1934, 470f; Bl-D, § 451.1).

polla...kai hetera 'many other things', accusative of content with *parakalōn*. *kai* is redundant in English.

heteros 'other', or 'different', here best understood in the former sense (cp. A-G s.v. 1 b β).

parakalōn 'exhorting'. The semantic problem involved here is the relationship between *parakalōn* and *euēggelizeto* 'he preached the good news'. The exhortations are either (1) part of John's preaching, or (2) identical with it, or (3) different from it, preferably (1).

parakaleō 'to exhort', 'to entreat', 'to comfort'.

euēggelizeto ton laon 'he preached the good news to the people', cp. on 1 : 19. The content of the preaching is to be supplied from the context, cp. preceding note.

Translation: *Many other exhortations*, or in a verbal clause, 'he was exhorting in many other ways' (cp. Kituba), 'John taught the people many more things' (Manobo), 'J. still used many other words to exhort the people' (Chinese UV). As shown in these examples the verb often requires an explicit reference to those who were exhorted, viz. 'the people', which may entail the shift to a pronominal reference with the next verb. — *Other* is referring here to non-specified examples of the same category; it may have to be rendered by 'more such', 'similar', 'of the same kind'. *Exhortations*. The verb 'to exhort' has been rendered 'to point-out' (East Toradja), 'to teach' (Javanese, Manobo), 'to remind-of' (Toba Batak), 'to stir' (Nyakyusa), 'to work upon the heart' (Sranan); cp. also *N.T.Wb./2*, ADMONISH.

He. The pronominal reference will often have to be specified, unless this has already been done in what precedes.

To preach the good news. This verbal phrase renders a Greek verb that is derived from the noun *eu-aggelion*, 'good news', 'gospel' (which noun, however, does not occur in Luke's Gospel); it refers to the news or message about man's salvation by God through Jesus the Messiah and about the kingdom he is establishing, the messenger being John the Baptist (here), the Messiah (4 : 18), Jesus (4: 43; 7 : 22; 8 : 1; 20 : 1), the twelve disciples (9 : 6), Jesus and/or the disciples (implied agents of the passive form in 16: 16). In a less specific sense the verb is used in 1 : 19 and 2 : 10, where an angel is the messenger. *To preach*, or, 'to tell/make-known/announce', 'to cause-to-be-heard' (Hindi). *Good news*, see *TH-Mk* on "gospel" in 1 : 1, ad (2).

The people, here referring to Israel, the people of God, as in 2 : 10; therefore, the rendering may have to differ from that in v. 15.

19 ***But Herod the tetrarch, who had been reproved by him for Herodias, his brother's wife, and for all the evil things that Herod had done,*** 20 ***added this to them all, that he shut up John in prison.***

Exegesis: *ho de Hērōdēs ho tetraarchēs* 'but Herod the tetrarch', cp. on v. 1. For *de* and the connexion with the preceding verse, cp. on *men oun* in v. 18. The verb of which *ho Hērōdēs* is the subject is *prosethēken* 'added', see below.

elegchomenos hup' autou 'being reproved by him', going with *ho Hērōdēs*. The present tense of the participle suggests that this reproving happened more than once.

elegchō (†) 'to reprove', 'to show somebody his fault'.

peri Hērōdiados...kai peri pantōn 'concerning Herodias...and concerning everything'. The idea of the clause appears to be that John used to reprove Herod because of every wicked thing he did but that his reproval of Herod because of Herodias (cp. Mt. 14 : 4) was what made Herod have John arrested.

tou adelphou autou. According to Josephus Herodias' first husband, referred to in this verse was Herod, son of Herod the Great and Mariamne (the second wife of that name). Herod the tetrarch was the son of Herod the Great and Malthake, whom he married after Mariamne, cp. *IDB* II, 586ff. Hence *adelphou* refers to an older brother of a different mother.

peri pantōn hōn epoiēsen ponērōn 'concerning all the wicked things he did'. *ponērōn* goes with *pantōn* and *hōn* is attraction of the relative pronoun into the case of its antecedent.

ponēros 'wicked', 'evil', 'bad', always with a moral connotation.

prosethēken kai touto epi pasin 'added also this to all (the wicked things he did)'. *pasin* refers back to the preceding clause *peri pantōn...ponērōn*. *kai touto* refers to the next clause. The clause represents John's arrest by Herod as the crowning of all his other wicked deeds, cp. NEB, Goodspeed.

prostithēmi 'to add', 'to grant'.

katekleisen ton Iōannēn en phulakē 'he shut up John in prison', asyndetic clause, taking up and explaining *touto*.

katakleiō (†) 'to lock up', 'to shut up'. For *phulakē*, here meaning 'prison', cp. on 2 : 8.

Translation: The syntactic structure will have to be changed more or less radically in some languages, e.g. 'John also reproved Herod...for Herodias, his brother's wife, and for all...done. After that/Then he/Herod added to all his crimes this (one): he shut up John in prison'.

To reprove, or, 'to rebuke' (for which cp. on 4 : 35), 'to scold' (Kituba, similarly East Toradja, using a verbal derivation of 'angry'), 'to hit-with words' (Toba Batak); or analytically, 'to say that he had done evil'.

For Herodias. Luke says less than he probably knew, and than we can know from Mk. 6 : 17f. Style, or decodability may require some clarification, e.g. "over the affair of...H." (NEB, similarly Chinese L.), 'for his doings with H.', 'because of what Herod did about the woman Herodias'

(Manobo, which has to add 'woman', because the proper name and the rendering of "brother's wife", viz. 'sibling's spouse', do not specify the sex), but Luke's allusive way of speaking should be preserved as far as possible; if one wishes to state the case overtly, one should do so in a footnote.

His. If Herod has been clearly in focus in the preceding clauses the pronoun will usually be sufficient as reference to him here; if not, one will have to use the proper name, or to change the sentence structure so as to keep one's references straight.

His brother's wife, or, 'whom his brother had married', 'who was married (or, had been given in marriage) to his brother'.

The evil things Herod had done, or, 'the crimes/misdeeds Herod (or, he) had done', 'Herod's (or, his) crimes/misdeeds/wicked doings'. Some versions (e.g. NEB, Kituba, Hindi) add 'other', to bring out that 'his doings with Herodias' were a crime also. For *evil* cp. also Nida, *BT*, 220f.

(V. 20) *Added this to them all*, or, 'to all his evil doings/crimes', 'to (lit. on top of) all other bad things he had done' (Kituba); or, 'extra added one item' (Chinese UV), 'did something even worse' (Tarascan, similarly TEV), 'put crime on top of crime' (Sranan). For *to add* cp. also *N.T.Wb.*/2.

He shut up John in prison, or, 'he imprisoned/locked-up J.', or, 'he gave J. rope in the rope house', as the idiom is in Gahuku. Cp. also *N.T.Wb.*/19f, CAPTURE. That Herod is not the direct agent, may lead to, 'he caused-to-be-put J. in prison' (Kituba, similarly Tarascan).

The connexion between "added this to them all" and "shut up J. in prison" is indicated by the forward pointing deictic element "this" in the first sentence, to which the next sentence is epexegetic. To express this relationship more overtly one may add a connective, e.g. 'namely', 'that is' (Chinese); elsewhere subordination is preferable, either of the second sentence, e.g. "by throwing J. in prison" (Rieu, similarly some other English versions, Bahasa Indonesia), or of the first sentence, e.g. 'locked-up J., in-addition-to all those crimes' (Balinese), 'imprisoned J., (as) the worst of all the evil things he did'.

21 ***Now when all the people were baptized, and when Jesus also had been baptized and was praying, the heaven was opened,***
22 ***and the Holy Spirit descended upon him in bodily form, as a dove, and a voice came from heaven, "Thou art my beloved Son; with thee I am well pleased."***

Exegesis: *egeneto de* 'and it happened', cp. on 1 : 8.

hapanta ton laon 'all the people', often in Luke in a context describing the reaction of the people upon, or attitude towards, John the Baptist (here) or Jesus (elsewhere). In these phrases *laos* is used not in a strictly religious sense. *pas* or *hapas* is not to be taken too literally; it expresses that a great number or a majority of those present takes the attitude which the clause describes. For *laos* cp. on 1 : 10.

aneōchthēnai ton ouranon 'that the heaven was opened'. The underlying picture may be that of a veil being rent (cp. Mk. 1 : 10 and *TH-Mk* there) or of a door of a temple or palace being opened (cp. Rev. 4 : 1), preferably the latter. It is to be noted that Luke describes the opening of the heaven and the coming down of the Spirit as something which everybody saw or could see, whereas Mark represents them as something which only Jesus saw.

katabēnai to pneuma to hagion...ep' auton 'that the Holy Spirit came down upon him'. Nowhere else is *katabainō* 'to come down' used in connexion with the Holy Spirit and it may well be that the verb is used here because of the fact that the Spirit shows the outward appearance of a dove. For *katabainō* cp. on 2 : 51.

sōmatikō eidei hōs peristeran 'in bodily form like a dove'. The addition *sōmatikō eidei* which is not in Mark stresses the fact that the Holy Spirit was in the appearance of a dove. The ambiguity of the Greek text in Mk. 1 : 10 (cp. *TH-Mk* there) is avoided by Luke. *peristera*, cp. on 2 : 24.

sōmatikos (†) 'bodily' with the connotation of 'real'.

eidos (also 9 : 29) 'outward appearance'.

phōnēn ex ouranou genesthai 'that a voice came from heaven'. For *phōnē* cp. on 1 : 44. Here the voice is the voice of God.

su ei ho huios mou ho agapētos 'you are my son, the beloved one', a public proclamation, not only for the sake of the person addressed but also for those present. *ho agapētos* may be interpreted as attributive to *ho huios mou* "my beloved Son" (RSV), or as an apposition to it, "My son, the Beloved One" (Rieu), or "my Son, my Beloved" (NEB). The latter interpretation is preferable since it brings out the two parts of the clause: *su ei ho huios mou* 'you are my son' (Ps. 2 : 7) a formula pertaining to the enthroning of a king, and *ho agapētos* reflecting Is. 42 : 1 (not a literal quotation!), which refers to the suffering servant.

agapētos (also 20 : 13) 'beloved', tending toward the meaning 'only-beloved'. Hence several commentators advocate the rendering 'only' (cp. *TH-Mk* on 1 : 11), but the great majority of translators favours 'beloved', which also fits the thought of Is. 42 : 1 better. This is to be preferred.

en soi eudokēsa 'in thee I am well pleased'. The aorist is best rendered as a present (cp. *TH-Mk* on 1 : 11).

eudokeō (also 12 : 32) 'take delight', especially of God's delight in somebody, with the connotation of favour (cp. NEB) and choice (cp. Goodspeed).

Translation: The verses link up with v. 18, not with vv. 19f, which are a kind of parenthesis. Consequently it may be necessary to use a transitional that suggests the resuming of the thread of the narrative, such as, 'it-is-told' (Javanese), "meanwhile" (Rieu), 'now'. For the same reason one may have to add a reference to the agent of the baptizing, where necessary shifting to active forms, e.g. 'at the time that all the people were baptized by John, Jesus was baptized also. Now, when Jesus was praying (afterwards), the heaven...'. Where a co-ordinating sentence structure is preferable one may say e.g., 'It is told further, Jesus received baptism/was baptized with all other people (or, John had baptized all the people and Jesus also). After that he (or, Jesus) was praying. At that very moment...' (cp. Chinese, Kituba).

All the people, where necessary qualified, e.g. 'all those people', 'all people there (or, which came to him)', 'all those present'.

The heaven was opened, intransitive, cp. "heaven opened" (NEB), or, 'the door of heaven opened' (Chuj for Acts 7 : 56, in which language a literal rendering would merely indicate a clearing away of the clouds).

(V. 22) *Descended upon him,* or, 'alighted upon him', as said of birds, 'came down. . . on top of his head' (Sranan).

Him. In some languages the use of a pronoun in referring to a person to whom reverence is due sounds impolite, vulgar, or is simply unidiomatic. Then one may have to substitute the name, or a title, such as 'the Lord' (which the Greek often employs of Jesus, e.g. in 7 : 13, cp. also on 1 : 6), or use some other device, such as a verbal form with implicit subject, or with a pronominal suffix (which in some languages is acceptable where the free form of the pronoun is not). Cp. also above on 1 : 8.

In bodily form, as a dove. Possible alternatives are, 'having-form like the body of a dove' (East Toradja), or, since the bodily form may be taken to be implied in the comparison, 'its shape like (that of) a dove', 'in the form of a dove' (Hindi, similarly Balinese), 'appearing to-have-a-form as a dove' (Javanese), 'looking like a dove', 'just like a dove'. When using the last mentioned rendering one should take care that the phrase does not qualify the process but the agent. — *Dove,* see above on 2 : 24; here probably symbolizing purity, innocence, peace.

A voice came from heaven, see *TH-Mk* on 1 : 10, and cp. 'there-was/ happened a voice from on-high' (Toba Batak), 'they heard a voice which originated in heaven' (Manobo), 'there-was a saying-in the ether' (Balinese, using an idiomatic phrase for a message of supernatural origin), 'someone called/spoke from heaven'.

Thou art my beloved son, with thee I am well pleased. In some honorific languages (e.g. Hindi, Marathi) the terms used, especially the pronouns, are the intimate, non-honorific ones that any father, royal or other, would use to his son, but others (e.g. Balinese) model their use of honorifics on the case of a royal father addressing his son in public. *My beloved son,* preferably, 'my son, the beloved (one)', as in 'my Son, the Chosen' in 9 : 35. For *beloved,* or, '(the one) whom I love', see on 6 : 27. In Kapauku the best rendering turned out to be 'own', which carries the meaning of especially one's own and beloved. For *well pleased* see *TH-Mk* on 1 : 11; Nida, *GWIML,* 127.

23 ***Jesus, when he began his ministry, was about thirty years of age, being the son (as was supposed) of Joseph, the son of Heli,***
24 ***the son of Matthat . . .*** 38 ***the son of Enos, the son of Seth, the son of Adam, the son of God.***

Exegesis: *archomenos* 'when beginning'. No object stated but to be supplied from what follows in ch. 4, viz. his service.

ēn. . .hōsei etōn triakonta 'was about thirty years (old)'. The main clause, to which is attached the long genealogy in the form of a participial clause, cp. next note.

hōsei with numbers 'about', 'approximately'.

ōn huios, hōs enomizeto, Iōsēph 'being the son, as was supposed, of

Joseph'. The participial clause introduces the subsequent genealogy. *hōs enomizeto* has no logical subject but a subject like 'people' may be supplied if necessary. *nomizō*, cp. on 2 : 44.

Vv. 23^b-38 present a genealogy of Jesus in the form of a series of genitives successively dependent upon one another. For a discussion of the theological and historical problems involved in these names the reader is referred to the commentaries. For translational purposes it will be sufficient to list the names in their Greek and Hebrew form. For the Greek form the text of *GNT* is followed. Variant spellings in the Greek are mentioned only when they have influenced the transliteration in English. For the Hebrew the spelling given by A-G is followed and the transliteration used in *Old Testament Translation Problems* is adopted. Latin transliterations are given only when they have influenced the transliteration in modern languages. Column 5 lists (a) the passages where the persons named in Luke are first mentioned in the Old Testament, and (b) the passages containing the name in question but referring to another person than the one meant in Lk. 3; category (b) is given in brackets.

	Greek	*Variant Gr.*	*Hebrew*	*Vulgate*	*Comp. in O.T.*
23	Iōsēph	—	yōsēp		(Gen. 30 : 24 etc.)
	Ēli		‘ēli(y)	Heli	(1 Sam. 1 : 9)
24	Matthat		mattat		
	Leui		lēwi(y)	Levi	(Gen. 29 : 34)
	Melchi		malki(y)		
	Iannai		—		
	Iōsēph (cp. 23^1)				
25	Mattathias		mattitya(h)		(Ezra 10 : 43)
	Amōs		‘amōs		(Am. 1 : 1)
	Naoum		naḥum	Nahum	(Nahum 1 : 1)
	Hesli		—		
	Naggai		—		
26	Maath		maḥat (?)		(1 Chr. 6 : 35)
	Mattathias = 25^1				
	Semeïn		šim‘i(y)	Semei	(1 K. 2 : 44)
	Iōsēch		—	Ioseph (!)	
	Iōda		—	Juda	
27	Iōanan		yōḥānān	Joanna	(1 Chr. 3 : 15; Jer. 40 : 13)
	Rēsa		—		
	Zorobabel		zerubbabel	= G	} Ezra 3 : 2 etc.
	Salathiēl		š^e'althī'ēl	= G	
	Nēri		nēr		(1 Sam. 14 : 50)
28	Melchi = 24^3				
	Addi		—		
	Kōsam		qāsam		
	Elmadam	Elmōdam	—		
	Ēr		‘er		(Gen. 38 : 3)

	Greek	*Variant Gr.*	*Hebrew*	*Vulgate*	*Comp. in O.T.*
29	Iēsous		yēšua‘/ y^{e}hōšua‘		(Ex. 17 : 9; Josh. 1 : 1 etc.)
	Eliezer		’ĕlī‘ezer		(Gen. 15 : 2)
	Iōrim		—		
	Matthat = 24^1	Maththat	mattat		
	Leui = 24^2				
30	Sumeōn		šim‘ōn		(Gen. 29 : 33 etc.)
	Iouda(s)		y^{e}hudah		(Gen. 29 : 35 etc.)
	Iōsēph = 23^1				
	Iōnam	Iōnan	—		
	Eliakim		’elyāqīm		(2 K. 18 : 18; Isa. 37 : 2)
31	Melea		—		
	Menna	Mainan	—		
	Mattatha		mattata(h)		(Ezra 10 : 33)
	Natham	Nathan	nātān	Nathan	2 Sam. 5 : 14
	Dauid		dawīd	David	1 Sam. 17 : 22 etc.
32	Iessai		yišay	Jesse	
	Iōbēd	Ōbēd	yōbēd	Obed	}
	Boos	Booz	bō‘az		}
	Sala	Salmōn	šelaḥ/šalmōn		}
	Naassōn		naḥšōn		} Ruth 4 : 18-22,
33	Aminadab		‘amīnādāb		} 1 Chr. 2 : 5-15
	Admin (cp. app. cr.)	Aram or omitted	—		}
	Arni	Aram			}
	Hesrōm		ḥeṣrōn		}
	Phares		pereṣ		ib., and Gen. 38 : 29
	Iouda = 30^2				Gen. 29 : 35 etc.
34	Iakōb		ya‘aqōb		Gen. 25 : 26 etc.
	Isaak		yiṣḥāq		Gen. 21 : 3 etc.
	Abraam		’abrāhām	Abraham	Gen. 17 : 5 etc.
	Thara		teraḥ		}
	Nachōr		nāḥōr		}
35	Serouch		ś^{e}rūg		}
	Ragau		r^e‘ū		} Gen. 11 : 13-26
	Phalek	Phaleg	peleg		}
	Eber		—		}
	Sala = 32^4				}
36	Kaïnam = 37^5				
	Arphaxad		’arpakšad		} Gen. 11 : 10-13
	Sēm		šem		}

	Greek	*Variant Gr.*	*Hebrew*	*Vulgate*	*Comp. in O.T.*
	Nōe		noaḥ		Gen. 5 : 1-32
	Lamech		lemek/lamek		
37	Mathousala		m^etūšelaḥ		
	Henōch		ḥ^enōk		
	Iaret	Iared	yered/yared		
	Maleleēl		mahalal^e'ēl		
	Kaïnam	Kainan	qē(y)nān		
38	Enōs		'ěnōs		
	Seth		šet		
	Adam		'ādām		

Translation: *Jesus, when he began... was...*, or, 'When Jesus began... he was...', or, 'Jesus was... when he began...'.

When he began his ministry, or, 'his work', 'his teaching', 'to preach (lit. to transmit the way, Chinese UV, L)', 'to act-as-*guru*' (East Toradja). Some languages possess an expression for a person's (first) appearance in a certain role, which requires no further qualification, e.g. 'raised his head' (Chinese BT), 'made-his-appearance' (Dutch, Zürich), cp. also *lors de ses débuts* (Jerusalem).

Jesus... was about thirty years of age, or, 'Jesus'/his age was about thirty (years)', 'Jesus/he was about thirty years old'. See also 2 : 42.

The position of *as was supposed*, or, 'as people saw it (i.e. according to people)' (Chinese UV), must be such that it qualifies the relationship between Jesus and Joseph only, and does not suggest a supposed son, or even a supposed Joseph (as has been the case in one older version); in many cases the phrase is better placed at the head of the sentence, e.g. 'people thought he was the child of Joseph' (Manobo). For the verb *to suppose* see on 2 : 44. — Several versions make some kind of incision after Joseph, e.g. 'people regarded him as the son of Joseph. Joseph (was) Heli's, he (was) Matthat's... Adam's, he (was) God's son' (Marathi), cp. also Javanese, quoted below.

The long series of proper names in vv. 23-38, connected with each other by the simple device of the genitive case, may have to be rendered less concisely, e.g. by appositional phrases, or relative clauses, of the type of, '(who was) the son/child of', in some cases even duplicating the names, e.g. 'Joseph, he the son of Heli, Heli, he the son of...' (Manobo). In honorific languages a high level honorific equivalent of 'son' may have to be used in the very last phrase, 'son of God' (e.g. in Balinese). Some versions have made a successful attempt to express the structure of the original by other means than genitives, cp. e.g. "Joseph whose line went back through Eli, Matthat,... to Adam, the son of God" (Rieu), '...was reckoned the son of Joseph, whose coming-forth (was) from H., from M., ..., from Adam, from Allah' (Javanese).

For general remarks on transliteration of proper names see above on the name "Luke" (pp. 3f), and references. The proper names in these verses present an additional problem in that most of them are themselves transliterations of Hebrew originals, cp. categories (a) and (b), as given in

Exegesis. In the case of the names in category (a) it is clear that Luke wants to refer his readers to persons known from the Old Testament; hence it may be supposed that he intended to reproduce their Hebrew names as faithfully as the Greek permitted him to do. Consequently one should not transliterate the Greek forms of the names in question (as several older and some new versions do), but their Hebrew models. (For a comparable case see above on Gr. *Kurēnios*—Latin 'Quirinius' in 2 : 2). In practice this means that the translator, by treating these names as they are treated in the Old Testament (or will presumably be treated when a translation of the O.T. passages concerned is made in the future) best fulfils Luke's purpose, viz. to help his readers to identify the Old Testament persons referred to. Names of category (b) can best be treated in analogy with (a). The remaining 14 names (probably transliterations also, but without known O.T. origin) should be treated as other New Testament names.

CHAPTER FOUR

1 ***And Jesus, full of the Holy Spirit, returned from the Jordan, and was led by the Spirit*** 2a ***for forty days in the wilderness, tempted by the devil.***

Exegesis: *Iēsous de* 'and Jesus' refers back to 3 : 21f after the genealogy of 3 : 23-38, as is shown by what follows, see below.

plērēs pneumatos hagiou 'full of the Holy Spirit', qualifies *Iēsous*. The omission of the article *tou* before *pneumatos* does not change the meaning of the phrase, cp. on 1 : 15. Here the Holy Spirit referred to is the Spirit who had descended upon Jesus after his baptism, cp. 3 : 22.

plērēs (also 5 : 12) 'full' (cp. also Acts 6 : 3; 7 : 55; 11 : 24). As contrasted with 'filled with the Holy Spirit' in 1 : 41, 67 the phrase 'full of the Holy Spirit' refers to a permanent condition, not a momentary experience.

hupestrepsen apo tou Iordanou 'returned from the Jordan', i.e. from the place where the events of 3 : 21f had taken place. It is not indicated whither he returned but the best assumption is to connect this clause with v. 14: Jesus left the place of his baptism in order to return to Galilee where he had come from (cp. Mk. 1 : 9), but on his way home he remained for 40 days in the wilderness.

kai ēgeto en tō pneumati en tē erēmō 'and he was led about in the Spirit in the wilderness'. The imperfect tense of *ēgeto* is durative. For *en tō pneumati* cp. on 2 : 27. The phrase does not mean that the Spirit is the agent (as it is viewed in Mk. 1 : 12) but rather the guiding principle or the instrument.

agō 'to lead', here in the passive, meaning 'to be led about': Jesus went, guided by the Holy Spirit, from place to place in the wilderness.

(V. 2[a]) *hēmeras tessarakonta* 'for forty days', goes either with *ēgeto* or with the subsequent *peirazomenos* 'being tempted', preferably with the former.

peirazomenos hupo tou diabolou 'being tempted by the devil'. *peirazomenos* is coextensive with *ēgeto* and the phrase refers to temptations preceding those described in vv. 4-13.

peirazō (also 11 : 16) 'to put to the test', 'to tempt', passive 'to be tested', here with hostile intent, cp. Richardson, *Word Book*, 253.

diabolos lit. 'the slanderer', cp. *N.T.Wb.*, 43/.

Translation: *Jesus, full of the Holy Spirit*, or, better to bring out the connexion with 3 : 22, 'full of the H. Sp. as he was now, Jesus', similarly but in co-ordinated sentences in Sranan; or, 'after Jesus had (thus) become full of the H. Sp. he'. For *full of the Holy Spirit* cp. on "filled with the H. Sp." in 1 : 15, where tense and aspect, however, are different.

Returned from the Jordan may require two verbs, 'left the J. and went back' (cp. Kituba, Sranan). *Jordan*, or, 'the bank/region of the (river) J.'.

And was led... If it is preferable to start a new sentence here, the existing relationship with what precedes (as indicated in *Exegesis*) may require the use of a transitional phrase such as e.g., 'As he went home he was led...'.

(He) *was led by the Spirit for...in...*, or, more explicitly, 'he was led about by the Spirit for...in...' (cp. Zürich, Jerusalem), 'he went about (or, he stayed) for...in...with the Spirit as his guide, or, and the Spirit guided him'.

(V. 2a) *For forty days*, or, 'during (a period of) forty days'. The phrase qualifies the verb 'was led', but indirectly also 'tempted', cp. "for forty days was led...and tempted..." (NEB). Even a rather small number like 40 may have to be expressed analytically, resulting in such a cumbersome phrase as, 'the number of a complete hand, the number of a complete foot, and the number of a complete hand, the number of a complete foot, such a number of days' (Auca, which, using hands and feet morphemes for 'five' and above, can count to 20 and in multiples of 10 or 20) (cp. Beekman, *NOT*, 50f).

Wilderness, see *N.T.Wb./*25, DESERT.

Tempted by the devil, or expressing the connexion more explicitly, 'during which days (or, where) he was tempted by the devil' (or, an active construction); the clause is sometimes better rendered as a co-ordinated one. For *to tempt*, i.e. 'to try to make a person sin', cp. *TH-Mk* on 1 : 13. For *the devil* cp. *N.T.Wb./*26; Nida, *BT*, 215f; *TBT*, 18.190f, 1967. Some versions use indigenous specific names, 'the avaricious one' (Tetelcingo Aztec), 'the malicious deity' (South Toradja); others have borrowed the name *Satan*, for which see on 10 : 18.

2b ***And he ate nothing in those days; and when they were ended, he was hungry.***

Exegesis: *kai ouk ephagen ouden* 'and he ate nothing'. The double negation *ouk...ouden* strengthens the negative aspect of the clause, cp. Bl-D, § 431.2. The aorist *ephagen* 'he ate' is probably used because the continued action is viewed as having reached its end, cp. Bl-D, § 332.

suntelestheisōn autōn 'when they had come to an end', absolute genitive; *autōn* refers to 'those days' in the preceding clause.

sunteleō (also v. 13) 'to bring to an end', here in the passive 'to be brought to an end', 'to be over', rather than 'to be completed'.

epeinasen 'he was hungry'. The aorist is ingressive: only after the 40 days of fasting did Jesus really feel that he was hungry.

Translation: *He*, or, 'Jesus', cp. on 1 : 8.

In those days, or, "all that time" (NEB), 'during that whole-period' (Balinese).

When they were ended, or, 'at the end of those days (or, of that time, of it)', or simply, "afterwards" (Phillips, similarly Sranan).

He was hungry, cp. on 1 : 53. Some idiomatic ways of expressing this phrase are, 'hunger killed him' (Sranan), 'he wanted to-begin-to eat' (Ponape).

3 ***The devil said to him, "If you are the Son of God, command this stone to become bread."***

Exegesis: *eipen de autō ho diabolos* 'the devil said to him'. *de* is connective and the clause implies that the devil had been present during the preceding 40 days.

ei huios ei tou theou 'if you are the Son of God', a supposition, not a recognition. The clause does not imply doubt concerning Jesus being the Son of God but a challenge to Jesus to prove that he really is the Son of God (cp. *TBT*, 13.223f, 1962). *huios* is separated from its complement *tou theou* by *ei*; this serves to emphasize *huios* as expression of the relationship between Jesus and God (cp. Plummer).

eipe tō lithō toutō hina genētai artos 'tell this stone to become bread'. *eipe* means here 'command', 'order' (cp. A-G s.v. 3 c). *tō lithō toutō* 'this stone', as if pointed at by finger (cp. Willibrord, 'that stone there'), because no previous identification of the stone occurs.

hina genētai artos lit. 'that he become bread', but *hina* has lost its final meaning and the construction substitutes an infinitive that supplements a verb meaning 'to order', cp. A-G s.v. *hina* II 1 a δ.

artos 'bread', 'loaf of bread', 'food'.

Translation: This dialogue between Jesus and the devil poses a problem for a translator in honorific languages, since he cannot find a model in the social scene. It is to be understood, therefore, that the solutions chosen may differ. In some languages both Jesus and the devil use honorifics, which suggests a certain recognition of each other's position; conversely in Shona honorifics are deliberately not used in this dialogue. Elsewhere the devil is represented as holding a decidedly lower rank than Jesus has, e.g. in Sinhalese, Marathi, Balinese, Javanese. In the last mentioned language the devil uses middle-class honorifics, expressing politeness but not reverence, as people do in ordinary life when addressing a stranger whose rank is unknown. In some cases existing myths or tales can be found that describe comparable situations. The translator should certainly study such material, but the chances are that the model which emerges from it may be unacceptable from the Christian point of view.

If you are, or, emphasizing the challenge, 'if it is a fact that you are'; or, if a conditional clause would be too strongly dubitative, 'you say that you are'.

The verb *to command* (also in 4:36; 5:14; 8:25, 29, 31; 9:21; 14:22; 17:9f; 18:40; 19:15) may have to be rendered analytically, using indirect or direct discourse, e.g. 'tell this stone to become (or, that it must become) bread', or, 'tell this stone, "Become bread"' (Marathi).

Become bread, or, 'change into bread' (cp. Goodspeed, Jerusalem, Trukese), or, 'become (or, change into) a loaf' (cp. Rieu, Ponape). For the rendering of *bread*, or, 'loaf (of bread)', by a generic term, e.g. 'food', 'lump/piece of food', or by the term for a local equivalent, cp. Nida, *BT*, 168; *N.T.Wb.*/38, FOOD; *TBT*, 18.82, 1967.

4 ***And Jesus answered him, "It is written, 'Man shall not live by bread alone.'"***

Exegesis: *gegraptai hoti* 'it is written (that)', introduces a quotation from the Old Testament, cp. on 3 : 4.

ouk ep' artō monō zēsetai ho anthrōpos 'not on bread alone shall man live', i.e. there are other things which are as important as bread for man. In the light of Jn. 4 : 34 it seems probable that Jesus here implicitly refers to obedience to God as being as important for man's life as bread. In *ep' artō monō* 'on bread alone', *epi* with dative indicates that on which life is based, cp. A-G s.v. *epi* II 1 b γ.

zēsetai 'shall live', has the force of a command, cp. Bl-D, § 362.

ho anthrōpos 'man', in English without article as a categorical indication; in other western languages the definite article is required in this meaning. The phrase is an implicit reply to the supposition of the devil 'if you are the Son of God': Jesus declines the challenge to prove that he is the Son of God but ranks himself with man. This is no denial of his sonship as such but a refusal to use its prerogatives in order to satisfy his human needs.

Translation: *It is written,* cp. on 2 : 23. A reference to the book may be required here, cp. 'in the Book of God it says' (South Toradja), 'it is written in the Scripture' (Marathi).

Man shall not live by (or, on) *bread alone.* The sentence structure often has to be recast, cp. 'man's life is not by-means-of bread only' (Javanese), 'bread alone cannot make people live' (Sranan), 'it is not just bread that people live by' (Ponape, similarly East Toradja), 'as though food (lit. what-is-eaten) only the life of man!' (Toba Batak). For *alone,* or, 'without anything else than', cp. *N.T.Wb./7*.

5 ***And the devil took him up, and showed him all the kingdoms of the world in a moment of time,***

Exegesis: *kai anagagōn auton* 'and after leading him up'. Subject is *ho diabolos*. For *anagō* cp. on 2 : 22. Commentators differ as to the nature of the event described in this phrase and the next. Some understand it as an inward imaginative, or, visionary experience (cp. Manson, Creed) or as an experience in thought (cp. Plummer) but others think of a real lifting up into the air (cp. Maclean Gilmour) or to some high place (cp. Grundmann, Klostermann). As Acts 8 : 39 shows for Luke (and his readers) such events are real and not experiences in mind or thought only. The same applies to vv. 9-12. Since *anagō* usually means 'to bring to a high place' and not 'to lift up in the air' it appears preferable to understand it here in that sense too.

edeixen autō pasas tas basileias tēs oikoumenēs 'he showed him all the kingdoms of the world'. For *basileia* cp. on 1 : 33; here in the local meaning of 'kingdom'; for *oikoumenē* cp. on 2 : 1; here in the literal meaning of 'the inhabited earth' and not restricted to the Roman empire.

deiknumi 'to point out', 'to show', 'to explain'.
en stigmē chronou 'in a moment of time'.
stigmē (††) 'prick', 'point', metaphorically of time 'moment', 'instant'.

Translation: *Took him up*, i.e. took him with him (or, led him) to a high place. For an honorific problem in the rendering of this phrase see *TBT*, 14.164, 1963.

Showed him, or, 'caused/gave him to see', 'pointed out to him'.

Kingdoms, i.e. regions ruled by a king (cp. on 1 : 33), but since the reference is rather to the locality than to the government such renderings as, 'countries', 'districts' (Ponape), 'dominions' (Balinese), are also acceptable.

World, or, 'earth'. That the reference is to the inhabited world (see *Exegesis*), need not be specified when the context implies a reference to human habitation, as does "kingdoms" here, or to human beings, as is the case in 21 : 26.

In a moment of time, or, 'in a very short time', "in a flash" (NEB).

6 ***and said to him, "To you I will give all this authority and their glory; for it has been delivered to me, and I give it to whom I will.***

Exegesis: *kai eipen autō ho diabolos* 'and the devil said to him'. The subject *ho diabolos* is also the subject to the preceding clause (where it is not mentioned). This tends to characterize v. 6 as the event to which v. 5 leads up.

soi dōsō tēn exousian tautēn hapasan 'to you I will give all this power'. *soi* is emphatic. *dōsō* 'I will give' does not mean unconditional giving as v. 7 shows.

exousia 'power', 'authority', in a concrete sense 'ruling power', or, 'domain in which the power is exercised'. As the demonstrative pronoun *tautēn* refers to 'the kingdoms of the world' of v. 5, *exousia* must mean here either 'the power, or, rule over these kingdoms', or, 'this domain'. The latter interpretation is preferable, cp. A-G s.v. 4 b.

kai tēn doxan autōn 'and their glory'. *autōn* refers back to 'the kingdoms', implied in *exousian* 'domain', which is in the singular.

hoti emoi paradedotai 'for to me it has been delivered'. *emoi* is emphatic. For *paradidōmi* cp. on 1 : 2; here it is used in a neutral sense without the implication of trust or right. Subject of *paradedotai* is *exousia*.

kai hō ean thelō didōmi autēn 'and to anyone I please I give it'. *hō ean thelō* scil. *didonai* 'to anyone I please to give (it)', conditional-relative clause (cp. Bl-D, § 380), stressing the assumption on the part of the devil that it is his privilege, and his only, to give away the power he holds.

didōmi means here 'I can give' or 'I am in a position to give', synonymous with *paradidōmi*.

Translation: *To you I will give all this authority and their glory*, or, following the interpretation preferred in *Exegesis*, 'all this domain (or, land to rule over) and their glory'. This incongruous use of the pronouns is unacceptable in many languages; hence,'and the glory of the kingdoms in it', or, 'and its glory'. The other possible meaning of Gr. *exousia* will result in something like, 'give you the authority over (or, the right to rule) all this (land) and (to possess) its glory (or, the glory of the kingdoms of it)'. The verb *to give* (or a synonym of it) may have to be repeated before the second object. The usual rendering of *glory* (for which see on 2 : 9) may not fit here, because the context is uncommon. Several of these points, and some further adjustments, are illustrated in the following quotations, 'I will give-you that you-will be-in-charge-of all these things, and I-will also give you their-beauty' (Trukese), 'you are the one I-will-cause-to-hold this, and included completely everything in it that always satisfies the breath of man (an expression covering fame, wealth, pleasures)' (Tagabili), 'I-will-give-you you-will-possess and I-will-give-you you-will-enjoy-its-goodness all this' (Tzeltal), '. . . the ruling of all this kingdom and its fame' (Shona).

It has been delivered to me, or, 'handed over to me', 'given to me' (East Toradja, same verb as used in the next clause); or in active construction, 'I have received it in my hands' (Sranan), 'it is in my possession'.

I give it to whom I will, or, 'to whom I want to give it, I am able to give it' (Tzeltal, similarly Cuyono), 'it is my pleasure now to cause-to-hold-it the person I choose' (Tagabili), 'if I want to give it to a person, I (can) do so'.

7 ***If you, then, will worship me, it shall all be yours."***

Exegesis: *su oun ean proskunēsēs enōpion emou* 'if you, then, will worship me'. *su* at the beginning of the clause before the conjunction *ean* again is emphatic. *oun* indicates that the clause draws an inference from what precedes. This inference is that the devil is in a position to dictate the terms on which he is willing to do what he promised in v. 6, 'to you I will give all this power'.

proskuneō lit. 'to prostrate oneself', hence 'to worship', usually with dative (cp. Mt. 4 : 9) or accusative (as in v. 8), here with *enōpion* with genitive (for which cp. on 1 : 15), which sounds somewhat more solemn than v. 8.

estai sou pasa 'it will all be yours'; subject is *exousia* understood. *sou* lit. 'of you' is predicate. *pasa*, grammatically going with the subject understood, modifies the predicate: it will be yours in its completeness, i.e. you will possess it completely.

Translation: *You will worship me* and *you shall worship the Lord* (v. 8). If the receptor language provides possibilities of variation, two expressions should be chosen that have virtually the same meaning but a slightly different form. In several cases, however, such differentiation would result in a rendering of the first phrase that is unidiomatic rather than solemn, or changes the connexion between action and goal, e.g. by making it too indirect (as in "you will worship before me", Moffatt), or is formally much more dissimilar than the two phrases are in the original. In such cases it is preferable to neglect the formal difference (cp. RSV, NEB and many other versions). For *worship* see *N.T.Wb.*/75; *TBT*, 5.92, 1954, Nida, *GWIML*, 24, 163. In several languages of Indonesia the term used refers to the gesture of worship or homage that is traditional in that region, viz., the hands with fingertips raised to the chin or higher while the body is in a bowing, squatting or kneeling position. Another interesting rendering is, 'to remember as holy' (Chontal of Tabasco).

It shall all be yours, or, 'it shall belong to you completely' (Jerusalem), 'all this shall be your property/possession/part', 'all this, you shall be its master' (South Toradja).

8 ***And Jesus answered him, "It is written,***
'You shall worship the Lord your God,
and him only shall you serve.'"

Exegesis: *kai apokritheis... eipen autō* 'and answering (he) said', cp. on 1 : 19.

gegraptai 'it is written', cp. on v. 4.

kurion ton theon sou proskunēseis 'you shall worship the Lord your God'. For *proskuneō* cp. on v. 7, for *kurion ton theon sou* cp. on 1 : 16.

kai autō monō latreuseis 'and you shall serve him alone'. For *latreuō* cp. on 1 : 74; with *proskuneō* it has in common that both refer to God as the one who is worshipped but *proskuneō* appears to imply a greater reverence for God than *latreuō* which is a more general term. *monō* 'alone' goes with *autō*.

Translation: *Worship* and *serve* are close synonyms in this context, cp. "do homage and worship" (NEB). In languages where the same word or phrase does duty for both verbs it may be preferable to mark the emphasizing function of the repetition, e.g. 'yes/indeed, him only shall you worship/serve'. For *to serve* see on 1 : 74.

For *the Lord your God* cp. on 1 : 16.

Only, or, 'and no one else', cp. *N.T.Wb.*/7, ALONE.

9 ***And he took him to Jerusalem, and set him on the pinnacle of the temple, and said to him, "If you are the Son of God, throw yourself down from here;***

Exegesis: *ēgagen de auton eis Ierousalēm* 'and he led him to Jerusalem'; subject again *ho diabolos* 'the devil'. For the character of the event described in this clause cp. on v. 5. For *Ierousalēm* cp. on 2 : 22.

estēsen epi to pterugion tou hierou 'he made him stand on the pinnacle of the temple'; object is *auton* understood from the preceding clause.

histēmi 'to set', 'to place', cp. A-G s.v. I 1 a α.

pterugion (†) lit. 'little wing', denotes "the tip or extremity of anything" (A-G s.v.), horizontal or vertical. As no 'little wing' of the temple is mentioned elsewhere the exact reference of the word is impossible to ascertain. For the translator's choice two considerations may be determining, viz. (1) that *to hieron* refers to the temple as a whole and not to the central building only, and (2) that *to pterugion* because of the article refers to something which was generally known and, as shown by the use of the word elsewhere (cp. L-Sc, s.v.), has a concrete meaning.

ei huios ei tou theou 'if you are the Son of God', cp. on v. 3.

bale seauton enteuthen katō 'throw yourself down from here'.

enteuthen (also 13 : 31) 'from here'.

katō (†) 'downwards'.

Translation: *He took him.* It may be preferable to specify one or both of the pronouns.

And set him, or, 'placed/put him', 'made him stand'.

Pinnacle. So long as it is not clear which specific part of the temple is meant it seems the wisest solution to use a generic rendering, e.g. "summit" (Goodspeed), 'top part' (Marathi), 'highest beam/pole/ridge/stone'. There is no serious loss of information then, since it is height rather than architectural detail that is important in this context.

Throw yourself down, or, 'cause-to-fall yourself (downwards)' (Trukese, some Indonesian languages), 'jump...downwards' (Ponape, Javanese).

10 ***for it is written,***
'He will give his angels charge of you, to guard you,'
11 ***and***
'On their hands they will bear you up,
lest you strike your foot against a stone.'"

Exegesis: *gegraptai gar* 'for it is written', cp. on v. 4. This time the quotation from the Old Testament comes from the devil in order to found the suggestion of v. 9.

tois aggelois autou enteleitai peri sou 'he will give his angels orders about you'. Subject of *enteleitai* is *ho kurios* 'the Lord' understood. The double reference to the person concerned, viz. *peri sou* and *se,* the object of *diaphulaxai* (cp. next note), is unidiomatic in Greek. This is due to the fact that the clause is a rather literal rendering of the Hebrew of Ps. 91 : 11, which is perfectly idiomatic in Hebrew.

entellomai (†) 'to command', 'to give orders'.

tou diaphulaxai se 'in order to guard you', independent articular infinitive with final force, cp. Bl-D, § 400 (5).

diaphulassō (††) 'to guard', in the Septuagint especially of God's care for man. Here the reference is rather to protection from danger.

(V. 11) *kai hoti* 'and' connects the second part of the quotation with the first, probably because the phrase 'on all your ways' is omitted in the quotation.

epi cheirōn arousin se 'on their hands they will bear you up'. Subject is *hoi aggeloi* 'the angels' understood from v. 10.

airō 'to lift up', 'to bear up', 'to carry along' as a continuation of bearing up. Different from Ps. 91 : 11f, the picture is here that of the angels lifting up somebody who throws himself down.

mēpote proskopsēs pros lithon ton poda sou 'lest you strike your foot against a stone'. This clause also applies only indirectly to the present situation, see above.

mēpote 'lest', emphatic form of *mē*, cp. A-G s.v. 2 b α, here in the sense of 'in order to prevent that'.

proskoptō (†) 'to strike'.

Translation: *Give his angels charge of you, to guard you.* Some renderings are more analytic, e.g. 'say to/command his angels, "Guard him/this man"', others more synthetic, e.g. 'cause-to-take-care-with-reference-to his angels you', i.e. cause his angels to take care of you (Ponape). For *to guard*, or, "to keep from harm" (Rieu), cp. *N.T.Wb.*/49, KEEP. — *You* here refers to man in general (as is clearly intended in the Psalm word quoted), not to the Messiah (as assumed in some versions). The repetition of this pronoun, is a literalism which should not be imitated at the cost of receptor language idiom.

(V. 11) The metaphorical meaning of the expressions used may have to be marked, e.g. by adding 'as it were', 'it will be as if'.

You strike your foot against a stone, or, 'stumble-over a stone' (Balinese); elsewhere 'the/your foot' has to become the subject of the clause.

12 ***And Jesus answered him, "It is said, 'You shall not tempt the Lord your God.'"***

Exegesis: *eirētai* 'it is said', introducing an Old Testament quotation like *gegraptai* in vv. 4, 8, 10; cp. also *to eirēmenon* in 2 : 24. There is no reason to differentiate between *gegraptai* and *eirētai* in this passage as is shown by the fact that all Old Testament quotations in this section are from the same book, viz. Deuteronomy and serve the same purpose.

ouk ekpeiraseis kurion ton theon sou 'you shall not put the Lord your God to the test'.

ekpeirazō (also 10 : 25) 'to put to the test', 'to tempt', 'to challenge' by doing something which one knows to be not the will of God.

Translation: *It is said* instead of "it is written" (vv. 4, 8, 10). If closely synonymous phrases are available (e.g. 'the Book says—Scripture says', or 'the Book says—the Book has it'), they should be used, of course; if not, one should neglect the variation. It is not advisable to use renderings that indicate an intentional difference between the two phrases, such as 'God says—Scripture has it', or, 'there is a word of God—there is written', suggesting that, whereas the devil appeals to the written word, Jesus appeals to the authority behind it.

To tempt...God. Translators often have tried their utmost to find a term that can cover the situation of v. 2[a] as well as the one in this verse. This is unnecessary, as even the Greek uses different (though cognate) verbs, and unadvisable, since the situations differ. Some renderings used here are, 'to push/urge-into-action God' (Lokele), 'to push God to do what you want' (Huanuco Quechua), 'to ask power of God without need' (Kekchi), 'to presume (i.e. go too far) in the presence of God' (Tzeltal, an idiomatic expression used of someone exceeding his rights).

13 ***And when the devil had ended every temptation, he departed from him until an opportune time.***

Exegesis: *suntelesas panta peirasmon* 'having brought to an end every (i.e. every kind of) temptation'. For *sunteleō* cp. on v. 2; it is best rendered in a neutral sense without implications of completing a prearranged plan.

peirasmos 'temptation', here in the active sense, 'tempting' (cp. A-G s.v. 2 a).

achri kairou lit. 'until a moment of time' is interpreted variously: (1) 'until a certain time', i.e. "for a while" (A-G s.v. 1), "for a time" (Kingsley Williams); (2) "until an opportune time" (RSV, Segond), i.e. "till a fit opportunity arrived" (Moffatt); (3) 'until a fixed time', i.e. "until the appointed time" (BFBS, NV, Willibrord, Jerusalem). The first interpretation seems preferable (cp. Acts 13 : 11).

Translation: *When the devil had ended every temptation.* In some cases it is necessary to add a reference to the actor or/and the goal of the tempting, e.g. 'all the temptations against him' (Bahasa Indonesia), 'all the temptations with which he tempted him' (Sranan), 'the devil's tricks to seduce Jesus' (East Toradja 1933). A shift to a verbal construction leads to a rendering such as, 'after the devil had tempted him/Jesus in every way'; and the conative aspect may better be made explicit as in, "when the devil had tried every kind of temptation" (Goodspeed), 'then the devil gave up all his attempts at seducing Him' (Willibrord).

Until an opportune time, or, following the interpretation preferred in *Exegesis,* "till another time" (Goodspeed, similarly Kituba), 'for the time being' (Leyden, East Toradja 1933), or, in a more expanded wording, 'he (i.e. the devil) said to himself, "There will be another day yet for that"' (Tagabili).

14 ***And Jesus returned in the power of the Spirit into Galilee, and a report concerning him went out through all the surrounding country.***

Exegesis: *kai hupestrepsen ho Iēsous en tē dunamei tou pneumatos eis tēn Galilaian* 'and Jesus returned in the power of the Spirit to Galilee'. This clause takes up and complements the first clause of v. 1, which see. Only in a secondary sense it says that Jesus returned from the place of his temptations. *en tē dunamei tou pneumatos* parallels *plērēs tou pneumatos* 'full of the Spirit' in v. 1. Both refer back to 3 : 22 and there is no reason to assume that the phrase means that Jesus was strengthened by the victory he had just won over the devil. The difference between *plērēs tou pneumatos* and *en tē dunamei tou pneumatos* is that the former refers to the state in which Jesus was after receiving the Spirit and that the latter brings out that the Spirit determines his actions. For the idiom cp. on 1 : 17 and 2 : 27.

kai phēmē exēlthen...peri autou 'and news about him went out', or 'news went out about him'. The former translation takes *peri autou* with *phēmē* 'news about him', the latter with the whole clause. Both are possible but the latter is preferable because of the place of *peri autou* at the end.

phēmē (†) 'report', 'news' as clearly in Mt. 9 : 26. The word has a rather neutral meaning and translations like 'fame' are not adequate.

kath' holēs tēs perichōrou 'throughout the whole neighbourhood', cp. on 3 : 3 and *TH-Mk* on 1 : 28, where, however, the situation is different, because a specific point of activity, viz. Capernaum, is mentioned previously. This is not the case here and this implies that the choice is between (1) Galilee and surrounding regions, and (2) the neighbourhood of Galilee, i.e. Galilee itself. The former is preferable.

Translation: *And Jesus returned...into* has a continuative aspect, 'then (or, from there) Jesus continued his return journey (or, went on) to', or a resultative aspect, cp. 'then Jesus came-back in' (Jerusalem, similarly Toba Batak).

In the power of the Spirit, or, 'directed/guided by the power of the Spirit', 'the one who was empowering him was the Holy Spirit' (Cuyono); and cp. on "in the power of" in 1 : 17.

A report concerning him went out, or, 'news about him spread'; or an equivalent expression such as, 'people/everyone spoke about him'.

All the surrounding country, or, in receptor languages where the implied central point has to be made explicit, 'in that region and in all those regions which were near-it' (Ponape), 'on the-whole-of all those regions which were around-it (i.e. around Galilee)' (Trukese).

15 ***And he taught in their synagogues, being glorified by all.***

Exegesis: *kai autos edidasken* 'and he taught', iterative imperfect. *kai autos* 'and he' unemphatic as in 1 : 17, cp. Bl-D, § 277.3.

didaskō 'to teach', in Luke always of the teaching of Jesus.

en tais sunagōgais autōn 'in their synagogues'. *autōn* refers by inference to the inhabitants of Galilee.

sunagōgē lit. 'the bringing together' (from *sunagō* 'to gather'), hence the place where people are brought together, has become the technical word for the local place for worship, religious teaching and for the administration of justice among the Jews. For a detailed account cp. *IDB* IV, 476-491.

doxazomenos hupo pantōn 'being glorified by all', participial phrase describing the result of Jesus' teaching in the synagogues. For *doxazō* cp. on 2 : 20.

Translation: *He taught.* For the verb 'to teach' (also in 4 : 31f; 5 : 3, 17; 6 : 6, 40; 10 : 39; 11 : 1; 12 : 12; 13 : 10, 22, 26; 19 : 47; 20 : 1, 21; 21 : 37; 23 : 5, and cp. on "teacher" in 2 : 46) cp. *N.T.Wb.*/70f; *TH-Mk* on 2 : 13. It may be obligatory to add a reference to those taught, e.g. 'the people (there)', or to the thing taught, e.g. 'the way of God' (cp. 20 : 21). Elsewhere 'to teach' is rendered by a causative form of 'to learn'; and in some languages (e.g. Dutch, Kapauku) one verbal form is used for both activities, which may make necessary the addition of an object to avoid ambiguity, compare 'those who learn/teach people' for 'teachers' with 'those who learn/teach' for 'disciples' (Kapauku). In Auca, where the concept is expressed by juxtaposing 'to speak' and 'to hear' in a cause-result relationship, 'he teaches' must be rendered by 'he speaks (that they may) hear'. In many Indonesian languages the common word for 'teacher' (*guru*, originally a borrowing from India) can have a religious connotation which the (non-cognate) verb 'to teach' has not, or has less clearly; hence, to indicate religious teaching a derivation of the former term may be preferable, e.g. 'to act-as-*guru*' (East Toradja).

Their synagogues, or, 'the synagogues of the people there' (cp. Javanese), or shifting to a locative qualification, 'the synagogues there' (cp. Balinese). For *synagogue* (also in 4 : 20, 28, 44; 6 : 6; 7 : 5; 8 : 41; 11 : 43; 13 : 10, 14; 20 : 46; and, referring not to the place but to the congregation in it, 12 : 11; 21 : 12) see *TH-Mk* on 1 : 21, and cp. 'place to talk God's talk' (Wantoat), 'house where God is remembered' (Chontal of Tabasco). The rendering 'place-of-teaching' will do only where 'to teach' clearly refers to religious education. Some Indonesian languages use their term for 'mosque', or for a Muslim building/institution of a less official type; in some cases, however, such a rendering has been replaced in revision by a term or descriptive phrase with a less strongly Muslim connotation, e.g. 'house of prayer' (Bahasa Indonesia).

Being glorified by all, or, 'and/so that all people praised/honoured him', 'all-of-them very good what they said about him' (Tzeltal). For *to glorify* see on 2 : 20.

16 ***And he came to Nazareth, where he had been brought up; and he went to the synagogue, as his custom was, on the sabbath day. And he stood up to read;***

Exegesis: *kai ēlthen eis Nazara* 'and he came to Nazareth'. *kai* marks here the transition from general description to a specific narrative, as brought out in "so he came to Nazareth" (NEB, cp. also Phillips, Schonfield, Willibrord, Menge). *Nazara* other form of the name Nazareth, cp. A-G s.v. and Bl-D, § 39.2.

hou ēn tethrammenos 'where he had been brought up'. The clause refers back to 2 : 39, 51f.

hou '(the place) where, or, whither'.

trephō 'to feed', 'to nourish', hence in the passive 'to be brought up', 'to grow up'.

kai eisēlthen...en tē hēmera tōn sabbatōn eis tēn sunagōgēn 'and he went on the day of the sabbath to the synagogue'. *kai* implies that what happened between his arrival and his going to the synagogue is irrelevant to the narrative.

sabbaton or *sabbata* (plural, without difference in meaning) 'sabbath', i.e. the last day of the week which was holy to God and destined for his worship, or 'week', cp. *IDB* IV, 135-141.

kata to eiōthos autō 'according to his custom', lit. 'according to what was customary for him', going with *eisēlthen...eis tēn sunagōgēn.*

eiōthos (†) participle of *eiōtha* 'to be accustomed', used as a substantive 'that which is customary', 'custom'. The following dative *autō* is due to the verbal origin of the word and indicates the person for whom it is customary (cp. also Acts 17 : 2).

kai anestē anagnōnai 'and he stood up to read'. *anistēmi* (cp. on 1 : 39) is used here literally, A-G s.v. 2 a. *anagnōnai* is final infinitive, 'in order to read'. Since Jesus was already widely known as a teacher, he may have been invited to read and expound the lesson in Nazareth too, but the fact that there is no hint at such an invitation seems to suggest that Jesus himself wanted to address the Nazarenes because he had a special message for them.

anaginōskō 'to read (aloud)'.

Translation: *He* (at the beginning of a new section, cp. also 4 : 31; 5 : 1, 17; 6 : 12, etc.). As often, the translator has to consider whether this pronominal reference must be specified. In doing so he should take into account that a pronoun referring to the principal character of a story sometimes has a wider range of occurrence than one referring to secondary characters. But even with this reservation, specification often is necessary. The use of an honorific form of the pronoun and/or the verb can often solve the problem, e.g. in Ponape, Balinese, East Toradja.

He came to Nazareth. If the receptor language distinguishes between intentional and unintentional acts, the first form can best be chosen here.

Where he had been brought up, or, 'in which he had grown up (lit. become big from little)' (Marathi), 'the town of his-bigness (i.e. his native town)' (Toba Batak). The indication of the past tense may go with 'place', cp. 'the former place (where) he was reared' (Balinese). *To bring up* is in this context sometimes expressed by 'to take-care-of' (Javanese), or, 'to take-care-of when young' (Malay).

And, often better a locative qualification, 'there', 'during his stay there', or a temporal one, 'on the sabbath day'.

As his custom was, or, 'as he used to do', "as he had always done" (Rieu). The phrase may better be transposed, to the end of the sentence, or to its beginning; or one may have to restructure the whole, e.g. 'he used to go (or, a habitual aspect form of that verb) to...on the sabbath day; so he did again now, or, there'.

On the sabbath day, or, 'on the next sabbath day', 'when the sabbath (day) came'; on a possible transposition of the phrase see above. For *sabbath* (also in 4 : 31; 6 : 1f, 5, 7, 9; 13 : 10, 14ff; 14 : 1, 3, 5; 23 : 54, 56) see *N.T.Wb.*/65; *TH-Mk* on 1 : 21.

Stood up here implies 'came to the front', as the lectern was close to the front seats.

To read. To make clear that reading aloud is meant Tzeltal renders, 'to say what God's Book says'. In some receptor languages the addition of a direct or an indirect object is obligatory, or desirable, e.g. 'to read the Scriptures' (Japanese Kogotai), 'to read to the people' (Sranan). In some

Muslim countries it is possible to use the technical term for reciting verses of the Koran (cp. e.g. Sundanese); the Toba Batak term for 'to read' is related to the conjunction 'if', probably because originally the principal reading material was to be found in manuals of magic, where each of the prescriptions began with 'if (such and such happens)'.

17 ***and there was given to him the book of the prophet Isaiah. He opened the book and found the place where it was written,***

Exegesis: *kai epedothē autō biblion tou prophētou Ēsaïou* 'and to him was given the book of the prophet Isaiah', viz. at his own request. This clause is in the Greek the beginning of a new sentence.

epididōmi 'to give', 'to hand over'.

biblion (also v. 20) 'book', 'scroll', here in the latter meaning as shown by *anaptuxas*, see below.

kai anaptuxas to biblion 'and having unrolled the scroll', cp. A-G s.v. *anaptussō* (††).

heuren ton topon hou ēn gegrammenon 'he found the place where it was written'. *heuren* means here that he found what he was looking for. *topos* 'place' means here 'passage', cp. A-G s.v. 2 a.

hou ēn gegrammenon 'where it was written'. The pluperfect tense of the Greek represents an adjustment to the historic (aorist) tense of the main verb *heuren*. The purpose of the clause is to connect *topon* with the following quotation.

Translation: *There was given to him*, or, 'the attendant (see v. 20) handed him', 'he received'.

The book of the prophet Isaiah, or, 'the writing(s) of the prophet I.', 'what (or, the book that) the prophet I. wrote', 'the book containing what the prophet I. had spoken'; cp. also on 3 : 4. —*Book*, or, 'writing', or the closer historical equivalent 'scroll', 'sacred roll' (Marathi). The specific term in the receptor language may refer to a quite different object, e.g. a long strip of bark folded plait-wise (Toba Batak 1885) or a bundle of loose palmleaves held together by strings between two wooden covers (Balinese).

He opened, or a more specific term that fits the distinctive features of the term rendering "book", e.g. 'unrolled', 'unfolded', 'loosened (the strings of)'.

He found, or indicating the implied search (cp. on 2 : 16), 'he selected' (Marathi), 'he sought and found', 'he found what he sought' (cp. below). The context clearly implies that Jesus read aloud the passage he had found. Usually this is sufficiently clear from the reference to reading aloud in v. 16; if not, one may have to say here, 'he found and read the place...', 'he found the passage he sought/wanted and read what was written there'; or one may have to add a reference to reading at the beginning of v. 20 (which see).

The place where it was written, or using one specific term, "this text" (Rieu), 'these verses' (Bahasa Indonesia RC, using a term that specifically refers to Koranic verses, and by extension to verses in the holy books of other religions). For the rendering of the relative clause see on 2 : 23. Balinese employs here one of its other formulas to introduce a quotation, viz. 'which its-wording (lit. its-being-pronounced) thus', thereby trying to suggest that the words quoted were read aloud.

18 ***"The Spirit of the Lord is upon me,***
because he has anointed me to preach good news to the poor.
He has sent me to proclaim release to the captives
and recovering of sight to the blind,
to set at liberty those who are oppressed,
19 ***to proclaim the acceptable year of the Lord."***

Exegesis: *pneuma kuriou ep' eme* 'the Spirit of the Lord is upon me', cp. on 2 : 25. The Spirit is the Spirit of prophetic inspiration, cp. Hos. 9 : 7; Micah 3 : 8; Ezek. 2 : 2; 3 : 24; 11 : 5.

hou heineken echrisen me 'because he has anointed me'.

hou heineken lit. 'because of the fact that', with the implication that the purpose of *echrisen me* 'he anointed me' is to bring about what the main clause refers to, as often in the Septuagint. *heineken* (here and 18 : 29), *heneken* (9 : 24; 21 : 12) or *heneka* (6 : 22) 'because of', 'on account of', cp. A-G s.v.

chriō (†) 'to anoint', in the New Testament only in figurative meaning, cp. *N.T.Wb.*, 20/. In view of the fulfilment to which v. 21 refers it appears that Jesus understands the descending of the Spirit upon him (3 : 22) as his being anointed with the Spirit.

euaggelisasthai ptōchois 'to preach good news to poor people'. For *euaggelizomai* cp. on 1 : 19. The phrase, which is dependent upon *echrisen*, serves to indicate God's commission implied in the anointing with the Spirit.

ptōchos lit. 'begging', hence 'poor'. Here as often in the Old Testament it does not denote people who are only economically poor but people who have little or nothing to expect from the circumstances wich determine their life and are therefore dependent upon God, cp. Richardson, *Word Book*, 168. The omission of the article before *ptōchois* (as before the other nouns in this verse) shows that the reference is not to one specific group but to people who are in this situation generally.

apestalken me 'he has sent me' cp. on 1 : 19. On this clause depend the subsequent infinitives *kēruxai* (twice) and *aposteilai*.

kēruxai aichmalōtois aphesin kai tuphlois anablepsin 'to proclaim release for captives and recovery of sight for blind'. For *kērussō* cp. on 3 : 3; for *aphesis* cp. on 1 : 77.

aichmalōtos 'captive', refers in Is. 61 : 1 perhaps to people who have been sold as slaves because of their debts and who were set free in the year of jubilee (see below), and may be taken here as referring to all people who are in some form of slavery, including that of sin.

tuphlos 'blind', here refers to blind people as socially weak and personally unhappy, cp. 14 : 13, 21. They are among the specific objects of Jesus' Messianic ministry of healing (cp. 7 : 21, 22 where also the *ptōchoi* are mentioned as those who receive the good news!).

anablepsis (††) 'recovery of sight', or, with a shift from the abstract to the concrete, "new eyes" (Rieu).

aposteilai tethrausmenous en aphesei 'to let go, or to send away, the down-trodden in liberty'. Here *apostellō* is used in a weaker meaning ('to let go' without indication of purpose or commission). *en aphesei* does not refer (as does *aphesin* above) to the release of prisoners but to a freedom in a social and religious sense which is the opposite of the state to which *tethrausmenous* (see below) refers.

tethrausmenous, from *thrauō* (††) 'to break', lit. 'the broken ones', fig. 'the oppressed', 'the down-trodden', socially and religiously.

(V. 19) *kēruxai eniauton kuriou dekton* 'to proclaim the Lord's year of favour', or 'the acceptable year of the Lord', dependent upon the interpretation of *dekton*. *eniautos* (†).

dektos (also v. 24) (1) 'acceptable', 'welcome' or (2) 'favourable'. In v. 24 only the former meaning is possible (see below), but here both may apply: (1) 'the acceptable, or, agreeable year of the Lord' (RSV, NV, Zürich, Rengstorf) must be understood as agreeable to men; (2) 'the favourable year of the Lord' i.e. the year of the Lord's favour, i.e. the year in which the Lord bestows his favour. The latter is preferable.

Translation: Here, again, the use of honorifics requires attention. In order to make the right choice the translator should carefully envisage the situation to which the quotation refers, viz. that of a messenger of God who tells the people what God has done to him and what he himself is going to do. The position of the messenger is such that he may be taken to address the people in non-honorific language.

The lines (a) and (b) may have to be co-ordinated, e.g. 'The Spirit of the Lord is upon me; for that purpose he has anointed me. He did so in order that I may preach...', or, 'The Lord has anointed me. Now his Spirit is upon me. This happens in order that I may preach...'.

The Spirit of the Lord. The relationship between 'the Lord' or 'God' and 'his Spirit' is not the same as that between 'man' and 'his heart/mind/soul'. To avoid misunderstanding one may have to say, 'the Spirit from God', 'the Spirit that God gives/sends'; in languages that distinguish between alienable and inalienable possessives, the first may be obligatory. For *Lord* see on 1 : 6, sub (c).

He has anointed me. For the verb, here used in a figurative sense, see *N.T.Wb.*/10. The words refer to Jesus' experience described in 3 : 22; hence in Foe the past tense referring to what happened before the day of speaking has to be used, and the aspect which indicates that the speaker describes something that he can see going on.

To preach good news, see on 3 : 18.

The poor (also in 6 : 20; 7 : 22; 14 : 13, 21; 16 : 20, 22; 18 : 22; 19 : 8; 21 : 2f), or, 'those who have very little'; or if such terms are too exclusively economic, 'the wretched/miserable' (Balinese), 'the pitiable'.

To proclaim release to the captives, or avoiding the verbal noun, 'to announce to the captives that they will be released' (Sranan), or, "You shall be (set) free!" In making his choice between possible restructurings the translator should take into account the parallelism with the next phrase, which makes the use of identical constructions preferable. — *To proclaim*, i.e. to make widely known with authority, has been rendered, 'to cause-to-be-heard-here-and-there' (Trukese), 'to spread by saying' (Tzeltal); cp. also on "to preach" in 3 : 3. For *captives* cp. *N.T.Wb.*/19f, CAPTURE. Where more than one term is available one should select the one that is most widely applicable and can also be used metaphorically. Some of the expressions used are, 'the tied-up ones' (Ponape, Kapauku), 'men that are-imprisoned' (Javanese), 'those taken and carried away' (Marathi), 'those who have become booty (lit. what-is-taken-as-plunder)' (Balinese).

And recovering of sight to the blind. For shifts that may be necessary in the syntactic structure, see above. *To recover sight*, or, 'to regain (one's) sight', 'to be able to see again'. For *blind* one says, '(having) eyes dark/night' in Kapauku, 'having no eyes' in Zarma, 'not seeing' in honorific Balinese. Some languages have distinctive terms for congenital and non-congenital blindness, the latter to be used here.

Lines (e) and (f) are dependent on "he has sent me" in line (c), which clause has to be repeated in some languages before (e) (as done in Sranan), and maybe also before (f).

To set at liberty, or, 'to set free', 'to deliver'. It may be necessary to add a reference to that which they were delivered from, e.g. 'to deliver the oppressed from their enemies', 'to help the oppressed against (or, to overcome) what oppresses them'.

Those who are oppressed, or, 'maltreated', 'defeated'.

(V. 19) The structure of *to proclaim the acceptable year of the Lord*, preferably, 'the favourable year of the Lord' (see *Exegesis*), usually will have to be changed, e.g. 'proclaim that the favourable year of the Lord has come' (cp. Sranan), or, 'that this is the year of the Lord's favour', "In this year the Lord will show his favour (towards man)!" — For 'favour' see references on 1 : 30.

20 ***And he closed the book, and gave it back to the attendant, and sat down; and the eyes of all in the synagogue were fixed on him.***

Exegesis: *kai ptuxas to biblion apodous tō hupēretē* 'and having rolled up the book (and) having given (it) back to the attendant', asyndetic clause of two conjunctive participles indicating two subsequent acts preceding the act of the main verb. Both participles have the same object, viz. *to biblion*. Most translations resolve the participles into two verbal clauses, co-ordinate with one another and with the main verb (cp. RSV).

ptussō (††) 'fold up', 'roll up', cp. Plummer.

apodidōmi 'give (away)', 'give back', cp. Plummer.

hupēretēs 'servant', cp. on 1 : 2, here 'attendant' of the synagogue, cp. *IDB* IV, 489 on *Hazzan*.

ekathisen 'he sat down', ingressive aorist of *kathizō* 'to sit', 'to sit down'. In the synagogue the teacher used to sit down on a chair while speaking.

kai pantōn hoi ophthalmoi en tē sunagōgē 'and the eyes of all in the synagogue', instead of *hoi ophthalmoi pantōn tōn en tē sunagōgē*, cp. Bl-D, § 275.1. *pantōn* is emphatic by position.

ēsan atenizontes autō 'were fixed on him', periphrastic construction without special meaning or emphasis, cp. Bl-D, § 353.

atenizō (also 22 : 56) with dative 'to look intently at'.

Translation: *And.* The transition may have to be rendered more fully, 'having done so', 'after he had read these verses'.

He closed the book, see on its counterpart in v. 17.

Attendant. Sometimes a specific term for 'attendant in church/mosque/temple' is employed, e.g. in Sranan, Sundanese. Where a rather generic term such as 'servant', 'guard', is used, a qualification may be required, e.g. 'guard of the meeting-house' (South Toradja).

He sat down, or, 'he sat down there', 'he sat down to teach' (Chontal of Tabasco), to show that he did not go back to where he had been sitting first.

The eyes of all...were fixed on him, or, 'everyone...peered, or, looked-intently at him'. In Marathi and Kapauku it is idiomatic to say that one 'nails, respectively, kills, one's eyes on a person'.

21 ***And he began to say to them, "Today this scripture has been fulfilled in your hearing."***

Exegesis: *ērxato de legein pros autous* 'then he began to say to them'.

archomai 'to begin', with following infinitive occurs 27 times in Luke. In some places it clearly refers to the beginning of an act, or event (e.g. 7 : 15; 9 : 12; 14 : 30). In others, however, the idea of beginning is almost completely absent, and *archomai* apparently has only the function of an auxiliary verb; or it has no specific meaning at all and may go untranslated. In a number of cases it appears to lend special emphasis to the main verb, or indicate a change in the situation. In every occurrence the context must determine in what sense it is used. Here it refers to a turning point in the situation.

hoti has the function of a semi-colon.

sēmeron peplērōtai hē graphē hautē en tois ōsin humōn 'today this scripture passage has been fulfilled in your ears'. For *peplērōtai* cp. on 1 : 20. Here the verb indicates that what the scripture passage says has come true and is happening now. *en tois ōsin humōn* may be taken (1) with *hē graphē hautē* 'this scripture', which results in 'the scripture in your ears', i.e. "the Scripture which you have heard" (Torrey, cp. Knox, Synodale, Segond, Menge, Bruns, Willibrord), or (2) with *peplērōtai* 'is fulfilled', which results in 'this scripture is fulfilled in your ears' i.e. "this Scripture has been fulfilled while you have been listening to it" (Phillips). The latter is preferable.

graphē 'scripture passage', in plural 'the scriptures'.

Translation: This is the first passage in the Gospel where Luke records a public speech of Jesus. The translator may have to decide here what honorifics to use in rendering the speech (cp. on 1 : 5). Since Jesus' general behaviour seems not to have been markedly different from that of the teachers of the law, it may be advisable to model his use of honorifics on what a religious teacher would use when speaking on an official occasion in a public place to persons of varying position, some socially his equals, some not. This may imply his employing polite forms, in contrast with what he would use in private conversation in the circle of friends or disciples. That he just has referred to his being anointed by the Spirit does not seem to be a reason for departing from this general rule.

And he began to say, or, 'thereupon (or, and then) he said'.

This scripture has been fulfilled in your hearing, or, "this passage of scripture has come true..., as you heard it being read" (TEV), 'you have heard these words completely confirmed' (Lokele). *This scripture,* or, 'this text', 'this wording of scripture' (Balinese), 'these matters that have been written in the Holy Book' (Kituba); and cp. on "the place where it was written" in v. 17. *To be fulfilled,* or, 'to reach-its-goal' (Bahasa Indonesia), 'to come to realization' (Kituba), 'to come right' (Sranan), 'to hit the very spot' (Shilluk, for John 17 : 12), 'to happen really/truly'.

22 ***And all spoke well of him, and wondered at the gracious words which proceeded out of his mouth; and they said, "Is not this Joseph's son?"***

Exegesis: *kai pantes emarturoun autō* lit. 'and all bore witness for him'.

martureō (†) with dative 'to bear witness to' (cp. Jn. 3 : 26), may here mean either 'to speak well of' (cp. RSV, BFBS, Goodspeed, more freely also NEB, Kingsley Williams), or 'to approve of' (Brouwer, cp. "to be well impressed with", TEV.) The latter is preferable.

epi tois logois tēs charitos tois ekporeuomenois ek tou stomatos autou 'at the words of grace coming from his mouth'. *charis* is best understood as 'graciousness' (cp. A-G s.v. 1). *tēs charitos* is a genitive of quality (cp. Bl-D, § 165). *tois ekporeuomenois ek tou stomatos autou* 'coming from his mouth' reflects common usage in the Septuagint, cp. e.g. Num. 32 : 24; Deut. 8 : 3 (quoted in Mt. 4 : 4). The idiom seems to imply that the words spoken are, as it were, a part of the speaker, revealing what is in him or binding him to the word he has spoken. Here the words that came from Jesus' mouth are representative of his personality.

kai elegon 'and they said', iterative imperfect.

ouchi huios estin Iōsēph houtos 'is not this Joseph's son?' This question expresses either astonishment at the fact that Joseph's son had become such a fine preacher or indignation at his presumption of speaking as a prophet, probably both. *houtos* may express contempt or amazement, cp. A-G s.v. 1 a α.

ouchi as an interrogative particle indicates that an affirmative answer is expected.

Translation: *Spoke well of him,* preferably, 'expressed their approval of him', 'said, "He is right!", or, "His words are true!"'

Wondered at, see on 1 : 21.

Gracious words, or, "winning words" (Goodspeed), 'sweet words' (Malay); or 'the loveliness (lit. fragrance), or, the eloquence (lit. smoothness) of his words' (Javanese, Balinese), 'how graciously he spoke'.

In some cases the clause *which proceeded out of his mouth* can be rendered rather literally, e.g. in Tagabili, which has, 'they were all completely absorbed in the things-told which dropped from his mouth'. In several receptor languages, however, idiom and/or decodability require another rendering, such as 'which fell/came from his lips', 'which flowed from in his mouth' (Ponape), 'that he uttered/spoke'. Neither the literal nor the other renderings express the specific shade of meaning discussed in *Exegesis*. This does not mean a serious loss of information here, since the context makes clear that the words were taken to be characteristic of Jesus' personality.

Is not this Joseph's son. If the receptor language cannot use an interrogative sentence in this sense, an affirmative sentence must express the astonishment or indignation of the speakers, e.g. 'and he merely is J.'s son', or, 'this fellow is nothing more than a son of J.'.

23 ***And he said to them, "Doubtless you will quote to me this proverb, 'Physician, heal yourself; what we have heard you did at Capernaum, do here also in your own country.'"***

Exegesis: *kai eipen pros autous* 'and he said to them', as an indirect reply to their question at the end of v. 22.

pantōs ereite moi tēn parabolēn tautēn 'no doubt you will say to me this proverb'. The connexion between these and the following words of Jesus, and the preceding thoughts and utterances of the people is expressed by *pantōs* (†). This word usually expresses a strong affirmation (cp. Acts 28 : 4, 1 Cor. 9 : 10) and therefore several translators render "no doubt". This implies that Jesus is sure that the proverb he will quote expresses the feelings of the people towards him. *ereite* 'you will say' indicates what Jesus thinks is in their minds, cp. Rom. 9 : 19; 11 : 19; 1 Cor. 15 : 35.

parabolē 'parable', 'illustration', here 'proverb', cp. *TH-Mk* on 3 : 23.

iatre, therapeuson seauton 'physician, heal yourself'. This must be understood against the background of Is. 61 : 1f, the fulfilment of which Jesus claimed for himself: when he who is the son of Joseph and a common man like all other people, thinks himself to be the prophet of Messianic salvation, let him understand that he is in no position to boast like that unless he establishes his claim by doing here what he did in Capernaum.

iatros 'physician', here in the literal sense; the proverb as a whole has a figurative meaning.

therapeuō 'to heal', 'to cure', always (except 9 : 1) with the sick as object.

hosa ēkousamen genomena eis tēn Kapharnaoum 'all the things we heard have happened in Capernaum', relative clause in which a verb of perception (*ēkousen*) is followed by a supplementary participle (*genomena*) which has the force of an infinitive (cp. Bl-D, § 416.1). *hosa* in plural without antecedent is stronger than the simple relative *ha*: 'all the things', cp. A-G s.v. *hosos* 2.

Kapharnaoum is also spelt *Kapernaoum* (which seems to represent a different pronunciation, cp. Bl-D, § 39.2) from which the usual transliteration Capernaum is derived. Versions in the Roman Catholic tradition appear to follow the Vulgate, which has a transliteration of *Kapharnaoum*.

poiēson kai hōde en tē patridi sou 'do (them) also here in your native place'.

hōde 'here', in the sense of 'in this place' or 'to this place'.

patris (†) 'native town'.

Translation: *Quote to me*, or, 'say to me, thus', 'speak to me, saying', or more polemically, 'confront me with' (Brouwer); in Sranan the idiomatic wording is, 'to cut a proverb to'.

Proverb, or, 'wise word' (Navajo), or more generically 'word', 'saying'. A figurative phrase is used in South Toradja, viz. 'bracelet of yarn'.

Physician, heal yourself; what we have heard...in your own country. These two sentences in quoted speech express what Jesus' audience are supposedly thinking but do not say. The proverb in the first part serves as general characterization of the situation; the next sentence (contrary to what the introductory words lead us to expect) does not form a part of the proverb, but is added to apply it to the particular situation. Therefore it is preferable not to use a semicolon but a full stop, and/or a suitable introducing verb before the second sentence, e.g. "..., and say, 'Do here also...'" (BFBS, similarly NEB). Cp. also "'Physician, heal yourself', and tell me to do here also..." (Rieu, who by giving the proverb as quoted, the following sentence as non-quoted speech, still more clearly distinguishes the two).

Linguistic forms to be used in proverbial sayings may be of a rather specific type; for instance, there may be a preference for somewhat archaic words, or/and for minor sentence types. The translator should attempt to use such forms here. In matters of honorifics a proverb is not usually subject to the linguistic etiquette ruling the conversation in which it is quoted. Hence, if honorifics are to be used in the present case, they may be not those fitting the social relationship of Jesus and his audience (see below), but those the receptor culture confers on a physician or medicine man—which often are rather high level ones.

For the second sentence matters are different. Though imaginary this quoted speech usually is to be treated in the same way as quoted real speech; this means that one has to use the honorifics which a general audience would normally employ in a (rather polemic) discussion with Jesus. There is, however, a complicating factor. As a rule honorifics are not used when the speaker is referring to what is connected with his own person. The fact that here the actual speaker and the supposed addressee are the same person may lead to avoidance of the honorifics that would have been used otherwise. For theological considerations that may influence the choice see *TBT*, 14.176, 1963. If conflicting tendencies would make the choice too complicated, matters can probably be made easier by a shift to non-quoted speech.

Physician, cp. *TH-Mk* on 2 : 17. Descriptive renderings may be, 'one who (habitually) treats sick people', 'one who (professionally) heals (people)' (see below); the Shilluk term, 'people of trees', refers to the healing medicines, which largely come from trees.

Often the term for *to heal* is a causative form built upon the word for 'well', 'recovered', etc., or, more negatively expressed, 'cause to be sick no longer'. It may be obligatory to use an object referring to the sick person, or to his disease, his body, or a part of his body. Some languages possess specific terms, distinguishing between the healing of internal or external disorders, sores or dislocations, organs of movement or organs of sense, wounds or diseases, congenital or non-congenital maladies, etc. For the healing of a specific disorder, such as paralysis, blindness, deafness, demon possession, a term that describes the result may be in use, e.g. 'cause to walk/see/hear', 'cause the demon to come out' (8 : 36). Generally speaking it is preferable to use a term that refers to indigenous medicine, but such a term should be checked as to its connotations and use; a word closely associated with magical charms and practices, and/or invocation of the spirits, though possible here, will not do when Jesus is the healer; and a verb referring to a treatment that the medicine man never applies to himself does not fit the present verse. Another problem in this verse may arise in languages that possess specific but no generic terms. Then one may have to use the specific term that is most commonly associated with the work of a physician or medicine man in the area, or shift to an expression such as, 'help yourself', 'apply your skill to yourself', 'go first to yourself'.

What we have heard you did at Capernaum, do here also, or with a shift towards co-ordination, 'We have heard of all that happened (or, all you did) at C.; do the same here' (cp. NEB); cp. also the rendering in non-quoted speech that is found in Tagabili, 'It is likely you have already heard what I did in C., and that which you desire now I do it here...'.

Your own country, or, 'your native country/place/town', 'the country/place/town of your-growing-up'. In some cases the rendering to be used here coincides with or converges towards the one used for "their own city" (2 : 39), and/or for "where he had been brought up" (4 : 16).

24 ***And he said, "Truly, I say to you, no prophet is acceptable in his own country.***

Exegesis: *eipen de* 'and he said', i.e. "he added" (Phillips), or "he went on" (Rieu).

amēn legō humin 'truly I say to you', cp. on 3 : 8.

amēn 'truly', always at the beginning of a solemn declaration. The introductory *amēn*-formula is a substitute for the Old Testament prophetic "Thus says the Lord" without the name of God. It serves to lend weight and authority to the statement which follows.

oudeis prophētēs dektos estin en tē patridi autou 'no prophet is acceptable in his native place'. This saying which has become a proverb and is today almost exclusively in use as a proverb, probably was not known as such in Jesus' time. For *dektos* cp. on v. 19.

Translation: *Truly, I say to you.* For the adverb see *N.T.Wb.*/8, AMEN and 71f, TRUTH; *TH-Mk* on 8 : 12. For the verbal phrase cp. on "I tell you" in 3 : 8.

The structure of *no prophet is acceptable in his own country* may have to be changed, e.g. 'a prophet is not accepted in (or, by the people of) his own country/place/town', 'the people in a prophet's own country/town (or, a prophet's fellow-countrymen/townsmen) never accept him'. *To be acceptable* has been rendered variously, e.g. 'to be well received (Sinhalese) or, welcomed', 'to be considered-good' (East Toradja), 'to be liked (Sundanese), or, cherished (Trukese), or, popular' (Ponape), 'to be believed with respect' (Lokele), 'to be listened to', cp. 'they do not always listen to a prophet if he tells something to his own people in his own country' (Tagabili).

25 ***But in truth, I tell you, there were many widows in Israel in the days of Elijah, when the heaven was shut up three years and six months, when there came a great famine over all the land;***
26 ***and Elijah was sent to none of them but only to Zarephath, in the land of Sidon, to a woman who was a widow.***

Exegesis: *ep' alētheias de legō humin* 'but in truth I say to you', cp. on 3 : 8.

ep' alētheias lit. 'on the basis of truth' (cp. A-G s.v. *epi* I 1 b β, the same expression in 20 : 21 and 22 : 59), 'in truth', though less solemn than *amēn* yet a strong expression which indicates, as it were, that the speaker vouches for the truth of what he is going to say.

en tais hēmerais Ēliou 'in the days of Elijah', a chronological indication.

en tō Israēl 'in Israel'. *Israēl* elsewhere denotes the nation, here the country where this nation lives.

hote ekleisthē ho ouranos epi etē tria kai mēnas hex, hōs egeneto limos megas epi pasan tēn gēn 'when the sky was closed for three years and six months, when there was a great famine over the whole land', two temporal clauses, the second with consecutive force, depicting the situation in Elijah's days. In this setting it happened that Elijah was not sent to one of the widows of Israel but to one outside. There is here no semantic difference between *hote* and *hōs*. In both clauses the verbs *ekleisthē* and *egeneto* are in the aorist, though the period of duration, three years and six months, is mentioned. But the aorist tense shows that the events are not viewed in their duration but as facts of the past.

ekleisthē ho ouranos 'the sky was closed', an obvious metaphor for "no rain fell" (Rieu). *kleiō* also 11 : 7.

egeneto 'there was', cp. on 1 : 5.

limos 'famine', 'hunger'.

epi pasan tēn gēn 'over the whole country', viz. of Israel; for *epi* cp. A-G s.v. III 1 a α.

(V. 26) *kai pros oudemian autōn epemphthē Ēlias* 'and (yet) to none of them was Elijah sent'. *kai* emphasizes as surprising the fact to which the clause refers, cp. A-G s.v. I 2 g.

ei mē lit. 'unless', here 'but', cp. A-G s.v. *ei* VI 8 b.

eis Sarepta tēs Sidōnias, scil. *chōras* 'to Sarepta in the Sidonian country'. *Sarepta* represents Hebrew *ṣār^{e}phat*, cp. 1 Kings 17 : 9f. The genitive *tēs Sidōnias* is a genitive of relationship.

pros gunaika chēran 'to a woman (who was a) widow', hence 'to a widow'. *chēra* 'widow' has here its original function of an adjective, cp. A-G s.v.

Translation: The principal feature of these two verses is the contrast between the many widows in Israel and the one outside. That the introductory formula, synonymous with the one used in v. 24, serves to call attention to this contrast, should become clear from its wording and position in the sentence, e.g. 'remember what happened in the days of E., when..., when...the land. I tell you there certainly were many widows in Israel then, yet E. was not sent to one of them but to a widow in Z....'.

Widows, cp. on 2 : 37.

When...when..., preferably, 'when...and...', or, 'when..., so that, or, with the result that...'.

The heaven was shut up, or with an equivalent metaphorical expression, 'the sky had drawn-up/withdrawn' (Toba Batak). Often a non or less metaphorical rendering is necessary, e.g. 'rain did not come' (Tzeltal), 'the sky refused to rain' (Shona 1966), or such a rendering has to be added, 'the heavens were closed up without rain' (Lokele).

Three years and six months, or, 'three and a half years' (Marathi, similarly in Kapauku, where the idiom is 'for the half of the fourth year').

There came a great famine, or, 'great was people's hunger' (East Toradja), 'people were very hungry, or, had not any food to eat', 'food became very scarce/expensive' (Low Malay), 'people died because they could not obtain any food'; in South Toradja the phrase 'the soil collapses' indicates 'crop failure', 'famine'.

(V. 26) *Elijah was sent to none of them*, or, in active construction, 'to no one of them God sent E.' (Sranan). It may be preferable to be more explicit, e.g. "sent to help" (Rieu).

To Zarephath..., to a woman who was a widow. Since it is the woman and not the locality which is in focus, it is usually better to reverse the phrase order. The verb has sometimes to be repeated, for reasons of grammar (Marathi, Balinese) or of emphasis, cp. 'but he *was* sent to a widow at Z....'.

27 ***And there were many lepers in Israel in the time of the prophet Elisha; and none of them was cleansed, but only Naaman the Syrian."***

Exegesis: *kai polloi leproi ēsan en tō Israēl* 'and (again), there were many lepers in Israel'. *kai* here connects two parallel stories, cp. NEB and Rieu. For *Israēl* cp. on v. 25.

lepros 'leprous', as a substantive 'leper'. For the exact reference of *lepros* and *lepra* cp. A-G s.v. *lepra*, *TH-Mk* on 1 : 40; *TBT*, 11.10-23, 69-81, 1960; 12.75-79, 1961.

epi Elisaiou tou prophētou 'in the time of the prophet Elisha'. Most translations have here the common Old Testament spelling of the name, not a transliteration of the Greek.

kai oudeis autōn ekatharisthē 'and (yet) none of them was cleansed'. For *kai* here cp. on v. 26.

katharizō 'to make clean', 'to cleanse', in Luke (except 11 : 39 where the cleaning of cups and dishes is referred to) always of the healing of leprosy which makes a person ceremonially unclean (cp. 17 : 14, the restoration of ceremonial cleanness had to be stated by the priests). Usually the verb is in the aorist (except 7 : 22) in order to stress the punctiliar nature of the cleansing.

ei mē Naiman ho Suros 'but only Naaman the Syrian'. For *ei mē* cp. on v. 26. Naaman is a transliteration of the Hebrew.

Translation: *And,* preferably, 'again', 'similarly', 'also'.

Lepers. The references given in *Exegesis* also provide material for possible solutions of the translational problems. Three points may be made, by way of summary. (1) A term exclusively or primarily referring to leprosy in the sense of Hansen's Disease should be avoided. If that is felt to be impossible (as seems, unfortunately, to be the case in most western versions), a footnote should explain that the meaning of Gr. *lepra,* as used in the New Testament, differs in many aspects from what now is meant by "lepra", "leprosy" (or equivalent terms in other languages), primarily in that it was considered curable (cp. Lev. 14 : 1-32), and that the socio-religious connotation was very important. (2) The use of a descriptive rendering, entirely unconnected with Hansen's Disease, is much to be preferred. (3) The use of an existing general term for a skin disease that can be serious and implies ostracism, even if it has Hansen's Disease amongst its possible referents, is acceptable as a second best solution.

Was cleansed, or, 'became clean'; cp. *N.T.Wb.*/59, PURE, rightly stressing that the term has both a socio-religious and a physical aspect. This is brought out e.g. in 'whose stain was-taken-away' (Balinese, in which 'stain' covers ritual impurity as well as disease or disaster). A more generic rendering, at least open to both aspects, may also be considered, e.g. 'received help' (Tzeltal), 'was released from his fearful state'. In some languages the negative term 'unclean/impure' is more frequent and productive than its opposite; hence, 'his-impurity was removed' (Javanese).

But only Naaman the Syrian. Here again repetition of the verb may be preferable, cp. '. . . ; but Naaman, . . ., became clean' (cp. Marathi). This may also serve to make clear that Naaman was not included among the lepers in Israel (Shona 1966 using two synonymous expressions, 'was cured', and 'had his leprosy taken away'); the same end may be reached by a locative rendering of 'Syrian', e.g. 'Naaman of Syria-country' (cp. Sranan).

28 ***When they heard this, all in the synagogue were filled with wrath.***

Exegesis: *kai eplēsthēsan pantes thumou en tē sunagōgē* 'and all who were in the synagogue were filled with rage'. *en tē sunagōgē* may go with *pantes* (as in v. 20) or with the main verb *eplēsthēsan thumou*, or with *akouontes tauta*, preferably the first. For the construction of *eplēsthēsan* with genitive cp. on 1 : 15. The phrase, which has lost the force of the original metaphor, serves here to indicate a high degree of anger. The aorist tense stresses the ingressive aspect.

thumos (†) 'rage'; as compared with *orgē* 'wrath' (cp. Eph. 4 : 31; Col. 3 : 8; Mk. 3 : 5), it is more passionate and of a more temporary nature, cp. Trench, *Synonyms of the New Testament*, 1880, p. 132.

Translation: *They... all in the synagogue.* Often it is necessary to reverse the order of these two subjects, or even of the clauses in which they occur.

Were filled with wrath, or, 'wrath overwhelmed them', 'they became heated' (cp. Marathi, implying great anger). For *wrath* see *N.T.Wb.*/9f, ANGER; *TH-Mk* on 3 : 5.

29 ***And they rose up and put him out of the city, and led him to the brow of the hill on which their city was built, that they might throw him down headlong.***

Exegesis: *kai anastantes exebalon...kai ēgagon* lit. 'and having risen they drove (him) out...and brought (him)'. Of the three acts referred to by these verbs the first is preparing for the other two. All three are due to their being filled with rage (v. 28). For *anastantes* cp. on 1 : 39 and 4 : 16; here it is used literally, since people used to sit down during the worship service (cp. *IDB* IV, 488f).

ekballō 'to drive out (forcibly)', 'to send out (without force)', here preferably the former, cp. *TH-Mk* on 1 : 12.

exō tēs poleōs 'out of the town'. *exō* 'outside', here used as preposition, cp. A-G s.v. 2 b.

heōs ophruos tou orous eph' hou hē polis ōikodomēto autōn 'to the, or a, brow of the hill on which their city was built'. The exact place to which this description refers is not identified with certainty. But the two places that seem to be probable are 1 and 2 kilometres away from the town, cp. Grundmann. From the few remains of the old town it appears that Nazareth was not built on the top of the hill but on its slope (cp. *IDB* III, 525).

ophrus (††) 'edge' (of a cliff), 'brow'.

hōste katakrēmnisai auton 'in order to throw him down'.

hōste introduces clauses which indicate result, either actual, or intended, as here. In the latter meaning it is hardly to be distinguished from *hina*, cp. A-G s.v. 2 b; Bl-D, § 391.3.

katakrēmnizō (††) 'to throw down from a cliff (Gr. *krēmnos*)'.

Translation: *Put him out*, preferably, 'expelled him', 'threw him out'.

Led him, or, in order to be in tune with the behaviour suggested by the preceding verb, 'drove' (Willibrord), 'seized-under-the-arms (as done when one runs in a prisoner)' (Javanese), 'dragged' (South Toradja).

City. The location of the city, mentioned in the next clause, may better be transposed to this part of the sentence, cp. '...outside their city which was built on a hill. They led him as-far-as to edge-of the hill, place which straight-up-and-down...' (Ponape), '...outside of the town. Their town was built on a hill, and they brought him to the edge of this hill...' (Cuyono; a comparable shift in Tagabili).

Brow of the hill, i.e. projecting upper part of a steep place on, not necessarily the top of, the hill. For *hill* cp. 3 : 5.

Built. The reference is to the situation rather than to the being built; hence, 'the site of their city' (Toba Batak), '(where) their city stood on' (Trukese).

That they might throw him down headlong, or, 'their intention (being), or, preparing to throw...', 'they would have thrown...'. *To throw down headlong,* preferably, "to throw down the cliff" (Rieu), "to throw down from it" (Goodspeed), 'push him over the edge' (cp. Marathi).

30 ***But passing through the midst of them he went away.***

Exegesis: *autos de* 'but he', emphatic.

dielthōn dia mesou autōn 'going through the middle of them'. This participial phrase carries the main weight in the whole sentence. It presupposes that Jesus had freed himself, and implies that Jesus did not flee but that all people watched him but did not dare to touch him again.

eporeueto 'he went his way', without suggesting that Jesus had a definite place in mind to which to go.

Translation: *Passing through the midst of them*...is often rendered as a co-ordinated sentence, "he walked straight through them all, or, through the whole crowd and..." (NEB, Phillips, similarly Balinese), 'he cut-straight-through the midst of those people, then...' (Javanese).

31 ***And he went down to Capernaum, a city of Galilee. And he was teaching them on the sabbath;***

Exegesis: *kai katēlthen* 'and he went down'. *kai* connects the following narrative with the preceding and marks it as a continuation.

katerchomai (also 9 : 37) 'to go down' or 'to go to a lower place'. Here the difference in height is approximately 1900 feet, that in distance, about 20 miles.

Kapharnaoum polin tēs Galilaias 'Capernaum, a town of Galilee'. *polin tēs Galilaias* is added as an identification. Capernaum was mentioned already in v. 23 but this first mentioning neither gave opportunity for nor required a geographical explanation.

kai ēn didaskōn autous en tois sabbasin 'and he taught them on the sabbath'. Two interpretations are possible which depend ultimately on the understanding of vv. 31-37 as a whole: (1) the clause refers to Jesus' consecutive teaching on several sabbath days; this also applies to v. 32 which describes the reaction of the people to this teaching. Then vv. 33-37 refer to what happens on presumably the last of these sabbath days;

(2) the reference is to a specific sabbath and this clause and the clauses in the imperfect tense in vv. 32f, as contrasted with the aorist tense of *anekraxen* 'he shouted' and subsequent verbs in vv. 32-36, describe as it were the setting in which the sudden outburst of v. 34 happens. The fact that v. 33 begins with *kai* and does not contain a reference or hint to a specific sabbath to be distinguished from sabbaths referred to previously, points to the second interpretation as being the more natural. This is also consistent with Mk. 1 : 21-23.

autous refers to the inhabitants of Capernaum who were present in the synagogue, though they have not been referred to previously and the synagogue itself is not mentioned until v. 33, though implied in "was teaching".

Translation: *He went down.* For movement to another level, cp. on "went up" in 2 : 4.

Capernaum, a city of Galilee, or, '(the city) C. (which is) in (the region) G.', cp. on 1 : 26.

And he was teaching them on the sabbath, or, to bring out interpretation (2), 'once he was teaching them (or, the people (there)) on the sabbath', 'on a certain sabbath he was... (etc.)'. That this happened in the synagogue may have to be stated explicitly.

32 ***and they were astonished at his teaching, for his word was with authority.***

Exegesis: *kai exeplēssonto epi tē didachē autou* 'and they were astonished at his teaching'. For *ekplēssomai* cp. on 2 : 48.

didachē (†) 'teaching' may refer to the act or to the content, cp. A-G s.v. 3. Here it probably includes both, but with an emphasis on content, rather than on form.

hoti en exousia ēn ho logos autou 'for his word was with authority'. *logos* is best understood as "what he said" (BFBS, NEB), because *exousia* would never apply to the act of speaking apart from what is said and apart from the person who speaks. *en exousia* therefore refers implicitly to Jesus himself as well.

exousia 'authority', cp. on v. 6. Here it has not the concrete sense but refers to the authority which Jesus' words command. German translations render *Vollmacht,* which is more than "authority" and less than "absolute power" (A-G s.v. *exousia* 3.) but refers to an authority derived from and bestowed by a higher power, here by God (cp. *TH-Mk* on 11 : 28).

Translation: *They were astonished,* see on "wondered" in 1 : 21.

At his teaching, or, 'at the things (or, at how) he taught them', 'when they heard him teach (them)'.

His word was with authority, or, 'what he said had authority', 'his word was that of one who has authority', 'he spoke as one who has authority'. For *authority,* which may be described as 'right (and power) to command, or, to do something', cp. also *TH-Mk* on 1 : 22; 2 : 10; Nida, *BT*, 197. The term occurs also in 4 : 6 (which see), 36; 5 : 24; 7 : 8; 9 : 1; 10 : 19; 12 : 11 (plural, referring to persons); 19 : 17; 20 : 2, 8, 20; 22 : 25.

33 ***And in the synagogue there was a man who had the spirit of an unclean demon; and he cried out with a loud voice,***

Exegesis: *echōn pneuma daimoniou akathartou* 'having (i.e. with) the spirit of an unclean demon'. The phrase looks like a contamination of *pneuma akatharton* 'unclean spirit' (cp. v. 36; 6 : 18; 8 : 29; 9 : 42; 11 : 24) and *daimonion* 'devil' (cp. v. 35; 8 : 27; 9 : 42), which are, as 9 : 42 shows, synonymous. *daimonion* never has a qualifying adjective (except 'many', or, 'all') and *pneuma,* when not referring to the divine or the human spirit, is always combined with *akatharton.*

daimonion 'demon', 'evil spirit'.

akathartos 'unclean', elsewhere of cultic or moral uncleanness, but in Luke only of evil spirits.

kai anekraxen phōnē megalē 'and he shouted in a loud voice'. Subject is *anthrōpos* 'man'.

anakrazō 'to cry out', 'to shout'.

Translation: *A man who had the spirit of an unclean demon.* That this expresses demon possession is clear, but the exact meaning of the uncommon collocation is not clear, as shown in *Exegesis.* This makes the clause difficult to translate. Matters are worse still in languages where the rendering of 'demon' coincides with that of '(evil) spirit' (NV) or of 'unclean spirit', or with both (Tzeltal, Bahasa Indonesia, Balinese); cp. also references on "demon" in v. 35 and on "unclean spirit" in v. 36. For a practical solution of this problem it is probably best for the translator to start from his usual rendering of demon possession and then try to expand it in such a way as to reflect the longer and more intricate wording of the Greek. In doing so he may use what is less common in the receptor language (since the Greek is uncommon), though not what is decidedly unidiomatic. This may lead to renderings such as, 'a person with an evil, unclean spirit' (NV), 'who had a bad, devilish spirit (lit. wind)' (Sranan), "possessed by a devil, an unclean spirit" (NEB); or simply, 'possessed by demons' (Balinese). For terms to express demon possession see *N.T.Wb.*/ 24f, DEMON; *TH-Mk* 1 : 23, 32; *TBT*, 3.167, 1952. In several Indonesian languages the rendering 'entered by a demon' is very common; the resulting expression has become so much a technical term that the qualification 'by a demon' is often omitted. Cp. also on "entered" in 8 : 30. In Marathi a term for demon possession is 'to be touched', and in Tagabili one can refer to it by a euphemism (used e.g. in 8 : 2), 'that which they always say, "Someone (or, something) is leading him"'.

Cried out with a loud voice, or, 'shouted loudly' (Willibrord), 'shrieking he shouted' (Balinese); and cp. on "exclaimed with a loud cry" in 1 : 42.

34 ***"Ah! What have you to do with us, Jesus of Nazareth? Have you come to destroy us? I know who you are, the Holy One of God."***

Exegesis: *ea* (††) 'ha!', exclamation of dismay.

ti hēmin kai soi 'what have you to do with us?', well known phrase in the Septuagint, cp. e.g. Judges 11 : 12. The corresponding Hebrew phrase means, 'why do you meddle with us?', cp. *TH-Mk* on 1 : 24, Goodspeed, *Problems* 100f and *TBT*, 7.149, 1956. The plural *hēmin* reflects the idea that an unclean spirit is a plurality in itself, cp. Mk. 5 : 2 (singular), 9, 12f (plural), and here *oida* 'I know' (singular).

Iēsou Nazarēne 'Jesus of Nazareth' or "Jesus the Nazarene" (Rieu). The reference to Nazareth does not imply contempt but serves as a means of identification.

ēlthes apolesai hēmas either 'have you come to destroy us?' or 'you have come to destroy us', preferably the former.

apollumi 'to destroy', 'to lose'.

oida se tis ei 'I know you who you are', anticipation of the subject of the subordinate clause by making it the object of the main clause, cp. Bl-D, § 480.6.

ho hagios tou theou 'the holy one of God' (cp. Mk. 1: 24 and *TH-Mk* there; Jn. 6 : 69), is to be understood as Messianic. The genitive *tou theou* is best interpreted as possessive, 'the holy one who belongs to God'.

Translation: For this verse cp. *TH-Mk* on the parallel passage 1 : 24, to which only a few points have to be added here.

What have you to do with us. An idiomatic expression used is, 'why do you fall among (i.e. interfere with) us?' (Marathi). To employ a reciprocal expression is not advisable.

Jesus of Nazareth, i.e. (originating) from N. Some languages use an appositional construction, 'Jesus, person-of N.' (Ponape), or a derivational term, as does the Greek, "Jesus the Nazarene" (Rieu, similarly Marathi), or, "Jesus, you Nazarene" (Goodspeed, adding the pronoun better to express the form of address).

I know who you are, the Holy One of God. The final phrase may have to be given a verb, 'you are the Holy One of God'; or the structure of the whole clause may have to be changed, e.g. 'I know you. You are the Holy One of God'. In the second case "to know" means 'to be acquainted with', in the first, 'to be aware of the fact that'. For *holy* see on 1 : 15. In languages that describe the word by 'of (i.e. belonging to) God' it may be possible to use a rendering such as, 'the one who comes from God and is dedicated (or, gives himself) to him (or, God)', 'the man who is God's very own'.

35 ***But Jesus rebuked him, saying, "Be silent, and come out of him!" And when the demon had thrown him down in the midst, he came out of him, having done him no harm.***

Exegesis: *epetimēsen autō ho Iēsous* 'Jesus checked him'. The meaning of *epetimēsen* is defined by the subsequent *phimōthēti* 'be silent', which suggests a command.

epitimaō 'to rebuke', 'to reprove', here "to speak seriously in order to prevent an action or to bring one to an end" (cp. A-G s.v. 1), hence 'to check', cp. *TH-Mk* on 1 : 25 and *TBT*, 7.6, 1956. This meaning also in vv. 39 and 41; 8 : 24; 9 : 42; 19 : 39, and probably also 9 : 21.

phimōthēti (†) 'be silent', cp. *TH-Mk* on 1 : 25.

exelthe ap' autou 'come out of him', not 'get away from him' as the preposition might seem to suggest. But Luke always has *apo* after *exerchomai* (cp. 5 : 8; 8 : 2, 29, 33, 35, 38; 9 : 5; 11 : 24).

kai ripsan auton to daimonion eis to meson exēlthen ap' autou mēden blapsan auton 'and having thrown him down in the midst the demon came out of him having done him no harm'. The sentence consists of (1) a main clause *to daimonion...exēlthen ap' autou* 'the demon came out of him', and (2) a participial clause *ripsan...meson* 'having thrown him in the midst', describing an event preceding that of the main clause, and (3) a participial clause *mēden blapsan auton* 'having done him no harm', which qualifies the event of (2) with regard to its consequences for the possessed.

ripsan auton...eis to meson 'having thrown him down in the middle'. For *eis to meson* cp. A-G s.v. *mesos* 2. The most natural explanation is that the man falls down where he stood in the middle of the people in such a way that it appears as if somebody throws him down. *riptō* also 17 : 2.

mēden blapsan auton (†) 'having done him no harm whatever', stronger than *mē blapsan auton* 'having done him no harm'.

Translation: For the first half of the verse cp. *TH-Mk* on the parallel passage in 1 : 25.

Rebuked him, or, 'the demon'. In the Gospel of Luke the Gr. verb *epitimaō* (with exception of 9 : 21 always rendered by 'to rebuke' in RSV) occurs with a non-personal object (for which see on 4 : 39; 8 : 24), or with a personal object, viz. demons (4 : 35, 41; 9 : 42), human beings (9 : 55; 17 : 3; 18 : 15, 39; 19 : 39; 23 : 40). In the latter case the verb is variously expressed, cp. e.g. 'to scold' (Bahasa Indonesia; similarly Toba Batak in 9 : 55, lit. 'to be hit with words by someone'), 'to reprimand' (Javanese, lit. 'to-be-angry-towards'), 'to threaten' (Jerusalem; similarly Sranan, lit. 'to peel one's eyes', i.e. to open one's eyes wide). Where, as in this case, the reference probably is to strict command rather than to censure it is preferable to use, 'to check', 'to bring to a stop', or making explicit the implied direct discourse, 'to say, "Stop doing so (immediately)"', which would result here in something like, 'he said to him, "Immediately stop speaking and get out of him"'.

Come out of him. The term to be used here for the cessation of demon possession should be the normal counterpart of the idiom that expresses the being in or beginning of that state, for which see on v. 33 and references.

The subsequent clauses may better be co-ordinated, e.g. 'then (or, on these words, or, when he heard this) de demon threw...and came...'.

For *demon* see *N.T.Wb.*/24; *TH-Mk* on 1 : 32; and cp. *TBT*, 1.87, 1950; 2.146, 1951; 3.167, 1952.

To throw down, or, 'cause-to-fall' (several Indonesian languages), 'cause to collapse'.

In the midst may have to be specified, 'in between the people' (Willibrord, Ponape), 'in front of all' (Jerusalem), 'in the sight of all present'.

Having done him no harm, or, 'injury'. This fact probably was contrary to expectation; this will influence the choice of connective when the clause has to be co-ordinated, e.g. 'but (he) did not hurt him at all'.

36 ***And they were all amazed and said to one another, "What is this word? For with authority and power he commands the unclean spirits, and they come out."***

Exegesis: *kai egeneto thambos epi pantas* 'and astonishment came upon all'. For a similar phrase cp. 1 : 65.

thambos (also 5 : 9) 'astonishment', 'awe', in the New Testament always of the feeling that comes over people when they witness an act of divine power.

kai sunelaloun pros allēlous 'and they talked to one another'. The imperfect tense has durative aspect.

sullaleō 'to talk', 'to talk with'.

tis ho logos houtos 'what is this word?' *logos* is best understood as referring to the imperatives of v. 35, 'be silent and get out of him'. This is supported by the fact that the subsequent clause introduced by *hoti* refers unequivocally to Jesus' power over the unclean spirits.

hoti introducing a clause which describes what *ho logos houtos* refers to, either 'because', 'for' (cp. RSV, BFBS, Goodspeed, Brouwer, NV) or 'that', preferably the former.

en exousia kai dunamei 'with authority and power'. The former refers to what cannot be contradicted, the latter to what cannot be resisted (cp. Bengel quoted by Plummer).

epitassei tois akathartois pneumasin, kai exerchontai 'he orders the unclean spirits and they come out'. The latter of the two co-ordinate clauses describes what is the result of the former.

epitassō 'to order', with the dative. Except 14 : 22 always of giving orders to more than human powers.

Translation: For the introductory sentence cp. *TH-Mk* on 1 : 27; for *amazed* see also above, on "wondered at" in 1 : 21.

Said to one another. Luke uses various phrases with reference to discussion or consultation taking place among Jesus' general audience and/or his opponents (4 : 36; 5 : 21; 6 : 11; 20 : 5, usually in reaction to what they hear him say or see him do), or among the disciples (9 : 46; 22 : 23), or between the two men on the way to Emmaus (24 : 14f), or among the tenants in 20 : 14 and the shepherds in 2 : 15. The particular nuance of the discussion may be that of wonder or questioning (4 : 36; 22 : 23), indignation (5 : 21), controversy (9 : 46), planning (for arrest or murder, 6 : 11; 20 : 14), deliberation (20 : 5; 22 : 4; 24 : 14). Some languages possess various specific terms for some or all of these nuances, cp. English "discussion", "dispute", "debate", "consultation", "planning", "argument", "questionings" etc., but elsewhere one may have to use a more generic rendering, viz. a reciprocal expression derived from or built upon 'to say' or 'to ask', leaving the specific nuance to be expressed by the following indication of the contents of the discussion (often given in direct discourse) or to be inferred from the context. A corresponding reflexive expression (e.g. 'to ask-oneself', 'to say to the heart') is in some of these languages used for inward reasoning and thought.

What is this word, or, 'how can he speak like that'. The interrogative clause has the force of an exclamation, cp. Jerusalem, *quelle parole!* and Balinese, which adds the exclamatory particle that indicates wonder.

One may have to make explicit that the relationship between the two next clauses is a consecutive one, e.g. 'with such authority and power he commands...that they come out', or transposing the prepositional phrase, 'he commands...with the result that they come out; so great is (or, that shows) his authority and power'.

With authority and power, or, 'with (or, as one who has) the right and power (to speak)'. Sranan combines the two terms in one expression, cp. 'in the way-of-a-boss he masters the bad spirits'.

He commands. If the verb must be rendered analytically and the contents of the command has to be specified, this may result in something like, 'he tells the unclean spirits to come out (or, in direct discourse), and they do so'.

Unclean spirits, see *N.T.Wb./*47, IMPURE; *TH-Mk* on 1 : 23; and cp. references on "demon" in v. 35.

37 ***And reports of him went out into every place in the surrounding region.***

Exegesis: *exeporeueto* 'went out', synonymous with *exēlthen* (cp. on v. 14).

ēchos (†, to be distinguished from *ēchos* in 21 : 25) 'report', 'news'.

eis panta topon tēs perichōrou 'to every place of the surrounding district', i.e. the district surrounding Capernaum.

Translation: This verse closely resembles v. 14, which see.

Place, a generic term for settlements of any kind, which may have to be rendered, 'where people live'.

In the surrounding region, i.e. in the area (that lies) around Capernaum.

38 ***And he arose and left the synagogue, and entered Simon's house. Now Simon's mother-in-law was ill with a high fever, and they besought him for her.***

Exegesis: *anastas de apo tēs sunagōgēs* 'after rising (and going away) from the synagogue'. *de* marks transition to a new part of the story. For *anistēmi* cp. on 1 : 39. In *anastas* the basic meaning 'to rise' is weakened; in connexion with *apo tēs sunagōgēs* it assumes the meaning 'to go away', or 'to leave'.

eis tēn oikian Simōnos 'into the house of a certain Simon', because of the omission of the article before *Simōnos.*

penthera de tou Simōnos ēn sunechomenē puretō megalō 'Simon's mother-in-law was suffering from a high fever'. *de* introduces a new phase of the story. *penthera* also 12 : 53. *puretos* also v. 39.

sunechō 'to press hard', 'to hold in custody', 'to distress', 'to torment'. In the passive 'to be hard pressed', 'to suffer'.

kai ērōtēsan auton peri autēs 'and they asked him concerning her'. The subject is not specified but may be taken to refer to the patient's relatives. Both *ērōtēsan* and *peri* are used in a pregnant sense: the former in the sense of 'asking for help' (cp. A-G s.v. 2.), the latter of 'on behalf of' (cp. A-G s.v. 1 f).

Translation: For possible problems concerning reference ties cp. *TBT*, 17.20f, 1966, on Mk. 1 : 29ff in Sateré.

And he arose and left, preferably, 'he left', 'he went away from', or to bring out the introductory function of the clause, 'on leaving', 'after going-out from'.

For the rest of v. 38 see *TH-Mk* on the parallel passage 1 : 30. A few additional remarks follow.

Mother-in-law, now see also *N.T.Wb.*/33, FAMILY.

Was ill with a high fever, or, 'had/was having a high/severe fever'. Luke does not say that the woman was lying down but this is implied in "she rose" (v. 39) and stated explicitly in some versions, e.g. Sranan, Kekchi. *Fever,* or a term derived from one of its symptoms, e.g. 'hot illness' (Balinese), 'warm-cold illness' (Javanese), 'be-shaking' (East Toradja), 'grabbing one's head' (Pame).

They besought him for her, or, 'they asked him to help (or, heal) her, or, that he would-kindly help her (Balinese), that he come and help her' (Sranan); or, 'they asked (or, said to) him, "Please, do help/heal her!"'. For *to beseech* cp. on 5 : 12.

39 ***And he stood over her and rebuked the fever, and it left her; and immediately she rose and served them.***

Exegesis: *kai epistas epanō autēs* 'standing over her', or, 'at her head'; the former is more consistent with the basic meaning of *epanō,* and hence to be preferred. For *epistas* cp. on 2 : 9. The aorist tense is ingressive and this makes the meaning of the whole clause complex: Jesus went to her and came to stand over her; *epistas* implies the idea of a movement towards and *epanō autēs* indicates a position.

epanō 'above', 'over', either used as an adverb or as a preposition with genitive.

epetimēsen tō puretō 'he checked the fever', cp. on v. 35 and references there.

kai aphēken autēn 'and it left her', sudden change of subject. For *aphiēmi* in the meaning 'to leave' cp. A-G s.v. 3 a.

parachrēma de anastasa 'after getting up at once'. Here *anastasa* has the basic meaning of 'rising', or, 'getting up', cp. on 1 : 39. For *parachrēma* cp. on 1 : 64. Often it is used by Luke with reference to an act of healing and suggests that no time elapsed between the word (or act) of healing and its effectuation (cp. also 5 : 25; 8 : 44, 47; 13 : 13).

diēkonei autois 'she served them', i.e. Jesus and those who had come with him.

diakoneō 'to serve', here of serving guests in the house, cp. Goodspeed, "waited on them".

Translation: *Stood over her*, preferably, "came and stood over her" (NEB, and cp. *Exegesis*), or, 'approached (or, came to her side) and bowed over (or, looked down on) her'.

Rebuked, or, 'stopped', 'checked', 'caused to cease'; or here a specific term for a comparable treatment by a medical man, e.g. 'chased-away' (Balinese).

And has consecutive force here, which is expressed in some languages, e.g. Balinese, Toba Batak.

It left her, or, 'it ceased' (Javanese), 'the fever went out' (Marathi); or, avoiding the change of subject, 'she became free from it' (Willibrord), 'she recovered'. For specific idioms see *TH-Mk* on 1 : 31.

Served them, or, "attended on them" (BFBS), "began to see to their needs" (Phillips), 'took care of them', 'gave them something to eat', 'prepared food' (South Toradja), 'entertained them (lit. treated-them-as-guests)' (East Toradja). One should avoid a rendering suggesting that she had the position of a servant in the house. The three Indonesian languages that use honorifics do not permit persons of different rank to be subjoined under one plural pronoun; hence the rendering 'she served the guests' was chosen in order to avoid a double rendering of "them", viz. by 'him (honorific) and them (common pronoun)', or 'Jesus and those with him'.

40 ***Now when the sun was setting, all those who had any that were sick with various diseases brought them to him; and he laid his hands on every one of them and healed them.***

Exegesis: *dunontos de tou hēliou* 'when the sun was setting', i.e. at the end of the same day. *dunō* (†).

hapantes hosoi 'all those who', stronger than *pantes hoi*.

eichon asthenountas nosois poikilais 'had people suffering from various diseases'. The phrase is neutral concerning the relationship between the sick and those who brought them to Jesus; it simply states that the latter 'had' the sick. This is best understood as that they had them in their homes and that they were relatives or responsible for them.

astheneō (†) 'to be sick', here with dative of relation 'to suffer from'.

poikilos (†) 'of various kinds', 'various'.

ēgagon autous pros auton 'brought them (i.e. the sick) to him'. Though this is done repeatedly the verb is in the aorist to bring out that it refers to every single act of bringing a sick person to Jesus.

ho de heni hekastō autōn tas cheiras epititheis 'and laying his hands on each of them'. The relationship between this participial clause and the subsequent main verb *etherapeuen autous* 'he healed them' is such that the former refers to the way in which the latter is brought about. The laying on of hands is generally interpreted as an act of transmission (cp. Plummer), here of the transmission of spiritual and physical wholeness, or vitality (cp. *IDB* II, 521). Other healings, however, do not depend upon the act of the laying on of hands (cp. 7 : 10; 17 : 14).

epitithēmi 'to lay upon', 'to put upon', lit. or figurative.

etherapeuen autous 'he healed them'. The imperfect tense *etherapeuen* points to the linear or even repetitive aspect of the healing.

Translation: *Now,* cp. on 1 : 57.

When the sun was setting, or, 'when the sun was entering/sinking/dying/descending/striking down' (cp. Bahasa Indonesia, South Toradja, Toba Batak 1885, Sranan, Enga respectively), or another idiom for 'when evening came'; cp. also *N.T.Wb.*/23, DAY.

All those who had any that were sick...brought them to him. In some languages it is preferable to make 'the sick' the object of the clause (as done in Leyden, Bahasa Indonesia RC), applying some further partial adjustments, e.g. 'all people brought to him the sick they had (or, the sick they looked after, or, the sick amongst them, or, their sick, or, their sick friends/relatives/housemates)...'; or as the subject of the clause (as done in Cuyono, some Indonesian languages), e.g. 'sick people...were brought to him by those who looked after them (or, by their friends)', 'sick people ...came before him; their friends brought them'; or again, assuming a conditional relationship, 'if people had any that were sick..., they brought them to him'. — *All,* i.e. the people of Capernaum; hence, 'all there', 'all inhabitants (of C.)', where necessary.

Any that were sick with various diseases, i.e. various sick people, each with a disease; hence, 'various ailing people', 'ill people whatever their illness' (Bahasa Indonesia RC). It may be necessary to change the pattern of subordination, e.g. 'any sick who were suffering of one disease or another', or to shift to co-ordination. For *sick* and *disease* see *N.T.Wb.*/67; Nida, *BT*, 156. In languages that have no generic term one may have to use a few specific terms for diseases most common in the area.

He laid his hands on. If the place touched has to be specified one can best say 'on their head'. The rendering chosen should preferably suggest a solemn act with symbolic function. An interesting cultural equivalent is used in East Toradja, which renders the whole phrase by 'He-pressed-down', a verb that in former times was used with the specific meaning of 'to press down one's hand on a person's head', in order to fortify his soul after a dangerous experience, but in Christian usage came to refer to the gesture made when blessing a person.

41 ***And demons also came out of many, crying, "You are the Son of God!" But he rebuked them, and would not allow them to speak, because they knew that he was the Christ.***

Exegesis: *exērcheto de kai daimonia apo pollōn* 'and demons also went out from many'. *de* is continuative, *kai* is used as an adverb, meaning 'also', cp. A-G s.v. II 1. *apo pollōn* is best understood as referring to a group different from those referred to in v. 40.

kraugazonta kai legonta 'shouting and saying'. The two participles refer to one act and hence *legonta* is often not translated, cp. RSV.

kraugazō (†) 'to shout', 'to cry out'.

kai epitimōn ouk eia auta lalein 'and checking them he did not allow them to speak'. *epitimōn* and *ouk eia* refer to the same act, cp. on v. 35.

eaō (also 22 : 51) 'to let', 'to permit', 'to let go'.

hoti ēdeisan ton Christon auton einai 'because they knew that he was the Messiah'. *hoti* may mean 'that' or 'because', preferably the latter.

Translation: For most expressions in this verse see on vv. 34f.

Many, or, "many others" (Rieu), 'many people that were there too' (cp. *Exegesis*).

He rebuked them (see on v. 35) is synonymous with *would not allow them*, which it seems to reinforce; hence renderings by an adverb(ial phrase) qualifying the next verb, e.g. 'did not allow them at all', 'sternly forbade them' (cp. Rieu, Leyden, Jerusalem). — The rendering of *to allow* is 'to give' in some Indonesian languages, and 'to give permission (lit. path)' in Sranan.

42 ***And when it was day he departed and went into a lonely place. And the people sought him and came to him, and would have kept him from leaving them;***

Exegesis: *genomenēs de hēmeras* 'when day came'. The phrase does not necessarily imply that the healing lasted the whole night.

exelthōn eporeuthē 'he left and went'. *exelthōn* probably refers to leaving the town.

eis erēmon topon 'to a lonely spot'.

kai hoi ochloi epezētoun auton 'and the crowds searched for him'. The imperfect tense *epezētoun* is durative, cp. "kept seeking" (Plummer). For *ochlos* cp. on 3 : 7.

epizēteō (also 12 : 30) 'to search for', 'to try to find'.

kai ēlthon heōs autou lit. 'they came as far as him', i.e. 'to where he was'. *ēlthon* is aorist because it refers to a punctiliar event as different from *epezētoun* and *kateichon* (see next note).

heōs here 'as far as', cp. A-G s.v. 2 a.

kai kateichon auton 'they tried to keep him'. The imperfect tense is conative.

katechō 'to hold back', 'to hold up', here with the implication of preventing from going away, cp. A-G s.v. 1 a. This implication is explicitly stated in what follows.

tou mē poreuesthai ap' autōn 'that he would not leave them'. Articular infinitive in the genitive after a verb of hindering to indicate the intended result, cp. Bl-D, § 400.4.

Translation: *When it was day,* preferably, 'when day came', is rendered by various idiomatic expressions, e.g. 'when it-sunned' (East Toradja), 'time of sun-rays' (Lokele), 'when sun is coming-out' (Kituba), 'when day dawned (lit. sprouted)' (Marathi), 'when space (referring to air or land) became white' (Tzeltal), 'when it/day became light' (Cuyono, Toba Batak); other possibilities are, 'early next morning', 'when the darkness had passed'.

Lonely place, or, 'uninhabited place', 'place where there are no people living', 'place where people seldom come'; in some cases one term covers 'silent/quiet' and 'lonely'.

The people is used here in its generic meaning, see on 1 : 17; cp. also on "multitudes" in 3 : 7, and references.

Sought him and came to him, or, 'went in search of him and (finally) came to where he was', cp. also, 'were-tracking (from a noun meaning 'footmark') until they reached him' (Javanese). Some versions (e.g. Rieu, NEB, Jerusalem, Bahasa Indonesia RC, Sundanese) subordinate the second clause to what follows, 'and when they came upon him they would have...'. *Came to him* may better be rendered, 'encountered him' (Bahasa Indonesia RC), 'found him' (East Toradja 1933).

Would have kept him from leaving them, or, 'tried to hold Him back that He would not leave them' (NV), 'tried to keep him, saying, "Do not leave us"', both reflecting the rather redundant wording of the Greek; or simply, 'tried to keep him with them', "did their best to make him stay with them" (Rieu).

43 ***but he said to them, "I must preach the good news of the kingdom of God to the other cities also; for I was sent for this purpose."***

Exegesis: *hoti* introduces direct speech here.

kai tais heterais polesin 'also to the other towns'; emphatic by position. The phrase refers to the other towns of Galilee, or of the whole country, preferably the latter as v. 44 seems to show.

euaggelisasthai me dei tēn basileian tou theou 'I must preach (the good news of) the kingdom of God'. For *euaggelizomai* cp. on 1 : 19. *dei,* impersonal verb 'it is necessary', denotes compulsion of some sort, cp. *TH-Mk* on 8 : 31.

basileia tou theou 'kingdom, or, rule of God', cp. *TH-Mk* on 1 : 15. The phrase has a dynamic and eschatological meaning. The kingdom of God comes (10 : 9, 11; 17 : 20), is near (21 : 31). It is Jesus' mission to preach this and to call people to surrender to the rule of God.

hoti epi touto apestalēn 'because for that I was sent', cp. on 1 : 19.

Translation: *I must,* cp. on 2 : 49.

Preach the good news of, or, 'about', or, 'that' (with following verbal clause, see below); and cp. on 3 : 18.

For *the kingdom of God* (also in 6 : 20; 7 : 28; 8 : 1, 10; 9 : 2, 11, 27, 60, 62; 10 : 9, 11; 11 : 20; 13 : 18, 20, 28; 14 : 15; 16 : 16; 17 : 20f; 18 : 16f,

24f, 29; 19 : 11; 21 : 31; 22 : 16, 18; 23 : 51) see Nida, *BT*, 196; *TH-Mk* on 1 : 14, 15; 4 : 11; 9 : 47; 10 : 15; *TBT*, 12.85f, 1961; 13.31f, 1962; and 11.177, 1960, on the dangers of the rendering meaning 'habitation of a king'; cp. also Beekman, *NOT*, 215-223, especially 218ff, giving the occurrences of the phrase in the Gospels together with the Mixtec renderings, some of which will be quoted below. Generally speaking renderings can best be modelled on a phrase such as, 'God's being king/chief/ruler', 'God's rule/government', or a corresponding verbal clause introduced by '(the fact) that', '(the time) when', '(the place) where', '(the way) how', as context requires. If an object is obligatory with the verb, it may be 'this world', 'men', or an appropriate pronoun. In the present verse this leads to 'news that God will be king/rule (over the world/men)'. For *kingdom* cp. also on 1 : 33.

Other cities, i.e. cities distinct from and additional to those that have been mentioned until now, viz. Capernaum and Nazareth.

I was sent for this purpose, or, "that is what I was sent to do" (Goodspeed, NEB), 'it is for this that God sent me', or more synthetically, "that is my mission" (Phillips, similarly Sranan).

44 ***And he was preaching in the synagogues of Judea.***

Exegesis: *tēs Ioudaias* 'of Judea'. This is appropriate if *Ioudaia* is understood as referring to the whole territory inhabited by the Jewish people, cp. on 1 : 5.

Translation: *He was preaching*. If an object is obligatory in the receptor language one may add a reference to what precedes, e.g. 'he was preaching this (news)', or a more generic term, e.g. "he continued proclaiming his message" (Phillips), and see *TH-Mk* on 1 : 38. For the verb see above on 3 : 3.

Judea, preferably, 'the Jewish country'.

CHAPTER FIVE

1 *While the people pressed upon him to hear the word of God, he was standing by the lake of Gennesaret.*

Exegesis: *egeneto de* 'and it happened', cp. on 1 : 8. Syntactically *en tō epikeisthai kai akouein* lit. 'during the pressing and listening' (see below) is subordinate to the connecting clause *kai autos ēn hestōs* 'and he was standing', but semantically both are introductory with regard to v. 2 *kai eiden* 'and he saw', cp. NEB, "One day as he stood by the Lake..., and the people crowded upon him...".

en tō ton ochlon epikeisthai autō kai akouein ton logon tou theou 'while the crowd was pressing around him and hearing the word of God', articular accusative and infinitive. In the light of what follows *epikeisthai* carries the main weight of meaning and *akouein* is secondary. For *ochlos* cp. on 3 : 7. *ochlous* (plural) in v. 3 refers to the same group.

epikeimai (also 23 : 23) 'to press around, or upon', with dative of the person. The verb carries a note of physical pressure (Plummer).

ho logos tou theou (also 8 : 11, 21; 11 : 28) 'the word of God', in Luke a fixed term for Jesus' preaching and (in Acts) the preaching of the apostles. The genitive *tou theou* is subjective: the word God speaks, or the message God sends. This message is transmitted by Jesus.

kai autos ēn hestōs 'and he was standing'. Here the force of the periphrastic construction *ēn hestōs* is descriptive. *autos* 'he' refers back to *autō*, not emphatic.

para tēn limnēn Gennēsaret 'by the lake Gennesaret', cp. A-G s.v. *para* III 1 b.

limnē 'lake', always of the lake Gennesaret which is called *thalassa* 'sea' by the other evangelists (cp. Mt. 13 : 1; Mk. 4 : 1).

Translation: Subordination of this verse to v. 2, as mentioned in *Exegesis*, is acceptable in several languages (e.g. in Ponape), but elsewhere it may be preferable to say something like, 'he was standing by the lake... and the people pressed...; (2) (then) he saw...' (cp. e.g. Trukese).

The people, see on "the crowd" in 5 : 19.

Pressed upon him, or, 'boisterously pushed-each-other around him' (Bahasa Indonesia RC), 'squeezed through and crushed him' (Santali), 'crowded/jostled against him' (Kapauku).

The word of God, i.e. 'what God has said', 'what God had to say (to them)', but a more specific term is often preferable, e.g. 'God's message' (Kapauku), cp. also on "the word" in 1 : 2. In several Muslim countries the phrase 'word of Allah' is common usage and may prove a good rendering, provided it does not refer exclusively to the Koran, or to divine words that have been written down.

By the lake. The preposition may have to be rendered, 'on the shore of', 'beside', 'close to'. *Lake.* The normal term for 'large inland body of water' should be used; in Trukese one has to say 'lagoon'; cp. also *N.T.Wb.*/51f, MARITIME. Sometimes the renderings of Luke's idiomatic expression, 'lake', and of Mark's and Matthew's semitism, 'sea' coincide—an entirely acceptable kind of harmonization. A few versions, however, harmonize the other way round: having used 'sea' more or less unidiomatically in Mark and Matthew, they introduce this term here also. Thus to "semiticize" Luke where he writes normal Greek is undesirable.

2 ***And he saw two boats by the lake; but the fishermen had gone out of them and were washing their nets.***

Exegesis: *kai eiden duo ploia hestōta para tēn limnēn* 'and he saw two boats standing by the lake'. This clause is the beginning of the story proper. *hestōta para tēn limnēn* means that the boats are on the shore of the lake, just as Jesus himself was (cp. v. 1). *hestōta* 'standing' is a very general word (cp. A-G s.v. *histēmi* II 2 b α) which means here little more than 'being'.

hoi de halieis ap' autōn apobantes eplunon ta diktua 'the fishermen having gone out of them were washing the nets'. *de* is best understood as continuative and the clause describes the second part of the picture: the boats on the shore and the fishermen washing the nets. *eplunon* is durative because it describes a situation.

apobainō (also 21 : 13) 'to go away', 'to get out', fig. 'to lead to', 'to result in' (21 : 13).

plunō (†) 'to wash', especially of clothes and material things, cp. Trench, *Synonyms of the New Testament*, 1880, p. 160f.

diktuon (also vv. 4f) 'net' for catching fish.

Translation: For nautical and fishing terms used in vv. 2ff see *N.T.Wb.*/56 and 37 respectively. Differences in cultural setting may cause considerable difficulties for the translator. Thus, if fishing in general is unknown in the receptor culture, he may have to coin short descriptive phrases, where necessary giving supplementary explanation in a footnote or picture. Or, if it is the particular method of fishing mentioned in the narrative that is unknown, he may have to adapt terms belonging to a method that, though different, is well known in the culture, carefully expanding their meaning by contextual conditioning, or combining description and adaptation (as in Navajo, see *TBT*, 13.30f, 1962). Or again, some kind of fishing may be known, but certain concomitant features do not fit, e.g. where fishing is done only by women (Kapauku), or at night (Rundi, see *TBT*, 1.19, 1950, on Mt. 4 : 18); in some such cases an explanatory note will again be required.

Boats. The reference probably is to rather small, relatively shallow boats, holding from six to twelve persons, propelled by oars and/or sail, cp. *TH-Mk* on 1 : 19. A descriptive phrase used in Chichimeca Pame is, 'that with which we can walk on water'. That these boats were fishing-boats may have to be made explicit, e.g. 'boats used for fishing, or, catching fish'.

By the lake. In some languages one has to add a verb to indicate how the boat lies moored, cp. 'tied' (viz. to a pole planted at the edge of the lake) (Kapauku), cp. also, "pulled up on the beach" (TEV).

Fishermen, cp. *TH-Mk* on 1 : 16. In some cases, especially if fishing has been referred to already, one may say, 'the sailors', 'the crew', 'those who owned/used them (or, the boats)'.

Washing, or, 'rinsing' (Sundanese, Dutch), 'making-clean' (Bahasa Indonesia).

Nets. Some descriptive phrases possible are, 'large fish traps made of strings', 'instruments for catching fish (or, to bring up out fish, cp. Navajo)'; if one has to choose between terms for 'dragnets' or 'casting nets', the former should be used.

3 ***Getting into one of the boats, which was Simon's, he asked him to put out a little from the land. And he sat down and taught the people from the boat.***

Exegesis: *embas de eis hen tōn ploiōn, ho ēn Simōnos* 'after stepping in one of the boats which was Simon's'; the genitive is possessive.

embainō 'to go in', 'to step in', in Luke always of going into a boat (cp. *N.T.Wb.*, 101/ NAUTICAL, III).

apo tēs gēs epanagagein oligon 'to put out a little from the shore', dependent upon *ērōtēsen auton* 'he asked him'. *gē* 'land' as opposed to sea, cp. A-G s.v. 4.

epanagō (†) 'to put out to sea', cp. *N.T.Wb.*, 100[a]/NAUTICAL (II).

kathisas de 'and after sitting down', going with *edidasken* 'he taught'. As 4 : 20 shows the usual way of teaching was sitting.

ek tou ploiou edidasken 'he taught from the boat'. The imperfect tense is continuative, cp. "he went on teaching" (NEB).

Translation: Shifting to co-ordination one may say, 'one of them was S.'s boat (or, one of the boats belonged to S.). He got into it and asked...'

To get into a boat, or synthetically, 'to embark', is variously expressed, e.g. 'to mount a boat' (East Toradja, same verb as used with horses), 'to ascend a boat' (Tagabili, same verb used when one comes up into a house on stilts), and cp. *TH-Mk* on 5 : 18.

Asked him to put out..., or more analytically, 'said to them, "Will you put out..., or, I want you to put out..."'; elsewhere more synthetically, 'he-let-her-be-pushed-off' (South Toradja); see also *N.T.Wb.*/12. In a language such as Balinese Jesus does not 'ask' but 'utters-a-wish'.

To put out...from the land. The aspect is momentaneous. Idiomatic equivalents may be viewing the event from another angle, 'to go-to-the-middle' (viz. of the lake) (Balinese), or built on the instrument used, 'to pole out (from the shore)' (Kapauku, East Toradja).

He sat down and taught...from the boat, or, if the first verb requires a locative qualification, 'he sat down in the boat and taught...from there' (Santali). *Sat down*, viz. on a beam or bench in the boat, or perhaps in its bow or stern.

4 ***And when he had ceased speaking, he said to Simon, "Put out into the deep and let down your nets for a catch."***

Exegesis: *hōs de epausato lalōn* 'when he stopped speaking'. *lalōn* here means 'addressing people'.

pauomai 'to stop (oneself) doing', 'to finish' usually with following participle.

epanagage eis to bathos lit. 'put out into the depth', i.e. to there where the water is deep. The use of the article does not imply that *to bathos* (†) refers to one particular spot. The command is addressed to Simon as in v. 3, which may imply that he was steering (cp. Plummer).

chalasate ta diktua humōn eis agran 'let down your nets for a catch'. Strictly speaking *chalasate* in the plural is still addressed to Simon. But the use of the plural implies that to let down the nets required more than one person (Plummer).

chalaō (†) 'to let down' the nets into the water, not 'to throw out', since the reference here is to a dragnet (cp. *IDB* II, 274).

agra 'catching', 'catch'. For the latter meaning cp. on v. 9. *eis agran* means 'in order to catch'.

Translation: *When he had ceased speaking,* or, 'being-finished his speaking' (Kapauku). Instead of 'speaking/speech' some versions (Malay, Sundanese) have 'teaching', because of v. 3.

Put out into the deep. The movement started in v. 3[a], and interrupted in v. 3[b], is now continued farther out into the lake, where the water is deeper. Some languages can use the same verb as in v. 3[a], e.g. 'pole (her) on to the deep' (East Toradja), 'cause the boat to go-to-the-middle further to the deep place' (Balinese), but in others the use of a different, sometimes rather specific, verb is required.

Put out (sing.) ... *let down* (plur.) *your* (plur.) *nets.* Where the shift from singular to plural cannot be brought out by simply using different pronominal and/or verbal forms some versions are content to leave it unexpressed, but in such cases one may consider a rendering like, 'put out (sing.) ..., you and your mates must let down the nets'.

For a catch, or, 'to get fish' (Sranan), 'to net (fish)' (cp. Santali), 'to fish' (East Toradja).

5 ***And Simon answered, "Master, we toiled all night and took nothing! But at your word I will let down the nets."***

Exegesis: *epistata* (always in the vocative and, except in 17 : 13, only used by the disciples) 'master!' Several commentators think that *epistata* carries a note of special authority, but as shown by the parallels quoted in Moulton-Milligan the emphasis is rather on an intimate, though respectful, relationship than on authority.

di' holēs nuktos kopiasantes ouden elabomen 'having toiled all night we caught nothing'. The participial phrase describes what they did, the main clause the result. Since the result is not in accordance with the work the participial phrase is implicitly concessive.

kopiaō (also 12 : 27) 'to work hard', 'to toil'.

epi de tō rēmati sou 'at your word'. *epi* here indicates that on which the subsequent action is based, cp. A-G s.v. II 1 b γ. *rēma* here 'order', 'direction', cp. A-G s.v. 1. The phrase expresses confidence in Jesus or merely reluctant obedience. The latter appears to be preferable.

chalasō 'I will let down', in the singular after *chalasate* (v. 4) in the plural.

Translation: *Master* can often best be rendered by the term for '(religious) teacher' (see 3 : 12); cp. also *TH-Mk* on 9 : 5. The use of the possessive, 'my master/teacher', may be helpful to suggest the more intimate connotation. This respectful intimacy is an important clue for the level of language to be used when one has to render the conversations between Jesus and his disciples in honorific languages.

We toiled... and took..., or, 'though we toiled..., we caught...', 'we toiled...and (yet) we caught...'. The verb has also been rendered, 'to try hard (lit. to-the-bone)' (Ponape), 'to seek with weariness' (Kapauku). In Trukese one has to add 'in-vain'; in Tagabili the work has to be specified, 'we worked...netting, but not even a little there was a catch we netted'.

All night, cp. *N.T.Wb.*/57. A reference to the past may have to be added, e.g. 'last night' (Trukese, similarly South Toradja). The night may be thought of as part of the preceding or of the present day. The latter is the case in Foe, which therefore uses near-past tense forms (see on 1 : 19).

At your word, or, '(only) because you say (or, tell me to do) so'.

I will let down the nets. Since more participators than one are implied Tagalog has to say, 'I will cause that the nets be let down'.

6 ***And when they had done this, they enclosed a great shoal of fish; and as their nets were breaking,***

Exegesis: *kai touto poiēsantes* 'and after having done this', refers (again in the plural) back to *chalasō ta diktua* 'I will let down the nets'.

sunekleisan plēthos ichthuōn polu 'they enclosed a great quantity of fishes'. The fact that *ichthuōn* stands between *plēthos* and attributive *polu* shows that semantically *plēthos ichthuōn* represents one concept.

sugkleiō (†) 'to enclose', without specific reference to fishing.

dierrēsseto de ta diktua autōn 'and their nets were breaking'. *de* is transitional. Semantically the clause describes the consequences of the preceding one, cp. e.g. Goodspeed ("...such a shoal of fish that their nets began to break"). Syntactically and semantically the clause goes with the preceding rather than with the following clause.

The force of the imperfect tense *dierrēsseto* is best brought out by such renderings as, 'were at breaking point', 'threatened to break', since an actual breaking of the nets did not happen.

diarrēssō (also 8 : 29) 'to tear', either intransitive or transitive.

Translation: *When they had done this*, a transitional phrase, which has also been rendered, 'this having been done', or, repeating the previous verb, 'having let down' (Kapauku).

They enclosed, or, 'they held/confined in it (or, in the net)', 'they brought together' (Ponape), or simply, 'they caught'.

A great shoal of fish, or simply, 'very many fish'. — *Fish* (cp. also *N.T.Wb.*/37) may have to be described, e.g. '(edible) things that live in the water'; or the name of one species must do duty for all, e.g. 'eel' (Wantoat).

Were breaking, or, 'almost tore' (South Toradja; similarly Balinese, where one has moreover to specify whether the threatening event did, or did not, take place afterwards).

7 ***they beckoned to their partners in the other boat to come and help them. And they came and filled both the boats, so that they began to sink.***

Exegesis: *kai kateneusan tois metochois en tō heterō ploiō* 'and they signalled to their partners in the other boat'.

kataneuō (††) 'to signal', 'to make signs'.

metochos (†) used as a substantive, 'partner', 'companion'. Here it has the same referent as *koinōnoi* in v. 10 (which see).

tou elthontas sullabesthai autois 'to come and help them', articular accusative and infinitive in the genitive, loosely connected with the preceding (cp. Bl-D, § 400.3), with final force. The subject is to be understood from *tois metochois*. *sullambanō* here the middle form with following dative, 'to come to the aid of', cp. A-G s.v. 2 b.

hōste buthizesthai auta 'so that they threatened to sink'. *hōste* with following accusative and infinitive indicates real or possible result (cp. Bl-D, § 391). Here the infinitive is in the present tense which implies that the sinking is not completed.

buthizō (†) 'to sink' (transitive), here in the passive with intransitive meaning.

Translation: *They beckoned,* or, 'gesticulated', 'waved their hands' (some Indonesian languages), etc., and cp. on "to make signs" in 1 : 22.

Partners, or, 'those of the same job', 'those who worked together with them' (Kapauku).

The other boat, or, 'the second boat', 'the boat (that was still) near the shore' (cp. South Toradja).

To come, or, to clarify the connexion with the main verb, 'trying-to-make (them) come' (Javanese), 'and thus requested them to come'.

Help them may require further qualification, e.g. 'assist them to draw up (the net)' (cp. Toba Batak 1885), 'help them with the catch' (Willibrord); and see on 10 : 40.

They came and filled both the boats. The pronoun is ambiguous in that it goes with both verbs, whereas actually only the other crew 'came' but both crews 'filled'. This ambiguity is acceptable in some languages but in others one has to differentiate, cp. 'they came and together they filled...', 'they came and the men (in the two boats) filled...'; or, shifting the subject of the second verb, 'they came and the two boats were filled' (cp. Toba Batak, Marathi). The emphasis is on the being full, hence, 'the boats were loaded (so) full that' (Javanese). It may be preferable to add 'with fish' (Balinese, Cuyono).

They began to sink, cp. on "were breaking" in v. 6; to express 'almost sinking' Tagabili says, 'just only a little left, their not sinking'.

8 ***But when Simon Peter saw it, he fell down at Jesus' knees, saying, "Depart from me, for I am a sinful man, O Lord."***

Exegesis: *idōn de Simōn Petros* 'and when Simon Peter saw it'. The object of *idōn* is to be understood from the preceding: the facts which vv. 6 and 7 describe. *de* is transitory. The two names *Simōn Petros* occur only here and in 6 : 14 together. The latter place refers explicitly to the fact that Jesus gave Simon the name Peter. This is, as it were, anticipated here.

prosepesen tois gonasin Iēsou 'he fell down at Jesus' knees', taking *Iēsou* as a genitive (cp. Plummer, Schlatter). The expression means that Peter knelt down, either bowing till his head was on a level with Jesus' knees, or clasping Jesus' knees in supplication (cp. Plummer, and L-Sc, s.v. *prospiptō* III). The former is preferable. *gonu* also 22 : 41.

exelthe ap' emou lit. 'go out of me', or 'go away from me', preferably the former, since it is consistent with Luke's use of the phrase elsewhere (cp. e.g. 4 : 35, 41).

hoti anēr hamartōlos eimi 'because I am a sinful man', motivates the preceding imperative. The meaning of the clause depends on the interpretation of *hamartōlos,* which is best understood in a general sense and refers to a class or group of people "who were not so careful in their observance of the Law...as were the Pharisees" (*TH-Mk* 2 : 15, cp. Richardson, *Word Book,* 228, and *TWNT* I, 331f). Simon knew that he belonged to that class and that he could not bear the presence of the one who had manifested his supernatural power beyond doubt.

kurie 'lord' (cp. on 1 : 6), stronger and more respectful than *epistata* 'master' in v. 5.

Translation: *Simon Peter* raises a problem in Tagabili, because the second name would always be the father's name; hence, 'Simon, the one Jesus named Peter'.

He fell down at Jesus' knees. In this context "to fall down" and its synonym "to fall on the face" mean 'to kneel down bowing the face towards the ground'; hence, 'to kneel (down)', 'to bow deep (down)' (Ponape), or a comparable idiom such as 'to throw himself against' (Santali), are possible renderings. Technical terms or phrases are usually available in Muslim countries, because the attitude in question occurs in the Muslim daily prayer. The phrase *at the knees of,* and its more common synonym 'at the feet of', may have to coincide in such renderings as 'before', 'in front of' (which in Kapauku idiom becomes 'at the nose of'); and cp. *N.T.Wb.*/17, BODY.

Depart from me, or, as advocated in *Exegesis,* 'go out of me', using a term that suggests the cessation of a mental state, viz. the being under the spell of Jesus' spirit.

A sinful man, see on "sinner" in *TH-Mk* on 2 : 15, and cp. on "sin", above, references on 1 : 77.

Lord, see on 1 : 6, sub (d).

9 ***For he was astonished, and all that were with him, at the catch of fish which they had taken;*** 10a ***and so also were James and John, sons of Zebedee, who were partners with Simon.***

Exegesis: *thambos gar perieschen auton* 'for astonishment had seized him'. The reference is to the state in which he speaks, hence 'he was astonished'. For *thambos* cp. on 4 : 36.

periechō (†) 'to seize', 'to come upon', cp. A-G s.v. 1 b.

kai pantas tous sun autō 'and all the men with him', i.e. the men who were with Simon in the same boat.

epi tē agra tōn ichthuōn hōn sunelabon 'at the catch of fishes which they had taken'. The relative pronoun goes with *ichthuōn* and *agra* has the same meaning as in v. 4 where it is to be understood in an active sense, and the genitive *ichthuōn* is objective. If the reading *hē* (cp. Nestle) is accepted *agra* is indirectly the object of *sunelabon* and is to be understood in a concrete sense, 'catch', i.e. the thing caught, and the genitive *ichthuōn* is genitive of content.

hoi ēsan koinōnoi tō Simōni 'who were partners of Simon's'. The phrase refers to the same persons as *tois metochois* in v. 7, viz. to the people who came in the other boat. The two terms are nearly synonymous, the difference being that *metochos* stresses the fact of having something in common and *koinōnos* (when used with dative) the fact of belonging together, but the difference should not be pressed, cp. Plummer on v. 7 and *N.T.Wb.*, 80f/JOIN and 117f/SHARE. *koinōnos* (†).

Translation: *For*, or, to make a better transition, 'thus his words, because' (Balinese).

He was astonished...at, see on "wondered at" in 1 : 21.

All that were with him, or, 'all his mates/companions', 'all those in his boat'.

The catch of fish which they had taken. The extraordinary character of the catch may be brought out by the use of a demonstrative pronoun, e.g. 'such a catch of fish...' (cp. Kapauku), or more explicitly by saying, 'their taking such-a-number of fish' (Javanese, similarly Santali), 'because they had caught so many fish'.

(V. 10[a]) *James and John, sons of Zebedee, who were partners with Simon.* Another phrase order may be more idiomatic in the receptor language, e.g. 'Simon's partners J. and J., Z.'s sons' (Toba Batak), 'the two children of Z., J. and J., the companions of S.' (South Toradja, similarly Kapauku). *Partners*, or, 'those associated with' (Balinese); the rendering often has to coincide with that of Gr. *metochoi* in v. 7, as e.g. in RSV, NEB, East Toradja, Santali.

10b ***And Jesus said to Simon, "Do not be afraid; henceforth you will be catching men."***

Exegesis: *mē phobou* 'do not be afraid', cp. on 1 : 13.

apo tou nun 'from now on', i.e., as the next verse shows, beginning immediately.

anthrōpous esē zōgrōn 'you will be catching men'. The place of *anthrōpous* at the beginning of the clause suggests emphasis and contrast with the fishes which he had been catching hitherto in his life. The periphrastic construction *esē zōgrōn* instead of the future indicative stresses the durative aspect: catching men will be his occupation. But v. 11 shows that this is not to be understood in a general sense. It is corollary to following Jesus.

zōgreō (†) 'to capture alive'.

Translation: *You will be catching men,* a metaphor, for which cp. *TH-Mk* 1 : 17; *N.T.Wb./*37; *TBT,* 19.114f, 1968, on the parallel phrase "become fishers of men". In some cases the metaphor can be rendered rather literally, cp. 'seeking for men' (Kekchi, where 'to seek fish' is the idiomatical rendering of 'to catch fish'). In several other languages, however, more radical adjustments are necessary, such as making explicit the underlying simile, 'you will catch men, so to say', 'you will not (or, no longer) catch fish, but men', cp. also 'you will catch men as if you were catching fish' (Barrow Eskimo); or a shift to a non-metaphorical rendering, sacrificing the play-on-words, e.g. 'you will be a bringer of men' (Gbeapo), 'you will be winning men', 'you will make others come to me'. In some cases the durative aspect of the construction is best expressed by an agent noun, e.g. 'you will act-as a catcher of men', or an occupational term, e.g. 'you will be one-whose-trade-is catching men' (East and South Toradja, Balinese). Some of the above mentioned adjustments may cause the wording of Lk. 5 : 10 and Mk. 1 : 17 to converge or even to coincide; this will have to be accepted, if idiom and/or intelligibility require the adjustments in question. — *Men.* Where the language distinguishes between 'men', i.e. individuals, and 'men', i.e. human as contrasted with other living beings (as e.g. in Balinese) the latter is to be used here, of course.

11 ***And when they had brought their boats to land, they left everything and followed him.***

Exegesis: *katagagontes ta ploia epi tēn gēn* 'when they had brought the boats to land'. The shift from the singular in vv. 8-10 to the plural here is remarkable and shows that v. 10 is understood by at least some of Simon's partners to refer to them also. *katagō* (†).

aphentes panta 'after they had left everything', with the implication of giving up, cp. 18 : 28. For *aphiēmi* cp. on 4 : 39.

ēkolouthēsan autō 'they followed him', i.e. they joined Jesus and became his disciples and followers.

akoloutheō 'to come after', 'to accompany', 'to follow' as a disciple.

Translation: *When they had brought their boats to land,* the opposite process of "to put out into the deep" (v. 4); some renderings used are, 'after the boats had been brought-to-the-side' (Balinese), 'they having tied their boats at shore' (Kapauku), 'when they had moved their boats beside/near the land' (Ponape). — *They*, or better to bring out the plural, 'Simon and those with him' (cp. v. 9).

They left everything, or, 'they abandoned/renounced all they had', 'they turned their back on all their possessions'; cp. also *TH-Mk* on 10 : 28.

Followed him, cp. the note on this verb in *TH-Mk* on 1 : 18, meaning (3). To express the inceptive-durative aspect a shift to 'they became his followers' may be useful. For the meaning intended here an idiomatic phrase may exist in the language, such as, 'followed in his footprints', used metaphorically of being a disciple (Santali). In some languages 'to follow' has the connotation of 'to do as told', 'to obey'. This may be an advantage here, but, when this connotation has become dominant the clause will only mean that they obeyed Jesus' command (e.g. his words in 10b), not that they accompanied him. Then some such expression as 'went with him', 'walked behind him' (Sranan) is preferable.

12 ***While he was in one of the cities, there came a man full of leprosy; and when he saw Jesus, he fell on his face and besought him, "Lord, if you will, you can make me clean."***

Exegesis: *kai egeneto* 'and it happened', cp. on 1 : 8.

en tō einai auton en mia tōn poleōn lit. 'during his being in one of the towns', of Galilee presumably, articular accusative and infinitive, cp. Bl-D, § 404.1. The numeral *mia* assumes the force of an indefinite article, cp. A-G s.v. *heis* 3 a.

kai idou anēr plērēs lepras lit. 'and behold, a man full of leprosy', hence "covered with leprosy" (Goodspeed, NEB, Willibrord, Jerusalem and others), stronger than *lepros* alone (cp. 4 : 27). For *kai idou* cp. on 1 : 20. *plērēs*, cp. on 4 : 1. *lepra* (†).

kai idōn ton Iēsoun pesōn epi prosōpon edeēthē autou legōn lit. 'and having seen Jesus, having fallen on his face he besought him saying'. The two participles *idōn* and *pesōn*, both in the aorist, have a different function; *idōn* refers to an act which precedes everything that follows, *pesōn epi prosōpon* describes an act which is intimately connected with *edeēthē* 'he besought', cp. "he prostrated himself in supplication...he said" (Rieu).

deomai 'to ask', 'to beg', 'to beseech', with following direct discourse (cp. A-G s.v. 2), here introduced by *legōn*.

kurie 'lord', cp. on v. 8.

ean thelēs "if only you will" (NEB).

katharisai 'cleanse', cp. on 4 : 27.

Translation: *In one of the cities*, or, 'in a city there', 'in a city of that region'.

Full of leprosy, or, 'who had leprosy all over' (Tagalog), 'suffering badly from leprosy' (Bahasa Indonesia). For *leprosy* cp. on "lepers" in 4 : 27.

He fell on his face, cp. on "he fell down at Jesus' knees" in v. 8.

Besought, or, 'begged', 'asked insistently'; cp. also *N.T.Wb.*/12f, ASK; *TH-Mk,* 1 : 40.

Lord, see on 1 : 6 (d).

If you will, you can make me clean, or, 'if (only) you want to make me clean, you have the power to make me clean, or, to do so'. For *to make clean* see on "cleansed" in 4 : 27.

13 ***And he stretched out his hand, and touched him, saying, "I will; be clean." And immediately the leprosy left him.***

Exegesis: *kai ekteinas tēn cheira* 'and stretching out his hand', with change of subject.

ekteinō 'to stretch out', always with a form of *cheir* 'hand'.

hēpsato autou legōn 'he touched him, saying', with following direct discourse.

haptō, in the middle 'to touch', 'to take hold of', often of touching as a means of conveying a divine blessing or healing (here; 18 : 15; 22 : 51), cp. A-G s.v. 2 b, or receiving it (6 : 19; 8 : 44-47).

thelō, katharisthēti 'I will, be cleansed', in the imperative as if an order was given to the leper, which is of course not the case. The imperative here has the force of a word of power which effects what it says.

hē lepra apēlthen ap' autou 'the leprosy left him', a very general and neutral expression.

Translation: *Stretched out his hand,* cp. on 6 : 10.

Touched him, see *TH-Mk* on 1 : 41.

I will may require a reference to what Jesus is willing, e.g. 'so I want' (Sranan), 'thus my will' (Balinese); see also *TH-Mk, l.c.*

Be clean. A passive imperative is a rather rare phenomenon; where an equivalent form (such as the "intentional" verbal form in Santali, used here with the force of 'be clean and be done with it') is not available, one may have to change the construction, e.g. 'throw-away your-impurity' (Javanese), or shift to an emphatic indicative, e.g. 'clean you are' (Bahasa Indonesia).

The leprosy left him, or, 'disappeared (lit. blew-away) from his body' (Sranan), 'disappeared from that man' (Trukese, Javanese), 'came loose from him' (Toba Batak); or, 'the leprosy ceased', 'that man was no longer leprous'; and cp. on "it left her" in 4 : 39.

14 ***And he charged him to tell no one; but "go and show yourself to the priest, and make an offering for your cleansing, as Moses commanded, for a proof to the people."***

Exegesis: *kai autos* 'and he', i.e. Jesus, indicating change of subject, without emphasis (cp. Bl-D, § 277.3).

parēggeilen autō mēdeni eipein '(he) ordered him to tell nobody', presumably that he had been cured by Jesus.

paraggellō 'to give orders', 'to order'; when used in connexion with a negative (as here *mēdeni*) sometimes translated 'to forbid'.

alla apelthōn deixon seauton tō hierei 'but (he said) go and show yourself to the priest', with a sudden shift from indirect to direct discourse (cp. Acts 1 : 4; 23 : 22). *apelthōn* (participle) *deixon* (imperative) are to be treated as two imperatives. For the rest cp. *TH-Mk* on 1 : 44.

kai prosenegke peri tou katharismou sou kathōs prosetaxen Mōüsēs lit. 'and present concerning your cleansing (an offering) as Moses prescribed'. For *katharismos* cp. on 2 : 14. Moses is here named as the author of the Pentateuch, i.e. of the law, and the clause is virtually equivalent to 'the law tells us'.

prospherō 'to bring', 'to present', often of gifts to be sacrificed by a priest. Here it is used without an object, 'to make an offering'.

prostassō (†) 'to order', 'to prescribe'.

eis marturion autois 'for evidence to them', cp. *TH-Mk* on 1 : 44. *autois* is best interpreted as referring to the people in general.

marturion 'testimony', 'proof', 'evidence', cp. A-G s.v. 1 a.

Translation: *He charged him to tell no one,* or, 'He forbade him to tell anyone' (cp. Javanese), 'he imposed-silence-upon him lest he should tell anyone' (Toba Batak), or where direct discourse is preferable, 'he ordered/told him, "Do not tell (this to) anyone"'.

But. For the way such an emphatic adversative following a negative assertion is rendered in Enga see *TBT*, 16.131, 1965.

Where an abrupt shift to direct discourse is stylistically undesirable it is usually best to insert 'he said' (cp. *Exegesis*), unless idiom requires direct discourse all through, see above. In receptor languages that have a graded system of honorific and reverential terms one may suppose that the leper was socially inferior to both Jesus and the priest, and that Jesus, in addressing the leper, referred to the priest in polite or reverential terms.

Go and show yourself to the priest, or, 'go to the priest and show yourself to him'. *Show yourself,* i.e. cause (or, ask) to look over, cp. "let him examine you" (TEV). For *priest* see on 1 : 5.

For *make an offering for your cleansing, as Moses commanded* cp. *TH-Mk* on 1 : 44. In Balinese the translator can use the verbal derivation mentioned in the note on 2 : 21, 'present your purification offering (lit. offering-of being-taken-away your stain) according to M.'s command'. — *Make an offering...as,* or, 'bring/present/put-down an offering...as (or, the offering...that)', 'bring/present/offer a sacrifice (see on 2 : 24)...as'. For *offering* a term for 'gift', 'what-is-given', can often be used, especially a gift offered in token of homage, as in Bahasa Indonesia (which uses a derivation of the word for the gesture mentioned in the note on 4 : 7), or South Toradja (lit. 'something-offered-on-the-palms-of-the hand'); some other renderings are, 'blessed thing' (Kpelle), 'gift to God from the heart' (Cuna). — *As Moses commanded* may have to be adjusted, e.g. 'as ordered/prescribed in the law of Moses' (for which cp. on 2 : 22f), or, 'as M. told us (inclus.)/the people to do'; and cp. on 4 : 3.

For a proof to the people, i.e. 'to the public', 'to everyone', usually requires rather radical adjustments, e.g. 'that people may be certain' (East Toradja 1933), 'so that the truth may be clear to the people' (cp.

Kekchi), "to prove to everyone that you are now clean" (TEV), and cp. the renderings that *TH-Mk, l.c.,* quotes. The phrase may better become a co-ordinated sentence, e.g. 'This will be a proof...'

15 ***But so much the more the report went abroad concerning him; and great multitudes gathered to hear and to be healed of their infirmities.***

Exegesis: *diērcheto de mallon ho logos peri autou* 'but the report about him spread all the more'. *de* means, notwithstanding Jesus' order to tell nobody. *mallon* 'all the more', i.e. as contrasted with Jesus' intentions (cp. A-G s.v. 3 a), or, 'now even more than ever' (cp. A-G s.v. 1). The latter is preferable. For *dierchomai* cp. on 2 : 15 and A-G s.v. 3. For *ho logos peri autou* cp. A-G s.v. 1 a β.

kai sunērchonto ochloi polloi 'and (as a result) great crowds gathered'.

sunerchomai (also 23 : 55) 'to come together', 'to gather'.

akouein kai therapeuesthai apo tōn astheneiōn autōn 'to hear (him) and to be cured (by him) of their diseases', final infinitives after *sunērchonto*. For *therapeuō* cp. on 4 : 23. The agent of the curing is Jesus. The fact that *polloi ochloi* is the logical subject of *therapeuesthai* does not imply that only sick people gathered.

astheneia 'sickness', 'disease'.

Translation: *The report went abroad concerning him,* cp. on 4 : 14.

Gathered, or, 'gathered around him'; or simply, 'came' (Marathi), 'came to him'.

To be healed of their infirmities often has to be adjusted, e.g. 'to get their diseases cured' (Marathi), 'to have-him-cure their illnesses' (East Toradja, using the verbal form mentioned on "be baptized" in 3 : 7), 'asked him that those who were ill amongst them be healed'; or again, 'those who were sick asked him to heal them', 'the sick-ones gave themselves to be made well' (Tzeltal). For *infirmity* see on "diseases" in 4 : 40.

16 ***But he withdrew to the wilderness and prayed.***

Exegesis: *autos de* 'but he', emphatic as contrasted with *ochloi polloi.*

ēn hupochōrōn en tais erēmois 'retired (and stayed) in the wilderness'. The imperfect may be iterative or durative, preferably the former: from time to time Jesus slipped away to the desert for prayer (cp. Rieu, NEB, BFBS). *en tais erēmois* (locative, not indicating a direction) anticipates the result of the retiring.

hupochōreō (also 9 : 10) 'to retire'.

kai proseuchomenos 'and was praying', goes also with *ēn.*

Translation: To make explicit the locative force of the preposition one may say, 'having withdrawn, he stayed and prayed in the wilderness (or, stayed in the wilderness and prayed there)'.

To withdraw, or, 'to go away (from them)', 'to isolate oneself' (Bahasa Indonesia RC).

Wilderness and *prayed,* see references on 1 : 80 and 1 : 10.

17 ***On one of those days, as he was teaching, there were Pharisees and teachers of the law sitting by, who had come from every village of Galilee and Judea and from Jerusalem; and the power of the Lord was with him to heal.***

Exegesis: *kai egeneto* 'and it happened', cp. on 1 : 8.

en mia tōn hēmerōn 'on one of the days', i.e. on a certain day, hence "one day" (NEB and others), cp. on v. 12.

kai autos ēn didaskōn 'and he was teaching', in a house, as v. 19 shows. *kai autos* unemphatic (cp. Bl-D, § 277.3).

kai ēsan kathēmenoi Pharisaioi kai nomodidaskaloi 'and there were sitting Pharisees and teachers of the law', presumably in the same house.

Pharisaioi 'Pharisees'; cp. *IDB* III, 774-781 for a detailed account of the Pharisees and their beliefs and practices. For translation purposes it is worth noting that the Pharisees were not a sect nor a clerical group but rather a lay movement for strict adherence to the law. Hence it often occurs together with *grammateis* 'scribes' (cp. e.g. 5 : 21, 30; 6 : 7; 11 : 53).

nomodidaskalos (†) 'teacher of the law', as v. 21 shows refers to the same persons as *grammateus* 'scribe'.

hoi ēsan elēluthotes 'who had come'; no special meaning is to be attached to the periphrastic form of the verb, cp. Bl-D, § 352.

ek pasēs kōmēs tēs Galilaias kai Ioudaias kai Ierousalēm 'from every village in Galilee and Judea and from Jerusalem'. As Plummer remarks, a hyperbolical expression. *Ierousalēm* is depending directly on *ek. Ioudaias* is best understood as dependent on *kōmēs*. For *Ioudaia* see on 1 : 5.

kōmē 'village', as contrasted with *polis* (cp. 8 : 1; 13 : 22).

kai dunamis kuriou ēn eis to iasthai auton 'and there was power of the Lord so that he could heal'. The preposition *eis* indicates result.

iaomai 'to heal', synonymous with *therapeuō* (cp. on 4 : 23, 40).

Translation: *Pharisees* (also in 5 : 21, 30; 6 : 2, 7; 7 : 30, 36f, 39; 11 : 37ff, 42f, 53; 12 : 1; 13 : 31; 14 : 1, 3; 15 : 2; 16 : 14; 17 : 20; 18 : 10f; 19 : 39) is a proper name, which should be transliterated. It may require a classifier, e.g. 'member of the religious group/party of the Pharisees', 'Jews called Pharisees', cp. *TH-Mk* on 2 : 16.

Teacher of the law, or, 'one who teaches the scriptures', 'causer to learn the commandments' (Yao, Lomwe, East Nyanja), and cp. on "teacher" in 2 : 46 and on "law" in 2 : 22. That the term is synonymous with "scribe" (see on 5 : 21) and "lawyer" (see on 7 : 30) is brought out nicely in some versions, compare e.g. 'expert (in) teaching the law' (here) with 'expert (in) law' (7 : 30) in Ponape, or, 'one who teaches (i.e. teaches how to read) the law' (here) with 'one who teaches (viz. by rote recitation) the law' (5 : 17) in Zarma. Where such closely synonymous expressions are not available the renderings of two or three of these terms should coincide rather than be so distinctive as to suggest an important difference in function or status (as probably is the case in one language, which uses 'superior scribe' here).

Were...sitting by, or, 'were sitting there (or, near him, or, where he was teaching)'; cp. also on 2 : 46.

Village (also in 8 : 1; 9 : 6, 12, 52, 56; 10 : 38; 13 : 22; 17 : 12; 19 : 30; 24 : 13, 28). Some languages have only one commonly used term for 'settlement', which must do duty for "village" and for "city/town" (see on 1 : 26). In passages where both terms occur together (e.g. 13 : 22) "village" may be distinguished as 'small settlement'; in such a case East Toradja and Toba Batak use a specific term for 'newly-founded-settlement', which is naturally small.

Judea, see on 1 : 65.

The power of the Lord was with him to heal may have to be restructured, e.g. 'Jesus was-made-strong by God to heal the sick' (East Toradja 1933), 'the strength of God was there, so that Jesus was-strong to heal people' (South Toradja), 'the power of the Lord caused him to be able to heal people' (Sundanese). For *Lord* see on 1 : 6, sub (c); some versions (Rieu, NEB, Leyden, East and South Toradja) substitute 'God'; this is advisable where it is necessary to avoid that the term would be mistaken for a reference to Jesus. — In several languages *to heal* requires an object, e.g. 'persons/people/the sick', cp. some of the above quotations.

18 ***And behold, men were bringing on a bed a man who was paralysed, and they sought to bring him in and lay him before Jesus;***

Exegesis: *kai idou andres pherontes* 'and behold, there were, or appeared, or came, men, carrying. . .', or 'and behold, men were bringing' (cp. RSV); the former rendering which treats *andres* as a nominal clause after *idou* and assigns to *pherontes* the role of a relative clause (cp. A-G s.v. *idou* 2) is preferable.

epi klinēs 'on a bed', 'on a stretcher', cp. A-G s.v.

anthrōpon hos ēn paralelumenos (also v. 24) 'a man who was paralysed'. The past participle *paralelumenos* points to a permanent situation.

kai ezētoun lit. 'and they sought', hence 'they tried' (cp. A-G s.v. 2 b γ). The imperfect tense stresses the conative meaning of the verb.

auton eisenegkein kai theinai [*auton*] *enōpion autou* 'to bring him in (scil. into the house) and to lay (him) before him (i.e. Jesus)'. *enōpion* (cp. on 1 : 15) here an indication of place.

eispherō 'to bring, or, to carry in', cp. A-G s.v. 1.

Translation: *Bringing on a bed*, or, 'carrying on a bed'. The language may possess a more specific verb which has to be used here, e.g. 'to carry-suspended-from-a-pole-on-the-shoulders' (Bahasa Indonesia, Balinese), 'to carry-with-some-people-together' (Javanese), 'to carry-on-a-stretcher' (East Toradja, thus dispensing with the prepositional phrase). *Bed* is sometimes rendered by a locative derivation, 'what-one-lies/sleeps-on'; here, since the context points to something light and easily transportable, it is also possible to say, 'mattress', 'mat', 'stretcher', 'litter'.

A man who was paralysed, cp. *N.T.Wb.*/68, SICKNESS; *TH-Mk* on 2 : 3.

They sought, or, 'they tried (hard)', 'they aimed-at' (Javanese in 19 : 47), 'they tried to find a way/means/an opportunity/a possibility'.

To bring him in, or, 'to take him in (or, into the house)', 'to cause-him-to-enter the house' (Sundanese, East Toradja).

19 *but finding no way to bring him in, because of the crowd, they went up on the roof and let him down with his bed through the tiles into the midst before Jesus.*

Exegesis: *kai mē heurontes*... 'and when they did not find...', *anabantes*... 'after they had gone up...', *kathēkan*... 'they let down...'. Semantically *anabantes* and *kathēkan* belong together closely and are dependent upon their not finding a way to bring the paralysed man in. This is usually brought out by a rendering as found in RSV. For a similar construction cp. on v. 12.

kai mē heurontes poias (scil. *hodou*) *eisenegkōsin auton* 'and when they did not find along which (way) they could bring him in', hence 'when they did not find a way to bring him in' (cp. RSV). *poias* scil. *hodou* is genitive of place, cp. Bl-D, § 186.

dia ton ochlon 'because of the crowd', goes with *mē heurontes*.

epi to dōma 'on the roof', presumably a flat roof. Usually a flat roof was covered with clay (cp. Mk. 2 : 4 and *TH-Mk* there) and Luke's reference to tiles (*dia tōn keramōn*) may be due to the fact that tiles were customary on pitch and on flat roofs in the Greek world.

dia tōn keramōn kathēkan auton sun tō klinidiō 'they let him down with the bed through the tiles', implying that they removed the tiles and let him down through the open space thus provided.

keramos (††) 'roof tile', of clay presumably.

kathiēmi (†) 'to let down'.

klinidion (also v. 24) diminutive of *klinē* (v. 18) but here synonymous with it.

eis to meson 'into the middle', viz. of the people gathered in the house.

emprosthen tou Iēsou 'in front of Jesus'.

emprosthen 'before', here synonymous with *enōpion* (v. 18).

Translation: *Because of the crowd* may better be given initial position, e.g. 'Now the people present there were many. Therefore those men could not find a way (or, were not able) to bring him in but went up...'. — *Crowd*, or, 'mass', 'gathering of people', 'many people' (cp. 6 : 17; 7 : 11f; 8 : 4; 9 : 37f; 22 : 47). With the definite article (here and in 6 : 19; 7 : 24 (plur.); 8 : 19, 40; 9 : 11 (plur.), 12, 16; 11 : 27, 29 (plur.); 19 : 3), it refers to the masses that gathered to see and hear Jesus, but did not belong to the circle of his disciples and followers. The force of the article may have to be expressed by a deictic locative element, e.g. 'great number of people there', or a qualifying phrase, e.g. 'many people (that were) around/near him', or by a term like 'the/his audience'.

The roof, i.e. a flat, or nearly flat, roof on which two or more people can stand. Where the normal term for 'roof' suggests a pitch roof, the expression will have to be adjusted, cp. e.g. 'the top of the house' (one Shona version, Zarma, Balinese), 'the flat house top' (Tzeltal), and cp.

'they climbed up on the house' (Marathi); or with a slight semantic shift, 'the loft of the house' (Bahasa Indonesia KB).

They...let him down...through the tiles. The verb may have to be specified, e.g. 'to hand-down' (Bahasa Indonesia), or, 'to lower-on-ropes' (Balinese). The prepositional phrase indicates that they made an improvised opening; hence such renderings as, 'having removed the tiles they let...' (Santali), or, where other material is used as a roofing, 'they parted the roof (of split bamboo, lit. 'roof which is split open')' (Tagabili); or again, without reference to the material, 'where the house top was opened by them' (Tzeltal). — *Tiles* has been described as 'flat stones' (Shona 1966), or more generically, 'covering' (Sinhalese), 'roofing' (Kapauku).

Him...with his bed, or, 'the sick man...bed-and-all' (Javanese), 'him...on his bed' (Toba Batak), since the paralytic and the bed were not let down separately.

Into the midst is often better specified, e.g. "into the middle of the group" (TEV, similarly Jerusalem, Sundanese).

20 ***And when he saw their faith he said, "Man, your sins are forgiven you."***

Exegesis: *kai idōn tēn pistin autōn* 'and when he saw their faith'. Whether *autōn* also refers to the paralytic cannot be decided, but it is not impossible.

pistis 'faith'; here and in 7 : 9, 50; 8 : 48; 17 : 19; 18 : 42 of faith or confidence in Jesus' power to heal, cp. A-G s.v. 2 b α.

anthrōpe 'man', here used without the note of reproach which is clearly present in 12 : 14; 22 : 58, 60; hence "friend" (Goodspeed, Willibrord, Jerusalem).

apheōntai soi hai hamartiai sou 'your sins have been forgiven you'. For the form of *apheōntai* cp. Bl-D, § 97.3. The agent of the forgiving is not mentioned, probably in order to leave room for the subsequent discussion with the Pharisees. As pointed out in *TH-Mk* 2 : 5 Jesus never says "I forgive your sins", and in v. 24 he speaks of his *exousia,* i.e. his authority derived from God to forgive sins (cp. on 4 : 32) and in the last analysis it is God who forgives the paralytic's sins. For *hamartiai* cp. on 1 : 77.

Translation: *When he saw their faith,* or, 'when he/Jesus saw this proof of their faith, or, realized/perceived that they believed in him'. For *their* cp. *TH-Mk* on 2 : 5; for *faith* (also in 7 : 9, 50; 8 : 25, 48; 12 : 28; 17 : 5f, 19; 18 : 8, 42; 22 : 32) see Nida, *GWIML,* 21f, 118-122; *TH-Mk, l.c.*; *TBT*, 7.127f, 1956; 11.28f, 1960; 13.33, 111-114, 1962.

Man has been rendered e.g. by, "(my) friend" (Goodspeed, Phillips), 'brother', a polite form of address (Bahasa Indonesia KB), 'my son' (Toba Batak), 'little-one' (Balinese, used by a father to his son, by a teacher to his pupil), an affective particle (Shipibo). In some receptor languages the word of address simply has to be omitted (cp. on "Theophilus" in 1 : 3), or it can only be represented by a particle or form used to call attention to what the speaker is about to say (cp. Santali).

Your sins are forgiven you. The clause is a difficult one to render in languages without passive verbal forms, since a shift to an active with 'God' as agent is usually unacceptable because of v. 21. In such cases one should preferably use a rendering that does not explicitly mention the agent, e.g. 'to receive forgiveness' (Sranan), 'forgiveness...has become' (Marathi). Where it is obligatory to mention the agent one may say something like, 'I declare to you, "God has forgiven your sins"' (which will require a corresponding adjustment of v. 21[c]).

21 ***And the scribes and the Pharisees began to question, saying, "Who is this that speaks blasphemies? Who can forgive sins but God only?"***

Exegesis: *kai ērxanto dialogizesthai hoi grammateis kai hoi Pharisaioi* 'and the scribes and the Pharisees began to question'. For *ērxanto* cp. on 4 : 21, and A-G s.v. 2 a β; here it expresses that the questioning was a reaction to what Jesus did. For *dialogizomai* cp. on 1 : 29. Here two interpretations are possible, viz. (1) that they began to debate or to argue among themselves, and (2) that they wondered in their own minds. Interpretation (1) appears to be preferable.

grammateus 'expert in the law', cp. on v. 17 and *TH-Mk* on 1 : 22.

tis estin houtos hos lalei blasphēmias lit. 'who is he who speaks blasphemies', with a note of contempt and indignation, hence "who is this fellow with his blasphemous talk" (NEB), the relative clause *hos lalei blasphēmias* serving to indicate the cause of the indignation.

blasphēmia 'blasphemy' i.e. impious talk about or concerning God. The plural here has no special meaning. *blasphēmias lalein* is synonymous with *blasphēmein* (Mk. 2 : 7).

tis...ei mē monos ho theos 'who...but only God', a combination of two phrases viz. *tis...ei mē* 'who but', and *monos ho theos* 'God alone', which reinforce one another.

Translation: *Scribe* (also in 5 : 30; 6 : 7; 9 : 22; 11 : 53; 15 : 2; 19 : 47; 20 : 1, 19, 39, 46; 22 : 2, 66; 23 : 10), or, 'one who knows the scriptures' (Timorese), or, 'studies/interprets the scriptures', 'scholar of the law' (colloquial Japanese). Terms existing in the culture for 'teacher of religion', 'religious scholar', such as, 'bearer-of-the-law' (Sinhalese), 'one-learned-in-the-Scriptures' (Marathi) may be used, where necessary with a further qualification, e.g. 'of Moses', or, 'Jewish'. Cp. also *TH-Mk* on 1 : 22. In some countries with a Muslim background Arabic terms, such as *ulama/ulema, katib, fakih,* have been used but proved unsatisfactory. Renderings such as, 'one who writes', 'one skilled in writing', 'a book-knower', 'a book-wise person', are acceptable where differentiation of function is unknown and such an expression refers to a position of learning comparable to that of the scribes, but in other circumstances a more specific term or phrase is preferable. In the New Testament 'scribe' and 'lawyer' (cp. on 7 : 30) are never used in the same sentence; therefore the two synonyms can acceptably be rendered by one expression, as done e.g. in Marathi; elsewhere 'scribe', 'lawyer' and 'teacher of the law' (5 : 17) are rendered by one and the same term, as done e.g. in Shona 1966 ('expert of the law'), Balinese ('expert of the books of Torah'), Kapauku ('one knowing paper/book'), Tagabili ('one who taught the law God before caused Moses to write', which in further occurrences in the same passage is shortened to 'one who taught the law of Moses').

The function of *began* may be rendered here by a transitional such as 'thereupon'.

To question, or, 'to make objections', 'to deliberate' (Santali), 'to consider (etym. to weigh)' (Bahasa Indonesia), all referring both to thought and to discussion. Where such happy ambiguity is not possible the translator following interpretation (1) has to choose a term referring to audible debate or discussion, for which cp. also "they said to one another" in 4 : 36. In honorific languages this will imply the use of polite terms common between persons who are colleagues but probably not intimates.

Who is this...? The interrogative clause, expressing the indignation felt by the scribes and Pharisees, may require modal forms, e.g. 'who possibly this one?', 'who can this be?'; or in an affirmative clause, 'I shall not allow this fellow to speak...'.

Speaks blasphemies, or, 'blasphemes', see *TH-Mk* on 2 : 7.

Who can forgive sins but God only, or shifting to the affirmative, "no man can forgive sins; God alone can" (TEV). If the person forgiven has to be mentioned, one may say, 'who can forgive man's sins', 'who can forgive us our (inclusive) sins' (Mazatec). If God had to be mentioned as agent in v. 20, one may say here something like, 'only God can declare that he has forgiven people's sins'.

22 ***When Jesus perceived their questionings, he answered them, "Why do you question in your hearts?***

Exegesis: *epignous de ho Iēsous tous dialogismous autōn* 'but Jesus perceiving their questionings'. For *epiginōskō* cp. on 1 : 4; it implies thorough knowledge but does not indicate in what way this knowledge is gained. *tous dialogismous autōn* refers to *dialogizesthai* in v. 21 and hence is to be interpreted along the same lines. For *dialogismos* cp. on 9 : 46.

apokritheis 'answering', cp. on 1 : 60.

ti dialogizesthe en tais kardiais humōn 'what, or why, are you questioning in your hearts', preferably the former. Since *dialogizesthe* refers to discussion the addition of *en tais kardiais humōn* suggests that the scribes and the Pharisees do not raise objections for the sake of argument but that Jesus' word of forgiveness is against their deepest convictions.

Translation: *Perceived their questionings*, or, 'perceived that they were in discussion, or, were speaking with each other'. *Perceived*, or, 'noticed', 'became aware', 'observed', 'came to know' (some Indonesian languages).

Why do you question in your hearts, preferably, 'what (matters) are you questioning in your hearts' (cp. *Exegesis*). The interpretation advocated in *Exegesis* will require adjustments of the phrase *in your hearts*, leading to renderings such as, 'what are you discussing with (all) your heart (or, so fervently)?', or even, 'what are you opposing so indignantly?'. The plural *hearts* is distributive, '(each) in/with your heart'.

The translation of vv. 21f will be different if *dialogizesthai* in v. 21 is rendered in accordance with interpretation (2). This may lead to a rendering of the verb "to question" by words referring to inward questioning, e.g. 'to ponder', and cp. on "considered in her mind" in 1 : 29; of "perceived" by such words as 'guessed' (Sranan, lit. 'Jesus went into their head'); and of "in your heart(s)" by 'in your mind(s)', 'inwardly', cp. 'why do you murmur-inside' (Ponape).

23 ***Which is easier, to say, 'Your sins are forgiven you,' or to say, 'Rise and walk'?***

Exegesis: *ti estin eukopōteron, eipein...ē eipein* 'which is easier to say, ..., or to say?' For this sort of question and the obvious answer cp. *TH-Mk* on 2 : 9.

eukopōteron 'easier' with following infinitive.

egeire kai peripatei 'get up and walk'. For *egeirō* cp. on 1 : 69. Here the active has intransitive meaning (also in 6 : 8; 8 : 54, cp. A-G s.v. 1 b); it is addressed to somebody who is lying down and is unable to get up (different in 6 : 8), which means that here *egeire* is part of the healing and in 6 : 8 it is preparing for it (cp. also *TH-Mk* on 1 : 31).

peripateō 'to walk', literally and figuratively; here it is to be taken in a strictly literal meaning.

Translation: For this verse see *TH-Mk* on 2 : 9; for renderings of a comparative construction cp. also the references on 3 : 16.

Easier, see *TH-Mk, l.c.*; in Kapauku 'easy' is expressed by 'do-able', i.e. what can be done.

Or may have to be rendered here by 'than' (Balinese, lit. 'compared with'), because of the comparative.

24 ***But that you may know that the Son of man has authority on earth to forgive sins"—he said to the man who was paralysed—"I say to you, rise, take up your bed and go home."***

Exegesis: *hina de eidēte* "but in order that you may know" (BFBS), final clause but not followed by a main clause as normally. One would expect a clause like 'I will do this' (cp. A-G s.v. *hina* I 6, *TH-Mk* on 2 : 10), but instead Jesus addresses himself to the paralytic and tells him to do that which will confirm what he had said to the scribes and the Pharisees.

hoti ho huios tou anthrōpou exousian echei epi tēs gēs aphienai hamartias 'that the Son of man has authority on earth to forgive sins'. For *exousia* in the sense of full, but derived authority, cp. on 4 : 32.

ho huios tou anthrōpou 'the Son of man', in the Synoptic Gospels always used by Jesus when referring to himself as distinguished from ordinary people. For a discussion of this title cp. Richardson, *Word Book*, 230ff, and *IDB* IV, 413-420. Idiomatically the phrase belongs to a group of expressions like 'son of peace', which mean 'one who has the essential quality of..., or, belongs to the group of...', but it has developed into a Messianic title and should be treated as such also when referring to Jesus in his earthly life (which is the case in many places), cp. *TH-Mk* on 2 : 10.

epi tēs gēs 'on earth', to be connected with *exousian echei* 'has authority', or with *aphienai hamartias* 'forgive sins', preferably the former.

eipen tō paralelumenō 'he said to the paralysed man', best treated as a parenthesis used to prepare a shift of the persons addressed.

soi legō 'to you I say', with emphasis in order to underscore the change of address.

egeire kai aras to klinidion sou poreuou eis ton oikon sou 'get up, take up your bed and go to your home'. *aras to klinidion sou* lit. 'after taking up your bed' is virtually an imperative.

poreuou eis ton oikon sou 'go to your home', stressing rather the action of going than its direction.

Translation: In many languages a rendering is possible that leaves the break in the sentence virtually as it is, and by a judicious use of punctuation marks indicates how it is to be understood, but this is, at the best, a help for the experienced reader only. Therefore it is often better for the translator not to depend on punctuation marks, but to change the sentence structure, cp. e.g. '"But I want you to know (or, I will prove to you, or, I will let you know) that the Son of man has authority on earth to forgive sins." So he/Jesus said to the paralysed man, "To you I say, get up..."' (cp. *The True Servant,* Toronto 1959; TEV); or, '..."Look here all of you so that you will know that..." Then Jesus said to that man who wasn't-able-to-go before, "Get up..."' (Tagabili). For changes in construction necessary in Enga see *TBT*, 16.136, 1965.

The Son of man (also in 6 : 5, 22; 7 : 34; 9 : 22, 26, 44, 58; 11 : 30; 12 : 8, 10, 40; 17 : 22, 24, 26, 30; 18 : 8, 31; 19 : 10; 21 : 27, 36; 22 : 22, 48, 69; 24 : 7), see *TH-Mk* on 2 : 10. Usually it is preferable to give a rather literal rendering, e.g. 'son/child of man'. Swahili has virtually the same rendering, viz. 'Son of Adam', used in contradistinction to the compound term 'Adam's-son', meaning 'human being'. Sometimes it is necessary to add a reference to the first person, 'I, the Son of man'. The rendering 'Son of men/mankind/people' may also be possible, but in some cases is unacceptable, e.g. in Zulu and Navajo (cp. *TBT*, 6.176f, 1955; 13.28, 1962), where it would mean 'son of our people/tribe', or in Zapotec, where it would suggest "that the father is unknown due to the indiscretions of the mother" and where 'he is the son of people' is used when one wants to disclaim responsibility for or relationship with a child caught in some mischief. For these and similar reasons some translators have had to shift to non-literal renderings, e.g. 'son (lit. child) descended in the world' (South Toradja, using a poetic verb, often found in songs that treat of the contacts between heaven and earth), 'the man appointed', i.e. the man to whom authority has been delegated (Tenango Otomi), 'Older Brother of everybody', expressing the dignity and authority of the Messiah and the universality of his work (San Andres Tzeltal), 'I, the elder-brother-man' (Guhu-Samane), 'I who have been stood up to help', usually but not exclusively used of appointment to a menial task (Tarahumara), 'he who is a relative/sibling of all people', or, 'I, the person who accompanies all people', expressing the universal character of Jesus' mission (Trique, Totonac, Cuicatec), see Beekman, *NOT*, 188ff, 192f.

In some languages there arise problems about honorifics. (1) Because the reference is to Jesus a language such as Balinese uses the honorific word for 'son', although this is felt to be incongruous when used with the word 'man/mankind' referring as it does to people of both high and low social position; this very incongruity, however, may help to signal the technical character of the title. (2) As a rule one never uses honorific terms for what concerns oneself; hence the use of honorifics with reference to 'the Son of man' may obscure the fact that the title refers to the speaker, i.e. Jesus. Yet honorifics have sometimes been employed, on the consideration that, when using 'the Son of man', Jesus referred to his own person in another function and a higher position than the one he occupied while speaking (see *TBT*, 14.162f, 176, 184, 1963). Such a solution, however, will be unacceptable where the use of honorifics would make the identification of 'the Son of man' as Jesus quite impossible. When investigating these and similar translation problems, one should remember that receptor language possibilities and requirements for the rendering of this title in passages referring to Jesus' earthly life may differ from those for passages about his *parousia* (9 : 26; 12 : 8, 40; 17 : 22ff; 18 : 8; 21 : 27, 36; 22 : 69); cp. also *TBT*, 18.78, 1967.

Earth stands here in contrast to heaven, the abode of God, cp. on 2 : 14.

Take up, i.e. 'lift up and carry away'. Here again a more specific verb may have to be introduced, e.g. 'lift-on-the-shoulder' (East Toradja), 'lift-up-with-the-hand' (Santali).

25 ***And immediately he rose before them, and took up that on which he lay, and went home, glorifying God.***

Exegesis: *kai parachrēma anastas..., aras...apēlthen* lit. 'and immediately having risen..., having taken up...he went away'. The three acts are grouped as rising on the one hand and taking up and going away on the other.

enōpion autōn "in front of them" (Phillips) i.e. so that they all could see him. *autōn* does not refer to participants in the preceding discussion only but to all present.

eph' ho katekeito 'that on which he lay', i.e. *to klinidion* 'the bed' mentioned in vv. 18, 19 and 24. Probably Luke's use of this paraphrase is intentional (cp. Mk. 2 : 12) and serves to avoid repetition.

katakeimai (also v. 29) 'to lie down' (here), 'to recline', hence 'to dine' (v. 29).

doxazōn ton theon 'praising God', cp. on 2 : 20.

Translation: *Before them*, cp. *TH-Mk* on 2 : 12.

That on which he lay. Often the antecedent has to be a noun, preferably a generic word or a synonym of "bed" (v. 18). One should handle the aspect carefully: the phrase indicates what he lay on previously but no longer now, which is made explicit e.g. in NEB, Balinese, Sundanese.

Glorifying God, or in co-ordination, 'and all the while he glorified God'. For the verb see on 2 : 20.

26 ***And amazement seized them all, and they glorified God and were filled with awe, saying, "We have seen strange things today."***

Exegesis: *ekstasis* (†) 'astonishment', cp. *existamai* (2 : 47).

kai eplēsthēsan phobou 'and they were filled with awe'. For the idiom of *pimplēmi* with genitive cp. on 1 : 15 and 4 : 28. For *phobos* cp. on 1 : 12.

legontes hoti 'saying'.

paradoxa (††) 'wonderful things'.

Translation: *Amazement seized them all,* or, 'they became all amazed', for which see on "wondered" in 1 : 21; and cp. *TH-Mk* on 2 : 12.

Filled with awe, see on "filled with fear" in 2 : 9.

Saying is reciprocal: they are speaking to each other.

Strange things, or, 'things we cannot believe, or, have never yet seen', 'what will be-denied by those who hear it' (East Toradja 1933), 'what never yet has happened' (Toba Batak), 'things we don't understand' (Kapauku), 'things causing-surprise' (Ponape).

27 ***After this he went out, and saw a tax collector, named Levi, sitting at the tax office; and he said to him, "Follow me."***

Exegesis: *kai meta tauta exēlthen* 'and after this he went out'. *tauta* refers to what has been told in vv. 17-26. *exēlthen* 'he went out', presumably out of the town as the parallel text Mk. 2 : 13 suggests.

kai etheasato telōnēn 'and he saw a tax collector'. For *telōnēs* cp. on 3 : 12. Here the word refers probably to a custom-house officer since the great commercial route from Acre to Damascus passed the lake near Capernaum and it may well be that on this route was the custom-office of Levi.

theaomai 'to see', often synonymous with *horaō*.

onomati Leuin 'named Levi'. In v. 29 the nominative *Leuis* occurs but the usual transliteration is 'Levi'.

kathēmenon epi to telōnion 'sitting at, or by, the custom-office'. The participle *kathēmenon* goes with *telōnēn* as an accusative and participle after a verb of perception (*etheasato* 'he saw'), cp. Bl-D, § 416.

telōnion (only here and the parallels Mk. 2 : 14 and Mt. 9 : 9) 'custom-office', 'revenue office'.

akolouthei moi 'follow me' without introductory words or an indication of the circumstances under which Levi was called to follow Jesus.

Translation: *He went out.* Where a literal rendering would restrict the meaning to leaving the house it may be preferable to say, 'he departed' (Sundanese), or more explicitly, "he left the town" (Rieu).

Saw a tax collector, . . ., sitting . . ., or, 'saw a tax collector, . . ., who was sitting, or, as he sat'. Because an unrelated character is introduced here (cp. on 1 : 5) the clause structure may have to be changed, e.g. 'Now there was a tax collector, . . ., sitting . . . ; Jesus saw him (or, looked at him) and said . . .'

Tax collector, see on 3 : 12.

Tax office, see *TH-Mk* on 2 : 14. Sometimes the rendering is a locative derivation built on the term for 'tax/customs' or 'to gather-tax/customs'. In the present verse, however, it is also possible simply to say, 'in his office' (East Toradja), the possessive serving to identify the kind of office meant.

Follow me, see on v. 11.

28 ***And he left everything, and rose and followed him.***

Exegesis: *katalipōn panta* lit. 'after leaving behind everything', realized by, not prior to, following Jesus.

kataleipō 'to leave (behind)'. Here it is synonymous with *aphentes* in v. 11. Cp. also v. 29.

anastas ēkolouthei autō lit. 'after rising he followed him', hence 'he rose and followed him'. *anastas* is here to be taken literally.

Translation: For this verse see on 5 : 11.

He left everything. To bring out the interpretation preferred in *Exegesis* one may better shift this clause, e.g. to final position, '. . . followed him, leaving (or, and so he left) everything behind'.

Rose. For reasons of transition or specification it may be better to say, 'rose from there', 'rose from where he was sitting'.

29 ***And Levi made him a great feast in his house; and there was a large company of tax collectors and others sitting at table with them.***

Exegesis: *kai epoiēsen dochēn megalēn Leuis autō en tē oikia autou* 'and Levi made a great feast for him in his house'. The word order (object before subject) tends to emphasize *dochēn megalēn* 'a great feast'. *en tē oikia autou* 'in his house' refers to Levi's house. The fact that Levi still had a house after leaving everything (v. 28) shows that the latter refers to his "whole mode of life" (Plummer), not to each of his possessions.

dochē (also 14 : 13) 'banquet', 'reception', 'feast', 'entertainment'.

kai ēn ochlos polus telōnōn kai allōn 'and there was a great crowd of tax collectors and other people', presumably of the same reputation as the tax collectors.

hoi ēsan met' autōn katakeimenoi 'who were dining with them'. *met' autōn* 'with them' is best understood as referring to Jesus and Levi (the only persons mentioned so far). For *katakeimai* cp. on v. 25.

Translation: *Made him a great feast*, i.e. 'arranged/organized a great feast in honour of him'. Where one has to choose between distinctive terms specifying the time of day (cp. *N.T.Wb.*/53, MEALS) one should use the term best suited to receptor culture customs, since the text does not say anything about this detail. In some languages, where an honorific word for 'meal/banquet/feast' is required because of its connexion with Jesus, the use of such a word would exclude other guests of lower social status; this leads in Balinese to, 'Levi offered Him a meal (honorific), great the reception (neutral in matters of honorifics)', thus suggesting that many persons more were present.

A large company, or, 'very many people', cp. on "multitudes" in 3 : 7.

Sitting at table with them, or, 'sitting/lying down to eat with them'. As shown in *TH-Mk* on 2 : 15 it is the function of the Greek verb, viz. 'to eat', 'to have a meal', that is important rather than the exact attitude; hence the rendering sometimes has to coincide with that of 'to eat (and drink) with', in 7 : 36 and 5 : 30. Another possible rendering of the verb here is 'to be guest', or, 'to be entertained', lit. 'to be-treated-as-guest' (Balinese).

30 ***And the Pharisees and their scribes murmured against his disciples, saying, "Why do you eat and drink with tax collectors and sinners?"***

Exegesis: *kai egogguzon...pros tous mathētas autou* 'and (they) grumbled at his disciples'.

gogguzō (†) 'to murmur', 'to grumble'; hence Schonfield translates "voiced their protests".

mathētēs 'disciple', 'follower', 'adherent', often referring to the twelve but sometimes to a larger or smaller circle. Here the reference is to a small group.

hoi Pharisaioi kai hoi grammateis autōn 'the Pharisees and their experts in the law', i.e. the experts who belonged to the party of the Pharisees, cp. Plummer and *hoi grammateis tōn Pharisaiōn* 'the experts of the Pharisees' (Mk. 2 : 16).

meta tōn telōnōn kai hamartōlōn 'with the tax collectors and sinners'. The fact that the substantives *telōnōn* and *hamartōlōn* both are determined by a single article (*tōn*) indicates that both belong to the same category (cp. Plummer). For *hamartōlos* cp. on v. 8.

esthiete kai pinete 'you eat and drink', stronger than eating alone. It occurs in places where the emphasis is on the idea of fellowship at meals (here and 10 : 7; 13 : 26; 22 : 30), or is used to denote normal non-ascetic life (5 : 33; 7 : 34; 17 : 27, 28) or even a wanton life (12 : 45).

Translation: *Murmured*, or, 'grumbled', "complained of this" (Phillips, in 15 : 2). Miskito has an idiomatic expression, 'to scrape off the lip'.

Disciples (also in 5 : 33; 6 : 1, 13, 17, 20, 40; 7 : 11, 18f; 8 : 9, 22; 9 : 14, 16, 18, 40, 43, 54; 10 : 23; 11 : 1; 12 : 1, 22; 14 : 26f, 33; 16 : 1; 17 : 1, 22; 18 : 15; 19 : 29, 37, 39; 20 : 45; 22 : 11, 39, 45), cp. *TH-Mk* on 2 : 15; Javanese has 'companion' (a borrowing from Arabic that is a technical term for Mohammed's close associates); the German rendering, 'the younger ones', may prove a useful model in societies where it is in the nature of things that 'the young' have to learn and to follow.

Why here expresses disapproval.

You (plural) refers to the disciples, but by implication also to Jesus.

Eat and drink with, cp. *N.T.Wb.*/31, *TH-Mk* on 2 : 16. In some languages one verb for 'to eat', 'to consume', 'to have-a-meal', covers the two, e.g. in Cuyono, and in Kapauku (where "to drink" is 'to consume water'); similarly in Navajo and Tagabili, where an explicit reference to drinking would suggest drinking in a saloon or to excess. Here the sharing of the meal is of importance; hence, 'eat-together-from-one-dish' (Balinese, using a verb which indicates so close an association that one's caste becomes involved).

Sinner (also in 5 : 32; 6 : 32ff; 7 : 34, 37, 39; 13 : 2; 15 : 1f, 7, 10; 18 : 13; 19 : 7), see *TH-Mk* on 2 : 15 and cp. above 1 : 77 references on "sin".

31 ***And Jesus answered them, "Those who are well have no need of a physician, but those who are sick;***

Exegesis: *apokritheis* 'answering', cp. on 1 : 60.

ou chreian echousin hoi hugiainontes iatrou 'those who are healthy have no need of a doctor', a proverbial saying, in v. 32 applied by Jesus to the specific situation of the moment.

hugiainō 'to be healthy', in Luke always of physical health.

chreia 'need', 'necessity', of personal or material needs.

alla hoi kakōs echontes 'but those who are sick'. *kakōs echō* (also 7 : 2) always of poor physical condition, cp. A-G s.v. *echō* II 1.

Translation: *Jesus answered them*, cp. on 3 : 16. The pronoun may have to be specified, e.g. 'those people', 'the Pharisees'; or adding a transitional phrase, 'hearing those murmurings/protests, Jesus said'.

Those who are well, or, 'healthy', 'not-sick', 'strong' (cp. Mk. 2 : 17), 'cheerful their-body' (East Toradja), 'good is the inside of their bones' (Mende), 'good the body' (Malay).

Have no need may have to be described otherwise, e.g. 'do not go looking for' (Subanen, similarly East Toradja), 'do not have to consult' (Barrow Eskimo); cp. also, 'with-reference-to those who are well there-is-no reason-for (a) doctor' (Trukese).

Physician, see on 4 : 23.

But those who are sick. The ellipsis may have to be filled out, e.g. 'need a physician', 'need one'. For *sick* see on 4 : 40.

32 ***I have not come to call the righteous, but sinners to repentance."***

Exegesis: *ouk elēlutha* 'I have not come' with following final infinitive, implying the sense of a mission (cp. A-G s.v. *erchomai* I 1 a η).

kalesai dikaious alla hamartōlous eis metanoian 'to call righteous but sinners to repentance'. *dikaious* and *hamartōlous* correspond to *hugiainon-*

tes and *kakōs echontes* respectively, in v. 31, but further application to one of the groups of the moment, viz. Pharisees and tax collectors, is omitted deliberately.

eis metanoian (cp. on 3 : 3) 'to repentance' goes with *kalesai* and indicates the purpose of the calling (cp. Phillips, Willibrord). Syntactically the latter has both *dikaious* and *hamartōlous* as its objects, but since righteous people do not need to repent, it refers semantically only to *hamartōlous*.

Translation: For this verse cp. *TH-Mk* on 2 : 17. The sentence structure may have to be changed and/or the ellipsis to be filled out, e.g. 'I have come to call sinners to repent, not (come to call) the righteous (to repent)'.

Call is used here in the sense of 'to summon to a particular activity'; it does not refer to loudness of voice.

The righteous, see references on 1 : 6; in Navajo the term has to be described, 'those who say, "I don't do evil"'; the specific connotation the word has here is brought out in TEV's "respectable people" (contrasting with "outcasts" for "sinners").

To repentance, often better as a verbal phrase, 'to (or, in order that they) repent'.

33 ***And they said to him, "The disciples of John fast often and offer prayers, and so do the disciples of the Pharisees, but yours eat and drink."***

Exegesis: *hoi de eipan pros auton* 'and they said to him'. *hoi* refers back to the subject of v. 30, viz. the Pharisees and their scribes.

hoi mathētai Iōannou 'the disciples of John (the Baptist)'.

nēsteuousin pukna kai deēseis poiountai 'fast often and offer prayers'. *pukna* goes with *nēsteuousin*, and *deēseis poiountai* appears to refer to prayers that accompany fasting (Schlatter); for *deēsis* cp. also 1 : 13; 2 : 37.

nēsteuō 'to fast', i.e. to abstain partly or completely from food for a certain time as a religious practice, cp. *TH-Mk* on 2 : 18; *N.T.Wb.*, 78/.

pukna (†) 'many times', 'often'.

homoiōs kai hoi tōn Pharisaiōn 'in the same way also the (disciples) of the Pharisees'. *hoi tōn Pharisaiōn* means either 'disciples (of unmentioned teachers) who belong to the party of the Pharisees', or 'disciples of teachers who belong to the party of the Pharisees', cp. on v. 30, probably the latter.

hoi de soi esthiousin kai pinousin 'but your (disciples) eat and drink', i.e. do not observe fasts at all, cp. v. 30.

Translation: For vv. 33-35 cp. *TH-Mk* on 2 : 18-20.

They may have to be specified, e.g. 'the Pharisees (and their scribes)', 'those people', 'Jesus' interlocutors/opponents', cp. on v. 31.

Fast often and offer prayers. Though going with the first verb, "often" qualifies the whole clause; hence it may be preferable to subordinate the second phrase, e.g. 'offering prayers', 'with prayers'. For *fast* see on 2 : 37. For *offer prayers*, or, 'say their prayers', 'hold their prayers' (Sranan), or simply, 'pray' (several Indonesian languages), cp. references 1 : 10.

And so do the disciples of... The verb may better be shifted to final position, 'and the disciples of...do the same'.

The disciples of the Pharisees. If one wishes to bring out the interpretation preferred in *Exegesis* it will usually be necessary to add a reference to 'teachers'.

Eat and drink. Here the fact of the actual eating and drinking is in focus, whereas in v. 30 the emphasis was rather on the having of a meal with others. In some receptor languages this leads to differentiation, e.g. 'just go on eating', viz. without interruption by fasting (Kapauku), 'take food (including drinking)' (Balinese); East Toradja uses the two verbs in the reduplicated form, which has intensive and/or iterative force, whereas in v. 30 the simple forms are employed.

34 ***And Jesus said to them, "Can you make wedding guests fast while the bridegroom is with them?***

Exegesis: *mē dunasthe...poiēsai nēsteusai* 'you cannot...make fast, can you?' *mē* indicates that a negative answer to the question is expected. *poiēsai* 'make' should not be pressed; it does not mean 'cause to fast' but is closer to "expect" (NEB). The aorist tense of *poiēsai* and *nēsteusai* suggests reference to occasional fasting as contrasted with habitual fasting to which v. 33 refers.

tous huious tou numphōnos lit. 'the sons of the bridal chamber'. *huioi* 'sons' often expresses a close relation of varying kinds, cp. A-G s.v. 1 b δ; 16 : 8; 20 : 34; Mt. 8 : 12; 13 : 38. The phrase is explained variously: (1) 'wedding guests', generally (RSV), or (2) 'the (special) friends of the bridegroom' (NEB), 'the bridegroom's attendants' (A-G). The latter is preferable.

numphōn (†) 'bridal chamber' (A-G), 'chamber of the bridegroom' (cp. *N.T.Wb.*, 92/ and *TH-Mk* on 2 : 19).

en hō ho numphios met' autōn estin 'while the bridegroom is with them'. *en hō* scil. *chronō*. The wording of the clause is determined by what follows; normally it is the friends who go away, not the bridegroom.

numphios (also v. 35) 'bridegroom'.

Translation: The rhetorical question may have to be rendered by an affirmative sentence, or elucidated by the adding of an answer, e.g. "of course not" (TEV).

Wedding guests, preferably, following interpretation (2) in *Exegesis,* 'friends/attendants of the bridegroom', also suggesting a wedding party and the festive eating and drinking associated with it. An appropriate rendering in several languages is, 'those who escort (the bridegroom)'. In Alangan, however, a similar expression, referring to the relatives who act as witnesses of the bridegroom, lacks the required associations, since in this culture the wedding ceremony does not include any festive meal. In such a case the translator will have to add a footnote explaining Jewish wedding customs. Some versions, e.g. RSV, NV, follow the other interpretation, 'wedding guests', or simply, 'guests', the word 'bridegroom' being sufficient to indicate the situation.

Bridegroom, often, 'the one who marries/takes a wife', 'the future husband' (Alangan). In Toba Batak the term etymologically means 'the-one-who-buys-a-wife', in Ponape, 'the man caused-to-sit'; in East Toradja the rendering is 'the-one who-is-escorted', a counterpart of the term for 'attendant of the bridegroom'.

35 ***The days will come, when the bridegroom is taken away from them, and then they will fast in those days."***

Exegesis: *eleusontai de hēmerai* 'but there will be days', introducing the announcement of some future significant event (cp. 17 : 22; 19 : 43; 23 : 29). Here the announcement itself follows in an independent sentence consisting of a temporal clause introduced by *hotan,* and a main clause in the future tense. *hēmerai* lit. 'days' means here 'time', 'period of time'. The absence of the article is intentional.

hotan aparthē ap' autōn ho numphios 'when the bridegroom is taken away from them'. The use of *apairō* may imply violence (cp. *TH-Mk* on 2 : 20).

tote nēsteusousin en ekeinais tais hēmerais 'then they will fast, in those days', double indication of time, the latter stressing *tote. en ekeinais tais hēmerais* intentionally recalls *eleusontai hēmerai* of the first clause.

Translation: *The days will come, when...*, or, making explicit what is somehow suggested by the break in the sentence "but other days will come, and when..." (Goodspeed, similarly NV).

When..., and then...in those days, preferably, '(and) when..., then..., in those days'. Often it is better to place the prepositional phrase closer to the word it is to stress, e.g. '...then, at that time, ...' (Willibrord); or indicating the stress otherwise, 'at that time only...' (Bahasa Indonesia). NEB shifts to co-ordination, cp. "but a time will come: the bridegroom will be taken..., and that will be the time for them to fast".

The bridegroom is taken away. Where an active form is required the subject can best be 'people', 'enemies'. For the verb see *TH-Mk, l.c.*

From them, or, 'from their side', 'from their midst'.

In those days. Stylistically it is preferable when the rendering of "days" can echo that of the same word in the first clause.

36 ***He told them a parable also: "No one tears a piece from a new garment and puts it upon an old garment; if he does, he will tear the new, and the piece from the new will not match the old.***

Exegesis: *elegen de kai parabolēn pros autous* 'he also told them a parable', added by Luke (cp. Mk. 2 : 16) to clarify the nature of what follows. For *parabolē* cp. on 4 : 23; here the meaning is rather 'illustration' than 'parable' (cp. Phillips, Schonfield). *autous* still refers to the same people as in vv. 34, 33, 31, 30.

epiblēma (only here and Mk. 2 : 21 and Mt. 9 : 16, in the N.T.) 'patch'. Syntactically it is object of *schisas* and *epiballei.* In the present context *epiblēma* is best understood to refer to exemption from fasting and the parable means that this exemption should neither be taken away from Jesus' disciples nor imposed upon John's disciples (cp. Plummer).

apo himatiou kainou schisas lit. 'after tearing (it) from a new garment'.

schizō (also 23 : 45) 'to tear off', 'to tear (apart)'.

epiballei epi himation palaion 'puts it on an old garment'.

epiballō 'to lay (hands) on' (cp. on 9 : 62); here 'to put on'. Luke uses this verb here instead of *epiraptō* 'to sew on' (Mk. 2 : 21), probably because of the alliteration with the formally related *epiblēma*.

ei de mēge lit. 'if not', here, because of *oudeis...epiballei*, 'if he does', with emphasis, cp. Plummer. For *ei de mē ge* cp. A-G s.v. *ge* 3 b.

kai (*to kainon*)...*kai* (*tō palaiō*) lit. 'and...and', here meaning, 'not only...but', '(first *kai* not rendered)...as well as'.

to kainon schisei 'he will both tear (apart) the new one'. Subject is the person implied in *oudeis*.

tō palaiō (scil. *himatiō*) *ou sumphōnēsei to epiblēma to apo tou kainou* 'with the old (garment) the patch from the new will not match'. *palaios* also v. 39.

sumphōneō (†) 'to match (with)'.

Translation: *Parable*, or, 'figure', 'illustration', 'lesson', when the usual rendering (see on 8 : 4) does not fit the context here.

Instead of Mark's "no one sews a piece of unshrunk cloth on an old garment" Luke has "no one tears a piece from a new garment", thus avoiding what *TH-Mk* calls the basic difficulty of Mk. 2 : 21.

No one tears, or, 'there is no man at all who tears' (Shona 1963, similarly Toba Batak); 'no one would tear' (Tagabili); or, using a pronoun in an indefinite sense, 'we (inclus.) do not tear' (Trique), 'you do not tear' (Cuyono). In Tzeltal the more idiomatic rendering is, 'it isn't done to tear'.

Tears a piece from a new garment and puts it upon an old garment. The second clause has final force, '...in order to put it...'. *Piece* stands here for 'patch', i.e. 'something that is (to be) sewn upon, or, added to'; hence, 'takes/tears something-to-become a patch from a new garment to-be-made to patch-up an old' (Javanese); this has the advantage of using a more expressive term, which also is more suitable in the second half of the verse. Other versions shift to, 'tears up a new garment and puts a piece of it (or, what is torn from it) upon an old garment', or, leaving more to the good understanding of the receptors, 'tears up...and puts it upon...' (cp. Marathi, Cuyono, Kituba, East Toradja, Toba Batak); thus the verb 'to tear' is used with approximately the same meaning as in the next sentence. — *New*...*old* refer to quality here, 'fresh', 'not (yet) used'...'worn out', 'used', 'threadbare'. For *garment* cp. *N.T.Wb.*/20, CLOTHE and below on 7 : 25; a generic term for a piece of clothing is meant. *To put upon*, or, 'to apply to', 'to be-used as means-to-patch-up' (Balinese), or simply, 'to patch up' (Tagabili, Tzeltal, Trukese).

If he does, elliptically stating the reverse case. Some versions echo the form of their rendering of "no one tears", cp. e.g. 'if that is what he would do' (Tagabili), 'if you do this '(Cuyono). Others use renderings such as, 'otherwise' (cp. Kituba, lit. 'if not'), 'in that case' (Zarma), or replace the transitional phrase by a causative conjunction, cp. 'because it is not only the new garment that he will tear...' (Sranan, similarly Ponape).

He will tear the new. Here the verb is used in the sense of 'to tear up', 'to make a hole in'. Because the pronoun has an indefinite function a passive or medial construction may be preferable, e.g. 'the new will be-torn-up/go-to-pieces/remain with a hole (in it)' (East Toradja; Toba Batak and Bahasa Indonesia; Tzeltal and Shona 1966).

The piece from the new, or, 'the piece that is taken from the new'; or more briefly, 'the new piece' (Bahasa Indonesia, Toba Batak), 'what-is-torn-off' (Balinese).

Will not match, or, 'will not be-the-same-as' (Ponape), 'will not form one whole with', or in the affirmative, 'will clash with' (Jerusalem), 'will deviate from' (Javanese). Trukese uses a reciprocal form, 'the new and the old will not agree-together'.

37 ***And no one puts new wine into old wineskins; if he does, the new wine will burst the skins and it will be spilled, and the skins will be destroyed.***

Exegesis: *kai oudeis ballei oinon neon eis askous palaious* 'and nobody pours new wine into old wineskins'. *kai* characterizes what follows as a continuation of the *parabolē* of v. 36. *ballei* is used here in the sense 'to put' or 'to pour' (of liquids, cp. Jn. 3 : 5; Mt. 26 : 12, A-G s.v. 2 b).

askos (also v. 38) 'leather bag', 'wineskin'.

rēxei ho oinos ho neos tous askous, kai autos ekchuthēsetai kai hoi askoi apolountai 'the new wine will burst the wineskins, and he will be spilt and the wineskins will be lost'. Of these three clauses the first stands apart, indicating an event of which the other two (which go closely together) describe the consequences, cp. "the new wine will burst the skins—the wine will be spilt and the skins ruined" (Phillips). *kai autos* refers to 'the wine' in contrast with 'the wineskins' mentioned in the next clause. *rēgnumi* (†).

ekcheō 'to pour out', here in the passive 'to be poured out', 'to be spilled'.

Translation: For this verse see *TH-Mk* on the closely parallel 2 : 22.

New...old, here in the sense of 'young/fresh/beginning to ferment' and 'old/worn out/rotten', etc.; since the use of the more specific among these renderings would lessen, or even spoil, the synonymity with the pair in v. 36, they should only be employed where strictly necessary for reasons of idiom.

Wine, see also on 1 : 15.

Wineskins. To the renderings mentioned in *TH-Mk, l.c.* may be added some cultural equivalents, viz. 'gourd', used in Guhu-Samane, or 'bamboo tube (for storing palmwine)', used in Toba Batak only in v. 38 (presumably because the wine is normally stored in new, not in old bamboo tubes), whereas in v. 37 the more generic word 'container' is preferred.

Will be spilled, or, 'will run out', 'will be wasted'.

Will be destroyed, or, 'will be lost/ruined', 'will go to pieces', 'will become-bad' (East Toradja).

38 ***But new wine must be put into fresh wineskins.***

Exegesis: *blēteon* (††) 'one must put', verbal adjective of *ballō*. It is used here as an impersonal verb with object (*oinon neon*), cp. Bl-D, § 65.3.

The meaning of vv. 37f is more general than that of v. 36: it says that old forms and new contents cannot go together; new contents require new forms.

Translation: *Must be put*. If an active construction is required it will usually be the positive counterpart of the construction used for 'no one tears/puts' in vv. 36 and 37.

Fresh wineskins. The adjective, in the Greek identical with the one rendered "new" in v. 36, refers to the strength and elasticity of the wineskins. Problems of specificity *versus* synonymity are similar to those in v. 37.

39 ***And no one after drinking old wine desires new; for he says, 'The old is good.'"***

Exegesis: [*kai*] *oudeis piōn palaion thelei neon* 'and nobody who has been drinking old (wine) wants new'. With *palaion* and *neon* is understood *oinon*. The clause, together with, and explained by what follows, is explained variously. Since, however, the parable seems to hinge on the taste of the old wine, rather than on the comparative merits of both, the most likely interpretation is that of Plummer viz. that it is only natural that those who have been brought up under the old are unwilling to abandon it for something untried.

ho palaios chrēstos estin 'the old is good'.

chrēstos (also 6 : 35) of things 'of good quality', 'pleasant', cp. A-G s.v. 1 a α.

Translation: The structure of the first sentence may have to be changed, e.g. 'no one desires new wine, after he has drunk old wine' (Balinese), or, 'no one drinks old wine, and then desires new (wine)'.

For *to desire* (also in 8 : 20; 10 : 24, 29; 16 : 21; 17 : 22; 22 : 15; 23 : 8, 20) see *N.T.Wb.*/25f. The rendering often coincides with that of 'to wish' or 'to want', although 'to desire' basically refers to a stronger emotion.

Old wine...new. The connotation 'old' has here is considerably more favourable than in vv. 36f, the 'old wine' being 'matured/mellow'; hence, 'dry (i.e. strong)' :: 'weak' (Bali). But in many languages the usual terms for 'old (of age)' and 'new/young' have proved satisfactory.

The old is good, or, 'tastes good' (cp. Kapauku, Balinese), implies comparison, and, therefore, may be rendered more idiomatically by a comparative form or construction, as e.g. in Santali.

CHAPTER SIX

1 ***On a sabbath, while he was going through the grainfields, his disciples plucked and ate some ears of grain, rubbing them in their hands.***

Exegesis: *egeneto de*... *diaporeuesthai auton dia sporimōn* 'and it happened that he was passing through grainfields'. In this form the *egeneto*-construction (cp. on 1 : 8) relates the introductory circumstances.

diaporeuomai 'to go, or, to walk through'.

sporima (†), plural, 'standing grain', 'grainfields', cp. *TH-Mk* on 2 : 23.

kai etillon hoi mathētai autou 'and his disciples were plucking', viz. *tous stachuas* (†) 'the heads of grain'. The imperfect tense indicates repeated action. *tillō* (†).

kai ēsthion tous stachuas psōchontes tais chersin 'and were eating the heads of grain, rubbing them with their hands'. Strictly speaking the rubbing comes before the eating but in a general sense both acts happen simultaneously. *psōchō* (††).

Translation: For vv. 1-5 cp. *TH-Mk* on 2 : 23-28.

While he was going through... Actually the agents are Jesus and his disciples; hence 'Jesus and his disciples walked in the midst of' (East Toradja 1933), or in honorific languages, to avoid double translation of the verb (cp. *TBT*, 14.162, 1963), 'while Jesus, accompanied by his disciples, was going through...', or with a further change, 'while the disciples followed Jesus through..., they...'. *Going through*, or, to bring out that he was not treading the grain under foot, 'taking his way through', 'walked between' (Ponape), 'going along a path through' (Ifugao).

Grainfields, or, 'cultivated-fields' (Shona 1966), 'fields' (Marathi). For "grain" in the sense used here see on "wheat" in 3 : 17.

Plucked and ate some ears of grain, rubbing them in their hands. It is usually better to take the noun object with the first verb, and to change the order of the second and third verb, cp. e.g. "pick the heads of wheat, rub them in their hands, and eat the grain" (TEV), or with a final construction, '...they rubbed it in their hands, to chew on' (Tagabili). When another cereal is chosen to render 'wheat' details will have to be adjusted to fit its characteristics and the more or less specific terms used with reference to it. In some cases the verb 'to pluck/pick' does not take 'ears of grain' as object, but 'the grains', or the name of the plant itself, as in South Toradja, Balinese, Tzeltal, Trukese. Then "rubbing" has to be taken in the sense of removing the husks of the grains. For *ears of grain* cp. *TH-Mk, l.c.*; some substitutes used are, 'corn cobs' (Lokele), 'fruits of the rice' (Tagabili). For *ate* some languages use a more specific term here, e.g. 'chewed/nibbled-on-rice-kernels' (Tagabili, which possesses still another term for chewing on kernels of corn).

2 ***But some of the Pharisees said, "Why are you doing what is not lawful to do on the sabbath?"***

Exegesis: *tines de tōn Pharisaiōn eipan* 'some of the Pharisees said'. Their presence in the grainfields is not explained; it is simply assumed that they are there.

ti poieite ho ouk exestin tois sabbasin 'why do you what is not allowed on the sabbath?', cp. *TH-Mk* on 2 : 24. The question is directed to the disciples.

exestin impersonal verb 'it is permitted', in Luke always of what is permitted, or, with negation, what is forbidden by the law.

Translation: *But some of the Pharisees said.* Since the Pharisees are new to what is narrated in this section, it may be necessary to introduce them as such, e.g. 'then there-were-present some Pharisees who said' (Malay), cp. also on 1 : 5.

Why are you (plur.) *doing what is not lawful to do* does not ask for information, hence, 'Why! (or another exclamation expressing indignation or disapproval) You are doing...' may be preferable. For similar reasons South Toradja restricts the question to the first clause, 'What are you doing? — It is not to be done'. For *what is not lawful to do,* or, with a further shift, 'what we (inclus.) should not do', see *TH-Mk* on 2 :24; 6 : 18; 10 : 2. In countries with a Muslim background a technical term used in connexion with Muslim law may be an appropriate rendering, e.g. 'what is not *halal* (i.e. permitted)' (Bahasa Indonesia), or, 'what is *haram* (i.e. forbidden)'.

3 ***And Jesus answered, "Have you not read what David did when he was hungry, he and those who were with him:*** 4 ***how he entered the house of God, and took and ate the bread of the Presence, which it is not lawful for any but the priests to eat, and also gave it to those with him?"***

Exegesis: *kai apokritheis pros autous eipen ho Iēsous* 'and in answer Jesus said to them'. As in 5 : 30 Jesus answers to a question which is directed to his disciples.

oude touto anegnōte ho epoiēsen Dauid 'have you not even read what David did?' The use of *oude* 'not even' (cp. A-G s.v. 3) in this question appears to imply slight reproach (cp. e.g. BFBS). Cp. also Mk. 12 : 10 and *TH-Mk* there.

hote epeinasen autos kai hoi met' autou [*ontes*] 'when he was hungry himself and those who were with him'. For the story to which Jesus refers cp. 1 Sam. 21 : 6.

(V. 4) [*hōs*] *eisēlthen eis ton oikon tou theou* 'how he went into the house of God'. The clause explains *touto ho epoiēsen Dauid* 'that which David did' in v. 3 and is also in the form of an indirect question.

ho oikos tou theou 'the house of God', in the time of David the Tabernacle, not the Temple.

kai tous artous tēs protheseōs labōn ephagen kai edōken tois met' autou 'and after taking the loaves of the presentation ate (them) and gave (them) to those with him'. For *tous artous tēs protheseōs* cp. *IDB* I, 464 and *TH-Mk* on 2 : 25f. As explained there the accurate meaning of the phrase is 'bread of the Presence (of God)'. *prothesis* (†).

hous ouk exestin phagein ei mē monous tous hiereis 'which it is not permitted to eat except only the priests'. *hous* refers back to *tous artous*. *tous hiereis* is the subject of *phagein*.

Translation: The two verses are variously read and punctuated, see *GNT* and punctuation apparatus. For translational purposes they are often best divided in two or more sentences, the first introducing, the rest stating and elaborating, the case referred to, e.g. 'you have read what D. did, haven't you? Once he and those with him were hungry. He entered ...' (cp. Kapauku).

Not, preferably, 'not even'. The emphasis on the negation can sometimes be expressed by a verbal form adverbially used, e.g. 'I-should-think' (Toba Batak), or by an intensifying affix (Enga, see *TBT*, 16.132, 1965).

Read, see on 4 : 16.

He was hungry, he and those who were with him. It is usually preferable to say, 'he and those (who were) with him (or, his companions) were hungry'. For *hungry* see on 4 : 2^{b}. In Balinese a double translation is required, 'when he was faint (honorific for 'hungry') and his followers were hungry (non-honorific)'.

(V. 4) *House of God*, or, 'house for God'; Balinese has, 'house lodging-place of God', adding the term for the shrines into which the gods are believed to descend during a temple festival. Cp. also on "my Father's house" in 2 : 49, and *TH-Mk* on 2 : 26. Where 'house of God' is used specifically, or even exclusively, with reference to the temple in Jerusalem a qualifying phrase may be useful, e.g. 'in (the city of) Nob'.

Bread of the Presence, see *TH-Mk, l.c.* A rather literal rendering is possible in South Toradja, which combines the word 'bread' with a derivation of the verb 'to stand-in-front-of/be-in-the-presence-of/wait-upon (someone in exalted position)'. Other, somewhat freer renderings are, 'bread to-do-homage' (East Toradja), 'holy bread' (Ponape, Trukese, cp. the Hebrew term in 1 Sam. 21 : 4ff), "consecrated loaves" (NEB), 'placed bread' (Kapauku), 'church-bread' (Sranan, where 'church' has acquired a more generic connotation). For *bread* in general cp. references on 4 : 3.

Which it is not lawful for any but the priests to eat is in the Greek separated from its antecedent, 'bread of the Presence', by 'and gave (it) to those with him'. By keeping too closely to the clause order of the original some translators have led the ordinary receptor to take David's men, and not the bread/loaves, as the object of the priests' eating. To avoid such a misunderstanding one may shift the relative clause so that it directly follows its antecedent (cp. e.g. RSV, Ponape), or repeat 'bread/loaves' directly before the relative clause (Jerusalem, Trukese, Sranan, Malay); or again, one may use a co-ordinated sentence, e.g. 'As-a-matter-of-fact nobody is allowed to eat it except...' (Javanese), "Yet it is against our

Law for anyone to eat it except..." (TEV). For *priests* see references on 1 : 5.

5 ***And he said to them, "The Son of man is lord of the sabbath."***

Exegesis: *kai elegen* 'and he said' or "he also said" (NEB), preferably the former, see below.

kurios estin tou sabbatou ho huios tou anthrōpou 'lord of the sabbath is the Son of man', i.e. if already David was exempted from the law, so much more the Son of man, which Jesus implicitly claims to be. The clause represents more a conclusion from what precedes than an addition to it. *kurios* 'lord', or 'master' with emphasis at the opening of the clause. For *huios tou anthrōpou* cp. on 5 : 24.

Translation: *Is lord of the sabbath* implies authority (for which cp. on 4 : 32) over the rules about the observance of the sabbath. Some possible renderings are, 'exercises-power-over' (Sundanese), 'rules'; and cp. *TH-Mk* on 2 : 28. In Toba Batak idiom requires another sentence structure, viz. 'the sabbath conforms to (or, is dependent on, lit. (has) a teacher/master in) the Son of man'. Formal identity or relationship of the expression used here with the term for 'Lord', when occurring as a Messianic title, is not of primary importance.

6 ***On another sabbath, when he entered the synagogue and taught, a man was there whose right hand was withered.***

Exegesis: *egeneto de...eiselthein auton eis tēn sunagōgēn kai didaskein* 'and it happened that he went into the synagogue (aorist, punctiliar event) and taught (present, linear event)'. Cp. on 6 : 1 and 1 : 8.

kai ēn anthrōpos ekei kai hē cheir autou hē dexia ēn xēra 'and there was a man there and his right hand was withered'. Co-ordination of two clauses where subordination would be normal in Greek. The emphasis is on the second clause.

xēros 'dry', of wood in 23 : 31, 'withered', i.e. incapable of motion (cp. A-G s.v. *xērainō* 2 b). In view of *ekteinon tēn cheira sou* 'stretched out your hand' (v. 10) *xēros* is best understood as referring to paralysis.

Translation: The introductory statement about time and place is often better rendered as an independent sentence.

A man was there, or, 'there happened to be a man there, or, in the congregation' (cp. NEB).

Whose right hand was withered, or, 'who had a withered right hand, or, a right hand that was withered'. For *withered* see *TH-Mk* on 3 : 1; the rendering should imply the impossibility to stretch out the hand, or arm, and the paralysis meant is a non-congenital ailment (cp. on v. 10). For *right hand* cp. *N.T.Wb./42, 63.*

7 ***And the scribes and the Pharisees watched him, to see whether he would heal on the sabbath, so that they might find an accusation against him.***

Exegesis: *paretērounto de auton...ei en tō sabbatō therapeuei* 'and (they) watched him (to see) whether he would heal on the sabbath'. The present tense of *therapeuei* has reference to habitual practice.

paratēreō 'to watch closely', here with following indirect question.

ei '(to see) whether', cp. A-G s.v. V 2 a.

hina heurōsin katēgorein autou 'in order that they might find a reason to bring a charge against him'. *heuriskō* with following infinitive, 'to get a chance', 'to find a reason' (cp. L-Sc, s.v. *heuriskō* II 2).

katēgoreō 'to accuse', 'to bring charges against (somebody)', with following genitive of the person; legal term.

Translation: To simplify the structure of this sentence one may say, 'some scribes...wanted to find an accusation against him. So they watched him to see if he would heal... (cp. TEV), or, watched him, asking themselves, "Will he heal...?"'

Watched him, i.e. Jesus, not the man of v. 6. *To watch,* or, 'to look-carefully-at' (South Toradja, using an intensive form of 'to see'), 'to fix-with-the-eyes' (East Toradja, using a derivation of 'eye'); or, better to bring out the pejorative meaning, 'to spy-on' (Bahasa Indonesia, similarly Sranan).

If *to heal* requires an object (cp. on 5 : 17), it should be indefinite, "anyone" (TEV), "people" (Goodspeed, similarly most Indonesian languages), 'the sick' (Toba Batak), not definite and referring to the man of v. 6 (as is the case in Mk. 3 : 2).

So that they might find an accusation against him, indicates the result their action aimed at; hence, 'their aim/intent/wish was to...'. *Find an accusation against him,* or, 'get a chance to accuse him'. Some of the expressions used to render this phrase are, 'find something which they will accuse him of (lit. make-sinner-about him)' (Ponape), 'be obtained what they might cause to be his sin' (Tzeltal), 'find (opportunity) to place blame on him' (Marathi). For "to accuse", i.e. to denounce before/to the authorities, see also *N.T.Wb.*/1.

8 ***But he knew their thoughts, and he said to the man who had the withered hand, "Come and stand here." And he rose and stood there.***

Exegesis: *autos de ēdei...eipen de...* 'but he knew ..., and (hence) he said...' Co-ordination of two clauses in order to give full emphasis to the first one. The first *de* marks contrast, the second continuation. *autos* is also emphatic.

tous dialogismous autōn 'their thoughts', i.e. "what was in their minds" (NEB). For *dialogismos* cp. on 9: 46.

tō andri tō xēran echonti tēn cheira 'to the man who had the withered hand', hence (bringing out the emphasis on *xēran* which takes up *xēra* in v. 6), 'whose hand was withered'.

egeire kai stēthi eis to meson 'get up and stand in the middle'. *egeire* probably has here a more general meaning, cp. A-G s.v. 1 b, and on 5 : 23, viz. 'get up', from a sitting position. *stēthi* is ingressive.

kai anastas estē lit. 'and he rose and took his stand (there)', ingressive aorist, cp. *stellte sich hin* (Zürich), and A-G, s.v. *histēmi* II 1 a.

Translation: *He knew*, or, 'he perceived/was aware of'.

Their thoughts, or, 'what they were thinking (or, asking themselves)', 'their disposition (lit. their way of mind)' (South Toradja).

Come and stand here, preferably, 'get up and (take your) stand in the midst', viz. of the group around Jesus, 'get up, come and stand here in the centre'. For 'in the midst' see on 4 : 35.

He rose and stood there, preferably, 'he got up and took his stand there' (see *Exegesis*). The repetition has the function to indicate that the man did as he was told.

9 ***And Jesus said to them, "I ask you, is it lawful on the sabbath to do good or to do harm, to save life or to destroy it?"***

Exegesis: *eperōtō humas, ei exestin* 'I ask you whether it is permitted'. For *eperōtō* cp. on 2 : 46; for *exestin* on v. 2.

agathopoiēsai ē kakopoiēsai 'to do good or to do harm'.

agathopoieō 'to do good', in the sense of helping.

kakopoieō (†) 'to do wrong' or 'to harm', here probably in the latter meaning.

psuchēn sōsai ē apolesai 'to save life or to destroy (it)', an explanation of what *agathopoiēsai ē kakopoiēsai* refer to. *psuchē* (cp. on 1 : 46) means here 'human life' (cp. A-G s.v. 1 a β) or 'living person' (cp. A-G s.v. 2). *apollumi* means 'to destroy', rather than "to let perish" (20th Century, cp. also NV and Willibrord).

Translation: *Said to them*. A specification of the pronoun may be necessary, e.g. 'to the men who were watching' (Javanese).

I ask you helps to bring out the decisive character of the subsequent question, hence 'I put this question to you' (cp. NEB, Balinese).

Is it lawful on the sabbath to do good or to do harm...?, a question anticipating the answer: only to do good (is lawful on the sabbath). Idiom may require finite verbal forms, e.g. 'that we do good or do harm' (cp. Tzeltal, Tagabili). A question, asking for a choice between two (or more) alternatives may require a specific connective, e.g. 'or-else' (lit. if not so) (Sranan), or an interrogative pronoun meaning 'which-one-out-of-two (or more)' (Javanese). *To do good or to do harm*, or, 'to do what is good or to do what is harmful/bad' (East Toradja, Toba Batak). It may be necessary to add an object, 'to do a person good or to do him harm'.

To save life, or, 'to save a person', 'to save a person's life'. The verb is used here in the sense of 'to deliver from bodily harm'. Some renderings used here are, 'to spare (lit. hide) a person's life' (Sranan), 'to snatch away life from danger' (Cuyono).

To destroy it, or, 'to destroy/kill him, or, that person'.

10 ***And he looked around on them all, and said to him, "Stretch out your hand." And he did so, and his hand was restored.***

Exegesis: *kai periblepsamenos* (†) *pantas autous* 'after looking around at them all', i.e. "after looking at each of them in turn" (Rieu).

eipen autō 'he said to him', i.e. the man with the withered hand.

ekteinon tēn cheira sou 'stretch out your hand', i.e. the hand which was withered. The act is best understood as a preparation for the subsequent healing.

ho de epoiēsen 'and he did (so)', i.e. as he had been told.

kai apekatestathē hē cheir autou 'and his hand was restored'. The use of the verb *apokathistēmi* (†) 'to restore' implies that the hand had been sound once and become withered afterwards (cp. e.g. Rieu, "his hand was made sound once more").

Translation: *He looked around on them all,* or, shifting 'around' so as to qualify the object, 'he looked in the face of the people that sat-around' (East Toradja, similarly Balinese).

Stretch out your hand, or, 'make your hand/arm long' (as idiom requires in Marathi). There is a difference with the identical phrase in 5 : 13, in that here the reference is to the act and attitude of stretching in itself, whereas the act in 5 : 13 is done with a certain aim and the specific attitude is less in focus. This may lead to differentiation, cp. 'to cause-to-be-astretch' (Bahasa Indonesia), 'to hold-up' (South Toradja), here, but 'to put-out' (same languages) in 5 : 13.

He did so, or, 'he/the man stretched-(it-)out' (Trukese, similarly several Indonesian languages).

Was restored, or, 'became well again' (Sranan, similarly Trukese), 'was sound as originally' (Balinese); or simply 'was healed', if the verb in question includes also the cure of non-congenital ailments.

11 ***But they were filled with fury and discussed with one another what they might do to Jesus.***

Exegesis: *autoi de eplēsthēsan anoias* 'but they (emphatic) were filled with (insane) fury' (cp. BFBS and Phillips). For *eplēsthēsan* with genitive cp. on 1 : 15 and 4 : 28.

anoia (†) 'fury', here of angry men, cp. A-G s.v. and *N.T.Wb.*, 19/ ANGER.

dielaloun pros allēlous ti an poiēsaien tō Iēsou 'they discussed with each other what they should/could do to Jesus'. The Greek covers both 'should' and 'could'; if a choice is necessary the former is slightly more probable. The imperfect tense is durative. For *dialaleō* cp. on 1 : 65.

Translation: *They were filled with fury.* Both the noun and the verbal construction (see on 4 : 28 and cp. on 1 : 15) indicate that they became very angry (for which word cp. *N.T.Wb.*/9f, and *TH-Mk* on 3 : 5).

Discussed with one another, cp. on "said to one another" in 4 : 36.

What they might do to Jesus, or, 'how they might treat (or, behave towards) Jesus'. Luke says only by implication what Mk. 3 : 6 states baldly. A rather literal rendering of the phrase often carries the required pejorative connotation (e.g. in Cuyono, Trukese, Ponape, South Toradja, Toba Batak, Sranan); elsewhere one can use a causative verb derived from 'how' or 'what' (e.g. in Sundanese, East Toradja). Where a more explicit rendering is necessary one should try still to preserve something of the veiled wording of the original, e.g. 'how they might trick him' (Balinese).

12 ***In these days he went out into the hills to pray; and all night he continued in prayer to God.***

Exegesis: *egeneto de* etc. 'and it happened', cp. on 1 : 8 and on v. 1.

en tais hēmerais tautais 'in those days', a very general indication of time without exact reference to the preceding events.

eis to oros lit. 'into the mountain', to be understood in a general meaning like "into the wood", etc., and best rendered as "into the hills" (RSV), cp. *TH-Mk* on 3 : 13.

proseuxasthai 'to pray', final infinitive dependent upon *exelthein.*

kai ēn dianuktereuōn en tē proseuchē tou theou 'and he spent the night in prayer to God'. The genitive *tou theou* is objective and indicates to whom the prayer was directed.

dianuktereuō (††) 'to spend the whole night', viz. in doing something.

Translation: *Went out*, or, 'went up', because of what follows (e.g. in Marathi, Toba Batak).

Into the hills, see *TH-Mk* on 3 : 13; and for the noun cp. above on 3: 5.

To pray, see references on 1: 10.

All night he continued in prayer to God, or, "(he) spent the night in prayer to God" (NEB), 'all-night-long he prayed to God'; the latter rendering may require a durative form, but in several languages this aspect is already sufficiently indicated by the temporal qualification. If the term for 'to pray' includes a reference to God, the rendering of this verse will have to be adjusted, cp. e.g. 'he went out/up...to speak to God; the whole night he spoke (or, he spoke to him, or, he did so)'. *Night*, cp. *N.T.Wb.*/57.

13 ***And when it was day, he called his disciples, and chose from them twelve, whom he named apostles;*** 14 ***Simon, whom he named Peter, and Andrew his brother, and James and John, and Philip, and Bartholomew,*** 15 ***and Matthew, and Thomas, and James the son of Alphaeus, and Simon who was called the Zealot,*** 16 ***and Judas the son of James, and Judas Iscariot, who became a traitor.***

Exegesis: The syntactic pattern of vv. 13-16 is broken, since *kai eklexamenos* 'and after selecting' is not followed by a main verb. Hence several editors include v. 17[a] in the sentence of vv. 13-16 and this makes *estē* 'he stood' the main verb (cp. *GNT* Punctuation apparatus and Nestle).

This, however, is not preferable and vv. 13-16 are best understood as an anacoluthon. The translational problem is best solved by rendering the participle *eklexamenos* as a main verb.

kai hote egeneto hēmera 'and when day came', rather than 'when it was day', because of the inceptive aspect of *egeneto.*

prosephōnēsen tous mathētas autou 'he called to him his disciples'. *mathētas* refers here to a larger group of followers from which the twelve are to be chosen.

prosphōneō 'to call out', 'to address', here 'to call to oneself', 'to summon', cp. A-G s.v. 2.

kai eklexamenos ap' autōn dōdeka 'and he selected from among them twelve'.

eklegomai 'to choose', 'to select', usually with implication of selecting for a certain purpose.

hous kai apostolous ōnomasen 'whom he also named apostles'. Whether this happened at the same time, or later is not stated. The latter is more probable, cp. *TWNT* I, 429. In either case *kai* marks the naming as a separate act. *onomazō* (†).

apostolos 'apostle', i.e. one who is especially commissioned for a certain task. In 11 : 49 this task is undefined but here it refers to the preaching of the kingdom of God and the performing of the accompanying signs such as healing (cp. 9 : 1f); in this meaning also in 9 : 10. In 17 : 5; 22 : 14; 24 : 10 the noun serves to denote a group without reference to the task.

(V. 14) *Simōna, hon kai ōnomasen Petron* 'Simon whom he also named Peter', at that same time or at some later occasion, probably the former. The use of *kai* here serves to mark the naming as a separate act.

(V. 15) *Iakōbon Halphaiou* 'James the son of Alphaeus'.

Simōna ton kaloumenon zēlōtēn 'Simon who was called the Zealot'.

zēlōtēs (†) here and Acts 1 : 13 used as a cognomen, probably referring to membership of a group which practised zeal for the law (cp. *IDB* IV, 936-939, esp. 938).

(V. 16) *Ioudan Iskariōth, hos egeneto prodotēs* 'Judas Iscariot who became a traitor'. *Iskariōth,* probably a transliteration of *'iš k^{e}riōt* 'man from Kerioth', cp. *TH-Mk* on 3 : 18 and A-G s.v. It is better to transliterate it, rather than to translate it.

prodotēs (†) 'traitor'. *egeneto* in this clause means 'became', not 'was' as e.g. 1 : 5.

It may be safely assumed that the names in the list are grouped two by two, but the reasons for this are only once (in the case of Peter and Andrew) indicated.

Translation: *And when it was day,* see on 4 : 42.

He called his disciples, preferably, 'he called his disciples to(wards) him' (cp. e.g. NEB, Javanese, Toba Batak). The verb does not have the meaning of 'calling for a certain vocation'.

Chose from them twelve. Some languages prefer to omit 'from them', cp. e.g. 'those chosen, only twelve persons' (Balinese). For *to choose,* i.e. to prefer (and take) one or some out of a bigger number, Sranan uses 'to take. . .pull'; in some cases expressions with 'to separate' do also duty for "to choose", cp. also *TBT*, 5.90, 1954.

Whom he named apostles, preferably, 'whom (or, these people/persons) he also named/called apostles'. To bring out the interpretation advocated in *Exegesis* one may say something like, 'whom he was to name also apostles', or, more (perhaps even too) explicitly, 'who at a similar/later occasion he named apostles'. For *apostle* see *N.T.Wb.*/10f; *TH-Mk* on 6 : 30. In Kapauku the descriptive term for "apostle", viz. 'one-who-is-made-to-tell' is partially cognate with that for "angel", viz. 'one-who-goes-and-tells-for-someone'. Some languages spoken in regions with a Muslim majority use the Arabic word *rasūl* 'messenger/envoy', a title of Mohammed expressing his function as apostle to the Arabs.

(V. 14) The enumeration that now follows is often better introduced by some such expression as 'namely', cp. also "they were" (Phillips). If the names in the list are taken two by two (see *Exegesis*), this may require the use of one kind of connectives between the names of each pair and another kind, or no connectives, between the pairs.

Whom he named Peter. Where a relative clause is impossible or undesirable, one may have to shift to something like, '. . .in the first place Simon; Jesus gave him the name Peter. Next Andrew, his brother, . . .'.

Andrew his brother, or, 'A., brother of Simon', 'A., who was Simon's brother'. — *Brother*, see *N.T.Wb.*/18f. Since the reference probably is to a younger brother of the same parents a term specifying one or both of these components is to be used where only such specific terms are available. In languages where specific and generic terms exist side by side translators tend to prefer the latter in order to avoid an uncertain choice. This is quite acceptable in some languages but not in all. In Balinese, for instance, which has distinctive terms for 'older' and 'younger brother', as well as a term for 'brother/sibling' indifferent to age, the latter term would be misleading in that it suggests a lack of intimate knowledge of the family relationship, and stylistically wrong because it has a somewhat solemn connotation.

(V. 15) *The son of Alphaeus*, a patronymic specification, in close apposition to "James", and forming part of his full appellation. In some languages, e.g. Malay, the lexical and syntactic features of the phrase in this context are different from those it would have in other contexts, such as, 'J. here is a/the son of A.'.

The Zealot, or, 'the zealous One', indicating a person with intense religious devotion. Cp. also *N.T.Wb.*, 137/76.

(V. 16) *Who became a traitor*, or, 'who later turned out to be a traitor' (Marathi), 'who at the end betrayed Jesus'. The concept 'to betray', i.e. to deliver to (or, cause to be arrested by) an enemy, violating allegiance and confidence, is idiomatically expressed in some languages by, 'to inform against' (East and South Toradja, lit. 'to point out'), 'to turn traitor (lit. story-man)' (Sranan, using a neutral term, which in this context has the pejorative sense of 'gossiper', 'slanderer', 'denouncer'), 'to eat-sell' (Pa-O, cp. also 'to sell', East Toradja 1933).

17 ***And he came down with them and stood on a level place, with a great crowd of his disciples and a great multitude of people from all Judea and Jerusalem and the seacoast of Tyre and Sidon, who came to hear him and to be healed of their diseases;***

Exegesis: *kai katabas met' autōn estē epi topou pedinou* 'and after coming down with them he took his stand on a level place'. *met' autōn* refers to the twelve. For *estē* cp. on v. 8.

pedinos (††) 'flat', 'level', contrasting either with 'uneven', 'steep' (here), or with 'high', 'elevated'. *topos pedinos* may refer to "level ground near the foot of the mountain" (Plummer) or to a level place somewhere on the slope of the mountain, preferably the former.

kai ochlos polus mathētōn autou 'and (there was) a great crowd of his disciples', with *ēn* 'was (there)' understood (cp. NEB, BFBS), since the situation appears to be that when Jesus and the twelve arrived from the summit the other disciples were still there (cp. v. 13). *ochlos* appears to denote a smaller group than *plēthos* 'multitude' in the next clause.

kai plēthos polu tou laou 'and a great multitude of people', cp. on 1 : 10. Here both *plēthos* and *laos* are used in a non-religious sense.

apo pasēs tēs Ioudaias kai Ierousalēm 'from all Judea and Jerusalem'. For *Ioudaia* cp. on 1 : 5.

kai tēs paraliou Turou kai Sidōnos 'and from the coastal region of Tyre and Sidon', i.e. the coastal region in which Tyre and Sidon lie, outside the Jewish country.

paralios (††) scil. *chōra*, lit. 'land by the sea', used as a substantive 'coastal region', 'seacoast'.

hoi ēlthon akousai autou kai iathēnai apo tōn nosōn autōn 'who had come to hear him and to be healed of their diseases'. This clause belongs to v. 18 in the Greek text. *ēlthon* 'had come' suggests that they were already there when Jesus came down. The infinitives *akousai* and *iathēnai* are final.

Translation: *Came down*, or, 'came down the hill' (e.g. in Sundanese).

Stood, preferably, 'took his stand', or, 'came to a stand', 'stopped' (Jerusalem, Malay, South Toradja).

With a great crowd of his disciples..., preferably, 'there were many of his disciples there', or, since the reference is to another group of disciples than in v. 13, 'many more/other disciples of His were (assembled) there'.

A great multitude of people, or, 'very many people/persons'.

From, or, 'native from', 'who had come from'.

All Judea, or, 'the whole Jewish country'.

And the seacoast of Tyre and Sidon, preferably, 'the region of T. and S. that is by-side-of the-sea' (Ponape), 'the coastal parts (or, the region along/near the sea), where (the cities) T. and S. are'. *Seacoast* often is, 'side/edge/bank of the sea, or, the big water' (cp. *N.T.Wb.*/52, MARITIME).

Who came..., often rendered as a co-ordinated sentence, 'they (or, all these people) had come...' (Sranan, Toba Batak).

To be healed of their diseases, see on 5 : 15.

18 ***and those who were troubled with unclean spirits were cured.***

Exegesis: *kai hoi enochloumenoi apo pneumatōn akathartōn etherapeuonto* 'and those who were troubled with unclean spirits were healed', mentioning a special category among those that had come to be cured. *apo pneumatōn akathartōn* goes with *enochloumenoi* and indicates the cause or the source of their being troubled (*apo* = *hupo*, cp. A-G s.v. *apo* V 6).

enochleomai (†), passive 'to be troubled', 'to be plagued'.

Translation: One should take care not to suggest a contrast between those who "came...to be healed" (v. 17) and those who actually "were cured" (here): vv. 18f intend to show that, and how, the people who came were healed.

Troubled with unclean spirits refers to demon possession (see on 4 : 33); for *unclean spirit* see on 4 : 36. For *cured* see on "heal" in 4 : 23.

19 ***And all the crowd sought to touch him, for power came forth from him and healed them all.***

Exegesis: *kai pas ho ochlos ezētoun haptesthai autou* 'and the whole crowd tried to touch him'. *pas ho ochlos* refers in a loose way to all people who were there; it is virtually plural, hence *ezētoun* 'tried' (cp. A-G s.v. *zēteō* 2 b γ) is in the plural. For *haptomai* cp. on 5 : 13.

hoti dunamis par' autou exērcheto 'for power came forth from him'. As in 5 : 17 and 8 : 46 the conception is that of a spiritual power or substance residing as it were in Jesus and becoming effective when Jesus addresses, or touches sick people, or is touched by them. In 8 : 46 the last happens even without Jesus knowing who touches him. *par' autou* is synonymous with *ap' autou* (cp. on 4 : 35 and 8 : 46). The imperfect tense *exērcheto* (as the subsequent *iato* 'healed') is durative.

kai iato pantas 'and (he) healed all'. The subject is *dunamis*, or Jesus himself, preferably the latter, since both *iaomai* and *therapeuō* occur always in the New Testament with a personal subject. The clause is governed by *hoti*.

Translation: For *to seek* see 5 : 18; for *to touch* and *power came forth from him* cp. *TH-Mk* on 5 : 28 and 30.

20 ***And he lifted up his eyes on his disciples, and said: "Blessed are you poor, for yours is the kingdom of God.***

Exegesis: *kai autos* 'and he', not emphatic, takes up the subject of v. 17.

eparas tous ophthalmous autou eis tous mathētas autou lit. 'having raised his eyes towards his disciples'. *mathētas* has the same reference as in vv. 13 and 17. The phrase indicates that Jesus' words which followed were addressed primarily to his disciples.

epairō 'to lift up', here, 16 : 23 and 18 : 13 metaphorically of lifting up, or raising the eyes.

makarioi hoi ptōchoi, hoti humetera estin hē basileia tou theou 'blessed (are you who are) poor, for yours is the kingdom of God', nominal clause followed by a subordinate causal clause which says what the blessedness involves. Unlike the well known beatitudes in Mt. 5 : 3ff, vv. 20f are in the second person as appears from the causal clauses. For *makarios* cp. on 1 : 45. For *ptōchos* cp. on 4 : 18.

In the clause *humetera estin hē basileia tou theou* the present tense *estin* suggests that they are, as it were, entitled to it. *hē basileia tou theou* refers here to the situation under the rule of God.

Translation: *He lifted up his eyes on*, or, 'towards', should not be rendered literally in most languages (cp. *N.T.Wb.*/60, RAISE); hence such adjustments as, 'Jesus raised his eyes, and looked at' (cp. Tzeltal), 'he fixed his sight on' (Marathi), 'he looked up gazed at' (Javanese); or an, often ingressive, form of the verb 'to look/gaze at' as in Kituba, Sinhalese, Tagabili; cp. also Kapauku, which uses the same verb as for "looked around" in v. 10.

For *blessed*, or, 'happy' see 1 : 45.

Yours is the kingdom of God, or, 'it is you who possess (or, your property is) the kingdom of God' (Javanese, Balinese), or, with further adaptations, 'you have already entered God's hand that he rule you' (Mixtec), 'you are inhabitants of God's place-of-ruling' (East Toradja 1933), 'you have-as-government God's government' (South Toradja), 'God is king over you, or, the one who is ruling you' (Cuyono), 'you are already included in God's reigning (lit. holding)' (Tagabili).

21 ***"Blessed are you that hunger now, for you shall be satisfied.***
"Blessed are you that weep now, for you shall laugh.

Exegesis: *hoi peinōntes nun* 'you who are hungry now'. *nun* emphatically contrasts with the future tense of *chortasthēsesthe*. For *peinaō* cp. on 1 : 53.

chortasthēsesthe 'you will be satisfied', here of men (cp. A-G s.v. 2 a).

hoi klaiontes nun 'you who weep now'.

klaiō 'to weep', here metaphorically of a feeling of sadness (cp. A-G s.v.).

gelasete 'you will laugh', of a feeling of gladness.

Translation: *You that hunger*, or, 'you who are hungry', cp. on 1 : 53.

Now reinforces the present tense. To emphasize the contrast with the next clause it may be advisable to add a comparable adverb there, e.g. 'afterward', 'presently' (Balinese, East Toradja 1933), or, 'again' (Toba Batak). The same is true in the next sentence.

You shall be satisfied, or, 'you shall receive to the full', 'you shall receive all food/goods you need'.

Weep. If the language has distinctive terms (cp. *N.T.Wb.*/73) the translator can best choose one that is commonly used for weeping as result of general disasters; in some cases it may be better to shift to a term for the emotion expressed by weeping, 'be sad'.

Laugh, or where necessary, 'be glad' (for which see on 1 : 14).

22 ***"Blessed are you when men hate you, and when they exclude you and revile you, and cast out your name as evil, on account of the Son of man!***

Exegesis: *makarioi este hotan*... 'blessed are you, when...', syntactically a different type of beatitude, because the subordinate clause is not causal but temporal or conditional and refers to the situation in which the subject of the main clause lives. It is this situation which receives full emphasis now. The blessedness implicit in *makarioi* is described in v. 23.

hotan misēsōsin humas hoi anthrōpoi 'when people hate you'. Because of *heneka tou huiou tou anthrōpou* 'to hate' here has a religious connotation, cp. on 1 : 71 where the connotation is different.

kai hotan aphorisōsin humas kai oneidisōsin kai ekbalōsin to onoma humōn hōs ponēron 'and when they exclude you and revile you and ban your name as evil'. The repetition of *hotan* suggests that the three clauses go together closely and refer to one and the same situation, viz. that of excommunication from the synagogue.

aphorizō (†) 'to exclude', 'to excommunicate', cp. Jn. 9 : 22; 12 : 42; 16 : 1.

oneidizō (†) 'to revile', 'to insult'. It is possible that it refers to the curses that belonged to excommunication from the synagogue, cp. Strack-Billerbeck IV, 1 p. 302. As object of *oneidisōsin* is best taken *humas* 'you'.

ekballō (cp. on 4 : 29) may be rendered 'to spurn', 'to ban' (cp. A-G s.v. 1), or less strongly, "to reject" (BFBS). For the historical problems involved cp. commentaries.

to onoma humōn 'your name', i.e. their own names, rather than their name as Christians.

heneka tou huiou tou anthrōpou 'on account of the Son of man', i.e. because of your allegiance to the Son of man, or, "because you are loyal to the Son of Man" (Phillips).

Translation: *Exclude you,* i.e. break off all intercourse with you; hence, 'outlaw/boycot you' (Balinese); the rendering in Ponape and Trukese literally means 'to separate-away', in South Toradja it is a derivation of 'to wean'.

Revile you, i.e. use abusive language about you, call you by ill names. Some possible renderings are here, "insult you" (TEV), 'curse you' (Sranan), "slander you" (Phillips), 'say bad things about you', 'say that you are evil'.

Cast out your name as evil, i.e. do not (or, no longer) mention your name, as though it were bad; hence such renderings as, 'consider your name as impure' (Balinese), 'discard your name as though it were evil' (Zarma), 'make your name that it be one of ill omen' (Shona 1966), 'ruin your name' (Sranan). For *evil* cp. also Nida, *BT*, 220f.

On account of the Son of man, or, 'because you are followers of (or, have believed on, Tzeltal) the Son of man'. One should make clear that the phrase qualifies the four verbs that precede it in the Greek, e.g. by placing it at the head of the first "when"-clause (cp. Rieu, Marathi, Bahasa Indonesia RC).

23 ***Rejoice in that day, and leap for joy, for behold, your reward is great in heaven; for so their fathers did to the prophets.***

Exegesis: *en ekeinē tē hēmera* 'on that day', i.e. "when that happens" (Goodspeed). The phrase refers to the circumstances described in v. 22. The demonstrative pronoun *ekeinē* is vaguer than *houtos*, which usually refers to the near future.

charēte...kai skirtēsate 'be glad and leap for joy'. The aorist tense is used because the imperatives refer to future events. *chairō* 'to be glad' is a very common word and *skirtaō* 'to leap' is very unusual when used of men (cp. on 1 : 41). It denotes here the tremendous joy which accompanies martyrdom (cp. Acts 5 : 41; Jas. 1 : 2; 1 Pet. 4 : 13).

idou gar ho misthos humōn polus en tō ouranō 'for behold, your reward is great in heaven'. *idou* emphasizes the clause as a whole. *en tō ouranō* denotes the place where the reward will be at the time of trial and where it will be kept till the day of granting.

misthos 'pay', 'wages', 'reward' (here and v. 35).

kata ta auta gar epoioun tois prophētais hoi pateres autōn 'for in the same way did their fathers treat the prophets' (cp. NEB). *gar* 'for' marks the clause as explanatory, which is best understood as a last explanation of *makarioi* in v. 22: it is because they share the prophet's fate that the persecuted disciples are blessed. For *poieō* with dative cp. on 1 : 25. *autōn* refers to *hoi anthrōpoi* in v. 22.

Translation: *Rejoice..., and leap for joy.* As the two verbs reinforce each other the phrase is also rendered, 'leap for gladness' (Willibrord), 'be so glad that you caper' (Balinese). If verbs for 'to leap/jump', 'to prance' (Tarascan) can be used to express joy, a rather literal rendering is possible; if not, it may be better to use one strong expression of joy, e.g. "exult" (Knox, Torrey).

Your reward is great in heaven, or, shifting to an active verbal construction, 'God is ready in heaven to reward you greatly/magnificently'. *Reward,* i.e. something that is given because of good done; hence e.g. 'the gift you receive because of it' (cp. Tzeltal).

So their fathers did to, or, 'the same things (or, that also is what) their fathers did to', 'in the same way the fathers of those men treated (or, behaved towards)'.

(Vv. 24-26) The four beatitudes of vv. 20-23 are followed by four woes, each of which corresponds closely with one of the beatitudes. Like the beatitudes the woes consist of a nominal clause followed by a subordinate causal clause except the last ones, where the structure is different, saying what the woe involves. Several words occurring in the nominal clause of a beatitude appear in the causal clause of the corresponding woe. It is advisable, therefore, to use the same words in those cases and, in general, to keep the syntactic patterns used in translating vv. 20-23, as much as possible.

24 ***"But woe to you that are rich, for you have received your consolation.***

Exegesis: *plēn ouai humin tois plousiois* 'but woe to you, rich people'. As different from v. 20 and v. 27 *humin* is here best understood as referring to people who are not present. The use of the second person is probably due to stylistic reasons, viz. Luke's intention to preserve the formal correspondence with vv. 20-23 as much as possible.

plēn 'but', usually marking a stronger contrast than *alla.*

ouai 'woe', 'alas', implying the thought of impending judgment (except 21 : 23), cp. Schonfield. It is construed with dative of the personal pronoun, followed by an apposition either in the dative (as here) or in the vocative (v. 25[a]), or it is construed with following vocative (v. 25[b]).

hoti apechete tēn paraklēsin humōn 'because you have (now already) your comfort in full'. *paraklēsis* cp. on 2 : 25.

apechō here transitive 'to receive, or, to have in full', i.e. 'to have had'. The emphasis is on the idea of 'now' implicit in the verb *apechete.*

Translation: *But,* or, 'on-the-contrary' (Sundanese).

Woe to you. The rendering should denote not pity, but displeasure, curse, judgment; hence, 'you will see misfortune/trouble' (Shona 1963, Tzeltal), 'rejection to you' (an idiom that can be used here in Marathi), 'disaster!', used as a curse (Malay), 'pain/trouble will come to you' (Kekchi, Zacapoaxtla Aztec), 'you shall suffer' (Ifugao), 'to-their-end your days!', an idiomatic expression for great distress and despair (South Toradja). The group referred to by *you,* though probably not present, is addressed as if it were present. The rendering may have to differ from the one used before, as e.g. in Balinese, which uses 'little-ones', a form of address to one's children or pupils, in vv. 20-23 but a generic, not intimate, form of address here.

You have received your consolation. The verb can also be rendered, 'you possess already', 'in your hands is already'. The verbal noun may be rendered, 'what comforts you' (Ponape), 'what satisfies you' (Kapauku, here using metaphorically the term that it uses in a literal sense in vv. 21 and 25), 'what gives you pleasure, or, makes you happy'; or simply, 'your pleasure/delight' (Shona 1966), 'your happiness' (Kituba, similarly Tagabili), 'all the joy you are going to get' (Cuyono). With further adjustments the whole clause may be rendered, 'your only riches (will be) the riches you possess at present' (Tzeltal). Some of the expressions mentioned on 2 : 25 and references will not fit here since they express or imply the taking away of already existing sorrow, which is not the case here.

25 ***"Woe to you that are full now, for you shall hunger.***
"Woe to you that laugh now, for you shall mourn and weep.

Exegesis: *ouai humin, hoi empeplēsmenoi nun* 'woe to you, you who are filled now'. For *empiplēmi* cp. on 1 : 53. Here the phrase refers to people who are "filled", i.e. have all they want (cp. *chortasthēsesthe* in v. 21).

hoti peinasete 'for (there will be a time when) you will be hungry'.

hoti penthēsete kai klausete 'for (there will be a time when) you will mourn and weep'.

pentheō (†) 'to mourn'; as compared with *klausete* it is of a more general meaning.

Translation: *You that are full.* The rendering may coincide with that of "satisfied" in v. 21. Sranan has here, 'you whose goods pass the mark'.

Mourn and weep, see *N.T.Wb./*73, WEEP. The first verb primarily refers to ritualized, collective expressions of sorrow because a death has occurred; terms used may mean, 'to sing-songs-for-the-dead' (Toba Batak), 'to emit loud cries' (Shona 1963). Some versions prefer a less specific term, e.g. South Toradja (lit. 'to cry "O mother!"', which expresses terror, pain, fear), or simply, 'to be sad-in-heart' (Tzeltal, similarly Cuyono, Shona 1966, Sranan, Sundanese, Tagabili). The second verb refers to the shedding of tears as a more private and personal expression of grief. Together the two verbs indicate intense grief, which in Kabba-Laka can be expressed by the phrase 'my soul is seeking me' (Nida, *GWIML,* 131).

26 ***"Woe to you, when all men speak well of you, for so their fathers did to the false prophets.***

Exegesis: *ouai hotan...* 'woe (to you) when...', with omission of *humin.* The clause introduced by *hotan* describes the situation to which *ouai* applies, cp. on v. 22.

hotan humas kalōs eipōsin pantes hoi anthrōpoi 'when all men speak well of you', i.e. 'praise you' or 'say good things about you'. For the reference of *humas* cp. on v. 24 *humin. kalōs* also 20 : 39.

tois pseudoprophētais (†) 'the false prophets', i.e. prophets who gave a wrong interpretation of the will of God.

Translation: *All men,* or, 'everyone', 'the land', i.e. people all over the country (Balinese).

False prophets, or, 'lying prophets' (Tarascan), 'those who spread false words' (Kapauku, where the usual term for 'prophet' does not allow the combination with 'false'); and cp. *N.T.Wb./*23f, DECEIVE.

27 ***"But I say to you that hear, Love your enemies, do good to those who hate you,*** 28 ***bless those who curse you, pray for those who abuse you.***

Exegesis: Vv. 27 and 28 consist of four asyndetic co-ordinate clauses which belong closely together in terms of subject matter. This is brought out by the punctuation in the Greek text and in modern versions.

alla humin legō tois akouousin 'but to you who are listening I say'. This introductory clause shows that what follows is meant for a different group from those addressed in vv. 24-26. For *humin legō* cp. on 3 : 8. Here the usual word order is inverted for reasons of emphasis. *tois akouousin* is best interpreted as 'you to whom I am talking', i.e. the disciples (cp. Creed).

agapate tous echthrous humōn, kalōs poieite tois misousin humas 'love your enemies, do good to those who hate you'. 'Enemies' and 'those who hate' are to be understood in the light of v. 22 where reference is made to people who hate the disciples because of the Son of man. The aspect of the verbal forms in these verses is habitual.

agapaō 'to love', cp. *N.T.Wb.*, 87ff/.

(V. 28) *eulogeite tous katarōmenous humas* 'bless those who curse you'. For *eulogeō* cp. on 1 : 42; its meaning is well brought out by Rieu, "call blessings down on..."

kataraomai (†) 'to curse', i.e. to call evil powers against somebody in order to consign him to destruction. As compared with enmity and hate cursing and, for that matter, abusing (see next note) are more specific acts in which enmity expresses itself.

proseuchesthe peri tōn epēreazontōn humas 'pray for those who abuse you'.

epēreazō (only here and 1 Pet. 3 : 16 in the N.T.) 'to abuse', either in deeds, i.e. 'to mistreat', or in words, i.e. 'to insult', probably the latter.

Translation: *You that hear,* or, 'you that hear me/my words', 'you, my hearers'.

Love, see *N.T.Wb.*/50f and cp. two Tagabili idioms used for "love" in some cases, 'use up one's breath for' (7 : 47), 'big one's breath toward' (10 : 27).

Enemies and *those who hate you,* see on 1 : 71.

Do good to, or, 'behave kindly towards', 'treat-kindly' (East Toradja).

(V. 28) *Bless,* see on 1 : 42 sub (3).

Curse is the direct opposite of 'to bless'. In Tzeltal the term has been described, 'to ask God to harm somebody'. The receptor language may possess a technical term that is associated with magical practices; in this context there is no objection against the use of such a term. Cp. also *TBT*, 7.87-90, 1956.

Pray for says by implication what the more specific 'to bless' indicates explicitly. For "to pray" see references on 1 : 10.

Abuse, in the meaning preferred in *Exegesis* synonymous with "revile" in v. 22.

29 ***To him who strikes you on the cheek, offer the other also; and from him who takes away your cloak do not withhold your coat as well.***

Exegesis: *tō tuptonti se epi tēn siagona pareche kai tēn allēn* 'to him who strikes you on the cheek, present the other also', cp. *N.T.Wb.*, 28/BODY II. Note that vv. 29f are in the singular as contrasted with what precedes and what follows. *tō tuptonti* is dative of advantage with *pareche.*

tuptō 'to strike', 'to beat', in Luke always literally.

siagōn (only here and Mt. 5 : 39 in the N.T.) 'jawbone', hence 'cheek'.

parechō 'to give', 'to present', 'to grant', 'to bring about'.

kai apo tou airontos sou to himation 'and from him who takes your upper-garment'. The phrase goes with the main verb *mē kōlusēs* 'do not keep back'. *kai* introduces the clause as a parallel to the preceding one. *sou* is possessive genitive with *to himation.* The latter refers here to the "upper and more valuable garment" (Plummer, cp. A-G s.v. 2).

kai ton chitōna mē kōlusēs 'do not keep back your undergarment as well'. For *chitōn* cp. on 3 : 11. *kai* 'likewise', 'as well' (cp. A-G s.v. II, 1).

kōluō 'to hinder', 'to prevent', 'to refuse'. Here with *apo* 'to keep back from' (cp. Bl-D, § 180.1).

Translation: The construction *to him who strikes..., offer...* may better be rendered, 'when someone strikes..., offer him'; similarly the constructions in vv. 29^b^, 30.

Who strikes you on the cheek, or, 'on one cheek' (BFBS, Balinese), 'on the cheek at one side' (some Indonesian languages); or, where the use of a specific verb is more idiomatic, 'who slaps-on-the-face/cheek you at one side'. *Cheek.* In Sranan the term literally means 'side-of-face', corresponding with 'the other side' in the next clause.

Offer the other, or, 'offer (him) the other cheek, or, (the cheek at) the other side'. Other possible renderings of the verb are, 'turn (to him)' (Goodspeed, NV, Sranan, Trukese), 'make (to be) in front of him' (Marathi), "let him hit" (TEV).

Also means 'in addition (to it)', 'to be treated similarly'.

Cloak and *coat,* referring to an outer and an inner garment; see *N.T.Wb.* /20, CLOTHE, and below on 7 : 25. To render *cloak* some versions have chosen a term referring to a non-indigenous piece of dress because it resembled the type of garment referred to in the original. This is advisable only, if the dress in question has been commonly accepted in the receptor culture. The *coat,* or, 'shirt' (for which cp. also on 3 : 11) is mentioned here as example of the necessities of life; therefore one should avoid the use of a term referring to a garment that is considered a luxury in the receptor culture.

Do not withhold, or, 'do not refuse', 'do not oppose his taking' (Marathi); or, positively stated, "let him have" (NEB, TEV), 'allow him to take' (East Toradja).

As well, or, 'in addition to it'.

30 ***Give to every one who begs from you; and of him who takes away your goods do not ask them again.***

Exegesis: *panti aitounti se didou* 'to everyone who asks you give'. That which is asked for and is to be given is not indicated and the clause is intended to be of the widest possible application, especially when compared with the more specific commandments of v. 29. *aiteō* 'to ask' does not have the connotation of requesting urgently or threateningly.

apo tou airontos ta sa mē apaitei 'from him who takes away your possessions, do not demand (it) back'. *airō* 'to take away' often has the connotation of taking by force, cp. A-G s.v. 4.

apaiteō (also 12 : 20) 'to ask back' something to which one is entitled, as e.g. a loan or stolen property.

Translation: The clause order in the first sentence may have to be reversed, 'to everyone who begs, give' (cp. Zürich, Balinese); objects may have to be added, e.g. 'if someone begs anything (from you), give it to him' (Sranan, East Toradja).

For *to beg* and *to ask again* cp. *N.T.Wb.*/12f, ASK. The participants are best taken as being of equal rank; in the case of the first verb an intention to give back is probably not implied. In some cases a shift to direct discourse is necessary, e.g. 'say, "Give me (that), please"', and 'say, "Give them/my goods back (to me)"'.

Your goods, or, 'your possessions', 'what you possess'.

31 ***And as you wish that men would do to you, do so to them.***

Exegesis: *kai kathōs thelete hina poiōsin humin hoi anthrōpoi* 'and as you wish that people do to you'. Again the number shifts to the plural as vv. 27-28 and also all following verses till v. 38. *kai* may mean, 'and in short' (cp. Plummer) or 'and further', introducing a rule which does apply to all human relationships (cp. Bruce, Weiss). The latter is preferable. *kathōs* corresponds with *homoiōs*, indicating a rather strong correspondence, as brought out by Phillips ("exactly as") and BFBS ("just as").

Translation: The imperative clause is sometimes better placed first, as done in several English versions, Balinese, Shona 1966, Kituba.

As...so..., or, 'that which...that is what...' (Tagabili), 'the things (that)...the same things...'. If the clause order is changed the connexion may be expressed only once, cp. e.g. 'do to men exactly as (or, just what) you wish...'.

To do to, or, 'to treat', 'to behave towards'.

Men, or, "your fellowmen" (Rieu), 'others' (cp. NEB, TEV, Sranan, Shona 1966, Tzeltal), better to bring out the contrast to 'you'.

32 ***"If you love those who love you, what credit is that to you? For even sinners love those who love them.***

Exegesis: In the form of a series of questions vv. 32-34 take up the theme of the love of enemies of v. 27 and, distinguishing it sharply from any form of mutual love or good treatment, lead clearly up to, and are contrasted with v. 35f.

kai ei agapate tous agapōntas humas 'and if you love those who love you', conditional clause stating the case to which the following question applies. *kai* is best taken as connecting a new subject with what precedes.

poia humin charis estin? 'what credit is that to you?' *poia* is here equivalent to *tis*, cp. A-G s.v. *poios* 2 a α. For *charis* two interpretations are given, viz. (1) 'favour', viz. with God or men, and (2) 'credit', viz. in the sight of God or in the judgment of men, preferably the latter.

kai gar 'for even', cp. A-G s.v. *gar* 1 b.
hoi hamartōloi 'sinners', cp. on 5 : 8. The article is generic.

Translation: A passive construction may be idiomatically preferable here, 'if (only) those who love you are loved by you', 'if you love (only) those by whom you are loved'.

What credit is that to you?, a rhetorical question anticipating a negative answer. The noun may be taken here in the sense of 'appreciation/respect (to be won)'; hence, 'what is there to-be-praised about you' (Sundanese, similarly Sinhalese), 'you would be able to be thanked for what' (Shona 1963, similarly Zarma, Cuyono); or of 'merit (to be deserved)', 'reward (to be received)'; hence, 'why do you think men/God should reward you for that', 'God will not repay that type of loving-one-another' (Tagabili), 'you would be able to deserve to be given what' (Shona 1966).

33 ***And if you do good to those who do good to you, what credit is that to you? For even sinners do the same.***

Exegesis: *kai* [*gar*], if adopted, is best rendered as simple *kai*.
ean agathopoiēte 'if you do good', cp. on v. 9. Here the meaning 'to help' is also adequate (cp. Goodspeed).

Translation: *For even*, preferably, 'even', as in v. 34.
The same, or simply, 'that' in an emphatic position (Willibrord) or form (East Toradja).

34 ***And if you lend to those from whom you hope to receive, what credit is that to you? Even sinners lend to sinners, to receive as much again.***

Exegesis: *kai ean danisēte par' hōn elpizete labein* 'and if you lend to those from whom you hope to receive'. As shown by what follows *labein* refers to receiving back what had been lent.

daneizō (also v. 35) 'to lend (upon interest)'.

hina apolabōsin ta isa 'in order to receive back the same amount'.

apolambanō 'to receive full', 'to receive in return', 'to receive back', more specific than *labein* (see above).

isos (†) 'equal'. *ta isa* appears to be a current financial term, 'the same sum' (cp. Moulton-Milligan).

Translation: *Lend.* Languages may distinguish between, (1) lending food, money, etc., expecting in return an equivalent quantity or sum; (2) lending objects such as tools, expecting the same object to be returned; (3) lending on interest. In the present context one may hesitate between (1) and (3), but (1) is preferable because "to receive as much again" excludes an explicit reference to interest. The concept meant here can be expressed in various ways, e.g. 'to give debt' (Javanese), 'to receive a debt' (Lokele, which uses 'to take a debt' for 'to borrow'), 'to give to-be-borrowed' (Tzeltal), a causative form of 'to borrow' (Kituba; similarly in Tagabili, which uses 'to have-a-debt' for 'to borrow', and in Balinese, where the term for 'to borrow' is related to that for 'to exchange/replace'); or, 'to give temporarily' (Kapauku).

Hope, see *N.T.Wb.*/45. A less pregnant rendering, 'think that you will' is preferred in Kapauku, South Toradja, Sranan.

Receive may require an object, e.g. 'something' (East Toradja), 'a return/substitute' (Balinese, using a term related to that for 'to lend').

Sinners lend to sinners, or, 'sinners lend to fellow sinners' (East and South Toradja), 'sinners lend-to-each-other' (Balinese, using a reciprocal verbal form).

As much again, or, 'the same quantity/sum', 'as much as has-been-lent' (Balinese), '(as-much-)as (their fellows) had borrowed' (Sundanese).

35 ***But love your enemies, and do good, and lend, expecting nothing in return; and your reward will be great, and you will be sons of the Most High; for he is kind to the ungrateful and the selfish.***

Exegesis: *plēn agapate tous echthrous humōn* 'but love your enemies', contrasting with v. 32, as do the subsequent two commandments with vv. 33f. This shows that the subsequent commandments may be understood as applications of the commandment to love the enemies. For *plēn* cp. on v. 24.

mēden apelpizontes 'expecting nothing in return'. *apelpizō* (††) usually means 'to despair' (cp. L-Sc, s.v.) which would lead to a translation 'despairing in no respect', i.e. "never despairing" (Goodspeed, cp. NEB, RSV footnote). But the context requires the meaning 'to expect in return' which appears only in later Greek (cp. A-G s.v. and Lampe, *A Patristic Greek Lexicon*, 1961, s.v. C.).

kai estai ho misthos humōn polus 'and your reward will be great', cp. on v. 23.

kai esesthe huioi hupsistou 'and you will be sons of the Most High'. The clause may specify the reward to which the preceding clause refers (cp. NEB), or refer to something different from that reward. The former is preferable (cp. Mt. 5 : 9 and 45).

For *hupsistos* cp. on 1 : 32. *huioi hupsistou* means 'people having the same nature as the Most High', cp. Leaney.

hoti autos chrēstos estin 'because he is kind', explaining why they will be sons of the Most High: "likeness proves parentage" (Plummer). *autos* 'he', not 'he himself'. For *chrēstos* (here used of God) cp. on 5 : 39.

epi tous acharistous kai ponērous 'towards the ungrateful and evil', looked upon as one group, as shown by the single article. *acharistos* (†).

Translation: *Expecting nothing in return,* or, 'and do not expect that anything will be given back to you, or, that you will receive anything back'; cp. also, 'I will get it back thought not thinking' (Kapauku). The verb is here virtually identical with 'to hope'.

Sons of the Most High. The plural should be made explicit, in order to distinguish this phrase from the title of Jesus (1 : 32; 8 : 28). The phrase is preferably rendered literally (cp. Wonderly, *BTPU*, 128), but it may be necessary to shift to a simile, 'sons, as it were, of (or, comparable to sons of) the Most High'.

Kind, or, 'friendly', 'good', 'good of heart' (East Toradja, Sranan), 'generous' (Bahasa Indonesia).

The ungrateful and the selfish, or a construction as, 'those who are ungrateful and wicked', 'wicked people who don't know gratitude' (Sranan). *Ungrateful,* or, 'not saying "Thank you"', 'not knowing gratitude/thanks'. For some idioms expressing 'thankfulness' see Nida, *GWIML*, 134f. In Bahasa Indonesia thanks towards men is expressed by the phrase 'to accept/acknowledge kindness', in South Toradja by a verb that has the basic meaning of well wishing (cp. on "hail" in 1 : 28), and in East Toradja by 'to praise'. — *The selfish,* preferably, 'evil men', 'the wicked'.

36 ***Be merciful, even as your Father is merciful.***

Exegesis: V. 36 may give "further development of the principle of Christian love" (Plummer), or be introduction to what follows, i.e. to vv. 37f (cp. Klostermann). The latter is preferable.

ginesthe oiktirmones 'be compassionate'.

oiktirmōn (†) 'merciful', 'compassionate', i.e. in judging people, as vv. 37f show.

kathōs [kai] ho patēr humōn oiktirmōn estin 'just as your father is compassionate'. *kai,* if adopted, reinforces *kathōs*.

Translation: *Merciful,* or, 'showing/having compassion', 'kind'. When the verse is taken with vv. 27-35 the word refers to gifts and deeds, cp. 'be a doer of merciful deeds' (Kekchi); when it goes with vv. 37ff the word implies kindness and forbearance in judgment. Cp. on "mercy" in 1 : 50.

Your Father. In languages that differentiate according to rank the disciples' own fathers would usually be referred to with a non-honorific term, but, since here (and in 12 : 30, 32) the reference is to their heavenly Father, an honorific term may be required, which often, but not necessarily always, is the same as the one used in 2 : 49. Another problem may arise in a language like Huixtec where the use of the pronoun of the second person would exclude Jesus; hence the rendering had to be 'our (inclus.) Father'.

37 ***"Judge not, and you will not be judged; condemn not, and you will not be condemned; forgive, and you will be forgiven;***

Exegesis: In vv. 37f four parallel clauses in the imperative are followed by clauses in the passive which describe what will be received or experienced in return. The agent of the passives is not stated (probably intentionally), but the description of 'good measure' (see on v. 38) makes clear that Luke thinks of God as the agent.

kai mē krinete 'and do not judge'.

krinō 'to judge'; here it is used metaphorically in the sense of 'to act as judge' (cp. Brouwer), 'to pass judgment on other people'.

kai ou mē krithēte 'and you will (certainly) not be judged', cp. on *ou mē* in 1 : 15 (cp. RSV). *kai* introduces result (cp. A-G s.v. I 2 f), 'and then' (cp. Willibrord, Zürich).

kai mē katadikazete 'and do not condemn'.

katadikazō (†) 'to condemn', here used in a non-technical sense.

kai ou mē katadikasthēte 'and you will (certainly) not be condemned', cp. on 1 : 15.

apoluete, kai apoluthēsesthe 'acquit, and you will be acquitted'.

apoluō (cp. on 2 : 29) may be rendered (1) 'to forgive' (cp. RSV), (2) 'to acquit' (cp. NEB), or (3) 'to pardon' (a debtor) (cp. BFBS, A-G s.v. 1). Since rendering (2), 'to acquit', is more consistent with *krinō* 'to judge', and *katadikazō* 'to condemn' than the others, it appears preferable.

Translation: The imperatives may require an object, e.g. 'others' (Sranan), 'people/men'. If passives, or other forms with indefinite agent, would suggest a human agent, it is better to add a reference to God, e.g. 'you will not be judged by your Father' (cp. Toba Batak 1885), or to shift to, "God will not judge you" (TEV), and a similar reference (name or pronoun) in the subsequent sentences.

The common legal term for *to judge* (cp. *N.T.Wb.*/48) may have a connotation that makes it unsuitable for use in a negative sentence, e.g. in Marathi where it implies settling a quarrel as arbitrator; then one may shift to 'to expose the faults of' (Marathi), 'to accuse' (Kapauku).

Condemn has been rendered by idiomatic or descriptive phrases such as, 'declare guilty' (Marathi), 'give (someone his) sin/blame' (Totonac, Mazahua), 'decide for punishment' (e.g. in Tagalog). Cp. also *N.T.Wb., l.c.*

Forgive, preferably, 'acquit', the direct opposite of the preceding verb, e.g. 'decide not to be guilty', 'to set free (from punishment)', etc.

38 ***give, and it will be given to you; good measure, pressed down, shaken together, running over, will be put into your lap. For the measure you give will be the measure you get back."***

Exegesis: *didote, kai dothēsetai humin* 'give and it will be given to you'. How much will be given is described in the following clause.

metron kalon pepiesmenon sesaleumenon huperekchunnomenon dōsousin eis ton kolpon humōn 'a good measure, pressed down, shaken together (and) running over they will give into the fold of your garment'. The reference is to corn being poured out into a fold of a garment overhanging a girdle. *dōsousin* may refer to human agents or be an impersonal construction used to avoid the name of God. The latter is preferable, since it is consistent with v. 36 and does justice to the fact that the description of the 'good measure' points to a more than human generosity (other examples of this impersonal construction in 12 : 20, 48 and 16 : 9).

metron (†) 'measure', here a measure of capacity. *metron kalon* 'good measure', i.e. generous, not scanty.

pepiesmenon (††) 'pressed down' (by hand rather than by treading), in order that the contents may fill all the space in the container.

saleuō 'to shake', 'to drive to and fro'. Here of grain which is shaken together, i.e. moved to and fro in order to make it shrink.

huperekchunnomenon (††) 'overflowing'. Note the present tense: after the grain has been properly pressed down and shaken together somebody pours more corn into the container to fill the empty space till it flows over.

kolpos (also 16 : 22f) 'bosom', or 'fold of a garment overhanging a girdle', used as a pocket (cp. A-G s.v. 2).

hō gar metrō metreite 'for with what measure you measure', i.e. the measure you use with regard to others, referring back to the imperatives of vv. 37f. *metron* here 'measuring instrument' (cp. A-G s.v. 1 a).

metreō (†) 'to measure', 'to give out'.

antimetrēthēsetai humin (††) "it will be measured to you in return" (BFBS). The clause is best understood as an implicit injunction: give as God gives, in abundance.

Translation: *Give*, or if objects are required, 'give others a gift/something/what they need'.

It will be given to you, or again, 'God will give it to you' (cp. TEV).

Good measure, or, 'full/complete measure', 'true measure' (East Toradja). The noun may be rendered by the name of any object used in the receptor culture as measure of capacity, e.g. 'half coconut-shell', 'sack' (Sranan).

Running over, or, 'full to overflowing' (Sranan), 'piled/heaped up' (East and South Toradja).

Will be put, or, 'poured/given'; or 'God/he will put (etc.)'.

Into your lap. Cultural equivalents may be available, e.g. 'in the fold of your garment' (Marathi), 'in your *klofoy* (a large fold of the skirt hanging down from the waist)' (Tagabili). Where this is not the case it usually is best simply to say, 'to you' (e.g. in Kapauku, Ponape, Lokele, East Toradja).

The measure you give will be the measure you get back, or, 'the measure you use for (or, to give something to) others will be used for (or, id.) you (by God)'; or, not to suggest exact reciprocity, 'use as full/good a measure for others, as God uses for you', 'measure/give out to others fully, as God measures/gives out to you'; and cp. *TH-Mk* on 4 : 24.

39 ***He also told them a parable: "Can a blind man lead a blind man? Will they not both fall into a pit?***

Exegesis: *eipen de kai parabolēn autois* 'he also told them a proverb'. The clause marks the beginning of a new section (vv. 39f) which is but loosely connected with what precedes, and contains implicit or explicit injunctions for the disciples (cp. v. 40). The chain of thought appears to be as follows: the disciples who have to give leadership may not be blind. If they are blind as are those whom they are to lead they will fail. But how can they be able to give leadership? Only when they are fully trained and have become like their teacher. For *parabolē* cp. on 4 : 23 and 5 : 36. Here the meaning is "parable-like proverb" (Grundmann). *autois* refers to the disciples (cp. v. 20).

mēti dunatai tuphlos tuphlon hodēgein 'can a blind man lead a blind man?'

mēti (also 9 : 13) interrogative particle used when a negative answer is expected.

hodēgeō (†) 'to lead', here literally, though the proverb as a whole has a figurative meaning.

ouchi amphoteroi eis bothunon empesountai 'will they not both fall into a pit?'

ouchi here an interrogative particle used when an affirmative answer is expected, cp. A-G s.v. 3.

bothunos (†) 'pit', 'hole', 'ditch'.

empiptō (also 10 : 36) 'to fall in, or into', here literally, in 10 : 36 figuratively.

Translation: *Parable*, or, 'proverb', 'figure/illustration' (see on 4 : 23 and 5 : 36).

Can a blind man lead a blind man, or, 'can a blind man lead (or, be guide to) another (blind man) or, his fellow (blind man)', or with a reciprocal verb, 'can two blind men lead-one-another'. For *blind* cp. on 4 : 18.

Both, or, 'the two of them', 'they together'.

Fall. Some languages use a specific verbal form for an event that is not expected or intended (e.g. Javanese), or for something that will inevitably happen (Kapauku).

40 ***A disciple is not above his teacher, but every one when he is fully taught will be like his teacher.***

Exegesis: *ouk estin mathētēs huper ton didaskalon* 'a disciple is not above his teacher'. The article *ton* has possessive force. The saying must be understood as having a bearing upon the leadership of the disciples, see below. *huper* means here 'surpassing', cp. A-G s.v. 2 and refers to authority and insight. *didaskalon* is best understood as referring to Jesus.

katērtismenos de pas estai hōs ho didaskalos autou 'every disciple, who is fully trained will be like his teacher'. The subject of *estai* is either 'he', to be understood from and referring back to *mathētēs* in the preceding clause (with *pas* going with *katērtismenos*), or *pas*, with *mathētēs* understood, 'every disciple' (cp. RSV). The latter seems preferable.

katartizō (†) 'to make complete', cp. A-G s.v. 1 b; here 'to train fully'.

Translation: *Is not above*, or, 'is not more/better/greater/higher than', in the sense of 'is not more important than'.

When he is fully taught, i.e. when he has been taught all things he has to know, or, when he has learned everything he has to learn (cp. Kekchi). In some languages one can use a rather technical term for having finished a course, or, graduated from a school (e.g. in Bahasa Indonesia RC).

Will be like here refers to equality in degree of authority or capability; hence, 'will be as great/high/important as', cp. also "will reach his teacher's level" (NEB).

41 ***Why do you see the speck that is in your brother's eye, but do not notice the log that is in your own eye?***

Exegesis: *ti de blepeis to karphos..., tēn de dokon...ou katanoeis?* 'why do you see the speck...but do not notice the beam...?' *ti* governs both interrogative clauses. Syntactically the clauses are co-ordinate but semantically the emphasis is distinctly on the second one. The saying has figurative meaning and refers to what a blind leader in the church (v. 39), who is not yet fully taught (v. 40), is likely to do and against which he has to be warned. *blepeis* and *katanoeis* in the next clause are synonymous and mean 'you see', 'you notice'.

to karphos to en tō ophthalmō tou adelphou sou 'the speck (which is) in the eye of your brother'. *adelphos* is used here and in v. 42 in the sense of fellow-member of one's own group.

karphos (also v. 42) 'speck', 'chip', i.e. any small piece of straw, chaff, wood, etc. (cp. Phillips, NEB, "speck of sawdust"). Here it is used in a literal sense but the figurative meaning of "something quite insignificant" (cp. A-G) is also present because of the figurative meaning of the saying as a whole.

tēn de dokon tēn en tō idiō ophthalmō 'but the beam (that is) in your own eye'.

dokos (also v. 42) 'beam of wood'. The phrase refers to something which, as contrasted with *karphos*, it is impossible not to notice.

idios 'one's own', here used as possessive pronoun of the second person (cp. A-G s.v. 2 b).

Translation: Human nature being what it is, proverbs with comparable intent are found in several languages, e.g. 'the ant in the eye of another one sees, the elephant in one's own eye one doesn't see' (Balinese; cp. also the literary proverb quoted in 13 : 19), 'you laugh at another but your own nose is running with snot' (Marathi). This is not to say that such proverbs should be used in the translation, but to show that a rather literal rendering of Luke's formally different wording can as a rule be easily understood, or where necessary explained.

Why expresses astonishment verging on indignation, 'how is it possible that', 'it is quite inconceivable that'.

Speck...log. Pairs expressive of a big difference in size are usually easy to find, e.g. 'hair (of an ear of rice)...beam' (Balinese), 'splinter...pole/mast' (Bahasa Indonesia RC), the name of a small seed of a certain kind of grass...'beam' (Marathi, where the two terms rime and the proverb has become common usage).

In several languages the term for bodily *brother* (cp. on 6 : 14) can also be used in the very general sense meant here (and in 17 : 3; 22 : 32), which in Kekchi is expressed by, 'big-brothers little-brothers', a term for a person of the same clan, and then for any neighbour. Elsewhere, however, one has to shift to 'fellow', 'companion', e.g. in East Toradja 1933, Toba Batak.

42 ***Or how can you say to your brother, 'Brother, let me take out the speck that is in your eye,' when you yourself do not see the log that is in your own eye? You hypocrite, first take the log out of your own eye, and then you will see clearly to take out the speck that is in your brother's eye.***

Exegesis: *pōs dunasai legein tō adelphō sou* 'how can you say to your brother?', implying that it is impossible, or, at least, does not make sense.

aphes ekbalō lit. 'permit, or, let that I remove', hence, 'let me remove', cp. Bl-D, § 364.1. For *ekballō* cp. A-G s.v. 3.

autos tēn en tō ophthalmō sou dokon ou blepōn 'you yourself not seeing the beam in your own eye', syntactically a conjunctive participial clause with *dunasai legein*. Most versions treat it as a subordinate circumstantial clause.

hupokrita (in Luke always in the vocative) 'pretender', 'hypocrite'. Here it is best understood as referring to pretending not to see the beam in one's own eye, i.e. to forget one's own failures and mistakes (cp. Grundmann).

prōton adverb of time 'first', i.e. before something else can happen.

kai tote diablepseis to karphos...ekbalein 'and then you will see clearly the speck...so as to/in order to remove (it)'. *tote* refers back to *prōton*. *karphos* is primarily object of *diablepseis* (†), and secondarily of *ekbalein*. This infinitive is either consecutive or final, probably the former (cp. Rieu, "you will see clearly enough to pull...out").

Translation: To simplify the structure of the first sentence one may say something like, 'You cannot say to your brother, "...". You yourself can't (or, You, who can't) even see the log in your own eye'.

To your brother is sometimes better omitted, because the following form of address is sufficient. The latter must agree with the rendering of 'brother' in the rest of the two verses, cp. e.g. 'my friend', the term normally used in East Toradja in addressing a 'companion'.

When is implicitly adversative: 'whereas', 'but'.

You hypocrite, or, 'hypocrite that you are', 'what a hypocrite you are'; for the noun see *N.T.Wb.*/46f and *TH-Mk* on 7 : 6 (the Balinese rendering mentioned there proved too literary an expression for use in the Bible translation). An interesting specialized idiom for 'hypocrisy' used in Kituba is 'eye under leaf'.

43 ***"For no good tree bears bad fruit, nor again does a bad tree bear good fruit;***

Exegesis: *ou gar estin dendron kalon poioun karpon sapron* 'for there is no good tree which bears rotten fruit', or, 'a tree is not good when it bears rotten fruit', taking *kalon* as predicate. The former is preferable. *gar* expresses here continuation, not explanation, cp. A-G s.v. 4.

sapros (†) 'rotten' (here of rotten fruit and a rotten tree), or, somewhat more general, 'bad'.

oude palin 'nor, on the other hand'. Several translations do not render *palin* (cp. e.g. BFBS, Goodspeed).

palin 'again', here 'in turn', 'on the other hand' (cp. A-G s.v. 4).

Translation: Another possible change in the structure is, 'a good tree does not bear bad fruit', etc. (cp. TEV).

For *good* or *bad trees* bearing *bad* or *good fruit* cp. *N.T.Wb.*/37, FLORA.

To bear fruit (for which cp. 3 : 8) is used here in a literal sense, but the sentence as a whole has figurative meaning.

44 ***for each tree is known by its own fruit. For figs are not gathered from thorns, nor are grapes picked from a bramble bush.***

Exegesis: *gar* 'for', introduces the principle which underlies the statements of v. 43.

ek tou idiou karpou ginōsketai 'is known by its own fruit'. The present tense is used in order to express a general truth. *ek* indicates the source of knowledge (cp. A-G s.v. 3 g β).

ou gar ex akanthōn sullegousin suka 'for one does not gather figs from thorns'. *gar* introduces self-evident facts as examples of the principle which v. 44ª expresses. *sullegousin* is used in an impersonal sense. *sukon* (†).

akantha 'thorn plant'. For varying opinions concerning its identification cp. A-G s.v., *IDB* II, 296 and *N.T.Wb.*, 63/FLORA.

sullegō (†) 'to collect', 'to gather', a very general word.

oude ek batou staphulēn trugōsin 'nor does one pick grapes from a thorn bush'.

batos (also 20 : 37) 'thorn bush', 'bramble bush'.

staphulē (†) 'bunch of grapes', 'grapes', usually referring to ripe grapes.

trugaō (†) 'to gather (ripe fruit)'. As compared with *sullegō* it is a much more specific term.

Translation: *Each tree is known by its own fruit* may have to be expanded, e.g. 'one knows trees by looking at the fruit that each (of them) bears', 'one knows a tree when one knows its fruit, or, the fruit it produces'.

The second *for* is best rendered, 'of course', 'as everyone knows'.

Figs. The reference is to an edible and valued kind of fruit. A more or less literal rendering is often possible (cp. *N.T.Wb.*/38, FLORA) but in some languages another fruit has to be substituted, either in all occurrences or specifically in this verse, e.g. in East Toradja 1933 ('bananas'), Huixtec Tzotzil ('apples').

Thorns. The name of any kind of thorny wild growth, shrub or tree with no fruits, or inedible fruits will do.

Grapes. Where 'wine' is known but 'grapes' are not one may say 'wine-fruits' (Bahasa Indonesia); elsewhere the name of edible berries, or of the fruits producing the beverage used instead of 'wine' (for which see on 1 : 15) may be acceptable, or again a local equivalent not connected with wine, e.g. 'peaches' (Huixtec Tzotzil), 'guava (Psidium Guajava)' (East Toradja 1933). Cp. also Nida, *BT*, 165f on "vine".

Picked, more specific than, but virtually synonymous with, "gathered". Where no synonymous verb is available it may be omitted in the second clause, as done in East Toradja.

Bramble bush, synonymous with "thorns", 'thorn-bush', symbol of unfruitfulness.

45 ***The good man out of the good treasure of his heart produces good, and the evil man out of his evil treasure produces evil; for out of the abundance of the heart his mouth speaks.***

Exegesis: *ho agathos anthrōpos* 'a good man'; the article has generic force (cp. A-G s.v. *ho* II 1 a β). V. 45 applies to man what has been said about trees in vv. 43f.

ek tou agathou thēsaurou tēs kardias 'from the good treasure of the (his) heart'.

thēsauros (1) 'place where something is kept', 'treasure-room'; (2) 'that which is kept', 'treasure'. Since *agathos* denotes the quality of that which is kept and not of the place where it is kept, interpretation (2) is preferable. *tēs kardias* 'of his heart' has locative meaning, viz. 'in his heart'.

propherei to agathon 'produces what is good'. The article *to* is generic. *propherei* (††) is used in a literal sense, viz. of bringing out, or, bringing to the fore (cp. Zürich, *bringt hervor*, and Jerusalem, *tire*).

ek tou ponērou scil. *thēsaurou tēs kardias* 'from the evil (treasure of the heart)', elliptic phrase.

ek gar perisseumatos kardias 'for out of the abundance of the heart'. *gar* introduces a statement of the general principle.

perisseuma (†) 'fullness', 'abundance', here in a concrete sense, 'that which fills and overflows the heart'.

Translation: *The good man*. If one receptor language term covers both 'good' and 'beautiful', some qualification will be required, e.g. 'of heart' (cp. South Toradja, Toba Batak). The same is true of "the bad man" in the next clause.

Out of the good treasure of his heart, or, 'from the good things stored/treasured up in his heart', "from the store of good within himself" (NEB); cp. also *N.T.Wb.*/49, KEEP.

Out of his evil treasure. If the ellipsis has to be filled out the terms used should preserve the parallel with the preceding clause, e.g. 'from the good things (stored/treasured up in his heart)', 'from the store of evil (within himself)'.

Out of the abundance of the heart his mouth speaks, a literalism against which no less a translator than Luther has already declaimed. More idiomatic renderings are, 'his mouth says only what his heart is (more than) full of' (cp. Goodspeed, Timorese), 'the mouth speaks what comes from the heart, where there is a fullness of it' (Shona 1966), 'it is what fills (or, overflows from) the heart that comes out at the mouth' (cp. Rieu), 'in our hearts arise/have-their-source all those things which come out of our mouth' (Tzeltal). For *abundance* cp. *N.T.Wb.*/1. — *Mouth* may in this context be more idiomatically rendered by 'lips', 'throat'. In Nyanja the word for 'mouth' (derived from 'to drink') cannot be the subject of 'to speak'; hence, 'in his mouth there is utterance out of...'. Another language distinguishes between 'mouth (as organ of eating)' and 'oral cavity (as organ of speaking)', used here; an older version in this language employed the former term—with catastrophic results!

46 ***"Why do you call me 'Lord, Lord,' and not do what I tell you?***

Exegesis: *ti de me kaleite, Kurie kurie* 'why do you call me, lord, lord'. The clause marks the transition to a new section, which deals with the problem of words and deeds. The double vocative *kurie kurie* is used when one tries to catch somebody's attention or to find where he is. For *kurios* cp. on 1 : 6 and on 5 : 8.

Translation: *Why* here gives the rhetorical question the meaning of 'it has no sense that...'.

Call me, or, 'address me, saying', 'say to me'.

Lord, see on 1 : 6 (d). The force the duplication has in the receptor language should be checked carefully; it may be found preferable to use the noun only once, together with an appropriate exclamatory particle.

What I tell you, or, 'what I tell/command you to do'.

47 ***Every one who comes to me and hears my words and does them, I will show you what he is like:***

Exegesis: *pas ho erchomenos* 'every one who comes', cp. A-G s.v. *pas* 1 c γ.

akouōn mou tōn logōn kai poiōn autous 'hears my words and does them', i.e. puts the words into practice (cp. Phillips), or acts according to them (cp. Rieu, Goodspeed). As contrasted with the aorist tense of *akousas* and *poiēsas* in v. 49 the present tense of the participles in this verse refers to an abiding attitude, whereas in v. 49 the reference is to a decision that has been made.

hupodeixō humin tini estin homoios 'I will show you whom he is like'. Syntactically the subject of *estin* is *pas ho erchomenos* etc. After introducing this subject at length in the nominative the writer as it were interrupts himself and begins anew with *hupodeixō* 'I will show', and takes up *pas ho erchomenos* in the clause which is dependent upon *hupodeixō*. Several translations render *tini estin homoios* as 'what he is like' (cp. RSV) but as v. 48 shows *tini* is to be understood as masculine in gender, "whom he is like" (Goodspeed).

Translation: Without interruption the sentence may run like this, 'I will show you whom everyone is like who comes...and does...', or to avoid subordination, 'persons come, ...and hear...and do... Whom are they like? I will show you that'.

My words, or, 'what I say (to him), or, tell (him)'; cp. also "this teaching of mine" (Goodspeed), "what I have to say" (Phillips).

Does them. The verb may have to be rendered less generically, e.g. 'obeys (cp. on 2 : 51) them', or, 'keeps/observes them'.

I will show you what (preferably, whom) *he is like*, or, 'who he is' (Sranan, where a literal rendering would suggest outward resemblance only). *To show*, or, 'to cause-to-see'; or, since the seeing is with the eye of the mind, 'to explain', 'to make clear', "to give an idea" (Rieu).

48 ***he is like a man building a house, who dug deep, and laid the foundation upon rock; and when a flood arose, the stream broke against that house, and could not shake it, because it had been well built.***

Exegesis: *anthrōpō oikodomounti oikian hos eskapsen kai ebathunen* 'a man building a house who dug deep'. The participle in the present tense *oikodomounti* refers to the general process, viz. that of building a house, in which the specific acts take place, to which *eskapsen kai ebathunen* (aorist tense) refer.

skaptō (also 13 : 8) 'to dig', here intransitive, cp. A-G s.v. 1.

bathunō (††) 'make deep', or, 'go deep', here used as a hendiadys together with *eskapsen* and expressing together one concept, viz. that of digging deep.

ethēken themelion epi tēn petran 'he laid the foundation on the rock'. The article *tēn* before *petran* is generic, cp. "upon rock" (RSV, BFBS).

themelios 'foundation', 'basis', here of the foundation of a building.

plēmmurēs de genomenēs 'when there came a flood'. *de* marks the transition to the next part of the story. *genomenēs* is inceptive, hence the translation 'came'. *plēmmura* (††). The picture is that of an overflowing river, as *ho potamos* shows.

proserēxen ho potamos tē oikia ekeinē 'the river broke against that house'.

prosrēssō (also v. 49), intransitive, 'to burst upon', 'to break against'. Here its meaning is determined by the picture of the overflowing river.

potamos (also v. 49) 'river'. The article does not imply a reference to a specific river but to the river which the parable presupposes.

kai ouk ischusen saleusai autēn 'and was unable to shake it'.

ischuō 'to have power', 'to be able', 'to be strong enough', with following infinitive.

dia to kalōs oikodomēsthai autēn lit. 'because of its having been well built', articular accusative and infinitive, cp. Bl-D, § 402.1.

Translation: In order to bring out that the point of comparison is not in the building but in the subsequent acts some adjustments may be necessary, e.g. 'he is like a housebuilder, who dug...' (Bahasa Indonesia RC;

similarly Marathi, which renders the relative clause as a co-ordinated sentence), 'he resembles a man who, when (he was) building a house, dug...' (cp. Jerusalem); or where co-ordination is preferable, 'his case is like this: a housebuilder dug..., or, a man was building a house; he dug...'. *To build* (also in 6 : 49; 7 : 5; 11 : 47f; 12 : 18; 14 : 28, 30; 17 : 28; 20 : 17) is sometimes rendered by a basically more generic term, e.g. 'to erect/cause-to-stand' (Bahasa Indonesia, Trukese, Ponape), 'to make' (Javanese, Barrow Eskimo), 'to bind/tie' (West Nyanja).

To dig deep, i.e. to make deep holes/cavities, to remove much earth.

And laid the foundation upon rock may require rather radical adaptations, e.g. 'caused it to receive strength on rock' (Tzeltal), 'till he reached rock' (Shona 1966, similarly South Toradja), 'its posts reaching-down to the rock' (East Toradja). *Foundation*, or, 'base', 'support' (Sranan, lit. stone-foot). *Upon rock*, or, 'upon strong stones' (Sranan). Where rock is unknown one may use 'upon a solid layer underneath' (such as sand under marshy ground); or, with more radical adjustments, 'deep the holes for his posts' (Tagabili, where all houses are built off the ground, and deep holes make sturdy houses).

A flood arose, or, 'flooding water came', 'a/the river started to flood/overflow'.

The stream, or, 'the river', 'the/its water', or simply, 'it', the pronoun referring back to the flood or river.

And could not shake it, or, 'but it (i.e. the flooding river) could not shake that house', or, 'it (i.e. the house) did not shake because of it' (Marathi, shifting to an intransitive construction). *Shake*, or, 'cause to totter' (NV), 'cause-to-move' (Toba Batak, Ponape).

Because it had been well built, or, 'because that man had built it/his house well'.

49 ***But he who hears and does not do them is like a man who built a house on the ground without a foundation; against which the stream broke, and immediately it fell, and the ruin of that house was great."***

Exegesis: *ho de akousas kai mē poiēsas* 'but he who has listened but not done', or, 'but he who hears but does not do' (treating the aorist as gnomic, i.e. expressing a general truth, cp. Bl-D, § 333.1). The former rendering is preferable.

anthrōpō oikodomēsanti oikian epi tēn gēn chōris themeliou 'a man who built on the ground without foundation', i.e. without digging at all and without laying any foundation. *chōris* (†).

hē proserēxen ho potamos 'against which the river broke'. *hē* refers to *oikian*.

kai euthus sunepesen 'and immediately it collapsed'. *sumpiptō* (††).

kai egeneto to rēgma tēs oikias ekeinēs mega 'and the ruin of that house was great'. *mega* is used here in a qualifying sense. Its position at the end is emphatic.

rēgma (††) 'ruin', i.e. the collapsing. It refers to the same event as *sunepesen*.

Translation: *Who hears and does not do them,* or, 'who has listened to my words and has not done them'. The aspect is momentaneous, as against the durative aspect in v. 47.

Who built a house on the ground without a foundation, the opposite of "who dug...upon rock", but worded more briefly. *On the ground,* or, 'simply on the ground/soil', i.e. without any digging (Malay, Sranan), 'not at all deep the holes for his posts' (Tagabili). *Without a foundation,* or, 'but had not made a foundation/basis (for it)', 'not having founded it, or, set it on a solid layer underneath'.

Against which the stream broke..., usually better in a new sentence, e.g. 'The flood/river broke against it and immediately it fell', cp. also "when the flood hit that house it fell at once" (TEV).

The ruin of that house was great, or, 'the total destruction of that house took place' (Marathi), 'it fell down, or, was destroyed, completely' (cp. Trukese, East and South Toradja).

CHAPTER SEVEN

1 *After he had ended all his sayings in the hearing of the people he entered Capernaum.*

Exegesis: *epeidē eplērōsen panta ta rēmata autou* 'when he had finished all his words'. The use of *autou* (where a demonstrative pronoun would be natural, cp. RSV) appears to be intentional as brought out in "all he wished to say" (Rieu, cp. Schonfield). For *plēroō* cp. on 1 : 20 and A-G s.v. 5.

epeidē (also 11 : 6) 'when', 'after'.

eis tas akoas tou laou 'in the ears of the people'. *akoē* (†) is here synonymous with *ous*, and the phrase has the same meaning as *en tois ōsin humōn* (4 : 21) and indicates that the people (*laos*) had heard what Jesus had to say. The phrase is best taken with the clause as a whole.

eisēlthen eis Kapharnaoum 'he went into Capernaum', without indicating how far he was from that place.

Translation: *After he had ended all his sayings,* or, 'after he had finished saying (or simply, had said) all he had/wished to say'.

In the hearing of the people, or, 'while (or, and) the people had been listening (to him)', 'listened-to by the people' (Javanese), 'to the people who-were listening-to him' (Kituba). In translation the phrase may better be taken with "his sayings", e.g. 'his words which those people should hear' (Trukese), 'everything he wanted the people to hear' (Shona 1966), or simply, 'all he had to say to the people'. Marathi uses an idiom, 'fallen in the ear of the people'. *The people,* here virtually the same as 'the crowd'.

2 *Now a centurion had a slave who was dear to him, who was sick and at the point of death.*

Exegesis: *hekatontarchou de tinos doulos* lit. 'and of some centurion a slave'. The position of *hekatontarchou* at the beginning is emphatic and indicates that he, and not his slave, is the main personality of the subsequent story. This is brought out by e.g. RSV by making 'a centurion' the subject of the sentence.

hekatontarchēs (also 23 : 47) 'centurion', a subaltern officer in the Roman army, cp. *IDB* I, 547ff.

doulos kakōs echōn ēmellen teleutan, hos ēn autō entimos lit. 'a slave, being ill, was about to die, who was very dear to him'. *hos ēn autō entimos* expresses another aspect of the relationship between the centurion and his slave, cp. NEB and RSV. For *kakōs echō* cp. on 5 : 31, and for *mellō* cp. on 3 : 7.

teleutaō (†) 'to end', euphemistically, 'to die'.

entimos (also 14 : 8) (1) 'honoured', 'respected', or (2) 'valuable'. The former is preferable, cp. 14 : 8 and Phil. 2 : 29.

Translation: The verse is usually better divided into two sentences, the first stating the relationship between the master and his servant, the second describing the state that servant was in, cp. TEV.

Centurion, see *N.T.Wb.*/54, MILITARY; the number of soldiers commanded actually varied between about 50 and 100.

Slave may be rendered or described as 'have-to-work-er', 'bought-servant', 'credit bondsman/pawner/peon' (i.e. one who is trying to work off a debt), 'a man owned by', 'one compelled to work without wages'. Such renderings, however, sometimes refer to degrading servitude, imply moral reprobation, are said only of persons performing menial tasks (Kituba), or reflect upon the slave's master as being cruel and merciless (Terena), none of which associations fits the situation in New Testament society. In such cases a less pejorative term is better used, e.g. 'servant' (for which see on 12 : 37), the usual rendering of Gr. *doulos* in RSV; cp. also *TBT*, 11.30, 1960; 13.145f, 1962; *TH-Mk* on 10 : 44.

Who was dear to him, or, 'who was precious/important to him' (Trukese, Ponape), 'whom he loved very much' (some Indonesian languages).

Who was sick..., or starting a new sentence, 'That slave/servant was *sick...*'.

Sick and at the point of death, or, 'so sick that he was at the point of death'. For *sick* see on 4 : 40. *At the point of death* indicates that the patient had been given up; cp. e.g. 'lay in agony', lit. 'was-tossing-to-and-fro (as a young buffalo calf)' (South Toradja); in Marathi the idiomatic expression is 'leaning on death'; and cp. on "was dying" in 8 : 42.

3 ***When he heard of Jesus, he sent to him elders of the Jews, asking him to come and heal his slave.***

Exegesis: *akousas de peri tou Iēsou* 'when he heard about Jesus', or 'since he had heard about Jesus' (cp. Willibrord, Brouwer, Zürich), preferably the former. *akousas* is used without object but this is implied in *peri tou Iēsou*, viz. what he had done to sick people.

apesteilen...erōtōn 'he sent (viz. Jewish elders), asking', implying that his request is transmitted by the people he sent (cp. NEB). *erōtōn* is singular.

presbuterous tōn Ioudaiōn 'elders of the Jews', without article; hence "some elders" (cp. among others Phillips).

presbuteros 'elder', i.e. member of a local religious and administrative council, or of the Sanhedrin in Jerusalem, cp. *IDB* II, 73.

hopōs elthōn diasōsē ton doulon autou 'that he would come and save his slave'. The participle *elthōn* denotes an event which has to precede the event to which the main verb *diasōsē* refers.

diasōzō (†) 'to save', i.e. to save the life (cp. NEB), or, 'to heal' (cp. RSV), preferably the former.

Translation: *Heard of*, or, 'heard the news about' (Javanese, Toba Batak), 'heard what people said about' (cp. Jerusalem).

He sent..., asking him to come, or, making explicit the implied direct discourse, 'he sent... (to Jesus), saying (or, and said), "Go and ask (the Lord), 'Please (or, we beg you to) come and heal the centurion's slave'"'. For problems that may arise in honorific languages cp. *TBT*, 14.161, 1963.

Elders of the Jews, or, 'Jewish elders'. *Elders*. Often a term for 'old men' implies a leading position in the community; Marathi uses a compound with collective meaning to indicate that official elders rather than old men are meant. Elsewhere one must say 'important men', e.g. in Sranan (lit. 'big-men'), Bamiléké (lit. 'those who take precedence'). For *Jews* the language may possess a traditional designation already. Where that is not the case one should build the rendering on the name *Yehuda*, using the form or phrase the receptor language employs for names of tribes called after a common ancestor, cp. e.g. *Yahudi* (Arabic, used also in some Indonesian languages).

Heal, preferably, 'save the life of' (Marathi), 'cause to remain living' (Sranan), or simply, 'save' (in the non-religious meaning), cp. on 1 : 47 and references.

4 ***And when they came to Jesus, they besought him earnestly, saying, "He is worthy to have you do this for him,***

Exegesis: *hoi de paragenomenoi pros ton Iēsoun* 'and they, when they came to Jesus'.

paraginomai 'to come', 'to arrive'.

parekaloun auton spoudaiōs 'they requested him earnestly'. The imperfect tense suggests duration. For *parakaleō* cp. on 3 : 18.

spoudaiōs (†) 'earnestly', 'strongly', cp. A-G s.v. 2.

axios estin hō parexē touto 'he deserves that you grant him this'. *axios* 'deserving' is followed here by a qualitative-consecutive relative clause (cp. Bl-D, § 379; this is a latinism), expressing that the centurion's quality is such that he deserves that his request should be granted.

Translation: *They*, i.e. 'the elders' (Sundanese), 'those sent' (Javanese).

Besought him earnestly, or, 'asked him urgently'. Some idiomatic expressions used are, 'to ask with the heart coming out' (Tzotzil), 'to give one a desire (viz. to do what the beseecher asks)' (Huichol in Mk. 1 : 40). Here again a shift to direct discourse may be preferable, e.g. 'they urged him, "Please, do help him/the centurion"'.

Saying..., usually better as a new sentence, 'they said (also)..', 'they added...'.

He is worthy to have you do this for him, or, "this man really deserves your help" (TEV). *He*, i.e. the centurion, not the slave. For *to be worthy* see on 3 : 16.

5 ***for he loves our nation, and he built us our synagogue."***

Exegesis: *agapa gar to ethnos hēmōn* 'for he loves our people', explains why he deserves what he asks. The present tense suggests that this is his permanent attitude. *to ethnos hēmōn* refers to the Jewish people in general, not to their nation as a political entity, or their race.

kai tēn sunagōgēn autos ōikodomēsen hēmin 'and he built the synagogue for us himself'. *autos* may mean '(he) himself', or 'he' (emphatic personal pronoun, cp. NEB), preferably the former. *ōikodomēsen* means here that he had made other people build the synagogue. The aorist tense, as contrasted with *agapa* (see above), implies a reference to one specific act proving his love for the Jewish people.

Translation: *He loves,* see on 6 : 27.

Our nation, or, 'our brothers/fellows' (Kabba-Laka, South Toradja, both using a term indicating persons of the same tribe, family or party as the speaker's); and see *TH-Mk* on 13 : 8. The pronoun has inclusive force.

He, preferably, 'he himself', indicating that the centurion acted on his own initiative and costs.

Built us our synagogue, or, 'built for us the synagogue' (the article signifying that the synagogue of Capernaum is meant), or simply, 'built our synagogue', or, because he is not the direct agent, 'caused our synagogue to be built'. One may hesitate whether to use an exclusive or an inclusive pronoun. The former is often used (e.g. in Mazatec, Ponape, Marathi, Malay), on the assumption that Jesus, being not native to Capernaum, was not a member of the group primarily associated with the synagogue there. The latter is used on the assumption that Jesus, having his permanent headquarters in Capernaum, could be taken as belonging to the local synagogue; or because the inclusive pronoun qualifies an object as known both to the speaker and the person addressed; or again, because the use of an exclusive pronoun may sound as though the speaker did not allow his collocutor the use of the synagogue. The inclusive pronoun is probably preferable. In some languages it is better to avoid the pronoun altogether, cp. 'the synagogue (for the people) here' (Balinese, Sundanese).

6 ***And Jesus went with them. When he was not far from the house, the centurion sent friends to him, saying to him, "Lord, do not trouble yourself, for I am not worthy to have you come under my roof;***

Exegesis: *ho de Iēsous eporeueto sun autois* 'and Jesus went with them'. The clause implies tacitly that Jesus complied with their request. The imperfect tense of *eporeueto* portrays Jesus' action of going with them as still lasting on when happens that which the subsequent clause describes.

ēdē de autou ou makran apechontos apo tēs oikias 'but when he was already not far from the house'. *ēdē* is emphatic: already he had reached a point where he was not far from the house. *makran* also 15 : 20.

epempsen philous ho hekatontarchēs legōn 'the centurion sent friends saying', viz. to Jesus (cp. RSV). For this construction cp. on v. 3.

mē skullou 'do not trouble yourself', in the present context implying 'do not trouble yourself any further' (cp. NEB).

skullō (also 8 : 49) 'to trouble'; hence in the passive 'to trouble oneself'.

ou gar hikanos eimi hina...eiselthēs 'for I am not worthy that you come...' For *hikanos* cp. on 3 : 16; here it is synonymous with *axios* in v. 4. For the construction cp. Bl-D, § 393.4.

hina hupo tēn stegēn mou eiselthēs 'that you come under my roof', i.e. into my house.

stegē (†) 'roof'.

Translation: *And,* or, 'so', 'accordingly'.

Not far from, preferably, 'already not far from', or, 'already close to', 'no longer far from'; cp. also "had nearly reached" (Rieu).

The house, or, 'his/the centurion's house'.

Saying to him, "....." In contrast to v. 3 the message (vv. 6[b]ff) is given in direct discourse and as though the centurion himself is speaking.

Friend, also in 7 : 34; 11 : 5f, 8; 12 : 4; 14 : 12; 15 : 6, 9 (feminine), 29; 16 : 9; 21 : 16; 23 : 12; and, as form of address, in 11 : 5[c] (which see) and 14 : 10. The noun indicates a relationship of mutual affection and/or obligations, dependent on personal choice or social circumstances (cp. *N.T.Wb.*/40), rather than on family ties, or on local circumstances (as is the case with 'relative/brother' and 'neighbour' respectively). The rendering may also cover the concepts 'companion' or 'associate', or be a descriptive phrase, e.g. here 'people who liked/esteemed him'.

Lord, cp. on 1 : 6 (d).

Do not trouble yourself, or, 'do not make-tired-yourself' (East Toradja), 'do not make-it-difficult (for) yourself' (Sranan). In Trukese the polite way to put this is, 'do not continue to do something you don't want to do', and cp. on 8 : 49.

I am not worthy to have you come..., or, 'my worthiness is not (so) much that you should come' (cp. Marathi), 'I am not fit to receive/welcome you' (Bahasa Indonesia KB); and cp. on "worthy" in v. 4[b]. In some cases, however, the negative phrase is more idiomatically rendered by giving it another turn, cp. "it is not for me to have you..." (NEB), 'I am not a person whose house you should enter' (East Toradja 1933).

Come under my roof, or, 'come under the roof of my house', 'enter my house' (Shona, where a literal rendering would suggest that a person has a roof attached to him), 'set-foot-on my-stair' (South Toradja); Sranan has 'under my roof', but 'under my verandah/porch' would have been a slightly more common idiom. Marathi has a word meaning both 'hut' and 'roof', and used, depreciatingly, for 'house'; with the same connotation Balinese uses 'shed', lit. 'what-is-supported-on-forked-stakes'.

7 ***therefore I did not presume to come to you. But say the word, and let my servant be healed.***

Exegesis: *dio oude emauton ēxiōsa pros se elthein* 'nor, therefore, did I consider myself worthy to come to you'. For *dio* cp. on 1 : 35. *oude* is a continuation of *ou* in the preceding clause and goes with *ēxiōsa. elthein* means here implicitly 'to come in person' (cp. NEB).

axioō (†) 'to consider worthy', cp. A-G s.v. 1 a.

alla eipe logō lit. 'but say, or, command with (only) a word', hence 'say (only) a word', or 'just say the word' (cp. A-G s.v. *logos* 1 a α), or "just give the order" (Phillips). For *eipe* meaning 'command' cp. A-G s.v. *legō* II 1 c. The clause implies that Jesus' personal presence is not necessary to heal the slave. It is sufficient when he speaks a word from a distance.

kai iathētō ho pais mou 'and let my slave be healed' (imperative, third person). This imperative is the word which the centurion wants Jesus to speak and, by saying it himself, he, as it were, anticipates Jesus' saying it. For *pais* cp. on 1 : 54; here it is synonymous with *doulos* (vv. 2, 10), though it sounds slightly more friendly.

Translation: *Therefore I did not,* preferably, 'therefore also I did not...', 'that also caused me not to...'.

Come to you, or, "approach you" (NEB), or very humbly, 'show myself in your presence (lit. approach the dust on your feet)' (Balinese).

And let my servant be healed. This difficult form may be rendered as a request, 'and, please, heal my servant', or as an utterance of confidence, cp. "and my servant will be cured" (NEB); the former is preferable though the latter is acceptable also. Or again, making explicit the implied direct discourse, one may use something like, 'and, please, say, "I want your servant to be well (again)"'.

Servant, see on 12 : 37. Sometimes differentiation from 'slave' in v. 2 is possible, e.g. 'boy' (Sranan, similarly Bahasa Indonesia KB), but often the two renderings have to coincide.

8 ***For I am a man set under authority, with soldiers under me: and I say to one, 'Go,' and he goes; and to another, 'Come,' and he comes; and to my slave, 'Do this,' and he does it."***

Exegesis: *kai gar* 'for indeed', 'for even', hence, "I know, for" (NEB), cp. on 1 : 66; introduces the explanation of what precedes (cp. Plummer).

egō anthrōpos eimi hupo exousian tassomenos 'I (too) am a man set under authority'. The main clause is *egō anthrōpos eimi*, 'I am a man', i.e. either, 'I am somebody', *anthrōpos* being almost equivalent to the indefinite pronoun, cp. A-G s.v. 3 a β, or, emphatically, 'I am an ordinary human being'. The latter appears preferable, cp. Plummer. The present tense of *tassomenos* (†) is durative, 'used to working under orders'.

hupo exousian tassō (†) 'to put under the command of', cp. A-G s.v. *exousia* 4 a. For *exousia* cp. on 4 : 6.

echōn hup' emauton stratiōtas 'having soldiers under me'. This participial clause and the preceding one are best understood as semantically co-ordinate (cp. RSV), each expressing one aspect of the centurion's position. *stratiōtēs* also 23 : 36.

kai legō toutō, Poreuthēti, kai poreuetai 'and I say to one, 'go', and he goes'. *houtos* has lost its force as a demonstrative pronoun when used in combination with *allos* as here, 'one...another'. No specific meaning is to be attached to the aorist tense of *poreuthēti*. The semantic pattern of the two co-ordinate clauses *kai legō..., poreuthēti* and *kai poreuetai* is that the latter presupposes the former, 'when I say..., go,...he goes'. The same is true of the subsequent clauses.

kai tō doulō mou, Poiēson touto, kai poiei 'and to my slave (I say), 'do this', and he does (it)'. *touto* does not refer to something specific.

Translation: *Set under authority, with soldiers under me,* i.e. 'under my authority'. The contrast may be expressed by using passive :: active forms, or a semantically equivalent pair of verbs, e.g. 'ordered by those in power and commanding soldiers' (Toba Batak), or simply, 'I am given orders and I give orders to (my) soldiers' (cp. Shona 1966, Tzeltal), 'I receive orders from those above (or, officers/superiors) and give orders to my soldiers', 'I obey orders from others and have soldiers under (my) orders' (Kituba); Tagabili has to expand the rendering, 'there is a person higher than I, our 'head', and that one we obey. And there are soldiers I lead, and they obey me'. Instead of the metaphor 'above :: below' some languages say 'in front :: behind'.

'Go,' and he goes. The imperative is sometimes rendered by an adverb indicating movement away from the speaker (e.g. in Toba Batak); similarly for 'come' an adverb for movement towards the speaker. In Tagabili the idiom is, '"There (distant) now!", true like the flash of a butterfly (i.e. he obeys in a flash)'.

And to another...and to my slave... The words 'I say' may have to be added, as in Tagabili, Sranan.

'Come,' and he comes. Here the Tagabili idiom is, '"Come!", before the blink-of-an-eye, he is already here'.

9 ***When Jesus heard this he marvelled at him, and turned and said to the multitude that followed him, "I tell you, not even in Israel have I found such faith."***

Exegesis: *ho Iēsous ethaumasen auton* 'Jesus marvelled at him', rather than 'admired him', as advocated by A-G s.v. 1 b β.

strapheis tō akolouthounti autō ochlō 'turning to the crowd that followed him'. *autō* is dependent upon *akolouthounti.*

strapheis (7 : 9, 44; 9 : 55; 10 : 23; 14 : 25; 22 : 61; 23 : 28) aorist participle of *strephomai* 'to turn' (cp. A-G s.v. *strephō* 2 a α), in Luke always in this form and always referring to Jesus, used to denote that Jesus turns his attention to others, or to some people specifically.

legō humin 'I say to you', cp. on 3 : 8.

oude en tō Israēl tosautēn pistin heuron 'not even in Israel have I found faith so great'. *Israēl* refers to the Jewish nation as a geographical and religious entity. *tosautēn* lit. 'so great', is best understood in a qualitative sense, cp. RSV. For *pistis* cp. on 5 : 20. *heuron,* aorist, expresses that the action is completed and now regarded as a whole in contrast with what Jesus found at that very moment (cp. Bl-D, § 332.1).

Translation: *Marvelled at,* see on "wondered at" in 1 : 21.

Turned and said to the multitude, or, 'turned (around) towards the multitude, saying/and said'. *To turn* (or, 'to turn the face', 'to look back'), viz. in order to address, hence in some cases, 'to address'.

Followed, or, 'went along with him', 'was/walked behind (him)', referring to accompaniment, not to discipleship. Cp. also *TH-Mk* on 3 : 7.

Not even in Israel have I found such faith, or, 'even in (the people) Israel I have not found a man who believed so strongly (in me)', or, 'this man believes very firmly (in me); even amongst Israelites I have not met/come-across the like of him'. — *Even* is often expressed by an intensive particle indicating what might not be expected, and/or by giving emphatic position to the word(s) it qualifies. — In Balinese *such faith* is idiomatically rendered as, 'faith that is so dense'.

10 ***And when those who had been sent returned to the house, they found the slave well.***

Exegesis: *hupostrepsantes eis ton oikon* lit. 'having returned to the house', viz. of the centurion.

hoi pemphthentes 'those who had been sent', viz. by the centurion (cp. Phillips), hence "the messengers" (Goodspeed, NEB, and others), refers to the friends of the centurion (v. 6).

heuron ton doulon hugiainonta 'they found the slave in good health'. The story implicitly assumes that Jesus did speak the healing word and did not go to the centurion's house.

Translation: *They found the slave well.* The verb 'to find' with accusative and following participle or adjective is often (cp. also 8 : 35; 11 : 25; 19 : 30) used of coming where somebody or something is and perceiving the action or state of being he or it is in. Here one may have to render it, 'they came where the slave was and saw that he was well (again)', or simply, 'and there they saw that the slave was well (again)'. Cp. also *TH-Mk* on 7 : 30. For *well*, or, 'in good health', see on 5 : 31. For complete and instant recovery the Tagabili idiom is, 'as if the *bal* has come-to-life-again', referring to a small animal that often shams dead but the next moment may scamper away like lightning.

11 ***Soon afterward he went to a city called Nain, and his disciples and a great crowd went with him.***

Exegesis: *kai egeneto* 'and it happened', cp. on 1 : 8.

en tō hexēs scil. *chronō* lit. 'in the subsequent time', hence '(soon) afterwards'.

hexēs (also 9 : 37) adv. 'next'.

eporeuthē..., kai suneporeuonto 'he went...and (with him) went'. The aorist *eporeuthē* describes the main event, the imperfect *suneporeuonto* describes the accompanying circumstances.

hoi mathētai autou 'his disciples', cp. on 6 : 13.

kai ochlos polus 'and a great crowd', as in 6 : 17 and 7 : 9.

Translation: *His disciples...went with him,* is sometimes better subordinated, e.g. 'accompanied by (or, together with) his disciples...'.

12 ***As he drew near to the gate of the city, behold, a man who had died was being carried out, the only son of his mother, and she was a widow; and a large crowd from the city was with her.***

Exegesis: *hōs de ēggisen tē pulē tēs poleōs* 'and as he approached the gate of the town'. *pulē* (†).

eggizō with following dative 'to approach', 'to come near'.

kai idou exekomizeto tethnēkōs '(and) behold a dead man was being carried out'. For *kai idou* cp. on 1 : 20. For *kai* introducing the apodosis cp. A-G s.v. I 2 d.

ekkomizō (††) 'to carry out', often used as here for the taking of a corpse to a burial-place outside.

tethnēka (also 8 : 49) lit. 'to have died', hence 'to be dead'. Here the participle *tethnēkōs* is used as an indefinite substantive.

monogenēs huios tē mētri autou 'an only son of (lit. for) his mother', apposition to *tethnēkōs*. For the dative *tē mētri autou* cp. Bl-D, § 190.4.

monogenēs, adjective, 'only', in Luke always of an only child.

kai ochlos tēs poleōs hikanos ēn sun autē 'and a large crowd of the townspeople (lit. of the town) was with her'. For *hikanos* meaning 'considerable' with reference to quantity cp. A-G s.v. 1 a.

Translation: *As he drew near..., behold, a man...*, or, 'just as (or, at the moment) he drew near, a man...'; cp. also on 1 : 20. *To draw near* with local object may be rendered, 'to come close to', 'to come in the neighbourhood of', 'to have nearly reached' (Javanese in 15 : 25).

Gate of the city, or, 'gate in the wall of the city' (Trukese). *Gate* can sometimes be rendered by the term for the entrance in an earthen wall, wooden palisade, or hedge of a settlement, which can be barricaded at night, e.g. in Marathi, East and South Toradja. Elsewhere a more generic word is used, e.g. 'entrance' (Kekchi), or, 'exit' (Balinese).

A man who had died was being carried out, or, 'people were/came carrying out a dead one' (cp. Trukese); or, introducing a technical term, "a funeral procession was coming out" (TEV). For *a man who had died*, or, 'a dead man/one', 'a corpse', cp. also *N.T.Wb.*/27. In the receptor language 'a dead man' may be thought of as a person or as an object, which will influence the selection of terms (cp. on 16 : 22), or of categories (e.g. personal :: non-personal, animate :: inanimate). For *to die* (also in 16 : 22; 20 : 28f, 31f, 36) cp. *N.T.Wb.*/27. — *To carry out.* Renderings may have to be specific as to the way of carrying (cp. on "bringing" in 5 : 18), or the occasion, viz. the burial (for which cp. also Nida, *BT*, 191).

The only son of his mother, and she was a widow. Often such a long apposition is better rendered as a new sentence, 'he/the dead man was the only son...'. More radical changes may be needed, e.g. 'an only son, his mother a widow' (Javanese), "the only son of a woman who was a widow" (TEV), 'the son of a widow, her only child' (Tzeltal), 'the child of a woman whose husband had died; this woman had no other sons' (Kituba), 'the mother of the dead man was a widow, having (as) son only him' (Balinese), 'he was the only one his mother had, and the mother was a widow' (Zarma); Tagabili has a euphemistic expression, 'he was the only child his father left his mother, a boy child'. For *widow* see above on 2 : 37.

A large crowd from the city was with her, or, 'very many people... accompanied/followed her, or, thronged-after her' (Toba Batak); 'a large crowd also from-with the woman in the-city (i.e. accompanied the woman as they came from within the city)' (Ponape).

13 ***And when the Lord saw her, he had compassion on her and said to her, "Do not weep."***

Exegesis: *idōn autēn ho kurios esplagchnisthē ep' autē* 'seeing her the Lord had pity for her'. For *ho kurios* referring to Jesus cp. on 1 : 6.

splagchnizomai 'to have pity', in Luke always with some form of *eidon* 'to see' which points to pity in a direct person to person encounter.

mē klaie 'do not weep', i.e. 'stop weeping' (cp. "weep no more", NEB).

Translation: For *the Lord* versions have a term characterizing Jesus as a king, or as a divine Lord, usually the latter, cp. on 1 : 6, sub (c), or (b).

Saw her, or, 'saw that woman, or, the just-mentioned widow' (Bahasa Indonesia, Javanese).

He had compassion on her, or, 'he pitied her'. Many idioms are on record, e.g. "his heart went out to her" (NEB), 'his heart sad with her' (Sranan), and see *N.T.Wb.*/54, MERCY.

Weep, cp. *N.T.Wb.*/73; the term does not refer here to a collective, more or less ritualized public demonstration, but to a private, individual expression of grief because of death.

14 ***And he came and touched the bier, and the bearers stood still. And he said, "Young man, I say to you, arise."***

Exegesis: *kai proselthōn hēpsato tēs sorou* lit. 'and after going (scil. to the bier) he touched the bier'. Because of the preposition *pros* in *proselthōn* a direction towards the bier is implied. For *haptomai* cp. on 5 : 13. Here the touching is, as the following clause shows, a means to stop the bearers and has no function in the subsequent raising which is performed by means of a word.

soros (††) 'coffin', 'bier', presumably the latter, cp. *IDB* I, 437 and Klostermann.

hoi de bastazontes estēsan 'and the bearers stopped, or, came to a stand', indicating the effect of the touching of the bier.

bastazō 'to carry', 'to bear', here in a literal sense (cp. A-G s.v. 2 a).

neaniske, soi legō, egerthēti 'young man, I say to you, rise up/arise'. *neaniskos* (†) is a (young) man between 24 and 40 years of age, cp. A-G s.v. *neanias*. *soi legō* serves to lend emphasis to the following imperative, as in 5 : 24. *legō* has the connotation of commanding, cp. on v. 7 and

Plummer. *egeiromai*, when used of people called back to life (here) or raised from the dead (e.g. 20 : 37), is rendered 'to rise', or 'to be raised' without difference in meaning, cp. A-G s.v. 2 b, c.

Translation: *He came and touched the bier*, preferably, 'he came up/forward and touched the bier', or, 'he came to the bier and touched it (viz. with his fingers)'. *Bier*, or, 'stretcher (lit. thing-to-be-carried-upon)' (Bahasa Indonesia).

Young man. If a literal rendering would sound standoffish, 'son' (Marathi), 'little-one' (Balinese), 'my brother/friend' (Kituba) may be preferable forms of address. Where a vocative is undesirable or impossible (see on 1 : 3), one may transpose the noun, e.g. 'he said to the young man, "I tell you: Arise!"'.

Arise, i.e. from a lying to a sitting position (in some languages to be distinguished from 'arise', i.e. from a lying to a standing position, as in 5 : 23), or, 'come to life (again)', cp. *N.T.Wb.*/60; *TH-Mk* on 6 : 14.

15 ***And the dead man sat up, and began to speak. And he gave him to his mother.***

Exegesis: *kai anekathisen ho nekros* 'and the dead man sat up'. The aorist tense is inceptive.

anakathizō (†) 'to sit up, or, upright'.

nekros 'dead', here used as a substantive 'the dead person'.

kai ērxato lalein 'and he began to speak', cp. on 4 : 21.

kai edōken auton tē mētri autou 'and he gave him to his mother', a literal quotation from 1 Kings 17 : 23 LXX; this explains the sudden change of subject between this clause and the preceding one.

Translation: *The dead man sat up* etc., logically impossible but stylistically effective because of the contrast, may be idiomatically unacceptable; hence the subject may have to become 'the man who had been dead' i.e. no longer is dead (Toba Batak), 'the (young) man' (cp. Tagabili, Balinese). For *dead*, i.e. having died (also in 7 : 22; 8 : 49, 52f; 9 : 7, 60; 10 : 30; 15 : 24, 32; 16 : 30f; 20 : 35, 37f; 24 : 5, 46) see *N.T.Wb.*/27, DIE.

And he gave him to his mother, or, 'then Jesus/the Lord gave him (back) to...'; in Tagabili one must say, 'then Jesus said to the mother, "Here is your child"'.

16 ***Fear seized them all; and they glorified God, saying, "A great prophet has arisen among us!" and "God has visited his people!"***

Exegesis: *elaben de phobos pantas* 'and fear seized them all', cp. on 1 : 12.

kai edoxazon ton theon 'and they praised God'. Note the durative imperfect tense after the aorist tense of *elaben* as in 5 : 26. *doxazō* (cp. on 2 : 20) is often used to describe the reaction upon some supernatural or miraculous event (cp. 5 : 26; 13 : 13; 17 : 15).

prophētēs megas ēgerthē en hēmin 'a great prophet has arisen among us', strictly speaking, not the content of the praise but the reason for it. For *egeirō* cp. on 1 : 69. The appearing of 'a great prophet' is a mark of the Messianic age.

epeskepsato ho theos ton laon autou 'God has visited his people', cp. on 1 : 68.

Translation: *Glorified,* or, 'praised', see on 2 : 20.

Saying, i.e. to one another, cp. on 4 : 36.

For *great* see on 1 : 15.

Has arisen among us, or, 'has come to be with us'. Other possible renderings of the verb are, 'has appeared' (Kituba, Trukese), 'has been seen', cp. 'now again our seeing a prophet...' (Tagabili), 'is-holding-office (lit. is-standing-up)' (Javanese); or, using a figurative expression, 'has come to a dawning/sunrise' (Marathi). In Foe this and the next verb are in the far past tense, thus bringing out that the reference is not only to the raising of the young man.

Has visited his people, see on 1 : 68.

17 ***And this report concerning him spread through the whole of Judea and all the surrounding country.***

Exegesis: *kai exēlthen ho logos houtos...peri autou* 'and this story went out about him'. For *peri autou* cp. on 4 : 14.

en holē tē Ioudaia...kai pasē tē perichōrō 'in the whole of the Jewish country and (in) all the surrounding region'. The preposition *en* modifies both phrases notwithstanding their separation by *peri autou.* For *perichōros* cp. on 3 : 3 and 4 : 14. Here it refers to the area surrounding Judea. For *Ioudaia* cp. on 1 : 5.

Translation: For this verse cp. 4 : 14[b].

This report concerning him spread, or, 'people told/spread this story about him', 'everywhere people talked about this thing he had done'.

Through the whole of Judea, or, 'in all the places/everywhere in the Jewish country', cp. 4 : 44.

All the surrounding country, or, 'all the countries around/near it'.

18 ***The disciples of John told him of all these things.*** 19 ***And John, calling to him two of his disciples, sent them to the Lord, saying, "Are you he who is to come, or shall we look for another?"***

Exegesis: *kai apēggeilan Iōannē hoi mathētai autou* lit. 'and to John his disciples reported'.

apaggellō 'to report', 'to tell', 'to proclaim', 'to confess'.

(V. 19) *proskalesamenos duo tinas tōn mathētōn autou* 'after summoning a certain two of his disciples'. The indefinite pronoun *tinas* with the numeral *duo* means here 'a certain two', or 'a certain pair', cp. Bl-D, § 301.1.

proskaleō, in Luke always in the middle, 'to call to oneself', 'to summon'.

epempsen pros ton kurion legōn 'he sent (them) to the Lord, saying'. For this phrase cp. on v. 3. For *kurion* cp. on 1 : 6. In *GNT* v. 19 begins here.

su ei ho erchomenos? 'are you the coming one?' *su* 'you' is emphatic. *ho erchomenos* probably is a Messianic designation (cp. Plummer).

ē allon prosdokōmen? 'or are we to expect somebody else?' There is no reason to stress *allon* as meaning 'another of the same kind' as contrasted with *heteron* 'another of a different kind' in Mt. 11 : 3. *prosdokōmen* (for this verb cp. on 1 : 21) is deliberative subjunctive; the problem whether it expresses doubt or astonishment is much discussed (cp. commentaries, esp. Plummer and Klostermann). The former appears to be preferable.

Translation: *John* refers to the main character in the subsequent section, as brought out in, 'John (too) was informed of all this by his disciples' (cp. NEB, Javanese), 'John (the Baptist) heard all this from his disciples'; then the subject of the next sentence may better be a pronoun, e.g. 'he called...and sent...'.

(V. 19) In matters of honorifics three grades can be distinguished: the disciples honour John as their teacher but know that he has viewed and probably still is viewing Jesus as his superior, cp. e.g. 'sent (non-honorific) to wait-upon and say (reverent forms)' (Javanese).

Two of his disciples, or, 'two (men) from among (or, taken from the group of) his disciples', usually sufficiently expressing the meaning discussed in *Exegesis.*

Sent...saying, or, 'sent...to ask him', "sent...with the question" (Rieu). The form of the question is as though John himself were addressing Jesus.

Are you he who is to come, or, 'are you the One who is destined/appointed to come' (Balinese), 'are you the one who people customarily say will come' (Kapauku); or, making explicit the implied direct discourse, 'People since long have said, "Someone/He will come"; are you that one, or, did they speak about you?' If the question threatens to be misunderstood (e.g. in Algeria where Muslims might take it as a reference to Mohammed, see *TBT*, 7.168, 1956), one may say something like, 'are you the Messiah who is to come', or use a footnote.

Shall we look for another, or, 'are we to wait that/till another comes' (cp. Sranan, Javanese). *We* is best taken as exclusive; the use of an inclusive pronoun (found in three of the versions investigated) would imply John's supposing that Jesus is not the Messiah and, therefore, including him among those who still have to look for the Messiah. For *to look for* see 2 : 25.

20 ***And when the men had come to him, they said, "John the Baptist has sent us to you, saying, 'Are you he who is to come, or shall we look for another?'"***

Exegesis: *paragenomenoi de pros auton* 'and after they came to him', cp. on v. 4.

Iōannēs ho baptistēs lit. 'John the Baptizer' (cp. the virtually equivalent *ho baptizōn* 'he who baptizes' in Mk. 1 : 4, cp. *TH-Mk* there). The traditional rendering 'John the Baptist' is more a transliteration than a translation.

Translation: *The men,* or, "the messengers" (NEB), 'those two' (Bahasa Indonesia).

To him. Often 'to Jesus' may be required.

John...has sent us to you has to become in Foe, 'because John...sent us we came to you', using the near past tense (cp. on 1 : 19). — *John the Baptist.* For construction and aspect cp. *TH-Mk* on 1 : 4 and 8 : 28; for 'to baptize' see above on 3 : 3.

Are you...another?' exactly repeats v. 19[b], but now as a quotation in a quotation. This may make preferable certain adaptations, e.g. a shift to indirect discourse (Sranan), or a specification of the source of the quotation, cp. *TBT*, 18.30ff, 1967, on quadruple quote in Warao.

21 ***In that hour he cured many of diseases and plagues and evil spirits, and on many that were blind he bestowed sight.***

Exegesis: *en ekeinē tē hōra* 'at that time', to be understood either in a more general, or, in a more specific sense, as e.g. Phillips, "at that very time". The latter is preferable because of the aorist tense of *etherapeusen* and *echarisato* (see below).

etherapeusen pollous apo nosōn kai mastigōn kai pneumatōn ponērōn 'he healed many people of diseases and ailments and evil spirits'. For *pneumatōn ponērōn* (also 8 : 2) Luke uses elsewhere *pneumata akatharta* (cp. e.g. 4 : 33, 36; 6 : 18; 9 : 42; always in Mt. and Mk.), without difference in meaning.

mastix (†) lit. 'whip', 'lash', here in a figurative meaning, 'torment', 'suffering', 'ailment', stronger than the rather general *nosos* and referring here to diseases that bring much suffering.

tuphlois pollois echarisato blepein 'on many blind people he bestowed sight', lit. 'seeing'.

charizomai here 'to bestow', 'to give as a favour', 'to grant' with infinitive, in v. 42 'to remit'.

Translation: *He cured many of diseases and plagues and evil spirits,* or, 'he cured many people who suffered from diseases and plagues and evil spirits, or, were sick and very ill, and demon-possessed'. For *to cure* see on "to heal" in 4 : 23. *Diseases and plagues.* The stronger term has been rendered "afflictions" (Rieu), 'suffering' (Bahasa Indonesia RC), 'incurable illness' (South Toradja). Where no two acceptable near-synonyms are available one may say 'various diseases' (Malay). Cp. also on 4 : 40 and references. *And evil spirits* is still dependent on 'cured' but in some languages a more specific verb for casting out, or exorcizing, evil spirits has to be inserted (e.g. in East Toradja 1933); to avoid this Marathi and Toba Batak shift from 'cure of' to 'deliver from', which fits the three dependent terms. For *evil spirits,* i.e. 'demons' or 'unclean spirits', and demon possession see 4 : 33, 35f.

On many that were blind he bestowed sight. Most versions try to bring out that the Greek verb characterizes the healing as a favour or gracious gift, e.g. 'he gave many blind-men the mercy to see' (Sranan), 'many blind men became seeing through his gracious help', but where this would result in a too heavy construction or in overtranslating, it may be wiser to say simply, 'he healed (or, caused-to-see/opened the eyes of) many blind people', as done e.g. in Kapauku, South Toradja, Bahasa Indonesia RC. For *blind* see on 4 : 18.

22 ***And he answered them, "Go and tell John what you have seen and heard: the blind receive their sight, the lame walk, lepers are cleansed, and the deaf hear, the dead are raised up, the poor have good news preached to them.***

Exegesis: *apokritheis* 'answering', viz. to their question of v. 20.

tuphloi anablepousin 'blind people are regaining sight'. The present tense is repetitive and refers to what happens regularly. This applies also to the subsequent clauses of v. 22. The fact that several of them reflect Old Testament prophecies concerning the Messianic age (cp. Plummer) is the implicit answer to John's question whether Jesus was 'the coming one'.

anablepō 'to look up', here, 'to gain, or, regain sight', preferably the latter.

chōloi peripatousin 'lame people are walking'. For *peripateō* cp. on 5 : 23.

chōlos 'lame', 'crippled', 'limping'.

leproi katharizontai 'lepers are cleansed', cp. on 4 : 27.

kai kōphoi akouousin 'deaf people are hearing (again)'. *kai* is best understood as being inserted for stylistic reasons, viz. in order to interrupt the series of asyndetic clauses.

nekroi egeirontai 'dead people are raised', cp. on v. 14.

ptōchoi euaggelizontai 'to poor people the good news is being brought'. For *ptōchoi* cp. on 4 : 18 and 6 : 20. *euaggelizomai* 'to proclaim good news' (cp. on 1 : 19 and 2 : 10) is used here in the passive with a personal subject indicating the person to whom the good news is brought (cp. A-G s.v. 2 b β).

Translation: *Go*, or, 'go back' (Javanese, Balinese).

What you have seen and heard. In Shona 1966 the so-called applied form of the verbs is used, giving the shade of meaning, 'what you have seen for yourselves and heard for yourselves'.

The blind receive their sight, or, 'can see (again)', or, 'become seeing (again)', or, 'see now' (Kekchi, 'now' indicating the change of former circumstances). For 'to see', when used intransitively in the sense of 'to have the faculty of sight', some languages have a specific form, e.g. Toba Batak; elsewhere the transitive verb can be used in this sense when a generic object, 'space', is added (Tzeltal).

The lame walk, or, 'the crippled/limping walk properly' (Bahasa Indonesia, Sundanese). The term for *lame* may lit. mean 'foot-dead' (Trukese); or, 'having just one foot/leg', cp. *TH-Mk* on 9 : 45.

Lepers are cleansed, or, 'lepers become clean', and see on 4 : 27.
The deaf, or, 'those who can't hear'; the Trukese term lit. means 'ear-closed'.
To hear, in the sense of, 'to have the faculty of hearing' is, again, expressed by a specific verbal form in e.g. Toba Batak, and by 'to hear space' and 'to hear the air (i.e. all that is in the air, or, in a person's surroundings)' in Tzeltal and East Toradja.
The dead are raised up, or, 'dead people arise, or, come to life (again), or, live again' (Sranan, East Toradja 1933); and see *N.T.Wb.*/60; *TH-Mk* on 6 : 14.
The poor have good news preached to them, or again, 'the poor receive/can hear the good news', 'someone preaches the good news to the poor'. For *to preach good news* see on 3 : 18.

23 ***And blessed is he who takes no offence at me."***

Exegesis: *makarios estin hos ean mē skandalisthē en emoi* 'blessed is he who does not take offence at me'. For *makarios* cp. on 1 : 45. *hos ean* with following subjunctive introduces a relative clause which is virtually the protasis of a conditional clause (cp. A-G s.v. *an* 2 b, Bl-D, § 380.1).
skandalizō (also 17 : 2) here in the passive and construed with *en* with dative 'to be repelled', 'to take offence'. It refers to him who misunderstands Jesus' acts referred to in v. 22 and fails to recognize him for what he is and hence does not believe in him. Cp. *TH-Mk* on 4 : 17 and *N.T.Wb.*, 123/.

Translation: *Blessed*, or, 'happy', see 1 : 45.
He who..., or, 'any one who...', 'a person/man, if he...'.
Takes no offence at me, see *N.T.Wb.*/69, STUMBLE.

24 ***When the messengers of John had gone, he began to speak to the crowds concerning John: "What did you go out into the wilderness to behold? A reed shaken by the wind?***

Exegesis: *tōn aggelōn Iōannou* 'John's messengers'. For *aggelos* cp. on 1 : 11.
ērxato legein 'he began to speak', referring to a change in the situation, cp. on 4 : 21.
ti exēlthate eis tēn erēmon theasasthai? 'what did you go into the desert to look at?' *ti* is the object of *theasasthai* and *exēlthate* is construed with final infinitive, cp. A-G s.v. *exerchomai* 1 a ζ. For *theaomai* cp. on 5 : 27. Here it denotes an intentional act. For *hē erēmos* cp. *N.T.Wb.*, 41f/DESERT.
kalamon hupo anemou saleuomenon lit. 'a reed driven to and fro by the wind', hence 'a reed swaying in the wind'. For *saleuō* cp. on 6 : 38. The phrase may have literal or figurative meaning. Literal interpretation appears to be preferable and it implies that Jesus means to say, 'you did not go to the desert for nothing'. *kalamos* (†).

Translation: *Messengers*, or, 'sent-ones', 'persons sent'.

What did you go out into the wilderness to behold?, or simplifying the clause structure, '(when) you went (out) into the wilderness, what did you want (or, what was it you intended) to see (there)?' (cp. Javanese, Shona 1966). For *wilderness* see *N.T.Wb.*/25, DESERT.

A reed shaken by the wind? It may be preferable to repeat the verb, or even the two verbs, e.g. 'used you to go to see a reed...?' (Shona 1963). The negative meaning of the rhetorical question may have to be made explicit, e.g. by adding the answer, 'of course not', or by shifting to a statement, e.g. 'it was certainly not (or, you did certainly not go) to see a reed...'. The phrase itself has been rendered, 'a reed swaying in, or, blown by, the wind' (cp. Goodspeed, Toba Batak), 'a leaf that the wind causes-to-move' (Kituba). *Reed*, or, 'blade/stalk of reed'; the name of any variety of reed, tall grass, wild sugarcane, bamboo, or more generically, 'leaf' (see above), may be used, provided it is flexible and fits the locality, and that it refers to something that is unimportant and valueless, if one follows the interpretation preferred in *Exegesis*. If, however, one takes the phrase as a figure of speech describing John's character, one may better shift to a simile, e.g. 'a man as weak as cogon grass which goes whatever direction the wind blows' (Cuyono), or, non-figuratively, 'a person easily persuaded' (Tagabili). *Wind*. Where no generic term exists (cp. Nida, *BT*, 159) the name of a specific kind of wind fitting the context may be used.

25 ***What then did you go out to see? A man clothed in soft raiment? Behold, those who are gorgeously apparelled and live in luxury are in kings' courts.***

Exegesis: *alla ti exēthate idein?* 'but what did you go out to see?' *alla* implies that the answer to the last question of v. 24 is, 'of course not'.

anthrōpon en malakois himatiois ēmphiesmenon 'a man dressed in soft garments'. Probably a contrastive allusion to John's way of dressing as described in Mk. 1 : 6 (cp. *TH-Mk* there) and Mt. 3 : 4. Again the implied answer to the question is, 'of course not'.

malakos (†) 'soft', has the connotation of 'luxurious', 'fine' (cp. Goodspeed).

amphiennumi 'to dress', 'to clothe'.

idou 'behold', serves to lend emphasis to what follows.

hoi en himatismō endoxō kai truphē huparchontes 'those who are in splendid apparel and in luxury'.

himatismos (also 9 : 29) 'clothing', 'apparel'.

endoxos (also 13 : 17) 'splendid', 'gorgeous', cp. A-G s.v. 2.

truphē 'luxury', 'splendour', cp. A-G s.v. 2.

huparchō 'to exist', 'to be at one's disposal', often simply a substitute for *eimi* 'to be' (cp. A-G s.v. 2 and Bl-D, § 414.1).

en tois basileiois eisin 'are, or, live in (royal) palaces'.

basileios (†) 'royal', here used as a substantive in the neuter plural, '(royal) palace'.

Translation: For remarks on syntax and clause structure cp. on v. 24.

In *what then did you...?*, or, 'but what did you... ?' the word 'then', or 'but', serves to introduce a further question that mentions a comparable possibility. If the preceding phrase has been rendered as a rhetorical question, it may be preferable to say, 'if that is not so (or, if not), what did you... ?'.

A man clothed in soft raiment, or, 'a man in (or, who wears) soft/fine/splendid clothes'; the reference probably is primarily to outer clothing or adornment. For *to clothe* cp. *N.T.Wb.*/20. The term for "clothes" may basically be a word meaning 'what covers the body' (East Toradja), 'what-is-used' (Javanese, Bahasa Indonesia).

Gorgeously apparelled is virtually synonymous with the preceding "clothed in soft raiment"; hence, the renderings may have to coincide, cp. e.g. 'having beautiful clothing/adornment' (South Toradja).

Live in luxury has been rendered by such phrases as, 'their lives are "choosy"', i.e. they have a wide choice of food and clothing (Trukese, Ponape), 'they enjoy themselves (by amusements etc.)' (Marathi), 'the big life of them is passing the mark' (Sranan), or, referring to food only, 'they continually eat nice food' (Tarascan), 'they receive all-kinds-of delicacies' (South Toradja).

Kings' courts, or, 'houses of princes/nobles' (Toba Batak, Balinese).

26 ***What then did you go out to see? A prophet? Yes, I tell you, and more than a prophet.***

Exegesis: *nai, legō humin* 'yes, I tell you'. *legō humin* (cp. on 3 : 8) goes with *nai* as answering the preceding question *prophētēn?* 'a prophet?', emphatically in the affirmative.

kai perissoteron prophētou 'and even more than a prophet', syntactically still object of the infinitive *idein*. *perissoteron* may be masculine ("someone even greater...", Rieu) or neutral ('something even more...'), preferably the latter (cp. *pleion Iōna* 'more than Jona' in 11 : 32). In both cases the reference is to a person.

Translation: Again cp. on v. 24.

A prophet, a rhetorical question expecting a positive answer—as given in the next sentence, "yes", or, 'that's it' (Toba Batak, Sranan).

And more than a prophet, or, 'even more than that'; Kapauku has, 'doubtless one incomparable to (i.e. surpassing) a prophet'.

27 ***This is he of whom it is written,***
'Behold, I send my messenger before thy face,
who shall prepare thy way before thee.'

Exegesis: *houtos estin peri hou gegraptai* 'this is he concerning whom it is written'. *gegraptai* does not imply a literal quotation (cp. Plummer). For the rest of the verse except the last two words see *TH-Mk* on 1 : 2.

kataskeuazō, cp. on 1 : 17.

emprosthen sou 'before you', either temporal ('before your arrival') or local ('in front of you'), preferably the latter.

Translation: *This is he of whom it is written.* The substitution of a noun or of the name 'John' is sometimes preferable; for the relative clause cp. on 4 : 4; hence, e.g. 'John is the one of whom it is written', 'about this man Scripture has said, or, a prophet has written', etc.

If *I send my messenger*, or, 'my sent-one', would become tautological, one may say, 'I send (or, order to go) my servant'. The source of the statement may have to be indicated, e.g. 'God says, "I send..."', cp. Nida, *TAPOT*, 166.

Before thy face, or, '(to go/walk) in front of you', 'to be herald before you' (Javanese), 'your forerunner' (Toba Batak); and cp. *TH-Mk* on 1 : 2.

Who shall prepare thy way, cp. on 3 : 4.

Before thee (not found in 3 : 4 and Mk. 1 : 2) is semantically less important than the synonymous phrase 'before thy face' is in its clause, since it only expresses what is already implied in the preceding part of the sentence. It is best taken as attributive to 'way', e.g. "the road ahead of you" (Goodspeed), 'the way that runs on in front of you'. Simply to say, 'prepare your way, or, the way for you' may be necessary in some cases, but does not do full justice to a feature that is characteristic of Luke's wording here.

28 ***I tell you, among those born of women none is greater than John; yet he who is least in the kingdom of God is greater than he."***

Exegesis: *legō humin* 'I tell you', cp. on 3 : 8.

meizōn...Iōannou oudeis estin 'greater than John is none'. *meizōn* is predicate.

en gennētois gunaikōn 'among men born of women'. *gennētos* (†) is used here as a substantive modified by a genitive. The phrase is a generic but expressive description of the "whole human race" (Plummer).

ho de mikroteros en tē basileia tou theou meizōn autou estin 'but the least in the kingdom of God is greater than he'. *en tē basileia* may go with *ho mikroteros*, or with the predicate, preferably the former, and the phrase refers to the situation of the kingship of God as preached and brought about by Jesus. John is prior to this situation. *mikroteros* is best understood as having the force of a superlative (cp. Bl-D, § 60.1). *meizōn autou estin* 'is greater than he', does not mean that John is excluded from the kingdom, but that he is a forerunner only.

Translation: *Among those born of women none*, or, 'among all persons whom mothers bore (lit. made) no one' (Sranan), 'there is no person whom a woman bore who' (Zarma). The reference to women may be tautological or even misleading; hence such renderings as, 'of all people (born) on the earth' (Tagabili, Cuyono), 'of all other people who-have been-born' (Kituba). A positive statement may sound more forceful, cp. "John is greater than any man ever born" (TEV).

He who is least, or, 'a very small/slight/unimportant person'.
Kingdom of God, or, 'now that God (or, where God) is king/rules'.

29 ***(When they heard this all the people and the tax collectors justified God, having been baptized with the baptism of John;***
30 ***but the Pharisees and the lawyers rejected the purpose of God for themselves, not having been baptized by him.)***

Exegesis: Vv. 29f may be viewed (a) as part of Jesus' words describing the reactions to John's preaching, or (b) as an inserted comment by Luke as to the various reactions to Jesus' words. Though the decision is difficult, (a) appears to be the more probable view.

(V. 29) *kai pas ho laos akousas kai hoi telōnai* 'and all the people who heard (him), and the tax-collectors...', with John understood as the object of *akousas*. *laos* (cp. on 3 : 21) refers here to the common people as contrasted with the Pharisees and the scribes. *kai hoi telōnai* (cp. 3 : 12) is added as if on second thought, since *akousas* is in the singular; *kai* is ascensive, i.e. means 'and even', cp. e.g. Goodspeed.

edikaiōsan ton theon 'acknowledged God, or, God's justice', cp. Goodspeed. A rendering like "praised God" (NEB, cp. BFBS) betrays a different interpretation of vv. 29ff.

dikaioō 'to justify', 'to treat as just', 'to acknowledge as just'.

baptisthentes to baptisma Iōannou lit. 'being baptized with the baptism of John', i.e. 'being baptized by John' (cp. 3 : 7, 16), to be understood as describing the way in which they had acknowledged God (cp. Goodspeed) or the result of it (cp. Phillips), preferably the former. *baptisma* (referring to the act of baptizing) is accusative of content (cp. Bl-D, § 153).

(V. 30) *hoi...Pharisaioi kai hoi nomikoi* 'the Pharisees and the experts in the law'. For *Pharisaioi* cp. on 5 : 17.

nomikos 'expert in the law', synonymous with *nomodidaskalos* (cp. on 5 : 17), and *grammateus* (cp. e.g. 5 : 21).

tēn boulēn tou theou ēthetēsan eis heautous 'rejected the will of God with reference to themselves'.

boulē (also 23 : 51) 'will', 'purpose'.

atheteō 'to nullify', hence 'to reject', viz. that which God wanted them to do, his will, or 'to thwart', viz. that which God had in mind to perpetrate, his purpose. The former is preferable. *eis heautous* is best understood as going with the clause as a whole.

mē baptisthentes hup' autou 'not being baptized by him', or preferably in the middle voice, 'not having themselves baptized by him', hence "by refusing to be baptized by him" (Goodspeed, cp. Rieu, Phillips).

Translation: On the basis of the interpretation preferred in *Exegesis* the following remarks have to be made.

For *all the people* cp. on 1 : 17, but for the people in contrast to its leaders some languages (e.g. in Indonesia) prefer a distinctive term, something like 'the common people'.

The tax collectors, see on 3 : 12.

Heard this, preferably, 'heard him/John, or, his/John's preaching/words'.

Justified God, or, more analytically, 'acknowledged that God is just', cp. 'gave God right' (Sranan), 'accepted the rightness of God by agreeing with it' (Trukese, Ponape); the Kapauku rendering lit. means, 'God is tremendous they thought'. Cp. also *N.T.Wb./*63, RIGHTEOUS, sub (5).

Having been baptized with the baptism of John, preferably, 'having had themselves baptized with the baptism of J.', which may result in such renderings as, 'having accepted/taken baptism of J.' (cp. Goodspeed, Jerusalem, Marathi, Sranan, Javanese, Toba Batak), 'having given themselves to be baptized by J.' (South Toradja), 'having asked J. to baptize them'; or, stressing John's role, 'they had themselves baptized by him—yes, by John himself' (Cuyono). Cp. also on 3 : 7 and 3. The descriptive connexion with the main clause is usually better made explicit, e.g. 'by having (or, when they) had themselves baptized...', or, changing the clause order, '...had taken John's baptism. By this means they justified...' (cp. Marathi).

(V. 30) *Lawyer*, i.e. 'expert/scholar of the law', 'one who knows/studies/interprets the law', 'one who knows the commandments' (Timorese), 'man of commandments' (East Nyanja, Lomwe, Yao). The rendering may have to coincide with that of "scribe" (see 5 : 21) and/or "teacher of the law" (see on 5 : 17). For 'law' cp. on 2 : 22.

Rejected...for themselves, or, 'concerning themselves'. Some descriptive renderings are, 'declared that...was not valid for themselves', 'showed that they did not reckon with...', 'in their hearts they had no use for...' (Tzeltal), 'waved, putting at the side...' (Sranan); cp. also *TH-Mk* on 7 : 9.

The purpose of God, or, 'what God wanted them to do', 'the way God would-fain have them follow' (Tagabili); or, 'God's will' (see on 12 : 47).

If the translator prefers to take these verses as a comment made by Luke (see e.g. RSV), this choice will influence some details of his translation: the tense of 'heard', 'justified', 'rejected' may have to be different, because the reference is to the near past; the object to be understood with 'heard' is 'Jesus', 'Jesus' words' (i.e. vv. 24ff); the participial phrases express reason not means; the shift from direct to indirect discourse after v. 28 and the reverse one after v. 30 may be indicated by some such device as brackets, or, preferably, by inserting 'thus he/Jesus said' after the former, and/or, 'then he/Jesus spoke again' after the latter verse.

31 ***"To what then shall I compare the men of this generation, and what are they like?***

Exegesis: *tini oun homoiōsō...kai tini eisin homoioi* 'to what then can I compare...and what are they like?' Rhetoric question, not in the sense that the answer is obvious, but introducing and preparing the way for the subsequent comparison. The repetition of the question in a slightly different form serves to strengthen this function. For *oun* cp. A-G s.v. I c γ. *tini* is neuter, and refers to the situation described in v. 32.

homoioō (1) 'to make like', hence in the passive 'to become like'; (2) 'to compare'.

tous anthrōpous tēs geneas tautēs 'the men of this (i.e. the present) generation', cp. A-G s.v. *genea* 2.

Translation: *To what...shall I compare the men...* may have to be given a somewhat expanded rendering, 'whose likeness/illustration have I to give the people' (Marathi); cp. also *TH-Mk* on 4 : 30. The shift from *what* to 'whom' is found also in Jerusalem, Toba Batak. For *compare* see *N.T.Wb.*/50, LIKE.

The men of this generation, or, 'the men of this time/age' (Bahasa Indonesia, Kapauku), 'people living now' (Ifugao), 'people of the present ways' (Balinese), 'those who are in space now' (Tzeltal); and cp. on 1 : 48.

To be like, again see *N.T.Wb.*/50.

32 ***They are like children sitting in the market place and calling to one another,***
'We piped to you, and you did not dance;
we wailed, and you did not weep.'

Exegesis: *homoioi eisin* 'they are like...'. The repetition of *homoioi* at the beginning of the clause strengthens the emphasis.

paidiois tois en agora kethēmenois kai prosphōnousin allēlois 'children sitting in the market place and calling out to one another'. The article *tois* serves to define *paidiois* as on afterthought. This appears to be a literary mannerism (cp. Bl-D, § 270.3). For the general interpretation of the parable see commentaries. For *prosphōneō* cp. on 6 : 13.

agora 'market place', 'bazaar', cp. *IDB* III, 278.

ha legei 'which say', referring back to *paidiois* and serving to introduce the words which the children call out to one another.

ēulēsamen humin kai ouk ōrchēsasthe 'we played the flute for you and you did not dance'.

auleō (†) lit. 'to play the flute', is often used of making music to dance.

orcheomai (†) 'to dance', a very general term.

ethrēnēsamen kai ouk eklausate 'we sang a dirge and you did not weep'.

thrēneō (also 23 : 27) lit. 'to wail', here probably of singing a dirge at a funeral (cp. A-G s.v. 1 b).

klauō 'to weep', here probably 'to mourn' at a funeral (cp. the parallel text Mt. 11 : 17).

Translation: *Market place,* or, 'place where people buy and/or sell' (cp. Ponape, Kapauku); in one of the Western Toradja languages the term lit. means, 'meeting-place'. Often such renderings have the connotation required here, i.e. place where the people of the village or town come together for social activities and amusements. Where this is not the case one must use another term, e.g. 'cross-roads' (as would be possible in Balinese, where the principal cross-roads in a village is its social centre), 'wide place' (in Trukese the common term for the central gathering place), 'plaza' (Latin America, cp. *TH-Mk* on 6 : 56).

We piped to you, or, 'for you'; or with a syntactic shift, 'you heard us pipe'. *To pipe,* or, 'to play the flute', 'to touch/beat the flute' (as is idiomatic in Spanish and Toba Batak), or more generically, 'to make music' (Ponape); or again, using a cultural equivalent, 'to drum' (South Toradja, Tagabili). If it is necessary to be specific as to the occasion, a wedding is probably the most obvious opposite of the funeral implied in the next sentence (cp. TEV, Marathi, Kituba).

Dance. Some versions have to use the name of a rather specific dance, e.g. Javanese, East and South Toradja, Toba Batak; if the dance in question is danced only by grown-up persons and/or on serious occasions, one may say 'play at dancing the... (name) dance'.

We wailed, and you did not weep, or, 'we wailed to/for you (or, you heard us wail), but you did not weep'. Both verbs (for which cp. *N.T.Wb.*/73) refer here to a public, collective demonstration of grief, as usual at funerals, the former indicating the loud, and probably rather ritualized lamentations of the leaders of the ceremony, the latter to some form of response of the followers. The playful character may again have to be made explicit, as done e.g. in East Toradja by using a reduplicated form of the first verb. *To wail,* or, 'to lament', 'to utter cries of grief, or, of mourning', 'to sing funeral songs', 'to sing songs that are sung at a death' (Tagabili). *To weep.* The rendering may refer to the shedding of tears, cp. e.g. 'why didn't your tears drop' (Tagabili), but it need not do so, since terms for another way of expressing grief may be a better cultural equivalent. If two appropriate terms for 'to wail' and 'to weep' are not available, the second may be rendered by, 'to wail/lament (etc.) together with us', 'to do the same', 'to join us'.

33 ***For John the Baptist has come eating no bread and drinking no wine; and you say, 'He has a demon.'***

Exegesis: *elēluthen gar Iōannēs ho baptistēs* 'for John the Baptist came'. *gar* implies that vv. 33f bring the application of v. 32. The perfect tense of *elēluthen* suggests that John's coming has created a situation which still exists and in connexion with which people have still to make up their mind.

mē esthiōn arton mēte pinōn oinon 'not eating bread nor drinking wine'. Semantically the participial clause carries the main weight in the sentence, because it describes John's way of life, and it is this way of life which calls forth people's reaction. In v. 34 the same participial clause occurs without *arton* and *oinon* (cp. also Mt. 11 : 18f, where *arton* and *oinon* do not appear at all), and this short form appears to be the basic form of the saying. In its negative form it describes the way of life of an ascetic, and in its positive form (v. 34) it refers to normal, non-ascetic life. *arton* and *oinon* are added for stylistic reasons.

kai legete 'and you say'. In the present context this is addressed to 'the crowds' that are there (v. 24), but the reference is to 'the men of this generation' (v. 31) in general.

daimonion echei 'he has a demon', i.e. 'he is in the power of a demon', 'he is possessed', cp. on 4 : 33.

Translation: *Has come.* The verb may have to be repeated with the second participle, as in Marathi.

Eating no bread and drinking no wine may better become the main clause, cp. e.g. 'when John...came, he ate no bread/food' etc. (cp. Goodspeed). If the hyperbolic negation would be misunderstood one may say, 'he suffered hunger and thirst', or, "he fasted (cp. references on 2 : 37) and drank no wine" (TEV). For *eat and drink* cp. on 5 : 30 and 33; for *bread* and *wine* see references on 4 : 3 and 1 : 15.

He has a demon, cp. references on demon possession in 4 : 33.

34 ***The Son of man has come eating and drinking; and you say, 'Behold, a glutton and a drunkard, a friend of tax collectors and sinners!'***

Exegesis: *ho huios tou anthrōpou* 'the Son of man', cp. on 5 : 24.

idou anthrōpos phagos kai oinopotēs 'look, a glutton and drunkard'. *idou* lends a note of emphatic contempt to what follows. Both *phagos* (†) and *oinopotēs* (†) are substantives, but are used here as adjectives with *anthrōpos. oinopotēs* (†) in the present context means 'drunkard', rather than (the more literal) 'wine-drinker'.

philos telōnōn kai hamartōlōn 'a friend of tax collectors and sinners', cp. on 3 : 12 and 5 : 8. The phrase sounds like an abusive expression used of Jesus (cp. Grundmann), since it is not an elaboration of the preceding phrase.

Translation: *Has come eating and drinking,* the positive, but not hyperbolic, counterpart of v. 33[a].

A glutton and a drunkard, or, expressing the pejorative meaning otherwise, 'only eating and drinking wine, is he content' (Kekchi). *Glutton.* A derivation of 'to eat' often has the pejorative meaning required here (cp. Yipounou, Balinese). Elsewhere a figurative expression or descriptive phrase is to be used, e.g. 'one who has just stomach' (Navajo), 'a stomach-for food' (Ponape), 'a very otter' (Isthmus Mixe, in Titus 1 : 12), 'a greedy fellow', 'one who eats-much' (Trukese), 'one who thinks only of eating' (Kapauku). *Drunkard.* The simple agent noun 'drinker' often has pejorative meaning, indicating excessive drinking of intoxicating liquor (cp. e.g. NEB, East Toradja). An express reference to 'wine', or, 'strong drink', may be superfluous then, or even misleading, since it is excessive drinking that is important, not the liquor drunk. Cp. also *N.T.Wb.*/31, DRUNK.

35 ***Yet wisdom is justified by all her children."***

Exegesis: *kai edikaiōthē hē sophia apo pantōn tōn teknōn autēs* 'and the wisdom is proved right by all its children'. The meaning of this saying in its present context is far from clear, and the interpretations vary considerably (see commentaries). There is no point in enumerating them. It will suffice to deal with a few questions which may influence the translation. (1) The clause sounds very much like a proverb which is applied by Jesus to the present situation in which both John the Baptist and he are rejected by their contemporaries. Since *edikaiōthē hē sophia* does not appear to refer to this rejection but rather to suggest some form of acceptance, it seems justified to interpret *kai* as a weak 'and yet', or 'but', though the (probable) proverbial nature of the saying does not commend an emphatic rendering of *kai*. (2) On the same grounds *sophia* seems to have some reference to Jesus himself, whether it is personified by him (cp. Richardson, *Work Book*, 283) or refers to the 'will of God' (v. 30), which is realized both in John and in Jesus. (3) *teknōn* 'children' of wisdom are those who accept wisdom as their true guide in life. They vindicate wisdom, i.e. they prove that wisdom is right, by their life, and/or by their acceptance of the message of John and of Jesus.

Translation: *Wisdom.* To avoid that the word be taken as a reference to human wisdom one may better add a qualification, e.g. 'God's wisdom', 'God's wise ways', 'that God is wise'. For the noun see on 2 : 40.

Is justified by all her children, or in active construction, 'all children of wisdom justify her, or, acknowledge/prove her to be right'. For the figurative use of 'children of' cp. *N.T.Wb.*/68f, SON, and such renderings as, 'people that spring from' (Balinese), 'those who belong to/accept', and cp. "all who are really wise" (Goodspeed).

Adjustments and shifts like those just mentioned may result in such renderings as, 'the knowledge of God receives right from all people that spring from it' (cp. Sranan), 'God's Wisdom is known to be right by the doing of it' (Lokele), 'God's wise ways are acknowledged as right by all those who follow them', 'all whom God has made wise acknowledge/prove him to be wise (or, the really wise One)'. Cp. also TEV.

36 ***One of the Pharisees asked him to eat with him, and he went into the Pharisee's house, and sat at table.***

Exegesis: *ērōta de tis auton tōn Pharisaiōn* 'one of the Pharisees asked him'. The new story begins without indication of place or time. The connexion with the preceding verses is that it illustrates what v. 34 says of Jesus, viz. *philos hamartōlōn* 'a friend of sinners'. The imperfect tense of *ērōta* represents the act of asking as incomplete until the invitation has been accepted (cp. Bl-D, § 328). The next sentence (*kai. . . kateklithē*) expresses the result of the asking and is, therefore, in the aorist tense.

hina phagē met' autou 'that he would have dinner with him', i.e. in his home, as the next clause shows.

kateklithē 'he reclined at table'. For the custom of reclining at table cp. *IDB* III, 317.

Translation: For the use of honorifics in this story cp. *TBT*, 14.164, 1963.

Asked him to eat with him, or, 'invited him at his table' (Jerusalem), 'invited Jesus to eat at his house' (Bahasa Indonesia RC), 'called him to come to eat with him' (Sranan). *To eat with him*, or, 'to share his meal', 'to eat from-the-same-dish with him' (Malay, cp. also Cuyono, lit. 'to use the same cup as he', and South Toradja, lit. 'to eat sitting-in-a-circle with him'), 'to be his guest'. Cp. also on "sit at table with" and "eat and drink with" in 5 : 29f.

Sat at table, indicating that Jesus accepted the invitation; hence several translations use an expression that comes close to, or is basically the same as, the one used in the invitation. A literal rendering of the Greek, 'reclined', is, as a rule, culturally unacceptable; the rendering 'sat at table' is contextually unacceptable because of v. 38, when it would suggest sitting with the feet under the table. Then renderings not specifying the attitude or the exact place are preferable, e.g. 'sat (down) at the meal, or, to eat' (cp. Marathi, TEV, Kapauku, Javanese), 'went at table' (Sranan), 'took his place (at table, or, for the meal)' (cp. NEB, Jerusalem).

37 ***And behold, a woman of the city, who was a sinner, when she learned that he was sitting at table in the Pharisee's house, brought an alabaster flask of ointment,*** 38 ***and standing behind him at his feet, weeping, she began to wet his feet with her tears, and wiped them with the hair of her head, and kissed his feet, and anointed them with the ointment.***

Exegesis: *kai idou* 'and behold', cp. on 1 : 20.

The syntactic structure is as follows: *gunē* 'a woman' is the subject of all verbal forms (except, of course, *katakeitai* 'he reclined'); it is followed by a relative clause (*hētis ēn...hamartōlos*) which serves to introduce the woman, and a participial clause (*epignousa*, etc.) which denotes something which prepares for what is coming. Then comes the chain of events in the house of the Pharisee in two participial phrases (*komisasa* and *stasa*; the present participle *klaiousa* goes with *stasa*, see below), preparing the way for the four verbal clauses (*ērxato brechein, exemassen, katephilei* and *ēleiphen*), which describe the main events.

gunē hētis ēn en tē polei hamartōlos 'a woman who was a sinner in the town', or 'a woman who was in the town, a sinner'. Both interpretations are possible but the former appears to be slightly preferable on stylistic grounds. The relative pronoun *hētis* is best understood as fully equivalent to the simple *hē*. *en tē polei* refers to the town where the Pharisee lived, as shown by the article. *hamartōlos* is here best understood as 'a prostitute'. For the general meaning cp. on 5 : 8.

kai epignousa hoti katakeitai 'and having found out that he reclined...'. *kai*, probably a Hebraism (cp. A-G s.v. 2 b), is omitted by all translations. For *epignousa* cp. on 1 : 4. Here it means 'to learn', 'to find out' (cp. A-G s.v. 2 b). For *katakeitai* cp. on 5 : 25.

komisasa alabastron murou lit. 'having brought an alabaster flask of ointment', describes the first of a series of acts which the woman does upon finding out where Jesus is.

komizō (†) 'to bring'. Here it almost means 'to come with' (cp. Brouwer, Willibrord).

alabastron murou 'an alabaster flask of ointment', cp. *TH-Mk* on 14 : 3.

(V. 38) *kai stasa opisō para tous podas autou klaiousa* lit. 'and having taken her place behind him at his feet weeping'. The guests used to recline supporting themselves by their left arm, their feet turned slightly backward. *opisō* is specified by *para tous podas autou.* For the meaning of *para* cp. A-G s.v. III 1 c. *klaiousa* qualifies not only *stasa* but also the following verbs. The woman's tears are explained as tears of repentance (Klostermann) or of gratitude (Grundmann), preferably the latter, see below.

ērxato brechein '(she) began to wet', cp. on 4 : 21. Here *ērxato* suggests that now the main act begins after the preparatory acts.

brechō here and v. 44 'to wet', in 17 : 29 'to rain' in a figurative sense.

tais thrixin tēs kephalēs autēs 'with the hair of her head', i.e. 'with her own hair' (cp. Rieu), implying that she had let down her hair for that purpose.

exemassen (also v. 44) 'she wiped', 'she dried', with shift to the imperfect which suggests duration.

katephilei tous podas autou 'she kissed his feet', also in the imperfect. The kissing of the feet was an act of reverence.

kataphileō 'to kiss', in Luke the general word, as *phileō* is in Mk. 14 : 44.

ēleiphen tō murō 'she anointed (them) with the ointment'. This is what she had come for. For *aleiphō* cp. *N.T.Wb.*, 20/.

Translation: Some changes in the syntactic pattern may be necessary or preferable, e.g. 'Now there was a woman who was a sinner in the city. As soon as she learned that Jesus was...in the Ph.'s house she came with...flask, and took her stand behind him at his feet, weeping. Thereupon she wetted his feet..., wiped them..., kissed them, and anointed them...'.

A woman of the city, who was a sinner, or, 'a woman who lived as (or, was known as) a sinner in the city'. *Sinner,* cp. on 5 : 30, but here in the sense of 'prostitute'; hence such, more or less outspoken, expressions as, 'woman leading an immoral/improper life' (cp. NEB, East Toradja 1933), 'a woman they always make jokes about' (Tagabili); and cp. on "harlot" in 15 : 30.

Learned, or, 'came to know', 'found out', 'discovered' (Sranan, lit. 'came see'), or simply, 'heard' (Kituba, Shona, Marathi, Tagabili, some Indonesian languages).

Brought. Renderings such as 'came with', 'came carrying', 'came and carried' have also the advantage of making a better transition to the subsequent events.

Alabaster flask. Some versions, preserving the borrowing, have, 'jar made of stone called alabaster', others have, 'jar of (white) stone' (Javanese, East Toradja), or simply, 'small-jar' (Bahasa Indonesia), 'small bottle' (Sranan), 'bottle' (Bamiléké), 'container' (Shona 1966). Such less specific renderings are usually preferable to a borrowing or a long descriptive phrase.

Of, or, 'full of', 'filled with', 'containing'.

Ointment, or, 'sweet smelling oil/ointment'; Tagabili describes the concept, 'expensive coconut oil, very beautiful odour'. What is in focus is the ointment rather than the container, cp. NEB's "brought oil of myrrh in a small flask".

(V. 38) When a new sentence is started here a transitional phrase may be required, cp. e.g. 'on her arrival' (Shona 1966), 'when she arrived there' (Tagabili), 'having entered (the house)'.

Standing behind him at his feet. Where Gr. *kateklithē* (v. 36) and *katakeitai* (v. 37) 'he reclined' have been rendered generically (cp. on v. 36) the words 'behind him' may better be omitted (unless the translator thinks the matter worth an explanatory note); hence 'she took her place at (or, near) his feet', 'she knelt down at his feet, or, close to him'. Tagabili uses a specific verb, indicating the (standing or sitting) attitude of a person who is so ashamed he can't hold up his head.

Weeping, or, 'while she wept', 'and wept', viz. in silence, as a private expression of emotion; cp. *N.T.Wb.*/73.

If the acts described in the following clauses are uncommon in the receptor culture or even offensive, a note stating that in the New Testament culture the woman's behaviour was expressive of grateful love will be advisable.

She began to wet his feet with her tears refers to an unintended consequence of the woman's weeping, as is brought out by, 'her tears dropped down, dropping on Jesus' feet' (Tagabili), 'her tears wetted his feet' (Javanese), 'His feet (became) wet from trickle of her tears' (Balinese). It may be preferable then to subordinate the clause to what follows, 'as her tears were falling on his feet, she wiped them...'. *Tear*, in Trukese, Ponape, some Indonesian languages literally, 'water of the eye'.

Wiped them with the hair of her head, or, 'used her (own) hair to wipe them off' (cp. Toba Batak). Some languages (e.g. Javanese) have distinctive terms for 'hair-on-the-head' and 'hair-on-the-body'.

Kissed. To avoid sexual associations one may say here, 'showed her reverence by kissing'. For *to kiss* see on 15 : 20, but some of the renderings mentioned there will not fit this context. Then one may say something like, 'touched (lovingly)', 'caressed'. An interesting cultural equivalent can be used in Bamiléké, viz. 'massaged his feet', as people do to show reverence to a chief, especially when imploring his protection or forgiveness.

Anointed them with the ointment, or, 'rubbed/poured/put the ointment on them'; see *N.T.Wb.*/10.

39 ***Now when the Pharisee who had invited him saw it, he said to himself, "If this man were a prophet, he would have known who and what sort of woman this is who is touching him, for she is a sinner."***

Exegesis: *ho Pharisaios ho kalesas auton* 'the Pharisee who had invited him', cp. A-G s.v. *kaleō* 1 b.

eipen en heautō 'he said to himself'.

houtos ei ēn prophētēs 'if this man were (really) a prophet', but, in the

Pharisee's judgment, he is not. *houtos* suggests contempt, cp. A-G s.v. 1 a α. As v. 16 shows, people considered Jesus a prophet.

tis kai potapē hē gunē hētis haptetai autou 'who and of what sort the woman is who clings to him', with *estin* understood. For *potapos* cp. on 1 : 29; here it is used with a note of contempt, as appears from the explanatory clause that follows, viz. *hoti hamartōlos estin* (see below).

hoti hamartōlos estin 'that she is a sinner', explaining *tis kai potapē.*

Translation: For *invited* see on 14 : 7. The rendering may have to coincide with that of "asked to eat with him" in v. 36.

Said to himself, cp. on 3 : 8.

If this man were... (etc.). The speaker does not expect his supposition to come true, as is indicated in some languages by the use of a modal verbal form, a comparable suffix joined to the verb or, as here, to the noun 'prophet' (Javanese), or a specific adverb, particle, or conjunction (Bahasa Indonesia RC), but in other languages (e.g. Toba Batak) the mood is left implicit and to be concluded from the context, viz. from the fact that in Jesus' behaviour towards the woman there is nothing to corroborate the supposition.

Know, i.e. realize, recognize.

Who and what sort of woman this is. The double predicate 'who and what sort' may make necessary that the introductory verb is repeated, as e.g. in, 'he would already know who this woman (is), he would also know the manner-of life of this woman', or with some variation, 'he knows this woman...and recognizes her behaviour' (Toba Batak). Shifting to a single predicate the rendering of the phrase may become, 'who this woman is' (Sranan), 'the doings (lit. the-like-this-and-like-that) of this woman' (Sundanese), 'what kind of individual this woman is'.

For she is a sinner, preferably, 'that (or, namely, that) she is a sinner'. This interpretation implies that this clause is also governed by the introductory 'he would have known'.

40 ***And Jesus answering said to him, "Simon, I have something to say to you." And he answered, "What is it, Teacher?"***

Exegesis: *apokritheis* 'answering', cp. on 1 : 60.

Simōn, echō soi ti eipein 'Simon, I have something to say to you', i.e. 'I want to say something to you', cp. A-G s.v. *echō* I 6 b.

ho de, Didaskale, eipe, phēsin 'and he said, master, say it, or, speak'. The words do not suggest much encouragement. *phēsin* is historical present, cp. Bl-D, § 321.

Translation: *And Jesus answering said,* or, "Jesus spoke up and said" (TEV), 'thereupon Jesus said' (Balinese); and see on 3 : 16.

I have something to say to you has the connotation of requesting attention; some idiomatic phrases used are, "may I put something to you?" (Rieu), 'there is a (small) matter we should discuss' (Shona), 'something must be discussed with Simon (the name doing duty for the pronoun of the second person)' (Balinese).

What is it? Here again several versions use an idiom indicating readiness to listen, e.g. 'speak (to me)' (Kituba, Marathi, Ponape), 'please, speak' (Sundanese), 'say what you have to say' (Shona), 'go ahead and speak/say it' (Zarma, Trukese), 'what is it, tell me' (Tagabili).

41 ***"A certain creditor had two debtors; one owed five hundred denarii, and the other fifty.***

Exegesis: *duo chreopheiletai ēsan daneistē tini* lit. 'two debtors (there) were to a certain money-lender', hence "two men were in debt to a money-lender" (NEB). *duo chreopheiletai* is emphatic by position.

chreopheiletēs (also 16 : 5) 'debtor'.

daneistēs (††) 'money-lender'.

dēnaria pentakosia. . .*pentēkonta* 'five hundred denarii. . .fifty'. *dēnarion* is estimated as equivalent to 18 cents of a dollar (cp. *IDB* I, 824). The important thing is the fact that the one debtor owes ten times the amount of the other.

Translation: The transition to the short parable is abrupt. Some translators, therefore, add an introductory phrase such as, '(then) Jesus said' (as e.g. in Javanese, South Toradja).

The wording of the sentence is redundant in that the terms "creditor", "debtor", "owed" refer to different participants in and aspects of the same process, especially so in languages which for two or more of these concepts use terms built on the same base, as e.g. in Tagabili and Cuyono, which use three derivations of the word 'debt'; hence such lexical simplifications as, 'There was a rich man; two people had borrowed from him. One had to pay 500. . .' (Sranan), 'There were two men who borrowed from one. Well, one of them borrowed 500. . .' (Trukese), 'A certain man lent money to two persons. To one of them (he lent) 500. . .'

A certain here indicates a reference to something specific but unspecified, which is a new item in the discourse. The corresponding Greek word (*tis*) is often used at the beginning of a parable (see 10 : 30; 12 : 16; 14 : 16; 16 : 1, 19; 18 : 2; 19 : 12), helping to mark the introduction of a story, and/or its imaginary character. In other languages one may have to do so by other means, cp. on 8 : 4.

Creditor, i.e. one to whom a debt is owed, or, one who has lent (something); or, as preferred in *Exegesis*, 'money-lender', i.e. one who professionally lends money on interest. East Toradja 1933 tried to describe this by 'a money trader', but the revision uses a modern borrowing, lit. meaning, 'one who manipulates money'. For 'to lend' cp. on 6 : 34.

Debtor, or, 'one who is in debt, or, has borrowed'. For 'to borrow' similar distinctions may exist as for 'to lend'.

Owed, or, 'had to pay' (Sranan), 'had-as-debt'; in Marathi the rendering lit. means 'had a giving', in Zarma, 'had it (i.e. the debt) on him' (as though carrying a burden).

Five hundred denarii, . . . fifty. For 'denarius' see on 10 : 35. It is neither the exact value of the coin nor the precise number that is important here but the proportion between the two sums; hence such shifts as in "a hundred dollars...ten" (Goodspeed, similarly South Toradja), "fifty pounds...five" (Rieu) are legitimate. Sometimes it is possible to omit the reference to a coin, 'one owed 500, the other 50', leaving it to the reader to supply the unit of currency, which will be the basic one used in his culture. *Five hundred* may have to be expressed approximately and analytically, e.g. 'eight times sixty', the closest natural equivalent in Kapauku.

42 ***When they could not pay, he forgave them both. Now which of them will love him more?"***

Exegesis: *mē echontōn autōn apodounai* 'since they were unable to pay back'. For *echō* with infinitive cp. A-G s.v. I 6 a.

amphoterois echarisato 'he cancelled (the debt) for both'. For *charizomai* cp. on v. 21.

tis oun autōn pleion agapēsei auton 'now which of them will love him more'. *oun* marks the clause as asking for the inference from what precedes. The parable rests on the idea that gratitude is proportionate to benefits received (cp. Klostermann).

Translation: *He forgave them both,* or, 'he cancelled what they owed him/their debt' (cp. Goodspeed, Bahasa Indonesia RC), 'he cleared them both' (South Toradja), 'he released them both (from) it (i.e. their debt)' (Marathi), or in direct discourse, 'he said, "Never mind; you don't have to pay it"' (Cuyono). Sometimes it is possible to use here the same verb as in the rendering of 'to forgive sins' (cp. on 1 : 77), e.g. in Shona, Kituba, Sinhalese; also in Lokele, 'to forgo/overlook a debt or a fault', and in Tzeltal, 'to lose a person's debt or sin out of one's heart'.

Now, introducing the concluding question, or, '(now) tell me' (cp. BFBS, South Toradja).

Love, see on 6 : 27.

More. Some languages express the comparative by, 'of these two, which one will love him much, which one (will love him) little', or, implying comparison without explicitly stating it, 'which of them will really love that man' (Trukese), 'which of these two men big will be his love to him' (East Toradja, similarly Ponape).

43 ***Simon answered, "The one, I suppose, to whom he forgave more." And he said to him, "You have judged rightly."***

Exegesis: *hupolambanō* (also 10 : 30 but in a different meaning) 'I suppose', 'I imagine', implying a certain caution on Simon's part, as to what Jesus' question may lead up to.

hō to pleion echarisato '(he) for whom he cancelled most', i.e. the greatest debt.

orthōs ekrinas 'you have judged correctly'. This conclusion prepares the way for Jesus' accusing application of the parable in v. 44.

Translation: The position of the asyndetic *I suppose* is rather free; in several languages (included the Greek) it is initial, in others final. Some other renderings are, 'I think' (Marathi), 'in my opinion' (Javanese), 'to (lit. as in) my mind' (Toba Batak). Otherwise than in 2 : 44 the verb does not suggest that what the speaker thinks is contrary to fact.

The rendering of *to whom he forgave more* should preferably echo v. 42, but if the expression used there cannot be fitted into the syntactic position here, one may shift to a more indirect statement, e.g. 'the one whose debt was much' (South Toradja).

You have judged rightly, or some other, idiomatic expression of approval, "You are right" (NEB), 'right your supposition/opinion/conjecture' (Bahasa Indonesia, South Toradja, Balinese), 'you speak truly' (East Toradja).

44 ***Then turning toward the woman he said to Simon, "Do you see this woman? I entered your house, you gave me no water for my feet, but she has wet my feet with her tears and wiped them with her hair.***

Exegesis: *kai strapheis pros tēn gunaika* 'and turning to the woman'. *kai* connects the parable of vv. 42f and its application. For *strapheis* cp. on v. 9, but here Jesus does not address the person to whom he turns, but continues to speak to Simon.

blepeis tautēn tēn gunaika 'do you see this woman?', implying that the parable applies to her and to Simon.

eisēlthon sou eis tēn oikian 'I came into your house', i.e. I came as your guest. The clause introduces a series of contrasts between Simon and the woman in their behaviour concerning Jesus.

hudōr moi epi podas ouk edōkas 'water for my feet you did not give me'. For the custom of footwashing cp. *IDB* II, 308. The clause is an asyndeton, just as the two subsequent clauses (vv. 45f) which criticize Simon's attitude towards Jesus. This lends them a note of sternness.

hautē de 'but she', emphatic, repeated at the beginning of each of the final clauses of vv. 44-46. This serves to bring out the contrast with Simon.

mou tous podas 'my feet'. The place of *mou* before *podas* is not uncommon, cp. Bl-D, § 284.1.

Translation: *Turning toward the woman,* or, describing the situation more exactly, "turning round to the woman, while still addressing Simon" (Rieu).

Do you see this woman, or, 'do you see what this woman is doing to me' (Tzeltal), 'you see that woman, don't you' (Marathi, cp. Toba Batak); Shona 1966 shifts to an imperative.

For most details of vv. 44b-46 cp. on v. 38.

You gave me no water, or, where the difference between initiator and agent is strictly to be observed, 'you did not order (people/your servants) to give me water'; the implied censure may be made explicit, e.g. 'you did not so much as give...' (cp. Willibrord).

Water for my feet, or, 'water to wash (my) feet' (e.g. in Tagabili, Sranan).

45 ***You gave me no kiss, but from the time I came in she has not ceased to kiss my feet.***

Exegesis: *philēma moi ouk edōkas* 'a kiss you did not give me'. *philēma* (also 22 : 48) at the beginning of the clause is emphatic. Kissing was a part of the ceremonial welcome to guests, cp. *IDB* III, 39f.

aph' hēs (scil. *hōras*) *eisēlthon* lit. 'from the moment I came in', cp. A-G s.v. *hōra* 3. When understood rigidly the clause seems to imply that the woman came in together with Jesus, but this does not transpire from vv. 36f. The phrase is, therefore, slightly hyperbolic.

ou dielipen kataphilousa '(she) has not stopped kissing'. For *kataphileō* cp. on v. 38. *dialeipō* (††).

Translation: *You gave me no kiss,* or to bring out the pejorative meaning, 'you could not bring yourself to kiss me' (South Toradja).

She has not ceased to kiss, or, 'continuously she has kissed' (Javanese).

To kiss my feet. When the normal rendering of the verb cannot be used with 'feet' as object (see on v. 38) the contrastive parallelism between what is said of Simon and of the woman will be lessened or lost. This may be remedied by making explicit the function of their acts or the intention of their behaviour, e.g. 'you did not (even) welcome me with a kiss (or, kiss me for a greeting) but...she has not ceased to show me her reverence by touching/caressing/massaging my feet (or, to touch (etc.) my feet to show that she revered me)'.

46 ***You did not anoint my head with oil, but she has anointed my feet with ointment.***

Exegesis: *elaiō tēn kephalēn mou ouk ēleipsas* 'with olive oil you did not anoint my head'. *elaiō* is emphatic. The anointing of the head was a gesture of hospitality. Cp. also on v. 38. There is a twofold correspondence between this clause and the next, viz. *elaiō* and *murō,* a cheap and a very expensive unguent, and *kephalēn* and *podas,* the usual spot of anointing and a rather unusual one.

Translation: *You did not anoint my head with oil,* or, better to bring out the pejorative connotation, "you did not anoint my head, even with oil" (Rieu); or, again making explicit the function, 'you didn't show me hospitality (or, give me a reception) by anointing my head'. The host usually did the anointing himself. For *to anoint with oil* cp. also *TH-Mk* on 6 : 13.

47 ***Therefore I tell you, her sins, which are many, are forgiven, for she loved much; but he who is forgiven little, loves little."***

Exegesis: *hou charin, legō soi, apheōntai hai hamartiai autēs* 'therefore, I tell you, her sins have been forgiven', or, punctuating with Nestle *hou charin legō soi,* 'therefore I tell you'. The former suggests a somewhat stronger connexion between the woman's behaviour and the forgiving of her sins, but it should be born in mind that the parable of vv. 41ff says that the measure of love shows the measure of forgiveness, instead of determining it. For *legō soi* cp. on 3 : 8. For *apheōntai* cp. on 5 : 20.

hai hamartiai autēs hai pollai lit. 'her sins, the many'. *hai pollai* is emphatic by position, cp. "her sins, her many sins" (Rieu).

hoti ēgapēsen polu 'because she loved much'. The clause refers to the evidence, or proof, of the fact that the woman's sins had been forgiven, as brought out by a rendering like 'her great love proves, or, shows it' (cp. BFBS), viz. that her many sins have been forgiven.

hō de oligon aphietai, oligon agapa 'he who is forgiven little, loves little', i.e. shows little love. The present tense conveys the idea of a general principle and tends to soften the obvious inference for Simon.

Translation: Some other renderings in line with the interpretation given in *Exegesis* are, 'her sins, which are many, are forgiven; the proof of it is that she loves much, or, that-is-why her love is great' (cp. Toba Batak), "the great love she has shown proves that her many sins have been forgiven" (TEV), 'if she shows much love, it is because she has been forgiven her many sins' (Jerusalem, note), 'this woman here has loved me greatly, that's how you can recognize that God has forgiven (lit. that no more at all God is following/noticing/making-her-accountable-for) her many sins' (Tagabili).

Her sins...are forgiven, or, to avoid a passive, 'she received forgiveness for her sins' (Sranan), 'God has forgiven her sins' (cp. East Toradja 1933, and Tagabili).

She loved. If an object is required it should be 'me', cp. Tagabili, Goodspeed.

He who is forgiven little, or, 'whoever the forgiveness of his-sins is small' (South Toradja), 'whoever receives small forgiveness' (Ponape), 'if God has forgiven a person only a few sins'.

48 ***And he said to her, "Your sins are forgiven."***

Exegesis: *eipen de autē* 'and he said to her'. This is the first time in this story that Jesus addresses the woman. It is, however, consistent with the story as a whole and with the parable in particular, to assume that the woman had received already previously some assurance of forgiveness (cp. Plummer). That Jesus now says so publicly may be intended to elicit the comments of those present and the comments come promptly (as in 5 : 20f, which see).

Translation: *To her,* or, 'to the woman' (e.g. in Ponape, Trukese, where the pronoun does not indicate gender).

Jesus' saying is the same as in 5 : 20; the double reference to the second person found there makes no difference for the meaning.

49 ***Then those who were at table with him began to say among themselves, "Who is this, who even forgives sins?"***

Exegesis: *ērxanto* 'they began', cp. on 4 : 21 and 5 : 21.

hoi sunanakeimenoi 'those (with him) at table', cp. *TH-Mk* on 2 : 15.

en heautois 'in themselves', or 'among themselves', preferably the former, cp. 3 : 8.

tis houtos estin hos kai hamartias aphiēsin? 'who is this man who even forgives sins?' For this type of clause cp. on 5 : 21. Here the clause has a note of marvel.

Translation: *Those who were at table with him,* see on 5 : 29; or, "his fellow-guests" (Rieu).

To say among themselves, preferably 'in themselves', hence, "to ask themselves" (NEB), and see on 3 : 8.

Who is this, who even forgives sins?, or, 'who (or, what kind of person) is this (man)? He even...' (cp. Balinese), 'who is this, that he even...' (Bahasa Indonesia RC); and see on 5 : 21.

50 ***And he said to the woman, "Your faith has saved you; go in peace."***

Exegesis: *eipen de pros tēn gunaika* 'but he said to the woman', without indication of the change of subject. *de* suggests that Jesus did not reply to what the other guests thought or said.

hē pistis sou sesōken se 'your faith has saved you'. This phrase usually occurs at the conclusion of some healing story (cp. 8 : 48; 18 : 42; Mt. 9 : 22; Mk. 5 : 34, where *TH-Mk* translates 'has made you well'). The present context requires a different meaning for *sesōken,* viz. has saved you from the power of sin.

poreuou eis eirēnēn 'go in peace', a quotation from 1 Sam. 1 : 17, occurring, with a different verb also in Mk. 5 : 34, cp. *TH-Mk* there.

Translation: *Your faith has saved you,* or, 'you are saved (or, God has saved you) because you have believed (in me)', and cp. *TH-Mk* on 5 : 34. In this context Tagabili renders "your faith" by 'that you did not doubt (lit. not being-two your breath)'; cp. also on 8 : 48.

Go in peace is to be rendered by an idiomatic expression of farewell, implying well-wishing, e.g. 'with one heart go', also used commonly as reassurance (Tzeltal), 'go well' (Zarma), 'there now, return now' (Tagabili), *salaam* (Lokele); and cp. *TH-Mk, l.c.* The translator should not try to bring in the term for 'peace' as used e.g. in 1 : 79 (which see), unless it fits the idiom.

CHAPTER EIGHT

1 ***Soon afterward he went on through cities and villages, preaching and bringing the good news of the kingdom of God. And the twelve were with him,*** 2 ***and also some women who had been healed of evil spirits and infirmities: Mary, called Magdalene, from whom seven demons had gone out,*** 3 ***and Joanna, the wife of Chuza, Herod's steward, and Susanna, and many others, who provided for them out of their means.***

Exegesis: Syntactically vv. 1-3 form one long sentence. The main verb *diōdeuen* 'he went about', or a related verb, is to be understood with *kai hoi dōdeka sun autō* 'and the twelve with him', and with *kai gunaikes tines* 'and (also) some women'. Semantically the sentence consists of three parts, concerning (a) Jesus who goes about among towns and villages preaching; (b) the twelve who are going with him, and (c) a group of women, also accompanying him and the disciples, and providing for them. Names and (some) details are added concerning some of these women.

kai egeneto 'and it happened', cp. on 1 : 8.

en tō kathexēs, scil. *chronō*, lit. 'in the subsequent time', hence '(soon) afterward' (cp. on 7 : 11). For *kathexēs* cp. on 1 : 3.

kai autos diōdeuen kata polin kai kōmēn 'he went about through town and village'. *autos* is unemphatic 'he' as often in *kai autos* (cp. on 2 : 28), and does not anticipate *hoi dōdeka*.

diodeuō (†) 'to travel about', 'to go about'.

kata polin kai kōmēn 'to (every single) town and village'. *kata* is distributive (cp. A-G s.v. II d). The phrase goes with *diōdeuen* but is also to be understood with the following participles.

kērussōn kai euaggelizomenos tēn basileian tou theou 'proclaiming and preaching (the good news of) the kingdom of God'. For *kērussō* cp. on 3 : 3, for *euaggelizomai* on 1 : 19. *tēn basileian tou theou* (cp. on 4 : 43) is object with both participles. *kērussōn* and *euaggelizomenos* supplement each other: *kērussōn* stresses the note of authority and *euaggelizomenos* implies the idea of the good tidings.

kai hoi dōdeka sun autō 'and the twelve (went) with him', see above. *hoi dōdeka* has the function of a title, or name, and identifies the disciples as a group.

(V. 2) *kai gunaikes tines* 'and some women (went with him, see above)'. *tines* is best understood to refer to the three women mentioned by name.

hai ēsan tetherapeumenai apo pneumatōn ponērōn kai astheneiōn 'who had been cured of evil spirits and illnesses', cp. on 7 : 21.

Maria hē kaloumenē Magdalēnē lit. 'Mary, who was called the one from Magdala', i.e. "Mary, who was called Mary of Magdala" (Goodspeed, cp. NEB), probably because in early Christian circles more than one Mary was known (cp. A-G s.v. *Maria*). For *Magdalēnē* cp. *TH-Mk* on 15 : 40 (where the reference to Lk. 7 : 2 must be to 8 : 2), and A-G s.v.

aph' hēs daimonia hepta exelēluthei 'from whom seven demons had come out'. The intransitive *exelēluthei* is virtually equivalent to the passive 'had been driven out' (cp. Goodspeed). *daimonia hepta* refers to possession of extraordinary malignity (cp. Plummer, Grundmann). Seven is a traditional number with evil spirits but there is no reason to attach a specific meaning to it here.

(V. 3) *Iōanna gunē Chouza epitropou Hērōdou* 'Jo(h)anna the wife of Chouza(s), the steward of Herod', presumably without further introduction known to the readers of Luke's Gospel. The same applies to Susanna.

epitropos (†) 'steward', 'manager', or 'governor', presumably the former (cp. Plummer, Grundmann).

kai heterai pollai 'and many others', probably differing from *gunaikes tines* in that they had not been healed by Jesus, but included in the same group, as also going with Jesus.

haitines diēkonoun autois 'who served them'. *haitines* is equivalent to the simple relative pronoun *hai* and does not have consecutive force (cp. Bl-D, § 293.3). Antecedent of *haitines* are both *heterai pollai* and *gunaikes tines*. *autois* refers to Jesus and the twelve.

diakoneō (cp. on 4 : 39) 'to serve', with dative means here 'to provide for', 'to support'.

ek tōn huparchontōn autais 'out of their means'. For *huparchō* cp. on 7 : 25. *ta huparchonta* lit. 'that which is at one's disposal' (hence with dative, here *autais*), is used here as a substantive 'means', 'possessions' (though the dative still reflects its verbal origin). In 11 : 21; 12 : 33, 44; 16 : 1; 19 : 8 it is followed by a possessive genitive (cp. A-G s.v. 1).

Translation: *Went on through cities and villages.* The distributive sense may be expressed in the prepositional phrase, e.g. 'in city (after) city and town (after) town' (Marathi), or in the verb, e.g. by the use of a verbal suffix with distributive force (Kapauku), or of a compound verbal phrase such as, 'travelled traversing' (Balinese).

Preaching and bringing the good news of the kingdom of God. The connexion with what precedes may be final, 'in-order-to preach...' (Bahasa Indonesia RC), temporal, e.g. 'and meanwhile (or, during these journeys) he preached...', or local, e.g. 'and there he preached...'. The two participles are sometimes better combined into one expression, e.g. 'and proclaimed/preached everywhere the good news of...' (cp. NEB, Brouwer, Sranan). For *to preach* see on 3 : 3; for *to bring* (or, preach) *the good news of the kingdom of God* see on 3 : 18 and 4 : 43.

The twelve, or, 'the twelve disciples'.

(V. 2) The intricate, almost confusing, structure of vv. 2f may have to be adjusted and clarified, e.g. 'Many women went with him also. Some among them had been healed of..., to wit, Mary, ..., ..., and Joanna, ..., ..., and Suzanna. All of them (or, All these women) provided for them...'.

Had been healed of evil spirits and infirmities, or, 'had been demon-possessed and ill, but Jesus had healed them'; see on 7 : 21. For *infirmity* see on 5 : 15.

From whom seven demons had gone out, cp. on 4 : 33, 35 and references.

(V. 3) *Joanna, the wife of Chuza, Herod's steward*. The double apposition may be ambiguous, e.g. where the word for "steward" is neutral as to sex; hence adjustments such as, 'J., the wife of H.'s steward, (called) Ch.', 'J., whose husband, Ch., served as steward to Herod' (Zarma). *Steward*, or, 'major-domo' (Tzeltal; similarly in Balinese, lit. the-one-who-prepares-the-betel-quid', then, the favourite courtier who manages the prince's palace and possessions), 'the-one who-is-trusted in the house' (South Toradja), 'the man who watches the house/goods' (Kapauku, Sranan), 'the head (lit. elder) of the house' (Sundanese).

Provided for them out of (i.e., taking from) *their means* (or, 'things'), 'giving a part from what they possessed' (cp. East Toradja); or, 'they used their possessions to pay-for their needs' (cp. Balinese). *Provided for them*, or, 'helped them' (cp. TEV), "attended to their needs" (BFBS), 'took care of them' (Toba Batak). It may be impossible, or unsuitable, to subjoin both Jesus and his disciples under one pronominal reference; hence, 'the group/party' (Bahasa Indonesia 1968), 'Jesus and his disciples' (Kapauku). For a comparable difficulty in connexion with honorifics see *TBT*, 14.162, 1963.

4 ***And when a great crowd came together and people from town after town came to him, he said in a parable:***

Exegesis: *suniontos de ochlou pollou* 'when a great crowd was gathering', without indication as to place or time, but placing the following event during (the course of) Jesus' going through towns and villages (cp. v. 1). *suneimi* (††).

kai tōn kata polin epiporeuomenōn pros auton lit. 'and the people from town after town were journeying to him', best understood as an elaboration of the preceding clause, and hence making clear that the crowd which was gathering were the people from town after town. The phrase *tōn kata polin* recalls *kata polin kai kōmēn* in v. 1.

epiporeuomai (††) 'to journey', 'to travel'.

eipen dia parabolēs 'he said in a parable' (cp. A-G s.v. *dia* A III 1 b), virtually equivalent to *eipen parabolēn* 'he told a parable' (cp. e.g. 4 : 23; 5 : 36; 6 : 39; 12 : 16, 41).

Translation: The second clause, containing the more general statement, may better be placed first, cp. TEV.

Came to him, he said. One of the pronouns will often have to be specified.

Town, see on "city" in 1 : 26.

He said in a parable, or, 'he said using a parable, or, by means (lit. on the way) of a parable' (East Toradja), 'he lined up and made even with a story' (Chontal of Tabasco), 'he told/uttered a parable', 'he used-a-simile/proverb/parable' (Toba Batak). For the noun see *TH-Mk* on 3 : 23. Some other descriptive renderings are, 'story with a meaning' (Barrow Eskimo), 'change, or, turned-about word' (Kekchi, Mixtec, referring to the metaphorical character of a parable); Sranan distinguishes between 'likeness story', traditionally used for 'parable' in the Bible, and 'experience story', which probably would be a better translation. — The narrative that forms the parable has sometimes to be introduced by some word or phrase, which serves to mark the beginning of a story and/or its imaginary character, e.g. 'once there was', 'it-is-told', cp. on 1 : 5, and on "a certain" in 7 : 41.

5 ***"A sower went out to sow his seed; and as he sowed, some fell along the path, and was trodden under foot, and the birds of the air devoured it.***

Exegesis: *exēlthen ho speirōn tou speirai ton sporon autou* 'a sower went out to sow his seed'. The clause has a ring of solemnity because of the threefold repetition of a word from the same root. In *ho speirōn* the force of the article is generic; hence 'a sower' in many translations (cp. RSV). *tou speirai* is final articular infinitive, 'in order to sow'.

sporos (also v. 11) 'seed'.

en tō speirein auton lit. 'during his sowing', i.e. 'as he sowed'. *auton* refers to *ho speirōn.*

ho men epesen 'some (seed) fell'. *ho* is neuter though it refers to the masculine *sporos.* For the use of the relative pronoun with demonstrative force cp. *TH-Mk* on 4 : 4 and A-G s.v. *hos* II 2. *ho men* is continued, not by *ho de,* but by *kai heteron* in vv. 6, 7, 8, also in the neuter (cp. *TH-Mk, l.c.*).

para tēn hodon 'by the side of the road', or 'on the road', preferably the latter, as the next verb shows (cp. also *TH-Mk, l.c.*).

katepatēthē 'was trodden on', 'was trampled', cp. on 12 : 1.

ta peteina tou ouranou katephagen auto 'the birds of the air ate it up'. For *ouranos* 'air' cp. A-G s.v. 1 d. The phrase *ta peteina tou ouranou* (also 9 : 58; 13 : 19; and cp. Gen. 1 : 26; Ps. 8 : 9) has become a stereotype in which the genitive *tou ouranou* has lost its specific meaning; hence the rendering 'birds'. For *katephagen* cp. A-G s.v. *katesthiō* 1. *auto* in the neuter refers to *ho men* at the beginning of v. 5.

Translation: For general remarks on vv. 5-8 see *TH-Mk* on 4 : 3-8.

A sower went out to sow his seed is redundant in specific references to the process; hence some of the terms may have to be rendered more generically, or even omitted, which results e.g. in, 'a man (or, farmer/husbandman) went out to sow his seed, or, to scatter-sow'. *Went out,* i.e. from his house or settlement towards his fields; the verb indicates ingressive aspect. *His seed.* Some languages distinguish between 'seed' (as found on the plant) and 'sowing-seed', e.g. East Toradja (lit. 'pip/grain' and 'what-has-been-threshed-out'); in others the normal object of 'to sow' is the name of the plant sown, i.e. here 'wheat/grain' (for the rendering of which cp. on 3 : 17). The possessive may have to be described, e.g. 'the seed he used', 'the seed for his fields', but more often the form, if rendered at all, is better left unpossessed. For *to sow* and *seed* see also *N.T.Wb.*/65; *TBT*, 13.31, 1962.

Some, or, 'some seed', 'a part (of the seed)'; in some Indonesian languages the idiom is, 'there-was seed that' (Bahasa Indonesia RC), 'there-was one part (lit. one-half, which can be used also when the item is divided into more than two parts)' (Malay). The fourfold 'some' in vv. 5-8 may require differentiation, e.g. 'there-was one-part that... (twice), there-was also one-part that..., there-was again one-part that...' (Bahasa Indonesia).

Along the path, preferably, 'on the path', or, 'towards the path' (Sundanese, Toba Batak). For *path* cp. on 3 : 4.

And was trodden under foot, or with an indefinite active form, 'and/there people (or, the passers-by) trod on it'.

The birds of the air, or simply, 'the birds' (see *Exegesis*), specifically the undomesticated birds (cp. 9 : 58), which is sometimes expressed 'wild birds', 'field birds'. Cp. also *TH-Mk* on 4 : 32.

Devoured, preferably, 'pecked up' (Javanese), cp. *TH-Mk* on 4 : 4.

6 ***And some fell on the rock; and as it grew up, it withered away, because it had no moisture.***

Exegesis: *heteron katepesen epi tēn petran* 'some fell upon the rock'. The article *tēn* is generic. *petra* means here 'rocky ground', i.e. rock with a thin covering of soil (cp. Plummer). *katapiptō* (†).

kai phuen exēranthē 'and after coming up, it withered'.

phuō (also v. 8) 'to grow', 'to come up'.

xērainō (†) 'to dry up', 'to wither'.

dia to mē echein ikmada lit. 'because of (its) not having moisture', i.e. 'because it had no moisture'.

ikmas (††) 'moisture of the soil'.

Translation: *On the rock*, or, 'in rocky soil', '(in ground) where stones were lying', 'in hard clay soil' (Fon).

As it grew up, it withered away, or, 'it sprouted (at first), but then it dried up' (cp. Willibrord). For *to grow* cp. *N.T.Wb.*/41f.

Because it had no moisture, or, 'because it (i.e. the seed) had/received no moisture' (Sranan, Bahasa Indonesia 1968), 'for there was no water-for-it' (East Toradja); or, 'because the soil had no moisture, or, was not humid' (cp. TEV).

7 ***And some fell among thorns; and the thorns grew with it and choked it.***

Exegesis: *en mesō tōn akanthōn* lit. 'in the midst of the thorns', hence 'among the thorns'. For *akantha* cp. on 6 : 44.

sumphueisai hai akanthai apepnixan auto 'as the thorns grew up with (the seed) they smothered it', implying that the thorns still had to come up at the time of the sowing, or, were at least very small (cp. Mk. 4 : 7 and Plummer). *sumphuō* (††).

apopnigō (also v. 33) 'to choke', 'to smother', synonymous with the simple verb *pnigō* (cp. A-G s.v. *pnigō* 1 c).

Translation: For this verse see *TH-Mk* on 4 : 7.

Among thorns, or, 'in the place where thorns habitually grow' (Fon). Tagabili uses a local equivalent, 'that area where *fet* (the weed that is most dreaded in the rice fields) will sprout again and grow (lit. will break out)'.

Choked it, or, 'pressed it to death' (Bahasa Indonesia KB), 'killed it' (Sranan), 'hindered its growth' (Marathi).

8 ***And some fell into good soil and grew, and yielded a hundredfold." As he said this, he called out, "He who has ears to hear, let him hear."***

Exegesis: *epesen eis tēn gēn tēn agathēn* 'fell into good soil'. The article, again, is generic. *agathēn* is somewhat emphatic by position.

hekatontaplasiona 'a hundredfold', adverb, going with the phrase *epoiēsen karpon* 'bore fruit' as a whole. Returns of hundredfold are not extraordinary (cp. Plummer).

tauta legōn ephōnei 'saying this he cried'. *ephōnei*, after *legōn*, indicates a raising of the voice (cp. Plummer).

ho echōn ōta akouein akouetō 'he who has ears to hear, let him hear', cp. *TH-Mk* on 4 : 9.

Translation: *Yielded a hundredfold*, or, 'it-bore-fruit so-that its grains were in-hundreds' (Balinese), '(it, i.e. its ears) became-full, one sowing-seed became hundred' (East Toradja 1933), 'it produced fruit a hundredfold (in-proportion-to what had been sown)' (East Toradja rev.); see also *TH-Mk* on 4 : 8. *A hundredfold* may have to be rendered analytically, e.g. 'ten-times-ten of fruit' (Lokele), and approximately, e.g. 'forty of a second sixty of fruits' (Kapauku), or generically, e.g. 'very many (fold)', and cp. 'when they fruit-ed, really heavy, to that extent the thickness of their fruit' (Tagabili), 'complete it gave grains' (Tzeltal).

As he said this, he called out, or, 'and in a loud voice he added' (Willibrord), 'thus he said, then he spoke again rather loudly' (Balinese).

He who has ears to hear, let him hear. A literal rendering may easily sound ridiculous; hence adjustments such as, 'those who not in vain have ears...' (Tzeltal), 'ear-road they-have those hear' (Enga, in *TBT*, 16.133, 1965), 'if you can hear at all you had better listen'. Toba Batak shifts to a restrictive sentence with the second person pronoun, 'you, all-who have-ears that can-hear, ear (imperative of a verb derived from the noun 'ear', and meaning 'to hear-intently', 'to grasp-the-sense-of') this parable'. At its first occurrence the verb (for which cp. on 1 : 41) refers to the faculty of hearing, at the second to the actual hearing of, or listening to something (viz. 'my words', or, 'this parable'). Cp. also *TH-Mk* on 4 : 9.

9 ***And when his disciples asked him what this parable meant,***

Exegesis: *epērōtōn* 'asked', imperfect tense, implying that the act of asking is incomplete in itself (cp. Bl-D, § 328).

hoi mathētai autou 'his disciples', i.e. the larger group of followers, cp. 6 : 13, 20.

tis hautē eiē hē parabolē 'what this parable was', i.e. meant. *hautē* goes with *hē parabolē* (hyperbaton).

Translation: *What this parable meant,* or, 'what (was) the meaning/intent of this parable'; or in direct discourse, e.g. 'What then (is) the meaning (lit. solution, as of a riddle) of this parable?' (East Toradja).

10 ***he said, "To you it has been given to know the secrets of the kingdom of God; but for others they are in parables, so that seeing they may not see, and hearing they may not understand.***

Exegesis: *humin dedotai gnōnai ta mustēria tēs basileias tou theou* 'to you it has been granted to know the secrets of the kingdom of God'. *humin* is emphatic as contrasted with *tois de loipois*. The agent of *dedotai* is God.

mustērion (†) 'secret', not something which is and remains a mystery, but a secret which is being disclosed by God to those to whom He grants it (cp. Richardson, *Word Book,* 156).

tois de loipois en parabolais 'but to the others in the form of parables'. The absence of a verbal clause is awkward and probably intentional (cp. Mk. 4 : 11); hence a rendering like, "but to the rest—parables" (Rieu). If necessary some verb like *lalō* 'I speak', or *dedotai* 'they are given', viz. the secrets of the kingdom of God (cp. BFBS) is to be understood. The former is preferable.

hina blepontes mē blepōsin 'that seeing they may not see'. For *hina* cp. *TH-Mk* on 4 : 12; if a choice between a final and a consecutive rendering is necessary, the former is preferable. *blepontes* refers to the physical act of seeing (cp. Phillips "with their eyes open"), *blepōsin* to conscious and understanding perception.

kai akouontes mē suniōsin 'and (that) hearing they may not understand', same differentiation between the physical act and conscious perception but this time brought out by different verbs.

Translation: For this verse cp. *TH-Mk* on 4 : 11f.

To know, i.e. to have understanding of; hence closely synonymous with the last verb of the verse.

The secrets of the kingdom of God, see *TH-Mk, l.c.* For *secrets of* Chol uses, 'truth about...which was not previously made known'.

For (or, to) *others,* viz. those who do not belong to Jesus' disciples or followers.

They are in parables, preferably, 'I speak in parables' (cp. on v. 4), 'they are told by parables' (Marathi).

Seeing they may not see. The style of this aphorism is best preserved when different forms of the same verb can be used, cp. e.g. 'seeing they don't really-see (perfective construction)' (Kapauku), 'not it is-to-be-seen to them, although they see' (Bahasa Indonesia KB), but often different verbs or verbal phrases must be employed, e.g. 'looking they may not perceive', 'while (they) appear to them, they may not look-at (them)' (Marathi), 'although they have their eyes wide open, they may not see'

(Sundanese). If an object must be added, it can be a pronominal reference to 'the secrets' (cp. Marathi), or, preferably, to the contents of the parables.

Hearing they may not understand. An interesting rendering is given in East Toradja, 'they turn-upwards (a verb often used of the mouth held upwards to catch water) the ear, they do not understand-it (lit. find-it with the heart)'. For *to understand* cp. on 2 : 47.

11 ***Now the parable is this: The seed is the word of God.***

Exegesis: *estin de hautē hē parabolē* 'now the parable is, or, means this'. *hautē* is predicate.

ho sporos estin ho logos tou theou 'the seed is the word of God'. *ho sporos* is subject. *estin* is best understood in the sense of 'stands for'. For *ho logos tou theou* cp. on 5 : 1.

Translation: For vv. 11-15 cp. *TH-Mk* on 4 : 14-20.

The parable is this, or, 'means this'. The rendering should preferably parallel the one used in v. 9.

The seed is the word of God, or as a simile, 'the seed is as/to-be-likened-to the word of God' (Low Malay). For *the word of God* see on 5 : 1.

12 ***The ones along the path are those who have heard; then the devil comes and takes away the word from their hearts, that they may not believe and be saved.***

Exegesis: *hoi...para tēn hodon* 'the people by, or, on the road' (cp. on v. 5), i.e. the people that can be compared to what became of the seed that fell on the road, cp. *TH-Mk* on 4 : 14.

eisin hoi akousantes, eita erchetai ho diabolos kai airei ton logon apo tēs kardias autōn '...are those who hear, (and) then the devil comes and takes away the word from their hearts', i.e. 'the people on the road are those from whose heart the devil takes away the word after they have heard it'. For *ho diabolos* cp. on 4 : 2[a].

hina mē pisteusantes sōthōsin 'in order that they may not believe and be saved'. The participle *pisteusantes* describes the way in which, or, the means by which, the event of *sōthōsin* is effected. *sōthōsin* is used here in the sense of 'attain salvation', cp. A-G s.v. *sōzō* 2 b.

Translation: The rather complex construction of the sentence may have to be changed, e.g. 'Thus are the ones on the path. They hear (the word), then the devil comes...'.

The ones along the path are those who may have to be expanded and/or changed into a simile, e.g. 'the people who are exemplified/illustrated by (or, whom we may call) the seed that fell on the path are those who', 'the seed that went to fall on the path is showing those who' (Kituba). — Similar adjustments may be necessary in vv. 13ff.

Who have heard sometimes requires an object, 'the word', or, 'it', which may entail the substitution of the object of the next clause by a pronoun.

Devil, see on 4 : 2[a].

Takes away the word from their hearts. To obtain a better transition one may say, 'takes away the word (that now is) in their hearts', or, transposing the reference to the heart, 'it (i.e. the word) is already there in their thoughts, but immediately Satan takes it away from them' (Tagabili).

Hearts. The plural is distributive.

That they may not... In some cases a shift to direct discourse may be desirable, e.g. 'thinking, "They should not..."'.

Not believe and be saved. To make clear that the negative goes with both verbs one may have to repeat the negative particle (as e.g. in Kituba, Sundanese), or to specify the connexion between them, cp. e.g. "not through their faith be saved" (Rieu), 'not believe with-the-result-of being-saved' (Javanese), 'not believe in him who can save them'. For *to believe* see references on "faith" in 5 : 20. *Be saved*, i.e. become safe (in the spiritual sense), reach the state of safety; for the form cp. *TH-Mk* on 10 : 26 (p. 325).

13 ***And the ones on the rock are those who, when they hear the word, receive it with joy; but these have no root, they believe for a while and in time of temptation fall away.***

Exegesis: *hoi de epi tēs petras* (scil. *eisin*) *hoi hotan akousōsin meta charas dechontai ton logon* 'the (people) on the rock (are) those who, when they hear (the word) receive it with joy'. For *hoi epi tēs petras* cp. on v. 12. *dechomai* here of receiving and acknowledging the word of God.

kai houtoi rizan ouk echousin 'and those have no root', as if the subject were the seed that fell on the rock, and not the people which can be compared with the seed that fell on the rock. *kai* is here 'and yet', or, 'but'. *riza*, cp. on 3: 9. *houtoi* refers back to *hoi epi tēs petras*.

hoi pros kairon pisteuousin 'who believe for a while'. This relative clause takes up *meta charas dechontai*, and, at the same time, applies the statement that they have no root: they believe for a while only.

kairos here '(short) period of time'. *pros kairon* 'for a short period', 'for a while'.

en kairō peirasmou aphistantai 'in a time of trial they fall away'. *kairos* has a somewhat wider scope here than in *pros kairon*. For *peirasmos* cp. on 4 : 13, but here the meaning is passive, and implies that the faith of the believers is put to the test.

aphistamai 'to become apostate', 'to fall away' (cp. 1 Tim. 4 : 1; Heb. 3 : 12).

Translation: *Receive it with joy*, cp. *TH-Mk* on 4 : 16. The verb implies mental consent, acceptance, approval. *With joy*, or, 'joyfully', 'and rejoice', 'while (or, and) their heart was glad', etc.

These have no root, or, 'do not root well' (cp. Tagabili); or, again making explicit the underlying simile, 'these are as though not (really) taking root', 'these are like seed that does not strike (much) root'.

In time of temptation, or, changing to a verbal clause, 'when they are tempted, or, put to the test' (cp. Balinese, East Toradja), or, where an active construction is preferable, 'when the devil tests them, or, tries to make them fall away'. For 'to tempt' see also on 4 : 2[a]. Renderings like 'hardship/trouble' are not advisable.

Fall away, or, 'draw back', 'go astray' (Marathi), 'turn away/aside' (Toba Batak, Sranan), 'desert', lit. 'fly back' (as a spring does) (South Toradja), 'become-renegades' (Javanese).

14 ***And as for what fell among the thorns, they are those who hear, but as they go on their way they are choked by the cares and riches and pleasures of life, and their fruit does not mature.***

Exegesis: *to de eis tas akanthas peson* 'and what fell among the thorns', or 'as for what fell among the thorns', taking *to...peson* as an accusative of reference (cp. RSV, BFBS). The latter is possible but not necessary. The shift from the masculine to the neuter is remarkable but hardly influences the meaning of the clause since *to...peson* is taken up by the masculine *houtoi*.

houtoi eisin hoi akousantes, kai...sumpnigontai 'those are the people who hear, and...they are choked'. Same structure as in v. 12, and best rendered in a similar way, e.g. 'those are the people who hear (the word) and (later on) are choked'.

hupo merimnōn kai ploutou kai hēdonōn tou biou 'by the worries and wealth and pleasures of life'. *tou biou* may go with all three nouns, or with *hēdonōn* only. The former is preferable, and *bios* is best understood in its most general meaning, viz. human, or, earthly life.

merimna (also 21 : 34) 'anxiety', 'worry'.

ploutos (†) 'wealth', 'riches'.

hēdonē (†) 'pleasure'.

poreuomenoi sumpnigontai 'going (their way), i.e. in the course of time, they are choked'. *poreuomenoi* serves to convey the idea that the choking is a gradual process which takes time (cp. Plummer).

sumpnigō 'to choke', in v. 42 'to press around somebody', here equivalent to *apopnigō* in v. 7.

kai ou telesphorousin 'and they do not bear (fruit) to maturity', rather than 'they do not come to maturity' (Willibrord, cp. Klostermann). *telesphoreō* (††).

Translation: *As they go on their way*, or, 'on the long run' (NV), 'the longer (it) lasts the-more' (Balinese), 'foot by foot' (Sranan), and cp. NEB, transposing the expression, "but their further growth is choked".

They are choked by the cares and riches and pleasures of life. Some adjustments that may be necessary are, (1) a shift to an active construction with the three nouns as subjects (e.g. in Sranan, Kituba, Zarma); (2) the repetition of the verb, or a synonym, which will lead to the use of two or three verbal clauses (e.g. in Cuyono and Tagabili respectively); (3) transposition and/or repetition of the term for 'life', cp. e.g. 'in (the pursuit of) worldly cares, wealth, and pleasures their growth is stunted' (Marathi), 'the business of this life and its riches, and the things of life's pleasure...

they choke it' (Zarma); (4) a shift from nouns to verbal phrases, e.g. 'by the fact that (or, because) they have cares (or, are anxious, or, worry), and are rich (or, have many possessions), and love pleasure (or, enjoy themselves) in life'. — *Choked,* used in its literal sense in v. 7, but metaphorically here; hence one may, again, have to make explicit the underlying simile, or shift to an expression that is better applicable to persons, e.g. 'overcome/defeated' (Cuyono, Tzeltal), 'strangled' (Sranan), 'cornered' (Toba Batak), and cp. Marathi (above). *Cares,* or, 'worries', or in a descriptive phrase, 'things which concern them very much' (Cuyono), 'thinking over the things they lack' (Tzeltal); cp. also *TH-Mk* on 4 : 19, and below on 21 : 34. *Of life* characterizes the cares etc. as belonging to human/earthly life only; hence, 'worldly'. The phrase "pleasures of life" has been rendered by, 'that which satisfies the breath' in Tagabili, and 'visible joys' (i.e. joys belonging to this visible world as opposed to the invisible, supernatural world) in Balinese.

Their fruit does not mature, or, 'become ripe', or, 'they do not bear/give ripe fruit' (Marathi); for 'to bear fruit' cp. on 3 : 8f. Non-metaphorically one may say something like, 'they do not produce good results', 'it does not come to completion (lit. is-not-able-to-finish)' (Tagabili), 'they do not develop fully'.

15 ***And as for that in the good soil, they are those who, hearing the word, hold it fast in an honest and good heart, and bring forth fruit with patience.***

Exegesis: *to de en tē kalē gē* 'but that (which is) in good soil'. Same structure as in v. 14.

houtoi eisin hoitines en kardia kalē kai agathē akousantes ton logon katechousin 'they are those who, having heard with a good and true heart, keep the word'. The phrase *en kardia kalē kai agathē* goes either with *akousantes* (cp. NEB), or with *katechousin* (cp. RSV), preferably the former because of its place immediately before *akousantes. en* has here instrumental meaning (cp. A-G s.v. III 1 a). *kalē* and *agathē* may perhaps be interpreted as reinforcing each other and rendered 'truly good' (cp. Grundmann).

katechō here 'to keep', of the Gospel message, as in 1 Cor. 11 : 2; 15 : 2; cp. Heb. 10 : 23.

karpophorousin en hupomonē 'they bear fruit with patience'. *karpophoreō* (†).

hupomonē 'patience', 'perseverance', 'constancy', especially in trial and tribulation (cp. 21 : 19). *en hupomonē* refers to the attitude of him who bears fruit.

Translation: *Hearing the word, hold it fast in an honest and good heart,* preferably, 'hear the word in an honest...heart, and hold it fast'. The prepositional phrase gives to the hearing a deeper meaning, indicating the heart as the means for considering and assimilating what is heard. *To hold fast,* i.e. to retain faithfully, to keep and obey. *Honest and good,* a pair of closely synonymous adjectives; hence, 'truly/really/very good', cp. also "in the true goodness of their hearts" (Rieu).

Bring forth fruit, or, 'bear fruit', or non-metaphorically, 'produce results'.

With patience, or, "by their perseverance" (NEB), 'because they have held through' (Sranan), and with a further shift, "persist until they bear fruit" (TEV). *Patience* in the sense of 'perseverance', 'steadfastness' has been rendered, 'firmness/toughness of heart' (Bahasa Indonesia RC, East Toradja), or by an expression built on 'brave' (Marathi, cp. also Ilocano in *TBT*, 11.29, 1960).

16 ***"No one after lighting a lamp covers it with a vessel, or puts it under a bed, but puts it on a stand, that those who enter may see the light.***

Exegesis: *oudeis de luchnon hapsas kaluptei auton* 'nobody, after lighting a lamp, covers it'. The clause is an injunction in the form of a negative statement: what is done by nobody ought not to be done by the disciples. The present tense *kaluptei* stresses the general character of the saying.

luchnos 'lamp', a wick lamp, the wick lying in a shallow bowl filled with oil (cp. *TH-Mk* on 4 : 21).

haptō 'to kindle', 'to light' (cp. A-G s.v. 1).

kaluptō (also 23 : 30) 'to cover', 'to hide'.

skeuei 'with a vessel'. *skeuos* (also 17 : 31) can mean any vessel: 'jar', 'dish', 'bowl', 'basin'.

ē hupokatō klinēs tithēsin 'or puts (it) under a bed'.

hupokatō (†) 'under'.

klinē here a bed on four legs.

epi luchnias tithēsin 'but he puts it on a lampstand', cp. A-G s.v. *luchnia* (also 11 : 33).

hina hoi eisporeuomenoi blepōsin to phōs 'so that those who come in may see the light'. *hoi eisporeuomenoi* are those that enter the house, or, the room. The clause probably refers to the Gentiles who must hear the Gospel message (cp. Plummer, Caird, Creed).

Translation: The structure may have to be changed in something like, 'a person (or, you) should not light a lamp, and then cover it...'.

Renderings of *to light* (viz. a lamp) have various basic meanings, e.g. 'to fix' (Bahasa Indonesia), 'to cause-to-burn' (Toba Batak), 'to cause-to-live' (other possibility in Bahasa Indonesia).

Lamp. The translator may use the name of anything that is commonly employed to give light in a house, e.g. 'torch' (East and South Toradja, Wantoat), 'candle'.

Covers it with a vessel, or, 'covers it with something' (South Toradja), or simply, 'covers it' (Balinese, using a verb specifically employed in connexion with concave things).

The usual rendering of *bed,* e.g. 'couch', 'what-one-lies/sleeps-on', may refer to something that is laid on the floor; hence shifts to, 'under a bench', 'under a sleeping/sitting-platform' (East Toradja), 'in the space-under-a-sleeping-platform' (Javanese); and see *TH-Mk* on 4 : 21.

But puts..., or in a new sentence, 'on the contrary he (or, you) should put...', or, 'of course (it) should-be-put...' (Balinese).

A stand, or, 'a lamp's foot' (Bahasa Indonesia), a locative derivation of 'lamp' (Toba Batak); or to be described as, 'an elevated/clearly-visible place', 'up where it is high' (Mazahua).

The light, referring to what emanates from a lamp, 'flame', 'radiance'; a shift to a verbal expression may result in, '...see it (or, the lamp) burn/give-brightness'.

17 ***For nothing is hid that shall not be made manifest, nor anything secret that shall not be known and come to light.***

Exegesis: *ou gar estin krupton ho ou phaneron genēsetai* 'for there is nothing hidden which will not become manifest', a general saying but here referring to the secrets of the kingdom of God, 'everything that is (now) hidden, will (in due time) become manifest'.

kruptos (also 12 : 2) 'hidden', 'secret', here used as a noun.

phaneros (†) 'plainly to be seen', 'manifest'.

oude apokruphon 'and (there is) nothing secret'. The clause introduced by *oude* is parallel to the preceding one; this combination serves to stress the truth of both clauses.

apokruphos 'hidden', 'secret', synonymous with *kruptos*.

ho ou mē gnōsthē kai eis phaneron elthē 'which will not be known and come to light'. For *ou mē* with subjunctive cp. on 1 : 15. In this context, however, the negation is inverted by the negative *oude* in the main clause, and the clause is a strong and definite positive statement. *eis phaneron elthē* literally means 'come into the manifest', hence 'come to light', or, 'become manifest'.

Translation: For this verse cp. *TH-Mk* on 4 : 22. A shift to an active form in the second person may be advisable (cp. Sranan in 12 : 2). To choose the right synonym in the right place is not always easy. To guide his choice the translator may assume that the first clause refers to sight, the second one to hearing, cp. e.g. 'no hidden thing that people will not hear...' (Sranan).

18 ***Take heed then how you hear; for to him who has will more be given, and from him who has not, even what he thinks that he has will be taken away."***

Exegesis: *blepete oun pōs akouete* 'take care, then, how you listen'. *oun* characterizes the clause as an inference from the preceding. For *blepō* meaning 'to take care', cp. A-G s.v. 4.

hos an gar echē, dothēsetai autō 'for (he) who has, to him will be given', referring either to faith (*pisteusantes*, v. 12; *pisteuousin*, v. 13), or, to the bearing of fruit (*karpophorousin*, v. 15), preferably the former. The agent of *dothēsetai* is God.

hos an mē echē, kai ho dokei echein arthēsetai ap' autou '(he) who has not, even what he thinks he has will be taken from him'. For *airō* cp. on 6 : 29f.
dokeō 'to believe', 'to think' (of subjective opinion), 'to seem'.

Translation: *Take heed then how you hear,* or, 'look to the manner you hear the word' (Sranan). For *take heed* cp. also *TH-Mk* on 4 : 24.
To him who has will more be given, or, 'he who has (some), he shall receive (or, to him God shall give) more (than that)'. Comparable changes will then be necessary in the next clause, using e.g. 'lose' or 'forfeit' (cp. Phillips, NEB), as the opposite of 'receive'.
What he thinks that he has, avoiding the paradoxical wording Mark has. Other possible renderings are, 'the things he supposed to be his' (Bahasa Indonesia), 'even what he called (or, said to be) his possessions' (cp. South Toradja). For *to think* cp. on "to suppose" in 2 : 44.

19 ***Then his mother and his brothers came to him, but they could not reach him for the crowd.***

Exegesis: *paregeneto de pros auton hē mētēr kai hoi adelphoi autou* 'and his mother and brothers came to him'. Though *paregeneto* is in the singular, its subject *hē mētēr* is closely connected with *hoi adelphoi* by the fact that *autou* goes with both nouns. It appears that the event of vv. 19-21 are to be understood as following the events of vv. 4-18.
ouk ēdunanto suntuchein autō 'they could not get to him, or, reach him'. The imperfect *ēdunanto* refers to a situation in which they find themselves.
suntugchanō (††) with dative 'to come together with', 'to get close to'.

Translation: One of the pronouns *his* or *him* may have to be specified.
In some older Indonesian languages *brothers* (cp. on 6 : 14) has been rendered by 'male siblings', but all more recent Indonesian translations investigated use 'sibling', because the specification would unduly emphasize the sex of the persons in question.
Came to him, or, 'came near to (the place/house) where he was', 'came to see him' (East Toradja 1933). Since they could not reach him, the aspect is conative, as made explicit in South Toradja.
For the crowd, or, 'because the people (present) were-closely-packed-together' (cp. Bahasa Indonesia), 'there-not-being a passage through the many people' (East Toradja 1933).

20 ***And he was told, "Your mother and your brothers are standing outside, desiring to see you."***

Exegesis: *apēggelē de autō* lit. 'it was reported to him', with a shift in syntactic structure 'he was told'. Cp. on 7 : 18.
hestēkasin exō 'are standing outside', i.e. outside the house.
idein thelontes se 'wishing to see you'.

Translation: *He was told,* or, 'people/somebody told him (or, informed him of this, saying)'.

Are standing outside, or, where idiomatically better, 'are outside (the house)': it is their presence, not their exact attitude that is relevant in this context.

To see you, or, 'to meet you' (Marathi, similarly South Toradja, lit. a reciprocal form of 'to see').

21 ***But he said to them, "My mother and my brothers are those who hear the word of God and do it."***

Exegesis: *apokritheis eipen* 'answering he said', cp. on 1 : 19.

mētēr mou kai adelphoi mou houtoi eisin... 'those are my mother and my brothers...'. The absence of the article with *mētēr* and *adelphoi* shows that these words are predicate, cp. "these...are mother and brothers to me" (Rieu).

hoi ton logon tou theou akouontes kai poiountes 'that hear the word of God and do it', cp. on 6 : 47.

Translation: *Said to them*, preferably, 'answered/replied', 'said in reply', since the words are spoken to the members of the crowd who addressed him (v. 20).

In order to give the right emphasis Jesus' saying may have to be adjusted, e.g. 'those who hear and do the word of God, that (with emphatic particle) my mother, that my younger-siblings' (Toba Batak), "My mother and my brothers? They are those who hear..." (NEB).

My mother and my brothers. To make explicit the metaphorical sense one may say, 'those I call/consider my mother...', and cp. Rieu's rendering quoted in *Exegesis*.

To hear the word...and do it, cp. on 6 : 47.

22 ***One day he got into a boat with his disciples, and he said to them, "Let us go across to the other side of the lake." So they set out,***

Exegesis: *egeneto de* lit. 'and it happened', cp. on 1 : 8.

en mia tōn hēmerōn 'on one of the days', cp. on 5 : 17.

kai autos enebē eis ploion kai hoi mathētai autou 'and he got into a boat and his disciples'. *autos* is not emphatic and *kai autos* has the same function and meaning as in e.g. 4 : 15. For *enebē* cp. on 5 : 3.

dielthōmen 'let us cross', hortatory subjunctive; cp. on 2 : 15.

eis to peran tēs limnēs 'to the other side of the lake', cp. on 5 : 1 and *TH-Mk* on 4 : 35. *peran* (†).

kai anēchthēsan 'and they put out'. For *anagō* cp. on 2 : 22 and for its meaning here A-G s.v. 3.

Translation: *He got into a boat with his disciples*, see on 5 : 3. It may be better to include the disciples in the subject, 'he and his disciples got...'. For *boat* see on 5 : 2.

Let us. Elsewhere expressions such as 'it is good' (South Toradja), 'come on' (Bahasa Indonesia) are used with hortative force.

Go across to the other side of the lake. In some languages one must be more specific about details, see *TH-Mk* on 4 : 35; but in others the idiom is more concise, cp. e.g. 'to cross the lake' (Kapauku, similarly Javanese, which expresses 'to cross' by a verbal derivation of 'the-opposite-side'), 'to break-through the lake' (Balinese), 'to cut to the opposite-side' (Sranan). For *lake* see on 5 : 1.

They set out, or such idioms as, "they set sail" (Goodspeed), 'they pushed (the boat) off' (Javanese, Sranan), 'they poled away' (East Toradja), or simply, 'they departed/left' (Toba Batak, Tagabili).

23 ***and as they sailed he fell asleep. And a storm of wind came down on the lake, and they were filling with water, and were in danger.***

Exegesis: *pleontōn de autōn* 'as they sailed (along)'. *autōn* refers to Jesus and his disciples. *pleō* (†).

aphupnōsen (††) 'he fell asleep'. Subject is Jesus.

kai katebē lailaps anemou eis tēn limnēn 'and a squall of wind came down upon the lake', as if descending from the surrounding mountains.

lailaps (†) 'whirlwind', 'hurricane', here with *anemou* 'a squall of wind'.

kai suneplērounto kai ekinduneuon lit. 'and they were filling and were in danger'. The subject of both verbs is Jesus and his disciples (as in *pleontōn autōn*), not the disciples only as in the first clause of v. 24. In *suneplērounto* (also 9 : 51 but in a different meaning) what happens to the ship is said to happen to the crew. The imperfect tense of both verbs serves to bring out the situation in which they find themselves due to the squall of wind.

kinduneuō (†) 'to be in danger'.

Translation: *They sailed,* or, 'they boat-ed' (e.g. in South Toradja, Toba Batak, just as in Greek), 'they were driving' (Marathi, same verb as used of carts, motor-cars etc.); or still more generically, 'they were going so' (Sranan).

He fell asleep. Other idiomatic expressions are, "he dropped off to sleep" (Phillips), 'his sleep stole Jesus' (South Toradja), 'his-eyes became-sleepy' (Toba Batak), and cp. *N.T.Wb.*/68, SLEEP.

A storm of wind, or, 'a heavy storm', 'a roaring wind', 'a gale', a term referring to heavy wind with rain, etymologically related with the word for 'west' (South Toradja), 'a very strong wind', lit. 'a mother of winds' (Tagabili, which has also another and more forceful idiom: 'a horse of winds').

Came down, or, 'began to blow/rage', 'came' (Sundanese), 'came suddenly (lit. broke came)' (Sranan), "struck" (NEB), 'released itself' (Marathi), as idiom may require; Tagabili shifts to, 'they ran into a very strong wind'.

They were filling with water, or, 'water began to fill the boat' (Marathi). Some idiomatic renderings are, 'they made water' (Willibrord), 'the(ir) boat was-entered-by water' (Bahasa Indonesia), 'the boat took water' (Sranan). Kapauku uses a specific word for water in a boat needing to be bailed.

And were in danger, or, 'and were in distress' (NV), 'so that they nearly perished' (some Indonesian languages), 'they were nearly sinking' (South Toradja, similarly Sranan, lit. 'they sought to sink').

24 ***And they went and woke him, saying, "Master, Master, we are perishing!" And he awoke and rebuked the wind and the raging waves; and they ceased, and there was a calm.***

Exegesis: *proselthontes de diēgeiran auton* 'after going (to Jesus) they woke him up'. For *proserchomai* cp. on 7 : 14.

diegeirō (†) 'to wake up (from sleep)'.

epistata epistata 'master, master'. The repetition makes the vocative more emphatic. For *epistatēs* cp. on 5 : 5.

apollumetha 'we are perishing', without indicating the way in which this happens.

epetimēsen tō anemō kai tō kludōni tou hudatos 'he checked the wind and the rough water', cp. on 4 : 35.

kludōn (†) with *hudatos* 'rough water'.

kai epausanto 'and they ceased', a general term.

egeneto galēnē 'there was a calm'.

galēnē (†) 'calm', always of the sea.

Translation: *They went*. Several versions indicate the goal, cp. 'having come to him' (Marathi), 'the disciples approached Jesus' (Balinese).

For *woke him* and *he awoke* see *N.T.Wb.*/14, AWAKE; for *Master* see on 5 : 5, and on the repetition cp. on 6 : 46.

We are perishing. For the choice between inclusive and exclusive 'we' cp. *TH-Mk* on 4 : 38. The translator should seek the idiomatic expression that people would commonly use in such a situation; in most cases this seems to require the inclusive pronoun. In honorific languages, however, linguistic etiquette may not allow that one includes one's betters in one's own situation; hence the exclusive pronoun, e.g. in Javanese, Sundanese. Sometimes the choice can be avoided, e.g. where an impersonal idiom is available, cp. 'brought-to-destruction now' (Balinese), 'having-sunk' (Marathi, using a past tense form without explicit pronoun and with a non-distinctive first person plural ending; on older renderings in this language cp. *TBT*, 3.26, 1952), or, 'the boat is being wrecked'. For the verb cp. *N.T.Wb.*/27[a], DIE; in this context a rendering that specifies the way in which they are perishing is also acceptable, cp. 'we will drown' (East Toradja, Sundanese).

Rebuked, or in this context, 'caused to cease, or, to be calm'.

The raging waves may have to be expressed variously, e.g. 'the high waves', 'the stormy/seething water', 'the water that-was-in-waves', 'the rolling of the waves'.

And is consecutive here; hence, 'so that' (Balinese, Toba Batak).

They ceased, and there was a calm. Subject of the first clause are the winds, the second clause refers to the water; hence one may have to say something like, 'the winds/storm ceased (or, ceased to blow, blew no more), and the water (or, waves/lake) became calm (or, still/smooth)'. For some renderings of *the wind ceased* cp. also *TH-Mk* on 4 : 39 and 6 : 51.

25 ***He said to them, "Where is your faith?" And they were afraid, and they marvelled, saying to one another, "Who then is this, that he commands even wind and water, and they obey him?"***

Exegesis: *pou hē pistis humōn* 'where (is) your faith'. Most probably this question refers to the attitude of the disciples which was one of anxiety and not of trust in Jesus.

tis ara houtos estin hoti... 'who then is this that he...' The question expresses their astonishment. The clause which is introduced by *hoti* may indicate to what the astonished question refers, viz. Jesus' power over the winds and the water, or the reason for the astonishment. The former is preferable. For other questions of this type cp. 4 : 36; 5 : 21.

kai tois anemois epitassei kai tō hudati 'he commands even the winds and the water', or 'he commands the winds and the water', preferably the former. In that rendering the first *kai* is ascensive (cp. A-G s.v. II 2), the second connective. For *epitassō* cp. on 4 : 36.

kai hupakouousin autō 'and (as a result) they obey him'. *hupakouō* also 17 : 6.

Translation: *Them,* i.e. the disciples, may have to be specified.

Where is your faith, or, 'why do you not have faith', 'why do you not trust (me)'; or, 'apparently you do not have faith, or, do not trust (me)'. If an object has to be supplied a reference to Jesus (hence, 'me') seems to agree better with the question in v. 25[b] than a reference to God (as advocated in *TH-Mk* on 4 : 40) would do.

For *marvelled* cp. on "wondered" in 1 : 21; and for *saying to one another* see on 4 : 36.

Who then is this. The interrogative pronoun may have to be qualified, see *TH-Mk* on 4 : 41. The force of the question has often to be specified by a modal or exclamatory particle or form expressing astonishment, e.g. 'who may he be, do-you-suppose?' (Bahasa Indonesia RC), 'what man is this!'

The next clause is often better rendered as an independent statement, 'He commands...and they obey (him)', 'He tells the winds...what to do and they do so, or, do what he says'. For *to obey* cp. on 2 : 51.

26 ***Then they arrived at the country of the Gerasenes, which is opposite Galilee.***

Exegesis: *kai katepleusan eis tēn chōran tōn Gergesēnōn* 'and they sailed to the country of the Gergesenes', cp. A-G s.v. *Gergesēnos.*

katapleō (††) 'to sail down (from the high seas) towards the coast'.

hētis estin antipera tēs Galilaias 'which is opposite Galilee', scil. across the lake.

antipera (††) adverb, here used as a preposition with following genitive 'across', 'opposite'.

Translation: *They arrived at*, or, "they made a landing in" (Goodspeed), 'they reached the shore of the lake at' (South Toradja), referring to the very end of the journey; other versions refer to the final stretch of the journey, e.g. 'they sailed on to' (Bahasa Indonesia), 'they headed for' (Bahasa Indonesia RC), 'their boat made-for-the-shore at' (Balinese), '(in) that boating-of-them, (they) went to' (East Toradja).

The country of the Gerasenes, preferably, *Gergesenes*, or, 'the country where the Gergesenes lived' (cp. *TH-Mk* on 5 : 1), or, shifting from persons to locality, 'the Gergesa country/region' (cp. East Toradja, Toba Batak).

Which is opposite Galilee, or, 'on the side (or, shore of the lake) opposite to the land G.' (East and South Toradja), 'which is across the lake (lit. having-in-between the lake) from the land G.' (Balinese); in Kapauku one must say, 'eastward of G.'.

27 ***And as he stepped out on land, there met him a man from the city who had demons; for a long time he had worn no clothes, and he lived not in a house but among the tombs.***

Exegesis: *exelthonti de autō epi tēn gēn* 'and when he went ashore', participle in the dative, going with *hupēntēsen* '(a man) met him'. Though the disciples who had come with Jesus are still with him *exelthonti* is in the singular and refers to Jesus alone.

hupēntēsen anēr tis ek tēs poleōs 'a man from the town met (him)'. *ek tēs poleōs* goes with *anēr*, 'a man from the town', i.e., in the light of the rest of the verse, a man who formerly used to live in the town.

hupantaō (also 14 : 31) 'to (come and) meet', or, 'to (come to) meet', with dative.

echōn daimonia lit. 'having demons', i.e. 'with demons', or, 'possessed by demons'.

chronō hikanō ouk enedusato himation 'for a long time he had worn no clothes'. *chronō hikanō* is temporal dative answering the question 'how long' (here and v. 29), cp. Bl-D, § 201.

enduō act. 'to dress', mid. 'to dress oneself', 'to put on', 'to wear', cp. *N.T.Wb.*, 33/CLOTHE.

kai en oikia ouk emenen all' en tois mnēmasin 'and in a house he did not live but in/among the tombs'. *emenen* is durative imperfect.

mnēma 'grave', probably referring to caverns in the rocks, cp. *TH-Mk* on 5 : 3.

Translation: *He stepped out on land.* For disembarkation various idioms are used, cp. e.g. "he stepped/went ashore" (NEB/BFBS), *il mettait pied à terre* (Jerusalem, similarly Shona 1966), 'he ascended to land/shore' (several Indonesian languages), 'alighting on the ground' (Marathi), 'Jesus jumped down from up in the boat' (Tagabili), 'he descended' (Balinese).

There met him a man, or, 'a man encountered him, or, came towards him' (Toba Batak). Where the language distinguishes between meeting by accident and by design (cp. *TH-Mk* on 14 : 13), the latter is to be chosen.

Who had demons, i.e. 'who was demon possessed', cp. on 4 : 33. If the expression in question does not permit an indication of plurality, it will usually allow an indication of high degree.

Had worn no clothes, or, 'had not been clothed', 'was-naked' (Balinese). For *clothes* or 'clothing' see on 7 : 25.

To live in a house, i.e. 'to stay/dwell in a house'.

Among the tombs, see *TH-Mk* on 5 : 2.

28 ***When he saw Jesus, he cried out and fell down before him, and said with a loud voice, "What have you to do with me, Jesus, Son of the Most High God? I beseech you, do not torment me."***

Exegesis: *idōn de ton Iēsoun anakraxas prosepesen autō* 'and when he saw Jesus he cried out and fell down before him'. For *anakrazō* cp. on 4 : 33 where a similar situation is referred to. For *prospiptō* cp. on 5 : 8; here it indicates an act of supplication.

phōnē megalē eipen 'he said in a loud voice'. *eipen* is best understood as taking up *anakraxas*, cp. 4 : 33.

ti emoi kai soi 'what have you to do with me', cp. on 4 : 34.

Iēsou huie tou theou tou hupsistou 'Jesus, son of the Most High God', cp. on 1 : 32.

deomai sou, mē me basanisēs 'I beseech you, do not torture me'. For *deomai* cp. on 5 : 12.

basanizō (†) 'to torture', cp. *N.T.Wb.*, 120/PAIN.

Translation: *He cried out.* The aspect is inceptive, 'he began to scream' (Sranan). The verb used need not refer to understandable speech.

Fell down before him, see on the synonymous phrase in 5 : 8.

Said with a loud voice, or, 'said loudly', 'shouted', cp. on 4 : 33. The verb or verbal phrase to be chosen must be applicable to understandable speech, and it should not suggest anger, as this would be incompatible with the following entreaty.

What have you to do with me, see on 4 : 34; for *Son of the Most High God* cp. on 1 : 32, 35; and for *I beseech you* see on 4 : 38.

Do not torment me. The verb may be rendered, 'cause to suffer', 'inflict-pain-on', 'cause-distress-to', 'give plague to', or, an expression carrying the idea of being twisted, figuratively spoken (Marathi); and cp. *N.T.Wb.* /57, PAIN.

29 ***For he had commanded the unclean spirit to come out of the man. (For many a time it had seized him; he was kept under guard, and bound with chains and fetters, but he broke the bonds and was driven by the demon into the desert.)***

Exegesis: *parēggeilen gar tō pneumati tō akathartō* 'for he had commanded the unclean spirit', implying that this had preceded the cry of the possessed man. Nestle reads *parēggellen* (imperfect) and with that reading the clause means 'for he was (already, i.e. while the man was approaching) commanding the unclean spirit'. For *paraggellō* cp. on 5 : 14. The singular *tō* *pneumati tō akathartō* takes up the plural *daimonia* (cp. also *daimonia polla* 'many demons' in v. 30) because an unclean spirit is considered a plurality of spirits, or demons, cp. on 4 : 34.

pollois gar chronois sunērpakei auton 'for on many occasions it had seized him', and this is what will happen when Jesus commands the unclean spirit to go out. *gar* indicates that this clause is also part of the explanation of the man's fear in the preceding clause. For *pollois chronois* cp. on v. 27.

sunarpazō (†) 'to seize by violence'.

kai edesmeueto halusesin kai pedais phulassomenos 'and then he was bound with chains and fetters being watched', iterative imperfect. The participle *phulassomenos* may either refer to an independent event (RSV) or indicate the intention with which he was bound (cp. NEB, "for safety's sake"); the latter is preferable. For *phulassomenos* cp. *N.T.Wb.*, 84/.

desmeuō (†) 'to bind'.

halusis (†) 'chain'.

pedē (†) 'fetter', 'shackle'.

diarrēssōn ta desma ēlauneto hupo tou daimoniou eis tas erēmous 'snapping his bonds he was driven by the demon to the desert'. For *diarrēssō* cp. on 5 : 6. For *eis tas erēmous* cp. on 1 : 80.

desmos (also 13 : 16, with plural *desma* in the neuter) 'bond'. As compared with *halusis* and *pedē* it is more general and comprehensive.

elaunō (†) 'to drive'.

Translation: *For,* or, to clarify the connexion with what precedes, 'he said so, because...' (cp. TEV, Balinese), 'the reason (why he did) so was because' (Bahasa Indonesia KB).

He, i.e. Jesus, usually has to be specified.

For *the unclean spirit* see 4 : 33, 36; for *come out* see 4 : 35.

(*For many a time...into the desert*) interrupts the narrative. It may have to be marked as such by the following linguistic means, (1) a tense form referring to what had been happening, or used to happen, in the past, as e.g. in Kapauku, Lokele, Marathi, or markers with similar meaning such as, 'usually/used to', 'often' (Sinhalese), 'formerly' (Cuyono), 'already how many times now' (Tagabili), 'for a long time already' (Tzeltal); (2) a more explicit introduction of the sentence, e.g. 'now the fact was that...' (cp. Zürich), 'it-should-be-known' (Bahasa Indonesia RC); or a combination of these means, cp. e.g. 'as to the demon, often already...' (Balinese).

It had seized him, or, 'it had taken possession of him', see on 4 : 33; cp. also *TH-Mk* on 9 : 18.

He was kept under guard, preferably, 'in order to keep him under guard' (cp. *Exegesis*). The verb has also been rendered "to keep prisoner" (TEV), 'to detain' (Willibrord), 'to keep him in the eye' (Sranan).

Bound with chains and fetters, or, 'he was chained and fettered' (Bahasa Indonesia), 'he was chained and put-in-the-stocks' (Toba Batak), or, since a reference to hands and feet is implied, 'his hands and feet were chained and fettered' (Balinese), 'bound by metal on hands and feet' (Kekchi), 'people had bound his-hands and his-feet' (East Toradja). In Wantoat "chains" has to be rendered 'vines', the normal binding material.

And was driven by the demon, or, 'and then the demon chased-away, or, led-away (the term used also of a thief that is run in) him, or, ran-away-with him' (cp. Bahasa Indonesia; Javanese; Balinese).

Desert, or, 'desolate/uninhabited place(s)', cp. *N.T.Wb.*/25.

30 ***Jesus then asked him, "What is your name?" And he said, "Legion"; for many demons had entered him.***

Exegesis: *epērōtēsen de auton ho Iēsous* 'then Jesus asked him'. *de* marks that after the explanatory clauses of v. 29 the story is resumed. For *eperōtaō* cp. on 2 : 46.

legiōn 'legion', military term and loanword from the Latin, here not denoting a specific large number but suggesting a multitude in general (cp. *daimonia polla*). Furthermore it is used to indicate supernatural powers, either demoniac (here) or heavenly (Mt. 26 : 53).

eisēlthen daimonia polla eis auton 'many demons had gone into him', i.e. 'had taken possession of him'. Here the verb with *daimonia* is in the singular, which is normal in Greek. In vv. 31f it is in the plural (*parekaloun, parekalesan*).

Translation: *Him*, i.e. the man, not the unclean spirit.

What is your name? or, 'who is your name?', and see *TH-Mk* on 5 : 9.

Legion has the function to describe a state, rather than to identify an individual; hence, translation is preferable to transliteration (unless, of course, the Latin word has been borrowed with approximately the same meaning, as is the case in several western languages). For various renderings used see *N.T.Wb.*/54f, MILITARY; *TH-Mk* on 5 : 9; Sinhalese can use a word (*senā*) that can function both as a proper name and as a noun meaning 'battalion'.

Many demons had entered him, referring to a high degree of demon possession, cp. on v. 27.

31 ***And they begged him not to command them to depart into the abyss.***

Exegesis: *kai parekaloun auton* 'and they besought him'. The imperfect tense may either suggest repetition (cp. Plummer, Rieu) or denote an act which may be without result (cp. Bl-D, § 328), preferably the latter (cp. *parekalesan* in v. 32 referring to a request which is granted). For *parakaleō* cp. on 3 : 18.

hina mē epitaxē autois eis tēn abusson apelthein 'that he would not order them to go away to the abyss'. For *epitassō* cp. 4 : 36; 8 : 25.

abussos (†) 'abyss', 'underworld', 'hell', 'bottomless pit', cp. *N.T.Wb.*, 73/HELL.

Translation: *Begged*, cp. *N.T.Wb.*/12f, ASK.

Command them to depart into, or because of the context, 'to command/tell them to plunge-into (Balinese), or, to descend into (Toba Batak), or, to come-out (of the man) and descend into' (Low Malay). The expression is sometimes rendered by one verb, cp. "order them off to" (Goodspeed), "banish them to" (NEB, similarly Javanese).

Abyss, or, 'hole/pit/well that has no bottom', 'unfathomably deep place' (Bahasa Indonesia). If such renderings would not have the required connotation, one may use terms as, 'abode of the wicked', 'place where they (i.e. the demons) dwell, or, are punished', 'land below' (Toba Batak, similarly Bahasa Indonesia KB, lit. 'layer below'); Sranan uses, 'the deep where the earth opens its mouth', a term well known from folktales.

32 ***Now a large herd of swine was feeding there on the hillside; and they begged him to let them enter these. So he gave them leave.***

Exegesis: *ēn de ekei agelē...boskomenē* 'now there was a herd...feeding'. The clause describes circumstances that are relevant to the event that follows. *ēn...boskomenē* is periphrasis of the imperfect and serves to stress the durative aspect.

boskō here passive 'to graze', 'to take food', in v. 34 active 'to give food', 'to tend'.

agelē choirōn hikanōn 'a herd of many pigs', or, with a shift in the syntactic pattern 'a large herd of pigs'.

agelē (also v. 33) 'herd'.

choiros (also 15 : 15f) 'pig', 'swine'.

en tō orei 'on the hillside' or 'on the hills'. The article does not refer to a specific hill, or mountain, but is used in the same loose way as in the English rendering.

kai parekalesan auton hina epitrepsē autois eis ekeinous eiselthein 'and they besought him that he would permit them to go into them'. For *parekalesan* (aorist, implying that the request would be granted) cp. on v. 31.

epitrepō 'to permit', 'to allow'.

Translation: For this verse see *TH-Mk* on 5 : 11-13[a].

Was feeding, or, 'was seeking (something) to eat' (Bahasa Indonesia); or, introducing an indefinite personal agent, 'they brought...swine there, to go seek food' (Sranan). The verb used in Kapauku lit. means 'rooting', i.e. seeking tiny sweet potatoes in a fallow garden.

On the hillside, or, 'on/along the hill'. For 'hill' cp. on 3 : 5.

They, i.e., the demons, may have to be specified.

Begged him to let them enter, or, 'asked him, "Please, allow us to enter"'. For the latter verb see v. 30, but since the demons use it here with reference to themselves, the rendering to be used should not have a decidedly pejorative connotation; hence differentiation may be necessary, e.g. in Bahasa Indonesia (RC and 1968), Balinese, Sranan.

33 ***Then the demons came out of the man and entered the swine, and the herd rushed down the steep bank into the lake and were drowned.***

Exegesis: *exelthonta de ta daimonia apo tou anthrōpou eisēlthon eis tous choirous* 'and after coming out of the man the demons went into the pigs'. For *exelthonta...apo tou anthrōpou* cp. on 4 : 35.

kai hōrmēsen hē agelē 'and the herd rushed'.

hormaō (†) 'to rush (headlong)'.

kata tou krēmnou 'down the steep slope'. The article *tou* has the same function as that in *en tō orei* in v. 32.

krēmnos (only here and parallels in the N.T.) '(steep) slope', 'bank', 'cliff'.

apepnigē 'and was drowned', from *apopnigō* 'to choke', cp. on v. 7.

Translation: For this verse see *TH-Mk* on 5 : 13.

Were drowned. Corresponding terms may require a reference to death, e.g. 'died sinking/choking' (Balinese, Bahasa Indonesia), or simply, 'died' (Sranan).

34 ***When the herdsmen saw what had happened, they fled, and told it in the city and in the country.***

Exegesis: *idontes de hoi boskontes to gegonos* 'when the herdsmen saw what had happened'. *hoi boskontes* is participle of *boskō* (cp. on v. 32) and used here as a substantive. For *to gegonos* cp. *TH-Mk* on 5 : 14.

apēggeilan 'they told (it)', here used without object.

eis tēn polin kai eis tous agrous 'in the town and in the (surrounding) fields, or, hamlets', preferably the latter, cp. *TH-Mk* on 5 : 14. *agros* denotes very small groups of farms out in the country.

Translation: For this verse cp. *TH-Mk* on 5 : 14; the "when"-clause may better be co-ordinated: 'the herdsmen saw what had happened (see on 2 : 15); so they came...'.

Herdsmen, i.e. those who were tending the swine.

In the city and in the country. The reference is to people in the biggest and the smallest local units. For the latter one may use 'villages', or, preferably, a term that also fits 9 : 12, e.g. 'hamlets', 'places-of-huts' (Balinese, using a word referring to a small cluster of huts or sheds, close to the fields and originally inhabited only in the periods of heavy work there), 'places of houses' (South Toradja, a term referring both to a small settlement containing houses of various owners, and to the premises of one owner containing several buildings), 'houses outside (it, i.e. the city)', 'farms' (cp. Sranan, with a word originally meaning 'plantation').

35 ***Then people went out to see what had happened, and they came to Jesus, and found the man from whom the demons had gone, sitting at the feet of Jesus, clothed and in his right mind; and they were afraid.***

Exegesis: *exēlthon de idein to gegonos* 'and they went out to see what had happened'. The subject is the people to whom the herdsmen had told their story.

kai ēlthon pros ton Iēsoun 'and they came to Jesus'. *ēlthon* denotes the result of *exēlthon* 'they went out'.

kai heuron kathēmenon ton anthrōpon...para tous podas tou Iēsou 'and they found the man sitting at Jesus' feet', i.e. as a disciple (cp. Acts 22 : 3).

himatismenon kai sōphronounta 'dressed and in his right mind', apposition to the noun in the participial clause in which it is inserted, and carrying the main semantic load.

himatizō (†) 'to dress', 'to clothe'.

sōphroneō (†) 'to be in one's right mind', of mental health.

kai ephobēthēsan 'and they were afraid', cp. on 1 : 13.

Translation: *People* may have to be specified, e.g. 'those who-had-been-told' (Javanese), 'those dwelling there', 'the inhabitants'.

If a break in the series of clauses is desirable, *they came* is best taken with what precedes, e.g. 'people went out to see...and came to Jesus (or, to where Jesus was). There they found...'.

And found the man...sitting..., or, 'and there they came upon the man...and saw him (or, saw how he was) sitting...', 'and there they perceived the man...; he was sitting...'. Cp. also on 7 : 10.

The man from whom the demons had gone, i.e. the man who was no longer demon possessed, the final result of what is told in vv. 29, 33.

Sitting at the feet of Jesus. The verb, suggesting an attitude of calm repose, contrasts with "driven" in v. 29. Where a literal rendering of the prepositional phrase would be misleading or unidiomatic it may be rendered, '(on the ground) before J.', 'near J.', 'beside J.' (Zarma, Tagabili), 'in the presence (lit. at the nose) of J.' (Kapauku). If the language possesses an idiom said of a disciple who sits listening attentively to his master its use should be considered here. — This and the following phrases may have to be rendered as separate clauses.

Clothed contrasts with "had worn no clothes" in v. 27.

In his right mind is rendered variously, e.g. 'come to his cleanness/purity' (Marathi), '(his) thoughts having become right' (Kapauku), 'his intelligence having-become clean again' (Sranan), 'having-mind' (Toba Batak), 'settled his mind' (East Toradja), or simply, 'settled/fixed' (Balinese), and cp. *TH-Mk* on 5 : 15.

36 ***And those who had seen it told them how he who had been possessed with demons was healed.***

Exegesis: *apēggeilan de autois hoi idontes* 'and those who had seen (it) told them'. Because *hoi idontes* has no object it is sometimes rendered as a substantive (cp. "the spectators", NEB, "eyewitnesses", BFBS).

pōs esōthē ho daimonistheis 'how the man who had been possessed was cured', syntactically dependent upon *apēggeilan*. For *sōzō* cp. on 7 : 50 and A-G s.v. 1 c.

daimonizomai (†) 'to be possessed by a demon'.

Translation: The sentence structure may have to be changed, e.g. 'those who had seen how he...was healed, told them this', or, 'those who had seen the healing of the man..., told them, how Jesus had done so'; cp. also *TH-Mk* on 5 : 16.

Them may have to be specified, e.g. 'those who came', "the others" (Phillips); for the same reason Javanese shifts to a passive form enabling the continuation of the subject of v. 35, 'they were informed by those who had seen'.

How he who...was healed, or, 'the way Jesus had healed the man who...' (Balinese), 'how he...became well' (cp. Marathi).

He who had been possessed, rendering the Greek aorist participle by a relative verbal clause in the past tense; most versions investigated, however, use (one of) their normal term(s) for 'the demoniac', not making explicit the past tense. Where this is stylistically preferable it usually is acceptable, since v. 35 precludes the possibility of misunderstanding.

Healed. The Greek verb used here is in other contexts rendered by 'to save' (for which see on 1 : 47), but in most languages idiom does not allow to preserve this formal identity.

37 ***Then all the people of the surrounding country of the Gerasenes asked him to depart from them; for they were seized with great fear; so he got into the boat and returned.***

Exegesis: *auton* 'him', refers to Jesus.

hapan to plēthos 'the whole crowd', 'all the people', cp. on 1 : 10.

tēs perichōrou tōn Gergesēnōn 'of the district of the Gergesenes', cp. on v. 26. *perichōros* 'neighbourhood', 'surrounding area' (cp. on 3 : 3 and 4 : 14) includes here the town Gergesa and is not restricted to the surrounding area.

phobō megalō suneichonto 'they were hard pressed with great fear' (cp. NEB). For *sunechō* cp. on 4 : 38.

autos de 'but he', emphatic.

embas eis ploion 'after getting into a boat', cp. on 5 : 3 and 8 : 22.

hupestrepsen 'he returned', viz. to Galilee.

Translation: *The surrounding country of the Gerasenes* (preferably, Gergesenes), here virtually the same as "the country of the G." in v. 26 (several Indonesian versions).

Asked him to depart from them, or, 'asked Jesus to leave them (or, their region), or, to depart from there, or, to go away from their "here" (as the idiomatic expression is in Marathi)'. The prepositional phrase may sound rather redundant; hence, "asked him to go (away)" (NEB, Rieu).

He got into the boat. Here again the pronoun is often better specified, 'Jesus'.

And returned. In some versions the rendering suggests that Jesus returned at once—with the result that the next verse becomes incomprehensible. To avoid this one may shift to a rendering that expresses intention, e.g. 'on the point of returning', 'in order to return' (Balinese,

Synodale), or to a verb that is less specific, cp. "and left them" (Rieu), or to a combination of both, cp. 'intending to depart' (Bahasa Indonesia RC).

38 ***The man from whom the demons had gone begged that he might be with him; but he sent him away, saying,***

Exegesis: *edeito de autou ho anēr* 'the man begged him'. The imperfect tense represents the act of begging as unfulfilled until the request has been granted (cp. on 7 : 36 and Bl-D, § 328).

einai sun autō lit. 'to be with him'. The final aspect of the infinitive is expressed by RSV. *einai* means here 'to be henceforth', 'to be continually', hence 'to stay'. Here to stay with Jesus implies to go with him.

apelusen de auton 'but he sent him away'. For *apoluō* cp. on 2 : 29. Here it has a stronger meaning, cp. A-G s.v. 2 b.

Translation: *That he might be with him,* or, 'that he might go with (or, accompany) him/Jesus', or, in direct discourse, 'let me stay with you' (Marathi), 'let us go together' (Enga).

He sent him away, implying that Jesus refused the man's request. Where a rather literal rendering would sound rude or would suggest rejection one may shift to something like, 'Jesus did not allow the man to stay/go with him', 'Jesus said to the man, "Stay here (or, in this country); (39) return to your home, ..."'.

39 ***"Return to your home, and declare how much God has done for you." And he went away, proclaiming throughout the whole city how much Jesus had done for him.***

Exegesis: *hupostrephe eis ton oikon sou* 'go back to your house'. *oikos* refers not so much to the building where he used to live but to the family who live in that building and of whom he used to be a part.

diēgou hosa soi epoiēsen ho theos 'tell all that God has done for you, or, to you', preferably the latter, since he is not only the recipient of God's blessing, but in the first place its object.

diēgeomai (also 9 : 10) 'to tell', 'to relate'.

kath' holēn tēn polin kērussōn 'proclaiming all over the town'. *kērussō* is a stronger and more specific word than *diēgeomai*. Here it has the connotation of proclaiming openly, or, loudly.

Translation: *Declare,* or, 'make-known/tell', if necessary adding an indirect object, e.g. 'to the people there'.

How much God has done for you, preferably, 'to you', or, 'God's big deed to you' (cp. Kapauku), 'how great things (or, all the great things that) God has done to you', 'that it is very good what God has done to you' (Tzeltal). For 'to do great things to' cp. also on 1 : 49.

Proclaiming throughout the whole city, or, "and told everyone in the town" (Rieu). For the verb see on 4 : 18.

40 ***Now when Jesus returned, the crowd welcomed him, for they were all waiting for him.***

Exegesis: *en de tō hupostrephein ton Iēsoun* 'when Jesus returned', articular infinitive in the present tense denoting an event which is simultaneous with the event to which the main verb refers, cp. Bl-D, § 404. Hence *hupostrephein* refers not to the journey back, but to the moment of arrival.

apedexato auton ho ochlos 'the crowd welcomed him'.

apodechomai (also 9 : 11) 'to welcome', 'to receive favourably'.

ēsan gar pantes prosdokōntes auton 'for they were all expecting him'. The periphrastic construction *ēsan...prosdokōntes* expresses duration. For *prosdokaō* cp. on 1 : 21.

Translation: *When Jesus returned,* i.e. to the other side of the lake (which has to be specified in Kituba), or, 'when J. arrived again' (Sundanese).

Welcomed, or, 'greeted joyfully' (Cuyono), 'came receive with pleasure' (Sranan); some Indonesian languages use 'met', 'came-to-meet'.

Waiting for him, cp. on 1 : 21. One may have to add the event waited for, e.g. 'waiting-for him to come' (Bahasa Indonesia), 'looked-out that he would arrive' (Sranan).

41 ***And there came a man named Jairus, who was a ruler of the synagogue; and falling at Jesus' feet he besought him to come to his house,*** 42a ***for he had an only daughter, about twelve years of age, and she was dying.***

Exegesis: *kai idou* lit. 'and behold', cp. on 1 : 20.

kai houtos archōn tēs sunagōgēs hupērchen 'and he was leader of the synagogue', or *archisunagōgos* (cp. on v. 49). The article *tēs* before *sunagōgēs* suggests that the reference is to the one local synagogue. Syntactically the clause is best understood as a free continuation of the (nominal) relative clause *hō onoma Iaïros* 'whose name was Jairus'. For *huparchō* cp. on 7 : 25.

pesōn para tous podas tou Iēsou 'falling at Jesus' feet'. Semantically there is no difference between this phrase (also 17 : 16 where *epi prosōpon* 'on his face' is added) and *prospiptein* with dative (cp. 5 : 8; 8 : 28, 47), 'to fall down before'. In both phrases it is implied that the face touches the ground before the feet of the other person involved.

parekalei auton eiselthein eis ton oikon autou 'he begged him to come to his house'. For the imperfect tense of *parekalei* cp. Bl-D, § 328. For *parakaleō* cp. on 3 : 18.

(V. 42[a]) *hoti thugatēr monogenēs ēn autō hōs etōn dōdeka kai autē apethnēsken* 'for he had an only daughter of about twelve years and she was dying', explaining Jairus' request. Syntactically the two clauses are coordinate but semantically the second clause is the most important, to which the first one is subordinate. *monogenēs* implies that the girl was an only child (cp. on 7 : 12 and Phillips). *apethnēsken* means that she was about to die.

Translation: *Ruler of the synagogue,* or, 'one who directed the affairs of the synagogue', 'the head/chief of the s.' (Sundanese, Sranan). Where *synagogue* has been rendered as 'mosque' a term denoting a comparable Muslim official has been used, e.g. in Malay; cp. also *TH-Mk* on 5 : 22.

Falling at Jesus' feet, cp. on "he fell down at Jesus' knees" in 5 : 8.

Besought him to come to his house. One or both pronouns may have to be specified. For *to beseech* cp. on 5 : 12; Tagabili shifts to direct discourse, 'appealed to Jesus, he said, "Would you call-in as-a-favour-to me at my house"'.

(V. 42[a]) Changing the sentence structure in agreement with its semantic value one may say, "for his daughter, an only child about twelve years old, was dying" (Phillips, similarly e.g. in Javanese), or, 'because his daughter was dying. She was his only child, about twelve years old'.

He had an only daughter may have to be described, cp. e.g. 'his daughter, he had no other child (or, no child but her)'; cp. also on 7 : 12. For *daughter* cp. *N.T.Wb.*/22.

About twelve years of age, cp. *TH-Mk* on 5 : 42.

Was dying is variously rendered, 'was nearly dead, or, near to dying' (Bahasa Indonesia), 'very ill, about to die' (Javanese), 'was (already) in her death agony' (Shona), 'already unconscious' (Tagabili), 'will only die (i.e. she cannot but die)' (South Toradja). Words with the general meaning of 'nearly', 'almost', 'about', have to be handled carefully in some languages (e.g. Lokele, Balinese), because they may imply an awareness of the speaker that the event referred to, though dreaded, did not actually happen. Cp. also on "at the point of death" in 7 : 2.

42b ***As he went, the people pressed round him.***

Exegesis: *en de tō hupagein auton* 'as he was going'.

hupagō 'to go', with the implication of going in a certain direction, here to the house of Jairus.

hoi ochloi sunepnigon auton 'the crowds pressed hard on him'. For *sumpnigō* cp. on v. 14. Here it has the connotation of almost crushing (cp. BFBS) or, of (nearly) suffocating a person (cp. NEB), preferably the latter.

Translation: *As he went,* or, 'while he/Jesus went there'.

The people pressed round him, or such a rendering as, 'his body came to be pressed/squeezed by the crowd' (Javanese). *The people,* cp. on "the multitudes" in 3 : 7; the verb is a slightly stronger synonym of the one used in 5 : 1.

43 ***And a woman who had had a flow of blood for twelve years and could not be healed by any one,*** 44 ***came up behind him, and touched the fringe of his garment; and immediately her flow of blood ceased.***

Exegesis: *kai gunē...hēpsato* 'and a woman...touched'. *gunē* and *hēpsato* are subject and main verb in a long sentence. With *gunē* go (a) *ousa en rusei haimatos apo etōn dōdeka* lit. 'being in a hemorrhage since twelve years', conjunctive participle, and (b) *hētis ouk ischusen ap' oudenos therapeuthēnai* 'who could not be healed by any one'; (a) and (b) together serve to identify the woman by describing her hopeless plight. With the verb *hēpsato* goes the participle *proselthousa opisthen* 'coming up behind', which describes the first stage of her action.

ousa en rusei haimatos 'being in a flow of blood', i.e. 'suffering from a hemorrhage'. For this phrase cp. *TH-Mk* on 5 : 25 and references there. *rusis* (†).

apo etōn dōdeka 'since twelve years' (cp. A-G s.v. *apo* II 2 a) implying that the illness had begun twelve years ago and had lasted ever since.

hētis...ouk ischusen ap' oudenos therapeuthēnai 'who could not be healed by any one', or, "whom nobody had been able to cure" (Goodspeed), in order to bring out the connotation of 'being able', which *ischuō* often has (cp. on 6 : 48). For *therapeuō* cp. on 4 : 23.

[*iatrois prosanalōsasa holon ton bion*] 'having spent all her property on physicians', cp. A-G s.v. *prosanaliskō* (††). The participle has concessive force.

bios 'life', here 'means of subsistence', 'property', cp. A-G s.v. 3.

(V. 44) *proselthousa opisthen* 'after coming up behind, or, from behind', in the latter case implying that she stayed behind him. *opisthen* also 23 : 26.

hēpsato tou kraspedou tou himatiou autou 'touched the hem, or, tassel of his garment'.

kraspedon (†) 'hem', or, 'tassel', cp. A-G s.v., *IDB* IV, 520 and *TH-Mk* on 6 : 56. The latter rendering is slightly preferable. Cp. also Num. 15 : 38ff and Deut. 22 : 12.

kai parachrēma estē hē rusis tou haimatos autēs 'and immediately her hemorrhage stopped', cp. A-G s.v. *histēmi* II 1 a. The possessive genitive *autēs* goes with *haimatos*.

Translation: For vv. 43-48 cp. also *TH-Mk* on 5 : 25-34. The sentence structure of vv. 43f may have to be simplified, e.g. 'among them (or, in the crowd) was a woman who had (or, a certain woman; she had) suffered from a flow of blood... ; nobody had been able to cure her. (V. 44) She came up...and touched...At once her flow of blood ceased'.

Who had had a flow of blood, cp. *TH-Mk* on 5 : 26. The Balinese non-vulgar term, 'illness (that makes) ritually-impure', expresses a religious view that closely parallels biblical concepts: impurity according to Jewish ritual law was one of the reasons why the woman did not act openly.

To heal, here, of course, the recovery from a non-congenital disease is meant. In some cases a hemorrhage is not said to be 'healed' but to be 'stopped' (South Toradja, and cp. the Greek in v. 44).

(V. 44) *Came up behind him*, or, 'approached him from behind', 'was able to come near to his back', or more contextually, 'made her way towards him from behind, or, at his back'.

Touched, see *TH-Mk* on 5 : 28. The verb or verbal form used should express or imply an intentional act.

The fringe of his garment. The loose end of the rather short square uppergarment was usually thrown over the left shoulder, so that it came to hang on the upper part of the back; it will have been the 'fringe' or 'tassel' attached to this end, that the woman touched, since it was only this part of Jesus' dress that could be reached in the situation described. A term suggesting a place low down (such as 'foot of his robe', found in one version), should not be used. If *fringe,* or, 'tassel', has to be described, one may say, 'the loose threads at (or, that adorned) the hem, or, the end of his uppergarment'. For *garment* cp. on "cloak" in 6 : 29.

Her flow of blood ceased, or, 'the blood stopped to flow', 'her blood dried-up' (Balinese), 'her hemorrhage ceased' (NV), 'her illness (or, she) was-healed' (East Toradja).

45 ***And Jesus said, "Who was it that touched me?" When all denied it, Peter said, "Master, the multitudes surround you and press upon you!"***

Exegesis: *tis ho hapsamenos mou* 'who (was it) that touched me', nominal clause in which the participle with article serves as predicate.

arnoumenōn de pantōn 'and when all denied', scil. having touched Jesus.

arneomai 'to refuse', 'to deny'.

epistata 'master', cp. on 5 : 5.

hoi ochloi sunechousin se kai apothlibousin 'the crowds are hemming you in and pressing upon you', answering Jesus' question by stating implicitly that no answer is possible.

sunechō (also 19 : 43) 'to crowd', 'to hem in', 'to surround'.

apothlibō (††) 'to press upon (somebody)', stronger than *sunechō.*

Translation: *Who was it that touched me?,* or, placing the participle clause first, 'someone touched me, who is it?'.

All denied it, or, 'there was no-one that admitted (it)' (Balinese, Bahasa Indonesia RC), 'they said all it was not they' (Sranan), 'everyone said, "It was not I who did so, or, who touched you"'.

The multitudes surround you and press upon you, implying astonishment, which may be indicated by the exclamatory form of the sentence, or, more explicitly, by preposing some such phrase as, 'how can you ask that!' The two verbs form a closely knit unit (as is shown by the fact that the object is only expressed with the first); hence renderings by one verb or verbal expression, e.g. 'push your person' (Sundanese), 'are rubbing-themselves-against you' (South Toradja), or by one verb to which the other is subordinated, cp. e.g. "you are surrounded by people jostling you" (Rieu, similarly Bahasa Indonesia RC). Such verbs or phrases are virtually synonymous with "pressed round him" in v. 42^{b}.

46 ***But Jesus said, "Some one touched me; for I perceive that power has gone forth from me."***

Exegesis: *egō gar egnōn dunamin exelēluthuian ap' emou* 'for I perceived that power had gone out from me'. For the meaning of *egnōn* cp. A-G s.v. *ginōskō* 4 a. For the construction *dunamin exelēluthuian* cp. Bl-D, § 416.2. The perfect tense of *exelēluthuian* does not refer to an event preceding that of the main verb but points to an accomplished situation.

Translation: *Some one touched me,* or better to mark the clause as a refutation, 'no, some one did touch me'. The verb, again, expresses an intentional act, whereas unintentional touching was implied in Peter's remark.

I perceive, or, 'I know/feel', 'I am aware'.

That power has gone forth from me, cp. *TH-Mk* on 5 : 30. If 'power' has to be possessed in this context, one may say, 'some power of mine', 'part of my power'. The healing is probably not to be envisaged as an intentional act on Jesus' part.

47 ***And when the woman saw that she was not hidden, she came trembling, and falling down before him declared in the presence of all the people why she had touched him, and how she had been immediately healed.***

Exegesis: *idousa...tremousa ēlthen kai prospesousa...apēggeilen* 'seeing ..., she came trembling and after falling down...she told...'. The first participle *idousa* denotes an event which precedes and determines all subsequent events; *tremousa* refers to an experience which occurs together with the event denoted by *ēlthen*; *prospesousa* describes an event which precedes that of the main verb *apēggeilen.*

hoti ouk elathen 'that she had not escaped notice', i.e. Jesus' notice.

lanthanō (†) 'to be hidden', 'to escape notice'.

tremousa ēlthen 'trembling she came (forward)', viz. to Jesus; hence "she approached" (Rieu). *tremō* (†).

prospesousa autō 'after falling down before him', or using a finite verbal form 'she fell down before him'. For the idiom cp. on 5 : 8 and 8 : 41.

di' hēn aitian hēpsato autou 'why she had touched him'. The aorist tense has here the force of a pluperfect. *di' hēn aitian* (*aitia* †) lit. 'for which reason', hence 'why'. The clause is dependent upon *apēggeilen.*

apēggeilen enōpion pantos tou laou 'she told before all the people', i.e. so that all people could hear. For *apaggellō* cp. on 7 : 18; for *enōpion* on 1 : 15; for *pas ho laos* on 3 : 21.

kai hōs iathē parachrēma 'and how she had been cured at once'. *hōs* is rendered 'that' by some translations (cp. BFBS, NV). This is possible though less probable. This clause is also dependent upon *apēggeilen.* This order of one dependent clause of indirect speech before, and one after the modifying verb is a characteristic of literary Greek.

Translation: For the "when"-clause see on v. 34.

Saw, or, 'realized', 'became aware', 'perceived'.

She was not hidden, or, 'she could not keep herself concealed', 'she could not keep concealed her deed (or, what she had done)' (cp. Balinese,

East Toradja, Toba Batak); or with a further shift, "she had been found out" (TEV).

Trembling, or, 'with trembling body', 'her body trembling' (Balinese); where 'trembling' does not indicate fear one may add a qualifying term, e.g. 'trembling with fear/terror', or shift to, 'very much afraid'.

Falling down before him may better become an independent clause, cp. TEV; for *to fall down before* cp. on "fell down at Jesus' knees" in 5 : 8.

Declared, or, 'told him'.

In the presence of all the people, or, 'before the ears of all the people', 'so that all the people could hear it'. For *all the people* see on 3 : 21.

Why she had touched him, or, "her reason for touching him" (Rieu), 'what had led/caused her to touch him'.

How she had been immediately healed, or (where necessary to avoid a rendering that would suggest an exact description), 'that she had been... healed', cp. also, 'her-being-healed at-once' (Toba Batak), 'about the-being-cured of her-illness at that very moment' (East Toradja). Where a shift to active form is necessary one should use 'how/that she had...recovered (or, become well) immediately, or, as soon as she had touched Jesus', rather than 'how/that Jesus had healed her...'.

48 ***And he said to her, "Daughter, your faith has made you well; go in peace."***

Exegesis: *thugatēr* 'daughter', a friendly greeting to a woman, cp. A-G s.v. 2 a and *TH-Mk* on 5 : 34. The nominative has here the force of a vocative.

hē pistis sou sesōken se 'your faith has made you well'; cp. on 7 : 50 and *TH-Mk* on 5 : 34.

poreuou eis eirēnēn 'go in peace', cp. on 7 : 50 and *TH-Mk* on 5 : 34.

Translation: *Daughter,* here serving as a general form for addressing women, cp. *N.T.Wb./22*. Toba Batak uses a vocative form 'you mother', which can even be used in speaking to a young girl; the same is true of several languages in Africa.

Your faith has made you well. For possibly necessary changes in the sentence structure cp. on "your faith has saved you" in 7 : 50. Here Tagabili renders *your faith* by 'your confidence (lit. the being hard your breath) in me'. For *made well* cp. on "healed" in 8 : 36.

Go in peace, see again on 7 : 50.

49 ***While he was still speaking, a man from the ruler's house came and said, "Your daughter is dead; do not trouble the Teacher any more."***

Exegesis: *eti autou lalountos* 'while he was still speaking', cp. *TH-Mk* on 5 : 35.

erchetai tis 'somebody came'. The historical present (cp. Bl-D, § 321) has a note of suddenness.

para tou archisunagōgou lit. 'from the leader of the synagogue', or, since he is with Jesus and not at home, 'from the house of the leader of the synagogue' (cp. Jerusalem, *de chez le chef*).

archisunagōgos (also 13 : 14) 'leader, or president of the synagogue', whose duty it was to take care of the arrangements for the worship services (cp. A-G s.v. and *TH-Mk* on 5 : 22).

legōn hoti 'saying', introducing direct speech.

tethnēken hē thugatēr sou 'your daughter has died', but in English better rendered 'your daughter is dead', cp. on 7 : 12.

mēketi skulle ton didaskalon 'do not trouble the teacher anymore'. For *skullō* cp. on 7 : 6. *didaskalos* as a title occurs usually in the vocative (cp. on 3 : 12), but here in the accusative.

Translation: For vv. 49-56 see *TH-Mk* on 5 : 35-43.

While he was still speaking, or, 'he was still speaking, there/suddenly...' (Balinese); the idea of continuance inherent in "still" may here be rendered otherwise, cp. "before he had finished speaking" (Rieu).

Your daughter is dead; do not trouble the Teacher any more. Supposing that the messenger is one of the ruler's servants, languages like Javanese, Sundanese will use honorific forms here. The first clause is the actual message, the second points to the consequences of the new situation; it expresses not a prohibition but an advice, 'you should not...', or 'there is no need now to...'. For *to trouble*, or, 'to bother', 'to put to inconvenience', 'to give labour' (Marathi), cp. also on the reflexive form in 7 : 6. Sometimes a circumlocutionary rendering of the verb must be given, cp. e.g. 'do not keep saying to the teacher, "Please, come (to my house)"', or, 'Why don't you say to the teacher, "You are not to come"?' (Auca). — If *Teacher* has to be possessed one may say 'our (inclus.) Teacher/Master'.

50 ***But Jesus on hearing this answered him, "Do not fear; only believe, and she shall be well."***

Exegesis: *ho de Iēsous akousas apekrithē autō* 'but when Jesus heard (this) he said to him', cp. on 1 : 60. The object of *akousas* which is not stated, are the words spoken by the man from Jairus' house. *autō* refers to Jairus.

mē phobou 'do not be afraid', cp. *TH-Mk* on 5 : 36.

monon pisteuson 'only believe'. The aorist tense of the imperative suggests the punctiliar nature of the injunction, 'have faith (or, believe) right now (or, at this very moment)', now that the sad message that she is dead has come. *monon* (†).

kai sōthēsetai 'and she will be well'; subject is the daughter.

Translation: *Answered him.* The pronoun refers to Jairus, not to the messenger; hence preferably, 'said to Jairus, or, to the ruler' (cp. Rieu, Balinese), 'interposed a word towards Jairus' (Javanese, and cp. NEB); see also on 3 : 16.

Only believe, or, 'do nothing except believe', 'have faith, nothing else'. For *only* cp. on 4 : 8; for the verb see the references on "faith" in 5 : 20.

She shall be well. The Greek verb does not contrast here with demon possession (v. 36) or illness (v. 48), but with death, which may make necessary another rendering, e.g. 'she shall live (again)' (Toba Batak), 'she shall have her spirit of life returned to her', or, 'she shall be snatched (back to life)' (two alternatives in Cuyono). A more generic expression is also used, e.g. 'it will again return good yet that (i.e. it is going to be all right)' (Tagabili).

51 ***And when he came to the house, he permitted no one to enter with him, except Peter and John and James, and the father and mother of the child.***

Exegesis: *elthōn de eis tēn oikian* 'when he came to the house'. The fact that all other people concerned accompany Jesus is taken for granted.

ouk aphēken eiselthein tina sun autō 'he let nobody go in with him'.

aphiēmi 'to permit', 'to let'.

kai ton patera tēs paidos kai tēn mētera 'and the child's father and mother'. *tēs paidos*, though syntactically going with *ton patera* only, refers to *tēn mētera* as well.

hē pais 'the girl'.

Translation: *He came to*, 'he arrived at', 'came near to', 'reached', 'was/stood at the entrance of'.

Permitted no one to enter, or expressing the prohibition otherwise, 'forbade everyone to enter', 'said to all the people (there), "You should not enter", or, "I want you not to go into the house"'.

No one...except may have to be expressed by, 'no one...only', 'only a few people, namely', or, with the shift discussed above, 'everyone...but not'; and cp. *TBT*, 16.131, 1965.

For the sequence of *father and mother* see on 2 : 33.

Child (see on 1 : 7), or, specifying the sex, 'girl', see *TH-Mk* on 5 : 39; cp. also *N.T.Wb.*/75, WOMAN.

52 ***And all were weeping and bewailing her; but he said, "Do not weep; for she is not dead but sleeping."***

Exegesis: *eklaion de pantes kai ekoptonto autēn* 'and all were weeping and beating their breasts for her'. Note the durative aspect of the imperfect tense. *pantes* is best taken to refer to the people in the house. For *klaiō* cp. on 7 : 32.

koptomai (also 23 : 27) 'to beat one's breast as an act of mourning', 'to mourn greatly', cp. A-G s.v. *koptō* 2.

mē klaiete 'stop weeping'.

ou gar apethanen alla katheudei 'for she has not died but she is asleep'. The difference between *apethanen* and *tethnēken* (v. 49) is that the former refers to the moment of dying as a punctiliar event and the latter to her being dead as a permanent situation. *katheudei* (also 22 : 46) may refer to natural sleep, or, figuratively to the sleep of death, preferably the former because of the contrast with *apethanen*. Cp. also *TH-Mk* on 5 : 39.

Translation: *Were weeping and bewailing her,* or, 'were weeping and wailing because of her', cp. 'called cried for her' (Sranan, using an idiom for loud lamentation). The pronoun goes with both verbs, which are closely connected syntactically, and also semantically, cp. on 7 : 32 and reference; one of them may better be subordinated, cp. e.g. 'wept-over her, wailing' (Balinese). *To bewail* must often be rendered by the same term as used for "to wail" in 7 : 32, although the Greek verb used here seems to refer to outward behaviour, gestures etc., suggestive of grief and mourning rather than to sounds or songs of lamentation.

Do not weep, or, 'stop weeping', 'weep no more', mentioning only one of the preceding verbs, but referring to the situation in its totality.

She is not dead but sleeping is strongly contrastive, cp. 'she has not died, (on-the-contrary) she is asleep'.

53 ***And they laughed at him, knowing that she was dead.***

Exegesis: *kai kategelōn autou* 'but they laughed at him'; durative imperfect.

katagelaō (only here and parallels in the N.T.) with following genitive of the person, 'to laugh at', 'to jeer at'.

eidotes hoti apethanen 'because they knew that she had died'. *eidotes* (participle of *oida* 'to know') refers to positive knowledge.

Translation: *They laughed at him,* or, 'they mocked him', and cp. *TH-Mk* on 5 : 40.

Knowing. They knew it to be an undeniable fact; hence more emphatical renderings, e.g. 'because they knew very well' (Bahasa Indonesia RC, similarly Balinese, Sundanese).

54 ***But taking her by the hand he called, saying, "Child, arise."***

Exegesis: *autos de* 'but he', emphatic.

kratēsas tēs cheiros autēs 'after seizing her hand', or 'taking her by the hand'.

krateō (also 24 : 16) 'to seize', 'to grasp', with the genitive of the part grasped.

ephōnēsen legōn 'he called out, saying'. For *phōneō* cp. on v. 8 and A-G s.v. 1 b.

hē pais, egeire 'child, get up'. *hē pais* is a nominative with the force of a vocative. For *egeire* cp. A-G s.v. 1 b and *TH-Mk* on 5 : 41.

Translation: *Taking her by the hand he called, saying,* or in co-ordinated clauses, 'he took her by the hand (or, took hold of her hand) and (he) called (or, said loudly, or, said in a loud voice)'. *Her* may have to be specified, e.g. 'the child/girl', 'the dead one' (Javanese).

Child, here in the vocative; some renderings used are, 'girl (lit. woman/ female)' (Balinese, employing a term for addressing a female person in a friendly way), or, a kind of name-substitute used by parents to their young daughter (South Toradja), or a term of endearment for little girls (Cuyono). Sometimes a pronoun of the second person is added, better to bring out the vocative force (e.g. Toba Batak).

Arise, or, 'get up', 'stand up'; and cp. *TH-Mk* on 5 : 41.

55 ***And her spirit returned, and she got up at once; and he directed that something should be given her to eat.***

Exegesis: *kai epestrepsen to pneuma autēs* 'and her spirit returned'. For *epistrephō* cp. on 2 : 39 and A-G s.v. 1 b α. *pneuma* means here 'life-spirit', and the clause implies that she came back to life from death, cp. A-G s.v. 2.

kai anestē parachrēma 'and she rose immediately', viz. from the bed.

kai dietaxen autē dothēnai phagein lit. 'and he ordered to be given to her to eat', i.e. 'he ordered to give her something to eat'. For *diatassō* cp. on 3 : 13. The infinitive *dothēnai* is in the passive since its subject is not explicitly stated. The infinitive *phagein* is best understood as having final force ('to give (something) in order to eat', i.e. that she might eat), but may also be interpreted as the object of *dothēnai* and be rendered as 'food' (cp. Phillips).

Translation: *Her spirit returned.* Since the concept of the life principle leaving the body at death is widespread, it will often be possible to use a rather close formal equivalent, using 'spirit', or, 'soul', 'breath', 'life', etc. Where, however, such a term can indicate also the vital force of a living person, such a literal rendering may have the wrong meaning, e.g. because the phrase is idiomatically used of a person who becomes strong or courageous again, after having been exhausted or afraid, or of a person who grows up/matures, as is the case in Tzeltal; then one may better say something like 'she became alive again'. For *spirit* cp. also on 1 : 47.

At once, cp. on "immediately" in 1 : 64.

He may have to be specified, e.g. 'Jesus'.

Directed that something should be given her to eat, or, 'said that they should give her something to eat'. *To give to eat* is sometimes rendered by a causative form of 'to eat', e.g. in South Toradja.

56 ***And her parents were amazed; but he charged them to tell no one what had happened.***

Exegesis: *kai exestēsan hoi goneis autēs* 'and her parents were astounded'. As a comparison with 2 : 47 shows this is a moderate phrase and less strong than the parallel Mk. 5 : 42.

parēggeilen 'he ordered', cp. on 5 : 14.

to gegonos 'what had happened', cp. *TH-Mk* on 5 : 14.

Translation: For *parents* see on 2 : 27, and for *amazed* on "wondered" in 1 : 21.

He charged them to tell no one, cp. on 5 : 14.

CHAPTER NINE

1 ***And he called the twelve together and gave them power and authority over all demons and to cure diseases,***

Exegesis: *sugkalesamenos...tous dōdeka* 'after calling together the twelve'. For *tous dōdeka* cp. 8 : 1.

sugkaleō 'to call together', i.e. to call a group of people to oneself, 'to summon'.

edōken autois dunamin kai exousian 'he gave them power and authority', cp. on 4 : 32 and 36.

epi panta ta daimonia 'over all the demons', dependent upon *dunamin kai exousian* (cp. Rieu, "to deal with every kind of demon"; cp. also NEB). For *daimonion* cp. on 4 : 33.

kai nosous therapeuein 'and to cure diseases', dependent upon *dunamin kai exousian* and parallel to *epi panta ta daimonia* (cp. RSV and others).

Translation: *He called the twelve together,* or, 'he caused-to-assemble the twelve disciples' (East Toradja); or, bringing out the implication mentioned in *Exegesis,* 'he called/ordered the twelve companions to assemble before him' (Javanese). *The twelve,* see on 8 : 1.

Power and authority, i.e. power, and the authority or right to use it.

Over demons, or, 'to dominate demons' (Javanese, similarly Sranan, lit. 'to boss demons'), 'to combat/expel demons' (Toba Batak, Balinese). For *demons* cp. references on 4 : 35.

To cure diseases. In order to make clear the syntactic structure one may have to repeat (part of) the preceding clause, e.g. 'also power (and authority) to cure...', 'also gave/enabled them to cure...' (East Toradja 1933), or, 'gave them power to cure...'. For *to cure* see on "to heal" in 4 : 23, for *diseases* see on 4 : 40.

2 ***and he sent them out to preach the kingdom of God and to heal.***

Exegesis: *kai apesteilen autous kērussein tēn basileian tou theou kai iasthai* [*tous astheneis*] 'and he sent them out to proclaim the kingdom of God and to heal the sick'. For *apostellō* cp. on 1 : 19. For *kērussein tēn basileian tou theou* cp. on 4 : 43f and 8 : 1. *tous astheneis* is omitted by Nestle.

asthenēs (also 10 : 9) lit. 'weak', hence 'sick', 'ill'.

Translation: *He sent them out.* The pronoun may have to be specified, e.g. 'those men', 'the twelve', 'his disciples'.

To preach, cp. on 3 : 3.

3 ***And he said to them, "Take nothing for your journey, no staff, nor bag, nor bread, nor money; and do not have two tunics.***

Exegesis: *mēden airete eis tēn hodon* 'do not take anything for the journey'. For *airō* cp. on 4 : 11; here it is used in the weakened meaning 'to take', or, 'to carry along'. For *eis tēn hodon* cp. A-G s.v. *hodos* 1 b.

mēte rabdon mēte pēran lit. 'nor a staff, nor a bag', elaborations of *mēden* (as are the following phrases).

rabdos (†) 'staff', 'rod', used in travelling.

pēra 'knapsack', 'traveller's bag', or (possibly but not preferably) 'beggar's sack' (cp. A-G s.v., *TH-Mk* on 6 : 8).

mēte arton mēte argurion lit. 'nor bread nor money'. They are to live on what will be given to them.

argurion 'money', cp. A-G s.v. 2 b, and *N.T.Wb.*, 97/.

mēte [*ana*] *duo chitōnas echein* lit. 'nor to have two undergarments each'. The infinitive *echein* may be an imperatival infinitive (Klostermann, cp. Bl-D, § 389), or represent a shift from direct to indirect speech (Plummer), in which case it is dependent on *eipen*. The latter is slightly preferable. For *ana* in its distributive meaning 'each', 'a piece', cp. A-G s.v. 3. For *chitōn* cp. on 3 : 11.

Translation: *Take nothing*, or, 'take nothing with you'. *Nothing*, or where this would be hyperbolical, 'no such things as', to be taken with the following negative phrases.

For your journey, or as a verbal clause, 'when you go (or, go-on-journey)', either at the end or at the beginning of the clause (South Toradja, Balinese).

No..., nor (thrice), repeating the negation in the elaborating phrases. Some languages prefer phrases governed by one negative particle, cp. e.g. 'do not take-with-you necessities for travel, as-there-are, staff, bag,...etc.' (Javanese, Sundanese), 'no..., or (thrice)' (Toba Batak, East Toradja). Elsewhere such a series is preferably given in pairs, 'staff (n)or bag, food (n)or money' (cp. South Toradja).

Bag, or, 'knapsack (lit. place for provisions)' (Bahasa Indonesia in 10 : 4), 'basket' (Toba Batak; similarly East Toradja 1933 in 10 : 4, lit. 'that-in-which-something-is-carried-on-the-back'), 'bundle' (Balinese, using a derivation of the verb 'to tie (up)', similarly Sranan in 10 : 4); or with a shift from the container to the contents, 'provisions' (Low Malay, East Toradja, in 10 : 4).

Bread, or, 'a piece of bread', see references on 4 : 3.

Money, or, 'some money', 'a sum of money'. Where a generic term for the means of payment locally in use (such as 'cowrie shells', in Kapauku) is lacking, a generic plural of a commonly accepted local coin may be possible.

Do not have two tunics, or, "nor are you each to have a second coat" (NEB). A shift from direct to indirect discourse (the interpretation preferred in *Exegesis*) will often be undesirable in the receptor language; then the other interpretation is to be followed, as done in RSV and the majority of the versions investigated; a few versions omit the verb, cp. TEV. *To have two tunics* may refer to the wearing of two tunics/shirts, the one over the other, or to taking one extra for change. If one must choose, the first is preferable. For the noun see on "coat" in 3 : 11.

4 ***And whatever house you enter, stay there, and from there depart.***

Exegesis: *eis hēn an oikian eiselthēte, ekei menete* 'whatever house you enter, stay there'. The clause appears to mean that in each place the disciples are to stay in the very first house which offers them hospitality.

kai ekeithen exerchesthe 'and (when you leave that place) go away from there', i.e. stay in that house as long as you stay in that town (cp. Rieu, "leave it only when you leave the town").

Translation: For this verse cp. also *TH-Mk* on 6:10. To avoid misunderstanding several terms will have to be specified.

Enter, i.e. 'enter to stay', cp. "go to stay in" (Goodspeed).

Stay there, i.e. settle in there, or, in that house, for the time of your visit to that town; hence, 'lodge there' (Balinese, Sundanese).

From there is emphatic, 'from that same place' (Kapauku), 'leaving from it (i.e. that house)' (Shona 1963).

Depart, i.e. 'depart to another town' (Sinhalese), 'continue your journey' (Shona 1963, Balinese).

5 ***And wherever they do not receive you, when you leave that town shake off the dust from your feet as a testimony against them."***

Exegesis: *hosoi an mē dechōntai humas* lit. 'as many as do not welcome you' (cp. A-G s.v. *hosos* 2) i.e. 'as for all those who do not welcome you' (cp. BFBS, NEB). The relative pronoun *hosoi* is not taken up by a corresponding demonstrative pronoun, but indirectly by *tēs poleōs ekeinēs* 'that town'. This shows that the clause *hosoi...humas* does not refer to the negative reactions of individuals but to the population of a certain town, or, towns, as a whole.

exerchomenoi apo tēs poleōs ekeinēs lit. 'when you leave that town' (cp. NEB); with a shift to an imperative because of *apotinassete* "leave that town" (Phillips).

ton koniorton apo tōn podōn humōn apotinassete 'shake the dust off your feet', cp. 10:11.

koniortos (also 10:11) 'dust', refers here to the dust in the streets.

apotinassō (†) 'to shake off'.

eis marturion ep' autous 'as a testimony against them'. For *marturion* cp. on 5:14 and A-G s.v. 1 a. The shaking off of the dust serves as a demonstration, or, a warning, or, a protest against those who do not receive the disciples.

Translation: *Wherever they do not receive you*, or, 'in a town where they do not receive you', 'if the people/inhabitants of a town reject you'. The verb *to receive* is used with personal object in the sense of 'to let a person come to one'; hence, 'to allow a person to approach' (in 15:2), 'to welcome a person (to one's house, or, as one's guest)' (9:5; 10:38; 16:4, 9, and cp. on "welcomed" in 8:40, and *TH-Mk* on 6:11), which may imply readiness to help (a child, 9 : 48[a]), or, when Jesus or his disciples are the guests, acceptance of and obedience to their words (9 : 48[b]; 10 : 8, 10; 19 : 6).

When you leave that town shake..., preferably two imperatives, 'leave (or, go away from) that town and shake...', or, better to bring out the simultaneousness, "leave their town, and as you do so shake..." (Rieu). For *town* cp. on "city" in 1 : 26.

Shake off the dust from your feet. The expression, as used by Jesus, is not a metaphor but refers to a well known custom, which may best be rendered literally. For a footnote, if required, cp. Plummer's "It signified that henceforth they had not the smallest thing in common with the place". — *Shake*, or, 'dust off' (Shona 1966), 'wipe off', if that is the more common gesture (Balinese, similarly Marathi). *Dust.* In some languages the same or cognate words are used to refer to 'dust' and to 'ash' (East Toradja, Sundanese), or to 'dust' and to 'powder/pollen' (Toba Batak, cp. Malay); in South Toradja the word lit. means 'what-is-like-husked-rice'. The phrase *from your feet* is in some cases better taken with the noun, e.g. 'the dust on your feet, or, that sticks to your feet' (cp. e.g. Trukese, Malay). Instead of 'your feet' one may have to use 'the soles of your feet' (e.g. in South Toradja), cp. also 'from underneath of your feet' (Kituba).

As a testimony against them, serving to indicate the meaning of the gesture just mentioned. Some more meaningful renderings are, 'as-breaking-off sign against those people' (Balinese, making use of a term commonly referring to the severing of relationships), 'to denounce (lit. to say-to-be-mistaken-to) those people' (East Toradja 1933), 'that it will be a sign of accusation to-them' (Trukese); and cp. *TH-Mk, l.c.*

6 ***And they departed and went through the villages, preaching the gospel and healing everywhere.***

Exegesis: *exerchomenoi de diērchonto kata tas kōmas* 'and setting forth they went from village to village', or, 'and they set forth and went'. Semantically *exerchomenoi* and *diērchonto* are not simultaneous but the latter follows the former. For *dierchomai* cp. on 2 : 15. For *kata* cp. on 8 : 1, 4.

euaggelizomenoi kai therapeuontes pantachou 'preaching (the good news) and healing everywhere'. *pantachou* (†) goes with both participles.

Translation: *They*, or, 'the disciples' (Sundanese).

Went through the villages, cp. on 8 : 1.

Preaching the gospel, or, 'announcing the good news', see on 3 : 18.

Everywhere, or, 'all-around' (Balinese), 'in all places (they visited)', 'wherever they came'.

7 ***Now Herod the tetrarch heard of all that was done, and he was perplexed, because it was said by some that John had been raised from the dead,*** 8 ***by some that Elijah had appeared, and by others that one of the old prophets had risen.***

Exegesis: *ēkousen de Hērōdēs ho tetraarchēs* 'Herod, the tetrarch heard'.

The loose connexion with the preceding is expressed by renderings like "now" (NEB), 'in the mean time' for *de*. For *Hērōdēs ho tetraarchēs* cp. on 3 : 1, 19.

ta ginomena panta 'all that was happening', i.e. all that Jesus did and said.

kai diēporei 'and he was perplexed', i.e. "and (he) did not know what to make of it" (NEB). *diaporeō* (†).

dia to legesthai hupo tinōn hoti...hupo tinōn de hoti...allōn de hoti... lit. 'because of it being said by some that..., by some that..., (by) others that...', i.e. 'because some people said...', etc.

Iōannēs ēgerthē ek nekrōn 'John had risen from the dead'. For the meaning of *egeirō* cp. 7 : 14.

ek nekrōn 'from (among) the dead', i.e. from the realm of the dead.

(V. 8) *hoti Ēlias ephanē* 'that Elijah had appeared'.

phainomai (also 24 : 11) 'to appear', here of someone who had not died but had been transferred to heaven (cp. 2 Kings 2 : 1-18).

hoti prophētēs tis tōn archaiōn anestē 'that one of the ancient prophets had risen', scil. from the dead. *anestē* is synonymous with *ēgerthē*. The reference is to the Old Testament prophets in general.

archaios (also in v. 19) 'ancient', 'of old times'.

Translation: For *now* see on 1 : 57, for *tetrarch* on 3 : 1.

Heard of, or, 'heard reports about/of' (Javanese), 'heard people speaking about'.

All that was done, or, 'all-things done by Jesus' (Javanese), or simply, 'all those events', 'all that was happening'.

Perplexed is expressed variously, e.g. by 'oppressed of heart' (East Toradja), or by a reduplicated derivation of the adverb 'how' (Toba Batak, thus rendering in one word what NEB says in a phrase). Cp. also on "perplexity" in 21 : 25, and *TH-Mk* on 6 : 20.

Because it was said by some, or in the active, 'because some people said'; similarly in the subsequent clauses.

The series *some...some...others* may have to be adjusted, e.g. 'some... others...still others', cp. on 8 : 5. The three clauses beginning with *that* may better be rendered in direct discourse.

Had been raised (or, had risen) *from the dead*, cp. on 7 : 22. The prepositional phrase is not explicitly rendered in several cases; if it is, one may have to say, 'from among dead people', 'from where dead people are' (South Toradja).

(V. 8) *Had appeared*, or, 'had shown himself (again)' (Sundanese, Sranan), 'had become-visible/been-seen (again)' (East Toradja). Some languages (e.g. Balinese) possess a specific term for gods or deified persons showing themselves (again) on earth.

Old prophets, cp. on 'prophets from of old' in 1 : 70.

Had risen, short for 'had risen from the dead', cp. above.

9 ***Herod said, "John I beheaded; but who is this about whom I hear such things?" And he sought to see him.***

Exegesis: *eipen de Hērōdēs* 'and (considering these statements) Herod said', scil. to himself.

Iōannēn egō apekephalisa 'John I have beheaded'. *egō* is emphatic (cp. NEB), the thought connexion being: it is impossible that he is John, I have seen to that (cp. Klostermann).

apokephalizō (†) 'to behead', 'to execute by beheading'.

tis de estin houtos peri hou akouō toiauta? 'who is this about whom I hear such things?' For this type of question and the meaning of *tis* cp. on 5 : 21 and A-G s.v. *tis* 1 a β. *toiauta* refers to *ta ginomena.*

kai ezētei idein auton 'and he tried to see him', i.e. he tried to find a way to meet him, cp. on 5 : 18.

Translation: *John I beheaded,* or, "John? I beheaded him" (Rieu). Herod is the initiator, not the direct agent, see *TH-Mk* on 6 : 16. The verb is in some languages rendered by a verbal derivation of 'head' (Greek, English, French, East Toradja), in some others by 'to cut (off) his head' (Toba Batak), 'to cut (through) his neck' (Sundanese).

But who is this about whom I hear such things? This sentence may better be divided in two, 'But who is this?' (for which cp. on 5 : 21), and, 'I hear strange (or, extraordinary) things about him', 'I hear reports about him which I cannot believe'.

He sought to see him, or, 'to meet him'. For the first verb cp. on 5 : 18.

10 ***On their return the apostles told him what they had done. And he took them and withdrew apart to a city called Beth-saida.***

Exegesis: *kai hupostrepsantes hoi apostoloi diēgēsanto autō hosa epoiēsan* 'and after returning the apostles told him all that they had done'. *kai* connects v. 10 with v. 6. *diēgeomai,* cp. on 8 : 39.

apostolos 'apostle', see on 6 : 13.

kai paralabōn autous hupechōrēsen kat' idian 'and taking them with him he withdrew privately'. For *hupochōreō* cp. on 5 : 16.

paralambanō 'to take along', 'to take with'.

kat' idian (also 10 : 23) 'privately', 'by oneself', including, of course, the disciples, as brought out e.g. in Brouwer, NV, 'alone with them'.

eis polin kaloumenēn Bēthsaïda 'to, or, in the direction of a town called Bethsaida', preferably the latter, since Jesus did not go to, or, into Bethsaida (cp. v. 12 'in a lonely place').

Translation: *On their return the apostles told him,* or in co-ordination, 'the apostles returned (or, came back to Jesus), and (then they) told him'. *Apostle,* see on 6 : 13.

He took them (or, took them with him, as in NEB and others) *and withdrew apart to* indicates that Jesus, taking the apostles with him, left the crowd, and went with the apostles alone to Bethsaida; *apart* says explicitly what is implicit in the rest of the utterance. The items mentioned are variously expressed and distributed over the sentence in the versions, cp. e.g. 'they were-told(-by-him) to accompany (him) on-their-own towards' (Javanese), 'the twelve disciples alone He took-with-him in leaving, and went to' (Balinese), 'he took them along (lit. carried them go) with him, he pulled himself from amongst the people, he with the apostles alone went to' (Sranan), 'Jesus having called them, them alone, took them to' (Kapauku), 'Jesus separated-them-from-all-others and took them there to' (Tagabili), 'he led-them-away and separated-them-away to' (Trukese, Ponape). For the first verb cp. also *TH-Mk* on 9 : 2.

City called Bethsaida, cp. on 1 : 26.

11 ***When the crowds learned it, they followed him; and he welcomed them and spoke to them of the kingdom of God, and cured those who had need of healing.***

Exegesis: *hoi de ochloi gnontes ēkolouthēsan autō* 'but when the crowds found out they went after him'. Object of *gnontes*, which is not stated, is the fact that Jesus withdrew with his disciples. *ēkolouthēsan autō* may be rendered 'they went after him', or, 'they followed him', preferably the former, as the latter verb may imply that Jesus was within the crowd's eyesight.

kai apodexamenos autous 'and after welcoming them', implying that when the crowds arrive Jesus is already there. For *apodechomai* cp. on 8: 40.

elalei autois peri tēs basileias tou theou 'he talked to them about the kingdom of God'. Since *laleō* is not used by Luke in the sense of preaching, it may refer here to teaching and to the telling of parables (cp. Mk. 6 : 34).

kai tous chreian echontas therapeias iato 'and those who were in need of healing he cured'. For *chreian echein* cp. 5 : 31. *therapeia* also 12 : 42, but in a different meaning.

Translation: *Learned*, see on 7 : 37; the verb used in Sranan basically means 'to smell'.

Followed him, or, 'went to seek him', cp. *TH-Mk* on 1 : 36.

He welcomed them, same verb as in 8 : 40 (which see), but the roles are reversed, which may lead to the use of a slightly different rendering, e.g. 'he received/accepted them' (some Indonesian languages), 'he received them with kindness' (Sranan), implying Jesus' readiness to help, cp. on "received" in 9 : 5.

Who had need of healing, or, 'who asked to be healed' (Bahasa Indonesia RC), 'who requested him to heal them', 'who suffered from illness' (Javanese), 'who were not well' (Toba Batak).

12 ***Now the day began to wear away; and the twelve came and said to him, "Send the crowd away, to go into the villages and country round about, to lodge and get provisions; for we are here in a lonely place."***

Exegesis: *hē de hēmera ērxato klinein* 'then the day began to decline'. A co-ordinate clause is employed here instead of the more common subordinate, temporal clause, because it is more vivid.

klinō here intransitive, 'to decline', 'to be far spent', cp. A-G s.v. 2.

apoluson ton ochlon 'dismiss the crowd', cp. on 2 : 29. *ton ochlon* takes up *hoi ochloi* in v. 11. To this group refers also the subject of *katalusōsin* (plural).

hina poreuthentes eis tas kuklō kōmas kai agrous katalusōsin 'that they, after going to the villages and farms around, find lodging'. For *agrous* cp. on 8 : 34. *kuklō* (†).

kataluō (also 19 : 7) 'to halt', 'to rest', 'to find lodging'.

kai heurōsin episitismon 'and find provisions'.

episitismos (††) 'provisions', 'food', a military term used also in the case of travellers.

hoti hōde en erēmō topō esmen 'for here we are in a lonely place'. For *erēmos* cp. *N.T.Wb.*, 41f/DESERT.

Translation: *The day began to wear away* may be variously expressed, cp. e.g. 'the time-of-day (was) close-to evening' (Bahasa Indonesia); and cp. on "the day is far spent" in 24 : 29.

Send the crowd away, to go into, or, 'give the crowd leave that they may go into', 'urge the crowd to go into'; renderings such as 'dismiss the crowd, and let them go into', or simply, "send the crowd away to" (Goodspeed), 'order the crowd to go to' (Balinese) are acceptable too, unless they would suggest a rejection or getting rid of.

Villages and country refers to local units of medium and smallest size; for the latter cp. on 8 : 34.

Round about (going with the two preceding nouns), or, 'that are nearby' (East Toradja, Sundanese), 'in the neighbourhood' (NV), 'to-the-left-and-right-from here' (Javanese).

To lodge and get provisions, or, 'to get a place to lodge and to get something-to-eat' (Sundanese), 'to seek/ask lodging (or, place-to-pass-the-night, East Toradja) and food', "to find food and shelter" (Goodspeed, changing the order in accordance with receptor language idiom). A syntactic shift sometimes useful is found in Toba Batak, '. . . to go to lodge in the villages and country to get something-to-eat'.

Lonely place, see on 4 : 42.

13 ***But he said to them, "You give them something to eat." They said, "We have no more than five loaves and two fish—unless we are to go and buy food for all these people."***

Exegesis: *dote autois humeis phagein* 'you give them (something) to eat', cp. on 8 : 55. *humeis* is emphatic: you give them to eat instead of letting them take care of themselves.

ouk eisin hēmin pleion ē artoi pente kai ichthues duo 'we have no more than, or, only, five loaves and two fish'.

ei mēti poreuthentes hēmeis agorasōmen eis panta ton laon touton brōmata 'unless we ourselves go and buy food for all this crowd'. Between this clause and the preceding one the train of thought is like this: so we are unable to feed them, unless... *hēmeis* is emphatic and takes up the emphatic *humeis* spoken by Jesus. For *ei mēti* cp. A-G s.v. *ei* VI 9. For *laos* cp. on 1 : 10; for *brōmata* on 3 : 11.

agorazō 'to buy', 'to purchase', in Luke only in a literal sense.

Translation: *You give them something to eat,* or, "give them...to eat yourselves" (NEB), '(it is) you that should give...' (Balinese).

We have. The pronoun is best taken to be exclusive (as e.g. in Mazatec, and most Indonesian versions), unless this would suggest an intention to exclude Jesus from the food.

Loaves, see on 4 : 3; Tagabili uses here, 'five wrappings of cooked rice', the normal provisions on a journey.

Fish, cp. on 5:6; here the reference is to 'cured (e.g. dried, or, salted) fish'.

Unless we are to go..., or, 'except only that (or, only if) we go' (Lokele, Kapauku), may have to be adjusted to bring out the right meaning, e.g. '..., unless you want us (emphatic) to go...' (Shona 1966), 'or maybe we should go' (East Nyanja), 'it would be necessary for us to go' (Tzeltal); or as a question, 'or shall we go?' (Zarma), 'you don't want us to go..., don't you?' (cp. Bahasa Indonesia RC); or again, filling out the elliptical utterance, 'only if we go..., there would be sufficient', 'we cannot give them enough, except if we go...'. Marathi reaches the same end by transposing this and the preceding clause, cp. 'if we don't buy and bring bread, then we have nothing besides five loaves and two fish'. Here *we* is best taken exclusive, otherwise the disciples would be implying that Jesus was to join them on their errand.

Food, see on 3 : 11.

All these people, i.e. "this whole crowd" (TEV), and cp. on 3 : 21.

14 ***For there were about five thousand men. And he said to his disciples, "Make them sit down in companies, about fifty each."***

Exegesis: *ēsan gar hōsei andres pentakischilioi* 'for there were about five thousand men'. The clause refers to *panta ton laon touton* in v. 13. The use of *andres* instead of *anthrōpoi* implies that women and children are not included in the number.

eipen de 'then he said', rather than 'but he said'. *de* is continuative, not contrastive.

kataklinate autous klisias [hōsei] ana pentēkonta 'make them sit down in groups of about fifty each'. For *kataklinō* cp. on 7 : 36; here it is transitive. For *hōsei* cp. on 3 : 23; for *ana* cp. on v. 3.

klisia (††) 'group of people eating together'. Here it is in the accusative plural, as an apposition which denotes the result of *kataklinate.*

Translation: *About.* Approximation may be expressed variously, e.g. 'perhaps' (South Toradja), a term related to the word for 'estimate' (Bahasa Indonesia, Toba Batak), 'more or less', or the indefinite article, cp. 'a five thousand'.

Five thousand. Terms for 1000 may be basically descriptive, cp. e.g. 'ant heap' (Shona), 'large/uncountable number' (East Nyanja, Yao). In some cases the rendering must be built on smaller units (cp. *TH-Mk* 5 : 13 on "two thousand"), and/or be expressed by approximation, cp. e.g. 'sixty sixties and more yet' (Kapauku, adding the last three words to distinguish the phrase from the one rendering "four thousand", in Mk. 8 : 9), or, 'very many'. In the former case it may be possible to indicate the number indirectly, viz. by using 'in hundred companies, about fifty men each' in the next clause.

Make them sit down, or, 'tell them all to sit on the ground'. The attitude may have to be specified, cp. on 2 : 46, and *TH-Mk* on 6 : 39.

In companies, about fifty each, or, 'forming-groups about fifty one-group' (Bahasa Indonesia), 'about fifty-fifty one-group' (Balinese, the repetition expressing the distributive use of the numeral); cp. also *TH-Mk, l.c.* If the category numbered must be indicated one may hesitate here between 'fifty male persons' and 'fifty persons (including men, women, and children)', but 'men/male persons' seems to be preferable, because the correlation 5000-50 suggests that in both cases the same category is meant.

15 ***And they did so, and made them all sit down.***

Exegesis: *kai epoiēsan houtōs kai kateklinan hapantas* 'and they did so, and made them all sit down'. *houtōs* means here, 'as they were told'.

Translation: *They* may have to be specified, 'the disciples'.

Did so, or, 'behaved according-to his word' (Balinese), 'obeyed' (Jerusalem), 'complied' (Javanese, Toba Batak).

16 ***And taking the five loaves and the two fish he looked up to heaven, and blessed and broke them, and gave them to the disciples to set before the crowd.***

Exegesis: *labōn..., anablepsas...eulogēsen...* 'after taking..., he looked up...and blessed'. Of the three acts to which the participles and the main verb refer the first stands apart and the second and the third go closely together as parts of the whole act of blessing.

anablepsas eis ton ouranon 'he looked up to heaven', as an act of silent invocation.

eulogēsen autous 'he blessed them', i.e. 'he said the blessing over them'. For *eulogeō* cp. on 1 : 42 and *TH-Mk* on 6 : 41. In the light of 24 : 30 (where also *eulogeō*) and 22 : 17, 19 (where *eucharisteō* is used) there is good reason to assume that in all places blessing and thanksgiving are identical.

kai kateklasen 'and broke (them) to pieces'.

kataklaō (†) 'to break to pieces'; elsewhere (e.g. 22 : 19) *klaō* is used for the same act.

kai edidou tois mathētais paratheinai tō ochlō 'and he gave (them) to the disciples to set before the crowd'. *edidou* is durative imperfect.

paratithēmi 'to set before', with following dative, hence 'to serve to', 'to pass to'.

Translation: For this verse cp. *TH-Mk* on 6 : 41. A co-ordinating structure may be preferable, e.g. 'thereupon he (or, Jesus) took the five loaves..., looked up..., and blessed them. Then he broke them and gave them to...'.

Blessed, see on 1 : 42, sub (4).

Them, i.e. the loaves and fish.

17 ***And all ate and were satisfied. And they took up what was left over, twelve baskets of broken pieces.***

Exegesis: *kai ephagon kai echortasthēsan pantes* 'and they ate and were all satisfied'. *pantes* may be the subject of both verbs (cp. RSV), or go with *echortasthēsan* only. The latter is preferable, and *pantes* serves to emphasize the climax already expressed in that verb: they ate (and not only that) they even were satisfied, all of them. For *chortazō* cp. on 6 : 21.

kai ērthē to perisseusan autois klasmatōn kophinoi dōdeka 'and what they left was picked up (by the disciples, presumably), twelve baskets of pieces'. *klasmatōn* may go with *to perisseusan,* or with *kophinoi dōdeka,* preferably the latter, and *klasmatōn kophinoi dōdeka* is best understood as an apposition to *to perisseusan autois.* For *airō* cp. A-G s.v. 3.

perisseuō 'to be abundant', 'to be more than enough', hence 'to be left over'. The agent, i.e. the person who leaves, follows in the dative (cp. Jn. 6 : 13), here *autois* referring to all people who were present.

klasma (†) 'piece', i.e. the result of breaking (*klaō*).

kophinos (†) 'basket', cp. *TH-Mk* on 6 : 43.

Translation: For this verse cp. *TH-Mk* on 6 : 42f.

All ate and were satisfied, preferably, "they ate and were all of them satisfied" (Rieu), or slightly more emphatic, 'they ate, and (or, so that) they were satisfied, everyone of them'. For *to be satisfied,* or, 'to get enough', cp. on 6 : 21, and 'to-the-very-fullest' (Auca, in Mk. 6 : 42).

They took up. East Toradja has, 'they gathered-in', suggesting a plurality as object.

What was left over, or, 'what they (i.e. those who ate) left over, or, did not eat'; or, in one word, 'its rest/remains' (several Indonesian languages).

Twelve baskets of broken pieces, or, '(this was) as much as twelve baskets...'. Some versions simply have, 'twelve baskets full its total' (e.g. Balinese), in order to avoid a cumbersome or intricate phrase; this is defensible, if it is clear that the reference is to the food that had been handed around after having been broken. *Broken pieces,* if translated, can sometimes be expressed by a resultative derivation of the verb used in v. 16; Sranan, using a more generic term, has to specify it: 'pieces of bread'.

18 ***Now it happened that as he was praying alone the disciples were with him; and he asked them, "Who do the people say that I am?"***

Exegesis: *kai egeneto* 'and it happened', cp. on 1 : 8, introduces an independent narrative without connexion with the preceding as to time and place.

en tō einai auton proseuchomenon kata monas lit. 'during his praying alone', hence 'when he was praying alone'. *kata monas* (cp. A-G s.v. *monos* 3) does not exclude the presence of the disciples as shown by what follows.

sunēsan autō hoi mathētai 'his disciples were with him', connecting clause after *kai egeneto*, best understood as implying that the disciples did not take part in the praying.

suneimi (†) with following dative 'to be with (somebody)'.

kai epērōtēsen autous 'and he asked them'. Here begins the narrative proper. For *eperōtaō* cp. on 2 : 46.

tina me legousin hoi ochloi einai? 'who do the people say that I am?' *hoi ochloi* is not to be understood as taking up *hoi ochloi* in v. 11 and later references (vv. 12, 13, 16); hence a general rendering like 'the people' is preferable.

Translation: The introductory sentence may have to be adjusted, e.g. 'once he/Jesus was praying alone and the/his disciples were with him (or, were near him/nearby, or, were there also, or, were at the same place)'.

Alone, or, "by himself" (Goodspeed), "in retirement" (Rieu, which may lead to a further shift, 'once Jesus had retired (from the crowd) for prayer...'); and cp. *N.T.Wb.*/7.

Who do the people say that I am, see *TH-Mk* on 8 : 27; cp. also, 'in the opinion of the people/crowd, who am I said (to be)' (cp. Balinese, Javanese).

19 ***And they answered, "John the Baptist; but others say, Elijah; and others, that one of the old prophets has risen."***

Exegesis: *Iōannēn ton baptistēn, alloi de Ēlian, alloi de hoti prophētēs tis tōn archaiōn anestē* 'John the Baptist, but others, Elijah, and others that one of the ancient prophets has risen'. For these three answers cp. on v. 7f. For the syntactic construction cp. *TH-Mk* on 8 : 28. The clause appears to suggest that the first answer is the one most generally given by 'the people' but that there are some who give different answers, cp. e.g. RSV, Goodspeed.

Translation: If the answer is to be preceded by an introductory phrase (see *TH-Mk* on 8 : 28), it can best be something like, 'many of them say'.

John the Baptist, see references on 7 : 20.

20 ***And he said to them, "But who do you say that I am?" And Peter answered, "The Christ of God."***

Exegesis: *humeis de* 'but you!', emphatic and contrasting with *hoi ochloi* (v. 18).

ton Christon tou theou 'God's Messiah', cp. on 2 : 11.

Translation: *Who...am?*, cp. also *TH-Mk* on 8 : 29.

The Christ of God. For the construction see on "the Lord's Christ" in 2 : 26.

21 ***But he charged and commanded them to tell this to no one,***

Exegesis: *ho de epitimēsas autois parēggeilen* lit. 'but he charging them, ordered', i.e. "he gave them strict orders" (NEB). For *epitimaō* cp. on 4 : 35 and A-G s.v. 1; for *paraggellō* cp. on 5 : 14.

mēdeni legein touto 'to tell nobody this'. *touto* refers to Jesus being the Messiah.

Translation: *He charged and commanded them to tell this to no one* is more emphatic than the expression used in 5 : 14 (which see), because of the use of two verbs, the one reinforcing the other, and often rendered by one verb or phrase such as, 'he commanded them strictly (or, on a severe tone) not to...' (cp. BFBS, Jerusalem), 'he forbade them emphatically/strongly to...' (cp. Willibrord, Bahasa Indonesia 1968), 'they were admonished, not allowed to spread-the-news to whomsoever' (Balinese); Javanese shifts to direct discourse with a strong prohibitive form in it, thus, 'he told the companions, "Do not at-all speak about this matter to anyone"'.

22 ***saying, "The Son of man must suffer many things, and be rejected by the elders and chief priests and scribes, and be killed, and on the third day be raised."***

Exegesis: *eipōn hoti* lit. 'saying', with following direct speech which is to be understood as an explanation of the injunction of v. 21, or, as additional information about the future destiny of the Messiah. The former appears to be more probable (cp. Klostermann).

dei with following accusative and infinitive 'it is necessary', cp. on 2 : 49. Here it expresses a divine necessity, cp. *TWNT* II, 23.

ton huion tou anthrōpou 'the Son of man', cp. on 5 : 24.

polla pathein kai apodokimasthēnai 'suffer much and be repudiated'. *polla* may mean 'many things' (cp. RSV) or be understood in an adverbial sense, 'much', 'greatly' (cp. A-G s.v. *polus* I 2 b β); the latter is slightly preferable.

apodokimazō 'to reject' (of materials which cannot be used), 'to repudiate' (of people whose claim is not accepted).

apo tōn presbuterōn kai archiereōn kai grammateōn 'by the elders, the chief priests and the scribes'. The phrase goes with both preceding infinitives; with *polla pathein* the preposition *apo* means 'at the hands of', with *apodokimasthēnai* it means 'by', cp. A-G s.v. *apo* V 6. The article *tōn* goes with all three nouns, expressing that over against the Son of man elders, high priests and scribes act as one group. For *presbuteros* cp. on 7 : 3. For *archiereus* cp. *TH-Mk* on 8 : 31; *N.T.Wb.*, 105/; A-G s.v. 1 b. In the plural it refers to the members of the high-priestly families as a group. In the singular it refers to the acting high priest, cp. on 3 : 2. For *grammateus* cp. on 5 : 21.

kai apoktanthēnai kai tē tritē hēmera egerthēnai 'and be killed and on the third day be raised (from the dead)'. For *tē tritē hēmera* cp. *TH-Mk* on 8 : 31. For *egeirō* cp. on 7 : 14.

apokteinō 'to kill'.

Translation: For the verse cp. *TH-Mk* on 8 : 31. For *must* see on 2 : 49.

Suffer many things, and be rejected by...seems to take the prepositional phrase with the second verb only. To bring out that the preposition introduces the persons who are the cause of the first and the agents of the second process (as advocated in *Exegesis*), one may seek two, passive or active, verbal forms that take the same agent or subject (e.g. 'be-caused-to-suffer much and be refused by...'), or refer twice to 'the elders' etc. (e.g. 'suffer many things at the hand of, or, from the side of, the elders..., and be rejected by them'). — *Suffer many things*, or, 'suffer greatly'. The verb refers to primarily physical suffering caused by violence. It is often rendered by expressions such as, 'to feel pain' (Lokele), 'to bear distress' (Javanese), 'to see/find (or, to pass through) pain/trouble' (Trukese, Tzeltal), 'to be-caused-sorrow' (South Toradja); cp. also *N.T.Wb.*/70. For *to reject* Sranan uses a combination of two verbs, 'to throw him away saying he is worth nothing'.

For *elders* see on 7 : 3; for *chief priests* cp. on "high-priesthood" in 3 : 2.

Be killed, implying a reference to the crucifixion; and cp. *N.T.Wb.*/49f.

On the third day is equivalent to "after three days" in 2 : 46. The original uses the numeral 'three' because it includes both the first and the last day of the period concerned. An expression that is formally the same seems to be acceptable as an indication of the same period in several languages, amongst them Tagabili, where it proved to be synonymous with 'on the tomorrow of two nights', but several other languages indicate the period in question by a formally different phrase (see on 2 : 46). Then a literal rendering of the Greek would bring the reader to the wrong day, and consequently make Jesus foretell something that did not come true. In principle it is preferable in such a case to use a current idiom in the receptor language, as is done in Kituba, 'after two days (lit. in behind-of two days)', 'two days later' (Today's Dutch Version in preparation). But rather often Bible translations (and creeds) in such languages seem to feel bound to render the phrase literally, thus allowing tradition to prevail over idiom and semantics. Where this cannot be altered the translator should at least give the idiomatic rendering in a footnote.

Be raised, or, 'arise', see on 7 : 22.

23 ***And he said to all, "If any man would come after me, let him deny himself and take up his cross daily and follow me.***

Exegesis: *elegen de pros pantas* 'then he said to all'. *pantas* may refer (1) to all the disciples, i.e. those present in vv. 18-22 and all other disciples (cp. on 6 : 13 and Mt. 16 : 24); or (2) to all people, i.e. the disciples and the crowd (cp. Mk. 8 : 34). The latter is slightly more probable.

For the rest of v. 23 cp. *TH-Mk* on 8 : 34. To that treatment one point must be added: to *aratō ton stauron autou* 'he must take up his cross' Luke adds *kath' hēmeran* 'daily', which makes the clause refer to daily acts of self-surrendering and not to actual death on a cross.

Translation: *All,* or, 'the many', 'the crowd' (Bahasa Indonesia RC), 'all the people there' (Balinese).

Would, here and in v. 24, preferably 'wants'.

Come after me, i.e. "be a follower of mine" (NEB), or an equivalent receptor language idiom, e.g. "walk in my footsteps" (Rieu), 'tie my back' (Guhu-Samane, see *TBT*, 16.199, 1965); cp. also on "followed" in 5 : 11.

Deny himself. The term for denying a fact usually cannot be employed in this context. For descriptive phrases and idioms used see *TH-Mk* on 8 : 34.

Take up his cross, as a metaphor for 'suffering like Jesus did', has its background and finds its explanation in the Gospel itself. This relationship should be preserved in translation, even if the noun sounds unfamiliar in the receptor language and requires explanation. *Take up,* or, 'carry (on shoulder)' (Trukese); the aspect is ingressive, cp. 'lift up and carry' (Shona 1966). *Cross,* as instrument for execution, is unknown in several cultures. Therefore, the translator may have to adapt a term, or form a descriptive phrase. In some languages such a term or phrase only refers to the form, e.g. in Shona, Toba Batak, East Nyanja and Yao (both using a term for 'ridge-pole of a hut-frame', similarly in Mongolian, see *TBT*, 5.76, 1954). Elsewhere it refers to the function, e.g. a coined term, made up of two Sanskrit words, meaning 'killing-pole' (Marathi revision), 'wood to-stretch-out-with' (South Toradja), 'nailing pole' (Zarma). A combination of the two seems to be used in Balinese, which employs a word for the crossbeams in a house, derived from a verb that can refer both to a beam that stretches from side to side under a roof, and to a person stretched out for torture. For a partly similar combination of concepts cp. *TBT*, 9.60, 1958. Very often a borrowing is employed, e.g. from 'cross' etc. (cp. *krus, krusha, kurusiya, kurisu* in some Indic languages), or from its equivalent in Arabic, as found in some other Indic and Indonesian languages (*salib*), and e.g. in Swahili (*msalaba*), etc. An available term, however, may have, or have acquired, an undesirable connotation. Thus the Tzeltal word originally refers to a fetish; to make possible its reinterpretation it is necessary to make explicit its connexion with death; hence here, 'let him obey dying on the cross, as it were'.

Follow me, i.e. 'accompany me', 'go the same way as I (go)'; cp. on 7 : 9.

24 ***For whoever would save his life will lose it; and whoever loses his life for my sake, he will save it.***

Exegesis: Again it may suffice to refer to *TH-Mk* on 8 : 35, and to notice the differences between Mark and Luke:

(1) Since Luke uses *psuchē* only in this verse and not in v. 25 = Mk. 8 : 36, and Mk. 8 : 37 has no counterpart in Luke, the interplay between *psuchē* as natural life and as spiritual life is less prominent in Luke. V. 24 is rather

dominated by the interplay between *sōsai* 'to preserve', 'to keep from danger and death', and *sōsei* 'he will save', in the theological sense.
(2) Luke omits *kai tou euaggeliou* 'and of the gospel' and in the next clause inserts *houtos*, which takes up emphatically the relative pronoun *hos*.
(3) Luke has *apolesē* (aorist subjunctive) instead of *apolesei* (future indicative). This is more correct from the point of view of Greek grammar but does not change the meaning.

Translation: For this verse cp. *TH-Mk* on 8 : 35. The stylistic pattern is as follows: the first sentence has two contrasting clauses, the second one has the same pair in reversed order, with a qualifying phrase inserted; the first verb of either pair is used in its literal, the second in a figurative meaning.

Whoever..., or, 'everyone who...', 'all those who...', may better be rendered by an 'if'- or 'when'-clause, 'if anyone (or, a person)..., he...', similarly in vv. 26, 48; 14 : 27, 33; 17 : 33; 18 : 17, etc., and in 10 : 16 for "he who...".

For *save* see also on 1 : 47.

Life. In some languages the use of the word for 'life', or such equivalents as 'soul', 'breath', would restrict the meaning to life as a function of the body only; hence shifts to 'himself', 'his own person' (cp. also v. 25, where *heauton* 'himself' is virtually interchangeable with 'his life'). This may result in such renderings of the verse as, "whoever wants to take care of himself will lose himself, but whoever...loses himself is saving himself'.

For my sake, or, 'for the benefit of me', 'in my behalf', 'to help me'.

25 ***For what does it profit a man if he gains the whole world and loses or forfeits himself?***

Exegesis: *ti gar ōpheleitai anthrōpos* lit. 'in what respect is a man profited', i.e. 'what profit does a man have'.

ōpheleō (†) pass. 'to be profited', 'to acquire profit'.

kerdēsas ton kosmon holon lit. 'having gained the whole world', cp. *TH-Mk* on 8 : 36. *kerdainō* (†).

heauton de apolesas ē zēmiōtheis lit. 'but having lost himself or being punished'. *heauton* may go with *apolesas* only, or with both *apolesas* and *zēmiōtheis*, the latter verb interpreted as 'to forfeit' (cp. Mk. 8 : 36). The former is more probable, since disjunctive *ē* suggests that the verbs are to be differentiated. Hence the phrase *heauton de apolesas* contrasts with *kerdēsas ton kosmon holon* and is best understood as referring to dying and *zēmiōtheis* (†) is to be understood as in 1 Cor. 3 : 15 and refers to punishment after death (cp. 12 : 5 and 16 : 23ff).

Translation: For the first two clauses of this verse see *TH-Mk* on 8 : 36.

Loses or forfeits himself, or, 'loses himself and is punished' (as advocated in *Exegesis*). The first phrase may also be rendered, 'ruins himself' (cp. Willibrord), 'causes his own destruction/perdition' (cp. Zürich), 'he himself perishes', "is himself lost" (TEV); or negatively expressed, 'does not preserve himself', 'does no longer possess his own self'. For 'to be punished', or, 'to suffer punishment', 'to suffer (pain) because of one's sins', cp. *N.T.Wb.*/59.

26 ***For whoever is ashamed of me and of my words, of him will the Son of man be ashamed when he comes in his glory and the glory of the Father and of the holy angels.***

Exegesis: *hos gar an epaischunthē me kai tous emous logous* 'for whoever is ashamed of me and of my words'. For *epaischunomai* (†) cp. *TH-Mk* on 8 : 38. *logous* is best understood as referring to both preaching and teaching.

hotan elthē en tē doxē autou kai tou patros kai tōn hagiōn aggelōn 'when he comes in his glory and (the glory) of the father and of the holy angels'. The reference is to the *parousia* of the Son of man (cp. 21 : 27). *en tē doxē* means 'surrounded by, or, clothed in', cp. A-G s.v. *en* I 4 b, and refers to the heavenly glory in which the Father and the holy angels live and in which the Son of man will live after his ascension. For *doxa* cp. on 2 : 9.

Translation: For this verse cp. *TH-Mk* on 8 : 38.

In his glory and the glory of the Father and of the holy angels. To avoid a rendering that could suggest the existence of two or three different entities called 'glory', one may say, 'in his glory, that is in the glory of...' (Bahasa Indonesia RC), 'possessing/having a glory, which is also that of...', '(being) glorious, so glorious as...'. For *glory* and *holy* see references on 2 : 9 and 1 : 15. *The Father*, or where this noun is obligatorily possessed, 'my Father', cp. on 2 : 49; for another solution see *TBT*, 13.28, 1962. In languages without a definite article the specifying force which *the* has here will have to be expressed otherwise, e.g. by using 'heavenly Father', or, 'Father (who is/lives) in heaven', or by treating the noun as a name or title, as done in Balinese, which preposes a name qualifier.

27 ***But I tell you truly, there are some standing here who will not taste death before they see the kingdom of God."***

Exegesis: *legō de humin alēthōs* 'I tell you truly', cp. on 3 : 8.

alēthōs 'truly', 'in truth', equivalent to *ep' alētheias* (cp. on 4 : 25).

For the rest of v. 27 cp. *TH-Mk* on 9 : 1. It should be noted that Luke reads *heōs an idōsin tēn basileian tou theou* 'until they have seen the kingdom of God', omitting *elēluthuian en dunamei* 'having come with power'. The Lucan clause, however, is best understood as referring also to the future consummation of the kingdom also. *geuomai* also 14 : 24.

Translation: For the whole verse see *TH-Mk* on 9 : 1, especially the warning to avoid, if possible, the "taking any overly decisive position" as to the interpretation of this verse.

But I tell you truly, see on 4 : 24f. *You,* i.e. the "all" of v. 23.

Taste death, or, 'see/experience death', 'encounter (a reciprocal form of 'to see') death' (South Toradja), or simply, 'to die'. Such renderings may coincide with that of "see death" in 2 : 26.

To render *until* in Enga one has to adjust the sentence, e.g. '...will not die right away; they will first see...' (cp. *TBT*, 16.134, 1965).

See the kingdom of God, i.e. see/know that God rules.

28 ***Now about eight days after these sayings he took with him Peter and John and James, and went up on the mountain to pray.***

Exegesis: *egeneto de* 'and it happened', cp. on 1 : 8.

meta tous logous toutous 'after these sayings', i.e. 'after he had said this' (cp. Goodspeed), rather than, 'after these things' (Klostermann). *logous* refers to vv. 23-27 as a whole.

hōsei hēmerai oktō 'about eight days', i.e. 'about a week' on the basis of Roman time-reckoning, and equivalent to Mk. 9: 2, 'after six days', on the basis of Jewish time-reckoning, cp. Grundmann. For the nominative of time cp. Bl-D, § 144.

[*kai*] *paralabōn* 'taking with him', cp. on v. 10.

eis to oros lit. 'to the mountain', but cp. on 6 : 12.

Translation: *About eight days after,* see also on 1 : 59.

He took with him...and went up... The main event is mentioned in the second clause. Therefore, it may be preferable to subordinate the first clause (Jerusalem, *prenant...il gravit la montagne*), and/or to shift it to the end of the verse, e.g. 'Jesus went up..., accompanied by (or, together with) his disciples'.

Went up on the mountain, i.e. 'went up into the mountains/hills', see on 6 : 12.

29 ***And as he was praying, the appearance of his countenance was altered, and his raiment became dazzling white.***

Exegesis: *kai egeneto...to eidos tou prosōpou autou heteron* 'and the appearance of his face became different, or, changed', without indicating the nature of the change. But according to v. 32 the disciples saw Jesus' *doxa*, i.e. 'his bright splendour' (cp. on 2 : 9). This is also consistent with what follows in v. 29. For *eidos* cp. on 3 : 21.

kai ho himatismos autou leukos exastraptōn scil. *egeneto* 'and his clothing became white (and) gleaming'. For *himatismos* cp. on 7 : 25. *leukos exastraptōn* without connective. Most translations render it as one phrase and treat *exastraptōn* as an adverb modifying *leukos* (cp. RSV). *leukos* (†).

exastraptō (††) 'to flash, or, gleam like lightning'.

Translation: The phrase *as he was praying* is more than a simple indication of time here; the verb is repeated to bring out the connexion between Jesus' communion with God in prayer and his transfiguration. The aspect is durative, 'during his prayer', 'there he prayed for a time, then...'

The appearance of his countenance was altered, or, 'the appearance of his face took another form, or, became different (lit. it one kind)' (East Nyanja, Trukese), 'the shadow/picture of his face was another one' (Yao).

To render 'appearance' one may have to shift to a verbal construction, 'his face was seen to have become different' (cp. East Toradja 1933), 'it became visible that his face had changed', 'his face appeared manner of otherness' (Kituba). Some versions slightly simplify the expression, e.g. 'his characteristic-appearance changed' (Balinese), 'his form/shape/appearance/face changed' (South and East Toradja, Shona 1966, Sinhalese, Kapauku, Sranan). Tagabili says 'he became different', because 'his face was changed' is an idiom to say that a person is dying. The translation to be used will often have to coincide with, or come close to, that of "he was transfigured", as discussed in *TH-Mk* on 9 : 2.

Raiment, or, 'clothing', cp. on 7 : 25. A more specific term may be used, where necessary, provided it refers to an outer garment.

Dazzling white, or, 'white and shining/sparking'; some versions render the phrase by one term expressing a high degree of splendour/brightness/whiteness.

30 ***And behold, two men talked with him, Moses and Elijah,***
31 ***who appeared in glory and spoke of his departure, which he was to accomplish at Jerusalem.***

Exegesis: *kai idou* 'and behold', focussing the attention strongly on what follows, cp. on 1 : 20.

andres duo sunelaloun autō 'two men were talking with him', durative imperfect. For *sullaleō* cp. on 4 : 36.

hoitines ēsan Mōüsēs kai Ēlias 'who were Moses and Elijah'; relative clause instead of apposition is more emphatic.

(V. 31) *hoi... elegon tēn exodon autou* 'who... spoke about his departure', relative clause which has *Mōüsēs kai Ēlias* as its antecedent. It takes up *sunelaloun autō* in v. 30 and specifies the subject of the conversation.

exodos (†) 'departure', here euphemistically, 'passing away', 'death'.

ophthentes en doxē lit. 'having appeared in glory', aorist tense, referring to an event which, in temporal sequence, precedes v. 30. For *ophthentes* cp. on 1 : 11; for *en doxē* cp. on v. 29.

hēn ēmellen plēroun en Ierousalēm 'which he was to fulfil in Jerusalem'. *ēmellen* means here 'he was destined', cp. A-G s.v. 1 c δ. For *plēroō* cp. on 1 : 20 and A-G s.v. 4 a. Its use here implies that Jesus' death is in some way a fulfilment of his mission.

Translation: *Talked with him,* often a reciprocal form of 'to speak'.

Moses and Elijah. One may have to add titles, e.g. 'prophet', and/or indicate that the reference is to persons that are no longer among the living, cp. *TH-Mk* on 9 : 4.

(V. 31) *Who appeared in glory,* or, as a new sentence, 'they, or, these (two) men, had appeared in glory'. If the linguistic sequence has to parallel the sequence of events, the clause must be shifted, e.g. 'two men had appeared in glory; these were M. and E. They were talking with him, and spoke of...'. *Appeared,* or, 'made their appearance', 'showed themselves'; cp. *N.T.Wb.*/11, sub (1).

His departure, which he was to accomplish at Jerusalem may have to be adjusted rather radically, e.g. 'the death of Jesus which he had-to die in J.' (Kituba), 'his last days, how he would take death in J.' (Sranan), "his departure, the destiny he was to fulfil in J." (NEB); or, more explicitly expressing the implication of Gr. *plēroō,* 'his dying there in J., for that was the whole purpose for which God sent him' (Tagabili), "how he would soon fulfil God's purpose by dying in J." (TEV); or again, shifting from verbal noun to verb, 'how he would depart/die, as (or, something that) he was destined to do in J., or, which was the task he had to perform in J.'. — *His departure.* Some other euphemisms for 'death' used are, 'his end' (South Toradja), 'his last going/journey' (Bahasa Indonesia KB), 'his going-home' (Balinese), 'he will go-away' (Ponape, similarly Timorese). Often, however, one must simply say, 'his dying' (Tagabili), 'his future death' (East Toradja, Kapauku). *Which he was to accomplish,* or, 'to fulfil', "to go through with" (Goodspeed), "to achieve" (Rieu), verbs that often do not go naturally with 'departure', or, 'death', because they imply activity and initiative on the part of the subject not compatible with the concept 'dying'; hence adjustments are usually necessary, see above.

32 ***Now Peter and those who were with him were heavy with sleep but kept awake, and they saw his glory and the two men who stood with him.***

Exegesis: *ho de Petros kai hoi sun autō* 'now Peter and those with him', instead of 'Peter and John and James' (v. 28), focussing the attention on Peter and thus preparing the reader for v. 33.

ēsan bebarēmenoi hupnō 'had (in the mean time) been weighed down with sleep', pluperfect tense, indicating a situation which had come into existence during the preceding events. *hupnos* (†).

bareō (also 21 : 34) 'to burden', here, in the passive, metaphorically of being weighed down with sleep (cp. Mt. 26 : 43).

diagrēgorēsantes (††) 'after waking up'. RSV has "but they kept awake" (cp. A-G s.v.), but this is less probable.

eidon tēn doxan autou 'they saw his glory', cp. on v. 29.

tous duo andras tous sunestōtas autō 'the two men who were standing with him', second object of *eidon.*

sunestōs (†, participle of *sunistamai,* cp. A-G s.v. II 1) 'standing (with somebody)'.

Translation: *Those...with him,* or, 'his (two) companions'.

Were heavy with sleep, when referring to actual being asleep, as preferred in *Exegesis,* "had been overcome by sleep" (Goodspeed, similarly several others), 'were very sleepy and took-a-nap' (Balinese), 'overcome by sleepiness (lit. closing of the eyes)' (East Toradja), 'had fallen asleep because their-eyelids-drooped' (South Toradja). Cp. also *N.T.Wb.*/68.

But kept awake, preferably, 'but they awoke', ingressive aspect, cp. *N.T.Wb.*/14 sub (1).

His glory, i.e. Jesus' glory, or, 'him/Jesus in his glory'.

With him, or, 'close to him', 'at his side' (Toba Batak), 'close by' (Javanese).

33 ***And as the men were parting from him, Peter said to Jesus, "Master, it is well that we are here; let us make three booths, one for you and one for Moses and one for Elijah"—not knowing what he said.***

Exegesis: *kai egeneto* 'and it happened', cp. on 1 : 8.

en tō diachōrizesthai autous ap' autou lit. 'at/during their parting from him', i.e. 'as they were (already) parting from him'.

diachōrizomai (††) 'to part from' (with *apo*), without indicating, or, implying how the departure took place.

epistata 'master', cp. on 5 : 5.

kalon estin hēmas hōde einai 'it is a good thing that we are here', a statement rather than an exclamation. *hēmas* refers to the three disciples.

kai poiēsōmen 'and let us make', hortatory subjunctive, explaining for what purpose it is good that they are there.

skēnas treis 'three booths', cp. *TH-Mk* on 9 : 5. *skēnē* also 16 : 9.

mē eidōs ho legei 'not knowing what he was saying', because he did not understand the situation.

Translation: The first clause may have to be co-ordinated, e.g. 'Next (or, another particle indicating transition without specifying the length of time elapsed) the men were parting. At that moment Peter...'

The men, i.e. Moses and Elijah; hence "these" (Rieu), 'the two men' (some Indonesian languages).

Were parting from him, or, "were leaving Jesus" (TEV), "were moving away from Jesus" (NEB), 'would withdraw from his presence' (Javanese, using a reverent form here, because Jesus is the person they were parting from).

Master, see on 5 : 5.

It is well that we are here, or, "it is a good thing that we are here" (Rieu), 'it is fortunate that we are at hand'. The pronoun has been taken as an inclusive (cp. *TH-Mk* on 9 : 5), but the exclusive is probably preferable (see *Exegesis*).

Let us make three booths. The pronoun is exclusive; in Kapauku the use of the exclusive form implies that the building is done for the benefit of others (i.e. Jesus, Moses, and Elijah) exclusive of the performer(s) (i.e. the disciples). The verb is often better rendered by 'to build', or by any other specific verb commonly used for the setting up of *booths* (or, 'huts', 'shelters'), for which see *TH-Mk, l.c.*

Not knowing what he said, or, resuming here the verb with which this phrase goes, 'but he spoke (or, said so) without knowing what he was saying' (cp. NEB). Of course Peter knew what he said, in the sense that he understood his own words, but he didn't realize that his proposal was out of place; hence more specific renderings such as, 'not conscious of...' (Bahasa Indonesia), '...the purport of these words of his' (Balinese), 'as-a-matter-of-fact this word-of-his was without thinking' (Javanese).

34 ***As he said this, a cloud came and overshadowed them; and they were afraid as they entered the cloud.***

Exegesis: *egeneto nephelē kai epeskiazen autous* 'a cloud came and (for some time) overshadowed them'. *egeneto* (aorist) refers to the punctiliar event of the appearing of the cloud, *epeskiazen* (imperfect) to the linear situation that followed. For *episkiazō* cp. on 1 : 35. *autous* may refer to all present, or to the three disciples only, preferably the former.

ephobēthēsan de en tō eiselthein autous eis tēn nephelēn 'and they (i.e. the disciples) were frightened after they (i.e. Moses and Elijah) went into the cloud'. *ephobēthēsan* describes the feeling of the three disciples at the end of the strange happening. For *ēn* with aorist infinitive cp. Bl-D, § 404.

Translation: Specifying the three pronouns of the third person plural in accordance with the interpretation preferred in *Exegesis* one may say, 'all of them', 'all (those who were) there/in that place' for *them*, 'the disciples' for the first *they*, whereas the second *they* may be replaced by 'Moses and Elijah' (Sranan), by 'they two' (Bahasa Indonesia KB), or by a deictic element indicating a group different from the group already referred to.

Came. 'Clouds' may not be said 'to come' but 'to be-there suddenly' (Balinese), 'to arrive-unexpectedly' (Jerusalem, *survint*), 'to appear', 'to emerge'.

Overshadowed, see on 1 : 35; of the two verbs mentioned there for Indonesian languages number (2) seems to be preferable here. Cp. also *TH-Mk* on 9 : 7.

Entered the cloud, or, 'disappeared into (or, were enveloped by) the cloud' (Javanese), 'the cloud encompassed/enveloped them' (Tagalog).

35 ***And a voice came out of the cloud, saying, "This is my Son, my Chosen; listen to him!"***

Exegesis: *phōnē* 'voice', cp. on 1 : 44.

ek tēs nephelēs 'out of the cloud'.

houtos estin ho huios mou ho eklelegmenos 'this is my son, the chosen one', cp. on 3 : 22. Here it is a proclamation in the third person, intended for those present, i.e. for the disciples.

eklelegmenos 'chosen', equivalent to *eklektos* (cp. 23 : 35), and both a Messianic title (cp. also Is. 42 : 1 LXX).

Translation: For *a voice came*... see on 3 : 22.

My Son, my Chosen, or, 'my Son, the One I have chosen', 'my Son, whom I have chosen' (cp. Balinese, Sranan). The appositional or relative construction has explicative, not distinctive or restrictive meaning, cp. on "your wife Elizabeth" in 1 : 13. For *to choose* cp. on 6 : 13.

For *to listen* cp. on "to hear" in 1 : 41.

36 ***And when the voice had spoken, Jesus was found alone. And they kept silence and told no one in those days anything of what they had seen.***

Exegesis: *en tō genesthai tēn phōnēn* lit. 'after the voice had happened, i.e., spoken', cp. RSV.

heurethē Iēsous monos 'Jesus was found (to be) alone', i.e. 'they (i.e. the three disciples) saw that Jesus was alone', implying that the others had gone (cp. Phillips).

kai autoi esigēsan 'and they kept silence'.

sigaō 'to be silent', 'to keep silence'.

oudeni apēggeilan...ouden hōn heōrakan 'they told nobody anything of what they had seen'. The two negatives reinforce one another.

en ekeinais tais hēmerais 'in those days', probably referring to the time that Jesus was with them.

Translation: *When the voice had spoken,* or, 'had-sounded' (East Toradja). The rendering should preferably echo the one of "a voice came" in v. 35.

Jesus was found alone. For the verb cp. on 7 : 10; for "Jesus...alone", i.e. no one but Jesus, cp. *N.T.Wb.*/7.

They, or, "the disciples", 'the three' (Malay, South Toradja), or again specification by a deictic element.

Kept silence. If an object is obligatory one may transpose the phrase 'what they had seen', e.g. 'the disciples kept-silent-about the things they had seen' (Balinese), or insert a generic object, e.g. 'they kept silence about it, or, the event'. Some versions shift to 'kept-it-secret' (Bahasa Indonesia RC), an acceptable means to avoid tautology in languages where the renderings of 'to keep silent' and 'not to tell, or, speak' coincide or closely resemble each other.

Told no one...anything. Other ways to express the strong negation are, 'told no single person...a word', 'told people...entirely nothing', etc.

For one possible transposition of *what they had seen* see above; another that may be necessary is, 'the disciples who had seen all this kept silence (about it) and told no one of it...'.

37 ***On the next day, when they had come down from the mountain, a great crowd met him.***

Exegesis: *egeneto de* 'and it happened', cp. on 1 : 8.

tē hexēs hēmera 'on the next day', cp. on 7 : 11.

katelthontōn autōn 'when they had come down', genitive absolute, serving as a complementary indication of time after *tē hexēs hēmera.* For *katerchomai* cp. on 4 : 31.

apo tou orous 'from the mountain', cp. v. 28.

sunēntēsen autō ochlos polus 'a great crowd met him', i.e. came to meet him. *sunantaō* also 22 : 10.

Translation: *On the next day,* or, 'on its to-morrow' (Bahasa Indonesia).

An expression for 'dawn' is sometimes idiomatically used to indicate 'the next morning, or, day', cp. e.g. '(when) the sun (is) big' (East Toradja), 'when day(light) broke' (Sranan).

They had come down. The pronoun may have to be specified, 'Jesus and those (or, the/his three) disciples'. In a language like Balinese one must say, 'when He descended (honorific)...accompanied by the disciples', cp. *TBT*, 14.160, 1963.

For *met him* see on 8 : 27.

38 ***And behold, a man from the crowd cried, "Teacher, I beg you to look upon my son, for he is my only child;***

Exegesis: *kai idou* lit. 'and behold', cp. on 1 : 20.

anēr apo tou ochlou eboēsen 'a man from the crowd shouted'. *apo tou ochlou* goes with *anēr* and has the function of a partitive genitive (cp. A-G s.v. *apo* I 6 and 19 : 39), cp. "a man in the crowd" (NEB). For a different interpretation cp. Rieu. For *boaō* cp. on 3 : 4.

didaskale 'teacher', cp. on 3 : 12.

deomai sou epiblepsai epi ton huion mou 'I beseech you to look at my son'. For *epiblepō* cp. on 1 : 48.

hoti monogenēs moi estin 'for he is my only child', cp. on 7 : 12.

Translation: *A man from the crowd,* i.e. from amongst the many people mentioned in v. 37.

Cried, or, 'shouted', 'spoke loudly'.

For *I beg you* cp. *N.T.Wb.*/12f, ASK.

For *to look upon* see on "to regard" in 1 : 48 and the closely synonymous "to look on" in 1 : 25; for *he is my only child* see on "child" in 1 : 7 and "only son" in 7 : 12.

39 ***and behold, a spirit seizes him, and he suddenly cries out; it convulses him till he foams, and shatters him, and will hardly leave him.***

Exegesis: *kai idou* 'and behold', emphatic introduction of the subsequent account of the boy's illness, cp. on 1 : 20.

pneuma lambanei auton 'a spirit takes, or, seizes him', viz. from time to time, not permanently.

kai exaiphnēs krazei 'and shouts suddenly'. Subject of *krazei* is either the spirit through the boy's voice (cp. NEB), or the boy (cp. RSV), probably the former. *exaiphnēs* also 2 : 13.

sparassei auton meta aphrou lit. 'convulses him with foam', i.e. so that he foames.

sparassō (†) 'to convulse', 'to pull to and fro', cp. *TH-Mk* on 1 : 26.

aphros (††) 'foam'.

kai mogis apochōrei ap' autou suntribon auton 'and it withdraws from him (only) with difficulty, mistreating him'. *suntribon auton* refers to an act which is simultaneous with *apochōrei* (cp. Willibrord) and it is best understood as supplementing *mogis*.

mogis (††) 'with difficulty', 'with toil and pain'.
apochōreō (†) 'to go away', 'to withdraw'.
suntribō (†) 'to mistreat', 'to wear out', 'to bruise'.

Translation: For *spirit,* i.e. 'evil/unclean spirit', 'demon', see on 4 : 33, 35f; for *seizes him* see on 8 : 29.

Convulses, cp. *TH-Mk* on 1 : 26; the rendering may make use of an idiom for a fit or convulsion, such as 'cut nose' (Kapauku), or for some of its characteristics, such as spastic movements of legs, arms, and/or body, cp. e.g. 'causes-to-be-contracted' (Toba Batak), 'torments him till he jerks' (Balinese), 'causes-him-to-turn-and-toss restlessly (lit. as-a-sun-hat)' (South Toradja), 'causes his body to break' (Sranan).

He foams, or, 'his mouth is (or, lips are) foaming' (East Toradja, Toba Batak; South Toradja), "he foams at the mouth" (Goodspeed), 'the foam is on his mouth' (NV).

Shatters him, and will hardly leave him, or, closer to the Greek word order, 'leaves him only with difficulty, wearing him out, or, and meanwhile it torments him horribly' (cp. BFBS, Willibrord); or, shifting from the act to the resulting state, "it leaves him, after a struggle, badly bruised" (Goodspeed), 'when it leaves him at last he is wholly broken', 'it leaves him only when (or, it does not leave him before) he is totally worn out'. In this context *to leave somebody* is virtually synonymous with "to come out of somebody", as used in 4 : 35 (which see).

40 ***And I begged your disciples to cast it out, but they could not."***

Exegesis: *hina ekbalōsin auto* 'that they cast him out'. *hina* points to the intended result. For *ekballō* cp. on 4 : 29.

kai ouk ēdunēthēsan 'and they could not'. The aorist tense, referring to a punctiliar event, implies that they tried but failed.

Translation: In Foe 'begged' and 'could' are in the near past tense, implying that the conversation referred to took place earlier on the day of speaking.

Cast out, or, 'caused to come out', see 4 : 35.

They could not, or, where necessary, 'they were not able to do so (or, to do what I asked, or, to cast it out)'.

41 ***Jesus answered, "O faithless and perverse generation, how long am I to be with you and bear with you? Bring your son here."***

Exegesis: *apokritheis de ho Iēsous eipen* 'Jesus answered'. Strictly speaking the first clause of what follows represents Jesus' reaction to v. 40, and the second takes up the father's request in v. 38.

ō genea apistos kai diestrammenē 'O faithless and perverse generation', best understood as being addressed to all people who are present and had failed to show faith enough for the healing of the boy. For *genea* cp. on 1 : 48 and A-G s.v. 2.

apistos (also 12 : 46) 'unbelieving', 'faithless'.
diestrammenē (past participle of *diastrephō* also 23 : 2) 'perverted', 'perverse', 'crooked'.
heōs pote esomai pros humas lit. 'till when, i.e., how much longer shall I be with you?' The future tense of *esomai* implies compulsion; hence the rendering "must I be" (Goodspeed and others). For *pros* meaning 'with' cp. A-G s.v. III 7.
kai anexomai humōn 'and shall I (have to) endure you'. For *anechomai* (†) cp. *TH-Mk* on 9 : 19.
prosagage hōde ton huion sou 'bring your son here', turning to the father. *prosagō* (†).

Translation: *Faithless and perverse generation* is used as a form of address and, therefore, often requires a reference to the second person plural, cp. e.g. "How unbelieving and wrong you people are" (TEV), 'you people of this time, there is no belief, your heart is corrupt' (Sranan). *Faithless*, or, 'who has no faith', cp. references on 5 : 20. *Perverse*, i.e. being what one ought not to be, has also been rendered, 'crooked' (Tagalog), 'gone-astray' (Bahasa Indonesia), 'mis-behaving' (Balinese), 'of reversed spirit' (South Toradja, the qualification being also used of words that pervert the truth), or simply, 'not good' (Kekchi). *Generation*, cp. on 1 : 48.

How long, or, as an exclamatory statement, 'I cannot... (much) longer'. Some receptor languages require that the words are repeated before 'bear with you'.

Be with you, or, 'remain with you (still)'; Bamiléké has, 'be I-plus-you', using a compound pronoun referring to a combination of an individual and a group or of two groups; Toba Batak shifts to 'how long (are) you my-companions'.

Bear with, or, 'put up with', "have patience with" (BFBS, similarly some Indonesian languages) 'hold-out in your midst' (Bahasa Indonesia 1968); in Balinese a verb used of catching trickling water in a receptacle can have the required figurative sense.

The last clause of this verse is no longer addressed to all present, but exclusively to the father, as is clear from the contents and from the singular verbal form and pronoun in the Greek. In languages not allowing such an abrupt transition from exclamation to imperative, and/or from third to second person, or second person plural (if that form has been used in the preceding clause) to second person singular, it is permissable to insert an explanatory clause like 'and then Jesus said to that man there' (Tagabili, cp. TEV).

Bring your son here, or, 'come here with your son', 'let your son come here' (Javanese, using a causative verbal form derived from an adverb indicating movement towards the speaker).

42 ***While he was coming, the demon tore him and convulsed him. But Jesus rebuked the unclean spirit, and healed the boy, and gave him back to his father.***

Exegesis: *eti de proserchomenou autou* 'while he, i.e. the son, was still coming (to him), or, on his way (to him)'.

errēxen auton to daimonion 'the demon threw him down'.

rēssō (†) 'to throw down', 'to dash to the ground'. Morphologically it is possible to derive *errēxen* from *rēgnumi* (cp. 5 : 37, and RSV) but this does not fit the context here.

sunesparaxen 'convulsed (him)', cp. on v. 39 and *TH-Mk* on 9 : 20. *susparattō* (†).

epetimēsen de ho Iēsous tō pneumati tō akathartō 'Jesus checked the unclean spirit', cp. on 4 : 35.

kai iasato ton paida 'and cured the boy', denoting the result of the preceding clause.

Translation: *He*, often better, 'the boy' (see below).

For *rebuked, demon* and *unclean spirit* see on 4 : 33, 35f.

And healed, or, 'and thus (he) healed'.

For *boy* (or, 'child') cp. on 2 : 43 and 1 : 7.

43a ***And all were astonished at the majesty of God.***

Exegesis: *exeplēssonto de pantes* 'and all were astonished', cp. on 2 : 48.

epi tē megaleiotēti tou theou 'at the majesty of God'.

megaleiotēs (†) 'grandeur', 'majesty', a rare word, here equivalent to *doxa* 'glory'.

Translation: *Astonished at*, see on "wondered at" in 1 : 21.

Majesty. Some renderings used are, 'the grand way' (Sranan), 'the great power' (Zürich), 'the greatness of power' (South Toradja).

43b ***But while they were all marvelling at everything he did, he said to his disciples,*** 44 ***"Let these words sink into your ears; for the Son of man is to be delivered into the hands of men."***

Exegesis: *pantōn de thaumazontōn* 'but while all were astonished'. *pantōn* may take up *pantes* in v. 43[a], or refer to 'all people' in general, preferably the latter (cp. Rieu and NEB), see next note.

epi pasin hois epoiei 'at all things he did'. The use of *pasin* and the imperfect tense of *epoiei* suggest reference to Jesus' mighty deeds in general. They form as it were the contrasting background against which the subsequent announcement of the passion must be placed. *pasin* 'all' (dative) echoes *pantōn* 'all' (genitive).

(V. 44) *thesthe humeis eis ta ōta humōn* lit. 'do you put into your ears', i.e. either, 'keep this in your minds/in mind' (cp. Goodspeed), or, 'listen carefully' (cp. Phillips); the latter rendering is here to be preferred. *humeis* 'you' is emphatic, referring to the disciples in contrast to the people in general who are lost in wonder about Jesus' mighty deeds.

tous logous toutous 'these words', pointing forward to what Jesus is going to say.

ho gar huios tou anthrōpou lit. 'for the Son of man' (cp. on 5 : 24). *gar* is used here in the meaning 'namely', 'to wit'.

mellei paradidosthai eis cheiras anthrōpōn 'is destined to be delivered into the hands of men', or, "is going to be handed over to men" (Goodspeed). *mellei* implies that it is God's will. It may also suggest that God is to be considered as the agent of *paradidosthai* (cp. A-G s.v. 1 b). The meaning of *paradidosthai* here is 'to hand over (into the custody of)', 'to give up', cp. A-G s.v. 1 b. In the phrase *eis cheiras anthrōpōn* the use of *anthrōpōn* contrasts with *ho huios tou anthrōpou. cheiras* is used in a figurative way and suggests 'power' (cp. A-G s.v. 1 b).

Translation: *Marvelling at,* see on "wondered at" in 1 : 21.

(V. 44) *Let these words sink into your ears,* or, 'let these words be established in your ears' (Yao), 'let these (very) words enter your ears' (Lokele, Zarma, East Nyanja), 'put it/these words into your ears' (cp. Shona 1966, Kapauku, Ponape, Trukese); or, shifting to another metaphor or a non-figurative expression, 'you (plur.), you take-hold well of these matters that I am telling you' (Kituba), 'listen to these-words-of-mine' (Toba Batak, similarly Tarascan).

Is to be delivered into. Both a passive construction and an active construction with indefinite subject may primarily suggest a human agent. On the other hand, an explicit reference to 'God' as agent may better be avoided; hence renderings such as 'will come into the hands of...' (Toba Batak 1885), and cp. *TH-Mk* on 10 : 33[a].

45 ***But they did not understand this saying, and it was concealed from them, that they should not perceive it; and they were afraid to ask him about this saying.***

Exegesis: *hoi de ēgnooun to rēma touto* 'but they did not understand this word'.

agnoeō (†) 'to understand not' (cp. Mk. 9 : 32).

kai ēn parakekalummenon ap' autōn 'and it was concealed/hidden from them', i.e. their not understanding what Jesus said was due to an influence beyond their control (cp. Plummer). *parakaluptō* (††).

hina mē aisthōntai auto 'in order that they might not comprehend it', indicating purpose, or, 'so that they might not comprehend it', indicating result, preferably the latter, since the perfect tense of *ēn parakekalummenon* suggests a situation which makes it impossible for the disciples to understand.

aisthanomai (††) 'to comprehend'; here used with negative it is synonymous with *agnoeō*.

ephobounto erōtēsai auton 'they were afraid to ask him', or 'they were ashamed to ask him' (cp. Bl-D, § 392.1b), preferably the former.

Translation: *They did not understand this saying*, cp. on 2 : 50.

It was concealed from them. A reference to God, or Jesus, as agent may be necessary in some cases, e.g. in Kituba, 'God had hid it (from them)', or in Tagabili, 'he did not cause-it-to-be-revealed to them', but it is preferable to be less explicit, cp. e.g. 'the word hid itself from them' (Lokele), 'it was a riddle to them' (Leyden), 'it still was-veiled (lit. having-its-peel, said of words that exalted characters use on the stage, incomprehensible for the common man)' (Balinese).

Perceive, or, "see its meaning" (BFBS), "grasp it" (Rieu, similarly Jerusalem), or some other synonym of 'understand'.

Were afraid, or negatively put, 'did not dare' (NV), 'did not have the courage'.

To ask, viz. for insight, cp. *N.T.Wb.*/12f; in Chontal the implied direct discourse is made explicit, cp. 'they were scared, so they didn't ask him, "What does your word say?"'

About this saying, or, 'what he/Jesus said (or, meant, or, meant to say)'.

46 ***And an argument arose among them as to which of them was the greatest.***

Exegesis: *eisēlthen de dialogismos en autois* lit. 'a discussion, or, a thought entered into them', hence—in order to fit *dialogismos* (either meaning, see below)—'came about', 'happened'.

dialogismos 'reasoning', 'deliberation', either outward and audible, i.e. 'discussion', 'argument', or inward and inaudible, i.e. 'consideration (in oneself)', 'thought', 'doubts'. Since a contrast with *ton dialogismon tēs kardias* ('reasoning of the heart', hence 'thought') in v. 47 appears to be present, the former rendering is preferable here.

en autois 'among them'.

to tis an eiē meizōn autōn 'as to which of them was the greatest' or 'as to who might be greater than they', indirect question indicating what the argument was about, introduced by the article *to*, cp. on 1 : 62. *autōn* is best understood as a partitive genitive, going either with *tis* ('which of them') or with *meizōn* ('the greatest of them'), preferably the former. *meizōn* is to be interpreted as a superlative (cp. Bl-D, § 60.1).

Translation: *An argument arose among them*, or, 'a deliberation grew/was-born among them' (Toba Batak), "they fell into an argument" (Rieu), 'they disagreed-with-each-other' (South Toradja), 'they fought in speech' (Sundanese). The expression is not neutral, as is "said to one another" (see on 4 : 36), but it implies less animosity than "a dispute arose" (22 : 24).

As to which of them was... The indirect question may have to become a direct one, 'which of us may be... ?', or, 'which of us is the greatest, do you think?' *Greatest.* Some languages use here 'most in front' (Javanese, Balinese), 'the highest' (Sranan); see also on 1 : 15. The superlative may be rendered by ascribing the qualification exclusively to one of the group, e.g. 'of/among all of them, which one (is) great'; and cp. *TH-Mk* on 9 : 34.

47 ***But when Jesus perceived the thought of their hearts, he took a child and put him by his side,***

Exegesis: *ho de Iēsous eidōs ton dialogismon tēs kardias autōn* 'but Jesus, knowing the thought of their heart', cp. on v. 46. Hence *eidōs* is best understood as 'knowing' (cp. 6 : 8), implying that Jesus did not need to hear their discussions in order to know what their deepest thoughts were.

epilabomenos paidion estēsen auto par' heautō '(after) taking a little child he made it stand by his side'. For *paidion* cp. on 1 : 59.

epilambanomai 'to take hold of', 'to catch', here in the sense of 'to draw to himself' (cp. Jerusalem).

par' heautō 'by his side', i.e. in a place where all attention would focus on the child.

Translation: *When*, temporal, or, 'because/as', causal conjunction; or, in co-ordinated clauses, 'then', or, 'therefore/so', introducing the second clause.

The thought of their hearts, or, 'what they were deliberating in their minds', 'what their hearts were considering' (Sranan), 'what (was) in their spirit' (South Toradja); or simply, 'their thoughts' (Sundanese), 'what they thought'.

Put him by his side, or, 'made-him-stand by his side/close-by' (some Indonesian languages).

48 ***and said to them, "Whoever receives this child in my name receives me, and whoever receives me receives him who sent me; for he who is least among you all is the one who is great."***

Exegesis: *hos an dexētai touto to paidion epi tō onomati mou* 'whoever receives this child on account of me'. *dechomai* probably is used here because of what follows where *dechomai* is appropriate (see below). For *epi tō onomati mou* cp. *TH-Mk* on 9 : 37. Here the rendering 'on my account' appears to fit the context best.

eme dechetai 'receives me'. *eme* is emphatic.

kai hos an eme dexētai dechetai ton aposteilanta 'and whoever receives me, receives him who has sent me'. *eme* is repeated from the preceding clause. *dechomai* is used here in the sense of 'acknowledge' or 'obey', cp. v. 5. For *apostellō* cp. on 1 : 19.

ho gar mikroteros en pasin humin huparchōn lit. 'for he who is the least among you all'. For *huparchō* cp. on 7 : 25. *mikroteros* has superlative force and is used metaphorically.

houtos estin megas 'he is (really) great'; *houtos* is emphatic. For *megas* cp. on 1 : 15.

Translation: *Receives* (4 ×), cp. on 9 : 5, and *TH-Mk* on 9 : 37; Tzeltal uses an expression meaning 'to take into account', 'to consider important' in all four occurrences.

This child, here, of course as an example of its kind, 'a little-one like this' (South Toradja).

In my name, or, 'because of my name (or, of me)', cp. *TH-Mk, l.c.*; or a descriptive phrase, such as, 'because he obeys me', 'because he is a follower of mine'.

Least, the direct opposite of "the greatest" in v. 46; hence, '(the) least important', '(the one) most to the back', 'the one who has little power' (Kekchi).

Great here refers to a deeper, spiritual reality; hence, "really great" (Goodspeed, similarly East Toradja 1933), 'the one who really has great power' (Kekchi), 'what-you-call great' (Toba Batak). Several versions (e.g. NEB, BFBS, Bahasa Indonesia RC) use the superlative, because the qualification refers to one out of many.

49 ***John answered, "Master, we saw a man casting out demons in your name, and we forbade him, because he does not follow with us."***

Exegesis: *apokritheis* 'answering', cp. on 1 : 60.

epistata 'master', cp. on 5 : 5.

eidomen tina en tō onomati sou ekballonta daimonia 'we saw somebody casting out demons in your name', i.e. "using your name" (Rieu), cp. *TH-Mk* on 9 : 38. *en tō onomati sou* recalls *epi tō onomati mou* in v. 48.

kai ekōluomen auton 'and we tried to stop him'; conative imperfect, cp. *TH-Mk* on 9 : 38.

hoti ouk akolouthei meth' hēmōn, scil. *soi* 'because he does not follow (you) with us', i.e. he is not together with us in following you.

Translation: *John answered*, lit. 'answering John said', or, 'thereupon John said', "here, J. said to him" (Rieu), 'then J. broke in' (Javanese).

We...we are best taken as exclusive (e.g. in East Toradja).

In your name has instrumental force; hence, "with your name" (Goodspeed), 'by-means-of your name' (Balinese, similarly Sranan, lit. taking your name). Other useful, more or less descriptive renderings are, 'borrowing your name' (East Toradja 1933), 'mentioning your name' (Sundanese), 'relying upon your name' (Toba Batak); and see *TH-Mk* on 9 : 38.

Forbade him, or, 'tried to stop/check/prevent him'; or, "told him not to do so" (Goodspeed), 'said, "Don't do that"' (Navajo).

Because. Enga conveys the causal idea by using 'seeing that', cp. *TBT*, 16.136, 1965.

He does not follow with us, or, 'he does not follow you as we do', 'he is not your follower as we are' (the pronoun 'we' having exclusive force), 'he does not join (us) in following you' (Bahasa Indonesia, Balinese); or, 'he is not with us, or, one of us' (cp. NEB, Subanen), 'us' having inclusive force, since the speaker himself is one of Jesus' followers. For *to follow* see on 5 : 11.

50 ***But Jesus said to him, "Do not forbid him; for he that is not against you is for you."***

Exegesis: *mē kōluete* "do not try to stop him" (Goodspeed).

kath' humōn 'against you', cp. A-G s.v. *kata* I 2 b γ.
huper humōn 'on your side', cp. A-G s.v. *huper* 1 a δ.

Translation: *He that is not against you is for you,* or rendering the prepositions otherwise, 'he that is not your adversary, he is your companion' (Bahasa Indonesia, using two closely similar forms, *lawan* and *kawan*), 'when a person does not oppose us, he helps us' (Sundanese), 'the man that does not oppose you, he is your partner' (Sranan); and cp. *TH-Mk* on 9 : 40.

51 ***When the days drew near for him to be received up, he set his face to go to Jerusalem.*** 52a ***And he sent messengers ahead of him,***

Exegesis: *egeneto de* lit. 'and it happened', cp. on 1 : 8.

en tō sumplērousthai tas hēmeras tēs analēmpseōs autou 'when the days of his ascension were fulfilled'. For this phrase cp. on 1 : 57 (where a related verb is used). *tas hēmeras* refers to a period which must elapse before the event to which *tēs analēmpseōs* refers, can take place. *sumplēroō,* cp. on 8 : 23.

analēmpsis (††) lit. 'taking up', here in a passive sense 'being taken up', with a shift to another word picture, 'ascension' (cp. the related verb *analambanomai* in Acts 1 : 2, 11, 22).

kai autos to prosōpon estērisen tou poreuesthai eis Ierousalēm lit. 'he set his face in order to travel to Jerusalem'. The meaning of the Hebraistic phrase *to prosōpon estērisen* is 'he resolved firmly', 'he decided definitely'. *tou poreuesthai eis Ierousalēm* is an independent genitive of the articular infinitive, loosely attached to the main clause in order to indicate its purpose (cp. Bl-D, § 400.5).

stērizō 'to fix', 'to set', 'to strengthen'.

(V. 52a) *aggelous* 'messengers'.

pro prosōpou autou lit. 'before his face', hence 'before him', 'ahead (of him)', cp. *TH-Mk* on 1 : 2.

Translation: Solemn wording and contents of v. 51 serve to mark the fact that a new major part of the narrative (9 : 50-19 : 27) begins here.

When the days drew near for him to be received up, or, 'that he/Jesus was to be received up, or, was to go up'; or focussing rather on the preceding period, 'as the days before he should be received up were running out' (cp. Phillips), 'when the time that had to elapse before his ascension was almost at its end' (Leyden). An interesting idiom for time that has elapsed is 'knot that is cut' (Kapauku, cp. the Tagabili rendering of "at the end of eight days" in 2 : 21). The idea that all this was preordained can usually be expressed in the phrase referring to the coming event (see above), but is sometimes better expressed (also) in the reference to the period, e.g. 'when the time-agreed-upon was at hand' (Balinese), 'when the time was due to come that...' (Sranan). *To be received up.* A locative qualification is often desirable, e.g. 'that Jesus would be taken-up/made-to-go-up (or, would go up) to heaven' (Tzeltal, Balinese, Sranan), 'that he should be taken away from this world' (Jerusalem). — Some translators have chosen a euphemism for 'to die', e.g. 'to go home', 'to pass away', or a term for 'elevation (to a higher rank)'; this is not to be recommended.

He set his face to go to, or, "he resolved to go to" (Phillips), 'Jesus decided to take-hold-of road to go to' (Kituba), 'he took resolutely the road to' (Jerusalem). Idioms used to express firm resolve are, 'to put into the head' (Sranan), 'to cause-to-be-fixed the heart' (Bahasa Indonesia RC), 'straight before the nose' (Kapauku), 'to hold-down the will' (Ponape, Trukese).

(V. 52ª) *He sent messengers ahead of him*, or, to avoid tautology, 'he sent some persons ahead of him', see on 7 : 27.

52b ***who went and entered a village of the Samaritans, to make ready for him;***

Exegesis: *kai poreuthentes eisēlthon eis kōmēn Samaritōn* 'and they (i.e. the messengers) went (scil. ahead of him) and entered a village of the Samaritans'. *poreuthentes* indicates the result of *apesteilen*. . .*pro prosōpou autou* of v. 52ª. For the Samaritans cp. *IDB* IV, 190-197. The route through Samaria was usually avoided by travellers to Jerusalem.

hōs hetoimasai autō 'in order to make preparations'. For *hōs* with infinitive cp. A-G s.v. IV 3 b. Nestle reads *hōste* instead of *hōs*, cp. on 4 : 29. For *hetoimazō* 'to prepare' cp. on 1 : 17.

Translation: *Who went*, preferably a co-ordinated sentence, "they set out" (NEB), 'they started on their way', or, specifying the subject, 'these (or, those sent-out, or, those that had-been-ordered) went in advance' (cp. Rieu, Balinese, Sundanese).

Samaritans, i.e. 'persons of Samaria', or, 'Samaria people'. The proper name is, of course, to be transliterated, not so its derivative affix; of this a meaningful receptor language equivalent should be given.

To make ready for him. If a direct object is required one may say, 'all things' (Sranan), 'lodging place' (Bahasa Indonesia), 'place-to-pass-the-night' (Toba Batak).

53 ***but the people would not receive him, because his face was set toward Jerusalem.***

Exegesis: *kai ouk edexanto auton* 'and they (i.e. the people of the village) did not receive him', or, 'they refused to receive him'. It is implied that this refusal came to light when the messengers tried to make arrangements, i.e. before Jesus came to the village himself (see on v. 54).

hoti to prosōpon autou ēn poreuomenon eis Ierousalēm lit. 'because his face was going to Jerusalem', a Hebraistic phrase cp. 2 Sam. 17 : 11 LXX. *to prosōpon autou* is here equivalent to the personal pronoun of the third person; its use makes the clause sound solemn.

Translation: *The people*, or more specifically, "the people there" (Goodspeed, Javanese), "the villagers" (NEB, similarly East Toradja 1933).

Would not receive him is intentional, referring to what they will do when Jesus arrives. For the verb see on 9 : 5.

His face was set toward, or more idiomatically rendered, "because he was making for" (NEB). It is stylistically preferable that the rendering should echo v. 51[b] exclusive of the concept of resolve, e.g. 'his face was toward', 'he had taken the road to'.

54 ***And when his disciples James and John saw it, they said, "Lord, do you want us to bid fire come down from heaven and consume them?"***

Exegesis: *idontes* 'seeing (this)', i.e. that the Samaritans in question refused to receive Jesus, probably when the messengers returned.

theleis eipōmen pur katabēnai apo tou ouranou kai analōsai autous 'do you want that we order fire to come down from heaven and consume them'. *eipōmen* is deliberative subjunctive introduced by asyndetic *theleis,* cp. Bl-D, § 366.3. James and John do not ask Jesus permission but expect that he wants them to call down fire from heaven (cp. Rieu, Phillips). The phrase *pur katabēnai,* etc. recalls 2 Kings 1 : 10. *analōsai* denotes the aim of the calling down of the fire (cp. Rieu).

analiskō (†) 'to consume', 'to destroy'.

Translation: *His disciples James and John.* The names in apposition are restrictive, indicating that the reference is to only two of the disciples; hence e.g. 'his disciples, that is those called J. and J.' (South Toradja).

Saw, or, 'perceived', 'became aware of', 'heard of', if 'saw' would suggest their having witnessed the Samaritans' refusal.

Do you want us to..., or, 'you certainly want us to', 'you wish us to..., aren't you'.

Bid fire come down. If it is impossible to address fire as though it were a person, one may shift to 'cause fire to come down'. The reference is probably to lightning.

Consume, i.e. "burn up" (NEB, similarly Bahasa Indonesia, East Toradja).

55 ***But he turned and rebuked them.*** 56 ***And they went on to another village.***

Exegesis: *strapheis* 'turning (round)', cp. on 7 : 9.

epetimēsen autois 'he reproved them'. For *epitimaō* cp. on 4 : 35.

(V. 56) *kai eporeuthēsan* 'and they went (on)'. Subject is Jesus and all that were with him (cp. Phillips).

eis heteran kōmēn 'to another village'. *heteros* may be referring to another Samaritan village, or to a non-Samaritan village, probably the former.

Translation: *He turned,* see on 7 : 9.

Rebuked them, i.e. 'the companions just-mentioned' (Javanese), 'those two' (Balinese). For the verb see on 4 : 35.

(V. 56) *They* is often better specified, e.g. "they all" (Phillips); Balinese has, 'he went (honorific), accompanied by his disciples' (cp. on v. 37).

57 ***As they were going along the road, a man said to him, "I will follow you wherever you go."***

Exegesis: *kai poreuomenōn autōn en tē hodō* 'and as they were going along the road'. Subject is Jesus and his disciples, as in v. 56. *poreuomenōn* is best understood as a continuation of *poreuesthai* in v. 51, since from that verse on till 19 : 27 Luke's theme is that of Jesus' journey from Galilee to Jerusalem (see commentaries, especially Grundmann).

akolouthēsō soi hopou ean aperchē 'I will follow you wherever you go'. For *akoloutheō* cp. on 5 : 11.

aperchomai here 'to go' with the implication of going to some place (cp. 17 : 23). Elsewhere usually 'to go away', 'to go back'.

Translation: *As they were going along the road,* or, "as they went on their way" (TEV), 'as they were travelling on', 'on their journey' (East Toradja).

Him, i.e. Jesus, who is referred to by his proper name in the next verse; this order may have to be reversed or otherwise adjusted.

Wherever you go may have to be translated, 'on all journeys you make', 'to all places that you go to'.

58 ***And Jesus said to him, "Foxes have holes, and birds of the air have nests; but the Son of man has nowhere to lay his head."***

Exegesis: *hai alōpekes phōleous echousin kai ta peteina tou ouranou kataskēnōseis* '(the) foxes have holes and (the) birds of the air have resting-places'. In such a proverbial saying the Greek uses the article where the English does not.

alōpēx (also 13 : 32, but in a figurative sense) 'fox'.

phōleos (†) 'den', 'lair', 'hole', of the dwelling place of animals.

ta peteina tou ouranou 'the birds of the air', cp. on 8 : 5.

kataskēnōsis (†) 'a place to rest', 'shelter', here 'nest'.

ho de huios tou anthrōpou ouk echei pou tēn kephalēn klinē 'but the Son of man has no (place) where he may lay his head'. For *ho huios tou anthrōpou* cp. on 5 : 24.

klinō here 'to lay down (the head) in order to sleep', cp. A-G s.v. 1 b.

Translation: *Foxes,* mentioned here as an example of a wild animal, roving far and wide, yet having his own place to rest. Some equivalents used where the fox is not known are, 'jackal' (Zarma, Shona, Bahasa Indonesia), 'wild cat' (Tagabili), 'civet cat' (South and East Toradja, Sundanese), 'coyote' (Tarascan, Navajo), 'wild dog' (Javanese, Balinese, Toba Batak, Sranan).

Have holes, or, 'have their (own) holes' (cp. NEB, some Indonesian languages), or more generically, 'have a place to live in, or, where they belong'.

Birds of the air, or, 'wild/field birds', cp. on 8 : 5.

Have nests, or, 'have their (own) nests/roosts'; or again a generic expression as mentioned above.

Nowhere to lay his head, or, 'no place where he can lay down his head'; or where a literal rendering would not convey the required meaning, 'no place where he can lie down to sleep', 'no place to rest'.

59 ***To another he said, "Follow me." But he said, "Lord, let me first go and bury my father."***

Exegesis: [*kurie*] 'lord', cp. on 1 : 6.

epitrepson moi 'let me', 'permit me', cp. on 8 : 32.

apelthonti prōton thapsai ton patera mou 'to go (away from here) and bury my father first'. *prōton* goes with the clause as a whole. The clause implies that the father was dying or had just died (cp. Plummer).

thaptō (also in next verse, and 16 : 22) 'to bury', without ceremonial implications.

Translation: *Another*, or, 'a second (man)'.

He said (2 ×) may have to be specified, e.g. 'Jesus said' (Bahasa Indonesia), and/or, "the man replied" (NEB).

Let me in the sense of 'give me permission to' is sometimes expressed by 'give me to' (East Toradja), 'give me opportunity (lit. path) to' (Sranan).

Go, or, 'go home' (Balinese).

To bury, i.e. to dispose of a dead person by depositing him in the earth. Terms used in other cultures may imply a different place or manner, e.g. 'to place-in-a-cave' (South Toradja), or be basically neutral as to place or manner, e.g. 'to do-as-to-a-dead-person' (East Toradja).

60 ***But he said to him, "Leave the dead to bury their own dead; but as for you, go and proclaim the kingdom of God."***

Exegesis: *aphes tous nekrous thapsai tous heautōn nekrous* 'let the dead bury their dead', i.e. 'leave it to the dead to bury their dead'. The meaning of *tous nekrous* is determined by the context. He who postpones the call of Jesus to the burying of the dead is, so to speak, dead himself. It is not advisable to press the figurative meaning of *tous nekrous* in such a way that it means 'spiritually dead'.

su de apelthōn diaggelle tēn basileian tou theou 'but you, go and proclaim the kingdom of God'. *apelthōn* takes up *apelthonti* in v. 59.

diaggellō (†) 'to proclaim (far and wide)', 'to preach', synonymous with *kērussō*, cp. 9 : 2.

Translation: *Leave the dead to bury their own dead* is sometimes better slightly simplified, e.g. 'the dead will take-care-of their dead' (East Toradja). *The dead*, or, as a simile, 'those who are like the dead'. *Their own dead.* The possessive may be taken to express the idea 'the dead that are related to them, or, for whom (or, for whose funeral) they are responsible'.

Some versions have taken it to carry the meaning 'those who are equally dead, or, as dead as they are', but this is not advisable. — The translator should avoid a rendering that will be understood to mean 'let the dead take care of themselves'.

Proclaim, cp. on "preach" in 3 : 3.

61 ***Another said, "I will follow you, Lord; but let me first say farewell to those at my home."***

Exegesis: *akolouthēsō soi* 'I will follow you' in the sense of 'I am going to follow you', implying that his decision has been made but that the implementation must wait.

prōton de epitrepson moi apotaxasthai tois eis ton oikon mou 'but let me first say farewell to those (that are) at home/in my house'; cp. on v. 59. For *eis* meaning 'in', cp. A-G s.v. 9.

apotassomai (also 14 : 33) with dative 'to say farewell to', cp. *TH-Mk* on 6 : 46; in 14 : 33 it means 'to give up'.

Translation: *Another*, or, 'still another', 'another again', 'a third one', cp. on "some" in 8 : 5.

Say farewell, or, "say good-bye" (NEB). Equivalent idiomatic expressions are, 'to beg' (Bahasa Indonesia RC), 'to beg (for) oneself' (Malay), both elliptic for 'to beg that one may be excused, or allowed, to depart', 'to leave behind words' (Toba Batak), 'to give (the) abide safely (a leave-taking formula)' (Bahasa Indonesia), or, a verb derived from 'to see' (Shona). The corresponding formula in Balinese is '(I am) leaving', which leads here to the rendering 'say to be leaving them'; and in Tagabili, 'I will make it known' (as courtesy demands before one enters a house, or leaves it).

Those at my home, or, "my people at home" (NEB), '(those of) my family' (Bahasa Indonesia RC, Balinese), 'the inmates of my house' i.e. my household (Bahasa Indonesia), 'up (i.e. up in the house)' (Tagabili).

62 ***Jesus said to him, "No one who puts his hand to the plough and looks back is fit for the kingdom of God."***

Exegesis: *oudeis...euthetos estin...* 'nobody...is fit...', subject and predicate of the clause. The subject is modified by a twofold participial clause, see next note.

epibalōn tēn cheira ep' arotron kai blepōn eis ta opisō lit. 'who has put his hand to the plough and is (still) looking behind (him)'. *epibalōn* is in the aorist and *blepōn* in the present. The clause is used in a metaphorical way and refers to the attitude of a person who has made a decision (punctiliar aspect) but does not live up to it (durative aspect, cp. NEB, "keeps looking back"). *arotron* (††).

euthetos...tē basileia tou theou 'fit for the kingdom of God', i.e. able to meet its demands.

euthetos (also 14 : 35) 'fit', 'suitable', 'usable'.

Translation: *No one who puts...is fit for* is sometimes better reversely expressed, 'anyone who puts...is unfit for...', or, 'if a person puts..., he is not fit for, or, not able to...'.

Puts his hand to the plough, or, 'takes hold of the plough' (Tarascan, similarly several Indonesian languages), 'starts ploughing', 'is ready to plough' (Bahasa Indonesia 1968), or more generically, 'has started working his fields' (cp. Sranan). Where *a plough* is unknown one may use the name of a tool used for the same kind of agricultural work, such as 'hoe' (Lokele), and cp. 'touches the helve of the hoe' (Bamiléké), 'takes the hoe into his hand' (Bali).

Is fit for the kingdom of God, or, 'is able to work under God's rule, or, where God reigns'; or, if the clause is reversely expressed (see above), 'is useless where God is king' (cp. Phillips).

CHAPTER TEN

1 ***After this the Lord appointed seventy others, and sent them on ahead of him, two by two, into every town and place where he himself was about to come.***

Exegesis: *meta de tauta* 'after this', i.e. the events told in 9 : 57-62.

anedeixen ho kurios heterous hebdomēkonta [*duo*] 'the Lord appointed seventy [two] others'. For *ho kurios* cp. on 1 : 6.

anadeiknumi (†) 'to appoint', 'to commission'.

ana duo 'two by two', cp. A-G s.v. *ana* 3.

pro prosōpou autou lit. 'before his face', cp. on 9 : 52 and *TH-Mk* on 1 : 2.

eis pasan polin kai topon 'to every town and place'. For *topos* meaning 'inhabited place' cp. A-G s.v. 1 a. It is less specific than *polis*.

hou ēmellen autos erchesthai 'where he intended to go himself/in person'. For *mellō* meaning 'to intend' cp. A-G s.v. 1 c γ.

Translation: *Appointed,* cp. *N.T.Wb.*/11, ad (1).

Seventy, or, "seventy-two". If it is deemed necessary to mention the two alternatives, one should go in the text of the translation, the other in a footnote; to combine them in the text, e.g. by using 'seventy[-two]', is not advisable.

Others, or, 'other disciples', viz. than the twelve mentioned in 9 : 1ff.

Two by two, or, 'in pairs', distributive, cp. *TH-Mk* on 6 : 7.

For *town* cp. on "city" in 1 : 26. For *place* cp. on 4 : 37; in this context a term for 'village' (East Toradja) is also acceptable.

2 ***And he said to them, "The harvest is plentiful, but the labourers are few; pray therefore the Lord of the harvest to send out labourers into his harvest.***

Exegesis: *ho men therismos polus* 'the crop is plentiful/abundant', first part of a saying in proverbial form. Its meaning depends on the meaning and connotation of *therismos*.

therismos (†) 'process of harvesting', or its result, 'harvest', 'crop', preferably the latter. Here it is best understood as a metaphor for the bringing in of those who are destined to enter the kingdom of God. The mission of the seventy is part of this bringing in.

hoi de ergatai oligoi 'but the workers are few'.

ergatēs 'worker', 'labourer', a general word which refers here to the work of reaping.

deēthēte oun tou kuriou tou therismou 'pray therefore to the master of the crop'. *ho kurios tou therismou* 'the master of the crop' is the owner of the crop on the fields who is responsible for the harvesting (cp. Goodspeed, NEB).

hopōs ergatas ekbalē eis ton therismon autou 'that he send out workers into his crop', scil. in order to reap it for him. For *ekballō* meaning 'to send out' without the connotation of force cp. A-G s.v. 2.

Translation: *Harvest,* or, 'crop', 'what is to be reaped/gathered-in', 'food ripe in the garden' (Neo-Melanesian); sometimes the term refers to the manner of harvesting, e.g. 'stuff to be cut' (Kapauku), 'what is plucked' (Tzeltal), or to the specific crop that is locally most important, e.g. 'rice-crop (lit. what-is-treated-with-a-small-knife)' (Javanese).

Labourers, or, 'harvesters', 'rice-reapers' (Javanese), 'cutters' (Kapauku).

Pray to, or a term without such religious connotation, 'beseech', 'beg' (cp. on 5 : 12).

Lord of the harvest, preferably, 'the owner of the harvest'; or, 'the owner of the field' (Melpa, a rendering with religious connotation, the phrase being used also of the spirits to whom sacrifices are offered before the beginning of the harvest).

To send out labourers into his harvest, or, 'to send harvesters/workers to harvest his field/seeds' (cp. Shona 1966, Kituba), "send out labourers to reap it for him" (Rieu), 'to order people to cut-together his-rice' (East Toradja 1933). In Zarma 'to harvest' is idiomatically rendered as, 'to kill the field'.

3 ***Go your way; behold, I send you out as lambs in the midst of wolves.***

Exegesis: *hupagete* 'go', 'be on your way', cp. on 8 : 42[b].

idou apostellō humas hōs arnas en mesō lukōn 'look, I am sending you like lambs among wolves'. For *idou* cp. on 1 : 20. *apostellō* takes up *apesteilen* of v. 1.

arēn (††) 'lamb' as a symbol of helplessness.

lukos (†) 'wolf' as a symbol of menacing danger.

Translation: *Go your way,* or, "set forth" (Rieu), '(now) go to where I told you'.

As lambs in the midst of wolves, or, 'as a lamb goes amongst wolves'. *Lamb,* usually, 'young sheep', or, 'child of sheep'. For 'sheep' see *TH-Mk* on 6 : 34; Nida, *BT*, 136; terms for species of 'sheep' and 'goat' may overlap. *Wolf,* an animal of depredation, fiercer than a fox. Local equivalents used are, 'hyena' (Yao), 'wild dog' (Shona; similarly Ponape, lit. 'dog-of uninhabited-place'), 'very fierce dog' (Tagabili), 'fierce coyote' (Mazahua), 'tiger' (Sranan, Toba Batak), 'leopard' (Lokele), 'jaguar' (Tzeltal). Some descriptive renderings are, 'wild animal that has teeth, or, that kills' (Kapauku, Huixtec), 'fierce wild animal' (Tepehua).

4 ***Carry no purse, no bag, no sandals; and salute no one on the road.***

Exegesis: *mē bastazete ballantion* 'do not carry with you a purse'.
ballantion 'money bag', 'purse'.
mē pēran, mē hupodēmata 'nor a knapsack, nor sandals'. For *pēra* cp. on 9 : 3 and for *hupodēma* on 3 : 16. The seventy [two] are not forbidden to wear sandals but to carry an extra pair with them (cp. Plummer, Klostermann).
kai mēdena kata tēn hodon aspasēsthe 'and do not greet any one on the road', because this would take too much time and would take them off their main duties (cp. Grundmann). *aspazomai*, cp. on 1 : 40.
kata tēn hodon 'along the road', i.e. while going along the road, cp. Acts 8 : 36.

Translation: *Purse*, or, 'small bag'. Where necessary one may replace the container by the contents, 'money'.
For *bag*, or, 'knapsack', see on 9 : 3; for *sandals* see on 3 : 16.
Salute no one. A literal rendering is possible in some languages where greetings take a notoriously long time, as in Zarma; or in Shona, where one might have used, 'do not greet with the full formula of greeting' (implying totem and praise names, inquiries about those at home and questions about whither the parties are bound). But elsewhere such a rendering would merely sound discourteous. To convey the intended meaning one may have to say then, 'do not delay for salutations' (Sinhalese), 'do not pause...to give even one person greetings' (Kituba), and in some cases one has almost or entirely to abandon the concept of greeting, cp. 'don't-waste-time talking to people you meet' (Tagabili), 'do not loiter...for useless words' (Navajo). For *to salute*, or, 'greet', see on 1 : 29, 40.
On the road, or, 'on (or, while making) your/this journey'.

5 ***Whatever house you enter, first say, 'Peace be to this house!'***

Exegesis: *eis hēn d' an eiselthēte oikian* lit. 'into whatever house you go', but the relative *hēn* is not taken up in the main clause.
prōton legete 'say first', i.e. before bringing your message.
eirēnē tō oikō toutō 'peace to this house', a well known Hebrew greeting (cp. e.g. Judges 19 : 20). Here it refers to the peace that characterizes the Messianic kingdom.

Translation: *Whatever house you enter*, or, 'when you go into (or, set foot in) a house' (cp. NEB, Sranan).
Peace be to this house, or, 'may peace be given to this house', 'may (the people in) this house receive peace', 'may God give peace to (all of) you who are in this house'; or, since wishing peace is a form of blessing, 'may God give you blessing, this whole household' (Tzeltal), cp. also East Toradja 1933, lit. 'pray-for those people that their life be well (a term for blessing)'. Where the optative mood cannot be expressed by position (as

here in the Greek), or by an optative verbal form or particle, one may prepose a phrase like, 'I want/wish that'. For *peace,* here used with positive aspect, see on 1 : 79. — Renderings in the line of those just mentioned will have to be used even in the considerable number of languages where the expression concerned does not function as, or even resemble, a formula of salutation, but it may be possible then to hint at that functional meaning, e.g. by rendering the introductory "first say" by, 'first say by way of greeting'.

6 ***And if a son of peace is there, your peace shall rest upon him; but if not, it shall return to you.***

Exegesis: *kai ean ekei ē huios eirēnēs* lit. 'and if there is a son of peace there', cp. A-G s.v. *huios* 1 c δ. Here 'son of peace' means a person who is destined to have/receive peace, cp. Strack-Billerbeck II, 166.

epanapaēsetai ep' auton hē eirēnē humōn 'your peace will rest upon him'.

epanapauomai (†) 'to rest (upon)' is used in Num. 11 : 25f of the spirit that rested upon the seventy elders (cp. also 2 Kings 2: 15). The picture is here that of a blessing, as it were released by the speaking of the word *eirēnē* (hence *hē eirēnē humōn* 'your peace') and subsisting apart from that word.

ei de mēge, scil. *ē huios eirēnēs ekei* 'if (there is) not (a son of peace there)'.

eph' humas anakampsei 'it will (turn around and) come back to you'. *anakamptō* (†).

Translation: *A son of peace.* The phrase may be rendered, 'one who can (or, is ready to) receive peace', 'one who has an expectation of peace' (Sinhalese), 'a man who is worthy of (or, to receive) peace' (cp. Bahasa Indonesia 1968). It is essential that both here and in the next clause the relationship with 'peace' in v. 5 be preserved in translation.

Your peace, i.e. the peace you have wished; hence, 'your greeting of peace' (Kituba), 'your saying of being-well' (Balinese), 'that prayer of you' (East Toradja 1933), 'the blessing you ask for him' (Tzeltal).

Rest upon him, or, 'stay with him', 'bless him'. Descriptive or idiomatic terms or phrases for 'peace' may influence the rendering of this clause, e.g. 'your wish of well-being will make him well'.

Return to you, or, "return and rest upon you" (NEB), 'come to rest upon you again', or further shifts in accordance with those in the preceding clause.

7 ***And remain in the same house, eating and drinking what they provide, for the labourer deserves his wages; do not go from house to house.***

Exegesis: *en autē de tē oikia menete* 'in that very house you must stay'. *autē* has the force of a strong demonstrative pronoun, cp. A-G s.v. 1 h.

esthiontes kai pinontes ta par' autōn 'eating and drinking what comes from them', i.e. 'what they offer you'. *ta par' autōn* is virtually equivalent to *ta paratithemena humin* (v. 8). *autōn* refers to the people who live in the house. For the phrase 'eating and drinking' cp. on 5 : 30.

axios gar ho ergatēs tou misthou autou 'for the worker is worth his pay'. Probably a proverbial saying which applies only indirectly to the present situation. The disciples are to consider the food and shelter they receive as payment for their service to the master of the crop.

mē metabainete ex oikias eis oikian 'do not move from one house to another', i.e. do not change quarters; stay where you are.

metabainō (†) 'to change one's residence'.

Translation: *Remain in the same house,* cp. on "stay there" in 9 : 4.

Eating and drinking what they provide, or, 'what those who live there offer you'. For *to eat and drink* cp. on 5 : 30.

The labourer, often better an indefinite form, e.g. 'a labourer', 'anyone who works'.

Deserves, or, 'is worthy of', 'is worthy to receive', cp. on 3 : 16.

Wages, i.e. what (or, the things) people give him in return for his services/work.

Do not go from house to house, stating negatively what the first clause has said positively.

8 ***Whenever you enter a town and they receive you, eat what is set before you;***

Exegesis: *kai eis hēn an polin eiserchēsthe kai dechōntai humas* 'and into whatever town you go and they receive you'. As in v. 5 the relative *hēn* is not taken up in the main clause. The second clause expresses a condition which must be met by the people of any town where the messengers come. Subject of *dechōntai* are the people of the town (cp. Phillips).

esthiete ta paratithemena humin 'eat what is put before you', cp. on 9 : 16 and on v. 7.

Translation: *Whenever you enter a town and they receive you,* or, 'if you enter a town and the people (there) receive you', 'if on entering a town its people receive you'; and cp. on 9 : 5.

What is set before you, or, 'what is offered you', 'what the people there offer you'.

9 ***heal the sick in it and say to them, 'The kingdom of God has come near to you.'***

Exegesis: *tous en autē astheneis* lit. 'the sick in it', i.e. in that town, or, there. For *asthenēs* cp. on 9 : 2.

kai legete autois 'and say to them', i.e. to the people of the town in question, not to the sick only.

ēggiken eph' humas hē basileia tou theou 'the kingdom of God has come close to you'. For *eggizō* cp. on 7 : 12. For *hē basileia tou theou* cp. on 4 : 43. The perfect tense of *ēggiken* indicates that the rule of God is a present reality then and there. *eph' humas* indicates the people for whom this reality is there.

Translation: For *sick* see on 4 : 40.

To them, or specifying the pronoun, 'to the people (there)', 'to the inhabitants/townspeople'.

The kingdom of God has come near to you, or, 'has come to you' (Toba Batak); or, 'the day that God rules has come near to you', 'here and now God is going to rule you'.

10 ***But whenever you enter a town and they do not receive you, go into its streets and say,*** 11 ***'Even the dust of your town that clings to our feet, we wipe off against you; nevertheless know this, that the kingdom of God has come near.'***

Exegesis: *eis hēn d' an polin eiselthēte kai mē dechōntai humas* 'into whatever town you go and they do not receive you', cp. on v. 8.

exelthontes eis tas plateias autēs eipate 'going out into its streets say'. *exelthontes* is equivalent to an imperative (cp. RSV).

plateia 'wide road', 'street'.

(V. 11) *kai ton koniorton ton kollēthenta hēmin ek tēs poleōs humōn eis tous podas* 'the very dust that sticks to us from your city to the feet', i.e. 'to our feet from your town'. *ek tēs poleōs humōn* goes with *kollēthenta,* and the picture is that of the dust which still sticks to the feet of the messengers when they leave the town which does not receive them. For *koniortos* cp. on 9 : 5. *hēmin* is dative of advantage. *eis tous podas* still has the suggestion of the dust finding its way to the feet of the messengers.

kollaō (also 15 : 15) here in the passive 'to cling to', 'to stick to'.

apomassometha humin 'we wipe off against you'. The dative *humin* is equivalent to *eph' humas* 'against you', i.e. 'in protest against you', cp. Acts 13 : 51, and *eis marturion ep' autous* 'as a witness against them' in 9 : 5, and *TH-Mk* on 6 : 11.

apomassomai (††) 'to wipe off', a more thorough act than shaking off (9 : 5).

plēn touto ginōskete 'but know this'. *plēn* is stronger than the common *alla,* cp. A-G s.v. 1 b.

Translation: *Go into its streets and say,* i.e. go out from the house that has lodged you and say in the streets you pass on your way out of the town (as implied in the wording of v. 11[a]). Hence, *go into* may better be rendered 'go out into', 'leave the house and go into/along'. *Streets,* or, better to bring out the public character, "open streets" (Goodspeed), *places publiques* (Jerusalem). Cp. also *N.T.Wb./72,* WAY.

(V. 11) The clause *even the dust of* (or, from, TEV) *your town that clings to our feet, we wipe off* has virtually the same meaning as the main clause of 9 : 5. Taking 'from the town' with the verb one may render the object phrase by, 'the very dust that clings/sticks to our feet in/from your town' (cp. Rieu, Brouwer), 'even the dust from your town on our feet' (Willibrord), 'the very dust on our feet, which comes from your town'. The rendering of *wipe off* may have to coincide with that of "shake off" in 9 : 5.

Against states briefly what "as a testimony against" has expressed more explicitly in 9 : 5.

Know here implies an act of will; hence, "take note of" (NEB), "understand" (Goodspeed).

The kingdom of God has come near, differing from v. 9[b] in not having 'to you'; it is preferable that this probably intentional difference should be preserved in translation.

12 ***I tell you, it shall be more tolerable on that day for Sodom than for that town.***

Exegesis: *legō humin* 'I tell you', cp. on 3 : 8.

Sodomois... anektoteron estai 'for Sodom it will be more tolerable'.

Sodoma (neuter plural) 'Sodom'.

anektos 'endurable', 'tolerable', especially with reference to judgment.

en tē hēmera ekeinē 'on that day', i.e. on the coming day of judgment, cp. v. 14.

Translation: This sentence does not continue the words Jesus tells the disciples to speak, but gives his judgment of the fate of a city that rejects his disciples.

It shall be more tolerable... for Sodom than for that town. Some changes of structure that may be required are: adding a term for 'suffering', 'punishment', e.g. 'there will be less suffering people in Sodom...' (Kekchi), 'the punishment of the city of S. will be lighter (or, less heavy/severe) than the punishment of that city' (several Indonesian languages), or more generically, 'what S. will experience shall be lighter than that town' (Javanese); taking 'Sodom' as subject, e.g. "Sodom will fare better than that town" (Goodspeed), 'S. will have a less severe fate than that city' (Jerusalem); making explicit the implied agent, e.g. 'God will punish Sodom less severely than that town'; or, transposing the parts of the comparison, e.g. 'that town will suffer more than S.' (cp. Navajo, in *TBT*, 13.29, 1962). Some ways to express the comparative here are, 'the Sodom people will suffer little (lit. eat comparatively little pain), while that town will suffer much (lit. eat much pain)' (cp. Melpa), 'it will be big, God's punishing that town. To-the-extent it is a lie (i.e. much less) his punishing... Sodom...' (cp. Tagabili).

On that day, or making explicit the specific meaning, e.g. 'at that great time' (Melpa), 'when the time of punishment arrives' (Tzeltal), 'when arrives that day of God's judging people' (Tagabili, similarly Kituba), 'on the day of judgment' (cp. Navajo, Lokele, Sinhalese), for which see *N.T.Wb.*/48f; *TH-Mk* on 6 : 11.

13 ***"Woe to you, Chorazin! woe to you, Bethsaida! for if the mighty works done in you had been done in Tyre and Sidon, they would have repented long ago, sitting in sackcloth and ashes.***

Exegesis: *ouai soi* (twice) 'woe to you', 'alas for you', cp. on 6 : 24.

Chorazin...Bēthsaïda 'Chorazin...Bethsaida' both close to Capernaum (v. 15).

ei en Turō kai Sidōni egenēthēsan hai dunameis...palai an...metenoēsan 'if the miracles...had happened in Tyre and Sidon, they would have repented long ago'. For this construction (unreal supposition in conditional clause, unreal case in main clause), cp. Bl-D, § 360, § 371.3.

palai (†) 'long ago', in view of the duration of Jesus' ministry in Galilee slightly hyperbolic and virtually equivalent to 'immediately'.

metanoeō 'to feel remorse', 'to repent', cp. *N.T.Wb.*, 109f/.

hai dunameis hai genomenai en humin 'the miracles that did happen in you', as contrasted with Tyre and Sidon where they did not happen. For *dunamis* cp. *TH-Mk* on 5 : 30, *TBT*, 7.42-47, 1956, and A-G s.v. 4.

en sakkō kai spodō kathēmenoi 'sitting in sackcloth and ashes', going with *metenoēsan*.

sakkos (†) 'sackcloth', a garment of goat's hair or camel's hair, cp. *IDB* IV, 147. *en sakkō* means 'clothed in sackcloth', and is a sign of remorse (here), or, mourning.

spodos (†) 'ashes'. *en spodō* means '(sitting) in/upon ashes', cp. Is. 58 : 5; Job 2 : 8, a sign of remorse (here), or, of mourning.

Translation: *Woe to you* (2 ×), see on 6 : 24. In South Toradja, which possesses two synonymous expressions, literary standards make the parallel use of these phrases more satisfactory than mere repetition of one phrase, 'to-their-end are your days, Chorazin! finished is what-is-measured-out to you, Bethsaida'.

If... etc., an unrealizable supposition, which may be expressed by a specific verbal form or construction (as e.g. in English, Javanese, Sranan) or by a modal particle (as e.g. in Balinese); or more explicitly by preposing a phrase meaning 'suppose that', or by first denying the supposed fact, and then stating it as a condition, which may result here in something like, 'the mighty works...have not been done in Tyre and Sidon, (but) if they had (been done there), they could have repented'. But there are languages also that use a construction that differs in nothing from the normal conditional sentence, thus leaving it to the receptor to deduce its unreal character from the fact that he knows the stated condition not to be true. See also on 7 : 39.

If the mighty works done in you had been done in T. and S., or, where an agent has to be mentioned, 'if someone had done in T. and S. the mighty works I have done in you'. *Mighty works*, cp. *TH-Mk* on 6 : 2; 9 : 39, and Phillips' rendering "demonstrations of God's power".

They, or, 'those cities', 'the people (who live) there', 'the people of those cities'.

Would have repented long ago, or, 'would not have waited long (or, delayed until now) to repent'.

Sitting in sackcloth and ashes, cp. *N.T.Wb.*/62[b], REPENT. Better to indicate the function of this expression and the rite it refers to one may explicitly state its relationship with the verb, cp. e.g. 'would long ago have been sitting in sackcloth and ashes to show that they repented'; cp. also TEV. Some cultures know of similar rites, sufficiently close in form and function to make the expression understandable. Thus amongst the Shona to dress in an equivalent of sackcloth and go unwashed as a beggar, forms part of a ritual to reconcile a person's parent who has died with a grievance against him. In other languages one of the two parts of the phrase "sitting in sackcloth and ashes" has such an equivalent, which could be used in the translation in order to clarify the function of the unknown part. In Sranan, for example, the first phrase is rendered by 'keep mat-mourning', i.e. show mourning by sitting and sleeping on a mat, a traditional Surinam rite of heavy mourning; and in Kapauku people smear their faces with ashes in grief and speak of sitting in ashes. Where this is not the case and the expression would not be understood, or could even be misleading (as it would be in Cuicatec, where 'sitting in ashes' refers to one who spends his day sitting by the fire instead of working), the function may have to be substituted, either for the whole phrase, e.g. 'they would surely have repented' (Tagabili), or for one of its parts, e.g. 'wear clothing-of sadness' (Ponape, Trukese). Some further, minor adjustments may be necessary: *sackcloth* is often rendered by a word referring to a coarse kind of cloth, or by 'clothing that hurts' (Otomi of Mexico), 'that which is scratchy' (Mazahua), 'rags' (East Toradja, Zarma); *in ashes* may have to become 'smeared, or, painted, themselves with ashes' (Shona 1966, Huixtec), 'having taken ash on their bodies' (Marathi).

14 ***But it shall be more tolerable in the judgment for Tyre and Sidon than for you.***

Exegesis: *plēn* 'yet', i.e. notwithstanding the fact that Tyre and Sidon have not repented (cp. Plummer).

anektoteron estai 'it will be more tolerable', cp. on v. 12.

en tē krisei 'in the judgment', i.e. 'on the day of judgment'.

krisis 'judgment', in Luke always (except 11 : 42) of the future day of eschatological judgment, cp. A-G s.v. 1 a α.

Translation: For this verse cp. on v. 12.

15 ***And you, Capernaum, will you be exalted to heaven? You shall be brought down to Hades.***

Exegesis: *kai su, Kapharnaoum* "and as for you, Capernaum" (NEB). *su* is emphatic. For *Kapharnaoum* cp. on 4 : 23.

mē heōs ouranou hupsōthēsē 'will you be exalted to heaven?', i.e. 'will you receive the place of the highest honour?' *mē* implies that a negative answer to this question is expected (cp. A-G s.v. C 1). For *hupsoō* cp. on 1 : 52. The language of v. 15 reflects closely Is. 14 : 13, 15 which apply to Babylon.

heōs tou hadou katabibasthēsē 'you will be brought down to the underworld'.

katabibazō (††) 'to bring down', 'to drive down', implying a note of violence, cp. Rieu. Nestle reads *katabēsē* 'you will go down', which is more general, cp. on 2 : 51.

hadēs (also 16 : 23) 'underworld', located in the depths of the earth, cp. *N.T.Wb.*, 72/HELL.

Translation: *Will you be exalted...*, i.e. do you really think/suppose that you will be exalted.... The negative answer expected is implied in the next sentence, which may in some cases better be introduced by 'no' (Shona 1966), or, 'on the contrary'.

Exalted to heaven...brought down to Hades. The agent or initiator is ultimately God, but where a passive form cannot be used, it is as a rule better to shift to forms that are neutral as to the cause, e.g. 'go up...go down...', 'become high...become low...', etc. For the figurative use of the verbs cp. *N.T.Wb.*/28, DIMENSIONS. *Heaven* and *Hades*, i.e. the highest and the lowest point of the universe; their other meaning, viz. 'abode of God' (cp. on 2 : 15) and 'abode of the dead' (cp. on 16 : 23) is of no, or only secondary importance in this verse; hence they are best rendered by 'sky', 'above/off the face of the earth' (East Nyanja, Yao), 'highest height' (Shona 1966), and, 'underworld', 'lowest layer (of the earth/cosmos)', 'depth of the ocean', 'depth of darkness' (Javanese), 'lowest point' (Shona 1966). Where elevation and its opposite do not have the required figurative meaning and one has to use 'to honour', 'to make big/heavy', and 'to humiliate', 'to make small/light' etc., one will have to replace the two qualifying prepositional phrases by some other indications of high degree.

16 ***"He who hears you hears me, and he who rejects you rejects me, and he who rejects me rejects him who sent me."***

Exegesis: *ho akouōn humōn emou akouei* 'he who listens to you listens to me'. Close of the commission to the seventy [two] and after vv. 13-15 addressed to them. *akouō* implies here acceptance of what is heard, as its contrast *atheteō* shows (see below).

ho athetōn humas eme athetei 'he who rejects you rejects me'. For *atheteō* cp. on 7 : 30. Here it is used with a personal object and refers to the rejection of the call to faith in, and allegiance to Jesus.

ton aposteilanta me 'him who has sent me', i.e. God. Jesus applies here to himself the word he applied to the messengers, cp. v. 3.

Translation: *Hears*, i.e. 'listens to' (cp. on 1 : 41), or, 'obeys' (cp. on 2 : 51).

You, i.e. the seventy [two] disciples.

Rejects, see on 7 : 30 (with a non-personal object) and on 9 : 22 (where the object is Jesus); or, 'does not receive' (for which cp. on 9 : 5).

17 ***The seventy returned with joy, saying, "Lord, even the demons are subject to us in your name!"***

Exegesis: *hupestrepsan de hoi hebdomēkonta* [*duo*] 'the seventy [two] returned', without indication of the time elapsed since Jesus sent them out. A period of some weeks may be safely assumed to have passed.

kurie 'lord', or, taking up *ho kurios* in v. 1, 'Lord', preferably the former, cp. on 1 : 6 and on 5 : 8.

kai ta daimonia hupotassetai hēmin 'even the demons subject themselves to us'. *kai* 'even', because they had not explicitly been sent to cast out demons (cp. v. 9). *hupotassetai* may be rendered (1) "are made obedient" (BFBS), passive; (2) 'subject themselves', or "submit" (Goodspeed, NEB), middle; (3) "are subject" (RSV), indicating a state of being. (2) is preferable (also in v. 20).

en tō onomati sou 'in your name', cp. *TH-Mk* on 9 : 38.

Translation: *The seventy returned with joy.* The reference to the return has transitional force in that it serves to bridge the time that has elapsed since the departure of the seventy. This is in some cases better brought out by changing the pattern of subordination, e.g. 'the seventy returned and rejoiced', 'on the return of the seventy sent-ones they all were glad' (Balinese). Some versions prefer to indicate the interval otherwise, e.g. 'later the seventy (disciples) came back full of joy' (cp. Phillips, Bahasa Indonesia 1968).

Demons, see references on 4 : 35.

Are subject to us, preferably, 'submit themselves to us' (see *Exegesis*), or, 'drop themselves for us' (Sranan), 'bow to us' (Balinese), and see *N.T.Wb.* /6, ALLOW. The pronoun is best taken as exclusive.

In your name, see on 9 : 49. A verbal clause is sometimes preferable, e.g. 'when we use/mention your name', 'when we name you' (Tagabili), or a shift to a causative construction, cp. 'your name makes even evil spirits obey us' (Shona 1966).

18 ***And he said to them, "I saw Satan fall like lightning from heaven.***

Exegesis: *etheōroun ton Satanan hōs astrapēn ek tou ouranou pesonta* 'I watched Satan fall like lightning from heaven'. *etheōroun* is durative imperfect. For the background of this saying see commentaries. Satan's fall from heaven means that he has lost his power, and this explains why the demons submitted to the disciples. *hōs astrapēn* 'like lightning' goes with *pesonta*. *ouranos* refers here to the abode of God.

theōreō 'to see', 'to watch'.

Satanas 'Satan', 'the devil', cp. *N.T.Wb.*, 43/DEVIL.

astrapē 'lightning'.

Translation: *I saw Satan fall*, or better to bring out the durative aspect, "I watched how Satan fell" (NEB), "I was watching and saw Satan fall"

(Phillips). *Satan* is usually transliterated, but the name may also be translated by the term for "devil" (for which see on 4 : 2[a]); the two designations do not occur in the same passage. In Muslim countries the Arabic form of the name, *Shaiṭān,* usually is well known, but it may have acquired a different meaning, e.g. in Bahasa Indonesia, Javanese, where it is a designation of 'demons' in general. Cp. also *N.T.Wb.*/26, DEVIL.

Like lightning, or to make clear what the comparison refers to, 'like lightning falls, or, goes down', or a more specific verb like 'strikes'. Toba Batak possesses distinctive terms for a 'flash-of-lightning (as seen in the sky)', and 'stroke-of-lightning (coming down to the earth)', used here.

19 ***Behold, I have given you authority to tread upon serpents and scorpions, and over all the power of the enemy; and nothing shall hurt you.***

Exegesis: *idou dedōka humin* 'behold, I have given you'. *idou* (cp. on 1 : 20) has here the force of a confirmative particle. *dedōka* points to an act in the past which is still effective.

tēn exousian tou patein epanō opheōn kai skorpiōn 'the authority to tread on snakes and scorpions', because of the article *tēn* referring to a specific authority. For *exousia* cp. on 4 : 6, 32. Here it is used in the sense of 'effective authority', or, 'power'.

pateō (also 21 : 24) here intransitive 'to walk', 'to tread', 'to trample', in 21 : 24 transitive.

epanō 'on', cp. on 4 : 39.

ophis (also 11 : 11) 'snake', general term, but here of dangerous snakes.

skorpios 'scorpion', cp. *IDB* IV, 245 and A-G s.v. Both *ophis* and *skorpios* (cp. also 11 : 11, 12), though here to be taken literally, symbolize harmful powers.

kai epi pasan tēn dunamin tou echthrou 'and (authority) over all the power of the enemy', with *exousian* understood from *tēn exousian.* As compared with the preceding phrase this is of a general and non-symbolic nature. *dunamis* may have the connotation of '(armed) forces'.

ho echthros 'the enemy' refers here to the devil, cp. A-G s.v. 2 b α.

kai ouden humas ou mē adikēsē 'and nothing will harm you', or 'and he will not harm you in any respect', preferably the former rendering which has *ouden* as subject of *adikēsē. ou mē* is a strong negation, cp. on 1 : 15, and reinforces *ouden...ou* which, by itself, is already stronger than *ouden* alone.

adikeō (†) 'to harm', 'to hurt'.

Translation: *I have given you authority to,* preferably, 'power to', or, with a syntactic shift, 'I have empowered/enabled you to', 'I have made you so strong that you can'.

Serpent, or, 'poisonous snake', or the name of a common local species or equivalent.

Where the *scorpion* is unknown, the name of another dangerous reptile will do, e.g. that of a poisonous lizard (Bamiléké), or a centipede whose bite causes a swelling (East and South Toradja).

And over, or, "and cope with" (Rieu), 'to subdue' (Balinese, South Toradja). The head of the construction may have to be repeated, 'and power over'.

The enemy. The referent may be suggested by marking the noun (for which see on 1 : 71) as a proper name (e.g. in TEV, Jerusalem), or made explicit, cp. 'the Evil-one' (East Toradja 1933), 'Satan' (Tagabili).

Hurt, or, 'cause harm/pain/evil to', 'make suffer'; or, 'to do-something-to' (a derivation of 'why' used in a clearly pejorative sense) (East Toradja, Toba Batak).

20 ***Nevertheless do not rejoice in this, that the spirits are subject to you; but rejoice that your names are written in heaven."***

Exegesis: *plēn* 'yet', i.e. 'though you have this authority'.

en toutō mē chairete hoti... 'do not rejoice over the fact that...'.

hoti ta onomata humōn eggegraptai en tois ouranois 'that your names have been enrolled in heaven', i.e. you are members of the heavenly community. For the background of this clause see commentaries, especially Plummer.

eggraphō (†) 'to write', 'to record', 'to enroll'.

Translation: Formally the two clauses are imperatives, expressing a negative and a positive command, but semantically they form a statement expressing preference; hence a rendering such as, 'you should, or may, not so much rejoice in that..., but rather you should/may rejoice in that...'. Further adjustments that may be necessary are: putting the positive clause first; using the verb only once (cp. NEB); or shifting to a conditional or concessive construction, e.g. 'if you rejoice, rejoice (or, do so) not so much in this, that..., but rather in that ...', 'you may rejoice, but rather because your names...than because the spirits...'.

For *spirits* see on 9 : 39 and references.

Your names are written in heaven, or, 'are enrolled in the book of heaven' (Lokele). The expression to be used should fit the way membership of a social group is recorded in the culture. The plural is distributive; the implied agent is God.

21 ***In that same hour he rejoiced in the Holy Spirit and said, "I thank thee, Father, Lord of heaven and earth, that thou hast hidden these things from the wise and understanding and revealed them to babes; yea, Father, for such was thy gracious will.***

Exegesis: *en autē tē hōra* 'at that very hour', 'at that moment', cp. on v. 7.

ēgalliasato [en] tō pneumati tō hagiō 'he rejoiced in the Holy Spirit', instrumental dative. For *agalliaō* (here in middle form) cp. on 1 : 47.

exomologoumai soi 'I praise you', or, 'I thank you', preferably the former. For *exomologeomai* (also 22 : 6) cp. A-G s.v. 2 a and c.

pater, kurie tou ouranou kai tēs gēs 'father, lord of heaven and earth', i.e. lord of all creation.

hoti apekrupsas tauta apo sophōn kai sunetōn 'that you have hidden these things from the wise and understanding'. *tauta* in the present context probably refers to the experiences of the messengers, viz. their power over the demons and their authority over the power of the enemy.

apokruptō (†) 'to hide'.

sophos (†) 'wise', 'learned'.

sunetos (†) 'intelligent'. As compared with *sophos, sunetos* refers more to intellectual capacities and *sophos* to knowledge and insight from learning and experience. In the present context *sophos* and *sunetos* refer to the spiritual and intellectual leaders of the Jewish people.

kai apekalupsas auta nēpiois 'and that you have revealed it to the simple', still dependent upon *hoti*. For *apokaluptō* cp. on 2 : 35. Here it has a religious connotation since God is subject.

nēpios (†) lit. '(young) child'. Here it contrasts with *sophos* and *sunetos* and this suggests the meaning "simple" (Rieu, NEB), or, 'innocent', cp. A-G s.v. 1 b β.

nai, ho patēr 'indeed, father'. *nai* resumes *exomologoumai*, cp. A-G s.v. *nai* 3. *ho patēr* is nominative with the force of a vocative.

hoti houtōs eudokia egeneto emprosthen sou lit. 'that thus it was well-pleasing in your sight', probably best understood as equivalent to *hoti houtōs eudokēsas* 'that you have chosen this way'. For *eudokia* cp. on 2 : 14.

Translation: *In the Holy Spirit,* or, 'through/because-of/under the influence of/in the power of the Holy Spirit' (Lokele, East Toradja, Jerusalem, Sinhalese); or one may take the Spirit as agent, cp. e.g. 'the Holy Spirit filled him with happiness' (Kituba).

I thank thee (see on 2 : 38), preferably, 'I praise thee' (see on 2 : 13).

Father, or, where this form of address is obligatorily possessed, 'my Father'; but cp. also *TBT,* 13.28, 1962. Although in languages that differentiate according to rank one usually addresses one's father in ordinary speech forms yet in this case (similarly in 22 : 42; 23 : 34, 46) linguistic usage may require an honorific word for 'father', and polite speech forms for the words addressed to him, because here the reference is to God, the heavenly Father. Cp. on 2 : 49.

Lord of heaven and earth is appositional, for which cp. on 1 : 13. *Lord of* may be rendered, 'Lord who possesses', 'the One who rules', cp. e.g. 'authority-exercising person' (Kapauku), or, expressing a personal relationship, 'lord (lit. revered-one) of all-who-live-in' (Balinese); cp. also on 6 : 5. *Heaven and earth* (also in 16 : 17; 21 : 32), or, 'sky/firmament and earth/land/world', or whatever pair of terms the receptor language normally uses to refer to the upper and lower strata of the universe; cp. also *TH-Mk* on 13 : 27 (*Exegesis*).

That, introducing the reason for Jesus' praise or thanksgiving, 'for the fact that', 'because'.

Hidden...from. The function of the preposition may have to be circumscribed, cp. e.g. 'so that the wise...cannot see (or, know) it'.

For *wise* see on the related noun "wisdom" in 2 : 40; for *understanding* see on 2 : 47.

To reveal, or here, 'to show'.

Yea. If no particle with resuming function is available, it may be preferable to repeat 'I praise/thank you (Father)'.

Such was thy gracious will, or, 'it pleased you' (Tarascan; similarly Sranan, lit. 'so it came sweet to you'), 'it has been your good pleasure to do so', 'you have been so kind to choose this way, or, to decide to do this'.

22 ***All things have been delivered to me by my Father; and no one knows who the Son is except the Father, or who the Father is except the Son and any one to whom the Son chooses to reveal him."***

Exegesis: *panta moi paredothē* 'everything has been handed over to me'. *panta* may mean 'all power', or 'all knowledge', preferably the latter. For *paradidōmi* cp. on 1 : 2.

oudeis ginōskei tis estin ho huios ei mē ho patēr 'nobody knows who the son is but the father'. Both *ho huios* and *ho patēr* have the force of a title.

kai hō ean boulētai ho huios apokalupsai 'and (he) to whom the son may choose to reveal', scil. who the father is.

boulomai (also 22 : 42) 'to be willing', 'to want', 'to choose'.

Translation: In this verse Jesus no longer addresses God but speaks to the seventy and other people present. This may have to be marked, e.g. by adding, "Then he went on" (Phillips), or more explicitly, 'And to the people he said'. In languages like Javanese and Balinese one has to shift from honorifics in v. 21 to a non-honorific form of address here.

For *delivered* cp. on 4 : 6.

The construction *no one knows who the Son is except the Father* may have to be recast, e.g. 'no one knows who the Son (really) is (or, knows the true nature of the Son), only the Father (knows him/it)' (cp. Kituba, Tzeltal), 'other people do not know who . . ., but the Father does', or reversely, 'the Father knows who . . ., no one else (knows him/it)'; cp. also *TH-Mk* on 6 : 4, 8. Similarly for the next clause, where 'to know' may have to be repeated.

Where *the Son* and *the Father* have to be possessed, or where third person reference to first person is impossible, one may have to shift to something like, '. . . who I am, except my Father, or who my Father is, except me, his Son'. For *the Son* cp. on "Son of God" in 1 : 35.

And, or, 'and also', 'and further', 'moreover'.

Any one to whom the Son chooses to reveal him, or, 'other persons only (or, in an expanded form, other persons can also know him/it, but only) if the Son chooses to reveal him/it to them'. — *Chooses,* or, 'is willing', 'wishes', 'sees fit'. *To reveal,* or here, 'to make known'.

23 ***Then turning to the disciples he said privately, "Blessed are the eyes which see what you see!***

Exegesis: *kai strapheis pros tous mathētas kat' idian* 'and turning to his disciples in private', i.e. probably, 'when they were alone'. For *strapheis* cp. on 7 : 9; for *kat' idian* cp. on 9 : 10.

makarioi hoi ophthalmoi hoi blepontes ha blepete 'blessed (are) the eyes that see what you see', nominal clause followed by a participial clause which explains the predicate *makarioi*. For *makarios* cp. on 6 : 20 and 1 : 45.

Translation: For *turning* cp. on 7 : 9.

Privately, or, 'when they were alone', may have to be transposed to form a better transition, e.g. 'when Jesus and his disciples were alone he turned to (or, addressed) them and said'.

Blessed are the eyes which see..., or shifting from the part to the whole, 'blessed are the people who see...'. For *blessed*, or, 'happy', see on 1 : 45.

24 ***For I tell you that many prophets and kings desired to see what you see, and did not see it, and to hear what you hear, and did not hear it."***

Exegesis: *legō gar humin* 'for I tell you', cp. on 3 : 8.

polloi prophētai kai basileis 'many prophets and kings', of Old Testament times.

ēthelēsan idein...kai akousai 'wished to see...and to hear'.

kai ouk eidan...kai ouk ēkousan 'but did not see...but did not hear'. *kai* has here the force of an adversative connective.

ha humeis blepete 'what you see', emphatic.

ha akouete 'what you hear', also emphatic though *humeis* is not added.

Translation: *Desired.* The reference to the past may have to be expressed not in the verb but otherwise, e.g. in the subject, cp. 'prophets and kings of old' (Balinese).

And to hear... This second clause may require repetition of the main verb, e.g. 'they desired to hear...'.

25 ***And behold, a lawyer stood up to put him to the test, saying, "Teacher, what shall I do to inherit eternal life?"***

Exegesis: *kai idou* 'and behold', cp. on 1 : 20. Here it introduces a new situation.

nomikos tis anestē 'an expert in the law got up'. For *nomikos* cp. on 7 : 30. *anestē* seems to suggest a situation in which people were sitting.

ekpeirazōn auton 'testing him', i.e., 'in order to test him'. For *ekpeirazō* cp. on 4 : 12.

ti poiēsas zōēn aiōnion klēronomēsō lit. 'what doing, or, by doing what shall I inherit eternal life?', i.e. 'what must I do to inherit eternal life?' The aorist tense of *poiēsas* points to one specific act (cp. Plummer).

zōē 'life', here with *aiōnios* of life in the period of final consummation, cp. A-G s.v. *zōē* 2 b β and *TH-Mk* on 10 : 17.

aiōnios 'eternal', i.e. 'without end'.

klēronomeō (also 18 : 18) 'to inherit', 'to come into the possession of'. Since the inheritance of eternal life is seen as depending on what man does, the meaning 'to inherit' is not to be pressed.

Translation: *Lawyer,* see on 7 : 30.

To put him to the test, or, specifying what is tested, 'to (put on the) test his wisdom/teaching'; cp. also *TH-Mk* on 10 : 2.

For *inherit eternal life* see *TH-Mk* on 10 : 17; *N.T.Wb.*/4f, AGE. A remarkable idiom used for 'life' is 'undyingness' (cp. *TBT*, 18.188, 1967).

26 ***He said to him, "What is written in the law? How do you read?"***

Exegesis: *en tō nomō* 'in the law', cp. on 2 : 22.

pōs anaginōskeis lit. 'how do you read', or, 'how do you recite', viz. in the worship service in the synagogue, a rabbinical formula used when a scripture quotation is called for. The latter rendering appears to be slightly preferable. *pōs* refers to the content of what is read, cp. BFBS.

Translation: *He said,* i.e. Jesus said/asked.

What is written in the law, see on 2 : 22f.

How do you read, or, "what do you read there" (BFBS), 'how/what do you (usually) read aloud, or, recite'. For *to read* cp. on 4 : 16.

27 ***And he answered, "You shall love the Lord your God with all your heart, and with all your soul, and with all your strength, and with all your mind; and your neighbour as yourself."***

Exegesis: *apokritheis* 'answering', cp. on 1 : 19.

agapēseis kurion ton theon sou 'you shall love the Lord your God'. The future tense of *agapēseis* has the force of an imperative. For the phrase *kurios ho theos sou* cp. on 1 : 16.

agapaō 'to love', cp. *N.T.Wb.*, 87ff/.

ex holēs [*tēs*] *kardias sou* 'with all your heart', or, 'with your whole heart'. For this and the following concepts cp. *TH-Mk* on 12 : 30; cp. also *TBT*, 4.36-40, 1953; 13.121-124, 1962. *kardia, psuchē, ischus* and *dianoia* together denote man in his totality; semantically they function together rather than separately. *ek* has instrumental force.

en holē tē psuchē sou 'with all your soul'. For *psuchē* cp. on 1 : 46 and A-G s.v. 1 b γ. *en* has instrumental force.

en holē tē ischuï sou 'with all your strength'. *ischus* (†).

en holē tē dianoia sou 'with all your mind'. For *dianoia* cp. on 1 : 51.

kai ton plēsion sou hōs seauton scil. *agapēseis* 'and (you shall love) your neighbour as yourself', cp. *TH-Mk* on 12 : 31. *ho plēsion* is to be distinguished from *hoi perioikoi*, i.e. 'those who live in the neighbourhood', cp. on 1 : 58.

Translation: For the first of the two commandments in this verse cp. *TH-Mk* on 12 : 30, which is identical, except for one difference in phrase order. Most versions give a rather literal rendering with only minor adjustments, e.g. substituting 'mind' for "heart" (Marathi), 'spirit', 'life', or, 'breath' for "soul" (e.g. in Lokele, Trukese; Marathi; Bamiléké), 'animation', or, 'ability' for "strength" (e.g. in Yao; Trukese), and 'thinking/thought(s)', or, 'intelligence' for "mind" (cp. e.g. Lokele, Trukese; Marathi). Such a rendering often is sufficiently idiomatic, but sometimes it has simply been accepted as a Biblical expression, even though it is decidedly unidiomatic as to its individual components, their combination, order and/or number, or to its construction (e.g. possession, impossible with the third and fourth term in some languages). Then one should preferably use the idiomatic way of referring to the totality of man's spiritual and emotional faculties. This may lead to rather radical shifts and changes. Thus Ponape and Trukese idiom would probably prefer an equivalent of the Biblical phrase 'with flesh and body', and in Tagabili, where a listing of the four faculties was first attempted but proved unsuccessful, the present translation of the sentence is, 'cause it to start from the very beginning of your stomach your loving God, for he is your place of holding'.

For *love* see on 6 : 27. In a language like Balinese one must use 'respectful love', since the object is God.

For *soul* see on 1 : 46.

Your neighbour as yourself, or filling out the ellipsis, 'you shall love your neighbour as yourself' (cp. Rieu, Bahasa Indonesia KB, Sundanese), 'you shall love your neighbour as you love yourself', where necessary shifting to plural forms, cp. *TH-Mk* on 12 : 31, or rendering the verb by a term for love between equals (Balinese). — *Your neighbour.* Some languages do as English, translating the noun by the term for a member of one's local group used also in 1 : 58, e.g. 'one who lives nearby' (cp. Lokele, Marathi), 'co-dweller' (Zarma), trusting to the context for making clear the expanded meaning the term has in the present verse. Several other versions use a term of wider application, such as 'your fellow-man' (Bahasa Indonesia, similarly East Toradja, using a reciprocal form built on 'man'), 'your fellow earth-dweller' (South Toradja), 'your companion as a person' (Tzeltal, which in 1 : 58 uses 'those at back and side'), 'another person like you' (Shona 1966).

28 ***And he said to him, "You have answered right; do this, and you will live."***

Exegesis: *orthōs apekrithēs* 'you have answered correctly', cp. 7 : 43.

touto poiei kai zēsē 'do that, and you will live'. The imperative has the force of a conditional clause, 'if you do that, you will live'. The present tense of *poiei* points to a continued attitude (cp. Plummer). In the present context *zēsē* refers to *zōē aiōnios* 'eternal life'.

Translation: *You have answered right,* or another idiomatic expression of approval, cp. "you are right" (Goodspeed), "quite right" (Phillips); and cp. on 7 : 43.

You will live, or, 'you will have/acquire eternal life'.

29 ***But he, desiring to justify himself, said to Jesus, "And who is my neighbour?"***

Exegesis: *thelōn dikaiōsai heauton* 'wishing to justify himself', i.e. 'to vindicate himself', or, 'to justify his question', i.e. to show that Jesus' apparently obvious answer was inadequate. The former is preferable. For *dikaioō* cp. on 7 : 29.

kai tis estin mou plēsion 'and who is my neighbour?' *kai* introduces a further question in a discussion (cp. Plummer).

Translation: *But he, desiring to...said*, or, 'but he (or, the lawyer/that man) desired/wished to.... Therefore he said (or, asked)'.

To justify himself, or, 'to vindicate himself', "to put himself in the right" (TEV), 'to show that his question had been right'. Sranan has, 'to pull himself out of the story', used when a person tries to withdraw from a discussion that becomes unpleasant; an English-Chinese equivalent would be, 'to save his face'.

30 ***Jesus replied, "A man was going down from Jerusalem to Jericho, and he fell among robbers, who stripped him and beat him, and departed, leaving him half dead.***

Exegesis: *hupolabōn ho Iēsous eipen* lit. 'taking up (scil. the question) Jesus said'. The answer to the question comes in the form of a story. Elsewhere *hupolambanō* means 'to assume' (cp. 7 : 43).

anthrōpos tis katebainen apo Ierousalēm eis Ierichō 'a man was going down from Jerusalem to Jericho', imperfect tense. For *katabainō* cp. on 2 : 51.

kai lēstais periepesen 'and fell into the hands of robbers', aorist tense, indicating a punctiliar event.

lēstēs 'robber', 'bandit'.

peripiptō (†, cp. v. 36, *empiptō*) with dative 'to fall into the hands of'.

hoi kai ekdusantes auton kai plēgas epithentes apēlthon aphentes hēmithanē 'who after stripping him and after inflicting blows went off, leaving him half dead'. *kai* after the relative pronoun serves to focus the attention on what follows (cp. e.g. Acts 1 : 11).

ekduō (†) 'to strip off (clothes)'.

plēgē (also 12 : 48) 'blow', 'stroke'.

epitithēmi (cp. on 4 : 40) here 'to inflict'.

aphiēmi 'to leave (behind)'.

hēmithanēs (††) 'half dead'.

Translation: *Replied*, or, "took this up and said" (Rieu), 'continued-the-discussion, saying' (Javanese, a verb lit. meaning 'to put-an-extension-to', then, 'to continue an activity started by someone else').

A man was going down from . . ., introductory clause, cp. on 8 : 4. For the verb cp. on "went up" in 2 : 4. Jericho is some 20 miles from Jerusalem, the road descending about 3000 feet from the neighbourhood of Bethany to the entrance into the plain of the Jordan (cp. Plummer).

He fell among robbers, or, 'he accidentally met robbers' (Tagalog), 'he-had-the-ill-luck to be-attacked (or, he was-set-upon) by robbers' (Javanese, Sundanese); or in active construction, 'on the way robbers surprised/attacked him'. *Robber*, or, "bandit" (Phillips), 'one-who-murders-to-rob' (South Toradja). In some cases one term covers both 'robbers', i.e. those who take away possessions by force, and 'thieves', who do so by stealth, e.g. in Sranan, or in East Toradja (etymologically 'one-who-lifts-up').

Stripped, or, 'cleaned-out', 'plundered' (Low Malay, lit. 'took-away all he had', and Sranan, lit. 'stole pulled from his hand').

Beat, probably with sticks or clubs; cp. also *N.T.Wb.*/15.

Leaving him (i.e. letting him remain there) *half dead*, or, 'they left him lying (on-the-ground, or, neglected) half/nearly dead' (cp. NV, Javanese, Bahasa Indonesia RC), 'leaving him like-one-dead (lit. dead-dead) on the road' (Sranan; a similar form in Toba Batak). In Conob the idiom for "half dead" is 'whirling in his head'.

31 ***Now by chance a priest was going down that road; and when he saw him he passed by on the other side.***

Exegesis: *kata sugkurian* (††) 'by coincidence'.

hiereus tis 'a priest', cp. *N.T.Wb.*, 104/.

katebainen en tē hodō ekeinē 'went down on that road', i.e. also from Jerusalem to Jericho. Note the durative imperfect.

kai idōn auton antiparēlthen 'and when he saw him he passed by on the opposite side' (with shift to the punctiliar aorist), perhaps because of Lev. 21 : 1. *antiparerchomai* (†).

Translation: *By chance*, or, "it so happened that" (NEB), serves to introduce another event happening, or, going to happen, at the same time and place; hence, 'at that very time' (Sranan), 'that being so' (East Toradja) are possible renderings also.

Priest, see on 1 : 5.

Was going down that road, or, 'was going (down) along that road'. For the noun cp. *N.T.Wb.*/72, WAY.

Saw him, or specifying the pronoun, 'saw that man', 'saw the man that had-been robbed' (Balinese).

Passed by on the other side, or, 'took the other side of the road and passed by' (Jerusalem), 'made a detour around him' (Willibrord, East Toradja), 'he cut the road (i.e. went to the other side) before him and passed' (Sranan).

32 ***So likewise a Levite, when he came to the place and saw him, passed by on the other side.***

Exegesis: *homoiōs de kai* 'and in the very same way'.

Leuitēs 'a Levite', a subordinate cultic officer, cp. *IDB* III, 859f.
[*genomenos*] (if read) 'coming on the scene', cp. TEV.
kata ton topon elthōn 'coming to the place', cp. A-G s.v. *kata* II 1 b.

Translation: *Levite,* or, 'a man of the tribe Levi' (Bahasa Indonesia), 'a descendant of L.' (Balinese, Kapauku). The Levite not having the rank of a priest may either be given no honorifics (as in Balinese), or middle class honorifics (as exist in some languages). Material for a footnote, if thought necessary, is to be found e.g. in 1 Chron. 23 : 28-32.

The place, or specifying the reference, 'the place of that man' (Balinese), 'the place where the unfortunate man (or, the victim) was (lying)' (cp. East Toradja 1933).

33 ***But a Samaritan, as he journeyed, came to where he was; and when he saw him, he had compassion,***

Exegesis: *Samaritēs de tis hodeuōn* 'but a Samaritan who was travelling'. *Samaritēs* is emphatic. For the Samaritans and the opinion held about them by the Jews see commentaries and *IDB* IV, 190-197.

hodeuō (††) 'to travel', 'to make one's way', without indication of direction or goal of the journey. That the Samaritan was not on his way home may be gathered from v. 35.

ēlthen kat' auton 'came upon him', unintentionally. For *kata* cp. on v. 32.

kai idōn esplagchnisthē 'and when he saw (him) he was moved with pity'. For *splagchnizomai* cp. on 7 : 13.

Translation: *Samaritan,* see on 9 : 52^{b}.

As he journeyed, or, 'who was on a journey' (Bahasa Indonesia RC, Balinese), 'a man from afar (lit. on a far journey)' (South Toradja, which has the advantage of suggesting that the Samaritan was a foreigner, which the priest and the Levite were not).

Came to where he was, but not yet at the man's side (see v. 34); hence, 'approached that man', or with further specification, 'came towards (or, passed) the place where he lay neglected, or, the place of the victim' (Bahasa Indonesia, Balinese).

He had compassion, or, 'he pitied (him)', see on 7 : 13.

34 ***and went to him and bound up his wounds, pouring on oil and wine; then he set him on his own beast and brought him to an inn, and took care of him.***

Exegesis: *kai proselthōn katedēsen ta traumata autou* 'and after going to him he bandaged his wounds'. *proselthōn* denotes a deliberate act as compared with *ēlthen kat' auton* (v. 33).

katadeō (††) 'to bind up', 'to bandage', 'to dress'.

trauma (††) 'wound'.

epicheōn elaion kai oinon 'pouring on (scil. the wounds) oil and wine', present participle denoting an act which is simultaneous with *katedēsen*, though in the normal order of things the bandaging follows the applying of oil and wine. For *elaion* cp. on 7 : 46. Here it serves to soften the pains. *oinos* 'wine' most probably was applied as a disinfectant (Grundmann).

epicheō (††) 'to pour on', 'to apply'.

epibibasas de auton epi to idion ktēnos 'and after putting him on his own beast'. *de* marks the transition to a new series of acts.

epibibazō (also 19 : 35) 'to cause to mount', 'to put', 'to load'.

ktēnos (†) 'beast', a generic term, here of an animal used for riding, probably a mule.

ēgagen auton eis pandocheion 'he brought him to an inn'.

pandocheion (††) 'inn', cp. on 2 : 7 (*kataluma*).

epemelēthē autou 'he looked after him', 'he took care of him'. *epimeleomai* also v. 35.

Translation: *Bound up . . ., pouring on . . .* Where this sequence is felt to be unacceptable one may say, 'bound up . . ., having poured on . . .' (Kapauku), or transpose the clauses, cp. e.g. TEV and many other versions. The second verb has been rendered 'to drip-on' (Balinese), 'to wash/bath with' (Shona 1966, NEB), and cp. below.

This medical use of *oil* (i.e. vegetable oil, cp. *TH-Mk* on 6 : 13) and *wine* (see above on 1 : 15) is sometimes uncommon or unknown. If so, the function may better be explained or substituted, cp. 'medicined (lit. cooled) them, with oil and wine' (East Toradja 1933, similarly Tzeltal), 'medicined his many wounds' (Tagabili).

Wounds, see *N.T.Wb.*/76.

Set him, or, "lifted him" (NEB, similarly South Toradja), 'made him ride' (Javanese).

His own beast, or, 'the animal he-was-riding-on himself' (Bahasa Indonesia KB).

Inn may be described, 'lodging house', 'house to pass (or, where travellers pass) the night', 'house where they receive travellers/guests'.

35 ***And the next day he took out two denarii and gave them to the innkeeper, saying, 'Take care of him; and whatever more you spend, I will repay you when I come back.'***

Exegesis: *epi tēn aurion* 'on the next day', cp. A-G s.v. *epi* III 2 a.

aurion adv. 'tomorrow', here with article *hē*, and substantive *hēmera* understood, 'the day of tomorrow', 'the next day'.

ekbalōn . . . duo dēnaria 'after taking out two denarii'. *ekballō* is used here without the usual note of violence, cp. Plummer. For *dēnarion* cp. on 7 : 41.

edōken . . . tō pandochei 'he gave (them) to the innkeeper' (*pandocheus* ††).

epimelēthēti autou 'look after him', effective imperative, i.e. not meant as an order for only once but for a period of time, cp. Bl-D, § 337.2.

ho ti an prosdapanēsēs egō . . . apodōsō soi 'whatever you spend in addition . . . I will repay you'. *egō* is emphatic. *prosdapanaō* (††).

en tō epanerchesthai me 'at my returning', i.e. 'when I come back to your place'. *epanerchomai* also 19 : 15.

Translation: *And the next day*, cp. on 9 : 37.

Took out, or, 'took from his pocket/purse/wallet'.

Two denarii. Generic renderings are, '(a sum of) money', 'two silver coins', 'two pieces of silver, or money'; local equivalents chosen are, "two dollars" (Goodspeed), "ten shillings" (Phillips), 'two guilders' (Toba Batak), 'two half guilders' (East Toradja 1933). Some versions in Muslim countries have used *d(j)inar*, an adaptation of the Arabic transliteration *dīnār*. This, however, is not advisable in at least some of the languages, since the term came to refer there to a gold coin worth up to a sovereign. For *denarius* cp. Nida, *BT*, 328; *TBT*, 10.167, 1959; *TH-Mk* on 6 : 38.

Innkeeper, or, 'master of the inn', 'the one who owns/runs the inn'. Where professional innkeeping is unknown the situation may require explanation.

Whatever more you spend, or, 'when you spend more', 'whatever you add to (it)' (Trukese), or with some further specification, 'when you lose more on him' (Sranan), 'if he (or, the care of him) costs you more (than this)', 'if you spend what goes beyond this money, or, more than I have already given you' (cp. Shona 1966, Tzeltal); or as co-ordinated sentence, 'perhaps this (money) is not enough; then...'.

Repay you may require an object, 'repay you that (sum/amount)', 'pay you your loss, or, what is lacking', 'exchange it for you' (Tagabili).

When I come back, or, 'when I pass here again', "on my way back" (NEB).

36 ***Which of these three, do you think, proved neighbour to the man who fell among the robbers?"***

Exegesis: *tis toutōn tōn triōn* 'which of these three?' Abrupt change from the narrative to a question addressed to the expert in the law.

plēsion dokei soi gegonenai '...seems to you to have been a neighbour'. *plēsion* without article *ho* as part of the predicate.

tou empesontos eis tous lēstas 'of him who fell into the hands of the robbers'. Here *empiptō eis* (cp. on 6 : 39) is equivalent to *peripiptō* with dative, cp. v. 30.

Translation: To mark the transition from the parable to the concluding question one may end v. 35 by a commonly used marker of the end of a narrative, as done e.g. in Tzeltal, using, '(thus) he said to him', similarly in Kapauku; or one may begin v. 36 by an exclamatory particle indicating a turn in the conversation (cp. Balinese, Marathi, Zarma); and/or one may shift the equivalent of "do you think" to initial position, cp. 'What do you say: ...' (Shona 1963), 'As you see it, which...' (Shona 1966), 'How do you judge? Who...' (Yao), 'So, how about your feeling/thought, who...' (Ponape, Trukese). In some cases a complete transitional sentence had to be inserted, cp. 'To finish, Jesus asked him' (Kituba), 'And now again Jesus spoke to the man who questioned him, he said' (Tagabili).

Which of these three, or, 'who among these three', 'there were three those men that passed by there, which of them...' (Tagabili).

Proved neighbour to..., or, 'has shown himself the nearest of...' (Jerusalem), 'behaved as his-fellow-man towards...' (Bahasa Indonesia RC), 'was/did like neighbour of...' (Shona 1966, Ponape), 'did in-order-to (be) neighbour of...' (Trukese). In some cases the expression used for "neighbour" in v. 27 requires some adjustment here; thus Tagabili and Sranan, which in v. 27 have, 'your companion/fellow Tagabili' and 'man at your side' respectively, here use, 'companioned that man...' and 'was at the side of the man...'.

37 ***He said, "The one who showed mercy on him." And Jesus said to him, "Go and do likewise."***

Exegesis: *ho de* 'he', i.e. *ho nomikos* 'the lawyer'.

ho poiēsas to eleos met' autou 'he who did the act of mercy for him', cp. on 1 : 72.

poreuou kai su poiei homoiōs 'you too go, do likewise'. *kai su*, best understood as 'you too' (cp. Plummer), may go with *poreuou* ('you too go'), or with *poiei* ('you too do'), preferably the former. For the asyndetic imperatives cp. Bl-D, § 461.1.

Translation: *Showed mercy on him*, or, 'had mercy on him', 'acted mercifully towards him', and cp. on 1 : 50.

Go, i.e. 'you too go...' (as advocated in *Exegesis*), paralleling the lawyer's going with that of the Samaritan; hence, 'you too proceed', 'you too continue your way'; the aspect is durative.

Do likewise, or, 'do the same', 'behave/do as he behaved/did'; the aspect again is durative.

38 ***Now as they went on their way, he entered a village; and a woman named Martha received him into her house.***

Exegesis: *en de tō poreuesthai autous* 'during their travelling', i.e. 'when they were on their way'. The use of *poreuesthai* (cp. 9 : 51-57 where it occurs five times) expresses that the journey to Jerusalem is continued. *autous* means Jesus and his disciples, probably not the small group of the twelve but a larger crowd.

eis kōmēn tina 'into a certain village', without indication of name or place.

gunē de tis...hupedexato auton 'a certain woman...received him'. Nestle adds *eis tēn oikian* 'into her house'.

hupodechomai (also 19 : 6) 'to receive', 'to welcome', always of receiving somebody as guest into the house.

Translation: *As they went on their way*, or, "as they continued their journey" (Goodspeed).

If the shift from *they* to *he* (or, 'Jesus') and *him* is to be avoided (e.g. because it would suggest that, while the disciples did one thing, Jesus did something else), one may say, 'as Jesus and (or, accompanied by) his disciples continued the(ir) journey he...him...', a rendering that is obligatory in some honorific languages.

And a woman...received, or better to link this clause to what precedes, 'there a woman...received', 'there lived a woman...who received' (cp. Javanese). For the verb cp. on 9 : 5. Some languages require a specification by a locative phrase such as 'in her house', which then is added not for textual but for linguistic reasons.

39 ***And she had a sister called Mary, who sat at the Lord's feet and listened to his teaching.***

Exegesis: *kai tēde ēn adelphē kaloumenē Mariam* 'and she had a sister called Mary'. The demonstrative pronoun *tēde* has the force of a personal pronoun.

[hē] kai parakathestheisa pros tous podas tou kuriou 'who, seated at the feet of the Lord'. *kai* after the relative pronoun serves to focus the attention on what follows (cp. also v. 30). *pros tous podas* may reflect the attitude of the pupil who listens to his teacher (cp. Acts 22 : 3), or is due to the situation at the table where Jesus was reclining (cp. Schlatter), probably the latter. For *ho kurios* cp. on 1 : 6.

parakathezomai (††) 'to sit down', 'to take one's place (beside somebody)'.

ēkouen ton logon autou 'listened to his word', i.e. to what he said. *ēkouen* is durative imperfect.

Translation: *She had a sister called Mary, who sat...,* or in two sentences, 'she had a sister called M.; this one sat...'; or, better to show that now Mary is in focus, 'her sister (or, a sister of hers), Mary, sat...' (cp. Toba Batak, Balinese). Mary probably was Martha's younger sister (by the same parents), which has been made explicit e.g. in East Toradja 1933, Toba Batak, and Navajo (*TBT*, 13.27f, 1962); cp. also on "brother" in 6: 14.

Sat at the Lord's feet, or, 'sat before/beside/near to Jesus', 'sat in Jesus' presence'; in Tzeltal idiom requires 'sat below/at-the-bottom-of the Lord's feet'.

For *listened* see on "to hear" in 1 : 41.

40 ***But Martha was distracted with much serving; and she went to him and said, "Lord, do you not care that my sister has left me to serve alone? Tell her then to help me."***

Exegesis: *hē de Martha periespato peri pollēn diakonian* 'but Martha was distracted by much service, i.e. by many duties'.

perispaō (††) lit. 'to drag around', here figuratively of duties that keep one going to and fro.

diakonia (†) 'service', here 'task', 'duty'.

epistasa 'approaching', cp. on 2 : 38.

ou melei soi hoti... 'is it nothing to you that...', 'don't you care/mind that...?' *melei* (†).

hoti hē adelphē mou monēn me katelipen diakonein 'that my sister has left me alone to serve'. *diakonein* is infinitive of result (cp. Bl-D, § 392.1f). *kataleipō* means here 'to leave without help'. The clause appears to imply that Mary did not help her sister from the beginning.

eipe oun autē hina moi sunantilabētai 'tell her then that she should help me'. *oun* 'then' is inferential and implies 'if you really care, then...'

sunantilambanomai (†) 'to help', 'to lend a hand', 'to come to the aid of'.

Translation: *Martha was distracted with much serving* refers to Martha's state of mind, viz. her feeling very busy, and to the correlated activity, viz. her doing many things for her guest(s). This has been variously expressed, e.g. 'all kinds of work to do had gone to M.'s heart' (Tzeltal), 'M. was wearing-herself-out how/the-way her feeding them' (Tagabili), 'because much work fell to M., her agitation flew/flared-up' (Marathi), 'M.'s mind was stirred up with excess of service' (Zarma), 'she danced to and fro in serving' (Timorese), 'much work overwhelmed M.' (Sranan). *To serve,* see on 4 : 39.

She went to him, or, better to bring out that Martha comes up to Jesus for a moment only (as indicated by the punctiliar aorist), 'she came-near for a moment' (Javanese, South Toradja).

Do you not care that, expecting a negative answer. The phrase has been expressed variously, 'do you feel it is good that' (Tzeltal), 'you haven't been thinking of the fact that' (Tagabili), and cp. *TH-Mk* on 4 : 38.

That my sister has left me to serve alone, or, 'that my sister has left me without help, so that now I must serve alone' (A-G s.v. 1 d), 'that my sister leaves to me (all) our (exclus.) work, or, (all) the work we (two) have to do', 'that my sister does not help me work'; or again, 'that I do all the work and my sister does not do anything (or, and my sister nothing)'.

Help, or, 'assist', 'work with'; or, 'do-together-with', a derivation of 'companion/associate' (Toba Batak).

41 ***But the Lord answered her, "Martha, Martha, you are anxious and troubled about many things;*** 42 ***one thing is needful. Mary has chosen the good portion, which shall not be taken away from her."***

Exegesis: *Martha Martha,* the repetition lends emphasis, cp. 22 : 31.

merimnas kai thorubazē peri polla 'you are anxious and troubled about many things'.

merimnaō 'to be anxious', 'to be worried', 'to fret'.

thorubazō (††) 'to be troubled', 'to be agitated'.

(V. 42) *henos de estin chreia* 'but one thing is needed'. For the textual problems see commentaries, esp. Klostermann. Nestle reads *oligōn de estin chreia ē henos* 'but a few things are needed, or rather one'. This one thing is, in the present situation, to listen to Jesus, and, in a more general sense, to have faith in him.

Mariam gar tēn agathēn merida exelexato 'for Mary has chosen the right portion'. *gar* implies that this clause illustrates the one thing that is needed.

meris (†) 'share', 'portion', sometimes of the portion one receives at a meal (cp. Plummer and references there), but here rather of the lot which one receives by virtue of divine grace (cp. Acts 8 : 21 where *meris* and *klēros* are used as synonyms).

hētis ouk aphairethēsetai autēs 'which shall not be taken away from her', viz. in the day of judgment.

Translation: *Martha, Martha.* Where repetition of a proper name does not convey the right meaning one will have to find an equivalent form, e.g. 'you, Martha, you are . . .', or, *E Marta* (Tagabili, expressing the emphasis by the use of a particle requesting close attention); cp. also Phillips' "Martha, my dear".

You are anxious and troubled about many things is rendered in Tzeltal, 'doing all kind of things has gone to your heart and you have difficulty because of it' (cp. v. 40). The two terms reinforce each other and express one idea. Some idiomatic renderings of *anxious*, or, 'worried', are, 'eating for oneself one's heart' (Shona 1966), 'black with worry' (East Nyanja), 'breaking one's head' (Sranan, cp. also 'our heads are breaking', Cuyono in 2 : 48), 'hanging up the heart' (Bulu), 'crumbling in one's abdomen' (Conob), 'one's stomach is rising up' (Gurunse), 'one's mind is killing one' (Navajo). Cp. also on 12 : 29. For *troubled* cp. *N.T.Wb./*71.

(V. 42) *One thing is needful*, or, 'needed', or, '(only) one thing you need, or, are in want of'.

Mary has chosen the good portion, i.e. has taken for herself the lot of one who expresses her devotion by listening to Jesus rather than that of one who does so by preparing his meal. Better to bring out the contrast one may say, 'it is M. who has chosen the good part' (cp. Jerusalem, similarly Shona 1966). *The good portion*, or, "the right thing' (Goodspeed), 'what is good' (South Toradja). Some versions prefer 'better', or, 'best' (e.g. NEB), since a comparison is implied.

Which shall not be taken away from her, or, 'that which no one will take from her' (Tagabili); often better co-ordinated, cp. 'there-is-not who will take (it) from her' (Ponape, similarly Tzeltal, Zarma).

CHAPTER ELEVEN

1 *He was praying in a certain place, and when he ceased, one of his disciples said to him, "Lord, teach us to pray, as John taught his disciples."*

Exegesis: *kai egeneto* 'and it happened', cp. on 1 : 8. No indications as to time and place are given beyond *en topō tini* 'in a certain place'.

hōs epausato 'when he stopped', cp. on 5 : 4.

kurie 'master', cp. on 5 : 8.

didaxon hēmas proseuchesthai 'teach us to pray'. *didaskō* here with double accusative, viz. the first of the persons to whom teaching is given (*hēmas*), the second of the thing taught (*proseuchesthai*). As vv. 2-4 show *proseuchesthai* refers to the words of prayer, rather than to the way of praying.

kathōs kai 'just as'. *kai* reinforces *kathōs*.

edidaxen tous mathētas autou 'taught his disciples', viz. 'to pray', with *proseuchesthai* understood.

Translation: *He was praying in a certain place,* or, better to bring out the introductory character of the clause, 'once he was praying at some place, or, somewhere'.

When he ceased, or, 'after he had finished', or with a syntactic shift, 'being-finished his prayer' (East Toradja 1933).

The construction *teach us to pray* may have to be expanded, e.g. 'teach us what/how we must pray, or, what (words) we should say in prayer (or, when we pray)'.

As John taught his disciples. What is compared is the agent and the recipients of the teaching, not its contents, of course. In some languages the reference to prayer has to be repeated here, cp. e.g. Bahasa Indonesia RC.

2 *And he said to them, "When you pray, say:*
"Father, hallowed be thy name. Thy kingdom come.

Exegesis: *eipen de autois* 'he said to them', viz. in reply to the request of v. 1 (cp. NEB). The answer is given to all disciples (*autois*), since the request included them all (*hēmas*).

Pater 'Father', Greek rendering of the Aramaic *Abba* (cp. Mk. 14 : 36 and *TH-Mk* there). It belongs to the language of every day life, and introduces a hitherto unknown element of tenderness into the language of prayer (cp. Grundmann, and Dalman, *Die Worte Jesu*, 1930, p. 157).

hagiasthētō to onoma sou 'your name be treated, or, acknowledged, as holy', or 'venerated' (cp. Plummer). *to onoma sou* 'your name' means 'you as you have revealed yourself', i.e. God in his revelation. The clause is an expression of adoration. *hagiazō* (†).

elthetō hē basileia sou 'your kingdom come'. For *basileia* cp. on 4 : 43 and reference there. The coming of the kingdom of God is the eschatological consummation and inauguration of the Messianic age. Hence Schonfield renders, "Let thy Kingdom be inaugurated".

Translation: *Father*, i.e. 'our (exclus. pronoun) Father'. The noun may have to be rendered by an honorific term; the case is comparable to that mentioned in the note on 6 : 36.

Hallowed be thy name. The optative mood may be expressed by a modal verbal form or particle, or by an introductory phrase such as, 'we pray/beg (you that)' (South Toradja). The implied agent is people in general. *To hallow*, or, 'to acknowledge/revere/honour as holy' (for which adjective see references on 1 : 15); for *name* see on 1 : 49.

Thy kingdom come, or, 'become visible' (East Toradja 1933), 'prevail' (South Toradja); or, 'let the day come that you rule' (Mixtec).

3 ***Give us each day our daily bread;***

Exegesis: *ton arton hēmōn ton epiousion* 'our daily bread'.

epiousios (only here and Mt. 6 : 11 in the N.T.) a very rare word of uncertain meaning. For the most important derivations and interpretations cp. A-G s.v. In the light of the great diversity of opinion the traditional rendering 'daily' is to be commended.

didou hēmin to kath' hēmeran 'give us each day'. *didou* is repetitive imperative. *to kath' hēmeran* is an adverbial phrase meaning 'day by day', 'each day' (cp. A-G s.v. *kata* II 2 c).

Translation: *Our daily bread*, i.e. the bread/food (we need) for this day. For *bread* see references on 4 : 3.

4 ***and forgive us our sins, for we ourselves forgive every one who is indebted to us; and lead us not into temptation."***

Exegesis: *kai aphes hēmin tas hamartias hēmon* 'and forgive us our sins'. For *aphiēmi* cp. on 5 : 20; for *hamartia* on 1 : 77. The aorist tense of *aphes* is best understood as referring to the eschatological forgiveness in the final judgment (cp. Grundmann).

kai gar autoi aphiomen panti opheilonti hēmin 'for we ourselves forgive anyone who owes us (anything)'. *autoi* means 'we ourselves', 'we on our part' and is emphatic. *aphiomen* 'we forgive' is habitual present.

opheilō 'to owe', 'to be in debt', here corresponding to an Aramaic term for 'sin' (cp. Black, *Aramaic Approach*, 102, and A-G s.v. *opheilō* 2 b β). The idea of debt is not to be pressed.

kai mē eisenegkēs hēmas eis peirasmon 'and do not bring us into temptation'. For *eispherō* cp. A-G s.v. 2. Here it is used in a figurative and weakened sense and denotes an unintentional act (cp. Plummer). For *peirasmos* cp. on 4 : 13. Here it is used in the passive sense (cp. A-G s.v. 2 b) and probably refers to the eschatological temptations (persecutions and tribulations) that precede the final consummation.

Translation: *Who is indebted to us,* or, 'our...debtor' (Marathi). Where words associated with debt (for which see on 7 : 41) cannot be used figuratively one may shift to, 'who is guilty towards us', 'who does us evil' (Kituba), 'who has offended us' (Shona 1966, rendering "sins" by 'things by which we have offended you').

Lead us not into temptation, or, 'do not subject us to temptation' (Jerusalem), "do not bring us to hard testing" (TEV), or, shifting to passive or active verbal forms, 'do not allow us to be tested' (cp. South Toradja), 'let us not fall into things that test us' (Shona 1966), 'do not permit that the evil One tempts/tests us, or, seduces us' (cp. East Toradja 1933); cp. also on 8 : 13.

5 ***And he said to them, "Which of you who has a friend will go to him at midnight and say to him, 'Friend, lend me three loaves;***
6 ***for a friend of mine has arrived on a journey, and I have nothing to set before him';*** 7 ***and he will answer from within, 'Do not bother me; the door is now shut, and my children are with me in bed; I cannot get up and give you anything'?***

Exegesis: *kai eipen pros autous* 'and he said to them', or, 'he also said to them', preferably the former.

tis ex humōn...kai poreusetai...kai eipē...kakeinos...eipē 'who of you will have..., and go...and say...and he will say'. The clause starts as an interrogative clause in the indicative of the future (*hexei, poreusetai*) but the question is never brought to an end, nor is a direct answer given. Instead mood and tense shift to *eipē* (aorist subjunctive, twice), as if *ean* 'if' preceded and the two clauses were conditional. To these conditional clauses v. 8 might be considered to be the main clause.

tis ex humōn hexei philon kai poreusetai pros auton 'which of you will have a friend and go to him', or, with change of subject, 'and he (i.e. the friend) will go to him', preferably the former. *tis ex humōn* usually introduces questions to which the obvious answer is, 'nobody' (cp. 12 : 25; 14 : 28; 15 : 4; 17 : 7). Also the future tense points to a self-answering question.

mesonuktiou 'at midnight', 'in the middle of the night'. *mesonuktion* (†).

chrēson moi treis artous 'lend me three loaves'.

kichrēmi (††) 'to lend', i.e. 'to allow the use of'.

(V. 6) *epeidē* here adverbial particle, 'for' (cp. on 7 : 1).

philos mou 'a friend of mine', undetermined as shown by absence of the article.

paregeneto ex hodou pros me 'has come to me from a journey'. For *paraginomai* cp. on 7 : 4. *ex hodou* means that he interrupts his journey (cp. A-G s.v. *ek* 1 a).

ouk echō ho parathēsō autō lit. 'I do not have (anything) which I may set before him', i.e. 'I have nothing to set before him'. For *paratithēmi* cp. on 9 : 16.

(V. 7) *kakeinos esōthen apokritheis eipē* 'and (if) he, or, that one, replies from inside'. *kakeinos* is contraction of *kai* and the demonstrative pronoun *ekeinos*.

esōthen (also vv. 39f) 'from inside', 'from within'.

mē moi kopous pareche lit. 'do not cause me troubles', hence 'do not bother me'.

kopos (also 18 : 5) 'trouble', 'difficulty'.

ēdē hē thura kekleistai 'already the door has been locked'. The perfect tense denotes a situation which is the result of the act of shutting. *thura* also 13 : 24f. *kleiō*, cp. on 4 : 25.

ta paidia mou met' emou eis tēn koitēn eisin lit. 'my children are with me in bed', i.e. 'my children and I have gone to bed'. *eis* is here equivalent to *en* (cp. A-G s.v. *eis* 9).

koitē (†) 'bed'.

ou dunamai anastas dounai soi 'I cannot get up and give you'. *anastas dounai* represents one event, hence *anastas* is also rendered as an infinitive. *dounai* is used without object, but a reference to *treis artous* 'three breads' may be understood with it.

Translation: To imitate the irregular structure of these verses is usually undesirable. If it has to be straightened out some of the possibilities are the following. (1) The use of one interrogative sentence all through the three verses (cp. e.g. BFBS, Marathi), or divided over two sentences, e.g. 'which of you...would go...and say, "... (v. 6) ..."; (v. 7) and would he answer then, "..." ?' Such a rendering may require that the anticipated answer be added, viz. 'no one (would have so bad a friend)', 'no (real) friend would answer thus'. (2) A shift to one or two affirmative clauses or sentences, introduced by 'if', 'suppose (that)', cp. e.g. Rieu, TEV; also Tzeltal, which introduces the conditional clause by 'is there anyone who does this?' (3) A combination of a suppositional sentence in vv. 5-6 with a rhetorical question in v. 7, to which v. 8 forms the reply, cp. e.g. 'For-example, you have a friend...you go and call, "... (v. 6) ...". (v. 7) Would it be possible that he replied, "..." ?' (cp. Balinese, Leyden, East Toradja 1933).

Which of you who has a friend will go to him, often better in the second person, cp. e.g. "suppose you have a friend and...you go to him..." (Rieu), 'would you go to a friend of yours...'.

For *friend* see on 7 : 6. Shona 1966 uses a term denoting a ritual friend to whom one would turn in an emergency in vv. 5^{bc}, 8, but another one in v. 6. The use of the former term puts the refusal in a very bad light; similarly in East Nyanja and Yao, which throughout the four verses use a term implying acceptance of reciprocal obligation. In v. 5^{c}, however, where "friend" is used as a form of address, the usual rendering often has to be possessed (e.g. in Kapauku), or is idiomatically unacceptable and, therefore, has to be replaced, e.g. by 'brother' (Tzeltal), 'elder-brother' (Balinese, which also uses 'elder' and 'younger brother' as substitutes for the pronouns of the first and the second person in v. 7), 'nephew' (Javanese), or to be omitted (Toba Batak).

For *lend* see on 6 : 34, sub (1), and cp. 'exchange' (Tzeltal). In some cultures, however, it is regarded as highly improper to hint at restitution, so that a phrase like 'please, give me', or, 'I ask you for', is the normal thing to say.

Three loaves, or, more generically 'some food'; and see on 4 : 3.

(V. 6) *Has arrived,* or a more specific word or phrase used in case of an unexpected, short visit, e.g. 'has-dropped-in-with me' (Javanese); cp. also "has just come to (or, turned up at) my house" (Goodspeed, NEB).

On a journey, or, 'from his travels', "who is travelling through" (Rieu), 'travelling around' (South Toradja).

Set before him is sometimes rendered by, 'to give him as a meal', or a causative form of the verb rendering 'eat'.

(V. 7) *He will answer from within,* shifting to another subject, as indicated by 'answer' and 'from within'. Yet further specification of the pronoun has been found necessary, e.g. 'the other one' (Jerusalem), 'that friend-of-his' (Bahasa Indonesia), 'that person' (cp. the Greek). Such specification is superfluous, however, if v. 5 has been shifted to the second person.

Do not bother me. The verb is slightly stronger than "to trouble" in 7 : 6; Tzeltal says, 'don't come and disturb my sleep'.

The door is now shut, or, 'I have shut the door' (Shona 1966); elsewhere one has to say, 'the doorway is blocked' (East Nyanja, Yao), 'the fence of the entrance has been shut' (East Toradja), 'my house is already closed' (Tzeltal, where huts have no doors but planks are set up and tied in the doorway); cp. also Rieu's "I locked up long ago".

Are with me in bed, or, 'are with me in the (bed)room (Sundanese), or, in the place where we sleep'; or, 'are lying down with me' (cp. Trukese, Marathi, Toba Batak), similarly in Tzeltal, which takes 'I' as subject, cp. also 'I and the children have gone to bed' (Shona 1966). For *bed* see on 8 : 16.

Anything, or, 'what (or, the things) you want/ask' (cp. NEB), 'them' (i.e. the loaves), 'it' (i.e. the bread/food).

8 ***I tell you, though he will not get up and give him anything because he is his friend, yet because of his importunity he will rise and give him whatever he needs.***

Exegesis: *legō humin* 'I tell you', cp. on 3 : 8.

ei kai ou dōsei autō anastas 'even if he will not get up and give him'. For *anastas* cp. on v. 7. Strictly speaking *ei kai ou* here is not introducing a supposition since it is clear from v. 7 that he will not give his friend because of their friendship.

dia to einai philon autou 'because of (his) being his friend', articular infinitive.

dia ge tēn anaideian autou 'because of his persistence'. *ge* emphasizes the substantive which follows, viz. *anaideian.*

anaideia (†) lit. 'shamelessness', or, 'persistence', preferably the latter.
egertheis dōsei autō hosōn chrēzei 'he will get up and give him whatever he needs'. *egertheis* is equivalent to *anastas*. The phrase *hosōn chrēzei* may imply that he gave more than was asked for at first. *chrēzō* also 12 : 30.

Translation: When vv. 5-7 have been rendered by conditional or suppositional clauses they are virtually elliptical; then the transition to v. 8 can best be made by indicating the ellipsis (e.g. by dots, Bahasa Indonesia RC), or by some phrase like, "Well, what then?" (TEV). To take v. 8 as the apodosis of vv. 5-7 results in a construction that is usually too heavy to be a practical solution.

It is important to keep straight the pronominal references, viz. to the one outside who has asked (A), and the one within who has been asked (B), respectively: B will not...give A anything because A is B's friend, yet because of A's importunity B will...give A whatever A needs. Probably the most practical way to do so is to refer to A by pronouns of the second person (as done by Moffatt, Rieu, cp. also on vv. 5ff). — The structure of the two clauses in this verse differs in the position of the two causal phrases; this is done in order to emphasize the contrast between them. Where a more parallel clause structure is required the emphasis must be brought out by other means.

Not goes with both 'to get-up/rise' and 'to give'.

Because he is his friend, or, 'because of their friendship', or with a reciprocal form, e.g. 'under name-of their being-friends-together' (Trukese, similarly Toba Batak, East Toradja 1933).

Because of his importunity may better be rendered as a verbal construction, 'because he (A) kept asking him (B)', 'because he insisted (or, asked persistently)'.

He will rise may require an emphasizer, e.g. 'he will certainly rise' (Balinese), 'he just has to rise' (Toba Batak).

Whatever he needs, or, 'all things he needs/wants/asks'.

9 ***And I tell you, Ask, and it will be given you; seek, and you will find; knock and it will be opened to you.***

Exegesis: *kagō humin legō* 'and I tell you' (cp. on 3 : 8), indicating that the inferences will be drawn from vv. 5-8, cp. 16 : 9.

aiteite, kai dothēsetai humin 'ask and (it) will be given to you'. *aiteite* is best understood as referring to prayer. The object of *aiteite* is not indicated, nor the subject of *dothēsetai*. The agent of *dothēsetai* is God, and the nature of what is sought and given is indicated by *pneuma hagion* in v. 13.

zēteite, kai heurēsete 'seek and you shall find', again without indication of the object.

krouete, kai anoigēsetai humin 'knock and (the door) will be opened to you'. For this picture cp. 13 : 24f, where the entrance into the kingdom of God is referred to.

krouō 'to knock at the door'.

Translation: *Ask.* If an object has to be added, one may use, 'what you need'.

It will be given you, or, 'you will receive it', 'God will give you what you ask'.

Seek. For an object, if required again, see above.

You will find, cp. on 2 : 12. Add, if necessary, 'it', or, 'what you seek'.

Knock and it will be opened to you, or, 'knock at the door and it will be opened to you', or, 'knock and the door will open to you, or, God will open the door for you'. Where it is not customary to ask admittance by knocking, one may have to use 'call' (some Mexican languages, and Zanaki, cp. Nida, *GWIML*, 45f), 'speak' (Tzeltal), 'clap' (Zarma), the normal terms for announcing one's arrival. The use of 'entrance/doorway' for 'door' may entail the use of 'to allow to enter' instead of *to open*. Cp. also on 12 : 36.

10 ***For every one who asks receives, and he who seeks finds, and to him who knocks it will be opened.***

Exegesis: *pas gar ho aitōn lambanei* 'for every one who asks receives'. A solemn and emphatic assurance, corresponding with the first clause of v. 9. Its nature is still further enhanced by *pas* and by the present tense of *lambanei*.

ho zētōn heuriskei 'he who seeks finds', without *pas* and hence less emphatic than the preceding clause.

tō krouonti anoigetai 'to him who knocks (the door) is opened'.

Translation: Cp. on v. 9; objects, if required, can usually be fewer and less explicit because of the parallelism between the two verses.

11 ***What father among you, if his son asks for a fish, will instead of a fish give him a serpent;*** 12 ***or if he asks for an egg, will give him a scorpion?***

Exegesis: *tina de ex humōn aitēsei ton patera ho huios ichthun, kai anti ichthuos ophin autō epidōsei* lit. 'whom of you, (being) the father, the son will ask for a fish, and will (he) give him a snake instead of a fish?' Semantically the first clause, referring to the son's asking, is subordinate to the second one, referring to the father's giving. Instead of connective *kai* Nestle reads interrogative *mē*, which makes the second clause asyndetic and stresses the fact that the anticipated answer will be in the negative. In *ton patera* and *ho huios* the article has the force of a possessive pronoun. *ton patera* is apposition to *tina*. *aiteō* is construed with double accusative, viz. that of the person who is asked, and the thing which is asked for. For *epididōmi* cp. on 4 : 17. *ophis*, cp. on 10 : 19.

(V. 12) *ē kai aitēsei ōon, epidōsei autō skorpion* 'or also (if) he asks for an egg, will he give him a scorpion?', continuation of v. 11 with omission of the interrogative pronoun. A scorpion with its limbs closed around it resembles an egg. *ōon* (††). For *skorpios* cp. on 10 : 19.

Translation: *What father among you, if..., will...give...* This rhetorical question may better be introduced by 'would any one of you that is a father...' (cp. Rieu), 'is there a father among you who...' (cp. NEB). In the rather long and involved sentence the clause *if...fish* may better be moved to final position, cp. '...will give his son a snake instead of the fish he asks him' (Sranan), or (with a further simplification), "...will offer his son a snake when he asks for fish" (NEB). Another possibility is to divide the sentence in two, e.g. 'Some of you are fathers. If your son..., would/do you give...' (cp. Phillips), 'Is this what a father among you does? If his son asks..., does he give...' or in the second person, '...you as father...' with corresponding shifts.

Father...his son, a double reference to the fater-son relationship, which seems to be undesirable in some languages, cp. 'suppose you are someone's father; if you would be-asked for a fish, would you give...' (Balinese), 'is this what you do? if your son or daughter asks you for...' (Tzeltal). The reference to the male sex is not relevant here; hence, 'child' in many versions, and cp. the Tzeltal quotation above.

Instead of a fish give him a serpent, or, "give him a snake instead" (Goodspeed), or, 'instead of it'; and see above. The meaning of *instead* may have to be circumscribed, e.g. 'as a substitute for', and cp. 'not give a fish but give a serpent' (Trukese, similarly Marathi). *Fish*, see on 9 : 13; a reference to food may have to be added, e.g. 'fish to eat' (Tzeltal). *Serpent*, or, 'snake', or the name of some local species or equivalent. Where snakes are used for food one should choose a term referring to an inedible snake, or still more generically, to something inedible.

(V. 12) *Egg* may have to be specified, 'egg of a hen' (East Toradja); in Toba Batak (where 'egg' can also mean 'testicle') a more respectable term is used (etym. 'what-is-put-in', viz., in the nest). Eggs are sometimes not thought of as food (e.g. formerly in East Nyanja and Yao), or are not permitted as food for women and children (as was the case amongst the Bamiléké); then one will have to seek some edible equivalent.

Scorpion, see on 10 : 19, but where a local equivalent is used the renderings may have to be different, because here the reference is not to something that is poisonous but to something that is inedible, and has a specific form (see *Exegesis*).

13 ***If you then, who are evil, know how to give good gifts to your children, how much more will the heavenly Father give the Holy Spirit to those who ask him!"***

Exegesis: *ei oun humeis* 'so if you...' *oun* indicates that now the inference is drawn from vv. 11f.

ponēroi huparchontes lit. 'being bad', i.e. 'bad as you are', or 'though you are bad', preferably the former. For *ponēros* cp. on 3 : 19.

oidate domata agatha didonai 'know, or, are able to give good gifts'. For this meaning of *oida* cp. A-G s.v. 3. *doma* (†).

posō mallon 'how much more'.

ho patēr [*ho*] *ex ouranou* lit. 'the father from heaven', i.e. 'your father in heaven'. *ho* has the force of a possessive pronoun. The use of *ex* instead of *en* brings out the fact that God gives from heaven (cp. Bl-D, § 437, and Plummer).

dōsei pneuma hagion 'will give the Holy Spirit', cp. on 1 : 15. For the theological meaning of the clause see commentaries.

Translation: The sentence may better be divided in two, cp. e.g. TEV, and 'You whose hearts are not good, know what good gifts you will give your children. Your father in heaven surpassingly knows...' (Huixtec, for Mt. 7 : 11). The Greek has plural forms, which here have distributive force.

Who are evil, or, 'evil men', in simple apposition (South Toradja, Toba Batak), 'bad (men) as you are' (viewing the statement as a generally known fact). For *evil* cp. also Nida, *BT*, 220f.

Know here in the sense of 'be versed in', 'have practical experience of'.

Give good gifts, or, 'give good things', 'give what is good'.

The heavenly Father, or, 'the Father (who lives/is) in heaven' (in which case one should make sure that the locative phrase is a qualification of 'Father', not an indication where the giving will take place). For the possessed form of 'father', if obligatory in the receptor language, cp. on "your Father" in 6 : 36.

Give, or, 'send (down)', 'cause-to-come', if 'to give' is used only when giver and receiver are in the same place.

Those who ask him, or, "ask him for it" (Goodspeed). Here again a shift to the second person is sometimes preferable, 'to you who (or, to you when you) ask him'.

14 ***Now he was casting out a demon that was dumb; when the demon had gone out, the dumb man spoke, and the people marvelled.***

Exegesis: *kai ēn ekballōn daimonion* 'and he was driving out a demon', without indication of time and place and no connexion with what precedes is stated. The clause and the next one describe the event which triggers off the subsequent story.

[*kai auto ēn*] *kōphon* 'and that was dumb', i.e. the demon is dumb, and by virtue of that fact the man who is possessed by the demon is also dumb, as the rest of v. 14 shows.

egeneto de 'and it happened', cp. on 1 : 8.

elalēsen ho kōphos 'the dumb man began to speak', ingressive aorist.

kai ethaumasan hoi ochloi 'and the crowds were astonished'. No previous indication of their presence is given.

Translation: *Now*, see on 1 : 57.

Casting out a demon, see on 9 : 40, and 4 : 33, 35.

That was dumb, or better to indicate the demon's function, 'who made dumb' (Toba Batak). For *dumb* see on 1 : 22.

The people, or, 'the multitudes', for which see on 3 : 7. *Marvelled*, see on "wondered" in 1 : 21.

15 ***But some of them said, "He casts out demons by Beelzebul, the prince of demons";***

Exegesis: *en Beelzeboul tō archonti tōn daimoniōn ekballei ta daimonia* lit. 'in (the power of) Beelzebul, the ruler of the demons, he drives out the demons'. *en Beelzeboul* is best understood as 'through', or, 'with the help of Beelzebul'. For *Beelzeboul* and the various transliterations of the name cp. *IDB* I, 374, *N.T.Wb.*, 43/, A-G s.v. and Plummer.

archōn 'ruler', here of the ruler of an hierarchy of evil spirits, or, demons, cp. A-G s.v. 3.

Translation: *By Beelzebul* should be given emphasis, cp. "it is through B., ..., that he casts demons out" (Rieu), or changing the sentence structure, 'because B., ..., gives him power (or, enables/helps him), he can cast out demons', 'B. he uses/takes to chase out demons' (Sranan), and cp. *TH-Mk* on 3 : 22, which see also for *prince*.

16 ***while others, to test him, sought from him a sign from heaven.***

Exegesis: *heteroi* 'others', viz. from among the crowds.

peirazontes scil. *auton* 'putting him to the test', or, 'trying to test him'. For *peirazō* cp. on 4 : 2.

sēmeion ex ouranou 'a sign from heaven'. *sēmeion* (cp. on 2 : 12) here refers to a miracle which Jesus was to perform in order to prove himself in the eyes of the people to be the Messiah.

ezētoun par' autou '(they) demanded from him', cp. A-G s.v. *zēteō* 2 c.

Translation: *To test him*, or, 'to (put on the) test his power', cp. *TH-Mk* on 10 : 2.

Sought from him, or, 'tried to get from him'; see also *TH-Mk* on 8 : 11.

17 ***But he, knowing their thoughts, said to them, "Every kingdom divided against itself is laid waste, and house falls upon house.***

Exegesis: *autos de* 'but he', emphatic.

eidōs autōn ta dianoēmata 'knowing their thoughts', i.e. understanding what really was behind their utterances in vv. 15f.

dianoēma (††) '(inner) thought'.

eipen autois 'said to them'. *autois* is best understood as referring both to *tines* (v. 15) and *heteroi* (v. 16).

pasa basileia eph' heautēn diameristheisa 'every kingdom divided against itself', i.e. the composing parts are divided against one another, rather than against the kingdom as a whole. Hence renderings like 'disunited' (cp. Goodspeed), or 'internally divided' (cp. Brouwer).

diamerizō 'to divide', both in a literal and in a figurative sense, 'to separate', 'to distribute'.

erēmoutai 'is ruined', 'becomes desolate'. For *erēmoō* (†) cp. *N.T.Wb.*, 42/.

kai oikos epi oikon piptei 'and (as a result) house falls on house', or, with *diameristheis* understood, 'and house, i.e. family, divided against house falls', preferably the former.

Translation: *To know,* i.e. 'to be aware of', 'not to be ignorant about' (Javanese).

Their thoughts, cp. on 6 : 8.

Every kingdom divided against itself is laid waste, or, 'every kingdom that is-divided, fighting the one the other, will be broken' (Sranan), "kingdoms are brought to ruin by internal strive" (Rieu). For the clause cp. *TH-Mk* on 3 : 24, for *divide* see *N.T.Wb.*/29f.

And, resultative, 'so that'.

House falls upon house, or e.g., 'the houses collapse, fall on each other' (Balinese, similarly Bahasa Indonesia RC).

18 ***And if Satan also is divided against himself, how will his kingdom stand? For you say that I cast out demons by Beelzebul.***

Exegesis: *ei de kai ho Satanas eph' heauton diemeristhē* 'and if Satan also is divided against himself'. *ei de kai* implies that the general principle expressed in v. 17 may also apply to the realm of Satan. *ho Satanas* stands for 'the kingdom of Satan' as the rest of v. 18 shows.

pōs stathēsetai hē basileia autou 'how will his kingdom stand firm?' The clause implies a negative answer to the question. For *stathēsetai* cp. A-G s.v. *histēmi* II 1 d.

hoti legete... 'for you say...', and what they say implies that Satan is divided against himself. The clause introduced by *hoti* is only implicitly an explanatory clause.

Translation: *Satan...is divided against himself,* or, 'Satan is fighting against himself', 'Satan fights Satan', 'Satan's subjects/followers/henchmen fight among themselves'. The rendering should parallel v. 17. For *Satan* see on 10 : 18.

How will his kingdom stand, or, 'hold out', 'last', 'continue to exist', 'exist any longer'; or, if one has to shift from the noun to a verb, 'how will he remain (or, go on) reigning?', 'he certainly cannot rule any longer'.

For you say that I..., or, "—since, as you would have it, I..." (NEB), reminding Jesus' interlocutors of their accusation (v. 15), which has been shown to be incompatible with facts everybody can know. This reminder, introduced by 'for', states the reason for things not explicitly expressed in vv. 17f; hence some versions use a dash or dots (NEB, Jerusalem), others make the reason explicit, cp. e.g. 'I spoke thus because you say that...' (Lokele, similarly Tzeltal, Rieu), or shift to 'but/yet you say...' (Balinese, Sinhalese).

19 ***And if I cast out demons by Beelzebul, by whom do your sons cast them out? Therefore they shall be your judges.***

Exegesis: *ei de egō* 'but if I...'. *de* marks here the shift to a different argument. *egō* is emphatic and contrasts with *hoi huioi humōn* 'your sons', see next note.

hoi huioi humōn en tini ekballousin 'by whom do your sons cast out (demons)?' *hoi huioi humōn* (emphatic by virtue of its position at the beginning of the clause) means 'your own people' viz. who practise exorcism.

dia touto autoi humōn kritai esontai 'because of this they shall be your judges'. *touto* refers to the fact that there are also Jewish exorcists (cp. 9 : 49; Acts 19 : 13), who know that they cannot exorcize demons with the help of Beelzebul. The clause means that their own exorcists are the people to judge their opinion about Jesus to be untrue, with the undertone that this will result in their condemnation.

kritēs 'judge', used here in a non-technical sense, cp. A-G s.v. 1 b.

Translation: *And,* preferably, 'again', 'what is more', 'at the same time', or another expression marking a new part of the argument.

If I cast out demons by Beelzebul, or, avoiding repetition, "if I do that" (Rieu), "if this is how I drive them out" (TEV).

Your sons, or, "your own people" (Rieu, NEB), "your own followers" (TEV).

They shall be your judges, or, 'the ones who judge/condemn you'; or better to emphasize the subject, 'it is they who will declare you guilty', 'they themselves will show/say that you are wrong'. Cp. also *N.T.Wb.*/48f.

20 ***But if it is by the finger of God that I cast out demons, then the kingdom of God has come upon you.***

Exegesis: *ei de en daktulō theou ekballō ta daimonia* 'but if I cast out demons by the finger of God...' The emphasis is on *en daktulō theou.* The accusation that Jesus casts out the demons by Beelzebul has been refuted. If it is not by Beelzebul then it must be by the finger of God.

daktulos 'finger', here symbolic of God's active power, cp. also Ex. 8 : 19.

ara ephthasen eph' humas hē basileia tou theou 'then (it is a sign that) the kingdom of God has come upon you'. *ara* is inferential.

phthanō (†) 'to have just arrived', 'to attain'. With *epi* 'upon' it is probably a rendering of an Aramaic idiom which implies that one cannot withdraw from the meeting.

Translation: *If it is by the finger of God,* an "if"-clause indicating what is not a hypothetical condition but an obvious fact (cp. Wonderly, *BTPU,* 143), as brought out in, "no, it is rather by means of God's power" (TEV).

The finger of God. Some versions can render *finger* in this context literally, e.g. Lokele, and Zarma (lit. 'offspring of the hand'); elsewhere one has to shift to 'arm', 'hand' (Gio), or to a non-metaphorical rendering such as, 'power/strength/authority' (Sinhalese, Kituba, Kapauku and several others); hence e.g. 'through the power of God', and with further shifts, 'because God's power helps/enables me to...', etc., cp. on v. 15.

Then, or, 'it-means-that' (Sundanese), "then be sure" (NEB); or, if the protasis has been restructured, "which proves that "(TEV), or, 'that means that'.

The kingdom of God has come upon you, or, 'among you all God is already ruling' (Mixtec).

21 ***When a strong man, fully armed, guards his own palace, his goods are in peace;***

Exegesis: *hotan ho ischuros* 'when the strong one, or, a strong man...'. The former is preferable because in the present context *ho ischuros* is best understood as a reference to Satan (cp. A-G s.v. 1 a).

kathōplismenos (††) 'fully armed', apposition to *ho ischuros.*

phulassē tēn heautou aulēn 'guards his own house'.

aulē (also 22 : 55) 'courtyard' (22 : 55), 'farm', 'house', 'premises', 'dwelling' (here).

en eirēnē estin ta huparchonta autou 'his possessions are in peace', i.e. are safe. For *ta huparchonta* cp. on 8 : 3.

Translation: *Strong,* see *TH-Mk* on 3 : 27.

Fully armed, or, 'equipped with (all) his weapons'. Some renderings of 'arms' are, 'fighting-things' (Sranan), 'that-which-hits' (South Toradja), 'equipment/tools of war' (East Toradja, Trukese), or the name of the most common kind of weapons, e.g. 'arrows' (Kapauku). One older version employed an existent phrase for 'weapons', lit. 'a man's equipment', which later was discovered to be also in use as a veiled expression for 'penis'!

Palace, preferably, 'dwelling', 'house', or 'premises' (rendered 'place-of-the-house' in Javanese, Balinese, and 'by the side of the house' in South Toradja).

Guards, or, 'keeps watch over', 'protects', and cp. *N.T.Wb.*/49, KEEP.

Are in peace, or, 'are safe/well-preserved/inviolate' (Sranan, Balinese), and cp. 'nothing will happen to all that is his' (East Toradja 1933).

22 ***but when one stronger than he assails him and overcomes him, he takes away his armour in which he trusted, and divides his spoil.***

Exegesis: *epan de ischuroteros autou* 'but when a stronger one than he...'. *ischuroteros* refers to Jesus himself.

epan 'when', equivalent to *hotan.*

epelthōn nikēsē auton lit. 'coming up overcomes him'. *epelthōn* has hostile meaning.

nikaō (†) 'to conquer', 'to overcome'.

tēn panoplian autou airei 'he takes away his armour'.

panoplia (†) 'full armour of a heavily armed soldier'.

eph' hē epepoithei 'on which he relied'. Subject is *ho ischuros* of v. 21.

ta skula autou diadidōsin 'he divides his spoils'. *autou* is best understood as referring to the same one as *autou* after *panoplian,* viz. to *ho ischuros* of v. 21. *ta skula* may refer to the spoils which the strong one had taken previously from others, or to the spoils which the stronger one takes off him now. In the former interpretation it takes up *ta huparchonta* in v. 21, in the latter *tēn panoplian autou*. The former appears to be slightly preferable.

skulon (††) armour and weapons taken from a slain enemy, then generally 'booty', 'spoils'.

diadidōmi (also 18 : 22) 'to divide'.

Translation: The pronominal references to "the strong man" of v. 21 (A) and the "one stronger than he" (B), who is in focus here, must be carefully handled to avoid confusion.

Assails, or, 'attacks', 'comes against' (Marathi), 'comes to fight with' (Sranan).

He takes away. The pronoun, referring to (B) may have to be specified, e.g. by a deictic element pointing further back than to the last mentioned person (Bahasa Indonesia RC). *To take away*, or, 'seize-by-force' (several Indonesian languages), 'seize-as-plunder' (Balinese).

His armour in which he trusted. The double pronominal reference may have to be simplified and specified, cp. "all the weapons the owner was depending on" (TEV, similarly East Toradja 1933). *Armour*. Some versions use a term indicating that defensive arms are included, cp. e.g. "arms and armour" (NEB, similarly in Gio, Bahasa Indonesia), 'weapons and shield' (Lokele), 'clothing-of war' (Ponape). *In which he trusted*. If a relative clause is unacceptable in this position, it may be possible to shift this piece of information to the end of v. 21, e.g. '...his goods are safe; he feels he can trust in his armour'. *To trust* is often rendered by forms of, or expressions with, 'to hope' (Trukese, Ponape), 'to believe' (cp. Marathi, 'to place faith on'), 'to be strong on' (Shipibo), 'to build upon' (Sranan), 'to place heart in' (Kituba), 'to use-as-substitute' (East Toradja), 'to die-absolutely-and-completely', i.e. 'to stake one's life on' (Luchazi), 'to have a thick heart' (Kaka), 'to put oneself upon' (Maya of Yucatan). If, however, such expressions only take a person as object, one may have to express the idea otherwise, e.g. 'to know to be good/efficacious', 'to feel safe with', 'to say: "I have my..."' (as Chontal does in Mk. 10 : 24), and cp. the rendering of this phrase used in Tzeltal, 'which he has caused others to consider him important because of'.

Divides his spoil, i.e. what he (A) had previously taken as plunder, as preferred in *Exegesis*; sometimes slightly simplified, "his goods" (Rieu, similarly Sranan). When the other interpretation is followed, i.e. what he (B) has taken from him (A) as plunder, especially referring to the armour, the reference is somewhat redundant; hence a simplification like, 'the armour...he takes away and divides' (cp. Balinese). *Divides*, i.e. distributes (among his companions/followers); cp. *N.T.Wb.*/29f.

23 ***He who is not with me is against me, and he who does not gather with me scatters.***

Exegesis: *ho mē ōn met' emou kat' emou estin* 'he who is not with me is against me', cp. A-G s.v. *meta* II 1 c δ, and s.v. *kata* I 2 b γ. The clause expresses that in the conflict between Jesus and Satan there is no neutral ground.

ho mē sunagōn met' emou skorpizei 'he that does not gather with me scatters'. The picture is that of gathering a flock, rather than a harvest (as in 3 : 17).

skorpizō (†) 'to scatter', of sheep (cp. Jn. 10 : 12).

Translation: For the first clause cp. on 9 : 50.

Who does not gather with me, or, 'join me to gather' (Javanese). If an object is required, one may use 'the sheep', or, 'the flock/herd' (for which see on 12 : 32). *To gather*, or, 'to cause to come together' (Sranan), 'to bring to the flock/herd'.

Scatters, or, 'causes (them/it) to run away (from the flock)', 'breaks up the herd'.

24 ***"When the unclean spirit has gone out of a man, he passes through waterless places seeking rest; and finding none he says, 'I will return to my house from which I came.'***

Exegesis: *hotan to akatharton pneuma exelthē apo tou anthrōpou* 'when an unclean spirit comes out of a man', i.e. when it is driven out. The articles *to* and *tou* are both generic. *akatharton pneuma* is synonymous with *daimonion* (cp. on 4 : 33).

dierchetai di' anudrōn topōn 'it goes through waterless places', i.e. it roams through the wilderness, the natural abode of demons.

zētoun anapausin 'seeking rest', or, 'a place to rest'.

anapausis (†) in a concrete meaning 'a resting place'.

hupostrepsō eis ton oikon mou hothen exēlthon 'I will return to my house from which I went out'. *oikos* 'house' here metaphorically for a person possessed by a demon (cp. Grundmann). The possessive pronoun *mou* suggests that the demon still considered the man whom he had possessed his own.

Translation: For *the* (preferably 'an') *unclean spirit* and *gone out* see on 4 : 33, 35f.

Passes through, or, 'goes through', see on 8 : 1.

Waterless places. The rendering often has to coincide with that of 'desert' (for which see *N.T.Wb.*/25).

My house from which I came. If this metaphorical use of 'house' would be incomprehensible, one may help the readers by saying in the preceding clause '...gone out of a man who was its house (or, in whom it dwelled), as it were'. The double reference to the first person has been avoided in some versions. But it should be remembered that it serves a purpose here, viz. to bring out that the demon, though he has left the house, still thinks of it as of his property.

25 ***And when he comes he finds it swept and put in order.***

Exegesis: *heuriskei sesarōmenon kai kekosmēmenon* 'he finds (the house) swept clean and in order', with *oikon* understood. That the house is also untenanted may be fairly inferred.

saroō (also 15 : 8) 'to sweep clean', 'to clean'.

kosmeō (also 21 : 5) 'to put in order', or 'to decorate', here preferably the former.

Translation: *He finds it swept,* or, 'sees/discovers that it is swept', cp. on 7 : 10. Explanation of the metaphorical use of 'house' in v. 24 may lead here to something like, 'he finds that man like a house swept' (Spanish VP). *Swept,* or, "swept clean" (NEB, adding the result), "cleaned" (Goodspeed, substituting the result). The verb is often a derivation of, or a phrase containing, 'broom/brush'. The implied agent is 'people', 'somebody'.

Put in order, i.e. all things (in it) put in their right place.

26 ***Then he goes and brings seven other spirits more evil than himself, and they enter and dwell there; and the last state of that man becomes worse than the first."***

Exegesis: *tote* 'then', i.e. when he sees that the house is untenanted.

poreuetai kai paralambanei 'it goes (away) and brings'. For *paralambanō* cp. on 9 : 10.

hetera pneumata ponērotera heautou hepta 'seven other spirits more evil than itself', cp. on 8 : 2.

eiselthonta katoikei ekei 'after going in they live there'. Subject is the spirits. For *eiselthonta* cp. on 8 : 30. *katoikeō* also 13 : 4.

kai ginetai ta eschata tou anthrōpou ekeinou cheirona tōn prōtōn 'and the last state of that man is worse than the first'.

eschatos 'last'. Here *ta eschata* refers to a period in a man's life as contrasted with an earlier period (*tōn prōtōn*), and not to his final, or, eternal state.

cheirōn (†) 'worse', 'more severe', without moral connotation.

Translation: *Brings,* or, 'causes, or, calls to accompany him' (East or South Toradja).

Other spirits here refers to additional specimens of the spirit class; hence, 'seven spirits more', 'seven more of his companions who are devils also' (Tzeltal). In this context, however, the comparison may be thought to imply that the items mentioned are in one class, and, therefore, the equivalent of "other" may be omitted, as in Ponape, Trukese, Toba Batak, and cp. 'in comparison to him seven very wicked spirits' (Kapauku). *Spirits,* see on 9 : 39.

Enter and dwell there, i.e. enter and stay permanently, or settle down, in that house; or without the metaphor, 'take possession of that man and hold him in their power'; cp. also on "enter" in 8 : 30.

The last state of that man becomes worse than the first, or, 'in the end the state of that man (or, the possessed man)...than in the beginning'. The clause is resultative.

27 ***As he said this, a woman in the crowd raised her voice and said to him, "Blessed is the womb that bore you, and the breasts that you sucked!"***

Exegesis: *egeneto de* 'and it happened', cp. on 1 : 8.

eparasa tis phōnēn gunē ek tou ochlou eipen autō 'raising her voice a woman in the crowd said to him'. *tis* and *gunē*, though separated by *phōnēn*, go together. *ek tou ochlou* may go with *tis...gunē* 'a certain woman in the crowd' (cp. A-G s.v. *ek* 4), or with *eparasa...phōnēn* 'raising her voice from the crowd', preferably the former.

makaria hē koilia hē bastasasa se 'blessed the womb that carried you'. For *makarios* cp. on 1 : 45. *bastazō* 'to carry', here of a pregnant woman.

kai mastoi hous ethēlasas with *makarioi* understood, 'and (blessed) the breasts which you have sucked'. *mastos* also 23 : 29.

thēlazō (also 21 : 23) 'to give suck' (21 : 23), 'to suck' (here).

Translation: *Raised her voice and said*, or, "called out" (Rieu, NEB), 'spoke with a loud voice (or, loudly)'.

Blessed, or, 'happy', see on 1 : 45.

The womb that bore you, and the breasts that you sucked, or making the clause structures parallel, "the womb that carried you and the breasts that suckled you" (NEB, similarly East Toradja). To use the parts ('womb', 'breasts') for the whole ('woman') is unacceptable in some languages; hence, 'the person/woman who bore you (in her womb) and suckled you' (Kapauku, Kituba, Tzeltal, Toba Batak, Balinese). *Womb*, see *N.T.Wb.* /18, BODY; the literal meaning of the South Toradja term used here is 'place of men'. For 'suckle', or, 'give suck to', cp. also *TH-Mk* on 13 : 17.

28 ***But he said, "Blessed rather are those who hear the word of God and keep it!"***

Exegesis: *autos de* 'but he', emphatic.

menoun (†) 'rather'. It does not question the truth of the preceding statement, but emphasizes the greater relevance of what follows.

hoi akouontes ton logon tou theou kai phulassontes 'those who hear the word of God and keep it', cp. the similar statements in 6 : 47 and 8 : 21. *phulassō* is used here in the metaphorical sense of 'keeping/observing' (cp. A-G s.v. 1 f), and is virtually equivalent to *poieō* in 6 : 47 and 8 : 21.

Translation: *Blessed rather are*, or, 'yes, but happier are', 'be that as it may, very much blessed are' (Shona 1966), 'that may be true, but those that are-called (i.e. really are) blessed are' (Balinese).

Hear the word of God, or, 'listen to what God says'. For the verb cp. on 1 : 41; for the noun phrase on 5 : 1.

Keep it, or, 'act in accordance with it', 'do what he commands'; and cp. *N.T.Wb.*/49.

29 ***When the crowds were increasing, he began to say, "This generation is an evil generation; it seeks a sign, but no sign shall be given to it except the sign of Jonah.***

Exegesis: *tōn de ochlōn epathroizomenōn* 'when the crowds were increasing', or, 'were crowding together', preferably the latter. *epathroizomai* (††).

ērxato legein 'he began to say', cp. on 4 : 21.

hē genea hautē 'this, i.e., the present generation'. For *genea* see A-G s.v. 2.

genea ponēra estin 'is an evil generation'. The repetition of *genea* is intentional and emphatic.

sēmeion zētei 'it demands a sign', cp. on v. 16.

kai sēmeion ou dothēsetai...ei mē to sēmeion Iōna 'and no sign will be given except the sign of Jonah', cp. on v. 30.

Translation: *Were increasing*, preferably, 'were crowding around Jesus'.

This generation is an evil generation, or, "how evil are the people of this day" (TEV), and cp. on 7 : 31.

No sign...except, or, 'no other sign...but', 'the only sign that...is', '(no more than) one sign..., namely'.

Shall be given. The implied agent is God.

The sign of Jonah, or, where necessary to clarify the relationship between noun and proper name, something like, 'the sign that (or, a sign like the one that) Jonah gave', 'the one Jonah showed/produced'. The rendering of *sign* should bring out the signifying, not the miraculous aspect.

30 ***For as Jonah became a sign to the men of Nineveh, so will the Son of man be to this generation.***

Exegesis: *kathōs gar egeneto Iōnas tois Nineuitais sēmeion* 'for just as Jonah became a sign to the Ninevites', viz. by his preaching (cp. Jonah 3 : 1-5).

houtōs estai kai ho huios tou anthrōpou tē genea tautē, with *sēmeion* understood, 'so too will the Son of man be (a sign) to this generation'. The future tense of *estai* and of *dothēsetai* in v. 29 are explained variously (see commentaries). Since the 'sign of Jonah' appears to refer to Jesus' preaching, *estai* and *dothēsetai* refer to the immediate future and not to eschatological judgment. For *ho huios tou anthrōpou* cp. on 5 : 24.

Translation: *Jonah became a sign*, or, 'Jonah's behaviour (or, what Jonah did) became a sign'. A similar specification will then be necessary in the next clause.

The men of Nineveh, or, 'the people/inhabitants (of the city) of N.'; the reference is not restricted to persons of the male sex.

Be to, or, 'be a sign to/for'.

31 ***The queen of the South will arise at the judgment with the men of this generation and condemn them; for she came from the ends of the earth to hear the wisdom of Solomon, and behold, something greater than Solomon is here.***

Exegesis: *basilissa notou* 'the queen of the south', without article but determined by the genitive *notou* (Hebraism). The reference is to the queen of Sheba (1 Kings 10 : 1-13).

basilissa (†) '(ruling) queen'.

notos 'south wind', 'south', 'a country in the south'.

egerthēsetai 'will rise', i.e. from the dead, or (more general), 'will appear', preferably the latter.

en tē krisei 'at the judgment', cp. on 10 : 14.

kai katakrinei autous 'and will condemn them', not because she is the one who judges, but by comparison. *katakrinō* also v. 32.

ēlthen ek tōn peratōn tēs gēs 'she came from the ends of the earth'. Sheba was located in the southern part of Arabia near the limits of the world then known (cp. Plummer). *peras* (†).

akousai tēn sophian Solomōnos 'in order to listen to the wisdom of Solomon', i.e. to the wise words of Solomon.

kai idou 'and behold', cp. on 1 : 20.

pleion Solomōnos hōde 'something greater than Solomon is here', an indirect reference to Jesus himself.

Translation: *Queen*, or, 'woman chief/ruler' (cp. Zarma, East Nyanja, Yao), 'woman who holds the country' (Kapauku), 'woman who has the office of ruler' (Tzeltal), 'woman ruling as king' (Kekchi). If the language possesses a feminine derivation of the word for 'king' one should make sure whether it covers both 'ruling queen' and 'wife of the king' (as in Marathi), or can mean only the former (as in Sinhalese, Shona), or the latter (in which case the term is not acceptable here).

The South, or, 'the South(ern) country', 'the land in/towards the South'. For *south* see *N.T.Wb.*/28f, DIRECTIONS; *TBT*, 7.104-113, 1956. In East Nyanja and Yao the name of the rain wind, which is south-easterly, is used for 'south'. The term used in Bahasa Indonesia originally meant 'region-of-the-straits (of Malacca)' but now is no longer bound to the local geographical situation. The Balinese equivalent (etym. 'region-of-the-sea'), however, is still bound so: it means 'south' in South Bali, but 'north' in North Bali; hence a footnote has to be added, giving the North-Balinese equivalent (etym. 'interior', which in South Bali means 'north'). Cp. also Safwa, where north of the watershed 'upstream' means 'south', but south of it the same term is used in the sense of 'north'. This kind of difficulty has often led to the use of a borrowing from a language of prestige, e.g. in Tzeltal, Kituba, East Toradja. In the present verse it is also possible to substitute 'Sheba' (as done in Lokele), which name, though more specific, is virtually synonymous to 'the South' in this passage.

Arise at the judgment with the men..., or, 'arise when the men...are judged, or, when God judges the men...'. *Arise with*, or, "appear against"

(NEB), 'appear in court together with' (Sundanese). For *judgment* see *N.T.Wb.*/48f; *TH-Mk* on 6 : 11.

Condemn them, or, 'accuse them' (Kekchi), 'show them to be guilty'. It may be preferable to connect the verb more closely with the preceding one, cp. e.g. "the Queen... will stand up and accuse the people of today" (TEV).

The ends of the earth. Comparable phrases used are, 'the fringes of the earth' (Kapauku), 'the cessation of the land' (East Nyanja), 'the "that's all" of here below' (Yao), '(one of) the border(s) of the earth' (cp. Marathi, Shona 1966). Elsewhere the meaning is described by, 'one of the farthest regions of the earth', or simply, '(a place) far away' (cp. Ponape, Trukese, Tzeltal).

The wisdom of Solomon, or, 'the wise words/sayings of S.' (Tzeltal, Zarma), 'how wisely S. spoke'. In Sinhalese one does not 'hear wisdom' but 'see wisdom'. For *wisdom* see 2 : 40. *Solomon* (following the Greek form), or 'Salomo' (cp. the Hebrew form, *Šelomo*), or 'Sulaiman' (cp. on 1 : 5).

Something, here referring to a person, often has to become 'somebody', 'a person'.

Greater. For the comparative see on "mightier" in 3 : 16 and references; for *great* see 1 : 15.

32 ***The men of Nineveh will arise at the judgment with this generation and condemn it; for they repented at the preaching of Jonah, and behold, something greater than Jonah is here.***

Exegesis: *andres Nineuitai* 'the men of Nineveh', 'the Ninevites' (cp. v. 30).

anastēsontai 'will rise', i.e. from the dead, or, 'will appear', preferably the latter.

metenoēsan eis to kērugma Iōna 'they repented at the preaching of Jonah'. *eis* is best understood as equivalent to *pros* 'with reference to', 'because of', cp. A-G s.v. *pros* 5 a and Bl-D, § 207.1. *kērugma* (†).

Translation: *This generation*, short for, 'the men of this generation', which often has to be used.

Repented at the preaching of Jonah, or, 'repented because (or, when) J. preached (to them)'. For *to preach* see on 3 : 3.

33 ***"No one after lighting a lamp puts it in a cellar or under a bushel, but on a stand, that those who enter may see the light.***

Exegesis: *oudeis luchnon hapsas* 'nobody, after lighting a lamp...' cp. on 8 : 16 and references there.

eis kruptēn tithēsin 'puts it in a cellar'.

kruptē (††) 'dark and hidden place', 'cellar'.

[*hupo ton modion*] 'under the peck measure', or, 'measuring vessel', cp. *TH-Mk* on 4 : 21. *modios* (†).

epi tēn luchnian scil. *tithēsin* '(he places it) on the lampstand', cp. on 8 : 16.

hina hoi eisporeuomenoi to phōs blepōsin 'so that those who come in may see the light', cp. on 8 : 16.

Translation: For the first and third parts of this verse see 8 : 16.

Cellar, or, 'hole' (Bahasa Indonesia), 'place-under-the-house', i.e. between the poles on which the floor of a house is built (Javanese, South Toradja), 'storeroom', '(place) where people put away (or, hide) things'.

Under a bushel. In some languages 'under' would suggest that the bushel is put on the light with the bottom down; hence, 'overarches (it) with a bushel' (cp. Javanese, East Toradja 1933), 'puts a vessel over it' (Sranan). For *bushel* one may use the term for any kind of vessel or basket, used to measure (or keep) cereals, and normally found in a house.

34 ***Your eye is the lamp of your body; when your eye is sound, your whole body is full of light; but when it is not sound, your body is full of darkness.***

Exegesis: *ho luchnos tou sōmatos estin ho ophthalmos sou* 'the lamp of the body is your eye', *ho ophthalmos* is predicate. The discourse shifts from the ordinary lamp, which gives light from the outside, to a figurative extension of the word 'lamp', here called 'the lamp of the body', which gives light from within.

hotan ho ophthalmos sou haplous ē 'when your eye is sound'.

haplous (†) lit. 'single', 'simple', hence 'sincere', 'sound'. Its opposite is *ponēros* 'evil', here 'unsound'. Probably both ideas (sincerity and soundness) are present here. For a different, though less probable interpretation, cp. A-G s.v.

kai holon to sōma sou phōteinon estin 'your whole body too is full of light'. *phōteinos* also v. 36.

kai to sōma sou skoteinon 'your body too is dark'.

Translation: *Your eye is the lamp of your body*, though worded as if addressed to Jesus' interlocutors, holds true of men in general. Accordingly the two possessive pronouns have a generic function, which may have to be expressed otherwise, e.g. by using pronouns of the first person plural inclusive (Huixtec in Mt. 6 : 22), or by substituting an article or equivalent form at one occurrence (e.g. "your eyes are like a lamp for the body", TEV), or at both (as in Javanese, Sundanese, Sranan). The preposition *of* may have to be rendered by a verb, e.g. 'the lamp that lights your/the body'. For *body* cp. also *N.T.Wb.*/16; in this context it may be necessary to shift to a term for 'inner being'.

Sound and *unsound*, or, "sound" and "bad" (NEB), 'healthy' and 'not healthy', 'clear' and 'turbid/dim' (Willibrord, Balinese, Sundanese).

Your whole body is full of light, or, changing the syntactic structure, 'your whole body has light, or, is bright', 'there is light in your whole body'. Parallel changes will then be necessary in *your body is full of darkness*. For *darkness* see *N.T.Wb.*/21.

35 ***Therefore be careful lest the light in you be darkness.***

Exegesis: *skopei oun mē to phōs to en soi skotos estin* 'consider, then, whether the light in you is not darkness', or, 'be careful lest the light in you be darkness', preferably the former since *estin* is in the indicative (cp. Plummer).

skopeō (†) 'consider', 'look out'.

skotos 'darkness', here used emphatically instead of the adjective *skoteinos*.

Translation: *Be careful lest*, preferably, 'consider whether', 'think (carefully) whether', 'ask yourself whether perhaps'.

The light in you, or, 'the light you have in you', 'what is bright about you' (NV).

36 ***If then your whole body is full of light, having no part dark, it will be wholly bright, as when a lamp with its rays gives you light."***

Exegesis: *ei oun to sōma sou holon phōteinon* 'if then your whole body (is) bright', taking up the first conclusion of v. 34.

mē echon meros ti skoteinon 'having no dark part', elaborating *holon*.

estai phōteinon holon 'it will be wholly bright', best understood as determined by what follows, viz. the reference to a light from outside: when the light from the inside is in order, then the body will enjoy also the light from the outside.

hōs hotan ho luchnos tē astrapē phōtizē se 'as when the lamp illuminates you by its light'.

astrapē here 'light', 'brilliance' (cp. 10 : 18).

phōtizō (†) 'to illuminate'.

Translation: *Having no part dark*, or, 'there-is not a bit in it dark' (Bahasa Indonesia RC).

A lamp with its rays gives you light, or, 'the rays/light of the lamp illuminate(s) you, or, cause(s) you to be bright', or simply, 'the lamp shines on you'.

37 ***While he was speaking, a Pharisee asked him to dine with him; so he went in and sat at table.***

Exegesis: *en de tō lalēsai* 'after his speaking', or, 'after he had spoken', because of the aorist tense of *lalēsai* (cp. Bl-D, § 404.2).

Pharisaios 'a Pharisee', cp. on 5 : 17.

hopōs aristēsē par' autō lit. 'that he would lunch with him', i.e. in his home.

aristaō (†) 'to have a meal', 'to lunch'.

eiselthōn de anepesen 'after going in, i.e. into the house, he sat at table'.

anapiptō 'to lie down', 'to take one's place at the table'.

Translation: *To dine with him*, or, 'to lunch (or, 'eat at noon', 'take the midday meal') with him (or, at his house)'. Several versions do not indicate the time of day, "to eat with him" (TEV), 'to come to his house to eat' (South Toradja). Cp. also "to eat with" in 7 : 36.

Went in. If the house has not been referred to already in what precedes, one may have to do so here, 'entered his house' (Bahasa Indonesia).

Sat at table, cp. 7 : 36.

38 ***The Pharisee was astonished to see that he did not first wash before dinner.***

Exegesis: *idōn ethaumasen hoti ou prōton ebaptisthē pro tou aristou* lit. 'seeing he wondered that he did not wash before the meal'. Though syntactically the clause introduced by *hoti* depends on *ethaumasen* only, it goes semantically with *idōn* in the first place. *prōton...pro tou aristou* lit. 'first...before the meal' (cp. RSV), but many translations do not render *prōton* specifically.

baptizō lit. 'to dip', here 'to wash', the hands presumably, cp. Mt. 15 : 2.

ariston (also 14 : 12) 'breakfast', 'noon meal', 'meal'.

Translation: *Was astonished to see*, or, "was surprised when he noticed" (TEV). For *astonished* cp. "wondered" in 1 : 21.

Wash. In some languages an object has to be added, 'wash hands' (Bahasa Indonesia), in others a derivational form of 'to wash' has the meaning 'to wash one's-hands-or-feet' (Sundanese), 'to wash-one's-hands' (Toba Batak). That the verb has a ritual connotation here is sometimes made explicit, cp. *faire des ablutions* (Jerusalem, similarly Zarma).

39 ***And the Lord said to him, "Now you Pharisees cleanse the outside of the cup and of the dish, but inside you are full of extortion and wickedness.***

Exegesis: *eipen de ho kurios* 'but the Lord said', in reply to his surprise. For *ho kurios* cp. on 1 : 6.

nun humeis hoi Pharisaioi 'indeed, you Pharisees', with emphasis on *humeis*. *nun* is best understood as equivalent to Hebrew *hinnēh* and as serving to lend emphasis to what follows.

to exōthen tou potēriou kai tou pinakos katharizete 'you clean the outside of the cup and the dish'. The article *tou* before *potēriou* and *pinakos* is generic. *exōthen* also v. 40.

potērion 'cup', 'drinking-vessel'.

pinax (†) 'platter', 'dish'.

to de esōthen humōn gemei harpagēs kai ponērias 'but the inside of you is full of greed and wickedness', hence, 'inside you are full...' (cp. RSV). As contrasted with *to exōthen* which is used in a literal sense, *to esōthen* is used metaphorically.

gemō (†) 'to be full'.

harpagē (†) 'greediness', 'rapacity', cp. A-G s.v. 3.
ponēria (†) 'wickedness', cp. the frequent *ponēros*.

Translation: *Cleanse,* see *N.T.Wb.*/59, PURE.

The outside of the cup and of the dish, or, 'cups and dishes at the outside'. For *cup* and *dish* instrumental or locative derivations of 'to drink' and 'to eat' are sometimes used, e.g. in Toba Batak (the first), and in South Toradja (both).

Inside you are full of extortion and wickedness, or, 'inside you are completely/very greedy (cp. *N.T.Wb.*/41) and wicked'. In several languages a word for *inside* can be used in the metaphorical sense required; where such is not the case one will have to shift to a term for the emotional centre of the personality, e.g. 'your heart is full of...' (Bahasa Indonesia, similarly Tzeltal). *Wickedness,* or, 'bad/evil thoughts'.

40 ***You fools! Did not he who made the outside make the inside also?***

Exegesis: *aphrones* 'you fools!'

aphrōn (also 12 : 20) 'fool', 'ignorant', here used as a substantive indicating culpable ignorance and carrying a strong note of reproach (cp. BFBS, Glossary, p. 79).

ouch ho poiēsas to exōthen kai to esōthen epoiēsen 'did not he who made the outside make the inside also?' *ouch* at the beginning of an interrogative clause suggests that an affirmative answer in expected.

Translation: *You fools,* or, 'fools that you are!', 'what fools you are!'. *Fools,* or, 'thought not (having) people' (Kapauku), 'people without sense/understanding/intelligence' (Kituba, Sinhalese, Marathi, Javanese), 'people having a dark liver' (Cuna), 'those short-of mind' (Toba Batak), mostly referring to stupidity or ignorance in general. Some versions use renderings more specifically expressing guilt and/or reproach, e.g. 'who don't know anything', a strong term of rebuke (Tzeltal), or a word indicating a person who refuses to use the intelligence he has (Zarma), or expressions implying intractability and wilful opposition to common interests or commonly accepted ideas (East Nyanja, Yao). Cp. also *TH-Mk* on 7 : 22.

Made...make. Since the implied agent is God some versions use their rendering for 'to create', e.g. Javanese, Toba Batak; cp. also "did not the Creator of the outside make the inside too?" (Goodspeed, similarly Bahasa Indonesia RC).

41 ***But give for alms those things which are within; and behold, everything is clean for you.***

Exegesis: *plēn* 'but', indicating a strong contrast.

ta enonta dote eleēmosunēn 'give as alms the things that are within'. If *dote eleēmosunēn* is not a mistranslation from the Aramaic (*zakki* 'give alms' read instead of *dakki* 'cleanse', cp. Creed, Manson, Leaney, Black, *Aramaic Approach*, 2, Dalman, *Worte Jesu*, 50), *ta enonta* (††) is best understood as referring to the content of the cups and the vessels, and the emphasis is on *dote eleēmosunēn* as contrasted with cleansing (cp. Rieu, NEB). For further details see commentaries, esp. Plummer.

eleēmosunē (also 12 : 33) 'kind deed', esp. 'alms'.

kai idou panta kathara humin estin 'and behold, all things are clean for you'. For *kai idou* cp. on 1 : 20. *panta* refers to all things that, in the opinion of the Pharisees, are in need of cleansing. *humin* 'for you', who are so easily worried about cleanliness.

katharos (†) 'ritually clean'.

Translation: *Give for alms*. The noun has been rendered 'presents of love' (Kituba), 'gifts of pity' (East Nyanja, Yao), a term combining the words 'gift' and 'religious duty' (Marathi). With some shifts the phrase may be expressed 'give freely' (Kapauku), 'give by way of kindness (lit. whiteness of heart)' (East Toradja; similarly Toba Batak, South Toradja, using a verb derived from 'kind' or 'compassion'), "give to the poor" (TEV), 'share with others, or, with the needy/pitiable' (Lokele, East Toradja 1933). In some Muslim countries the commonly known Arabic term for 'alms' (*ṣadaḳah*) is borrowed, e.g. in Bahasa Indonesia.

Things which are within, or, "what is *in* your cups and dishes" (Rieu, and cp. *Exegesis*).

Everything, or more specifically, 'all vessels', 'every utensil'.

Clean, cp. *N.T.Wb.*/59, PURE. What is ceremonially clean may also be called 'allowed for use', 'good for you' (Shona 1963).

42 ***"But woe to you Pharisees! for you tithe mint and rue and every herb, and neglect justice and the love of God; these you ought to have done, without neglecting the others.***

Exegesis: *alla ouai humin tois Pharisaiois* 'but woe to you Pharisees'. *alla* indicates transition, rather than contrast. For *ouai* cp. on 6 : 24; for *Pharisaioi* cp. on 5 : 17.

hoti apodekatoute to hēduosmon kai to pēganon kai pan lachanon 'for you pay tithes (even) on mint and rue and every kind of garden herb', though tithing on these herbs was not prescribed in the Law. *hoti* introduces the clauses which explain the woe to the Pharisees, and goes also with *parerchesthe*, etc.

apodekatoō (also 18 : 12) 'to give one tenth of', 'to pay tithes on', 'to tithe', cp. *IDB* IV, 654f.

hēduosmon (†) 'mint', an aromatic plant, cp. *IDB* III, 392. The article *to* before *hēduosmon* is generic.

pēganon (††) 'rue', a strong smelling perennial shrub, cp. *IDB* IV, 129.

lachanon (†) 'garden herb', 'vegetable'.

kai parerchesthe tēn krisin kai tēn agapēn tou theou 'and (yet) you disregard justice and the love of God'.

parerchomai 'to go, or, pass by', here figuratively 'to disregard', 'to neglect'.

krisis here 'justice', 'righteousness'. The article is generic.

agapē (†) 'love'. The genitive *tou theou* is objective and the phrase *agapē tou theou* recalls the commandment to love God (10 : 27).

tauta de edei poiēsai scil. *humas* 'these things you should have done'. *tauta* refers to *tēn krisin kai tēn agapēn tou theou.*

kakeina mē pareinai 'and those things (you should) not neglect'. *kakeina* is a contraction of *kai* and *ekeina. ekeina* points back to the things the Pharisees already do as mentioned in vv. 39-42.

Translation: *Woe to,* see 6 : 24.

Tithe, or, 'pay/offer a tenth of', or, to bring out that the term refers to a religious duty, 'of every ten...give one to God' (cp. e.g. Sranan, Melpa). In some Muslim countries the Arabic term (*zakāt*) has been borrowed, e.g. in Javanese, Sundanese.

Mint and rue, or the names of locally known plants that have the same function and are of little value, as e.g. in Yao, 'scented millet and bitter leaves'. The function and/or an indication of the value may have to be added (as in Kituba, 'leaves that give taste/flavour to food'), or substituted, e.g. 'little scented plants and little plants for flavouring food' (East Nyanja), or, 'the tiniest and cheapest of the herbs'.

Herbs, or, 'vegetables' (East Toradja, lit. 'what-is-cooked'), 'edible herbs' (Marathi), 'leaves' (Kituba), 'cultivated plants (lit. kinds-of plant-of garden)' (Ponape, Trukese).

Neglect, or, "have no care for" (NEB), 'omit/fail to (do)'.

Justice and the love of God, or, to avoid the verbal nouns, 'to be just and to love God', or, if the first verb requires an object, 'to be just to men and to love God'. For *justice,* in the sense of 'just behaviour', 'fair/equitable treatment' see *N.T.Wb.*/63f, RIGHTEOUS; for *love* see above 6 : 27.

These...the others, i.e. the latter/second-mentioned (things/deed/duties) ...the former/first-mentioned (ones).

Without neglecting, or, 'although you should not omit/fail to do', 'although you should continue to care for'.

43 ***Woe to you Pharisees! for you love the best seat in the synagogues and salutations in the market places.***

Exegesis: *agapate tēn prōtokathedrian en tais sunagōgais* 'you love the front seat in the synagogues', cp. *TH-Mk* on 12 : 39, and Plummer. *agapaō* is used here with regard to human ambition. *prōtokathedria* also 20 : 46.

tous aspasmous en tais agorais 'the salutations in the market places', cp. on 1 : 29 and *TH-Mk* on 12 : 38. For *agora* cp. on 7 : 32.

Translation: *You love,* or, 'you want', 'you like it to have', 'you desire' (for which cp. *N.T.Wb.*/25f); Tzeltal has 'your hearts are glad'.

The best seat, or, 'the front seat', 'the seat of honour'; or in a verbal construction, 'to sit on the best seat', 'to sit in front', etc. Cultural equivalents are e.g. 'the seat at the head end, or, at the inland/upstream side, or, at the right side, or, towards the east'.

Salutations, or, 'to be greeted' (e.g. in Shona 1963), 'that people greet you' (e.g. in Zarma); cp. "greeting" in 1 : 29, 40. Some terms for greeting imply already a showing of respect, as e.g. in Tzeltal, 'to have the backs of your hands kissed', or in Marathi, 'to take *namaskar* (an obeisance originally given to Brahmins only)'; elsewhere this has to be explicitly stated, either in addition to the term for "salutation", e.g. 'to be given praise greetings' (Shona 1966, cp. also Goodspeed), or instead of it, 'people to honour you' (Kapauku), 'to be-asked-permission' (Balinese, referring to the custom that, on meeting a person of higher position, one has to ask to be allowed to pass him).

In the market places, or, 'in public (places)', 'where people have gathered together' (Shona 1966); and see on 7 : 32.

44 ***Woe to you! for you are like graves which are not seen, and men walk over them without knowing it."***

Exegesis: *este hōs ta mnēmeia ta adēla* 'you are like unmarked graves'. The article *ta* is generic. Since contact with graves makes ritually unclean, graves used to be whitewashed so as to be conspicuous (cp. Mt. 23 : 27).

adēlos (†) 'not clear', 'unseen', 'unmarked'.

hoi anthrōpoi [*hoi*] *peripatountes epanō* 'the people who walked over', scil. the graves.

ouk oidasin 'do not know', scil. that they walk over graves.

Translation: To bring out that the comparison is between the hidden uncleanness of graves and the unknown evil in the hearts of the Pharisees one may specify the object of the last verb, e.g. 'without knowing how bad/unclean/filthy they (i.e. the graves) are inside', choosing for the adjective a term that can be used both of ritual and of moral badness. Further explanation, if required, can better go into a footnote referring to Mt. 23 : 27f, where the simile is elaborated.

Graves which are not seen, or, 'are unmarked'; or, 'graves which people cannot see (for what they are), or, have not marked (as such)'. For *grave* one may have to use a descriptive rendering, e.g. 'hole in the ground where a corpse is buried/put', or a locative derivation of 'to inter/inhume' (South Toradja). In Bali the place where a corpse is buried (either permanently or awaiting cremation) is marked by mounds that rise a few inches above ground level; therefore the phrase has been rendered, 'mounds that have become flat'.

And men walk over them without knowing it, or, 'and men who walk over (or, tread upon) them do not know it'; and cp. above. The clause is resultative.

45 ***One of the lawyers answered him, "Teacher, in saying this you reproach us also."***

Exegesis: *apokritheis* 'answering', cp. on 1 : 60.
tis tōn nomikōn 'one of the experts in the law', cp. on 7 : 30.
didaskale 'teacher', cp. on 3 : 12.
tauta legōn 'saying that', i.e. 'by saying that'.
kai hēmas hubrizeis 'you insult us too', because the experts in the law belonged as a rule to the party of the Pharisees.
hubrizō (also 18 : 32) 'to mistreat', 'to insult'.

Translation: For *lawyers* see on 7 : 30.
Reproach, or, 'insult', 'affront', 'offend'; South Toradja uses an idiomatic phrase, lit. 'you lay nothing on your lips', i.e. 'you do not take care what you say', 'you speak rude words'.
Us also, or, 'us as well as them'.

46 ***And he said, "Woe to you lawyers also! for you load men with burdens hard to bear, and you yourselves do not touch the burdens with one of your fingers.***

Exegesis: *kai humin tois nomikois ouai* 'to you, experts in the law also woe'. *humin* is emphatic as its position before *ouai* shows.
phortizete tous anthrōpous phortia dusbastakta 'you burden people with burdens hard to bear'.
phortizō (†) 'to cause (someone) to carry', hence 'to burden', 'to load'.
phortion (†) 'burden', 'load', here figuratively of the burden of keeping the law as laid down by the experts.
dusbastaktos (††) 'hard to carry, or, to bear'.
kai autoi 'and you yourselves', emphatic.
heni tōn daktulōn humōn ou prospsauete tois phortiois 'with (so much as) one of your fingers you do not (even) touch the burdens'.
prospsauō (††) 'to touch (lightly)'.

Translation: *You load men with burdens hard to bear,* or, 'you cause/order men to carry very heavy loads/burdens', i.e. you compel men to do things (or, impose on men duties) that are very difficult to perform.
Touch the burdens with one of your fingers, viz. in order to bear/perform those burdens/duties yourselves.

47 ***Woe to you! for you build the tombs of the prophets whom your fathers killed.***

Exegesis: *hoti oikodomeite ta mnēmeia tōn prophētōn* 'for you build the tombs of the prophets'. The present tense of *oikodomeite* is best understood as habitual. *mnēmeion* means here 'tomb', 'memorial' (cp. A-G s.v. 1), elsewhere in Luke (e.g. v. 44) 'grave'.

Translation: *Build the tombs of the prophets,* or, 'build tombs for the prophets'. Where 'tombs' in the sense of 'sepulchral monuments' are unknown, one may say 'make beautiful the graves of...' (Sranan), 'erect/make a building (or, put high stones) where the prophets have been buried'.

Whom your fathers killed, or better to bring out the contrast, "the very prophets your ancestors murdered" (TEV). For *to kill* cp. *N.T.Wb.*/49f.

48 ***So you are witnesses and consent to the deeds of your fathers; for they killed them, and you build their tombs.***

Exegesis: *ara martures este* 'so you are witnesses', viz. to the fact that their fathers killed the prophets, or, taking the clause to refer to what follows, to their approval of the deeds of their fathers. The former appears to be slightly preferable. *martus* also 24 : 48.

kai suneudokeite tois ergois tōn paterōn humōn 'and you approve of the deeds of your fathers'.

suneudokeō (†) 'to agree with', 'to approve of'.

ergon (also 24 : 19) 'work', 'deed', 'act'.

hoti autoi...apekteinan autous 'for they killed them'. *autoi* is emphatic.

humeis de oikodomeite 'you build', scil. their memorials. *humeis* is emphatic.

Translation: *You are witnesses,* i.e. you give testimony, you state that you know, or, since the testimony is not by word but by deed, 'you show/prove that you know', or, with transposition of the object of the next verb, 'you show/prove that you know what your fathers did'. If one follows the alternative interpretation, testimony and consent or approval go together, and one may say e.g. 'you testify and consent to (or, you show/prove that you approve of) what your ancestors did'. For *witness* cp. also *N.T.Wb.*/74f.

Them, i.e. the prophets.

49 ***Therefore also the Wisdom of God said, 'I will send them prophets and apostles, some of whom they will kill and persecute,'***
50 ***that the blood of all the prophets, shed from the foundation of the world, may be required of this generation,*** 51 ***from the blood of Abel to the blood of Zechariah, who perished between the altar and the sanctuary. Yes, I tell you, it shall be required of this generation.***

Exegesis: *dia touto kai hē sophia tou theou eipen* 'therefore then the wisdom of God said'. *kai* reinforces *dia touto.* Whether *hē sophia tou theou* is the title of an (unknown) book, or refers to a place in an (unknown) book, in which the personified wisdom of God speaks is uncertain. The meaning 'God in his wisdom' is improbable.

apostelō eis autous prophētas kai apostolous 'I will send to them prophets and apostles'. For *apostellō* cp. on 1 : 19. For *apostolos* cp. on 6 : 13.

kai ex autōn apoktenousin kai diōxousin 'and (some) of them they will kill and persecute', or, 'and (some) of them they will kill and (some others) they will persecute', preferably the latter. *ex autōn* stands for *tinas ex autōn* 'some of them', cp. A-G s.v. *ek* 4 a γ.

diōkō 'to run after', 'to persecute'.

(V. 50) *hina ekzētēthē to haima pantōn tōn prophētōn...apo tēs geneas tautēs* 'so that the blood of all the prophets will be required of this generation', i.e. the present generation will be charged with the crimes of the preceding generations.

ekzēteō (also v. 51) 'to seek out', hence 'to require as a debt', 'to charge with'.

haima 'blood', see next note.

to ekkechumenon apo katabolēs kosmou, going with *haima,* '(the blood) that has been shed since the foundation of the world'. To shed somebody's blood means to kill him, cp. A-G s.v. *haima* 2 a.

katabolē (†) 'foundation', 'beginning'.

kosmos here 'created world', 'creation'.

(V. 51) *apo haimatos Habel heōs haimatos Zachariou* 'from the blood of Abel to the blood of Zechariah', a specification of *apo katabolēs kosmou,* stating the slaying of the first and the last prophet of the Old Testament that were killed (cp. Gen. 4 : 1ff and 2 Chron. 24 : 20f, the last book in the Hebrew Bible).

tou apolomenou metaxu tou thusiastēriou kai tou oikou, going with *Zachariou* (Zechariah), 'who perished between the altar and the temple building'. For *apollumai* cp. A-G s.v. 2 a α. The verb implies violence. For *thusiastērion* cp. on 1 : 11. Here the reference is to the altar of burnt offering in the inner forecourt of the temple in Jerusalem in front of the temple building itself (to which *oikos* refers). *metaxu* also 16 : 26.

nai, legō humin 'indeed, I tell you' (cp on 3 : 8), marks the end of the quotation from the wisdom of God (v. 49) and introduces the emphatic repetition of its main words by Jesus himself. In that repetition the emphasis is on *apo tēs geneas tautēs* 'of this generation'.

Translation: *The Wisdom of God said,* or, 'it is written (for which cp. 2 : 23) in (the) book of (i.e. called) Wisdom of God' (Kituba), following the first interpretation. If the other interpretation is preferred, it may be unidiomatic to take an abstract noun ('Wisdom') as subject of 'said'; then one may shift to something like, 'the One called Wisdom of God said'.

I will send them. The first pronoun refers to (the Wisdom of) God, the second presumably to Israelites of preceding generations, virtually identical with "your fathers" in vv. 47f.

Apostles, or, 'personal messengers' (Zarma), 'persons sent' (Trukese, Ponape), and cp. the descriptive renderings mentioned in 6 : 13 and references, most of which can be used also in the more general sense meant here.

Some of whom, or co-ordinated, 'some of (or, from among) them', referring to the prophets and apostles.

They (same reference as "them" has in "send them") *will kill and persecute.* To keep the references clear it may be better to shift to a passive construction, e.g. 'some of whom will be killed and persecuted' (cp. Shona 1966, some Indonesian languages), or to specify the agent, e.g. 'those men' (Balinese), unless this has been done already in the preceding clause. When *kill and persecute* are taken as having the same group as object the more logical sequence is 'persecute and kill' (followed e.g. in Tzeltal, Trukese, Ponape); this transposition is not necessary, however, when two different groups are envisaged, as advocated in *Exegesis*. The verb *to persecute*, i.e. to pursue (or, run after) with enmity and injury, has also been rendered 'to harass', 'to maltreat' (Bahasa Indonesia, Tzeltal).

(V. 50) *That* is resultative, hence in co-ordination e.g. 'the consequences/ result (of this) will be thus: ...'.

The intricate pattern of the subsequent clause may require several adjustments. The agent implied in "may be required" is God, that in "blood...shed" is the preceding generations, or, the fathers. *To shed* (or, cause to flow) *the blood of...* may have to be rendered by, 'to cause the death of', 'to kill/murder', and *the blood of...may be required of this generation* by, 'the blood of...has been avenged on...' (South Toradja, Toba Batak), 'this generation may be caused to pay for the blood/death of... (or, to pay because their fathers killed...)', "the people of this time will be punished for the murder of..." (TEV), 'the blood of..., its account may be taken from this generation' (Marathi). When an active construction is necessary or preferable, one may say, 'God will require (etc., as above) of this generation the blood shed (or, which their fathers shed)', or shift to, 'this generation will be responsible for the blood of...'; cp. also 'the killing of..., this generation must pay(-for-it)' (cp. Kituba).

From the foundation of the world, or, 'from the (very) beginning of the world onward' (cp. Trukese, Tzeltal), 'since the world was made' (Sranan), 'from the oldest times onward' (cp. Ponape).

(V. 51) The first half of this verse also may better be co-ordinated and recast, e.g. 'as the first they killed A. and as the last they killed Z., who...'.

Perished, see *N.T.Wb./27*, DIE.

The altar. To make explicit what was implied in this expression for the original receptors one may have to add some specification, e.g. 'in the courtyard of the temple' (Tzeltal). For the noun see *N.T.Wb./7*; some other possible renderings are, 'where they place the gifts to God' (cp. Huixtec), 'place where the (killed) gifts to God are burned'.

For *sanctuary* see "temple" in 1 : 9.

It refers to 'the blood, or, murder, of all the prophets'.

52 ***Woe to you lawyers! for you have taken away the key of knowledge; you did not enter yourselves and you hindered those who were entering."***

Exegesis: *ērate tēn kleida tēs gnōseōs* 'you have taken away the key to knowledge'. *airō* means here 'to take away from its proper place, so that it cannot be used' (cp. 8 : 12). The phrase *kleis tēs gnōseōs* is best understood metaphorically as the key that opens the way to the understanding of

Scripture which is the way of salvation (cp. *gnōsis sōtērias* 'knowledge of salvation', 1 : 77). The experts in the law have a wrong interpretation of the Old Testament and this makes it impossible for them to find salvation. *kleis* (†).

autoi ouk eisēlthate '(consequently) you have not gone in yourselves', scil. into the knowledge of salvation. This metaphorical use of *eiserchomai* (cp. also 22 : 40, 46; Mt. 25 : 21) is a Hebraism. The asyndeton indicates that this clause, and also the next one, are the result of the taking away of the key.

tous eiserchomenous ekōlusate 'those who wanted to enter you have stopped'. The participle *tous eiserchomenous* is best understood as conative. For *kōluō* cp. on 6 : 29.

Translation: *The key of knowledge,* preferably, "the key to (the door of) knowledge" (Rieu, Goodspeed), "the key that opens the door to the house of knowledge" (TEV). The function of *key* may have to be described, e.g. 'unlocker' (East Nyanja, Yao), 'means to open', 'what opens the way to', and *knowledge,* or, 'house of knowledge' may have to be explained, e.g. 'the place where people can acquire knowledge, or, can learn to understand the Scriptures'.

Hindered, or, "kept out" (Goodspeed), 'stopped' (Shona 1963), 'did not allow' (Tzeltal).

53 ***As he went away from there, the scribes and the Pharisees began to press him hard, and to provoke him to speak of many things,*** 54 ***lying in wait for him, to catch at something he might say.***

Exegesis: *kakeithen exelthontos autou* 'as he went away from there', i.e. from the house of the Pharisee who had invited him (cp. v. 37).

kakeithen contraction of *kai* and *ekeithen* 'from there'.

ērxanto hoi grammateis kai hoi Pharisaioi 'the scribes and the Pharisees began...'. It is probable that *ērxanto* is to be understood in the same (weakened) sense as 3 : 8. For *grammateis* cp. on 5 : 21; for *Pharisaioi* on 5 : 17.

deinōs enechein 'to watch closely', or 'to be terribly hostile', preferably the latter, cp. *TH-Mk* on 6 : 19. *deinōs* (†).

apostomatizein auton peri pleionōn 'to draw him out on many subjects'. In *peri pleionōn* the comparative has the force of a somewhat reinforced positive.

apostomatizō (††) 'to draw out', or 'to watch closely', or 'to catechize', preferably the first.

(V. 54) *enedreuontes auton* (†) 'lying in wait for him', here metaphorically.

thēreusai ti ek tou stomatos autou lit. 'in order to catch something out of his (own) mouth', i.e. to catch him "with his own words" (NEB), cp. 19 : 22.

thēreuō (††) 'to hunt', 'to catch'.

Translation: *To press him hard*, or, 'to attack him fiercely' (NV), 'to pester/harass him' (several Indonesian languages).

To provoke him to speak of many things, or, 'to try to make him speak on (or, give his opinion about) many subjects', 'put to him all kinds of thorny questions' (Willibrord), 'pumped him on many things' (Sranan, lit. asked him many things go/thither, asked him come/hither).

(V. 54) *Lying in wait for him*, or, 'trying/wanting to take him unawares', or, with another metaphor, "laying snares" (NEB, similarly NV, Javanese, East Toradja, Sranan); and cp. *N.T.Wb.*/14, AWAIT.

To catch at something he might say, i.e. to catch/seize him because of something he might say, or more explicitly pejorative, "and catch him in something wrong he might say" (TEV).

CHAPTER TWELVE

1 ***In the meantime, when so many thousands of the multitude had gathered together that they trod upon one another, he began to say to his disciples first, "Beware of the leaven of the Pharisees, which is hypocrisy.***

Exegesis: *en hois episunachtheisōn tōn muriadōn tou ochlou* 'meanwhile, when the (usual) thousands of people gathered'. *en hois*, lit. 'during which', with relative pronoun, has demonstrative force and is equivalent to *en toutois* lit. 'during these things', i.e. the things reported in 11 : 37-54.

episunagō 'to bring together', 'to gather', here in the passive with intransitive force.

murias (†) 'myriad', 'then thousand', here in the plural, of a very large number without exact definition. The article before *muriadōn* points to what is usual. The phrase *tōn muriadōn tou ochlou* is hyperbolical (as in Acts 21 : 20).

hōste katapatein allēlous 'so that they actually were treading upon one another'. *hōste* with following infinitive indicates the actual result, cp. A-G s.v. 2 a β.

katapateō (also 8 : 5) 'to tread upon', 'to trample' (8 : 5), here of treading upon each other's feet, or, of trampling under foot, preferably the latter.

ērxato legein pros tous mathētas autou prōton 'he began to say to his disciples first of all'. For *ērxato* cp. on 4 : 21. *prōton* does not refer to order but to degree: the crowds are listening too.

prosechete heautois apo tēs zumēs, hētis estin hupokrisis, tōn Pharisaiōn 'be on your guard against the yeast, that means, the hypocrisy of the Pharisees'.

prosechō lit. 'to turn one's mind to', with dative of the reflexive pronoun, 'to be on one's guard', here followed by *apo* as indication of that against which one is on one's guard.

zumē (also 13 : 21) 'yeast', 'leaven', a substance to produce fermentation, here in a figurative sense, explained by the subsequent relative clause.

hupokrisis (†) 'hypocrisy', 'outward pretense'.

Translation: The structure of the introductory clause may have to be recast, e.g. 'meanwhile (or, while all this happened) the crowd was gathering; there were so many thousands (or, so very many people) that they... Then Jesus...'.

Had gathered together, or, 'had come together (where Jesus was)'.

Trod upon one another, or, 'trampled each other under foot', 'crowded each other out' (NV), 'pushed/elbowed each other aside', or any other idiom the receptor language uses for an accumulation of people in a crowded place.

First, or, 'in the first place' (Sranan), "speaking primarily" (Phillips).

Beware of the leaven of the Pharisees, which is hypocrisy. The metaphor indicates here an all-pervading evil influence. This function may have to be made explicit, e.g. 'the leaven of the Pharisees, that is (or, I mean), their all-pervading hypocrisy', or as a simile and with further shifts, 'the hypocrisy of the Pharisees which pervades all things like leaven (does)'. The utterance does not warn the disciples against tricks of the hypocritical Pharisees but against their becoming hypocrites themselves. Hence *beware of* (for which cp. also *N.T.Wb.*/13f, AVOID) may better be rendered by 'have nothing to do with' (Shona 1966), 'watch-out-for' (East Toradja), 'keep away from', 'do not become involved in', or, again with further shifts, 'do not become such hypocrites as the Pharisees; their hypocrisy is like an all-pervading leaven'. For *leaven,* or, 'yeast', see *TH-Mk* on 8 : 15; *N.T.Wb.*/39, FOOD; in Wantoat one has to substitute 'salt'. For *hypocrisy* see on 6 : 42.

2 ***Nothing is covered up that will not be revealed, or hidden that will not be known.***

Exegesis: *ouden de sugkekalummenon estin* 'but nothing is covered up'. *de* is transitional (cp. A-G s.v. 2), and the clause explains the warning of v. 1.

sugkaluptō (††) 'to veil completely', 'to cover up'.

ho ouk apokaluphthēsetai 'that is not going to be uncovered'. For *apokaluptō* cp. on 2 : 35. The verse recalls 8 : 17 but has a different point because of the preceding verse: hypocrisy is useless (cp. Plummer).

kai krupton ho ou gnōsthēsetai 'and (nothing is) secret that is not going to be known'. *kruptos* (cp. on 8 : 17) is adjective here.

Translation: For this verse cp. 8 : 17; Sranan renders it, 'you can't cover anything so that it doesn't come out; you can't hide anything so that people don't know it'.

Revealed, or, 'uncovered', 'brought to light', 'made (publicly) known'.

3 ***Whatever you have said in the dark shall be heard in the light, and what you have whispered in private rooms shall be proclaimed upon the housetops.***

Exegesis: *anth' hōn* 'for', cp. on 1 : 20, here used in a somewhat weakened sense.

hosa en tē skotia eipate 'whatever you have said in the dark'. *hosa* is stronger than the simple relative pronoun which is used in the next clause.

skotia (†) 'darkness', here used in the sense of 'night'.

en tō phōti akousthēsetai 'will be heard in the light', viz. because it will be repeated. *en tō phōti* means 'in the light of the day'.

ho pros to ous elalēsate en tois tameiois 'what you have said into the ear (of somebody) in the inner rooms'. *pros to ous* qualifies *elalēsate* as meaning 'you have whispered', cp. RSV.

tameion (also v. 24) 'storeroom', here 'secret room', or 'inner room'.

kēruchthēsetai epi tōn dōmatōn 'will be proclaimed on the housetops'. *kērussō* is here (as in 8 : 39) to be understood in the sense of telling publicly. For *dōma* cp. on 5 : 19. The housetops are mentioned here as the place from which a speaker is heard best.

Translation: *Whatever...*, or, 'when you have said something it shall be heard...'.

In the dark...in the light, or, 'at night time...in day time' (Kekchi, similarly East Toradja).

Shall be heard...proclaimed, or, 'people will hear...people/they will proclaim'.

In private rooms, or, 'behind closed doors' (Spanish VP), 'in the sleeping-room' (Sranan, South Toradja, Javanese), 'in the sleeping-house' (Balinese, using the term for the only closed building in a compound), 'underneath the granary' (Shona 1966, there being no really private rooms in traditional Shona houses).

Whispered, i.e. spoken softly and to one or only a few persons.

Proclaimed. The reference is to speaking loudly (cp. "shouted", NEB) and publicly to many persons, cp. also note on 4 : 18.

The housetops, or, 'the roof(-top)/upper-storey, or, the ridge of the house/hut-roof' (cp. e.g. Tzeltal, Bahasa Indonesia; Lokele, Lomwe). Such renderings, however, will not do where people cannot imagine a person proclaiming on or from such a place; hence functional renderings such as, 'the meeting places' (Shona 1966), 'where you meet your fellowmen' (Mazahua), or cultural equivalents, e.g. 'the streetcorners' (Sranan), 'the place-under-the-tree' (Toba Batak, i.e. a place outside the village, where people gather to discuss public matters).

4 ***"I tell you, my friends, do not fear those who kill the body, and after that have no more that they can do.***

Exegesis: *legō de humin tois philois mou* 'I tell you, my friends' (cp. on 3 : 8), takes up emphatically *pros tous mathētas autou prōton* in v. 1.

mē phobēthēte apo tōn apokteinontōn to sōma 'do not be afraid of those who kill the body'. *phobeomai apo tinos* with genitive may imply the idea of turning away from the person one is afraid of (cp. Plummer). The participle *tōn apokteinontōn* refers to actual, not potential killing.

kai meta tauta mē echontōn perissoteron ti poiēsai 'and after that cannot do anything more'. *meta tauta* means 'after they have actually killed the body'. For *echō* with following infinitive, meaning 'to be able', cp. A-G s.v. I 6 a.

perissoteron ti 'something more'.

Translation: *You, my friends,* or, better to bring out that this is more than a mere form of address, "you who are my friends" (NEB).

The body may have to be possessed, 'your body'; cp. also *N.T.Wb.*/16.

And after that have no more that they can do, or, 'but cannot afterward do (to you) anything worse (than that)' (cp. TEV, Willibrord).

5 ***But I will warn you whom to fear: fear him who, after he has killed, has power to cast into hell; yes, I tell you, fear him!***

Exegesis: *hupodeixō de humin tina phobēthēte* 'I will show you whom you have to fear'. For *hupodeiknumi* cp. on 3 : 7. *phobēthēte* is aorist subjunctive, here used in a subordinate clause, see below.

phobēthēte ton...echonta... 'fear him who has...'. Here *phobēthēte* is aorist imperative, used in a main clause. It is followed by an accusative and this may suggest that here a different type of fearing is implied, viz. the fear of God, to whom *ton...echonta* is best understood to refer.

meta to apokteinai 'after killing', takes up *meta tauta* in v. 4.

exousian embalein eis tēn geennan 'power to throw into hell', dependent upon *echonta*. The phrase refers to the power to condemn, not the power to destroy. For *exousia* cp. on 4 : 32.

emballō (††) 'to throw into', with *eis* following.

geenna (†) 'hell', place of eschatological punishment, cp. *N.T.Wb.*, 72/.

nai, legō humin 'yes, or, indeed, I tell you', cp. on 3 : 8. *nai* is added in order to stress that the subsequent statement serves to affirm emphatically the preceding one.

Translation: *Warn*, or, 'make clear/explain' (South Toradja), or simply, 'tell'.

Whom to fear, or, "the only One you need to fear" (Phillips), 'who (it is) that you really should fear' (Balinese). For *fear* with reference to God see 1 : 50.

Who, after he has killed, has power to cast, or, 'who has power (first) to kill and then to cast', 'who not only kills, but also has power to cast'. *Kills*, or, 'causes to die'; in Balinese God cannot be said 'to kill a person', but 'to take-away a person's life'. The verb may require an object, e.g. 'you', 'a man' (Balinese), 'your-body' (East Toradja 1933). *Cast*, or, 'hurl down', 'send', 'cause to descend/fall/go'. Since the persons in question are envisaged now as dead, an object, if required, may have to be a specific term used to refer to dead persons, cp. e.g. East Toradja 1933.

Hell, cp. *N.T.Wb.*/42f. *Yes*, or, 'indeed', 'once more'.

6 ***Are not five sparrows sold for two pennies? And not one of them is forgotten before God.***

Exegesis: *ouchi pente strouthia pōlountai assariōn duo* 'are not five sparrows sold for two cents', i.e. "do not sparrows sell five for two cents" (Goodspeed). The clause means that sparrows are of very little value. For *ouchi* cp. on 6 : 39.

strouthion (also v. 7) 'sparrow', or, in a more general sense, 'bird', cp. *IDB* IV, 430f.

pōleō 'to sell', here in the passive.

assarion (†) a Latin loanword, cp. *TBT*, 10.167f, 1959. It is one of the smallest coins used in Roman coinage and best rendered as 'cent', 'penny', etc.

kai hen ex autōn ouk estin epilelēsmenon enōpion tou theou 'and (yet) not one of them is forgotten in the sight of God'. *kai hen* with following negation is emphatic, 'not even one...'. For *enōpion* cp. on 1 : 15.

epilanthanomai (†) 'to forget', 'to overlook'. The perfect tense refers to a state, or, situation in which one is overlooked.

Translation: In the interrogative sentence the price is in focus rather than the process of selling; hence some idiomatic renderings omit the verb, e.g. 'isn't the price of five sparrows two pennies?' (cp. East Toradja 1933), "are not sparrows five for twopence?" (NEB). The force of the question is, 'everyone knows that...'.

Sparrow, or the name of a common small bird, e.g. a rice-eating finch (some Indonesian languages), or simply 'small bird' (Sranan).

Penny should preferably be rendered by the name of a small coin used in the culture, but not the smallest one, for which see "copper coin" (21 : 2). Where no distinctive names are available or usable one may say 'small coin', 'piece of money of small value'. Cp. also Nida, *BT*, 328f, 338, 341; *N.T.Wb.*/55, MONEY.

Forgotten before God, or not to obscure the fact that God is the implied agent, "forgotten in the thoughts of God" (Rieu), or simply 'forgotten by God', 'God forgets' (cp. e.g. Shona 1966, Sranan). For some idioms rendering the verb see *TH-Mk* on 8 : 14.

7 ***Why, even the hairs of your head are all numbered. Fear not; you are of more value than many sparrows.***

Exegesis: *alla kai* serves to introduce a clause which contrasts with, and goes beyond, the preceding clause, 'but (more than that), even...' (cp. NEB), or 'not only this but even...' (cp. A-G).

hai triches tēs kephalēs humōn 'the hairs of the head of (each of) you'.

pasai ērithmēntai 'are all counted', scil. *enōpion tou theou* 'in the sight of God', also in the perfect tense, cp. v. 6.

arithmeō (†) 'to count', 'to number'.

mē phobeisthe 'do not fear', i.e. 'stop fearing', cp. on 1 : 13.

pollōn strouthiōn diapherete "you are of more value than many sparrows" (RSV). The plural form of the verb has distributive meaning, since each single person is of more value than many sparrows.

diapherō (also v. 24) 'to be worth more', 'to be superior', with genitive of that to which one is superior, cp. A-G s.v. 2 b.

Translation: *The hairs of* (or, on) *your head are all numbered*, or, 'the number of all the hairs...is known', 'God knows how many hairs there are on your head'. For *hairs of the head* see 7 : 38.

You are of more value than many sparrows, i.e. your value (figurative) is more than the value/price (literal) of many sparrows, and cp. 'you are in-all-respects above...' (East Toradja), 'you are better than...' (Toba Batak). The contrast between one human being and many sparrows may be made more explicit, e.g. 'even if only one, you are...' (cp. East Toradja 1933), or, '...sparrows, many as they may be' (Balinese).

8 ***"And I tell you, every one who acknowledges me before men, the Son of man also will acknowledge before the angels of God;***
9 ***but he who denies me before men will be denied before the angels of God.***

Exegesis: *legō de humin* 'I say to you', cp. on 3 : 8.

pas hos an homologēsē en emoi 'everyone who acknowledges me'.

homologeō (†) 'to acknowledge', 'to confess', here with *en*, probably an Aramaism (cp. A-G s.v. 4). To acknowledge Jesus means to acknowledge allegiance to Jesus.

emprosthen tōn anthrōpōn 'before, or, in the presence of men', i.e. publicly, here and now.

kai ho huios tou anthrōpou 'the Son of man on his part...'. For *ho huios tou anthrōpou* cp. on 5 : 24.

homologēsei en autō emprosthen tōn aggelōn tou theou 'will acknowledge him before the angels of God', i.e. in the eschatological judgment the Son of man will answer for him.

(V. 9) *ho de arnēsamenos me enōpion tōn anthrōpōn* 'he who disowns me before men'. *de* marks transition and contrast. *arnēsamenos* is in the aorist because, from the standpoint of the final judgment, it refers to an act in the past. *enōpion* is equivalent to *emprosthen* (v. 8). For *arneomai* cp. on 8 : 45. To disown Jesus means to deny allegiance to him.

aparnēthēsetai enōpion tōn aggelōn tou theou 'will be disowned before the angels of God', in the eschatological judgment Jesus will not answer for him. *aparneomai* is equivalent to *arneomai*.

Translation: *Every one who acknowledges me..., the Son of man also will acknowledge...* The structure of this verse may have to be recast, e.g. 'when a person acknowledges me..., the Son of man on his part will acknowledge him...', or in co-ordination, e.g. 'let anybody acknowledge me..., and I the Son of man will acknowledge him...' (cp. Rieu).

Acknowledges me is often rendered by a descriptive phrase, cp. e.g. "confesses publicly that he belongs to me" (TEV), 'say openly...that they have believed on me' (Tzeltal), 'approves me' (West Nyanja, a term explained as "to utter response in chorus, or in a speech approve, by word of mouth or by clapping of hands, the words of the speaker, to...do the part of an approver and say, 'yes, yes, we say so too'"; also used for 'to confess', in the sense of reciting the Creed); or by comparable expressions in direct discourse; or again by, 'declares/mentions my name' (Kekchi, Sranan), 'talks my good name' (Gbeapo), 'testifies to me' (cp. e.g. Zarma, Ponape), 'takes my side' (Shona 1966), 'speaks for me' (Kapauku).

(V. 9) *He who denies me...will be denied...*, or, 'when a person disowns/

rejects me..., he will be disowned/rejected, or, I will disown/reject him...'. *To deny* can often be rendered by the opposite or negative of the expression used for "to acknowledge", e.g. 'not be willing to acknowledge' (Thai 1967), 'say I do not (or, don't want to) believe', etc., 'pretend not to know' (Kapauku); in Zarma one uses 'to take oath', nearly always with negative connotation: to swear that it is not true, or that one will not.

10 ***And every one who speaks a word against the Son of man will be forgiven; but he who blasphemes against the Holy Spirit will not be forgiven.***

Exegesis: *kai pas hos erei logon eis ton huion tou anthrōpou* 'and everyone who will speak a word against the Son of man'. For the interpretation of this difficult verse see commentaries. *pas* may have the same referent as *pas* in vv. 8 and 9, viz. the disciples of Jesus, or refer to people in general, probably the latter. *pas hos erei* (future indicative) is in the nature of a general statement and may be rendered as a present. *erei logon* is a neutral expression, but has implications of rejection, or, blasphemy by virtue of its use in the present context. On the same grounds *eis* assumes here a hostile meaning (cp. A-G s.v. 4 c α).

aphethēsetai autō lit. '(it) will be forgiven to him', the subject of the verb being the speaking against the Son of man. The future tense, again, refers to final judgment.

tō de eis to hagion pneuma blasphēmēsanti 'him who has blasphemed against the Holy Spirit'. For the aorist tense of the participle *blasphēmēsanti* cp. on v. 9. The dative *tō...blasphēmēsanti* goes syntactically with *aphethēsetai*.

blasphēmeō 'to blaspheme', 'to revile', cp. *TH-Mk* on 3 : 28.

ouk aphethēsetai '(it) will not be forgiven', the subject being the blaspheming against the Holy Spirit.

Translation: *Speaks a word against*, or, 'says something opposing' (Bahasa Indonesia RC), 'speaks to-the-detriment-of'; more generic than 'blaspheme', and less pejorative.

Every one who...will be forgiven, or with a shift as discussed above (v. 8), 'when a person..., he will be forgiven, or, this (sin of him) will be forgiven (him)', or in active construction with 'God' as subject.

Blasphemes against the Holy Spirit, or, 'insults (or, spoils the name of) the Holy Spirit', etc., cp. *TH-Mk* on 2 : 7.

11 ***And when they bring you before the synagogues and the rulers and the authorities, do not be anxious how or what you are to answer or what you are to say;***

Exegesis: *hotan de eispherōsin humas epi tas sunagōgas kai tas archas kai tas exousias* 'when they drag you to the synagogues and the magistrates and the authorities'.

eispherō lit. 'to bring (in)to', here of forceful bringing, 'to drag', 'to hale'.

sunagōgē 'synagogue', here of the synagogue in its function of a local court.

archē here in a concrete sense, 'ruler', 'magistrate' (cp. A-G s.v. 3).

exousia (cp. on 4 : 6) here in a concrete sense 'ruler', 'authority' (cp. A-G s.v. 4 c α). There is little or no difference between *exousia* and *archē* in the present context. Both words refer to judicial officers before whom the disciples may be brought.

mē merimnēsēte 'do not worry', cp. on 10 : 41.

pōs [ē ti] apologēsēsthe ē ti eipēte 'how you are to defend yourself, or what you are to say'. [*ē ti*] is best disregarded for translational purposes.

apologeomai (also 21 : 14) 'to answer', 'to say in one's defense', 'to defend oneself'. As shown by *pōs* the verb refers here to the manner of the defense, as contrasted with *eipein* which refers to the actual wording.

Translation: *Bring you before*, i.e. 'bring you up', 'bring you to be tried before' (cp. TEV); specific terms are available in some languages, e.g. Javanese, Sundanese (lit. 'to escort'), South Toradja (see on 21 : 12).

Synagogues, here, 'the councils, or, those assembled, in the synagogue' (cp. Bahasa Indonesia, South Toradja).

Rulers and authorities here usually best rendered by two rather common synonyms, e.g. "governors or rulers" (TEV), 'princes and/or kings', 'chiefs low and/or high', or, interpreted as a hendiadys, "state authorities" (NEB).

Do not be anxious, see 10 : 41. The connexion with what follows may have to be clarified, e.g. by inserting, 'asking yourself (or, saying within yourself, or, thinking)' before the dependent clauses.

How . . . you are to answer or what you are to say. The first verb has been rendered, 'say-in-reply' (Lokele, a "reversive" form of 'to reply', implying that an accusation has been made), 'defend-oneself' (West Nyanja), 'say back' (Kapauku). Since "answer" and "say" refer to virtually the same act the two verbs have sometimes been combined into one verb or verbal expression, e.g. 'how or what you are to reply', 'how or what you must speak to defend yourself (NV), or, answer to pull yourself out from it' (Sranan, using an idiomatic expression for 'preservation of life').

12 ***for the Holy Spirit will teach you in that very hour what you ought to say."***

Exegesis: *to gar hagion pneuma didaxei humas . . . ha dei eipein* 'for the Holy Spirit will instruct you what you must say', i.e. the Holy Spirit will put the right words in your mind and mouth.

en autē tē hōra 'at that very hour, or, moment', cp. on 10 : 21 and reference there.

Translation: *In that very hour* may be given a more emphatic position, cp. e.g. "for when the time/moment comes, the Holy Spirit . . ." (NEB, Rieu).

What you ought to say, or, "what is the right thing for you to say" (Phillips), or simply, 'the suitable word(s)'.

13 ***One of the multitude said to him, "Teacher, bid my brother divide the inheritance with me."***

Exegesis: *tis ek tou ochlou* 'somebody in the crowd', cp. on 11 : 27.

didaskale 'master', cp. on 3 : 12.

merisasthai met' emou tēn klēronomian 'to share the inheritance with me', dependent upon *eipe* 'tell'. The infinitive *merisasthai* has obligatory force, i.e. 'that he must share'.

merizomai (†) 'to share with', followed by *meta* with genitive, cp. A-G s.v. 1 b.

klēronomia (also 20 : 14) 'inheritance', 'estate', i.e. what is left after the father's death.

Translation: *Bid,* or, 'please, tell/say-to/order'.

Brother, see 6 : 14. If one has to choose between terms for different kinds of brothers, the decision must be made on the basis of the situation most likely to occur in the receptor culture; hence 'son of my father' (cp. *TBT*, 11.177, 1960, and 12.86, 1961), 'elder-brother' (many cultures), 'youngest brother' (as might be preferable in some parts of Bali, since there the youngest brother usually stays to live with the father after his brothers have gone off to live on their own), 'brother-of-the-same-mother' (in some matrilineal societies), and so on.

Divide...with me, or, 'give me my part of' (East Toradja 1933); and cp. *N.T.Wb.*/29f.

The inheritance may be described here, if necessary, 'the property our (exclusive) father left (us) at his death'.

14 ***But he said to him, "Man, who made me a judge or divider over you?"***

Exegesis: *anthrōpe* 'man!', a harsh form of address implying disapprobation (cp. Plummer).

tis me katestēsen kritēn ē meristēn eph' humas 'who appointed me judge or arbitrator over you?', the obvious answer being: nobody. For *kritēs* cp. on 11 : 19 and A-G s.v. 1 a α. *eph' humas* 'over you' implies the idea of having power over someone, cp. A-G s.v. *epi* III 1 b α.

kathistēmi 'to appoint', 'to put in charge as'.

meristēs (††) lit. 'divider', hence 'arbitrator'.

Translation: *Man.* In some languages a form of address has been chosen that is only used towards strangers, and as such expresses distance and aloofness; in others omission may be the best solution, because the available words of address have the wrong connotation.

Who made me a judge or divider over you, or, 'who appointed me to be judge and inheritance divider for you' (Thai 1967), 'who gave me the task to judge (between) you (or, to decide your case) and to divide your property/inheritance'. The two nouns qualify each other; hence e.g. 'who appointed me to decide about the division (or, how you should divide) your property'. Where a shift to a statement is preferable one may begin the sentence with, 'nobody made me...', 'it is certainly not my task to...'. For *judge* cp. also on the verb in *N.T.Wb.*/48f.

15 ***And he said to them, "Take heed, and beware of all covetousness; for a man's life does not consist in the abundance of his possessions."***

Exegesis: *eipen de pros autous* 'he said to them'. *autous* may refer to all present (cp. *ochlos* in v. 12), or to the disciples, preferably the former.

horate kai phulassesthe apo pasēs pleonexias 'take care, and be on your guard against every form of greed'. *horate* may stand alone, or, like *phulassesthe*, go with *apo* (cp. A-G s.v. *horaō* 2 b), preferably the former. For *phulassō* cp. on 2 : 8 and A-G s.v. 2 a. In *pasa pleonexia* the adjective *pasa* means 'every kind, or form', cp. A-G s.v. 1 a β.

pleonexia (†) 'greed', 'greediness', cp. *N.T.Wb.*, 69f/GREED.

ouk en tō perisseuein tini lit. 'not (even) when there is an abundance for somebody', i.e. 'not (even) when somebody has in abundance'. For *perisseuō* cp. on 9 : 17.

hē zōē autou estin ek tōn huparchontōn autō 'his life belongs to his possessions'. For *ta huparchonta* cp. on 8 : 3 and reference there. For the meaning of *ek* cp. A-G s.v. 4 a δ.

zōē 'life', here of man's natural life as contrasted with death, cp. A-G s.v. 1 a.

Translation: *Take heed*, or, 'Attention!', "Watch out" (TEV).

Beware of all covetousness, or, 'evil longing', 'envious-desire' (cp. Zarma, Ponape). The clause often has to be adjusted, e.g. 'do not be loving riches', 'may wealth not take possession of your heart' (Tzeltal), 'do not desire to gather all kinds of goods' (East Toradja 1933), 'do not give-the-reins to a greedy mind' (Balinese). For the noun cp. also *N.T.Wb.*/41, GREED; and /25f, DESIRE.

A man's life does not consist in the abundance of his possessions, or, as preferred in *Exegesis*, 'a man's life does not belong to (or, is not part of, or, does not depend on) his possessions, even when he has (them) in abundance, or, even when he possesses more than he needs'; or again 'a man is not master of his own life, even when he is master of many goods', 'a man may be very rich, but this does not mean that he will live long, or, but this does not give him the right/power to live long'. For *abundance* see also *N.T.Wb.* /1, ABOUND.

16 ***And he told them a parable, saying, "The land of a rich man brought forth plentifully;***

Exegesis: *eipen de parabolēn pros autous* 'and he told them a parable'. *de* marks continuation since the ensuing parable serves to illustrate the saying of v. 15. For *parabolē* cp. on 4 : 23. *autous* refers to the same group as *autous* in v. 15.

anthrōpou tinos plousiou euphorēsen hē chōra lit. 'of a certain rich man the land yielded well'. *anthrōpou* etc. is possessive genitive with *chōra* but is placed emphatically at the beginning of the clause because the man is the main personality of the parable.

euphoreō (††) 'to bear a good crop', 'to yield well'. The aorist tense refers to a punctiliar event, i.e. to one good crop (cp. Rieu, "one year").

chōra (cp. on 2 : 8) here 'cultivated land', 'farm land', 'farm', cp. A-G s.v. 4.

Translation: *Parable,* see 8 : 4.

The land of a rich man..., or, since the man rather than the land is in focus, 'there was once a rich man who had produced for him very much by his field' (cp. Shona 1966), 'once there was a rich man. His lands...', 'a certain (see on 7 : 41) rich man had land which...'.

The land...brought forth plentifully, or, 'gave heavy crops', 'plentiful was his crop (lit. the strength of his-field)' (Toba Batak), 'the field...made much food' (Sranan).

17 ***and he thought to himself, 'What shall I do, for I have nowhere to store my crops?'***

Exegesis: *kai dielogizeto en heautō* 'and he debated with himself', durative imperfect. For *dialogizomai* cp. on 1 : 29.

hoti ouk echō pou sunaxō tous karpous mou lit. 'for I have not where I shall store my crops', i.e. 'I have no place to store my crops'. For *echō* cp. A-G s.v. I 2 d.

sunagō (cp. on 3 : 17) here 'to store'.

karpos 'fruit', here in the plural of grain/corn crops.

Translation: *He thought to* (or, within) *himself,* or, 'he deliberated', 'he asked (in) his heart', or simply, 'he thought'.

What shall I do, or, 'what am I to do'. Some idiomatic renderings are, 'what-now my-tactics' (Malay), 'how am I to devise now' (Balinese), 'how the plan' (Javanese).

Nowhere to store..., or, 'no place where I can put-away...' (Sranan), 'not enough place for-storing...' (East Toradja). Some versions (e.g. East Toradja 1933) use the more specific term rendering "barn" in v. 18.

My crops may have to become, 'the crops (or, the produce/yield) of my farm/fields' (e.g. in some Indonesian languages).

18 ***And he said, 'I will do this: I will pull down my barns, and build larger ones; and there I will store all my grain and my goods.***

Exegesis: *kai eipen* 'and (at last) he said'. After *dielogizeto* (v. 17, imperfect tense) *eipen* (aorist) marks the end of his deliberations and the reaching of a decision.

touto poiēsō 'this (is what) I will do', introductory clause. *touto* is emphatic.

kathelō mou tas apothēkas 'I will tear down my barns'. For *kathaireō* cp. on 1 : 52. For *apothēkē* cp. on 3 : 17.

kai meizonas oikodomēsō 'and I will build bigger ones', with *apothēkas* understood.

ekei 'there', i.e. in the new bigger barns.

panta ton siton kai ta agatha mou 'all my grain/corn and goods'. *panta* goes with *siton* only. *agatha* refers to movable possessions in general.

Translation: *Pull down,* referring probably not to mere destruction, but to the deliberate taking down of the barns in such a way that the material can still be used, as indicated e.g. in Balinese, which uses a word lit. meaning 'to untie/loosen'.

Barns, or, 'storehouses', in Indonesia often a term that basically means 'rice barn', then 'granary', 'storehouse (for any kind of food and goods)'. A generic descriptive phrase, 'place/building where are stored', may coincide with the expression employed in v. 17.

All my grain and my goods, or, 'all this grain (of mine) and my other goods/possessions'. For *grain* cp. on "wheat" in 3 : 17.

19 ***And I will say to my soul, Soul, you have ample goods laid up for many years; take your ease, eat, drink, be merry.'*** 20 ***But God said to him, 'Fool! This night your soul is required of you; and the things you have prepared, whose will they be?'***

Exegesis: *kai erō tē psuchē mou* 'and I will say to my soul', i.e. 'I will say to myself' (cp. A-G s.v. *psuchē* 1 f). This reflexive use of *psuchē* is also true of the following vocative *psuchē* as a way of self-addressing (cp. Ps. 103 : 1, 2, 22 and other places). But in v. 20 *psuchē* means 'life' as something which is given to man and can be taken away from him (cp. *TBT*, 2.74, 1951). This ambiguous use of *psuchē* is intentional.

echeis polla agatha keimena eis etē polla 'you have many goods laid up for many years'. *eis etē polla* goes with *polla agatha* primarily, meaning 'enough for many years'. *polla agatha* here includes *panta ton siton kai ta agatha mou* of v. 18, i.e. *agatha* has a wider meaning here than in v. 18.

keimai here 'to be stored up', 'to be laid by, or, up'.

anapauou (†) 'take your rest, or, ease', 'relax', imperative.

euphrainou 'be merry', 'enjoy yourself', 'have a good time'.

(V. 20) *eipen de autō ho theos* 'but God said to him', contrasting with, and interrupting what he said to himself (v. 19).

aphrōn 'you fool', vocative, cp. on 11 : 40.

tautē tē nukti 'this very night', emphatic.

tēn psuchēn sou apaitousin apo sou 'they demand your life from you', present tense expressing the imminence of what will happen. *tēn psuchēn sou* (cp. on v. 19) is emphatic by position. For *apaiteō* cp. on 6 : 30. The agent implied in *apaitousin* is God.

ha de hētoimasas 'what you have prepared', relative clause serving as subject of the main clause *tini estai*. For *hetoimazō* cp. on 1 : 17.

tini estai 'for whom shall it be?', i.e. 'to whom shall it go?'

Translation: *My soul* (1), *Soul* (2)...(v. 20)...*your soul* (3). By using the same term thrice Luke effectively brings out the contrast between what the rich man thinks to be the case, viz. that he is master of his soul just as he seems to be of his goods, and what God knows it to be, viz. that he is to lose both. In some languages one has the translational luck that one term is idiomatic in the three occurrences, e.g. 'life', in Zarma; 'soul/breath (of life)' in Tzeltal, and in Shona 1966, which in (2) personalizes the term; 'heart' in Bamiléké, and in Sranan, which in (3) has 'your heart will cease to beat'. The contrast is also sufficiently preserved when the term in question occurs only once in v. 19, e.g. 'say to my soul, "Now you have..." (20) ..., "...your soul is required of you..."'. Often, however, it would be so unidiomatic to use the same term twice or thrice that differentiation is obligatory. Cp. e.g. Thai 1967: (1) 'inner being (lit. mind-heart)'—(2) 'inner being (id.)'—(3) 'life'; East Toradja 1933: 'soul—you here—breath-of-life'; Toba Batak: 'soul—soul—breath-of-life'; Kapauku: 'self—you—(living) soul (lit. thought-word)'; Kituba, Leyden: 'self'—left untranslated—'life'; NEB, Willibrord, or TEV: 'self—man, or, lucky man—life'. In such languages one may try to bring out the contrast in another way, e.g. by rendering (3) as 'the soul *you* think is yours', or by emphasizing the contrast between the two forms of address, saying e.g. 'you lucky man' for (2) and 'you foolish man' in v. 20. For *soul* see also 1 : 46 and references.

Laid up for many years, or, 'which have been (or, which I have) laid up (for you) for many years', 'enough for years on end' (Balinese, cp. also 'many years not-yet exhausted', in East Toradja 1933).

Take your ease, or, "take life easy" (TEV), can better be rendered as a proposal or permission, e.g. '(now) you should/may take your ease'. The same holds true of the subsequent imperatives.

Eat, drink, cp. "eat and drink" in 5 : 30; the reference is to feasting, as shown by the subsequent *be merry*, or, "enjoy yourself" (NEB), "have a good time" (Phillips).

(V. 20) *Fool*, or, 'you fool(ish man)'; and see 11 : 40.

Assuming these words to be spoken by day, *this night* refers to the coming night, which implies a reference to the next day in languages where the day is taken to begin at sunset. For *night* cp. also *N.T.Wb.*/57.

Your soul is required of you. A literal rendering of the Greek by 'they require', 'somebody requires' may suggest God as agent (e.g. in Zarma, Kapauku), but will more often be taken as referring to unmentioned human beings; hence shifts to the passive (in some European versions and in Lomwe, Shona, Lokele, Thai 1967, Tzeltal), or to 'I require' (cp. Kituba, Trukese), or to renderings such as, "you will have to give up your life" (TEV), 'your-spirit will drift-away from you' (Ponape). *To require of*, or, 'to ask (back) from', 'to call/take from', 'to reclaim from (as one does a loan)' (Rieu, Bahasa Indonesia KB, Toba Batak), and cp. 'you will have these words addressed to you, "Give me here your soul"' (Shona 1966).

The things you have prepared is emphatic by position. If emphasis has to be expressed otherwise, one may say something like, '(all) those things you have been preparing up till now'. *To prepare*, or, 'to set/make ready', or, in this context, 'to store up' (Bamiléké), 'to collect' (Sranan), since the reference is to the goods rather than to the barns.

Whose will they be, or, 'who will acquire/possess them'. This clause may better come first, cp. e.g. 'to whom will you leave the things you have collected' (Sranan), 'who will call-his-own all that you prepared' (South Toradja).

21 ***So is he who lays up treasure for himself, and is not rich toward God."***

Exegesis: *houtōs* 'so', 'in this way', here used elliptically, 'this is how it is with...', 'this is the situation of...', and it points to the moral after the parable, cp. A-G s.v. 1 b.

ho thēsaurizōn heautō kai mē eis theon ploutōn 'he who stores up treasure for himself and is not rich toward God'. The article *ho* governs both participles. *plouteō,* cp. on 1 : 53.

thēsaurizō (†) 'to store up', here implying 'to store up treasure', as explicitly in Mt. 6 : 19.

eis theon lit. 'toward God', i.e. 'with reference to', hence "where God is concerned" (Phillips), or "in the sight of God" (NEB), "from God's point of view" (TEV).

Translation: *To lay up treasure,* or, 'to pile up riches' (TEV, similarly Balinese); and cp. 12 : 33.

Is not rich toward God. Where the models given in *Exegesis* won't do one may say, 'whom God knows to be not rich', 'God knows that he is poor, or, has no treasures'. The metaphorical use of *rich* may have to be signalled, e.g. 'truly rich', 'having treasures that really count'.

22 ***And he said to his disciples, "Therefore I tell you, do not be anxious about your life, what you shall eat, nor about your body, what you shall put on.***

Exegesis: *eipen de pros tous mathētas* 'and he said to his disciples', after having addressed the crowds in vv. 15-21. The clause introduces a second inference from the parable in vv. 16-20, as shown by *dia touto* 'therefore'. For the subsequent *legō humin* cp. on 3 : 8.

mē merimnate tē psuchē ti phagēte 'do not worry about the (i.e. your) life, what you are to eat'. For *merimnaō* cp. on 10 : 41. *tē psuchē* (dative of reference) refers to physical life to be sustained by food, cp. A-G s.v. 1 a β.

mēde tō sōmati ti endusēsthe 'nor about the (i.e. your) body, what you are to put on', with *merimnate* understood. The syntactic structure is the same as in the preceding clause. For *enduō* cp. on 8 : 27.

Translation: *To be anxious,* see 10 : 41; the expression may have to be repeated before the clause about clothing, e.g. in Tzeltal.

About your life, what you shall eat, or with two verbs, 'how to live and what to eat'. To bring out that life has to be sustained by what one eats some versions have, 'about your life, that is, what will be-used-as means-to-support-life (or, livelihood)' (Balinese), or, more radically recasting the sentence structure, "about food to keep you alive" (NEB), 'concerning the food that you must get in-order to live-by' (Kituba). For *food* see 3 : 11.

About your body, what you shall put on. The structure should preferably parallel that of the preceding clause. *To put on*, or, 'to wear (clothes)', 'to be clothed with'.

23 ***For life is more than food, and the body more than clothing.***

Exegesis: *hē gar psuchē pleion estin tēs trophēs* 'for life is something more important, or, valuable, than food'. Both times the article (*hē* and *tēs*) is generic. *pleion* is substantive, cp. A-G s.v. *polus* II 2 c. *psuchē* has the same meaning as in v. 22, and v. 23 emphasizes the difference in value and meaning between physical life and that which is needed to sustain it.

kai to sōma tou endumatos 'and the body (is something more important, or, valuable) than clothing', with *pleion estin* understood, see above.

Translation: *Life* and *body* may have to be possessed, 'your life', 'your body'.

For *clothing* see 7 : 25.

24 ***Consider the ravens: they neither sow nor reap, they have neither storehouse nor barn, and yet God feeds them. Of how much more value are you than the birds!***

Exegesis: *katanoēsate tous korakas* 'consider the crows'.

katanoeō 'to notice', here 'to consider', 'to look intently at', cp. A-G s.v. 2.

korax (††) 'crow', cp. *IDB* IV, 13.

hoti ou speirousin oude therizousin 'that they neither sow nor reap'. Sowing and reaping represent labouring to provide for food. Both words also together in 19 : 21f.

hois ouk estin tameion oude apothēkē '(the crows) who have no storehouse and no barn', i.e. who cannot store food for the time that there is no food to be obtained. For *tameion* cp. on v. 3; for *apothēkē* on 3 : 17.

kai ho theos trephei autous 'and God feeds them'. *kai* has concessive force, 'and yet'. The underlying thought is, 'and yet they do not starve, for God feeds them'.

posō mallon humeis diapherete tōn peteinōn 'by how much are you more important than the birds'. For *diapherō* cp. on v. 7. The comparative meaning of *diapherō* is strengthened by *mallon* which is, in itself, redundant, cp. Bl-D, § 246. *posō* is dative of degree.

peteinon 'bird', here used generically of all birds, of which the crows are representative.

Translation: *Sow* (or, 'sow seeds') and *reap* (or, 'reap crops', "gather a harvest", TEV), are sometimes rendered by a term specifically referring to the sowing and reaping of the local staple food, e.g. 'plant rice-seedlings' and 'cut-rice'. For *sow* see 8 : 5.

Storehouse and *barn* are close synonyms; the phrase as a whole means, 'storehouses of any kind'. *Storehouse,* or, 'place/house for food' (East Toradja, Sranan), 'big-basket', used for storing corn or rice (Zapotec of Villa Alta, South Toradja).

Feeds, or, 'gives food' (Javanese), 'rears/takes-care-of' (Bahasa Indonesia), 'causes to eat', cp. *N.T.Wb.*/36.

Of how much more value are you than the birds, or, "you are worth far more than the birds" (NEB); or describing the comparison in another way, 'what-is-the-quantity (in the sense of 'how trifling') the life of birds in-comparison-with your life' (East Toradja 1933). See also v. 7.

25 ***And which of you by being anxious can add a cubit to his span of life?***

Exegesis: *tis...ex humōn* 'which of you?' cp. on 11 : 5.

merimnōn 'by worrying', 'by being anxious'.

dunatai epi tēn hēlikian autou prostheinai pēchun 'can add a cubit to his lifetime'. For *hēlikia* cp. on 2 : 52. In view of v. 20 and of the meaning of *pēchus* (see below) the rendering 'life', 'lifetime' is here preferable. For *prostithēmi* cp. on 3 : 20.

pēchus (†) lit. 'cubit', 'ell', a measure of length (length of a forearm, about 18 inches = 46.2 centimetres) here used to indicate a short span of time (cp. A-G s.v.).

Translation: *Which of you,* or, 'is there anyone among you who', 'certainly no one among you'.

By being anxious, or, 'by-means-of his worrying' (Toba Batak), "however much he worries about it" (Phillips), sometimes better placed at the end of the sentence. Further shifts or expansions may be necessary, e.g. 'even if you are anxious can you ever add...', 'however much you worry how to make yourself live longer you cannot add...' (cp. Tzeltal).

Can add a cubit to his span of life, or, 'can cause his life to become one span longer' (Sranan), 'can live a day more/longer'. A term for *cubit* exists in most languages (e.g. 'an axe handle long' in Gio, and cp. Nida, *BT*, 341; *N.T.Wb.*/73f, WEIGHTS and MEASURES); but in many of them it cannot be used as a measure of time in this context; hence, 'short space of time', "a single hour" (Goodspeed), 'a day', but better not 'an instant/second', since the 'cubit' is not the smallest measure of length. *His span of life,* or, 'the length/duration of his life', "his years" (Rieu), 'his-days' (Toba Batak). Brouwer and Bahasa Indonesia RC use 'path-of-life', in the sense of 'length of life', with which term 'cubit' (as measure of length) fits in nicely.

26 ***If then you are not able to do as small a thing as that, why are you anxious about the rest?***

Exegesis: *ei oun oude elachiston dunasthe* 'if then you cannot (do) even a very small, or, insignificant thing'. The reference to what precedes is brought out in "as small a thing as that" (RSV). The rendering 'the smallest thing' appears to be too emphatic. The clause is conditional in form but inferential in meaning.

peri tōn loipōn 'about the rest', i.e. about physical necessities.

Translation: *If then you...*, preferably, 'since you...', 'thus it is certain that you...', cp. the remark on the "if"-clause in 11 : 20.

As small a thing as that, or, 'such a small thing', 'such a trifle' (Javanese).

The rest, or, 'the other things', "anything else" (Phillips).

27 ***Consider the lilies, how they grow; they neither toil nor spin; yet I tell you, even Solomon in all his glory was not arrayed like one of these.***

Exegesis: *katanoēsate ta krina pōs auxanei* 'consider the lilies how they grow', i.e. 'consider how the lilies grow'. *ta krina* is emphatic by position. For *auxanō* cp. on 1 : 80.

krinon (†) 'lily', cp. *IDB* III, 133f and *N.T.Wb.*, 63/FLORA.

ou kopia oude nēthei 'they do not toil or spin', referring to human efforts towards the sustaining of life in an agricultural setting. *kopiaō* (cp. on 5 : 5) refers to the (hard) work on the land (usually done by men), and *nēthō* (†) 'to spin' to domestic work (usually done by women).

legō de humin 'but I tell you', cp. on 3 : 8.

oude Solomōn en pasē tē doxē autou 'not even Solomon in all his splendour'. *doxa* refers here to the magnificence which surrounds a king in every respect.

periebaleto hōs hen toutōn 'was dressed like one of them'. The aorist tense does not refer here to an event, but to a situation of the past (cp. Bl-D, § 332).

periballō (also 23 : 11) 'to put on', in middle form 'to dress (oneself)'.

Translation: *Lilies,* or, the name of some brightly coloured flower, especially the purple, or scarlet, wild anemone; or more generically, '(wild) flowers' (Toba Batak, Huixtec, Mazahua), 'blooms'.

How they grow refers here to the result of their growth, i.e. their outward appearance, rather than to the process of growing; it has, therefore, sometimes been omitted, i.e. left to be understood from the context, e.g. in Shona 1966. For *to grow* cp. *N.T.Wb.*/41f.

To spin, or, 'to spin thread', or some term referring to an equivalent feminine activity, e.g. 'to weave cloth(es)' (Tzeltal, similarly in Shona 1963; and in one West Nyanja version, lit. 'to beat cloth', i.e. to beat the threads into position in the loom), or a term for rolling fibres to make thread (Shona 1966), twisting bark threads on the thigh to make strings (Kapauku, similarly another West Nyanja version), beating out bark-cloth (Lokele); or more generically, "make clothes for themselves" (TEV).

Even Solomon in all his glory was not arrayed like one of these. The sentence structure often has to be recast, e.g. 'not even S., as glorious (or, rich) as he was, had clothes as beautiful as one of these flowers' (cp. TEV), or, if a term for 'array', 'clothing' cannot be applied to flowers, 'although the clothes of S. were very beautiful, their beauty did not equal the beauty of one flower' (Tzeltal). *Glory,* here referring to a human being's outward appearance, may be rendered, 'pomp', 'splendour', 'magnificence', 'beauty', 'greatness of life' (East Toradja 1933); such a rendering will often differ from the one used for '(heavenly or divine) glory' in 2 : 9. *Arrayed,* or, 'attired', especially said of princely dress, or simply, 'clothed' (for which see *N.T.Wb.*/20).

28 ***But if God so clothes the grass which is alive in the field today and tomorrow is thrown into the oven, how much more will he clothe you, O men of little faith!***

Exegesis: *ei de* 'and if...', introducing the inference to be drawn from v. 27.

en agrō ton chorton onta sēmeron 'in the field the grass that is today', or, 'the grass that is in the field today', preferably the latter. *ton chorton* is emphatic by position. *chorton* (†) 'grass' takes up and interprets *ta krina,* since even the lilies belong to the grass that is alive today and is dead tomorrow. *onta* means 'is present', 'is alive'. For *agros* cp. *TH-Mk* on 5 : 14.

kai aurion eis klibanon ballomenon 'and is thrown into the furnace tomorrow'. *ballomenon* is present, as if it were happening already.

klibanos (†) 'furnace', 'oven'.

(*ei*)...*ho theos houtōs amphiazei* '(if)...God so clothes...', indicating the premiss from which the inference is to be drawn in the exclamation that follows. *houtōs* points back to v. 27.

amphiazō (††) 'to dress', 'to clothe'.

posō mallon humas 'how much more you', with some verb meaning 'to clothe', or, 'to take care of' understood.

oligopistoi (†) 'you men of little faith', vocative, implying a severe criticism of the disciples' trust in God.

Translation: *But if...,* cp. v. 26.

So clothes, or, 'gives such (beautiful) clothing to', 'makes so beautiful'.

Grass, or, 'weeds' (Toba Batak), 'field-herbs' (Willibrord), or some other rather high level generic term for (non-cultivated, short-living) vegetation that includes the term for "lilies" in v. 27. Cp. also *N.T.Wb.*/37f, FLORA.

Is alive, or, 'is there', 'grows' (cp. NEB, East and South Toradja), 'stands' (Toba Batak).

Field. The rendering should refer to uncultivated land, or to arable land at the time it is not tilled.

Thrown into the oven, "burned up in the oven" (TEV), 'used as fuel'; in Balinese one has to say, 'thrown into the mouth of the oven'. The reference is to a possibility; hence, 'may-be burned up' (Toba Batak).

How much more will he..., or, '(then) he will certainly...', '(then) it is much more certain that he will...'; cp. also, '...won't the clothes God gives you be more beautiful than this?' (Tzeltal).

O men of little faith usually requires adjustments, e.g. 'you who are short-of faith' (Bahasa Indonesia), 'who don't believe thoroughly' (Kapauku), 'you, owners of small faith' (Zarma), 'you who believe little (or, only a bit, or, feebly)'; or as a full clause, "how little is your faith" (TEV), 'really you believe half-heartedly/reluctantly' (Shona 1966), 'why difficult your hearts believe?' (Tzeltal). The phrase may have to be transposed, e.g. to a position before 'how much...' (Thai 1967).

29 ***And do not seek what you are to eat and what you are to drink, nor be of anxious mind.***

Exegesis: *kai humeis* 'and you', with continuing emphasis.

mē zēteite lit. 'do not seek'. *zēteite* (here and v. 31) and *epizētousin* (v. 30) have approximately the same meaning, viz. 'be intent on', 'be preoccupied with'.

mē meteōrizesthe (††) 'do not live in a state of anxiety' (cp. Phillips).

Translation: *And do not seek,* contrasting those who know God's care and "the men of little faith" who do not; hence, "and so you are not to set your mind on" (NEB), 'so do not always be looking for' (cp. TEV).

Of anxious mind, or, "all upset" (TEV), referring to the emotion that accompanies the seeking. Some idiomatic renderings used here are, 'divided your-spirit' (South Toradja), 'irresolute (a reduplicated form of 'why') your mind' (Toba Batak), 'receive jump-of-heart' (Sranan).

30 ***For all the nations of the world seek these things; and your Father knows that you need them.***

Exegesis: *tauta gar panta ta ethnē tou kosmou epizētousin* 'all these things the peoples of the world are pursuing' (taking *tauta panta* together), or 'these things all the people of the world are pursuing' (taking *panta ta ethnē* together), preferably the former. *tauta panta* refers to such things as eating and drinking. *ta ethnē* refers to the peoples of the world that live outside the covenant-relationship between God and Israel. The present tense of *epizētousin* is habitual. *epizēteō,* cp. on 4 : 42.

humōn de ho patēr 'your father', with continuing emphasis on *humōn,* 'you as distinct from the peoples of the world'.

oiden hoti chrēzete toutōn 'knows that you need these things'. *toutōn* refers to the same things as *tauta panta. chrēzō,* cp. on 11 : 8.

Translation: *The nations of the world* has the same reference meaning as "the Gentiles" in 2 : 32 (which see); it may be translated, 'the heathen' (South Toradja), "the pagan world" (Rieu), 'the other (or, non-Jewish) peoples in the world'.

Your Father, cp. on 6 : 36.

You need them, i.e. you are in need/want of them, or since the implied reference is to food, 'you live-on those things' (South Toradja).

31 ***Instead, seek his kingdom, and these things shall be yours as well.***

Exegesis: *plēn zēteite tēn basileian autou* 'instead, pursue/seek his kingdom'. *zēteite* takes up *zēteite* (v. 29) and *epizētousin* (v. 30) without difference in meaning. Hence the clause may be paraphrased as follows, 'what you should pursue instead (*plēn*) is his kingdom'. For *basileia* cp. on 4 : 43 and references there. The phrase 'to pursue/seek the kingdom of God' means to prepare oneself for the coming of the kingdom of God and to try to live according to its requirements.

kai tauta prostethēsetai humin 'and these things will be given to you in addition'. *tauta*, again, refers to *tauta panta* in v. 30. For *prostithēmi* cp. on 3 : 20. Here it has the connotation of giving in addition. The agent of *prostethēsetai* is God.

Translation: *Instead*, or, 'in place of this', 'as a substitute for this', or, 'do not do this, but'.

Seek his kingdom. If 'kingdom' cannot be the direct object of 'to seek', one may say something like, 'seek the things of (or, that belong to, or, are important in) God's kingdom, or, where God rules'.

These things shall be yours as well, or, 'you will be given (or, will receive) those (i.e., the previously mentioned) things as well', 'God will give you those things also'.

32 ***"Fear not, little flock, for it is your Father's good pleasure to give you the kingdom.***

Exegesis: *mē phobou, to mikron poimnion* 'do not be afraid, you little flock'. The article *to* points to a vocative (Hebraism, cp. Bl-D, § 147). *to mikron poimnion* takes up *tous mathētas* in v. 22, as an indication of the persons addressed.

poimnion (†) 'flock', figurative for a small group.

hoti eudokēsen ho patēr humōn 'for your father has resolved'. *ho patēr humōn* takes up *humōn ho patēr* of v. 30. *eudokeō* (cp. on 3 : 22) means here 'to resolve', 'to choose'.

dounai humin tēn basileian 'to give you the kingdom', i.e. to grant you participation in the divine rule, cp. 22 : 29-30.

Translation: *Little flock.* The vocative is sometimes to be marked as such by an exclamatory particle, or by 'you'. Elsewhere the phrase cannot be used as a vocative; hence e.g. 'though you are a little flock'. Where the term for *flock* (for which see 2 : 8) cannot be used figuratively of people one can say, 'little group', 'small band', 'men few in number' (South Toradja), preferably seeking a term that suggests a fellowship of persons following a leader.

It is your Father's good pleasure, i.e. 'your Father has resolved/chosen, or, has considered good' (Sranan, lit. 'found for good').

To give you the kingdom, or, if syntactic shifts are required, 'to allow you to reign where he reigns', 'to make you kings/rulers/chiefs as he is'.

33 ***Sell your possessions, and give alms; provide yourselves with purses that do not grow old, with a treasure in the heavens that does not fail, where no thief approaches and no moth destroys.***

Exegesis: *pōlēsate ta huparchonta humōn* 'sell your possessions', cp. on 8 : 3.

kai dote eleēmosunēn 'and give alms', i.e. give the money that you make on your possessions as alms. For *eleēmosunē* cp. on 11 : 41.

poiēsate heautois 'make for yourselves'. *poiēsate* goes with *ballantia* and *thēsauron*. With the former *poiēsate* means 'make', with the latter 'gather'. *heautois* 'for yourselves' contrasts with the giving of alms to other people.

ballantia mē palaioumena, thēsauron anekleipton en tois ouranois 'purses that do not wear out, an inexhaustible treasure in heaven'. *ballantia* is best understood to refer to that which is contained in the purses, as e.g. *thēsauros* can mean both 'treasure' and 'treasure-box', cp. A-G s.v. *thēsauron anekleipton* is an explicative apposition to *ballantia mē palaioumena.*

palaioomai (†) lit. 'to grow old', here 'to wear out'.

hopou kleptēs ouk eggizei 'where no thief comes near', i.e. where no thief can get near it, viz. the treasure.

oude sēs diaphtheirei 'and where no moth destroys', i.e. can destroy it. *sēs* and *diaphtheirō* (†).

Translation: *Give alms,* or, "give the money to the poor" (TEV); and see 11 : 41.

Provide yourselves with, or, "get yourselves" (Goodspeed), 'try to acquire/possess'.

Purses that do not grow old, or, 'become bad', 'decay'; the interpretation given in *Exegesis* may result in, 'money that does not run short/give out'.

With a treasure in the heavens that does not fail, explaining the metaphor found in the preceding phrase; hence e.g. 'that is, with a treasure...', 'which form, as it were, a treasure...'. *Treasure,* i.e. that which is stored up (see 6 : 45), 'wealth' (Tzeltal), '(precious) possessions', 'important goods' (Ponape), 'a lot of things that are valuable' (Mazahua in Mt. 13 : 44). The term to be used here should include, or at least not exclude, clothes and fabrics liable to be eaten by insects. *That does not fail,* or, 'that will not give out/decrease', 'that will suffice for ever', 'that no one can use up'.

The clause *where...destroys* may better be co-ordinated, e.g. 'there (or, in that place)...'.

No thief approaches (it), or, 'no thief can reach it', 'no one can come near to steal it, or, take it away secretly', 'it is not stolen'. The term for *thief* often is derived from 'to steal'.

No moth destroys (it), or, 'devours/eats it', or, 'it is not termite-eaten' (Tzeltal). *Moth,* or the name of some other destructive insect or grub, e.g. 'weevil/borer' (Shona), '(house) cricket' (Lomwe, Yao, Zarma), 'termite', or generically, 'insect' (Kituba, Thai 1967).

34 ***For where your treasure is, there will your heart be also.***

Exegesis: *hopou gar estin ho thēsauros humōn, ekei kai hē kardia humōn estai* 'for where your treasure is there your heart also will be', expressing the general principle underlying the injunction of v. 33. The future tense of *estai* is consequential. *kardia* is here used in the sense of the seat of emotions, wishes and desires, cp. A-G s.v. 1 b ε.

Translation: It may be preferable to reverse the clause order, e.g. 'your heart will be in the place where your wealth is, or, in the same place as your goods/riches are (stored up)'.

There will your heart be also, or, 'there your heart will return' (Zarma, viewing the persons in question as having been there first to deposit the treasure). If one has to shift to the emotion implied in "heart", one may say something like, 'to that place also your desire will go out', 'there you (yourselves) will wish to be also'.

35 ***"Let your loins be girded and your lamps burning,***

Exegesis: *estōsan humōn hai osphues periezōsmenai* 'your waists must be girded', i.e. 'you must be prepared for action'. *estōsan* is imperative 3rd person plural. *humōn* is emphatic and indicates implicitly the agents of the girding.

osphus (†) 'waist', 'loins' as the place where a belt or girdle is worn, cp. A-G s.v. 1.

perizōnnumi 'to gird about', i.e. to tuck up one's long garment by pulling it through a belt, here in the passive, with the part of the body where the belt is worn as subject.

kai hoi luchnoi kaiomenoi 'and your lamps (must be) burning', with *estōsan* understood, implying that it is night and anticipating the events told in vv. 36f. For *luchnos* cp. on 8 : 16. *kaiō* also 24 : 32.

Translation: *Let your loins be girded*. A rather literal rendering sometimes conveys the required meaning, e.g. 'tighten your belt' (Kapauku), 'tighten the belt about your loins' (Lokele). Elsewhere the term for a similar act has the same metaphorical meaning, e.g. 'have (it)-tucked-in' (Balinese), 'have (it)-rolled-up' (South Toradja, similarly Yao), 'have your clothing tucked up' (Shona 1966), i.e. make ready for work at hand, by pulling up the long skirt-like garment between the legs and tucking it into the belt at the back, or by rolling or pulling it up around the waist. But in several languages only a non-figurative, functional rendering is acceptable, e.g. 'be ready always' (Tzeltal), 'be prepared' (Gio), 'prepare yourselves', or a combination of a functional rendering of this (and the next) phrase with a literal one, e.g. "be ready for action, with belts fastened and lamps alight" (NEB, cp. also TEV, Rieu).

Your lamps burning, or, 'and let your lamps give light', 'keep/have your lamps shining'. A non-figurative rendering of this phrase is both undesirable and unnecessary because of the short parable in vv. 36ff. For *lamp* see 8 : 16; the rendering chosen may also influence that of the verb, e.g. if the language distinguishes between the burning or light of a lamp and of a torch.

36 ***and be like men who are waiting for their master to come home from the marriage feast, so that they may open to him at once when he comes and knocks.***

Exegesis: *kai humeis homoioi anthrōpois prosdechomenois ton kurion heautōn* 'and you (must be) like men waiting for their master', with *este* understood. *humeis* is emphatic. For *kurios* cp. on 1 : 6. For *prosdechomai* cp. on 2 : 25.

pote analusē ek tōn gamōn lit. 'when he will return from the party'. *pote* introduces here an indirect question, depending on some verb of asking, implied in *prosdechomenois*. The article *tōn* does not refer to a specific occasion.

analuō (†) 'to depart', 'to return', here preferably the latter.

gamos (also 14 : 8) 'marriage', in the plural 'wedding celebration', 'wedding-party', or 'party', 'banquet', here preferably the latter (cp. A-G s.v. 1 b).

hina elthontos kai krousantos eutheōs anoixōsin autō 'so that when he comes and knocks on the door they may open the door for him at once'. With *elthontos kai krousantos* is understood *autou* (absolute genitive). *krouō* means 'to knock on the door', and *anoigō* means here 'to open the door' (cp. 11 : 9f).

Translation: *Be like,* or, '(you should) be/act/behave like', 'do like this, like' (Kapauku).

Men, or, because of their relationship to a master, 'servants', 'a man's servants' (Kapauku).

Who are waiting for their master to come home, or, 'for their master's return', 'until their master returns'; 'who are awaiting their master asking themselves (or, each other), "When will he (or, the/our master) come home?"', 'who are (awake) at home and ask themselves (or, each other), "When will the/our master return?"' *Master,* cp. the note on "Lord" in 1 : 6, sub (a).

From the marriage feast, preferably, 'from a feast/banquet', cp. *N.T.Wb.* /53, MEALS.

So that they may open to him, or, "ready to let him in" (NEB), 'and are ready to open the door for him'. For *to open* cp. 11 : 9; a different cultural situation may lead to renderings like, 'open the house' (Tzeltal), 'go to meet him' (East Toradja 1933).

At once when (or, as soon as) *he comes and knocks* is sometimes better transposed, cp. e.g. "when he comes..., they will open...at once" (TEV). For *to knock* see 11 : 9. A Malay idiom used here is 'asks-for the door'.

37 ***Blessed are those servants whom the master finds awake when he comes; truly, I say to you, he will gird himself and have them sit at table, and he will come and serve them.*** 38 ***If he comes in the second watch, or in the third, and finds them so, blessed are those servants!***

Exegesis: *makarioi hoi douloi ekeinoi*...(38)...*makarioi eisin ekeinoi* 'blessed those servants...blessed are those'. *makarioi* and *ekeinoi* are emphatic by virtue of their position both at the beginning and the end of vv. 37f and mark the content of both verses as belonging together.

hous elthōn ho kurios heurēsei grēgorountas 'whom the master when he comes will find awake'. *ho kurios* here takes up *ton kurion* in v. 36.

grēgoreō (also v. 39) 'to be awake', 'to stay awake'.

amēn legō humin 'truly I say to you', cp. on 3 : 8 and 4 : 24.

perizōsetai 'he will gird himself', cp. on v. 35. Here *perizōnnumi* is used in the middle voice with reflexive meaning, cp. A-G s.v. 2.

anaklinei autous 'he will make them sit, or, lie down at the table', cp. on 2 : 7.

kai parelthōn diakonēsei autois 'and after coming he will serve them, or, wait on them'. *parelthōn* is best understood as referring to coming to the place where the servants are reclining. For *diakoneō* cp. on 4 : 39.

V(. 38) *kan en tē deutera kan en tē tritē phulakē elthē* 'and whether he comes in the second or even in the third watch...'. *kan...kan* lit. 'and if...and if' is best understood as 'whether...or even'; it does not refer to two contrasting possibilities, but rather has ascensive meaning, since the time of the second night watch is already very late. For *phulakē* cp. on 2 : 8. The reference is here probably to the Jewish and Greek division in three (cp. A-G s.v. 4).

kai heurē houtōs 'and finds (them) so', with *autous* understood. *houtōs* means *grēgorountas*.

Translation: If the structure of the first sentence is too heavy one may shift to, 'if he/the master comes and finds those (or, his) servants awake, blessed are they'.

For *blessed*, or, 'happy', see 1 : 45.

Servant. The RSV uses this term for Gr. *pais*, lit. 'child', 'boy' (1 : 54, 69; 7 : 7; 15 : 26), *oiketēs*, lit. 'domestic (slave)' (16 : 13), *doulos*, lit. 'slave' (2 : 29; 12 : 37-47; 14 : 17-23; 15 : 22; 17 : 7-10; 19 : 13-22; 20 : 10f), and in the expressions "menservants and maidservants" (*paidas kai paidiskas*, 12 : 45), "hired servants" (*misthioi*, 15 : 17, 19). Gr. *doulos* is rendered "slave" in two passages (7 : 2-10; 22 : 50); *diakonos*, the word most closely corresponding to 'servant', does not occur in Luke. Juridically speaking each of these 'servants', with exception of the *misthioi*, probably was a 'slave' in that his person and work were at the disposal of another, viz. his owner or master, but in most New Testament passages this juridical aspect does not predominate. Socially speaking the slave played an important role in New Testament times; he did all and any kind of work, from labour on the field and menial jobs in- and outside the house to the task of manager or agent (cp. 12 : 42f; 19 : 13ff; 20 : 10ff) and he had a recognized social status; possession of slaves was not subject to moral reprobation. Accordingly Gr. *doulos* did not have the bad connotation that 'slave' has in languages reflecting other norms. In such languages the term for 'slave' (for which see above 7 : 2) can better be reserved for those passages where the juridical aspect comes to the fore (cp. *TBT*, 13.146); in other passages a word for 'servant' (i.e. one who exerts himself for the benefit of another, viz. his employer), will be preferable, e.g. 'one who is sent here and there' (Navajo), 'one who does errands' (Zoque, for Mk. 9 : 35), 'one-who-works-for-you' (Kapauku), 'helper' (Zacapoaxtla Aztec). In some languages one may have to choose between distinctive terms according to the task the servant has to do, e.g. 'labourer', 'domestic servant', etc.

When he comes, i.e. comes home/returns.

For *finds* see 7 : 10, for *awake* cp. *N.T.Wb.*/14, sub 2 (a), and for *truly, I say to you* see references above on 4 : 24.

The rendering of *he will gird himself* may be basically the same as in v. 35[a], but in some cases a distinction must be made, e.g. in Balinese, where one who is waiting upon persons at a meal would not wear a tucked-in sarong (which is informal dress) but 'wraps-himself-in a *saput* (i.e. a garment worn over the sarong, covering the body from the breast to the knees)'; similarly in Toba Batak, 'puts-on his-ceremonial-dress'.

Have them sit at table, or, "make them take their places at table" (Goodspeed), 'cause them to sit down to eat', 'seat them at the place of food' (Zarma), 'invites them to take the meal', 'tell them to come and sit to eat' (Kapauku); and see 5 : 29.

Serve them, here in the sense of, 'wait upon them (at the meal)', 'serve the meal, or, the food to them'. The verb used often has to differ from the one occurring in the rendering of "servant", see above.

(V. 38) *In the second watch, or in the third,* or, "even if it is the middle of the night or before dawn" (NEB, similarly Lokele), "as late as midnight or even later" (TEV), 'before or after noon of night' (Kituba, similarly Kekchi); and cp. *TH-Mk* on 6 : 48 and 13 : 35.

39 ***But know this, that if the householder had known at what hour the thief was coming, he would have been awake and would not have left his house to be broken into.***

Exegesis: *touto de ginōskete* 'this you must know', or 'this you know', presumably the former.

hoti...ouk an aphēken dioruchthēnai ton oikon autou 'that...he would not have let his house be broken into'. For *aphiēmi* cp. on 8 : 51.

diorussō (†) lit. 'to dig through', here of digging through the sun dried brick wall of a house, hence, 'to break into', cp. A-G s.v.

ei ēdei ho oikodespotēs 'if the master of the house had known', cp. Bl-D, § 360. The picture changes rather abruptly from the servants waiting for the return of their master to the master expecting a thief but not knowing when he will come. The common element in vv. 36-38 and v. 39 is that of watchfulness.

poia hōra ho kleptēs erchetai 'at what time the thief would come'. *erchetai,* though in the present tense, has future meaning. *poia* lit. 'of what kind' is here equivalent to *tini* 'what', cp. A-G s.v. *poios* 2 a β.

Translation: *But know this, that,* or as a co-ordinate sentence, "and remember this!" (TEV), 'Take notice also of this!'.

The subsequent sentence may better be divided into two, e.g. 'a householder cannot know (or, no householder knows) at what hour a thief will come; if he did/knew, he would not have let...'.

The householder, or, 'the master of the house', 'the one who owns the house'.

Would not have left (or, let) *his house to be broken into,* or, 'would not have allowed him (or, that thief) to break into his house' (cp. Toba Batak, TEV). *To break into a house* is variously rendered, e.g. 'to enter a house with force' (Kituba, similarly Tzeltal), 'make a hole through (the wall of) a house' (Zarma, Thai 1967; Lokele, East Toradja 1933), 'to pierce through the wall to enter a house', 'to steal (the contents of) a house' (Trukese).

40 ***You also must be ready; for the Son of man is coming at an hour you do not expect."***

Exegesis: *kai humeis ginesthe hetoimoi* 'you too must be ready', i.e. like the servants of vv. 37f and the master of the house of v. 39.

hetoimos 'ready', 'prepared'.

hoti hē hōra ou dokeite ho huios tou anthrōpou erchetai 'for at the time you do not believe (him to come) the Son of man will come'. *hē hōra* lit. 'at which time', stands for *tē hōra hē* 'at the time at which'. For *dokeō* cp. on 8 : 18, for *erchetai* on v. 39.

Translation: *You also must be ready; for the Son of man is coming...* The first clause may require a qualification, which may result in something like, 'you also must be ready to receive/welcome the Son of man, for he will come...'. *You also,* or, 'you likewise', 'you just as he (or, that householder)'.

At an hour you do not expect, or, adding a qualification again, 'at a moment you do not expect him', 'when you think, "He will not come now"'. For the verb cp. *N.T.Wb.*/14, AWAIT; in South Toradja it is rendered by a reduplicated verbal derivation of the word for 'perhaps/probably'.

41 ***Peter said, "Lord, are you telling this parable for us or for all?"***

Exegesis: *kurie* 'lord', cp. on 1 : 6.

pros hēmas 'with reference to us', emphatic by position. For *pros* cp. A-G s.v. III 5 a.

ē kai pros pantas 'or with reference to all as well'. *kai* implies that the parable applies to the disciples in any case.

Translation: *Are you telling this parable for us,* or, 'that you tell this parable is it aiming at us' (Javanese), 'is this parable intended for (or, aimed at) us' (Bahasa Indonesia, Balinese), 'were you thinking of us when you told this parable' (Sranan). For *parable* see 8 : 4. To bring out the emphasis on *for us* one may say 'only/especially for us'.

42 ***And the Lord said, "Who then is the faithful and wise steward, whom his master will set over his household, to give them their portion of food at the proper time?***

Exegesis: *kai eipen ho kurios* 'and the Lord said', cp. on 1 : 6.

tis ara estin... 'well, who is...'. *ara* is used to enliven the question, cp. A-G s.v. 2. The question is an indirect answer to Peter's question in v. 41. It is meant as an injunction to follow the example of the steward and to identify oneself with him (cp. Grundmann).

ho pistos oikonomos ho phronimos lit. 'the faithful manager, the wise (one)', best rendered as 'the faithful, wise steward'. There is no reason to treat *ho phronimos* as emphatic.

pistos 'faithful', 'reliable', 'dependable', cp. A-G s.v. 1 a α.

oikonomos 'steward', 'manager', in a private position, cp. A-G s.v. 1 a.

phronimos (also 16 : 8) 'wise', 'sensible', 'thoughtful', 'prudent'.

hon katastēsei ho kurios epi tēs therapeias autou 'whom the master will put in charge of his servants'. For *kathistēmi* cp. on v. 14. The clause serves as a further identification of the *oikonomos* in that it refers to his responsibilities.

therapeia here synonymous with *hoi therapontes* 'the servants' (abstract for concrete).

tou didonai en kairō [*to*] *sitometrion* 'to give the rations at the proper time', articular infinitive clause supplementing *katastēsei*. For *en kairō* cp. A-G s.v. 2.

sitometrion (††) 'measured allowance of food', 'ration'.

Translation: Where this construction, an interrogative sentence with embedded relative clause, is too heavy, it may be preferable to shift to the use of two sentences, e.g. 'Who is the...steward? Who is the man whom his master will set over his household to give...'. Other adaptations that may be required are a shift from metaphor to simile, and/or from question to injunction, e.g. 'be like a...steward, like a man whom his master will set (or, who will be set by his master) over...'; and/or, with a further shift from relative to resultative clause, 'be like a steward who is so faithful and wise that his master will put him in charge of the household to give...'.

Faithful may be rendered by, "trustworthy" (BFBS), 'to be trusted', 'honest/straight' (South Toradja), 'unchangeable' (Barrow Eskimo), 'who fulfils' (Totonac). For 'to trust' cp. also on 11 : 22.

Steward, i.e. a slave who is a kind of agent, foreman or caretaker; hence, 'overseer' (Shona 1963), 'watcher' (one West Nyanja version), and cp. the renderings mentioned in 8 : 3, unless specific to princely households. Since the man's task is described in the next clause a generic rendering, e.g. 'servant' (Tzeltal, TEV), 'man' is also acceptable.

Set over, or, 'put in charge over', 'appoint to rule/manage'.

His household, or, 'his servants/slaves'; or, to help the reader realize that the steward is himself part of the household, 'the other servants/slaves'. The possessive pronoun refers to the master.

Their portion of food, or, 'their rightful share of food', 'what they should be given to eat', 'the (quantity of) food he (i.e. the master) has assigned to them'.

At the proper time, or, 'at the appointed/right time', 'at its-time' (Toba Batak), 'regularly'. Rieu combines this phrase with the preceding one in, "their daily rations".

43 ***Blessed is that servant whom his master when he comes will find so doing.***

Exegesis: *makarios ho doulos ekeinos* 'blessed (is) that servant', referring to *oikonomos* in v. 42; cp. on v. 37.

poiounta houtōs 'doing so', i.e. as described in v. 42.

Translation: *Whom his master...will find so doing*, or, as a temporal clause (cp. 12 : 9) and adjusting the verb (see 7 : 10), 'when his master... will see that he is doing so (or, those things, or, as told)'.

When he comes (home), or, 'at his return', interrupts the connexion between subject and verb, and may, therefore, better be transposed to final position (cp. TEV, Sranan, Bahasa Indonesia), or to the head of the sentence, e.g. 'if his master comes (home) and finds him doing so'.

44 ***Truly I tell you, he will set him over all his possessions.***

Exegesis: *alēthōs legō humin* 'truly I tell you', cp. on 3 : 8 and 9 : 27.

epi pasin tois huparchousin autou katastēsei auton 'he will put him in charge of all his possessions'. Subject of *katastēsei* is *ho kurios*. For *ta huparchonta* cp. on 8 : 3.

Translation: *Truly I tell you*, see 4 : 24.

Will set him over all his possessions, repeating the verb used in v. 42[b], and preferably to be rendered alike, unless the presence of a non-personal object compels one to use a different rendering.

45 ***But if that servant says to himself, 'My master is delayed in coming,' and begins to beat the menservants and the maidservants, and to eat and drink and get drunk,*** 46 ***the master of that servant will come on a day when he does not expect him and at an hour he does not know, and will punish him, and put him with the unfaithful.***

Exegesis: *ho doulos ekeinos* 'that servant', i.e. the one referred to in v. 43.

en tē kardia autou 'in his heart', i.e. 'to, or, in himself'.

chronizei ho kurios mou erchesthai 'my master is a long time in coming'. For *chronizō* (here with the infinitive) cp. on 1 : 21.

kai arxētai tuptein tous paidas kai tas paidiskas 'and (when) he begins to beat the menservants and womenservants', dependent on *ean. tuptō* (cp. on 6 : 29) here has a more general meaning, viz. 'to bully', cp. NEB.

paidiskē (also 22 : 56) 'maid', 'servant-girl', 'woman-servant'.

esthiein te kai pinein kai methuskesthai 'to eat and drink, and to get drunk', dependent on *arxētai. esthiein te kai pinein* is one phrase and denotes gluttony (cp. on 7 : 33 where a different meaning prevails).

methuskomai (†) 'to get drunk'.

(V. 46) *ho kurios tou doulou ekeinou* 'the master of that slave', emphatic repetition of *ho doulos ekeinos* in v. 45.

en hēmera hē ou prosdoka 'on a day on which he does not expect (him to return)'. For *prosdokaō* cp. on 1 : 21.

kai en hōra hē ou ginōskei 'and at a time at which he does not know', i.e. he had not been informed about the time of his master's return.

kai dichotomēsei auton 'and will cut him in two', as execution of death penalty, cp. A-G s.v. *dichotomeō* (†).

kai to meros autou meta tōn apistōn thēsei lit. 'and (he) will put his share with the unbelievers', i.e. 'will make him share the lot of the unbelievers' with implicit reference to the final judgment. *apistos*, cp. on 9 : 41.

meros 'part', here 'share', 'lot', 'allotted place', 'place of destiny'.

Translation: V. 45 expresses a suppositional case: 'but suppose now...'; v. 46 is to be introduced then by a consecutional connective, e.g. 'so, then' (Trukese).

Says to himself, or, 'says in his heart', 'thinks'.

My master is delayed in coming, or, describing the verb, 'my master does not come (home) quickly/shortly, or, stays away fairly long'; or, 'it will take a long time before my master returns'.

Beat, probably with hand or stick, cp. *N.T.Wb.*/15.

Menservants and maidservants, or, 'servants, both men and women'.

To eat and drink and get drunk here refers to feasting; cp. 5 : 30 and *N.T.Wb.*/31, DRUNK. In Trukese excessive eating and drinking is expressed by reduplicated forms of the verbs, and "get drunk" by 'become-foolish'.

(V. 46) *On a day when he does not expect him*, or, 'does not await him, or, does not think he will come'.

At an hour he does not know closely parallels the preceding phrase, using a more specific indication of time, and a verb that, in this context, is rather synonymous with 'to expect'. Hence the two phrases can better be combined in some languages, cp. e.g. 'at a day and an hour that are not to-be-known' (Balinese), 'at an hour when his heart is forgetful, and he is not expecting him'.

Will punish him, preferably, 'will punish him by death (or, very severely)'; or in languages that prefer to make explicit indirect agency, 'will have him punished (or, will order someone to punish him) severely/by death'. For *to punish* cp. also *N.T.Wb.*/59.

Put him with the unfaithful (preferably, 'the unbelievers'), or, 'put him where the unbelievers are, or, in the same place as the unbelievers', 'let him suffer what the unbelievers suffer'. The term 'unbelievers', i.e. those who do not believe in the God of Israel, refers to the non-Jews in general; hence some versions render 'heathen' (Jerusalem, Bahasa Indonesia). For 'to believe' cp. the references on "faith" in 5 : 20; for 'heathen' cp. on "Gentiles" in 2 : 32.

47 ***And that servant who knew his master's will, but did not make ready or act according to his will, shall receive a severe beating.*** 48a ***But he who did not know, and did what deserved a beating, shall receive a light beating.***

Exegesis: *ekeinos de ho doulos* 'but that servant...', referring forward to *ho gnous*, etc., and to be distinguished from the one to whom vv. 43, 45f refer.

ho gnous to thelēma tou kuriou autou 'who did know what his master wants'.

thelēma 'will', i.e. what is willed, here of that which one wants to be brought about by somebody else, cp. A-G 1 c.

kai mē hetoimasas ē poiēsas pros to thelēma autou 'and who has not made preparations or acted according to what he wants'. *autou* refers to *tou kuriou*. For *pros* cp. A-G s.v. III, 5 d. For *hetoimazō* cp. on 1 : 17.

darēsetai pollas (scil. *plēgas*) 'will be beaten with many (strokes)', hence 'severely' (cp. NEB).

derō 'to beat', here with accusative of content.

(V. 48a) *ho de mē gnous* 'but he who did not know', viz. 'what his master wants', with *to thelēma tou kuriou autou* understood from v. 47.

poiēsas de axia plēgōn 'but who did what deserves strokes', i.e. what deserves punishment. *plēgē*, cp. on 10 : 30.

darēsetai oligas (scil. *plēgas*) 'will be beaten with few (strokes)', hence 'lightly'.

Translation: Again a change in the sentence structure may be preferable, e.g. 'if a servant knows..., he will receive...'.

Did not make ready or act according to his will. Where the verbs to be used are obligatorily transitive one may say, 'did not make ready or do what he (i.e. his master) wanted him to do'.

Shall receive a severe beating. Such constructions with 'receive' can often be rendered as passives, e.g. 'will be beaten severely', then, with a further shift, 'his master will beat him severely'. For indirect agency cp. the remark on v. 46. *Beating* here probably refers to beating with a stick or whip.

(V. 48a) *He,* referring to another hypothetical servant.

Did what deserved a beating, or, 'did what is repaid/punished with blows' (cp. Yao), 'did something that properly brings (lit. causes-to-come) blows' (Bahasa Indonesia RC); or introducing a reference to the person to be beaten, 'did things for which he deserved a beating, or, ought to be beaten', 'acted so that his master must beat him', etc., see above.

48b ***Every one to whom much is given, of him will much be required; and of him to whom men commit much they will demand the more.***

Exegesis: *panti de hō edothē polu, polu zētēthēsetai par' autou* 'from everyone who has been given much, much will be required'. *panti* is in the dative under the influence of the case of the relative pronoun *hō* that goes with it (inverse attraction, cp. Bl-D, § 295). *par' autou* takes up *panti*. The repetition of *polu* is intentional. The implied agent is God.

hō parethento polu, perissoteron aitēsousin auton 'from him to whom much has been entrusted, even more will be demanded'. *parethento* and *aitēsousin*, though both in 3rd person plural, are best understood as impersonal plurals equivalent to passives. *paratithemai* means here 'to entrust', 'to commend', 'to deposit' (cp. A-G s.v. 2 b α). *polu* and *perissoteron* lit. 'much' and 'more', are best understood in their literal sense. For the meaning of the verse, see commentaries.

Translation: An 'if'- or 'when'-clause may be preferable again, cp. 9 : 24.

Of him will much be required, i.e. he will be asked/expected to give much, 'God will expect him to give much'. Cp. also *N.T.Wb.*/12f, ASK.

Demanded of is closely synonymous here with 'required of'.

More, viz. than has been committed or deposited.

49 ***"I came to cast fire upon the earth; and would that it were already kindled!***

Exegesis: *pur ēlthon balein epi tēn gēn* 'I came to cast fire upon the earth'. *pur* is emphatic by position (cp. Plummer). The fire is the fire of judgment (cp. 3 : 16f).

kai ti thelō ei ēdē anēphthē 'and what do I want if it is already kindled?', or, 'how I wish it were already kindled!' The latter is preferable (cp. Bl-D, § 299.4).

anaptō (†) 'to kindle'.

Translation: *I came to cast fire upon the earth.* The final force of the construction should not be pressed; hence one may say also 'my coming will cast...' (Balinese), 'I come and will cast...'. *To cast fire upon the earth*, or, 'to start (or, cause to burn) a fire on earth', then, "to set the earth on fire" (TEV), 'to cause the earth to burn'.

Would that, or, 'how I wish that', 'I very much wish that', 'my whole soul desires that' (cp. Toba Batak).

Were...kindled, or, 'were...lighted', 'had...started burning', 'were... burning/aflame'.

50 ***I have a baptism to be baptized with; and how I am constrained until it is accomplished!***

Exegesis: *baptisma de echō baptisthēnai* 'but I have a baptism to be baptized with'. *baptisma* is emphatic: before the fire can be kindled Jesus has to undergo a baptism. For baptism as a metaphor of suffering cp. *TH-Mk* on 10 : 38.

pōs sunechomai heōs hotou telesthē 'how I am distressed till it is accomplished!', i.e. 'till it is over'. For *sunechomai* cp. on 4 : 38. The subject of *telesthē* is *baptisma,* and the clause refers to a situation that is to come about. For *teleō* cp. on 2 : 39.

Translation: *I have a baptism to be baptized with,* or, 'I have a baptism to undergo/receive', 'I have to be baptized in a certain way', or shifting to a simile, 'I have to be immersed/bathed as at baptism (or, as though I were baptized)', cp. 'I must begin by being submerged by the baptism I shall be done' (Shona 1966). If the term and/or the ritual do not have a clear association with immersion in water, an explanatory note referring the reader to Mk. 1 : 9f, Acts 8 : 36-39, may be useful. Where the figure of speech would be incomprehensible the non-figurative meaning may have to be added, e.g. 'I have to be plunged in suffering as a person is plunged in water when he is baptized' (or in active construction with indefinite agent). For *baptism, baptized* see 3 : 3.

I am constrained, or, 'I feel oppressed', 'my mind is-in-straits' (Balinese), 'my-heart (is) restless' (Bahasa Indonesia RC).

Until, cp. 1 : 20.

51 ***Do you think that I have come to give peace on earth? No, I tell you, but rather division;***

Exegesis: *dokeite hoti eirēnēn paregenomēn dounai en tē gē* 'do you think that I have come to establish peace on earth?' For *dokeō* cp. on 8 : 18. For *paraginomai* on 7 : 4; here it expresses coming with a purpose. *eirēnēn* (emphatic by position) is best understood as referring to a realm of peace, and hence *dounai* may be rendered 'to establish'.

ouchi, legō humin, all' ē diamerismon 'no, I tell you, but rather division'. For *ouchi,* a strong negation, cp. on 1 : 60. Here it is reinforced by the parenthetical *legō humin. all' ē* (from *alla ē*) is here equivalent to a stronger *alla* (cp. Bl-D, § 448.8).

diamerismos (††) 'division'. Here it prepares the reader for the forms of the verb *diamerizō* which dominates vv. 52f.

Translation: *Do you think,* or, 'are you of the opinion', 'do you suppose' (for which see 2 : 44).

To give peace on earth, or, 'to establish (a realm of) peace on earth' (see *Exegesis*), 'to make the earth a peaceful place', 'to produce peace on earth' (Tarascan), 'to cause the people on earth to be at peace (with each other)'. For *peace* see 1 : 79; the reference here is primarily to lack of strife, unruffled social intercourse.

No, I tell you, but. The function which the phrase *I tell you* has here is sometimes better expressed by emphasizing the negation, 'No!' (Balinese), "No indeed" (NEB), 'no, not peace'.

Division, or, repeating the verb, 'I give division/dissension', or in a verbal phrase, 'I cause people to be divided (against each other)', cp. on v. 52.

52 ***for henceforth in one house there will be five divided, three against two and two against three;*** 53 ***they will be divided, father against son and son against father, mother against daughter and daughter against her mother, mother-in-law against her daughter-in-law and daughter-in-law against her mother-in-law."***

Exegesis: *esontai gar apo tou nun pente en heni oikō diamemerismenoi* 'for from now on five (people) in one house will be divided', or, 'there will be five (people) in one house divided', preferably the former (cp. "...if there are five people...they will be divided", Goodspeed). For *apo tou nun* cp. on 1 : 48. The number five results from the enumeration of relatives, where mother and mother-in-law are one and the same person. *en heni oikō* means 'in one house' (where they live together), or, 'in one family' (cp. A-G s.v. *oikos* 2), probably the former.

treis epi dusin 'three against two', viz. son, daughter and daughter-in-law against father and mother, referring to the second, the fourth and the sixth line in v. 53 as printed in *GNT*.

duo epi trisin 'two against three', inverted order, referring to the first, the third and the fifth line.

(V. 53) *diameristhēsontai* 'they will be divided', taking up *esontai... diamemerismenoi*. Subject of *diameristhēsontai* are the following nouns in the nominative. In the subsequent enumeration *epi* with dative changes into *epi* with accusative without change of meaning.

penthera also 4 : 38.

numphē (†) here 'daughter-in-law'.

Translation: *In one house there will be five divided*, preferably, 'five (people/persons) will be divided in one house'. The verb (also in v. 53) is reciprocal, 'divided against one another', 'quarrelling with each other', 'fighting/opposing-each-other' (East Toradja, Bahasa Indonesia), 'not agreeing-with-each-other' (Shona 1966), or a verb combining the constituents 'come-apart/break' and 'separate(-oneself-from)' (Thai).

The four pairs of phrases with *against* (one pair here, three in v. 53) are dependent on "divided", but the relationship between the members of each phrase is not reciprocal (otherwise each two phrases would be tautological) but one-directional; hence the preposition has been rendered by such verbs as, 'opposes' (Bahasa Indonesia, similarly in Trukese, lit. 'stands toward'), 'sides against' (cp. Rieu in v. 53), 'fights' (East Toradja), 'is enemy of' (cp. Kituba), 'hates' (Kekchi), in several cases a transitive form of the verb which, in a reciprocal form, serves as rendering of "divided".

(V. 53) *They will be divided* is omitted as redundant in several versions (esp. those that render the phrases with "against" as verbal clauses), but it should be remembered that the repetition of this verb is emphatic.

The group of five persons envisaged here comprises father, mother, their son and daughter, and the son's wife, a quite common pattern in societies where a married couple usually lives with the man's family.

Some examples of adjustments that these three pairs of phrases may require are the following. (a) The terms, some or all, may be obligatorily possessed in the receptor languages; or possession, though not obligatory, is idiomatically preferable in some cases or positions, e.g. with the second term of each phrase (several Indonesian languages, Sranan). (b) Since the two terms in each phrase refer to the same relationship, but viewed from different angles, it may be preferable to indicate the relationship only once, e.g. 'a man against his son, a young man against his father', etc. A comparable point is that in some languages 'son' and 'daughter', since they presuppose a relationship with the parents, can only be used, if the term for 'father', or, 'mother' is in focus; hence e.g. 'a father against his male child and a young man against his father' (cp. South Toradja), and similar differentiation with (some of) the other terms. (c) The rendering of the last pair of phrases may present specific problems, cp. *N.T.Wb.* /33, FAMILY. In Toba Batak, where, ideally, a man's mother and his wife are from the same clan and a wife's mother-in-law accordingly is her paternal aunt, these two phrases have been rendered, 'a mother-in-law against her-daughter-in-law, a daughter-in-law against her-father's-sister'; in Kapauku, which possesses a term for in-laws but does not distinguish between mother- and daughter-in-law, the two phrases had to be combined into one, lit. 'female reciprocal-in-laws-two quarrel with-each-other'.

54 ***He also said to the multitudes, "When you see a cloud rising in the west, you say at once, 'A shower is coming'; and so it happens.*** 55 ***And when you see the south wind blowing, you say, 'There will be scorching heat'; and it happens.***

Exegesis: *elegen de kai tois ochlois* 'he also said to the crowds', marking the transition to a new point.

hotan idēte [*tēn*] *nephelēn anatellousan epi dusmōn* 'when you see a cloud coming up in the west'. *nephelē* is used here in the sense of rain-cloud. The article *tēn* (if read) is generic.

anatellō (†) 'to rise' (of the sun), here 'to come up'.

dusmē (also 13 : 29) lit. 'going down', 'setting' (of the sun), in the plural 'the west', 'the western horizon'. For *epi* 'in the area of', 'in', cp. A-G s.v. I 1 a γ.

eutheōs legete 'you say at once, or, promptly'.

hoti Ombros erchetai 'a rain-storm is coming', i.e. 'it is going to rain'. *hoti* introduces direct speech. *erchetai*, present tense, refers to the immediate future.

ombros (††) 'rain-storm', 'thunder-storm'.

kai ginetai houtōs 'and so it happens', i.e. as expressed in *ombros erchetai*.

(V. 55) *kai hotan noton pneonta,* scil. *idēte* 'and when (you see) the south wind blowing'. For *notos* cp. on 11 : 31.

pneō (†) 'to blow'.

legete hoti Kausōn estai 'you say: there will be heat'.
kausōn (†) 'burning', 'heat', 'heat wave'.
kai ginetai 'and it happens', viz. what you have said.

Translation: *When you see . . ., you say at once,* or, 'as soon as you see . . ., then you say' (Balinese, similarly in v. 55).

A cloud rising in the west, or, 'that clouds are rising in (or, from) the west'. In Palestine the west, i.e. the side of the Mediterranean, is the normal place for rain-clouds to gather (cp. e.g. 1 Kings 18 : 44); where the situation is entirely different an explanatory note may be required. The same holds true for "south wind" and "heat" in v. 55. Some idiomatic expressions for rain-clouds rising are, 'air becomes closed (viz. with clouds)' (Tzeltal), 'sky makes hedges' (Zarma). For *west* see *N.T.Wb./*28f, DIRECTIONS; and cp. 'where the sun pours-out' (Tzeltal), 'down-river' (Lokele).

A shower is coming, or, 'heavy rain is coming/near', 'a rain-storm is-passing' (South Toradja).

And so it happens, or repeating the term in the preceding clause, 'and rain it does' (cp. NEB), 'and the rain really comes (presently)'.

(V. 55) *See,* or, 'know/notice' (Javanese), "feel" (TEV).

The south wind blowing. Idiom may require, 'it is blowing from the south', 'a wind coming from the south' (Sundanese), 'a strong wind from the south' (Javanese). For *south* see 11 : 31.

There will be scorching heat, or, 'it will be very hot', 'the sun will hurt very much' (Tzeltal), 'the heavens will become scorching-hot' (Lokele). In some cases the term for 'dry season' can be used (East Toradja, Toba Batak; also in South Toradja, which speaks of 'the time when the rains cease, or, stay away').

And it happens, or, again repeating the preceding term, 'and hot it is' (cp. Rieu).

56 ***You hypocrites! You know how to interpret the appearance of earth and sky; but why do you not know how to interpret the present time?***

Exegesis: *hupokritai* 'you hypocrites' (cp. on 6 : 42). The word implies here that they only pretend not to know how to interpret the present time.

to prosōpon tēs gēs kai tou ouranou 'the appearance of the earth and the sky'. For this meaning of *prosōpon* cp. A-G s.v. 1 d. Here it refers to signs that forecast changes in the weather.

oidate dokimazein 'you know to interpret (correctly)'. For this use of *oida* cp. on 11 : 13.

dokimazō (also 14 : 19) 'to examine', 'to interpret', here with the connotation of interpreting correctly.

ton kairon de touton pōs ouk oidate dokimazein 'but how (is it possible that) you do not know to interpret this present time?' *ton kairon touton* is strongly emphatic. *kairos* refers here to the time in which God is acting, now in Jesus.

Translation: *You hypocrites,* see 6 : 42.

You know how to, or, 'you can', 'you are able to'.

Interpret..., or analytically, 'recognize the meaning of...' (Lokele), 'understand/explain/discover what...means'. Often specific verbs are available, e.g. 'recognize-the-signs-of' (Trukese, similarly Balinese), 'judge-after-observation' (Tzeltal).

Appearance of earth and sky, or, 'face of earth and sky' (East Nyanja, Yao), 'shape (lit. circuit) of-sky together-with earth' (South Toradja, the first part being a standing phrase to which 'earth' has been joined); or more analytically, 'the things that appear on...', 'what earth and sky show, or, give you to see', 'what you see on earth (lit. underneath) and what you see in the sky' (Shona 1966); cp. also, "you can look at the earth and the sky and tell what it means" (TEV). *Earth and sky.* The reverse order may be obligatory or preferable, e.g. in Lokele.

57 ***"And why do you not judge for yourselves what is right?***

Exegesis: *ti de kai aph' heautōn ou krinete to dikaion* 'why then (is it) not of yourselves (that) you judge what is right?' *de kai* serves to emphasize *aph' heautōn.*

aph' heautōn 'of yourselves', i.e. 'out of your own judgment', contrasting with the external signs of the time, or with being taught by Jesus or somebody else, preferably the latter.

to dikaion 'what is right', i.e. 'what you ought to do'. It refers to the implication of vv. 58f (see below).

Translation: *You judge for yourselves,* or, 'you yourselves decide', 'you take your own decision'. The verb (for which see *N.T.Wb.*/48f) is used here in a non-legal context, but it anticipates the example given in v. 58, which is in a legal sphere; hence a term that is appropriate in both spheres is preferable, such as e.g. 'to weigh/consider' (Javanese), 'take/give a decision' (cp. Bahasa Indonesia).

58 ***As you go with your accuser before the magistrate, make an effort to settle with him on the way, lest he drag you to the judge, and the judge hand you over to the officer, and the officer put you in prison.*** 59 ***I tell you, you will never get out till you have paid the very last copper."***

Exegesis: Vv. 58f supplement v. 57 by means of a parable-like story without proper introduction, in the 2nd person singular. The implication of vv. 58f is: do what v. 57 suggests before it is too late. Even in the singular the parable applies to the crowds (v. 54).

hōs gar hupageis meta tou antidikou sou ep' archonta 'for while you are going to the magistrate with your opponent'. For *hōs* with present tense, 'while', 'as long as', cp. A-G s.v. IV 1 b; for *hupagō* cp. on 8 : 42.

antidikos (also 18 : 3) 'opponent in a lawsuit'.

archōn here 'magistrate', 'judge'.

en tē hodō dos ergasian apēllachthai ap' autou 'do your best to come to terms with him (while still) on the/your way'. *en tē hodō* is emphatic by position. *dos ergasian* (†) probably is a Latinism (cp. A-G s.v. *didōmi* 7) and means 'make an effort', 'do your best'.

apallassomai apo tinos (†) lit. 'to get rid of somebody', i.e. 'to settle, or, to come to terms, with somebody'.

mēpote katasurē se pros ton kritēn 'lest he should drag you before the judge'. *mēpote* is somewhat stronger than *mē* with subjunctive and lends a touch of threat to what follows (cp. A-G s.v. 2 a). The subject of *katasurē* is *ho antidikos* and *ton kritēn* refers to the same officer as *archonta.*

katasurō (††) 'to drag away by force'.

kai ho kritēs se paradōsei tō praktori 'and the judge will hand you over to the bailiff'. The clause is no longer dependent upon *mēpote,* as shown by the future indicative of *paradōsei,* and describes what will be the sure outcome when the opposing parties have appeared before the judge. For *paradidōmi* cp. on 1 : 2.

praktōr (††) here an official of the court who executes the sentences of the court and is in charge of the prison, 'bailiff', 'constable', cp. A-G s.v.

kai ho praktōr se balei eis phulakēn 'and the bailiff will throw you into prison'. For *phulakē* cp. on 2 : 8. For the future tense of *balei* see above.

(V. 59) *legō soi* 'I tell you', cp. on 3 : 8.

ou mē exelthēs ekeithen 'you shall not come out from there'. For *ou mē* with subjunctive cp. on 1 : 15.

heōs kai to eschaton lepton apodōs 'until you have paid back even the last cent'. For *apodidōmi* cp. on 4 : 20.

lepton (also 21 : 2) lit. 'small', 'thin' (adjective), here a neuter substantive denoting a small copper coin of little value.

Translation: The case envisaged in this parable is like this. Two persons, in dispute about a debt, take the matter to the magistrate that usually settles such disputes. The party that is in the wrong will do well, then, to propose satisfactory terms and thus get the other party to release him before they are in the court. If not, his case will be tried and decided with unpleasant consequences for him. Jesus compares his collocutors, i.e. "the multitudes", with the party that has to give in: in spiritual matters they should act as quickly as he advises them to do in this juridical matter.

For... It may be desirable to mark the following advice as a metaphor or simile, e.g. 'for it is like this...', "for instance" (Phillips).

As you go with your accuser before... Probably the initiative was not with the party that was in the wrong (i.e. the party referred to by 'you'); hence, 'when you and the one opposing you are on your way together to...' (Kapauku), 'if you are called to-be-arranged (i.e. to have a dispute settled) with one-who-is-against-you in presence of...' (Tzeltal), or even, "if a man brings a lawsuit against you and takes you to..." (TEV). *You,* i.e. someone amongst you, as expressed by the singular form. *Accuser,* 'adversary/opponent', 'dispute-partner' (Zarma), 'he who calls the lawsuit' (an idiom found in West Nyanja), 'he who brings the case' (Shona 1963). For 'to accuse' cp. also 6 : 7.

Magistrate, slightly more generic synonym of 'judge' (next clause); 'chief', 'headman' are amongst the acceptable renderings, provided these authorities have some kind of juridical function.

To settle with him, or, 'to be-good-with-each-other(-again)' (East Toradja 1933), "to obtain a release from him" (BFBS). Versions tend to use 'to be released/set-free/delivered from' (probably because this is close to the literal meaning of the Greek); such renderings may, however, suggest a narrow escape by running away, rather than a release because the matter in dispute has been settled.

On the way, preferably renderings like, "while you are still on the way" (NEB, similarly Bahasa Indonesia RC, East Toradja), "before you get there" (Rieu); the phrase, indicating the period before the decisive event, is basic to the understanding of the parable.

Lest he drag you to the judge, or, 'in order that he may not drag you (or, compel you to come/appear) before the judge'; or, with a non-subordinate clause, 'otherwise, or, if (you do) not, he will drag you...'. For *the judge* cp. on the verb in *N.T.Wb.*/48f.

To bring out that *and the judge hand you over...* is not dependent on "lest" one may start a new sentence here, 'Then the judge will hand you over to (or, deliver you in the hands of)'.

Officer has been rendered, 'jailer' (because of the next clause), cp. also, 'watcher (i.e. guard)' (Kapauku), 'warden' (Thai 1967), or, 'soldier' (Lomwe), '(village) policeman' (Zarma); where such terms are not available or would not fit the context one may describe the function as 'his (i.e. the judge's) helper/assistant', 'his subordinate' (cp. Shona 1963).

To put in prison, see "shut up in prison" in 3 : 20.

(V. 59) For *till* see 1 : 20.

You have paid the very last copper, viz. of your debt, a reference to which may have to be added, cp. e.g. 'you-have-paid that debt-of-yours, not one half-cent lacking' (South Toradja), 'your debt is-paid-off, not one cash still being-left-over' (Balinese). For *copper,* or, 'mite', 'farthing', cp. 21 : 2. There may exist idiomatic phrases for the smallest amount one can imagine, e.g. 'one penny split in seven' (Malay); elsewhere idiom prefers an expression not mentioning a specific coin, cp. e.g. 'you have cleared your debt to-the-very-end-of-it' (Bahasa Indonesia), 'you have paid your debt to its-being-cleared entirely' (Javanese).

CHAPTER THIRTEEN

1 *There were some present at that very time who told him of the Galileans whose blood Pilate had mingled with their sacrifices.*

Exegesis: *parēsan de tines en autō tō kairō* 'at that very time some people came up', or, 'were present', preferably the former, cp. A-G s.v. *pareimi* 1 a and Plummer. *kairos* means here 'moment of time' without the theological implications it has in 12 : 56.

apaggellontes autō peri tōn Galilaiōn 'telling him about the Galileans', denoting the purpose of their coming. As shown by the article *tōn* the clause refers to a commonly known fact. For *apaggellō* cp. on 7 : 18.

hōn to haima Pilatos emixen meta tōn thusiōn autōn 'whose blood Pilate had mixed with (the blood of) their sacrifices', with *tou haimatos* understood after *meta*. The reference is to people who were killed by Roman soldiers when they were slaughtering the beasts they had brought as sacrifices. The phrase 'to mix blood with blood' is a Hebraism. *thusia* (cp. on 2 : 24) refers here to sacrificial animals.

Translation: *At that very time,* i.e. in the same point of time, 'at the same occasion'.

Told him of the Galileans whose..., or, 'told Jesus about (or, the story of) the G. whose...', 'told Jesus that there were G. whose...' (or in direct discourse).

The Galileans whose blood Pilate had mingled with their sacrifices. The clause structure often has to be changed, cp. e.g. 'the G. whose blood had-been-shed by P., so-that it got-mixed with their sacrifices' (Toba Batak), or, making explicit the function of the Hebraistic expression, 'there-are G. killed by P...., mixed-together (is) their blood and the blood of the animals they slaughtered' (East Toradja 1933), or again, substituting the function, 'the G. whom P. killed while they were sacrificing' (Gio, cp. TEV). *Galileans,* i.e. men from the land Galilee, and see below on 22 : 59. *Sacrifices,* or, 'animals they had slaughtered (in the temple), or, killed as a gift (for God)'; and cp. 2 : 24. *Pilate.* For a title, if required with the name, cp. "governor" in 2 : 2.

2 *And he answered them, "Do you think that these Galileans were worse sinners than all the other Galileans, because they suffered thus?*

Exegesis: *kai apokritheis eipen autois* 'and answering he said to them'. *apokritheis* implies that the story about the killing had intimated some question or statement about the sinfulness of the people who had been killed.

dokeite hoti hoi Galilaioi houtoi hamartōloi para pantas tous Galilaious egenonto 'do you think that these Galileans were sinners, more than all (other) Galileans', i.e. greater sinners than all other Galileans. For *dokeō* cp. on 8 : 18. For *hamartōlos* cp. on 5 : 8. For *para* with accusative meaning 'beyond', 'more than' cp. A-G s.v. III 3. *egenonto* is equivalent to the (non-existing) aorist of *eimi*.

hoti tauta peponthasin 'because they suffered these things'. *tauta* is pronominal accusative of content, cp. Bl-D, § 154. The perfect tense refers to an event which was irrevocable.

Translation: *Do you think*, see 12 : 51.

Were worse sinners than..., or, 'were more sinful than...', 'sinned more (gravely) than...'.

Because they suffered thus gives the reason of what Jesus understands the people to be thinking. To bring this out it is sometimes sufficient to place the phrase nearer to 'do you think' (cp. Goodspeed, Rieu), but often further adjustment is required, e.g. 'is it because these men suffered thus that you think they are worse...', 'do you think: that these men suffered thus (or, what these men suffered) proves that (or, is because) they are worse...'. The verb *to suffer* here means, 'to experience (or, to be subjected to) something bad', 'have something bad happen to one', hence, "because this happened to them" (Goodspeed); the thing suffered was death, cp. "because these G. were killed" (TEV), 'their death' (East Toradja 1933).

3 ***I tell you, No; but unless you repent you will all likewise perish.***

Exegesis: *ouchi, legō humin* 'no, I tell you', emphatic rejection of what had been intimated by his opponents, rather than an introduction of what follows.

all' ean mē metanoēte 'but unless you repent...', a warning instead of an answer. For *metanoeō* cp. on 10 : 13.

pantes homoiōs apoleisthe 'you will all perish similarly', i.e. you will perish as they perished. *homoiōs* does not refer to the way in which they will perish (e.g. killing, accident, etc.) but to the fact that they also will perish.

Translation: *I tell you, No*, or, "I tell you they were not" (NEB), and cp. 12 : 51.

But unless you repent you will..., or, 'but (as to) you, if you do not repent, you will...', 'but you, you must repent, otherwise (or, if not) you will...'.

Perish, cp. *N.T.Wb./27*, DIE.

4 ***Or those eighteen upon whom the tower in Siloam fell and killed them, do you think that they were worse offenders than all the others who dwelt in Jerusalem?***

Exegesis: *ē* 'or', introduces a clause which, again in the form of a question, describes a similar case, cp. A-G s.v. 1 a β.

ekeinoi hoi deka oktō 'those eighteen people', the subject of *egenonto* but for the sake of emphasis placed at the beginning of the sentence and hence taken up by *autoi* (after *hoti*). The demonstrative pronoun and the article show that Jesus referred to people whom everybody knew about.

eph' hous epesen ho purgos en tō Silōam 'on whom the tower fell at Siloam'. *en tō Silōam* is best understood to mean 'in the neighbourhood of Siloam', and to go with the whole clause. For *Silōam* cp. *IDB* IV, 352ff. *purgos* also 14 : 28.

dokeite hoti autoi opheiletai egenonto para pantas tous anthrōpous tous katoikountas Ierousalēm 'do you think that they were offenders, more than all people who live in Jerusalem?', same structure as the corresponding interrogative clause in v. 2. *katoikeō*, cp. on 11 : 26.

opheiletēs (†) lit. 'debtor', here corresponding with, and equivalent to *hamartōloi* 'sinners' in v. 2 (cp. also 11 : 4).

Translation: The introductory words (*or those...killed them*) can often best be rendered as an independent question or statement, introduced by a phrase like, "again, take" (Rieu), "what about... ?" (TEV); or, 'you remember how... ?', which may require some of the shifts mentioned in the next entry.

Those eighteen upon whom the tower in Siloam fell and killed them, or, 'those eighteen men who were killed when/because the tower fell on them (or, by/at the falling down of the tower) in S.', or, 'the eighteen people who died fallen-upon-by the tower in S.' (Bahasa Indonesia, Javanese). *Tower* sometimes has to be rendered by a descriptive term, e.g. 'built upward house' (Kapauku), 'high house/building' (Kekchi, Zarma), 'far-visible house' (East Toradja 1933), 'house/building one looks out from'; Tzeltal suggests not height but strength by using a word designating any kind of edifice or wall made of stones put together with mortar, in contrast with the usual buildings made with poles and vines. Since the tower may have been part of the fortifications, Toba Batak uses the term for an observation-post on the walls around the settlement, cp. also, 'house-of war' (Trukese, Ponape). For *to be killed*, here accidentally, cp. *N.T.Wb.*/49f.

Were worse offenders than, see the synonymous phrase in v. 2. *Offender*, or, 'wrong doer', 'transgressor', 'sinner'.

The others who dwelt in, or, 'the other inhabitants of', implying that the eighteen also lived in Jerusalem.

5 ***I tell you, No; but unless you repent you will all likewise perish."***

Exegesis: *ouchi, legō humin*, 'no, I tell you', cp. on v. 3.

hōsautōs lit. 'in the same way', here 'similarly', equivalent to *homoiōs* in v. 3.

Translation: See the note on v. 3.

6 ***And he told this parable: "A man had a fig tree planted in his vineyard; and he came seeking fruit on it and found none.***

Exegesis: *elegen de tautēn tēn parabolēn* 'and he told this (i.e. the following) parable'. The parable states that, unless the repentance to which vv. 3 and 5 call comes shortly, it will be too late. For *parabolē* cp. on 4 : 23.

sukēn eichen tis pephuteumenēn lit. 'a certain man had a fig tree planted', or "had a fig tree growing" (Goodspeed). *sukēn* (also 21 : 29) is emphatic by position. The past participle *pephuteumenēn* going with *sukēn* refers to a prevailing situation, not to an act or event of the past.

en tō ampelōni autou 'in his vineyard'.

ampelōn 'vineyard', in Palestine not exclusively a plantation of grape vines, but including also other kinds of fruit-trees, cp. Strack-Billerbeck I, 873.

kai ēlthen zētōn karpon en autē 'and he came seeking fruit on it', i.e. 'he came and sought', rather than 'he came to seek'. The participle *zētōn* denotes the main act and the verb *ēlthen* leads up to the main act.

kai ouch heuren 'and he found none', lit. 'and he did not find (any)'.

Translation: *Parable,* see 8 : 4.

A man had a fig tree planted in his vineyard, or, to show that the tree is in focus, 'there was a fig tree, which stood planted (or, was growing) in someone's vineyard, or, which someone had growing in his vineyard'; in some cases it is better to render the relative clause as a co-ordinate sentence. With a further shift one may say, 'there was a fig tree that stood planted in a vineyard. Once its owner came...'. In some languages the reference to being planted is better omitted; hence, 'there-was(-standing)' (Malay, similarly in Shona 1966, South Toradja). For *fig tree* see 6 : 44. The term chosen should refer to a tree with edible fruits, which is taken care of in some manner or other. For *vineyard* see 20 : 9. In this context, however, it is acceptable to use a more generic term, e.g. 'garden', 'field', since the specific concept 'vine(yard)' plays no role in what follows.

He came seeking fruit on it, or, 'for its fruit', 'for fruit(s) on the/his tree'; or, 'he came and looked whether there was fruit on it, or, whether it had (or, had borne) fruit'. For the generic *fruit* (cp. *N.T.Wb.*/40) one may substitute the specific, i.e. the name of the fruit of the tree in question.

Found none. For the verb see 2 : 12.

7 ***And he said to the vinedresser, 'Lo, these three years I have come seeking fruit on this fig tree, and I find none. Cut it down; why should it use up the ground?'***

Exegesis: *eipen de pros ton ampelourgon* 'and he said to the vinedresser'.

ampelourgos (††) 'vinedresser', 'gardener'.

idou 'look here', emphatic introduction of what follows, cp. on 1 : 20.

tria etē aph' hou lit. '(it is) three years since', meaning here 'for the last three years'.

erchomai zētōn lit. 'I come seeking', here denoting acts (viz. coming and seeking) that have been done during the last three years and are still in process. For the relationship between participle and main verb, cp. on v. 6.

ekkopson [*oun*] *autēn* 'so cut it down'. For *ekkoptō* cp. on 3 : 9.

hinati kai tēn gēn katargei 'why does it waste the soil?', rhetoric question to which the answer is, "there is no reason".

hinati lit. 'for what reason', hence 'why'. Here it is reinforced by *kai.*

katargeō (†) 'to make ineffective', here of a tree, 'to use up', 'to waste', cp. A-G s.v. 1 a.

Translation: *Lo,* see "behold" in 1 : 20.

These three years, or, 'already as-long-as three years' (Bahasa Indonesia RC), 'these three years successively/time-and-again' (South Toradja).

For *to cut down* (a tree) see 3 : 9.

Why should it use up the ground? has been rendered variously, e.g. 'why does it occupy room (or, spread-itself here, or, on the land) uselessly?' (cp. Lokele, Ponape; South Toradja, Malay), 'why does it keep other things out of the place?' (Shona 1966), 'why does it use-up food in earth?' (Kituba), 'why does it exhaust (lit. continually-eat-up) the soil?' (one West Nyanja version, similarly Jerusalem), 'is not this occupying good soil?' (Lomwe), 'why should it merely take-away the fertility of the soil?' (Balinese); or, as a statement, 'in vain it takes-up (lit. covers) space' (Tzeltal), 'it is making the soil worthless' (Yao).

8 ***And he answered him, 'Let it alone, sir, this year also, till I dig about it and put on manure.***

Exegesis: *kurie* 'sir', cp. on 1 : 6.

aphes autēn kai touto to etos 'leave it also this year', i.e. 'this one year more'.

heōs hotou skapsō peri autēn kai balō kopria lit. 'until I have dug around it and put on manure'. As the subjunctives *skapsō* and *balō* show the clause has final meaning, and denotes the gardener's plans concerning the fig tree. For *skaptō* cp. on 6 : 48.

koprion (††) 'dung', 'manure'.

Translation: *Let it alone,* cp. *N.T.Wb.*/6, ALLOW; in this context one may say, "don't touch it" (Phillips), 'allow it to go on growing, or, to stand here'.

Sir, or, 'master', or an equivalent term commonly used by a servant or slave when addressing his employer or master, or by a labourer towards the owner of the garden he takes care of. Cp. on "Lord" in 1 : 6 sub (a).

Till I dig..., or, "while I dig..." (NEB); or, to bring out the propositive force of the clause, 'then (or, in the meanwhile) I will dig...', 'let me first dig...' (Willibrord).

Dig about it and put on manure may be quite foreign to local agricultural methods. If so, one may consider a generic rendering like, 'give it the best care I can'. *Dig about it* may require an object, 'dig-up/break-up the ground at its base' (East Toradja), 'hoe the soil around it' (Bahasa Indonesia 1968). *Put on manure.* One may describe the material, 'put faeces of cattle (or, dirt of animals) on it' (East Toradja, Kituba), 'fill its foot with rotten-earth (i.e. compost)' (Tzeltal), or the function, 'make the soil more fertile', 'give-to (it) its food' (Ponape).

9 ***And if it bears fruit next year, well and good; but if not, you can cut it down.'"***

Exegesis: *kan men poiēsē karpon eis to mellon* 'and if it bears fruit for the future,...' with aposiopesis following. *kan* is contraction of *kai* and *an*. *eis to mellon* 'for the future', i.e. '(for) next year', cp. Plummer.

ei de mēge lit. 'but if not', i.e. 'otherwise', cp. on 5 : 36.

ekkopseis autēn 'you will cut it down', i.e. 'you can cut it down'.

Translation: *To bear fruit*, cp. 3 : 8.

Next year, i.e. next (fig) season, next (fig) harvest.

Well and good, or, "so much the better" (TEV), 'then it is all right' (Zürich), added to complete the thought that is left incomplete in the Greek. Another solution is to change the conditional clause into a sentence in the potential or optative mood, cp. e.g. "perhaps it will bear fruit next year" (Goodspeed, similarly Jerusalem, Javanese, Sundanese), or, 'may it (or, I hope it will) bear fruit in the future' (Toba Batak).

You can cut it down. In some languages a form showing that the subject is not the direct agent is preferable or obligatory, e.g. 'let it be cut down' (Shona 1966, similarly Tzeltal, Kituba, South Toradja), 'you can order me to cut it down'.

10 ***Now he was teaching in one of the synagogues on the sabbath.***

Exegesis: *ēn de didaskōn* 'he was teaching', introductory description of the situation in which the healing of a crippled woman occurs. No connexion with what precedes is stated.

en mia tōn sunagōgōn 'in one of the synagogues', hence, 'in a synagogue', cp. on 5 : 12, 17.

en tois sabbasin 'on the sabbath', cp. on 4 : 16. The reference is here not to a specific sabbath day, hence, "on a sabbath day" (Rieu).

Translation: For *now* see on 1 : 57.

11 ***And there was a woman who had had a spirit of infirmity for eighteen years; she was bent over and could not fully straighten herself.***

Exegesis: *kai idou gunē* lit. 'and behold, a woman...', hence, 'and there was a woman'.

pneuma echousa astheneias lit. 'having a spirit of sickness', i.e. 'possessed by a spirit that caused sickness', or, 'having a sickness caused by a spirit'. The spirit and the sickness are conceived as being one, cp. 11 : 14.

etē deka oktō 'eighteen years', accusative of duration.

kai ēn sugkuptousa (††) 'and she was bent double', i.e. as a result of the sickness.

kai mē dunamenē anakupsai eis to panteles 'and completely unable to straighten herself up'. *eis to panteles* is best understood as going with *dunamenē.*

anakuptō (also 21 : 28) 'to raise oneself up', 'to straighten oneself', less probably 'to lift up the head' (cp. Lagrange, Rieu).

eis to panteles (†) 'completely', 'wholly', 'at all', cp. A-G s.v. *pantelēs.*

Translation: *To have a spirit of infirmity* often is to be described by, 'to have (or, to be possessed/entered by) a spirit/demon that makes (a person) ill', or with a resultative clause, 'so that one becomes ill' (cp. East and South Toradja), cp. also, 'to be the host of a spirit that took away her strength' (Shona 1966). In Tzeltal the idiom is, 'to be molested by the devil'; Kapauku uses a form that may mean both 'having seen a spirit' and 'a spirit having seen her', either event being thought of as a cause of illness. For *spirit* cp. 9 : 39, for *infirmity* see "disease" in 4 : 40.

She was bent over..., sometimes introduced by, 'because of that', 'so that'. Idiom may require another subject, e.g. 'her back was bent' (Bahasa Indonesia, similarly Sranan, lit. 'was-broken'), 'her body was crooked' (Toba Batak).

Straighten herself, or, 'her body/back', or, "stand up straight" (NEB, similarly Sranan).

12 ***And when Jesus saw her, he called her and said to her, "Woman, you are freed from your infirmity."*** 13 ***And he laid his hands upon her, and immediately she was made straight, and she praised God.***

Exegesis: *idōn de autēn ho Iēsous prosephōnēsen kai eipen autē* 'when Jesus saw her he called (her) to him and said to her'. *prosephōnēsen* and *eipen* are best understood as referring to two different acts. For *prosphōneō* cp. on 6 : 13.

apolelusai tēs astheneias sou 'you are released from your sickness'. The perfect tense of *apolelusai* refers to a new and permanent situation, cp. Plummer. For *apoluō* cp. on 2 : 29.

(V. 13) *kai epethēken autē tas cheiras* 'and he laid his hands on her', best understood as happening simultaneously with Jesus' words. For the laying on of hands cp. on 4 : 40.

kai parachrēma anōrthōthē 'and at once she became erect/stood upright'. Note the change of subject.

anorthoō (†) in the passive 'to become erect', probably a medical term.

kai edoxazen ton theon 'and she praised God', imperfect tense denoting a prolonged act. For *doxazō* cp. on 2 : 20.

Translation: *Woman.* The corresponding Greek word, used here in the vocative, is a form of address that does not sound unkind and even may function "as a term of respect or affection" (L-Sc, 363). The same is true of some other languages, e.g. Lokele, Zarma, Balinese. Elsewhere a literal rendering is impossible and one has to use an indigenous vocative word for kindly or respectfully addressing a woman without mentioning her name (Trukese, Ponape, similarly Tzeltal; also Sundanese, the same term being used for "daughter" and "child" in 8 : 48 and 54), or a particle used to call the attention of women (Kapauku, its masculine counterpart occurring in 12 : 20); in several languages the word in question lit. means '(my) mother', e.g. in South Toradja (applicable to middle-aged married women), Shona (to women that are married or of marriageable age but not yet grandmother), Toba Batak (cp. on "daughter" in 8 : 48). See also *N.T.Wb.* /75[b].

You are freed from your infirmity, or, 'now your illness is-healed', 'from now on you are no longer sick'.

(V. 13) For *he laid his hands upon her* cp. 4 : 40.

She was made straight, or again, 'her back/body became straight (or, stood upright)'. The aspect is inceptive-durative.

Praised God, see on "glorifying God" in 2 : 20.

14 ***But the ruler of the synagogue, indignant because Jesus had healed on the sabbath, said to the people, "There are six days on which work ought to be done; come on those days and be healed, and not on the sabbath day."***

Exegesis: *apokritheis de ho archisunagōgos...elegen tō ochlō* 'but the leader of the synagogue answering...said to the crowd'. For *apokritheis* cp. on 1 : 60. For *archisunagōgos* cp. on 8 : 49. *tō ochlō* refers to the people who are in the synagogue and attend the worship service, i.e. 'the congregation'.

aganaktōn (†) 'being angry, or, indignant', placed between the introductory participle *apokritheis* and the main verb *elegen* (which go usually very closely together) in order to bring out the mood in which he spoke.

hoti tō sabbatō etherapeusen ho Iēsous 'because (it was) on the sabbath (that) Jesus had healed'. *tō sabbatō* is emphatic and the article is generic.

hex hēmerai eisin en hais dei ergazesthai 'there are six days on which work ought to be done'. *dei* 'it is necessary' means here 'it is prescribed in the law'.

ergazomai (†) 'to do work', 'to work'.

en autais oun erchomenoi therapeuesthe 'so come and be healed on them'. *en autais* is emphatic by position. *oun* is inferential. The saying rests on the assumption that healing is to be classified as work. *erchomenoi* has the force of an imperative.

kai mē tē hēmera tou sabbatou 'and not on the day of the sabbath'.

Translation: *But* can be said to represent here Gr. *apokritheis*; similarly "whereupon" (BFBS). Other versions use a verb, e.g. "intervened" (NEB), or verbal phrase, e.g. "took the matter up" (Rieu). Cp. also the note on "answered" in 3 : 16.

The ruler of the synagogue, see 8 : 41.

Indignant because Jesus had healed on the sabbath may better be rendered as a clause in initial position, cp. TEV. For *indignant* see *N.T.Wb.*/9f, ANGER; *TH-Mk* on 3 : 5. An object with *healed*, if required, may be indefinite, e.g. 'some one' (Leyden, Bahasa Indonesia), 'sick people' (Javanese), 'sickness' (Toba Batak), or a reference to the preceding case, e.g. "her" (Goodspeed), 'this illness'.

The people, or, 'the (many) people present (there)', cp. "crowd" in 5 : 19.

There are six days on which work ought to be done, or, simplifying the clause structure, "there are six days in which we should work" (TEV), 'during six days (or, six days long) it is lawful (see 6 : 2) for people to work, or, that we (inclusive, Toba Batak) do-work'. The higher unit 'in each week', or 'in each seven days' may have to be made explicit. Shorter, more synthetical renderings are, 'six days are for working' (Sranan), "there are six working-days" (NEB, similarly East Toradja 1933).

And be healed, cp. 5 : 15.

And not, or, 'but don't do so'.

15 ***Then the Lord answered him, "You hypocrites! Does not each of you on the sabbath untie his ox or his ass from the manger, and lead it away to water it?***

Exegesis: *apekrithē de autō ho kurios kai eipen* 'but the Lord answered him and said'. For *apekrithē* cp. on 1 : 60; for *ho kurios* on 1 : 6.

hupokritai 'hypocrites', cp. on 6 : 42 and 12 : 56. The fact that Jesus uses the plural, though addressing one man, means that all who tacitly agree with the leader of the synagogue are involved.

hekastos humōn tō sabbatō ou luei ton boun autou ē ton onon apo tēs phatnēs 'does not each one of you on the sabbath untie his ox or donkey from the manger?' *hekastos humōn* and *tō sabbatō* are emphatic by position. Interrogative *ou* suggests that the obvious answer to the question is 'yes', cp. A-G s.v. 4 c. For *luō* cp. on 3 : 16. For *phatnē* cp. on 2 : 7.

kai apagagōn potizei 'and does not (each of you) lead (it) away and water (it)?', continuation of the interrogative clause.

apagō 'to lead away', with the connotation of leading to a certain goal; here the goal is indicated by the following verb. The aorist tense of *apagagōn* suggests an act preceding that expressed by the main verb *potizei*.

potizō (†) 'to water', 'to give drink to (an animal)'.

Translation: For *you hypocrites* see 6 : 42.

Does not each of you ... untie ..., or better to bring out the emphasis, "is there a single one of you who does not loose ..." (NEB), or, as a statement, 'no doubt any one of you would untie ...' (cp. TEV). *Untie*, or, 'loose the tie/bond of'.

Ox and *ass*, cp. *N.T.Wb.*/34f, FAUNA. For *ox* one may use the name of, or a generic designation for, a comparable domestic animal commonly known in the culture, such as 'buffalo' (e.g. in South Toradja), 'head of cattle' (Shona, West Nyanja). The word is used here in its general sense not in that of 'castrated bull'. *Ass* may have to become 'horse', 'mount', 'riding-animal'.

Manger, see 2 : 7. Several versions prefer the meaning 'stall', '(compartment of a) stable'; then the verb 'to untie' is sometimes rendered by 'to release' (BFBS, Bahasa Indonesia), or, 'lead out' (South Toradja), implying that there is no bond to be untied, but an enclosure to be opened.

To water it, or, 'to cause-to-drink it' (Sundanese); or, taking the animal as subject, 'that it may drink', 'to drink (water)' (Toba Batak, Sranan); or again, as a locative, 'towards the watering-place' (Willibrord).

16 ***And ought not this woman, a daughter of Abraham whom Satan bound for eighteen years, be loosed from this bond on the sabbath day?"***

Exegesis: *tautēn de thugatera Abraam ousan* 'this (woman), a daughter of Abraham', emphatically placed at the beginning of the clause. *tautēn* is demonstrative pronoun used as a substantive. *thugatēr Abraam* denotes a female descendant of Abraham, i.e. a member of God's people (cp. on 1 : 5).

hēn edēsen ho Satanas idou deka kai oktō etē 'whom Satan has kept bound, mind you, for eighteen years'. For *Satanas* cp. on 10 : 18. *idou* serves to focus the attention on the eighteen years.

deō (also 19 : 30) 'to bind', here in the figurative meaning of being bound by sickness. The aorist tense has the force of a pluperfect and refers to a situation which only now has come to an end.

ouk edei luthēnai apo tou desmou toutou lit. 'was it not necessary that (this woman) should be released from this bond'. *edei* denotes obligation. *luthēnai* is equivalent to *apolelusai* in v. 12.

desmos (cp. on 8 : 29) 'bond', here in the same figurative sense as *deō*.

Translation: The sentence is often better divided in two sentences, one stating the case, e.g. "and here is this woman, ..., who has been kept prisoner by Satan for...years" (NEB), 'but this woman, ..., well, already...years Satan has kept her fettered' (cp. Balinese), and the other containing the rendering of the rhetorical question, e.g. 'ought she not be freed... ?', "surely she should be released..." (Phillips).

Ought not this woman... be loosed, or, 'was it not right that this woman... be loosed'; or as a statement and shifting to an active construction, 'surely it is my duty to (or, certainly I should) loose this woman...'.

For *daughter of Abraham* cp. on 1 : 5, for *Satan* 10 : 18.

Bound...loosed from this bond. Because of v. 15 it is preferable to preserve the metaphor, if necessary shifting to a simile, or adding a reference to its meaning, cp. e.g. 'bound with this sickness...loosed from this sickness' (Spanish VP). Where this is impossible one must shift to a non-metaphorical rendering, e.g. 'made ill...cured from this illness'. Tzeltal combines two solutions, cp. 'bound as it were by Satan...be helped'.

For eighteen years. The emphasis (expressed by the Gr. *idou*) has also been brought out by such renderings as, "for eighteen long years" (NEB), 'a time up-to eighteen years' (Javanese).

17 ***As he said this, all his adversaries were put to shame; and all the people rejoiced at all the glorious things that were done by him.***

Exegesis: *kai tauta legontos autou* 'when he was saying this', or, 'because he said this', preferably the former.

katēschunonto pantes hoi antikeimenoi autō 'all his adversaries were put to shame'.

kataischunō (†) 'to put to shame', 'to humiliate'.

antikeimenos (also 21 : 15) 'opposing', then 'adversary', 'opponent', here with dative of the person opposed.

pas ho ochlos 'all the crowd', refers to the same people as *ochlos* in v. 14.

epi pasin tois endoxois tois ginomenois hup' autou 'at all the glorious things that were done by him'. For *endoxos* cp. on 7 : 25; here it is used as a substantive in the plural, meaning 'glorious things, or, deeds'. *ginomenois* 'happening', is virtually equivalent to the passive of *poieō* 'to do'.

Translation: *Adversaries,* or, 'enemies', 'opponents' (East Toradja), 'the men that were criticizing him' (Sranan, similarly Sundanese).

Were put to shame, or, 'felt ashamed', 'were embarassed' (Tzeltal); TEV shifts to an active construction, "his answer made all his enemies ashamed of themselves". In Kituba one 'sees shame', in East Toradja one's 'eyes are-ashamed', in East Nyanja and Yao 'shame is done to, or, poured upon' one, and in West Nyanja one can 'do shame'. Some figurative expressions for 'be ashamed' are, 'the body is cold' (Kabba Laka), 'to have to sell face' (Thai 1967).

All the people, cp. on 3 : 21.

At all the glorious things that were done by him, or, 'because Jesus did such glorious things/deeds'. *Glorious things,* or, 'deeds that have-glory' (East Toradja, cp. "glory" in 2 : 9), "wonderful things" (NEB, Jerusalem) 'wonders' (Javanese, using the same term as for Gr. *terata* in Mt. 24 : 24), 'big works' (Sranan, using the same term as for "mighty works" in 10 : 13).

18 ***He said therefore, "What is the kingdom of God like? And to what shall I compare it?***

Exegesis: *elegen oun* 'then he said', or 'he said therefore', depending on whether *oun* is interpreted as continuative or inferential. The former is preferable.

tini homoia estin hē basileia tou theou, kai tini homoiōsō autēn? 'what is the kingdom of God like, and with what shall I compare it?' For the function of these questions cp. on 7 : 31. For *hē basileia tou theou* cp. on 4 : 43. For *homoioō* cp. on 7 : 31.

Translation: *He said therefore,* preferably, "next, he said" (Rieu), "he continued" (NEB).

For the wording of the two subsequent questions see 7 : 31, which is in the reverse order, however.

19 ***It is like a grain of mustard seed which a man took and sowed in his garden; and it grew and became a tree, and the birds of the air made nests in its branches."***

Exegesis: *homoia estin kokkō sinapeōs* 'it is like a mustard seed', cp. *TH-Mk* on 4 : 31. *kokkos sinapeōs* also 17 : 6.

hon labōn anthrōpos ebalen eis kēpon heautou 'which a man took and put in his garden'. *ballō* lit. 'to throw', is used here in a weakened sense, 'to put', cp. A-G s.v. 2 b. The aorist tense of *ebalen* and the other verbs in v. 19 is gnomic and due to the parable-character of the passage. It does not refer to a past event but to a present reality (cp. Bl-D, § 333.1).

kēpos (†) 'garden'.

kai ēuxēsen 'and it grew', change of subject. For *auxanō* cp. on 1 : 80.

kai egeneto eis dendron 'and it became a tree'. *ginomai eis* with accusative means 'to become', cp. A-G s.v. I 4 a.

kai ta peteina tou ouranou kateskēnōsen en tois kladois autou 'and the birds of the air nested in its branches'. For *ta peteina tou ouranou* cp. on 8 : 5.

kataskēnoō (†) 'to nest', cp. *TH-Mk* on 4 : 32.

klados (†) 'branch'.

Translation: *A grain of mustard seed,* i.e. a single seed of the mustard plant; cp. *TH-Mk* on 4 : 31. One should keep in mind that in Rabbinic literature the mustard seed was proverbial for an insignificant size or amount (also in the Koran, S. 21 : 47; 31 : 16). A close equivalent in Indonesia is the *Brassica juncea* (or, *rugosa*), which is botanically related with the *Sinapis nigra,* has an equivalent function (its leaves being used for spicing food), can reach a length of 1.25 M., and is typical for insignificance (it being said, for instance, in a Malay literary work that heaven and earth are "no bigger than a seed of the *brassica* when compared with Allah's Throne", and in a Balinese proverb that bad people "see the sins of the righteous, although they are as *Brassica*-seeds, but do not see their own sins, although they are as *madja*-fruits"). In some cases, however, a reference to mustard seed, or to a close botanical and functional equivalent does not fit the context, e.g. because its plant is small, so that it would be ridiculous to say that the birds nestle in its branches, or because another seed is proverbial for insignificance. Then one may consider a generic rendering, such as 'tiny seed', or a cultural equivalent, e.g. seed of a fig tree (used in Yao), or of a *banyan* tree (suggested but not used in Gujarati)—with an explanatory footnote, if thought necessary. For *seed* see 8 : 5.

Which a man took and sowed in his garden is sometimes better changed into a conditional or temporal clause going with what follows, 'when a man takes it (or, that seed) and sows it in his garden, it grows...'. *A man,* or, where sowing is not done by men, 'somebody', the sex not being relevant here. For *to sow* see references on 8 : 5. *Garden,* or, 'field', 'plot of ground'.

It grew, or, using a more specific verb, 'it sprouted' (Balinese), or shifting to what comes from the seed, 'the plant grew'. Cp. also 1 : 80.

And became a tree, or, 'till it had-a-stem' (Balinese). That *tree* is used rather hyperbolically may be indicated by saying 'a tree so to say', but a word for 'bush', or, 'shrub' may be more appropriate for the plant in question. Cp. also *N.T.Wb.*/37, FLORA.

The birds of the air, see 8 : 5.

To make nests, or, 'to nest', 'to make/have a place to live', 'to live'.

In its branches, or, 'among its branches/twigs/leafstalks', 'under its leaves', etc. depending again on what is normally said in connexion with the plant chosen, or even, 'in its shade' (Malay).

20 ***And again he said, "To what shall I compare the kingdom of God?***

Exegesis: *kai palin eipen* 'and again he said', indicating not only repetition (v. 20), but also continuation, here the addition of a similar parable (v. 21).

Translation: *Again he said*, or, 'furthermore he said', "he went on" (Goodspeed). For the rest of the verse see again 7 : 31, first question.

21 ***It is like leaven which a woman took and hid in three measures of meal, till it was all leavened."***

Exegesis: *homoia estin zumē* 'it is like yeast', cp. on 12 : 1.

hēn labousa gunē enekrupsen eis aleurou sata tria 'which a woman took and hid in three measures of flour'. For the aorist tenses in v. 21 cp. on v. 19.

egkruptō (†) 'to hide', 'to cover up', or, 'to put into', since here the hiding of the yeast is not the purpose, but the result of the woman's act. The purpose is indicated by the subsequent clause.

aleuron (†) 'wheat flour'.

saton (†) transliteration of Aramaic *ṣata* or *seah*, a measure of capacity, of a little less than three gallons, or about thirteen L. (cp. Strack-Billerbeck I, 669f).

heōs hou ezumōthē holon 'till it was all leavened'. *holon* is adjective. It is modified by the subject of *ezumōthē*, viz. *aleuron* understood from the preceding clause, and indicates that the leavening affected all of the flour.

zumoō (†) 'to ferment', 'to leaven'.

Translation: *Leaven*, see 12 : 1; here used as a metaphor for an all-pervading good influence.

Which a woman took... may have to become a conditional or temporal clause as in v. 19.

Hid, preferably 'put', or more specifically, 'mixed' (e.g. Javanese), 'kneaded', or another term by which the receptor language normally refers to this activity.

Three measures, or, 'three baskets' (South Toradja), "a bushel" (Goodspeed, TEV), 'one barrel' (Sranan), or any other expression designating a fairly large quantity of meal. Cp. also Nida, *BT*, 330f; *N.T.Wb.*/73, WEIGHTS and MEASURES.

Meal, or, 'wheat-flour', 'rice-flour', has sometimes to be described, cp. 'dry seed (that is) ground' (Trique for Rev. 18 : 13).

Till here introduces an event that takes place some time after and as the result of the preceding act; hence, '(and) after-some-time' (Bahasa Indonesia RC), or, 'so-that' (Malay).

It...all, i.e. 'all the flour, or, bread dough'.

Was...leavened, or, 'became sour', 'had fermented', 'was swollen up', 'became salted'; often dependent on the term for 'leaven/yeast'.

22 ***He went on his way through towns and villages, teaching, and journeying toward Jerusalem.***

Exegesis: *kai dieporeueto kata poleis kai kōmas* 'and he went on through towns and villages'. The imperfect tense of *dieporeueto* suggests duration. *diaporeuomai* is here equivalent to *dierchomai* (cp. on 9 : 6). For the phrase *kata poleis kai kōmas* cp. on 8 : 1.

poreian poioumenos eis Hierosoluma 'making his way to Jerusalem', or, 'headed for Jerusalem', taking up the main verb *dieporeueto* in order to indicate the goal of Jesus' journey, and thus marking Jesus' going as a continuation of the journey begun in 9 : 51.

poreia (†) 'journey', 'trip'.

Translation: *He went on his way through towns and villages,* see 8 : 1; for *towns* cp. on "city" in 1 : 26.

Journeying toward Jerusalem, or as a new sentence, '(thus/so doing) he continued his journey toward J.', which may better be given initial position, cp. e.g. 'he continued his journey toward J., and on the way he passed through...and taught (there)'.

23 ***And some one said to him, "Lord, will those who are saved be few?" And he said to them,***

Exegesis: *eipen de tis autō* 'somebody said to him', without indication of place or time or occasion.

kurie 'lord', cp. on 1 : 6.

ei oligoi hoi sōzomenoi 'are those who are saved few?', with *eisin* understood. *ei* introduces here a direct question, cp. A-G s.v. V 1, but does not anticipate whether the answer will be in the affirmative or not. For *sōzō* cp. on 8 : 12.

ho de eipen pros autous 'he said to them'. *autous* is best understood as referring to all present, cp. on 12 : 15.

Translation: *Those who are saved,* cp. the note on 8 : 12.

To them, or, in order to bring out the interpretation preferred in *Exegesis,* 'to the people', 'to those present'.

24 ***"Strive to enter by the narrow door; for many, I tell you, will seek to enter and will not be able.***

Exegesis: *agōnizesthe eiselthein dia tēs stenēs thuras* 'struggle to go in through the narrow door'. The saying of entering the kingdom of God (cp. 18 : 17) is here modified by the picture of entering a house. The article *tēs* seems to imply that the phrase *dia tēs stenēs thuras* is a generally known saying. *stenos* (†).

agonizomai (†) with following infinitive, 'to struggle', 'to strive', 'to strain every nerve'.

hoti polloi, legō humin, zētēsousin eiselthein 'for many, I tell you, will try to get in'. *legō humin* is inserted to emphasize *polloi*. For *zētēsousin* cp. on 5 : 18. *eiselthein* takes up *eiselthein dia tēs stenēs thuras*.

kai ouk ischusousin 'and they will not be able'. For *ischuō* cp. on 6 : 48.

Translation: *Strive*, or, "do your utmost/best" (Phillips, TEV), 'try hard'.

To enter may require a goal, viz. 'the kingdom of God', anticipating v. 28.

By the narrow door, or, making explicit the concessive force, e.g. 'how narrow the door may be'. If the metaphor would be incomprehensible, one may say, 'along the difficult path', 'how difficult the way (to get in) may be'. *Narrow* has been described as, 'which hole/width-small' (Trukese, Ponape), or by a reciprocal form of 'to close-in-on' (Shona), or an adjective derived from 'to squeeze through' (West Nyanja).

For *seek* see 5 : 18.

Enter, or, 'enter it', 'get in there'.

And will not be able, or, filling out the ellipsis, 'will not be able to enter (it), or, to do so'.

25 ***When once the householder has risen up and shut the door, you will begin to stand outside and to knock at the door, saying, 'Lord, open to us.' He will answer you, 'I do not know where you come from.'***

Exegesis: V. 25 begins with a subordinate temporal clause. The main clause is either *kai apokritheis erei humin* 'he will answer and say to you', or does not begin till v. 26, *tote arxesthe legein* 'then you will begin to say'. The former interpretation is more probable.

aph' hou an 'when once' (cp. A-G s.v. *apo* II 2 c), modifies three verbs, viz. *egerthē, apokleisē* and *arxēsthe*.

egerthē ho oikodespotēs '(when once) the master of the house has got up'. *egerthē* refers here to getting up after sitting down at table.

kai apokleisē tēn thuran 'and has locked the door'.

apokleiō (††) 'to lock', synonymous with *kleiō* (11 : 7).

kai arxēsthe exō hestanai 'and you begin to stand outside'. Strictly speaking they were outside all the time, and *arxēsthe* indicates a new situation, viz. that of their being locked out.

kai krouein tēn thuran legontes 'and to knock at the door, saying'.
kurie, anoixon hēmin 'sir, open (the door) for us'.
kai apokritheis erei humin 'he will answer and say to you'. *kai* at the beginning of the apodosis is a Hebraism, cp. A-G s.v. I 2 d.
ouk oida humas pothen este 'I do not know where you come from', i.e. 'I do not know of any relationship with you'.

Translation: The sentence *when once . . ., 'Lord, open to us'* (rendering a Greek subordinate clause) may better be rendered as two co-ordinate sentences, e.g. 'the moment/time will come that the householder . . . shuts the door; then you will begin . . ., saying, "Lord, open to us" '.
The householder, i.e. the one who has authority in the place referred to in v. 24; hence 'the one who rules there, or, owns that place', may help to bring out the connexion with what precedes.
Shut the door, cp. 11 : 7.
You will begin to stand outside and to knock . . ., or, to bring out the new situation, "you may find yourselves standing outside and knocking . . ." (Phillips). *Outside,* or, 'at-the-other-side', viz. than the householder who is inside (East Toradja).
For *knock at the door* and *open to us,* or, "let us in" (NEB), cp. 11 : 9.

26 ***Then you will begin to say, 'We ate and drank in your presence, and you taught in our streets.'***

Exegesis: *tote arxesthe legein* lit. 'then you will begin to say'. *tote* 'then', i.e. when the master of the house has denied the relationship (v. 25). *arxesthe* indicates that the activity of those whom Jesus addresses takes a new turn in that they attempt to prove their relationship to the householder, cp. on 4 : 21.
ephagomen enōpion sou kai epiomen 'we ate and drank in your presence', i.e. 'we had fellowship with you at table', cp. on 5 : 30. *enōpion sou* goes with both verbs which form one expression. For *enōpion* cp. on 1 : 15.
en tais plateiais hēmōn edidaxas 'you taught in our streets', i.e. in the streets of the towns in which we live, implicit reference to Jesus' activity as a teacher.

Translation: *We ate and drank in your presence,* preferably, 'with you'; or, 'we sat at table (or, had meals) with you' (cp. NEB, Phillips); and cp. the note on 5 : 30.
In our streets, or, 'in the roads/paths/trails of our towns and villages', 'in our village-squares' (cp. Lokele, one West Nyanja version), 'on the cross-roads of our villages', or simply, 'in our settlements' (East Toradja); cp. on 10 : 10.

27 ***But he will say, 'I tell you, I do not know where you come from; depart from me, all you workers of iniquity!'***

Exegesis: *kai erei legōn humin* 'and he will say to you'. RSV does not follow *GNT* in that it reads: *kai erei, Legō humin.* The participle *legōn* as usual introduces direct speech though it has the same meaning as *erei.*

ouk oida [humas] pothen este 'I do not know where you come from,' emphatic repetition of v. 25.

apostēte ap' emou 'go away from me', 'withdraw from me'.

pantes ergatai adikias 'all you workers of wickedness', indicating the reason for their rejection. *ergatēs* (cp. on 10 : 2) is used here in a neutral sense, 'doer', 'one who does', cp. A-G s.v. 2, and its colour is determined by the following substantive.

adikia 'wickedness', 'unrighteousness'.

Translation: *Depart from me,* or, '(get) away from me' (cp. TEV, Rieu), "out of my sight" (NEB); comparable idioms e.g. in Balinese (lit. 'away go-off').

All you workers of iniquity, i.e. "all evil-doers" (Rieu), 'all you customarily bad-doing people' (Kapauku); or, shifting from address to causal clause, 'for all of you have done evil'.

28 ***There you will weep and gnash your teeth, when you see Abraham and Isaac and Jacob and all the prophets in the kingdom of God and you yourselves thrust out.***

Exegesis: *ekei estai ho klauthmos kai ho brugmos tōn odontōn* 'there will be the weeping and the gnashing of teeth'. *ekei* may have local or temporal meaning, preferably the former, since v. 28[a] is a well known description of the place where the rejected are after the final judgment (cp. Mt. 8 : 12). The weeping and the gnashing of teeth may express contrition and anxiety, or anger because of being excluded from the kingdom of God to which they thought themselves to be entitled, preferably the latter (cp. Grundmann).

klauthmos (†) 'weeping', 'crying'.

brugmos (†) 'gnashing', 'chattering'.

hotan opsesthe...en tē basileia tou theou 'when you see...in the kingdom of God', i.e. when you see that they have entered and are now in the kingdom of God. As v. 29 shows the reference is to a banquet in the kingdom of God.

humas de ekballomenous exō 'but (when you see) yourselves being thrown out', i.e. when they try to get in they are excluded (cp. Plummer).

Translation: *Weep,* see 6 : 21; Tzeltal uses a reciprocal form suggesting crying over one's state.

Gnash your teeth. In several languages (e.g. Tzeltal, Shona, Lokele, South Toradja) 'to gnash/grind/bite one's teeth' has the required associations, but in others it suggests illness, or the enduring of pain without flinching, etc. In such cases one will better add an indication of the function, e.g. 'because you are angry', 'to show (your) anger', or shift to a cultural equivalent, as done in Yao, which uses a reference to a grimace that in English can be described as 'clenching the teeth', or, 'biting the tongue', as in a war-snarl of rage.

For *Abraham* see 1 : 55.

Kingdom of God is locative here; hence 'the settlement where God rules' (a Mixtec dialect).

You yourselves thrust out, or, "kept outside" (TEV), "shut out" (Phillips), or, 'that you yourselves have to stand/remain outside'. The verb 'to see' may have to be repeated, cp. e.g. Sranan, 'you shall see how they chased you yourselves outside', cp. also Jerusalem.

29 ***And men will come from east and west, and from north and south, and sit at table in the kingdom of God.***

Exegesis: *kai hēxousin* 'and (in addition to those mentioned in v. 28) people will come'.

apo anatolōn kai dusmōn 'from east and west'. For *anatolē* (here in the plural without difference in meaning) cp. on 1 : 78; for *dusmē* cp. on 12 : 54. The omission of the article with the points of compass is usual, cp. Bl-D, § 253.5.

kai apo borra kai notou 'and from north and south'. For *notos* cp. on 11 : 31.

borras (†) 'north'.

anaklithēsontai en tē basileia tou theou 'they will sit, or, lie down at the table in the kingdom of God'. For *anaklinō* cp. on 2 : 7.

Translation: *From east and west, and from north and south,* the usual order for the points of the compass in the Bible (cp. e.g. 1 Chron. 9 : 24, Ps. 107 : 3); if in the receptor language another order is usual, that order should be followed. For the four terms see *N.T.Wb.*/28f, DIRECTIONS, *TBT*, 7.104-113, 1956, and for *west* cp. also 12 : 54. East Toradja renders the pair *north* and *south* (see also 11 : 31) by an idiomatic phrase, lit. 'the beams of heaven on-either-side', i.e. the northern and southern orbit of the sun, then the northern and the southern hemisphere. South Toradja has here, 'the north (etym. inland), the head of the river, and the south (etym. seaward), the estuary of the water/river', using a double designation, so to say. Where 'north-south', or the phrase as a whole, cause difficulties one may say, 'from east and west and from (all) other directions', or, 'from each and every direction, or, place (on earth)'.

Sit at table, see 5 : 29, or more specifically, in accordance with the context here, 'take their places at the feast' (Jerusalem).

30 ***And behold, some are last who will be first, and some are first who will be last."***

Exegesis: *kai idou* 'and behold', cp. on 1 : 20.

eisin eschatoi hoi esontai prōtoi 'some are (now) last who will be first', viz. when the kingdom comes. The clause refers to the people of v. 29.

eisin prōtoi hoi esontai eschatoi 'some are (now) first who will be last'. The people referred to are the Jews whom Jesus addresses.

Translation: For *last* and *first* see *TH-Mk* on 9 : 35 and 10 : 31.

31 ***At that very hour some Pharisees came, and said to him, "Get away from here, for Herod wants to kill you."***

Exegesis: *en autē tē hōra* 'at that very hour', 'just then', indicating that the events of vv. 31-35 follow immediately upon Jesus' words of vv. 24-30.

tines Pharisaioi 'some Pharisees', cp. on 5 : 17.

exelthe kai poreuou enteuthen 'go away from here and continue your journey'. *enteuthen* (also 4 : 9) goes with both verbs. *exelthe* (aorist) denotes the punctiliar event of Jesus' going away from that region; *poreuou* (present) refers to the continuing of Jesus' journey.

Hērōdēs thelei se apokteinai 'Herod wants to kill you'. *thelei* refers to a purpose, cp. A-G s.v. 2.

Translation: *Get away from here.* The imperative may better be rendered not as a command but as a friendly advice, 'you had better...' (cp. Rieu).

Wants to kill you, or, 'wants/intends to have you killed', since Herod is the initiator, not the direct agent. For *to kill* cp. *N.T.Wb.*/49f.

32 ***And he said to them, "Go and tell that fox, 'Behold, I cast out demons and perform cures today and tomorrow, and the third day I finish my course.***

Exegesis: *poreuthentes eipate tē alōpeki tautē* 'go and tell that fox'. *poreuthentes* has the force of an imperative since it is subordinate to the imperative *eipate*.

alōpēx (also 9 : 58) 'fox', here in a figurative sense, viz. 'crafty, or, cunning man', and referring to Herod.

idou lit. 'behold', serves to focus the attention on what follows.

ekballō daimonia kai iaseis apotelō 'I am casting out demons and performing cures', i.e. I am continuing my work, cp. 7 : 22. *iasis* and *apoteleō* (†).

sēmeron kai aurion 'today and tomorrow', meaning either 'a definite time' (Plummer), or 'a short time' (Klostermann, Grundmann), probably the latter.

kai tē tritē teleioumai 'and on the third day I reach my goal'. *tē tritē* denotes the time that follows immediately upon the time to which *sēmeron kai aurion* refers. The exact meaning of *teleioumai* is difficult to ascertain; it may be (1) middle, and mean 'I complete, or, bring to a close', with the casting out of demons and the healing as object understood; it may be (2) passive and mean either (a) 'I am made perfect' (cp. Plummer), or (b) 'I reach my goal' (cp. A-G s.v. 1, Grundmann), both referring probably to Jesus' death in Jerusalem. Since *plēn* at the beginning of v. 33 (which refers to Jesus' death) suggests a contrast between v. 32 and v. 33 it seems better to interpret *teleioumai* as not referring to Jesus' death. Hence (1) is preferable. *teleioō*, cp. on 2 : 43.

Translation: *Fox.* The rendering used in 9 : 58 often has also the figurative meaning required here (e.g. in Bahasa Indonesia, Balinese, where the jackal plays a treacherous part in fables), but elsewhere another animal must be chosen, e.g. 'civet cat' (Javanese); or one must shift to a simile or to a non-metaphorical rendering, e.g. 'one who deceives' (East Toradja 1933, Tagabili), 'tricky one' (Spanish VP). In the Caribbean it is the spider who often has the role of a trickster, and in several parts of Africa either the spider or the hare. The names of these animals may be considered as acceptable cultural equivalents of 'fox' here.

The subsequent message ('*behold, I...my course*') is quoted speech embedded in Jesus' own quoted speech; Jesus is, of course, the actual speaker of both but the Pharisees are the presumed speakers on the second level, telling Herod what Jesus said. Where the use of a first person in such a position is not acceptable the sentence will have to be recast, by specifying the speaker, e.g. 'go to that fox and bring him this message from me (or, and tell him that I have said): "Behold I..."', cp. 'go and tell...for me, "Listen here, I..."' (Kapauku); or by shifting to the third person, cp. e.g. Tzeltal, using quotative particles indicating that the speaker is recounting what some one else has said, 'he will cast out demons' (quot. part.), 'he will heal the sick' (id.), '...he will finish his work' (id.); or, again, by shifting to indirect discourse, '...and say (or, tell him) that I cast out...'.

Cast out demons, cp. on 9 : 40 and 4 : 33, 35.

Perform cures, or, 'cure/heal people', cp. "heal" in 4 : 23.

Today and tomorrow often can have the expanded meaning required here; if not, one must use an expression for, 'during a few days', 'for some time'.

Similarly *the third day*, or, 'the day after tomorrow' (East Toradja, and cp. on 9 : 22) often can be used in a more expanded sense; if not, one will have to say something like, '(soon) after that time/those days', 'and then', 'and afterwards'.

I finish my course, or, following the interpretation preferred in *Exegesis*, 'I am (or, my work is) ready' (NV, Balinese), 'I (shall) finish my work' (cp. Bahasa Indonesia, Tzeltal, TEV).

33 ***Nevertheless I must go on my way today and tomorrow and the day following; for it cannot be that a prophet should perish away from Jerusalem.'***

Exegesis: *plēn* 'but', cp. on 6 : 24. Here its use suggests that v. 33 is no longer part of the message to Herod.

dei me sēmeron kai aurion kai tē echomenē poreuesthai 'I must continue my journey today and tomorrow and the next day'. *poreuesthai* refers to the journey to Jerusalem. *sēmeron kai aurion kai tē echomenē* refers to the same time as the partly identical partly synonymous words in v. 32.

hē echomenē, scil. *hēmera* 'the immediately following day', cp. A-G s.v. *echō* III 3.

ouk endechetai prophētēn apolesthai exō Ierousalēm 'it is impossible that a prophet should perish outside Jerusalem'.

endechetai (††) 'it is possible', 'it is right', 'it is thinkable'.

Translation: *Nevertheless*, or, 'however', 'yet'. To mark the message to Herod as ended, Rieu has, "yet to you I admit that".

I must, see 2 : 49.

The day following, or, 'the day-after-tomorrow' (Sranan, lit. 'the-other tomorrow'; also several Indonesian languages), in some cases coinciding with the rendering of 'the third day' in v. 32.

Perish, cp. *N.T.Wb.*/27.

Away from, or, "anywhere except in" (TEV), 'if not in' (Bahasa Indonesia 1968), 'in any other place than' (Sranan), focussing on what must happen in Jerusalem, rather than on what cannot happen outside it (a meaning conveyed by some literal renderings).

34 ***O Jerusalem, Jerusalem, killing the prophets and stoning those who are sent to you! How often would I have gathered your children together as a hen gathers her brood under her wings, and you would not!***

Exegesis: *Ierousalēm Ierousalēm* 'Jerusalem, Jerusalem', vocative; the repetition lends emphasis, cp. 10 : 41.

hē apokteinousa tous prophētas 'you that kill the prophets', continuation of the vocative. The present tense denotes a habitual situation, cp. Plummer.

kai lithobolousa tous apestalmenous pros autēn 'and stone those that have been sent to her', also dependent on the article *hē* before *apokteinousa* and continuation of the vocative. *tous apestalmenous* is best understood as referring to the same people as *tous prophētas* (cp. Plummer). *pros autēn* 'to her', refers to Jerusalem in the third person though the clause addresses it in the second person; this is a Semitism. For *apostellō* cp. on 1 : 19.

lithoboleō (†) lit. 'to throw stones', hence 'to kill by throwing stones', 'to pelt to death with stones'.

posakis ēthelēsa episunaxai ta tekna sou 'how often have I longed to gather your children'. *ta tekna sou* does not refer to the inhabitants of Jerusalem only but implicitly to all that belong to the people of God.

posakis (†) 'how often', 'how many times'.

episunagō (also 17 : 37) 'to gather', synonymous with *sunagō*, cp. on 3 : 17.

hon tropon ornis tēn heautēs nossian hupo tas pterugas 'just as a hen (gathers) her brood under her wings', with *episunagei* understood (cp. the parallel Mt. 23 : 37). *hon tropon* lit. 'in the (same) way as', hence 'just as', cp. A-G s.v. 1.

ornis (†), generally, 'bird', here 'hen', 'cock', as a symbol of protecting care.

nossia (††) 'brood' (cp. *nossous* in 2 : 24), here 'chickens'.

kai ouk ēthelēsate 'and you were not willing', 'you would not have it'.

Translation: *O Jerusalem, Jerusalem*, the city standing for its inhabitants, which may lead to, 'O you, people of Jerusalem'. The subsequent phrase (*killing...sent to you*), usually rendered as a relative clause, 'you that (use to) kill...', may also be rendered as a sentence, e.g. 'when(ever) prophets are sent (or, God sends prophets) to you, you kill and stone them'.

I would have gathered, or, 'I have wanted/longed to gather'. Cp. *N.T.Wb.* /25f, DESIRE. *To gather...together*, preferably, "to gather...around (or, to) me" (Goodspeed, Rieu).

Your children, or, 'your people', 'your inhabitants'; or simply 'you', if the city's people have been mentioned already.

Gathers...under her wings, or, 'shelters...under her wings', 'habitually covers its nest with its wings' (one West Nyanja version). Some languages can render the phrase by a specific verb, e.g. Thai (lit. 'to cover', said also of a hen that sits on its eggs), similarly Balinese.

You would not, or filling out the ellipsis, 'you would not let me do so', 'you did not want to be gathered (thus)'.

35 ***Behold, your house is forsaken. And I tell you, you will not see me until you say, 'Blessed is he who comes in the name of the Lord!'"***

Exegesis: *idou* 'behold', cp. on v. 32.

aphietai humin ho oikos humōn 'your house is abandoned to you', i.e. is left to your own care without protection from God. *oikos* may refer to the city of Jerusalem or to the temple, preferably the former.

legō [de] humin 'I tell you', cp. on 3 : 8.

ou mē idēte me heōs [hēxei hote] eipēte 'you will not see me till (the time) will come when you say', as if Jesus had already left Jerusalem for the last time in his earthly life. *hēxei* is impersonal, cp. A-G s.v. 2.

eulogēmenos ho erchomenos en onomati kuriou 'blessed is he who comes in the name of the Lord', a Messianic exclamation and greeting, here referring to the (eschatological) moment when Israel will acknowledge Jesus as its Messiah. *en onomati kuriou* means 'as one who is sent and authorized by the Lord', i.e. by God, cp. *TBT*, 14.78f, 1963.

Translation: *Your house is forsaken*, or, 'God will leave your house to you' (Sranan), 'God no longer concerns himself about your house'. *House*, literally translated, often has too restricted a meaning here; hence, "home" (TEV), 'habitation' (Jerusalem), 'place where you (plur.) live'.

For *blessed* see on 1 : 42, sub (1).

He who comes in the name of, or, 'supported by (lit. having-as-bridge) the name of' (South Toradja), 'with/carrying the name of'. Where such a rather literal rendering would be incomprehensible one will have to describe the meaning of the phrase, e.g. 'the one sent by' (cp. Tzeltal, Shona 1966), 'the one who comes as the Lord's namesake (cp. Guhu-Samane, *TBT*, 16.200, 1965), or, as the representative of the Lord, or, to represent the Lord'.

CHAPTER FOURTEEN

1 ***One sabbath when he went to dine at the house of a ruler who belonged to the Pharisees, they were watching him.***

Exegesis: *kai egeneto* 'and it happened', cp. on 1: 8. The connecting clause begins either with *kai autoi* (cp. RSV), or with *kai idou*, in v. 2 (cp. Rieu), preferably the former.

en tō elthein auton 'after his going', or, 'when he had gone', because of the aorist tense of *elthein*, cp. Bl-D, § 404.2.

eis oikon tinos tōn archontōn [*tōn*] *Pharisaiōn* 'into the house of one of the leaders of the Pharisees' (cp. Rieu, Phillips, NEB), or, 'into the house of one of the rulers who were Pharisees' (cp. RSV, Goodspeed), preferably the former. *archontes* is to be understood in the more general sense of 'leaders', 'leading personalities'. For the Pharisees cp. on 5 : 17.

sabbatō 'on a sabbath', goes with *elthein*.

phagein arton lit. 'in order to eat bread' (final infinitive), i.e. 'to take a meal', 'to dine'.

kai autoi ēsan paratēroumenoi auton 'and they were watching him closely', durative imperfect. *kai* at the beginning of the apodosis is due to Hebrew idiom, cp. A-G s.v. I 2 d. *autoi* refers to those present at the meal as if they had been mentioned already previously. For *paratēreō* cp. on 6 : 7.

Translation: *He went to dine...*, preferably, 'he/Jesus had gone into (or, entered)...to dine (there)'; the attention is on the moment when the guests are arriving.

To dine in the house of, cp. 11 : 37. Since an invitation is implied, one should avoid a rendering suggesting that Jesus went on his own initiative.

A ruler who belonged to the Pharisees, preferably, "one of the leading Pharisees" (Rieu, and see *Exegesis*), 'a prominent/important (lit. most-in-front) Ph.' (Bahasa Indonesia RC), 'one of the notable Pharisees' (cp. Bamiléké), 'one of the big men of the Pharisee group'.

They were watching him. The pronoun refers to the host and his friends. For the verb see 6 : 7; Sranan uses here 'they held him good in the eye'.

2 ***And behold, there was a man before him who had dropsy.***

Exegesis: *kai idou* 'and behold', cp. on 1 : 20.

anthrōpos tis ēn...emprosthen autou 'there was a man in front of him'. *tis* has the force of an indefinite article, cp. A-G s.v. 2 a α.

hudrōpikos (††) 'suffering from dropsy' (apposition to *anthrōpos*), i.e. from effusion of watery fluid into the tissues or cavities of the body, cp. *IDB* I, 872.

Translation: *Who had dropsy.* The name of some kind of oedema, such as beri-beri, can often be used (as in some Indonesian languages, Kapauku), or of a rheumatic ailment causing swellings (Zarma); or a descriptive phrase, e.g. 'swollen all over' (Tzeltal), 'whose whole body was swollen' (East Toradja), "whose legs and arms were swollen" (TEV, similarly in Kituba).

3 ***And Jesus spoke to the lawyers and Pharisees, saying, "Is it lawful to heal on the sabbath, or not?"***

Exegesis: *apokritheis* 'answering', cp. on 1 : 60.

pros tous nomikous kai Pharisaious 'to the experts in the law and the Pharisees', cp. on 7 : 30.

exestin tō sabbatō therapeusai ē ou 'is it permitted to heal on the sabbath or not?' For *exestin* cp. on 6 : 2, for *therapeuō* cp. on 4 : 23. The article *tō* with *sabbatō* is generic.

Translation: *Spoke to,* cp. the note on "answered" in 3 : 16.

For *lawyers* see 7 : 30; for *is it lawful* see 6 : 2.

Or not, or filling out the ellipsis, 'or is it not allowed/fitting' (Toba Batak, Sranan), 'or is it forbidden'.

4 ***But they were silent. Then he took him and healed him, and let him go.***

Exegesis: *hoi de hēsuchasan* 'but they were silent', i.e. "they made no answer" (Goodspeed).

hēsuchazō (also 23 : 56) 'to be quiet', 'to rest', 'to be silent'.

kai epilabomenos iasato auton 'and taking him he cured him'. *epilabomenos* describes an act which precedes the healing. For *epilambanomai* cp. on 9 : 47 and A-G s.v. 1.

kai apelusen 'and he dismissed him', cp. on 2 : 29.

Translation: *They were silent,* or, 'they kept silent' (NV, Jerusalem), 'they would not say a word'.

He took him. The pronouns may have to be specified, e.g. 'Jesus', and/or, 'the man', 'the sick man' (Jerusalem, Indonesian languages), 'the dropsical one' (cp. Sundanese).

And let him go, or, 'and he dismissed him', 'after that he gave him permission to go away, or, to go home'.

5 ***And he said to them, "Which of you, having an ass or an ox that has fallen into a well, will not immediately pull him out on a sabbath day?"***

Exegesis: *kai pros autous eipen* 'and to them he said'. *pros autous* is emphatic by position.

tinos humōn etc. lit. 'of whom of you will the son or ox fall into a well, and will he not immediately pull him out on the day of the sabbath?', interrogative clause consisting of two co-ordinate clauses of which the former is not interrogative semantically, but serves to describe a situation to which the second clause refers. This second clause contains the question proper. RSV follows the text read by Nestle, which has *onos* 'ass' instead of *huios*.

phrear (†) 'well', dug for the purpose of supplying water.

anaspaō (†) 'to draw up', 'to pull up'.

Translation: Recasting the sentence structure one may say, e.g. 'if any of you had a son or an ox that (or, if your son or your ox) happened to fall into a well, would you not (or, would you hesitate to) pull him out...'; or as a statement, 'if..., you would certainly pull him out'; or in two sentences, e.g. 'suppose any one of you..., what will he do? He immediately pulls...'. Cp. also the constructions in 11 : 5-7 and 11.

For *ass* (RSV) and *ox* see 13 : 15; for 'son' (*Exegesis*) cp. on 1 : 13.

Well, cp. *N.T.Wb.*/72, WATER. Any common term for 'well', 'pond', 'fountain', 'cistern' is acceptable here, provided that falling into it implies the danger of drowning. In Toba Batak 'to fall into a well' is expressed by a passive verbal derivation of 'well/moat'.

Pull him out, or, 'pull him up', 'lift him up from in that hole' (Trukese, Ponape).

On a sabbath day, or, 'even though it were on sabbath' (e.g. in Shona 1966, Sundanese), 'even if you must do so on a sabbath' (Sranan); cp. also "...fall in a well on a Sabbath, would you not pull him out at once on the Sabbath itself" (TEV).

6 ***And they could not reply to this.***

Exegesis: *kai ouk ischusan antapokrithēnai pros tauta* 'and they were not able to make a reply to this'. For *ischuō* cp. on 6 : 48.

antapokrinomai (†) 'to make a reply', here of making a reply to a question in an argument.

Translation: *Could not reply to this*, or, 'could not answer (or, meet) this question', 'had nothing to say against this, or, to refute this (viz. the criticism implied in Jesus' question)'; or again, emphasizing their inability, 'could not answer, not a single word (lit. one-movement-of-the-lips not)' (East Toradja).

7 ***Now he told a parable to those who were invited, when he marked how they chose the places of honour, saying to them,***

Exegesis: *elegen de pros tous keklēmenous parabolēn* 'then he told those who had been invited a parable'. Presumably the incident recorded in vv. 1-6 took place before the guests took their places. For *kaleō* meaning 'to invite' cp. A-G s.v. 1 b. For *parabolē* cp. on 4 : 23. Strictly speaking Jesus does not tell a parable-story but gives an injunction or advice (cp. Phillips, "a little word of advice"). This advice is called a parable because it interprets the present situation metaphorically.

epechōn pōs tas prōtoklisias exelegonto 'noticing how they were selecting the places of honour for themselves'. *pōs* refers more to the fact that, than the way in which they selected the places. For *eklegomai* cp. on 6 : 13. The imperfect tense is both durative and conative.

epechō (†) 'to fix one's attention', 'to notice', 'to mark'.

prōtoklisia (also 20 : 46) lit. 'first place at a meal', 'place of honour'. To what place the word actually refers is not sure, cp. Plummer.

legōn pros autous 'saying to them', taking up the beginning of the clause.

Translation: Since the "when"-clause is the reason for and base of Jesus' "parable", it is often better to give it the initial position, e.g. 'now he/Jesus marked how those who were invited chose... Therefore he told them...'.

He told a parable. The use of "parable" is to show that the subsequent injunctions are not mere rules for politeness (vv. 7-11) and hospitality (12-14) but means to teach true humility and unselfishness. To bring this out one may have to say, 'taking this (referring to what Jesus marked) as parable/illustration/comparison, he told them', 'starting from this (example) he gave them this lesson/teaching'. For *parable* see 5 : 36.

Those who were invited, in some languages simply, 'the guests'. The verb is often rendered, 'to call' (e.g. Zarma, West Nyanja), where necessary specified, e.g. 'to call to come at table' (Sranan), 'to come to eat' (Tzeltal, which in v. 8 uses 'to call to see'—viz. the wedding); elsewhere, 'to ask to come (to eat, etc.)'.

Marked, or, 'noticed', "observed" (Rieu), 'saw'.

Chose, or, "picked out" (Goodspeed), 'sought to sit in' (Sranan); and see 6 : 13.

The places of honour, similarly e.g. in Zarma, East and West Nyanja, Lomwe; also in South Toradja (where it refers to places on a mat on the platform between the posts of the rice-barn, less important guests sitting on mats on the ground); also rendered as, 'seats occupied by senior elders' (Shona 1966), 'places of the great' (Yao). Locative qualifications occur also, cp. e.g. 'upper seats' (Kapauku, but in v. 8 'good place'), 'first seats at the table', i.e. front row (Tzeltal), 'before table' (Ponape), 'places at the head of the table', i.e. where the ritual speaker starts to speak (Timorese, but 'place of the famous people' in v. 8). Another possible way to express the concept is, 'where one is served first'.

Saying to them, or, 'and he said to them', 'as follows', can sometimes better be omitted.

8 ***"When you are invited by any one to a marriage feast, do not sit down in a place of honour, lest a more eminent man than you be invited by him;*** 9 ***and he who invited you both will come and say to you, 'Give place to this man,' and then you will begin with shame to take the lowest place.***

Exegesis: *hotan klēthēs hupo tinos eis gamous* 'when you are invited by somebody to a banquet'. For *gamos* cp. on 12 : 36. The rendering 'wedding-party' is also possible though less probable.

mē kataklithēs eis tēn prōtoklisian 'do not recline at the place of honour', or, somewhat simplified, 'do not take the place of honour'. For *kataklinomai* cp. on 7 : 36.

mēpote entimoteros sou ē keklēmenos hup' autou (v. 9) *kai elthōn ho se kai auton kalesas erei soi* 'lest (i.e. in order to avoid that) a more respected person than you be invited by him, and he who has invited (both) you and him, will come and say to you'. Both clauses are modified by *mēpote.* The change from the usual subjunctive (*ē keklēmenos*) to the indicative (*erei*) does not constitute a change of meaning, cp. Bl-D, § 370.2. The first clause describes a situation which, if it occurs, will cause the host to remove one from the place of honour. *ho se kai auton kalesas* is emphatic and stresses the fact that both have been invited by him. For *entimos* cp. on 7 : 2. For *mēpote* cp. on 4 : 11.

dos toutō topon 'give place (i.e. your place) to this man', cp. A-G s.v. *topos* 1 e.

kai tote arxē meta aischunēs ton eschaton topon katechein 'and then you will begin with disgrace to occupy the lowest place', no longer modified by *mēpote. arxē* denotes here the fact that he will find himself in a new and unexpected situation, cp. on 4 : 21. *ton eschaton topon* 'the lowest place', i.e. the least honourable place, probably the place farthest away from the host.

aischunē (†) 'shame', 'disgrace', 'ignominy', i.e. not a feeling one has but an experience which comes to someone, cp. A-G s.v. 2, and Rieu, "to your shame".

katechō here 'to occupy', cp. A-G s.v. 1 c.

Translation: *When you are invited by any one,* or, 'when someone has invited you' (cp. e.g. Tzeltal, Kapauku, Kituba), or focussing on the result, i.e. the being a guest, 'when you come as a guest'.

Marriage feast, preferably, 'banquet', see 12 : 36.

Sit down in a place of honour, or more generically, 'take/occupy the place of honour', the exact attitude not being relevant.

Lest a more eminent man. . . be invited by him; (9) *and he who invited you both will come. . .*, or, to bring out that "lest" semantically goes with the second clause only, 'lest, if a man. . . has been invited by him, (9) he. . . will come. . .'. Usually the sentence is better divided into two, e.g. 'there might be somebody called. . . (9) Then the one who called you both would come. . .' (Kapauku, similarly Kituba, TEV), cp. also 'someone. . . might be caused to sit there. (9) The one who called you to eat, and him, "make a place for this other to sit down", might say to you. Thus. . .' (Tzeltal). *More eminent,* or, 'higher' (Sranan), 'who (is) above you' (East Toradja), 'surpassing you in importance/honour' (Kituba). *Invited by him,* or otherwise expressed, 'amongst his/the guests', or simply, 'present', because his being invited is clear from what follows. *He who invited you both* (or, "him as well as you", Rieu); or again, 'his host and yours'. *Come,* or, 'come towards (or, approach) you', or, 'enter (the house/room)', implying that the host makes his entrance after those he invited have taken their places.

Give place to this man, or, 'give this/your seat to this man' (cp. NEB, Balinese), 'you move on, this place (lit. here) will be used by this man' (Javanese). The command may have to be softened, cp. e.g. "I am afraid you must" (Phillips, similarly in Balinese).

And then, or, 'in that case', 'consequently' (e.g. in Toba Batak), introducing the expected result.

You will begin...to take, or, "you...would find yourself in occupation of" (Rieu), cp. 13 : 25.

With shame, or, changing the phrase into a clause in different position, 'which will cause you to be/feel ashamed', or, 'and so you will be put to shame'. For the term cp. 13 : 17.

Lowest place contrasts with "place of honour" in v. 7. Some locative renderings used are, 'farthest place' (viz. farthest from the principal guests), 'at the far end', 'at the lower end (also called, the leg) of the table' (Timorese), 'place at the very back, or, towards the side end' (West Nyanja versions), 'last seat' (Tzeltal), 'downstream side' (Balinese); functional renderings are "poorest/humblest place" (Goodspeed, Phillips), 'where the ordinary people sit' (Shona 1966, similarly Ponape), 'place that surpasses in-not-having honour' (Kituba).

10 ***But when you are invited, go and sit in the lowest place, so that when your host comes he may say to you, 'Friend, go up higher'; then you will be honoured in the presence of all who sit at table with you.***

Exegesis: *poreutheis anapese eis ton eschaton topon* 'go and lie down on the lowest place', or 'take the lowest place'. For *anapiptō* cp. on 11 : 37. It is equivalent to *kataklinomai* (v. 8).

hina...erei soi 'so that...he may say to you', indicating the intended result.

phile, prosanabēthi anōteron 'friend, come up higher', i.e. probably 'approach to where the host is sitting', cp. Plummer. *prosanabainō* (††).

tote estai soi doxa 'then you will have honour', i.e. 'you will be honoured', contrasts with the last clause of v. 9, *tote arxē* etc. 'then you will begin...'. For *doxa* cp. on 2 : 9 and A-G s.v. 3.

enōpion pantōn tōn sunanakeimenōn soi 'in the presence of all who sit with you'. For *enōpion* cp. on 1 : 15, and for *sunanakeimai* cp. *TH-Mk* on 2 : 15.

Translation: *But*, or a stronger adversative, "no" (Rieu, NEB), 'instead' (cp. TEV and several others).

So that...he may say to you, or non-subordinated, 'if you do that your host will come (in) and say to you', or, 'then your host will say to you, when he comes (in)'.

Go up higher, or, 'go to (or, go and sit in) a higher place', 'move closer to the highest place', the opposite of "the lowest place" in v. 9.

You will be honoured (or, "this will bring you honor", TEV) *in the presence of all,* or with some shifts, 'the eyes of all... will see that you are considered important' (cp. Tzeltal), 'you certainly will get a good name among all' (Timorese, similarly Trukese), 'you will see (i.e. receive/have) honour...' (one West Nyanja version). For the verb cp. *TH-Mk* on 6:4; 7:6.

All who sit at table with you, cp. 7 : 49.

11 ***For every one who exalts himself will be humbled, and he who humbles himself will be exalted."***

Exegesis: *hoti pas ho hupsōn heauton tapeinōthēsetai* 'for everyone who exalts himself will be humbled'. For *hupsoō* cp. on 1 : 52. For *tapeinoō* cp. on 3 : 5; here it is used in a figurative sense. The agent of *tapeinōthēsetai* is God, since the saying and the preceding parable are to be understood as referring to a religious attitude.

ho tapeinōn heauton hupsōthēsetai 'he who humbles himself will be exalted'. For the agent of *hupsōthēsetai* see above.

Translation: One may have to shift to an 'if'-clause (cp. 9 : 24), and/or to an active form, 'God will humble him, ...exalt him' (cp. 6 : 37).

Exalts himself... humbles himself, or, 'tries to reach a high position (or, makes his own power great, Kekchi)..., accepts (or, is ready to be in) a low position'. For *to exalt* see 1 : 52; for *to humble* see *N.T.Wb.*/45f, category (2).

12 ***He said also to the man who had invited him, "When you give a dinner or a banquet, do not invite your friends or your brothers or your kinsmen or rich neighbours, lest they also invite you in return, and you be repaid.***

Exegesis: *elegen de kai* 'and he said also', introducing an additional statement.

tō keklēkoti auton 'to the man who had invited him', 'to his host'.

hotan poiēs ariston ē deipnon 'when you give a midday meal or an evening meal'. For *poieō* in this connexion cp. A-G s.v. 1 b ζ. For *ariston* cp. on 11 : 38.

deipnon 'meal', 'dinner', 'evening meal'.

mē phōnei tous philous sou 'do not invite your friends'. *phōneō* is here synonymous with *kaleō* (cp. vv. 7ff).

mēde tous suggeneis sou 'nor your relatives', cp. on 1 : 36, 58.

mēde geitonas plousious 'nor rich neighbours', without article and possessive genitive *sou* following. This suggests the absence of personal relationships.

geitōn 'neighbour' in a general sense.

mēpote kai autoi antikalesōsin se 'lest they on their part invite you in return'. For *mēpote* cp. on 4 : 11. *kai autoi* lit. 'they also', means 'they on their part'. *antikaleō* (††).

kai genētai antapodoma soi 'and you get/receive repayment', still modified by *mēpote.*

antapodoma (†) 'repayment', 'reward'.

Translation: *Give a dinner or a banquet*, or, 'give/arrange a large meal (or, a feast) at noon or evening' (see *Exegesis*); and cp. *N.T.Wb.*/53, MEALS.

Friends...brothers...kinsmen...neighbours are masculine, because only men would normally attend such a party, but this is not of special relevance in the context; hence, where the terms are neutral as to sex, specification may be unnecessary or even undesirable (cp. also the remark on "friends" in 15 : 9). *Brothers* (cp. 6 : 14) may refer to bodily brothers or close relatives, and *kinsmen* (cp. "kinsfolk" in 1 : 58) to less close relatives. For *neighbour* see 1 : 58.

The two clauses governed by *lest* are on the same level, the second is consecutive; for the rest same construction as in v. 8, cp. e.g. 'it might happen that they...invite you and you are consequently repaid' (Willibrord).

Also (or, 'on their part') and *in return* serve here to emphasize the reversal of the roles of host and guest.

You be repaid, or, 'you get your payment' (Sranan); or changing the subject, 'they give you something in exchange' (Tzeltal), 'they can do-to you the same (lit. kind one)' (Kituba), 'they give-what-is-due to-you' (Ponape). Available renderings should be carefully handled, because the expression in question may also occur in the unfavourable sense of 'to revenge' (e.g. in Shona, Kapauku, Bahasa Indonesia).

13 ***But when you give a feast, invite the poor, the maimed, the lame, the blind,*** 14 ***and you will be blessed, because they cannot repay you. You will be repaid at the resurrection of the just."***

Exegesis: *all' hotan dochēn poiēs* 'but when you give an entertainment'. For *dochē* cp. on 5 : 29. Here it takes up in a general way *ariston* and *deipnon* (v. 12).

kalei ptōchous, anapeirous, chōlous, tuphlous 'invite the poor, the cripple, the lame, the blind', not intended as an exhaustive enumeration but as illustration of explicit or implicit social handicaps. For *ptōchos* cp. on 4 : 18. For *chōlos* cp. on 7 : 22.

anapeiros (also v. 21) 'crippled', 'cripple' (subst.).

(V. 14) *kai makarios esē* 'and you will be blessed', scil. if you do that. For *makarios* cp. on 1 : 45.

hoti ouk echousin antapodounai soi 'because they have not (the means) to repay you', i.e. 'they cannot repay you', cp. A-G s.v. *echō* 6 a.

antapodidōmi (†) 'to repay', 'to reward' (cp. *antapodoma* in v. 12).

antapodothēsetai gar soi lit. 'for it will be repaid to you', i.e. 'for you will be repaid'. The agent is God.

en tē anastasei tōn dikaiōn 'at the resurrection of the righteous, or, the just'. For *anastasis* cp. on 2 : 34.

Translation: For *the blind* see 4 : 18.

Maimed, or, 'mutilated', covering an area of reference in which *lame* (see 7 : 22) is included; also rendered, 'having a bodily defect' (Javanese), 'deformed' (South Toradja), 'missing-a-limb' (Balinese).

(V. 14) *You will be blessed,* or, 'happy', see 1 : 45.

Because they cannot repay you, or, 'they cannot do-to you things that you have done-to them' (Kituba), expresses the reason of the preceding statement in negative terms, the next clause does the same in positive terms: what the poor etc. are not able to do now God will do in a more splendid way at the resurrection; hence, the two clauses are sometimes more closely connected, e.g. 'because they cannot repay you, but you will be repaid (cp. NEB, Phillips, Malay, Toba Batak), or, but God will repay you'. Since at its third occurrence *to repay* has another nuance of meaning, pointing beyond the human sphere, a different rendering may be required.

At the resurrection of the just, or, 'when the righteous arise from death' (Thai 1967), 'when those people who righteous they-will live-up (i.e. return to life)' (Trukese, Ponape). For *resurrection* see Nida, *BT*, 230f; *N.T.Wb.* /60, RAISE, and cp. *TH-Mk* on 6 : 14. *The just,* or, 'the just/righteous ones', or, sometimes, 'the righteous dead ones', 'the dead ones that have been righteous'; and cp. the references on "righteous" in 1 : 6.

15 ***When one of those who sat at table with him heard this, he said to him, "Blessed is he who shall eat bread in the kingdom of God!"***

Exegesis: *tis tōn sunanakeimenōn,* see v. 10.

makarios hostis phagetai arton en tē basileia tou theou 'blessed (is the man) who will eat bread in the kingdom of God'. For *makarios* cp. on 1 : 45. Here it takes up *makarios* in v. 14, to which *tauta* refers. For *phagein arton* cp. on v. 1. *phagetai* is future tense, cp. Bl-D, § 74.2. There appears to be no reason to understand the phrase in a different sense from v. 1. For *en tē basileia tou theou* cp. on 13 : 28f.

Translation: *To eat bread,* or, 'to have the meal', 'to be entertained(-as-guest)' (Bahasa Indonesia, Balinese).

16 ***But he said to him, "A man once gave a great banquet, and invited many;*** 17 ***and at the time for the banquet he sent his servant to say to those who had been invited, 'Come; for all is now ready.'***

Exegesis: *anthrōpos tis epoiei deipnon mega* 'a man was giving a big dinner'. The imperfect tense of *epoiei,* as contrasted with the aorists *ekalesen* and *apesteilen* (v. 17), is durative and refers to both the preparations and the actual giving of the dinner. For *poiein deipnon* cp. on v. 12.

kai ekalesen pollous 'and invited many people'. The clause refers to a first invitation, to be followed by a second call when the appointed time had come. It is possible to render *ekalesen* 'he had invited' as expressing an act prior to that denoted by *apesteilen* in v. 17.

(V. 17) *kai apesteilen ton doulon autou...eipein tois keklēmenois* 'and he sent his servant...to say to those who had been invited'. For *apostellō* with following infinitive cp. on 1 : 19.

tē hōra tou deipnou 'at the time of the dinner', cp. A-G s.v. *hōra* 3.

erchesthe, hoti ēdē hetoima estin 'come, for things are (or, it is) ready now'. *ēdē* is used without emphasis. The subject of *hetoima estin* is not stated but refers to the preparations for the dinner.

Translation: *He*, i.e., Jesus.

Gave a great banquet, or, since the banquet is not yet begun, 'made-preparations-for a big meal' (East Toradja), 'was-to entertain on-a-big-scale' (Balinese).

Invited many, i.e. 'many people/guests'. Toba Batak possesses a verb implying that those invited have been requested to remain at home on the day of the feast awaiting the announcement that everything is ready, which fits this context admirably.

(V. 17) *At the time for the banquet*, or, 'shortly-before the banquet' (Bahasa Indonesia 1968), 'when the feast was about to begin', 'at the time they were-to sit-down' (Balinese).

Sent his servant to say to those who..., or, 'sent his servant to those who...with the message'. In honorific languages it may be the status of the master, who causes the message to be sent, rather than that of the servant, who actually conveys it, that is decisive for the level of language to be chosen. The former probably requires a polite form of address, as would be used towards equals one wishes to honour, whereas in the latter case the servant would address his master's guests as his superiors, using reverent honorifics. *To those who*... The plural is basically distributive, 'to say to each of those who...'; cp. also Goodspeed's less explicit "he sent around...to say to those who...".

Come. A form of request may be preferable, e.g. "please come" (NEB, similarly Bahasa Indonesia RC), 'be so kind as to come along'.

All is now ready, or, 'everything is just waiting' (Shona 1966), 'the food has now been prepared' (Shona 1963); in Yao the idiom is, 'things are matured'.

18 ***But they all alike began to make excuses. The first said to him, 'I have bought a field, and I must go out and see it; I pray you, have me excused.'***

Exegesis: *kai ērxanto apo mias pantes paraiteisthai* 'and they all with one accord began to excuse themselves'. *apo mias* may mean 'at once', or, with *gnōmē* 'mind' understood, 'with one mind', 'with one accord', 'unanimously'.

paraiteomai lit. 'to beg off', here with reference to an invitation, 'to excuse oneself', 'to make excuses'.

ho prōtos eipen autō 'the first one (to whom the servant came) said to him', i.e. to the servant, but through him implicitly to the host as well.

agron ēgorasa 'I have bought a piece of land'. For *agros* cp. *TH-Mk* on 5 : 14. For *agorazō* cp. on 9 : 13.

echō anagkēn exelthōn idein auton 'I must go out (of town) and look at it'.

anagkē (also 21 : 23 but with a different meaning) 'necessity', 'compulsion', here with *echō* and following infinitive, 'I must'.

erōtō se, eche me parētēmenon 'I beg you, consider me as having excused myself, or, as excused', i.e. 'accept my excuses'. What he begs, is expressed in an asyndetic clause in the imperative, cp. Bl-D, § 471.1. For *echō* meaning 'to consider', cp. A-G s.v. I 5.

Translation: *They all* is basically distributive, again.

Alike, or, 'as with one accord', 'with a sameness (i.e. as though by agreement)' (Kapauku); they act in the same way, but not together at the same time, as some renderings seem to suggest.

To make excuses, i.e. to produce reasons why they should be released from their promise to come. Renderings may be built on the formula for excusing oneself used at the end of the verse; or the language may possess an idiomatic phrase, e.g. 'to seek what words to cover-up with' (Tzeltal); or one may describe the concept, e.g. 'to say they could not come/had no time', 'to ask a way to refrain-from arriving at that feast' (Kituba); or, somewhat pejoratively, 'to seek pretexts/subterfuges' (e.g. in Toba Batak). Kapauku uses a rather generic expression, 'to say every sort of thing (lit. this word that word)', leaving its specification to what follows.

The first said to him, or, 'the one visited first said to the servant' (Balinese). The subsequent speech may be envisaged as addressed simply to the servant (hence non-honorifics, e.g. in Balinese), or to the master, though *via* the servant (hence honorific terms, e.g. in Javanese). To indicate the latter choice Willibrord has, 'the first told him to say'.

Field, probably a piece of arable land.

I pray you, (or, Please) *have me excused.* Some expressions used address the master, e.g. 'I ask your forgiveness' (Javanese), 'I ask (for) myself (viz. to be released from the obligation), please' (Thai 1967); others ask the servant's mediation with his master, e.g. 'ask-for(-me) pardon' (Balinese), 'please (lit. ruler you!), intercede-for me' (Toba Batak), 'I beg your master: may he not be offended (lit. small his-heart)' (East Toradja 1933), 'may he (i.e. the master) forgive me that I do not go' (Tzeltal), 'I ask you to go and speak for me' (Shona 1963); still others seem rather to apologize to the servant himself, e.g. 'I beg you, don't take me for bad (i.e. don't take it ill)' (Sranan), 'let me be, I ask you' (Kapauku).

19 ***And another said, 'I have bought five yoke of oxen, and I go to examine them; I pray you, have me excused.'***

Exegesis: *kai heteros eipen* 'and another (of those invited) said'.

zeugē boōn ēgorasa pente 'I have bought five yoke of oxen'. For *zeugos* cp. on 2 : 24.

poreuomai dokimasai auta 'I am on my way to examine them'. The servant finds the man when he is about to go. For *dokimazō* cp. on 12 : 56.

Translation: *Another,* not necessarily 'the next one', but referring to a second example out of the many mentioned previously.

Five yoke of oxen, or, 'five pairs (or, five twos, Lomwe) of oxen', 'ten farming bulls' (Zarma); where the use of oxen as draught-animals is unknown it may be possible to say, 'ten cows' (Kapauku, Trukese). For *ox* see 13 : 15.

Examine, or, 'inspect', 'try (out)' (cp. NEB, Jerusalem, Kapauku, several Indonesian languages).

20 ***And another said, 'I have married a wife, and therefore I cannot come.'***

Exegesis: *gunaika egēma* 'I have married a wife', i.e. "I have just got married" (NEB).

gameō 'to marry', with a man as subject.

kai dia touto ou dunamai elthein 'and therefore I cannot come'.

Translation: *Another,* or, 'yet another', i.e. a third example.

I have married a wife, or, 'I have married', since 'a wife' is unduly redundant here. Elsewhere 'to marry' may be rendered e.g. by, 'to take a spouse' (e.g. in Kapauku, which, when a woman is the subject, uses, 'to go-with a spouse'), 'to take a woman' (Toba Batak, which says of the woman, 'to go-home', or, 'to go-home to the village', viz. of her husband); or by an idiomatic phrase, e.g. in Maya (lit. 'to end one's road', viz. as bachelor), or in South Toradja (lit. 'to establish-a-fireplace'). Cp. also *N.T.Wb.*/52; *TH-Mk* on 10 : 12.

21 ***So the servant came and reported this to his master. Then the householder in anger said to his servant, 'Go out quickly to the streets and lanes of the city, and bring in the poor and maimed and blind and lame.'***

Exegesis: *paragenomenos* lit. 'after coming', i.e. 'when he came', here in the sense of, 'when he came back to his master'. For *paraginomai* cp. on 7 : 4.

ho doulos apēggeilen tō kuriō autou tauta 'the servant reported this to his master'. For *apaggellō* cp. on 7 : 18. *tauta* refers to vv. 18-20 and presumably to similar answers from the other invited people.

tote orgistheis ho oikodespotēs eipen 'then the master of the house became angry and said'. *tote* means 'when he heard that'. For *oikodespotēs* cp. on 12 : 39.

orgizomai (also 15 : 28) 'to be angry', in both places ingressive aorist, 'became angry'.

exelthe tacheōs eis tas plateias kai rumas tēs poleōs 'go out quickly into the streets and alleys of the town'. Note that the article *tas* goes with both *plateias* and *rumas*. Hence also the genitive *tēs poleōs* refers to both preceding substantives. For *plateia* cp. on 10 : 10. *tacheōs* also 16 : 6.

rumē (†) 'narrow street', 'lane', 'alley'.

kai tous ptōchous kai anapeirous kai tuphlous kai chōlous eisagage hōde 'and bring in here the poor, the cripple, the blind and the lame'. Note that the article *tous* goes with all four substantives. This suggests that they are to be considered as one group. For the poor, etc. cp. on v. 13.

Translation: For *master*, and for "sir" in v. 22, cp. the note on "Lord" in 1 : 6, sub (a). For *householder* see 12 : 39; in this context 'host' is also possible.

In anger, or, 'becoming angry', 'became angry and'; cp. *N.T.Wb.*/9f and *TH-Mk* on 3 : 5.

Quickly is often rendered by a verb, e.g. 'do-quick/make-haste' (Balinese), 'hurry', 'run along'.

To the streets and lanes of the city, or, 'to market places and streets (or, to streets and slums, or, to streets and narrow-passages) of the town' (Kituba, Sranan, Shona 1966). In non-urbanized areas one may have to use, 'into the village, on the roads big and small' (East Toradja), 'to wide and narrow places/passages between the houses (or, past all the houses and hovels) of this city/settlement'. For *street* see 10 : 10.

22 ***And the servant said, 'Sir, what you commanded has been done, and still there is room.'***

Exegesis: *kurie, gegonen ho epetaxas* 'master, what you ordered has been done'. This assumes tacitly that there is an interval in time between v. 21 and v. 22 in which the master's orders are carried out. For *kurios* cp. on 1 : 6; for *epitassō* cp. on 4 : 36.

kai eti topos estin 'and still there is room', scil. for more people. For *topos* cp. on v. 9.

Translation: When one does not clearly indicate an interval between v. 21 and v. 22 the latter may easily be taken to mean that the servant had already gone out to the streets, anticipating his master's orders, an impression actually made in some versions. To avoid this one may have to use a transitional word or phrase, e.g. 'when (he was) back' (Bahasa Indonesia RC), 'after a while' (Shona 1966, similarly Kituba, TEV), 'after that' (Balinese); or to make the command more specific, as in 'the things you have sent me to do I have done' (Sranan); or, again, to change the sentence structure, cp. "reporting to him that these orders had been carried out, 'Sir', said the servant, 'there is still room for more'" (Rieu).

And still there is room, or, "and there are still empty places" (Phillips), 'but the room/house is not yet full'.

23 ***And the master said to the servant, 'Go out to the highways and hedges, and compel people to come in, that my house may be filled.***

Exegesis: *eis tas hodous kai phragmous* 'to the roads and hedgerows'. The article *tas* goes with both *hodous* and *phragmous* although they differ in gender. *hodous* denotes here roads outside the town, or, highways.

phragmos (†) 'fence', 'hedge', here parallel with *hodos* and probably referring to hedgerows in the country where vagabonds and beggars are to be found.

anagkason eiselthein 'make (people) come in'.

anagkazō (†) 'to compel', 'to force', here 'to urge strongly'.
hina gemisthē mou ho oikos 'that my house may be filled'.
gemizō (†) 'to fill', here in the passive 'to become full'.

Translation: *Go out,* i.e. not only out of the house (as in v. 21), but also out of the city.

To the highways and hedges. The nouns may require different prepositions, cp. e.g. 'on the roads and among (or, along) the hedges' (cp. Goodspeed, Javanese). The phrase refers to roads and lanes or places outside the towns; hence, 'small trails and cornfields' (Tzeltal), 'roads and bushes' (Shona 1966), 'paths and bushtrails' (Zarma), '(built) roads and gardenpaths' (one West Nyanja version), 'small roads and shacks (in the fields)' (Toba Batak). In some cases, e.g. East Toradja, the rendering coincides with that of "the streets and lanes", only the absence of the phrase 'of the town/settlement' indicating that the reference is to the countryside.

Compel people to come in, viz. those found in the countryside; hence, 'urge (or, demand strongly) the people there to come in (or, into my house)' (cp. Balinese).

That my house may be filled. One may render the conjunction by 'so that' (resultative), or, 'in order that' (final).

24 ***For I tell you, none of those men who were invited shall taste my banquet.'"***

Exegesis: *legō gar humin* 'for I tell you', cp. on 3 : 8. The subject of *legō* is either the master of the house, or, Jesus, preferably the former.

oudeis tōn andrōn ekeinōn tōn keklēmenōn 'none of those men who were (originally) invited'. *tōn keklēmenōn* defines the reference of the demonstrative pronoun *ekeinōn*.

geusetai mou tou deipnou 'shall taste my dinner', i.e. 'shall eat of my dinner'. For possessive *mou* cp. on v. 23. *geuomai* also 9 : 27.

Translation: *Those men who were invited,* or, specifying which group is intended, 'the men who were first invited' (e.g. in Willibrord, Javanese), 'the men I invited previously'.

Taste my banquet, or, 'eat/partake of the banquet/feast I give, or, the meal I (caused to be) prepared'.

25 ***Now great multitudes accompanied him; and he turned and said to them,***

Exegesis: *suneporeuonto de autō ochloi polloi* 'great crowds were travelling with him'. The clause presumes that Jesus had resumed his travelling after the meal at the house of the Pharisee.

kai strapheis eipen pros autous 'and turning to them he said to them'. For *strapheis* cp. on 7 : 9. *pros autous* goes with *strapheis* and *eipen*.

Translation: The implied reference to Jesus' journey, last mentioned in

13 : 22, is made explicit in some versions, e.g. 'many people followed Him on his journey' (East Toradja), 'then Jesus went on, accompanied by a big crowd' (Javanese).

For *turned and said to* cp. on 7 : 9.

26 ***"If any one comes to me and does not hate his own father and mother and wife and children and brothers and sisters, yes, and even his own life, he cannot be my disciple.***

Exegesis: *ei tis erchetai pros me kai ou misei ton patera heautou* 'if any one comes to me (viz. to become a disciple) and does not hate his own father'. Syntactically the two clauses are co-ordinate but semantically the latter is more important, since it stipulates the condition which he who wants to become a disciple must meet. For *miseō* cp. on 1 : 71. Here it refers to renouncing natural affections for the sake of Jesus Christ, cp. 9 : 23f; 16 : 13. *heautou* goes with all the subsequent nouns as well.

eti te kai tēn psuchēn heautou 'and even his own life also'. For *psuchē* cp. on 9 : 24.

ou dunatai einai mou mathētēs 'he cannot be my disciple'.

Translation: One may have to adjust the first part of the clause, e.g. 'if a man who comes to me does not hate...', or to transpose the last, e.g. 'when a man comes to me, he cannot (or, a man who comes to me cannot) become my disciple, if he does not hate...'.

Hate. In several languages the term commonly used for 'to hate' (cp. 1 : 71) implies emotions of aversion and malice that make its use unacceptable in this context; hence renderings as 'put out of his heart (i.e. disregard)' (Tzeltal), 'keep-away-from' (West Sumbanese), 'turn his back on' (Sranan, Shona 1966, East Toradja 1933), 'be-indifferent-toward' (Javanese), 'reject' (Zarma); or, 'love less...than (he loves) me'.

His own. Often the simple possessive will do.

The following enumeration may better be rendered as a series of three pairs.

For the sequence of *father and mother* cp. on 2 : 33.

The order of *wife and children* has sometimes to be reversed, e.g. in Balinese.

Brothers and sisters, cp. on "brother" in 6 : 14. Differences in kinship system and/or in terminology may lead to shifts such as 'siblings male and female' (e.g. in some Indonesian languages), 'older and younger siblings' (Lokele), 'his elder brother and his younger brothers and his sisters' (Shona 1966), 'older brothers, older sisters and younger siblings' (Tzeltal), 'male mother's children and sisters' (Zarma), 'brothers (generically used of all male relationships of equality) and siblings' (West Nyanja). Where terms differ according to the sex of the person in question (as e.g. in Yao, 'younger brothers and all sisters' and 'younger sisters and all brothers', respectively) it may be preferable to say, 'all that person's kin'.

Yes, and even..., or, "not only them but..." (Rieu), "and...as well" (TEV), 'what-is-more...'.

His own life, or, 'his (own) soul', 'his own self', 'himself' (cp. 9 : 24) is dependent on "does not hate"; the rendering chosen for that verb may have to be repeated with this last object.

27 ***Whoever does not bear his own cross and come after me, cannot be my disciple.***

Exegesis: *hostis ou bastazei ton stauron heautou* 'whoever does not carry his own cross'. For *bastazō* cp. on 7 : 14; for *stauros* cp. on 9 : 23 and *TH-Mk* on 8 : 34.

kai erchetai opisō mou 'and (does not) come after me', cp. *TH-Mk* on 8 : 34. *erchesthai opisō* is virtually equivalent to *akolouthein*, cp. 9 : 23.

Translation: For this verse see the note on 9 : 23.

Bear, ingressive aspect, and virtually synonymous with "take up" in 9 : 23.

28 ***For which of you, desiring to build a tower, does not first sit down and count the cost, whether he has enough to complete it?***

Exegesis: *tis gar ex humōn* 'for who of you... ?' *gar* connects what follows with the preceding statements. This connexion is that the very requirements for discipleship make a conscious decision necessary. *tis* introduces a rhetoric question, the obvious answer being: no one.

thelōn purgon oikodomēsai 'planning to build a tower'. *thelō* implies here purpose. *purgos* may refer here to a tower of a vineyard (cp. Grundmann).

ouchi prōton kathisas psēphizei tēn dapanēn 'does not first sit down and calculate the cost'. For *ouchi* cp on 4 : 22; for *prōton* cp. on 6 : 42. *kathisas* goes with *psēphizei* and suggests serious and prolonged consideration (cp. Plummer).

psēphizō (†) 'to count', 'to calculate'.

dapanē (††) 'cost', 'expenses'.

ei echei eis apartismon '(to see) if he has (enough) for completion (of the building)'.

apartismos (††) 'completion'. *eis apartismon* is virtually equivalent to final *apartizein* 'to complete'.

Translation: For shifts to a suppositional or conditional clause, or to second person forms, cp. on 11 : 5.

Tower. The reference is to something relatively big; other semantic components of the term e.g. that a tower is high, or serves as a look-out, are not specially relevant in this context. Therefore a generic rendering, such as 'big building', may be preferable in cases where the rendering used in 13 : 4 does not fit.

Count the cost (i.e. the building cost), or, 'calculate what it will cost', 'considers what he must pay' (Sranan).

To connect the clause *whether he...complete it* with what precedes one may have to insert, 'asking himself', 'in order to know' (Kituba), 'to see'

(Thai 1967, similarly Lomwe, one West Nyanja version). *Whether* may have to be rendered by a positive-negative expression, 'whether or not' (Shona, similarly Ponape). In some cases a shift to a direct question will be preferable.

He has enough to complete it, or, 'he has what is needed to finish it', 'he has that which will finish building it' (Zarma), 'he is with all the money that-will-be-required' (one West Nyanja version).

29 ***Otherwise, when he has laid a foundation, and is not able to finish, all who see it begin to mock him,*** 30 ***saying, 'This man began to build, and was not able to finish.'***

Exegesis: *hina mēpote...pantes hoi theōrountes arxōntai autō empaizein* 'lest surely...all the onlookers began to make fun of him', syntactically a final clause in the subjunctive, dependent upon v. 28, describing what would happen if the answer to the question of v. 28 were not in the negative. *hina mēpote* is somewhat stronger than *hina mē,* cp. A-G s.v. *mēpote* 2 b α and on 12 : 58. For *theōreō* cp. on 10 : 18.

empaizō with dative 'to mock', 'to ridicule', 'to make fun of'.

thentos autou themelion kai mē ischuontos ektelesai 'when he has laid the foundation and (then) is unable to finish', temporal clause in the genitive absolute. The aorist tense of *thentos* denotes a fact preceding that denoted by *ischuontos* in the present tense. For *themelios* and *ischuō* cp. on 6 : 48.

ekteleō 'to complete', 'to finish'.

(V. 30) *houtos ho anthrōpos* 'this man', with a note of contempt, cp. Plummer.

ērxato oikodomein kai ouk ischusen ektelesai 'began to build but was unable to finish', aorist tense expressing that the onlookers regard the story as an event of the past.

Translation: Changing the structure of this sentence one may say, 'if not (or, if he does not do so), it may happen (that) he lays the foundation but is not able to finish its-building; then all who see...'.

To lay a foundation, or, 'to place/make/build the base, or, the supporting stones/beams, or, what is to support it (i.e. the tower)'.

Finish, or, 'finish it (i.e. the tower)'. The verb is synonymous with 'complete' in v. 28.

To mock, or, 'to make fun of', 'to laugh at'. Some languages prefer to use here a distinctive term in accordance with the specific kind of mockery indicated in the next verse, e.g. 'to jeer/taunt'.

31 ***Or what king, going to encounter another king in war, will not sit down first and take counsel whether he is able with ten thousand to meet him who comes against him with twenty thousand?***

Exegesis: *ē tis basileus...* 'or what king?', another rhetoric question.

poreuomenos heterō basilei sumbalein eis polemon 'going/setting out to wage war on another king'. *poreuomenos* does not mean that he is already marching but intends to do so. *polemos* also 21 : 9.

sumballō (cp. on 2 : 19) here intransitive 'to meet', 'to fall in with', for the purpose of war (*eis polemon*), i.e. 'to wage war on', cp. A-G s.v. 1 b.

ouchi kathisas prōton bouleusetai 'will not first sit down and consider', cp. on v. 28.

bouleuomai (†) 'to consider'.

ei dunatos estin 'whether he is able', with infinitive (*hupantēsai*).

en deka chiliasin 'with ten thousand (men)', cp. A-G s.v. *en* I 4 c α.

hupantēsai tō meta eikosi chiliadōn erchomenō ep' auton 'to meet him who comes against him with twenty thousand (men)', implying that 'the other king' is really the one who starts the war. For *hupantaō* cp. on 8 : 27. In *ep' auton* the preposition *epi* is used in a hostile sense.

Translation: Adjustments in v. 31, where required, will usually parallel those in v. 28.

Or does not introduce an alternative but a parallel example; hence e.g. 'but listen again' (Sranan), 'so again' (Javanese).

To go to encounter...in war, i.e. 'to go/intend to fight against...', 'to go war against...' (Trukese), 'to go meet to fight with...' (Sranan). Some renderings are built on 'enemy/adversary', e.g. in South Toradja, using a reciprocal verbal form.

Another king, i.e. distinct but of the same category; hence 'a fellow king/chief' (Javanese, one West Nyanja version), 'one-who-is-chief-like-him' (East Toradja).

To take counsel, with oneself, hence, 'to consider', 'to think' (Trukese, Ponape), 'to ask himself' (Shona).

He is able with ten thousand to meet, or, 'he is strong enough to meet with ten thousand (men)', 'he who has (or, he although he has) only 10.000 (men) is able to meet'; or changing the subject, 'his 10.000 soldiers will be-able-to war against' (Ponape). *Ten thousand* may have to be rendered analytically, e.g. '100 companies', or generically, 'very many soldiers', 'large army', which will probably entail the use of 'twice as many', 'twice as large an army', or, 'two such (large) armies' in the subsequent clause. *To meet* here is virtually synonymous with 'to encounter in war'.

To come against, or, 'to come to fight', 'to attack'.

32 ***And if not, while the other is yet a great way off, he sends an embassy and asks terms of peace.***

Exegesis: *ei de mēge* scil. *dunatos estin* 'and if (he is) not (able)', 'if he cannot'.

eti autou porrō ontos 'while he is still far away'. *autou* refers to the other king. *porrō* also 24 : 28.

presbeian aposteilas erōta ta pros eirēnēn 'he sends an embassy and asks for terms of peace'. For *apostellō* cp. on 1 : 19. *ta pros eirēnēn* lit. 'that which belongs to/has to do with peace' (cp. A-G s.v. *pros* III 5 b), hence 'terms of peace'.

presbeia (also 19 : 14) 'embassy', here abstract for concrete, 'ambassadors', 'envoys'.

Translation: *While the other is yet a great way off,* or, "long before the enemy approaches" (NEB), may better be transposed after the first or the second verbal phrase of the main clause, with ensuing adjustments.

Sends an embassy (or, envoys/messengers) *and asks,* or, 'orders some representatives (or, some spokesmen, cp. Lokele; or, some of his servants/officers/counsellors) to go (to the other king) to ask'.

To ask terms of peace, or, 'to beg agreement about peace' (Yao), 'to ask about the becoming-good-with-each-other again' (East Toradja); or, more descriptively, 'to ask on what conditions he (i.e. the other king) will make peace' (cp. Goodspeed), 'to ask, "What must we (exclus.) do in order that there may be peace, or, that the war may come to an end?"'. Some idiomatic phrases used are, 'to ask to be friends with each other' (Thai 1967), 'to ask-ask-as-a-favour time good' (Ponape), 'to make his heart willing-to-be-reconciled in order that thus will be calmed down the trouble started by them' (Tzeltal, combining two such phrases). For *peace* cp. also 1 : 79.

33 ***So therefore, whoever of you does not renounce all that he has cannot be my disciple.***

Exegesis: *houtōs oun* lit. 'in this way, then', here 'in the same way', referring back to vv. 26f.

pas ex humōn hos ouk apotassetai pasin tois heautou huparchousin lit. 'everyone of you who does not give up all his possessions'. For *apotassō* cp. on 9 : 61 and reference there. For *ta huparchonta* cp. on 8 : 3.

Translation: *To renounce,* or, 'to leave behind', 'to let go', 'to say farewell to, or, to take leave of' (same term as in 9 : 61, but used metaphorically). In South Toradja the idiom is 'to cause his soul to miss it', i.e. to turn away one's desire from.

34 ***"Salt is good; but if salt has lost its taste, how shall its saltness be restored?***

Exegesis: *kalon oun to halas* 'salt is good'. *oun* is difficult to interpret as to its reference, and best left untranslated.

halas (†) 'salt', here probably referring to discipleship.

ean de kai to halas mōranthē 'but if even the salt becomes tasteless'.

mōrainō (†) in the passive 'to become tasteless', 'to lose strength/flavour'.

en tini artuthēsetai 'with what can it (viz. the salt) be seasoned?'. *artuō* (†).

Translation: Jesus concludes by referring to a general truth, leaving it to his hearers to draw the inference; this may make advisable the use of some such introductory expression as, 'remember', 'you all know'.

Salt is good; but if..., or, 'even though salt is good, if it...'.

Has lost its taste, or, 'no longer has its taste/flavour', 'has become insipid' (Bahasa Indonesia, using the opposite of 'salt-ish'), "loses its strength" (Goodspeed, similarly East Toradja); in Sranan the idiom is, 'becomes dead'.

How shall its saltness be restored?, or, 'how will it be given flavour again?', 'how can it be made salt/salt-ish again?', 'what will you take to awaken/raise it again?' (Sranan); or as a statement, "there is no way to make it good again" (TEV). If an active construction has to be used, the subject can best be 'people', or, 'we' (inclusive). For this and the preceding entry cp. also *TH-Mk* on 9 : 50.

35 ***It is fit neither for the land nor for the dunghill; men throw it away. He who has ears to hear, let him hear."***

Exegesis: *oute eis gēn oute eis koprian eutheton estin* 'it is fit neither for the ground nor for the manure-heap'. For *euthetos* cp. on 9 : 62. The clause is best understood as meaning, 'it is neither directly nor indirectly useful as manure' (cp. Klostermann, Grundmann).

kopria (††) 'dungheap', 'manure-heap' (cp. 13 : 8).

exō ballousin auto 'they throw it away', without specific indication of place or agent.

ho echōn ōta akouein akouetō 'he who has ears to hear, let him hear', cp. on 8 : 8.

Translation: The negative of *it is fit* has been rendered, 'it cannot (or, can nowhere) be used', "it is no good" (Phillips, similarly Ponape, Sranan), 'it is worthless' (Kapauku, similarly Zarma), 'it is useless' (one West Nyanja version, lit. 'is without work'; similarly Shona 1963, lit. 'it has no work to do').

For the land, i.e. the farmland, the fields. The meaning of the preposition may have to be stated more explicitly, cp. e.g. 'to manure (lit. fatten) the soil' (Sranan).

For the dunghill, or, again more explicitly, 'to keep (it) on the dunghill' (Sranan), 'to mix (it) with manure, or, compost, dry grass' (cp. 13 : 8).

He who...hear, see the note on 8 : 8.

CHAPTER FIFTEEN

1 ***Now the tax collectors and sinners were all drawing near to hear him.***

Exegesis: *ēsan de autō eggizontes pantes hoi telōnai kai hoi hamartōloi* 'now all the tax-collectors and sinners were drawing near to him'. No connexion as to time and place with 14 : 25-35 is indicated and it is preferable to leave that connexion undefined. The periphrastic form *ēsan... eggizontes* is best understood as referring to a specific occasion. *pantes* may refer to all tax-collectors and sinners of a specific place, or may be used hyperbolically and mean 'very many', preferably the latter. For *telōnēs* cp. on 3 : 12; for *hamartōlos* cp. on 5 : 8. The repetition of the article *hoi* before *hamartōloi* suggests that Luke does not consider the tax-collectors and sinners as one group, as contrasted with inarticulate *hamartōlous* in v. 2.

akouein autou 'in order to hear him (speak)', 'to listen to him'.

Translation: *Now,* or, "one time" (TEV), cp. 1 : 57.

The tax collectors and sinners, preferably, '(both) the tax-collectors (see 3 : 12) and the sinners' (cp. *Exegesis*).

To draw near, or, 'to approach', 'to come towards him'; or here, since they were many, "to crowd up, or, in" (Goodspeed, NEB).

2 ***And the Pharisees and the scribes murmured, saying, "This man receives sinners and eats with them."*** 3 ***So he told them this parable:***

Exegesis: *diegogguzon* 'grumbled', presumably in Jesus' presence.

diagogguzō (also 19 : 7) 'to murmur', 'to grumble', synonymous with *gogguzō* (cp. on 5 : 30).

hoi te Pharisaioi kai hoi grammateis 'the Pharisees and the experts in the law', cp. on 5 : 17 and 21. By *te...kai* they are represented as belonging very closely together.

houtos 'this man', contemptuously.

hamartōlous prosdechetai 'welcomes sinners', viz. into his company, cp. A-G s.v. *prosdechomai* 1 a. For the inarticulate *hamartōlous* cp. on v. 1.

sunesthiei autois (†) 'and eats with them', presumably at their invitation and in their homes.

(V. 3) *eipen de pros autous tēn parabolēn tautēn* 'then he told them this parable', i.e. as an answer to their grumbling. Strictly speaking Jesus does not tell them one parable, but two parables in question-form, which closely resemble each other and from which the same application is drawn in vv. 7 and 10.

Translation: *Murmured*, cp. on 5 : 30.

For *receives* see 9 : 5. In this context Sranan has: 'sides (lit. keeps/holds) with', Français Courant: *fait bon accueil à*.

For *eats with them* see 7 : 36; for *parable* see 8 : 4.

4 ***"What man of you, having a hundred sheep, if he has lost one of them, does not leave the ninety-nine in the wilderness, and go after the one which is lost, until he finds it?***

Exegesis: *tis anthrōpos ex humōn...ou kataleipei* 'what man of you... does not leave?', rhetorical question, the obvious answer being: everyone. *anthrōpos* is virtually redundant.

echōn hekaton probata kai apolesas ex autōn hen lit. 'having a hundred sheep and having lost one of them'. *echōn* denotes a prevailing situation (present tense) and *apolesas* a punctiliar event (aorist tense). The latter does not suggest want of care.

en tē erēmō 'in the pasture land', cp. *N.T.Wb.*, 42/.

poreuetai epi to apolōlos '(does not) go in search of the lost (sheep)', modified by interrogative *ou*, as *kataleipei* (see above). For *epi* indicating goal cp. A-G s.v. III 1 a δ.

heōs heurē auto 'till he finds it', denoting the tenacity of the seeker.

Translation: For possibly necessary changes of structure cp. 14 : 5.

A hundred sheep...the ninety-nine. Exact arithmetical equivalence may be undesirable, as may be clear from the following remarks. In the Greek the first numeral, a basic unit in the numerical system, functions as a round number for a considerable quantity; hence in Kapauku (where the highest basic unit is 'sixty', and the arithmetical equivalent of "hundred" would be 'forty of the second sixty') the closest natural equivalent of the phrase is 'sixty sheep...fifty-nine' (to which this version adds a footnote giving the exact number). In some African languages "ninety-nine" has to be rendered as 'five (tens) and four tens and five and four', a rather cumbersome phrase which moreover does not go too well with the term used to translate "hundred". In such a case a more generic rendering is probably preferable, e.g. 'many sheep...the others', 'a flock (cp. 2 : 8) of sheep...the rest (of the flock)'. For *sheep* cp. Nida, *BT*, 136; *TH-Mk* on 6 : 34.

He has lost one of them, i.e. he finds that one sheep is missing from his flock, referring to inadvertent loss. In several receptor languages the corresponding verb, if used in a transitive-active form, suggests a deliberate act, which is acceptable e.g. in "loses his life for his sake" (9 : 24) but not here; or it implies wastefulness (e.g. in Zarma, which therefore uses such a form for "squandered" in v. 13). In such languages intransitive-passive forms are often to be used here and in v. 8, cp. e.g. 'he suffered-the-loss of one...' (Bahasa Indonesia, similarly Shona 1963), or, changing the subject, 'one...gets-lost (with regard) to him' (East Nyanja, Zarma). Elsewhere 'to lose/get-lost' can be said only of lifeless objects, but animals and/or human beings are said 'to go-astray', cp. also Toba Batak, which in v. 4^b says 'the one not to-be-seen'; the same two renderings are used (in expositions, not in the Bible translation) in East Nyanja, Lomwe, Yao. Similar adjustments may be required in v. 6 and/or vv. 24, 32. If that is the case demands of idiom will interfere with demands of style, since the differentiation required for an idiomatic translation does not allow the preservation of the repeated occurrence of forms of 'to lose', which is a characteristic stylistic feature of this chapter.

Leave, or, 'go-away-from' (Balinese, East Toradja).

Wilderness, cp. *N.T.Wb.*/25, DESERT; in seeking an appropriate rendering one should remember that the term refers here to a place fit for pasturage (cp. NEB's "open pasture").

Until, i.e. seeking until, or, not stopping before.

For *to find* see 2 : 12.

5 ***And when he has found it, he lays it on his shoulders, rejoicing.***
6 ***And when he comes home, he calls together his friends and his neighbours, saying to them, 'Rejoice with me, for I have found my sheep which was lost.'***

Exegesis: *kai heurōn epitithēsin epi tous ōmous autou chairōn* 'and when he has found (it) he puts it on his shoulders rejoicing'. The question of v. 4 changes into a story, describing what happens when the lost sheep is found and leading up to the application in v. 7. *chairōn* serves to colour the whole clause (cp. 19 : 6; Acts 8 : 39), and explains the rather unusual act of carrying the lost sheep (cp. Lagrange).

(V. 6) *kai elthōn eis ton oikon* 'and when he has come home', without paying further attention to the sheep left behind in the pasture land.

sugkalei tous philous kai tous geitonas 'he calls together his friends and neighbours', viz. for a celebration. For *sugkaleō* cp. on 9 : 1.

sugcharēte moi 'rejoice with me', cp. on 1 : 58.

to probaton mou to apolōlos 'my sheep which was lost'. *to apolōlos* is emphatic.

Translation: *To lay on the shoulders,* or, 'to carry on the shoulder(s) (or, on the back of the neck, or, on the back)' is expressed by one verb in some languages.

Rejoicing, or, 'because he-rejoices' (Sundanese); or with a further shift, "he is so happy that he puts it on his shoulders" (TEV); "how delighted he is then! He lifts it on to his shoulders..." (NEB).

(V. 6) *He calls together,* viz. 'in his house'; hence 'he invites' (Bahasa Indonesia) is possible also.

For *neighbours* and for *rejoice with me,* sometimes a reciprocal expression, e.g. 'let us rejoice with each other', cp. also 1 : 58.

7 ***Just so, I tell you, there will be more joy in heaven over one sinner who repents than over ninety-nine righteous persons who need no repentance.***

Exegesis: *legō humin* 'I tell you', cp. on 3 : 8.

houtōs 'in just that way', 'in the same way'.

chara en tō ouranō estai 'there will be joy in heaven'. No distinctive meaning is to be attached to the shift to the future tense (cp. v. 10, *ginetai*).

epi heni hamartōlō metanoounti 'over one sinner who repents', cp. A-G s.v. *epi* II 1 b γ. For *metanoeō* cp. on 10 : 13.

ē 'more than', cp. A-G s.v. 2 b α.

epi enenēkonta ennea dikaiois 'over ninety-nine righteous persons'. *dikaios* contrasts here with *hamartōlos*; both words are to be understood in terms of relationship to God.

hoitines ou chreian echousin metanoias 'who do not need repentance', probably meant ironically. For *metanoia* cp. on 3 : 3.

Translation: *There will be...joy in heaven*, or, when a personal subject is required, 'those in heaven will have joy'.

Over one sinner who repents expresses the reason of the joy; hence e.g. 'because (of) one sinner (who) repents' (Thai 1967, East Toradja 1933), 'because/when they perceive (or, see) that one sinner has repented'.

More joy...over one...than over ninety-nine... The reference to 'joy' may have to be repeated, e.g. '...than joy in heart because of 99' (Tzeltal), '...than they will have joy over 99...' (Sranan). Radical changes of structure may be necessary, cp. e.g. 'in comparison with the 59, one bad person having repented, in heaven surpassing joy' (Kapauku).

Righteous, cp. 5 : 32.

Who need no repentance. If the saying is interpreted in accordance with what *Exegesis* thinks probable, the irony may have to be made explicit, e.g. 'who think they do not need to repent', 'who seem not to need repentance'.

8 ***"Or what woman, having ten silver coins, if she loses one coin, does not light a lamp and sweep the house and seek diligently until she finds it?***

Exegesis: *ē tis gunē* 'or what woman... ?' *ē* introduces the second parable in question form, cp. on v. 3.

drachmas echousa deka, ean apolesē drachmēn mian 'who has ten drachmas, if she has lost one'. *ean apolesē* is equivalent to *apolesas* (cp. on v. 4).

drachmē (also v. 9) 'drachma', Greek silver coin worth about 17 cents of a dollar. Ten drachmas is a very small possession.

ouchi haptei luchnon 'does not light a lamp... ?', cp. on 8 : 16. Interrogative *ouchi* (cp. on 4 : 22) introduces a rhetorical question as *ou* in v. 4. It also modifies the subsequent verbs *saroi* and *zētei*.

kai saroi tēn oikian 'and (does not) sweep the house', cp. on 11 : 25.

kai zētei epimelōs 'and (does not) search carefully'. The object understood of *zētei* is the lost drachma. *epimelōs* (††).

heōs hou lit. 'till the time when', equivalent to *heōs* (v. 4).

Translation: *Or*, cp. 14 : 31.

Silver coins, or, 'pieces of silver (money)', or a local equivalent, e.g. 'half-guilder' (Toba Batak); in Muslim countries it may be possible to borrow or adapt the Arabic transliteration *dirham*. Cp. also Nida, *BT*, 328f.

Light a lamp (see 8 : 16) and *sweep the house* (see 11 : 25) serve to show that all is done to make the search referred to in the next clause successful. The rendering of the verb should express that the dust (or, dirt) on the floor is swept together to facilitate the search (not that it is simply swept out of the house, as is the case in one version).

9 ***And when she has found it, she calls together her friends and neighbours, saying, 'Rejoice with me, for I have found the coin which I had lost.'***

Exegesis: *kai heurousa* 'and when she has found (it)', same transition as in v. 5 (see there).

hēn apōlesa 'which I lost', cp. on *apolesas* in v. 4.

Translation: In the Greek the word for *friends* is in the feminine form, but this is not of specific relevance in this context. Therefore, if the normal term to be employed in the receptor language is neutral as to gender, no specification of sex is needed, as a rule; it may even be undesirable where the specification 'woman-friends' would suggest the existence of boy-friends better not mentioned—as is the case in some versions. The same is true where 'woman neighbours' would have such implications.

The coin which I had lost. This construction, though formally different, has the same meaning as 'my sheep which was lost' (v. 6).

10 ***Just so, I tell you, there is joy before the angels of God over one sinner who repents."***

Exegesis: *houtōs, legō humin* 'in the same way, I tell you'. Here *legō humin* is inserted in the main clause but has the same function as in v. 7.

ginetai chara enōpion tōn aggelōn tou theou 'there is joy among the angels of God'. *ginetai* is equivalent to *estin*. For *enōpion* cp. A-G s.v. 5 a. The phrase *enōpion tōn aggelōn tou theou* is virtually equivalent to *en tō ouranō* in v. 7.

Translation: *There is joy before the angels of God.* A personal subject is usually preferable, 'the angels of God will have joy'.

11 ***And he said, "There was a man who had two sons;*** 12 ***and the younger of them said to his father, 'Father, give me the share of property that falls to me.' And he divided his living between them.***

Exegesis: *eipen de* 'and he said', introducing a parable in the proper sense. The situation is the same as before.

(V. 12) *kai eipen ho neōteros autōn tō patri* 'and the younger one of them said to his father'. *kai* marks here the transition from description (v. 11) to action.

dos moi to epiballon meros tēs ousias 'give me the part of the property that falls to me'. *epiballō* means here 'to fall to', or 'to belong to' (cp. A-G s.v. 2); hence *to epiballon meros* is 'the part, or, share that is due' (cp. BFBS, "my due share"). For *meros* cp. on 12 : 46.

ousia (also v. 13) 'property', equivalent to *bios* (below). For the much debated question whether a son could claim his part of an estate when his father was still alive, cp. commentaries. For translational purposes it is best to take the present tense of *epiballon* at face value and to understand the share as due at the time of claiming.

ho de dieilen autois ton bion 'and he divided the property among them'. For *bios* cp. on 8 : 43.

diaireō (†) 'to divide', 'to distribute'.

Translation: *And he said*, or, 'again he/Jesus said'.

(V. 12) *The younger of them*, or, 'the/his younger son', 'the younger-brother' (e.g. in Toba Batak), 'the second one' (Gbeapo).

Give me the share of property that falls to me presupposes that their property is to be divided, which may have to be made explicit, e.g. 'divide the property and give me the part that I am entitled to', 'gather up my birth portion and give me' (Moré, see *TBT*, 15.11f, 1964). *Give.* A polite form is sometimes required, cp. e.g. 'please-hand-out-now' (West Nyanja). *The share of property that falls to me*, or, 'my share of the/our (inclus.) property', 'as many things as will become mine by you' (Tzeltal), 'the part of the good I must receive' (Sranan), 'our things that will be mine' (Bamiléké), 'the things (in contrast with somebody else's things in the context) I am to have' (Kapauku); or making explicit the reference to inheritance, 'my share of the things that I shall inherit' (Shona 1966), 'my part of what I inherited from my grandfather/ancestors' (cp. East Toradja 1933). In some cultures, e.g. Lomwe, Yao, a father can only make a gift, but never can assign such a right; a slightly more generic rendering will be preferable then, e.g. 'a part of the/your property'. Elsewhere a man can leave his property only to his eldest son not to the younger ones, or to his sister's not to his own sons. In such cases a note may be advisable to explain that according to Jewish custom sons normally inherited their father's property, the eldest obtaining double the portion assigned to his younger brothers, cp. Deut. 21 : 17.

He, i.e. the father, which usually has to be specified.

Divided his living between them, or, 'between the two of them', 'gave to each of them (or, of his sons) a part of his property/possessions'.

13 ***Not many days later, the younger son gathered all he had and took his journey into a far country, and there he squandered his property in loose living.***

Exegesis: *kai met' ou pollas hēmeras* 'and after not many days', i.e. 'not many days later', hence, "a few days later" (NEB). The phrase goes with *apedēmēsen* 'went abroad'.

sunagagōn hapanta 'having gathered everything', probably by turning it into cash, cp. A-G s.v. 1.

ho neōteros huios apedēmēsen eis chōran makran 'the younger son went abroad to a distant country'.

apodēmeō (also 20 : 9) 'to go abroad', 'to go on a journey'.

makros 'far away', 'distant'.

dieskorpisen tēn ousian autou 'he squandered his property'.

diaskorpizō here 'to squander', 'to waste'.

zōn asōtōs 'by living extravagantly', going with *dieskorpisen.*

asōtōs (††) 'extravagantly', i.e. as a spendthrift, or 'recklessly', probably the former.

Translation: *Gathered all he had,* or, 'sold the whole of his share' (cp. e.g. TEV, East Toradja).

Took his journey into, or, 'left home and went to' (cp. TEV and NEB).

Squandered, i.e. spent lavishly and/or foolishly, 'flung about'; Toba Batak uses a compound verb built on 'finished' and 'clean'; Zarma has, 'caused-to-be-lost'.

His property has the same reference as "all he had"; hence, "it" (NEB), "his money" (TEV).

In loose living, or, 'by extravagant behaviour', 'giving-rein-to (his) desires' (Balinese, similarly Toba Batak).

14 ***And when he had spent everything, a great famine arose in that country, and he began to be in want.***

Exegesis: *dapanēsantos de autou panta* 'but when he had spent it all'. *panta* points back to *ousian* in v. 13.

dapanaō (†) 'to spend', a neutral term (cp. *dapanē* in 14 : 28).

egeneto limos ischura kata tēn chōran ekeinēn 'there arose a severe famine throughout that country'.

ischuros lit. 'strong', here figuratively, 'severe'.

kai autos ērxato hustereisthai 'and he began to be in want'. *autos* is not emphatic but resumes the subject of *dieskorpisen* (v. 13). For *archomai* with infinitive cp. on 4 : 21.

hustereomai (also 22 : 35) 'to be in want', 'to be needy', with following genitive, 'to lack', 'to be in need of'.

Translation: *When he had spent everything,* or, 'all that he possessed'. *To spend,* or, 'to use-up/finish' (Bahasa Indonesia, similarly Sranan, lit. 'to eat').

A great famine arose, cp. "there came a great famine" in 4 : 25.

And he began to be in want, i.e. to lack the things that he needed to live, especially food, cp. 'then he had nothing' (Kapauku), "and he faced starvation" (Rieu).

15 *So he went and joined himself to one of the citizens of that country, who sent him into his fields to feed swine.*

Exegesis: *kai poreutheis ekollēthē heni tōn politōn tēs chōras ekeinēs* 'he went and attached himself to one of the citizens of that country'. *poreutheis* refers to a change of place and, implicitly, of situation.

kollaomai lit. 'to cling to' (cp. 10 : 11), here 'to associate with', 'to join oneself to'.

politēs (also 19 : 14) 'citizen'.

kai epempsen auton eis tous agrous autou 'and he (i.e. the citizen) sent him to his fields', change of subject not indicated. For *agros* cp. *TH-Mk* on 5 : 14 (here in literal meaning).

boskein choirous '(in order) to tend pigs', cp. on 8 : 32.

Translation: *Joined himself,* i.e. begged to be allowed to work, probably for nothing more than some food. The verb has been rendered by, "to hire oneself out" (Goodspeed), 'to seek work with' (Sranan), an idiom meaning 'to hang around (in the hope of getting something)' (Zarma), 'to enter the service of, or, work with' (cp. Jerusalem, Malay); or by a specific term for comparable relationships that come close to serfdom or peonage (e.g. in South Toradja, Toba Batak). In Tzeltal the usual phrase in such circumstances is 'to talk', the specification having to be supplied from the context.

Citizens of that country is not used here in a political sense; hence, 'people of (or, living/residing in) that country', cp. also "local landowners" (NEB).

Fields, cp. 2 : 8; 12 : 28.

To feed swine, i.e. 'to tend/look-after/guard the pigs while they are, or, were feeding' (cp. 8 : 32).

16 *And he would gladly have fed on the pods that the swine ate; and no one gave him anything.*

Exegesis: *kai epethumei* 'and he desired, or, longed', here, 'he would gladly have...' with infinitive. Durative imperfect.

chortasthēnai ek tōn keratiōn hōn ēsthion hoi choiroi 'to be satisfied', i.e. 'to fill himself with the carob pods the pigs were eating'. *ek* after verbs meaning 'to fill' means 'with'.

keration (††) 'carob pod', i.e. fruit of the carob tree, or locust tree.

kai oudeis edidou autō 'and nobody gave him (anything)', scil. from the carob pods, a durative imperfect.

Translation: The first clause expresses the degree of his hunger, cp. "he got to the point of longing to..." (Phillips), 'his hunger (was) such (that) very-much he wanted to...' (cp. East Toradja 1933), or, 'he would not have hesitated to...'.

To feed on, i.e. 'to appease one's hunger with' rather than merely 'to eat'.

For *pods* the translator may use any local term for what pigs commonly eat, e.g. 'residue-of-coco-nut (after the oil has been pressed out)' (Sranan), 'bran (of the rice)' (East Toradja 1933), or a generic rendering, as in "the food the pigs were eating" (Phillips, similarly Balinese).

And no one gave him anything, or, 'but no one gave him any, or, it' (cp. TEV, Bahasa Indonesia RC).

17 ***But when he came to himself he said, 'How many of my father's hired servants have bread enough and to spare, but I perish here with hunger!***

Exegesis: *eis heauton de elthōn* lit. 'having come to himself', i.e. 'when he came to his senses' (cp. Phillips, NEB, TEV), 'when he recognized his situation for what it was'.

posoi misthioi tou patros mou perisseuontai artōn 'how many paid servants of my father have more than enough food', exclamative statement introduced by an interrogative noun. *perisseuontai* may be middle voice with the same meaning as the active, or passive voice, meaning 'receive abundantly' (cp. A-G s.v. 1 b α and 2 b), preferably the former. For *artos* (plural) meaning 'food' cp. A-G s.v. 2.

misthios 'paid servant', 'hired worker'. Though not a slave the paid worker would expect less affection from his master than a slave.

egō de limō hōde apollumai 'but here I am dying of hunger'. *limos* 'hunger', 'starvation', different in meaning from v. 14. *egō* and *hōde* are emphatic, 'here I am'.

Translation: *He came to himself*. Other idioms are, 'he came to get himself' (Sranan), 'his heart arrived' (Tzeltal), 'he sensed himself', implying realization that he had done wrong (Thai 1967), 'it fell into his heart' (Kekchi), 'his self came back' (Tagalog), 'he came to wisdom, or, became wise' (Kiyaka, Trukese, Ponape), 'he understood himself' (Kituba), 'his heart came to life again' (Timorese), 'he came out of his stupor' (Cakchiquel), 'he was turned, or, aroused (as from sleep), in his heart' (Lomwe, Yao); or, 'he became-aware of his own condition' (Javanese), 'he thought again about his affair' (Lokele).

He said, viz. to himself. This has to be made explicit in Kapauku, which therefore adds '(he) thought' at the end of this verse and of v. 19.

Hired servants, or, 'paid servants/labourers', 'men working for pay, or, food' (Balinese, South Toradja). The rendering should refer to people of low social status and precarious living.

Have bread enough and to spare, or, "have more food than they can eat" (NEB), 'have food enough and some left over' (cp. Tagalog); cp. also *N.T.Wb.*/1, ABOUND. For *bread*, or, 'food', see references on 4 : 3.

I perish...with hunger, or, 'I am dying of hunger', 'I die suffering-from hungry stomach' (Balinese). For *hunger* cp. 1 : 53.

18 ***I will arise and go to my father, and I will say to him, "Father, I have sinned against heaven and before you;***

Exegesis: *anastas poreusomai pros ton patera mou* 'I will set out and go to my father'. For *anastas* cp. on 1 : 39.

hēmarton eis ton ouranon kai enōpion sou 'I have sinned against heaven and against you'. *enōpion sou,* lit. 'in your sight', is here parallel with *eis ouranon*; hence *enōpion* is here equivalent to *eis*; *ouranon* is equivalent to God.

hamartanō 'to sin', 'to do wrong', followed by *eis* to indicate against whom is sinned.

Translation: *I will arise and go,* or, 'let me arise and go', in the propositive mood. For the two verbs see 1 : 39.

Though the following quoted speech is not actually addressed to the father, languages such as Javanese use the same honorifics in it as in v. 21 (which see).

Sinned, to be rendered by a verbal form or phrase built on 'sin'. A verb that fits the first object may not fit the second; then differentiation is needed, cp. e.g. 'sinned against heaven and misbehaved against you'.

Against heaven. This metonymical use of "heaven" easily leads to misunderstanding; hence, 'against the One in heaven', "against God" (e.g. in NEB). Similarly in 15 : 21; and cp. 20 : 3, 5.

Before, preferably, 'against', 'to(wards)'.

19 ***I am no longer worthy to be called your son; treat me as one of your hired servants."'***

Exegesis: *ouketi eimi axios klēthēnai huios sou* 'I am no longer worthy, or, I no longer deserve, to be called your son'.

poiēson me hōs hena tōn misthiōn sou lit. 'make me as one of your paid servants', i.e. 'put me in the same position' or 'take me on', rather than 'treat me as one of your paid servants'.

Translation: *I am no longer worthy,* cp. 3 : 16.

To be called your son, or, 'that you call me your son' (Français Courant); if a more analytical rendering is required, this may be, 'that you say, "He is my son"'.

Treat me as, preferably, 'please take me on as' (cp. *Exegesis*), or, 'make me' (Kapauku), 'allow me to become', 'please let me work for you as'; in Kiyaka one says, 'write me up as'.

20 ***And he arose and came to his father. But while he was yet at a distance, his father saw him and had compassion, and ran and embraced him and kissed him.***

Exegesis: *kai anastas ēlthen pros ton patera heautou* 'and he set out and went to his father'. *heautou* is equivalent to the simple possessive *autou.* For *anastas* cp. on v. 18.

eti de autou makran apechontos 'while he was still far away', scil. from his father's house. The range of *makran* (also 7 : 6) 'far away' is determined by the fact that he is already within eyeshot.

eiden auton ho patēr autou 'his father saw him'. *auton* takes up preceding *autou. eiden* is best understood as ingressive, cp. Jerusalem.

esplagchnisthē 'he was filled with pity', "his heart went out to him" (Phillips, NEB), cp. on 7 : 13.

dramōn epepesen epi ton trachēlon autou 'he ran and fell on his neck', i.e. 'he threw his arms around him', 'he embraced him', cp. A-G s.v. *epipiptō*, cp. on 1 : 12. *trachēlos* also 17 : 2.

katephilēsen auton 'he kissed him', cp. on 7 : 38.

Translation: *While he was yet at a distance*, or, "while he was still a long way off" (NEB). *To be at a distance* is sometimes rendered by a verbal form derived from 'far/distant'.

Saw him, sometimes better, 'saw him coming' (cp. e.g. Javanese).

Had compassion, see 7 : 13.

And ran..., or, as a new sentence, 'he went to meet him' (Sranan); or specifying the participants, e.g. 'his father ran...' (Bahasa Indonesia KB), 'he-ran-toward his child' (Balinese).

Embraced him and kissed him, indicating an affectionate greeting. Descriptive renderings of the first verb may come close to the Greek expression, 'he put his arms around him, or, around his neck/shoulders/body'; the function, if unknown, usually will become clear from what follows. The verb *to kiss* often is difficult to render (cp. *TH-Mk* on 14 : 44). Some descriptive or idiomatic renderings used are, 'to smell (the face of)' (Kapauku, Kekchi), an intensive form of 'to suck' (West Nyanja, habit and term a novelty amongst the young and more or less westernized people, the traditional term for greeting a friend after a long absence being, 'to clap in the hands and laugh happily'), 'to hug' (Shona 1966), 'to caress' (Balinese); Bamiléké uses 'suck the cheek', a novelty again, the traditional term being 'to embrace'—which might have been considered here also, as rendering of the two verbs. A generic rendering may be, 'to greet/welcome affectionately', which, again, may have to serve for the two verbs.

21 ***And the son said to him, 'Father, I have sinned against heaven and before you; I am no longer worthy to be called your son.'***

Exegesis: *eipen de ho huios autō* 'but his son said to him', i.e. notwithstanding this unexpected welcome.

Translation: In languages such as Javanese the son uses honorifics in addressing his father, thus showing that he knows to have forfeited the right to employ the non-honorific terms which are appropriate to intimate family relationships.

22 ***But the father said to his servants, 'Bring quickly the best robe, and put it on him; and put a ring on his hand, and shoes on his feet;***

Exegesis: *eipen de ho patēr pros tous doulous autou* 'but his father said to his slaves', presumably when both had reached the house (cp. Plummer).

tachu exenegkate stolēn tēn prōtēn kai endusate auton 'bring out quickly a robe, the best one, and put it on him'. *tachu* goes with all imperatives in

vv. 22f. *stolēn tēn prōtēn* may mean 'the best robe' (assuming the omission of *tēn* before *stolēn*), or, 'a robe, the best one', hence, 'the best we have'. The latter is preferable.

ekpherō (†) 'to bring out', 'to fetch'.

stolē (also 20 : 46) 'robe' '(long) garment'.

enduō 'to clothe', 'to put a garment on somebody', cp. on 8 : 27.

kai dote daktulion eis tēn cheira autou 'and put a ring on his finger', or 'give him a ring for his finger', preferably the former. *cheir* lit. 'hand', here 'finger'.

daktulios (††) 'ring' as a sign of honour and, perhaps, even authority (cp. Plummer).

kai hupodēmata eis tous podas 'and (put) shoes on his feet', with *dote* understood. For *hupodēma* cp. on 3 : 16.

Translation: *Quickly*, cp. 14 : 21.

Best, i.e. 'the most beautiful'.

Robe, or, 'cloak', a long outer garment, see on 6 : 29.

Put it on him, or, 'dress him in/with it', 'let him clothe himself in it', 'cause him to wear it'; cp. also *N.T.Wb.*/20, CLOTHE. *Him*, or, 'my son'.

Put a ring on his hand may require specification somewhere, e.g. 'put/do/fit a ring on his finger', 'put a finger ring on his hand/finger', or as a single verb, 'put-a-finger-ring-on (him)' (Balinese). In some cultures 'bracelet... arm' may have to be substituted, e.g. Kapauku.

And (put) *shoes on his feet*, sometimes a specific verb, e.g. 'shoe his-feet' (Sundanese), or, 'shoe (him)' (cp. Balinese). For *shoes*, or, 'sandals', cp. 3 : 16.

23 ***and bring the fatted calf and kill it, and let us eat and make merry;***

Exegesis: *kai pherete ton moschon ton siteuton* 'and get the fatted calf', i.e. the calf fatted for a special occasion.

moschos 'calf', 'young bull'.

thusate 'kill (it)'.

thuō 'to sacrifice', hence 'to slaughter', 'to kill'.

kai phagontes euphranthōmen 'and let us eat and enjoy ourselves, or, celebrate', both acts occurring together, cp. Bl-D, § 420.3. For *euphrainomai* cp. on 12 : 19.

Translation: *The fatted calf*, or, 'the fattest/best calf', "the prize calf" (TEV); Goodspeed has an active finite form, "the calf we are fattening" (and in vv. 27 and 30, "the calf he has, resp. you have, been fattening"). *Calf*, or, 'young bull', cp. on "ox" in 13 : 15; the generic 'beast' is sometimes a sufficient designation, e.g. in East Nyanja, Lomwe, Yao. If the whole concept is foreign to the receptor culture one may say, 'the very best food I, or, we (inclus.), keep in supply'.

Eat and make merry, or, 'let-us(inclus.)-eat having-a-feast' (East Toradja), or in a single verb, 'let-us(inclus.)-be-feasting' (South Toradja); and cp. 12 : 19.

24 ***for this my son was dead, and is alive again; he was lost, and is found.' And they began to make merry.***

Exegesis: *hoti houtos ho huios mou nekros ēn kai anezēsen* 'for this son of mine was dead and has come to life again'. *houtos* here points to somebody who is present. *nekros* and *anazaō* (†) are used here metaphorically; they either refer to moral death and rebirth, or mean 'thought to be dead', and 'to come back alive', preferably the latter.

ēn apolōlōs kai heurethē 'he was lost and has been found', repeating the thought expressed in the preceding clause.

ērxanto euphrainesthai 'they began to celebrate', cp. on 4 : 21.

Translation: For *was lost,* used also metaphorically here, cp. the note on v. 4.

Is found, here not the result of a previous search (as it is in vv. 5f, 8f), cp. note on 2 : 12; hence one may have to say, 'has come home' (e.g. Kapauku), or, 'I have got him back'.

25 ***"Now his elder son was in the field; and as he came and drew near to the house, he heard music and dancing.*** 26 ***And he called one of the servants and asked what this meant.***

Exegesis: *ho huios autou ho presbuteros* 'his elder son'. *autou* refers back to *ho patēr* in v. 22.

en agrō 'in the field' (cp. v. 15), presumably at work there. For *agros* cp. *TH-Mk* on 5 : 14.

kai hōs erchomenos ēggisen tē oikia 'and when going home he approached the house'. *erchomenos* lit. 'going', here implicitly 'going home', hence, 'on his way home', 'on his way back'. For *hōs* cp. A-G s.v. IV 1 a.

ēkousen sumphōnias kai chorōn 'he heard music and dancing'.

sumphōnia (††) either abstract, 'music', or concrete, 'instrument', preferably the former; cp. A-G s.v.

choros (††) 'dance', here in the plural 'dancing'.

(V. 26) *proskalesamenos hena tōn paidōn* 'after calling one of the servants'. For *proskaleō* cp. on 7 : 18. For *pais* cp. on 7 : 7; *pais* and *doulos* (v. 22) are synonymous.

epunthaneto ti an eiē tauta 'he enquired what this was'. For *punthanomai* (also 18 : 36) cp. *N.T.Wb.*, 23/ASK. The imperfect tense is conative. The indirect question with the unusual optative with *an* may express astonishment on the part of the speaker.

Translation: *Now,* see 1 : 57, and cp. 'in the meantime' (Willibrord), 'while such-things-were-happening' (East Toradja 1933).

His elder son, or, 'that (old) man's elder son', 'the elder son', 'the first-born son' (Bahasa Indonesia); or, 'his (or, that young man's) elder brother' (cp. Sranan).

Was in the field, i.e. 'was (working) in the field', here probably referring to arable land that he tilled or reaped.

Drew near to, cp. 7 : 12.

Music and dancing, or, 'noise of merry-making' (Kapauku, not specifying the manner). *Music*, or, 'sound of music' (Trukese, Ponape), 'singing' (West Nyanja, similarly East Toradja, Toba Batak), 'music and clapping' (Zarma, where dancing unaccompanied by clapping is unthinkable). Idiom may require a reference to the instruments and/or persons making the music, e.g. 'drums being beaten' (Shona 1966), 'persons beating-the-drum' (South Toradja), 'sound of flutes' (Timorese), 'sound of a (percussion) orchestra' (Javanese, Thai 1967), 'making-music' (Tzeltal). *Dancing*, or, 'sound of dancing, or, of a dance' (cp. e.g. Timorese), 'people dancing' (Shona 1966). Terms used are sometimes more generic, e.g. 'making-party', which includes dancing (Tzeltal), or more specific, e.g. 'people performing the *simbong* (round dance with chorus, performed at a feast usually given after a person's long absence)' (South Toradja). Connotations of available terms for dancing may range from solemn (ritual or temple dance) to frivolous; one should choose a term referring to a folk dance, culturally regarded as an acceptable form of merry-making.

(V. 26) *What this meant*, or, 'what this might be', 'what was happening'; or as a direct question, "What's going on?" (TEV), 'What are those people doing?' (Balinese).

27 ***And he said to him, 'Your brother has come, and your father has killed the fatted calf, because he has received him safe and sound.'***

Exegesis: *ho adelphos sou hēkei* 'your brother has come', stating the situation that caused the event mentioned in the next clause.

kai ethusen ho patēr sou ton moschon ton siteuton 'and (therefore) your father has killed the fatted calf'. Note the shift from perfective present tense (*hēkei*) to aorist denoting a punctiliar act.

hoti hugiainonta auton apelaben 'because he has got him back safe and sound'. *hugiainonta* (cp. on 5 : 31) is emphatic by position. For *apolambanō* cp. on 6 : 34.

Translation: *Brother*, or, 'younger brother'.

Has killed. The father certainly was not the direct agent (cp. v. 23); hence, 'has had killed', 'has ordered (us, exclus.) to slaughter' may be preferable.

He has received him, or, "he has (gotten) him back" (Goodspeed, NEB), 'he has met again with the son' (Javanese, where the use of the pronoun would sound impolite), does not imply an activity on the part of the father; hence one may shift to, 'he, or, his son has been given back to him, or, has been found/met again' (Balinese, Sundanese), 'he has returned' (Kapauku).

Safe and sound, or, "alive and well" (Goodspeed); and cp. "well" in 5 : 31.

28 ***But he was angry and refused to go in. His father came out and entreated him,***

Exegesis: *ōrgisthē de kai ouk ēthelen eiselthein* 'but he became angry and would not go in', with sudden change of subject. For *orgizomai* cp. on 14 : 21. *ouk ēthelen* (imperfect tense) denotes a lasting unwillingness, caused by his anger, not a momentary refusal to go into the house.

exelthōn parekalei auton 'came out and pleaded with him'. For *parakaleō* cp. on 3 : 18. The imperfect tense suggests duration.

Translation: *He was* (or, became) *angry,* cp. *N.T.Wb./*9f; *TH-Mk* on 3 : 5. The pronoun may have to be specified, e.g. 'the elder son/brother'.

Entreated him, or, 'begged him', 'tried-to-persuade/coaxed him' (some Indonesian languages), 'asked him urgently' (East Toradja), 'didn't stop begging him' (Sranan). One may have to make explicit the aim, e.g. "begged him to come in" (TEV), or the implied direct discourse, e.g. 'said to him, "Please, please, come in (or, do not stay/remain outside)"'.

29 ***but he answered his father, 'Lo, these many years I have served you, and I never disobeyed your command; yet you never gave me a kid, that I might make merry with my friends.***

Exegesis: *apokritheis* 'answering', viz. to his father's pleading.

idou 'behold', emphatic introduction of what follows.

tosauta etē douleuō soi lit. 'so many years I am serving you', i.e. 'so many years I have served you, and am still serving you'. *tosauta etē* is accusative of duration.

douleuō (also 16 : 13) 'to serve as a *doulos,* i.e. as a slave, or, servant'.

kai oudepote entolēn sou parēlthon 'and I never once disobeyed an order of yours'. The aorist tense of *parēlthon* is punctiliar. For *parerchomai* cp. on 11 : 42.

kai emoi oudepote edōkas eriphon 'and to me you never once gave a kid'. *emoi* is emphatic.

eriphos (†) 'kid', 'young he-goat', cheap as compared with the fatted calf.

hina meta tōn philōn mou euphranthō 'that I might enjoy myself with my friends', i.e. by means of a meal together.

Translation: Honorifics, again, in Javanese and related languages, but now with another intention than in v. 21: the honorific form of the elder son's words is sarcastic rather than respectful, treating the father as a stranger.

Lo, cp. on "behold" in 1 : 20.

I have served you, or, 'I have kept on working for you' (Kapauku), 'I have been your servant, or, like a servant of yours'.

I never disobeyed your command, or, 'I never transgressed your command/word', 'I never failed to do what you commanded/told me (to do)'; in Sranan the idiom is, 'never I passed your mouth'. Cp. also on "disobedient" in 1 : 17.

A kid, or, more disdainfully, "so much as a kid" (NEB), "even a goat" (TEV).

That I might make merry with my friends, or, 'to-be-used by me to feast together-with' (Sundanese).

30 ***But when this son of yours came, who has devoured your living with harlots, you killed for him the fatted calf!'***

Exegesis: *ho huios sou houtos* 'this son of yours', contrasting with *emoi* in v. 29. *houtos* here with obvious contempt, as shown by what follows.

ho kataphagōn sou ton bion meta pornōn 'who has devoured your possessions with prostitutes'. *katesthiō* means here 'to destroy', 'to consume', 'to eat up', cp. A-G s.v. For *bios* cp. on 8 : 43; here it is used hyperbolically since the younger son spent only his part of his father's possessions.

pornē (†) 'prostitute', 'harlot'.

Translation: One may have to change the sentence structure, e.g. 'this son of yours has devoured...with harlots; but when (or, as soon as) he (emphatic) came, you killed...'.

Devoured. A verb meaning 'to eat up' can sometimes be used in the metaphorical sense required here, e.g. in Sranan; where that is not the case one may say, 'to spend all', 'to waste', 'to squander' (see v. 13).

Harlots. Some idiomatic expressions used are, "women of the street" (Goodspeed), 'single (woman) of the-state/government' (Kituba), 'women who live like dogs' (Cakchiquel), 'ten pence women' (Timorese), 'bad women' (Thai 1967, Trukese, Ponape), 'lustful/debauched women' (South Toradja, Yao), 'ones-who-walk' (Bamiléké). Often a generic term is used, e.g. "his women" (NEB), *les femmes* (Jerusalem, similarly East Toradja 1933), in this context the mere plural being enough to give the word a clearly pejorative meaning. Cp. also on "sinner" in 7 : 37.

31 ***And he said to him, 'Son, you are always with me, and all that is mine is yours.***

Exegesis: *ho de eipen autō* 'but he said to him', change of subject.

su pantote met' emou ei 'you are always with me'. *su* is emphatic. *met' emou* contrasts with *nekros* and *apolōlōs* in v. 32.

panta ta ema sa estin 'all I have is yours', since his brother's part had already been spent.

Translation: *And he said to him.* The speaker may have to be specified, e.g. 'his father answered' (Balinese).

Son, see 2 : 48.

All that is mine is yours, or, 'all my things belong to you only' (Kapauku), 'all I have/possess you have/possess too' (Malay, Balinese).

32 ***It was fitting to make merry and be glad, for this your brother was dead, and is alive; he was lost, and is found.'"***

Exegesis: *euphranthēnai de kai charēnai edei* 'but we had to enjoy ourselves and to be glad', with *hēmas* 'we' (i.e. 'we in the house') understood; the clause refers to the inner compulsion which the coming home of the younger son caused, cp. A-G s.v. *dei* 4. *euphranthēnai* refers to external celebration, *charēnai* to inner feeling (cp. Plummer).

ho adelphos sou houtos 'your brother here', echoes *ho huios sou houtos* in v. 30, and implicitly criticizes the note of contempt in those words.

ezēsen 'he began to live again', synonymous with *anezēsen* in v. 24.

apolōlōs '(he was) lost', with *ēn* understood.

Translation: *It was fitting to,* or, "but we *had* to" (Rieu, TEV), 'how would it have been possible not to', the personal pronoun to be taken as exclusive, where that distinction is obligatory.

Be glad, or, 'rejoice', see 1 : 14.

CHAPTER SIXTEEN

1 ***He also said to the disciples, "There was a rich man who had a steward, and charges were brought to him that this man was wasting his goods.***

Exegesis: *elegen de kai pros tous mathētas* 'he said also to the disciples', though the Pharisees heard it too (cp. v. 14). This means that what follows is primarily intended for the disciples as contrasted with what precedes (cp. 15 : 3).

anthrōpos tis ēn plousios hos eichen oikonomon 'there was a rich man who had a manager'. Of the two facts related in this sentence, viz. that the man was rich, and that he had a manager, the latter is the more relevant to what follows. *plousios* is attributive to *anthrōpos tis*. For *oikonomos* cp. on 12 : 42.

kai houtos dieblēthē autō hōs diaskorpizōn ta huparchonta autou 'and this one was reported to him as squandering his property'. *houtos* refers to the manager, and *autō* and *autou* refer to the rich man. For *diaskorpizō* cp. on 15 : 13; for *ta huparchonta* cp. on 8 : 3.

diaballō (††) 'to accuse', 'to bring charges against someone', usually with hostile intent.

Translation: *There was a rich man who had a steward,* or, 'a certain (cp. on 7 : 41) rich man had a steward'. For *steward,* or, 'manager', 'secretary/bookkeeper' (Sranan), see on 12 : 42.

Charges were brought to him that this man was wasting his goods, usually to be recast, and the participants to be specified, cp. e.g. 'people came bringing charges to the rich man, saying the steward was wasting his (i.e. the master's) goods' (Thai 1967), 'he was told that one was using-up what belonged to his master' (Tzeltal), 'who was exposed to him because he was wasting his (unambiguous, since a reference to the steward would require another pronoun) goods' (Fulani 1964), 'some people accused the steward, may be he was wasting the goods of that man' (Trukese, Ponape); or, in direct discourse, 'people told him, "Your steward is wasting your property", or, "He is causing your wealth to fly away"' (Marathi). For *to bring charges against* cp. *N.T.Wb.*/1f, ACCUSE; for *wasting* cp. on "squandered" in 15 : 13.

2 ***And he called him and said to him, 'What is this that I hear about you? Turn in the account of your stewardship, for you can no longer be steward.'***

Exegesis: *kai phōnēsas auton eipen autō* 'and he summoned him and said to him'. For *phōneō* as synonymous with *kaleō* cp. on 14 : 12.

ti touto akouō peri sou lit. 'what this I hear about you', with demonstrative *touto* loosely appositive to interrogative *ti*, implying that the question concerns something which both parties know about.

apodos ton logon tēs oikonomias sou 'render the account of your managing', cp. A-G s.v. *logos* 2 a. As the article *ton* shows the reference is here to some specific account, viz. the final account, as the rest of this verse shows.

oikonomia (also vv. 3 and 4) 'the function of a manager', 'stewardship', 'agency', cp. on v. 3.

ou gar dunē eti oikonomein 'for you cannot be manager any longer'.

oikonomeō (††) 'to act as manager', 'to be manager'.

Translation: *He called him*, or, 'had him called', 'caused(-someone)-to-fetch that man' (East Toradja 1933). Again the subject may have to be specified, cp. e.g. 'the rich man sent to call him' (Sranan).

Turn in the account of your stewardship may be described by, 'write down what you received and spent', 'count-for-me all that came-in, went-out' (East Toradja 1933), 'show the books of your stewardship' (Kituba, similarly Trukese, Ponape), 'give me so that I can hear about your supervision' (Shona 1966). *Your stewardship*, or as a verbal phrase, 'the way you managed my property', 'what you did as my steward/manager'.

You can no longer be steward, or, 'you cannot remain (or, continue as) my steward'.

3 ***And the steward said to himself, 'What shall I do, since my master is taking the stewardship away from me? I am not strong enough to dig, and I am ashamed to beg.***

Exegesis: *eipen de en heautō ho oikonomos* 'the manager said to (lit. 'in') himself', i.e. debated inwardly.

ti poiēsō 'what shall I do', i.e. 'what am I to do', viz. with a view to his future, not with regard to the rendering of his account.

hoti ho kurios mou aphaireitai tēn oikonomian ap' emou 'since my master is taking the stewardship from me'. *hoti* means here 'since', 'now that', as the clause refers to causes which are already known. For *kurios* cp. on 1 : 6. *oikonomia* refers here and in v. 4 to the function, or, the job, in v. 2 to the way in which the function is performed.

skaptein ouk ischuō 'I cannot dig', i.e. 'I am not strong enough to dig', a proverbial saying, indicating that one cannot do heavy manual labour.

epaitein aischunomai 'I am ashamed to beg', i.e. to be a professional beggar, obviously the alternative for one who cannot earn his living with his own hands.

aischunomai (†) 'to be ashamed', 'to be too proud to', with following infinitive.

Translation: For *said to himself* see 3 : 8; for *master* see on "Lord" in 1 : 6, sub (a).

Is taking the stewardship (or, this/my work) *away from me*, or, 'dismisses (lit. causes-to-cease) me as steward' (Balinese, similarly Tzeltal), 'will let-me-go' (Kapauku, East Toradja 1933), 'will remove me from (my) steward's duties' (Thai 1967, similarly Shona 1966), 'has decided that I can no longer be his manager, or, cannot continue to manage his property'.

I am not strong enough to dig, or, continuing, as it were, the initial question, 'Dig? I have not the strength for it' (Jerusalem). *Dig*, or, 'hoe' (Indonesian languages, Jerusalem); some specification may be required, e.g. 'dig in the fields', 'till the soil'.

I am ashamed to beg, i.e. begging will cause me shame, 'beg? I would be ashamed' (Jerusalem); or, worded reversely, "I am...too proud to beg" (NEB). Cp. also "shame" in 13 : 17. *To beg*, or, 'to ask for money/gifts', 'to ask-for alms (cp. 11 : 41), or, pity' (Bahasa Indonesia, East Toradja), 'to go (around) begging' (Sranan); and cp. *N.T.Wb.*/12f, ASK.

4 ***I have decided what to do, so that people may receive me into their houses when I am put out of the stewardship.'***

Exegesis: *egnōn ti poiēsō* 'I know what I am to do'. The aorist tense of *egnōn* suggests that he suddenly gets an idea.

hotan metastathō ek tēs oikonomias 'when I am removed from the stewardship'.

methistēmi (†) 'to remove', 'to dismiss'.

hina...dexōntai me eis tous oikous heautōn 'so that...people will welcome me in their homes'. *hina* refers to the intended result. The subject of *dexōntai* are his master's debtors, as vv. 5-7 show.

Translation: *I have decided...*, or, better to bring out the suddenness, 'ah, (or, now) I know...', 'I know already...'.

What to do, so that people receive me, or, "how to make them welcome me" (Rieu). *Receive me*, cp. 9 : 5.

I am put out of the stewardship, a counterpart of the phrase used in v. 3, but in passive construction. The phrase, in the Greek inserted between "so that" and "receive...", often is better transposed to initial or final position (e.g. TEV, or RSV, Sranan, Sundanese).

5 ***So, summoning his master's debtors one by one, he said to the first, 'How much do you owe my master?'***

Exegesis: *kai proskalesamenos hena hekaston tōn chreopheiletōn tou kuriou heautou* 'after summoning each of his master's debtors', i.e. he called all of them one by one. For *proskaleō* cp. on 7 : 18. *chreopheiletēs* (cp. on 7 : 41) refers here either to tenants who are behind with the rent, or, to merchants who are behind in settling their accounts, preferably the former.

poson opheileis tō kuriō mou 'how much do you owe my master?' *opheilō* (also 7 : 41) refers to what one has to pay, not what one has purchased, and hence, to pay for.

Translation: *Summoning*, or, 'having called' (cp. v. 2).

His master's debtors, or, 'those (who were) in debt, or, who had to pay (something) to his master'; or, following the interpretation preferred in *Exegesis,* "his employer's tenants" (Rieu).

The first, or, 'the one who came first' (e.g. in Toba Batak).

How much do you owe, cp. 7 : 41; or, "what rent do you have to pay" (Rieu).

6 ***He said, 'A hundred measures of oil.' And he said to him, 'Take your bill, and sit down quickly and write fifty.'***

Exegesis: *hekaton batous elaiou* 'a hundred bats of (olive) oil', with *opheilō* 'I owe' understood.

batos (††) 'bat', a Hebrew liquid measure of capacity, about 8 gallons, or 37 litres. 800 gallons of olive oil appears to be a great debt.

dexai sou ta grammata 'take your bill', implying that the manager handed it to him.

grammata (also v. 7) plural, 'written agreement', here 'bill', 'account'.

kathisas tacheōs grapson pentēkonta 'sit down and write quickly fifty'. *tacheōs* goes with both *grapson* and *kathisas*. *grapson* is best understood as referring to writing a new account.

Translation: On *hundred* cp. 15 : 4. For "hundred" and "fifty" (here) and "hundred" and "eighty" (v. 7) Kapauku has to say, 'sixty' and 'thirty', 'sixty' and 'fifty', respectively.

Measure, preferably to be rendered by the designation of a common local measure for liquids, e.g. "barrel" (TEV), 'jar' (Bahasa Indonesia 1968), 'jug' (Toba Batak), 'bottle' (East Toradja 1933). Where the quantity designated considerably differs from that of Gr. *batos,* one may adjust the renderings of "hundred" and "fifty" in such a way that the sum total approximately agrees with the original. See also *N.T.Wb.*/73f, WEIGHTS and MEASURES.

Oil, cp. *TH-Mk* on 6 : 13.

Take, or, 'here is', 'this here (is)', or whatever phrase is idiomatically used when handing over something.

Bill, or, 'debt letter' (some Indonesian languages), 'paper on which your payment is written' (Sranan), 'evidence of your debt' (Kekchi), 'small paper of agreement' (Shona 1963), 'letter to-acknowledge your-debt' (East Toradja).

Fifty. The measure may have to be added, e.g. 'fifty barrels/jars' (Sranan, Bahasa Indonesia 1968).

7 ***Then he said to another, 'And how much do you owe?' He said, 'A hundred measures of wheat.' He said to him, 'Take your bill, and write eighty.'***

Exegesis: *epeita heterō eipen* 'then he said to another'. *heterō* instead of *tō deuterō* 'the second one' implies that vv. 6 and 7 relate only examples of what the manager did.

hekaton korous sitou 'a hundred kors of wheat'.

koros (††) 'kor', a Hebrew dry measure of capacity, about 10 bushels or 370 litres, also a very considerable amount.

grapson ogdoēkonta 'write eighty', cp. on v. 6.

Translation: Cp. on v. 6. For *another* cp. also 14 : 19.

Measure, or, 'bag', 'sack' (Shona 1963, Sranan), or a similar designation for a common local dry measure much larger than the preceding one; and cp. on v. 6.

Wheat, see on 3 : 17.

8 ***The master commended the dishonest steward for his prudence; for the sons of this world are wiser in their own generation than the sons of light.***

Exegesis: *kai epēnesen ho kurios ton oikonomon tēs adikias* 'and the master praised the dishonest manager'. Whether *ho kurios* refers to the master of the manager, or to Jesus is hard to decide (see commentaries). On the whole the former appears slightly preferable. *oikonomos tēs adikias* (qualifying genitive) is equivalent to *oikonomos adikos,* and refers to dishonesty, rather than unrighteousness, cp. on v. 10.

epaineō (†) 'to praise', 'to approve', 'to commend'.

hoti phronimōs epoiēsen 'because he had acted shrewdly'. *hoti* may mean here 'that', or, 'because', preferably the latter. *phronimōs* does not refer to the moral aspects of the manager's dealing but to the fact that he knew how to act in the face of imminent crisis. This is the point of the parable.

hoti hoi huioi tou aiōnos toutou 'for the sons of this age', as contrasted with the people of the age to come (cp. 18 : 30), i.e. people whose main concern is the here and now, as contrasted with the people whose main concern is the kingdom of God. The clause is best understood as a parenthetical comment by Jesus on the reaction of the master, and the meaning appears to be that the sons of this age are more shrewd in dealing with their own kind than the sons of light in dealing with their situation *vis à vis* the imminent coming of the kingdom. For *aiōn* cp. on 1 : 33.

phronimōteroi huper tous huious tou phōtos...eisin 'are more shrewd than the sons of light'. *huper* lit. 'beyond' means here '(more) than'. The sons of light are the people who belong to the kingdom of God, of which the light is the symbol (cp. Jn. 12 : 36, Eph. 5 : 8, 1 Thess. 5 : 5).

eis tēn genean tēn heautōn 'in dealing with their own generation', i.e. "in dealing with their own kind" (NEB), goes with *hoi huioi tou aiōnos toutou.*

Translation: *Commended* (or, praised) *the dishonest steward,* i.e. said that the...steward had done well. *Dishonest,* or, 'deceitful', 'who didn't do right' (Sranan). Words for 'crooked', 'not straight' can often be used in the figurative sense required here.

For his prudence, or, 'because he had acted prudently/shrewdly/carefully, or, with (so) much forethought'.

The sons of this world, or, 'those who belong to this world/age'. The expression has pejorative force, since the contrast with "the sons of light" characterizes the sphere of this world or age as darkness. Some renderings used are, 'heirs of visible-pleasures' (Balinese, cp. 8 : 14), 'people who seek this world, or, value-highly the life in the world' (East Toradja 1933, South Toradja), 'lovers of the earth' (proposed for Shona).

Wiser, i.e. more prudent (see above).

In their own generation, or, 'regarding those of their own kind' (Marathi), 'the way they live with each other' (Sranan), 'towards their-fellows (of-the-same-mind)' (East and South Toradja, Toba Batak).

The sons of light, or, 'people belonging to the light', 'people characterized by light', 'those who are in the realm of daylight' (existing figurative expression in Tzeltal).

9 ***And I tell you, make friends for yourselves by means of unrighteous mammon, so that when it fails they may receive you into the eternal habitations.***

Exegesis: *kai egō humin legō* 'and I tell you', cp. on 3 : 8. Here it introduces the application of the parable.

heautois poiēsate philous 'make friends for yourselves'. *heautois* is emphatic by position. As apparent from what follows the clause is not to be understood literally, but refers rather to acts of goodwill and charity which last beyond this age.

ek tou mamōna tēs adikias 'by means of dishonest wealth'. For this type of phrase cp. on *oikonomos tēs adikias* (v. 8), and *en tō adikō mamōna* (v. 11). Here the genitive *tēs adikias* refers to the way in which the wealth is acquired.

mamōnas from Aramaic *māmōna'*, of uncertain derivation, often occurring in the Targum and the Talmud with reference to money made in dishonest ways, or spent for dishonest purposes. The phrase *ho mamōnas tēs adikias* seems almost to imply that wealth as such is morally or religiously bad (cp. Phillips).

hina...dexōntai humas eis tas aiōnious skēnas 'so that...they may welcome you into the eternal dwellings'. The subject of *dexōntai* is not the friends of the preceding clause, and the verb is best understood as a Hebraistic way of rendering the passive with God as agent of the welcoming (cp. on *aitousin* in 12 : 20). The eternal dwellings are best understood as dwelling places in the age to come. *skēnē*, cp. on 9 : 33.

hotan eklipē 'when it comes to an end'. Subject of *eklipē* may be *ho mamōnas tēs adikias*, or the verb may be impersonal, preferably the former.

ekleipō 'to fail', 'to come to an end', here probably in the sense of being no longer of any use.

Translation: *Make friends... by means of unrighteous mammon*, i.e. 'use...Mammon to make-friends' (cp. South Toradja). *Unrighteous*, i.e. 'gained dishonestly', "ill-gotten" (Goodspeed), and cp. "'Money', tainted as it is" (Phillips). *Mammon*, preferably, 'property', 'wealth', 'riches', 'money'; if transliterated, an explanatory note is required.

So that when it fails they may receive..., or, starting a new sentence, 'then (or, the result will be that, or, if you do so) they will receive...when (or, at the moment that) it fails'. *It fails*, or, 'it lets you down' (Balinese), 'it is-there no longer' (East Toradja), "money is a thing of the past" (NEB).

They may receive you into the eternal habitations. In many cases the preservation of the third person plural would be misleading since it suggests a reference to 'friends'; hence, 'God may receive...', or somewhat less explicitly, 'those who are, or, he who is, in the eternal habitations will welcome you there'. *Eternal habitations*, or, 'everlasting dwellings', 'places where people dwell forever, or, without end', see *N.T.Wb.*/4f, AGE, and cp. *TH-Mk* on 3 : 29; 10 : 17.

10 ***"He who is faithful in a very little is faithful also in much; and he who is dishonest in a very little is dishonest also in much.***

Exegesis: *ho pistos en elachistō kai en pollō pistos* 'he who is trustworthy in a very little is also trustworthy in much', a general statement, reinforced by its opposite (see below), preparing the way for the two rhetorical questions in vv. 11f. For *en* meaning 'with regard to', hence, 'in the use of', cp. A-G s.v. 2. For *pistos* cp. on 12 : 42. *elachistō* and *pollō* are without specific reference; they indicate degrees of importance.

ho en elachistō adikos 'he who is untrustworthy in a very little'. The meaning *adikos* is determined by its being the opposite of *pistos* (cp. *ho oikonomos tēs adikias* in v. 8).

Translation: *He who is faithful in a very little*, or, 'he who one can trust in (or, with, or, to take care of) a very little', 'he to whom a very little can be entrusted', cp. 'he in whose hands you can leave the very small things, in his hand you can leave the great things' (Sranan). For a shift to an 'if'-clause see the note on "whoever" in 9 : 24; for *faithful* cp. also 12 : 42. *A very little*, or, if a noun has to be added, 'a very small matter/property', 'very few goods' etc.; similarly in the case of *much* in the next clause.

Dishonest, or, 'unfaithful', 'not to be trusted'.

11 ***If then you have not been faithful in the unrighteous mammon, who will entrust to you the true riches?***

Exegesis: *ei oun en tō adikō mamōna pistoi ouk egenesthe* 'if then you have not been trustworthy in dishonest wealth'. *oun* introduces the inference from the general principle of v. 10. *ho adikos mamōnas* has the same meaning as *ho mamōnas tēs adikias* in v. 9.

to alēthinon tis humin pisteusei 'who will entrust to you what is genuine?' *to alēthinon* is used here as a substantive, contrasting with *ho adikos mamōnas* and hence refers implicitly to wealth which is genuine. But here the concept of wealth is to be taken metaphorically referring to spiritual wealth.

alēthinos (†) 'true', 'genuine'.

pisteuō here 'to entrust'. The future tense of *pisteusei* may refer to some future event, or be due to the interrogative nature of the clause, preferably the latter.

Translation: *Who will...?* The rhetorical question has negative force, and may have to be rendered, '(there is) no one (who) will...'.

Entrust to, i.e. commit something in confidence to; 'to put something into the hands of' (Sranan).

The true riches, or, 'genuine wealth', 'what is really valuable' (Kapauku). For the adjective cp. *N.T.Wb.*/71.

12 ***And if you have not been faithful in that which is another's, who will give you that which is your own?***

Exegesis: *en tō allotriō* (†) 'in what belongs to another', refers to *ho adikos mamōnas* and interprets wealth as something one does not own. No thought about the person, or nature of the owner is implied.

to humeteron 'that which is yours', i.e. what God gives to you as inheritance.

Translation: *That which is another's*, or, following the interpretation advocated in *Exegesis*, 'what does not belong to you', 'wealth/riches/property you do not possess'.

That wich is your own, or, 'what is to belong to you yourselves', 'what really is to become your own' (Tzeltal), 'wealth/riches/property you are to possess yourselves', again to be taken metaphorically.

13 ***No servant can serve two masters; for either he will hate the one and love the other, or he will be devoted to the one and despise the other. You cannot serve God and mammon."***

Exegesis: *oudeis oiketēs dunatai dusi kuriois douleuein* 'no slave can serve two masters'. For *douleuō* cp. on 15 : 29.

oiketēs (†) 'slave', added in order to make clear that the reference is not to serving in general but to a slave's serving.

ē gar ton hena misēsei kai ton heteron agapēsei 'for either he will hate the one and love the other'. *miseō* and *agapaō* are used here in the meaning 'reject strongly' and 'prefer strongly'. The future tense of both verbs expresses that this is what may be naturally expected.

ē henos anthexetai kai tou heterou kataphronēsei 'or he will be devoted to the one and despise the other'. *antechomai* and *kataphroneō* are as strong as *agapaō* and *miseō*.

antechō (†) 'to cling to', 'to be devoted to'.

kataphroneō (†) 'to despise', 'to treat with contempt'.

ou dunasthe theō douleuein kai mamōna 'you cannot serve God and money', personal application of what hitherto was stated in general terms. *mamōnas* is represented here as a power which may lay hold of people.

Translation: *No servant can serve two masters* is redundant in that the relationship between the participants is indicated thrice, in "servant", or 'slave', in "serve", or 'be the slave of', and in "master", or 'owner'. Less redundant renderings may be more idiomatic, e.g. 'no slave can have two masters, or, can have-as-master two men' (Bahasa Indonesia), 'no one can be the slave of two masters', 'there is no slave who can hold two servitudes, or, can make himself slave of two men' (Javanese, East Toradja). For 'slave' see 7 : 2.

For *hate* see on 1 : 71; for *love* on 6 : 27.

He will be devoted to the one and despise the other, using verbs that are approximately synonymous with the preceding ones, but in reversed word order, a well known stylistic device in Greek, but unacceptable in some receptor languages, which prefer parallel order. *To be devoted to* has also been rendered by "to be attached/loyal to" (BFBS, TEV, cp. Phillips), 'to make-common-cause-with' (Toba Batak), 'hold strongly to the side of' (Sranan), and *to despise* by 'to make-light-of' (Bahasa Indonesia), 'to neglect' (Balinese), 'to be indifferent to', 'not to count' (Sranan).

You cannot serve God and mammon. Although the verb is preferably to be rendered as in the first occurrence, differentiation may be required, e.g. because here 'God' is one of the objects; hence, 'have-as-lord' (Bahasa Indonesia), 'worship' (Balinese); or because it is used metaphorically here, hence e.g. "serve" instead of "be the slave of" (NEB). Where no verb is available that fits both objects an appropriate synonym may have to be inserted, e.g. 'to worship God and be a slave of Riches/Wealth/Property/ Money'. *Mammon* functions here as a person. If possible one should keep to the noun used in vv. 9, 11 (see above), marking it as a proper name. Where such personification is idiomatically unacceptable, it may be possible to use the name of the god of wealth (as in an older Balinese version); or one may transliterate the Greek word (cp. Rieu's "Mammon" here, "world" in vv. 9, 11), where necessary adding a footnote that equates the translation in vv. 9 and 11 with this transliteration. Or, again, one may shift to a non-personifying rendering, where necessary adjusting the verb, cp. e.g. 'strive-after property' (South Toradja), 'be devoted to...riches' (Javanese).

14 ***The Pharisees, who were lovers of money, heard all this, and they scoffed at him.***

Exegesis: *ēkouon de tauta panta hoi Pharisaioi* 'now the Pharisees heard all this'. *tauta panta* is best understood as referring to vv. 1-13 which Jesus spoke to the disciples (cp. v. 1), but in the presence of the Pharisees. For *hoi Pharisaioi* cp. on 5 : 17.

philarguroi huparchontes 'who were fond of money', going with *hoi Pharisaioi*. The participle *huparchontes* suggests here a permanent characteristic, cp. Plummer.

philarguros (†) 'fond of money', 'avaricious'.

kai exemuktērizon auton 'and they were sneering at him'. The imperfect tense is durative and suggests that the Pharisees sneered at Jesus while listening to him.

ekmuktērizō (also 23 : 35) 'to sneer', 'to ridicule'.

Translation: *Who were lovers of money*, or, 'who loved money, or, were (very) fond of money/wealth'; and cp. *N.T.Wb.*/25f, DESIRE. The relative clause does not have restrictive force; it suggests a reason for the Pharisees' behaviour, and is, therefore, sometimes rendered as a causal clause going with 'scoffing', cp. e.g. TEV, Bahasa Indonesia RC.

Heard all this, or, 'heard these words, or, what Jesus was saying'.

They scoffed at him. Some idiomatic renderings used describe or suggest a gesture or facial movement that expresses contempt in the culture, e.g. 'to turn-up-the-nose' (Toba Batak), 'to make the mouth long', suggesting 'to suck the lips', an indication of contempt that was felt to be too vulgar for use in this context (Sranan).

15 ***But he said to them, "You are those who justify yourselves before men, but God knows your hearts; for what is exalted among men is an abomination in the sight of God.***

Exegesis: *humeis este hoi dikaiountes heautous* 'you are the people who justify yourselves', i.e. 'you are characterized by the fact that you justify yourselves'. *dikaioō* means here 'to claim to be just', 'to present as just'.

enōpion tōn anthrōpōn 'in the sight of men', going with *hoi dikaiountes heautous*.

ho de theos ginōskei tas kardias humōn 'but God knows your hearts', contrasting with *enōpion tōn anthrōpōn*.

hoti to en anthrōpois hupsēlon lit. 'for that what is high among men', in the present context, 'that which is highly regarded among men without foundation'.

hupsēlos (†) 'high', here figuratively, 'highly regarded', 'esteemed', cp. *N.T.Wb.*, 47/DIMENSIONS.

bdelugma enōpion tou theou '(is) an abomination in the sight of God', with *estin* understood.

bdelugma (†) 'abomination', 'detestable thing'.

Translation: *Justify yourselves before men*, or, 'pose as just/righteous (cp. on 1 : 6) before men', 'give yourselves the appearance of straight hearts' (Kekchi), 'want people to regard you as (take you to be) righteous', cp. "like the world to look at you and say, "What upright men!"" (Rieu).

Knows your hearts, or, 'your mind/inward-being/thoughts'; or, 'knows who you (really) are', cp. "sees through you" (NEB).

What is exalted among men, or, 'what people regard as exalted' (cp. on 1 : 52).

Is an abomination in the sight of God, or, 'is detested by God' (East Toradja), 'brings-disgust-in God's heart' (Balinese), 'God regards as filthy things' (Sranan).

16 ***"The law and the prophets were until John; since then the good news of the kingdom of God is preached, and every one enters it violently.***

Exegesis: *ho nomos kai hoi prophētai mechri Iōannou* lit. 'the law and the prophets (were) until John'. No connexion with what precedes or with what follows (vv. 17f) is indicated or suggested. *ho nomos kai hoi prophētai* is a well known phrase denoting the old covenant, or the Old Testament (cp. e.g. Acts 13 : 15; 28 : 23; Mt. 5 : 17). The clause states that the old covenant existed and had authority until John the Baptist.

apo tote hē basileia tou theou euaggelizetai 'from then the (good news of the) kingdom of God has been preached'. *euaggelizetai* in the present tense implies that the preaching has been going on and is still going on, cp. on 4 : 43. The emphasis is here on *hē basileia tou theou* as the new situation that exists since John the Baptist.

kai pas eis autēn biazetai 'and everyone forces his way into it', i.e. everyone tries hard to enter it, in response to the proclaiming of the kingdom.

biazomai (†) here 'to enter forcibly', 'to force one's way into', cp. A-G s.v. 2 d.

Translation: *The law and the prophets,* or, 'what is written in the law and the books of the prophets', 'the law and the words of the prophets', 'what the law commands and the prophets say'. For *law* see 2 : 22.

Were until John, or, 'up to the time J. came', not including the time of John's ministry. A more specific rendering of the verb may be necessary, e.g. 'were preached' (Fulani), 'were important to believe/obey' (Tzeltal), 'were valid'.

Since then, or, 'beginning at that moment' (South Toradja).

The good news of the kingdom of God is preached, see on 4 : 43. The passive has probably been used here to leave the agent ambiguous, but where an active construction is required and the translator is compelled to name an agent, it is probably best to say, 'I preach the good news...' (cp. *TBT*, 19.163, 1968).

Enters it violently. The pronoun refers to the 'kingdom of God', but now taken in its locative sense; hence e.g. 'fights to get into that place, or, into the place where God rules', and cp. 'all people do great effort to enter God's hand (viz. in order that He rule them)' (a Mixtec dialect).

17 ***But it is easier for heaven and earth to pass away, than for one dot of the law to become void.***

Exegesis: *eukopōteron de estin ton ouranon kai tēn gēn parelthein* 'but it is easier for heaven and earth to pass away'. *de* 'but' implies a contrast with v. 16, and suggests probably that the new situation to which v. 16 refers does not imply that the law is no longer valid. *parerchomai* means here 'to come to an end', 'to disappear'.

ē tou nomou mian keraian pesein lit. 'than that one hook of the law falls down'. *tou nomou* is emphatic by position.

keraia (†) lit. 'hook' as part of a letter, i.e. some insignificant part, dot, stroke, comma.

piptō lit. 'to fall', here 'to become invalid', cp. A-G s.v. 2 b δ.

Translation: For *easier* cp. 5 : 23; for *heaven and earth* see 10 : 21.

To pass away, or, 'to be destroyed', 'to go to ruin', 'to die' (used metaphorically), 'to become dead, as it were' (as simile), 'to cease to exist'.

Dot. The rendering should preferably be the name of a small item in the script best known in the culture, cp. e.g. "dotting of an *i*" (Goodspeed), "comma" (Rieu), 'period' (Thai 1967, Fulani), 'tilde' (Tzeltal), 'dash', indicating a vowel (in Arabic script, Zarma), 'dot', indicating the *ng* (in Balinese script). Other versions use a descriptive rendering, e.g. 'part of a letter' (Kituba), 'tiniest word' (Kapauku), 'small (thing) written' (Lomwe), 'small mark' (Ponape), "smallest detail" (TEV); cp. also, 'were it only something very small (lit. like the dirt in a nail)' (South Toradja).

18 ***"Every one who divorces his wife and marries another commits adultery, and he who marries a woman divorced from her husband commits adultery.***

Exegesis: *pas ho apoluōn tēn gunaika autou kai gamōn heteran moicheuei* 'everyone who divorces his wife and marries another woman commits adultery'. As this teaching is not found in the Old Testament law (cp. Mk. 10 : 1-12), v. 18 is not to be regarded as an exemplification of v. 17. The relationship between the two participial clauses is that the latter presupposes the former: he who after divorcing his wife remarries, commits adultery.

apoluō 'to send away', here 'to divorce'.

moicheuō (also 18 : 20) 'to be an adulterer', 'to commit adultery'.

he apolelumenēn apo andros gamōn 'he who marries a woman divorced from, or, by her husband'. The former is preferable though no presumption is implied as to the initiative in bringing about the divorce. The perfect tense of the participle *apolelumenēn* points to a situation in which a woman finds herself after having been divorced from her husband.

Translation: *Every one who divorces*, for the construction cp. on 9 : 24; for the verb cp. *N.T.Wb.*/30. A formal, legal separation is probably meant here (cp. Mk. 10 : 4). Balinese expresses this by, 'break-off having-a-wife'.

Marries another (or, another woman), or, 'marries again'. *To marry*, see 14 : 20.

Commits adultery, or, 'is (or, acts as) an adulterer', 'breaks the marriage' (Sranan). For *adultery* cp. Nida, *BT*, 193; *TH-Mk* on 7 : 21; *N.T.Wb.*/66f, SEX; *TBT*, 3.93f, 1952.

And, or here, 'so', 'similarly'.

A woman divorced from her husband, or, where the prepositional phrase would sound unduly redundant, 'a woman who has been divorced', or simply, 'a-divorced-one' (Balinese, her sex to be understood from the context).

19 ***"There was a rich man, who was clothed in purple and fine linen and who feasted sumptuously every day.***

Exegesis: *anthrōpos de tis ēn plousios* 'there was (once) a rich man'. No connexion with the preceding is indicated or suggested. Cp. also on v. 1.

kai enedidusketo porphuran kai busson 'and he used to dress in purple and fine linen'. The imperfect tense suggests habitual conduct.

endiduskomai (†) 'to dress oneself'.

porphura (†) 'purple', hence 'purple garment', here referring to the upper garment.

bussos (††) 'fine linen', hence 'fine linen cloth', here referring to the undergarment. Both words suggest expensive clothing.

euphrainomenos kath' hēmeran lamprōs 'enjoying himself splendidly every day'. The participial clause is syntactically subordinate to the preceding clause but semantically of the same order. *euphrainomenos* refers probably to the feasts which the rich man gives.

lamprōs (††) 'splendidly', 'luxuriously'.

Translation: *Who was clothed* (or, used to dress) *in purple and fine linen*, or, 'his garments were of purple (cloth) and fine linen', cp. *N.T.Wb.*/20, CLOTHE. One may have to shift to terms for garments and/or material known in the culture as expensive and luxurious, e.g. 'in silk and satin' (East Toradja 1933), or to make that connotation explicit, e.g. '...in expensive red and white cloth' (cp. Kekchi), 'beautifully dressed in a smooth sarong of fine cloth' (cp. South Toradja), 'in a luxurious robe and shirt', "in the most expensive clothes" (TEV).

Feasted sumptuously, or, 'was having (lit. eating) big feasts' (Sranan), and cp. the note on "make merry" in 12 : 19.

20 ***And at his gate lay a poor man named Lazarus, full of sores,***
21 ***who desired to be fed with what fell from the rich man's table; moreover the dogs came and licked his sores.***

Exegesis: *ptōchos de tis onomati Lazaros* 'a beggar named Lazarus'. For *ptōchos* cp. on 4 : 18. The religious connotation is also present here. No special meaning is to be attached to the name Lazarus even though this is the only time that a personal name occurs in a parable.

ebeblēto pros ton pulōna autou lit. 'had been laid at his gate'. The pluperfect tense of *ebeblēto* denotes the result of the laying down, rather than the act, cp. Bl-D, § 347.1, "(had been prostrated and) lay".

pulōn (†) 'gate', 'entrance', of the gate of a large house or palace.

heilkōmenos 'covered with sores', past participle of *helkoō* (††) 'to cause sores'.

(V. 21) *epithumōn chortasthēnai apo tōn piptontōn apo tēs trapezēs tou plousiou* 'longing to satisfy himself with that which fell from the rich man's table'. *epithumōn* is syntactically co-ordinate with *heilkōmenos*. *ta piptonta* lit. 'that which falls' refers to that which was thrown away after the meals, or to that which fell from the table during the meals, preferably the former.

alla kai hoi kunes erchomenoi epeleichon ta helkē autou 'but (not only that,) even the dogs used to come and lick his sores', adding another touch of sorrow to the picture of the poor man's situation.

epileichō (††) 'to lick'. The imperfect tense points to a habitual situation.

helkos (†) 'sore', 'abscess'.

Translation: *At his gate lay a poor man..., who...*, introducing a second character, which may require something like 'there was (also) a poor man..., lying at his (or, the rich man's) gate/door. He...'. *At his gate,* or, 'at the entrance of his house', 'in front of his house (lit. at his opening)' (West Nyanja). In other cultural situations one may have to say e.g. 'at the lower-end of the rich man's stairs', or, 'at the place where-one-steps-inside(i.e. the upper end of the stairs)-of-him' (East or South Toradja, where houses are built on poles), 'at the gate of the fence around his house' (Thai 1967, similarly Shona 1966), 'at the entrance of the other's compound' (Zarma).

Full of sores. For *full of* see 5 : 12; for *sores,* or, 'ulcers', cp. *N.T.Wb.*/76, WOUND.

(V. 21) *Desired to be fed with,* or, 'desired to be given (to eat)', 'longed to receive (for food)', 'wished to satisfy his hunger with'.

What fell from the rich man's table, i.e. 'scraps/bits (thrown away) from the...table/meal', 'what the servants threw away from the...meal', 'the leftovers from the rich man's food' (Toba Batak).

Moreover the dogs came..., the climax in this description of Lazarus' misery, as brought out in, 'he was even forced to put up with the dogs who used to come...' (cp. Rieu). For *dogs* cp. also *N.T.Wb.*/34f, FAUNA.

22 ***The poor man died and was carried by the angels to Abraham's bosom. The rich man also died and was buried;***

Exegesis: *egeneto de apothanein ton ptōchon* 'it happened that the beggar died', cp. on 1 : 8. As to its function *egeneto de* may be placed under (2) or (4) of the list given there, preferably the latter.

kai apenechthēnai auton hupo tōn aggelōn eis ton kolpon Abraam 'and that he was carried by the angels to Abraham's bosom', dependent upon *egeneto.*

apopherō (†) 'to lead away', 'to carry away', here of the carrying away of the soul after death. The identity of a man and his soul is expressed by the fact that *auton* is subject of *apenechthēnai.*

kolpos (cp. on 6 : 38) here 'bosom'. The phrase *eis ton kolpon Abraam* is best understood as referring to the place next to Abraham while reclining at table, cp. Mt. 8 : 11, Jn. 13 : 23.

apethanen de kai ho plousios kai etaphē 'the rich man also died and was buried', without details or indication of place. No significance is to be attached to the fact that the rich man's burial is mentioned and the beggar's not.

Translation: *Was carried by the angels to* goes with "the poor man". But it may be impossible thus to refer to a deceased person in the same way as to a living person, e.g. in South Toradja, where the subject of the sentence must be 'his soul' (i.e. what leaves the body at death, and continues the deceased's personality in the Land of the Souls). *To carry* (away) *to* is sometimes better rendered by two verbs, cp. e.g. 'to take-up/away..., (and) bring to' (Malay), and in some languages only things can be said 'to be carried', whereas personal entities, including 'souls', require another verb, cp. e.g. 'to lead/take-with-one, or, to accompany..., (and) put-(down-)at' (Balinese, South Toradja).

To Abraham's bosom is, as a rule, better not rendered literally; hence, 'put in Abr.'s hands' (Sranan), 'to sit with Abr.' (East Toradja), "to Abr.'s side" (TEV), 'near Abr.' (Kekchi).

Buried, cp. on 9 : 59.

23 ***and in Hades, being in torment, he lifted up his eyes, and saw Abraham far off and Lazarus in his bosom.***

Exegesis: *kai en tō hadē* 'and in Hades', going with all verbs of v. 23. For *hadēs* cp. on 10 : 15 and *N.T.Wb.*, 72f/HELL.

eparas tous ophthalmous autou 'raising his eyes', preparing the way for *hora*, etc. Cp. also on 6 : 20.

huparchōn en basanois 'being in torment', parenthetical insertion, describing his situation in Hades. *huparchōn* is equivalent to *ōn*.

basanos (also v. 28) 'torment', 'torture'.

hora Abraam apo makrothen 'he saw Abraham far away', yet within hearing distance.

kai Lazaron en tois kolpois autou 'and Lazarus at his bosom', dependent upon *hora*.

Translation: For *Hades*, i.e. the abode of the dead, see *N.T.Wb.*/43, HELL; *TBT*, 4.181f, 1953; for *he lifted up his eyes* cp. 6 : 20.

Being in torment, or, 'while/where he was in torment, or, underwent suffering, or, suffered great pain'. For 'to torment' cp. 8 : 28.

Far off here sometimes best taken with 'Abraham', e.g. 'saw Abr. who was far away (from him)'.

24 ***And he called out, 'Father Abraham, have mercy upon me, and send Lazarus to dip the end of his finger in water and cool my tongue; for I am in anguish in this flame.'***

Exegesis: *kai autos phōnēsas eipen* 'and he raising his voice said', hence, 'and he called out'.

pater Abraam 'father Abraham', cp. on 3 : 8.

eleēson me 'have pity on me'; the aorist tense points to a specific act of pity as indicated by *pempson*, etc.

pempson Lazaron 'send Lazarus', i.e. send him over to this place.

hina bapsē to akron tou daktulou autou hudatos '(in order) to dip the tip of his finger in water'. Strictly speaking the dipping precedes the going over. This implies that *pempson* means not only 'order to go' but also 'order to do'.

baptō (†) 'to dip', here with genitive of that into which something is dipped (*hudatos*), cp. Bl-D, § 172.

akron (†) 'tip' of a finger, 'top' of a mountain.

kai katapsuxē tēn glōssan mou 'and to cool my tongue', only a very small alleviation. *glōssa*, cp. on 1 : 64.

katapsuchō (††) 'to cool off', 'to refresh'.

odunōmai en tē phlogi tautē 'I am in agony in these flames', cp. on 2 : 48.

phlox (†) 'flame', here in a collective sense, 'flames', 'fire'.

Translation: *Called out*, or, "called to him and said" (Goodspeed), 'cried out, saying' (Indonesian languages).

Have mercy upon me, cp. on 1 : 50.

To dip the end of his finger, stressing the smallness of the matter requested: immerse/moisten for a moment only a small part of the smallest finger.

To cool has in many languages been rendered by causative verbs built on 'cool/cold/fresh', elsewhere by 'to ease' (Toba Batak), 'to alleviate the pain/heat of', 'to besprinkle' (East Toradja, designating the act itself instead of its result).

I am in anguish, or, 'I suffer pain', referring to the emotion felt by him while "being in torment" (v. 23), which refers to what happened to him.

25 ***But Abraham said, 'Son, remember that you in your lifetime received your good things, and Lazarus in like manner evil things; but now he is comforted here, and you are in anguish.***

Exegesis: *teknon* 'child', i.e. 'my child', implying that he is still considered as belonging to the people of Abraham.

mnēsthēti 'remember', pointing to what he was supposed to know.

apelabes ta agatha sou en tē zōē sou 'you received to the full your good things during/in your lifetime'. *apolambanō* means usually 'to receive back', but here 'to receive to the full' (cp. *apechō* in 6 : 24). *ta agatha sou* does not mean 'your possessions' (cp. 12 : 18) but 'the good things that were your share', 'your share of blessings' (cp. Goodspeed). For *zōē* meaning 'lifetime' cp. A-G s.v. 1 a.

kai Lazaros homoiōs ta kaka 'and Lazarus likewise the bad things', with *apelaben* understood. *homoiōs* is best understood as corresponding to *en tē zōē sou* in the preceding clause.

nun de hōde parakaleitai 'now he is being comforted here'. *nun* goes with this and with the next clause and indicates the contrast with the life of Lazarus and the rich man before dying; *hōde* refers to the place where Abraham now is.

su de odunasai 'and you are in agony'.

Translation: *Remember*, or, 'think again', 'bring back to mind'; and cp. the note on "remembrance" in 1 : 54.

In your lifetime, or, 'while you were (still) alive' (cp. NEB, Balinese).

You...received your good things, or, 'you were very greatly favoured'

(Tzeltal), 'you saw good' (Kituba). In Foe the verb is rendered in the far past tense, referring to yesterday and before, and in the aspect used when a speaker describes what he observed. *Your good things*, or, 'your share of good things, or, good-fortune (Javanese), or, pleasure (Bahasa Indonesia RC), or, happiness (Marathi), or, joy', 'whatever which good to-you' (Trukese), 'things that pleased you (Shona 1966), or, gave you joy'.

And Lazarus in like manner evil things, taken as the opposite of the preceding "that"-clause but in elliptical form, sometimes has to be filled out entirely, 'but that L. in his lifetime received his evil things' (or equivalent expressions, see above, and cp. e.g. 'great his suffering he lived in the world', Tzeltal), but more often partially, only some of the corresponding terms being repeated, or rendered by a synonym, as required by idiom. See also Wonderly, *BTPU*, 188. For *evil* cp. also Nida, *BT*, 220f.

Comforted, cp. on "received...consolation" in 2 : 25.

26 ***And besides all this, between us and you a great chasm has been fixed, in order that those who would pass from here to you may not be able, and none may cross from there to us.'***

Exegesis: *kai en pasi toutois* 'and besides all this', i.e. the moral aspects described in v. 25.

metaxu hēmōn kai humōn 'between us and you'. The plural *humōn* shows that the reference is to the deceased rich man and those that are with him in *Hades*. *metaxu* also 11 : 51.

chasma mega estēriktai 'a great chasm has been fixed'. The perfect tense of *estēriktai* points to a permanent and unchangeable situation. For *stērizō* cp. on 9 : 51.

chasma (††) 'chasm', 'gulf'.

hopōs hoi thelontes diabēnai enthen pros humas mē dunōntai 'in order that those who want to pass from here to you may not be able', final clause to indicate the intended result, semantically very close to a consecutive meaning (cp. Phillips). *diabainō* (†). *humas* is used here in the sense of 'the place where you are'.

(*hopōs*) *mēde ekeithen pros hēmas diaperōsin* 'and (in order that) they may not cross from there to us'. The subject of *diaperōsin* is not specified. *hēmas* is used here in the sense of 'the place where we are'.

diaperaō (†) 'to cross', here virtually synonymous with *diabainō*.

Translation: *Besides all this*, or, 'moreover' (Balinese), "but that is not all" (NEB).

Between us (referring to Abraham and those with him) *and you*, or, more economically, 'between us (inclusive, covering both parties)' (Mazatec, Toba Batak).

Great chasm, or, 'wide ravine' (Bahasa Indonesia KB), 'a great trench/ditch (as around a village)' (Bamiléké).

Has been fixed, or simply, 'exists', 'is', or more expressively, 'yawns' (Willibrord), 'is-extended' (Bahasa Indonesia KB).

Pass from here, or, 'cross (or, go over, or simply, go) from here'. *Here*, i.e. 'where we (exclus.) are'.

None may cross from there, or, more fully, 'nobody may be able to cross (or, come over, or simply, come) from there, or, from where you (plur.) are'. For *pass* and *cross* cp. also Wonderly, *BTPU*, 187.

27 ***And he said, 'Then I beg you, father, to send him to my father's house,*** 28 ***for I have five brothers, so that he may warn them, lest they also come into this place of torment.'***

Exegesis: *eipen de* 'he said', change of subject.

erōtō se oun 'then I beg you'. *oun* means 'in that case'.

hina pempsēs auton eis ton oikon tou patros mou 'that you send him to my father's house', i.e. 'family', implying a restoring to life. *oikos tou patros mou* refers to his brothers, as v. 28 shows, not to his father.

(V. 28) *echō gar pente adelphous* 'for I have five brothers', parenthetical clause explaining 'my father's house'.

hopōs diamarturētai autois 'in order to warn them', final clause dependent upon *pempsēs*.

diamarturomai (†) 'to warn', or, 'to testify', i.e. 'to inform fully', preferably the former.

hina mē kai autoi elthōsin 'lest they too may come', final clause dependent upon *diamarturētai*.

eis ton topon touton tēs basanou 'to this place of torment'. *tēs basanou* (cp. on v. 23) is qualifying genitive.

Translation: *He said*. The speaker often has to be specified.

Beg, cp. *N.T.Wb.*/12f, ASK.

My father's house, or, 'those who live in my father's house', 'my nearest kin', 'my family'.

(V. 28) Where a more specific term for *brothers* (see 6 : 14) is obligatory they may be taken to have been younger brothers and/or of the same parents.

So that he may warn them, often better as a new sentence here, 'cause him to warn them', or, 'let him (go and) warn them' (cp. e.g. Sranan, East Toradja, TEV). *Warn them*, or more analytically, 'tell them not to do as I did'.

Lest they...come, or, 'in order that they...may not come', viz. once they will have died; hence some adjustments may be required, cp. v. 22.

Place of torment, or, 'place where I (or, we, exclus.) suffer torment/pain'.

29 ***But Abraham said, 'They have Moses and the prophets; let them hear them.'***

Exegesis: *echousi Mōüsea kai tous prophētas* 'they have Moses and the prophets', i.e. they have the written word of God which is read and expounded in the synagogue, cp. 4 : 16ff; 16 : 16; Acts 28 : 23.

akousatōsan autōn 'let them listen to them', presumably in the synagogue. *akouō* implicitly means here 'to listen and obey'.

Translation: *Moses and the prophets,* or, 'the books/writings of M. and the prophets' (several Indonesian versions), 'what M. (or, the prophet M., cp. on 2 : 22) and the (other) prophets have written'.

Hear them, or, 'hear their words', 'listen to (or, obey) what they say'. The verb 'to hear' often can be used also with reference to books/writings, but sometimes adaptation is needed, cp. e.g. 'they should listen to their-sound (i.e. to what is written in them)' (Malay).

30 ***And he said, 'No, father Abraham; but if some one goes to them from the dead, they will repent.'***

Exegesis: *ouchi* 'no', i.e. they will not listen to Moses and the prophets.

all' ean tis apo nekrōn poreuthē pros autous metanoēsousin 'but if someone comes to them from the dead, they will repent'. For *apo nekrōn* (going with *poreuthē,* not with *tis*) cp. on 9 : 7. For *metanoeō* cp. on 10 : 13 and reference there.

Translation: *Goes to them from the dead,* or, 'goes to them from the-midst-of the dead' (Bahasa Indonesia KB), 'visits them from the land of the dead, or, from where the dead are'.

31 ***He said to him, 'If they do not hear Moses and the prophets, neither will they be convinced if some one should rise from the dead.'"***

Exegesis: *eipen de autō* 'but he (i.e. Abraham) said to him', change of subject.

oud' ean tis ek nekrōn anastē peisthēsontai 'not even if someone rises from the dead, will they be convinced'. *anistamai* occurs only here and 24 : 46 in Luke together with *ek nekrōn* and is synonymous with *egeiromai ek nekrōn,* cp. 9 : 7.

peithō 'to persuade', 'to convince'.

Translation: *Neither will they be convinced if some one...,* or, in an active construction, 'then no one will convince them, even if he (or, even a person who)...', 'even some one who...will not gain them over so-that they believe' (Sranan). *Be convinced,* or, "pay heed" (NEB); or, linking-up with v. 28, 'be-warned' (Bahasa Indonesia KB), 'accept warning' (Malay), 'accept (it)' (South Toradja).

Rise from the dead, see on 9 : 7f.

CHAPTER SEVENTEEN

1 ***And he said to his disciples, "Temptations to sin are sure to come; but woe to him by whom they come!***

Exegesis: *eipen de pros tous mathētas autou* 'then he said to his disciples', implying that what precedes was addressed to a larger audience. No indication as to sequence in time or place is given.

anendekton estin tou ta skandala mē elthein lit. 'it is impossible that the temptations should not come', i.e. 'the temptations are bound to come'. For the syntactic construction (articular infinitive in the genitive after an impersonal verb) cp. Bl-D, § 400.4.

anendektos (††) 'impossible', cp. *ouk endechetai* in 13 : 33.

skandalon (†) 'temptation to sin', 'enticement to apostasy', cp. A-G s.v. 2. The article *ta* is best understood as generic.

plēn ouai di' hou erchetai 'but alas (for him) through whom they come', with *toutō* understood. For *ouai* cp. on 6 : 24.

Translation: *Temptations to sin are sure to come,* or, 'without doubt there will come/arise/happen things that cause people to sin'. For *temptations to sin* cp. *N.T.Wb.*/69, STUMBLE; *TH-Mk* on "causes...to sin" in 9 : 42.

For *woe to* see on 6 : 24.

(He) *by whom they come,* or, 'he who is the means of (lit. the road for) their coming' (cp. Javanese, Balinese), 'the one who causes them to come/arise/happen'.

2 ***It would be better for him if a millstone were hung round his neck and he were cast into the sea, than that he should cause one of these little ones to sin.***

Exegesis: *lusitelei autō ei...ē hina* 'it would be better for him if...than that'. The clause introduced by *ei* refers to an event, which, had it happened, would have prevented the event denoted by the clause introduced by *hina.*

lusitelei (††), impersonal, 'it is good', 'it is useful'. Here it is used comparatively (as indicated by *ē* 'than'), and the present tense denotes a supposition, hence, 'it would be better'.

ei lithos mulikos perikeitai peri ton trachēlon autou 'if a millstone had been placed around his neck', cp. *TH-Mk* on 9 : 42 for the tense and meaning of *perikeitai.*

mulikos (††) 'belonging to a mill', here with *lithos* means 'a millstone', a more general term than *mulos onikos* (Mk. 9 : 42, cp. *TH-Mk* there).

kai erriptai eis tēn thalassan 'and (if) he had been thrown into the sea', with change of subject. A violent and gruesome death is better than causing someone to yield to temptation. *riptō* also 4: 35.

ē hina skandalisē tōn mikrōn toutōn hena 'than that he causes one of these little ones to stumble'. *hina* is used in a weakened sense and refers to a fact, cp. A-G s.v. II 1 b. In *tōn mikrōn toutōn hena* the last word is emphatic by position, 'even one'. *tōn mikrōn toutōn* is best understood as referring to the disciples in the broad sense.

skandalizō (also 7 : 23) 'to cause to stumble', 'to entice to sin', cp. *TH-Mk* on 4 : 17 and *N.T.Wb.*, 123/STUMBLE.

Translation: It may be necessary to change the sentence structure, e.g. 'suppose (or, if) a millstone were to be hung round the neck of such a man, that would be good for him, for then he would not be able to cause...'.

If a millstone were hung round his neck, or, 'if his neck had-been-weighted-with a millstone' (Balinese, specifying the aim); cp. also *TH-Mk* on 9 : 42. NEB and Rieu subordinate this clause to the next one, cp. "thrown into the sea with a millstone (tied) round his neck". The implied agent is 'people'. *Millstone* stands here for something large and heavy; some cultural equivalents are, 'blacksmith's stone' (Gio), 'supporting-stone', i.e. a big stone under the main pole of a house (South Toradja); a more generic rendering used is 'large(-sized) stone' (Lokele, Trukese).

Cast into, or, indicating the result, 'immersed' (Toba Batak).

Sea, i.e. 'ocean', cp. *N.T.Wb.*/51f, MARITIME.

Cause...to sin. The rendering should preferably be built on the same terms as used to render "temptation to sin" in v. 1.

Little ones is used here metaphorically in the sense of 'weak/feeble ones', 'people of humble rank'.

3 ***Take heed to yourselves; if your brother sins, rebuke him, and if he repents, forgive him;***

Exegesis: *prosechete heautois* 'be on your guard', cp. on 12 : 1, best understood as an introduction to the exhortation that follows (cp. Plummer, Lagrange).

ean hamartē ho adelphos sou 'if your brother sins (against you)', with *eis se* understood from *hamartēsē eis se* in v. 4, hence "if your brother wrongs you" (Goodspeed). For *adelphos* cp. on 6 : 41.

epitimēson autō 'rebuke him', 'take him to task'.

kai ean metanoēsē aphes autō 'and if he repents, forgive him', syntactically parallel to *ean hamartē* etc. but semantically the point of the exhortation: if your brother wrongs you and if, upon being rebuked by you, he repents, you shall forgive him. For *metanoeō* cp. on 10 : 13.

Translation: *Take heed to yourselves*, or, "keep watch on yourselves" (NEB), 'take care what you do'.

For *sins* (viz. against you) see on v. 4; for *to rebuke* see on 4 : 35.

4 ***and if he sins against you seven times in the day, and turns to you seven times, and says, 'I repent,' you must forgive him."***

Exegesis: *heptakis tēs hēmeras* 'seven times a day' tantamount to 'countless times'.

kai (*ean*) *heptakis epistrepsē pros se* 'and if he turns to you seven times'. *epistrephō* may mean intransitively, 'to turn', or 'to return', preferably the former. It denotes the act of one person addressing another.

aphēseis autō 'you shall forgive him'. The future tense has the force of an imperative.

Translation: *Sins against you,* not used in a primarily religious sense, since it refers to a relationship between men rather than to one between God and man; hence, "wrongs you" (NEB, similarly Sranan), "offends you" (Phillips).

Seven times in the day, or, where the numeral would be taken as a limitation, 'many times a day'.

Turns to you, or, "comes to you" (TEV, similarly some Indonesian languages).

I repent, also used here in the context of a human relationship, but even so stronger in connotation than 'I am sorry', or an equivalent polite expression of apology/excuse.

5 ***The apostles said to the Lord, "Increase our faith!"***

Exegesis: *kai eipan hoi apostoloi tō kuriō* 'and the apostles said to the Lord'. For *apostolos* cp. on 6 : 13. Here *hoi apostoloi* is best understood as referring to a smaller group that is part of the larger circle of *mathētai* 'disciples' to whom vv. 1-4 are addressed. For *kurios* cp. on 1 : 6, sub (3).

prosthes hēmin pistin lit. 'add for us faith', i.e. either 'add to our faith', 'give us more faith', or 'give us faith in addition (to other gifts of grace)', 'give us faith as well', preferably the latter, cp. Plummer and A-G s.v. *prostithēmi* 2. For *pistis* cp. on 5 : 20. Here it refers to faith in the miracle-working power of Jesus, cp. 1 Cor. 13 : 2.

Translation: *Increase our faith,* preferably, 'give us faith as well/also', cp. *Exegesis.* If 'faith' has to be rendered by a verbal expression one may say something like, 'also help/cause us to believe in your power, or to trust in you (cp. 11 : 22)'.

6 ***And the Lord said, "If you had faith as a grain of mustard seed, you could say to this sycamine tree, 'Be rooted up, and be planted in the sea,' and it would obey you.***

Exegesis: *ei echete...elegete an* 'if you had...you would say', implying that they do not have faith even like a mustard-seed.

pistin hōs kokkon sinapeōs 'faith like a mustard seed', i.e. a very small amount of faith. For *kokkos sinapeōs* cp. on 13 : 19.

tē sukaminō [*tautē*] 'to this mulberry tree', presumably a tree close to the speaker.

sukaminos (††) 'mulberry tree', cp. A-G s.v. and *IDB* IV, 470; exact meaning uncertain.

ekrizōthēti kai phuteuthēti en tē thalassē lit. 'be uprooted and be planted in the sea', here best understood as reflexive, 'pull up yourself by the roots and plant yourself in the sea'.

ekrizoō (†) 'to uproot', 'to pull out by the roots'.

kai hupēkousen an humin 'and it would obey you at once'. The shift from the imperfect (*elegete an*) to the aorist points to an immediate result. *hupakouō*, cp. on 8 : 25.

Translation: *As a grain of mustard seed,* or making explicit the reference to (small) size, 'the size of a mustard seed' (Kekchi), '(even) as little as a (grain of) mustard seed'. For *mustard seed* see 13 : 19.

Sycamine tree. Simply to say 'tree' (Leyden, Sranan, one West Nyanja version), 'big tree' (East Toradja), is acceptable here because the kind of tree is not of special relevance in the context.

Be rooted up, and be planted in the sea, or, to avoid an imperative and/or apassive form, 'you shall be uprooted and shall be planted', 'you must pull yourself out by the roots and plant yourself in the sea'. *To uproot,* or, 'to pull out' (Bahasa Indonesia, Balinese), 'to pull loose from the ground' (Sranan). *Be planted* may have to be rendered, 'be set' (Zarma), 'go and stand', 'grow' (South Toradja).

For *to obey* see on "obedient" in 2 : 51.

7 ***"Will any one of you, who has a servant ploughing or keeping sheep, say to him when he has come in from the field, 'Come at once and sit down at table'?***

Exegesis: *tis de ex humōn... hos... erei* lit. 'who of you (is there)... who will say?', with *estin* understood, more emphatic than 'who of you will say?' The expected answer is: no. *humōn* points back to *pros tous mathētas autou* in v. 1.

doulon echōn arotriōnta ē poimainonta 'having a slave ploughing or tending sheep', describing the background circumstances of the subsequent narrative. The emphasis is on *doulon* as shown by its position before *echōn*.

arotriaō (†) 'to plough'.

poimainō (†) 'to tend (sheep)'.

hos eiselthonti ek tou agrou erei autō 'who when he comes in from the field will say to him'. *eiselthonti* goes with *autō*, which refers to *doulon*.

eutheōs parelthōn anapese 'come along at once and lie down (at the table)'. *parerchomai* means to go to the place where one is going to do something, cp. on 12 : 37. For *anapiptō* cp. on 11 : 37.

Translation: For the rendering of such rhetorical questions with suppositional force cp. on 11 : 5.

A servant ploughing or keeping sheep (viz. as his habitual duty) may have to be recast, e.g. 'a slave working for him at the plough or with the sheep, or, who ploughs for him and tends his sheep' (cp. NV), 'the servant he employs as ploughman and herdsman' (Willibrord); and cp. below, the quotation from Tzeltal. *Ploughing,* or, 'who hoes' (West Nyanja), 'tilling the fields', 'who turns the soil for him' (Sranan), 'who works the garden (with a hoe)' (Lokele), 'farming' (Zarma). *To keep the sheep*, i.e. 'to be a shepherd' (cp. 2 : 8), or more generically, 'to tend the flock (cp. *ibid.*), or, the (small) cattle'. For *sheep* see references on 15 : 4.

Field here refers both to the fields tilled (cp. 15 : 25) and those used for pasturage (cp. 2 : 8); to cover both by one term one may say, 'the open' (Fulani), 'where he had been working' (cp. Kapauku), 'his work' (East Toradja, similarly in Tzeltal, which, moreover, transposes the reference to the jobs, cp. 'if your servant arrives from work, from ground-breaking or caring-for-cattle for you...').

At once, or, 'without delay', 'quickly'.

Sit down at table, cp. on 7 : 36.

8 ***Will he not rather say to him, 'Prepare supper for me, and gird yourself and serve me, till I eat and drink; and afterward you shall eat and drink'?***

Exegesis: *all' ouchi erei autō* lit. 'but will he not rather say... ?' with a shift to a different type of interrogative clause.

hetoimason ti deipnēsō lit. 'prepare what I will eat', i.e. 'prepare something for me to eat'. The aorist tense of *hetoimason* refers to the punctiliar act that precedes the more durative act of serving at the table (*diakonei* present tense).

deipneō (also 22 : 20) 'to have a meal' (*deipnon*, cp. on 14 : 12), i.e. 'to eat', 'to dine'.

perizōsamenos diakonei moi 'gird yourself and serve me'. For *perizōnnumi* (here in the middle voice with reflexive meaning) cp. on 12 : 35. For *diakoneō* cp. on 4 : 39.

heōs phagō kai piō either 'while I eat and drink', or, 'till I have finished eating and drinking', preferably the latter. Here eating and drinking refers to a full meal.

kai meta tauta phagesai kai piesai su 'and after that, i.e. after you have served me, you will eat and drink yourself'. *su* is emphatic by position.

Translation: The verse indicates the negative answer anticipated by the rhetorical question in v. 7, but by implication only; it may be better to make this explicit, e.g. by inserting, 'No, you won't!', "Of course not!" (TEV). V. 8 itself is a rhetorical question anticipating a positive answer, sometimes better rendered as a statement, cp. e.g. "Instead, you say to him..." (TEV).

Gird yourself, as a servant does who is to wait on his master at table. Some cultural equivalents are, 'wrap your waist-cloth about you', as is obligatory when approaching a person of superior rank (Balinese), 'have-the-upper-garment-tied-together-on-the-breast', as one does when bringing an offering (Toba Batak), 'wear clothes' (Lokele), cp. also, "dress yourself" (Goodspeed). The rendering may have to differ from the one in 12 : 35, because the expression is used there metaphorically, and the circumstances envisaged as the basis of the metaphor are different.

For *serve* see on 12 : 37[c], for *eat and drink* on 5 : 30.

9 ***Does he thank the servant because he did what was commanded?***

Exegesis: *mē echei charin tō doulō* 'is he grateful to the servant?' *mē* presupposes an answer in the negative, cp. A-G s.v. C 1. *echei* has the same subject as *erei* in vv. 7 and 8. *charin echō* lit. 'to have thanks' means 'to thank', 'to be thankful', cp. A-G s.v. *charis* 5.

hoti epoiēsen ta diatachthenta 'because he has done what was ordered', i.e. 'what he was told to do'.

Translation: *Does he thank the servant?* or, 'he will not thank the servant'; or with further shifts, "the servant does not deserve thanks..., does he?" (TEV). For *to thank* cp. on "ungrateful" in 6 : 35.

He did what was commanded, or, 'he (i.e. the servant) did as he (i.e. the master) had commanded him, or, told him to do'. One or both pronouns may require specification.

10 ***So you also, when you have done all that is commanded you, say, 'We are unworthy servants; we have only done what was our duty.'"***

Exegesis: *houtōs kai humeis...legete* 'so you also...must say'. It is also possible to take *houtōs kai humeis* as independent, 'so you also', i.e. 'so with you too', "it is the same with you" (TEV), but this appears less probable. *houtōs kai* draws a parallel between the servant of v. 9 and Jesus' hearers.

panta ta diatachthenta humin 'all you were told to do'.

douloi achreioi esmen lit. 'we are useless servants'. For the various interpretations of *achreioi* cp. commentaries, especially Plummer, Lagrange. Here it refers to servants who are aware that they have done only what they ought to do, and no more. Hence *achreioi* (†) is best understood as expressing the servant's modesty, cp. Grundmann, and NEB, "deserve no credit".

ho ōpheilomen poiēsai pepoiēkamen 'we have (only) done what we ought to do'. The perfect tense of *pepoiēkamen* denotes an act that has been accomplished.

Translation: *Say,* viz. to each other; hence the subsequent pronouns are taken as inclusive, e.g. in Mazatec.

Unworthy servants, i.e. 'undeserving servants' (see *Exegesis*), 'servants who do not deserve (or, are not worthy of) praise/thanks/reward/credit'.

Only, or, 'nothing more than', cp. on 4 : 8.

11 ***On the way to Jerusalem he was passing along between Samaria and Galilee.***

Exegesis: *kai egeneto* 'and it happened', cp. on 1 : 8.

en tō poreuesthai eis Ierousalēm lit. 'during the journeying to Jerusalem'. The subject of *poreuesthai* may be 'they', i.e. Jesus and his disciples, or 'he', i.e. Jesus. The latter is preferable because no reference is made to the disciples in the subsequent story.

kai autos diērcheto dia meson Samareias kai Galilaias 'he passed between Samaria and Galilee'. *kai autos* is here not emphatic. For *dierchomai* cp. on 2 : 15. *dia meson* with following genitive is very awkward (cp. Bl-D, § 222 and commentaries). Here it may mean either 'through the midst of', or 'between', i.e. 'through the borderlands' of Samaria and Galilee, preferably the latter.

Translation: *On the way to Jerusalem,* or, 'on his journey to J.', 'while he was travelling to J.', cp. 9 : 51 and 13 : 22.

12 ***And as he entered a village, he was met by ten lepers, who stood at a distance***

Exegesis: *eiserchomenou autou eis tina kōmēn* 'when he was entering a village'. Since lepers were not admitted to the community the clause is best understood as, 'when he was on the point of entering', or, 'when he was approaching a village'.

apēntēsan [autō] deka leproi andres lit. 'ten lepers met him', but, as *idōn* 'when he saw them' in v. 14 shows, Jesus did not immediately notice them.

apantaō (†) 'to meet', 'to come towards'.

hoi estēsan porrōthen lit. 'who took their stand', i.e., 'who stopped at a distance', cp. on 6 : 8.

porrōthen (†) lit. 'from a distance', hence 'at a distance'.

Translation: *He was met by ten lepers,* or, 'ten lepers encountered him, or, came towards him', cp. on 8 : 27. For *leper* see 4 : 27.

At a distance, or, 'some way off (but within hearing distance)'; and cp. on 15 : 20.

13 ***and lifted up their voices and said, "Jesus, Master, have mercy on us."***

Exegesis: *kai autoi ēran phōnēn* 'and they raised their voices'. *autoi* is unemphatic.

Iēsou epistata 'Jesus, master'. For *epistatēs* cp. on 5 : 5. Here it suggests submission rather than intimate relationship.

eleēson hēmas 'have pity on us', implicitly a request to be healed, cp. on 16 : 24.

Translation: *Lifted up their voices and said,* or, 'shouted' (cp. TEV, Tagalog), "called across to him" (Rieu); and cp. on 11 : 27.

Master, cp. on 5 : 5.

Have mercy on us, cp. on 1 : 50. The supplicatory mood of the imperative is sometimes more explicitly expressed, e.g. by a word meaning 'please' (Javanese, Balinese).

14 ***When he saw them he said to them, "Go and show yourselves to the priests." And as they went they were cleansed.***

Exegesis: *kai idōn eipen autois* 'and when he saw (them) he said to them', cp. on v. 12.

poreuthentes epideixate heautous tois hiereusin 'go and show yourselves to the priests', cp. on 5 : 14. The order is implicitly a promise of healing, cp. on v. 19. *epideiknumi* (†).

kai egeneto en tō hupagein autous ekatharisthēsan 'and as they were going they were made clean'. For *kai egeneto* cp. on 1 : 8. Here it introduces the climax of the story. For *hupagō* cp. on 8 : 42b.

Translation: *Go and show yourselves to the priests,* see on 5 : 14.

As they went, or, 'while they were on their way, or, went there' (cp. NEB, Jerusalem).

They were cleansed, or, 'became clean', cp. on 4 : 27.

15 ***Then one of them, when he saw that he was healed, turned back, praising God with a loud voice;*** 16 ***and he fell on his face at Jesus' feet, giving him thanks. Now he was a Samaritan.***

Exegesis: *hupestrepsen* 'returned', scil. to Jesus. Presumably before he had shown himself to the priests.

meta phōnēs megalēs doxazōn ton theon 'praising God with a loud voice', durative participle. *meta phōnēs megalēs* is best understood as instrumental, cp. *phōnē megalē* (instrumental dative) in 4 : 33. For *doxazō* cp. on 2 : 20.

(V. 16) *kai epesen epi prosōpon para tous podas autou* 'and he fell on his face at his (i.e. Jesus') feet'; for this expression cp. 5 : 12 and on 8 : 41.

eucharistōn autō 'thanking him', durative after the punctiliar *epesen* 'he fell'.

eucharisteō 'to give thanks', 'to thank', usually with God as object but here the thanking is to be distinguished from the praising of God.

kai autos ēn Samaritēs 'and he was a Samaritan'. *autos* has here demonstrative force, cp. A-G s.v. 2. For *Samaritēs* cp. on 9 : 52b.

Translation: The subordinate clause *when he saw that he was healed,* separating subject and verb of the main sentence, may better be transposed, cp. e.g. 'one of them turned back when he saw that he (or, his body) was healed', 'seeing himself healed one of them turned back'. If one has to shift to co-ordination, one should remember that this leper was not exceptional in his seeing that he was healed but in his turning back to Jesus; hence, 'they saw that they were healed (or, became aware of their recovery). Then one of them returned'. *He was healed,* or, 'he had become well'.

Praising God, cp. on "glorifying...God" in 2 : 20. *With a loud voice,* cp. on 4 : 33.

(V. 16) *He fell on his face at Jesus' feet,* cp. the note on "he fell down at Jesus' knees" in 5 : 8.

Samaritan, see 9 : 52b.

17 ***Then said Jesus, "Were not ten cleansed? Where are the nine?***

Exegesis: *apokritheis* 'answering', cp. on 1 : 60.

ouchi hoi deka ekatharisthēsan 'were not all ten made clean?' *ouchi* implies an affirmative answer. *hoi deka* lit. 'the ten' views the group in its totality.

hoi de ennea pou 'the (other) nine, where are they?' *pou* is emphatic by position.

Translation: *Were not ten cleansed,* or, where active voice is preferable, 'didn't I make ten (men/lepers) clean'.

18 ***Was no one found to return and give praise to God except this foreigner?"***

Exegesis: *ouch heurethēsan hupostrepsantes...ei mē ho allogenēs houtos* lit. 'were there found none returning...except this foreigner?' The clause is best understood as a question. *heuriskomai* with adjective or participle means 'to be found' in the sense of 'to appear' (cp. A-G s.v. 2); that which appears is expressed by the adjective or participle, cp. Rieu and Plummer.

allogenēs (††) 'foreigner' in the sense of 'non-Israelite'.

dounai doxan tō theō 'in order to give praise to God', final infinitive; the phrase is equivalent to *doxazō* with accusative.

Translation: The force of this question is sometimes brought out by the use of introductory phrases such as, 'is it really so that...', "can it be true that..." (Rieu).

Was...found, or, 'did appear', 'was-seen' (South Toradja), often simply 'was there'.

No one...except this foreigner. Adjustments in the line of the notes on 8 : 51 and 10 : 22 may lead here to something like, 'is there no other who returns and gives...than this foreigner' (East Toradja), 'is this foreigner the only one to come back and give...'; or in two clauses, e.g. 'This foreigner here comes back and gives... Why could the others (or, the nine) not come also?', or, 'Does this one who is not an Israelite return and give..., but do the Israelites not do so, or, not come back to do so?'. *Foreigner,* or, 'man-from-outside' (Sranan, Bahasa Indonesia), 'man from another people' (Javanese), 'man who is not of our (inclus.) people (East Toradja 1933), or, not of (the people) Israel'.

19 ***And he said to him, "Rise and go your way; your faith has made you well."***

Exegesis: *anastas poreuou* 'stand up and go'. *anastas* is used literally here. *poreuou* is expression of dismissal.

hē pistis sou sesōken se 'your faith has saved you', cp. on 7 : 50. The clause refers to his faith in Jesus' implied promise of healing (v. 14) and its fulfilment.

Translation: *Rise,* i.e. "stand up" (NEB), viz. from kneeling.

Go your way, or, 'go home', or another formula used to give a person leave to go.

Your faith has made you well, see references on 8 : 48.

20 ***Being asked by the Pharisees when the kingdom of God was coming, he answered them, "The kingdom of God is not coming with signs to be observed;*** 21 ***nor will they say, 'Lo, here it is!' or 'There!' for behold, the kingdom of God is in the midst of you."***

Exegesis: *eperōtētheis de hupo tōn Pharisaiōn* 'when he was asked by the Pharisees', without indication of place or time and without connexion with the preceding narrative. For *eperōtaō* cp. on 2 : 46; for *Pharisaios* on 5 : 17.

pote erchetai hē basileia tou theou 'when the kingdom of God would come'. *erchetai* is used with future meaning. For *hē basileia tou theou* cp. on 4 : 43. The coming of the kingdom refers to the moment when God will exercise his royal power in full.

apekrithē autois kai eipen 'he answered them and said', i.e. 'he answered them by saying', or 'he said to them in reply'.

ouk erchetai hē basileia tou theou meta paratērēseōs lit. 'the kingdom of God will not come with observation'.

paratērēsis (††) 'observation' (cp. *paratereō* 6 : 7; 14 : 1). *meta paratērēseōs* may mean either 'in such a way as to be seen', or 'in such a way as to be predictable by signs', preferably the latter.

(V. 21) *oude erousin, Idou hōde; ē, Ekei* 'nor will people say, look here, or there', i.e., neither will the kingdom come in such a way that people can say, 'look here, or there'.

idou gar hē basileia tou theou entos humōn estin 'for behold, the kingdom of God is among you'. *idou* contrasts emphatically with the preceding *idou* and introduces the clause which explains why the preceding delimitations of the coming of the kingdom are to be rejected. The meaning of *entos humōn* (†) is much discussed, cp. commentaries, esp. Creed. The following renderings are possible: (1) 'within you', i.e. 'within your heart', taking *basileia tou theou* in a non-eschatological sense; (2) 'among you', i.e. 'in your midst', either now or in the future; (3) 'within your reach', cp. *TBT*, 4.7f, 1953; 9.162f, 1958, and Leaney ad loc. Of these (2) seems to be preferable.

Translation: *Being asked by the Pharisees,* or, 'once the Ph. asked him/Jesus'.

When the kingdom of God was coming, or, 'when the time would come that God reigns'.

The kingdom of God is not coming with signs to be observed. The prepositional phrase has also been rendered by, 'so that one/you can calculate it, or, divine it, or, see it beforehand' (cp. NV, Balinese, Sranan), 'with signs (lit. things-that-may-be-seen)' (one West Nyanja version). Further adjustments may lead to, 'you/people cannot tell by observing signs when the kingdom of God will come' (cp. NEB), 'there are no signs that can tell you when God is going to rule', 'no sign will be seen to appear when God begins to give orders' (Tzeltal), 'when the power of God comes there will not be a visible sign' (Kekchi).

(V. 21) *Nor will they say,* or, 'and no one will say' (cp. TEV).

'Lo, here it is!' or 'There!'. An equivalent of "lo" is often better omitted, since the next words sufficiently express the demonstrative force of Gr. *idou*; cp. on "behold" in 1 : 20.

For behold, or, "for in fact" (NEB); or more strongly contrastive, 'No!'.

The kingdom of God is in the midst of you, or, 'already God is ruling among you, or, giving orders in your midst' (a Mixtec dialect, Tzeltal), cp. interpretation (2) in *Exegesis*. A term covering both 'within' and 'amongst', cp. interpretation (1) and (2), is recorded for Shona, East Nyanja, Yao, Lomwe, Marathi.

22 ***And he said to the disciples, "The days are coming when you will desire to see one of the days of the Son of man, and you will not see it.***

Exegesis: *eipen de pros tous mathētas* 'then he said to his disciples', with shift of audience.

eleusontai hēmerai hote epithumēsete...idein lit. 'days will come when you will long to see'. For *hēmerai* cp. on 5 : 35.

mian tōn hēmerōn tou huiou tou anthrōpou idein 'to see one of the days of the Son of man', i.e. either of the period when he was with them in the past, or the time of his Messianic glory in the future, preferably the latter. The phrase 'one of the days' has the value of 'a very short moment', or 'only a single moment'.

kai ouk opsesthe 'and you will not see it'. Presumably the sentence refers to a time of tribulation or even persecution.

Translation: *You will desire to see...,* or, 'to experience/to (be) witness (of)...', 'you will long for...'. Where a personal object is preferable one may say, 'you will desire to see the Son of man, if only for one of his days'.

One of the days of the Son of man, or, 'the time/period of the Son of man even if only for not more than one day/moment'. The connexion between "days" and "Son of man" may have to be clarified, e.g. 'the time/period when the Son of man will be visible (or, will show himself, or, will be present) again'.

23 ***And they will say to you, 'Lo, there!' or 'Lo, here!' Do not go, do not follow them.***

Exegesis: *kai erousin humin, Idou ekei*; [*ē*,] *Idou hōde* 'and people will say to you, look there, or, look here', cp. v. 21. *ekei* and *hōde* refer to places where the Son of man was alleged to have appeared.

mē apelthēte mēde diōxēte 'do not go off (viz. from your ordinary occupation), and do not run after (them)', viz. the people that say 'here', or 'there'. The clause is asyndetic. For *diōkō* cp. on 11 : 49 and A-G s.v. 4 a.

Translation: *'Lo, there!' or 'Lo, here!'*, or, '"There he is!" or, "Here (he is)!"'

Go, or, 'go off', 'go away'.

Follow them, i.e. 'follow where they lead you', or, 'go with them'.

24 ***For as the lightning flashes and lights up the sky from one side to the other, so will the Son of man be in his day.***

Exegesis: *hōsper gar hē astrapē astraptousa...* 'for just as the lightning when it flashes...'. The comparison explains why the Son of man will not appear 'here' or 'there': his coming will be as sudden and as universally visible as the shining of the lightning, cp. Plummer and Lagrange.

astraptō (also 24 : 4, but with figurative meaning) 'to flash', of the same root as *astrapē* and used here for that reason in order to stress the idea of very bright lightning. *astraptousa* is best taken by itself and not in connexion with the subsequent phrase that goes with *lampei*, see below.

ek tēs hupo ton ouranon eis tēn hup' ouranon lampei '(the lightning) shines from one region under the sky to another under the sky', with *chōran* 'region' understood, cp. A-G s.v. 1 a. *ouranos* means here 'the sky that overarches the earth', cp. A-G s.v. 1 b. Hence *hupo ton ouranon* virtually means 'on earth', here, 'on a part of the earth'.

houtōs estai ho huios tou anthrōpou [*en tē hēmera autou*] 'so the Son of man will be in his day'. *en tē hēmera autou* refers to the day of his glorious appearance in the future.

Translation: The clause order may better be reversed, e.g. 'the Son of man...will be like lightning that...'; similarly in vv. 26 and/or 28-30.

As the lightning flashes and lights up, or, 'as the lightning, when it flashes, lights-up/shines'. The combination of two rather similar verbs such as 'to flash' and 'to light up' may make necessary some adaptation, cp. "like the lightning-flash that lights up" (NEB), 'as lightning shines flashingly' (Leyden), or, with some simplification, 'as the lightning that shines on, or, flashes over, or, lights up'. Toba Batak uses here its specific term for 'flash-of-lightning', cp. on 10 : 18.

Tke sky from one side to the other, preferably, 'from one region/side/point under the sky to the other', "from one horizon to the other" (BFBS, similarly Leyden, Brouwer), 'over all(-that-is)-under-the-sky from end to end' (Balinese, where 'all-under-the-sky' is a common expression for 'the whole earth'), or simply, 'across the sky' (Navajo).

25 ***But first he must suffer many things and be rejected by this generation.***

Exegesis: *prōton de* 'but first', i.e. before it comes to that. For the rest of this verse cp. on 9 : 22. *genea* means 'generation' and refers here to Jesus' contemporaries.

Translation: *This generation* (corresponding to "the elders and chief priests and scribes" in the parallel verse 9 : 22[a]) is virtually identical with "the men of this generation" in 7 : 31, which see.

26 ***As it was in the days of Noah, so will it be in the days of the Son of man.***

Exegesis: *kai kathōs egeneto...houtōs estai* 'and as it was...so it will be'. Both parts of the comparison refer to a situation existing for some time and suddenly brought to an end. Hence *egeneto* is best understood as equivalent of *ēn. kathōs* and *houtōs* define two situations as similar.

en tais hēmerais Nōe 'in the time of Noah', i.e. the time before he went into the ark.

en tais hēmerais tou huiou tou anthrōpou 'in the days of the Son of man', best understood as analogous to *hai hēmerai Nōe* and as denoting the period, or time preceding the appearing of the Son of man.

Translation: *In the days of Noah,* or, 'in the (former) day/time of N.', 'when N. lived'.

27 ***They ate, they drank, they married, they were given in marriage, until the day when Noah entered the ark, and the flood came and destroyed them all.***

Exegesis: *ēsthion, epinon, egamoun, egamizonto* 'they ate, drank, married, were married'. The asyndetic verbs in the imperfect tense depict the steady flow of normal life. For eating and drinking cp. on 5 : 30. For *gameō* cp. on 14 : 20.

gamizomai (also 20 : 35) 'to be given in marriage', 'to be married', of women.

achri hēs hēmeras 'till the day on which', cp. on 1 : 20, and note the singular *hēmeras* as contrasted with the plural *hēmerais* in v. 26.

eis tēn kibōton 'into the ark'.

kibōtos (†) 'ark', i.e. a floating house, cp. *IDB* I, 222.

kai ēlthen ho kataklusmos kai apōlesen pantas 'and the flood came and destroyed all'. The clause is best understood as being independent and not modified by *achri hēs hēmeras,* cp. Plummer. *pantas* refers to the subject of *ēsthion* etc.

kataklusmos (†) 'flood', 'deluge'.

Translation: *They,* or, 'everybody', 'people', referring to Noah's contemporaries.

The series of verbs may better be rendered in pairs; similarly in the next verse.

They married, they were given in marriage, describing the event from the viewpoint of the man and of the woman, respectively. Some renderings used lit. mean, 'married and caused-to-marry' (Bahasa Indonesia), 'took-wife and were-caused-to-take-husband' (South Toradja), 'acquired (wives) and were-acquired (by husbands)' (Shona 1963), 'paid-the-bride-price and had-the-bride-price-paid-for-them' (Shona 1966, similarly Toba Batak), 'took-wife, took-husband' (East Toradja 1933, and, in reversed order, Javanese); or, using one verb, 'men and women married' (Sranan), 'they married-each-other' (Trukese, Ponape, Kituba). The reference is not to marriages arranged by the partners themselves *versus* marriages contracted through intermediaries (as a literal rendering would mean in Tagalog), nor to two stages in the marriage process, the actual marriage and the negotiations leading up to it. For various renderings of *to marry* cp. also 14 : 20, and references.

Entered, cp. on "getting into" in 5 : 3.

Ark, or, 'big boat/ship', *N.T.Wb.*/56, NAUTICAL.

The flood came, or, 'overflowing water, or, a sweeping flood, or, a heavy rainstorm, or, much rain came' (cp. East Nyanja, Yao, Trukese, Shona). Elsewhere a specific term for a mythical flood is available, e.g. in Marathi, Zarma, West Nyanja. Further necessary adjustments may lead to something like, 'it flooded' (Tagalog), 'the water (of the sea/rivers) rose (or, overflowed the land)'.

Destroyed them, or, 'made-perish/killed/drowned them'.

28 ***Likewise as it was in the days of Lot—they ate, they drank, they bought, they sold, they planted, they built,*** 29 ***but on the day when Lot went out from Sodom fire and brimstone rained from heaven and destroyed them all—*** 30 ***so will it be on the day when the Son of man is revealed.***

Exegesis: *homoiōs kathōs egeneto* 'in the same way, as it was...' *homoiōs* may either be taken together with *kathōs* 'in the same way as' (cp. A-G s.v. *homoiōs*), or connect the comparisons of vv. 26f and vv. 28ff, preferably the latter. Hence a rendering like "also" (NEB).

ēsthion, epinon, ēgorazon, epōloun, ephuteuon, ōikodomoun 'they ate, drank, bought, sold, planted, built', cp. on v. 26. The description is more extensive here and partly different, but no special meaning is to be attached to the differences.

(V. 29) *hē de hēmera exēlthen Lōt apo Sodomōn* 'but on the day on which Lot went out of Sodom, or, left Sodom'.

ebrexen pur kai theion ap' ouranou 'it rained fire and sulphur from heaven', or 'he (i.e. God) made it rain fire and sulphur from heaven', preferably the latter, cp. A-G s.v. *brechō* 2 a, and Gen. 19 : 24. *ebrexen* is punctiliar aorist after the descriptive imperfects in v. 28.

theion (†) 'sulphur', 'brimstone'.

kai apōlesen pantas 'and destroyed all'. For *pantas* cp. on v. 27. The subject of *apōlesen* is the same as that of *ebrexen*.

(V. 30) *kata ta auta estai* 'in the same way', or 'so it will be', taking up *kathōs* in v. 28.

hē hēmera ho huios tou anthrōpou apokaluptetai 'on the day on which the Son of man is revealed'. *apokaluptō* here of the glorious manifestation of the Son of man at his coming, cp. A-G s.v. 4.

Translation: *Likewise* (introducing a second comparison), or, 'similarly', 'or again', and cp. "so too, what happened in the time of Lot will be repeated" (Rieu).

The final clause (v. 30) may better be rendered as an independent sentence, e.g. 'similarly, in the days of Lot everybody ate, . . . , but on the day when Lot went out from S. fire. . . destroyed them all. So will it be (or, that will happen also) on the day when the Son of man is revealed'; or, it may be transposed to initial position, 'or again, when the Son of man is revealed, the situation will be as it was in the time of Lot: people ate. . .'.

They bought, they sold, or, 'they bought and sold goods' (cp. Ponape). That the two processes are basically reciprocal is sometimes made explicit, e.g. in Navajo; since they view the same process, though from different sides, they may be rendered by one expression, e.g. 'they traded-with-each-other' (Yao; similarly in Javanese, lit. a compound form, 'sold-bought').

They planted may, again, require an object, e.g. 'they planted seedlings', 'they sowed seed'; elsewhere it is more idiomatic to use two verbs, '(they) sowed planted' (Thai 1967).

They built, or, 'they built houses' (Trukese). Thai 1967, again, uses a double rendering, '(they) built made'.

(V. 29) *Fire and brimstone rained,* preferably, 'he/God made it rain fire and brimstone', 'he/God caused to fall/descend/come a rain of fire and brimstone (or, fire and brimstone as a rain)'. *Brimstone,* or, 'sulphur', may be described as 'fiery stones' (Gio), 'burning/inflammable stones (or, stuff)'.

(V. 30) *Is revealed,* or, "is brought into the light" (Rieu), "appears" (Goodspeed), 'shows himself', 'becomes-visible' (cp. Javanese).

31 ***On that day, let him who is on the housetop, with his goods in the house, not come down to take them away; and likewise let him who is in the field not turn back.***

Exegesis: *en ekeinē tē hēmera* 'on that day', referring back to *hē hēmera* in v. 30, and emphatic because of its position at the beginning of the clause, even before the relative pronoun *hos.*

hos estai epi tou dōmatos kai ta skeuē autou en tē oikia '(he) who will be on the house-top/roof and his belongings in the house', or, removing the syntactic incongruity between the two parts, 'whose belongings are in the house'. For *dōma* cp. on 5 : 19.

skeuos (cp. on 8 : 16) here in the plural in the general meaning 'property', 'belongings', 'things', cp. A-G s.v. 1 a.

mē katabatō arai auta 'he must not go down (scil. into the house) to pick them up'. *arai* is final infinitive and has the general meaning 'to take', 'to pick up', 'to get'.

ho en agrō homoiōs mē epistrepsatō eis ta opisō 'he who is in the field must, in the same way, not turn around to what is behind'. The common thought of both parts of v. 31 appears to be that on the day of the Son of man there is no point in turning to, or caring about, things which might otherwise be important. For *agros* cp. *TH-Mk* on 5 : 14. *eis ta opisō* lit. 'to what is behind', may refer either to what is behind him on the field (cp. 9 : 62), or to his house and what is in it. The former is preferable.

Translation: Here again a shift to an 'if'-clause may be preferable, cp. 9 : 24.

On the housetop, see "roof" in 5 : 19, and cp. *TH-Mk* on 13 : 15; if renderings as discussed there would suggest a decidedly abnormal place to stay, one will have to seek a functional equivalent, e.g. 'outside', suggesting 'in the yard' (Amuzgo), with ensuing shift from 'go down' to 'go in'.

With his goods in the house, or, 'but has his belongings in the house', 'but his possessions are in the house'.

To be in the field, cp. 15 : 25.

Turn back, preferably, 'turn around to what is behind' (see *Exegesis*), 'turn to look at/for the things he left behind' (Sranan).

32 ***Remember Lot's wife.***

Exegesis: *mnēmoneuete tēs gunaikos Lōt* 'remember Lot's wife', who did turn back.

mnēmoneuō (†) 'to remember' refers here to something taken to be known generally.

Translation: *Remember*, or, 'think of', 'bring back to your mind', and cp. on 1 : 54.

Lot's wife, or, 'the case/story of Lot's wife', "what happened to Lot's wife" (Phillips).

33 ***Whoever seeks to gain his life will lose it, but whoever loses his life will preserve it.***

Exegesis: *hos ean zētēsē tēn psuchēn autou peripoiēsasthai* 'whoever tries to preserve his life'. For *zēteō* in this meaning cp. on 5 : 18. For *psuchē* cp. A-G s.v. 1 a β, and 9 : 24.

peripoieō (†) 'to preserve', 'to save', here in the middle voice, implying that the preserving is to the benefit of the subject of the clause.

hos d' an apolesē zōogonēsei autēn 'but whoever loses (it) will preserve it'. *hos d' an apolesē* may mean either, 'he who is prepared to lose', or 'he who actually loses', preferably the latter.

zōogoneō (†) 'to preserve alive'.

Translation: The verse closely parallels 9 : 24, which see.

Seeks (cp. 5 : 18) differs from the verb used in 9 : 24 in that it implies some effort.

Gain his life (or, 'cling to his life', Navajo) and *preserve it* are closely synonymous, and they parallel 'save his life' in 9 : 24; the renderings of the three verbs coincide in several versions, e.g. in TEV, Sranan, East Toradja.

34 ***I tell you, in that night there will be two men in one bed; one will be taken and the other left.***

Exegesis: *legō humin* 'I tell you', cp. on 3 : 8.

tautē tē nukti 'on that night'. The shift from 'that day' in v. 31 to 'that night' here is due to the situation that is envisaged here and does not imply that the coming of the Son of man will take place during the night, cp. Plummer.

esontai duo epi klinēs mias 'there will be two people in one bed', probably to be understood as two men, cp. *ho heis* and *ho heteros*. For *klinē* cp. on 8 : 16.

ho heis paralēmphthēsetai 'one will be taken', probably to be understood as 'taken along', viz. by the angels who gather the elect (cp. Mk. 13 : 27 and *TH-Mk* there).

ho heteros aphethēsetai 'the other will be left (behind)', cp. A-G s.v. *aphiēmi* 3 a.

Translation: *In that night,* i.e. at that time, in the night. To avoid the implication rejected in *Exegesis* it may be wise to say something like, 'then, or, at that time, there will be two men in one bed at night'. For *night* cp. also *N.T.Wb.*/57.

There will be two men in one bed, or, 'there will be two men lying/sleeping in one (or, in the same) bed'; or where this would have undesirable associations, 'two men will both be lying/sleeping'.

One will be taken and the other left. Where no passive form can be used one may have to say, 'the angels will take one (of them) and will leave behind the other', or, 'God will choose one (of them), reject the other'.

35 ***There will be two women grinding together; one will be taken and the other left.***

Exegesis: *esontai duo alēthousai epi to auto* 'there will be two women grinding at the same place', because the mills are usually operated by two persons, cp. A-G s.v. *alēthō* (†).

epi to auto 'on the same spot', hence here 'together'.

Translation: *Grinding* may require the cereal as object, cp. e.g. "grinding corn" (NEB), or the result, cp. e.g. 'grinding meal' (TEV, Malay; and Ponape, 'rub flour'); in South Toradja the verb used is a derivation from 'meal'. A common cultural equivalent is 'to pound rice' (e.g. in Balinese, Lokele). Sometimes a generic rendering is preferable, e.g. because grinding or pounding is not a daily task of women; hence, 'to work' (Trukese).

Together, or, 'at the same place', may be taken as referring to working the same instrument, e.g. 'mill' (Rieu), or, 'mortar/pounding-block', or to working two instruments at the same spot, as is normal e.g. in Shona and Fulani.

[36 Two men will be in the field; one will be taken and the other left.]

Text: This verse, read by *Textus Receptus*, is rejected by all modern editors. The expressions used in it are all to be found in the preceding verses, see on v. 31 and v. 34.

37 ***And they said to him, "Where, Lord?" He said to them, "Where the body is, there the eagles will be gathered together."***

Exegesis: *kai apokrithentes legousin autō* 'and they answered and said to him', presumably the disciples. *apokrithentes* means here 'reacting, or, commenting upon what Jesus had said', or 'taking up Jesus' words'.

pou, kurie 'where (will this be), Lord', referring either to the place where the events of vv. 31-35 will happen, or to the place where those will be who are left behind, preferably the former.

hopou to sōma, ekei kai hoi aetoi episunachthēsontai 'where the body (is) there also the vultures will gather', probably a proverbial saying, meaning that there will be no mistaking the place. At the same time this is not an answer to the question, and it appears that Jesus declines to give a forthright answer. For *episunagō* cp. on 13 : 34.

sōma 'body', hence 'corpse'.

aetos (†) 'eagle', here 'vulture', cp. A-G s.v.

Translation: *And they said to him,* or, 'thereupon they said to him', "at this point they asked him" (Rieu), cp. on "answered" in 3 : 16.

Where?, or, 'where will it/that happen?' (cp. Rieu, Toba Batak).

He said to them, or, in order to provide a clue that what follows must be taken metaphorically, 'he spoke to them (or, he answered them with) a saying/proverb'.

In the following saying it is sometimes better to shift to a conditional clause, cp. 'if a body is lying somewhere, the vultures...' (Navajo).

Body, preferably, 'dead body', 'corpse', 'carrion', 'dead animals' (Kekchi).

Eagle, preferably, 'vulture', or a comparable bird of prey eating carrion, e.g. 'raven' (Balinese); South Toradja uses the name of a grey bird (lit. 'meat-fetcher'), which preys on the sacrificial meat at places where a religious feast is held.

Will be gathered, or, 'will come together', cp. *TH-Mk* on 2 : 2.

CHAPTER EIGHTEEN

1 ***And he told them a parable, to the effect that they ought always to pray and not lose heart.***

Exegesis: *elegen de parabolēn autois* 'then he told them a parable'. *autois* refers to the disciples to whom 17 : 22-37 was addressed. *de* marks continuation.

pros to dein pantote proseuchesthai autous kai mē egkakein 'to show that they must always pray and not give up'. The clause is best understood as going with *elegen* and indicating Jesus' intention in telling the parable. The impersonal *dei* marks necessity.

egkakeō (†) 'to become tired', here either in an absolute sense, 'to lose heart', 'to become discouraged', or, with the participle *proseuchomenous* understood (cp. 2 Thess. 3 : 13), 'to give up', scil. praying. The latter is preferable.

Translation: *Parable,* see on 8 : 4.

To the effect, or, "to make it clear" (Rieu), "to teach them" (TEV); or, 'its-contents, or, its-gist (being)' (Balinese, Javanese). The following clause may better be shifted to direct discourse, "You should always pray and never lose heart, or, give up".

Always, or, 'again and again'.

To lose heart, or, '(to become) desperate (lit. hope being-broken-off)' (Bahasa Indonesia); cp. also *TH-Mk* on the opposite expression "to take heart" in 6 : 50. Following the interpretation preferred in *Exegesis* one may say, "to slacken" (Rieu), 'to weary' (Sranan, similarly Jerusalem).

2 ***He said, "In a certain city there was a judge who neither feared God nor regarded man;***

Exegesis: *legōn* 'saying', takes up *elegen* after the long interruption in the rest of v. 1.

kritēs tis ēn 'there was a (certain) judge'. For *kritēs* cp. on 11 : 19. Here it is used in a technical sense, cp. A-G s.v. 1 a.

ton theon mē phoboumenos 'not fearing God', cp. on 1 : 50.

kai anthrōpon mē entrepomenos 'and not respecting man'. *anthrōpon* refers to man in general.

entrepomai 'to have respect for', 'to respect'.

Translation: For *a certain* see on 7 : 41, and for *judge* cp. *N.T.Wb./*48f.

Neither feared God nor regarded man. The two verbs are closely synonymous in this context; hence a contracted rendering, combining one verb with the two objects, is sometimes preferable, as in "cared nothing for

God or man" (NEB). For *feared God* cp. on 1:50. *Nor regarded man*, or, 'nor took-notice-of man' (Sundanese), *se moquait des hommes* (Jerusalem), or in an idiomatic phrase, 'he had no business with anyone', i.e. he didn't care about anyone's opinion (Sranan).

3 ***and there was a widow in that city who kept coming to him and saying, 'Vindicate me against my adversary.'***

Exegesis: *chēra de ēn...kai ērcheto pros auton* 'there was a widow...and she constantly came to him'. The imperfect tense of *ērcheto* marks repetition.

ekdikēson me apo tou antidikou mou 'protect me from my opponent'. For *antidikos* cp. on 12:58.

ekdikeō (also v. 5) 'to avenge', 'to procure justice for', 'to protect juridically'.

Translation: *Widow*, cp. on 2:37.

Vindicate me against my adversary, i.e. take a just decision in the lawsuit I have with my opponent, implying that the decision would be in the favour of the speaker. Various idiomatic or descriptive renderings are used, e.g. 'arrange the matter between my adversary and me' (Tzeltal), 'please make-straight for us this affair' (South Toradja); or, making more explicit the favourable connotation, 'make-me-true before my enemy' (Fulani), 'cause-to-win(-out) me against my enemy' (Kituba), 'take my case and make justice against my legal opponent' (Marathi), 'judge for me, let me get my right against my enemy' (Sranan), and, distributing direct and indirect discourse differently, "pleading for her rights: 'Help me against my opponent'" (TEV).

4 ***For a while he refused; but afterward he said to himself, 'Though I neither fear God nor regard man,*** 5 ***yet because this widow bothers me, I will vindicate her, or she will wear me out by her continual coming.'"***

Exegesis: *kai ouk ēthelen epi chronon* 'and for a while he was not willing', scil. to protect the widow, with *ekdikein* understood. *epi chronon* refers to an undefined length of time, cp. A-G s.v. *epi* III 2 b.

meta de tauta eipen en heautō lit. 'but after that he said in himself, or, to himself'. As a rule *meta tauta* is used with reference to a specific moment or period previously mentioned, but after an indefinite expression such as *epi chronon* it is to be rendered 'afterward', or 'in the end'.

ei kai ton theon ou phoboumai 'even though I do not fear God', etc., implying that fear of God and respect for men would have required him to protect the widow.

(V. 5) *dia ge to parechein moi kopon tēn chēran tautēn* 'at least because of the fact that this widow gives me trouble', articular accusative and infinitive. *ge* serves to emphasize what follows as contrasted with the fact that he does not fear God or respect man. For *kopon parechein* cp. on 11:7.

ekdikēsō autēn 'I will protect her'.

hina mē eis telos erchomenē hupōpiazē me 'lest by coming here till the end/continually she wears me out'. *hina* may denote intention or expected result, preferably the latter. *eis telos* lit. 'till the end', here 'continually', or 'again and again', goes with *erchomenē*.

hupōpiazō (†) lit. 'to strike under the eye' (in prize fighting), here in a weakened sense, 'to wear out'. The present tense here suggests duration.

Translation: *He said to himself,* see on 3 : 8.

Though I neither fear . . . , yet . . . The first clause is sometimes better not subordinated, e.g. '(true,) I neither fear . . . ; yet (or, nevertheless/however) . . .'.

(V. 5) *Because this widow bothers me, I will vindicate her* may have to be restructured, e.g. 'this widow so bothers me that I will vindicate her' (cp. NEB), or, 'I will vindicate her, but (I will do so) only because she bothers me'.—*Bothers me,* or, 'causes me trouble', "is so great a nuisance" (NEB), and cp. *N.T.Wb.*, 71/TROUBLE. *I will vindicate her,* propositive mood, 'I had better vindicate her' (cp. Balinese).

Or, i.e. 'if not', 'if (I do) otherwise'.

She will wear me out by her continual coming, or, 'she will come continually (or, again and again) and wear me out (or, till she has worn me out)', 'she will tire me by her coming and coming' (Lomwe, similarly Nyanja, Zarma, Lokele). *To wear out,* i.e. to make tired by persistence.

6 ***And the Lord said, "Hear what the unrighteous judge says.***

Exegesis: *eipen de ho kurios* 'then the Lord said', introducing Jesus' application of the parable. For *ho kurios* cp. on 1 : 6.

akousate ti ho kritēs tēs adikias legei 'hear what the unrighteous judge says', pointing to what has been said, not, as usually to what will be said. In *ho kritēs tēs adikias* the genitive *tēs adikias* is qualifying and equivalent to an adjective.

Translation: *Hear* asks for the audience's attention; the rendering should not suggest advice to imitate the judge's example!

Unrighteous, or, 'unjust', 'violating justice'. In several languages the basic meaning of words for 'unjust' or 'dishonest' is 'crooked', 'not straight'; the South Toradja rendering, however, basically means 'not-exactly-spherical', also said e.g. of a coconut that has a protuberance.

7 ***And will not God vindicate his elect, who cry to him day and night? Will he delay long over them?***

Exegesis: *ho de theos ou mē poiēsē tēn ekdikēsin tōn eklektōn autou* 'and will not God protect his elect ?' *de* is contrastive. *ou mē* with subjunctive in an interrogative clause expects an answer in the affirmative. *poiein tēn ekdikēsin* with following genitive is equivalent to *ekdikein* with accusative (cp. on v. 3).

eklektos (also 23 : 35) 'chosen', here in the plural referring to the people of God as his chosen community.

tōn boōntōn autō hēmeras kai nuktos 'who cry to him day and night', going with *tōn eklektōn.* The clause refers to a situation of persecution and affliction. *boaō* with dative means here 'to cry out in prayer'. *hēmeras kai nuktos,* temporal genitives, means here virtually 'continually', 'uninterruptedly'.

kai makrothumei ep' autois 'and will he delay over them'. This difficult clause (see commentaries, esp. Plummer) is best understood as part of the interrogative clause, the expected answer being now in the negative. *makrothumeō* (†) is best understood as meaning 'to be long in helping', 'to delay'; *autois* refers to the chosen.

Translation: The answer to the two interrogative clauses is to be found in v. 8, to the first an explicit, positive answer, viz. "he will vindicate them", to the second one that implies a negation, viz. "speedily", i.e. not delaying long. The form to be given to the clauses in translation must be in accordance with the subsequent answer. Cp. for the first clause e.g. 'how about God? won't he certainly arrange (cp. on v. 3) as many as have been chosen by Him...' (Tzeltal), 'God will-he-not-reveal-as-true his chosen ones, won't he?' (Fulani, anticipating 'no, he will reveal them as true' in reply).

His elect, or, 'his chosen ones', 'the ones he has chosen', 'those he has pulled from amongst others' (Sranan). The aim of the choice may have to be specified, e.g. '...chosen to belong to him, or, to be his people/children'. Cp. also on "chose" in 6 : 13.

Cry to him, or, "appeal to him" (Phillips), 'cry, or, call to him for help' (cp. TEV), 'pray to him fervently (for help)'.

Day and night, see on 2 : 37.

Will he delay long over them, or, 'and will He-cause-to-be-long the waiting of those people' (East Toradja), 'will he delay in responding to them' (Tagalog), 'he will-be-long in-helping them, will he' (Fulani, anticipating 'no, he will not be long...' in reply), 'won't He immediately answer their words' (Tzeltal, this positive wording being felt to be more forceful).

8 ***I tell you, he will vindicate them speedily. Nevertheless, when the Son of man comes, will he find faith on earth?"***

Exegesis: *legō humin* 'I tell you', cp. on 3 : 8.

en tachei (†) lit. 'with speed', hence 'quickly', 'speedily'.

plēn 'but', here marking stronger contrast than *alla,* or *de.*

ho huios tou anthrōpou elthōn 'the Son of man, when he comes', implying that the coming of the Son of man is God's way of providing justice for his elect. The place of the subject with the participle that goes with it, before the interrogative particle *āra* which modifies the subsequent clause, is awkward and suggests strong emphasis.

āra heurēsei tēn pistin epi tēs gēs 'will he find the faith on earth?' *āra* (†, to be distinguished from *ara,* cp. e.g. 1 : 66) suggests a note of anxiety.

The article *tēn* before *pistin* is either generic and then better left untranslated (cp. RSV), or points to a specific form of faith, viz. the faith that is expecting the Son of man. This is preferable.

Translation: *When...earth.* Transposition of the two clauses may be preferable, e.g. "will the Son of Man find faith on earth when he comes" (TEV, similarly Bahasa Indonesia, Toba Batak).—*Find faith,* or, "find men...who believe in him" (Phillips, similarly East Toradja 1933).

9 ***He also told this parable to some who trusted in themselves that they were righteous and despised others:***

Exegesis: *eipen de kai...tēn parabolēn tautēn* 'he also told...this parable'. *kai* 'also' means 'in addition to what he had said before'.

pros tinas tous pepoithotas eph' heautois hoti eisin dikaioi 'to some people who were confident of themselves to be righteous'. *pros* may mean 'to', or 'with a view/with reference to', preferably the former. This implies the presence of a wider audience. *eph' heautois* indicates the foundation of the confidence. *hoti eisin dikaioi* refers to the content of the confidence. For *dikaios* cp. on 15 : 7.

kai exouthenountas tous loipous 'and who despised others', still modified by the article *tous* before *pepoithotas.* In *tous loipous* the article is generic, and the phrase means 'all other people', 'every one else'.

exoutheneō (also 23 : 11) 'to despise', 'to look down upon', 'to treat with contempt'.

Translation: *He also told this parable to,* or, 'and here is another parable of his. He told it to...' (cp. NEB).

Trusted in themselves that they were righteous, or, 'were sure that they themselves were righteous', 'thought of themselves: "We are the upright ones"' (Shona 1966), 'looked on themselves as people who do right' (Sranan), 'thought that their hearts were straight, theirs-only' (Tzeltal), 'believed regarding themselves: we meet the measure' (East Nyanja). For *righteous* see references on 1 : 6.

Despised others, or, "thought nothing of others" (Goodspeed), "looked down on everyone else" (NEB); or, 'said/thought of every body else, "He is worth nothing (or, is not righteous, or, is inferior to me)"'.

10 ***"Two men went up into the temple to pray, one a Pharisee and the other a tax collector.***

Exegesis: *anthrōpoi duo anebēsan eis to hieron proseuxasthai* 'two men went up to the temple to pray'. *anebēsan* 'went up' from the lower city to the temple mount. For *to hieron* cp. on 2 : 27. *proseuxasthai* final infinitive in the aorist tense, pointing to a punctiliar event.

ho heis Pharisaios kai ho heteros telōnēs 'one a Pharisee and the other a tax-collector', apposition to *anthrōpoi duo.* For *Pharisaios* cp. on 5 : 17; for *telōnēs* on 3 : 12.

Translation: The verse must be given the form used to mark the beginning of a narrative, e.g. '(once) there were two men who...'.

Went up, see on 2 : 4. Though in this situation a word expressing 'ascent' can often be used, some versions are somewhat more generic, e.g. 'went', 'entered' (cp. Low Malay, Sranan).

One a Pharisee and the other a tax collector, or, since the number has already been limited to two, simply, 'a Pharisee and a tax collector'. The appositional phrase sometimes can better be rendered as a clause, 'one was...the other/second (was)...'. For *tax collector* see on 3 : 12.

11 ***The Pharisee stood and prayed thus with himself, 'God, I thank thee that I am not like other men, extortioners, unjust, adulterers, or even like this tax collector.***

Exegesis: *statheis* lit. 'having taken his stand', in Luke always used of a person who is about to make an important statement (v. 40; 19 : 8; Acts 2: 14; 5 : 20; 17 : 22; 27 : 21), and meaning either that the person stood up from sitting, or that he took a position, or a place from which to speak. Here it may suggest that the Pharisee took a position where he could be seen by the public.

pros heauton tauta proseucheto 'prayed to himself this'. *pros heauton* is here equivalent to *en heautō* 'in himself' (cp. *TH-Mk* on 9 : 10), i.e. 'silently'.

ho theos, eucharistō soi 'O God, I thank you'. *ho theos* is nominative with the force of a vocative.

hoti ouk eimi hōsper hoi loipoi tōn anthrōpōn 'that I am not like the rest of men'. *hoi loipoi* takes up *tous loipous* in v. 9.

harpax (†) 'robber', or 'swindler', probably the latter, cp. A-G s.v.

adikoi lit. 'unrighteous (people)', here used as a substantive, 'law breakers', 'criminals'.

moichoi (†) 'adulterers'.

ē kai hōs houtos ho telōnēs 'or, for that matter, like that tax-collector'. *kai* means that the tax-collector is in the same class as the other people named.

Translation: *Prayed...with himself,* or, "silently prayed" (Rieu), 'prayed in his heart/mind', 'prayed, thus his-unuttered-thought' (Javanese).

I thank thee, see on 2 : 38.

Extortioners, unjust, adulterers. The appositional construction has equational force; it implies that the Pharisee declares all people other than himself and his group to be extortioners etc. It is sometimes better to shift to a relative clause, e.g. '...the rest of men, who are extortioners...'.—*Extortioners,* or, 'robbers' (cp. on 10 : 30), preferably 'swindlers', i.e. persons who take other people's property away by fraud or deceit. For *unjust,* or, 'evil/bad men', cp. *N.T.Wb.*/63f, RIGHTEOUS sub (7), for *adulterers* cp. references on "adultery" in 16 : 18.

Or even like..., preferably, 'or also like...', 'or again like...' (Jerusalem) (see *Exegesis*). The phrase is dependent on 'that I am not', or, 'I thank you...that I am not', which may better be repeated, cp. TEV.

12 ***I fast twice a week, I give tithes of all that I get.'***

Exegesis: *nēsteuō dis tou sabbatou* 'I fast twice a week'. The present tense suggests habit. For *nēsteuō* cp. on 5 : 33. Fasting twice a week was more than the law required. For *to sabbaton* cp. on A-G s.v. 2 and on 4 : 16. *dis* (†).

apodekatō panta hosa ktōmai 'I pay tithes on all I get', i.e. on all my income. This was also more than the law required. *apodekatoō* (*GNT*) or *apodekateuō* (Nestle) 'to tithe', 'to give one tenth (of income, or, profits) to God'; cp. also on 11 : 42.

ktaomai (also 21 : 19) 'to procure for oneself', 'to acquire'.

Translation: *Fast,* see references on 2 : 37.

A week, or, 'every week', 'every seven days', or, following another calculation, 'every eight days' (Javanese).

I give tithes of..., see on 11 : 42. Some descriptive renderings used here are, 'I divide...in ten (parts) and bring one part to the Temple (East Toradja 1933), or, give-in-charity one-part-of-it' (South Toradja).

13 ***But the tax collector, standing far off, would not even lift up his eyes to heaven, but beat his breast, saying, 'God, be merciful to me a sinner!'***

Exegesis: *ho de telōnēs makrothen hestōs* 'but the tax-collector, standing at a distance'. As contrasted with *statheis* (v. 9) *hestōs* is a neutral term. *makrothen* is used with reference to the Pharisee, or, to those present in the temple in general, preferably the latter.

ouk ēthelen oude tous ophthalmous eparai eis ton ouranon 'would not even raise his eyes to heaven'. The double negation *ouk...oude* goes with the clause as a whole (cp. Plummer). Eyes were raised in the direction of those that were going to be addressed (cp. 6 : 20; 16 : 23; Jn. 4 : 35; 6 : 5), hence before a prayer they were raised upward.

etupten to stēthos autou 'he kept beating his breast', iterative imperfect. The beating of the breast was a gesture of sorrow, or contrition.

hilasthēti moi tō hamartōlō 'have mercy on me, the sinner, i.e. sinner that I am'. As contrasted with *eleēson* 'have pity on me' (16 : 24; 17 : 13; 18 : 38f) *hilasthēti* refers not to some physical need or distress, but to a spiritual predicament, the nature of which is indicated by *tō hamartōlō* (cp on 5 : 8), in apposition to *moi,* the object of *hilasthēti.*

hilaskomai (†), in the passive 'to be merciful, or, gracious', 'to have mercy'.

Translation: *Standing far off,* or, 'kept at a distance and', 'did not dare to come near (or, to the front) and'.

Lift up his eyes to heaven, or, 'look towards the sky, or, upwards', for which several languages possess a specific verb; cp. also *N.T.Wb.*/60, RAISE.

Beat his breast is expressive of sorrow, contrition, or remorse in some languages (e.g. Marathi, Zarma, Timorese, Toba Batak) but in several others it indicates something quite different, e.g. delight (Gio), anger (Mezquital Otomi), self-congratulation, or boasting (Sranan, Cuicatec of Teutila, Chokwe, Kapauku, some European languages); hence, cultural equivalents such as 'beat his head' (Gio), 'got low' (Kapauku), 'beat his heart' (Sranan, which uses an equivalent, but slightly archaic idiom, 'laid his hand on his head', in 23 : 48), or a literal rendering followed by an indication of its functional meaning, e.g. 'beat-himself on his chest to show his sorrow' (Kituba, similarly Chokwe), or again non-symbolic renderings, cp. "with a gesture of despair" (Phillips). See also *N.T.Wb.*/15, BEAT.

Be merciful to me, or, 'have mercy on me', cp. on "mercy" in 1 : 50. Here the reference is to compassion that is ready to forgive offenses.

Sinner, see references on 5 : 30.

14 ***I tell you, this man went down to his house justified rather than the other; for every one who exalts himself will be humbled, but he who humbles himself will be exalted."***

Exegesis: *legō humin* 'I tell you', cp. on 3 : 8.

katebē houtos...eis ton oikon autou 'this man went down to his home'. *katebē* contrasts with *anebēsan* in v. 10.

dedikaiōmenos...par' ekeinon 'in the right relationship with God, more than the other', or, 'rather than the other', i.e. 'instead of the other', preferably the latter, cp. A-G s.v. *para* III 3. The past participle *dedikaiōmenos* points to a situation that will last henceforth. The passive appears to imply God as agent.

dikaioō 'to justify', 'to set right with God'.

For the rest of v. 14 cp. on 14 : 11.

Translation: *This man...rather than the other*, or, "it was he who...and not the other" (Goodspeed, and similarly several other versions), 'this man..., in contrast to the other' (NV), 'this man..., but this did not happen to the other one' (Sranan).

Went down to his house, or simply, 'went home', 'went back'.

Went...justified, or, 'went...(as) a justified man' (Bahasa Indonesia RC), 'was a justified man, when he went...' (cp. TEV). For *justified* cp. *N.T.Wb.*/64, RIGHTEOUS (4). The relation with God is often better made explicit, e.g. "justified in God's sight" (Phillips), cp. also "approved by God" (Rieu), "in the right with God" (TEV); a rendering that is more directly related to the preceding prayer is, "went...acquitted of his sins" (NEB).

For v. 14[b] see remarks and references on 14 : 11.

15 ***Now they were bringing even infants to him that he might touch them; and when the disciples saw it, they rebuked them.***

Exegesis: *prosepheron de autō kai ta brephē* 'they brought to him also the little children'. *prosepheron* and *epetimōn* in the next clause are descriptive imperfect. *kai* may mean 'even', or 'also', i.e. 'in addition to the sick', preferably the latter. *ta brephē* (cp. on 1 : 41) refers here to children who are able to walk, as *erchesthai* 'to come', and *ta paidia* in v. 16 suggest. Subject of *prosepheron* is implicitly the parents.

hina autōn haptētai 'that he might touch them', final clause. For *haptomai* cp. on 5 : 13.

idontes de hoi mathētai epetimōn autois 'but the disciples, when they saw it, stopped them'. *epetimōn* may mean 'they scolded, or, reproved (them)', or 'they checked, or, stopped (them)', preferably the latter, cp. on 4 : 35 and *TH-Mk* on 1 : 25 and 10 : 13. *autois* is best understood as having the same referent as *autōn* above, and *auta* in v. 16, viz. the children.

Translation: For *now* see on 1 : 57.

They were bringing...to him, or, '(some) people were leading/taking-with-them...to him' (Balinese, South Toradja).

That he might touch them, or, 'saying, "Please touch my little one"'. The people probably expected that Jesus' touch had the power to bless. The verb cannot be rendered literally in some cases, e.g. in Tzeltal, where 'to touch' is the technical term for a shaman's rite of curing the sick; hence, 'that He might place His hand on their heads one-after-the-other'. Elsewhere it is thought undesirable for a stranger to touch children; then one may use the term rendering 'to bless', for which cp. on 1 : 42, sub (1) or (3), preferably (1).

Rebuked them, cp. on 4 : 35.

16 ***But Jesus called them to him, saying, "Let the children come to me, and do not hinder them; for to such belongs the kingdom of God.***

Exegesis: *ho de Iēsous prosekalesato auta* 'but Jesus called them to him'. The aorist tense of *prosekalesato* after two imperfects indicates the beginning of the main part of the narrative. *auta* refers to *ta brephē*. For *proskaleō* cp. on 7 : 18.

legōn lit. 'saying', i.e. either 'by saying', or 'meanwhile saying to the disciples', preferably the former.

aphete ta paidia erchesthai pros me 'let the children come to me', cp. 8 : 51.

tōn gar toioutōn estin hē basileia tou theou 'for to such (as these) belongs the kingdom of God', i.e. people such as these will have the right to share in the kingdom of God. *toioutos* means here 'having the same qualities as little children', cp. A-G s.v. 3 a α. For *hē basileia tou theou* cp. on 4 : 43.

Translation: *Called them to him*, or, 'called out for them to (or, that they should) be brought to him' (cp. Phillips, to indicate that the children are not addressed directly, see *Exegesis*). *Them* is often better specified, 'those (little) children'.

Saying, or, 'and said', 'with the words'.

Let the children come, i.e. allow the children to come.

Hinder, i.e. '(try to) stop', sometimes coinciding with the rendering of "rebuke" in v. 15.

To such belongs the kingdom of God, or, '(it is) they (who) possess the kingdom of God'. The structure of this clause may have to be changed more radically, e.g. 'as are these children, so are the people who can enter God's hand that he rule over them' (a Mixtec dialect), 'their-place shall become where God is governing' (Tzeltal).—*Such,* or, "such as these" (NEB), 'people who are like these (children)' (Bahasa Indonesia).

17 ***Truly, I say to you, whoever does not receive the kingdom of God like a child shall not enter it."***

Exegesis: *amēn legō humin* 'truly I say to you', cp. on 3 : 8 and 4 : 24.

hos an mē dexētai tēn basileian tou theou hōs paidion 'whoever does not accept the kingdom of God like a child', elaborating the thought implied in the preceding clause. The phrase 'to accept the kingdom of God' is best understood as 'to accept God's rule over men'.

ou mē eiselthē eis autēn 'shall not enter it'. For *ou mē* cp. on 1 : 15. To enter the kingdom of God means to share in its blessings at the final consummation.

Translation: *Truly, I say to you,* cp. the references on 4 : 24.

Whoever does not receive...shall not enter may, again, better be rendered as an 'if'-clause (cp. on 9 : 24), and/or as a positive sentence, e.g. 'only people who receive...will enter'.

For the rest of the verse see *TH-Mk* on 10 : 15.

18 ***And a ruler asked him, "Good Teacher, what shall I do to inherit eternal life?"***

Exegesis: *kai epērōtēsen tis auton archōn* 'a certain man of the ruling class asked him'. For *eperōtaō* cp. on 2 : 46. *archōn* is used here in a general sense and denotes a person who belongs to the important and influential groups that have the ruling functions in society.

didaskale agathe 'good teacher', cp. *TH-Mk* on 10 : 17.

ti poiēsas zōēn aiōnion klēronomēsō lit. '(by) doing what shall I inherit eternal life?', cp. on 10 : 25.

Translation: *Ruler,* preferably, "a man of high standing" (Rieu), 'a prominent man' (Leyden, NV), *un notable* (Jerusalem).

Good Teacher, or shifting to an attributive clause, 'teacher, you who are good', cp. *TH-Mk* on 10 : 17. In this verse *good* is used in the sense of 'kind', 'generous', but in v. 19 it refers to moral perfection. Where one term covering both meanings is not available considerable difficulty may arise, since Jesus' reply in v. 19 takes up the same term but gives it a slightly different meaning. It may then be possible, however, to qualify the term in v. 18, e.g. 'good of heart', i.e. kind (Toba Batak), but to use it without qualification and in a more absolute sense in v. 19. If this also proves impossible, the term for moral goodness, or perfection, is best used in both verses.

Inherit eternal life, see on 10 : 25 and references.

19 ***And Jesus said to him, "Why do you call me good? No one is good but God alone.***

Exegesis: *ti me legeis agathon* lit. 'what do you call me good?' Interrogative *ti* may inquire after the cause and be rendered, 'why', or express astonishment at what has been said or done and mean, 'what!', i.e. 'how could you', preferably the latter. For *agathon* cp. *TH-Mk* on 10 : 18.

oudeis agathos ei mē heis ho theos 'no one is good except one, viz. God', cp. *TH-Mk* on 10 : 18.

Translation: *Call me good* may have to be rendered 'say that I am good' (Sranan, where a more literal rendering would cause 'good' to be taken as a name or title).

No one is good but God alone, or, '(only) God is good, no one else (is good)'; or, in order to avoid classifying God as a human being, 'not any man is good, only God is (good)'; cp. *TH-Mk, l.c.,* and *N.T.Wb.*/7.

20 ***You know the commandments: 'Do not commit adultery, Do not kill, Do not steal, Do not bear false witness, Honour your father and mother.'"***

Exegesis: Except for the place of the first two commandments which occur in Mark in the inverse order, and for the omission of *mē aposterēsēs* by Luke, v. 20 is identical to Mk. 10 : 19, cp. *TH-Mk* there.

Translation: For the whole verse see again *TH-Mk, l.c.*; for *commandment* and *commit adultery* see also above on 1 : 6 and 16 : 18 respectively; for *kill* see also *N.T.Wb.*/49f.

To bear false witness, or, 'to give false testimony', i.e. to state, as though one has seen or heard them personally, things that are not true; or, less specifically, 'to tell lies'.

For the sequence of *father and mother* see above on 2 : 33.

21 ***And he said, "All these I have observed from my youth."***

Exegesis: *tauta panta ephulaxa* 'I have kept all these'. For the general meaning of this verse cp. *TH-Mk* on 10 : 21. For *phulassō* meaning 'to keep', 'to observe', cp. A-G s.v. 1 f.

ek neotētos 'from boyhood', probably referring to the age of twelve, cp. on 2 : 42.

neotēs (†) 'youth', 'childhood'.

Translation: *He* may have to be specified, e.g. "the man" (NEB), *celui-ci* (Jerusalem), 'the ruler (just-mentioned)' (Javanese, Tagalog).

All these I have observed, cp. *TH-Mk* on 10 : 20; *N.T.Wb.*/49, KEEP. In Sranan the idiom is, 'I have put my eye on all these things'.

From my youth, or, 'since I became a boy'.

22 ***And when Jesus heard it, he said to him, "One thing you still lack. Sell all that you have and distribute to the poor, and you will have treasure in heaven; and come, follow me."***

Exegesis: *eti hen soi leipei* 'there is still one thing lacking for you', or 'you lack only one thing', i.e. either 'there is one thing which you do not yet have', or 'there is one thing which you must do yet', hence "you still need to do one thing" (TEV), preferably the latter, as the subsequent imperatives suggest. *leipō* (†).

panta hosa echeis pōlēson 'sell everything that you have'.

diados ptōchois 'distribute (the proceeds) to the poor'. For *diadidōmi* cp. on 11 : 22; for *ptōchos* (here without specific religious connotation) cp. on 4 : 18.

kai hexeis thēsauron en [tois] ouranois 'and (as a result) you will have treasure in heaven', cp. *TH-Mk* on 10 : 21.

deuro akolouthei moi 'come, follow me', present tense of *akolouthei* 'follow' suggests duration as compared with the aorist tense of *pōlēson* and *diados*.

deuro (†) lit. 'hither', when followed by an imperative, 'come (here)'.

Translation: *Distribute to,* or, "divide...among" (Goodspeed), cp. *N.T.Wb.*/29, DIVIDE. Where an object is required one may use 'the proceeds (of the sale)', 'the money', or, illogically, 'it' (NV, Jerusalem, Zürich, some Indonesian languages).

Treasure in heaven, cp. on 12 : 33.

And come, or, 'after that (or, then) come'. The verb may require some specification, 'come here' (NV, similarly Bahasa Indonesia, Javanese), "come back" (Goodspeed).

Follow, see on 5 : 11.

23 ***But when he heard this he became sad, for he was very rich.***

Exegesis: *perilupos egenēthē* 'he became very sad'. *egenēthē* is best understood as ingressive aorist. *perilupos* (†).

ēn gar plousios sphodra 'for he was very rich'. *sphodra* (†) 'very', modifies *plousios* though placed after it.

Translation: *Sad.* For terms to express sorrow, cp. *N.T.Wb.*/73, WEEP, and *TH-Mk* on "sorrowful" in 10 : 21.

He was very rich, or, 'he was a very rich man'.

24 ***Jesus looking at him said, "How hard it is for those who have riches to enter the kingdom of God!***

Exegesis: *idōn de auton...[perilupon genomenon]* 'seeing him to be very sad'.

pōs duskolōs 'with how much difficulty', going with *eisporeuontai* 'enter'. For *pōs* cp. A-G s.v. 3.

duskolōs (†) adverb 'with difficulty'.
hoi ta chrēmata echontes 'those who have property'.
chrēmata (†) 'property', 'wealth'. The article *ta* is generic.
eis tēn basileian tou theou eisporeuontai 'enter the kingdom of God', cp. on v. 17.

Translation: *Looking at him,* preferably, 'seeing him so sad' (Zürich), 'seeing that he had become very sad'.

Enter the kingdom, or, 'come into the place where God is king', 'enter where God rules', cp. 'enter God's hand that he rule over them' (a Mixtec dialect).

For the rest of the verse cp. *TH-Mk* on 10 : 24.

25 ***For it is easier for a camel to go through the eye of a needle than for a rich man to enter the kingdom of God."***

Exegesis: *eukopōteron...estin kamēlon...dielthein ē plousion...eiselthein* lit. 'it is easier that a camel passes through...than that a rich man enters...', hence, 'it is easier for a camel to pass through...than for a rich man to enter...', cp. *TH-Mk* on 10 : 25 on details of syntax. For *eukopōteron* cp. on 5 : 23.

kamēlon dia trēmatos belonēs dielthein 'for a camel to pass through the eye of a needle'. For the meaning of this saying cp. *TH-Mk* on 10 : 25.
kamēlos (†) 'camel'.
trēma (†) 'opening', 'hole'.
belonē (††) 'needle', instrument used for sewing.

Translation: For this verse see *TH-Mk* on 10 : 25. Moreover, for "easy" cp. above on 5 : 23.

For *camel* see also *TBT*, 12.2 and 7, 1961. Where a borrowing is used, because the animal is unknown in the culture, it may be useful to indicate the point of comparison, cp. e.g. Tzeltal, which uses *camello* but makes explicit that the reference is to its bigness. In some regions another animal is proverbial for bigness, e.g. 'elephant' (Toba Batak).

The eye of a needle is elsewhere called its 'face' (Kekchi), 'loop' (East Toradja), 'foot' (Tzeltal). A term for some sort of *needle* seems usually to be available, e.g. a coarse bone or bamboo needle used to sew pandanus-leaves to make raincapes or mats (Kapauku), or for stitching reed mats with bark fibres (Nyanja).

26 ***Those who heard it said, "Then who can be saved?"*** 27 ***But he said, "What is impossible with men is possible with God."***

Exegesis: *eipan de hoi akousantes* 'those who heard (this) said', to each other, or, to Jesus, preferably the latter.

kai tis dunatai sōthēnai 'then who can be saved'. *kai* at the beginning of a question expresses astonishment, cp. A-G s.v. I 2 h. *sōthēnai* means here 'to attain salvation', cp. on 8 : 12.

(V. 27) *ta adunata para anthrōpois* 'the things which are impossible with men, i.e. for men', cp. A-G s.v. *para* II 2 c.

adunatos (†) 'impossible', here used as a substantive.

dunata para tō theō estin 'are possible for God', cp. A-G s.v. *dunatos* 2 c. The clause is an answer to the question of v. 26 in the form of a general pronouncement.

Translation: *Who can be saved,* or, 'who can reach/acquire salvation' (Balinese, Javanese), and cp. *TH-Mk* on 10 : 26.

(V. 27) *What is impossible with men is possible with God,* or, 'things men cannot do, God can (do)', or, 'God is able to do what no men can do'.

28 ***And Peter said, "Lo, we have left our homes and followed you."***

Exegesis: *idou* 'see', emphatic introduction of what follows.

hēmeis aphentes ta idia ēkolouthēsamen soi 'we having given up our possessions have followed you'. *hēmeis* is emphatic and contrasts the disciples with the 'ruler' of vv. 18ff. For the general meaning of the clause cp. on 5 : 11.

ta idia (†) lit. 'the own things', i.e. 'the things one owns', either in a specific sense, 'home' (cp. Goodspeed, *Problems* 87f), or in a more general sense, 'property' (including wife and children), preferably the latter.

Translation: *Lo,* cp. on "behold" in 1 : 20.

Left our homes, preferably, 'given up our possessions, or, what was ours' (cp. Rieu, NV).

For *left* and *followed* see on 5 : 11.

29 ***And he said to them, "Truly, I say to you, there is no man who has left house or wife or brothers or parents or children, for the sake of the kingdom of God,*** 30 ***who will not receive manifold more in this time, and in the age to come eternal life."***

Exegesis: *amēn legō humin* 'truly I say to you', cp. on 3 : 8 and 4 : 24.

oudeis estin hos aphēken...hos ouchi mē apolabē... 'there is no one who has given up...who will not receive...'. *oudeis estin...hos* is equivalent to an emphatic *oudeis*: 'absolutely no one'. The clause *hos aphēken...*, subordinate to the main clause, has the function of a conditional clause.

adelphous 'brothers', implying sisters.

heneken tēs basileias tou theou 'for the sake of the kingdom of God', i.e. in order to serve the cause of the kingdom.

(V. 30) (*oudeis*)...*hos ouchi mē apolabē* '(no one) who will not receive...'. Together with, and because of the preceding *oudeis, ouchi mē* serves to express a strongly positive assertion, which is in the nature of a promise. For *apolambanō* cp. on 6 : 34.

pollaplasiona (†) 'many times as much', 'many times more'.

en tō kairō toutō 'in this time', *en tō aiōni tō erchomenō* 'in the coming age', cp. *TH-Mk* on 10 : 30, and *N.T.Wb.*, 13/AGE.

zōēn aiōnion 'eternal life', cp. on 10 : 25.

Translation: *There is no man who has left...who will not receive,* or, 'everybody who has left (or, if a man has left..., he) will be sure to receive...'; cp. also on 9 : 24.

House...children, cp. on 14 : 26. Each or some of the terms used may obligatorily be possessed. For *parents* see on 2 : 27.

For the sake of the kingdom of God, or shifting to a verbal clause, 'in order that God may rule (the world/people)'.

(V. 30) *Receive,* or, "get back" (Rieu), 'receive in return' (Thai), 'come to have in return', 'be given in exchange' (Tzeltal).

Manifold more, or, 'many times as much'; the idioms used in Fulani and Timorese lit. mean 'pile surpassing in quantity', and 'in layers', respectively. The ellipsis may have to be filled out, '...more than he has left' (Shona 1966), '...more than all he had, or, than all his family and property'.

The age to come, cp. *TH-Mk* on 10 : 30; *N.T.Wb.*/4, AGE.

31 ***And taking the twelve, he said to them, "Behold, we are going up to Jerusalem, and everything that is written of the Son of man by the prophets will be accomplished.***

Exegesis: *paralabōn de tous dōdeka* 'and after taking aside the twelve', i.e. taking them away from the other people around them, in order to talk to them privately.

idou anabainomen eis Ierousalēm 'see, we are going up to Jerusalem'. *idou* (cp. on 1 : 20) does not primarily focus the attention on *anabainomen* (which denotes a fact well known since 9 : 51) but on *telesthēsetai* etc. For *anabainō* cp. on 2 : 4.

kai telesthēsetai panta ta gegrammena dia tōn prophētōn tō huiō tou anthrōpou 'and (when we are there) all that has been written through the prophets about the Son of man will be accomplished'. For *teleō* cp. on 2 : 39. Here the idea of fulfilment is also implied. *dia tōn prophētōn* depicts the prophets as transmitters of a divine message of which God is the author, cp. A-G s.v. *dia* A III 2 a. The dative *tō huiō tou anthrōpou* (cp. on 5 : 24) may go with *telesthēsetai* (cp. NEB), or with *gegrammena* (cp. RSV), preferably the latter.

Translation: *Taking,* i.e. 'taking aside', suggesting that they remained in the same place, or, 'taking with him' (cp. on 9 : 10), implying that they moved along with Jesus.

For *the twelve* see on 8 : 1, and for *going up* on 2 : 4.

Everything that is written...by the prophets, or, 'through the agency of the prophets' (Marathi); or, 'everything that is written...in (or, stands in, or, forms the contents of) the books of the prophets'. In cases like this, however, the difference between primary and secondary agency is negligible; hence, renderings like RSV, and 'all that the prophets wrote...' (Yao). For equivalent formulas cp. also on "as it is written" in 2 : 23.

Will be accomplished, or, 'fulfilled' (cp. on 4 : 21), 'will become a fact'; or transposing the first part of the clause, 'everything will happen exactly in accordance with what (or, as it) is written in...'.

32 ***For he will be delivered to the Gentiles, and will be mocked and shamefully treated and spit upon;*** 33 ***they will scourge him and kill him, and on the third day he will rise."***

Exegesis: *paradothēsetai gar tois ethnesin* 'for he will be handed over to the heathen'. For *paradidōmi* cp. on 1 : 2 and 9 : 44. *ta ethnē* (cp. *TH-Mk* on 10 : 33) refers here specifically to the Roman authorities in Jerusalem. The agent of the verbal action may be God (as in 9 : 44) or the Jews, presumably the former because the handing over is a fulfilment of prophecy.

empaichthēsetai kai hubristhēsetai kai emptusthēsetai 'he will be ridiculed and insulted and spat upon'. The agent of these actions are the Romans. For *empaizō* cp. on 14 : 29; for *hubrizō* cp. on 11 : 45.

emptuō (†) 'to spit upon', as an act of humiliation.

(V. 33) *kai mastigōsantes apoktenousin auton* 'and after flogging him they will kill him', shift from the passive to the active, the agent being the same.

mastigoō (†) 'to whip', 'to flog', cp. *TH-Mk* on 10 : 34.

tē hēmera tē tritē anastēsetai 'on the third day he will rise', cp. on 9 : 7f and *TH-Mk* on 8 : 31.

Translation: For *he will be delivered* and *the Gentiles* see 9 : 44 and 2 : 32 respectively.

And will be mocked and shamefully treated and spit upon. Because the implied agent is different this part of the verse is usually better treated as a separate clause or sentence, where preferable in an active construction, e.g. 'who (going with 'the Gentiles') will mock him...', or, 'they/these people will mock him...'.—*To mock*, or, 'to ridicule', "to jeer at" (Phillips), "to make fun of" (TEV). *To treat shamefully*, or, 'to insult', 'to treat with arrogance/insolence'. *To spit upon*, see *TH-Mk* on 10 : 34.

(V. 33) For *to scourge* cp. *N.T.Wb.*/15, BEAT. For *to kill* in this context and for *on the third day* see on 9 : 22; for *he will rise* see on 9 : 7f.

34 ***But they understood none of these things; this saying was hid from them, and they did not grasp what was said.***

Exegesis: *kai autoi ouden toutōn sunēkan* 'and they did not understand any of this'. *autoi* refers to *hoi dōdeka* in v. 31 and is slightly emphatic. For *suniēmi* cp. on 2 : 50; it often refers to the understanding of a word or an action of Jesus.

kai ēn to rēma touto kekrummenon ap' autōn 'and this word was concealed from them', explaining the preceding clause: it was not their own fault that they did not understand Jesus' word. The agent of the verb is not stated and this is here clearly intentional.

kai ouk eginōskon ta legomena 'and they did not know his sayings', taking up and repeating in other words what was said in the first clause after the explanation given in the second. *ta legomena* is virtually equivalent to *to rēma touto.*

Translation: *They understood none of these things,* cp. on 2 : 50.
This saying was hid from them, or, "the significance of the saying was hidden from them" (Rieu), 'this saying (or, what he said) was/remained obscure to them' (cp. Willibrord); cp. also on "it was concealed from them" in 9 : 45.
And has consecutive force here, 'so', 'accordingly'.
They did not grasp what was said, synonymous with the first clause. Some renderings used are, "they did not know what Jesus was talking about" (TEV), 'the things spoken did not enter their attention/perception' (Marathi), 'they did not find the sense of that saying' (cp. Timorese).

35 ***As he drew near to Jericho, a blind man was sitting by the roadside begging;***

Exegesis: *egeneto de* 'and it happened', cp. on 1 : 8.
en tō eggizein auton eis Ierichō lit. 'at his approaching Jericho', i.e. 'as he approached Jericho'. *eggizō eis* followed by the name of a town means 'to approach', 'to come into the neighbourhood of'.
tuphlos tis ekathēto para tēn hodon epaitōn 'a blind man was sitting by the road, begging'. *tis* has the force of an indefinite article. *epaitōn* adds a secondary trait to the picture and plays no part in what follows.

Translation: *Drew near,* cp. on 7 : 12.
A blind man was sitting by the roadside begging tends to lend emphasis to the last verb; to avoid this one may better say e.g. "a certain blind man was sitting and begging by the road" (TEV), 'a blind man who was begging (or, a blind beggar) sat by the side of the road'. For *blind* cp. on 4 : 18, for *road* cp. *N.T.Wb.*/72, WAY, for *to beg* cp. on 16 : 3; the verb may require an object, 'to beg for something' (Sranan).

36 ***and hearing a multitude going by, he inquired what this meant.***

Exegesis: *akousas de ochlou diaporeuomenou* 'when he heard a crowd going by'. *akousas* refers to judgment based on his own observation. *ochlou* 'a crowd', without article. *diaporeuomai* here 'to go by', 'to go along', elsewhere (cp. 6 : 1) 'to pass through'.
epunthaneto ti eiē touto 'he inquired what this was', cp. on 15 : 26.

Translation: *Hearing a multitude going by,* or, 'as soon as he heard the noise of a crowd that went by' (Javanese, specifying by the use of the non-honorific pronoun that the reference is now to the beggar). Elsewhere one may have to use, 'this one' (NV), 'the (blind) man', 'the beggar'.
Inquired what this meant, cp. on 15 : 26 and *N.T.Wb.*/12, ASK. If the persons asked have to be specified, one may say, 'asked those near him'.

37 ***They told him, "Jesus of Nazareth is passing by".***

Exegesis: *apēggeilan de autō* 'they told him', without indication of subject.

Iēsous ho Nazōraios parerchetai 'Jesus the man from Nazareth is passing by', direct speech introduced by *hoti*. *parerchomai* is virtually equivalent to *diaporeuomai* in v. 36. *Nazōraios* is best understood as equivalent to *Nazarēnos* (cp. 4 : 34).

Translation: *They told him.* The subject may have to become, 'people', 'those near him', if not specified already in v. 36.
Jesus of Nazareth, cp. on 4 : 34.

38 ***And he cried, "Jesus, Son of David, have mercy on me!"***

Exegesis: *kai eboēsen* 'and he cried out'. When *boaō* is compared to *krazō* (v. 39), the latter is the stronger in meaning.
Iēsou, huie Dauid 'Jesus, Son of David'. *huios* means here 'male descendant'. The phrase 'Son of David' is a Messianic title.
eleēson me 'have pity on me', cp. on 17 : 13.

Translation: *Cried,* or, 'shouted', 'called out loudly'.
Son of David, see *TH-Mk* on 10 : 47. For *David* cp. on 1 : 27.
Have mercy on me, cp. on 1 : 50.

39 ***And those who were in front rebuked him, telling him to be silent; but he cried out all the more, "Son of David, have mercy on me!"***

Exegesis: *hoi proagontes epetimōn autō hina sigēsē* 'those who were in front told him sharply to be silent', i.e. "to hold his tongue" (NEB). For *epitimaō* cp. on 4 : 35.
proagō (†) 'to go before', 'to walk ahead'.
autos de pollō mallon ekrazen 'but he (emphatic) shouted out much more', i.e. 'all the more, or, the louder'. The imperfect tense of *ekrazen* is repetitive.

Translation: *Those who were* (or, walked) *in front,* viz. 'of the group/caravan'.
Rebuked him, telling, see on 4 : 35.
He cried out all the more, or, 'he shouted even louder because of it' (Tzeltal), 'he began to scream more than ever' (Yao). The concept "all the more" is expressed in several versions by the use of verbs indicating excessive, increasing or surpassing activity (cp. e.g. Shona, Kapauku, Nyanja, Kituba, Fulani).

40a ***And Jesus stopped, and commanded him to be brought to him;***

Exegesis: *statheis de ho Iēsous* 'Jesus stood still', cp. on v. 11. Though Jesus actually stopped (cp. RSV) *statheis* at the same time has the function of preparing the way for what Jesus is about to do.

ekeleusen auton achthēnai pros auton 'he ordered him to be brought to him'. The first *auton* refers to the blind man, the last to Jesus.

keleuō (†) 'to command', 'to order'.

Translation: *Commanded him to be* (or, that he should be) *brought to him*, or, 'had-(him-)brought to where-he-was' (East Toradja, using the prefix discussed in the note on "to be baptized" in 3 : 7). The first pronoun may have to be rendered as, 'the (blind) man', and/or the rendering of the second pronoun must make clear that the person referred to is identical with the one who gives the command. Further shifts may lead to something like, 'ordered/told them (or, those people, or, those close by), "Bring him to me"'. *To bring*, or, 'cause-to-come', in this context sometimes more specific 'to lead (by the hand)'.

40b ***and when he came near, he asked him,*** 41 ***"What do you want me to do for you?" He said, "Lord, let me receive my sight."***

Exegesis: *eggisantos de autou* 'when he drew near', 'when he came up'.

(V. 41) *ti soi theleis poiēsō* lit. 'what do you want I should do for you?', i.e. 'what do you want me to do for you?' *poiēsō* is deliberative subjunctive, here asyndetically introduced by *theleis*, cp. Bl-D, § 366.3. *soi* may mean 'for you', or, 'to you', preferably the former.

hina anablepsō 'that I may recover my sight', final clause, indirectly dependent upon *poiēsō*, and virtually equivalent to a wish, or a request.

Translation: In v. 40^b specification of the pronoun or pronouns may be necessary again.

(V. 41) Jesus' question may sometimes better be rendered in two clauses, e.g. 'What shall I do for you? What is your wish?'

Let me receive (preferably, 'recover', or, 'receive again') *my sight*, or to bring out the dependence upon the preceding question: "to make me see again" (Rieu), 'that my eyes become-clear' (East Toradja), 'I want to see again' (Kituba); or, as an independent clause, 'grant that I may see' (Thai), 'cause me to see (again)', 'let me please be able to see' (Javanese). Cp. also on 7 : 22 and *TH-Mk* on 10 : 51.—The terms employed in this clause can usually be echoed in vv. 42 and 43, e.g. in Shona (a hortative, an imperative and an indicative form of 'to see'), Marathi (two optative and one indicative forms of 'sight comes again to'), or in Tzeltal, which has, 'I want that you might open my eyes—be opened your eyes (3rd person imperative)—his eyes opened (intransitive verb)'. But sometimes idiom requires differentiation, cp. e.g. 'make-seeing my eyes—eyes look (imperative)—his eyes became-seeing' (Kapauku), 'that I may get-back my sight—be-unblinded (one word)—he got-back his sight' (Fulani), 'that I may obtain seeing—see—at once he made eye' (Zarma, the last phrase being an idiom for to become sighted; a blind man is said 'not to have eyes', a seeing man is an 'eye-owner').

42 ***And Jesus said to him, "Receive your sight; your faith has made you well."***

Exegesis: *anablepson* 'recover your sight', imperative, yet not requiring or commanding any activity of the blind man, but rather due to the fact that he is healed by the powerful word of Jesus.

hē pistis sou sesōken se 'your faith has made you well', cp. on 7 : 50 and *TH-Mk* on 5 : 34.

Translation: *Your faith has made you well,* see on 8 : 48 and references.

43 ***And immediately he received his sight and followed him, glorifying God; and all the people, when they saw it, gave praise to God.***

Exegesis: *kai parachrēma aneblepsen* 'and (as a result) he recovered his sight at once'.

kai ēkolouthei autō doxazōn ton theon 'and he followed him glorifying God'. The imperfect tense is durative. For *doxazō* cp. on 2 : 20.

pas ho laos idōn edōken ainon tō theō 'when they saw (it) all the people gave praise to God'. For *pas ho laos* cp. on 3 : 21. The aorist tense of *edōken* refers to the immediate reaction of the people as contrasted with the lasting reaction of the healed man. *edōken ainon* (†) is virtually equivalent to *ēnesan* (from *aineō,* cp. on 2 : 20).

Translation: *And followed him* is usually better rendered as a new sentence. The verb here has the meaning 'went with him', 'accompanied him'.

Glorifying God, simultaneous with the preceding act: and, as he went (or, while he did so) he glorified God. For *to glorify* see on 2 : 20; Goodspeed and TEV render "giving thanks to God".

For *all the people* cp. on 3 : 21.

To give praise to God, or, 'to praise God', closely synonymous with 'to glorify God', cp. on 2 : 20. If no suitable synonym is available one may say, 'praising God—they too praised God'.

CHAPTER NINETEEN

1 ***He entered Jericho and was passing through.***

Exegesis: *kai eiselthōn diērcheto tēn Ierichō* 'and after entering Jericho he passed through it'. *diērcheto* is durative imperfect. The verse sets the scene for the subsequent events. For *dierchomai* cp. on 2 : 15.

Translation: *Was passing through,* or, 'made his way through it', 'passed in the midst of the town' (East Toradja), implying that Jesus did not stay in the city but entered it only to leave it at the other end.

2 ***And there was a man named Zacchaeus; he was a chief tax collector, and rich.***

Exegesis: *kai idou anēr* lit. 'and behold, (there was) a man', nominal clause introduced by emphatic *kai idou,* denoting that Zacchaeus' appearance on the scene was rather surprising.

onomati kaloumenos Zakchaios 'named Zacchaeus', pleonastic since *onomati* (cp. A-G s.v. I 1, 2 b) and *kaloumenos* (cp. A-G s.v. 1 a γ) are synonymous.

kai autos ēn architelōnēs 'and he was a chief tax-collector'. *autos* is unemphatic.

architelōnēs (††; not found elsewhere in Greek) 'chief tax-collector', cp. on 3 : 12 where *telōnēs* is used. *architelōnēs,* either the head of the local *telōnai,* or merely higher in rank.

kai autos plousios 'and he (was) rich', explicit addition of what might be presumed in the case of a chief tax-collector and preparing the way for v. 8.

Translation: *Chief tax collector,* i.e. 'one of the great/principal tax collectors', or, 'the head (Bahasa Indonesia), or, the father (Bamiléké) of the tax collectors'. For *tax collector* see on 3 : 12.

And rich, sometimes better appositional, 'a rich man', or as a new sentence, 'he was a rich man'.

3 ***And he sought to see who Jesus was, but could not, on account of the crowd, because he was small of stature.***

Exegesis: *kai ezētei idein ton Iēsoun tis estin* 'and he tried to see who Jesus was', implying that he had heard about Jesus but had never seen him. For the imperfect tense of *ezētei* cp. on 5 : 18. *tis estin* may mean 'which of all the people Jesus was', or "how Jesus looked" (Rieu), preferably the former.

ouk ēdunato apo tou ochlou 'he could not (see him) because of the crowd', cp. A-G s.v. *apo* V 1.

hoti tē hēlikia mikros ēn 'because he was small of stature'. *tē hēlikia* (cp.

A-G s.v. 2) is dative of respect, indicating that to what *mikros* refers.

Translation: *He sought*, cp. on 5 : 18.

But could not, on account of the crowd, because he was small of stature, or, "but being short he could not see him for the crowd" (Rieu), or, 'But he was a little/short man, and (therefore) he could not see him/Jesus because of the crowd, or, because he was kept-from-seeing by the crowd (cp. Javanese), or, because people stood-packed' (cp. Balinese).—Zacchaeus' attempt to see Jesus will have been made inside the city, but their actual meeting (vv. 5ff) probably took place outside.

4 ***So he ran on ahead and climbed up into a sycamore tree to see him, for he was to pass that way.***

Exegesis: *prodramōn eis to emprosthen* lit. 'after running on ahead'. *eis to emprosthen* lit. 'to the front' (cp. A-G s.v. 1 a), hence 'ahead', which is pleonastic since *protrechō* (†) means 'to run ahead'.

anebē epi sukomorean hina idē auton 'he climbed up a fig-mulberry tree in order to see him'.

sukomorea (††) 'ficus sycomorus', 'fig-mulberry tree', a fig tree whose leaves resemble those of a mulberry tree, cp. *IDB* IV, 470f, *N.T.Wb.*, 62/FLORA (B/6).

hoti ekeinēs ēmellen dierchesthai 'because he was going to pass that way', with *hodou* 'way' understood with *ekeinēs*.

Translation: *He ran on ahead*, viz. some distance in front of Jesus and his companions.

Sycamore tree. Where the exact species is unknown the term for '(wild) fig tree' (cp. *N.T.Wb.*/38, FLORA), is an acceptable rendering; or simply, 'a tree' (East Toradja 1933), the kind of tree not being of specific relevance here.

For he (or, Jesus) *was to pass that way*, stating explicitly what has been implied already in the words "ran on ahead", viz. that Zacchaeus could foresee along which road Jesus would come; hence, 'expecting that Jesus was going to take that way' (cp. Rieu) is an acceptable rendering also.

5 ***And when Jesus came to the place, he looked up and said to him, "Zacchaeus, make haste and come down; for I must stay at your house today."***

Exegesis: *hōs ēlthen epi ton topon* 'when he came to the spot', with change of subject. The article *ton* has demonstrative force.

anablepsas ho Iēsous eipen pros auton 'Jesus looked up and said to him'. For *anablepō* cp. on 7 : 22.

speusas katabēthi 'come down with haste'. The participle *speusas* lit. 'hurrying', does not denote an act of its own but qualifies the imperative *katabēthi*. For *speudō* cp. on 2 : 16.

sēmeron gar en tō oikō sou dei me meinai 'for today I must stay at your home'. *sēmeron* is emphatic by position and is taken up by *sēmeron* in v. 9. *dei* implies that Jesus considered his staying at Zacchaeus' home as part of his mission. *meinai* 'to stay' includes staying overnight (cp. *katalusai* in v. 7).

Translation: *He looked up and said to him.* In some languages the person has to be mentioned earlier in the sentence, e.g. 'he looked up towards him/ Zacchaeus, and said', or even, '...came to where he/Zacchaeus was, he looked up (towards him), and said'.

Make haste and come down, or, 'come down quickly'. Similarly in v. 6.

I must stay at your house, or, 'I must descend at your home' (Zarma), 'I must lodge with you', 'I must be your guest, or, guest in your house' (cp. Phillips, Willibrord, East Toradja); or with further shifts, "you must be my host" (Rieu). For *must* cp. on 2 : 49.

6 ***So he made haste and came down, and received him joyfully.***

Exegesis: *speusas katebē* 'he came down with haste', cp. on v. 5.

hupedexato auton chairōn 'he welcomed him with joy'. For *hupodechomai* cp. on 10 : 38. The participle *chairōn* denotes the mood in which Zacchaeus welcomed Jesus (cp. 15 : 5).

Translation: One or both of the pronouns may have to be specified as references to Zacchaeus and Jesus respectively.

Received him, viz. in his house as guest, cp. on v. 5.

Joyfully, or, 'with joy', cp. on 8 : 13.

7 ***And when they saw it they all murmured, "He has gone in to be the guest of a man who is a sinner."***

Exegesis: *kai idontes pantes diegogguzon* 'when they saw this they all grumbled'. *pantes* refers to all the people who watched Jesus go into Zacchaeus' house. For *diagogguzō* cp. on 15 : 2.

para hamartōlō andri eisēlthen katalusai 'he has gone to be the guest of a sinful man'. *para hamartōlō andri* is emphatic by position, and goes with *katalusai.* For *kataluō* cp. on 9 : 12. For *hamartōlos* cp. on 5 : 8.

Translation: For *murmured* see on 5 : 30.

To go in to be the guest of, virtually synonymous with, but slightly more specific than "to stay in the house of" in v. 5[d]. Some renderings used are, 'to go to sleep in the house of' (Shona 1966, similarly Lokele), 'to enter (lit. ascend) for the night into the house of' (cp. East Toradja 1933); several versions, however, use the same rendering in both verses.

8 ***And Zacchaeus stood and said to the Lord, "Behold, Lord, the half of my goods I give to the poor; and if I have defrauded any one of anything, I restore it fourfold."***

Exegesis: *statheis* lit. 'having taken his stand', cp. on 18 : 11. Here it could mean that Zacchaeus took a position where everyone could hear him.

pros ton kurion 'to the Lord', cp. on 1 : 6.

idou 'behold', emphatic introduction of what follows.

ta hēmiseia mou tōn huparchontōn 'half of my possessions'. *ta hēmiseia*, or *ta hēmisē* (Nestle) (†). Possessive *mou* goes with *huparchontōn* (cp. on 8 : 3).

tois ptōchois didōmi 'I give to the poor', best understood as a pledge and hence often rendered in the future (cp. BFBS).

ei tinos ti esukophantēsa 'if I have defrauded anyone of anything', implicit admission. For *sukophanteō* cp. on 3 : 14.

apodidōmi tetraploun (††) 'I make fourfold restitution', also a pledge.

Translation: *Stood*, or, "took his stand" (Rieu), or, 'came forward', 'stood in front of all'.

I have defrauded any one of anything, or, 'I have taken anything from (or, things belonging to) any one by deceit' (for which cp. *N.T.Wb.*/23), 'from any person I have taken wrongfully' (Kapauku, using a combination of the verbs 'to clutch-a-prey' and 'to take'), 'there are some I have deceived (by taking) their money' (Tzeltal).

I restore it fourfold, or, 'I give-instead-of-it fourfold' (Balinese, Bahasa Indonesia RC), 'I pay (or, give) back four times as much' (cp. Goodspeed, Sranan).

9 ***And Jesus said to him, "Today salvation has come to this house, since he also is a son of Abraham.***

Exegesis: *sēmeron sōtēria tō oikō toutō egeneto* 'today salvation has come (lit. has happened) to this house'. For *sēmeron* cp. on v. 5. For *sōtēria* cp. on 1 : 77. It is best understood as consisting of forgiveness of sins. *oikos* is used here in the meaning 'family', cp. A-G s.v. 2.

kathoti kai autos huios Abraam estin 'since he also is a son of Abraham'. *kathoti* (cp. on 1 : 7) introduces a clause that states grounds which are supposed to be known. *autos* refers emphatically to Zacchaeus in the third person, notwithstanding the fact that, strictly speaking, Zacchaeus is addressed by Jesus. This implies that the causal clause is spoken also for the benefit of those present. For *huios tou Abraam* cp. on 13 : 16.

Translation: *Salvation has come to this house*, or, 'has been given to this house' (cp. NV), 'this house has received salvation' (Sranan); or, where a shift to a passive or active verbal construction is required, 'this house has been saved, or, has received the one who saves it'. *House* has been rendered "household" (Rieu), 'the-whole-family' (Balinese), 'all-who-are-in the house' (Bahasa Indonesia).

Since, cp. on "inasmuch" in 1 : 1.

He also. Where a third person reference to the person addressed is unacceptable one may shift to the second person (as in Tzeltal), or change the introductory words into, 'thereupon Jesus said', or, 'Jesus replied to this'.

Is a son of Abraham, or, 'is one of (or, belongs to) the sons/descendants of Abraham'.

10 ***For the Son of man came to seek and to save the lost."***

Exegesis: *ēlthen gar ho huios tou anthrōpou* 'for the Son of man has come' with following infinitive indicating the purpose of his coming. For *ho huios tou anthrōpou* cp. on 5 : 24.

zētēsai kai sōsai to apolōlos 'to seek and save what is lost'. *to apolōlos* refers to people who have gone astray; hence *sōsai* means to save them from their predicament and to restore their relationship with God and men.

Translation: For *the lost* cp. on 15 : 4.

11 ***As they heard these things, he proceeded to tell a parable, because he was near to Jerusalem, and because they supposed that the kingdom of God was to appear immediately.***

Exegesis: *akouontōn de autōn tauta* 'while they were listening to this', connecting the subsequent parable with what happened in Zacchaeus' house. *autōn* refers to those present there; *tauta* is best understood as referring to Jesus' words in vv. 9f.

prostheis lit. 'adding', i.e. in addition to what he had already told them.

dia to eggus einai Ierousalēm auton kai dokein autous 'because (of the fact that) he was near Jerusalem and that they thought', double articular accusative and infinitive. For this meaning of *dokeō* cp. A-G s.v. 1 d. *eggus* also 21 : 30f.

hoti parachrēma mellei hē basileia tou theou anaphainesthai 'that the kingdom of God was going to appear at once'. *parachrēma* (emphatic by position) presumably means as soon as he entered Jerusalem. For *hē basileia tou theou* cp. on 4 : 43.

anaphainomai (†) 'to appear', cp. 17 : 20 for a similar phrase with reference to the kingdom of God.

Translation: *As they heard these things, he proceeded to tell a parable* may have to be recast, e.g. 'while they (or, the people) were listening to these words (or, to what Jesus was saying), he/Jesus told (them) a parable also, or, he/Jesus went on by telling (them) a parable'; or in co-ordinated clauses, connected by 'then'. For *parable* see on 8 : 4.

They supposed, or, 'they thought', 'it was their opinion', and cp. on 2 : 44.

The kingdom of God was to appear, or, 'the fact that God rules was to become visible', 'all people were to see that God rules'.

12 ***He said therefore, "A nobleman went into a far country to receive kingly power and then return.***

Exegesis: *eipen oun* 'so he said', takes up *eipen* in v. 11.

anthrōpos tis eugenēs 'a nobleman'.

eugenēs (†) 'well born', 'high born'.

eporeuthē eis chōran makran labein heautō basileian 'travelled to a far country in order to receive for himself a kingship'. The picture is that of a vassal king to be appointed by the Roman emperor. For allusions to contemporary events see commentaries, esp. Plummer p. 438. For *basileia* 'kingship', cp. 1 : 33 and A-G s.v. 1.

kai hupostrepsai 'and (then) to return', viz. to his country over which he would have received the kingship, still dependent upon *eporeuthē. hupostrepsai* is added explicitly because the parable hinges on his return.

Translation: *A nobleman,* or, 'a certain nobleman', see on 7 : 41. If a specific term is not available, one may render the noun by, 'a man of a chief's family', 'a descendant of chiefs', 'a man of high position' (cp. Sranan; similarly Kapauku, lit. 'a person having a name').

Went, preferably 'was about to go', 'planned to travel'.

To receive kingly power, or, 'power to rule the kingdom' (Thai), 'authority of a chief' (Lokele). The phrase structure may have to be changed, e.g. "to be appointed king" (NEB), 'to be installed as chief' (East Toradja 1933), 'that the emperor might appoint/grant him to be king/chief of his land'. Some versions add a locative specification, 'there to receive...' (cp. Sranan, Sundanese, Jerusalem). For *kingly power* cp. also on "kingdom" in 1 : 33 and references.

Then return, or with a more explicit transition, 'after that (or, having received it) to come back home'; or as a new sentence, 'he intended to come back after that (or, after he had been appointed)'.

13 ***Calling ten of his servants, he gave them ten pounds, and said to them, 'Trade with these till I come.'***

Exegesis: *kalesas de deka doulous heautou* lit. 'after calling ten slaves of his', i.e. 'ten of his slaves'.

edōken autois deka mnas 'he gave them ten minas', i.e. one each.

mna (††) 'mina', a Greek monetary unit of about eighteen to twenty dollars.

pragmateusasthe en hō erchomai 'do business until I come back'.

pragmateuomai (††) 'to conduct business', 'to trade'.

en hō lit. 'during (the time) which', 'while', here equivalent to *heōs* 'until', cp. Bl-D, § 383.

Translation: *Calling..., he gave,* or, "he summoned...and gave" (Rieu). *To call* is used here in the sense of, 'to order to appear before one'.

He gave them ten pounds, preferably, "he...gave them a pound each" (NEB). *Pound.* One may transliterate the Greek word, or the Hebrew word it represents (*maneh*); or one may translate it by an expression built on the rendering of Gr. *dēnarion* (cp. on 10 : 35), e.g. 'hundred pieces of silver'. Some other renderings are, 'a sum of money' (Navajo), 'a gold piece of money' (Sranan), 'silver money one catty' (cp. Balinese). Cp. also Nida, *BT*, 328f, and 338; *N.T.Wb.*/55, MONEY.

Trade with these, i.e. use this to trade/do-business. Most languages possess a specific word for 'to trade with', which in Toba Batak is a causative derivation of 'market'; some other renderings used are, 'to work with' (Sranan), 'to buy and sell' (cp. Javanese).

Till I come (i.e. come back), or, "while I am away" (NEB).

14 ***But his citizens hated him and sent an embassy after him, saying, 'We do not want this man to reign over us.'***

Exegesis: *hoi de politai autou emisoun auton* 'but his citizens hated him', again an allusion to contemporary events. *politai* refers to the people of the country over which he was to be appointed king.

apesteilan presbeian opisō autou legontes 'they sent a delegation after him, saying', i.e. 'to say', implying that the delegates were to transmit what the citizens had said. For *presbeia* cp. on 14 : 32.

ou thelomen touton basileusai eph' hēmas 'we do not want this man to become king over us'. *touton* is slightly contemptuous. *basileusai* is ingressive aorist.

Translation: *His citizens,* or, 'the people of (or, living in) his country' (Shona), 'those of the same land as he' (Tzeltal).

Hated, see on 1 : 71; Sranan has here, 'did not like him at all'.

Sent an embassy after him, 'ordered messengers to go after him, or, to follow him (several Indonesian languages), or, to go to that country also'. *To send an embassy,* see on 14 : 32; Fulani shifts from messengers to a message (lit. 'a sending'); the Tzeltal rendering of "embassy" is coloured by the contents of the message, 'those-who-make-a-complaint'.

Saying is often better taken with the messengers, e.g. 'who were to say' (cp. Jerusalem), 'with the message' (NV). Some further qualification may be necessary, cp. e.g. 'who were to go and on arrival say' (Shona 1966), 'to say there (i.e. in the far country)', 'to inform the emperor/ruler/government (there)'. Since the message is to be addressed to persons of high rank languages such as Javanese and Balinese use honorific forms.

15 ***When he returned, having received the kingly power, he commanded these servants, to whom he had given the money, to be called to him, that he might know what they had gained by trading.***

Exegesis: *kai egeneto* 'and it happened', cp. on 1 : 8.

en tō epanelthein auton labonta tēn basileian 'when he returned after receiving the kingship'. The aorist tense of *epanelthein* points to an event preceding that of the main verb *eipen* (cp. Bl-D, § 404). *labonta* (aorist) refers to an event prior to his return. For the development of the parable, however, the return is the important event.

kai eipen phōnēthēnai autō tous doulous toutous hois dedōkei to argurion 'he ordered to be called to him those slaves to whom he had given the money'. The passive form of *phōnēthēnai* implies that the order to summon the slaves is given to one or more intermediaries. For *phōneō* cp. on 14 : 12. *dedōkei* (pluperfect) points to an event in the past which is still valid in the present. For *to argurion* cp. A-G s.v. 2 b.

hina gnoi ti diepragmateusanto 'that he might learn what they had accomplished in business'. *gnoi* is ingressive aorist.

diapragmateuomai (††) 'to accomplish by doing business', hence 'to make profit'.

Translation: Because Gr. *kai egeneto* here marks a turning point in the narrative some versions begin a new paragraph, others indicate a certain contrast, cp. "But he *was* made king, and on his return..." (Rieu).

The clause *having received the kingly power* bridges the time-gap between vv. 12-14 and vv. 15ff. It is often better rendered as a full sentence in initial position, cp. Rieu.

He commanded these servants...to be called to him, or more synthetically, "he...sent for the servants..." (NEB); or more analytically, 'he said they (indefinite) should summon those slaves' (Zarma, similarly Fulani), 'he ordered somebody to tell those servants that they should come to him'. The implied direct discourse (cp. on 4 : 3) may have to be made explicit on one or two levels.

To whom he had given the money, or, 'who had received (from him) the money', or more specifically, 'the pound (cp. v. 13)'.

That he might know, or, 'in order to find out'; or non-subordinated, 'He intended/wanted to know' (cp. Sranan). The main verb can also be rendered, 'to hear' (East Toradja), or, 'to be told', which with a further shift may lead to, 'that they (i.e. the ten servants) could tell him'.

What they had gained by trading is again distributive, cp. "what profit each had made" (NEB, similarly Sundanese), 'how much the yield of the trade of each of them' (Bahasa Indonesia RC).

16 ***The first came before him, saying, 'Lord, your pound has made ten pounds more.'***

Exegesis: *kurie* 'master', cp. on 1 : 6 (2).

hē mna sou deka prosērgasato mnas 'your mina has made/gained ten minas in addition', hence, 'has made ten more minas'.

prosergazomai (††) 'to make in addition', here of making money, usually with a personal subject.

Translation: *Your pound has made ten pounds more*, or, 'increased to ten pounds' (cp. Lokele), 'earned (lit. netted), or, made-a-profit-of ten pounds' (Fulani, Balinese). Some languages use a specific term for making profit on an investment, e.g. a derivation of 'head' (Tzeltal), or of 'flower' (Timorese). If a personal subject is obligatory with the verb, one may say something like, 'by means of the one pound you gave me I got ten (pounds) more'.

17 ***And he said to him, 'Well done, good servant! Because you have been faithful in a very little, you shall have authority over ten cities.'***

Exegesis: *euge, agathe doule* 'well done, good slave!', expression of approval.

hoti en elachistō pistos egenou 'because you have been faithful in a very small matter', cp. on 16 : 10 and 12 : 42. The clause indicates the cause of the following statement.

isthi exousian echōn epanō deka poleōn lit. 'be having authority over ten towns', hence 'have authority'. For *epanō* cp. on 4 : 39; here it is used in a figurative sense, cp. A-G s.v. 2 b.

Translation: *Well done,* or some other exclamation of approval, e.g. 'Splendid!' (cp. Phillips).

Good servant, or, shifting from vocative to statement, 'you are a good servant'.

You have been faithful in a very little, or, 'I know now that I can trust you in a very small matter'; and cp. on 16 : 10.

You shall have authority over. The imperative of the Greek can sometimes be preserved (e.g. in Sranan, 'go to govern'), but in many languages one must use an indicative (cp. RSV), e.g. 'you (shall) have, or, I (shall) give you, the right to rule'.

18 ***And the second came, saying, 'Lord, your pound has made five pounds.'*** 19 ***And he said to him, 'And you are to be over five cities.'***

Exegesis: *hē mna sou...epoiēsen pente mnas* 'your mina has made five minas'. *epoiēsen* is equivalent to *prosērgasato* in v. 16.

(V. 19) *kai su epanō ginou pente poleōn* 'you too, be over five towns'. *kai* 'too' is used because the second slave is also rewarded in proportion to what he gained. *epanō ginou* is equivalent to *isthi exousian echōn epanō* in v. 17.

Translation: (V. 19) *And you,* preferably, 'you too', 'you similarly'.

You are to be over, or, 'rule over', 'you (shall) rule over', cp. on v. 17.

20 ***Then another came, saying, 'Lord, here is your pound, which I kept laid away in a napkin;*** 21 ***for I was afraid of you, because you are a severe man; you take up what you did not lay down, and reap what you did not sow.'***

Exegesis: *kai ho heteros ēlthen* 'and the other came', as if there were only three instead of ten (v. 13). But the first two and the third represent the two different attitudes of diligence and negligence respectively.

idou hē mna sou 'behold your mina', i.e. 'here is your mina'.

hēn eichon apokeimenēn en soudariō 'which I kept put away in a face-cloth'. *eichon* is durative imperfect.

apokeimai (†) 'to be put away', 'to be stored up'.

soudarion (†) 'face-cloth', cp. A-G s.v.

(V. 21) *ephoboumēn gar se* 'for I was afraid of you', durative imperfect.

hoti anthrōpos austēros ei 'because you are an exacting man'. This statement is illustrated by the subsequent asyndetic sentence.

austēros (also v. 22) 'hard', 'severe', 'exacting'.

aireis ho ouk ethēkas 'you take away what you did not put down', a proverbial saying, which refers probably to taking away from the threshing floor corn which one had not brought in and put down for threshing, cp. parallels quoted by Creed. Here it is used in the more general meaning of taking what one has not laboured for, cp. Phillips. This is in accordance with *therizeis ho ouk espeiras* (cp. on 12 : 24) 'you reap what you did not sow'. In both clauses the present tense is habitual.

Translation: *Another,* or, 'yet another' (Javanese); or, "the next" (Rieu), "the third" (NEB). To use a term that expresses not serial but qualitative differentiation (cp. *N.T.Wb.*/28, DIFFERENT) is not advisable.

Which I kept laid away in a napkin, often better rendered as a new sentence, e.g. 'I kept it put away in a napkin', 'I wrapped it up in a face-cloth and (so) kept it safe'. For the verb cp. also *N.T.Wb.*/49. — *Napkin,* or, 'face-cloth', 'handkerchief', often simply 'piece of cloth'.

(V. 21) *I was afraid of you.* The phrase *of you* is sometimes omitted, as virtually redundant.

You are a severe man, or, 'your character (lit. the you-ness) is severe' (East Toradja). Some renderings of *severe* basically mean 'hard' (Toba Batak), 'hard hearted' (Kapauku), 'hard-livered' (Bahasa Indonesia), 'rigid' (South Toradja), 'stinging' (East Toradja).

You take up what you did not lay down, or to stress the illustrative character of the sentence, 'you are (like) a man who takes up what he did not lay down, or, what is not his' (cp. TEV). Other pairs of contrastive terms used are, "draw out—put in" (NEB), 'claim back—deposit' (Willibrord). An equivalent English saying is, "getting something for nothing" (Phillips).

For *to reap* and *to sow* see on 12 : 24 and 8 : 5, and references.

22 ***He said to him, "I will condemn you out of your own mouth, you wicked servant! You knew that I was a severe man, taking up what I did not lay down and reaping what I did not sow?***

Exegesis: *legei autō* 'he said to him'; change of subject without indication.

ek tou stomatos sou krinō se lit. 'out of your own mouth I condemn you', i.e. on the basis of your own words, cp. TEV. *krinō* may be interpreted as present (so *GNT*), or as future (so Nestle), depending on the accentuation in Greek. The latter is preferable. *krinō* is a judicial term, here used in a non-judicial situation meaning either 'to condemn', or 'to judge', preferably the former, cp. A-G s.v. 4 a α.

Translation: *He said to him,* or to specify the reference, 'the master (or, king) said/replied'.

I will condemn you out of your own mouth, or, "by your own words" (NEB), 'in accordance with what you yourself just said', 'by what comes-out of your mouth, or, lips' (cp. Kituba, South Toradja); or recasting the sentence structure, "I will use your own words to condemn you" (TEV), 'you yourself are saying with your own mouth what you will be judged by' (Tzeltal); or again, taking a non-personal subject, 'the word you uttered condemns you' (Kapauku, similarly Shona 1966). For *condemn* see on 6 : 37.

You wicked servant may have to be transposed to the beginning of the discourse, and/or rendered as a statement.

You knew...sow?, a rhetorical question that may have to become a statement, e.g. 'you said that you knew...sow'.

23 ***Why then did you not put my money into the bank, and at my coming I should have collected it with interest?'***

Exegesis: *kai dia ti* 'why then?' *kai* expresses astonishment, cp. A-G s.v. I 2 h.

epi trapezan lit. 'on a table', here 'in the bank'. *didonai epi trapezan* means 'to put in the bank', cp. A-G s.v. *trapeza* 4.

kagō elthōn sun tokō an auto epraxa 'and on my return I should have reclaimed it with interest'. The clause describes an event which did not happen because the act which should have preceded it did not happen. This is expressed by *an*, cp. Bl-D, § 360.

tokos (†) 'interest'.

prassō here 'to reclaim', 'to collect', cp. A-G s.v. 1 b.

Translation: *Put my money into the bank.* The verb can also be rendered more specifically, 'to deposit with', 'to lend to'. *Bank* may be described, 'place where people trade-with money' (Bahasa Indonesia), 'house of lenders' (Fulani); or shifting to the persons that do the job, 'money changers' (Zarma, East Toradja), 'money traders' (Bahasa Indonesia RC), 'those who put-on-interest money' (e.g. South Toradja), 'those who make gain with money' (a Tzotzil dialect).

The interrogative sentence can best be taken to end after 'bank'. The next sentence may be opened by a transitional, e.g. 'then'; its unreal character is sometimes expressed by specific verbal forms (cp. English, Javanese), or by a modal particle (cp. Greek), or by an introductory phrase such as, 'if may-be thus, then certainly I...' (e.g. in Balinese).

I should have collected it with interest, or, 'I should have received it back (or, claimed the repayment of it, or, caused them to repay it) together with its interest'. For *interest* see *N.T.Wb.*/55, MONEY. The term used in some Malaio-Polynesian languages is, 'flower (of money)' (e.g. in Timorese, Bahasa Indonesia), or, 'child (of money)' (e.g. in Tagabili, or in Balinese, where 'mother' is used for 'principal sum'); Sranan describes the concept by 'money that is gained (lit. worked) upon it'.

24 ***And he said to those wo stood by, 'Take the pound from him, and give it to him who has the ten pounds.'***

Exegesis: *kai tois parestōsin eipen* 'and to those standing by he said'.

tois parestōsin refers to those who were standing by in attendance, i.e. attendants, cp. 1 : 19 and A-G s.v. *paristēmi* 2 b α.

arate ap' autou tēn mnan 'take the mina from him', implying that he is still standing before his master with the money in his hand.

Translation: *Those who stood by*, or, 'those waiting upon him', 'his attendants/servants'; cp. also on "stand in the presence of" in 1 : 19.

25 ***(And they said to him, 'Lord, he has ten pounds!')***

Exegesis: *kai eipan autō* 'and they said to him'. Subject of *eipan* are the attendants, or the audience of Jesus, preferably the former.

kurie, echei deka mnas 'master, he (already) has ten minas'. *echei* is emphatic. For the textual problems cp. *GNT* and commentaries.

Translation: *He has ten pounds* expresses the speakers' astonishment at the king's unexpected, and in their eyes unfair decision, cp. "he *has* ten pounds" (Rieu), "he has ten already" (NEB, similarly in many other versions).

26 ***' I tell you, that to every one who has will more be given; but from him who has not, even what he has will be taken away.***

Exegesis: *legō humin* 'I tell you', cp. on 3 : 8. Subject of *legō* is Jesus (as e.g. in 18 : 8 in a similar context), or the king of the parable (cp. v. 27). The latter is preferable.

panti tō echonti dothēsetai 'to every one who has will (more) be given', cp. 8 : 18. The clause brings the application of the parable into the context of the kingdom of God. The object of *echonti* and the subject of *dothēsetai* is best understood as the fruit of obedience to God.

apo de tou mē echontos kai ho echei arthēsetai 'from him who has not, even what he has will be taken away', paradoxical statement, describing the opposite of the preceding clause, cp. 8 : 18, where instead of *ho echei* it reads *ho dokei echein* 'what he thinks he has'.

Translation: For the two clauses see on the less paradoxically worded passage in 8 : 18, and cp. *TH-Mk* on 4 : 25.

27 ***But as for these enemies of mine, who did not want me to reign over them, bring them here and slay them before me.'"***

Exegesis: *plēn* 'but', cp. on 18 : 8.

tous mē thelēsantas me basileusai ep' autous 'those who did not want me to become king over them', cp. on v. 14. The phrase is emphatic by position. The aorist tense of *thelēsantas* refers to their rejection of him in the past. What they think now is not considered.

katasphaxate autous emprosthen mou 'slaughter them before my eyes, i.e. in my presence'.

katasphattō (††) 'to slaughter', 'to slay', 'to kill by violence'.

Translation: *But as for*, here indicating a sudden turn in the discourse, which now proceeds to discuss a different subject.

These enemies of mine. The demonstrative assumes that the hearers know about these persons and their deeds, mentioned in v. 14. For *enemies* cp. on 1 : 71.

Bring them here implies their being arrested; hence some versions use a verb for 'to lead captive' (cp. Balinese).

Slay them, viz. with a sword, referring to an act of revenge from the side of the king rather than to a judicial act. Cp. also *N.T.Wb.*/49, KILL.

28 ***And when he had said this, he went on ahead, going up to Jerusalem.***

Exegesis: *kai eipōn tauta* 'after he had said this', i.e. in Jericho in Zacchaeus' house.

eporeueto emprosthen 'he went on ahead, or, ahead of them', depending upon the interpretation of *emprosthen* as an adverb, or as a preposition with *autōn* understood, cp. A-G s.v. 1 b, 2 e. The former is preferable.

anabainōn eis Hierosoluma lit. 'ascending to Jerusalem', defining the rather general *eporeueto* as to direction and goal of his journey, cp. 18 : 31. For *Hierosoluma* cp. on 2 : 22.

Translation: *He went on ahead*, or, "Jesus went forward" (NEB), 'Jesus travelled on'.

Going up to Jerusalem, or, "on his way to Jerusalem" (Goodspeed), or simply "to Jerusalem" (TEV). For the verb cp. on 2 : 4.

29 ***When he drew near to Bethphage and Bethany, at the mount that is called Olivet, he sent two of the disciples,*** 30 ***saying, "Go into the village opposite, where on entering you will find a colt tied, on which no one has ever yet sat; untie it and bring it here.***

Exegesis: *kai egeneto* 'and it happened', cp. on 1 : 8.

hōs ēggisen eis Bēthphagē kai Bēthania 'when he approached Bethphage and Bethany', two villages on the eastern slope of the Mount of Olives.

pros to oros to kaloumenon Elaiōn 'at the mountain called (Mount) of Olives', or, with different accentuation of *Elaiōn* (cp. Nestle), 'Olive-grove' (hence RSV's "Olivet"), preferably the former. The phrase *pros to oros* is directly dependent on *ēggisen* and hence parallel to *eis Bēthphagē kai Bēthania*.

(V. 30) *hupagete eis tēn katenanti kōmēn* 'go to the village opposite (you)'. For *hupagō* cp. on 8 : 42.

katenanti (†) adverb 'opposite', here used as an adjective with a noun.

en hē eisporeuomenoi heurēsete 'in which you will find when you enter', taking *en hē* with *heurēsete*.

heurēsete pōlon dedemenon 'you will find a colt tethered, or, tied up', preferably the latter.

pōlos 'colt (of a horse)', or 'foal of an ass', or, in a more general meaning, 'young animal', cp. A-G s.v. Though the exact meaning is difficult to ascertain, the first of the above interpretations appears preferable.

eph' hon oudeis pōpote anthrōpōn ekathisen 'on which no one has ever sat (with the purpose of riding it)', hence 'which no one has ever ridden'.

kai lusantes auton agagete 'and, after you have untied it, bring it'. *kai* connects the future *heurēsete* 'you will find' and the imperative *agagete*. *lusantes* has also the force of an imperative.

Translation: *Draw near*, see on 7 : 12.

At the mount that is called Olivet, preferably, 'to the mount (or, hill, or, place) called the Mount of Olives', the phrase "of Olives" characterizing the mountain or hill as a place well known for its olive trees. The rendering of this geographic name is sometimes a transliteration of the form used in the language of prestige in the area, cp. e.g. *Olèfbergi* in Sranan, but often it is some kind of translation, cp. '(the mount) of the olive-trees' (Jerusalem), 'the hill with the oil-trees' (East Toradja). For 'olive' cp. *N.T.Wb.* /37f, FLORA; in predominantly Muslim countries it may be better not to use a term built on the borrowing 'olive', but on the borrowing *zaitūn*, the Arabic name for this fruit and its tree.

(V. 30) *Opposite*, or, "that lies in front of you" (Goodspeed), 'there before us' (Leyden).

Where on entering you will find a colt tied, usually better a new sentence, 'when you enter (it) you will come upon (or, you will see there) a colt that is tied'. For *find* cp. on 7 : 10. *A colt*. Where horses are unknown, one may use a descriptive rendering, e.g. 'a young riding-animal', or a borrowed term with or without classifier. *Tied*, or, 'that is (or, is standing) tied up'. The term used in some Indonesian languages refers to the pole or post to which the animal is tied up, e.g. Balinese (lit. 'having-a-post').

On which no one has ever yet sat, or, 'no one has ever used it yet to ride upon'.

Untie it, or, 'untie (or, make loose) its rope' (Bahasa Indonesia).

Bring, sometimes a specific term, e.g. for leading an animal by a rope (East Toradja 1933).

31 ***If any one asks you, 'Why are you untying it?' you shall say this, 'The Lord has need of it.'"***

Exegesis: *dia ti luete* 'why are you untying it?', implying that this question is asked while they are untying the colt.

houtōs ereite hoti 'you will speak thus', with *hoti* introducing direct speech.

ho kurios autou chreian echei 'the Lord needs it'. *autou* is placed before *chreian* on which it depends, as an objective genitive. For *kurios* cp. on 1 : 6 (3). For *chreian echein* cp. on 5 : 31.

Translation: *'The Lord has need of it'*. These words spoken by Jesus are a case of quotation on two levels. This somewhat intricate pattern requires careful handling in some languages, e.g. in Warao, see *TBT*, 18.30-33, 1967. — *The Lord* is used by the disciples as a reverent title for Jesus, but in the Gospel of Luke Jesus never explicitly and expressly declares himself to be the Lord. A specific problem arises in honorific languages, which ususally do not allow a speaker to refer to himself with reverent terms, even if he does so in an utterance of which others are the presumed speakers. The translator may feel himself compelled, then, to use a rendering that is more or less contrary to the linguistic etiquette in the receptor language (cp. *TBT*, 14.176, 1963, on "The Teacher says" in Mk. 14 : 14 = Lk. 22 : 11); or he may have to reword the passage in such a way that Jesus becomes the presumed speaker on the second level also, e.g. (in indirect discourse), '...say, that I, the one whom you call the Lord, have need of it', or (in direct discourse), '...give him this message from me, or, this is my message (to him), "I, whom people call the Lord, have need of it"'. If the rendering of "the Lord" has to be a possessed form, one may say 'our Lord' (inclusive, if the owner is assumed to be one of Jesus' adherents; or exclusive, if this is not the case, or if the inclusive would reveal too much of the owner's relation with Jesus). — *Has need of*, or, 'must use it', 'wants to ride on it', 'has business with it' (Zarma), or with a shift, 'it will serve for our Lord' (Tzeltal).

32 ***So those who were sent went away and found it as he had told them.***

Exegesis: *hoi apestalmenoi* lit. 'the sent', i.e. the messengers.

heuron kathōs eipen autois '(the messengers) found (it) just as he had told them'. The object of *heuron* is not stated specifically. From the context an object like 'the situation', or, 'the colt', may be understood. *eipen* (aorist) has the force of a pluperfect.

Translation: *Those who were sent.* Bahasa Indonesia RC has, 'the two disciples', to avoid a rather cumbersome literal rendering.

Found it as, or, 'what they found (was) as/in-accordance-with' (cp. Javanese). For the verb cp. on 7 : 10.

33 ***And as they were untying the colt, its owners said to them, "Why are you untying the colt?"*** 34 ***And they said, "The Lord has need of it."***

Exegesis: *luontōn de autōn ton pōlon* 'as they were untying the colt', describing the situation as presumed by Jesus, cp. on v. 31.

hoi kurioi autou 'its owners', cp. on 1 : 6 (1).

(V. 34) *hoti* cp. on v. 31.

Translation: The first part of v. 33 may be rendered better as two coordinated sentences, e.g. 'they untied (or, began to untie) the colt, but then the owners said to them'.

(V. 34) *The Lord has need of it.* The disciples now actually say what in

v. 31 Jesus told them to say; the discourse structure is one degree less intricate. The wording should echo v. 31[d] as closely as possible.

35 ***And they brought it to Jesus, and throwing their garments on the colt they set Jesus upon it.***

Exegesis: *kai ēgagon auton pros ton Iēsoun* 'and they brought it to Jesus', either the close of the preceding part of the story (cp. NEB, TEV), or the beginning of a new part (cp. RSV), preferably the latter. Agents of this and the following acts in this verse are the two disciples.

kai epiripsantes autōn ta himatia epi ton pōlon 'and after throwing their clothes upon the colt'. *himatia* means here 'top clothes'.

epiriptō (†) 'to throw (something) upon (something)'. Here its meaning is close to 'spreading'.

epebibasan ton Iēsoun 'they mounted Jesus (on it)'. For *epibibazō* cp. on 10 : 34.

Translation: *It. . .the colt.* The sequence of pronominal before nominal reference may have to be reversed.

Throwing, or, 'laying', 'spreading', if 'to throw' would suggest violence.

Garments, see on "cloak" in 6 : 29. The plural is distributive.

On the colt, sometimes preferably, 'on the back of the colt'.

They set Jesus upon it. If a literal rendering would suggest a child, or an invalid (as in 10 : 34), one may say, 'they caused Jesus to mount it' (Tagalog), 'helped Jesus get on it, or, on the animal' (cp. TEV, Sranan, Bahasa Indonesia 1968). Cp. also *TH-Mk* on 11 : 7.

36 ***And as he rode along, they spread their garments on the road.***

Exegesis: *poreuomenou de autou* 'as he went on', or, in a more specialized meaning, 'as he rode on'.

hupestrōnnuon ta himatia autōn en tē hodō 'they spread their clothes on the road'. The subject of *hupestrōnnuon* is best understood as referring to the people that were present.

hupostrōnnumi (††) 'to spread out under'.

Translation: *They spread their garments on the road* viz. in token of reverence. If it would not be understood as such, an explanatory note will be necessary, cp. *TH-Mk* on 11 : 8. — *They*, having indefinite force here, is often better rendered 'people' (Kapauku, Kituba), 'there were some who' (Tzeltal). *On the road*, or, "before him on the road" (Rieu), 'on the road he went/rode over' (Javanese). For *road* cp. *N.T.Wb./72*, WAY.

37 ***As he was now drawing near, at the descent of the Mount of Olives, the whole multitude of the disciples began to rejoice and praise God with a loud voice for all the mighty works that they had seen,***

Exegesis: *eggizontos de autou ēdē pros tē katabasei tou Orous tōn Elaiōn* 'when he was already approaching (viz. Jerusalem), at the descent of the Mount of Olives', taking *pros tē katabasei* as an apposition to *eggizontos autou* (cp. Plummer, RSV), or, 'when he approached the slope of the Mount of Olives' (cp. A-G s.v. *katabasis*, BFBS), preferably the former. *ēdē* may go with *eggizontos*, or with *pros tē katabasei*, preferably the former.

katabasis (††) 'descent', hence 'road leading down', 'slope'.

ērxanto hapan to plēthos tōn mathētōn chairontes ainein ton theon phōnē megalē 'the whole throng/company of the disciples began to praise God with joy with a loud voice'. For *plēthos* cp. on 1 : 10. For *ērxanto* with infinitive cp. on 4 : 21; here the phrase serves to stress the unexpectedness of the following event. *ērxanto* and *chairontes* are in the plural because *plēthos*, as collective singular, has plural force. *chairontes* denotes the mood of the disciples, *phōnē megalē* 'with a loud voice', denotes the mode, or way of their praise.

peri pasōn hōn eidon dunameōn 'for all the miracles they had seen'. *peri* lit. 'concerning' refers here to the ground of their praise. For *dunameis* (plur.) cp. on 10 : 13.

Translation: *As he was now drawing near, at the descent of the Mount of Olives*, introductory clause stating where the events of vv. 37b-40 took place. It may be better to make explicit the goal of 'drawing near' and/or to use a verb instead of the verbal noun "descent", e.g. 'he was already approaching Jerusalem (or, the city), at the place where the road goes down, or, where people are accustomed to go down from the M. of O.', or, transposing the prepositional phrase, 'he was about to go down from the M. of O. and was already coming near to Jerusalem (or, Jerusalem was coming near, or, in sight already)'.

The whole multitude of the disciples, or, 'all the crowd of the disciples', 'his many disciples no one excepted'. Here *disciples* is referring to the widest circle of Jesus' followers.

Began. The force of this auxiliary verb is sometimes brought out by introducing the clause by a connective marking an unexpected event (Balinese), or by using a specific rendering of the main verb, e.g. 'burst out in praise'.

Since *rejoice* qualifies the next verb it may be rendered by an adverbial construction, 'with joy', cp. on 8 : 13.

Praise and *with a loud voice*, see on 2 : 13 and 4 : 33 respectively.

For all the mighty works that they had seen, or, 'because of the marvellous things they had seen him do' (cp. Phillips), 'because they had seen him perform mighty deeds'. For *mighty works* see on 10 : 13.

38 ***saying, "Blessed is the King who comes in the name of the Lord! Peace in heaven and glory in the highest!"***

Exegesis: *eulogēmenos ho erchomenos ho basileus en onomati kuriou* 'blessed (is) the coming one, the King, in the name of the Lord', cp. on 1 : 42. Since *ho erchomenos* is virtually a title (cp. on 7 : 19), *ho basileus* is in apposition to it. *en onomati kuriou* goes with *ho erchomenos*. For the meaning of the phrase cp. *TH-Mk* on 11 : 9.

en ouranō eirēnē kai doxa en hupsistois 'in heaven (is) peace, and glory in the highest', chiastic clause. For *eirēnē* cp. on 1 : 79. Here it refers to the eschatological peace after the expulsion of Satan from heaven (cp. 10 : 18). For *doxa en hupsistois* cp. on 2 : 14.

Translation: *Blessed is the King who comes in the name of the Lord,* preferably, 'blessed is he who comes, the King, in the name of the Lord'. Cp. also on 13 : 35.

Peace in heaven. For *peace* see on 1 : 79; the positive aspect of the term is dominant here.

Glory in the highest, i.e. glory/honour/praise is in the highest (heaven). A personal referent may be preferable or obligatory here, e.g. 'to God in the highest (heaven)', 'to the Most High', or simply, "to God" (TEV); and one may have to shift to a verbal construction, e.g. 'praised/exalted/honoured is' (cp. Tzeltal), or, 'we praise/exalt/honour'. For *glory* and *in the highest* see on 2 : 14.

39 ***And some of the Pharisees in the multitude said to him, "Teacher, rebuke your disciples."***

Exegesis: *tines tōn Pharisaiōn apo tou ochlou* 'some of the Pharisees in the crowd'. *apo tou ochlou* has the function of a partitive genitive with *tines tōn Pharisaiōn* taken as a whole, cp. on 9 : 38 and A-G s.v. *apo* I 6.

epitimēson tois mathētais sou 'check, or, stop your disciples', cp. on 4 : 35.

Translation: *Rebuke your disciples,* or, 'tell your disciples that they must not do so (or, must be silent)'; cp. on 4 : 35.

40 ***He answered, "I tell you, if these were silent, the very stones would cry out."***

Exegesis: *legō humin* 'I tell you', cp. on 3 : 8.

ean houtoi siōpēsousin lit. 'if they were silent, or, will be silent' (preferably the latter), conditional clause in the future, equivalent to an aorist subjunctive and hence to be rendered in the present, cp. Bl-D, § 373. *siōpaō,* cp. on 1 : 20.

Translation: *If these were silent,* preferably, 'if these are silent', 'if these (people) say nothing, or, do not shout', 'if these shut their mouth' (Sranan).

The very stones would cry out, preferably, 'will cry out, or, shout'. Emphasizers like 'without-doubt' (Bahasa Indonesia) are often added to bring out better the contrast with the preceding clause, as does "very" in the RSV.

41 ***And when he drew near and saw the city he wept over it,***

Exegesis: *kai hōs ēggisen* 'and as he came near', viz. to the city, temporal clause denoting what precedes the events to which *idōn* and *eklausen* refer.

idōn tēn polin eklausen ep' autēn 'when he saw the city he wept over it'. For *epi* meaning 'over' with a verb denoting emotions, or expressions of emotion, cp. A-G s.v. III 1 b ε.

Translation: *And when he drew near*, or, 'still nearer', as some versions have in view of v. 37. The reference to 'the city' is usually better transposed to this introductory clause; hence, 'when he drew still nearer to the city and looked at it'.

He wept over it, i.e. 'he wept because of (grief over) it, or, because he pitied it', in view of the disasters that would come over it. For the verb see on 6 : 21.

42 ***saying, "Would that even today you knew the things that make for peace! But now they are hid from your eyes.***

Exegesis: *legōn* 'saying', here denoting an act to be distinguished from that to which the main verb *eklausen* refers.

ei egnōs en tē hēmera tautē kai su ta pros eirēnēn 'if only you too had known, on this day, the things which make for peace', with no main clause following, and hence virtually equivalent to a wish which cannot be fulfilled, cp. Bl-D, § 482 and Plummer. *en tē hēmera tautē* refers to the day of Jesus' glorious entry. *kai su* may mean 'even you', i.e. 'you yourself', or, 'you too', i.e. as well as the disciples, preferably the latter. *ta pros eirēnēn* lit. 'the things that have to do with peace', cp. A-G s.v. *pros* III 5 b, hence, 'the things that make for peace'.

nun de ekrubē apo ophthalmōn sou 'but as it is they are hidden from your eyes'. *nun* means 'as things are now', 'as it is', and refers to the spiritual state in which Jerusalem is. The clause as a whole may refer to inability or to prohibition, preferably the former. Subject of *ekrubē* is *ta pros eirēnēn*.

Translation: *Saying*, preferably, 'and (he) said'.

Would that even today you knew, preferably, 'if only you too had known today'. The sentence is often introduced by a particle or phrase with desiderative or supplicatory force, e.g. in Sundanese, Sranan. *You* (sing.) refers to the city of Jerusalem. Where idiom is such that one cannot address a city but only the people in it, one may have to shift to 'you (plur.)', or more explicitly, 'your inhabitants'. *To know* is used here in the sense of 'to have understanding of', 'to recognize the nature of'.

The things that make for peace, or, "the way that leads to peace" (NEB), "what is needed for peace" (TEV), 'the things which cause-to-happen peace, or, cause peace to come to you, or, assure peace' (cp. Trukese, Shona 1966, Zarma). In languages that use distinctive terms for the positive and the negative meaning of 'peace' (see on 1 : 79) the choice is difficult here. Some versions, e.g. Bahasa Indonesia RC, Toba Batak use the latter because they view the term as primarily referring to reconciliation, the end of the strife between God and his people; others (e.g. Bahasa Indonesia, Javanese) prefer the positive term (which, of course, may imply the concept of being reconciled to God). The latter is preferable, as a rule.

But now, preferably, 'but as it is'; or bringing out the implied disappointment more strongly, "but no" (NEB), *mais hélas* (Jerusalem).

They are hid from your eyes, or, 'they are kept from your sight', 'you are unable to see/perceive these things'.

43 ***For the days shall come upon you, when your enemies will cast up a bank about you and surround you, and hem you in on every side,*** 44 ***and dash you to the ground, you and your children within you, and they will not leave one stone upon another in you; because you did not know the time of your visitation."***

Exegesis: *hoti hēxousin hēmerai epi se kai...* 'for days will come upon you and...', i.e. 'a time is coming upon you when...', co-ordination instead of the normal subordination of the following clauses (cp. 17 : 22). For *epi* referring to the object of unpleasant experiences, cp. A-G s.v. III 1 b γ.

parembalousin hoi echthroi sou charaka soi 'your enemies will throw up a palisade against you'. *soi* is dative of disadvantage.

paremballō (††) 'to throw up', 'to cast up'.

charax (††) 'stake', here 'palisade', 'rampart'.

perikuklōsousin se 'they will encircle you'. *perikukloō* (††).

sunexousin se pantothen 'they will hem you in from all sides'. *sunechō* (cp. on 8 : 45) may mean 'to hem in', 'to close in', or, 'to press hard', preferably the former.

(V. 44) *edaphiousin se kai ta tekna sou en soi* 'they will dash you and your children within you to the ground'.

edaphizō (††) 'to raze' (of buildings), 'to dash to the ground' (of people), cp. A-G s.v.

ouk aphēsousin lithon epi lithon en soi 'they will not leave one stone upon another within you', expressing complete destruction. *aphiēmi* means 'to leave where it belongs'.

anth' hōn ouk egnōs ton kairon tēs episkopēs sou 'because you did not know/perceive the time of your visitation'. *egnōs* takes up *egnōs* in v. 42.

episkopē (†) 'visitation', i.e. demonstration of God's grace, cp. on *episkeptomai* in 1 : 68.

Translation: *The days shall come upon you,* or more clearly pejorative, 'days of your-ill-luck will come' (South Toradja), or with a syntactic shift, 'you will live to see days', 'you will have to endure a time'.

Enemies, see on 1 : 71.

Cast up a bank, or, 'pile up earth/soil, or, a wall' (cp. East Toradja, Timorese), 'build a mud wall' (Zarma). *Bank,* or, 'war-stockade' (Lokele), "barricades" (TEV), "earthworks" (Goodspeed), 'fortifications', or any term that refers to strongholds for the protection of besiegers against attacks from those besieged.

About you, or, 'around you', 'against you', 'to fight you' (cp. Thai).

Surround you, describing what the banks are cast up for, hence 'besiege you', 'shut you in completely' (cp. Tzeltal), "blockade you" (TEV), 'surround you so that you cannot go out' (Navajo, where an unqualified rendering of the verb would imply 'to guard', hence 'to help').

Hem you in is referring to movement, viz. the attacks of the besiegers.

On every side, or, 'from all sides', 'all-around-it' (Sundanese).

(V. 44) *Dash you to the ground, you and your children within you.* If the verses must be addressed not to the city but to its inhabitants (cp. on v. 42), adjustments will have to be made, e.g. 'dash to the ground yourselves and your city, or, the buildings in your city'. *Dash to the ground,* or, 'smash' (Sranan), or more generically, "destroy" (TEV), all of which can do duty with both objects. Where such a zeugma is impossible a double rendering of the verb will be required, cp. e.g. 'level you to the ground and smash your children within you' (Zürich). — *Your children within you,* or, "the people within your walls" (TEV), 'your inhabitants' (East Toradja 1933, lit, 'the people your contents'); and cp. on 1 : 7.

They will not leave one stone upon another in you, vividly depicting the ruin of the city. Some other renderings are, "not a single stone will they leave in its place" (TEV), 'they will not let be stone still affixed to its-fellow-stone' (East Toradja, using a reciprocal affix at the second occurrence of 'stone'), 'they will not leave two stones lying-on-each-other' (Toba Batak); and see *TH-Mk* on 13 : 2.

Know, here in the sense of 'be aware of'.

The time of your visitation, or shifting to a verbal clause, 'the time when God comes to visit you, or, to save you' (cp. Thai, Kituba), 'when you came to be favoured by God' (Tzeltal). For 'to visit' see on 1 : 68.

45 ***And he entered the temple and began to drive out those who sold,***

Exegesis: *eis to hieron* 'into the temple', cp. on 2 : 27.

ērxato ekballein tous pōlountas 'he began to drive out those who were selling'. For *ērxato* with infinitive cp. on v. 37.

Translation: The event is to be located in the outer court of the temple, called the Court of the Gentiles.

Those who sold may require an object and/or a locative qualification, e.g. "those who were selling things there" (Goodspeed), 'those who were trading there/in-it' (cp. Rieu, Sranan, several Indonesian languages); elsewhere the phrase is rendered by a noun 'the merchants' (e.g. in Toba Batak).

46 ***saying to them, "It is written, 'My house shall be a house of prayer'; but you have made it a den of robbers."***

Exegesis: *legōn autois* 'saying to them', cp. on v. 42.

gegraptai 'it is written', introducing an Old Testament quotation.

kai estai ho oikos mou oikos proseuchēs 'my house will be a house of prayer'. *kai* may be left untranslated.

humeis de auton epoiēsate spēlaion lēstōn 'but you (emphatic) have made it a robbers' den'.

spēlaion (†) 'cave', 'den'.

Translation: *It is written*, see on 4 : 4. It may be necessary to indicate the speaker of the quoted words, e.g. 'it is written that the Lord (or, God) has said'.

My house, cp. on "house of God" in 6 : 4, but the fact that God is referring here to what is his own may make necessary some adjustments, especially in honorific languages (cp. *TBT*, 14.162 and 176, 1963).

House of prayer, or, 'place (for) praying' (Balinese), 'house/place where people pray (to me)'.

Den of robbers, or, 'a cave hideout-of robbers' (Javanese), 'a thieves' camp' (Sranan), 'a cave/place where robbers hide/meet'. For *robbers* see on 10 : 30.

47 ***And he was teaching daily in the temple. The chief priests and the scribes and the principal men of the people sought to destroy him;***

Exegesis: *kai ēn didaskōn to kath' hēmeran* 'he taught daily', referring to a period of teaching following the events of vv. 45f.

to kath' hēmeran 'day after day', 'daily'.

hoi de archiereis kai hoi grammateis... kai hoi prōtoi tou laou 'the chief priests and the experts of the law and the leaders of the people', together the subject of *ezētoun*. For *hoi archiereis* see on 9 : 22. But the fact that *hoi prōtoi tou laou* is separated from the other two by the predicate is an indication that *hoi prōtoi tou laou* are not in the same way involved as the chief priests and the experts, being involved either to a lesser degree, or only recently (this is the first time they are mentioned), preferably the latter.

ezētoun auton apolesai '(they) were seeking to destroy him', iterative imperfect referring to a situation which had existed for some time.

Translation: For *chief priests* see on "high-priesthood" in 3 : 2.

And the principal men of the people. This phrase is better given a more independent position (see *Exegesis*); hence e.g. 'and so did (or, similarly) the leading citizens' (cp. Rieu, Jerusalem, Balinese, which give this phrase at the end of the sentence). Whereas the two preceding terms refer to the religious authorities, this one refers to persons whose importance is felt in the more secular sphere.

For *sought* cp. on 5 : 18, for *destroy*, or, 'cause-to-perish', 'kill', cp *N.T.Wb./27*, DIE.

48 ***but they did not find anything they could do, for all the people hung upon his words.***

Exegesis: *kai ouch heuriskon to ti poiēsōsin* 'and they did not find what they should do', i.e. 'they did not find a way to do it'. Iterative imperfect, cp. on v. 47. *to ti poiēsōsin* is an indirect question made into a substantive by prefixing the article, cp. 1 : 62 and Bl-D, § 267.2.

ho laos gar hapas exekremato autou akouōn 'for all the people were hanging upon him while listening', i.e. "all the people were listening to Him with close attention" (BFBS), or 'all the people were hanging on his words'.

ekkremannumi (††) 'to hang on', with genitive.

Translation: For *all the people* cp. on 3 : 21.

Hung upon his words. Non-figurative renderings used are, "kept listening to him, not wanting to miss a single word" (TEV), 'desired very much to hear his words' (East Toradja).

CHAPTER TWENTY

1 ***One day, as he was teaching the people in the temple and preaching the gospel, the chief priests and the scribes with the elders came up***

Exegesis: *kai egeneto* 'and it happened', cp. on 1 : 8.

en mia tōn hēmerōn 'one day', cp. on 5 : 17.

didaskontos autou ton laon en tō hierō kai euaggelizomenou 'while he was teaching the people in the temple and preaching the good news'. Both teaching and preaching have the good news of the kingdom of God as content, the difference being that with teaching the emphasis is on explaining and understanding, and with preaching on appeal and acceptance. For *en tō hierō* cp. on 2 : 27.

epestēsan hoi archiereis kai hoi grammateis 'the chief priests and the experts of the law came up'. For *ephistamai* cp. on 2 : 9; for *hoi archiereis* cp. on 9 : 22; for *grammateis* cp. on 5 : 21.

sun tois presbuterois 'together with the elders', virtually equivalent to *kai hoi presbuteroi*. For *presbuteros* cp. on 7 : 3.

Translation: For the whole section cp. *TH-Mk* on the parallel passage 11 : 27-33.

The verse may better be divided into two sentences, e.g. 'One day he was...gospel; then (or, as he was doing so) the chief priests...came up'. For *preaching the gospel*, or, "telling them the good news" (NEB), see on 3 : 18; for *the elders* see on 7 : 3.

Came up, or, 'came to stand by/around him', i.e. joined the audience.

2 ***and said to him, "Tell us by what authority you do these things, or who it is that gave you this authority."***

Exegesis: *eipon hēmin* 'tell us', imperative, either modifying indirect questions (cp. punctuation of *GNT*), or introducing direct questions (cp. punctuation of Nestle), preferably the latter.

en poia exousia 'by what authority'. *poios*, lit. 'of what kind?', may be equivalent to *tis* and mean 'what?' (cp. A-G s.v. 2 a α), or take the place of the genitive of interrogative *tis* and mean 'whose?' (cp. A-G s.v. 2 a γ). Here the former is preferable (cp. also *TH-Mk* 11 : 28). For *exousia* cp. on 4 : 6, 32.

tauta poieis 'are you doing these things'. *tauta* may either refer to Jesus' behaviour generally (cp. Goodspeed, Phillips) or to his teaching and preaching specifically, probably the latter.

ē tis estin ho dous soi tēn exousian tautēn 'or who it is who gave you this authority?' *ē* introduces a second question (cp. A-G s.v. 1 d δ), which refers to the origin of Jesus' authority.

Translation: *By what authority you do these things*, or, 'what (sort of) authority/right you have (or, you received) to do this, or, to do what you are doing here', 'what authority you-have-as-authority to do these things' (South Toradja), 'what authority you rely-on to do these-your-deeds' (Toba Batak).

3 ***He answered them, "I also will ask you a question; now tell me,***
4 ***Was the baptism of John from heaven or from men?"***

Exegesis: *erōtēsō humas kagō logon* 'I too will ask you a question'. For *logos* meaning 'question' cp. A-G s.v. 1 a β.

kai eipate moi 'and tell me'; *kai* is semantically redundant. The imperative calls for an answer to the direct question of v. 4.

(V. 4) *to baptisma Iōannou ex ouranou ēn ē ex anthrōpōn* 'was the baptism of (i.e. preached and administered by) John from heaven or from men (i.e. of divine or human origin, due to divine or human initiative)?'; cp. *TH-Mk* on 11 : 30.

Translation: Since Jesus replied with another question a literal rendering of *he answered them* is sometimes unacceptable; hence, 'he spoke to them again' (Navajo).

I also will ask you a question, or, 'now let me ask you a question' (cp. TEV). The combination 'ask a question' is too redundant in some languages; hence, 'I too will ask you something' (cp. Sranan, Javanese, South Toradja). Cp. also *N.T.Wb.*/12.

(V. 4) *Was the baptism of John from heaven or from men*, or, "did John's right to baptize come from God or from man" (TEV), 'when John baptized, was his power from heaven or from man' (Kekchi), 'the baptism of John, (was) its origin from heaven or from man' (some Indonesian languages), 'who caused/sent/told John to baptize (people), God (in heaven) or men?' For *baptism* see on 3 : 3.

5 ***And they discussed it with one another, saying, "If we say, 'From heaven,' he will say, 'Why did you not believe him?'*** 6 ***But if we say, 'From men,' all the people will stone us; for they are convinced that John was a prophet."***

Exegesis: *hoi de sunelogisanto pros heautous* 'they discussed among themselves'. *sullogizomai* (††) is here synonymous with the expression used in 5 : 21 and 20 : 14, and cp. Mk 11 : 31.

ean eipōmen 'if we say', 'suppose we say', hypothetical.

dia ti ouk episteusate autō 'why did you not believe him', cp. *TH-Mk* on 11 : 31. *autō* may refer to John, or to his baptism, preferably the former.

(V. 6) *ho laos hapas katalithasei hēmas* 'the whole people will stone us to death'. *laos* refers not only to the people present but to the whole nation, cp. on 3 : 21; 7 : 29.

katalithazō (††) 'to stone to death', synonymous with *lithoboleō* in 13 : 34.

pepeismenos 'convinced', here denoting subjective conviction, not referring to objective fact.

Translation: *They discussed it with one another,* cp. on "said to one another" in 4 : 36. The pronoun may have to be specified, e.g. 'the-ones-who were-questioned' (Balinese).

Believe, see on 1 : 20.

(V. 6) *The people,* cp. on 7 : 29.

Stone us, i.e. 'kill us by throwing stones', 'pelt us to death with stones'.

They are convinced, or, '(they) are-certain in their heart' (East Toradja), 'all of them vouch for the truth (lit. dare to confirm)' (Balinese).

7 ***So they answered that they did not know whence it was.***

Exegesis: *kai apekrithēsan mē eidenai pothen* lit. 'and they answered not to know from where', i.e. 'that they did not know where it came from'.

Translation: *Whence it was,* or, 'who caused/sent/told him (to baptize)', 'from where its origin', cp. on v. 4.

8 ***And Jesus said to them, "Neither will I tell you by what authority I do these things."***

Exegesis: *oude egō legō humin* 'nor do I tell you', or, 'then I too do not tell you', implying that Jesus, just as his opponents, refuses to answer their question.

Translation: *By what authority I do these things,* cp. on v. 2.

9 ***And he began to tell the people this parable: "A man planted a vineyard, and let it out to tenants, and went into another country for a long while.***

Exegesis: *ērxato de pros ton laon legein tēn parabolēn tautēn* lit. 'he began to tell the people this parable'. For *archomai* with infinitive, cp. on 4 : 21; here it refers to a new turn in Jesus' activity, cp. "He went on to tell" (NEB). *pros ton laon* is emphatic by position and brings out a change in Jesus' audience after vv. 1-8, cp. "then he turned to the people" (Phillips). For *parabolē* cp. on 4 : 23.

exedeto auton geōrgois 'he let it to tenants'.

ekdidomai (†) 'to lease', 'to let (out)'. For the form *exedeto* instead of *exedoto* cp. Bl-D, § 94.1.

geōrgos 'farmer', here 'tenant', cp. *TH-Mk* on 12 : 1.

apedēmēsen chronous hikanous 'he went abroad for a considerable time'. For *apodēmeō* cp. on 15 : 13 and *TH-Mk* on 12 : 1. *chronous hikanous* is accusative of duration. *chronoi* in the plural denotes a longer period. For *hikanos* cp. A-G s.v. 1 b.

Translation: *Parable*, see on 8 : 4.

Planted a vineyard. The verb 'to plant' in some languages may only take 'plant(s)' or 'tree(s)', or the name of a specific plant/tree as object, but not 'vineyard' or 'garden'; hence, 'made (or, laid out) a vineyard' (Javanese, Willibrord); in Bahasa Indonesia the technical term is 'to open', referring primarily to the clearing of the jungle, then also to the laying-out of a garden in the area cleared. — *Vineyard*, or, 'field/garden with vines', 'grape garden' (Thai), 'place-for-grapes' (Tzeltal), 'wine (fruit) garden' (several Indonesian languages); cp. also 'a man possessed a field; he planted vines (a transliterated term) in it' (Fon, in Mk. 12 : 1; cp. *TBT*, 19.115, 1968). For 'vines', or, 'grape-plants' (Spanish VP), see Nida, *BT*, 165f; *N.T.Wb.*/38, FLORA. Where a cultural equivalent for 'wine' (for which see on 1 : 15) is used, it may be possible to employ a term connected with the beverage chosen, e.g. 'field/garden of palmwine-trees'. Such a rendering, however, requires careful consideration, because it must fit the concomitant features mentioned in the parallel passages (Mt. 21 : 33, Mk. 12 : 1). Thus in Bamiléké, where 'wine' is rendered by *ndu*', i.e. the fermented juice of the raffia-palm (*nkùà*), the translator may feel that he cannot say 'field of *nkùà*' (since such a field has neither a wall or hedge, nor a tower) but must coin a descriptive phrase, 'plantation of *ndu*' trees'.

Let it out to tenants, or, "leased it (or, rented it out) to tenants" (Goodspeed, TEV), 'left it to be taken care of by renters-of-land' (Tzeltal), and cp. *TH-Mk* on 12 : 1. What is probably meant here is a long lease, and payment in kind, either a fixed amount of the product, or a third or fourth part of it. Renderings of *tenants* may be rather generic (as is the Greek), e.g. 'farmers' (Shona), 'field-workers' (Toba Batak), 'gardeners' (Trukese, Ponape), 'those who hoe' (Fulani, Balinese); or more specific, referring to the men's having the vineyard in lease, e.g. "tenants" (RSV, similarly Sranan, South Toradja), 'caretakers' (Kapauku), or to their job, e.g. "vine-growers" (NEB, similarly Jerusalem).

Went into another country for a long while, or, 'went to another (or, a far/foreign) country (or, to the country of other/foreign/far-away people) and stayed there for a long time'.

10 ***When the time came, he sent a servant to the tenants, that they should give him some of the fruit of the vineyard; but the tenants beat him, and sent him away empty-handed.***

Exegesis: *kairō* 'at the proper time', cp. *en kairō* (12 : 42) and A-G s.v. 2.

hina apo tou karpou tou ampelōnos dōsousin autō lit. 'in order that they might give him from the fruit of the vineyard', final clause denoting the owner's intention in sending the slave and virtually equivalent to his message to the tenants. *apo tou karpou* is equivalent to a partitive genitive, cp. A-G s.v. *apo* I 6; it is best rendered 'a share of' or 'a part of'. *karpos* is used in a more general meaning, 'produce', 'proceeds'. *autō* is best understood as referring to the servant.

hoi de geōrgoi exapesteilan auton... kenon 'but the tenants sent him away empty-handed', cp. on 1 : 53.

deirantes lit. 'after beating (him) up', denoting an act which takes place before the sending away.

Translation: *When the time came,* or more explicitly, 'at the season of grapes' (cp. Bahasa Indonesia), 'at the time for harvesting the grapes' (cp. Balinese).

The construction *sent a servant...that they should give* has to be adjusted in some languages, so as to avoid the change of subject, e.g. 'sent a servant...to ask-for/collect/receive' (Tzeltal, Balinese, Rieu), or to make explicit the implied message, e.g. 'he ordered a servant to go...and to tell (them), "You must give..."'.

Some of the fruit of the vineyard, or, "his (i.e. the owner's) share of the harvest" (TEV), "his share of the produce (of the vineyard)" (NEB, Rieu), 'the produce (lit. the strength) of the vineyard a part' (Toba Batak), 'a part from what they had gained with the vineyard' (Sranan, where a more literal rendering would suggest that the owner sent his servant for some grapes). *Fruit,* cp. also *N.T.Wb.*/40.

Empty-handed, see on "empty" in 1 : 53.

11 ***And he sent another servant; him also they beat and treated shamefully, and sent him away empty-handed.***

Exegesis: *kai prosetheto heteron pempsai doulon* lit. 'and he went on to send another slave', i.e. 'again he sent a slave', cp. A-G s.v. *prostithēmi* 1 c.

atimasantes lit. 'after humiliating (him)'.

atimazō (†) 'to dishonour', 'to treat shamefully', 'to humiliate'.

Translation: *He sent another* (or, a second) *servant,* or, 'again (or, for the second time) he sent a servant (of his)'.

Treated him shamefully, cp. *TH-Mk* on 12 : 4.

12 ***And he sent yet a third; this one they wounded and cast out.***

Exegesis: *hoi de kai touton traumatisantes exebalon* 'but him too they wounded and threw him out'. *kai touton* suggests that this one was treated along the same lines as the other two, yet *traumatizō* and *ekballō* have a stronger connotation of violence than the verbs used in vv. 10f, cp. Plummer.

traumatizō (†) 'to wound', 'to hurt'.

Translation: *He sent yet a third,* or, 'for the third time he sent a servant (of his)'.

Wounded, probably referring to heavy, but non-fatal, bruises or wounds, inflicted by some instrument; cp. *N.T.Wb.*/76, also /43, HIT.

Cast out may have to be specified, e.g. 'cast/flung/pushed out of the vineyard'.

13 ***Then the owner of the vineyard said, 'What shall I do? I will send my beloved son; it may be they will respect him.'***

Exegesis: *ho kurios tou ampelōnos* 'the owner of the vineyard', cp. on 1 : 6.

ti poiēsō 'what shall I do?', deliberative question.

pempsō ton huion mou ton agapēton 'I shall send my beloved son', cp. on 3 : 22.

isōs touton entrapēsontai 'perhaps they will respect him'. For *entrepomai* cp. on 18 : 2 and *TH-Mk* on 12 : 6.

isōs (††) 'perhaps' (as usual in Greek), or, 'surely', preferably the former.

Translation: *Said,* i.e. in himself, or, 'asked himself', 'thought'.

My beloved son, or, 'my son, the one I love'. If in 3 : 22 a rather literary or archaic phrase, or honorific forms have been used, the more colloquial context here may require a more common expression, cp. e.g. "my Son, my Beloved" (3 : 22), and, "my own dear son" (here) in NEB.

They will respect, or, 'they will have regard (or, show consideration) for', 'they will not dare to touch/maltreat'.

14 ***But when the tenants saw him, they said to themselves, 'This is the heir; let us kill him, that the inheritance may be ours.'***

Exegesis: *hoi geōrgoi dielogizonto pros allēlous* 'the tenants discussed among themselves', cp. A-G s.v. *dialogizomai* 2. The imperfect is durative and implies that it took some time before they came to the decision expressed in what follows.

houtos estin ho klēronomos 'this is the heir'. *klēronomos* (†).

hina hēmōn genētai hē klēronomia 'in order that the inheritance be ours', i.e. 'may come to us'. *hēmōn* is possessive genitive and goes with the predicate. *genētai* is ingressive aorist.

Translation: *Said to themselves,* or, 'to one another', see on 4 : 36.

For *this is the heir* and *that the inheritance may be ours* see *TH-Mk* on 12 : 7, and cp. 'he (it is who) will own the garden later' and 'that his garden be our (inclus.) share' (East Toradja 1933), 'he will receive the property of his father' and 'that the property come in our hands' (Sranan), 'to him his father will leave the property' and 'that we may possess what-is-his (South Toradja), or, the property/vineyard'.

15 ***And they cast him out of the vineyard and killed him. What then will the owner of the vineyard do to them?***

Exegesis: *ti oun poiēsei autois ho kurios tou ampelōnos* 'what then will the owner of the vineyard do to them?' This question interrupts the parable since it is addressed to the listeners. No answer from them is expected or given and the question serves to enliven the parable and focus attention on its main point. It is in the future tense as if Jesus and the listeners are witnesses of the events.

Translation: *Cast him out... and killed him*: the victim is cast or pushed out of the vineyard while still alive, and then killed outside.

What then will the owner... do...? The force of this question may have to be brought out by saying, 'what then do you expect the owner... will do...?', or as a statement, 'you all, or, we (inclus.) all, know what the owner... will do, of course...'. *Then*, or, 'therefore', 'so', indicates that the question draws the inference from the parable, and as such marks its end. If this is still felt to be too abrupt a transition, one may add, "Jesus asked" (TEV), or, 'thereupon Jesus said'.

16 ***He will come and destroy those tenants, and give the vineyard to others." When they heard this, they said, "God forbid!"***

Exegesis: *eleusetai kai apolesei... kai dōsei* 'he will come and destroy (or, put to death)... and give'. The end of the parable is told in the future as if it is yet to come.

akousantes de eipan 'when they heard it they said'. Subject is the people (v. 9).

mē genoito lit. 'let it not happen', expressing strong rejection, in Paul always in response to a question, here in reaction upon the preceding statement, 'never!', or 'God forbid', cp. Bl-D, § 384. This strong reaction of the people is understandable only when it is assumed that the people know the application of the parable.

Translation: For the first part of this verse see *TH-Mk* on 12 : 9.

God forbid!, or, "heaven forbid!" (Goodspeed), 'by no means!', 'not at all!', 'surely not!', 'far from it!' (Balinese), 'may God hinder it, or, protect us from it' (Fulani, Zarma), 'oh, God, perhaps not' (the usual Tzeltal way of remonstrating).

17 ***But he looked at them and said, "What then is this that is written:***
'The very stone which the builders rejected
has become the head of the corner'?

Exegesis: *ho de emblepsas autois eipen* 'he looked at them and said'. *emblepsas* (also 22 : 61) denotes a meaningful look; the verb is often used to introduce an act of special meaning, cp. e.g. Mk. 10 : 21.

ti oun estin to gegrammenon touto 'than what does this text of Scripture mean?' *oun* is inferential and means, 'if you don't want this to happen', cp. Plummer. *to gegrammenon* lit. 'that which is written', hence 'text of Scripture'.

For the rest of v. 17 cp. *TH-Mk* on 12 : 10.

Translation: *He*, or, 'Jesus'.

Looked at, or, 'fixed-his-eyes-on' (East Toradja), 'observed-closely/intently' (Bahasa Indonesia RC).

What then is this that is written, i.e. how then do you explain/interpret/understand this text? (cp. Plummer). For *this that is written* cp. on "the place where it is written" in 4 : 17.

Builders, or, 'those who build/make the house'.

The head of the corner, or, "the main corner-stone" (NEB), 'the post of the corner' (Javanese), 'the stone that-strengthens the corner of the wall' (Balinese). Some renderings make use of cultural equivalents, e.g. 'principal stone' (South Toradja, employing the name of the big stones on which the main poles of a house are erected), 'stone which combines the house' (Kipsigis in 1 Peter 2 : 6, in analogy to the term for the centre pole of the hut), 'the root of the house at the corner' (Kekchi), 'stone heavy pole' (East Toradja, qualifying 'stone' by the term that refers to the four big corner-poles of a house), 'the main pole' (Aguaruna, without any reference to a stone, since stones are never used in the region for the building of a house). Some descriptive renderings used are, 'place/thing-where-the-house-corner-receives-strength' (Tzeltal), 'the chief stone that carries the whole house' (Sranan), 'the thing joining the walls' (Shona 1966). Cp. also *TH-Mk* on 12 : 10.

18 ***Every one who falls on that stone will be broken to pieces; but when it falls on any one it will crush him."***

Exegesis: *pas ho pesōn ep' ekeinon ton lithon sunthlasthēsetai* 'every one who falls on that stone will be dashed to pieces'. The clause is an expansion of v. 17 but it changes the picture considerably since it refers no longer to a cornerstone, but a stone which is in such a position that one can fall upon it, or, as the rest of v. 18 shows, it can fall upon somebody.

sunthlaō (†) 'to crush together', 'to dash to pieces', here of people.

eph' hon d' an pesē, likmēsei auton '(the man) on which it falls, him it will crush'.

likmaō (†) 'to winnow' (so usually in Greek), hence 'to scatter (like chaff)', or 'to crush to powder', 'to pulverize', preferably the latter.

Translation: The translator should not feel called upon to set right the incongruity that exists between v. 17 and v. 18 (as shown in *Exegesis*).

Every one who... may better become 'when a person...he', cp. on "whoever..." in 9 : 24.

Will be broken to pieces, or, 'will go to (or, break into) pieces', 'will shatter himself on it' (Jerusalem), 'will break his body' (Sranan).

When it falls on any one it will crush him, or, 'the man whom the stone falls upon, that one it will smash completely' (Sranan); or, keeping the same subject, and using a passive form of the first verb, or of both, 'he who is-fallen-upon by it (or, by the stone) will turn-to-pulp, or, will be shattered' (Javanese, Malay).

19 ***The scribes and the chief priests tried to lay hands on him at that very hour, but they feared the people; for they perceived that he had told this parable against them.***

Exegesis: *ezētēsan* 'they tried', cp. 19 : 47, here in the aorist because v. 19 describes the immediate reaction upon Jesus' words in v. 18 (cp. *en autē tē hōra,* see below).

hoi archiereis, cp. on 9 : 22.

epibalein ep' auton tas cheiras 'to lay/get their hands on him', cp. 9 : 62. Here it is used in a hostile sense.

en autē tē hōra 'at that very time', hence by extension, 'then and there'.

kai ephobēthēsan ton laon 'and they were afraid of the people'. *kai* is used here because the clause is more or less a parenthesis between what precedes and its explanation, cp. A-G s.v. *kai* 2 i. *egnōsan gar* 'for they perceived, or, understood', cp. *TH-Mk* on 12 : 12.

pros autous 'with reference to them', cp. *ibid.*; emphatic.

Translation: *Tried,* cp. on "sought" in 5 : 18.

To lay hands on, or, "to arrest" (TEV), 'to take-hold-of/seize' (Balinese; similarly Sranan, lit. 'stretch forth the hand and seize'), or, since they will not be agents but initiators, 'to cause to be seized'.

They feared the people. For the position of the clause see next entry. *People,* cp. on 7 : 29.

For they perceived... This clause (c) goes with clause (a), "they tried to lay hands on", not with (b), "they feared". If such a sentence structure is unacceptable, (c) may have to come before (b) (as e.g. in NEB, TEV, Thai, Trukese, Tzeltal, South Toradja), or before (a), see *TH-Mk* on 12 : 12; or one may repeat part of (a) before (c) in order to help the reader to make the right connexion, e.g. 'they tried that, or, they tried to do so, because they perceived...'.

He had told this parable against them, or, 'he had aimed this parable at them, or, at their behaviour' (cp. Balinese, South Toradja), 'he had spoken this parable touching (i.e. causing embarrassment to) them' (Thai), 'Jesus had exposed/unmasked them in the parable' (Lokele), 'he had been speaking about them in telling this parable' (Shona 1966). In Javanese, where the term for 'parable' also means 'allusion', one can use here a related verb, 'they-themselves were-parabled/alluded-to by these words'.

From this verse onward some versions in honorific languages (such as Bengali, see *TBT,* 14.185, 1963) no longer use honorifics with reference to the Jewish leaders, because their malevolence has now become manifest; often, however, linguistic etiquette is such that all leaders, even malevolent ones, are entitled to honorifics.

20 ***So they watched him, and sent spies, who pretended to be sincere, that they might take hold of what he said, so as to deliver him up to the authority and jurisdiction of the governor.***

Exegesis: *paratērēsantes* lit. 'after watching', either with *auton* 'him', i.e.

Jesus, understood, or without object in an absolute sense, i.e. 'watching their opportunity', preferably the latter, cp. A-G s.v. 1 b.

egkathetous hupokrinomenous heautous dikaious einai 'spies who pretended to be righteous'. *dikaious* is best interpreted, 'scrupulous', 'conscientious', since it is a matter of doing the right thing.

egkathetos (††) lit. 'suborned, or hired', viz. to perform a secret commission, hence 'secret agent'. Here the commission is to try to catch Jesus in his words.

hupokrinomai (††) 'to pretend'. The participial clause *hupokrinomenous...einai* refers to the method which the agents were to use.

hina epilabōntai autou logou 'in order that they (i.e. the agents) might catch him in/on a word'. *epilabōntai* is best understood as construed with two genitives viz. the genitive of the person (*autou*), and the genitive of the thing in which (*logou*), cp. A-G s.v. 2 a, and Plummer.

hōste paradounai auton tē archē kai tē exousia tou hēgemonos 'so as to hand him over to the jurisdiction and the authority of the governor'. *hōste* with infinitive refers here to the intended result, cp. A-G s.v. 2 b. *archē* and *exousia* are probably best understood as a hendiadys.

hēgemōn (also 21 : 12) 'governor', in itself a general term and applicable to the Roman emperor and his underlings (cp. *hēgemoneuō* in 2 : 2, and *hēgemonia* in 3 : 1).

Translation: *They watched him,* preferably, 'they looked out for an opportunity', "they watched for the right time" (TEV).

An existing receptor language term for *spies* often does not fit the situation; a term for 'secret agent' may not exist in the language. Then one may have to use a descriptive phrase, e.g. 'men secretly commissioned/told/persuaded', 'people hired/bribed'; such a phrase may have to be connected with the following 'that'-clause, which indicates what they were commissioned (etc.) to do.

Pretended to be sincere, or, 'posed as conscientious people', 'played the conscientious' (Jerusalem), 'acted as conscientious though they were not'. *Sincere,* preferably, 'conscientious', 'strict/punctilious (in their behaviour)', especially in their observance of the religious law.

That they might take hold of what he said, or, 'to ensnare him in an utterance-of-his' (Bahasa Indonesia RC), 'to catch-him-like-a-fish with-reference-to his words' (Trukese, Ponape), 'to spy on him till he would miss his mouth (i.e. make a mistake in speaking)' (Sranan), 'that they would be able to find his sin if his words became bad' (Tzeltal); cp. also above on 11 : 54 and *TH-Mk* on 12 : 13, where synonymous expressions are used.

So as to, or, 'so that they could', 'which would enable them'; usually better as a new sentence, e.g. 'Thus they expected to be able to...', 'Thus they might...' (Leyden).

Deliver him up, or, 'turn/hand him over', 'seize and bring him'. The verb, in itself neutral, has in this context a pejorative meaning, but less so than 'to betray' (cp. on 6 : 16), since it does not presuppose a violation of allegiance.

The authority and jurisdiction of the governor, or, 'the power and authority of the governor', 'the hand(s) (in the sense of 'power') and authority of the governor', 'the supreme-power of the governor' (Willibrord). If the verb only takes a personal indirect object, one may shift to, 'the governor, who had authority and jurisdiction (over him)', cp. 'the governor, he being the one who had power and authority' (Shona 1966), 'the one in authority' (Zarma), 'those who (were) in power (to) watch over the land' (Kapauku). For *governor* see on 2 : 2.

The rather intricate sentence pattern may have to be recast, especially where "spies" has to be rendered by a descriptive phrase, and/or the linguistic and historical order should closely parallel each other. This may result e.g. in, 'They watched their chance and intended (or, hoped to be able) to deliver him to...the governor. Therefore they secretly commissioned some men, who were to pose as conscientious people, and sent them to catch him in his words (or, commissioned some men and sent them to catch him in his words. To do so these men were to pose as conscientious people)'.

21 ***They asked him, "Teacher, we know that you speak and teach rightly, and show no partiality, but truly teach the way of God.***

Exegesis: *kai epērōtēsan auton* 'and they asked him'. The question they ask does not come until v. 22; it is preceded by a flattering statement concerning Jesus.

didaskale 'teacher', cp. on 3 : 12.

oidamen hoti orthōs legeis kai didaskeis 'we know that you speak and teach correctly'. *orthōs* may refer to the manner of Jesus' speaking and teaching, 'forthrightly' (cp. Willibrord), or to the content of his speaking and teaching. The latter is preferable.

ou lambaneis prosōpon lit. 'you do not accept a person,' a very strong Hebraism quite frequent in the Septuagint (cp. A-G s.v. *prosōpon* 1 b). It means 'to show partiality', 'to show favouritism'.

ep' alētheias 'truly', cp. on 4 : 25.

tēn hodon tou theou didaskeis lit. 'you teach the way of God', cp. *TH-Mk* on 12 : 14.

Translation: *They asked him.* The verb 'to ask' is in some cases better avoided, because a question does not follow directly; cp. 'they told him' (Kituba), "these spies said to Jesus" (TEV, which introduces v. 22 by "tell us").

Rightly, preferably, 'what is right', cp. "what you...teach is right" (TEV).

You...show no partiality, or, 'you do-not choose-choose people' (Trukese), 'there exists no preference of one over another with you' (Zarma), 'you do not make-difference-between people' (South Toradja), 'you do not observe hairs-on-the-body' (Bahasa Indonesia RC, using an idiom for discrimination). See also *TH-Mk* 12 : 14 on "care for no man".

Truly refers to the truth of his teaching; hence 'in a true way', 'with true words', and cp. *N.T.Wb.*/71f.

The way of God, or, 'the commandments/instructions of God' (Balinese); and see *TH-Mk, l.c.*

22 ***Is it lawful for us to give tribute to Caesar, or not?"***

Exegesis: *exestin*...*ē ou* 'is it lawful..., or (is it) not?' For *exestin* cp. on 6 : 2.

Kaisari phoron dounai 'to give, i.e. to pay, taxes to Caesar'. For *kaisar* cp. on 2 : 1; here it is used as a title.

phoros (also 23 : 2) 'tribute', 'taxes', probably referring to direct taxes on land, or personal property, cp. *IDB* IV, 520ff.

Translation: For the whole verse cp. *TH-Mk* on 12 : 14.

Is it lawful for us to give... *or not*, or, 'shall-we-give, (or on the contrary) shall-we-not-give...' (Enga, see *TBT*, 16.132, 1965). In some languages it is preferable to state the case first, e.g. 'that we all pay taxes to the King-of-kings, is it right or not' (Balinese). For *lawful* see also on 6 : 2. *Us.* One may hesitate here between exclusive and inclusive; the former is probably preferable because of the clearly exclusive 'we' in v. 21, and the contrasting 'you' implied in the imperative in v. 25.

Tribute, preferably, '(personal) taxes', cp. *N.T.Wb.*/70.

Caesar, or, 'the emperor/big-chief/king-of-kings'.

23 ***But he perceived their craftiness, and said to them,*** 24 ***"Show me a coin. Whose likeness and inscription has it?" They said, "Caesar's."*** 25 ***He said to them, "Then render to Caesar the things that are Caesar's, and to God the things that are God's."***

Exegesis: *katanoēsas*...*autōn tēn panourgian* 'seeing through their trickery'. For *katanoeō* cp. on 12 : 24; here it means 'to see through', 'to perceive what is hidden'.

panourgia (†) 'trickery', 'cunning'.

(V. 24) *deixate moi dēnarion* 'show me a denarius', cp. on 7 : 41.

tinos echei eikona kai epigraphēn 'whose likeness and inscription does it have?' *tinos* goes with both *eikona* and *epigraphēn*.

eikōn (†) 'image', 'likeness', 'head' on a coin.

epigraphē (also 23 : 38) 'inscription', 'legend' on a coin.

(V. 25) *hoi de eipan, Kaisaros* 'they said, Caesar's'. In Nestle these words belong to v. 24 (cp. RSV and other versions).

toinun apodote ta Kaisaros Kaisari 'then give Caesar what belongs to Caesar'. *toinun* introduces a strong inference. *apodidōmi* 'to give, or, to pay what is due'. *ta Kaisaros* lit. 'the things of Caesar', i.e. 'what is due to Caesar', 'what Caesar is entitled to receive'.

Translation: For these verses cp. also *TH-Mk* on 12 : 15-17.

He, i.e. Jesus, may have to be specified; similarly in v. 25.

Perceived their craftiness, or, "saw through their trick" (NEB); in Sranan the idiom is 'bored through their head and came to know their trick', in Javanese 'not ignorant of their deceit'.

(V. 24) *Coin*, or, 'piece of silver, or, money', 'silver coin', see references on "denarii" in 10 : 35; cultural equivalents as mentioned there are not advisable here, because the reference is not to the value but to the object and its historic details; see also *TBT*, 9.88, 1958. Sometimes a coin of the same value cannot be used because it has no effigy or legend, but one of different value has the details required and hence is the closest natural equivalent, e.g. in Sranan.

Whose likeness and inscription has it, or with a syntactic shift, 'who is portrayed on it? Whom does the inscription mention?' (cp. Leyden). *Likeness*, or, "portrait" (Rieu), "face" (TEV). *Inscription*, or, 'writing' (Toba Batak), 'stamp/seal' (Bahasa Indonesia), "name" (TEV), 'name mark' (Javanese), 'written mark'.

Caesar's, or, 'those of (or, they belong to, or, the likeness and inscription are of) the Emperor'; or, 'the Emperor' (Leyden, cp. above). The answer may have to be introduced by an affirmative expression, without which it would sound impolite, 'indeed (or, yes, or, you are right), Caesar's' (Javanese, Sundanese).

(V. 25) *Then*, or, 'well, then', 'because that is so', 'for that reason'.

26 ***And they were not able in the presence of the people to catch him by what he said; but marvelling at his answer they were silent.***

Exegesis: *ouk ischusan epilabesthai autou rēmatos* 'they could not catch him in (one) word', cp. on v. 20. For *ischuō* cp. on 6 : 48.

enantion tou laou 'in the presence of the people', i.e. 'with the people present', or 'in public'.

thaumasantes epi tē apokrisei autou 'astonished at his answer', here with negative connotation, 'taken aback'. *apokrisis*, cp. on 2 : 47.

esigēsan 'they fell silent', ingressive aorist.

Translation: *In the presence of the people*, cp. also on 8 : 47.

Marvelling at, cp. on "wondered at" in 1 : 21.

His answer refers to the contents, 'what he had answered', 'the things he had said in reply'.

They were silent, or, 'they said nothing more', 'they became speechless', is a resultative clause: 'so amazed that they fell silent'.

27 ***There came to him some Sadducees, those who say that there is no resurrection,*** 28a ***and they asked him a question, saying,***

Exegesis: *proselthontes de tines tōn Saddoukaiōn* 'some of the Sadducees came (to him)'.

Saddoukaios (†) 'Sadducee', i.e. a member of the religious group called Sadducees, cp. *TH-Mk* on 12 : 18; for a detailed treatment cp. *IDB* IV, 160-163.

hoi antilegontes anastasin mē einai 'who deny that there is a resurrection', qualifying the entire group of Sadducees, not the few of them who came to Jesus. For *antilegō* cp. on 2 : 34; here it is construed with *mē* and infinitive to indicate that which is denied. *anastasis* (cp. on 2 : 34) refers here and in vv. 33, 35, 36 to the eschatological resurrection, cp. *TH-Mk* on 12 : 18.

(V. 28a) *epērōtēsan* '(they) asked'. As in v. 21f the actual question is preceded by two statements, viz. of the principle involved (v. 28b), and of the case (vv. 29-32).

Translation: For vv. 27-33 cp. *TH-Mk* on 12 : 18-23.

Sadducees, or, 'Sadducee men', 'members of the (priestly) party/group of the Sadducees', 'Jews called Sadducees'. In transliteration the *c* may become *s* or *k*; the latter is preferable, where possible.

That there is no resurrection, or, 'that the dead do not rise, or, come to life again', etc., cp. on 14 : 14.

(V. 28a) *They asked him a question, saying,* or, "they set him a problem" (Rieu), or simply, 'they said to him', cp. on "they asked him" in v. 21. In the latter case v. 33 may have to be introduced by, 'then they asked him'.

28b ***"Teacher, Moses wrote for us that if a man's brother dies, having a wife but no children, the man must take the wife and raise up children for his brother.***

Exegesis: *didaskale* 'teacher', cp. on 3 : 12.

Mōüsēs egrapsen hēmin 'Moses wrote for us', viz. in Deut. 25 : 5-10, cp. on 5 : 14.

ean tinos adelphos apothanē echōn gunaika 'if a man's brother dies having a wife'. *echōn gunaika* means 'having a wife at the time of his death', hence 'leaving a wife'.

sperma 'offspring', cp. on 1 : 55.

kai houtos ateknos ē 'and (if) this one (i.e. the brother) is childless', still modified by *ean. ateknos* also v. 29.

For the rest of v. 28 cp. *TH-Mk* on 12 : 19.

Translation: *Moses wrote for us,* or, 'M. ordered us in the law, or, in Scripture', "M. wrote this law for us" (TEV, similarly Balinese), 'the law of Moses (see on 2 : 22f) tells us'. *Us,* preferably inclusive.

If a man's brother dies...the man must... The components of the sentence may have to be distributed differently, e.g. 'if an older brother dies...the/his younger brother must...', 'if a man has a brother who (or, and that brother) dies..., he (or, that man) must...' (cp. Jerusalem); or one may have to introduce first some of the persons concerned, e.g. "if there are brothers, and one dies..., then the next should..." (NEB), 'if there is a married couple, and the husband (lit. the male-one-of-it) dies... then the brother of the deceased must...' (Balinese).

...brother dies, having (or, leaving) *a wife but no children,* or, '...brother dies, who is married but has/leaves no children', '...married brother dies childless'.

Take the wife, or, 'marry the deceased's wife, or, the widow', or, 'take his sister-in-law as his wife' (Thai). For 'marry' see on 14 : 20 and references. Where comparable customs are known a specific term for a levirate marriage may be available, e.g. in Javanese, where a verbal derivation of 'pillow' is used (probably referring to the pillow on which the first husband laid his head), or in Toba Batak, 'to act-as-substitute-with-reference-to the wife'. Elsewhere the custom described may be actually shocking, e.g. in Zarma, where marrying one's brother's wife is strictly forbidden. In such a case an explanatory note will be required.

And raise up children for his brother. Descriptive renderings used are, "and carry on his brother's family" (NEB), 'in order to continue his older brother's family line' (Thai), "so they can have children for the dead man" (TEV), 'in order that thus his older brother's offspring may not be lost' (Tzeltal), 'that he may make flowers alive for his older brother' (Timorese), 'the children of that woman will be called the children of her dead husband' (East Toradja 1933).

29 ***Now there were seven brothers; the first took a wife, and died without children;*** 30 ***and the second*** 31 ***and the third took her, and likewise all seven left no children and died.*** 32 ***Afterward the woman also died.***

Exegesis: *hepta oun adelphoi ēsan* 'now there were seven brothers'. *oun* marks the transition to the exposition of the case.

ho prōtos labōn gunaika apethanen ateknos 'the first took a wife and died childless'. For *ho prōtos* cp. *TH-Mk* on 12 : 20; for *labōn gunaika* cp. *TH-Mk* on 12 : 19.

(V. 30) *kai ho deuteros* (V. 31) *kai ho tritos elaben autēn* 'and the second and the third took her'. *elaben* is in the singular because the marriage with the second and with the third brother are two distinct events. The clause implies that the second brother also died childless, and the same is to be inferred with regard to the third brother.

hōsautōs de kai hoi hepta ou katelipon tekna kai apethanon 'in the same way also the seven left no children and died', short for, 'in the same way also the rest of the seven brothers took her and left no children and died', i.e. died without leaving children.

(V. 32) *husteron* (†) 'afterward', or, 'last of all', preferably the latter, cp. A-G s.v. *husteros* 2 b.

Translation: *Now,* or, 'now, once there was', 'it-happened' (Javanese), introducing the statement of the (fictional) case.

Seven brothers may have to become, 'seven men related-as-siblings' (Balinese), 'seven men related-as-older-sibling-younger-sibling' (Toba Batak), 'seven men with the same father and mother' (Tzeltal).

(V. 30ff) *And the second and the third took her* may have to be adjusted and/or expanded in order to be comprehensible, e.g. 'then the second married her and died, and then (or, after him) the third (married her and died)'.

Likewise all seven..., or, 'up to the seventh, all...' (East Toradja 1933), 'the same happened with the rest of them, they...', 'thus one by one all seven complete' (Tzeltal).

Left no children and died is usually better rendered in inverted order, e.g. 'died and left no children', 'died without leaving line of descent' (Shona

1966), 'died childless, or, having had no children with her', and may have to be expanded, see *Exegesis*.

33 ***In the resurrection, therefore, whose wife will the woman be? For the seven had her as wife."***

Exegesis: *hē gunē oun en tē anastasei tinos autōn ginetai gunē* 'the woman then, the wife of which of them is (she) at the resurrection?' *oun* marks the transition to the question proper. *hē gunē* 'the woman', emphatically placed at the beginning of the clause because the question concerns her. *ginetai,* though in the present, refers to a future event. *gunē* is used in two meanings, viz. 'woman' and 'wife'.

hoi gar hepta eschon autēn gunaika 'for the seven, i.e. all seven, had her as wife'. *eschon* (aorist) refers to a series of events that have come to an end.

Translation: The structure of the first sentence may have to be recast, e.g. 'now, as to that woman, or, now we (exclus.) ask you about that woman (cp. on v. 21): whose wife will she be in the resurrection?'

In the resurrection, or, '(at the time) the dead rise, or, come to life again' etc.

Whose wife will the woman be?, or, 'which one's wife will she be?', 'which one will she have as (her) husband?', 'with which one will she be-in-married-state?'; or, changing the subject, 'which one will have-her-as-his-wife?' (Toba Batak).

The seven had her as wife, or, 'all (those) seven (brothers) had married her'; or changing the subject, "she was married to all seven of them" (Rieu).

34 ***And Jesus said to them, "The sons of this age marry and are given in marriage;***

Exegesis: *hoi huioi tou aiōnos toutou* 'the children of this age', cp. on 16 : 8. Here it is used in a temporal sense. The phrase refers to both men and women, see below.

gamousin kai gamiskontai 'marry and are given in marriage'. The former refers to men, the latter to women, cp. 17 : 27. *gamiskō* (††) is synonymous with *gamizō* (v. 35).

Translation: *The sons of this age,* preferably, 'the children of (or, people belonging to) this age', 'those who live in the present age/time', without the pejorative connotation the phrase has in 16 : 8.

Marry and are given in marriage, see on 17 : 27.

35 ***but those who are accounted worthy to attain to that age and to the resurrection from the dead neither marry nor are given in marriage,***

Exegesis: *hoi de kataxiōthentes tou aiōnos ekeinou tuchein kai tēs anastaseōs* *tēs ek nekrōn* 'but those who are judged worthy to attain that age and the resurrection from the dead'. *kataxioō* (†). *ho aiōn ekeinos* is the age to come, cp. on 18 : 30. It is to be viewed in terms of temporal sequence. For *ek nekrōn* cp. on 9 : 7.

Translation: *Those who are accounted* (or, thought/called) *worthy*, or slightly simplified, 'those who are worthy', 'those who are allowed' (Bahasa Indonesia RC). The agent to be understood with this passive form is God. — *Those*, or, because of the subsequent reference to marriage, "the men and women" (TEV). For *worthy* see on 3 : 16.

To attain to, or, 'to reach/gain/find/experience', 'to share in' (cp. Balinese), 'to be participants in' (cp. Navajo).

To that age and to the resurrection from the dead is basically a hendiadys, the second phrase modifying or explaining the first; hence e.g. 'that age, when the dead come to life again'. — *That age*, i.e. 'the age to come', see *TH-Mk* on 10 : 30 and *N.T.Wb.*/4f. *The resurrection from the dead* has virtually the same meaning as "the resurrection" in vv. 27 and 33.

36 ***for they cannot die any more, because they are equal to angels and are sons of God, being sons of the resurrection.***

Exegesis: *oude gar apothanein eti dunantai* 'for they also cannot die any more', stating the reason why there is no marriage in the age to come. *oude* suggests correspondence with what precedes. *dunantai* means that dying has become impossible.

isaggeloi gar eisin 'for they are like angels', explaining why they cannot die.

isaggelos (††) 'like an angel', substantive.

kai huioi eisin theou, tēs anastaseōs huioi ontes 'and they are children of God, being children of the resurrection'. *huioi theou* refers to a relationship with God which goes beyond the relationship with God in this life. For the phrase *tēs anastaseōs huioi* cp. on 10 : 6; here *huioi* means 'belonging to', 'sharing in'. *ontes* is causal participle.

Translation: *They are equal to angels*, or, specifying the point of comparison, 'they exist like angels', 'they live on like angels do'.

Sons of God, or as a simile, cp. on "sons of the Most High" in 6 : 35.

Being sons (or, children) *of the resurrection*. This metaphor, even if marked as a simile, is unacceptable in many languages; hence such renderings as, 'because (they are) heirs of the resurrection' (cp. Balinese), "because they have been raised from death" (TEV), 'because they (are) people who have-been-brought-to-life again, or, have risen from the dead' (South Toradja, Gio).

37 ***But that the dead are raised, even Moses showed, in the passage about the bush, where he calls the Lord the God of Abraham and the God of Isaac and the God of Jacob.***

Exegesis: *hoti de egeirontai hoi nekroi* 'but that the dead are raised' i.e.

that there is a resurrection of the dead, indirect speech dependent upon *emēnusen* but placed at the opening of the sentence for reasons of emphasis. For *egeirō* cp. on 7 : 14.

kai Mōüsēs emēnusen epi tēs batou 'also Moses indicated in the passage concerning the thornbush'. Moses is envisaged here as the author, not as participating in the event. For *epi tou batou* cp. *TH-Mk* on 12 : 26. *mēnuō* (†).

hōs legei kurion ton theon Abraam kai theon Isaak kai theon Iakōb 'when he calls the Lord the God of Abraham, the God of Isaac and the God of Jacob'. *kurios* (cp. on 1 : 6) is without article as if a personal name. *hōs* is used here in a temporal sense (cp. A-G s.v. IV 1 b).

Translation: *But that the dead are raised.* Jesus shifts the topic of the discussion, from the situation in which the risen dead will find themselves to the fact that the dead will really arise. This introductory statement, in Greek and English an object-clause dependent on 'showed', is in some other languages given a more independent position, cp. 'as-to-the-fact-that the dead are-raised, that matter is made-clear...' (Balinese, Jerusalem); cp. also *TH-Mk* on 12 : 26. For *the dead are raised* see above on 7 : 22.

Showed, or, 'indicated', 'made known', 'made clear'.

The passage about the bush, or, "the chapter on the Bush" (Rieu, similarly Balinese), 'the chapter/story/section called "the Bush" (or, "the burning bush", NEB, TEV, better to bring out that the reference is to Ex. 3 : 1ff)'. For *bush* cp. on "bramble bush" in 6 : 44.

Where. Though the Gr. *hōs*-clause is temporal, going with 'showed', it may be preferable to do as RSV and render it as a locative clause going with "the passage".

Calls the Lord, or, 'speaks of the Lord as', 'mentions the Lord as being'.

The God of Abraham and the God of Isaac and the God of Jacob may be unidiomatic and even misleading; hence, 'the God of A. and I. and J.' (South Toradja), 'the one who is God (in relation) to A., (is God) to I. and (is God) to J.'.

38 ***Now he is not God of the dead, but of the living; for all live to him."***

Exegesis: *theos de ouk estin nekrōn alla zōntōn* 'he is not God of dead people but of living people', or, 'God is not (God) of dead people but of living people', preferably the former.

pantes gar autō zōsin 'for all men are alive to him'. *pantes* means 'all people regardless of their being alive or dead'. *autō* may mean 'in relationship with him', or 'in his judgment'. The former is preferable.

Translation: The argument runs thus: God has revealed himself to Moses as the Lord of Abraham, Isaac and Jacob, which proves that these patriarchs are still alive, since such a relationship presupposes living partners; *ergo,* there is a resurrection of the dead. The objection that all people know that the patriarchs have died is countered by the next sentence: this may seem so in reference to men, in the human sphere, but in reference to God, in the divine sphere, they are alive. By this Luke provides a help towards the right interpretation of the preceding clause. For the first sentence see also *TH-Mk* on 12 : 27. The second sentence may prove misleading in its brevity. Then it will have to be adjusted and expanded, e.g. 'if the Lord is a person's God, that person is not dead but alive', 'those whom God has called are not dead, they are living' (Tzeltal).

Live. The term used should preferably be the same as used in the rendering of "eternal life", for which cp. references on 10 : 25.

39 ***And some of the scribes answered, "Teacher, you have spoken well."***

Exegesis: *apokrithentes* lit. 'answering', cp. on 1 : 60.

tines tōn grammateōn 'some of the experts in the law', cp. on 5 : 21. They were the theological and religious opponents of the Sadducees.

kalōs also 6 : 26.

Translation: *You have spoken well,* or, "that was a fine answer" (Goodspeed), expressing approval of Jesus' confutation of the Sadducees.

40 ***For they no longer dared to ask him any question.***

Exegesis: *ouketi...ouden* 'not...any more', the two negations reinforcing each other.

etolmōn (†) 'they dared', subject the Sadducees.

Translation: *No longer...any,* or, 'not...any more/further'; or an expression denying continuation, e.g. 'they did not dare to go on asking...'.

To dare, cp. *N.T.Wb.*/21, COURAGE; used with a negation the verb may be rendered by 'to fear', e.g. 'they feared to ask any more questions'.

To ask a question, cp. on v. 3.

41 ***But he said to them, "How can they say that the Christ is David's son?***

Exegesis: *pros autous* 'to them', without indication to whom it refers. In the light of the preceding section the reference is to the Sadducees, or to the scribes, preferably the latter.

pōs legousin ton Christon einai Dauid huion 'how (is it possible that) they say that the Messiah is David's son?'. The subject of *legousin* is either 'people' in general, or the teachers, preferably the former. For *pōs* cp. on 1 : 34; for *christos* on 2 : 11 and 26; for *Dauid huios* on 18 : 38. For the meaning of vv. 41-44 and the translational aspects cp. *TH-Mk* on 12: 35-37[a].

Translation: No further comments.

42 ***For David himself says in the Book of Psalms,***
'The Lord said to my Lord,
Sit at my right hand,
43 ***till I make thy enemies a stool for thy feet.'***

Exegesis: *en biblō psalmōn* 'in the book of psalms'. For *biblos* cp. on 3 : 4.

psalmos (also 24 : 44) 'song of praise', 'psalm', in Luke in the plural and referring to the Old Testament book of Psalms.

For a detailed treatment of the rest of vv. 42f, containing the quotation from Psalm 110 : 1, cp. *TH-Mk* on 12 : 36. The text of Mark and Luke is identical with the one exception that Luke following the Septuagint reads *hupopodion tōn podōn sou* instead of *hupokatō*. For *kurios* and *tō kuriō mou* cp. on 1 : 6, sub (4) and (3) respectively.

hupopodion (†) 'footstool'.

Translation: *In the Book of Psalms*, or, 'in the part of Scripture called the Psalms', or simply, 'in the Psalms'. For *book* see on 4 : 17. *Psalms*, often transliterated, may be translated as 'chanting' (Kapauku), 'songs' (Shona 1966, East Toradja), 'Holy Songs' (Trukese), 'holy songs of old' (Timorese), 'songs of worship/praise'. In some predominantly Muslim countries one of the Arabic terms for the Psalms, viz. *zabūr*, or *mazmūr* (etymologically related to Hebr. *mizmōr*), has been transliterated.

For *the Lord* and *my Lord* see on 1 : 6, sub (c) and (b). If the term for "Lord" is obligatorily possessed, the first phrase may have to become 'our Lord' (Gio).

Sit, the aspect is ingressive and continuative: sit down (or, take a seat) and remain seated.

My right hand, cp. also on 1 : 11, ad (1) and references.

(V. 43) *Till* here has the meaning of 'during the time that', 'and in the meanwhile'; cp. also *TBT*, 16.134, 1965.

Enemies, see on 1 : 71.

A stool for thy feet. In this metaphor, which sometimes is better rendered as a simile, any term will do that refers to something that is put under the feet of a person sitting in state, such as, 'cushion', 'carpet', 'small-bank' (Sranan), 'footstick' (Totonac). It may be preferable, however, to use a culturally equivalent figure of speech for subjection of enemies; or to shift to a non-figurative rendering, e.g. 'I subject your enemies to you', 'I defeat your enemies for you'; or to combine a figurative and a non-figurative rendering, e.g. 'I beat down to the ground your enemies and put them underneath your feet like grass' (Lengua).

44 ***David thus calls him Lord; so how is he his son?"***

Exegesis: *Dauid oun kurion auton kalei* 'so David calls him lord'. *oun* is inferential and means here, 'as scripture shows', 'as we have seen'.

pōs autou huios estin 'how (is it possible that) he is his son?'

Translation: *Calls him Lord*, or, 'causes/says-(him-)to-be-lord' (South

Toradja, using a causative-declarative verbal derivation of 'lord'). *Him,* or to avoid ambiguity, 'the Messiah'.

His son, or, 'David's son', again for the sake of clarity.

45 ***And in the hearing of all the people he said to his disciples,***

Exegesis: *akouontos de pantos tou laou* 'while all the people were listening'. For *pas ho laos* cp. on 3 : 21.

Translation: No further comments.

46 ***"Beware of the scribes, who like to go about in long robes, and love salutations in the market places and the best seats in the synagogues and the places of honour at feasts,*** 47 ***who devour widows' houses and for a pretence make long prayers. They will receive the greater condemnation."***

Exegesis: *prosechete apo tōn grammateōn* 'beware of the experts in the law'. For *prosechō* with *apo* cp. on 12 : 1; for *grammateus* cp. on 5 : 21.

For the rest of v. 46 cp. *TH-Mk* on 12 : 38f. It should be noted, however, that Luke inserts *philountōn* before *aspasmous,* thus avoiding Mark's incongruous construction of *thelontōn* (with following infinitive, and with substantives as object). *prōtokathedria,* cp. 11 : 43.

phileō (also 22 : 47, but in a different meaning) 'to love', 'to like'.

(V. 47) *hoi katesthiousin...kai...proseuchontai* 'who eat up/devour... and...pray'. For this verse cp. *TH-Mk* on 12 : 40. Note that Luke restores the syntactical concordance which is lacking in Mk. 12 : 40 by changing the participles into relative clauses.

Translation: *Beware of,* or, "be on your guard against" (Phillips), see on 12 : 1.

Long robes, or to make clear the function, 'long coats/clothes to show their importance'.

For *salutations in the market places and the best seats in the synagogues* and *places of honour at feasts* see also on 11 : 43 and 14 : 7ff respectively.

(V. 47) *Who devour...make long prayers,* see *TH-Mk* 12 : 40.

They will receive the greater condemnation is elliptical in that it does not mention the point of comparison, a reference to which may have to be added, e.g. 'they will be condemned/punished more heavily than others (who have not done so)'. For 'condemn(ation)' cp. *N.T.Wb.*/48f, JUDGE, and again *TH-Mk, l.c.*

CHAPTER TWENTY-ONE

1 *He looked up and saw the rich putting their gifts into the treasury;*

Exegesis: *anablepsas* 'looking up', or 'looking closely', preferably the latter; it suggests an attentive look (cp. *TH-Mk* on 16 : 4).

eiden tous...plousious 'he saw the rich'. *plousious* is stressed by its position at the end of the participial phrase that goes with it (see below).

ballontas eis to gazophulakion ta dōra autōn 'dropping their gifts into the treasury', participial phrase going syntactically with *tous...plousious*. *ballō eis* may mean 'to drop into', or 'to put into', here preferably the former.

gazophulakion (†) 'treasury', 'contribution box', cp. *TH-Mk* on 12 : 41.

dōron (also v. 4) 'present', 'gift'.

Translation: *Saw the rich putting*, or, 'saw the rich (who) put'. The aspect is iterative: Jesus saw that again and again one of the rich came to bring a gift.

Gifts, or, 'offerings', 'the money they-offered' (Balinese). To use a term for 'alms' is not advisable.

Treasury, or, 'box (for) gifts' (Balinese), 'money-box of the church/temple' (Sranan), 'place/box where people put in the money'.

2 *and he saw a poor widow put in two copper coins.*

Exegesis: *eiden de tina chēran penichran* 'he saw (also) a needy widow'. 'Also' is expressed not by a specific word but by the repetition of *eiden* after v. 1.

penichros (††) 'poor', 'needy', a not very common word and hence somewhat stronger than *ptōchē* (v. 3).

ballousan ekei lepta duo 'dropping there two small coins'. For *lepton* cp. on 12 : 59 and *TH-Mk* on 12 : 42.

Translation: *Poor*, or, "very poor" (TEV), "poverty-stricken" (Rieu).

Widow, see on 2 : 37.

Put in, or, 'put into it, or, into the (offering) box'.

Copper coin should preferably be rendered by the name for the smallest coin known in the culture, and distinguished from "penny" (12 : 6). Where no distinctive names are available one may say, "tiny coin" (NEB), 'smallest coin', 'piece of cheapest kind of money'. Cp. also Nida, *BT*, 328f, 338, 341; *N.T.Wb.*/55, MONEY.

3 ***And he said, "Truly I tell you, this poor widow has put in more than all of them;***

Exegesis: *alēthōs legō humin* 'I tell you truly', cp. on 3 : 8 and 9 : 27.

pleion pantōn ebalen '. . . has put in more than all'. *pantōn* refers to *tous plousious* in v. 1, as is brought out in v. 4.

Translation: *Truly I tell you,* cp. references on 4 : 24f.

More than all of them, or, 'most of all'. *More,* of course, does not mean here 'more coins' but 'something more valuable'; to make the reader aware of this one may have to add a cue, cp. e.g. "has really put in more than all the others" (TEV).

4 ***for they all contributed out of their abundance, but she out of her poverty put in all the living that she had."***

Exegesis: *ek tou perisseuontos autois* 'out of what is present for them in abundance', i.e. 'out of their abundance'. The phrase may be interpreted as a periphrasis for the partitive genitive, 'part of their abundance', or as indicating the source from which their gifts come, preferably the latter. This applies also to *ek tou husterēmatos autēs,* see below.

ebalon eis ta dōra lit. '(they) put into the gifts', viz. the gifts that were already in the treasury.

ek tou husterēmatos autēs 'out of her want'.

husterēma (†) lit. 'that which is lacking', hence, 'want', 'need', 'poverty'.

panta ton bion hon eichen ebalen '(she) has put in (viz. into the gifts, with *eis ta dōra* understood) all the means of subsistence/livelihood she has'. For *bios* in this meaning cp. on 8 : 43.

Translation: *Contributed,* more lit. 'put/threw into the gifts', using the verb with a more generic meaning than in vv. 1ff. This results in renderings like, 'added to the offerings' (South Toradja), 'gave as their share of the gifts, or, the gifts to God'. An object may be required: 'something', '(some) money'.

Out of their abundance, or, '(taking it) from their surplus (lit. more-ness)' (cp. Javanese), '(out) of their left-over money' (cp. Tzeltal), '(which came) from what they had to spare' (cp. Goodspeed), or with a further shift, 'money they did not need'. It may be preferable to give the phrase a different position and construction, cp. e.g. "all of these have more than they need, and they contributed from that" (Rieu), "those others who have given had more than enough" (NEB). For *abundance* cp. also *N.T.Wb.*/1.

The syntactic structure of the second part of the verse should parallel that of the first part as closely as possible, cp. the examples in the following two entries.

Out of her poverty, or, '(taking it) from her shortage/need (lit. less-ness)' (cp. Javanese), 'from what she had not to spare', 'money she needed', '(though) she has less than she needs', etc.

Put in, preferably a rendering which (partly) echoes that of "contributed", e.g. 'added (to the offerings)', 'gave as her share (of the gifts)', etc.

All the living that she had, or, 'all she had to live on', 'her all, even that too on which she depended' (Lokele), 'what she intended to buy food with' (Tzeltal), and see *TH-Mk, l.c.*

5 ***And as some spoke of the temple, how it was adorned with noble stones and offerings, he said,***

Exegesis: *kai tinōn legontōn peri tou hierou* 'and when some people said about the temple...'. No direct connexion with what precedes as to time and place is stated, nor is it indicated to whom *tinōn* refers.

hoti lithois kalois kai anathēmasin kekosmētai '...that it was adorned with beautiful stones and votive offerings'. *lithois kalois* refers to materials used when the buildings were erected, *anathēmasin* to later decorative additions.

anathēma (††) 'votive offerings', refers to special gifts from individuals.

kosmeō (cp. 11 : 25) here 'to decorate', 'to adorn'.

Translation: *As some spoke...he said*, or co-ordinated, 'Some spoke... Then he/Jesus said', addressing himself to those present in general, probably.

How it was adorned with noble stones... gives the contents of what they said about the temple. Making explicit the implied direct discourse one may say, therefore, something like, 'saying (or, and they said), "Look, it is adorned with noble stones...!"'. An alternative solution is to shift from a clause to a noun with qualifying clause or phrase, e.g. 'and (of) its decoration with costly stones...' (cp. Goodspeed), 'and (about) the fine stones with which it was adorned (cp. NEB), or, which made it beautiful'.

Offerings, or, 'gifts for God' (Sranan), 'beautiful things people had given to honour God'.

6 ***"As for these things which you see, the days will come when there shall not be left here one stone upon another that will not be thrown down."***

Exegesis: *tauta ha theōreite* lit. 'these things which you see', aposiopesis, since it is not taken up by a clause of which *tauta* is a part. It is best rendered independently, 'as to these things which you see'.

eleusontai hēmerai en hais 'days will come in which...', cp. on 5 : 35.

en hais ouk aphethēsetai lithos epi lithō 'in which, i.e., when no stone will be left upon another'. For *aphiēmi* cp. on 19 : 44.

hos ou kataluthēsetai 'that shall not be thrown down', as if preceded by *ouk estin lithos* 'there is no stone...'. As the clause stands it has the semantic function of stating positively what was expressed negatively by *ouk aphethēsetai lithos epi lithō*.

kataluō here 'to throw down', 'to detach from its place', cp. A-G s.v. 1 a.

Translation: *As for these things which you see.* The subsequent break in the sentence structure is best marked by a dash or dots. Where such a break would be unacceptable one may connect the phrase with what follows, cp. e.g. 'what you see there, the days will come that no stone of it...' (Leyden), 'such days will come, that what you are looking at, of it no stone...' (cp. Marathi).

There shall not be left here one stone upon another, or in active construction, 'they (or, the enemies) will not leave...', cp. on 19 : 44.

That will not be thrown down is often better translated as a new sentence, e.g. 'everything (or, every stone) will be cast down'.

7 ***And they asked him, "Teacher, when will this be, and what will be the sign when this is about to take place?"***

Exegesis: *epērōtēsan de auton* 'they asked him'. In view of vv. 12ff the subject is presumably the disciples.

didaskale 'teacher', cp. on 3 : 12.

pote oun tauta estai 'then when will these things be, or, happen?' *oun* points back to v. 6 to which also *tauta* refers.

ti to sēmeion hotan mellē tauta ginesthai 'what will be the sign when these things are about to happen?', with *estai* understood. The underlying idea is that events due to divine intervention are announced by a sign. To know the sign means to know that the events are about to happen. For *sēmeion* cp. on 2 : 12; for *mellei* cp. A-G s.v. *mellō* 1 c α.

Translation: *They,* or, 'his disciples/followers'.

The sign when (or, that) *this is about to take place,* or more explicitly, 'the sign which will show that this is about (or, that the time has come for this) to happen' (cp. TEV).

8 ***And he said, "Take heed that you are not led astray; for many will come in my name, saying, 'I am he!' and, 'The time is at hand!' Do not go after them.***

Exegesis: *blepete mē planēthēte* 'beware lest you are led astray', cp. *TH-Mk* on 13 : 5.

planaō (†) 'to mislead', here in the passive 'to be misled', 'to be deceived', 'to be led astray', cp. A-G s.v. 2 c δ.

polloi gar eleusontai epi tō onomati mou 'for many will come under my name'. *eleusontai* means here 'to appear on the scene'. For *epi tō onomati mou* cp. *TH-Mk* on 13 : 6.

egō eimi 'I am he', cp. *TH-Mk, l.c.*

ho kairos eggiken 'the time has drawn near', or, 'is at hand'. *kairos* is the moment appointed by God for the eschatological events to happen. *eggizō* (cp. 7 : 12) is used here in a temporal sense.

mē poreuthēte opisō autōn 'do not go after them', 'do not follow them'. *opisō* (cp. 9 : 23) here implies following as a disciple, or an adherent.

Translation: *Take heed that you are not led astray.* What is to be avoided is the being led astray, of course, but in some languages a literal rendering of the negation in the dependent clause may suggest that it is the opposite, viz. the not being led astray. To prevent this a rendering by two co-ordinated imperatives may be advisable, 'take heed; don't be led astray'. — *Take heed,* or, 'take care', 'be on your guard', 'watch out'. — *That you are not led astray,* or, 'deceived/misled', or, 'that you do not go astray, or, err, or, believe lies'; Sranan has an idiomatic phrase, 'that people do not turn your head'.

For *in my name,* or more descriptively, 'as though they were I (or, were representing me)', and for *I am he* cp. *TH-Mk* on 13 : 6.

The time, or, making explicit what this term implies in this context, 'his time', 'the time that he/the Christ comes'. In Kapauku the appropriate idiom is, '(the time when) the knots will be untied' (cp. the Tagabili rendering of "at the end of" in 2 : 21).

Go after, see on "come after" in 9 : 23.

9 ***And when you hear of wars and tumults, do not be terrified; for this must first take place, but the end will not be at once."***

Exegesis: *hotan de akousēte polemous kai akatastasias* 'but when you hear of wars and insurrections'. *de* contrasts v. 9 with v. 8; the clause takes up the question of the sign in v. 7.

akatastasia (†) 'disorder', 'insurrection', 'revolution'.

mē ptoēthēte 'do not be frightened, or, startled'.

ptoeomai (also 24 : 37) 'to be terrified', 'to be frightened', indicating a strong feeling of terror.

dei gar tauta genesthai prōton 'for it is necessary that these things happen first'. For *dei* cp. on 2 : 49 and 9 : 22. *prōton* (not occurring in the parallel text Mk. 13 : 7) is added by Luke to stress the thought of the next clause.

all' ouk eutheōs to telos 'but the end will not come immediately', i.e. will not immediately follow the wars and insurrections, with *hēxei* or a similar verb understood. *eutheōs* is emphatic by position. For *to telos* 'the end', i.e. the end of this age, cp. A-G s.v. 1 b.

Translation: *War,* probably referring to external strife; South Toradja uses a reciprocal derivation of 'to fight'.

Tumults, probably referring to internal riots, cp. also, 'disdain for one's chief' (East Toradja 1933).

Do not be terrified, or, 'do not let people make you afraid, or, cause you to fear' (for which see on 1 : 12).

The end will not be at once, or, 'the end will not follow them at once', 'they do not indicate that the end is near' (cp. TEV), 'it is not immediately so that it-is-finished' (Sranan). *The end,* or more specifically, 'the final hour' (Tzeltal), 'that this age (or, everything) comes to an end', cp. also *TH-Mk* on 13 : 7. The use of adjustments as discussed may lead to further changes in the sentence structure, e.g. 'these things must happen before this age ends, but they do not indicate that this will happen (or, that it will end) at once'. *At once*, or, 'immediately', 'at the very moment', 'right then'.

10 ***Then he said to them, "Nation will rise against nation, and kingdom against kingdom;*** 11 ***there will be great earthquakes, and in various places famines and pestilences; and there will be terrors and great signs from heaven.***

Exegesis: *tote elegen autois* 'then he said to them', introductory formula which serves not to introduce a new discourse, but to emphasize the significance of what follows.

For the rest of v. 10 cp. *TH-Mk* on 13 : 8.

(V. 11) *seismoi te megaloi* 'and there will be great earthquakes', going with *esontai*. *seismos* (†). *te* corresponds with *kai* before *kata topous*, and the second *kai* serves to connect *limoi* and *loimoi*, 'there will be both great earthquakes and plagues and famines', thus bringing out that two groups of events are envisaged, viz. catastrophes in nature, and human afflictions.

kata topous 'in various places', cp. A-G s.v. *kata* II 1 a, and s.v. *topos* 1 d. Syntactically the phrase goes with what follows, but not to the extent that the earthquakes do not occur in various places.

limoi kai loimoi esontai 'there will be famines and plagues'.

loimos (†) 'pestilence', 'plague', 'contagious disease'.

phobētra te kai...sēmeia megala estai 'there will be terrors and...great signs'. *te kai* connects *phobētra* and *sēmeia* as belonging closely together. Hence *megala* goes with both substantives.

phobētron (††) 'terror', 'terrible event', here probably referring to cosmic catastrophes.

ap' ouranou 'from heaven', 'from the sky', going with both *phobētra* and *sēmeia*.

Translation: *Then he said*, preferably, "he went on to say" (TEV).

Nation will rise against nation, or, 'nations will defy each other' (Bahasa Indonesia RC). Instead of *nation*, or, 'people/tribe', one may have to use 'men of a nation, or, tribe, or, country' (cp. East Toradja, Tarascan).

(V. 11) *In various places*, or, 'now here, then there' (NV), should be given such a position in the sentence that it can qualify the three nouns, e.g. at the very end (some English versions), or at the very beginning (Javanese).

Famines, see on 4 : 25.

Pestilences, or, 'spreading illness (i.e. epidemic)' (East Toradja), 'the bowing-down of stalks-of-reed' (South Toradja using a figurative phrase, comparing the people falling down in an epidemic with broken rushes).

Terrors and great signs, or, 'great terrifying things and signs'; or, because of the close relationship between the two nouns, 'terrifying and great signs', 'great signs that cause people to fear' (East Toradja 1933). *Signs*. Some languages have a distinctive term for things that foreshadow coming events, e.g. "portents" (Rieu, similarly Balinese).

For the rest of the two verses see *TH-Mk* on 13 : 8.

12 ***But before all this they will lay their hands on you and persecute you, delivering you up to the synagogues and prisons, and you will be brought before kings and governors for my name's sake.***

Exegesis: *pro de toutōn pantōn* 'but before all these things', points back to the signs and events foretold in vv. 10f.

epibalousin eph' humas tas cheiras autōn 'they will lay/get their hands on you', cp. on 20 : 19. The subject is not stated but the rest of v. 12 shows that Luke thinks in terms of a general persecution, not one restricted to the Jews.

kai diōxousin scil. *humas* to be understood from *eph' humas*, 'and they persecute you'.

paradidontes eis tas sunagōgas kai phulakas 'handing (you) over to synagogues and prisons', with *humas* understood. For *paradidōmi* cp. on 9 : 44 and A-G s.v. 1 b; for the meaning of *sunagōgē* here, cp. on 12 : 11. The clause is best understood as referring to an aspect, or to the consequences of the persecutions and could be rendered, 'and hand you over . . .'.

apagomenous epi basileis kai hēgemonas lit. 'being brought to kings and governors', with *humas* understood from *diōxousin* (*humas*), see above. The clause is best interpreted and rendered in the same way as the preceding participial clause, viz. 'and you will be brought before . . .'. *apagō* means here (with *epi*) 'to bring before a judicial authority in order to be tried'. For *hēgemōn* cp. on 20 : 20.

heneken tou onomatos mou 'on account of my name', 'because of my name', i.e. 'on my account', 'because of me', or, 'on account of your allegiance to me', preferably the former.

Translation: *Before all this*, or, 'before all these things happen'.

For *they* (or, people) *will lay their hands on you* see on 20 : 19, for *persecute* on 11 : 49.

Delivering you up to the synagogues and prisons. The verb 'to deliver up' (see on 20 : 20) often requires a person as recipient. This causes no difficulties with the first noun, since one may say 'the leaders/councils of the synagogues' (cp. on 12 : 11), but it does with the second. If necessary, one may either insert a different verb, resulting in 'put in prison' (Zarma, Tzeltal) or, 'imprison' (cp. Willibrord), or choose a (usually more generic) verb that can go with both nouns, e.g. 'to cause to be sent' (Lokele), "to drag to" (Rieu), 'to bring', cp. e.g. 'bringing you to the judgment councils of the synagogues and to the jails' (Shona 1966).

You will be brought before, or, 'they will bring you before'. South Toradja uses a technical term literally meaning, 'you will be-caused-to-ascend before'.

For *governors* see on 2 : 2; for *name* cp. on 1 : 49, and for the prepositional phrase cp. on "for my sake" in 9 : 24.

13 ***This will be a time for you to bear testimony.***

Exegesis: *apobēsetai humin eis marturion* 'it will result for you in a testimony'. For *apobainō* cp. on 5 : 2.

marturion (cp. on 5 : 14) here either in a passive sense, 'testimony for you', i.e. it will bring you a good reputation, or in an active sense, 'testimony', 'testifying', i.e. it will bring you an opportunity to testify. The latter is preferable.

Translation: *This will be a time for you,* preferably, 'this will lead you', 'its-consequence (will be) that you' (cp. Balinese), 'these things will carry you' (Sranan), 'this will give you the opportunity' (cp. NEB).

To bear testimony, i.e. to tell publicly about the things you have experienced while being with me; hence, 'give testimony in my favour' (cp. Bahasa Indonesia), 'speak on my behalf before them' (Lokele); or, shifting to the contents of the testimony, "declare your faith" (Rieu), "tell the Good News" (TEV). For *testimony* cp. also *N.T.Wb.*/74, WITNESS.

14 ***Settle it therefore in your minds, not to meditate beforehand how to answer;***

Exegesis: *thete oun en tais kardiais humōn* lit. 'so lay to your hearts'. For this phrase cp. on 1 : 66, but here its meaning is 'to resolve', 'to make up one's mind', 'to come to a decision' (cp. Acts 5 : 4).

mē promeletan apologēthēnai 'not to prepare beforehand (how) to defend yourselves'. For *apologeomai* cp. on 12 : 11. Here it refers to the wording of their defence.

promeletaō (††) 'to practise beforehand', 'to prepare beforehand'.

Translation: *To meditate beforehand,* or, 'to think-out before it happens' (East Toradja).

How to answer, cp. on 12 : 11. Toba Batak uses here, 'your-justification (lit. being-cleansed)'.

15 ***for I will give you a mouth and wisdom, which none of your adversaries will be able to withstand or contradict.***

Exegesis: *egō gar dōsō humin stoma kai sophian* lit. 'for I will give you a mouth and wisdom'. *egō* is very emphatic. *stoma* is used in a figurative sense, and it may either refer to power of speech (Plummer) or eloquence (A-G), or go with *sophian* as a hendiadys and mean 'words of wisdom'. The latter appears to be preferable.

hē ou dunēsontai antistēnai ē anteipein 'which cannot resist or contradict. . .'. *hē* (dative) refers, strictly speaking, to *sophian* alone, but is to be understood as taking up the one concept of *stoma kai sophian.*

anthistamai (†) 'to resist', 'to withstand', here referring to resisting the power or strength of their speaking.

anteipon (†) 'to speak against', 'to contradict', here used in the sense of arguing against the defence of the disciples.

hapantes hoi antikeimenoi humin 'all your opponents', cp. on 13 : 17.

Translation: *For I will,* or to bring out the emphasis, 'for it is I who will'.

Give you a mouth and wisdom, or, following the interpretation preferred in *Exegesis*, 'give you words of wisdom (or, words which are wise)', 'cause/help you to speak wise words, or, wisely'. For *wisdom* see on 2 : 40.

Which none...will be able to withstand or contradict has resultative force, 'so that no one...will be able to withstand or contradict them, or, such words'. If in the receptor language one or both verbs require a personal object, one may say e.g. 'resist you and refute such words', or, 'resist and oppose you (when you speak so)'. — *To withstand*. In Sranan the idiom is here, 'to put to one side'. — *To contradict*, i.e. to oppose (a person) in argument, or, to deny the truth (of something that is said).

Adversaries, or, 'opponents/enemies/accusers'.

16 ***You will be delivered up even by parents and brothers and kinsmen and friends, and some of you they will put to death;***
17 ***you will be hated by all for my name's sake.***

Exegesis: *paradothēsesthe de kai hupo goneōn* 'you will also be delivered up by (your) parents', i.e. apart from being persecuted by the opponents just mentioned; for *paradidōmi* cp. on v. 12.

kai thanatōsousin ex humōn 'and they will put to death (some) of you'. The subject is either the parents etc. named in the preceding clause (which would require the rendering, 'they will cause to be put to death'), or those to whom the disciples will be turned over, viz. the persecuting authorities. The latter is preferable. *thanatoō* (†). For *ex humōn* cp. on *ex autōn* in 11 : 49.

(V. 17) *kai esesthe misoumenoi* 'and you will be hated', periphrasis for the future passive.

dia to onoma mou 'because of my name', 'on account of my name', equivalent to *heneken tou onomatos mou*, cp. on v. 12.

Translation: The recipients of *delivered up* may have to be mentioned, cp. e.g. 'even parents...will hand you over to the court-of-justice' (Sranan).

Parents, see on 2 : 27.

And (thrice) here indicates alternatives; hence 'or' may be better (cp. Balinese).

For *brothers and kinsmen* see on 14 : 12.

If *some of you they will put to death* is translated literally, 'they' will be taken as a reference to the 'parents', etc., not to the persecuting authorities (as preferred in *Exegesis*). To avoid this misunderstanding some versions shift to a passive construction, suggesting indefinite agents that as such must be different from the definitely named 'parents', etc.; where this is apt to be still rather ambiguous one may render "put to death" by a technical term that implies persecuting authorities as its agents, e.g. 'sentence to death', cp. also, "send to their death" (Rieu), or one may explicitly refer to the agents, replacing "they" by 'the judges/authorities/those-in-power'.

(V. 17) For *hated* see on 1 : 71.

All refers to people in general.

18 ***But not a hair of your head will perish.***

Exegesis: *thrix ek tēs kephalēs humōn ou mē apolētai* 'not a hair of your head will perish', proverbial saying promising that they will be invulnerable. This may be understood in a spiritual sense, viz. that their souls will be absolutely safe (cp. Plummer), or in the sense that though some will be killed, as a whole or as a community the disciples will be safe (cp. Grundmann). The latter is preferable. *ek tēs kephalēs* stands for the simple partitive genitive used in 7 : 38 and 12 : 7, cp. A-G s.v. *ek* 4 a α. For *ou mē* cp. on 1 : 15.

Translation: *Not a hair of your head will perish* (or, 'be harmed/lost'), or trying better to bring out the emphasis, 'you will not lose a single one of your hairs-of-the-head' (Javanese); or again, shifting from negative to positive, and focussing on the person, 'you will be entirely safe, even to (a single) one of the hairs of your head'. For *hair of one's head* cp. also on 7 : 38.

19 ***By your endurance you will gain your lives.***

Exegesis: *en tē hupomonē humōn* 'by your endurance', cp. on 8 : 15. *en* here with instrumental meaning, cp. A-G s.v. III 1 a.

ktēsasthe tas psuchas humōn 'gain your lives'. Nestle reads *ktēsesthe* 'you will gain', which is followed by the majority of translations. The clause may, like v. 18, be interpreted in a spiritual, or in a physical sense, here preferably the former. For *ktaomai* cp. on 18 : 12. For *psuchē* cp. A-G s.v. 1 c, and *TH-Mk* on 3 : 4 (3).

Translation: *By your endurance,* or, "by standing firm" (NEB), 'the holding that you hold through, will make that' (Sranan, making use of a construction the language commonly employs to indicate emphasis); cp. also on "patience" in 8 : 15. The implied exhortation to endure may be made explicit, e.g. "never give up, for in this way you will..." (TEV).

You will gain your lives, or, 'you will win/acquire/obtain life (or, true life) for yourselves' (cp. NEB), 'you will find real life' (Timorese), 'you will become really able to live', the qualifications 'true' or 'real' being added to indicate that this is a reference to what transcends earthly life, cp. *TH-Mk* on 8 : 36.

20 ***"But when you see Jerusalem surrounded by armies, then know that its desolation has come near.***

Exegesis: *hotan de idēte kukloumenēn hupo stratopedōn Ierousalēm* 'but when you see Jerusalem being surrounded by armies'.

kukloō (†) 'to surround', 'to encircle'. Note the present tense: the encircling is not yet completed, otherwise some of the following injunctions would be pointless.

stratopedon (††) 'army camp', hence 'army', 'army corps', 'legion'.

tote gnōte 'then you must know', referring to a future time.

hoti ēggiken hē erēmōsis autēs 'that the time of her devastation has drawn near'. For *ēggiken* cp. on v. 8.

erēmōsis (†) 'devastation', 'desolation', cp. *N.T.Wb.*, 42/DESERT.

Translation: *Jerusalem surrounded by armies*, or, 'that armies are engaged in surrounding J., or, on the point of surrounding J.' *Armies*, or, '(troops of) soldiers'; if the word for 'to surround' does not clearly express the hostile intention, one may have to say 'enemy armies'.

Then know, i.e. "then you may be sure" (NEB), 'you must realize then' (cp. Jerusalem).

That its desolation has come near, or, 'that the time for it to fall desolate has come near' (Marathi), 'that the hour has come for it to be destroyed' (Tzeltal), 'that it is about to be destroyed (cp. Kapauku, Shona 1963), or, will soon perish/fall/go-to-ruin', 'that far-off not, they will destroy it' (Kituba).

21 ***Then let those who are in Judea flee to the mountains, and let those who are inside the city depart, and let not those who are out in the country enter it;***

Exegesis: *tote* 'then', takes up *tote* in v. 20.

hoi en tē Ioudaia pheugetōsan eis ta orē 'those who are in Judea must fly to the hills'. *Ioudaia* is used here in the proper sense, cp. on 1 : 5. *pheugetōsan* is an imperative. *ta orē* refers to the hills or mountains in the southern part of Judea.

hoi en mesō autēs ekchōreitōsan 'those who are inside her must leave'. *autēs* refers to Jerusalem.

ekchōreō (††) 'to go out', 'to leave'.

hoi en tais chōrais 'those who are in the country', cp. A-G s.v. *chōra* 2.

mē eiserchesthōsan eis autēn 'must not enter her', i.e. Jerusalem. To seek refuge in Jerusalem would be the normal procedure in case of war.

Translation: *The mountains*, or, 'the hill country', see on 1 : 39.

Flee to, or, "take refuge in" (Rieu, similarly Javanese; and Sranan, lit. 'run into hiding').

Depart, or, 'leave (it)', 'get out of it'.

Out in the country, in opposition to what is in the city; hence, 'in the fields' (Javanese), 'where the ricefields are' (South Toradja), 'in the villages' (Malay), 'outside the city' (Balinese), 'not in the city' (East Toradja 1933); cp. also on 8 : 34.

22 ***for these are days of vengeance, to fulfil all that is written.***

Exegesis: *hoti hēmerai ekdikēseōs hautai eisin* 'for those are the days of vengeance'. *hautai* is subject. *hēmerai ekdikēseōs* is emphatic by position.

ekdikēsis (also in 18 : 7f, in a different meaning) 'vengeance', 'punishment'.

tou plēsthēnai panta ta gegrammena 'that all that has been written be fulfilled', articular accusative and infinitive in the genitive loosely dependent upon the preceding clause, either complementing it and defining the idea of vengeance expressed by *hēmerai ekdikēseōs* as a fulfilment of prophecy (cp. e.g. NEB), or (in a consecutive sense) denoting that the vengeance will result in the fulfilment of prophecy (cp. e.g. TEV). The former appears to be preferable. For *pimplēmi* cp. on 1 : 15; here it is used in a meaning for which Luke elsewhere uses *teleō* (cp. 18 : 31; 22 : 37), or *plēroō* (cp. 4 : 21; 24 : 44). *ta gegrammena* refers to what is written in the Scriptures.

Translation: *Days of vengeance.* Terms for *vengeance,* or, 'to avenge, or, revenge oneself', etc. usually have a connotation of 'paying back in kind', implying malice and ill will; hence 'days of punishment' (cp. TEV, Jerusalem), or, 'time when God punishes Israel/his-people' is usually preferable. For 'to punish' cp. also *N.T.Wb.*/59.

To fulfil all that is written, preferably, 'which is the fulfilment of (or, which fulfils) all that is written', "when all...is to be fulfilled" (NEB), or, as a co-ordinated sentence, 'at this time all...will be fulfilled'. For *to fulfil* see on 4 : 21. For *all that is written* see on 4 : 4. That *all* has limited application, as shown by the context, may have to be stated explicitly, 'all that is written about it, or, about those days, or, about the coming judgment'.

23 ***Alas for those who are with child and for those who give suck in those days! For great distress shall be upon the earth and wrath upon this people;***

Exegesis: *ouai tais en gastri echousais kai tais thēlazousais* 'alas for those who are with child and for those who are nursing (children)', cp. *TH-Mk* on 13 : 17. *ouai* here implies the thought of sudden danger. For *en gastri* cp. on 1 : 31. For *thēlazō* cp. on 11 : 27.

en ekeinais tais hēmerais 'in those days', goes with the whole clause. It refers to the same time as *tote* in vv. 20f.

anagkē megalē 'great distress', cp. A-G s.v. *anagkē* 2.

epi tēs gēs 'on earth', or, 'in the land', preferably the latter. The land referred to is Palestine.

orgē 'wrath', cp. on 3 : 7. Here it refers to God's impending judgment.

tō laō toutō 'for this people', 'upon this people', i.e. the Jewish nation.

Translation: *Alas,* or an equivalent exclamative particle indicating pity for suffering, or some such expression as, 'poor/miserable (are)', 'you should pity', 'what misfortune will this be for'; cp. *TBT*, 19.26f, 1968.

Those who are with child, see on 2 : 5.

Those who give suck, referring to the situation mothers with babies will be in rather than to the process of suckling; hence, "women...who have children at the breast" (NEB, similarly Sranan), 'women who have babies to suckle/nurse', "mothers with little babies" (TEV). For *to give suck* cp. *TH-Mk* on 13 : 17.

Great distress shall be upon the earth, or, 'will come over, or, will harass this earth'; or recasting the syntactic structure, 'this earth will suffer great distress, or, will greatly be-distressed'. For *distress*, primarily referring to physical disasters and suffering cp. *N.T.Wb.*/57, PAIN. *The earth*, or, 'all men in (or, inhabitants of) this land'.

Wrath (will come) *upon this people* may have to be recast in the same way as the preceding phrase. For *wrath*, or, 'judgment', 'punishment', cp. on 3 : 7; for *this people* on 1 : 17.

24 ***they will fall by the edge of the sword, and be led captive among all nations; and Jerusalem will be trodden down by the Gentiles, until the times of the Gentiles are fulfilled.***

Exegesis: *pesountai stomati machairēs* 'they will fall by the edge of the sword'. The subject of *pesountai* is best interpreted as the members of the Jewish people.

piptō 'to fall', here, 'to be slain', 'to be killed'.

stoma lit. 'mouth', here, 'point', or, 'edge', cp. A-G s.v. 2.

aichmalōtisthēsontai eis ta ethnē panta 'they will be scattered as prisoners over all the peoples'. *ethnē* may refer here to 'nations' or 'peoples' in a neutral sense, or, like in *hupo ethnōn* in the same verse, to 'gentile people' or 'Gentiles'. The former appears to be preferable.

aichmalōtizō (†) 'to take captive', here in the passive with *eis ta ethnē panta* to denote the scattering of the captives over the earth.

Ierousalēm estai patoumenē hupo ethnōn 'Jerusalem will be trampled over by Gentiles', not denoting an event but a situation in the future. For the periphrasis of the future cp. on v. 17. For *pateō* cp. on 10 : 19.

achri hou plērōthōsin kairoi ethnōn 'till the times of the Gentiles are fulfilled'.

achri hou 'till the time when', with *chronou* understood.

kairoi ethnōn 'the times of the Gentiles', probably referring to the time in which the Gentiles exercise judgment, though the exact meaning of the phrase is very uncertain, cp. commentaries.

Translation: *Fall by the edge of the sword*, or, 'fall, being cut down by the sword' (Kapauku), or, 'sharp choppers will cut them down (lit. cut-and-kill them)' (Sranan); or simply, "be killed by the sword" (TEV, similarly East Toradja), 'the enemy will kill them with the sword', 'perish in war'. Some idiomatic phrases used are, 'die eaten by the sword' (Malay), 'be passed along the thread of the sword' (Jerusalem). *Sword*, cp. below on 22 : 36.

And introduces an alternative future event here; hence 'or' may be preferable.

Be led captive among all nations, or, "carried off as prisoners among all nations" (Goodspeed), 'be taken captive and led away among all nations'; if an active construction is required, 'the enemy' is best taken as agent. *Among all nations*, or more explicitly locative, 'everywhere among the nations', "into all countries" (NEB), 'all over the earth'. For *captive* see on 4 : 18.

Trodden down, or non-figuratively, 'utterly destroyed' (cp. Bahasa Indonesia RC).

Gentiles, see on 2 : 32.

Until, or, '(and this will go on) up to the moment that', 'and this will not end before'.

Times of the Gentiles. If the connexion between the two nouns must be specified, one may say, 'the period the Gentiles (or, they) (still) have power', 'the time it is in the hands of people-from-other-places' (Tzeltal), 'time-of those governments-of men Gentile' (Trukese).

Are fulfilled, or, 'have run their full course', 'has come to an end' (cp. Balinese), 'is complete' (Bahasa Indonesia).

25 ***"And there will be signs in sun and moon and stars, and upon the earth distress of nations in perplexity at the roaring of the sea and the waves,***

Exegesis: *kai esontai sēmeia* 'and (then) there will be signs', i.e. probably after the times of the Gentiles (cp. Lagrange). For *sēmeion* cp. on v. 7 and reference there. The event to which the signs here point is described in v. 27.

en hēliō kai selēnē kai astrois 'in sun and moon and stars', without article and hence denoting together the sky in its entirety. *selēnē* and *astron* (†).

kai epi tēs gēs sunochē ethnōn 'and on earth (there will be) anguish of the nations', with *estai* understood, i.e. the nations will be in anguish. *epi tēs gēs* here different from v. 23.

sunochē (†) 'anguish', 'dismay', 'distress' (cp. *sunechō* 4 : 38).

en aporia ēchous thalassēs kai salou lit. 'in perplexity of the sound and the rolling of the sea', i.e. because of a perplexity due to the sound and the rolling of the sea. *thalassēs* may go with *ēchous* or with both *ēchous* and *salou*. The latter is preferable.

aporia (††) lit. 'being at a loss', 'bewilderment', 'perplexity'. Together with what follows it takes up and explains *sunochē*.

ēchos (†) 'sound', 'noise', 'roaring'.

salos (††) 'rolling or tossing motion, especially of waves'.

Translation: *There will be signs*. A verb like 'appear/be-seen/become-visible' may better fit the noun here.

Distress of nations in perplexity, or, 'nations will be distressed, because they are perplexed', or simply, 'nations will be distressed and perplexed'. Some versions treat the two nouns as a hendiadys, e.g. 'perplexed distress', 'desperate fright' (NV). *Nations* probably refers here both to the Gentiles and to the Jewish people. The concept *perplexity* may be expressed by such idioms as 'the heart jumps up' (Gio), 'speech vanishes' (Malay), 'spirit/mind at-its-end' (South Toradja, cp. also English "at their wits' end"), 'no longer knowing what to do' (Sranan), 'tying up the head' (Zarma); cp. also on 9 : 7.

At the roaring of the sea and the waves, or, taking 'sea' with both other nouns (see *Exegesis*), 'at the roaring and the rolling of the sea', 'because the sea is roaring and (its waves are) rolling'. The expression refers to excessive sound and movement of the sea. The movement, being the producer of the sound, may better come first, cp. Rieu's "surge and thunder of the sea". Cp. also *N.T.Wb.*/51f, MARITIME.

26 ***men fainting with fear and with foreboding of what is coming on the world; for the powers of the heavens will be shaken.***

Exegesis: *apopsuchontōn anthrōpōn* 'while men are fainting', absolute genitive elaborating the theme of *sunochē ethnōn.*

apopsuchō (††) lit. 'to stop breathing', hence 'to faint', 'to swoon'.

apo phobou kai prosdokias tōn eperchomenōn tē oikoumenē lit. 'because of fear and of expectation of what is coming upon the world'. *phobou* and *prosdokias* are perhaps best understood as a hendiadys, viz. 'fearful expectation'. For *eperchomai* cp. A-G s.v. 1 b β. For *oikoumenē* cp. on 2 : 1.

prosdokia (†) lit. 'looking toward (something)', hence 'expectation'.

hai gar dunameis tōn ouranōn saleuthēsontai 'for the powers of the heavens will be shaken', cp. *TH-Mk* on 13 : 25. It seems advisable to understand *hai dunameis* to refer to the stars, cp. Plummer. For *saleuō* cp. on 6 : 38.

Translation: Often the verse is better not rendered as a dependent clause but as a new sentence, e.g. 'and men will faint/be fainting...'.

Fainting can sometimes be rendered by, '(as it were) dying', 'almost dying' (Balinese). Some versions have used a receptor language idiom, which resembles the Greek term (such as, 'losing heart', 'whose soul disappears', 'whose spirit fails them') but which on further investigation proved to have the wrong meaning, e.g. referring to discouragement.

With fear and with foreboding of, or, 'because they fear and expect'. If the two nouns are interpreted as a hendiadys (see *Exegesis*), one may take the first one as head of the construction (cp. e.g. "from fear as they wait for", TEV), or the second one (e.g. 'fearfully expecting'). *Foreboding*, i.e. expecting non-beneficial events, cp. *N.T.Wb.*/14, AWAIT.

What is coming on the world, or more clearly pejorative, 'what will threaten the world' (Jerusalem), 'the disasters that will come over the world'. For *world* cp. on 4 : 5.

The powers of the heavens, or, "the forces in the sky" (Goodspeed), 'the strong (ones, or, things) in the sky'. Cp. also *TH-Mk* on 13 : 25. The rendering of the phrase should not suggest that the supports of (the vault of) heaven are shaken, as it does in some versions.

Shaken, i.e. moved from their proper place, cp. "driven from their course" (TEV).

27 ***And then they will see the Son of man coming in a cloud with power and great glory.***

Exegesis: V. 27 is almost completely identical with Mk. 13 : 26, cp. *TH-Mk* there. The differences between Mark and Luke are that the former has *en nephelais* in the plural and the latter *en nephelē* in the singular, without appreciable difference of meaning; and that Mark reads *meta dunameōs* *pollēs kai doxēs* 'with great power and glory', and Luke, *meta dunameōs kai doxēs pollēs* 'with power and great glory'. In both cases *pollēs* goes with both substantives.

Translation: *See the Son of man coming*, or, 'see how the Son of man comes', 'see the Son of man, who will be coming', and cp. *TH-Mk* on 13 : 26.

In a cloud, i.e. enveloped in a cloud, in the midst of a cloud.

Glory, see references on 2 : 9.

28 ***Now when these things begin to take place, look up and raise your heads, because your redemption is drawing near."***

Exegesis: *archomenōn de toutōn ginesthai* 'when these things begin to happen'. *toutōn* refers to the events announced in vv. 25f.

anakupsate kai eparate tas kephalas humōn 'stand up and lift up your heads', expressing an attitude of expectation. *anakuptō* may mean here 'to look up', or 'to stand upright', preferably the latter, cp. 13 : 11. For *epairō* cp. on 6 : 20.

dioti eggizei hē apolutrōsis humōn 'because your deliverance is drawing near'. For *dioti* cp. on 1 : 13. *eggizei* here as in vv. 8 and 20 in a temporal sense.

apolutrōsis (†, cp. *lutrōsis* in 1 : 68; 2 : 38) 'redemption', 'deliverance', 'liberation' in an eschatological sense, cp. *N.T.Wb.*, 109/RANSOM.

Translation: *Raise your heads*, or, 'look up(ward)' (several Indonesian languages).

Your redemption is drawing near, or, 'you are to be delivered soon', 'God will soon redeem you' (cp. Zoque); see also references on 1 : 68. Some versions use "salvation" (TEV, similarly Sranan), or a related verbal form, shifting from the process to the result.

29 ***And he told them a parable: "Look at the fig tree, and all the trees;***

Exegesis: *kai eipen parabolēn autois* 'and he told them a parable', introductory formula marking the addition of an independent part, cp. 6 : 39. For *parabolē* cp. on 4 : 23. *autois* refers to the disciples.

idete tēn sukēn kai panta ta dendra 'look at the fig-tree and all the trees'. The addition *kai panta ta dendra* (not in Mk. 13 : 28) brings out that the parable is of a general nature and that no special meaning is to be attached to the fig-tree.

Translation: *He told them a parable*, or, if the common term for "parable" implies a story, preferably something like, "gave them an illustration" (Goodspeed), 'made a comparison' (Willibrord); and cp. on 5 : 36.

Look at, or, 'think of', "remember" (TEV).

Fig tree, cp. on "figs" in 6 : 44.

And all the trees, preferably, "or any other tree" (NEB).

30 ***as soon as they come out in leaf, you see for yourselves and know that the summer is already near.***

Exegesis: *hotan probalōsin ēdē* 'when they already put out leaves', i.e. 'when they have begun to put out leaves'.

proballō (†) 'to put out (leaves)', 'to bud'.

blepontes 'when you see (it)'.

aph' heautōn ginōskete lit. 'you know from yourselves', i.e. 'without being told'. It is also possible though rather improbable to take *aph' heautōn* with *blepontes*.

hoti ēdē eggus to theros estin 'that already summer is near'. *eggus* is used in a temporal sense like *eggizō* in vv. 8, 20, 28. *theros* (†).

Translation: *They come out in leaf*, or, 'their leaves begin to appear' (cp. TEV). One often can use a specific verb, related to the word for 'bud', 'sprout', 'young leaf'; cp. "it buds" (NEB).

You see is often better taken with the preceding clause, 'as soon as (or, when) you see that they come out in leaves'.

For yourselves, when taken with "know" (see *Exegesis*), 'by yourselves', "without anybody telling you" (Phillips).

Know, i.e. 'are aware', 'realize', 'are sure'.

Summer is already near, see *TH-Mk* on 13 : 28.

31 ***So also, when you see these things taking place, you know that the kingdom of God is near.***

Exegesis: *hotan idēte tauta ginomena* 'when you see these things happening'. *tauta* takes up *toutōn* in v. 28 and refers to the events announced in vv. 25f.

hoti eggus estin hē basileia tou theou 'that the kingdom of God is near', i.e. 'that the coming of the kingdom of God is near'. For *hē basileia tou theou* cp. on 4 : 43.

Translation: *So also...you know*, or, "in the same way...you may be sure" (NEB), 'so yourselves also...then you know' (Sranan).

The verbs *see, know* and *is* may better be rendered as futures, cp. *TH-Mk* on 13 : 29.

The kingdom of God is to be taken as a temporal phrase, 'the time when God rules'.

32 ***Truly, I say to you, this generation will not pass away till all has taken place.*** 33 ***Heaven and earth will pass away, but my words will not pass away.***

Exegesis: *amēn legō humin* 'truly I say to you', cp. on 3 : 8 and 4 : 24.

ou mē parelthē hē genea hautē heōs an panta genētai 'this generation shall not pass away till all things have happened', implying that the present generation will live to see all things happen, cp. *TH-Mk* on 13 : 30. For the strong negation *ou mē* cp. on 1 : 15. *panta* refers to all that has been announced in the preceding verses.

(V. 33) *ho ouranos kai hē gē pareleusontai* 'heaven and earth shall pass away', cp. on 16 : 17, and *TH-Mk* 13 : 31.

hoi de logoi mou ou mē pareleusontai 'but my words shall not pass away'. *hoi logoi mou* refers to Jesus' words in vv. 6-28. *parerchomai* means here 'to lose force', 'to become invalid', cp. A-G s.v. 1 b α.

Translation: For *truly, I say to you* see on 4 : 24; for *this generation*, or, 'people of (or, living in) this generation' see on 7 : 31.

Pass away. A term that fits both here and in the two occurrences in v. 33 is stylistically preferable, of course, and apparently can often be found; if not, one will have to differentiate according to meaning, e.g. 'die'—'come-to-an-end' (twice) (Kituba), 'be-lost'—'not be-present' (twice) (Kapauku), 'die—end—become invalid', and cp. 'their (life)time comes to an end... Heaven shall end, earth shall end, but my word shall remain unchanged' (Tzeltal). See also on 16 : 17.

Not...till..., if rendered literally, may imply a condition. In such a case one can better use, 'not...before...' (Balinese), or, invert the clause and shift to a positive wording, cp. e.g. "all these things will take place before the people now living have all died" (TEV).

(V. 33) *Heaven and earth*, cp. on 10 : 21.

For the two verses cp. also *TH-Mk* on 13 : 30f.

34 ***"But take heed to yourselves lest your hearts be weighed down with dissipation and drunkenness and cares of this life, and that day come upon you suddenly like a snare;***

Exegesis: *prosechete de heautois* 'be on your guard', cp. on 12 : 1, here followed by *mēpote* and subjunctive to indicate that against which one has to be on one's guard.

mēpote barēthōsin humōn hai kardiai 'lest your hearts be weighed down'. For *mēpote* cp. on 4 : 11. For *bareō* cp. on 9 : 32; here it is used in the sense of being no longer sensitive to what is happening, cp. A-G s.v. The meaning *kardia* has here is 'mind'.

en kraipalē kai methē kai merimnais biōtikais 'by dissipation and drunkenness and anxieties of this life'. For *merimna* cp. on 8 : 14.

kraipalē (††) 'intoxication', 'dissipation', 'carousing'.

methē (†) 'drunkenness'.

biōtikos (†) 'belonging to daily life'.

kai epistē eph' humas aiphnidios hē hēmera ekeinē 'and (lest) that day come upon you suddenly', still dependent upon *mēpote*. The clause indicates what may be the consequences of the attitude described in the preceding clause. For *ephistamai epi* with accusative cp. on 2 : 9; here its meaning is almost 'to set upon', 'to catch', cp. A-G s.v. 1 b. *hē hēmera ekeinē* is the day of the coming of the Son of man, cp. 17 : 30f.

aiphnidios (†) 'sudden'. Here it goes with the predicate and means, 'as a sudden one', hence to be rendered emphatically.

Translation: *Take heed to yourselves lest*..., or, 'take care that...not...', or in two sentences, 'be on your guard; do not let...', and cp. on v. 8.

Lest your hearts be weighed down with dissipation and drunkenness and cares of this life, or, taking the nouns as subjects, 'lest dissipation, etc. weigh down your hearts' (cp. Sranan). A further shift to verbal clauses may lead to, 'that you are not dissipated, etc.; if you do that (or, if you are so), your hearts will be weighed down'. The phrase *your hearts* (are) *weighed down* contrasts with "look up and raise your heads" in v. 28: so occupied that they are not on the look-out for the coming of the Son of man; hence, 'your hearts...closed for anything else', "your minds...dulled" (NEB, BFBS), "yourselves...occupied" (TEV), 'your hearts die' (Lokele), 'your hearts...made unfeeling' (Shona 1966); or with a syntactic shift, 'making-fiesta...has gone-to-your-hearts' (Tzeltal, using an idiom for being engrossed in something, usually with unfavourable connotation). Some renderings used for *dissipation,* i.e. intemperate, or loose living (cp. on 15 : 13), are, 'much-eating' (Shona 1963, using an intensive form of the verb), 'feasting' (Balinese, similarly Tzeltal, see above), 'fullness of bellies' (Zarma, using an idiom for satisfying all kinds of physical desires). For *drunkenness* see *N.T.Wb.*/31; cp. also on 12 : 45. *Cares of this life,* i.e. excessive care for the daily necessities of life; hence, 'worries/anxiety for your livelihood', 'much-thinking (intensive verbal form) about what is of this life' (Shona 1966), 'worrying/fretting over what you have to live on'. Cp. also on 8 : 14 and 12 : 22.

That day, or less generically, 'that awful day'; or quite explicitly, 'the day the Son of man comes'.

Come upon you suddenly, or, "takes you by surprise" (Goodspeed). In the receptor language a 'day' may not 'come', however, but 'break', 'dawn', etc., or a personal subject may be required, e.g. 'you shall see the day dawn'. *Suddenly,* or, 'quite unexpectedly', 'when you do not expect it at all'.

Like a snare, see v. 35.

35 ***for it will come upon all who dwell upon the face of the whole earth.***

Exegesis: *hōs pagis* 'like a trap', goes with the preceding clause in Nestle; this is followed in the majority of modern translations, cp. e.g. RSV, BFBS, NEB. The punctuation and reading of *GNT* are followed by AV and TEV.

hōs pagis gar epeleusetai 'for like a trap it will come'. Subject is *hē hēmera ekeinē. eperchomai* followed by *epi* (cp. on 1 : 35) is equivalent to *eperchomai* with dative (cp. on v. 26).

pagis (†) 'trap', 'snare', here figuratively for a sudden and unexpected danger.

epi pantas tous kathēmenous epi prosōpon pasēs tēs gēs lit. 'upon all who are sitting on the (sur)face of the whole earth', i.e. 'all who are living on the whole earth', cp. A-G s.v. *kathēmai* 1 b, and s.v. *prosōpon* 1 e. *epi prosōpon* meaning 'upon' is a Hebraism.

Translation: The reading of *GNT* will result in a rendering like, 'for like a snare it will come upon all...', or, if one has to be quite explicit, e.g. 'just as a snare seizes a bird/animal, so will the day come upon all...'. For *snare* one may have to use, 'noose', 'trap', or 'net' (Bamiléké) for catching birds or wild animals.

The rendering of *come upon* may be coloured by the metaphor, e.g. 'close upon', 'catch', 'fall upon'.

All who dwell upon the face of the whole earth, or, "all men, wherever they are, the whole world over" (NEB); in Balinese the equivalent idiom is, 'all men under-the-vault-of the sky'.

36 ***But watch at all times, praying that you may have strength to escape all these things that will take place, and to stand before the Son of man."***

Exegesis: *agrupneite de* 'be alert, then', taking up the command of v. 34.

agrupneō (†) 'keep awake', 'be alert', 'be vigilant'.

en panti kairō deomenoi 'praying at all times'. *en panti kairō* may go with *agrupneite*, or, with *deomenoi*, preferably the latter.

hina katischusēte ekphugein tauta panta ta mellonta ginesthai 'that you may have the strength to escape all these things that are about to happen', the content of *deomenoi*. *tauta panta* etc. refers to the events announced in vv. 6-28. For *mellonta* cp. on v. 7.

katischuō (also 23 : 23 but in a different meaning) 'to be strong'; with infinitive, 'to have the strength', or in a somewhat weaker sense, 'to be able', preferably the former.

ekpheugō (†) 'to escape', here, 'to pass safely through'.

stathēnai emprosthen tou huiou tou anthrōpou 'to stand before the Son of man', dependent upon *katischusēte*. *stathēnai* is best understood as ingressive aorist, viz. 'to take one's stand'. The picture is probably that of appearing before a judge. For *ho huios tou anthrōpou* cp. on 5 : 24.

Translation: *Watch*, or, 'be watchful', 'be on the look-out (for danger)'.

At all times, here in the sense of 'again and again'.

Praying, often better rendered as a second imperative.

Have strength to escape, or, "be strong enough to come safely through" (Phillips), 'have strength to suffer/endure safely'.

To stand before, or, 'appear before', 'come to be tried by'.

37 ***And every day he was teaching in the temple, but at night he went out and lodged on the mount called Olivet.***

Exegesis: *ēn de tas hēmeras en tō hierō didaskōn* 'during the days he taught in the temple'. The periphrastic imperfect *ēn...didaskōn* expresses duration. *tas hēmeras* is accusative of extent. For *to hieron* cp. on 2 : 27.

tas de nuktas 'but during the nights', parallel to *tas hēmeras* and going with *ēulizeto* (see below).

exerchomenos ēulizeto lit. 'going out he spent the night', i.e. 'he went out and spent the night'. *exerchomenos* refers to leaving Jerusalem, not only the temple.

aulizomai (†) 'to spend the night', 'to lodge during the night'.

eis to oros to kaloumenon Elaiōn 'on the mountain called (Mount) of Olives', cp. on 19 : 29. *eis* is used for *en*, cp. A-G s.v. *eis* 9.

Translation: *At night*, or, 'every night'; for the noun cp. also *N.T.Wb.*/57.

He went out and lodged, or, 'he left (the city) and stayed', 'he stayed/lodged outside (the city)'. The reference is to habitual action, habitual, that is to say, during the period in view.

Mount called Olivet, cp. on 19 : 29.

38 ***And early in the morning all the people came to him in the temple to hear him.***

Exegesis: *pas ho laos* 'all the people', cp. on 3 : 21.

ōrthrizen pros auton lit. 'rose early toward him', i.e. 'rose early and came to him', hence, 'came to him early in the morning'. *ōrthrizen* (††) is habitual imperfect.

en tō hierō akouein autou 'to listen to him in the temple'. *en tō hierō* may go with *ōrthrizen*, or with *akouein*, preferably the latter.

Translation: *Early in the morning*, or, 'at dawn'; South Toradja says, 'when-it-was-no-longer night'.

All the people, here referring to the many people who formed his usual audience in this week.

CHAPTER TWENTY-TWO

1 ***Now the feast of Unleavened Bread drew near, which is called the Passover.***

Exegesis: *ēggizen...hē heortē tōn azumōn* 'the feast of the unleavened bread was drawing near', durative imperfect. For *ta azuma* see below.

hē legomenē pascha 'which is called Passover'. For *pascha* and *ta azuma* cp. on 2 : 41; *TH-Mk* on 14 : 1; and A-G s.v. *pascha,* and *N.T.Wb.*, 58/ FEASTS.

Translation: *Feast of Unleavened Bread,* see *TH-Mk* on 14 : 1; Sranan has 'feast of the matzos', making use of the Yiddish term for 'pieces of unleavened bread'. For *unleavened* cp. also on "leaven" in 12 : 1; for *bread* cp. references on 4 : 3.

Drew near, or, 'was to happen soon'.

Passover, see on 2 : 41, and references.

2 ***And the chief priests and the scribes were seeking how to put him to death; for they feared the people.***

Exegesis: *kai ezētoun...to pōs anelōsin auton* 'and (they) investigated as to how they might do away with him'. For *zēteō* cp. A-G s.v. 1 c. Here it is followed by an indirect question denoting the purpose of the investigation (*pōs anelōsin auton*). This indirect question has been made into a substantive by prefixing the article *to* (cp. on 1 : 62).

anaireō (also 23 : 32) 'to do away with', 'to get rid of', 'to destroy', generally implying the use of violence.

hoi archiereis 'the chief priests', cp. on 9 : 22.

hoi grammateis 'the experts of the law', cp. on 5 : 21.

ephobounto gar ton laon 'for they were afraid of the people', implying that they looked for a way to do away with Jesus without attracting the attention of the people (cp. *ater ochlou* in v. 6). For *laos* cp. A-G s.v. 1 c α.

Translation: For *chief priests* see on "high-priesthood" in 3 : 2.

Were seeking how, or, 'were trying to find some way to', and cp. on 5 : 18.

To put him to death, or, since the priests and scribes are probably not to be the direct agents, 'to have him put to death', 'to cause people to kill him'.

For *the people* see on 7 : 29.

3 ***Then Satan entered into Judas called Iscariot, who was of the number of the twelve;***

Exegesis: *eisēlthen de Satanas eis Ioudan* 'then Satan entered into Judas', i.e. 'took possession of J.', elsewhere in the sense of demon possession (cp. on 8 : 30), but here in a somewhat weaker sense, since Judas does not henceforth appear as a demoniac who is not acting of his own will (cp. Plummer). For *Satanas* cp. *N.T.Wb.*, 43/DEVIL.

ton kaloumenon Iskariōtēn 'called Iscariot', cp. on 6 : 16.

onta ek tou arithmou tōn dōdeka 'belonging to the number of the twelve'. For *onta ek* cp. A-G s.v. *ek* 4 a γ. *tou arithmou* (†) may be taken as semantically redundant (cp. A-G s.v. 1), or as meaning 'group', preferably the former. For *hoi dōdeka* cp. on 8 : 1.

Translation: *Satan entered into Judas.* A term for demon possession (cp. on "had...demon" in 4 : 33) is often also acceptable in this context, but if one has the choice between a technical term and a less specific one, the latter is to be preferred, cp. e.g. 'come upon', as against 'jump upon' in 8 : 30 (Sranan). Elsewhere a term referring to an emotional seizure or a bad influence is used, e.g. in Shona 1966, where the verb 'to enter' can have this figurative meaning. In Tzeltal the rendering is built on an idiomatic phrase, 'he has the devil in his heart', which is used both for demon possession and for badness. For *Satan* see on 10 : 18.

Called Iscariot, or, since the reference is not to Judas' proper name but to an additional name, "surnamed I." (Rieu, similarly Jerusalem, South Toradja), 'named also I.' (Balinese).

Who was of the number of the twelve, preferably, "one of the Twelve" (NEB), cp. on 8 : 1.

4 ***he went away and conferred with the chief priests and captains how he might betray him to them.***

Exegesis: *apelthōn* lit. 'after going off', i.e. after leaving Jesus and his fellow-disciples.

sunelalēsen tois archiereusin kai stratēgois 'he discussed with the chief priests and the captains'.

stratēgos (also v. 52) 'captain', 'officer', here referring to the captain of the temple police, cp. *stratēgous tou hierou* in v. 52.

to pōs autois paradō auton '(the question) as to how he might hand him over to them', same construction as in v. 2, see there. For *paradidōmi* cp. on 9 : 44 and A-G s.v. 1 b.

Translation: *Conferred with,* cp. on "said to one another" in 4 : 36.

Captains. It is usually preferable to employ the fuller designation of v. 52, which see.

For *betray* see on "traitor" in 6 : 16; but a less pejorative term like 'deliver up', 'hand over' (see on 20 : 20) is preferable.

5 ***And they were glad, and engaged to give him money.***

Exegesis: *echarēsan* 'they were delighted'. Subject is the chief priests and the captains.

sunethento autō argurion dounai 'they agreed with him to pay (him) money'.

suntithemai (†) 'to agree', 'to covenant', 'to promise'.

Translation: *They were glad*, or, "greatly pleased" (NEB), or, 'they rejoiced' (for which see on 1 : 14).

They...engaged to give him money, preferably, 'they came to an agreement with him to give him money'. Judas' part of the agreement has been indicated in v. 4; the part of the chief priests and their associates is indicated by this last clause of v. 5; hence one may have to render it, 'they came to an agreement with him, saying (or, promising) that they would give him money, or, pay him for it'. For *money* see on 9 : 3.

6 ***So he agreed, and sought an opportunity to betray him to them in the absence of the multitude.***

Exegesis: *exōmologēsen* 'he consented', 'he agreed'. *exomologeō* in 10 : 21 in a different meaning.

ezētei eukairian 'he sought an opportunity', 'he looked for a chance'. The imperfect tense of *ezētei* is durative.

eukairia (†) 'favourable opportunity'.

tou paradounai auton...autois 'to hand him over to them', articular infinitive in the genitive, dependent upon *eukairian* (cp. Bl-D, § 400.1).

ater ochlou lit. 'without a crowd', i.e. 'without a crowd being present', or 'without tumult', preferably the former.

ater (also v. 35) 'apart from', 'without'.

Translation: *He agreed*, preferably, 'he consented', 'he accepted their proposal' (Willibrord), 'he said it was all right'.

In the absence of the multitude, or, 'without the crowd knowing about it' (cp. TEV), 'when the crowd would not be present, or, aware of it'.

7 ***Then came the day of Unleavened Bread, on which the passover lamb had to be sacrificed.***

Exegesis: *ēlthen...hē hēmera tōn azumōn* 'the day of the (feast of the) unleavened bread arrived'. *ēlthen* contrasts with *ēggizen* 'was drawing near' in v. 1. For *ta azuma* cp. references on v. 1.

[*en*] *hē edei thuesthai to pascha* 'on which the Passover lamb had to be slaughtered'. For *to pascha* in this meaning cp. A-G s.v. 2 and *TH-Mk* on 14 : 12. For *thuō* cp. on 15 : 23. *edei* denotes religious compulsion.

Translation: For most of this verse cp. *TH-Mk* on 14 : 12.

On which, or starting a new sentence, 'this is (the day) when'.

Lamb, see on 10 : 3.

Sacrificed. Though the slaughtering of the passover lambs took place in the temple it was not a sacrifice to God. Accordingly a verb for (ritual) slaughtering is best used, or simply, 'to kill'.

8 *So Jesus sent Peter and John, saying, "Go and prepare the passover for us, that we may eat it."* 9 *They said to him, "Where will you have us prepare it?"*

Exegesis: *apesteilen* 'he sent off', 'he despatched', implying the idea of a commission. Subject is Jesus.

eipōn 'saying', i.e. 'instructing', 'ordering'.

hetoimasate hēmin to pascha hina phagōmen lit. 'prepare for us the passover meal that we may eat (it)'. *hina phagōmen* describes the potential result of *hetoimasate* in the form of a final clause. For the meaning of *to pascha* 'passover meal', cp. A-G s.v. 3 and *TH-Mk* on 14 : 12.

(V. 9) *pou theleis hetoimasōmen* 'where do you want us to prepare (it) ?'. For the construction cp. on 18 : 41. The emphasis is on *pou*.

Translation: *Prepare the passover for us, that we may eat it*, or, "get our Passover supper ready for us to eat" (TEV), or simply, 'prepare the passover meal for us, or, our passover meal' (cp. NEB).

(V. 9) *Where will you have us prepare it?*, or, 'where do you want (or, would you like) us to prepare it ?', or in a more expanded form, 'what is your wish as to (the place) where we must prepare it ?'; or in two clauses, 'where must we prepare it ? What do you wish, or, do you command (us) ?'.

10 *He said to them, "Behold, when you have entered the city, a man carrying a jar of water will meet you; follow him into the house which he enters,*

Exegesis: *idou* lit. 'behold' (cp. on 1 : 20), here calling their attention to what follows, hence 'listen'.

eiselthontōn humōn eis tēn polin sunantēsei humin anthrōpos 'when you have entered the city a man will meet you'. *sunantēsei* does not imply that the man would come with the purpose of meeting them and the intention of the Greek text is better brought out by rendering 'you will meet' or 'you will find'. *sunantaō* also 9 : 37.

keramion hudatos bastazōn 'carrying a jug/jar of water', i.e. filled with water. *keramion* (†).

akolouthēsate autō eis tēn oikian eis hēn eisporeuetai 'go after him into the house into which he goes', or, 'which he enters'.

Translation: If the manner of *carrying* has to be specified, as is often the case, one should conform to what is normal in the receptor culture, e.g. 'carry-on-the-shoulder' (East Toradja), 'carry-on-the-head' (Timorese), 'carry-on-the-back' (Tzeltal). Kapauku, not specifying how the water was carried, has, 'a person who has gone to fetch water'.

Jar. The Bamiléké rendering refers to a gourd serving as water-vessel, elsewhere this may be a bamboo tube. Some languages use an instrumental noun derived from 'to fetch-water' (East Toradja, Toba Batak), or simply say, 'place-of water' (Trukese).

Meet. The non-purposive meaning the verb has here is in some languages rendered by a reciprocal expression, e.g. 'will come-to-each-other you and a man...' (East Toradja).

Follow him into the house which he enters, or, 'go along with him and enter the house which he enters'.

11 ***and tell the householder, 'The Teacher says to you, Where is the guest room, where I am to eat the passover with my disciples?'***

Exegesis: *ereite tō oikodespotē tēs oikias* 'you must say to the master of the house'. *ereite* is future with the force of an imperative. *oikodespotēs* itself means 'master of the house' (cp. 12 : 39), and the addition of the genitive *tēs oikias* has deictic function.

legei soi ho didaskalos 'the teacher says to you', i.e. 'sends this message to you', or 'asks you'.

pou estin to kataluma 'where is the room ?'. For *kataluma* cp. on 2 : 7 and *TH-Mk* on 14 : 14.

hopou to pascha...phagō 'where I may eat the passover meal'. The subjunctive *phagō* has final implication.

Translation: The verse contains quotation on three levels. On level (1) Jesus speaks to the two disciples about the householder; on levels (2) and (3) the actual speaker, of course, is Jesus also, but on (2) the presumed speakers are the two disciples, who speak to the householder about Jesus, whereas on (3) the presumed speaker is Jesus, but now speaking by the mouth of his disciples. In some cases it is preferable to reword the sentence in such a way that the disciples are the presumed speakers both on level (2) and on level (3), e.g. 'tell the householder, "The Teacher orders us to ask you where the room is in which he will/may eat...with his disciples"', or that Jesus is the actual speaker on all three levels, '...that I, whom people call the(ir) Teacher, ask him, "Where...in which I will/may eat... with my disciples"'; cp. also, "tell the owner...that the Master wishes to know which is the room where he...can eat...with his disciples" (Rieu). For a comparable case (with two levels) and for problems of honorifics cp. on "The Lord has need of it" in 19 : 31 and references.

The householder, or, 'the master/owner of that house', 'the head of the household there'.

The Teacher may have to become 'our teacher', cp. on "the Lord" in 19 : 31.

Guest room, or simply, 'room', 'place'; which may lead to further simplification of the clause, e.g. 'where is it that I am to eat', 'where am I to eat'.

I am to eat...with my disciples, or, as a compound subject, 'I and my disciples are to eat'. Requirements of linguistic etiquette may make it preferable, then, to reverse the word order, cp. "my disciples and I will eat" (TEV).

12 ***And he will show you a large upper room furnished; there make ready."***

Exegesis: *anagaion mega estrōmenon* (†) 'a large furnished room upstairs', cp. *TH-Mk* on 14 : 15.

Translation: *Make ready*, or, 'make the/our (inclus.) meal ready'.
For the rest of the verse see *TH-Mk, l.c.*

13 ***And they went, and found it as he had told them; and they prepared the passover.***

Exegesis: *heuron kathōs eirēkei autois* 'they found (it) as he had told them'. The object of *heuron* is not stated but is here to be understood as referring to the situation in general.

Translation: *Found it as he had told them* repeats part of 19 : 32.

14 ***And when the hour came, he sat at table, and the apostles with him.***

Exegesis: *hote egeneto hē hōra* 'when the hour came'. *hē hōra* probably refers to the traditional hour of beginning the passover meal.
anepesen 'he sat down', 'he took his place at the table', cp. on 11 : 37.
hoi apostoloi sun autō 'the apostles (sat down) with him', with *anepeson* understood. For *apostolos* cp. on 6 : 13.

Translation: *When the hour came*, or, 'when it was time to eat (it/the passover meal)'.
Sat at table, i.e. 'sat down to eat', cp. on 5 : 29. The aspect is ingressive.
And the apostles with him, or, 'sat down with him'; or, in apposition to the subject, 'he..., together with the apostles'. *Apostles* (see on 6 : 13) is rather exceptional in this context, but to render it by the more usual 'disciples', as some versions do, is not advisable.

15 ***And he said to them, "I have earnestly desired to eat this passover with you before I suffer;***

Exegesis: *epithumia epethumēsa* lit. 'with desire I desired', hebraistic phrase in which the dative *epithumia* (†) serves to strengthen the meaning of the main verb *epethumēsa*, cp. Bl-D, § 198.6.
touto to pascha phagein 'to eat this passover meal', cp. on v. 8.
pro tou me pathein 'before my suffering', 'before I suffer', articular accusative and infinitive in a temporal construction. The infinitive *pathein* is used in the same unspecified way as in 9 : 22, but it is implied that this suffering will end in death (cp. NEB).

Translation: *I have earnestly desired*, or, "I have wanted so much"

(TEV), 'with the desire of my heart I wanted' (Bahasa Indonesia RC).
To eat... with you, or, 'that I should eat... with you'. In some languages (e.g. Huixtec) 'I... with you' is better rendered by inclusive 'we'.
Suffer, cp. on 9 : 22.

16 ***for I tell you I shall not eat it until it is fulfilled in the kingdom of God."***

Exegesis: *legō gar humin* 'for I tell you', cp. on 3 : 8.
ou mē phagō auto 'I shall not eat it', strongly negative statement, cp. on 1 : 15. Here it refers not to the present situation but to the future.
heōs hotou plērōthē en tē basileia tou theou 'until (the time) when it is fulfilled in the kingdom of God'. The subject of *plērōthē* is probably *to pascha* (see commentaries) and this is here best understood in the wider sense of the feast of passover. The underlying idea appears to be that the passover feast and the redemption to which it refers are still imperfect and that they will become perfect *en tē basileia tou theou*, i.e. when the kingdom of God has come.

Translation: *Until*, cp. on 1 : 20.
It is fulfilled. Some useful descriptive or explanatory renderings are, "it is given its real meaning" (TEV), "the day of the perfect Passover" (Rieu), 'it has reached its mark', i.e., it has finished its task (Sranan), 'the future-day of its-coming-true' (Javanese), 'its-being-realized' (Sundanese). For the verb cp. also on 4 : 21.
I shall not eat it. This refers to future passovers not to the present one, which Jesus is eating. To make this clear one may have to say, 'I shall not eat it again', 'after this one I shall not eat any more passovers'.
In the kingdom of God, or, 'when the time comes that God rules'.

17 ***And he took a cup, and when he had given thanks he said, "Take this, and divide it among yourselves;***

Exegesis: *dexamenos potērion eucharistēsas eipen* 'when he had received a cup he gave thanks and said'. The lack of a connective between the two participles *dexamenos* and *eucharistēsas* shows that the latter is to be taken closely with the main verb *eipen*. *dexamenos* implies that Jesus was handed a cup. For *eucharisteō* cp. on 17 : 16 and *TH-Mk* on 14 : 23.
labete touto 'take this', in the plural, implying that the cup will be taken by each in turn.
diamerisate eis heautous 'distribute it among yourselves', referring to the content of the cup, and implying that each was to drink from the cup in turn. For *diamerizō* cp. on 11 : 17.

Translation: *He took a cup*, preferably, 'he received/accepted a cup', 'after having-been-offered a cup' (Javanese), 'after they had handed him a cup'. For *cup* one may use local equivalents such as, 'half coconut shell for-drinking' (East Toradja), 'hollowed-out gourd' (Shona 1966); and cp. on 11 : 39.

When he had given thanks, viz. to God, which may have to be made explicit. For the verb cp. on 2 : 38.

Divide (or, share) *it among yourselves*, or, 'drink-it-together' (Shona 1966), 'pass-it-round in-order-that all (of-you) partake (of it)' (Balinese), 'pass-this-from-one-to-another for you all to drink' (Tzeltal), 'drink it and give-to-each-other' (Zarma); cp. also *N.T.Wb.*/67, SHARE (3). The rendering chosen should not give the impression that Jesus himself did not drink from the cup.

18 ***for I tell you that from now on I shall not drink of the fruit of the vine until the kingdom of God comes."***

Exegesis: *legō gar humin* 'for I tell you', cp. on 3 : 8.

apo tou nun 'from now on', i.e. after this time.

apo tou genēmatos tēs ampelou 'from the fruit of the vine', i.e. from the wine that is in the cup.

genēma (†) 'product', 'fruit'.

heōs hou hē basileia tou theou elthē 'till the kingdom of God has come', cp. on 17 : 20.

Translation: *From now on...not...until*, or, "not...again until" (Goodspeed); or in two clauses, 'I will not drink...; I will do it again only when' (cp. Kekchi).

The fruit of the vine, or, 'the product of the vine', 'what the vine produces', or simply, 'wine' (for which cp. on 1 : 15, and references). What is drunk in church at the celebration of the Lord's supper may influence the translator's choice. For that reason he may, for instance, prefer a borrowed foreign term for 'wine' here to the cultural equivalent he uses in other texts. For *vine* see in the note on "vineyard" in 20 : 9.

19 ***And he took bread, and when he had given thanks he broke it and gave it to them, saying, "This is my body [which is given for you. Do this in remembrance of me].***

Exegesis: *labōn arton eucharistēsas eklasen* 'when he had taken a loaf of bread he gave thanks and broke it', cp. on v. 17 where the semantic structure is the same. *klaō* also 24 : 30.

edōken autois 'he gave it to them', i.e. he gave each a piece.

touto estin to sōma mou 'this is my body', cp. *TH-Mk* on 14 : 22.

to huper humōn didomenon 'that is being given for you'. For the historical and textcritical problems of this phrase and the rest of v. 19 and v. 20 cp. commentaries. *huper humōn* 'in your behalf', not, 'in your place' or, 'as a substitute for you'. *didomenon* is best understood in a sacrificial sense, viz. 'being offered up as a sacrifice'. The present tense of *didomenon* expresses that Jesus' being offered up is viewed as happening already. The agent may be Jesus himself, or God, preferably the former.

touto poieite eis tēn emēn anamnēsin 'do this (from now on) in remembrance of me'. *touto* refers to the breaking and the eating of the bread. *eis tēn emēn anamnēsin* (†) is best rendered in such a way that it implies no allusions to a memorial of a dead man.

Translation: *Bread*, or, 'a loaf (of bread)', cp. on 4 : 3.

He broke it, or, 'broke-it-to-pieces', 'divided-it-in-pieces' (Bahasa Indonesia, South Toradja, Sundanese, using reduplicated form of 'to break', 'to pinch-off' and 'to divide', respectively).

This is my body. The verb indicates an equation between two objects; this is often expressed by simple juxtaposition of the two nouns. Such constructions can usually cover some of several kinds of relationship, such as identity, comparison, representation, association, which is all right here, since the rendering should not be unduly interpretative. On the other hand the translator may have to avoid such an equational construction, for instance because it would exclusively indicate identification of two objects; hence e.g. 'this represents (lit. is a sign of) my body' (Tzeltal, chosen to avoid the suggestion of identification similar to indigenous ideas of magic). For *body* (not 'corpse'!) see *N.T.Wb.*/16.

In remembrance of me, or, 'in order to remember me, or, to keep me in mind'; and see on 1 : 54.

*[20 **And likewise the cup after supper, saying, "This cup which is poured out for you is the new covenant in my blood.**]*

Exegesis: *kai to potērion hōsautōs* 'and in the same way the cup'. *hōsautōs* refers to acts with reference to the cup comparable to what v. 19 says about the bread, viz. taking, blessing and giving it to the disciples. The article *to* is best understood as referring to the cup mentioned in v. 17.

meta to deipnēsai lit. 'after the eating of the meal/supper', hence, 'after the supper', implying the elapse of some time between v. 19 and v. 20. For *deipneō* cp. on 17 : 8 and 14 : 12.

touto to potērion hē kainē diathēkē en tō haimati mou 'this cup (is) the new covenant in my blood'. For translational purposes the following considerations are relevant: (1) *touto to potērion* refers to that which the cup contains, viz. wine. (2) The relationship between the covenant and the blood, indicated by the preposition *en*, is that the covenant is inaugurated by the sprinkling of sacrificial blood (cp. *IDB* IV, 151). The new covenant is inaugurated by the shedding of Jesus' blood. (3) There is the same relationship between the wine and the blood of Jesus as there is between the bread and his body. For *diathēkē* cp. on 1 : 72; for *kainos* cp. A-G s.v. 3 b.

to huper humōn ekchunnomenon 'which is being shed for you'. Grammatically the phrase goes with *potērion* but semantically it refers to the blood. As 11 : 50 shows *ekchunnō* is not a sacrificial term but has the connotation of murder. For the present tense cp. on v. 19, *didomenon*.

Translation: *Likewise*, or, 'he did the same with'.

After supper, or, 'when they had finished eating, or, finished the meal/supper'. Cp. also *N.T.Wb.*/53, MEAL. The phrase modifies the event as a whole, not 'the cup' only.

This cup which is poured out for you is the new covenant in my blood, preferably, "this cup is the new covenant in my blood, which is being shed for you" (see *Exegesis*). For *is* see on v. 19. — *New* contrasts here with 'old', 'former' and implies that the Mosaic covenant has become obsolete and should be replaced by the superior new one. *Covenant,* see on 1 : 72. *In* is instrumental here; hence 'through', 'by means of', 'made by' (Gbeapo), "sealed by/with" (NEB, TEV), 'put in force by' (Totonac), 'established/made-strong/confirmed by'; this may lead to further shifts, cp. e.g. 'this the cup that-establishes (lit. plants)...' (South Toradja). Actually it is not the object, the blood, but the process, the shedding of the blood, through which the new covenant is being established; therefore 'my blood which is being shed' may have to become, 'shedding my blood' (cp. Gbeapo), 'the fact that I shed my blood', 'the fact that I allow my blood to be shed, or, allow people to kill me (cp. on 11 : 50)'.

21 ***But behold the hand of him who betrays me is with me on the table.***

Exegesis: *plēn idou* 'yet see'. For *plēn* cp. on 6 : 24; for *idou* emphatic introduction of what follows cp. on 1 : 20.

hē cheir tou paradidontos me met' emou 'the hand of him who hands me over is with me', i.e. his hand receives bread and wine from my hand. The phrase denotes intimate fellowship. For *paradidōmi* cp. on 9 : 44 and A-G s.v. 1 b.

Translation: *The hand of him who...is with me on the table* is stylistically incongruous in that it first mentions the part of the whole ("hand of him" implying a reference to the person), next the whole itself, i.e. the person referred to by "me". It may be better idiom to mention the part twice, "the hand of the man who...is on the table with mine" (Rieu, and cp. NEB), or, '...is beside my hand on the table', or to mention the whole twice, "the one who...is here at the table with me" (TEV), 'the one who...is here eating with me' (Navajo, similarly Tzeltal). A combination of the two solutions may also be possible, cp. 'the one by whose hand I will be delivered up is with me at the table' (Willibrord).

22 ***For the Son of man goes as it has been determined; but woe to that man by whom he is betrayed!"***

Exegesis: *hoti ho huios men tou anthrōpou...poreuetai* 'for the Son of man goes (his way)'. Despite *hoti* the clause offers no explanation of v. 21. Rather it reaffirms the truth of the divine necessity of Jesus' suffering which might, perhaps, be doubted after the revelation that one of the twelve was to deliver up Jesus. *men* is not followed by the usual *de,* instead of which the subsequent clause is introduced by the stronger *plēn.* This lends to the first clause of the verse almost the force of a concessive protasis, e.g. 'though it remains true that the Son of man goes (his way)'.

kata to hōrismenon poreuetai '...goes (his way) in accordance with what has been determined', hence, 'goes his determined, or, appointed way', referring to the fact rather than to the manner of Jesus' death.

horizō (†) 'to determine', 'to appoint', 'to decree'. The agent is God.

plēn ouai tō anthrōpō ekeinō 'but, woe to that man'. For *plēn* and *ouai* cp. on 6 : 24.

di' hou paradidotai 'through whom he is handed over'. The present tense suggests that the handing over is already under way. For *dia* cp. A-G s.v. A III 2 a.

Translation: *Goes*, or, 'goes his way' can often have the sense of 'to pass away'; if not, one may have to say, 'goes to his death' (Tzeltal), "will die" (TEV).

As it has been determined, or, 'in accordance with the (or, God's) decree', 'as God put it beforehand concerning him' (Sranan); or, 'which is what God has decided beforehand'.

Woe, see on 6 : 24.

By whom he is betrayed, preferably, 'who is handing him over, or, delivering him up'.

23 ***And they began to question one another, which of them it was that would do this.***

Exegesis: *kai autoi ērxanto suzētein pros heautous* 'and they began to discuss among themselves'. *kai autoi* (not emphatic) indicates the change of subject. For *archomai* with infinitive cp. on 4 : 21. Here it refers implicitly to a reaction to the startling communication of Jesus in v. 21.

suzēteō (also 24 : 15) 'to discuss', 'to debate', cp. *TH-Mk* on 1 : 27.

to tis ara eiē ex autōn 'as to who of them might be...'. The indirect question is made into a substantive by prefixing the article *to* (cp. on 1 : 62), and this substantive is the object of *suzētein*. For *ara* cp. on 1 : 66. *ex autōn* stands for the partitive genitive.

ho touto mellōn prassein 'the one who was to do this'. *mellō* with infinitive is somewhat more definite than the simple future.

Translation: *They began to question one another*, cp. on "said to one another" in 4 : 36.

Would do this, or, 'planned/intended to do thus' (Bahasa Indonesia).

24 ***A dispute also arose among them, which of them was to be regarded as the greatest.***

Exegesis: *egeneto de kai philoneikia en autois* 'an argument also arose among them'. *de kai* marks the transition to a new event in the same situation.

philoneikia (††) in a concrete sense, 'dispute', 'argument', 'quarrel'.

to tis autōn dokei einai meizōn 'as to who of them was accounted the greatest'. The interrogative clause is substantivized by prefixing the article *to* in order to connect it with *philoneikia*. *dokei* is used here in the specific sense of being recognized, having the reputation, cp. A-G s.v. 2 b. *meizōn* means here, 'greater than the rest', cp. Plummer.

Translation: *A dispute...arose among them,* or, 'a quarrel/dissension broke out among them' (cp. NV; also East Toradja, using a reciprocal form of 'to be-at-fault'); and cp. on "an argument arose" in 9 : 46.

Which...was to be regarded as the greatest, or to avoid a passive construction, 'which...people would consider the greatest', 'who...would have the highest position'; cp. also, "who...should rank highest" (NEB). For *the greatest* see again on 9 : 46.

25 ***And he said to them, "The kings of the Gentiles exercise lordship over them; and those in authority over them are called benefactors.***

Exegesis: *hoi basileis tōn ethnōn kurieuousin autōn* 'the kings of the nations lord it over them'. *tōn ethnōn* may refer to the nations or peoples of the world in general, or to the Gentiles as contrasted with Israel, preferably the former, cp. A-G s.v. 1. The clause refers to what is considered a normal situation in the world, to which the situation of Jesus and his disciples will be contrasted in vv. 26f.

kurieuō (†) 'to be lord of', 'to exercise lordship over', 'to lord it over', with genitive.

hoi exousiazontes autōn euergetai kalountai 'those who exercise authority over them are called benefactors'.

exousiazō (†) 'to have power, or authority over', with genitive.

euergetēs (††) 'benefactor', here best understood as a title which kings and princes claim for themselves. Hence *kalountai* is best understood as middle, 'have themselves called', cp. Plummer.

Translation: *The kings of the Gentiles,* preferably, "the kings of the nations". To bring out better that the contrast is between what is customary among the nations and what should be the rule among the disciples (v. 26) one may give the prepositional phrase a more prominent position, cp. e.g. "in the world, kings..." (NEB).

Exercise lordship over them, or to bring out the pejorative meaning, "lord it over them", i.e. exercise overbearing authority over them, 'domineer/tyrannize over them', and see *TH-Mk* on 10 : 42. The pronoun is in some cases better specified, e.g. 'their (i.e. the kings') peoples/subjects'.

Those in authority over them, or, 'those who have power over them', 'their rulers'.

Are called benefactors, preferably, 'have themselves called (or, want people to call them) benefactors', "claim the title Benefactor" (Rieu). Some renderings of *benefactor* are, 'benevolent (lit. whitehearted) Lord' (East Toradja 1933), 'generous one' (Kapauku), 'doer of favours to others' (Marathi), 'one who causes good to happen' (Zarma, built on an exclamation used when in trouble, 'may God cause good to happen', i.e. cause it to come out well); or an equivalent complimentary title, e.g. 'protector'

(Bahasa Indonesia RC), "Friend of the People" (TEV). If such a title does not exist, or such a descriptive term cannot be easily coined, one may have to shift to, 'want people to speak well of them' (cp. Tzeltal), 'want their subjects to say about them, "He does good" (cp. Lokele), or, "He is benevolent/generous"'.

26 ***But not so with you; rather let the greatest among you become as the youngest, and the leader as one who serves.***

Exegesis: *humeis de ouch houtōs* 'but you (should) not (be) like this', hence, 'it should not be so with you'. With this clause may be understood an indicative (cp. BFBS), or an imperative, preferably the latter.

ho meizōn en humin ginesthō hōs ho neōteros 'the greatest among you must become like the youngest'. *ho meizōn* takes up *meizōn* in v. 24. *ginesthō* may be rendered 'be', or, 'become', preferably the latter. *ho neōteros* may be understood in terms of rank, or age, preferably the former. For the meaning of the comparative cp. on *meizōn* in v. 24.

ho hēgoumenos hōs ho diakonōn 'the one who leads (must be) like the one who serves'. *hēgoumenos* (†) is best understood as referring to leadership in the community of believers, cp. Hebr. 13 : 7, 17, 24. In the same way *diakonōn* refers to service in the community in general though in v. 27 the role of the servant is illustrated from table service.

Translation: *Rather*, or, "on the contrary" (NEB, Jerusalem); or as an separate exclamation, "far from it" (Rieu).

Greatest...youngest, both referring to position and honour. It may be preferable to use a pair of more directly opposite words, e.g. 'greatest—smallest', 'highest—lowest', 'most in-front—most at-the-end' (Balinese), or, if age and rank are closely associated, 'senior—junior'.

Let...become, or, "must become" (Phillips), "must take the...role" (Rieu), 'must start to behave as'.

Leader...one who serves, again a pair of terms that are not each other's exact opposite. *Leader*, or, 'the one who governs' (Jerusalem), 'the one who orders/commands' (Balinese). *One who serves* (here and in the second occurrence in v. 27 referring to service in general), cp. the verbs mentioned in the note on "servant" in 12 : 37, but one may also consider a rendering that is a more direct opposite of the word for "leader", e.g. 'one who follows/obeys' (Toba Batak, East Toradja 1933), 'one who is-subordinate' (Sundanese).

27 ***For which is the greater, one who sits at table, or one who serves? Is it not the one who sits at table? But I am among you as one who serves.***

Exegesis: *tis gar meizōn* 'for who is greater?' As shown by what follows the standard by which to answer this question is that of the normal situation in life, to which the situation of Jesus is contrasted.

ho anakeimenos ē ho diakonōn 'the one who reclines at table, or the one who serves (at table)?' For *anakeimai* (†) cp. on 5 : 25 (*katakeimai* with which it is synonymous).

ouchi 'is it not?', interrogative particle suggesting an answer in the affirmative.

egō de 'but I (who am your master)'.

en mesō humōn 'in your midst', 'among you'.

eimi hōs ho diakonōn 'I am like the one who serves', takes up *ho diakonōn* in the preceding clause but leads back to the general idea of service in v. 26.

Translation: The structure of the first sentence may have to be recast, e.g. 'when there is (or, when you compare) one who...and one who..., which of the two is greater (than the other), or, which of them is great, which is not great?'

Who serves (first occurrence), same term as used in vv. 26 and 27[b], but with the more restricted meaning it has also in 12 : 37[c], 'who waits upon (him) at the meal', 'who serves the meal, or, the food' (Shona 1966).

Is it not?, or in the affirmative, "surely" (NEB), "of course" (TEV).

28 ***"You are those who have continued with me in my trials;***

Exegesis: *humeis de este hoi diamemenēkotes met' emou en tois peirasmois mou* 'you are those who have stood by me in my trials'. *humeis* is emphatic but no other persons with whom the disciples are contrasted, are named. The periphrastic construction stresses the idea of permanence more strongly than the indicative of the perfect would have done. For *peirasmos* cp. on 4 : 13 and 8 : 13; here it is used in a passive sense.

diamenō (also 1 : 22) 'to remain', 'to stay with', 'to stand by', with *meta* and genitive.

Translation: *Continued with me in,* or, 'remained faithful/loyal (to me)' (cp. Willibrord), 'persevered together-with me' (Bahasa Indonesia); or negatively expressed, 'never left me' (East Toradja 1933). The phrase refers to holding out while having the same experience as Jesus had (*not* to helping him when he was tested).

In my trials. The noun here refers to a being put to the test by difficulties and suffering; hence, 'in my hardships' (Ponape), 'in my afflictions' (Bahasa Indonesia RC), 'in all that I have suffered', 'while I have been tried/afflicted'. Further shifts may lead to something like, 'you and I have experienced the same trials (or, we have suffered equally), and you have held out (or, stood by me)'.

29 ***as my Father appointed a kingdom for me, so do I appoint for you*** 30 ***that you may eat and drink at my table in my kingdom, and sit on thrones judging the twelve tribes of Israel.***

Exegesis: *kagō diatithemai humin...basileian* 'and I assign to you dominion'. *kagō* means here 'I on my part'. *basileian* is object of both *diatithemai* and *dietheto* and has in both cases the same general and abstract meaning, viz. 'dominion', 'royal power'.

diatithemai (†) 'to ordain', 'to decree', 'to assign'.

kathōs dietheto moi ho patēr mou 'just as my father assigned (dominion) to me'.

(V. 30) *hina esthēte kai pinēte epi tēs trapezēs mou* 'in order that you may eat and drink at my table', i.e. that you have fellowship with me at the Messianic banquet, cp. on 5 : 30. The clause indicates the intended result of the assigning of the royal power to the disciples: they will reign in fellowship with Christ in his kingdom.

en tē basileia mou 'in my kingdom', i.e. 'when my Messianic kingdom has come'.

kai kathēsesthe epi thronōn 'and you will sit on thrones', syntactically no longer dependent upon *hina* and describing, together with what follows, the situation in which the royal power will be exercised.

tas dōdeka phulas krinontes tou Israēl 'judging the twelve tribes of Israel', referring to the eschatological judgment. *phulē* also 2 : 36.

Translation: One may have to render v. 29 in two sentences, e.g. 'my Father appointed a kingdom for me; I on my part appoint (it) for you in the same way', or to keep to the clause order of the Greek, e.g. 'I appoint a kingdom for you in the same way as my Father (on his part) appointed it for me', 'I determine that you receive kingship, just as the Father granted it to me' (cp. Balinese, where an honorific term for God's act is required).

My Father, cp. on 2 : 49.

Appointed a kingdom for me, i.e. caused me to be king/ruler, or, to have royal power/rule/dominion, cp. "made me King" (Rieu), 'gave me to rule' (Chol), 'gave me the right (or, the position) to rule' (cp. TEV, Otomi).

I appoint for you will require similar adjustments, 'I cause you to be king', etc., or, 'the same (or, that also) I cause you to be', etc.

(V. 30) *That you may eat...*, or as a new sentence, '(so/then) you shall eat...'.

Eat and drink at my table, or, 'eat and drink at-the-same-table (or, from-the-same-dish) with me' (Bahasa Indonesia RC, Malay), and cp. on "eat (and drink) with" in 7 : 36.

Sit on thrones. For the noun see on 1 : 32. If a literal rendering is impossible or culturally irrelevant, one may say, 'to reign in splendour'.

Judging, cp. *N.T.Wb.*/48.

Twelve tribes of Israel, cp. on 2 : 36; in Huixtec one must say, 'twelve groups of our (inclus.) people, we who are descendants of (the patriarch) Israel'.

31 ***"Simon, Simon, behold, Satan demanded to have you, that he might sift you like wheat,***

Exegesis: *Simōn Simōn* 'Simon, Simon', emphatic repetition of Simon's original name, as contrasted with *Petre* in v. 34, the name given to Simon by Jesus as a name of honour, cp. 6 : 14. The absence of a clause, or phrase to indicate the transition is awkward.

idou 'look' (cp. on 1 : 20), strengthens the emphasis on what follows.

ho Satanas exētēsato humas 'Satan has claimed you'. For *ho Satanas* cp. *N.T.Wb.*, 43/DEVIL. *humas* (plural) refers to Simon and the other disciples (see also on v. 32).

exaiteomai (††) 'to ask for', 'to claim (with success)', 'to obtain by asking', cp. *N.T.Wb.*, 23/.

tou siniasai hōs ton siton 'in order to sift (you) like wheat', final articular infinitive in the genitive (Bl-D, § 400.5), with *humas* understood.

siniazō (††) 'to shake in a sieve', 'to sift', here in the figurative meaning of putting to the test, or, on trial.

Translation: *Satan*, see on 10 : 18.

Demanded to have you, preferably, "obtained permission" (Goodspeed), "has been given leave" (NEB). The translator should not hesitate to mention God as the one who gives the permission, if the linguistic structure of the receptor language requires it.

Sift you like wheat, or, 'sift you like people sift wheat', 'shake you many times as people do to wheat' (cp. Kekchi). *To sift*, i.e. 'to shake in a sieve' (Zürich), or, 'to winnow' (cp. on 3 : 17), 'to sort' (Tzeltal). For *wheat* see on 3 : 17. Rieu prefers a non-metaphorical rendering, "to put you all on trial"; Kituba has a rendering that combines non-metaphorical meaning with simile, 'to put-to-the-test you, as a woman sifts kernels of corn'; cp. also TEV.

32 ***but I have prayed for you that your faith may not fail; and when you have turned again, strengthen your brethren."***

Exegesis: *egō de* 'but I...', contrasting with *humas*.

edeēthēn peri sou 'I have prayed for you'. For *deomai* cp. on 5 : 12. *peri sou* lit. 'with regard to you', hence, 'for you'.

hina mē eklipē hē pistis sou 'that your faith may not fail'. For *ekleipō* cp. on 16 : 9.

kai su 'and you (on your part)', contrasting with *egō*. It should be noted that Simon is here singled out from the disciples addressed in *humas*, because he will receive a special commission with regard to the others.

pote epistrepsas 'when once you have turned back', scil. 'to me', after having been sifted by Satan. *pote* (†) refers to an undefined moment in the future. For *epistrephō* cp. on 1 : 16. Here it is intransitive, cp. A-G s.v. 1 b β.

stērison tous adelphous sou 'strengthen your brothers', i.e. your fellow-disciples. *stērizō* (cp. on 9 : 51) is used here in the figurative sense of strengthening somebody's faith, or, courage.

Translation: *I have prayed for you*. For the verb see on 1 : 10. The reference is probably to something that happened on the day of speaking; in a language like Foe, therefore, one would use the near past tense. To bring out that *you* is singular one may say, "for you, Simon" (Rieu, TEV).

That your faith may not fail, or, 'that you do not stop (or, that you persevere/persist in) believing (in me)'. *Fail* has also been rendered in this context by 'collapse' (Balinese), 'disappear' (East Toradja), 'be-extinguished' (Toba Batak).

Strengthen, or, 'make strong/firm', or marking the figurative meaning, 'make-strong the heart/mind of' (East Toradja, Toba Batak).

Brethren, see on "brother" in 6 : 41.

33 ***And he said to him, "Lord, I am ready to go with you to prison and to death."***

Exegesis: *kurie* 'lord', cp. on 1 : 6 sub (2[b]).

meta sou 'with you', emphatic by its position at the beginning of the clause but going with *poreuesthai*.

hetoimos eimi kai eis phulakēn kai eis thanaton poreuesthai 'I am ready to go even to prison and to death'. The phrase 'to go to death' is formed by analogy to the more common 'to go to prison', and is equivalent to 'to die'. For *phulakē* cp. on 2 : 8.

Translation: *I am ready to go with you.* To bring out that the emphasis is on the prepositional phrase it may be preferable to move it towards the beginning of the sentence, 'if only it is accompanying you, I am...' (Balinese), 'if it is a matter of going with you, I would go' (Shona 1966), 'with one heart I will accompany you' (Tzeltal); or to render it twice, cp. e.g. 'I am ready to go to prison with you and even to die with you' (Sranan). *I am ready* indicates here that Peter is willing to suffer what Jesus has to suffer, *not* that he has completed his preparations to meet all emergencies (as the terms used in some versions seem to suggest); the concept is expressed by such idioms as, 'my-heart is-willing' (Bahasa Indonesia), 'it will be my-inner-being' (East Toradja), 'I-cause-to-be-willing my soul' (South Toradja), 'with one heart' (Tzeltal).

To go...to prison and to death, or, 'to be imprisoned and put to death', 'to let people lock me up and kill me'. Grammatically the reference is to Peter's going, but Jesus' going is implied. In Bamiléké, therefore, one has to use a dual 'we', including the speaker and the hearer, and the Tzeltal rendering quoted above continues in the second person, 'even though you are taken prisoner, even though you are taken to be killed'. For *prison* see *N.T.Wb.*/19f, CAPTURE.

34 ***He said, "I tell you, Peter, the cock will not crow this day, until you three times deny that you know me."***

Exegesis: *legō soi, Petre* 'I tell you, Peter', cp. on 3 : 8. Note the change from 'Simon' (v. 31) to 'Peter', which possibly serves to bring out the contrast between the solemn statement of v. 33 and the announced denial.

ou phōnēsei sēmeron alektōr 'the cock will not crow today'. Since the day goes from sunset to sunset, the clause means, 'before dawn', 'this night'. See also *TH-Mk* on 14 : 30. *ou...heōs* 'not...until', hence, 'before', with change of the syntactic pattern.

phōneō 'to produce a sound', here 'to crow'.

alektōr (also v. 60) 'cock', 'rooster'.

heōs tris me aparnēsē eidenai 'until you have three times denied that you know me'. *aparneomai* (cp. on 8 : 45) is used here with following infinitive.

Translation: *The cock,* cp. *TH-Mk* on 14 : 30.

Crow, often a specific, basically onomatopoeic term, cp. e.g. *kongkorongok* (Sundanese), *makakrujuk* (Balinese), *martatahuak* (Toba Batak), but elsewhere a more generic one, cp. 'sing' (Jerusalem), 'sound' (Greek, South Toradja), 'shout' (Sranan).

This day, according to Jewish reckoning, refers to the period of 24 hours that has just begun at sunset; the words must be rendered by the expression commonly used in the culture to refer in the evening to (a part of) the night that is beginning, e.g. '(in) this night' (Kituba, Toba Batak), "tonight" (NEB); in some cases 'tomorrow' may be the closest equivalent. Cp. also *TH-Mk, l.c.* on "this very night".

Not...until refers to sequence in time; it does not have conditional function (as suggested by some literal renderings, cp. *TBT,* 4.61, 1963). To make this clear one may have to shift the conjunction, e.g. 'before the cock crows (or, 'the cock will not yet have crowed', Tzeltal)...you will deny...', and/or to change the clause order, 'you will deny...before the cock crows...', a construction that will coincide with that of v. 61 and Mk. 14 : 30, 72.

Deny that you know me, or, 'say, "I do not know him"'. Tzeltal uses an idiomatic phrase, 'you will cover-me-up-in-your-heart'.

35 ***And he said to them, "When I sent you out with no purse or bag or sandals, did you lack anything?" They said, "Nothing."***

Exegesis: *kai eipen autois* 'and he said to them', marking the transition to a new subject.

hote apesteila humas 'when I sent you out', referring to one specific event in the past (as brought out by *hote* and by the aorist tense of *apesteila*), viz. that of 10 : 3ff.

ater ballantiou kai pēras kai hupodēmatōn 'without a purse and a knapsack and sandals', cp. on 10 : 4.

mē tinos husterēsate 'did you lack anything?', cp. on 15 : 14. *mē* in interrogative clauses does not presume an affirmative or negative answer.

outhenos (scil. *husterēsamen*) '(we lacked) nothing'.

Translation: *With no purse or bag or sandals,* or, 'not taking with you a purse or bag or sandals', or using different verbs, 'not having with you a purse, not carrying-on-the-back a knapsack, not wearing sandals'. For the nouns see on 10 : 4 and references.

Did you lack anything, or, 'were you ever short of anything', 'was there anything you wanted but could not get' (East Toradja 1933).

Nothing, or, filling out the expression, 'we lacked nothing'.

36 ***He said to them, "But now, let him who has a purse take it, and likewise a bag. And let him who has no sword sell his mantle and buy one.***

Exegesis: *eipen de autois, Alla nun* 'then he said to them, "But now . . ." '. The introductory clause serves to emphasize the contrast between then and now to which *alla nun* refers.

ho echōn ballantion aratō 'he who has a purse must take it along', cp. A-G s.v. *airō* 2.

homoiōs kai pēran 'in the same way also a knapsack', short for *homoiōs kai ho echōn pēran aratō* 'and in the same way he who has a knapsack must take it along'.

kai ho mē echōn 'and he who has not . . .' with either *ballantion* 'purse', i.e. 'money', or, *machairan* 'sword' understood. The latter is preferable.

pōlēsatō to himation autou kai agorasatō machairan 'must sell his cloak and buy a sword'. For *himation* cp. on 6 : 29.

Translation: *Let him who has . . . take,* or, 'if a man has . . . he must take', "if you have . . . take" (Rieu).

Sword may be described as, 'huge knife', 'large knife of war'.

Mantle, see on "cloak" in 6 : 29.

37 ***For I tell you that this scripture must be fulfilled in me, 'And he was reckoned with transgressors'; for what is written about me has its fulfilment."***

Exegesis: *legō gar humin* 'for I tell you' (cp. on 3 : 8), introduces the explanation of v. 36. The situation has changed and become more dangerous because people will deal with Jesus in the way implied in the subsequent scripture quotation.

touto to gegrammenon lit. 'this, which is written', hence 'this scripture saying'.

dei telesthēnai en emoi 'must be fulfilled in me', 'must find its fulfilment in me'. *dei* suggests a divine compulsion. For *teleō* cp. on 2 : 39. *en emoi* 'in me', i.e. 'in my fate', 'in what happens to me'.

to Kai meta anomōn elogisthē 'the (saying), and he was counted among the law-breakers'. The article *to* serves to introduce a direct quotation.

anomos (†) 'lawless', here referring to people who break the law of God, hence 'godless', 'wicked'.

logizomai (†) 'to consider', 'to reckon', here with *meta* and genitive, 'to count among'.

kai gar to peri emou telos echei 'for that which concerns me has an end'. *to peri emou* may mean 'that which concerns me' (cp. 24 : 19; Acts 1 : 3), or, with *gegrammenon* understood (cp. 24 : 44), 'that which is written about me', preferably the former; hence the clause is best understood as meaning, 'my life is drawing to an end' (cp. Klostermann and Rieu). *telos* is used here in the sense of 'end'.

Translation: The clause order in this verse may be better changed, e.g. 'It has been written, "..."; this, I tell you, must be fulfilled in me. ...'.
This scripture must be fulfilled, cp. on 4 : 21; for *must* also cp. on 2 : 49 and for *fulfilled* on "accomplished" in 18 : 31.
And can usually better be omitted.
He was reckoned with transgressors, or, "they numbered him among the criminals" (Rieu), 'they numbered him one way with the sinners' (Sranan), 'people said that he was just (or, no other than) a wicked/godless man'.
What is written about me has its fulfilment, preferably, 'what concerns me reaches/has its end' (Jerusalem, Balinese), "for me the course is run" (Rieu), 'my end is drawing near' (cp. Leyden), 'my life is nearly ended'.

38 ***And they said, "Look, Lord, here are two swords." And he said to them, "It is enough."***

Exegesis: *machairai hōde duo* 'here (are) two swords', taking up v. 36.
hikanon estin 'it is enough', referring either to the two swords, or, expressing the fact that Jesus wants to stop the conversation about the swords (cp. NEB, BFBS), preferably the latter.

Translation: *Here are two swords*, or, 'we (inclus.) have two swords here'.
It is enough, or, "Enough of this!" (Goodspeed), or more explicitly expressing the meaning preferred in *Exegesis*, 'Finished!' (Bahasa Indonesia), 'Well, have-done!' (Balinese).

39 ***And he came out, and went, as was his custom, to the Mount of Olives; and the disciples followed him.***

Exegesis: *exelthōn* lit. 'after going out', either of the house, or, of the city, preferably the latter.
eporeuthē kata to ethos 'he went according to (his) custom', i.e. as usual, cp. 21 : 37. For *to ethos* cp. on 1 : 9.
eis to Oros tōn Elaiōn 'to the Mount of the Olives', cp. on 19 : 29.
ēkolouthēsan de autō kai hoi mathētai 'and his disciples followed him', rendering *ēkolouthēsan* as usual and omitting *kai*. *kai hoi mathētai* lit. 'his disciples too' as if a synonym of *eporeuthē* preceded.

Translation: *He came out*, or, 'he left the city'.
As was his custom, or, 'as he used to do'; or, transposing the phrase to the end of the sentence, 'that was where he habitually-went, or, went often', cp. on 4 : 16.
Mount of Olives, see on "mount...Olivet" in 19 : 29.
Followed him, cp. on 7 : 9.

40 ***And when he came to the place he said to them, "Pray that you may not enter into temptation."***

Exegesis: *genomenos de epi tou topou* 'when he reached the place'. No previous reference to the place has been made and *epi tou topou* may be taken to mean either, 'the usual place', or, 'the place he had in mind', preferably the latter.

proseuchesthe mē eiselthein eis peirasmon lit. 'pray not to come into temptation', i.e. 'that you may not come into temptation'. *proseuchomai* here with final infinitive to indicate that which is prayed for. The phrase *eiselthein eis peirasmon* is used in a figurative way (cp. 11 : 4). For *peirasmos* cp. A-G s.v. 2 b.

Translation: *That you may not enter into temptation,* though formally active, is semantically passive; hence renderings of the verb such as, "not be subjected" (Goodspeed), "be spared" (NEB), 'not fall into' (Marathi), 'not find/experience' (Tzeltal); cp. also, 'that you will not be made heavy' (Kekchi, using an idiom for being tempted). Here God is the implied agent or initiator; in 11 : 4 God's role is more explicitly indicated, because the prayer is addressed to him.

41 ***And he withdrew from them about a stone's throw, and knelt down and prayed,***

Exegesis: *kai autos apespasthē ap' autōn* 'and he withdrew from them'. *kai autos* may mean 'and he himself', or, without emphasis, 'and he', probably the latter.

apospaō (†) 'to draw away', here in the passive, either with intransitive meaning, 'to withdraw', or with passive meaning, 'to be drawn away' (viz. by the violence of his emotions, cp. Plummer), preferably the former.

hōsei lithou bolēn 'about a stone's throw', accusative of extent, cp. Bl-D, § 161.

bolē (††) 'throw', here of the distance covered by throwing a stone, approximately 30 yards.

theis ta gonata lit. 'after bending his knees', hence 'kneeling down', denoting a less common position of praying, standing being the more common position, cp. 18 : 11. For *gonu* cp. on 5 : 8.

prosēucheto 'he prayed for some time', durative imperfect.

Translation: *He withdrew from them,* cp. on 5 : 16.

About a stone's throw, or, 'as far as one/you may throw a stone' (cp. Tarascan, Sranan), or not specifying the object, 'a throw its-distance' (Balinese, South Toradja).

To kneel down, or, 'to fall on one's knees' (Phillips, similarly Sranan, lit. 'to fall with one's knees on the ground'). For 'knee' cp. also *N.T.Wb.*/17, BODY. The usual rendering should be used even when referring to a position that is not the normal one for prayer in the culture.

42 ***"Father, if thou art willing, remove this cup from me; nevertheless not my will, but thine, be done."***

Exegesis: *ei boulei* 'if you will', i.e. 'if you decide so', not 'if you are willing to grant me what I want', cp. Plummer. *boulomai*, cp. on 10 : 22.

parenegke touto to potērion ap' emou 'take this cup away from me', cp. *TH-Mk* on 14 : 36. *parapherō* (†).

plēn 'but', cp. on 18 : 8.

mē to thelēma mou alla to son ginesthō 'not my will but your (will) be done'. For *to thelēma* cp. on 12 : 47. It should be noted that *mou* is a less emphatic possessive pronoun than *to son*. *ginesthō* lit. 'must happen', is a very general expression.

Translation: *Remove this cup from me.* One may have to add a reference to the intention of the act, cp. e.g. 'take this can/mug from my hand that I need not drink it' (Sranan); or to explain the metaphorical meaning of *cup*, 'cup of heaviness' (Guhu-Samane), 'trouble bowl' (Zarma), and see *TBT*, 8.110f, 1957); or to substitute a non-metaphorical rendering, e.g. 'take away this pain/affliction from me' (East Toradja 1933, similarly in a Zoque dialect), 'free me from having to suffer this trial' (Spanish VP), and cp. 'if there were some way in which you would not allow suffering to come to me' (Tzeltal).

Not my will, but thine, be done, or, 'not what I wish/desire be done but (only) what you wish/desire', 'do not do what (or, do not let it happen just as) I want...', cp. *TH-Mk* on 14 : 36.

43 ***And there appeared to him an angel from heaven, strengthening him.***

Exegesis: For the textual problems of v. 43f cp. *GNT* apparatus criticus, and commentaries. The treatment of these verses here does not imply a decision as to their authenticity.

ōphthē de autō aggelos ap' ouranou 'there appeared to him an angel from heaven', cp. on 1 : 11. *ap' ouranou* may go with *ōphthē*, adding an idea of 'coming' to 'appearing', or with *aggelos* 'an angel from heaven', preferably the former.

enischuōn auton 'strengthening him', denoting the purpose of the appearing.

enischuō (†) 'to give, or inspire strength', hence 'to strengthen', of moral strength.

Translation: *There appeared to him an angel from heaven*, or, 'coming from heaven', cp. on 1 : 11.

44 ***And being in an agony he prayed more earnestly; and his sweat became like great drops of blood falling down upon the ground.***

Exegesis: *kai genomenos en agōnia* 'and becoming greatly distressed, or, anguished'.

agōnia (††) 'anxiety', 'anguish', 'distress'.

ektenesteron proseucheto 'he prayed more fervently'.

ektenōs (†) 'eagerly', 'fervently'.

kai egeneto ho hidrōs autou hōsei thromboi haimatos 'and his sweat became like drops of blood'.

hidrōs (††) 'sweat', 'perspiration'.

thrombos (††) 'small amount of blood', 'clot', here 'drop'.

katabainontos epi tēn gēn lit. 'going down to the ground', hence 'falling on the ground', going with *haimatos*.

Translation: *Being in an agony*, or, 'in great anguish/distress', 'his heart was oppressed' (Timorese); and cp. *N.T.Wb.*/57, PAIN. The vehemence of the emotion may colour the rendering of the verb, cp. e.g. 'broken with anguish' (cp. Navajo). The phrase indicates cause, cp. 'his agony made him pray' (Sranan).

More earnestly, or, 'even more intensely and seriously', viz. than previously.

Falling down upon the ground, though grammatically going with 'blood', may in translation often better be taken with 'drops', and then be rendered, 'trickled/dripped to the ground' (Balinese).

45 ***And when he rose from prayer, he came to the disciples and found them sleeping for sorrow,***

Exegesis: *anastas apo tēs proseuchēs* lit. 'after rising from prayer', i.e. either 'from the position of prayer' (cp. v. 41), or 'from the act of prayer', i.e., 'after the prayer', taking *apo* in a temporal sense. The latter is preferable.

elthōn pros tous mathētas 'after going to the disciples', without connective between *anastas* and *elthōn* because the latter denotes an act which is, as it were, part of the event to which the main verb *heuren* refers.

heuren koimōmenous autous apo tēs lupēs 'he found them sleeping because of their grief'. For *apo* with causal meaning cp. A-G s.v. V 1. The article *tēs* should be noted and is best understood as possessive.

koimaomai (†) 'to sleep', here equivalent to *katheudō* (v. 46).

Translation: *He...found them sleeping*, or, 'perceived (or, saw, or, became aware) that they were sleeping'; cp. on 7 : 10.

For sorrow, or, 'worn out (or, overwhelmed) by grief' (cp. NEB, East Toradja 1933), "so great was their grief" (TEV), 'because they were very sad'. For the noun see *N.T.Wb.*/73, WEEP.

46 ***and he said to them, "Why do you sleep? Rise and pray that you may not enter into temptation."***

Exegesis: *ti katheudete* 'why are you sleeping?', expressing astonishment rather than inquiring after a reason. *katheudō*, cp. on 8 : 52.

anastantes proseuchesthe 'rise and pray', i.e. rise from your lying position and stand on your feet, cp. on v. 41.

Translation: *Why do you sleep?*, or, 'how is it possible that you are asleep?', 'do you really sleep now?'.

47 ***While he was still speaking, there came a crowd, and the man called Judas, one of the twelve, was leading them. He drew near to Jesus to kiss him;***

Exegesis: *eti autou lalountos idou ochlos* 'while he was still speaking behold, (there appeared) a crowd', suggesting a sudden appearing of the crowd.

ho legomenos Ioudas 'the one called Judas', 'the man called Judas'.

heis tōn dōdeka 'one of the twelve', cp. on 8 : 1.

proērcheto autous 'went ahead of them', 'was at their head', cp. on 1 : 17 and A-G s.v. 2. As contrasted with *ēggisen* (aorist) *proērcheto* (imperfect) describes the situation.

ēggisen tō Iēsou philēsai auton 'he drew near, or, he came up to Jesus to kiss him', describing the first specific act that happened in the new situation. *philēsai* is final infinitive. Whether Judas actually kissed Jesus is not stated or intimated. For *phileō* meaning 'to kiss', cp. A-G s.v. 2.

Translation: *While he was still speaking*, see on 8 : 49.

A crowd (cp. on 5 : 19), or a slightly more military term, 'a band/troop' (Leyden, Jerusalem, Malay).

And...Judas...was leading them, or, 'was walking in front'. The sentence is often better subordinated, 'headed by...Judas', "with...Judas...at their head" (Goodspeed, NEB).

For *to draw near to* see on 15 : 1, for *to kiss* on 15 : 20.

48 ***but Jesus said to him, "Judas, would you betray the Son of man with a kiss?"***

Exegesis: *philēmati ton huion tou anthrōpou paradidōs* 'is it with a kiss that you deliver up the Son of man?' *philēmati* (cp. on 7 : 45) is emphatic. For *huios tou anthrōpou* cp. on 5 : 24; for *paradidōmi* cp. on v. 4.

Translation: *Would you betray...with a kiss?*, or, 'are you betraying... by giving him a kiss?', 'you are kissing...in order to deliver him up?' (Sranan). If the indirect object has to be mentioned explicitly, one may say, 'to his enemies', or, 'to those who arrest (him)' (East Toradja 1933).

For *betray* see on 22 : 4.

49 ***And when those who were about him saw what would follow, they said, "Lord, shall we strike with the sword?"***

Exegesis: *hoi peri auton* lit. 'those around him', i.e. 'his disciples'.

to esomenon lit. 'that which will be', here, 'what was going to happen'.

kurie 'lord', cp. on 1 : 6 sub (2^b).

ei pataxomen en machairē 'shall we strike with a sword?', direct question introduced by *ei* cp. on 13 : 23. *en machairē* in the singular is used in a collective sense, cp. "with our swords" (BFBS), and 'with the sword' (Jerusalem).

patassō 'to strike', 'to hit'.

Translation: *Those who were about him*, or, specifying the reference, 'the people beside/near Jesus' (Kapauku), "his followers" (NEB, similarly Balinese), 'Jesus' companions' (Toba Batak).

Strike with the sword, or, 'strike them with this sword' (Balinese), 'fight (them) with (our) swords'. For *strike* see *N.T.Wb.*/43, HIT. The intention probably is to rout the assailants rather than to kill them.

50 ***And one of them struck the slave of the high priest and cut off his right ear.***

Exegesis: *kai epataxen heis tis ex autōn* 'and (indeed) one of them struck...', without waiting for Jesus' answer to the question of v. 49. *heis tis* is equivalent to *heis* alone, cp. A-G s.v. *heis* 3 c.

tou archiereōs ton doulon 'the slave of the high priest'. *tou archiereōs* is emphatic by virtue of its position before *ton doulon.*

kai apheilen to ous autou to dexion 'and cut off his right ear'. *aphaireō* lit. 'to take away' is used here in a more specific meaning, viz. 'to cut off', 'to shear off'.

Translation: For *slave* see on 7 : 2, for *high priest* see references on 3 : 2.

His right ear. In several languages one has to say, 'his ear at the right side'. For *right* see *N.T.Wb.*/63, and cp. /42, HAND; for *ear* see *ibid.*/16f, BODY.

51 ***But Jesus said, "No more of this!" And he touched his ear and healed him.***

Exegesis: *apokritheis* 'answering', cp. on 1 : 60.

eate heōs toutou lit. 'let go/be as far as this', a very ambiguous saying, best understood as addressed to the disciples and expressing Jesus' wish that no more violence be done, cp. RSV, and on 4 : 41.

hapsamenos tou ōtiou 'touching the ear'. For *haptomai* 'to touch' as a gesture of healing cp. on 5 : 13. *ōtion* (†) is equivalent to *ous.*

iasato auton 'he healed him', shifting from the part of the body to the person in question.

Translation: *But Jesus said*, cp. on "answered" in 3 : 16.

No more of this, or, "Stop! No more!" (BFBS), 'leave off, this is enough' (Jerusalem), 'let it remain till so far', i.e. 'no more' (Sranan), or quite unambiguously, 'no more fighting' (Navajo).

He touched his ear, or, 'he touched that man's/slave's ear'. The noun refers here not to the outer ear, or shell of the ear, but rather to the place of the head where the organ (inner and outer ear) is situated. In most languages a literal rendering seems to be sufficient to express this, where necessary with slight adjustments, cp. e.g. *lui touchant l'oreille* (Jerusalem), but one may consider also a more precise rendering, e.g. 'he touched the place of his ear, or, where-had-been his ear' (as was considered in Balinese). Some translators, however, have taken 'ear' as referring to the part of the ear that had been cut off, cp. e.g. 'he took up the ear', but this is not advisable.

Healed him. If a personal object would be unidiomatic, a reference to the ear, in the sense of the whole organ, or the place where it is situated, may be substituted. Some languages use here a verb meaning 'to restore', 'to make as it was before' (Balinese, Kapauku).

52 ***Then Jesus said to the chief priests and captains of the temple and elders, who had come out against him, "Have you come out as against a robber, with swords and clubs?***

Exegesis: *pros tous paragenomenous ep' auton* 'to the ... who had come out against him', going with the three subsequent nouns. For *paraginomai* cp. on 7 : 4. *epi* with accusative indicates hostile intent, here to have him arrested.

archiereis kai stratēgous tou hierou kai presbuterous '...chief priests, temple officers and elders', cp. on 9 : 22 (*archiereis*), 22 : 4 (*stratēgoi*) and 7 : 3 (*presbuteroi*).

hōs epi lēstēn 'as if against a robber', with emphasis. For *lēstēs* cp. on 10 : 30.

meta machairōn kai xulōn 'with swords and clubs'.

xulon (also 23 : 31) lit. 'wood', here, 'club', 'cudgel', 'stick', cp. A-G s.v. 2 b.

Translation: For *chief priests* see on "high-priesthood" in 3 : 2; for *elders* see on 7 : 3.

Captains of the temple, or, 'officers/commanders/leaders of the temple guard, or, of those who guard the temple'.

Who had come out against him, or, 'who had come (or, who were) there to attack him, or, to seize/arrest him'.

Have you come out as against a robber..., or, to bring out better the meaning of this rhetorical question, "Do you take me for a bandit, that you have come out..." (NEB), 'have you come as-though to oppose a rioter...' (Kapauku, using a connective with the meaning 'as though it were but it isn't'). For *robber* see on 10 : 30.

With swords and clubs, cp. *TH-Mk* on 14 : 48.

53 ***When I was with you day after day in the temple, you did not lay hands on me. But this is your hour, and the power of darkness."***

Exegesis: *kath' hēmeran* 'daily', 'day by day', with emphasis, going with the following absolute genitive.

ontos mou meth' humōn en tō hierō 'when I was with you in the temple'. *meth' humōn* does not imply personal contact. For *hieron* cp. on 2 : 27.

ouk exeteinate tas cheiras ep' eme 'you did not stretch out your hands against me', hence either 'you did not lay hands on me' (as a reference to an act), or, 'you did not raise a hand against me' (as an expression of hostile intent), preferably the latter.

all' hautē estin humōn hē hōra 'but this is your hour', meaning either 'now at this time and this place you dare to arrest me', or 'this is your appointed time', i.e. appointed by God. The latter is preferable.

kai hē exousia tou skotous 'and (this is) the power of darkness', i.e., now the power of darkness is at work. For detailed interpretations of this clause and its relationship to *hautē estin humōn hē hōra* see commentaries. For translation purposes it seems advisable to understand the clause as expressing a complementary aspect of the situation: not only the hour of Jesus' human adversaries but also of the activity of the power of darkness, i.e. of the devil, cp. A-G s.v. *exousia* 4 c β.

Translation: *You did not lay hands on me,* preferably, 'you did not raise a hand against me', or, 'you did not even try/dare to touch me' (cp. East Toradja 1933). For the rendering of the phrase according to the other interpretation see on 20 : 19.

This is your hour, or more explicitly, 'this is the moment for you to act', 'now you are allowed (or, God allows you) to do this'.

And the power of darkness, i.e. 'and (this is the moment) for the power of darkness to act', 'it is also the time of darkness when it has strength' (Shona 1966), parallel to the preceding phrase. *Power of darkness,* i.e. the powerful/mighty/strong one who is characterized as dark, or, where idiomatically preferable, the reversed construction, 'the dark one who is powerful'. If the phrase would not be understood as referring to the devil, such a reference has to be added, e.g. 'the devil who rules in darkness'. For *darkness* cp. also *N.T.Wb.*/21f.

54 ***Then they seized him and led him away, bringing him into the high priest's house. Peter followed at a distance;***

Exegesis: *sullabontes de auton ēgagon* 'after arresting him they led (him) away'. Subject is probably the persons mentioned in v. 52. *agō* is used here in the meaning 'to lead away', 'to take into custody', cp. A-G s.v. 2.

eisēgagon eis tēn oikian tou archiereōs 'they brought him to the house of the high priest'. *eisagō* is a general term without specific judicial connotation. *oikia* refers to the official residence of the high priest. For *archiereus* cp. on 3 : 2.

ho de Petros ēkolouthei makrothen 'and Peter followed at a distance', descriptive imperfect, denoting an act which accompanied the events related in the preceding clause. The range of *makrothen* 'at a distance' is determined by the fact that he had to keep far enough away to remain unnoticed, i.e. outside the light of the torches.

Translation: *They seized him and led him away.* Since the persons mentioned in v. 52 are initiators rather than direct agents the clause may have to be rendered, 'had him seized and led away', 'ordered their men to take hold of him and lead him away'. For *to lead away* cp. *TH-Mk* on 15 : 1.

Bringing him to often better as a main clause, e.g. "They brought him to" (NEB), or, 'they had him brought to'.

Followed, i.e. went along after the crowd, see *TH-Mk* on 14 : 54, and cp. a rendering such as, 'walked far behind in coming' (Sranan, similarly Zarma). If an object is obligatory, one can best add 'them' or another reference to those who led Jesus away.

At a distance, cp. on 15 : 20.

55 ***and when they had kindled a fire in the middle of the courtyard and sat down together, Peter sat among them.***

Exegesis: *periapsantōn de pur en mesō tēs aulēs kai sugkathisantōn* 'after they had kindled a fire in the middle of the courtyard and (after) they had sat down together'. Genitive absolute without a subject, which is to be supplied from v. 54. For *aulē* cp. on 11 : 21 and *TH-Mk* on 14 : 54.

periaptō (††) 'to kindle', 'to light'.

sugkathizō (†) lit. 'to sit down together with somebody else', here 'to sit down together as a group'.

ekathēto ho Petros mesos autōn 'Peter sat down among them'. *mesos* does not mean that Peter sat in the centre of the group but is used in a more general meaning, viz. 'among'.

Translation: *Kindled a fire*, or, 'caused-to-burn/flame/blaze a fire', 'laid/made a fire' (NV, Sranan), 'caused-to-live/grow a fire' (East Toradja).

The courtyard. The closest cultural equivalent often is the term for an open space in front of, or around the house, which, though not enclosed by buildings, walls or porches, is part of the premises. A rendering suggesting a room under the roof of the house should be avoided.

Sat down is ingressive aspect, but *sat* describes the resulting situation. A more specific verb may be required by local custom, e.g. 'squatted' (Toba Batak); cp. also on 2 : 46.

56 ***Then a maid, seeing him as he sat in the light and gazing at him, said, "This man also was with him."***

Exegesis: *idousa de auton...kathēmenon pros to phōs* 'when (she) saw him...sitting by the light'. *pros to phōs* may mean 'in the firelight', or 'by the fire', preferably the former. It is best understood as going with *kathēmenon*.

paidiskē tis 'a servant-maid'. For *paidiskē* cp. on 12 : 45. *tis* has approximately the function of the indefinite article.

kai atenisasa autō eipen 'she stared at him and said'. Though both *idousa* and *atenisasa* are participles in the aorist and syntactically co-ordinate, the latter goes more closely with the main verb *eipen*. For *atenizō* cp. on 4 : 20.

kai houtos sun autō ēn 'this man was with him too', implying that Jesus was usually accompanied by a group of people. *sun autō* 'with him' may refer to a specific occasion or to a more general relationship between Jesus and Peter, preferably the latter.

Translation: *Then a maid, seeing him as he sat...* Reasons of focus or transition may make preferable a transposition, e.g. 'while he was sitting there..., a maid saw him' (Bahasa Indonesia KB), or, 'there was a maid there, who (or, she) saw him sitting...'. Cp. also on 5 : 27. — *Maid* can usually be rendered by a word for 'servant' (cp. on 12 : 37) or 'slave' (cp. on 7 : 2), with indication of female sex. In some languages the term employed refers to a job that is characteristic in the society for female slaves, e.g. 'grinder' (Totontepec Mixe).

In the light, preferably, 'in the firelight', 'shone-upon by the fire' (cp. South Toradja).

Gazing at him. The preceding "seeing" referred to initial perception, here "gazing" (see on "fixed" in 4 : 20) indicates further, more accurate observation.

This man also was with him, or, 'with Jesus', or, 'this man also was one of his companions, or, of Jesus' followers'. Languages with evidential aspect pose a problem here. Thus in Huli the translator must decide whether he will use the speculative aspect, expressing that the slave's, statement is based on a supposition, or the factual aspect, indicating that her statement is founded on what she saw herself. If one chooses the latter, as seems preferable, a second decision must be taken, i.e. between remote or near past, indicating respectively that the seeing has happened before, or, on the day of speaking, preferably the former.

57 ***But he denied it, saying, "Woman, I do not know him."***

Exegesis: *ouk oida auton, gunai* 'woman, I don't know him', denying the possibility of any relationship with Jesus.

Translation: *He denied it, saying, "Woman..."*, or simply, 'he said, "No, woman, ..."'; cp. on v. 34. *Woman.* The translator should seek a term that is culturally appropriate in the given situation: a stranger addressing a female servant belonging to the household, cp. on 13 : 12.

58 ***And a little later some one else saw him and said, "You also are one of them." But Peter said, "Man, I am not."***

Exegesis: *meta brachu* lit. 'after a short (time)', hence, 'a little later', 'presently'.

heteros idōn auton ephē 'somebody else saw him and said'. *heteros* does not mean that he was a slave like the servant-maid, but only that he was a different person.

kai su ex autōn ei 'you too are one of them'. For *kai* cp. on v. 56. *ex autōn* refers to Jesus' followers, though they are not mentioned explicitly in the preceding verses. For *ex* as periphrasis for the partitive genitive, cp. A-G s.v. *ek* 4 a δ.

anthrōpe, ouk eimi 'man, I am not', a flat denial.

Translation: *Some one else.* If a literal rendering would suggest 'another female slave', it is preferable to say, 'a man' (Tzeltal, Kituba), 'a certain man' (Zarma), 'one of the men who sat/were there'.

One of them, or, '(one) of their group', '(one) of his friends' (Malay), 'a companion of that man', and cp. *TH-Mk* on 14 : 69f.

Man, a form of address between strangers, here having a connotation of reproach.

I am not. The ellipsis may have to be filled out, e.g. 'I am not one of them', but one should remember that the shortness of the phrase serves to express Peter's annoyance; hence the rendering should be as snappy a phrase as idiom permits.

59 ***And after an interval of about an hour still another insisted, saying, "Certainly this man also was with him; for he is a Galilean."***

Exegesis: *diastasēs hōsei hōras mias* lit. 'when about one hour had passed', genitive absolute.

diistamai (also 24 : 51) 'to go away', 'to part', here 'to pass', of time.

allos tis 'somebody else', synonymous with *heteros* in v. 57.

diischurizeto legōn 'affirmed strongly, or confidently, saying'. *legōn* is used to introduce direct speech.

diischurizomai (†) 'to affirm strongly'. It does not imply a reference to a previous statement.

ep' alētheias 'verily', 'without doubt', cp. on 4 : 25.

kai houtos met' autou ēn 'this man was with him too', cp. on v. 56.

kai gar Galilaios estin 'for he is a Galilean', best understood as an additional indication that Peter belonged to Jesus, cp. Rieu.

Translation: *After an interval of about an hour*, or, 'about an hour later'. *Hour* refers here to 1/12 of the period of daylight, but the exact duration is not to be pressed. South Toradja uses 'one betel chewing', an idiomatic expression for an unspecified period of time which in actual fact is rather shorter than an hour.

Still another, or, 'another (or, a second) man'; cp. on v. 58.

Insisted, or, 'made himself strong' (Timorese), 'spoke emphatically/heavily' (Kapauku, Trukese); or simply, 'said', since the idea of strong affirmation is sufficiently expressed in the following direct discourse.

Certainly, or, more adapted to the present context, "of course" (NEB), "there isn't any doubt that" (TEV), 'right indeed' (Bahasa Indonesia KB); and cp. references on "truly" in 4 : 24.

He is a Galilean, or, 'he is a Galilee-man, or, one-who-hails-from Galilee' (Balinese, here and in 23 : 6 respectively), 'he is from Galilee', 'Galilee is his (native) country'. The statement probably is a deduction from what the man had heard, viz. Peter's Galilean accent (cp. Mt. 26 : 73); this is of importance where one has to decide which evidential aspect is to be used (cp. on v. 56).

60 ***But Peter said, "Man, I do not know what you are saying." And immediately, while he was still speaking, the cock crowed.***

Exegesis: *anthrōpe, ouk oida ho legeis* 'man, I don't know what you are saying, or, talking about', i.e. it is absolutely not true what you say.

parachrēma eti lalountos autou 'and immediately, while he was still speaking'. The genitive absolute *eti lalountos autou* stresses *parachrēma* which goes with the main verb *ephōnēsen.*

ephōnēsen alektōr 'the cock crowed', cp. on v. 34.

Translation: *I do not know what you are saying,* or, 'I do not know (or, understand) what you are talking about, or, what your words (can possibly) mean'.

Immediately and *while he was still speaking,* or, "just as he spoke" (Goodspeed), 'before he had finished (speaking)' (cp. Rieu), both serve to express the concept of immediacy; the renderings may have to be combined into one phrase.

61 ***And the Lord turned and looked at Peter. And Peter remembered the word of the Lord, how he had said to him, "Before the cock crows today, you will deny me three times."***

Exegesis: *strapheis ho kurios eneblepsen tō Petrō* 'the Lord turned around and looked at Peter'. The clause implies that Jesus is within sight. For *strapheis* cp. on 7 : 9; for *ho kurios* cp. on 1 : 6 sub (3); for *emblepō* cp. on 20 : 17.

hupemnēsthē ho Petros tou rēmatos tou kuriou 'Peter remembered the word of the Lord'. *rēma* means here 'saying', 'utterance'.

hupomimnēskō (†) 'to remind', here in the passive 'to remember', with genitive.

hōs eipen autō 'how he had said to him', connects *rēma* with the subsequent direct quotation and has no semantic function of its own.

prin alektora phōnēsai sēmeron aparnēsē me tris 'before the/a cock will have crowed today, you will disown me three times', cp. on v. 34, though the structure of the saying is different here.

Translation: *Turned,* or, 'turned around', 'turned his head'.

For *looked at* see on 20 : 17 and cp. East Toradja 1933, 'meeting eyes with Peter' / '(his) eye meeting Peter's'; for *remembered* see on 16 : 25.

The word of the Lord, how he had said to him, or, 'the word(s) the Lord had said to him', or simply, 'what the Lord had said a while ago', 'the Lord's word(s)'.

For the last sentence of this verse see on v. 34; where an analytical rendering of *deny* is necessary, e.g. 'you will say that you do not know me', 'you will say, "No, I do not know him"', it may have to coincide with that of "you...deny that you know me" in v. 34.

62 ***And he went out and wept bitterly.***

Exegesis: *exelthōn* 'after going outside', i.e. out of the high priest's house.

eklausen pikrōs 'he wept bitterly', a well known metaphor referring not to the way in which one weeps but expressing the deep anguish/sorrow which causes the weeping.

Translation: *And,* or, 'then', 'thereupon'.

Wept, cp. *N.T.Wb.*/73, i.e. in private.

Bitterly, or, 'sorrowfully' (Bahasa Indonesia), 'sobbing-violently' (Balinese); or a generic term for high degree, cp. e.g. 'wept very much' (Sranan, Sundanese).

63 ***Now the men who were holding Jesus mocked him and beat him;*** 64 ***they also blindfolded him and asked him, "Prophesy! Who is it that struck you?"***

Exegesis: For a correct understanding of these verses it should be noted that the mocking and beating related in v. 63 are understood to be going on in v. 64. The latter represents as it were one specific moment in the events related in v. 63.

hoi andres hoi sunechontes auton 'the men who were holding him in custody'.

sunechō 'to hold in custody', 'to guard'.

enepaizon autō derontes lit. 'mocked him beating (him)' with *auton* understood. *derontes* (cp. on 12 : 47) may refer to the same act as *enepaizon* (cp. Phillips), or to a separate act (cp. RSV), preferably the latter.

(V. 64) *kai perikalupsantes auton epērōtōn legontes* 'and after blindfolding him they asked him'. *epērōtōn* in the imperfect tense may be iterative.

perikaluptō (†) 'to cover', 'to conceal', here with personal object, 'to blindfold', probably with a cloth.

prophēteuson, tis estin ho paisas se 'prophesy, who is it that struck you?'. For *prophēteuō* cp. on 1 : 67. Here it may be used in an ironical sense ('Play the prophet! Who is it...', Jerusalem, cp. NEB) or in a less specific meaning, viz. 'to tell what one cannot see' (cp. *TH-Mk* on 14 : 65), preferably the former.

paiō (†) 'to strike', 'to hit'.

Translation: For *mocked him* see on 14 : 29, for *beat him,* i.e. struck him repeatedly, probably with fist or stick, cp. *N.T.Wb.*/15.

(V. 64) *Blindfolded him,* or, 'covered his face/eyes/head'.

Prophesy. Where an ironical use of the verb or the cognate noun (see on 1 : 67, 70) is undesirable one may shift to a more generic term, cp. "guess" (TEV, similarly Shona 1966, Colloquial Japanese), 'make-known' (South Toradja, Trukese). Phillips combines the two solutions, "Now, prophet, guess who...".

65 ***And they spoke many other words against him, reviling him.***

Exegesis: *kai hetera polla blasphēmountes elegon eis auton* 'and they said many other insulting things with regard to him'. *blasphēmountes* and *elegon* are to be taken together.

blasphēmeō (cp. on 12 : 10), here of one human being towards another, 'to revile', 'to infame', 'to insult'.

Translation: *Spoke many other words against him, reviling him,* or, 'to revile him, or, with which they reviled him'; or, 'said many other insulting things at his expense, or, to his discredit'. For *to revile* see on 6 : 22.

66 ***When day came, the assembly of the elders of the people gathered together, both chief priests and scribes; and they led him away to their council, and they said,***

Exegesis: *hōs egeneto hēmera* 'when day came'. In this phrase *hēmera* means 'daylight', 'dawn', cp. 6 : 13; Acts 27 : 29.

sunēchthē to presbuterion tou laou, archiereis te kai grammateis 'the council/elders of the people met, the chief priests and the experts in the law'. The clause may be interpreted in two ways: (1) *archiereis te kai grammateis* indicate of what kind of members the council was composed (cp. Phillips, BFBS, RSV); (2) *to presbuterion* is used here in the concrete sense of *hoi presbuteroi* 'the elders' (cp. NEB), preferably the latter. *presbuterion* (†).

sunagō 'to bring together', here in the passive with reflexive meaning, 'to meet', 'to assemble', 'to gather'.

apēgagon auton eis to sunedrion autōn lit. 'they brought him before their council', but in view of the context here best understood as 'they had him brought before their council'. *apagō* is used here in a judicial sense, cp. A-G s.v. 2 a.

sunedrion (†) 'high council', 'Sanhedrin', highest religious and civil body among the Jews, cp. A-G s.v. 2 and *TH-Mk* on 14 : 55.

Translation: *When day came,* see on "when it was day" in 4 : 42.

The assembly of the elders of the people gathered together, both chief priests and scribes, preferably, 'the elders of the people, chief priests, and scribes came together', mentioning some of the officials found also in vv. 2 and 52. For *the people,* here referring to the Jewish nation, see on 1 : 17.

Their council, i.e. the council formed by them, or, of which they were members. For *council* cp. *TH-Mk* on 15 : 1, and 'place for speech-making/discussion' (Kapauku), 'great assembly' (East Toradja), or more juridically, '(high) tribunal' (Sranan, Jerusalem, Javanese), 'assembly of their Judgment-court' (Marathi).

67 ***"If you are the Christ, tell us." But he said to them, "If I tell you, you will not believe;*** 68 ***and if I ask you, you will not answer.***

Exegesis: *legontes* 'saying', here referring to an act distinct from the verb with which it goes, viz. *apēgagon.*

ei su ei ho Christos, eipon hēmin 'if you are the Messiah, tell us (so)'. *ei* is conditional, not interrogative 'whether'.

ean humin eipō ou mē pisteusēte 'if I tell you (viz. that I am the Messiah), you will not believe me'. For *ou mē* cp. on 1 : 15.

(V. 68) *ean de erōtēsō* 'if I ask you', either in a general sense (cp. NEB) and referring to situations like e.g. 20 : 41, or specifically, 'whether you think I am the Messiah', preferably the former.

ou mē apokrithēte 'you will not answer', cp. on 1 : 15. Like *ou mē pisteusēte* in v. 67 the clause expresses strong conviction on the part of Jesus.

Translation: *If you are.* In languages like Thai and Javanese the high priest, by not using honorifics, shows his conviction that Jesus cannot be the Christ; cp. *TBT*, 8.57, 1957. The same holds true for v. 70.

For *believe,* i.e. 'believe me (or, it, or, my words)', cp. on 1 : 20.

(V. 68) *Ask you,* or, 'ask (you) questions', 'ask you something' (East Toradja 1933).

69 ***But from now on the Son of man shall be seated at the right hand of the power of God."***

Exegesis: *apo tou nun* 'from now on', not to be pressed as to its immediacy, since the clause refers to the exaltation after the resurrection (cp. Acts 1 : 11; 2 : 33).

estai ho huios tou anthrōpou kathēmenos 'the Son of man will be seated', referring not to a future event, but to a future situation. For *ho huios tou anthrōpou* cp. on 5 : 24.

ek dexiōn tēs dunameōs tou theou 'at the right hand of the power of God', a combination of *ek dexiōn tou theou* 'at the right hand of God', and *ek dexiōn tēs dunameōs* 'at the right hand of the power', cp. *TH-Mk* on 14 : 62.

Translation: *Shall be seated,* or, 'will be sitting', 'will have the seat', cp. 'will sit-stay' (Kapauku).

The right hand of, cp. on "the right side of" in 1 : 11, ad (1); the idiom Zarma has here is, 'at the much hand (i.e. the hand most used)'.

The power of God often has to be changed, e.g. into 'God who has power', 'Almighty God' (e.g. in Marathi).

70 ***And they all said, "Are you the Son of God, then?" And he said to them, "You say that I am."***

Exegesis: *eipan de pantes* 'all said', i.e. all members of the Sanhedrin.

su oun ei ho huios tou theou 'so you are the Son of God?', drawing the inference from v. 69, and implying that the concept of the Son of man and that of the Son of God are here virtually identical.

humeis legete hoti egō eimi 'you say that I am', with emphasis on *humeis,* 'you, not I', but not implying a denial.

Translation: *You say that I am,* or, 'you yourselves say that I am he'

(NV). By changing the question just uttered by his opponents Jesus represents them as having said that he is the Son of God (which actually is his opinion, not theirs). A too literal rendering may easily suggest that Jesus has another, or no opinion on the matter. To avoid this some versions give slightly adjusted renderings such as, 'you say rightly, I am he' (Jerusalem), 'as you say: I am He' (Balinese), 'as you said to me, I am that' (Kapauku).

71 ***And they said, "What further testimony do we need? We have heard it ourselves from his own lips."***

Exegesis: *ti eti echomen marturias chreian* 'what do we still need testimony?'. No witnesses are needed any more.

marturia (†) 'testimony', here with passive force, 'things said by witnesses in court', 'testimony given in court'.

apo tou stomatos autou 'from his mouth', cp. on 19 : 22.

Translation: *Said* is reciprocal: they are speaking to each other.

What further testimony do we need, or, describing the noun, 'what do we still need words/declarations of witnesses', 'why should we still need to hear things that witnesses can tell us (or, that other people know) about him'. For *testimony* cp. *N.T.Wb.*/74, WITNESS.

Heard it...from his own lips, or, 'mouth'; or, "heard his very own words" (TEV, similarly East Toradja 1933), 'heard him say it himself' (cp. Toba Batak).

CHAPTER TWENTY-THREE

1 *Then the whole company of them arose, and brought him before Pilate.*

Exegesis: *hapan to plēthos autōn* 'the whole body of them', hence 'they in a body', cp. Goodspeed. For *plēthos* cp. on 1 : 10. *autōn* refers to those mentioned in 22 : 66.

anastan . . . *ēgagon* 'after rising . . . they brought'. *anastan* is in the neuter singular as it goes with *plēthos*, but *ēgagon* is in the plural as if *anastantes* preceded, because *plēthos* refers to a collective body.

ēgagon auton epi ton Pilaton 'they brought him before Pilate'. *agō* is here equivalent to *apagō* in 21 : 12 and 22 : 66.

Translation: *The whole company of them arose,* or, 'they all arose together (or, in a body)', or more specifically, 'the whole council/tribunal (cp. on 22 : 66) arose', viz. from their seats, indicating the end of their deliberations, cp. "the Council rose" (Rieu).

Brought him before, or, 'had him (or, caused him to be) brought before'. For the verb see on 12 : 11.

2 *And they began to accuse him, saying, "We found this man perverting our nation and forbidding us to give tribute to Caesar, and saying that he himself is Christ a king."*

Exegesis: *ērxanto de katēgorein autou* 'they began to accuse him'. For *archomai* with infinitive cp. on 4 : 21. Here it is best understood as denoting the beginning of an act. For *katēgoreō* cp. on 6 : 7.

touton heuramen diastrephonta to ethnos hēmōn 'we found this man subverting our people'. *touton* is emphatic and contemptuous. *heuramen* may mean 'we found out', or 'we caught', implying intentional search, preferably the latter because of the fact that a participle is following and not an infinitive. *to ethnos hēmōn* may refer to the Jewish nation in the political sense, or be used in the same general sense as in 7 : 5, probably the latter.

diastrephō (also 9 : 41) here 'to subvert', in a political sense.

kōluonta phorous Kaisari didonai 'forbidding to give taxes to Caesar'. For this phrase cp. on 20 : 22.

legonta heauton Christon basilea einai 'saying that he is the Messiah, a king'. For *Christos* cp. on 2 : 11. *basilea* is best understood as an apposition to *Christon* added as a clarification of the meaning of *Christos*.

Translation: *Accuse,* see on 6 : 7.

We found this man perverting our nation, i.e. we caught this fellow while he was perverting our nation. For *found* cp. on 7 : 10. *To pervert,* or, 'to instigate to rebellion' (Willibrord), 'to stir-up' (Malay). *Our nation*, cp. on 7 : 5; the pronoun has exclusive force.

Forbidding us to give tribute to Caesar, see on 9 : 49 and on 20 : 22 and references.

Saying, or a more specific verb, coloured by the context, "claiming" (e.g. Goodspeed), 'pretending' (Jerusalem).

A king, or, 'that means, a king'.

3 ***And Pilate asked him, "Are you the King of the Jews?" And he answered him, "You have said so."***

Exegesis: *su legeis* 'you say so'. *su* is emphatic: you, not me!, and the phrase is best understood as a refusal to answer the question directly, cp. *TH-Mk* on 15 : 2.

Translation: *Are you*. Thai uses here, in contrast to 22 : 67, a polite form for the pronoun, thus leaving Pilate in a formally neutral position.

For *the Jews* see on 7 : 3.

You have said so, or, "the words are yours" (Rieu, NEB), '(it is) you (that) say it'. The expression resembles the one used in 22 : 70 but is slightly more evasive.

4 ***And Pilate said to the chief priests and the multitudes, "I find no crime in this man."***

Exegesis: *pros tous archiereis kai tous ochlous* 'to the chief priests and the crowds'. *tous archiereis* refers back to, and stands for, those who had brought Jesus before Pilate, i.e. those mentioned in 22 : 66. *tous ochlous* is added as if the gathering of the crowds before Pilate's palace (a natural thing to happen in the present situation) had been mentioned before (cp. Plummer).

ouden heuriskō aition 'I find no guilt', i.e. no reason to condemn, or, no ground for a charge.

en tō anthrōpō toutō 'in this man', i.e. in the case of this man, not, in his heart, or, inner being.

Translation: For *chief priests* see on "high-priesthood" in 3 : 2.

I find no crime in this man, or, "I do not find this person guilty" (Rieu), 'I do not discover anything for which this man should be punished'; or with a syntactic shift, 'what I find/see, this person has no guilt' (Balinese). For *crime* see *N.T.Wb.*/1f, ACCUSE. The concept 'guilt' is sometimes rendered by such an idiom as, 'something connected with a person (as though tied by a string)' (Navajo, in James 2 : 10), cp. 'to have deed on your neck' (Uduk).

5 ***But they were urgent, saying, "He stirs up the people, teaching throughout all Judea, from Galilee even to this place."***

Exegesis: *hoi de epischuon legontes* 'but they insisted saying', i.e. 'by saying'.

epischuō (††) lit. 'to be strong', here 'to insist', 'to persist'.

anaseiei ton laon 'he stirs up the people'. For *laos* cp. on 1 : 10.

anaseiō (†) 'to stir up', 'to incite', probably somewhat stronger than *diastrephō* in v. 2.

didaskōn kath' holēs tēs Ioudaias 'teaching throughout all Judea'. *didaskōn* may mean 'while teaching' (temporal) or 'by teaching' (causal), preferably the latter. *Ioudaia* is used here to indicate the area of Pilate's jurisdiction.

kai arxamenos apo tēs Galilaias heōs hōde lit. 'and having begun from Galilee till here', attached to the indication of Jesus' present area of activity in order to indicate the origin of his operations. It is best rendered as an independent clause.

Translation: *They were urgent.* The pronoun may have to be specified, cp. e.g. 'the accusers' (Javanese). The verb expresses that they firmly and stubbornly kept on accusing Jesus, repeating and pressing their charge against him, cp. 'they held yet more determinedly to their earnest demand' (Marathi), 'they kept on pressing (the matter)' (Zarma), 'they repeated-stubbornly' (Ponape).

The people, cp. on 7 : 29.

Teaching, preferably, 'by, or, with his teaching', 'because he teaches them these/such things'.

Throughout all Judea, cp. on 7 : 17 and 4 : 44.

From Galilee even to this place, or as a new sentence, "He started in G. and now he has come here" (Rieu, similarly Goodspeed), "It (referring to Jesus' teaching and to the disaffection it causes) started from G. and has spread as far as this city" (NEB).

6 ***When Pilate heard this, he asked whether the man was a Galilean.***

Exegesis: *Pilatos de akousas* 'when Pilate heard (this)', viz. that Jesus originally came from Galilee.

epērōtēsen ei ho anthrōpos Galilaios estin 'he asked (the accusers) whether the man was a Galilean'. *ho anthrōpos* may have here a depreciatory sense but this is not necessary.

Translation: *Whether the man was a Galilean,* often better in direct discourse, 'Is this man a Galilean?' Cp. also on 22 : 59.

7 ***And when he learned that he belonged to Herod's jurisdiction, he sent him over to Herod, who was himself in Jerusalem at that time.***

Exegesis: *epignous* 'when he learned', 'when he discovered', cp. A-G s.v. 2 b.

hoti ek tēs exousias Hērōdou estin 'that he was from the region ruled by Herod'. *exousia* lit. 'authority', means here, 'area, or region of rule', cp. on 4 : 6.

anepempsen auton pros Hērōdēn 'he sent him up to Herod'.

anapempō 'to send up', to a higher authority, 'to send on', to the proper authority (here), or 'to send back' (vv. 11 and 15).

onta kai auton en Hierosolumois 'who himself was also in Jerusalem', going with *Hērōdēn*, implying that for Pilate too Jerusalem was not his customary place of residence.

en tautais tais hēmerais 'in those days', best understood as referring to the time of the feast.

Translation: For *learned* see on 7 : 37.

He belonged to Herod's jurisdiction, or, 'he was from the country that was ruled by H.' (Shona 1963), 'he had come from where H. was the ruler' (Tzeltal), 'Jesus was-subject to (lit. was-governed by) H.' (Balinese), 'he was a person of H.'s area of responsibility (lit. watched place)' (Kapauku), 'he originated from H.'s holding' (Fulani).

Sent him over to Herod, preferably, 'sent him on to H.', 'sent him to his presence' (Tzeltal), 'had him taken to have his case heard by H.' (Shona 1966), 'ordered to bring him to H.' (cp. South Toradja).

Who was himself in Jerusalem, or, since it gives the reason of what precedes, 'for Herod was himself also/likewise staying in Jerusalem'.

8 ***When Herod saw Jesus, he was very glad, for he had long desired to see him, because he had heard about him, and he was hoping to see some sign done by him.***

Exegesis: *echarē lian* 'was very glad', 'was very pleased'.

ēn gar ex hikanōn chronōn thelōn idein auton lit. 'for he was eager to see him for a long time', i.e. he had been and still was eager to see him; *ex hikanōn chronōn* lit. 'since a long time', means here in connexion with the durative imperfect *ēn...thelōn*, 'for a long time' (cp. A-G s.v. *ek* 5 a). For *hikanos* cp. A-G s.v. 1 b, for *chronoi* (plural) denoting a rather long period, cp. A-G s.v.

dia to akouein peri autou lit. 'because of the hearing about him', i.e. 'because he used to hear about him', also to be understood in a durative sense.

kai ēlpizen ti sēmeion idein hup' autou ginomenon 'and he hoped to see some miracle being performed by him'. *ēlpizen* is coextensive in time with *ēn...thelōn*. *ti* is virtually equivalent to the indefinite article. For *sēmeion* cp. on 2 : 12. *ginomenon* lit. 'happening', here 'being performed'.

Translation: For *glad* see on "joy" in 1 : 14.

Because he had heard about him, or, 'because he had heard many stories (or, many people speak) about him', cp. also 'the hearing he heard of him made that he wanted to see him' (Sranan, similar construction to that used in 21 : 19).

The clause *he was hoping* etc. is dependent on "for". As to the verb see *N.T.Wb.*/45; the component 'desire' is more in focus here than the component 'confidence'.

See some sign done by him, or, 'see him perform a miracle', cp. NEB, TEV.

9 ***So he questioned him at some length; but he made no answer.***

Exegesis: *epērōta de auton en logois hikanois* 'he questioned him with many words', durative imperfect. *en* has instrumental meaning, cp. A-G s.v. III 1 a.

autos de ouden apekrinato autō 'but he gave him no answer'. The aorist tense *apekrinato* implies that he did not answer one single word. *autos* indicates change of subject.

Translation: One or more of the three pronouns, referring first to Herod, then twice to Jesus, may have to be specified.

10 ***The chief priests and the scribes stood by, vehemently accusing him.***

Exegesis: *heistēkeisan de hoi archiereis kai hoi grammateis eutonōs katēgorountes autou* 'the chief priests and the experts in the law stood there, vigorously accusing him'. *heistēkeisan* at the beginning of the clause is emphatic and stresses the action denoted by the subsequent participial phrase.

eutonōs (†) 'vigorously', 'vehemently', referring either to the content of the accusation, or to the tones of their accusing, preferably the latter.

Translation: *Stood by...accusing him,* cp. also, "stepped forward and pressed the case against him..." (TEV).

Vehemently, or, 'with violent words', 'speaking/shouting violently'.

11 ***And Herod with his soldiers treated him with contempt and mocked him; then, arraying him in gorgeous apparel, he sent him back to Pilate.***

Exegesis: *exouthenēsas...kai empaixas peribalōn...anepempsen* 'after treating (him) with contempt and after mocking (him) he put on...and sent back'. Of the three participles of this clause the first and the second go together and refer to acts without direct connexion with the act denoted by the main verb *anepempsen*; the third, however, is directly connected with the sending back of Jesus since it is a preparation for it. For *exoutheneō* cp. on 18 : 9; for *empaizō* on 14 : 29.

ho Hērōdēs sun tois strateumasin 'Herod together with his troops'.

strateuma (†) 'army', in the plural 'troops', 'soldiers'.

peribalōn esthēta lampran 'after putting on (him) a splendid robe', probably some mock royal robe or cloak. For *periballō* cp. on 12 : 27.

esthēs (also 24 : 4) 'clothing', in a general sense, here, 'robe', 'cloak'.

lampros (†) 'splendid', 'gorgeous', cp. Plummer.

anepempsen auton tō Pilatō 'he sent him back to Pilate', cp. on v. 7.

Translation: Grammatically only Herod is the subject of the whole sentence; semantically Herod and his soldiers are the agents of "treated...

with contempt" and "mocked"; of the arraying the same may be true, but it is probably preferable to take Herod as the initiator; of the sending back Herod alone is the direct agent. These differences may have to be made explicit in the translation, e.g. in Fulani, or in Timorese, which has, 'H. slandered him together with his officers, they all mocked him. Then he ordered to array him..., and he sent him back to P.'. Tzeltal has 'Herod and his soldiers' as subject of the first three verbs, 'Herod' as subject of 'sent him back'.

To treat with contempt, or, 'to look down upon', 'to despise', and cp. *TH-Mk* on "to treat shamefully" in 12 : 4. *To mock*, see on 14 : 29.

Arraying him in gorgeous apparel, he sent him back, or in co-ordination, 'Herod had him arrayed, or, they arrayed him..., and so he/Herod sent him back'. For *to array* cp. on 12 : 27. *Gorgeous apparel* (cp. on 7 : 25), or, 'splendid cloak' (cp. on 6 : 29), 'kingly clothes' (Shona).

12 ***And Herod and Pilate became friends with each other that very day, for before this they had been at enmity with each other.***

Exegesis: *egenonto de philoi...met' allēlōn* '(they) became friends with one another'. *met' allēlōn*, which is virtually redundant semantically, is best understood as strengthening *philoi*.

en autē tē hēmera 'that very day'.

proüpērchon gar en echthra ontes pros hautous 'for previously they were at enmity between themselves'.

proüparchō (†) 'to exist before', here virtually an auxiliary verb denoting that the event or situation to which the following participle refers, happened in the past.

echthra (†) 'enmity'.

Translation: *Became friends with each other*, or, 'became friends', or, 'they came to like (or, to be on good terms with) each other'.

For introduces explanatory matter, not cause or reason, and must therefore not be rendered literally, cp. "...became friends; they had been enemies before this" (TEV), "Herod and Pilate, who had been at enmity, ..." (Rieu), *H. et P. devinrent amis, d'ennemis qu'ils étaient auparavant* (Jerusalem), 'whereas before the two had been each other's enemy' (Bahasa Indonesia).

They had been at enmity with each other, or, 'they had been enemies' (cp. on 1 : 71), 'they had not liked each other', etc., the opposite of the preceding clause. Both 'to be friends' and 'to be enemies' indicate a reciprocal relationship; hence they are often rendered by reciprocal verbal forms, e.g. in Balinese, South Toradja.

13 ***Pilate then called together the chief priests and the rulers and the people,*** 14 ***and said to them, "You brought me this man as one who was perverting the people; and after examining him before you, behold, I did not find this man guilty of any of your charges against him;***

Exegesis: *sugkalesamenos tous archiereis kai tous archontas kai ton laon* 'after summoning the chief priests and the rulers and the people'. For *sugkaleō* cp. on 9 : 1. *ton laon* (cp. on 1 : 10) is to be interpreted in the same sense as *tous ochlous* in v. 4.

archōn 'ruler', 'leader', here best understood as referring to the members of the Sanhedrin, cp. on 22 : 66.

(V. 14) *prosēnegkate moi ton anthrōpon touton* 'you brought this man before me'. *prospherō* with following accusative and dative means here, 'to bring before a judge'.

hōs apostrephonta ton laon 'as one who is misleading the people'. *hōs* with participle implies that it is not an established fact but their subjective allegation, cp. Bl-D, § 425.3. For *laos* cp. A-G s.v. 1 c α.

apostrephō (†) lit. 'to turn away', viz. from allegiance or obedience, hence 'to mislead', 'to cause to revolt', 'to subvert'. The phrase repeats in a condensed form the accusations of v. 2, and *apostrephō* is virtually equivalent to *diastrephō*.

kai idou 'and behold' (cp. on 1 : 20), emphasizing the contrast between the allegations of the priests and the result of Pilate's examination.

egō enōpion humōn anakrinas 'I (for one) having examined (him) in your presence'. *egō* is emphatic.

anakrinō (†) 'to question', 'to examine', with personal object (here understood), or in an absolute sense, 'to conduct an examination', preferably the former.

outhen heuron en tō anthrōpō toutō aition 'I have found no guilt in this man', repeating v. 4.

hōn katēgoreite kat' autou lit. 'of the things of which you accuse him', going with *outhen...aition*, 'no guilt of', i.e. 'no ground for the accusations you make against him'.

Translation: *Called together*, or, 'summoned', i.e. ordered the Jewish leaders and crowd (who probably were still, or again, standing around in the neighbourhood of Pilate's palace) to come together again at the place where Jesus' case was to continue.

The rulers, cp. on 18 : 18; or here, more specifically, "the...councillors" (NEB), 'the other members of the Jewish council'.

(V. 14) *Said to them.* The pronoun refers to all the groups mentioned in v. 13; if one has to use honorifics with reference to the leaders, one should take care to render Pilate's address in such a way that the crowd is not excluded from the persons addressed.

You brought me this man, preferably, 'you brought this man before me', cp. on 12 : 11.

As one who was perverting the people, or, bringing out the force of "as" in another way, 'you-were-saying: he is perverting the people' (cp. East Toradja 1933).

To examine, or, 'to interrogate', 'to investigate'.

Before you, or, 'in your presence', 'while you were standing by, or, heard it'.

I did not find this man guilty of any of your charges against him may require rather radical changes of structure, cp. e.g. 'I did not find that he has committed any of the crimes you say he has done', 'bad thing not even one concerning him have I found like you accuse him' (Kapauku), 'I did not find any case at all in those (things) you accuse him of' (Shona 1966); or, expressing a concessive connexion, "I have found nothing criminal about him, in spite of all your accusations" (Phillips), cp. also, 'he has no sin, I found, although he has much sin, you say' (Tzeltal); or again, taking "charges" with "to examine", 'I held an investigation concerning the charges you brought forward, but I did not find any crime/fault in Him' (Bahasa Indonesia RC, similarly Marathi). For *charge* cp. on "accusation" in 6 : 7. — The first part of the sentence echoes Pilate's words in v. 4 and is echoed again in v. 22, a stylistic trait which should preferably be preserved.

15 ***neither did Herod, for he sent him back to us. Behold, nothing deserving death has been done by him;***

Exegesis: *all' oude Hērōdēs* 'but (not only I), neither (did) Herod', viz. find any guilt in him, cp. A-G s.v. *alla* 3.

anepempsen gar auton pros hēmas 'for he has sent him back to us', takes up the end of v. 11.

kai idou 'and behold', cp. on 1 : 20. Here it serves to introduce the concluding statement, cp. "obviously" (Phillips).

ouden axion thanatou lit. 'nothing worth death', i.e. 'nothing deserving capital punishment'.

estin pepragmenon autō 'has been done by him'. The use of the perfect tense suggests that the statement is final.

Translation: *Neither did Herod.* Even if the ellipsis has to be filled out, the rendering should preserve something of the forceful terseness of the original.

To us. The plural does not refer to Pilate only, as a plural of majesty, but to Pilate, the Jewish leaders and the people together; hence the pronoun has inclusive force; cp. also, 'me and you' (Javanese).

Nothing deserving death. Idiom may require some adjustments, cp. e.g. 'nothing fit to suffer death-penalty' (Marathi), 'nothing in-keeping-with a sentence of death' (Bahasa Indonesia RC), 'nothing worthy (lit. to reach) death' (Zarma), 'no affair for making-him-die' (Kapauku), 'nothing that causes him to have-as-debt life' (Toba Batak), 'not anything which could ever kill him' (Fulani), 'nothing...which could be said: let him die' (Shona 1966).

16 ***I will therefore chastise him and release him."***

Exegesis: *paideusas oun auton apolusō* 'so after disciplining him I shall release (him)'. *oun* is inferential and the clause represents a concession to the accusers. Hence the clause is sometimes rendered as a proposal (cp. e.g. NEB), but it appears preferable to understand it as Pilate's decision.

paideuō (also v. 22), 'to educate', here 'to discipline', by means of whipping, or scourging, cp. A-G s.v. 2 b γ; probably meant as a euphemism.

Translation: *I will...chastise him*, or, using a corresponding euphemism for beating or punishment, "teach him a (sharp) lesson" (Goodspeed, Phillips), "after due correction" (Rieu). Where such a rendering is not possible one can best say, 'I will...scourge him, or, have him scourged', cp. on 18 : 33.

Release him, or, 'make him go free', 'let him go out (from prison)'.

17 ***Now he was obliged to release one man to them at the festival.***

Exegesis: *anagkēn de eichen apoluein autois kata heortēn hena* lit. 'he had the compulsion, i.e. he was obliged, to release for them one (person) at a feast'; here *anagkē* refers to a compulsion by tradition. For *kata heortēn* cp. *TH-Mk* on 15 : 6.

Translation: *To them*, referring to the beneficiaries, may have to be described, e.g. by 'as-a-kindness-to them' (cp. Balinese), 'according to their choice' (Willibrord), 'as they requested'. The pronoun refers to the inhabitants of Jerusalem, hence 'the populace' (Bahasa Indonesia RC), 'the crowd' (Javanese), or to the whole people, as represented by their leaders and the populace of Jerusalem, hence 'the Jews', or, 'the Jewish people' (Sundanese, Balinese).

At the festival, or more specifically, "at each Passover Feast" (TEV); cp. also *TH-Mk* on 15 : 6, and above on 2 : 41.

18 ***But they all cried out together, "Away with this man, and release to us Barabbas"—***

Exegesis: *anekragon de pamplēthei* 'but they shouted out all together'.

pamplēthei (††) lit. 'with the whole multitude', adverb, 'all together'.

aire touton lit. 'take him away', 'remove him', hence 'away with him'.

apoluson de hēmin ton Barabban 'release Barabbas for us'. For *Barabbas* cp. *TH-Mk* on 15 : 7.

Translation: *They all cried out together*, or, "the whole crowd shouted" (BFBS).

Away with this man, implying that he should die; hence, 'kill this man, or, him' (cp. Goodspeed, TEV, Jerusalem, Toba Batak), or, 'destroy this man' (Javanese).

Release to us Barabbas, or, if the force of "to us" has to be described,

"We want B. set free" (Phillips, similarly Sundanese), "...let us have B." (Rieu). *Us* has exclusive force.

19 ***a man who had been thrown into prison for an insurrection started in the city, and for murder.***

Exegesis: *hostis ēn...blētheis en tē phulakē* 'who had been thrown into prison'. The relative clause is attached to the direct speech of v. 18, but is not part of it. It is added in order to give information about Barabbas after his name has been mentioned, and is best treated as an independent clause in parentheses. The periphrastic construction *ēn...blētheis* is equivalent to a pluperfect, cp. Bl-D, § 355. *en* is here equivalent to *eis*, cp. A-G s.v. *en* I 6.

dia stasin tina genomenēn en tē polei kai phonon 'on account of a rising that had happened in the city and of murder', implying that Barabbas had something to do with the riot and was responsible for a murder committed during the riot. For *stasis* (also in v. 25) cp. *TH-Mk* on 15 : 7.

Translation: *A man who had been...*, or as a new sentence, '(This) Barabbas (or, This man) had been...', 'Barabbas was a man who had been...'. In some cases it is preferable to start the sentence with the description of the situation, e.g. 'There had been an insurrection in the city and a murder, and as a result (or, and for this reason) this man had been...' (cp. Rieu, Toba Batak).

Thrown into prison, or, 'imprisoned', cp. on "shut up...in prison" in 3 : 20. If an active construction is required, one can best use an indefinite agent (cp. e.g. Sranan, 'they'), or take Pilate, the Romans, or the Roman authorities as agent(s) or initiators.

For an insurrection started in the city, or in a verbal clause, 'because people had begun to riot in the city', 'because people in the city had fought the ruler' (cp. East Toradja 1933); see *TH-Mk* on 15 : 7.

Murder, or, 'someone had been killed' (East Toradja 1933), 'he had committed a murder, or, had killed a person'. Cp. also *N.T.Wb.*/49, KILL.

20 ***Pilate addressed them once more, desiring to release Jesus;***

Exegesis: *palin de ho Pilatos prosephōnēsen autois* 'once more Pilate called out to them', without stating what he said. For *prosphōneō* cp. on 6 : 13. Note the punctiliar aorist tense of *prosephōnēsen* as contrasted with *epephōnoun* in v. 21.

thelōn apolusai ton Iēsoun 'wanting to release Jesus', indicating his intention in calling out to the people.

Translation: *Desiring*. The reason may better be mentioned first, cp. e.g. "P. wanted to set Jesus free, so he called out to the crowd again" (TEV).

21 ***but they shouted out, "Crucify, crucify him!"***

Exegesis: *hoi de epephōnoun legontes* 'but they shouted out'. The imperfect tense is durative.

epiphōneō (†) 'to shout out', 'to cry out'.

staurou, staurou auton 'crucify, crucify him', emphatic repetition of the imperative.

stauroō 'to nail to the cross', 'to crucify'.

Translation: *They shouted out,* or because of what precedes, "they shouted back" (TEV).

Crucify, crucify him. The verb is usually rendered by an expression built on, or derived from the term for "cross" (for which see on 9 : 23), cp. e.g. 'to the cross he must go' (Sranan), 'stretch him' (Balinese, South Toradja), 'hang him on a crossbeam' (Sundanese); cp. also *TH-Mk* on 15 : 13.

22 ***A third time he said to them, "Why, what evil has he done? I have found in him no crime deserving death; I will therefore chastise him and release him."***

Exegesis: *triton* adverb, 'for the third time'.

ti gar kakon epoiēsen houtos 'why, what evil has he done?' *gar* has lost its causal meaning and is used here in an inferential or transitional sense, cp. A-G 1 f.

ouden aition thanatou lit. 'nothing guilty of death', i.e. 'no ground for capital punishment'.

Translation: *Why, what evil has he done?,* or, 'now tell me, what crime (or, bad deed, or, evil thing) has he done?', "What is his crime, then?" (Phillips, similarly Javanese). For *evil* cp. also Nida, *BT*, 220f.

The next two sentences combine parts of vv. 4, 15 and 16 (which see).

23 ***But they were urgent, demanding with loud cries that he should be crucified. And their voices prevailed.***

Exegesis: *hoi de epekeinto...aitoumenoi* 'but they persisted in demanding'. For *epikeimai* cp. on 5 : 1; here it is used of applying mental pressure, with following participial clause indicating what was pressed for, viz. that Jesus should be crucified.

phōnais megalais 'with loud voices', elsewhere in the singular (cp. 19 : 37), in a clause with plural subject, here in the plural, without difference in meaning.

katischuon hai phōnai autōn 'their voices, i.e. their shouting prevailed'.

katischuō here 'to prevail', 'to win the day'.

Translation: *They were urgent, demanding,* or, 'they insisted on their demand', 'they pressed (lit. made to walk) their earnest entreaty' (Marathi), 'they kept on demanding', cp. "they kept on shouting" (TEV, choosing a verb more in tune with the next phrase). The person to whom the demand is addressed may have to be indicated, cp. e.g. 'they pressed him (or, Pilate) and asked', or, shifting the main verb, 'they demanded him/Pilate urgently'.

With loud cries, or, 'shouts', 'crying/shouting loudly'. The phrase may better become the main clause, cp. e.g. 'they made-loud (lit. blazing) their voice to press him, asking' (Toba Batak).

That he should be crucified, or, 'that he (i.e. Pilate) should crucify him/Jesus, or, should have him/Jesus crucified'.

Their voices prevailed, or, 'won-the-victory' (Ponape), is variously rendered, cp. e.g. 'their noises defeated him' (Fulani), 'their words conquered, or, were obeyed' (cp. Shona 1963, Tzeltal), 'their voices made authority' (Zarma, an idiom for a pronouncement one is forced to obey whether right or wrong), 'success came to their yelling' (Marathi), 'they won-out' (Kituba).

24 ***So Pilate gave sentence that their demand should be granted.***

Exegesis: *kai Pilatos epekrinen genesthai to aitēma autōn* 'and (consequently) Pilate decided that their request, i.e. what they requested, should be done'.

epikrinō (††) 'to decide', 'to determine', not a specific judicial term.
aitēma (†) 'request', here referring to the content of the request.

Translation: *Gave sentence*, or, 'pronounced/passed sentence', and cp. *N.T.Wb.*/48, JUDGE.

That their demand should be granted, or, 'that he (i.e. Pilate) would do what they asked for', 'to comply with their request' (Balinese, East Toradja).

25 ***He released the man who had been thrown into prison for insurrection and murder, whom they asked for; but Jesus he delivered up to their will.***

Exegesis: *hon ētounto* 'whom they kept demanding', iterative imperfect.

ton de Iēsoun paredōken tō thelēmati autōn lit.'but Jesus he delivered up to their will', i.e. as they wished, but in fact the execution of Jesus is not performed by the high priests or, for that matter, the people, but by Roman soldiers.

Translation: *Whom they asked for*, or, where a second relative clause would be undesirable, 'because they kept asking for him', 'as they had demanded'.

Jesus he delivered up to their will. If one wishes to avoid the suggestion that Jesus was handed over to the Jews (see *Exegesis*), one may specify the meaning of verb and preposition, e.g. 'Jesus he abandoned/gave-up, in accordance with their desire' (Leyden, similarly Bahasa Indonesia), or more explicitly, 'Jesus he gave up to his death (or, as to Jesus, he had him put to death), since they wished so', 'he ordered his men to execute Jesus, in accordance with the wishes of the Jews'.

26 ***And as they led him away, they seized one Simon of Cyrene, who was coming in from the country, and laid on him the cross, to carry it behind Jesus.***

Exegesis: *hōs apēgagon auton* 'as they led him away', viz. in order to be executed, cp. A-G s.v. 2 c. The subject (not stated) is the Roman soldiers.

epilabomenoi Simōna tina Kurēnaion 'after taking hold of a certain Simon, a Cyrenaean'. For *epilambanō* cp. on 9 : 47; here a note of violence is implied. *tina* may go with *Simōna* or with *Kurēnaion,* preferably the former, cp. also *TH-Mk* on 15 : 21.

erchomenon ap' agrou 'coming in from the country', or, 'from the field', preferably the former, cp. *TH-Mk, l.c.*

epethēkan autō ton stauron 'they put the cross upon him'. *epitithēmi* does not imply violence. For *stauros* cp. *TH-Mk* on 8 : 34.

pherein opisthen tou Iēsou 'in order to carry it after Jesus', final infinitive. *opisthen* also 8 : 44.

Translation: *As they led him away.* The direction may have to be specified, e.g. 'from Pilate's palace', or, 'to (the place of) execution'. For the verb cp. *TH-Mk* on 15 : 1. — The clause may better become a co-ordinate sentence, the next sentence being introduced then by a transitional phrase, e.g. 'on the(ir) way' (cp. TEV), 'as-they-led-him thus' (East Toradja 1933).

Simon may have to be properly introduced; hence e.g. 'Now, a certain Simon was coming. . . . They seized him. . .' (cp. Marathi), 'They met a man named S. . . . They seized. . .' (cp. Tzeltal).

Of Cyrene, i.e. 'a man hailing-from C.' (Balinese), 'native from (the town of) Cyrene', 'who originally had lived in C.'.

From the country, i.e. the countryside, see on 21 : 21.

Laid on him the cross, to carry it behind Jesus, cp. "take up his cross daily and follow me" in 9 : 23, using in a figurative sense what here refers to actual fact. The sentence is sometimes better rendered in two or three clauses, e.g. 'they laid the cross on him and compelled/ordered/caused him to carry it behind Jesus (cp. Rieu), or, walking after Jesus'. In translation one may have to use more specific verbs, e.g. 'to lay-on-the-shoulder/back/back-of-the-neck', and/or, 'to carry-on-the-shoulder' etc.

27 ***And there followed him a great multitude of the people, and of women who bewailed and lamented him.***

Exegesis: *ēkolouthei de autō polu plēthos tou laou* 'him followed a great crowd of the people'. *ēkolouthei* is emphatic by position. The imperfect tense is descriptive and refers to a situation which forms the background of the subsequent events and words. For *plēthos* and *laos* cp. on 1 : 10, but both are used here without religious implications; *laos* refers to the people of Jerusalem in general.

kai gunaikōn 'and of women', depending on *plēthos* and mentioned separately because of Jesus' words to them.

hai ekoptonto kai ethrēnoun auton 'who were beating (their breasts) and weeping for him'. *auton* goes with both verbs, cp. on 8 : 52. For *thrēneō* cp. on 7 : 32. As a comparison with these two places shows the women acted as if attending a burial.

Translation: For *followed* and *the people* cp. on 7 : 9 and 29 respectively.

And of women, or, 'and also (or, amongst them also) several women'.

Who bewailed and lamented him, or, 'who were mourning and weeping because of him'. For the first verb, lit. 'to beat (the breast)' cp. on 18 : 13. A cultural equivalent expressing sorrow or sorrowful commiseration can sometimes be used, e.g. 'who put their hands on their head' (Sranan), but many versions do as RSV and employ a non-symbolic or non-figurative expression such as 'to wail over', 'to bewail'. For this verb and for *to lament* see *N.T.Wb.*/73, WEEP; the pair may be treated as a hendiadys.

28 ***But Jesus turning to them said, "Daughters of Jerusalem, do not weep for me, but weep for yourselves and for your children.***

Exegesis: *strapheis...pros autas* 'turning to them', cp. on 7 : 9.

thugateres Ierousalēm 'daughters of Jerusalem', cp. on 1 : 5. Here *thugateres* means 'female inhabitants'.

mē klaiete ep' eme lit. 'do not weep toward me', i.e. 'do not weep for me'. *epi* refers to the object of the emotion expressed in the weeping, cp. A-G s.v. III 1 b ε.

plēn 'but', expressing strong contrast.

Translation: *Turning to them,* or, 'to these women' (Javanese); for the phrase cp. also on 7 : 9.

Daughters of Jerusalem, preferably, '(you,) women of (or, who live in) Jerusalem'.

But weep, or more strongly contrastive, 'on the contrary weep', "...; no, weep" (NEB).

29 ***For behold, the days are coming when they will say, 'Blessed are the barren, and the wombs that never bore, and the breasts that never gave suck!'***

Exegesis: *hoti idou erchontai hēmerai* lit. 'for behold days come'. *idou* focusses the attention on what follows. For *erchontai hēmerai* cp. on 5 : 35; *erchontai* is best understood as referring to the future.

hēmerai en hais lit. 'days in which', i.e. 'a time when'.

erousin 'they will say', 'people will say'.

makariai hai steirai 'happy (are) the barren ones', cp. on 1 : 45 for *makarios*, and on 1 : 7 for *steira.*

kai hai koiliai hai ouk egennēsan 'and (happy are) the wombs which never bore (children)'. Note the punctiliar aorist tense, 'never once'.

kai mastoi hoi ouk ethrepsan 'and (happy are) the breasts which never nursed/fed (children)'. For the aorist tense see above. *mastos* also 11 : 27.

Translation: For the clauses in quoted speech cp. on 11 : 27 and 21 : 23. *The barren* (cp. on 1 : 7) refers to those who cannot bear children, *the wombs that never bore* to those who do not bear children.

30 ***Then they will begin to say to the mountains, 'Fall on us'; and to the hills, 'Cover us.'***

Exegesis: *tote arxontai legein* 'then they will begin to say', cp. on 4 : 21. *arxontai* has here no meaning of its own and may go untranslated.

tois oresin...kai tois bounois 'to the mountains...and to the hills', often occurring together as in 3 : 5, here, however, also personified. This personification is poetic and not mythical.

pesete eph' hēmas...kalupsate hēmas 'fall on us...cover us up', expressing either a request for protection, or the wish to be killed in order to miss the imminent terror. The latter is preferable, cp. Plummer. *kaluptō*, cp. on 8 : 16.

Translation: If addressing mountains and hills as though they were persons is unacceptable in the receptor language, even in poetical passages, one may have to shift to something like, 'then they will begin to say, "We should be better as dead as people are when mountains have fallen upon them and hills are covering them'.

For *mountains* and *hills* see on 3 : 5.

Fall on. A literal rendering may not fit this context; hence e.g. 'collapse-on' (Javanese), 'crash-down hitting' (Bahasa Indonesia RC), 'lie-down-on-top-of' (East Toradja), 'press-down-upon' (South Toradja); or shifting from the process to its result, 'put an end to' (Tzeltal).

Cover, here in the sense of, 'pile up over', 'form a heap over', 'bury'.

31 ***For if they do this when the wood is green, what will happen when it is dry?"***

Exegesis: *hoti* 'for', introducing Jesus' explanation of the quotation in v. 30.

ei en tō hugrō xulō tauta poiousin 'if they do this to the green wood'. *tauta* refers to what is being done to Jesus. *poiein en* means 'to do to', i.e. 'affect by doing', here used in a pejorative sense.

hugros (††) 'moist', 'pliant', here of wood ,'green', 'fresh'. For this metaphor see below.

en tō xērō ti genētai 'what will happen to the dry (wood)?' *ginesthai en* lit. 'to happen in the case of', hence 'to happen to', is equivalent to the passive of *poiein en* (see above). The subjunctive has the force of an interrogative future. *xēros* contrasts with *hugros*. Since the latter, because of *tauta* and of the underlying contrast between Jesus and the women (v. 28), refers to Jesus, *xēros* must refer to the generation that will have to go through the ordeals implied in v. 29f. The saying appears to be proverbial (see commentaries) and implies that when the innocent Jesus has to suffer death how much more will the far from innocent Jews have to suffer.

Translation: Where the metaphor would be unacceptable a shift to a simile will be helpful, e.g. 'if they do this to me, who am comparable to green wood, what will happen to you, who are comparable to dry wood'; where one has to adjust the "if"-clause (cp. on 11 : 20) and the rhetorical question, the result will become something like, '(you see that) they are doing this when the wood is green (or, to me who am..., etc., see above); they certainly will do worse when the wood is dry (or, to you who are..., etc.)'.

Green wood and *dry wood*, or, 'live tree' and 'dry tree' (Kapauku), 'wet tree' and 'dry one' (Marathi).

32 ***Two others also, who were criminals, were led away to be put to death with him.***

Exegesis: *ēgonto de kai heteroi kakourgoi duo* 'two other criminals were also led out'. *ēgonto* is semantically equivalent to *apēgagon* in v. 26. As v. 33 shows the phrase *heteroi kakourgoi duo* does not suggest that the word *kakourgos* applies to Jesus also. But even without this clarification the phrase is not likely to be misunderstood (cp. Plummer).

kakourgos (also v. 39) 'evil-doer', 'criminal', of a person who commits serious crimes, cp. A-G s.v.

sun autō anairethēnai 'to be put to death with him', final infinitive. *anaireō* (cp. on 22 : 2) is used here in the meaning, 'to kill by execution'.

Translation: *Two others also, who were criminals, were led away*, restricting the qualification "criminals" to the "two others"; similarly, 'they (or, the soldiers) took away two others, both of them criminals' (cp. TEV), 'there were two other men led away, viz. two evildoers' (Bahasa Indonesia 1968).

Put to death, or, 'executed' (Jerusalem), 'punished by death' (Javanese, Balinese), or, in this context, 'crucified' (Bahasa Indonesia RC).

33 ***And when they came to the place which is called The Skull, there they crucified him, and the criminals, one on the right and one on the left.***

Exegesis: *hote ēlthon epi ton topon ton kaloumenon Kranion* 'when they came to the place called Skull'. The subject of *ēlthon* is the same as that of *estaurōsan*.

kranion (†) 'skull', here the name of a hill after its shape, Greek rendering of Aramaic Golgotha.

estaurōsan auton kai tous kakourgous 'they crucified him and the criminals'. Subject of *estaurōsan* is the Roman soldiers charged with the execution (cp. on v. 26).

hon men ek dexiōn hon de ex aristerōn 'one on the right and one on the left', with *merē* 'side' (cp. A-G s.v. 1 b δ) understood with *dexiōn* and *aristerōn*; *aristeros* (†). The relative pronoun functions here as a demonstrative. *men* and *de* have distributive function.

Translation: *The Skull.* The designation used in some languages is basically descriptive, e.g. 'coconutshell, or, gourd, of the head' (Balinese, South and East Toradja), 'head-bone' (Sranan).

Right and *left*, cp. *N.T.Wb.*/42, HAND.

34 ***And Jesus said, "Father, forgive them; for they know not what they do." And they cast lots to divide his garments.***

Exegesis: *aphes autois* 'forgive them'. For the concept of forgiveness cp. on 1 : 77, *autois* may refer to the Jewish high priests or to the Roman soldiers. The latter is preferable.

ou gar oidasin ti poiousin 'for they do not know what they are doing'. *oida* means here 'to realize', 'to understand'. *poiousin* refers to what they are doing there and then, not to what they usually do.

diamerizomenoi...ta himatia autou 'dividing (among themselves) his clothes'. For *diamerizō* cp. on 11 : 17.

ebalon klēron 'they cast lots', cp. A-G s.v. *klēros* 1. The semantic relationship between *diamerizomenoi* and *ebalon klēron* is that the latter denotes the way in which the former is accomplished, cp. NEB. *klēros* (†).

Translation: *And*, preferably, 'but', viz. in contrast to what the soldiers did.

They cast lots to divide his garments, i.e. "they parcelled out his clothing and cast lots for the shares" (Rieu), or, to bring out the instrumental relationship, 'they/the soldiers divided his clothes by casting lots (amongst themselves)'. For *to cast lots* cp. on "by lot" in 1 : 9; and *TH-Mk* on 15 : 24. Some versions use a term with the pejorative connotation of gambling here, e.g. "to throw dice" (TEV), 'to do like spinning acorns' (Kapauku), 'to cast-hollow-bamboo-chips' (South Toradja), but another term in 1 : 9 and Acts 1 : 26. For *garments* see on 5 : 36.

35 ***And the people stood by, watching; but the rulers scoffed at him, saying, "He saved others; let him save himself, if he is the Christ of God, his Chosen One!"***

Exegesis: *kai heistēkei ho laos theōrōn* 'and the people stood there watching'. For *ho laos* cp. on v. 27. *theōrō* means here 'to watch', 'to look on', 'to stare', as at a spectacle, cp. Plummer.

exemuktērizon de kai hoi archontes 'also the rulers sneered'. *de kai* implies that the attitude of the people was also contemptuous. For *ekmuktērizō* cp. on 16 : 14. As compared with *empaizō* in v. 36 it has a stronger connotation of contempt. For *hoi archontes* cp. on 23 : 13.

allous esōsen, sōsatō heauton 'he saved others, let him save himself'. *sōzō* is used here in the meaning, 'to save from death'.

ei houtos estin ho Christos tou theou ho eklektos 'if this man is the Anointed One of God, the chosen one'. *houtos* is used here contemptuously. For *ho Christos tou theou* cp. on 2 : 26. For *ho eklektos* cp. on *ho eklelegmenos* in 9 : 35. *ho eklektos* may be attributive to *ho Christos* ('God's chosen Messiah'), or in apposition to it. The latter is preferable.

Translation: *Scoffed*, see on 16 : 14.

To save, or, 'to rescue', 'to save (lit. help) the life of' (Balinese), not used in a specifically religious sense here.

The Christ of God, his Chosen One, cp. on 2: 26 ("the Lord's Christ") and on 9 : 35. Comparable adjustments may lead here to, 'the Messiah God has sent (or, given) and chosen', 'the One whom God has anointed and elected (or, especially loved, cp. Sranan)'.

36 ***The soldiers also mocked him, coming up and offering him vinegar,*** 37 ***and saying, "If you are the King of the Jews, save yourself!"***

Exegesis: *enepaixan de autō kai hoi stratiōtai* 'the soldiers also made fun of him'. For *empaizō* cp. on 14 : 29. The aorist tense is best understood as being for the sake of variety. *stratiōtēs* also 7 : 8.

proserchomenoi, oxos prospherontes autō kai legontes 'coming up, offering sour wine and saying'. The mocking by the soldiers consists of (1) the offering of the sour wine, and (2) their words related in v. 37. The act denoted by *proserchomenoi* leads up to (1) and (2).

oxos (†) 'wine vinegar', 'sour wine', cp. A-G s.v. As this is a cheap and common beverage, to offer it to someone who pretended to be king was, in the eyes of the soldiers, an act of mockery.

(V. 37) *ei su ei ho basileus tōn Ioudaiōn* 'if you are the king of the Jews', same construction and meaning as in 4 : 3, which see.

Translation: *Mocked*, see on 14 : 29.

Coming up and offering...and saying, often better as a co-ordinated sentence, 'they came up, offering...and saying', 'they came up and offered...and said'. *To come up*, or, 'near', 'to come closer to Jesus'.

Vinegar, or, 'sour wine'; for 'wine' cp. on 1 : 15.

(V. 37) *If you are*, or, 'if you really are', 'you say that you are', cp. 4 : 3.

Jews, see on 7 : 3.

38 ***There was also an inscription over him, "This is the King of the Jews."***

Exegesis: *ēn de kai epigraphē ep' autō* 'there was also a notice above him'. For *epigraphē* cp. on 20 : 24. Here it is used in the meaning 'notice', 'placard'. *ep' autō* 'above him', or 'above his head', cp. A-G s.v. *epi* II 1 a α.

ho basileus tōn Ioudaiōn houtos 'this is the king of the Jews', not a statement but a charge.

Translation: *There was...an inscription*, or, 'a writing', 'these words (or, letters) were written' (cp. TEV, Tzeltal), 'they had written' (cp. Fulani).

Over him, or, 'above his head'; Tzeltal shifts to, 'at the top of the cross'.

39 ***One of the criminals who were hanged railed at him, saying, "Are you not the Christ? Save yourself and us!"***

Exegesis: *heis de tōn kremasthentōn kakourgōn* 'one of the criminals who had been hung', or, with a shift from the act to the result, 'who were hanging'.

kremannumi (†) 'to hang', here of crucifixion and equivalent to *stauroō* (vv. 21, 33).

eblasphēmei auton legōn 'reviled him by saying'. For *blasphēmeō* cp. on 22 : 65.

ouchi su ei ho Christos 'are you not the Christ?'. *ouchi* indicates that an affirmative answer is expected, and this reveals the question as mockery.

Translation: *Who were hanged,* or, 'who were being crucified', 'who were hanging on the cross'.

Railed at, or, 'reviled' (see on 6 : 22).

Are you not the Christ, or, 'you are the Messiah, aren't you' (cp. BFBS), better to suggest the affirmative answer expected.

Save yourself and us. The second pronoun has exclusive force. Balinese has to say here, 'save your life (honorific) and the life (non-honorific) of the two of us'; in South Toradja it is preferable to repeat the verb before the second object.

40 ***But the other rebuked him, saying, "Do you not fear God, since you are under the same sentence of condemnation?***

Exegesis: *apokritheis de ho heteros epitimōn autō ephē* lit. 'answering the other said, checking him'. For the use of *apokritheis* see on 1 : 60. For *epitimaō* cp. on 4 : 35 and reference there.

oude phobē su ton theon 'do you not even fear God', not to speak of feeling remorse (cp. Klostermann), or, taking *oude* with *su,* 'do not even you fear God'. The former is preferable.

hoti en tō autō krimati ei 'since you are under the same sentence'. The clause is to be taken and understood together with v. 41: the fact that they are suffering what they deserve but that Jesus is suffering what he does not deserve should have kept him from reviling Jesus. For *krima* cp. *TH-Mk* on 12 : 40.

Translation: For *rebuked* see on 4 : 35, for *fear God* on 1 : 50.

Since, or, 'in view of the fact that', 'now that'; the relationship may also be expressed by an appositional construction, '..., you who are...', or an asyndetic sentence, cp. TEV.

You are under the same sentence of condemnation, or, 'you receive the same punishment (as he receives)' (cp. Marathi, Lokele, East Toradja, Sranan), 'they have condemned (or, are punishing) you like him (or, as they have done him)', 'you and he are both condemned to death' (Shona 1966). Of course the speaker does not mean to exclude himself; hence it is more idiomatic in some languages to say, 'we (inclus.) are under the same sentence' (Toba Batak). For *sentence of condemnation* cp. *N.T.Wb.*/48, JUDGE.

41 ***And we indeed justly; for we are receiving the due reward of our deeds; but this man has done nothing wrong."***

Exegesis: *kai hēmeis men dikaiōs* 'and we (are) justly (condemned)', 'for us it is just'.

axia gar hōn epraxamen apolambanomen 'for we receive worthy of what we have done', i.e. 'we get what we deserve'. *apolambanō* means here 'to receive what is due'.

houtos de ouden atopon epraxen 'but this man has done nothing wrong'.

atopos (†) lit. 'out of place', here in a moral sense, 'improper', 'wrong', 'wicked'.

Translation: *We* refers to the speaker and the one addressed, but should not include Jesus. Kapauku makes this clear by saying 'we two'; elsewhere one may have to use, 'you and I'.

We are receiving the due reward of our deeds (or, 'our works' salary', in Zarma, or, 'a judgment matching our works', in Fulani) may have to be variously recast, cp. e.g. 'we are getting (or, they give us) what we deserve for what we did' (cp. TEV), 'what (or, the punishment) we suffer is in-accordance-with what we did', 'we are being caused to pay for as many sins as we sinned' (Tzeltal), "we deserved what we have got" (Rieu).

This man has done nothing wrong. In Huli one would use here a suffix denoting that the statement is made on the grounds of visible evidence, such as what the man had seen during the trial, or, of Jesus' behaviour earlier.

42 ***And he said, "Jesus, remember me when you come in your kingly power."***

Exegesis: *mnēsthēti mou* 'remember me', i.e. 'remember me graciously', 'show me your grace'.

hotan elthēs en tē basileia sou 'when you come in your kingship/reign', i.e. either, 'when you come into your kingdom', 'when you become king', or 'when you come with your kingship', 'when you come as king', cp. Mt. 16 : 28 and Plummer and Klostermann. The latter is preferable.

Translation: The words express a reverent request; hence, where honorific forms exist they will have to be used, and an honorific name qualifier may have to be added.

Remember me, cp. also on 1 : 54.

When you come in your kingly power, or, 'when you come as king' (see *Exegesis*), 'when you come with the authority of the Kingdom' (Coll. Japanese), 'when you come (with the power) to rule'.

43 ***And he said to him, "Truly, I say to you, today you will be with me in Paradise."***

Exegesis: *kai eipen autō* 'and he said to him', change of subject.

amēn soi legō 'truly I say to you', cp. on 4 : 24.

sēmeron met' emou esē en tō paradeisō 'today you shall be with me in paradise'. *sēmeron* contrasts with the future of Jesus coming as king. The predicate with *esē* may be *met' emou*, or, *en tō paradeisō*, preferably the latter. Then *met' emou* refers to the situation in which he will find himself in paradise, viz. 'in the company of Jesus'. For the theological implications cp. commentaries.

paradeisos (†) 'paradise', here of the place where the redeemed are after death and before the coming of the kingdom, best envisaged as being in heaven, cp. A-G s.v. 2.

Translation: *Truly, I say to you,* see references on 4 : 24.

Paradise is often transliterated on the base of the Greek, or of the language of prestige in the region; in Muslim countries, for instance, the base is usually the Arabic form, *Firdaus*. Translating the word one may say e.g. 'Place of well-being' (South Toradja, Tzeltal), 'abode of happiness, or, of happy people' (Marathi), 'beautiful garden' (cp. Fulani *aljanna,* borrowing another Arabic name, lit. 'garden'), 'garden of eternal life' (Timorese), or, the name of a place where you don't have to work and fruits drop ripe in your hand (Kapauku).

44 ***It was now about the sixth hour, and there was darkness over the whole land until the ninth hour,*** 45 ***while the sun's light failed; and the curtain of the temple was torn in two.***

Exegesis: *kai ēn ēdē hōsei hōra hektē* 'by now it was about the sixth hour', i.e. 'noon'.

skotos egeneto eph' hōlēn tēn gēn 'darkness came over the whole land'. *gē* may denote the earth, or the country of Palestine, preferably the latter. For *epi* '(spreading) across' cp. A-G s.v. III 1 a α.

heōs hōras enatēs '(lasting) till the ninth hour', i.e. three o'clock in the afternoon.

(V. 45) *tou hēliou eklipontos* 'after the sun had failed', i.e. 'grown dark'. It is possible, though less probable to render, 'after the sun had been eclipsed', cp. Plummer.

eschisthē de to katapetasma tou naou meson 'and the veil of the temple was rent down the middle'. No material or chronological connexion with what precedes is indicated. It may have taken place during, or after the three hour period of darkness, presumably after. For *schizō* cp. on 5 : 36; for *to katapetasma tou naou* cp. *TH-Mk* on 15 : 38; for *naos* cp. on 1 : 9. *meson* lit. '(in the) middle', goes with *katapetasma* (†) and indicates where the rending took place.

Translation: *The sixth hour...the ninth hour.* Where the Jewish way of indicating the hours of the day is unknown one may use a literal rendering and add the explanatory phrase 'after sunrise', or shift to the equivalent receptor language idiom, cp. *TH-Mk* on 15 : 33. In Bali the period of daylight was traditionally divided into eight parts (*dauh*); hence, '*dauh* four... *dauh* six'; nowadays, however, a rendering in accordance with modern Western terminology is probably preferable, 'twelve (at noon)...three o'clock (in the afternoon)'.

There was darkness over the whole land, or, 'the whole country became dark, or, was darkened'. Cp. also *N.T.Wb.*/21f.

(V. 45) *While the sun's light failed* (or, 'was lost', Kapauku). The phrase is sometimes better placed before the reference to 'darkness over the whole land', cp. TEV. Possible rewordings are, "the sun stopped shining" (TEV), 'the sun/day became-dark' (South Toradja).

For *the curtain of the temple* (preferably "before the sanctuary", Goodspeed) *was torn in two* cp. *TH-Mk* on 15 : 38.

46 ***Then Jesus, crying with a loud voice, said, "Father, into thy hands I commit my spirit!" And having said this he breathed his last.***

Exegesis: *phonēsas phōnē megalē* 'calling out with a loud voice', going with *eipen*, not referring to a separate act.

eis cheiras sou paratithemai to pneuma mou lit. 'into your hands I place my spirit' (cp. Ps. 31 : 6 LXX). The phrase 'to place into the hands of (somebody)' has here the connotation of 'giving over', 'commending', 'entrusting'. For *to pneuma* in the anthropological sense of the word cp. on 1 : 47.

exepneusen (†) lit. 'he breathed out', hence, 'he expired', 'he died'.

Translation: *Crying with a loud voice*, cp. on 4 : 33.

Spirit, cp. on 1 : 47; more often than not the term to be used is different from the one rendering '(Holy) Spirit'.

He breathed his last, or, 'he died' (e.g. in Kituba, Trukese). Equivalent idioms are, 'his life-force broke-off' (Bahasa Indonesia, Balinese), 'his breath stopped, or, was-exhausted' (Kapauku, Sranan; East Toradja 1933), 'his breath (and body) parted-with-each-other' (South Toradja).

47 ***Now when the centurion saw what had taken place, he praised God, and said, "Certainly this man was innocent!"***

Exegesis: *idōn de ho hekatontarchēs to genomenon* 'when the centurion saw what had happened'. For *ho hekatontarchēs* cp. on 7 : 2. The article *ho* does not refer to a previous mention of the centurion but depicts him as the man who was naturally supposed to preside over the execution. *to genomenon* refers to all events and circumstances of Jesus' death, cp. Plummer.

edoxazen ton theon legōn 'he praised God (by) saying...'; it implies that he praised God unwittingly, cp. Plummer. For *doxazō* cp. on 2 : 20.

ontōs (also 24 : 34) 'really', 'certainly'.

ho anthrōpos houtos dikaios ēn 'this man was righteous'. *dikaios* is used either in a judicial sense ('innocent'), or in a moral sense ('good'), preferably the latter.

Translation: *The centurion,* see on 7 : 2. The force of the definite article may lead to a rendering such as 'the commander (of the soldiers) present there'.

For *what had taken place* cp. on "thing that has happened" in 2 : 15; for *praised* on 2 : 13.

Certainly, cp. on 22 : 59. The word characterizes the centurion's words as an affirmation of the good reports he had heard previously about Jesus.

Innocent, preferably, '(a) good/honest/upright (man)'; see also references on 1 : 6.

48 ***And all the multitudes who assembled to see the sight, when they saw what had taken place, returned home beating their breasts.***

Exegesis: *pantes hoi sumparagenomenoi ochloi epi tēn theōrian tautēn* 'all the crowds who had assembled for this spectacle'.

sumparaginomai (††) 'to come together', 'to assemble', 'to gather'.

theōria (††) 'spectacle', 'sight', denoting that which is to be seen, not the act of seeing.

theōrēsantes ta genomena 'after/when they had seen what had happened'. *theōrēsantes* (of the same root as *theōria*) is used deliberately to express that they had seen what they had come for. *ta genomena* has the same referent as *to genomenon* in v. 47.

tuptontes ta stēthē hupestrephon 'went home beating their breasts'. The imperfect tense is durative and suggests that they left the place slowly. For the phrase *tuptontes ta stēthē* cp. on 18 : 13.

Translation: If partial co-ordination is preferable one may shift e.g. to, 'very many people had gathered (there) to see the sight; after they had seen what had taken place, they returned home beating (or, and on their way they beat) their breast'.

To see the sight, or, "to watch the spectacle" (TEV). Several languages (e.g. Javanese, Toba Batak) possess one specific verb for 'to see/gaze-at a spectacle/performance'.

Beating their breasts, see on 18 : 13; the plural is distributive.

49 ***And all his acquaintances and the women who had followed him from Galilee stood at a distance and saw these things.***

Exegesis: *heistēkeisan de...* 'but...stood there'. Subject is *hoi gnōstoi autō* and *gunaikes*. *de* may be continuative ('and'), or contrastive ('but'), preferably the latter. The contrast is between the crowds that went home and the friends who remained behind.

pantes hoi gnōstoi autō lit. 'all who were known to him', hence, 'all his acquaintances', cp. on 2 : 44. *pantes* is used here hyperbolically.

gunaikes hai sunakolouthousai autō apo tēs Galilaias 'the women who were following him from Galilee'. The present tense implies that the following is not envisaged as something of the past only but as still continuing.

sunakoloutheō (†) 'to follow', equivalent to *akoloutheō.*

horōsai tauta 'seeing this', best understood as going with both *hoi gnōstoi* and *gunaikes. tauta* has the same referent as *ta genomena* in v. 48 and *to genomenon* in v. 47.

Translation: *All,* or, 'many of'.

Acquaintances, see on 2 : 44, but here the term probably refers to a rather more intimate relationship; hence, "those who knew Jesus personally" (TEV), "friends" (NEB).

Followed, i.e. were his followers, cp. on 5 : 11.

At a distance, cp. on 15 : 20. Neither the phrase itself nor the context gives a clear indication as to the distance; they must have been within eyeshot but probably had not ventured close to the soldiers guarding the cross.

Saw, here in the sense of looking with deep concern, not in that of 'watching, or gazing, at a spectacle', as in v. 48.

50 ***Now there was a man named Joseph from the Jewish town of Arimathea. He was a member of the council, a good and righteous man,*** 51 ***who had not consented to their purpose and deed, and he was looking for the kingdom of God.*** 52 ***This man went to Pilate and asked for the body of Jesus.*** 53 ***Then he took it down and wrapped it in a linen shroud, and laid him in a rock-hewn tomb, where no one had ever yet been laid.***

Exegesis: These verses comprise a long elaborate sentence, introduced by *kai idou* ('and behold', cp. on 1 : 20). The structure of this sentence is as follows: the subject *anēr onomati Iōsēph* is followed by three appositions *bouleutēs huparchōn, anēr agathos kai dikaios* and *apo Arimathaias poleōs tōn Ioudaiōn* which serve to identify him as to his position, his moral character and his local origin, and by the relative clause *hos prosedecheto tēn basileian tou theou* which identifies him as to his religious conviction. Between the second and third apposition a parenthetical clause is inserted (*houtos . . . autōn*) in order to explain his relationship with the trial of Jesus. At the beginning of v. 52 the main clause begins, the subject being resumed by the demonstrative pronoun *houtos*; it consists of three co-ordinate verbs *ētēsato, enetulixen* and *ethēken,* the first two being preceded by a subordinate participle (*proselthōn* and *kathelōn*). In each case participle and main verb denote closely connected acts. Finally *mnēma* is more precisely defined by the closing relative clause *hou . . . keimenos.* For details cp. subsequent notes on each verse.

(V. 50) *bouleutēs huparchōn* lit. 'being a council member', i.e. a member of the Sanhedrin, cp. on 22 : 66. For *huparchō* cp. on 7 : 25. Here *huparchōn* is virtually redundant. *bouleutēs* (†).

anēr agathos kai dikaios 'a good and just man', used in a moral sense, and explained by what follows.

(V. 51) *houtos ouk ēn sugkatatetheimenos tē boulē kai tē praxei autōn* 'this man had not agreed with their plan and their action', parenthesis serving to explain how he, a member of the Sanhedrin, in the present situation with regard to Jesus could be called good and just. The periphrastic pluperfect has no special meaning. *autōn* refers to the members of the Sanhedrin, though they are not mentioned in the preceding clauses. *boulē*, cp. on 7 : 30.

sugkatatithemai (††), with dative, 'to agree with', 'to consent to', 'to vote for'.

boulē here 'plan', 'purpose', 'policy'.

praxis (†) 'action', 'act'.

apo Arimathaias poleōs tōn Ioudaiōn lit. 'from Arimathea a town of the Jews', best understood as identifying him as a native, not an inhabitant, of Arimathea (cp. Plummer). *tōn Ioudaiōn* has the name of the people instead of that of the country.

hos prosedecheto tēn basileian tou theou 'who expected the (coming of the) kingdom of God'. For a similar use of *prosdechomai* cp. on 2 : 25, 38. For the coming of the kingdom of God cp. on 17 : 20.

(V. 52) *ētēsato to sōma tou Iēsou* '(he) asked for the body of Jesus'. *sōma* means here '(dead) body', 'corpse'.

(V. 53) *kai kathelōn enetulixen auto sindoni* 'and after taking it down (from the cross) he wrapped it in a linen cloth'. *auto*, referring to *sōma* 'corpse', goes with both verbs.

entulissō (†) 'to wrap', 'to wrap up'.

sindōn (†) 'linen', 'linen cloth', 'linen sheet'.

ethēken auton en mnēmati laxeutō 'he laid him in a rock-hewn tomb'. Note *auton* 'him', referring to a person, i.e. Jesus, after *auto* 'it' in the preceding clause.

laxeutos (††) 'hewn in the rock'.

hou ouk ēn oudeis oupō keimenos 'where no one had yet been laid'. The accumulation of the negations strengthens the negative aspect of the clause. Periphrastic *ēn keimenos* is to be rendered as a pluperfect, not as an imperfect.

Translation: The main clause, vv. 52f, can usually be rendered as two or more separate sentences; the real difficulty is in the introductory clauses, vv. 50f, because of the parenthesis in v. 51. Some translators change the syntactic structure rather radically, redistributing the clauses and phrases according to a clearer, more logical sequence, cp. e.g. TEV. This has the drawback of suggesting relationships which Luke may not have had in mind. Most translators, therefore, think it wiser to restrict themselves to subdividing vv. 50f into two or more sentences, if necessary elucidating the relationships, e.g. 'Now there was a man called Joseph, a member of the (Jewish) council, a good and just man, who had (or, He was a good and just man; as such he had) not agreed with their... deed. He came from the Jewish town of A. He expected the kingdom of God. This man (or, Joseph) went to Pilate...', cp. e.g. NEB, Jerusalem; also Marathi (which puts the locative apposition directly behind the name, as does TEV). It may be necessary to transpose part of the main clause to the first sentence, e.g. 'Look, a man who was called Joseph, a member of the council, a good and upright man, went to Pilate. He had not agreed with...what they did. He was a man from A., ... He was expecting the kingdom of God. Well, he went to Pilate, he asked...' (Sranan).

(V. 50) *From the Jewish town of Arimathea*, or, 'native from A., a town in the region Judea (Bahasa Indonesia RC, Balinese), or, in the Jewish country'. For the force of the preposition *from* see on "of Cyrene" in v. 26, for *town* cp. on "city" in 1 : 26.

A member of the council, or, 'a man of the (or, elder in their) council' (cp. Balinese, Zarma), 'one of the men who sat in council' (cp. East Toradja); or a derivation of the word for council, e.g. 'one of the speechmakers/discussers' (Kapauku). For *council* see on 22 : 66; the term may have to be specified, cp. "Jewish council" (Phillips).

Righteous, cp. references on 1 : 6.

(V. 51) *Who had not consented to their purpose and deed*, or, 'who had not approved of what they had decided and what they had done (cp. Sranan), or, what the other members had designed and done', or, 'he had not agreed with the other men about the things they had planned and done'. In Kapauku *consented*, or, 'agreed' is rendered by the phrase 'one thought decided'.

He was looking for, or, 'expecting', see on 2 : 25.

The kingdom of God, or, 'the day to come that God rules' (Mixtec), 'the time when the hour of God's governing would arrive' (Tzeltal).

(V. 52) *Went to*. In this context an honorific term may be preferable or obligatory, e.g. 'waited upon' (Balinese, cp. also "went into the presence of", TEV).

Asked for, cp. *N.T.Wb.*/12f; in some cases better in direct discourse, 'said, "Please, give me the body of Jesus"'.

Body, or, 'corpse', 'dead body', as is obligatory in several languages.

(V. 53) *He took it down*. A locative specification may be preferable, and/or an indication that Joseph probably was not the direct agent, e.g. 'he had it taken down (or, caused people to lower it) from the cross'.

A linen shroud, or, 'a grave cloth'; or less specifically, 'a (good, or, linen) cloth'.

Laid him. In several languages the use of a personal pronoun would suggest a reference to a living person, and therefore one has to neglect the difference and use "it", or a similar non-personal reference.

A rock-hewn tomb, or, 'a tomb hewn (or, cut/dug) out of a rock (or, a rock cliff)', 'a stone-hole grave' (Sranan). If *tomb* has to be described, one may say here, 'hole/cave to place dead people in', or simply 'hole/cave', the function being sufficiently clear from the context.

54 ***It was the day of Preparation, and the sabbath was beginning.***

Exegesis: This verse has the function of a parenthetical indication of time.

kai hēmera ēn paraskeuēs 'and it was the day of preparation', cp. *TH-Mk* on 15 : 42. *paraskeuē* (†).

sabbaton epephōsken lit. 'the sabbath was shining forth'.

epiphōskō (†) 'to shine', 'to shine forth'. Since according to Jewish custom the new day was reckoned from sunset the verb cannot refer to the shining forth of the sun at dawn; hence it may refer to the custom of lighting lamps at the beginning of the sabbath (Klostermann, Lagrange) or it may be used in a weakened and general meaning, viz. 'to dawn', 'to begin'. The latter is preferable, cp. Plummer.

Translation: *The day of Preparation*, or, 'the day for preparing (or, when people prepare)', or, if an object and a reference to the occasion have to be added, 'the day when people prepare things (or, what is necessary) for the sabbath' (in which case 'sabbath' in the next clause is better replaced by a pronominal reference, e.g. '. . ., which was beginning', '. . . ; it was about to begin'). Some versions render "day of Preparation" by the term used for Friday; a closer rendering is usually preferable, however, since it reminds the receptor better of the regulations for the sabbath, which play a role in v. 56b.

55 ***The women who had come with him from Galilee followed, and saw the tomb, and how his body was laid;*** 56a ***then they returned, and prepared spices and ointments.***

Exegesis: The syntactic structure is as follows: *katakolouthēsasai* (subordinate participle) *hai gunaikes* (subject)...*etheasanto* (main verb); *hupostrepsasai* (subordinate participle) *hētoimasan* (second main verb, same subject).

katakolouthēsasai de hai gunaikes 'the women, having followed', viz. Joseph. The placing of the participle before the subject at the beginning of the clause is for stylistic reasons. The participle denotes the act that connects the events of these verses with the preceding story.

katakoloutheō (†) 'to follow', 'to follow after (somebody)', with the implication of following at some distance.

haitines ēsan sunelēluthuiai ek tēs Galilaias autō 'who had come with him from Galilee', identifying the women as those referred to in v. 49.

etheasanto to mnēmeion kai hōs etethē to sōma autou '(they) saw the tomb and how his body was laid'. Note the twofold object of *etheasanto*, viz. a noun (*to mnēmeion*) and an indirect question (*hōs etethē*...), which denotes the act of the burial, rather than the manner. For *to sōma* cp. on v. 52. As implied in the story as a whole the women saw the grave with a view to coming back later. Hence *etheasanto* may be rendered, 'they noted', 'they took note'.

(V. 56a) *arōmata kai mura* 'spices and ointments'. For *arōma* (†) cp. *TH-Mk* on 16 : 1.

Translation: For *followed* see on 7 : 9. A specification of the person followed may be preferable, or of the place reached, 'followed to-that-place' (Balinese, Toba Batak 1885).

Saw. The verb may have to be repeated, cp. e.g. 'saw the grave and burial affair saw' (Kapauku), 'looked at the grave: saw how they had put his body' (Sranan).

(V. 56[a]) *Then they returned,* or, 'after that they went back home', viz. to their lodgings in Jerusalem, not to Galilee.

For *spices* see *TH-Mk* on 16 : 1, for *ointment* above on 7 : 37.

56b ***On the sabbath they rested according to the commandment.***

For this clause see next page, the note on 24 : 1.

CHAPTER TWENTY-FOUR

1 ***But on the first day of the week, at early dawn, they went to the tomb, taking the spices which they had prepared.***

Exegesis: 23 : 56[b] may be taken as a part of the sentence of v. 56[a] (cp. NEB), or as an independent clause (cp. e.g. RSV), or as one sentence with 24 : 1 (cp. e.g. BFBS). The third alternative is preferable.

to men sabbaton 'during the sabbath', accusative of time, cp. Bl-D, § 161.3.

hēsuchasan 'they rested', cp. on 14 : 4.

kata tēn entolēn 'according to the commandment', scil. of the Law of Moses.

(24 : 1) *tē de mia tōn sabbatōn* 'but on the first day of the week', cp. *TH-Mk* on 16 : 2.

orthrou batheōs 'at early dawn', genitive of time, cp. Bl-D, § 186.2.

orthros (†) 'dawn', 'early morning'.

bathus (†) 'deep', here in a figurative sense 'early'.

epi to mnēma ēlthon 'they went to the tomb'.

pherousai ha hētoimasan arōmata 'bringing (with them) the spices they had prepared'. The word order (relative clause before the antecedent) does not influence the meaning.

Translation: (23 : 56[b]) *They rested.* The verb may have to be expressed by 'not to work'; an idiomatic rendering found in Tzeltal is, 'to let the heart live'.

According to the commandment, or, "in obedience to the commandment" (Goodspeed, NEB), "as the Law commanded" (TEV), 'as the law says' (Sranan). For the noun see on 1 : 6.

(24 : 1) *On the first day of the week,* cp. *TH-Mk* on 16 : 2. Where a literal rendering of the phrase would present difficulties one may shift to 'on the next day', 'on the day after (the sabbath)'.

At early dawn, or, 'very early'; cp. also *N.T.Wb.*/23, DAY. South Toradja uses an idiomatic phrase, lit. 'night not yet (probably elliptical for, not yet ended)'.

Taking, i.e. 'taking/carrying with them'.

2 ***And they found the stone rolled away from the tomb,*** 3 ***but when they went in they did not find the body.***

Exegesis: *heuron de ton lithon apokekulismenon apo tou mnēmeiou* 'but they found the stone rolled away from the grave'. The article *ton* before *lithon* is best understood as identifying the stone as well known, cp. Plummer. *apokulizō* (†). *mnēmeion* is equivalent to *mnēma*.

(V. 3) *eiselthousai de* 'but after going in', viz. into the chamber of the tomb.

ouch heuron to sōma tou [kuriou] Iēsou 'they did not find the body of the Lord Jesus'. For *sōma* cp. on 23 : 52; for *kuriou* cp. on 1 : 6.

Translation: For *they found* see on 7 : 10.

The stone rolled away, or, where an active construction is preferable, 'that someone had rolled the stone away'. *The stone,* or, making explicit what for the original receptor was too self-evident to need mentioning, 'the closing stone', or, 'the stone that served to close the tomb' (if necessary shifting to pronominal reference in the following phrase).

From the tomb, i.e. 'from before the tomb' (Jerusalem), 'from the entrance/mouth/outlet of the tomb' (cp. East Toradja 1933, Low Malay, Balinese).

(V. 3) *Went in,* or, 'entered it', 'went inside the tomb (or, cave)'.

They did not find. The verb refers to finding as a result of seeking (cp. on 2 : 12), as shown by v. 5c; cp. also Rieu's "they looked in vain for".

4 ***While they were perplexed about this, behold, two men stood by them in dazzling apparel;***

Exegesis: *kai egeneto* 'and it happened', cp. on 1 : 8. The main clause is introduced by *kai idou* for which cp. on 1 : 20.

en tō aporeisthai autas peri toutou lit. 'during their being at a loss about this', articular accusative and infinitive, cp. Bl-D, § 404. *toutou* refers to v. 3.

aporeō (†) 'to be at a loss', 'to be uncertain', 'to be perplexed' (cp. *aporia* in 21 : 25).

andres duo epestēsan autais 'two men came upon them', cp. on 2 : 9.

en esthēti astraptousē 'in dazzling clothing', cp. on 23 : 11. For *astraptō* cp. on 17 : 24.

Translation: For *perplexed* cp. on 9 : 7 and 21 : 25.

Stood by them, cp. on 2 : 9.

In dazzling apparel, or, 'dazzlingly clothed', 'wearing dazzling garments'. For *dazzling,* i.e. 'shining brilliantly', cp. also on 9 : 29.

5 ***and as they were frightened and bowed their faces to the ground, the men said to them, "Why do you seek the living among the dead?***

Exegesis: *emphobōn de genomenōn autōn kai klinousōn ta prosōpa eis tēn gēn* 'when they became afraid/terrified and were bowing their faces to the ground'. *genomenōn* is ingressive aorist and denotes the reaction to the appearance of the two men; *klinousōn* is present tense and denotes the attitude of the women at the moment when the men began to speak.

emphobos (also v. 37) 'afraid, startled', 'terrified'.

ti zēteite ton zōnta meta tōn nekrōn 'why are you seeking the living one among the dead?' The clause may express rebuke or mild criticism, preferably the latter. The use of the articles *ton* and *tōn* is probably due to the fact that the clause reflects proverbial sayings, though its meaning here is to be taken literal.

Translation: A shift from pronoun to noun and/or from subordination to co-ordination may be preferable, e.g. 'The women became afraid and bowed...to the ground; (then/thereupon) the men said...'.

They were frightened, see on "fear" in 1 : 12.

Bowed their faces to the ground, or, 'they turned/made their faces towards the ground' (Lokele, Marathi). The phrase is sometimes rendered by one verb (several Indonesian languages). The rendering should express fear or confusion, rather than reverence or worship; hence, "lowered their eyes" (Rieu), "stood with eyes cast down" (NEB, similarly Toba Batak).

Why do you seek, or, 'you should not seek, or, look for, or, try to find'.

The living, or, 'the living one', 'the person who lives'.

Among the dead, or, 'among dead people', 'among corpses', 'in the place of dead people' (several Indonesian languages), 'where dead people (or, corpses) are/lie'.

6 ***[He is not here, but has risen.] Remember how he told you, while he was still in Galilee,*** 7 ***that the Son of man must be delivered into the hands of sinful men, and be crucified, and on the third day rise."***

Exegesis: *ouk estin hōde* 'he is not here', i.e. in the tomb.

alla ēgerthē 'but he has risen', cp. on 7 : 14.

mnēsthēte hōs elalēsen humin 'remember how he said to you'. *hōs* does not refer to the mode of speaking but to what was said.

(V. 7) *legōn ton huion tou anthrōpou hoti dei paradothēnai* 'saying that the Son of man must be delivered up'. *ton huion tou anthrōpou,* though syntactically the object of *legōn*, is the subject of *paradothēnai. dei* denotes the divine compulsion. For the phrase about the Son of man cp. on 9 : 44.

anthrōpōn hamartōlōn 'of sinful men'. Here *hamartōlos* is used in the meaning 'wicked', 'evil'.

kai tē tritē hēmera anastēnai 'and rise on the third day', cp. on 9 : 7 and *TH-Mk* on 8 : 31.

Translation: For *has risen* and *rise* cp. on 9 : 7f.

Remember, see on 16 : 25.

How he told you, or, 'what (or, the things) he told you', 'his words to you'. V. 7 may become then, 'that is, "The Son of man must..."', or, as a new sentence, 'He said...', followed by the verse in indirect or direct discourse.

Still, cp. on 8 : 49.

(V. 7) For *must* cp. on 2 : 49, for *delivered into the hands of sinful men* on 9 : 44. *Sinful,* i.e. 'evil' (for which cp. Nida, *BT*, 220f).

And be crucified, or, 'and these will crucify (see on 23 : 21) him'.

For *on the third day* see on 9 : 22.

8 ***And they remembered his words,*** 9 ***and returning from the tomb they told all this to the eleven and to all the rest.***

Exegesis: *kai emnēsthēsan tōn rēmatōn autou* 'and (indeed) they remembered his words'.

(V. 9) *hupostrepsasai apo tou mnēmeiou* 'after returning from the tomb', viz. to the city.

apēggeilan tauta panta tois hendeka kai pasin tois loipois 'they reported all this to the eleven and to all the others'. For *apaggellō* cp. on 7 : 18. *tauta panta* refers to what they had seen and heard. For *tois hendeka* cp. *TH-Mk* on 16 : 14. The relationship of 'all the others' to the eleven is not stated but presumably the phrase refers to disciples, or followers of Jesus in the wider sense.

Translation: (V. 9) *Returning,* or, 'after they had come back'.

The eleven, or, 'the eleven disciples'.

All the rest, or, 'all the remaining (ones)' (Marathi), 'all the other followers (of Jesus)', cp. also *TH-Mk* on 16 : 13; or again, 'all their (referring to the eleven) associates/companions' (Javanese, Toba Batak), 'all those with them'.

10 ***Now it was Mary Magdalene and Joanna and Mary the mother of James and the other women with them who told this to the apostles;***

Exegesis: *ēsan de hē Magdalēnē Maria kai Iōanna kai Maria hē Iakōbou* 'they were Mary of Magdala and Joanna and Mary the mother of James'. For *Magdalēnē* cp. on 8 : 2.

kai hai loipai sun autais elegon...tauta 'and the other women with them also told these things'. *sun autais* may go with *elegon,* or with *hai loipai,* preferably the latter. This somewhat redundant phrase implies that the preceding clause does not mean that the three women named were the only ones who went to the grave. *tauta* takes up *tauta panta* in v. 9.

pros tous apostolous 'to the apostles', cp. on 6 : 13.

Translation: *Now it was,* preferably, "the women concerned were" (Rieu), 'they, or, the(se) women were' (cp. *Exegesis*).

...and the other women with them...told, preferably a new sentence, '... ; the other women with them also told'. *The other women with them,* or, 'the other women, who were with, or, had gone with them, or, had accompanied them'.

The apostles, see on 6 : 13.

11 ***but these words seemed to them an idle tale, and they did not believe them.***

Exegesis: *kai ephanēsan...hōsei lēros ta rēmata tauta* 'and these words appeared...as nonsense'. Notwithstanding *ta rēmata tauta* being neuter plural *ephanēsan* is in the plural, cp. Bl-D, § 133.3. *phainomai*, cp. on 9 : 8.

lēros (††) 'nonsense', 'idle talk'.

enōpion autōn 'in their sight', equivalent to dative *autois* going with *ephanēsan*.

ēpistoun autais 'they did not believe them', denoting the situation that existed as a result of what the preceding clause related.

apisteō (also v. 41) 'to disbelieve', here used in a non-religious sense, in v. 41 with the connotation of being unable to believe.

Translation: *These words seemed to them*, or, specifying the participants, "the apostles thought that what the women said was" (TEV).

An idle tale. Some idioms used are, 'empty talk' (Zürich, Timorese), 'wind talk' (Bahasa Indonesia), 'carried-around story' (Kapauku), 'purposeless talking' (Lokele), 'words that-frighten without-reason' (South Toradja), 'talk without-foundation' (Ponape, Trukese).

Believe them, or, 'their words'; cp. on 1 : 20.

[12 But Peter rose and ran to the tomb; stooping and looking in, he saw the linen cloths by themselves; and he went home wondering at what had happened.]

Exegesis: *parakupsas blepei ta othonia mona* 'stooping down he saw only the linen clothes'. *mona* may be taken as predicate (cp. RSV, Phillips) or as attributive to *othonia*, 'the clothes alone', i.e. 'only the clothes' (cp. BFBS, TEV). The latter is preferable.

parakuptō (†) 'to stoop down', 'to peer in'.

othonion (†) 'linen cloth', 'bandage', used in preparing a corpse for burial, cp. A-G s.v.

pros heauton thaumazōn to gegonos 'wondering in himself (at) that which had happened'. *pros heauton* may go with *apēlthen*, or with *thaumazōn*, preferably the latter.

Translation: *Stooping and looking in, he saw*, or, 'when he stooped to look (or, when he peered in), he saw/noticed'.

The linen cloths by themselves, preferably, 'only the linen cloths', "nothing but the linen wrappings/clothes" (Rieu, BFBS), 'the linen bandages and nothing else'; cp. also *N.T.Wb./7*, ALONE. — *The linen cloths* refers to what in 23 : 53 is called "a linen shroud".

He went home wondering, preferably, 'he went away wondering in himself' (NV). The qualification 'in himself' is redundant; it should not be rendered where idiom is against it. For *wondering* see on 1 : 21.

13 ***That very day two of them were going to a village named Emmaus, about seven miles from Jerusalem,*** 14 ***and talking with each other about all these things that had happened.***

Exegesis: *kai idou* 'and behold', cp. on 1 : 20.

duo ex autōn 'two of them', either of the apostles (cp. v. 10), or of the disciples in general. The latter is preferable, as shown indirectly by v. 33.

ēsan poreuomenoi eis kōmēn apechousan stadious hexēkonta apo Ierousalēm 'were going to a village sixty stades distant from Jerusalem'. The periphrastic imperfect *ēsan poreuomenoi* is durative.

apechō 'to be distant from', with *apo* and genitive, cp. A-G s.v. 2. Here it goes with *stadious hexēkonta* as accusative of extent.

stadion (with masculine plural; †) 'stade', as a measure of distance, about 607 English feet, or 185 metres, cp. Bratcher, *TBT*, 10.170, 1959.

(V. 14) *kai autoi hōmiloun pros allēlous* 'and they were talking to each other'. *autoi*, not emphatic, is used to resume the subject after the identification of Emmaus in v. 1.

homileō (†) 'to converse', 'to talk'.

peri pantōn tōn sumbebēkotōn toutōn 'about all these things that had happened'. The things referred to are mentioned in vv. 19ff; hence *toutōn* has a temporal connotation.

sumbainō (†) 'to happen'. The perfect participle in the neuter is virtually equivalent to a noun meaning 'event'.

Translation: *Two of them,* i.e. 'two of Jesus' followers' (East Toradja 1933).

About seven miles from, or, '(which was situated) at a distance of about seven miles from, or, eleven kilometres from (East Toradja 1933), or, two hour's walk from (Leyden, Sranan, Timorese), or, two leagues from' (Tzeltal, where 'a league' is commonly explained as 'one hour's walk'). Cp. also *N.T.Wb.*/73f, WEIGHTS and MEASURES.

(V. 14) *And* (they were) *talking with each other,* cp. on "said to one another" in 4 : 36.

All these things that had happened, or, 'all these events' (cp. also on 2 : 15), or, to bring out the temporal force the pronoun has here, 'all that had recently happened'.

15 ***While they were talking and discussing together, Jesus himself drew near and went with them.*** 16 ***But their eyes were kept from recognising him.***

Exegesis: *kai egeneto* 'and it happened', cp. on 1 : 8, sub (2).

en tō homilein autous kai suzētein lit. 'during their conversing and discussing', articular accusative and infinitive, cp. Bl-D, § 404. For *suzēteō* cp. on 22 : 23.

kai autos Iēsous 'Jesus himself'.

eggisas suneporeueto autois lit. 'after drawing near went along with them', hence 'drew near and went along with them'. *eggisas* is used here in the sense of overtaking, cp. Plummer.

(V. 16) *hoi de ophthalmoi autōn ekratounto tou mē epignōnai auton* lit. 'but their eyes were held back so as not to recognize him', hence, 'their eyes were kept from recognizing him'. *krateō* 'to hold back', or, 'to restrain from', 'to hinder'; pass. 'to be prevented' (here). The agent of *ekratounto* is God. *krateō,* cp. on 8 : 54. *tou mē epignōnai* is consecutive articular infinitive in the genitive, cp. Bl-D, § 400.4. For *epiginōskō* meaning 'to recognize' cp. A-G s.v. 1 b.

Translation: *They were talking and discussing together.* The second verb is stronger than the first; hence the sequence is a bit of a climax, e.g. 'they were talking and even debating with each other' (cp. Bamiléké), 'they were questioning each other, even heatedly'.

Drew near and went with them, or, "came up and walked along with them" (NEB); or simply, 'joined them' (cp. East Toradja 1933).

(V. 16) *Their eyes were kept from,* implying that, though their eyes perceived a person, their minds were not able to realize who he was, and that this was not their own doing but because of some outside agent, ultimately God. An explicit reference to God, however, should preferably be avoided, cp. e.g. 'something covered their eyes that they not' (Trukese), "a spell was on their eyes" (Rieu). Similar idioms appear to exist in several languages, e.g. 'their eyes were clouded, or, shrouded/blindfolded' (Shona 1966, 1963), 'their eyes were misty' (Timorese). Elsewhere one has to shift to a simile, 'their eyes were just as if they had been caused to be shut' (Marathi), but sometimes more radical changes are necessary, e.g. 'they were prevented from', cp. also, "they saw him, but somehow did not recognize him" (TEV). Cp. also below on v. 31.

Recognising him may be described here as 'seeing who he was'.

17 ***And he said to them, "What is this conversation which you are holding with each other as you walk?" And they stood still, looking sad.***

Exegesis: *tines hoi logoi houtoi hous antiballete pros allēlous* 'what are these words which you cast at each other?'

antiballō (††) lit. 'to cast against', here of words, hence 'to exchange'.

peripatountes 'walking', hence 'as you walk along'.

kai estathēsan "they came to a halt" (Rieu), 'they stood still', ingressive aorist.

skuthrōpoi (†) 'gloomy', 'downcast'.

Translation: *What is this conversation which you are holding with each other,* or simply, 'what affair are you talking about' (Kapauku), 'what are you discussing' (cp. Goodspeed).

Looking sad, or, "with sad faces" (TEV), '(their) faces clouded' (Kapauku). For *sad* see references on 18 : 23.

18 ***Then one of them, named Cleopas, answered him, "Are you the only visitor to Jerusalem who does not know the things that have happened there in these days?"***

Exegesis: *heis onomati Kleopas* 'one (of them) called Cleopas', or, 'the one called Cleopas', preferably the former.

su monos paroikeis Ierousalēm kai ouk egnōs ta genomena en autē lit. 'you alone stay in Jerusalem and do not know what has happened in her?', meaning 'you alone of those who stay in Jerusalem do not know... ?', i.e. 'are you the only one of those staying in Jerusalem who does not know... ?' *monos* is emphatic and goes with both *paroikeis* and *egnōs.*

paroikeō (†) 'to live as a stranger in', 'to stay in' (cp. A-G s.v. 1), or 'to live in', 'to inhabit' (cp. A-G s.v. 2). The former is slightly preferable.

en autē 'in her', i.e. 'there'.

en tais hēmerais tautais 'in these days', 'lately', 'recently'.

Translation: In languages with obligatory honorifics Cleopas and his companion will have to use the polite terms common in addressing a stranger; these may be of a lower level of honorifics than those they would have used had they known that they were speaking to Jesus.

Are you the only visitor...who does not know the things...? The sentence may have to be recast, e.g. in order to describe the force of "only": 'do you not know the things...although all other strangers in J. know them'; or avoiding a rhetorical question: 'it appears that you are the only traveller who does not know the things...' (Marathi); or using a non-subordinate clause structure: 'among the visitors to J. you alone do not know... ?' (cp. Kituba).

19 ***And he said to them, "What things?" And they said to him, "Concerning Jesus of Nazareth, who was a prophet mighty in deed and word before God and all the people,*** 20 ***and how our chief priests and rulers delivered him up to be condemned to death, and crucified him.***

Exegesis: *poia* (with *genomena* 'the things that happened' understood) 'what kind of thing?' or simply 'what?' The latter is preferable, cp. A-G s.v. 2 b α.

ta peri Iēsou tou Nazarēnou 'the things about Jesus of Nazareth'. This general phrase is elaborated by (1) the relative clause *hos egeneto* 'who was...', and (2) the indirect question *hopōs te paredōkan*, etc., 'and how handed him over...'. It is also possible to understand both *ta peri Iēsou tou Nazarēnou* and *hopōs te paredōkan,* etc., as object of *egnōs* in v. 18, but this is less probable.

hos egeneto anēr prophētēs 'who was a man, a prophet', i.e. 'who was a prophet'.

dunatos en ergō kai logō 'powerful in deed and word', in apposition to *prophētēs*. *en ergō* refers to miracles and healings, *logō* to teaching and preaching. For *ergon* cp. on 11 : 48.

enantion tou theou kai pantos tou laou 'in the judgment of God and of all the people', cp. on 1 : 6. The phrase means that God confirmed Jesus' power in word and deed by its outcome and that all the people recognized it as such.

(V. 20) *hopōs te paredōkan auton...eis krima thanatou* 'how (they) handed him over to a sentence of death', i.e. 'to be sentenced to death'. *hopōs* refers to the facts related in the clause rather than to their mode. For *krima* cp. *TH-Mk* on 12 : 40.

hoi archiereis kai hoi archontes hēmōn 'our chief priests and rulers', cp. on 9 : 22 (*hoi archiereis*) and on 23 : 13 (*archōn*).

kai estaurōsan auton 'and (how) they had him crucified', still dependent on *hopōs*.

Translation: *Concerning Jesus*, or, 'the things concerning (or, about, or, that happened to) Jesus'; if the preceding question has been rendered 'what?' (see *Exegesis*) another antecedent may be preferable, e.g. 'what happened to Jesus', "all this about Jesus" (NEB). The two subsequent subordinate clauses may better become co-ordinate sentences, e.g. 'he (or, this man/this Jesus) was a prophet, ..., but our chief priests...crucified him' (cp. Kilega).

Mighty in deed and word, or, 'mighty in what he did and said'; or changing the phrase structure, 'whose (or as a new sentence, his) deeds and words were mighty/strong' (cp. Balinese, Kapauku), 'who/he acted and spoke powerfully', 'who/he performed mighty deeds and spoke powerful words'.

(V. 20) *Our chief priests and rulers*. The pronoun has exclusive force, presumably. For *chief priests* see on "high-priesthood" in 3 : 2, for *rulers* see on 23 : 13.

Delivered him up, see on 20 : 20. If idiom requires a reference to the other participant(s), one may add 'to Pilate', or, 'to the Roman authorities'.

To be condemned to death, or, 'to receive the death sentence', 'in order that Pilate/the Roman authorities (or, a pronominal reference, if these persons have been mentioned already in the preceding clause) would sentence him to death, or, to be killed'; cp. *TH-Mk* on 14 : 64, and for 'to condemn/sentence' see *N.T.Wb.*/48, JUDGE.

And crucified him, or, 'and had him (or, caused him to be) crucified' (see *Exegesis*). If an active construction is obligatory a difficulty may arise in that Pilate or the authorities in their turn are also initiators. This may result in 'and caused him/them to order the soldiers to crucify him'. As a rule a rendering that is less explicit as to participants will be possible, e.g. 'and (so) caused him to die on the cross'.

21 ***But we had hoped that he was the one to redeem Israel. Yes, and besides all this, it is now the third day since this happened.***

Exegesis: *hēmeis de* 'but we', emphatic and contrasting with the people mentioned in v. 20.

ēlpizomen '(we) were hoping', durative imperfect, referring to the time preceding the events related in v. 20.

hoti autos estin ho mellōn lutrousthai ton Israēl 'that he was the one who was to redeem Israel'. *autos* 'he' is emphatic. For *ho mellōn* 'he who is (destined) to' with infinitive, cp. A-G s.v. 1 c δ. For *lutroō* (†) cp. *N.T.Wb.*, 108f/RANSOM, and *lutrōsis* in 1 : 68; 2 : 38.

alla ge kai sun pasin toutois 'but even in addition to all this'. *alla ge kai* is best taken as reinforcing *sun pasin toutois* (cp. Bl-D, § 439.2). *sun* may mean 'in addition to', or, 'apart from', cp. A-G s.v. 5. The former is preferable. *pasin toutois* refers to the whole of what is related in vv. 19-21[a].

tritēn tautēn hēmeran agei aph' hou tauta egeneto lit. 'he is spending this day as the third since these things happened', with *ho Iēsous* as subject of *agei* understood (cp. A-G s.v. *agō* 4 and Bl-D, § 129). For translational purposes, however, it may be necessary or advisable to shift to an impersonal rendering like 'this is the third day'.

Translation: *But we had hoped*, or, 'as for us, we had hoped'. The pronoun is exclusive, of course; for the verb cp. *N.T.Wb.*/45.

That he was the one to redeem, or, 'that he was the man destined/sent (or, whom God had destined/sent) to redeem'; or again, 'that God had destined/sent him (emphatic) to redeem'. For the latter verb see references on 1 : 68.

It is now the third day since this happened, i.e. this happened the day before yesterday. For *the third day* in this connexion see on 9 : 22; and cp., in this occurrence, *voilà deux jours que* 'it is now two days ago that' (Jerusalem). For *since* see on 16 : 16; the clause thus introduced is sometimes better transposed, e.g. 'beginning from that these things happened, now it is already...' (Balinese).

22 ***Moreover, some women of our company amazed us. They were at the tomb early in the morning*** 23 ***and did not find his body; and they came back saying that they had even seen a vision of angels, who said that he was alive.***

Exegesis: *alla kai* lit. 'but (in spite of this,) also', here expressing strong contrast with what precedes, 'yet despite this' (cp. Plummer).

gunaikes tines ex hēmōn exestēsan hēmas 'some women of our group have astounded us'. *ex hēmōn* 'of our group' implies a wider reference for *hēmōn* than the speaker and his friend, viz. the followers of Jesus in general. As for the punctuation cp. *GNT*. A major punctuation after *hēmas* is preferable.

existēmi lit. 'to drive out of one's senses', hence 'to confuse', 'to astound'.

genomenai orthrinai epi to mnēmeion 'when they went early/at dawn to the tomb'. *ginomai epi* with accusative implies the idea of motion, cp. A-G s.v. *ginomai* I 4 c γ. *orthrinai* (††) is an adjective going with the subject of the clause but serves to indicate the time of the event denoted by *genomenai...epi to mnēmeion* and hence to be rendered as an adverb, 'early', 'at dawn' (cp. *orthros* in v. 1).

(V. 23) *kai mē heurousai to sōma autou* 'and when they did not find his body', continuing the preceding participial clause and carrying the main semantic weight: the fact that they did not find the body made them go back. For *to sōma* cp. on 17 : 37.

ēlthon legousai kai optasian aggelōn heōrakenai 'they came saying that they had also seen a vision of angels'. *ēlthon* means 'they came to us, or, to our group'. *kai* may mean 'actually', or 'also', i.e. besides the fact that they did not find the body. The latter is preferable. For *optasia* cp. on 1 : 22. *aggelōn* is genitive of content.

hoi legousin auton zēn 'who said that he lives, or, is alive'.

Translation: *Moreover*, preferably, "yet there is this" (Rieu), 'nevertheless', 'true enough' (Jerusalem).

Some women of our company is rendered variously, e.g. 'some women among (or, out of) us' (e.g. in Trukese, Marathi), 'some women our companions/associates' (Sundanese, South Toradja), 'two or three of our women' (Tzeltal), but one may have to be more explicit, e.g. 'some women who are (Jesus') followers like us'.

Amazed us, or, 'confused/alarmed/startled us', or, a causative form or phrase built on one of the more forceful expressions for 'amazement' or 'wonder' (mentioned in the note on 1 : 21).

They were at... (v. 23) *and did not find*...; *and they came*..., or, 'they went to...but did not (emphatic) find...; therefore/thereupon they came...'.

That they had...*seen a vision of angels*, or, 'that they had seen a vision, or, a (supernatural) appearance, namely angels', 'that they saw (supernatural) things, that is to say angels' (Sranan), 'that they saw something which appeared to them: some angels (lit. people of heaven)' (Trukese); or with further shifts, 'that they had seen angels showing-themselves' (Sundanese), 'we clearly saw angels', implying that something normally invisible is revealed (Kapauku). For *see a vision* cp. on 1 : 22.

Who said..., often as a new sentence, cp. 'and these (angels) said' (Sranan, Marathi, Kapauku).

24 ***Some of those who were with us went to the tomb, and found it just as the women had said; but him they did not see."***

Exegesis: *kai apēlthon tines tōn sun hēmin epi to mnēmeion* 'and some of our group went to the tomb'. *tōn sun hēmin* means literally 'of those with us', hence, 'of our group'.

kai heuron houtōs kathōs kai hai gunaikes eipon 'and found (things) exactly as the women had said'. *kai* is to be taken with *houtōs kathōs*. *eipon* has the force of a pluperfect.

auton de ouk eidon 'but him they did not see'. *auton* is emphatic by position.

Translation: *Who were with us* is synonymous with "of our company" in v. 22.

25 ***And he said to them, "O foolish men, and slow of heart to believe all that the prophets have spoken!***

Exegesis: *kai autos eipen pros autous* 'and he said to them'. *autos* is emphatic and stresses the change of subject.

ō anoētoi kai bradeis tē kardia tou pisteuein epi pasin hois elalēsan hoi prophētai 'you foolish men and slow in mind to believe all that the prophets said'. *anoētos* (†) 'foolish', is explained by what follows: it points to a lack of understanding. For *kardia* meaning 'mind', cp. *TH-Mk* on 2 : 6. *tou pisteuein* goes with *bradeis* (†) and denotes that which they are slow in, cp. Bl-D, § 400.8. *pisteuō epi* with dative means 'to believe' in the sense of being convinced of the truth of something. As v. 27 shows the reference is not to the prophetic writings only but also to the Law.

Translation: The structure may have to be changed, e.g. 'O (you) foolish men, (you who are) so slow of heart that you cannot believe...', 'O (you) foolish men, you are too slow of heart to believe...', 'How foolish you are and how slow (you are) to believe...' (cp. Goodspeed, NEB, TEV). Jesus is still incognito, hence in a language like Balinese he does not use the non-honorific forms common from teacher to pupil, but the honorific, polite forms common between strangers.

Foolish, cp. on "fools" in 11 : 40.

Slow of heart. The qualification 'heart' serves to indicate that 'slow' is used here metaphorically, in the sense of 'lacking spiritual alertness'. The phrase is variously rendered, e.g. 'the heart is hard' (Zarma), 'very heavy in heart' (Timorese), 'blocked-hearted' (Bahasa Indonesia), 'lazy to think' (East Toradja), 'having a heart that delays' (Shona 1963), 'failing-heart-people' (Fulani). In Tzeltal 'not with one's heart' is a common idiom for reluctance; hence, 'you have not believed with your hearts' as the rendering of RSV's "slow of heart to believe".

26 ***Was it not necessary that the Christ should suffer these things and enter into his glory?"***

Exegesis: *ouchi tauta edei pathein ton Christon* 'was it not necessary that the Messiah should suffer these things?' For *ouchi* cp. on 4 : 22. For *edei* and for the idea which the clause expresses cp. on 9 : 22. For *ho Christos* cp. on 2 : 11, 26.

kai eiselthein eis tēn doxan autou 'and to enter into his glory', syntactically also dependent upon *edei* but semantically of a different nature. It may be taken in a final sense, 'in order to enter', in a temporal sense, 'before entering', or in a consecutive sense, 'and so to enter'. The last is preferable. The phrase *eiselthein eis* (to be understood primarily in a spatial sense, as *doxa* denotes the heavenly realm of glory, cp. A-G s.v. 1 b) means 'to come into', hence 'to come to share in', 'to come to enjoy'.

Translation: *Was it not necessary that the Christ should suffer*, rhetorical question anticipating an affirmative answer; hence, as a statement, e.g. 'it certainly was (or, you should know that it was) necessary that...'. For *to be necessary*, indicating divine necessity, cp. on "must" in 2 : 49, for *the Christ* see on 2 : 11, and for *to suffer* on 9 : 22.

Enter into his glory, or, 'so to come to enjoy his glory', 'thus He would begin to be considered great/honoured' (Tzeltal). For *glory* see references on 2 : 9.

27 ***And beginning with Moses and all the prophets, he interpreted to them in all the scriptures the things concerning himself.***

Exegesis: *arxamenos apo Mōüseōs kai apo pantōn tōn prophētōn* lit. 'beginning with Moses and with all the prophets', but to be understood as, 'beginning with Moses and proceeding to all the prophets'.

diermēneusen autois...ta peri heautou 'he explained to them the things concerning himself'.

diermēneuō (†) 'to explain', 'to expound'.

en pasais tais graphais 'in all the scriptures', i.e. 'in all the parts, or, books of scripture', cp. A-G s.v. *graphē* 2 b α.

Translation: *Beginning with Moses and all the prophets*, or, 'beginning with (the books of) M. and proceeding with (the books of) all the prophets', 'first quoting (passages) from (the books of) M., next from (the books of) all the prophets'; cp. also on 16 : 29, and on "book of the prophet Isaiah" in 4 : 17. The phrase is sometimes better transposed to the end of the sentence.

He interpreted, or, 'explained', 'made clear, or, gave the meaning of' (cp. Kapauku), 'expounded' (which in Chokwe is rendered by a term literally meaning 'to take-apart-a-pile', see *TBT*, 5.94, 1954).

In all the scriptures the things concerning himself, or, "the passages which referred to himself in every part of the scriptures" (NEB), 'what was said/written about him in all the scriptures' (cp. TEV). For *the scriptures* cp. *TH-Mk* on 12 : 10; sometimes (e.g. in Bahasa Indonesia) an Arabic borrowing (lit. 'the Book'), which amongst Muslims is a common designation of the Koran.

28 ***So they drew near to the village to which they were going. He appeared to be going further,***

Exegesis: *kai ēggisan eis tēn kōmēn hou eporeuonto* 'and they came near the village to which they were going'. Subject of *ēggisan* are the two disciples and Jesus, of *eporeuonto* the two disciples alone. For *eggizō eis* cp. on 18 : 35. *hou* is an adverb of place meaning 'where', or 'whither', here the latter, cp. A-G s.v. 2.

kai autos prosepoiēsato porrōteron poreuesthai 'and he acted as though he were going on'. *autos* stresses the change of subject.

prospoieomai (††) 'to act as though', 'to give the impression', with following infinitive.

porrōteron 'further', with *poreuomai* 'to go on'.

Translation: The first sentence may be better subordinated to what follows (e.g. in Javanese, East Toradja), or the second sentence may require a transitional, 'then' (Sranan), 'being close by'.

They drew near, see on 7 : 12.

He appeared to be going further. The specific aspect is brought out in various ways, cp. e.g. 'Jesus was like a man who would go further' (Balinese), 'Jesus, it seemed, wanted to continue his journey' (Javanese, similarly Kituba), or a suffixed form of 'to pass on' which indicates that they thought he would pass on, but he did not do so (Lokele). *To go further* may have to be specified, e.g. 'to go-on-beyond from them' (Trukese), 'to pursue the journey past the place' (Shona).

29 ***but they constrained him, saying, "Stay with us, for it is toward evening and the day is now far spent." So he went in to stay with them.***

Exegesis: *kai parebiasanto auton legontes* 'and they urged him strongly saying'. *parebiasanto* qualifies *legontes*, i.e. the urging is not denoted by the meaning of the words but by the way in which they are spoken.

parabiazomai (†) 'to urge strongly', 'to press', here of moral pressure.

meinon meth' hēmōn 'stay with us'. For *menō* meaning 'to stay overnight as a guest', presumably in the house of one of them, cp. on 19 : 5.

pros hesperan estin lit. 'it is toward evening', hence, 'it is getting toward evening', or, 'it is almost evening'. *hespera* (†).

kekliken ēdē hē hēmera 'the day is already almost over', cp. on 9 : 12.

kai eisēlthen tou meinai sun autois 'and he went in (the house) in order to stay with them'. *tou meinai* is final articular infinitive, cp. Bl-D, § 400.5.

Translation: *They constrained him*, or, 'they (or, the two men) urged him strongly/invited him earnestly'; or, specifying their intent, "they urged him not to" (Goodspeed), "they held him back" (TEV, similarly Kilega, Javanese), 'they didn't allow him to go on' (Tzeltal).

With us, or, 'in our (exclus.) company'; or, if a locative qualification is required, 'in the house we (exclus.) are lodging in (or, going to)', or simply, 'here' (Balinese).

It is toward evening and the day is now far spent, or, 'night is coming, day has already passed' (Sranan), 'it is already evening, the world is dark already' (Bamiléké). For the second clause see also on "the day began to wear away" in 9 : 12. The two clauses are so closely synonymous that the translator may have to combine them in order to avoid a tautology, cp. e.g. 'nearly dark is the day' (Toba Batak 1885), 'the day is already evening, is already dark' (Kilega).

30 ***When he was at table with them, he took the bread and blessed, and broke it, and gave it to them.***

Exegesis: *kai egeneto* 'and it happened', cp. on 1 : 8. Here it serves to indicate the climax of vv. 13-32.

en tō kataklithēnai auton met' autōn 'after he had sat down with them', cp. Bl-D, § 404.2. For *kataklinomai* cp. on 7 : 36.

labōn ton arton eulogēsen lit. 'after taking the bread he blessed it'. The wording of this clause and the next recalls the last supper of Jesus and his disciples (22 : 19), but is not specifically liturgical, since all words are in common usage with regard to ordinary meals. The point, however, is that

Jesus acts as though he were host. *eulogeō* is used here with an impersonal object and means 'to say the blessing (over something)', cp. on 9 : 16.

klasas epedidou autois lit. 'after breaking it he gave it to them'. *epididōmi* is equivalent to simple *didōmi*.

Translation: For *when he was* (or, sat, or, had sat down) *at table* see on 7 : 36, for *bread* see on 4 : 3, and for *blessed* on 1 : 42, sub (4).

31 ***And their eyes were opened and they recognized him; and he vanished out of their sight.***

Exegesis: *autōn de diēnoichthēsan hoi ophthalmoi* lit. 'of them the eyes were opened'. *autōn* is emphatic by position. The opening of the eyes is to be understood in a metaphorical way. Its result is expressed non-metaphorically in the following clause. As in v. 16 the agent is God.

dianoigō 'to open', in a figurative sense of the opening of the eyes, i.e. of making people recognize (here), of the opening of the scriptures, i.e. of making people understand them (v. 31), of the opening of the mind, i.e. of making people understand (v. 45, also with reference to the scriptures).

epegnōsan auton 'they recognized him', ingressive aorist.

kai autos aphantos egeneto ap' autōn 'and he became invisible from them', i.e. 'he disappeared from their sight'.

aphantos (††) 'invisible'.

Translation: The sentence *their eyes were opened and they recognized him* is in meaning the opposite of v. 16 (which see), and closely corresponds to it in form. This formal similarity can quite often, it seems, be preserved in translation without discarding the requirements of idiom and clarity, e.g. 'the spell was taken from their eyes', 'their eyes/sight became clear', etc. The preservation of another stylistic feature, however, viz. the repetition of 'opened' in vv. 32 and 45, appears often to be incompatible with such requirements.

And he vanished out of their sight, or, 'then (or, at that very moment) he became invisible to them' (cp. Ramabai's Marathi version: 'he became he could not be seen by them'). In Lokele the idiom is, 'he no longer appeared before their eyes', and in Tzeltal, 'he was lost to their eyes'.

32 ***They said to each other, "Did not our hearts burn within us while he talked to us on the road, while he opened to us the scriptures?"***

Exegesis: *ouchi hē kardia hēmōn kaiomenē ēn* 'was not our heart burning, or glowing'. For *ouchi* cp. on 4 : 22. For *kardia* as the seat of emotions cp. A-G s.v. 1 b ε. *kaiomenē* is used metaphorically and indicates both enthusiasm and expectation.

hōs elalei hēmin en tē hodō 'while he talked to us on the road'. *elalei* is durative imperfect. *en tē hodō* 'on the road', i.e. 'while/as we were going along' (cp. also *peripatountes* in v. 17).

hōs diēnoigen hēmin tas graphas 'while he opened up the scriptures to us', temporal clause co-ordinate with the preceding clause and explaining it.

Translation: *Our hearts burn within us* (or, "glow", Goodspeed), or, 'a boiling comes to our hearts inside' (Marathi, an idiom for joy and enthusiasm), a metaphor that has to be handled with caution. In Bahasa Indonesia, for instance, 'a burning heart' and 'a hot heart' indicate anger (similarly in Zarma), but 'a flaming heart' refers to fervour. Often terms for fire, glow, or heat must be discarded altogether; hence e.g., 'drawn, as it were, our mind' (Balinese), 'hurt (i.e. longing) our hearts' (Kapauku), 'something was-consuming in our-heart' (East Toradja, an idiom for 'we were profoundly moved'), 'we have our hearts captivated' (as might have been said in Shona), 'our heart was beating for joy' (Sranan). *Our hearts* is distributive, 'the heart of each of us', or, since they are speaking to each other, "your heart" (Phillips 1952).

He opened to us the scriptures, or, 'opened-for-us the meaning of the words of God's book' (Lokele), 'was making clear to us the books' (Fulani). In Zarma a literal rendering is possible since in this language one uses 'to open' in the sense of 'to interpret (a foreign language)' or 'to explain (a written message)'.

33 ***And they rose that same hour and returned to Jerusalem; and they found the eleven gathered together and those who were with them,*** 34 ***who said, "The Lord has risen indeed, and has appeared to Simon!"***

Exegesis: *anastantes autē tē hōra* 'getting up at that very hour, i.e., immediately', referring to rising up from the table.

heuron ēthroismenous tous hendeka kai tous sun autois 'they found the eleven and their adherents gathered together'. For *hoi hendeka* cp. on v. 9. *hoi sun autois* lit. 'those with them', i.e. 'their adherents', or, 'the others of the group', cp. on v. 24.

athroizō (††) 'to collect', 'to gather', here of people that are gathered together.

(V. 34) *legontas* 'saying', going both with the eleven and with all the others.

hoti 'that', or, introducing direct speech, preferably the latter.

ontōs ēgerthē ho kurios 'indeed the Lord has risen', cp. on 7 : 14. For *ontōs* cp. on 23 : 47; for *ho kurios* cp. on 1 : 6.

ōphthē Simōni 'he has appeared to Simon', cp. on 1 : 11.

Translation: *That same hour*, or, 'at once', 'without (a moment's) delay'.

Found, cp. on 7 : 10.

(V. 34) *Who said*, or, 'and these said (to them)'.

Indeed, here indicating affirmation, more specifically rejection of previous doubts.

Appeared to Simon, or, 'showed himself to Simon' (Balinese, South Toradja, Bamiléké), 'caused S. to see him' (Sranan). Some translators, taking Simon to be in focus, render, 'Simon has seen him', but this is less advisable.

35 ***Then they told what had happened on the road, and how he was known to them in the breaking of the bread.***

Exegesis: *kai autoi exēgounto* 'and they on their part, or, in their turn, reported'. *autoi* stresses the change of subject.

exēgeomai (†) 'to explain', here, 'to report', 'to tell'.

ta en tē hodō 'the things on the road', i.e. 'what had happened on the road', cp. on v. 32.

kai hōs egnōsthē autois en tē klasei tou artou 'and how he was recognized by them at the breaking of the bread', still dependent on *exēgounto. hōs* refers to the fact rather than to the mode. Here *ginōskō* is used in the meaning 'to recognize', cp. A-G s.v. 7. *en tē klasei* is temporal.

klasis (†) 'the (act of) breaking'.

Translation: *They,* or, specifying the pronoun, 'in their turn, or, thereupon they', 'the two (men/disciples)' (cp. TEV, Kapauku, and several others).

How he was known to them, or, 'that they had recognized him (or, realized that it was Jesus)'.

In the breaking of the bread, or, 'when he broke the bread', or, 'at the moment they saw him break the bread'.

36 ***As they were saying this, Jesus himself stood among them [and said to them, "Peace to you!"].***

Exegesis: *tauta de autōn lalountōn* 'while they were still telling these things'. *tauta* at the beginning of the clause refers back to v. 35. *autōn* takes up *autoi* in v. 35.

autos estē en mesō autōn 'he himself stood in their midst'. For *estē* cp. on 6 : 8 and A-G s.v. *histēmi* II 1 b. *en mesō autōn* does not suggest that Jesus is in the very centre of the group but that he is among them, cp. on 2 : 46. *autōn* refers to the whole group, not to the two disciples that had come from Emmaus.

eirēnē humin 'peace to you', cp. on 10 : 5, here without eschatological connotation.

Translation: *As they were saying this,* or, 'as they were telling (them) their story' (cp. Rieu, TEV).

Jesus himself stood among them, an unexpected event; hence, "there he was, standing among them" (NEB), 'suddenly Jesus stood in their midst' (Bahasa Indonesia). *Stood.* One should not employ a term specifically used to indicate the appearance of disembodied spirits.

Peace to you. Several versions use a literal rendering of this formula of salutation, for which see on 10 : 5; Tarascan prefers an equivalent formula, 'God guard you'.

37 ***But they were startled and frightened, and supposed that they saw a spirit.***

Exegesis: *ptoēthentes de kai emphoboi genomenoi* 'startled and terrified'. For *ptoeomai* cp. on 21 : 9, for *emphobos* cp. on v. 5. There is little difference between the two and they serve to reinforce one another.

edokoun pneuma theōrein 'they thought that they were looking at a ghost'. For *dokeō* cp. on 8 : 18. *pneuma* (in this meaning †) means here 'ghost', i.e. a bodyless being yet perceptible to the eye.

Translation: *Startled and frightened,* or, "full of fear and terror" (TEV), 'very much frightened'. For terms rendering the concept 'fear' see on 1 : 12.

Supposed, see on 2 : 44.

Spirit, or, 'ghost', in the sense of that portion of the personality which leaves the body at death and is believed to appear to the living in bodily likeness; cp. also *TH-Mk* on 6 : 49.

38 ***And he said to them, "Why are you troubled, and why do questionings rise in your hearts?***

Exegesis: *ti tetaragmenoi este* 'why are you perturbed?', cp. on 1 : 12.

dia ti dialogismoi anabainousin en tē kardia humōn 'why do doubts arise in your heart?' *dia ti* is slightly more emphatic than *ti*. For *dialogismos* cp. on 9 : 46; here it denotes unspoken thoughts concerning the truth of what they see, hence 'questionings', 'doubts'. *anabainō* is used in a metaphorical sense, cp. A-G s.v. 2.

Translation: For *troubled* see on 1 : 29.

Why do questionings rise in your hearts, 'why are you asking yourselves, "Who/What is this"', 'why do you doubt'. The concept 'to doubt' is often rendered by an idiomatic expression comparable to English 'to be in two minds', e.g. 'to stand two' (Zapotec of Juarez), 'one's heart is made two' (Kekchi), 'one's heart is forked' (Kapauku). Some other idioms used do not have such an English equivalent, e.g. 'to whirl words in one's heart' (Chol), 'to place it on one's heart' (Huave), 'not to be able to get things in the proper order', a repetitive form of the verb 'to spread out in order' (Chokwe, see *TBT*, 5.94f, 1954), 'not to think (or, to become without thought) in one's heart' (Bulu, Kaka, see *TBT*, 10.3, 1959). Cp. Nida, *GWIML*, 123f.

39 ***See my hands and my feet, that it is I myself; handle me, and see; for a spirit has not flesh and bones as you see that I have."***

Exegesis: *idete tas cheiras mou kai tous podas mou* 'look at my hands and my feet'. The repetition of possessive *mou* is emphatic and prepares for the next clause which expresses what will be the result of looking at Jesus' hands and feet.

hoti egō eimi autos 'for it is I myself', or, 'that it is I myself', preferably the latter.

psēlaphēsate me kai idete 'feel me and see'. Implicitly *me* goes with *idete* also.

psēlaphaō (†) 'to touch' (in order to investigate), 'to feel'.

hoti pneuma sarka kai ostea ouk echei 'for a ghost does not have flesh and bones'. For *sarx* cp. on 3 : 6.

osteon (†) 'bone' of the human body.

kathōs eme theōreite echonta 'as you see that I have'. *eme* is emphatic by form and position.

Translation: *That it is I myself,* or as an asyndetic sentence, leaving the relationship with what precedes implicit, cp. e.g. 'look at my hands. . . : it is I myself' (cp. NEB); if that relationship has to be made explicit one may say something like, 'look. . . ; then you will realize that it is I myself'.

Handle me, or, 'touch me', 'feel me all over'; or, 'pass/move your hands over me (or, over my body)'.

And see, i.e. 'and look at me'.

Flesh and bones, characteristic for a body, and as such incompatible with a disembodied spirit. The phrase seems to exist in many languages; it may even be the normal term for a person's body (Mixtec), in some cases in reversed word order, 'bone (and) meat/flesh' (Marathi, similarly Balinese). In other languages one has to say 'body (and) bones' (Tzeltal, East Toradja), or simply 'body'.

As you see that I have, or better to bring out the contrast, 'but I do have them (or, have flesh and bones), as you see'.

[*40 *And when he had said this, he showed them his hands and his feet.]* 41 *And while they still disbelieved for joy, and wondered, he said to them, "Have you anything here to eat?"

Exegesis: (V. 41) *eti de apistountōn autōn* 'because they could not yet believe'. The genitive absolute may be temporal, or causal, preferably the latter. For *apisteō* cp. on v. 11.

apo tēs charas 'because of their joy', cp. A-G s.v. *apo* V 3. The article *tēs* has possessive force. The phrase goes with both *apistountōn* and *thaumazontōn.*

echete ti brōsimon enthade 'do you have anything to eat here'.

brōsimos (††) 'eatable', here in the neuter with *ti* 'something to eat', 'food'.

enthade (†) 'here', 'on/at this place'.

Translation: (V. 41) For *disbelieved,* or, 'could not believe (what he said)' cp. on 1 : 20, and for *wondered* on 1 : 21.

For joy does not seem to fit in this context; perhaps it may be taken to mean, 'this was such joyful news to them that they could not believe it'; hence, "for it seemed too good to be true" (NEB).

42 ***They gave him a piece of broiled fish,*** 43 ***and he took it and ate before them.***

Exegesis: *ichthuos optou meros* 'a piece of cooked fish'.
meros 'part', 'portion', 'piece'.
optos (††) 'cooked', 'broiled'.
(V. 43) *labōn enōpion autōn ephagen* lit. 'after taking (it) he ate (it) before their eyes', i.e. while they watched him, with *meros* understood with both verbs.

Translation: *Broiled fish,* or, 'grilled/roasted fish'. The verb refers to cooking by direct exposure to fire or burning coals, but what is relevant here is the fact that the fish had been prepared for food rather than the way this had been done. For *fish* see on 5 : 6.

44 ***Then he said to them, "These are my words which I spoke to you, while I was still with you, that everything written about me in the law of Moses and the prophets and the psalms must be fulfilled."***

Exegesis: *eipen de pros autous* 'he said to them', either at that same time, or at some later meeting. The latter is preferable, cp. Plummer.
houtoi hoi logoi mou 'these are my words'. Since this does not refer to words spoken in the preceding verses it means either 'these are my words which I said to you when I was still with you and which I repeat now, viz. that...', or, 'to these things that have happened refer the words which I said to you...' etc. The latter is more probable, cp. Klostermann.
eti ōn sun humin 'when I was still with you', i.e. before his death and resurrection. It implies that his presence now among them was of a different nature from what it had been before his death.
hoti dei plērōthēnai 'viz. that must be fulfilled', summarizing what Jesus had told the disciples during his lifetime. For *dei* cp. on 9 : 22; for *plēroō* cp. on 1 : 20.
panta ta gegrammena...peri emou 'all that has been written...about me'.
en tō nomō Mōüseōs 'in the law of Moses', i.e. the Pentateuch.
tois prophētais kai psalmois '(in) the (books of the) prophets and the (book of) psalms'. For the latter cp. on 20 : 42.

Translation: *These are my words which I spoke to you, ..., that everything...*, or, following the interpretation preferred in *Exegesis*, "these are the very things I told you...: everything..." (TEV), 'this is the thing-I-meant, which I...pointed-out to you, namely, that everything...' (Bahasa Indonesia RC).
While I was still with you, or, 'while still I-had-as-companion you' (cp. East Toradja 1933), 'when we (inclus.) were still together' (South Toradja).
For *everything written in,* or, 'everything that stands in, or, is found in, or, forms the contents of', or equivalent formulas for reference to scripture

passages, and for *the law of Moses* see on 2 : 22f; for *psalms* see on 20 : 42, and for *to be fulfilled* on 4 : 21.

45 ***Then he opened their minds to understand the scriptures,***

Exegesis: *tote diēnoixen autōn ton noun* 'then he opened their minds', cp. on v. 31.

nous (†) 'mind', i.e. seat of the intellectual capacities, cp. A-G s.v. 1.

tou sunienai tas graphas 'to understand the scriptures', either final, 'in order to...', or consecutive, 'so as to...', preferably the latter; cp. Bl-D, § 400.5.

Translation: *He opened their minds to understand,* or with another metaphor, 'he enlightened their mind (or, clarified their thoughts) that they could understand' (Balinese, Shona 1966); or again non-metaphorically, 'he made them able to understand', 'he caused them to know well' (Tzeltal); and see on v. 31. For *to understand* cp. on 2 : 47.

The scriptures, or, 'the meaning/contents of the Holy Book' (Balinese), 'what God's book says' (Tzeltal).

46 ***and said to them, "Thus it is written, that the Christ should suffer and on the third day rise from the dead,*** 47 ***and that repentance and forgiveness of sins should be preached in his name to all nations, beginning from Jerusalem.***

Exegesis: *kai eipen autois* 'and he said to them', best understood as a continuation of the preceding clause.

houtōs gegraptai 'thus it is written', i.e. 'this is what is written'.

pathein ton Christon kai anastēnai 'that the Messiah should suffer and rise'. Although in the aorist the infinitives refer to prophecies to be fulfilled in the future. For the phrase itself cp. on v. 7.

(V. 47) *kai kēruchthēnai...metanoian kai aphesin hamartiōn* 'and that repentance and forgiveness of sins should be proclaimed', still dependent upon *gegraptai.* For *kērussō* and *metanoia* cp. on 3 : 3; for *aphesis* and *hamartia* cp. on 1 : 77.

epi tō onomati autou lit. 'upon his name', hence, 'on the basis of (all that) his name (implies)', cp. Plummer, and Acts 5 : 28, 40.

eis panta ta ethnē 'to all nations', going with *kēruchthēnai,* cp. *TH-Mk* on 13 : 10. In contrast to 12 : 30 and 21 : 24 *ta ethnē* here includes Israel.

arxamenoi apo Ierousalēm 'beginning from Jerusalem', either to be understood as going with *kēruchthēnai* as a rather strong anacoluthon, implying that the unnamed agents of the preaching are to be the disciples, or to be taken with v. 48, 'beginning from Jerusalem you are witnesses to these things'. The former is preferable, cp. Plummer.

Translation: *Rise from the dead,* see on 9 : 7f.

(V. 47) *That repentance and forgiveness of sins should be preached...to all nations,* cp. on 3 : 3; where rather radical changes in sentence structure are required one may say, 'that you should preach to all nations, "Repent and God will forgive you your sins."' — *All nations*, or, 'all (different) peoples/races/tribes', 'the people of all (different) countries, or, places', cp. *TH-Mk* on 13 : 10. In South Toradja a poetic idiom emphasizing totality is used, viz. 'all inhabitants (lit. contents) of the world, covered by the sky and supported by the earth'.

In his name, or, 'calling upon his name' (see *Exegesis*). In several languages 'name' cannot be used here (cp. on 1 : 49); then one may say something like, 'appealing to him, or, to all that he has said and done', 'because of what he has promised'.

Beginning from Jerusalem, i.e. that preaching should begin (or, you should start preaching) in J. and from there go further.

48 ***You are witnesses of these things.***

Exegesis: *humeis martures toutōn* 'you (are) witnesses of these things'. *humeis* is emphatic and brings out what was implied in v. 47. For *martus* cp. on 11 : 48, and Acts 1 : 8, 21f. The clause refers to the future.

Translation: *You are witnesses of these things*, or, 'you are to give testimony about these things', 'you are to tell the things you have seen', 'you have seen these things and will tell people about them'; cp. *N.T.Wb.*/74.

49 ***And behold, I send the promise of my Father upon you; but stay in the city, until you are clothed with power from on high."***

Exegesis: *kai* [*idou*] 'and behold', cp. on 1 : 20.

egō apostellō tēn epaggelian tou patros mou eph' humas lit. 'I send the promise of my father upon you'. *egō* is emphatic and contrasts with *humeis* in v. 48 and v. 50. For *apostellō* cp. on 1 : 19. The present tense has future meaning, cp. Bl-D, § 323.

epaggelia (†) 'promise', here in the concrete sense, 'that which is promised'. As in Acts 2 : 33 the reference is to the Holy Spirit; hence *epi* is to be interpreted as in 1 : 35.

humeis de 'but you' takes up *humeis* in v. 48 and *humas* in v. 49.

kathisate en tē polei 'stay in the city', i.e. Jerusalem. For *kathizō* in this meaning cp. A-G s.v. 2 a β.

heōs hou endusēsthe ex hupsous dunamin 'till you are clothed with power from on high'. For *enduō* cp. on 8 : 27. Here it is used in a metaphorical sense of the receiving of the Holy Spirit, cp. A-G s.v. 2 b. For *dunamis* as a virtual synonym of *pneuma* cp. on 1 : 17. *ex hupsous* may go with *endusēsthe* or with *dunamin*, preferably the latter. *hupsos* (cp. on 1 : 78) may be interpreted as a circumlocution for God, or for heaven, preferably the latter, cp. A-G s.v. 1 b.

Translation: *I send...upon you*, or, 'I will order to descend upon you', 'I will bring down upon you' (Kapauku), 'I will cause-to-come to you' (cp. Balinese); cp. also on "come upon you" in 1 : 35.

The promise of my Father, or, 'the gift promised by my Father' (Shona 1966), 'what my Father has said He will give you' (Tzeltal). For *my Father* see on 2 : 49.

Until, i.e. 'waiting for the moment that', 'as long as not yet', cp. on 1 : 20.

You are clothed with, or, 'you are equipped-with' (Bahasa Indonesia), 'you put on as (one puts on) a garment' (cp. Trukese), or simply, 'you are given' (Sundanese), 'you receive' (Malay); cp. also 'till the strength...will cover your body like a garment' (Sranan).

On high, cp. on 1 : 78.

50 ***Then he led them out as far as Bethany, and lifting up his hands he blessed them.***

Exegesis: *exēgagen de autous* 'he led them out (of the city)'. *exagō* (†).

heōs pros Bēthanian 'as far as Bethany', or 'as far as over against Bethany', preferably the former, cp. Plummer and A-G s.v. *heōs* II 2 c. The phrase does not mean that they went into Bethany. For *Bēthania* cp. on 19 : 29.

eparas tas cheiras autou lit. 'after lifting up his hands', usually as a gesture of prayer, here of blessing.

eulogēsen autous 'he blessed them', i.e. 'he called God's gracious power upon them', cp. on 1 : 42.

Translation: *As far as Bethany*, or, 'to the vicinity of' (cp. NV, Javanese).

Lifting up his hands, or, 'holding his hands over them' (Javanese), 'having made his hands high' (Marathi), 'stretched up his hands' (Trukese).

He blessed them, see on 1 : 42, sub (1). South Toradja uses a poetic idiom here, lit. 'he sprinkled-upon them a favourable countenance'.

51 ***While he blessed them, he parted from them [and was carried up into heaven].***

Exegesis: *kai egeneto* 'and it happened', cp. on 1 : 8.

en tō eulogein auton autous lit. 'during his blessing of them', cp. Bl-D, § 404.

diestē ap' autōn 'he parted from them', without indication of direction. For *diistamai* cp. on 22 : 59.

anephereto eis ton ouranon 'he was carried up into heaven', if retained in the text, supplements the preceding clause as to direction and destination. *anapherō* (†).

Translation: For *he parted from them* cp. on 9 : 33.

Was carried up into heaven, or, if no passive form is available, 'ascended/went-up to heaven' (East Toradja 1933), 'rose above' (Zarma). *Heaven*, here used in the sense of 'God's abode', cp. on 2 : 15.

52 ***And they [worshipped him, and] returned to Jerusalem with great joy,*** 53 ***and were continually in the temple blessing God.***

Exegesis: *kai autoi* 'and they', indicating change of subject.

proskunēsantes auton 'after worshipping him', cp. on 4 : 7.

meta charas megalēs 'with great joy'. *meta* with genitive here expresses accompanying emotions, cp. A-G s.v. A III 1.

(V. 53) *kai ēsan dia pantos en tō hierō* 'and they were constantly in the temple'. *dia pantos* scil. *chronou*, lit. 'during all the time', 'constantly'. For *hieron* cp. on 2 : 27.

eulogountes ton theon 'praising God', cp. on 1 : 64 and 42.

Translation: For *to worship* see on 4 : 7; for *with great joy*, or, 'very joyfully', cp. on 8 : 13.

(V. 53) *Were continually in the temple*, or, "spent all their time in the temple" (NEB), or, stated negatively, 'did not cease being (or, stayed without interval) in the temple' (Sundanese, East Toradja). The expression is hyperbolical, like the comparable one in 2 : 37.

Blessing God, i.e. praising God, see on 1 : 42, sub (2).

LISTS AND INDICES

PROPOSED SECTION HEADINGS

The user of this list of section headings should bear the following points in mind.

(1) As regards the division of the text into sections and the general contents of the headings this list conforms, as a rule, to the Bible Societies' *Greek New Testament*, edition 1966, which itself closely follows the division found in *Section Headings for the New Testament* (in *Helps for Translators*, Vol. IV, UBS, London, 1961), Part 2, pp. 7-11. As regards the wording, however, the proposed headings differ considerably from those in *GNT*, the principal reason being that they try to anticipate translation problems.

(2) To achieve this end the proposed headings are rather simple in their vocabulary and their grammatical and semantic structures, keeping close to "kernel sentences". In some cases it may be advisable for a translator to take the proposed wording as his model, even though it may result in a rather long and explicit sentence, and sometimes in monotony. But more often he will have to reckon with a specific style for headings, aiming at brevity and pointedness (of which TEV gives good examples). Such a style may prefer, for instance, nominal to verbal forms, passive to active constructions, variety to repetition, the specific to the generic, fragmentary phrases to full sentences, and the use of special markers. It must be left to each individual translator to investigate the linguistic possibilities and stylistic preferences of the receptor language, in order to decide how the kernel sentences should be "forward-transformed". In this process of "forward-transformation" questions of focus and line of thought through a sequence of sections should be carefully kept in mind, lest confusion arise, e.g. when, by choosing a passive or a nominal construction, the focus shifts to the goal, or to the event, whereas it should be on the actor; when the figure selected as agent of the heading is not the principal actor of the section; or when a pronoun (which presupposes a previous context) is used, whereas headings imply a beginning (even if the section is one of a sequence). For all this cp. Will. A. Smalley, "Preparation and Translation of Section Headings" (*TBT*, 19.149-158, 1968), to which article the present list owes much.

(3) In honorific languages one must decide whether to use honorific or ordinary forms. As discussed above, in the first translational note on 1 : 1-4, Luke, as narrator of the Gospel story, can often be envisaged as addressing his hearers or readers in ordinary, non-honorific language; if so, the translator must simply follow him in this. In the section headings, however, it is not Luke who is speaking, but the translator himself, of whom politeness towards his readers is usually expected. Therefore the headings (and, likewise, preface or notes) are, as a rule, best given in polite language.

(4) The section headings in this list are meant as helps to those translators who have to compose new headings, or to change or correct unsatisfactory existing ones. If, however, a section is already known in the receptor language by an appropriate heading, the translator may find it better to keep to it and ignore the heading which this list proposes for such a section. If, for instance, 12 : 13-21 is always referred to as "The (parable of the) rich fool", there is no point in changing this into, 'The (parable of the) rich man who acted like a fool'; or if 9 : 28-36 is commonly known under an intelligible heading built on the concept 'transfiguration', or, 15 : 11-32 under the heading 'The (parable of the) prodigal son', one should leave it so.

(5) The headings often use terms occurring in the section concerned. For problems that the rendering of these terms may pose, compare the translational notes in the body of this Handbook.

1 : 1-4, 'Introduction', or a comparable term, which may literally mean, 'foreword' (Bahasa Indonesia), 'opening' (Javanese), 'its-head' (East Toradja), etc. If such a specific term does not exist, the translator may use a descriptive heading, e.g. 'Luke (or, The author) tells how and why he wrote this book'.

1 : 5-25, 'Zechariah will have (or, Z.'s wife will give birth to) a son, John (the Baptist)'. It may be necessary to indicate that this was an announcement. Some languages possess a particle to mark a phrase as being quoted; elsewhere one will have to introduce the heading, cp. e.g. 'The angel Gabriel tells Z., "You will ..."', or, shifting to indirect discourse, '...tells Z. that he will...'. A shorter alternative is, 'The angel G.'s message to Z.' — N.B. The following headings will usually be given in direct discourse. In some languages shifts to indirect discourse, similar to the one just given, will be necessary; such shifts will, as a rule, not be specifically mentioned.

1 : 26-38, 'Mary will give birth to a son, Jesus (the Saviour)', etc., cp. on the preceding heading; or again, 'G.'s message to Mary'.

1 : 39-45, 'Mary visits Zechariah's wife, Elizabeth'.

1 : 46-56, 'Mary praises God', or, 'Mary's song of praise'.

1 : 57-66, 'Elizabeth gives birth to a son', or ,'John (the Baptist) is born', 'The birth of John (the Baptist)'.

1 : 67-80, 'Zechariah speaks of God's great deeds', or, 'Z.'s song of praise'.

2 : 1-7, 'Mary gives birth to a son', or, 'The birth of Jesus', or, 'Jesus is born'.

2 : 8-21, ('Angels tell the shepherds',) "The Saviour has been born"; or without the introductory words, cp. on the heading of 1 : 5-25.

2 : 22-40, 'Jesus' parents go with him (or, with their son, or, with the child) to the temple in Jerusalem'. — *GNT* takes vv. 39f as a separate section, but the longer section, taking v. 39 as closely connected with what precedes and v. 40 as marking the end of a section (cp. 1 : 80 and 2 : 52), seems preferable.

2 : 41-52, 'Jesus, as a boy, in the temple in Jerusalem'.

3 : 1-20, 'John tells the Jews to repent, and baptizes them', or, 'The work of J. the B.'.

3 : 21f, 'Jesus baptized, and proclaimed the Son of God', or, 'John baptizes Jesus also; God proclaims him his Son'.

3 : 23-38, 'The human forefathers of Jesus'.

4 : 1-13, 'Jesus tempted (in the wilderness)', or, 'The Devil tempts Jesus (in the wilderness)'.

4 : 14f, 'Jesus begins his work in Galilee'.

4 : 16-30, 'Jesus and the people of Nazareth'.

4 : 31-37, 'Jesus heals a demon-possessed man in Capernaum'.

4 : 38-41, 'Jesus heals many other people'.

4 : 42-44, 'Jesus preaches all through the country of the Jews'.

5 : 1-11, 'Jesus chooses three fishermen to become fishers of men', or, where a concise and idiomatic rendering of this play-on-words is impossible, 'Jesus chooses three fishermen to be his disciples'.

5 : 12-16, 'Jesus makes a leper clean'.

5 : 17-26, 'Jesus forgives the sins of a paralyzed man and heals him'.

5 : 27-32, 'Jesus chooses Levi to be his disciple'.

5 : 33-39, 'Jesus explains why his disciples need not fast'.
6 : 1-5, 'On the Sabbath Jesus' disciples pluck grain'.
6 : 6-11, 'On the Sabbath Jesus heals a man with a crippled hand'. Because in both sections the observance of the Sabbath is at issue some translators prefer to combine vv. 1-11 in one section, headed e.g. 'Jesus tells (and shows) what one is allowed to do on the Sabbath'.
6 : 12-16, 'Jesus appoints the twelve apostles'.
6 : 17-19, 'Jesus teaches and heals (many people)'.
6 : 20-26, 'Jesus teaches (his disciples), who is blessed/happy and who is not (blessed/happy)', or, '(Jesus' teaching about) happiness and sorrow'.
6 : 27-35, ('Jesus teaches his disciples',) "Love your enemies"; for the introductory words cp. on the heading of 1 : 5-25.
6 : 36-38, ('Jesus teaches his disciples',) "Do not judge others (or, your fellow men)".
6 : 39-49, 'Parables'. — A different division of vv. 27-49 is found in *GNT*, i.e. vv. 27-36 (which may be headed, "Love your enemies"); 37-42 (to be headed as 36-38 above); 43-45 ('A tree and its fruit', TEV); 46-49 ('The two house builders', TEV).
7 : 1-10, 'Jesus heals the slave of a Roman officer'.
7 : 11-17, 'Jesus raises the son of a widow (in Nain) from death'.
7 : 18-23, 'Jesus and the messengers from John the Baptist'. — *GNT* has a longer section, vv. 18-35 under a similar heading.
7 : 24-35, 'Jesus speaks to the people about John the Baptist'.
7 : 36-50, 'Jesus at the home of Simon the Pharisee' (TEV).
8 : 1-3, 'Women who accompanied Jesus'.
8 : 4-8, 'The parable of the seed (or, of the sower)'.
8 : 9f, 'Why Jesus uses (or, teaches by means of) parables', or, 'The purpose of the parables' (TEV).
8 : 11-15, 'Jesus explains the parable of the seed (or, of the sower)'.
8 : 16-18, 'Jesus' saying about the lamp under a bowl'.
8 : 19-21, 'Jesus' mother and brothers'.
8 : 22-25, 'Jesus calms a storm'.
8 : 26-39, 'Jesus heals a demon-possessed man in Gergesa'.
8 : 40-56, 'Jesus raises Jairus' daughter from death, and heals a woman who touches his cloak'.
9 : 1-6, 'Jesus sends out his twelve disciples to preach and to heal'.
9 : 7-9, 'Herod is perplexed (or, is in doubt) about Jesus', or, 'Herod asks himself who Jesus is'.
9 : 10-17, 'Jesus feeds five thousand people'.
9 : 18-20, 'Peter says to Jesus, "You are the Christ"', or, 'Peter acknowledges Jesus as the Christ'.
9 : 21f, 'Jesus tells his disciples, "I have to die but shall rise again"'. — *GNT* has one section, covering vv. 21-27, 'Jesus foretells his death and resurrection'.
9 : 23-27, 'Jesus tells his followers, "You have to suffer also"'.
9 : 28-36, 'Jesus appears (or, is seen) in heavenly glory', or, 'Three disciples see Jesus' glory'.
9 : 37-43a, 'Jesus heals a demon-possessed boy'.
9 : 43b-45, 'Jesus again tells his disciples, "I have to suffer"', or, 'Jesus speaks again about his death'.
9 : 46-48, ('Jesus tells his disciples',) "Do not want to be the greatest", or, 'Jesus' disciples quarrel-over greatness' (South Toradja). For the introductory words in parenthesis here and in several headings below cp. on the heading of 1 : 5-25.

9 : 49f, ('Jesus tells his disciples',) "Who is not against you is for you", or, 'About one who acts in Jesus' name but is not his follower'.

9 : 51-56, 'The people of a village in Samaria do not receive Jesus as guest'.

9 : 57-62, 'What Jesus demands of people who profess to be (or, desire to become) his followers', or, 'About people who desire to become followers of Jesus'.

10 : 1-16, 'Jesus sends out seventy (or, seventy-two) other disciples to heal and to preach'. — *GNT* has two sections, viz. vv. 1-12, 'The mission of the seventy-two', and 13-16, 'Woes to unrepentant cities'.

10 : 17-24, 'The seventy(-two) disciples return'. — *GNT* has two sections, vv. 17-20, 'The return of the seventy-two', 21-24, 'The rejoicing of Jesus'.

10 : 25-37, 'The parable of the good (or, merciful) Samaritan'.

10 : 38-42, 'Jesus visits Martha and Mary'.

11 : 1-13, 'Jesus teaches his disciples (what and how) to pray', or, 'Jesus' teaching on prayer' (TEV).

11 : 14-23, 'Jesus and Beelzebul', or, 'People say, "Jesus casts out demons by (or, with the help of) the chief of demons"'.

11 : 24-26, ('Jesus warns the people',) "Demons that have gone out of a man are liable to return".

11 : 27f, 'Jesus explains who should be called truly blessed/happy', or, 'True happiness' (TEV).

11 : 29-32, ('Jesus tells the people',) "You should not demand a sign".

11 : 33-36, 'Jesus' saying about the light of the body'.

11 : 37-54, 'Jesus accuses (or, points out the wrongs of) the Pharisees and lawyers'.

12 : 1-3, 'Jesus warns his disciples against hypocrisy', or, ('Jesus tells his disciples',) "Do not behave like hypocrites".

12 : 4-7, ('Jesus teaches his disciples',) "Do not fear men but (fear) God".

12 : 8-12, ('Jesus tells his disciples',) "Acknowledge me publicly". — Several versions have one section covering vv. 1-12, headed e.g. ('Jesus tells his disciples',) "Be sincere and courageous".

12 : 13-21, 'The parable of the foolish rich man, or, of the rich man who acted like a fool'.

12 : 22-34, ('Jesus teaches his disciples',) "Trust in God". — Some versions add "and gather riches in heaven", or take vv. 32-34 as a separate section with a similar heading.

12 : 35-48, ('Jesus tells his disciples',) "Behave like watchful and faithful servants", or, "Be ready when the Lord returns" (cp. Jerusalem).

12 : 49-53, ('Jesus says to his disciples',) "I cause people to be divided", or, "I do not bring peace but division".

12 : 54-59, ('Jesus tells the people',) "Realize how important/decisive the present time is". — TEV has two sections, vv. 54-56, headed 'Understanding the time', and vv. 57-59, 'Settle with your opponent'; same division in *GNT*.

13 : 1-5, ('Jesus tells the people',) "You must repent or perish", or, 'Call to repentance'.

13 : 6-9, 'The parable of the fig tree that did not bear fruit'.

13 : 10-17, 'On the Sabbath Jesus heals a crippled woman'.

13 : 18-21, 'The parables of the mustard seed and the leaven'.

13 : 22-30, ('Jesus tells the people',) "Try hard to enter the kingdom of God though the door is narrow".

13 : 31-35, 'Jesus says openly, "I am soon to die in Jerusalem", or, "The people of Jerusalem will soon kill me"'.

14 : 1-6, 'On the Sabbath Jesus heals a man who has dropsy'.

14 : 7-14, 'A lesson to guests and a host'.

14 : 15-24, 'The parable of the great banquet' (*GNT*, keeping to the traditional designation of this section), but a better characterization of the main subject is, 'The parable of the excuses (NV), or, of the invited-ones who excused themselves, or, who did not want to come (cp. Jerusalem, Bahasa Indonesia RC); or, of the guests that had no time to come' (cp. Sranan).

14 : 25-35, 'Jesus describes those who cannot be his disciples', or, 'The conditions for becoming a disciple of Jesus'. *GNT* has vv. 34f as a separate section, headed 'Tasteless salt'.

15 : 1-7, 'The parable of the lost sheep'.

15 : 8-10, 'The parable of the lost coin'.

15 : 11-32, 'The parable of the lost son'.

16 : 1-13, 'The parable of the dishonest steward'.

16 : 14-18, 'Jesus admonishes (or, earnestly warns) the Pharisees'.

16 : 19-31, 'The parable of the rich man and (the poor man, called) Lazarus'.

17 : 1-10, 'Some sayings of Jesus'. Several versions prefer to use four sections (vv. 1f; 3f; 5f; 7-10), which may be headed, ('Jesus tells his followers',) "Do not cause others to sin"; "Be quick to forgive"; "Have a strong faith"; and, "You are servants who do only what they ought to do".

17 : 11-19, 'Jesus makes ten lepers clean'.

17 : 20-37, 'Jesus speaks about the coming of the kingdom of God', or, 'Jesus answers the question, "When will the kingdom of God come?"'.

18 : 1-8, 'The parable of the widow and the judge'.

18 : 9-14, 'The parable of the Pharisee and the tax collector'.

18 : 15-17, 'Jesus and the children'.

18 : 18-30, 'Jesus and the rich ruler'.

18 : 31-34, 'Once more (or, For the last time) Jesus tells his disciples, "I have to die but shall rise again"', cp. on 9 : 21.

18 : 35-43, 'Jesus heals a blind man near Jericho'.

19 : 1-10, 'Jesus and Zacchaeus'.

19 : 11-27, 'The parable of the pounds'.

19 : 28-44, 'Jesus enters Jerusalem as Messiah'.

19 : 45-48, 'Jesus in the temple', or, 'Jesus drives-away the people who trade in the temple and teaches (there)' (Javanese).

20 : 1-8, 'Jesus answers a question about his authority', or, 'Jesus answers the question, "What authority do you have (to do these things)?"'.

20 : 9-19, 'The parable of the wicked tenants, or, of the man who let out his vineyard to tenants'.

20 : 20-26, '(Jesus answers) the question about paying taxes to Caesar, or, "Is it lawful for us to pay taxes to Caesar?"'.

20 : 27-40, '(Jesus answers) the question about the resurrection, or, "How will things be when the dead arise?"'.

20 : 41-44, 'Jesus asks (the scribes) about the Messiah, or, "How can the Messiah be the son (of David) and also the Lord of David?"'.

20 : 45-47, 'Jesus warns his disciples to beware of the scribes'.

21 : 1-4, 'Jesus compares the offerings of the rich with that of a poor widow', or, 'The widow's offering'.

21 : 5-38, 'Jesus speaks about the things that will happen before the end of this age'. — *GNT* has six sections, viz., vv. 5f; 7-19; 20-24; 25-28; 29-33; 34-38. The first four may be headed, ('Jesus says',) "The temple will be destroyed"; "There will be wars and troubles"; "Jerusalem will be destroyed"; "Signs must happen before the Son of man will come"; the fifth may be headed, 'The lesson of the fig tree'; and the sixth,

('Jesus tells his followers',) "Watch for the day (of the Son of man)".

22 : 1-6, 'Judas agrees to deliver Jesus up'.

22 : 7-13, 'Jesus sends two of his disciples to prepare the passover meal', or, 'Jesus has the passover meal prepared'.

22 : 14-23, 'Jesus eats the passover meal with his disciples', or, 'Jesus has supper with his disciples for the last time', 'The last supper'. Several versions, however, prefer a heading built on the liturgical passage in vv. 19f, such as 'Jesus institutes (or, tells his disciples to celebrate, or, starts (Kituba)) the Lord's Supper'. For the latter term languages may use expressions lit. meaning e.g. 'the Holy Meal' (Balinese), 'the holy ceremony' (Toba Batak), 'the great-good' (Sranan), 'Feast of Chief' (Lokele), 'Our Lord's Table' (Tzeltal, similarly Kituba).

22 : 24-30, 'Jesus points out who is great in his eyes', or, 'True greatness'.

22 : 31-34, 'Jesus says to Peter, "You will deny me"', or, 'Jesus foretells that Peter will deny him'.

22 : 35-38, 'Jesus tells his disciples, "You must prepare for strife/opposition"'.

22 : 39-46, 'Jesus prays on the Mount of Olives'.

22 : 47-53, 'Jesus is arrested', or, 'The Jewish leaders arrest Jesus'.

22 : 54-62, 'Peter denies Jesus'.

22 : 63-65, 'Jesus is mocked and beaten', or, 'Jesus' guards mock and beat him'.

22 : 66-71, 'Jesus is led before the Council', or, 'The Jewish council tries Jesus'.

23 : 1-5, 'Jesus is led before Pilate', or, 'P. tries Jesus'.

23 : 6-12, 'Jesus is led before Herod', or, 'Pilate sends Jesus on to Herod'.

23 : 13-25, 'Jesus is sentenced to death', or, 'Pilate pronounces sentence that Jesus must die'.

23 : 26-43, 'Jesus is crucified', or, 'The Roman soldiers crucify Jesus'.

23 : 44-49, 'Jesus dies', or, 'The death of Jesus'.

23 : 50-56[a], 'Jesus is buried', or, 'Joseph of Arimathea buries Jesus'.

23 : 56[b]-24 : 12, 'The women and Peter do not find Jesus in the tomb'.

24 : 13-35, 'Jesus appears to two of his disciples going to Emmaus'.

24 : 36-49, 'Jesus appears to other disciples of his in Jerusalem'.

24 : 50-53, 'Jesus takes leave of his disciples'. Many versions have 'The ascension', 'Jesus ascends (or, is taken up) to heaven', cp. the last part of v. 51; this, however, is not to be recommended when v. 51[c] is thought to be of dubious authenticity.

LIST OF BOOKS QUOTED MORE THAN ONCE IN THE HANDBOOK

1. Greek texts

GNT: *The Greek New Testament*, ed. by Kurt Aland, Matthew Black, Bruce M. Metzger and Allen Wikgren, Stuttgart, 1966.

Nestle, Erwin, and Aland, Kurt, *Novum Testamentum Graece* (*editio vicesima quinta*), Stuttgart, 1963.

Westcott, B. F., and Hort, F. J. A., *The New Testament in the Original Greek*, London, 1890.

LXX: *Septuaginta* (*editio quarta*), ed. Alfred Rahlfs, Stuttgart, 1950.

2. Translations in English and other western languages

AV: *The New Testament of our Lord and Saviour Jesus Christ. Authorized Version*, 1611.

BFBS: *Luke, A Greek-English Diglot for the use of Translators*, London, 1962.

Brouwer: *Het Nieuwe Testament, vertaald door Prof. Dr. A. M. Brouwer*, Leiden, 1925.

Bruns: *Das Neue Testament, neu übertragen von Hans Bruns*, Giessen, 1959.

Français Courant: *La naissance et l'enfance de Jésus* (pre-publication edition of Lk. 1 : 5-2 : 40).

Goodspeed: *The New Testament, An American Translation*, by Edgar J. Goodspeed, Chicago, 1923 (ed. 1948).

Jerusalem: *La Sainte Bible, traduite en français sous la direction de L'École Biblique de Jérusalem*, Paris, 1956.

Kingsley Williams: *The New Testament in Plain English*, by Charles Kingsley Williams, London, 1952.

Knox: *The New Testament of our Lord and Saviour Jesus Christ. A New Translation*, by Ronald P. Knox, New York, 1952.

Leyden: *Bijbel in de Leidse Vertaling*, Zaltbommel, 1912.

Menge: *Die Heilige Schrift*, übersetzt und neu bearbeitet von D. Dr. Hermann Menge, Stuttgart, 1927 (ed. 1951).

Moffatt: *The Bible, A New Translation*, by James Moffatt, New York and London, 1935.

NEB: *The New English Bible, New Testament*, Oxford and Cambridge, 1961.

NV: *Bijbel in de nieuwe Vertaling van het Nederlandsch Bijbelgenootschap*, Amsterdam, 1939 (ed. 1962).

Phillips: *The Gospels translated into Modern English*, by J. B. Phillips, London, 1952.

Rieu: *The Four Gospels, A New Translation from the Greek*, by E. V. Rieu, Penguin Classics, 1958.

RSV: *The New Testament of our Lord and Saviour Jesus Christ. Revised Standard Version*, New York, 1946 (ed. Great Britain, 1964).

Schonfield: *The authentic New Testament, edited and translated from the Greek* by Hugh J. Schonfield, London, 1962.

Segond: *La Sainte Bible, traduite d'après les textes originaux hébreu et grec* par Louis Segond, éd. revue, Paris, 1959.

Spanish VP: *Dios Llega al Hombre, El Nuevo Testamento de nuestro Señor Jesucristo (Versión Popular)*, Sociedades Bíblicas en América Latina, 1966.
StV: *Bijbel in de Statenvertaling*, 1637 (ed. 1948).
Synodale: *Le Nouveau Testament. Version Synodale* (7e édition entièrement revisée). Paris, 1952.
TEV: *Good News for Modern Man, The New Testament in Today's English Version*, ABS, New York, 1966 (ed. 1967).
Torrey: *The Four Gospels, A New Translation*, by C. C. Torrey, London, without year.
20th Century: *The Twentieth Century New Testament, A Translation into Modern English*, London, 1904.
Weissäcker: *Das Neue Testament* übersetzt von Carl Weissäcker, Tübingen, 1903.
Weymouth: *The New Testament in Modern Speech*, by R. F. Weymouth, 4th ed., London, without year.
Willibrord: *Het Nieuwe Testament van onze Heer Jesus Christus*, Katholieke Bijbelstichting St. Willibrord, Boxtel, 1961.
Zürich: *Die Heilige Schrift des Alten und Neuen Testaments*, Verlag der Zwingli-Bibel, Zürich, 1931.

3. Commentaries on Luke

Caird, G. B., *The Gospel of St. Luke* (*The Pelican Gospel Commentaries*), Harmondsworth, 1963.
Creed, J. M., *The Gospel According to St. Luke*, London, 1953.
Grundmann, W., *Das Evangelium nach Lukas* (*Theologischer Handkommentar zum Neuen Testament*), Berlin, 1961.
Klostermann, E., *Das Lukasevangelium* (*Handbuch zum Neuen Testament*), Tübingen, 1929.
Lagrange, M. J., *Évangile selon Saint Luc*, Paris, 1927.
Leaney, A. R. C., *A Commentary on the Gospel according to St. Luke* (*Black's New Testament Commentaries*), London, 1958.
Maclean Gilmour, S., *The Gospel according to St. Luke. Introduction and Exegesis* (*The Interpreter's Bible*, vol. VIII), New York, 1952.
Manson, W., *The Gospel of Luke* (*Moffatt New Testament Commentary*), London, 1930.
Plummer, A., *A Critical and Exegetical Commentary on the Gospel according to St. Luke* (*International Critical Commentary*), Edinburgh, 1922.
Rengstorf, K. H., *Das Evangelium nach Lukas* (*Das Neue Testament Deutsch*, vol. I, 2), Göttingen, 1937.
Schlatter, A., *Das Evangelium des Lukas*, Stuttgart, 1960.
Weiss, B., *Die Evangelien des Markus und Lukas* (*Kritisch Exegetischer Kommentar über das Neue Testament*, Vol. I, 2), 8th edition, Göttingen, 1892.
Zahn, Th., *Das Evangelium des Lukas* (*Kommentar zum Neuen Testament*, vol. III), 4th edition, Leipzig, 1920.

4. Lexicons, Grammars, and Other Philological Literature

Arndt, William F., and Gingrich, F. Wilbur, *A Greek-English Lexicon of the New Testament and Other Early Christian Literature*, Chicago, 1957 [cited as A-G].
Black, M., *An Aramaic Approach to the Gospels and Acts*, 2nd edition, Oxford, 1954.
Blass, F., and Debrunner, A., *A Greek Grammar of the New Testament and Other Early Christian Literature*, translated and revised by Robert W. Funk, Chicago, 1961 [cited as Bl-D].
Dalman, G., *Die Worte Jesu*, Leipzig, 1930.

Interpreter's Dictionary of the Bible, The, 4 volumes, New York, 1962 [cited as *IDB*].
Kittel, G., and Friedrich, G. (edd.), *Theologisches Wörterbuch zum Neuen Testament*, Stuttgart, 1933- [cited as *TWNT*].
Liddel, H. G., and Scott, R., *A Greek-English Lexicon. A New Edition revised and augmented throughout*, by H. S. Jones, Oxford, 1948 [cited as L-Sc].
Moule, C. F. D., *An Idiom Book of New Testament Greek*, Cambridge, 1953.
Moulton, J. H., and Milligan, George, *The Vocabulary of the Greek Testament illustrated from the Papyri and other non-literary sources*, London, 1914-1929.
Richardson, A. (ed.), *A Theological Word Book of the Bible*, London, 1950.
Strack, H. L., and Billerbeck, P., *Kommentar zum Neuen Testament aus Talmud und Midrasch*, München, 1922-1961.
Trench, R. C., *Synonyms of the New Testament*, London, 1880.
TWNT, see above on Kittel-Friedrich.

5. Translational and Linguistic Literature

Beekman, John (ed.), *Notes on Translation with Drills*, Summer Institute of Linguistics, 1965 [cited as Beekman, *NOT*].
Bible Translator, The, UBS, London, 1950- [cited as *TBT*, followed by the number of volume, page, and year].
Bratcher, Robert G., and Nida, Eugene A., *A Translator's Handbook on the Gospel of Mark*, UBS Helps for Translators, vol. 2, Leiden, 1961 [cited as *TH-Mk*, followed by the number of chapter and verse; and in *Exegesis* referring to the exegetical, in *Translation* to the translational part of the *TH-Mk* note on that verse unless stated otherwise].
Goodspeed, Edgar J., *Problems of New Testament Translation*, Chicago, 1945.
Indian Wordlist: *Greek New Testament Terms in Indian Languages* (*a comparative word list*), compiled by J. S. H. Hooper, BSIC and BFBS, Bangalore, 1957 (to be used together with its mimeographed Supplement, giving the translation of Sanskrit words, by W. Perston, BFBS, London).
Nida, Eugene A., *Bible Translating*, ABS, New York, 1947 [cited as Nida, *BT*].
——, *God's Word in Man's Language*, New York, 1952 [cited as Nida, *GWIML*].
——, and Taber, Charles R., *The Theory and Practice of Translation*, UBS Helps for Translators, Vol. 8, Leiden, 1969 [cited as Nida, *TAPOT*].
——, *Toward a Science of Translating*, Leiden, 1964 [cited as Nida, *Science*].
N.T.Wb.: *A New Testament Wordbook for Translators*, (1) *Some Exegetical Articles in Preliminary Form*, ABS, New York, 1964, (2) *Some Translational Articles in Preliminary Form*, ABS, New York, 1966 [cited as *N.T.Wb.* followed by page number, slant line and (where necessary) catchword when referring to (1), and by slant line, page number and (where necessary) catchword when referring to (2)].
TH-Mk: see above on Bratcher-Nida.
Wonderly, William L., *Bible Translation for Popular Use*, UBS Helps for Translators, vol. 7, 1968 [cited as Wonderly, *BTPU*].

GREEK WORD LIST

The Index is based on the text of *GNT* and disregards words mentioned in the critical apparatus. Not included in the Index are:

(a) words occurring only once or twice (cp. p. X);
(b) proper names;
(c) pronouns;
(d) the following prepositions: *apo, dia, eis, ek, en, epi, meta, para, pros, sun, huper, hupo*;
(e) the following particles or conjunctions: *alla, an, ean, ei, gar, ge, de, ē, idou, hina, kai, men, mē, hotan, hoti, ou, oun, oute, te, hōs*;
(f) numerals;
(g) the following nouns: *anthrōpos, hēmera, theos*;
(h) the following adjectives: *heteros, pas, polus*;
(i) the following verbs: *ginomai, eidon, eimi, eipon, eiserchomai, erchomai, echō, legō, poieō*.

The alphabetical order of this Index is that of the Greek alphabet: a - b - g - d - e - z - ē - th - i - k - l - m - n - x - o - p - r - s - t - u - ph - ch - ps - ō. Words beginning with h (in the Greek a spiritus asper) are to be sought under the following vowel.

ENGLISH WORD LIST

Listed are, (1) words that often occur in the RSV text (e.g. "behold", "power", "scribe"), and (2) some grammatical catchwords (e.g. "*honorifics*", "*pronouns*"), together with a reference to the passage(s) where they have been dealt with.

LIST OF LANGUAGES

Aguaruna (Indian language of Peru) 20 : 17.
Alangan (northern Central Mindoro; a Philippine language) 5 : 34.
Amuzgo (Indian language of southern Mexico) 17 : 31.
Apache (i.e. the western Apache dialect group, in southern central Arizona, USA; a member of the Athabaskan family) ch. 1.
Arabic (references are to classical Arabic as spread by Islam) 1 : 28, 7 : 3, 9 : 23, 10 : 18,35, 11 : 41f, 16 : 17, 20 : 42, 23 : 43, 24 : 27.
Auca (Indian language of Ecuador) 4 : 15, 8 : 24,49, 9 : 14,17.
Aymara (Indian language of Bolivia and southern Peru) 1 : 41, 2 : 25.
Aztec: group of related Indian languages of Central Mexico belonging to the Nahuatlan branch of the Uto-Aztecan family; see on Tetelcingo, and Zacapoaxtla Aztec.
Bahasa Indonesia (national language of Indonesia; a member of the Indonesian family of languages; quotations are from the version of 1938, except those with the addition *KB*, which refers to *Kabar Baik*, Djakarta, 1955, a provisional edition of selections in the new translation, or with the addition *RC*, which refers to the Roman Catholic version of the Gospels and Acts, *Kitab Kudus Perdjandjian Baru, Kitab Indjil dan Kisah Rasul-Rasul*, Ende, 1955, or again those with the addition 1968, which refers to the checked draft of the new translation) chs. 1-24.
Bali (western Cameroun; a Bantu language) 5 : 39, 9 : 62.
Balinese (Bali; an Indonesian language) chs. 1-24.
Bambara (Sudan, and groups in Senegal, Upper Volta and Ivory Coast, West Africa; a member of the Mande branch of the Niger-Congo family) 1 : 28,32,50.
Bamiléké (collective name for a group of Bantu languages in western Cameroun) chs. 1-24; some lexical items are taken from "Manuel de Traduction Orale", ed. J. de Waard (mimeographed), Yaounde, 1967 (part I, A-I).
Bantu languages: members of the Benue-Congo branch of the Niger-Congo family, in central and southern Africa.
Barrow Eskimo (Alaska; a member of the Eskimo-Aleut family) 1 : 55,59, 2 : 32, 5 : 10,31, 6 : 48, 8 : 4, 12 : 42.
Bengali (Eastern India; a member of the Indic branch of the Indo-European family) 5 : 24, 20 : 19.
Bolivian Quechua (see on Quechua) 1 : 2,7,33f,51,66,74, 2 : 10,14,52.
Bulu (southern Cameroun; a Bantu language) 1 : 21, 2 : 40,48, 10 : 41, 24 : 38.
Cakchiquel (highlands of Guatemala; a Mayan language) 15 : 17,30.
Cashinahua (a Pano language spoken in eastern Peru and adjacent Brazilian regions, on tributaries of the Purus and Jurua rivers) 1 : 5.
Chichimeca Pame (see on Pame) 5 : 2.
Chinese (quotations are from UV, i.e., the Mandarin Union Version, 1919; from RC, i.e., the translation of the Franciscan Fathers, 1960; from L, i.e., Rev. Lü Chen-chung's revised draft translation, 1952; from BT, i.e., the "Bible Treasury Version", third tentative edition, 1958) chs. 1-3.
Chokwe (eastern Angola and western Congo, at home in Kasai Valley; a Bantu language) 1 : 33, 18 : 13, 24 : 27,38.
Chol (Chiapas, southern Mexico; a Mayan language) 22 : 29, 24 : 38.
Chontal (*of Tabasco*) (southern Mexico, a Mayan language) 1 : 21, 2 : 20,40, 4 : 7,15,20, 8 : 4, 9 : 45, 11 : 22.

Chuj (*de San Sebastián Coatán*) (Guatemala, a Mayan language) 2 : 37, 3 : 21.
Conob (Guatemala; a Mayan language) 1 : 72, 2 : 48, 10 : 30,41.
Cuicatec (an Indian language of southern Mexico) 2 : 51, 5 : 24, 10 : 13, 18 : 13.
Cuna (Indian language of San Blas Islands and Panama) 2 : 13,25, 5 : 4, 11 : 40.
Cuyono (Cuyo Islands and Palawan; a Philippine language) chs. 1, 2, 4-8; v. 10 : 41.
Dravidian languages (southern India and Ceylon; in this book used as a common denomination for Kanarese, Telugu and Tamil) 1 : 28f,62, 2 : 26, 3 : 7,15.
East Nyanja (see on Nyanja) 6 : 45; chs. 9-18.
East Toradja, also called *Pamona*, or *Bare'e* (eastern central Celebes, an Indonesian language; quotations are from the 1954 revision, unless marked as taken from the first version, of 1933) chs. 1-24.
Enga (central highlands, Territory of New Guinea; a Papuan language) 4 : 40, 5 : 14,24, 6 : 3, 8 : 8,38, 9 : 27, 14 : 34, 20 : 22.
Foe (central highlands, Territory of New Guinea; a Papuan language) 1 : 19, 2 : 11, 4 : 18, 5 : 5, 7 : 16,20, 9 : 40, 16 : 25, 22 : 32.
Fon (main centre in southern Dahomey; a language of the Kwa branch of the Niger-Congo family) 8 : 6f, 20 : 9.
Fulani (West Africa; a member of the West-Atlantic branch of the Niger-Congo family; the references are to a translation in Eastern Fulani (ed. 1964), based largely on Cameroun dialects but with modifications for use in Niger, Nigeria, Dahomey, Chad) chs. 16-20, 23, 24.
Gahuku (eastern highlands, Territory of New Guinea; a Papuan language) 3 : 20.
Gbandi, or *Bandi* (north-western Liberia; a member of the Mande branch of the Niger-Congo family) 1 : 35.
Gbeapo, or *Gbewapo* (on River Cavally in western Liberia; dialect of Bakwe, a Kru language, a member of the Kwa branch of the Niger-Congo family) 1 : 79, 5 : 10, 12 : 8, 15 : 12, 22 : 20.
Gio, or *Dan* (western Ivory Coast, on Liberian border; a member of the Mande branch of the Niger-Congo family) 1 : 41, 2 : 1,52, 3 : 3, 11 : 20,22, 12 : 25,35, 13 : 1, 17 : 2,29, 18 : 13, 20 : 36,42, 21 : 25.
Guaica (Indian language of southern Venezuela) 1 : 3.
Guhu-Samane (spoken inland along the Waria River, Territory of New Guinea; a Papuan language) 2 : 27, 5 : 37, 9 : 23, 22 : 42, 24 : 24.
Gujarati (western India; an Indic language) 13 : 19.
Gurunse, or *Grusi* (Upper Volta and Ghana; a member of the Gur branch of the Niger-Congo family) 2 : 48, 10 : 41.
Hindi (national language of India; a member of the Indic branch of the Indo-European family) chs. 1, 3.
Huanuco Quechua (central Peru; cp. on Quechua) 1 : 17,28,42, 2 : 1,25, 4 : 12.
Huastec (east coast of Mexico; a Mayan language) 1 : 72.
Huave (Indian language of southern Mexico) 24 : 38.
Huichol (Sierra Madre Occidental, in the Nayarit and Jalisco states of north-western Mexico; a member of the Uto-Aztecan family) 2 : 25, 7 : 4.
Huixtec (a dialect of Tzotzil, which see) 1 : 54, 6 : 44, 10 : 3,13, 11 : 13,34,51, 12 : 27, 22 : 15,29f.
Huli (central highlands, Territory of New Guinea; a Papuan language) 2 : 11, 22 : 56, 23 : 41.
Ifugao (northern Luzon; a Philippine language) 1 : 42, 2 : 40, 6 : 1,24, 7 : 31.
Ilocano (one of the major Philippine languages, originally at home in northern Luzon) 1 : 79, 8 : 15.
Indian languages: general designation of indigenous languages in the Americas; also designated as American Indian or Amerindian languages.
Indic languages: languages of India that are members of the Indo-European family.

Indonesian languages: all languages of Indonesia mentioned in this book, except the Papuan languages; members of the Malayo-Polynesian family.
Isthmus Mixe (see on Mixe; Indian language of southern Mexico) 7 : 34.
Isthmus Zapotec (see on Zapotec) 1 : 11.
Japanese (quoted is the Kogotai, or colloquial, version, 1954) 4 : 16, 5 : 21,24, 22 : 64, 23 : 42.
Javanese (central and eastern Java; an Indonesian language) chs. 1-24.
Kabba-Laka (eastern Cameroun, on the border of the Chad Republic; a member of the Adama-Eastern branch of the Niger-Congo family) 1 : 12, 6 : 25, 7 : 5, 13 : 17.
Kaka, or *Kako* (Cameroun; a Bantu language) 2 : 40, 11 : 22, 24 : 38.
Kanarese, or *Kannada* (around Mysore, South India; a Dravidian language) chs. 1-3.
Kapauku, or *Ekari* (Wissel Lakes in central West New Guinea, Indonesia; a Papuan language) chs. 1-24.
Karré, or *Kare*, or *Kari* (Ubangi-Chari district of Chad Republic; a member of the Chari-Nile branch of the Saharan family) 1 : 54,79.
Kekchi (Alta Verapaz state of Guatemala; a Mayan language) chs. 1-24.
Kikongo, or *Kongo* (western Congo; a Bantu language) 1 : 53.
Kilega, or *Lega* (eastern Congo; a Bantu language) 24 : 19,29.
Kipsigis (Kenya; a dialect of Nandi, a Bantu language) 2 : 51, 20 : 17.
Kirundi, or *Rundi* (Ruanda-Urundi; a Bantu language) 5 : 2.
Kituba (western Congo; a creole language based on Kikongo and Lingala; the quotations are from a translation made by a committee which was using the first draft of this handbook; the translation concerned has not yet been published) chs. 1-24.
Kiyaka, or *Yaka* (western Congo on the Angola border; a Bantu language) 1 : 72, 15 : 17,19.
Korku (a Munda language spoken throughout the hills of Maharashtra State, Berar, Madhya Pradesh) 3 : 17.
Kpelle (central Liberia and Guinea; a member of the Mande branch of the Niger-Congo family) 2 : 13, 5 : 14.
Lahu (southern Yunnan, China; Kengtung and Wa States, Burma; northern Thailand and Laos; a member of the Lolo branch of the Sino-Tibetan family) 1 : 49,64,71,74f.
Lengua (Indian language spoken in the eastern part of Gran Chaco, Paraguay) 2 : 7,23, 20 : 43.
Lokele, or *Kele* (upper Congo River, around Stanley Falls; a Bantu language) 3 : 14, and chs. 4-24.
Lomwe (Mozambique coast; a Bantu language) chs. 12-18.
Low Malay (name given to a local variety of Malay spoken in Java; quotations are from the version made in Semarang, northern central Java, in 1863, edition 1941) chs. 1-24.
Luchazi, or *Chazi* (a lingua franca of Southern Angola; a Bantu language) 11 : 22.
Machiguenga (an Arawak language spoken on the Urubamba river in central Peru) 1 : 3.
Malay (former trade language of the East Indian Archipelago, at home in Sumatra, Malaya and adjacent islands, ancestor of Bahasa Indonesia, and national language of Malaysia; an Indonesian language; for one of the many local varieties, see on Low Malay) chs. 1-24.
Malayalam (Kerala, west coast of South India; a Dravidian language) 1 : 35.
Manobo (western Bukidnon in central Mindanao; a Philippine language) ch. 3.
Marathi (western India; a member of the Indic branch of the Indo-European family; the notes are based on the revision of 1962) chs. 1, 3-11, 16-18, 21-24.

Shipibo, or *Shipibo-Conibo* (north-eastern Peru; an Indian language of the Pano group) ch. 1; vv. 5 : 20, 7 : 31, 11 : 22.
Shona (union language centring in southern Rhodesia; a Bantu language. Quotations are from versions of 1963, in Central Shona but having a chi-Karanga bias, and of 1966, also in Central Shona but with a chi-Zezuru bias) 3 : 2, and chs. 4-24.
Sinhalese (chief language of Ceylon; a member of the Indic branch of the Indo-European family) chs. 1-11.
South Toradja, also called *Tae'* (south-western central Celebes; an Indonesian language) chs. 1-24.
Sranan (creole language, formerly called Negro-English, of Surinam, northern Latin America) chs. 1-24.
Subanen (south-western Mindanao; a Philippine language) 1 : 15,38,42,50,52, 5 : 31, 9 : 49.
Sundanese (West Java; an Indonesian language) chs. 1-24.
Tagabili (south-western Mindanao; a Philippine language) chs. 1, 2, 4-10; vv. 13 : 32, 19 : 23, 21 : 8.
Tagalog, or *Pilipino* (national language of the Philippines, at home in Luzon) chs. 1, 2; vv. 5 : 5,12, 6 : 37, 9 : 34,41, 10 : 30, 15 : 17, 17 : 13,27, 18 : 7,21, 19 : 35.
Tamil (South India and Ceylon; a Dravidian language) chs. 1-3.
Tarahumara (north-western Mexico; a member of the Uto-Aztecan family) 1 : 21, 5 : 24, 7 : 31.
Tarascan (Indian language of western central Mexico) 1 : 7,14,17,35,59,74, 2 : 13,25, 3 : 20, 6 : 23,26, 7 : 25, 9 : 44,58,62, 10 : 21, 12 : 51.
Tchien (eastern Liberia; a tribal variety of Kran, which is a dialect of Kru, member of the Kwa branch of the Niger-Congo family) 1 : 72.
Telugu (central and eastern South India; a Dravidian language) chs. 1-3.
Tenango Otomi (see on Otomi) 5 : 24.
Tepehua (Indian language of eastern central Mexico) 1 : 14, 2 : 13, 10 : 3.
Terena (Indian language of Brazil) 7 : 2.
Tetelcingo Aztec (see on Aztec) 1 : 59, 4 : 2.
Thai (national language of Thailand; a member of the Chinese-Thai branch of the Sino-Tibetan family) chs. 1, 2, 12-20; vv. 22 : 67, 23 : 3.
Timorese, or *Dawan* (Timor; an Indonesian language) chs. 1-3, 9-24; and v. 6 : 45.
Toba Batak (centre of northern Sumatra; an Indonesian language; quotations are from the revision of 1932, unless marked as taken from the first version, of 1885) chs. 1-24.
Totonac (Indian language of eastern central Mexico) 1 : 9,32,79, 2 : 13, 5 : 24, 6 : 37.
Totontepec Mixe (see on Mixe) 22 : 56.
Trique (Indian language of southern Mexico) 5 : 24,36, 13 : 21.
Trukese (Caroline Islands, Micronesia; a member of the Malayo-Polynesian family) chs. 1-24.
Tzeltal (in the state Chiapas of Southern Mexico; a Mayan language; from ch. 4 onward the references are mainly to the translation in the Bachajón dialect, ed. 1964) chs. 1-24.
Tzotzil (Southern Mexico; a Mayan language closely related to Tzeltal) 1 : 12,59, 7: 4, 19 : 23.
Uduk (Sudan, along Ethiopian border; a member of the Koman branch of the Nilo-Saharan family) 1 : 12, 2 : 48,51, 23 : 4.
Vai (south-western Liberia and Sierra Leone; a member of the Mande branch of the Niger-Congo family) 1 : 48,50f,72,79f, 2 : 13,23,26,37, 3 : 6.
Valiente (Indian language of north-western Panama) 1 : 12,15,42,50, 2 : 34, 3 : 8.
Wantoat (Huon peninsula, Territory of New Guinea; a Papuan language) 4 : 15, 5 : 6, 8 : 16.

DATE DUE
